Culturally Alert
COUNSELING

—— SECOND EDITION ——

To the victims of Black 47, may their descendants speak truth to power.

Culturally Alert
COUNSELING
A COMPREHENSIVE INTRODUCTION

—— SECOND EDITION ——

GARRETT McAULIFFE & ASSOCIATES
Old Dominion University, USA

Los Angeles | London | New Delhi
Singapore | Washington DC

Los Angeles | London | New Delhi
Singapore | Washington DC

FOR INFORMATION:

SAGE Publications, Inc.
2455 Teller Road
Thousand Oaks, California 91320
E-mail: order@sagepub.com

SAGE Publications Ltd.
1 Oliver's Yard
55 City Road
London EC1Y 1SP
United Kingdom

SAGE Publications India Pvt. Ltd.
B 1/I 1 Mohan Cooperative Industrial Area
Mathura Road, New Delhi 110 044
India

SAGE Publications Asia-Pacific Pte. Ltd.
3 Church Street
#10-04 Samsung Hub
Singapore 049483

Acquisitions Editor: Kassie Graves
Editorial Assistant: Courtney Munz
Production Editor: Laura Stewart
Copy Editor: Sarah J. Duffy
Typesetter: C&M Digitals (P) Ltd.
Proofreader: Jennifer Thompson
Indexer: Teddy Diggs
Cover Designer: Glenn Vogel
Marketing Manager: Lisa Sheldon-Brown
Permissions Editor: Adele Hutchinson

Copyright © 2013 by SAGE Publications, Inc.

Printed in the United States of America

Library of Congress Cataloging-in-Publication Data

Culturally alert counseling : a comprehensive introduction / editor, Garrett McAuliffe. — 2nd ed.

p. cm.
Includes bibliographical references and index.

ISBN 978-1-4129-8135-4 (pbk.)

1. Cross-cultural counseling. I. McAuliffe, Garrett.

BF636.7.C76C853 2013
158′.3—dc23   2012017345

This book is printed on acid-free paper.

13 14 15 16 10 9 8 7 6 5 4 3 2

Contents

PART III SOCIAL GROUPS

PART IV IMPLICATIONS FOR PRACTICE

Preface to the Second Edition

Garrett McAuliffe

Does the world change for the better? Can we be as hopeful as the father of counseling Frank Parsons's expectation that our work results in "social improvement?" That optimistic early 19th century concept sometimes can fall prey to cynicism, as unnecessary suffering continues to plague human societies. And yet, we have seen remarkable social changes in the past 50 years. Who would have thought that race relations would have improved so much since the 1960s, even if the struggle continues? Who could imagine that consciousness of women's rights would become a mainstream assumption, if not a reality? Who would have thought that marriage for persons who are gay would be a reality in some states?

Thus change does happen. And we can give credit to the counselors, writers, and activists of each era for the changes we see today. So we have cause for hope, even optimism. However, we must be vigilant. We must be ever restless in order to ensure that the dominant groups do not reign supreme as they once did, and still do in many cases. As author Robert Kegan says, social change does not pass on through the genes, but it requires constant education. And those in power do not often willingly give up their power. So the public conversation about who is at the equity table must continue. Counselors are central players in that conversation.

Culturally alert counseling is a moral enterprise. It is an effort at *tikkun olam,* the Hebrew term that refers to renewing or repairing the world. Culturally alert counseling is an attempt to include all other human beings in the great work of helping and healing, with no exceptions. That work is done daily in counselors' attention to clients' cultural assumptions, in counselors' outreach to nondominant groups. Unfortunately, much counseling in the past has been the province of the mainstream, leaving poor persons, gay persons, and people of color out of the picture.

Counselors cannot in good conscience leave anyone out. But inclusion has not been easy for human beings over the centuries. Class, race, gender, sexual orientation, ability, ethnicity, and religion have been used as dividers. Counselors, above all professionals, are asked to look into those great divides, to see themselves in others, to see others in others, to know the rich differences among mixed-up human beings, and to relish the great similarities. The philosopher Richard Rorty (1989) explains this obligation as

> reminding ourselves to keep trying to expand our sense of "us" as far as we can . . . [to include] the family in the next cave, then of the tribe across the river, then of the tribal confederation beyond the mountains, then of the unbelievers beyond the seas (and, perhaps last of all, . . . the menials who, all this time, have been doing our dirty work). This is a process that counselors must engage in. We should stay on the lookout for marginalized people—people whom we still instinctively think of as "they" rather than "us." (p. 196)

Rorty asks us to stretch our vision. To know others as they are, by knowing them well, is our obligation as counselors. And that is a central purpose of this book.

FOUR GUIDING DIMENSIONS BEHIND THE BOOK

This book is a beginning text for emerging counselors and psychotherapists of all kinds. It has been written with four guidelines in mind: depth, breadth, readability, and applicability. The contributors hope that these dimensions make this book both useful and moving.

Depth refers to two levels. First is the personal conceptual depth, or framework, that is presented in the notion of constructivism. Constructivism is here defined as the simple idea that each human being makes meanings in her or his own culturally influenced way. Constructivism reminds counselors to be humble, to realize that they are always making sense, and to take responsibility for the sense that they are making. To aid in that sense-making, this book provides further conceptual frameworks for the journey. In the first two chapters, the notions of critical consciousness, ethno- or culture-centrism, privilege, social stratification, pluralism, dominance and nondominance, and oppression are examined in hopes that they might guide you, the reader, through the remaining chapters.

The second dimension of depth lies in the content of subsequent chapters on ethnic and social groups. Chapter authors who are known experts on each culture or topic were recruited to pen the particulars. Those chapters are therefore characterized by accurate and meaningful insights into the human conditions of each cultural group.

Breadth is the second of the four impulses that led to this book. The notion of culture can be writ large, and it is here. Thus, culture no longer refers only to race or ethnicity. Our worlds are also culturally constructed through the lenses of social class, gender, sexual orientation, and religion. This book therefore honors those topics with corresponding chapters.

Readability is the third major impulse behind this book. Much textbook and academic writing on culture and counseling suffers from the malady of academic prose: It is overly abstract, insufficiently illustrative, and often wooden. To remedy this problem, I selected writers who could bring out the power of this material in vital, rich ways. Thus the text is littered with vignettes, anecdotes, figures, and exercises that make the concepts come alive.

Finally, *applicability* guided the writing of these chapters. The book presents actual skills to be used in culturally alert counseling. Counselors are practical people; they must act. Multicultural counseling skills have not been very fully articulated up until now, so this book tries to stretch that boundary by presenting explicit sets of counseling skills that might be used with culture in mind. The two final chapters and the complementary demonstration DVD set sum up the current practices of multicultural counseling skills so that readers might counsel right away in a culturally alert way.

OUTLINE OF THE BOOK

The book begins with the more tender topic of yourself—the cultural being that you are. You are asked to know yourself better in order to know others. At the end of the first two chapters, you will perhaps be less likely to project your cultural assumptions onto others; you will be more likely to listen and wait. Then Chapter 3 launches into the topic of human equality, with a description of social stratifications and how to challenge those that are harmful through advocacy.

The journey then leads in Chapters 4 and 5, to explorations of ethnicity and race—topics that involve all readers. No one is left out of this book, whether she or he is in a dominant/majority group or in a less powerful minority. The following seven chapters (Chapters 6–12) describe specific ethnic groupings. In those pages, you will come to better know both yourself and others. Next, Chapters 13–17 present readings and activities devoted to exploring the wide worlds of social class, gender, sexual orientation, religion, and disability.

The book ends with a depiction of the key skills for doing culturally alert counseling. This topic has been scarcer in the counseling literature, and Chapters 18 and 19 are an attempt to remedy that omission. With exposure to actual counseling skills, you will be better equipped to apply the understandings that you have learned and try them out in solidarity with those now-familiar "others." These skills are vividly illustrated by the complementary six-part training DVD series *Culturally Alert Counseling: Working With African*

American, Asian, Latino/Latina, Conservative Religious, and Gay/Lesbian Youth Clients. One of the six videos parallels Chapters 18 and 19 and comes with this text. That video, Key Practices, provides an overview of the skills required for doing culturally alert counseling.

ENHANCEMENTS TO THE SECOND EDITION

This second edition of *Culturally Alert Counseling,* after 5 years of feedback, triumph, reconsideration, and pondering, continues to be a labor of love for me and all of the authors.

A revision should significantly enhance a prior version of a book. And so I expect that we, the authors, have done so. Change for change's sake only speaks to restlessness. Change for improvement's sake speaks to a responsible enhancement in a book. We have chosen the latter route. Many of the authors are the same experts on each topic from the successful first edition. They have revised their work with the wisdom of 5 years of living, reading, and testing.

So we have built on the first edition, with wisdom that can be gained only from experience. Here are examples of the improvements that this second edition offers:

- A brand-new, comprehensive **chapter on counseling individuals with disabilities**. This topic has long been in need of more coverage. The chapter is the result of a national recruiting effort to find two top experts on disabilities and counseling. And coauthors Yvette Getch and Adrianne Johnson have lived up to their established reputations. They define specific disabilities, sprinkle the chapter with applications to a case, and highlight new practices that are responsive to clients with disabilities.
- A radically revised chapter on **equity, advocacy, and social justice**, one that gives counselors the skills to be advocates for clients. The chapter explicitly spells out specific strategies for advocacy and the rationale for such a counselor role.
- A separate chapter on the **clarifications and complications of culture** that spells out foundational

concepts related to this complex topic—including cultural identity development, intersectionality, and salience—and offers a revised **cultural decentering activity** based on recently published research on the notion of self-authorizing culture.

- A thorough exposition on **stages of faith development** so that counselors might assess their own faith journey and help clients with theirs.
- Continuing treatment of **bisexuality and transgender** as frontier topics in the field.
- A new section on **microaggressions and gender** as well as expanded treatment of **nature and nurture** in the development of sex and gender.
- A **class genogram** activity for counselors to use and an expanded treatment of class-alert counseling practices, including presentation of a new section on **class-alert client assessment.**
- Expanded descriptions of the **growing South Asian, Middle Eastern, and Latino/Latina ethnic groups** in the United States and counseling practices for these groups.
- A completely revised chapter on **Native Americans.**

THE CHALLENGE TO COUNSELORS

But why is there a book on culturally alert counseling at all? The work of counseling is like almost no other work. It is difficult. Complex. Personally challenging. Ambiguous. Emotional. Concrete. Abstract. It takes a particular kind of person to encounter other human beings in their uncertainty and pain, to hold them, and to journey with them on the bumpy road to becoming more fully human. As my brother says, "How can you do this work? Isn't it too hard? You have to be so engaged all the time." To each her or his own, said the philosopher. Those of you who have chosen to accompany other human beings through their doubts and discoveries must therefore be prepared. There is much to learn and try, and try again, and learn.

It used to be simpler. Counselors worked with the supposedly autonomous individual to "cure" her or him. Now we have acknowledged the inextricable cultural dimension in the life of the individual. Counselors have to acknowledge that, metaphorically speaking, there are hundreds of people in the room with the individual client or family, to paraphrase Paul Pedersen. Clients bring with them ancestors, parents, religious teachers, ethnic models, neighborhood friends. There are films seen and lyrics heard. There are the aunts and uncles of childhood, the siblings of yesterday and today, the weddings, the memorial services, the dinner table conversation. All are represented in clients' memories, in their strivings, in their manners, and in their morals. All sit with the client before you. Thus the work of counseling is now made larger by our recognition of these "people in the room."

It is not the purpose of the multicultural counseling movement to unnecessarily daunt the novice counselor. The field did slog on for many years without a full appreciation of these silent, and noisy, presences in clients' lives. But there was a cost. Minority group members and poor folks didn't seek counseling, or dropped out early, when the field was seen as a white middle-class endeavor. I know this fact personally—no working-class Irish kid from Queens had access to counseling, nor would go for it, even if he were lost, anxious, scared, confused, or addicted. And we were all of those. The community didn't support personal exploration or vulnerability. The working-class environment didn't usually value probing for personal meanings and seeking right relations with others. But to counseling I did go—only after it seemed acceptable to tell all to a stranger. Although we feared that these counselors wouldn't understand our ethnic group, our religion. And sometimes they didn't. Counselors of the time rejected religion as superstition, but prayed to the god of analysis and insight. They didn't know that they were engaged in a great classist enterprise of trying to heal the white upper middle class. Counseling must now be bigger than that. It must embrace the complexity that culture brings. That is the only way to do this good work. With the inclusion of culture into the work of counseling, we extend the possibility of human solidarity that we so long for.

REFERENCE

Rorty, R. (1989). *Contingency, irony, and solidarity.* Cambridge, UK: Cambridge University Press.

PART I

INTRODUCTION

CHAPTER 1

Culture and Diversity Defined

Garrett McAuliffe

Old Dominion University

*If indeed we could sustain a life in which we would only meet people from our own culture . . .
we might need to learn only the rules of our own culture and adhere to them. But such a world is
rapidly disappearing if not already gone.*

Robert Kegan (1998, p. 208)

*[My book] celebrates hybridity, impurity, intermingling, the transformation that comes of new and
unexpected combinations of human beings, cultures, ideas, politics, movies, songs. It rejoices in
mongrelization and fears the absolutism of the Pure. . . . It is the great possibility that mass migration gives to the world, and I have tried to embrace it. . . . Throughout human history, the apostles
of purity, those who have claimed to possess a total explanation, have wrought havoc among mere
mixed-up human beings. Like many millions of people, I am a bastard child of history. Perhaps
we all are, black and brown and white, leaking into one another, . . . like flavors when you cook.*

Salman Rushdie (1992, p. 394) on his novel *The Satanic Verses*

Nothing human is alien to me.

The Roman writer Terence

The three quotes that open this chapter capture the fundamental message of this book: Counselors
must embrace the kaleidoscope that is human diversity while at the same time remembering that
humans have much in common. With that paradox in mind, the counselor can be prepared to do
ethical, culturally alert counseling.

The field of counseling cannot be separated from the study of culture. After all, counseling began in the
early 20th century with an earnest attempt at social reform by helping poor, orphaned youth make good life
choices. In that tradition, the work of counseling can be seen as a hopeful, and a moral, enterprise. Through

counseling, the disempowered find strength and resources. Counselors embrace a world of possibility, as difficult as that may be at times.

Clients come to counselors wounded by the slings and arrows of living. Some of those wounds are created by other humans, humans who find "the other" to be distasteful, foreign, dismissable. Some humans say, "After all, they are 'not like us,' and we cannot understand them because they are . . . gay, black, disabled, Jewish, Christian, poor, white, rich, Asian, Mexican, female, Arab, atheist, or Anglo." And the list goes on. Counselors imagine a world in which there are fewer such wounds. Counselors embrace a moral vision of human solidarity; they commit themselves to principles that go beyond any particular group or place. Counselors cherish the "unexpected combinations of human beings," to quote Salman Rushdie, that is the world and always has been. Those combinations include the Latino migrant worker in North Carolina, the African American father in Oregon, the gay adolescent in Louisiana, the Muslim immigrant in Michigan, the evangelical Christian in Texas, and the white Southerner in Georgia. And those are but a few descriptors for the inevitability of human diversity. The previous individuals do not fit into "pure" categories; each individual carries her or his own constellation of cultures with her or him, based on unique experiences and individual temperament.

So the counselor is hereby welcomed to a world of mélange and hotchpotch, a world in which her or his own point of view must be continually extended as newness enters. This book is indeed a "love song to our mongrel selves." The following vignettes demonstrate the themes and movements of that song. It is a song that you must learn to sing, sometimes while improvising, but always with great heart.

The counselor is a middle-aged American white male of second-generation Irish ancestry who was raised Catholic in a working- to lower-middle-class neighborhood in Boston. He is middle class and heterosexual. His client is a 53-year-old Boston fire captain who is also Irish and Catholic.

The counselor and his client probably share many cultural similarities, such as a tendency to suppress negative feelings, especially sadness and pain; appreciation of having fun with groups of people (called "good craic," pronounced "crack" in Irish); an inclination to liberally drink alcohol at social gatherings; enthusiasm for a good song or a sentimental occasion; appreciation of "the talk" as a means of elaborating on experience; a predisposition to indirectness in expressing feelings; and the use of humor, especially sarcasm ("slagging"), as a substitute for intimacy. The counselor may, therefore, make some assumptions about his client without asking. Although the counselor will need to confirm these hunches, they will give him a head start in probing his client's worldview.

Yet the counselor and client, for all their similarities, may not see the world through the same eyes. In each of the following areas, counselor and client differ. For example, when discussing his marital difficulties, the client cannot conceive of divorce. In addition, he does not expect his wife to be interested in sex. Unlike the counselor, he does not like to show his feelings or even tell them to anyone. He hides physical discomforts, even from himself. He believes that drinking to excess is an acceptable social practice. He considers his age to be "old," and therefore he engages in no physical exercise. He is uncomfortable with "darker people," as he calls them, and considers immigrants to be ruining the city he loves. He belongs to Irish organizations and trumpets Irish accomplishments whenever he can. Finally, he is anti-gay, saying that being gay is unnatural and forbidden by his church. Each of these views contrasts significantly with the counselor's perspectives, as the counselor has questioned the inherited norms of his traditional ethnic culture and attempted to construct a more multicultural set of values.

A Korean couple and their 15-year-old son come into the public school counseling office unannounced one morning as the children are arriving at school. These recent arrivals to this rural community in Kansas moved from Los Angeles for a job opportunity. Their son has been in the school for 2 months and seems morose, commenting that he has no friends among the largely Anglo-American student body.

The school counselor, who is a heterosexual European American, immediately begins making empathic responses to their concerns, mixed with exploratory open questions about their feelings and the meanings of the situation to them. The counselor probes into how the parents are feeling about the move and about leaving their homeland. The parents respond with few words and many silences.

The counselor then tells them that she would like to meet with their son alone in order to understand his perspective more clearly. She has been taught to encourage students to think for themselves and to express their views in these situations. After hearing the son describe his hesitance at engaging other students in conversation and banter, or about joining any student organization, the counselor calls the parents back into the room.

She then suggests that the parents teach their son assertive behavior and that the family members practice direct communication of needs and requests at home so that the son will learn how to have his needs met. She teaches them basic assertiveness principles about believing in one's individual rights, making eye contact, having a firm vocal tone, and clearly stating one's needs without necessarily apologizing or empathizing with others' situations. She further directs them to keep a daily record of successful assertive exchanges. The counselor hopes that this will help their son, and them, adjust to life in this new area. She asks them to come back the following week at 9 A.M. to tell her how it has worked. However, the parents do not show up. Furthermore, they take their child out of the public school the week after and send him to a nearby religious private school.

As demonstrated by the first vignette, culture pervades all counseling exchanges. Even though the counselor and client share the same ethnic culture, gender, social class, sexual orientation, and religion of origin in name, they are having a cross-cultural encounter because their experiences of those cultures differ significantly. The counselor and client have been enculturated into the same Irish Catholic ethnic group, but each has a different relationship to that culture. There is clearly more to culturally alert counseling than meets the eye.

The second vignette also demonstrates the complexity of culturally alert counseling because the counselor's presumption of Western communication styles and individualism likely resulted in the clients not returning. Here the culture clash was more obvious—an individualistic, direct European American style encountering (unsuccessfully) a collectivist Asian tradition. The counselor lost the clients by promoting an individual, rights-oriented, confrontational communication style that is better suited to the European American notion of assertiveness. The Korean clients instead saw their primary allegiance as being to the group, namely the family and the community. The counselor also expressed no knowledge of Korean culture. That is unfortunate because such knowledge might have engendered trust. In addition, the counselor did not acknowledge the family's cultural isolation and failed to connect the clients with Korean persons and resources in the community. Finally, she did not acknowledge the social prejudice that is likely adding to some of the isolation and feelings of displacement.

In these two examples, the themes that will permeate this book emerge. A primary theme is that all counseling encounters are multicultural, in that the cultures of gender, ethnicity, race, sexual orientation, religion, and social class are always present. In these two vignettes, each of the following important counseling-related themes are embedded: attitudes toward health maintenance, sexuality, alcohol use, expectations of intimacy with a life partner, socialized gender roles, the valuing of emotional expressiveness versus emotional control, the level of acculturation to a dominant culture, ethnic identity, and being in a nondominant culture versus a more privileged one. And these are only two vignettes. The contemporary counselor is likely to be confronted with many more culturally saturated situations, for culture is everywhere in each human being's life. Culturally alert counseling is therefore defined as *a consistent readiness to identify the cultural dimensions of clients' lives and a subsequent integration of culture into counseling work.*

This chapter establishes a foundation for culturally alert counseling by responding to two of the three fundamental questions that must be asked of culturally alert counseling. First, the question "Why are culture and culturally alert counseling important?" is examined. The second question discussed is "What is culture and culturally alert counseling?" The third and most critical question, namely, "How does one actually do culturally alert counseling?" will be addressed in subsequent chapters, especially in Chapters 18 and 19 on key culturally alert practices.

The current chapter is divided into three major sections. It begins with the aforementioned *why* and *what* segments, followed by a presentation of the fundamental multicultural counseling competencies.

WHY CULTURALLY ALERT COUNSELING?

Whenever two people meet, it is a multicultural encounter. All individuals see the world, and are seen, through lenses of ethnicity, race, social class, gender, sexual orientation, religion, and ability status, to name some discourse lenses. Each client, and counselor, also brings a family-of-origin discourse to the encounter. Two individuals never meet purely as individuals, for all humans are socially constructed, that is, they make meaning through their socialization lenses. Thus, infusing culture into counseling should be nothing new. Nevertheless, until relatively recently, little attention has been paid to culture by mental health professionals. And while the multicultural dimension of counseling has been maturing in the past two decades, there is still much to be learned (D'Andrea & Heckman, 2008).

There are at least two arguments for culturally alert counseling. One argument relates to the inevitability of cross-cultural contact. More than ever before, people encounter cultural diversity daily, in their schools and neighborhoods and through media. The quote from Robert Kegan (1998) that opens this chapter describes this sea change. He goes on to iterate the inevitability of cross-cultural encounters: "Diversity of cultural experience may once have been the province of the adventurous, the open-minded, and those too poor to live where they wished. Tomorrow it will be the province of all" (p. 208).

Counselors can no longer assume that all they need to do is treat clients as somehow "pure" individuals. If that were the case, then culture wouldn't matter. But these words from sociologists Carol Aneshensel and Jo Phelan (1999) give the lie to the extreme individualist position:

> There are pronounced group differences in the course and consequences of mental illness, . . . differences that . . . point to the . . . powerful influence of the social factors that differentiate one group from another. The impact of gender, race, age, and socioeconomic status are apparent at virtually every juncture. (p. xii)

A second argument for culturally alert counseling concerns equity and inclusiveness. The counseling field is dedicated to equity, that is, access for all people to the things that matter in society, like good education and jobs (see Chapter 3 for a discussion of this topic). That is a long tradition, dating to the origin of the field in the early 20th century. Inclusiveness is closely related to equity. Who creates the counseling practices? From what perspective? With whom in mind? Counseling cannot be an exclusive endeavor for middle-class dominant-group members. Counseling theory and practice bias are products of culture, despite their being considered universal. Counseling practice has been embedded in a largely heterosexual, male, middle-class, European, and European American perspective, which emphasizes such cultural notions as self-actualization, human rights, achieved identity, choice theory, and autonomy.

These towering Western ideas have produced much good for some, reducing human suffering and increasing human potential, and are therefore to be honored. However, they have left others out. As recently as 2002, Stanley Sue and Amy Lam noted the inequality in mental health practice:

> Women, ethnic minorities, gay/lesbian/bisexuals, and individuals from lower social classes . . . have been subjected to detrimental stereotypes, have not been targeted for much psychological research, and are often underserved or inappropriately served in the mental health system. . . . There is an increasing urgency to provide effective treatment to these groups, as reflected in the "cultural competency" movement, which tries to identify the cultural knowledge, skills, and awareness that permit one to effectively work with clients from diverse populations. (p. 401)

Examples of being "inappropriately served" include the following: Lesbians and gay men have been treated as maladjusted. Women have been seen as overly dependent and emotional and were encouraged to follow limiting life paths. Many persons of color have been ignored; they, in turn, viewed counseling with suspicion.

That dominant-group bias is no longer possible. Nondominant groups of people have asserted their rights to be heard and to be dealt with. There is no going back to the previously mentioned "bad old days" of white, male, middle-class hegemony over cultural norms, values, and assumptions. "We are everywhere" is the refrain of formerly silent and voiceless minorities.

Here are some of the facts about diversity and culture in the United States:

- African Americans comprise about 12.6% of the U.S. population (U.S. Census Bureau, 2010b).
- Nationally, students of color constituted a majority in the public schools in 11 states and are a majority overall in the Southeast (Suitts, 2010).
- Seventy-five percent of people entering the U.S. labor force are women and racial/ethnic minorities (Lee & Mather, 2008).

- Gay, lesbian, and bisexual persons make up at least 7% of the population and seek out counselors at high rates (Kane & Green, 2009; Rivers, McPherson, & Hughes, 2010).
- In 2009, there were 1,482 hate crime offenses against gays and lesbians (Federal Bureau of Investigation, 2010).
- Men's and women's roles have become unclear for many, leading to distress over family and career commitments (Williams, 2003).
- Religion is a central enterprise for 70% of the U.S. population, with 90% of the population believing in God (Harris Interactive, 2003).
- Asians are the largest recent immigrant group to the United States, comprising 40.5% of new immigrants (U.S. Department of Homeland Security, 2010).
- Latinos have become the largest "mega-minority" in the United States (U.S. Census Bureau, 2010a).
- African Americans continue to experience segregation and bias in housing and jobs, and their poverty rate is double that of European Americans, despite significant economic gains over the past 30 years (Parisi, Lichter, & Taquino, 2011).
- The median wealth of white households is 20 times that of black households and 18 times that of Hispanic households (Kochhar, Fry, & Taylor, 2011).

These facts matter for two reasons. One is ethical responsibility and the other is professional self-interest. In the case of ethical responsibility, counselors must have an internal commitment to equity in their life. To undergird that stance, the American Counseling Association's (2005) *Code of Ethics* preamble states, counseling members "recognize diversity and embrace a cross-cultural approach in support of the worth, dignity, potential and uniqueness of people within their social and cultural contexts" (p. 3). Therefore, counselors must ask themselves: Whom are we serving? Are these statistics important for our work? Are we part of the problem of, or the solution to, social inequity? How are we acting to change the conditions that lead some people to have fewer obstacles while others must scramble through the thicket of hidden and overt bias, limited opportunities, and legacies of deficit?

The second reason for the urgency of culturally alert counseling is professional self-interest. If counselors are not convinced of its importance, their credibility will be challenged by both clients and employers (D. W. Sue & Sue, 2008). Clients will ask, "Can you be trusted to help me?" A counselor's livelihood may depend on the answer. For example, counselors who adhere to an insight-oriented practice may lose clients from cultural groups that eschew public emotional expression and expect direct problem-solving action for life concerns. Such can be the case for many people from so-called collectivist cultures, such as traditional American Indian and East Asian cultures, in which individual emotions are often considered secondary to group welfare.

This section on the *why* of culturally alert counseling should end with a reminder: Culturally alert counseling is for all people, not only members of nondominant groups. *All* counselors and clients are cultured. Every reader of this book has been constructed through many discourses that surround her or him, including various white European American discourses, middle-class discourses, male discourses, heterosexual discourses, and Christian discourses. Culturally alert counseling is a way of recognizing the social influence in human life. That will become clearer in upcoming chapters of this book.

THE *WHAT* OF CULTURE AND CULTURALLY ALERT COUNSELING: KEY NOTIONS

This section explores the key notions of *culture* and *diversity*. These two notions are foundational. They pervade all chapters of this book. First, definitions are provided. Then related concepts are discussed, including the pervasiveness and invisibility of culture and the notion of discourse.

Defining Culture

Culture is defined here as *the attitudes, habits, norms, beliefs, customs, rituals, styles, and artifacts that express a group's adaptation to its environment*—that is,

ways that are shared by group members and passed on over time. There are two parts to this definition, representing internal and external dimensions to culture. Most obvious are the external expressions, the customs, rituals, and styles. But the internalized dimensions of culture are especially important for the work of counseling. They are represented by "attitudes, habits, norms, and beliefs" in the above definition. Those internalized assumptions inform clients' expectations about relationships, their career aspirations, and their self-esteem, to name just a few impacts of internalized culture. Internal aspects of culture that counselors might encounter include the following. In each case, the counselor needs to be mindful of the cultural dimension and bring it into the work.

- A middle-class African American teacher is uncertain about how to express herself in a culturally congruent way in the largely European American school in which she teaches.
- A man is so bottled up emotionally that he drinks, broods, and isolates himself because he doesn't feel able, as a male, to ask for help or to show sadness.
- A working-class 20-year-old woman can't imagine pursuing a medical career because she just "doesn't know where to start" and can't imagine delaying paid work for school, plus she doesn't know where the money would come from for her training anyway.
- A Chinese American daughter of immigrants cannot figure out how to put together family loyalty and her desire to move across the country on her own to try an acting career.
- A gay 16-year-old boy is infatuated with another boy in the high school but is terrified of being found out.
- A Southern Anglo-American woman would like to express her negative feelings directly but has learned "proper manners" so well that she finds herself being angry at herself for not saying what she feels.

In each of these cases, culture can be both an opportunity and a barrier. Either way, culture is a consistent presence in the counseling room. In order to start the personal journey, you are invited to explore your cultural identities in a beginning way by completing Activity 1.1, Introductory Cultural Self-Awareness.

This activity begins your exploration of the realm of culture by asking you to define your current understanding of your own cultures.

Description of Activity

This introductory exercise occurs in three phases. You will respond to each cultural group in terms of two notions: its name and general status. After you put your responses in the boxes, write your thoughts about doing each phase on the second page of this activity, in the spaces provided, or as otherwise directed by your instructor.

First, complete Phase 1 on the following "Cultural Group Memberships Worksheet" by naming the cultural groups that you belong to, across seven categories. Then write down your thoughts on doing this phase.

Cultural Group Memberships Worksheet

Directions for Phase 1: Below are seven cultural categories. As you consider each of the categories in the far left column, name your own particular group identity in the second column, Phase 1. Use whatever label makes sense to you currently. Do Phase 1 first and then read the directions for Phase 2 below. (Note: You may be asked to share as many of these as you are comfortable with.)

Cultural Group Categories	Phase 1: NAMES	Phase 2: STATUS	Phase 3: IMPACT
	A name for your current group membership(s):	Whether this group is generally dominant or nondominant in many contexts	One way in which each social group membership affects your life
Ethnicity			
Race			
Social class, or SES (e.g., upper middle class, poor, working class)	Of origin:		
	Current:		
Gender			
Sexual orientation			
Ability/disability (e.g., generally abled, disabled)			
Religion	Of origin:		
	Current:		

Comments on Phase 1: What thoughts came to you as you tried to name your cultural groups?

(Continued)

(Continued)

Directions for Phase 2: When directed, note in the next column on the Worksheet whether you see each of your groups as dominant (for example, generally in a position of greater power and/or favor at the current time and place) or nondominant (access to significant social power is generally limited or denied) in most contexts (e.g., occupations, standards for language, beauty, power, presence, access to resources). The issue of dominance/nondominance will be taken up more extensively in Chapter 3.

Comments on Phase 2: What thoughts do you have on naming your groups' statuses?

Directions for Phase 3: Think of one way in which each cultural group membership affects, or has affected, your life. This can be a general effect or a specific event from the recent past.

This cultural group membership activity is aimed at stimulating your awareness of your being culturally constituted, that is, being made up by your cultures. It is meant to begin your movement toward what Paulo Freire (1974/2005) called *critical consciousness*, which is one of the major aims of this book. That topic is discussed later and in Chapter 3.

Culture: Pervasive and Invisible

Culture is so pervasive in people's lives that it can be likened to the water that surrounds a fish or the air that humans breathe—in other words, an ambient element outside of their consciousness. Much of what individuals assume to be individual choice is instead culturally constructed and automatic. This invisibility can lead to individuals being ignorant about how saturated a dominant culture is in a society. For example, what were once seemingly universal standards in American life are now seen as culturally male, European American, middle class, Christian, and heterosexual. This dominant cultural monolith has been toppled by other communities in U.S. society clamoring to be recognized. However, U.S. society was never so monolithic in a fundamental sense, because the nation has always been culturally diverse to a great extent. Women, gay people, non-Christians, Africans, Asians, American Indians, non-English-speaking people, poor persons, and individuals with disabilities have always been a part of American life (Takaki, 1993; Zinn, 2003). However, they are no longer background to the dominant culture but are, more and more, foreground on the American cultural landscape in numbers and in public voice.

Culture as Discourse

Another way to describe the pervasiveness of culture and its importance is to understand culture as an expression of a discourse. *Discourse* is a general term for a system of thought, a network of historically, socially, and institutionally held beliefs, categories, statements, and terms that give meaning to the world. The term comes from linguistics, where it refers to the connection between sentences and their social context. To understand discourse, as it relates to culture, it may be helpful to keep in mind that every sentence a person utters reflects her or his historical, social, and institutional context, from the words themselves being part of a language to the ideas being a product of a time and place. A discourse is like the lens in a pair of glasses. People actually wear many discourse "lenses." Cultures are groups of people who share particular discourses.

A person is always influenced by many discourses. A person's gender, ethnicity, and religious expression, for example, inform the way she or he views issues, situations, and people; they implicitly affect how individuals think and act. You might think about fashion in hair style and clothing. What is beautiful to one group can be unattractive to another. Individuals are caught up in a discourse that automatically affects what they see as attractive.

Such discourses set the foundation for the argument that one might make on what is valued in life. That is a dangerous situation for counselors. For example, if a male counselor speaks from within his own gender discourses, he might see an expressive and nurturing female client as emotionally labile and dependent. Or a working-class client as loud and aggressive instead of being less concerned about respectability and propriety.

There is a solution to this embeddedness in one's discourses. A counselor can be aware of the discourses from which she or he is speaking or acting. Or not. In Kegan's (1998) terms, she or he can "have" the discourse rather than it "having" her or him. Indeed, a major aim of this book is to help counselors become aware of how their discourses are influenced by the groups to which they belong, that is, to know the discourses through which they are thinking and acting. It might be some combination of their middle-class discourse, their Christian discourse, their conservative discourse, their feminist discourse, to name a few sets of assumptions that individuals might speak through. By being alert to the discourse that is informing their thinking, counselors can see their "truths" as perspectives, not monopolies on the one "right" way to view an issue. Counselors can then imagine alternate perspectives, ones that are informed by other gender, ethnic, social class, sexual orientation, and religious viewpoints.

History of the Term Culture

Culture is an often-used, yet elusive, term. The earliest known use of the word referred to care for the earth (e.g., "culturing the soil") so that it would produce (Dictionary.com, 2012). The extension of the term to human customs is credited to the Roman writer and orator Cicero, who wrote of the "culture of the soul," that is, taking care to live well in general. Thus, culture came to refer to the human creation of ways to live well through establishing social norms, roles, and customs.

Through the years, culture became associated with the notion of civilization itself, until in 1871 Edward Tylor, one of the great early anthropologists, offered an inclusive definition of the term: the "capabilities and habits acquired by [a person] as a member of society" (p. 1). For Tylor, "knowledge, belief, arts, morals, law, and customs" were expressions of culture. The definition given earlier in this chapter is parallel to Tylor's concept of culture. Each makes reference to the human creation of ways of living well in community. Those means include rituals, languages, celebrations, and hierarchies in relationships.

Culture Broadly Applied

The notion of culture, in this book, is used broadly. It is not restricted to the traditional anthropological usage, in which culture is equivalent only to ethnicity. Culture includes the customs, norms, and values of nations, region, generations, and organizations. For example, in academia there is often a less formal dress code than in retail businesses. And in the military, strict hierarchy and obedience are norms. In academia, equality and critiquing the status quo are norms. Culture also refers to social groups that are identified by race, ethnicity, gender, class, sexual orientation, and religion. Culture in this broad sense can be translated into such notions as youth culture, disability culture, school culture, male culture, gay culture, working-class culture, and agency culture. In each case, culture refers to how a group establishes behaviors and values that help members to achieve shared aims and therefore to live well. The resulting particular expressions of culture, such as accents, dialects, rituals, expressions, and family structures, are human ways of coping, each deserving consideration and respect.

This book explores culture as it is expressed through six cultural categories—race, ethnicity, social class, gender, sexual orientation, and religion. These categories are described in Box 1.1.

Box 1.1   The Six Major Categories of Culture

The six categories of culture defined here are neither exclusive nor final. For example, age and ability/disability are not explicitly included, despite their importance in counseling. Those two concepts are usually addressed in other areas of counselor education.

1. *Race.* Race is an especially contested and indeed controversial notion. What is uncontestable, however, is its power to affect human relations and individual lives. The most basic definition of race is *a group of people of common ancestry, distinguished from others by physical characteristics, such as hair type, color of eyes and skin, and stature.* Like other cultural categories, it is a social construction—the creation of people in a language, a time, and a place. As such, it takes on many meanings, depending on the era, the society, and the speaker. The notion of race is especially intertwined with power and intergroup conflict.

2. *Ethnicity.* Ethnicity, too, carries many definitions. Here it is defined as *the recognition by both the members of a group and by others of common social ties among people due to shared geographic origins, memories of a historical past, cultural heritage, religious affiliation, language and dialect forms, and/or tribal affiliation* (Pinheiro, 1990, p. 7). As might be seen, it also is an elusive and loose notion. Ethnicity matters for two reasons. First, it is a source people's standards, beliefs, and behaviors, even when they are unaware of its impact. Second, for those people from nondominant ethnicities, it is an external marker, one that defines their opportunities or lack thereof.

3. *Social Class/Socioeconomic Status.* One powerful factor in a person's aspirations and experiences is socioeconomic status, sometimes also called social class. Socioeconomic status inevitably influences many life roles and choices, including religious affiliation, gender roles, career aspirations, diet habits, entertainment choices, health, housing, self-esteem, dress, and recreation.

   Class is defined here as *the position in a society's hierarchy occupied by a person, based on education, income, and wealth.* This definition is external; here the status is given by others. Yet social class also is an internalized set of assumptions and an identity. Clients bring internalized expectations and self-images to counseling based on their social class. Counselors also need to know their own class-based assumptions.

4. *Gender.* Gender is often conflated with the term *sex.* Anthropologists, however, now reserve *sex* for references to biological categories and *gender* for culturally defined categories. Here the term gender refers to *a socially constructed set of roles ostensibly based on the sex of individual*s. Gender stems largely from the division of labor roles in a society, not the physiological differences between men and women. As cultural creations, gender roles can and do shift with social, economic, and technological change. Influences on gender are the formal legal system, which reinforces customary practices; sociocultural attitudes such as ethnic-based obligations; and religious beliefs and practices. Like all cultural constructions, gender is both externally imposed and internalized to a greater or lesser extent by individuals. The culturally alert counselor needs to be aware of both.

5. *Sexual Orientation.* The American Psychological Association defines sexual orientation as *an enduring emotional, romantic, sexual, or affectional attraction to either gender or both genders.*

Sexual orientation is a complex notion because it refers to a continuum of affectional attractions, ranging from exclusive homosexuality through various forms of bisexuality to exclusive heterosexuality. Sexual orientation does not imply particular behaviors. Indeed, the exact origins of sexual orientations are uncertain at this time. The American Psychological Association has declared that sexual orientation is shaped in most people at an early age and that biology plays a significant role in it. Being in a sexual minority can be a source of significant stress and self-doubt. Counselors have a particular role in reaching out to sexual minorities in order to provide advocacy and support.

6. *Religion and Spirituality.* Religion is also fraught with definitional difficulties. Religion is defined here as *the organized set of beliefs that encode a person's or group's attitudes toward, and understanding of, the essence or nature of reality*. By this definition, religion does not require belief in a higher power or a deity. Spirituality can be distinguished from religion by its locus in the individual rather than the group. Spirituality refers to a mindfulness about the existential qualities of life, especially the relationship between self, other, and the world. Religion and spirituality are powerful sources of meaning, esteem, and social life to many, but not all, individuals. Religion is an especially powerful force in American life, as compared to other industrialized nations. It is part of the culturally alert counselor's task to evoke clients' relevant religious and spiritual beliefs and practices, as well as any related communities to which they might belong. Clients can draw strength from religious and spiritual sources. Such sources can also result in maladaptive attitudes.

Defining Diversity

Diversity is a word that is heard regularly. Diversity is, most simply, *the existence of variety in human expression, especially the multiplicity of mores and customs that are manifested in social and cultural life.* When used with terms like *celebrate* and *embrace*, diversity represents an appreciation of multiple perspectives, a recognition of the contribution that many cultures make to a community.

In contrast to much of the United States today, there are places where diversity is minimal. Members of isolated groups are often unaware of alternative cultural expressions and frequently are surprised by and disapproving of them (Kegan, 1998). If group members only associate with their group, they might consider their ways to be "the" ways to think, judge, and act. But even within monoethnic societies, there is diversity.

For example, all societies have diversity in gender and sexual orientation.

When members of a group encounter other groups, they become aware of differences between their way of life and those of others. That encounter might be about religious beliefs, culinary customs, communication styles, or sexual behavior, to name a few possible expressions of diversity. An American in India becomes vividly aware of diversity as she or he walks the colorful, filled streets of Mumbai. An African American who moves to a largely Haitian neighborhood in Brooklyn, New York, becomes similarly aware of her own and other such expressions.

Before reading further, you are invited to check in on your experiences with cultural diversity by completing Activity 1.2, Encounters With Cultural Diversity. This activity is best done privately, so that you may be completely honest in your responses.

Activity 1.2   Encounters With Cultural Diversity

By now you have read about how pervasive culture is in the sensitive work of counseling. However, perhaps you are still not sure about the power of culture in human lives.

Review your life, looking for times when you were aware of culture in a situation. This may have occurred when you were in a nondominant status. Brainstorm as many occasions as possible. Then list up to three examples of situations in which you were aware of cultural differences between you and those around you. Remember, culture includes ethnicity/race, gender, sexual orientation, social class, and religion:

1. _____

2. _____

3. _____

Answer the following questions about one or more of the examples listed above:

- What were your automatic assumptions and/or behaviors during the situation? Were your beliefs challenged in any way?

- If you were in a nondominant or minority group, did you experience any discomfort in this role?

You might use the feelings you had in these situations to remind yourself of the possible confusion and discomfort experienced by others when they are in a culturally unfamiliar situation, such as counseling itself.

- What did you learn about yourself from this situation?

Perhaps it is at first unsettling to experience cultural newness; however, it might be exciting, if you open up to it.

Perhaps you had trouble coming up with experiences when you were aware of culture. That in itself might be an invitation for you to expose yourself to additional culturally different experiences. Try to turn any confusion into curiosity. This book aims to engender that curiosity and encourage such experiences.

Attitudes Toward Diversity

Proponents of diversity argue that it makes communities stronger. In that vein, novelist Salman Rushdie (1992), in the opening quote in this chapter, refers to "the transformation that comes of new and unexpected combinations of human beings, cultures, ideas, politics, movies, songs." Robert Kegan (1998) connects diversity with healthy organisms and societies in this way:

> Biologists tell us that the ongoing variability of the gene pool is a key to the health of any organism. . . . The more a family intermarries, for example, and succeeds at preserving the "purity" of its line, as has happened throughout history with several dynasties, the greater the likelihood of physical and mental debilities in its issue. Psychologists tell us that the single greatest source of growth and development is the experience of difference, discrepancy, anomaly. So it is for a society—an encounter with some new custom is a challenge for us to accommodate, to see the power of alternate ways of living. . . . These images . . . raise the possibility that diversity is best conceived not as a problem in need of a solution, but as *an opportunity or a necessity, to be prized and preserved as a precious resource.* (pp. 210–211; italics added)

The "precious resource" that is diversity doesn't always feel so appealing on a day-to-day level. Instead, many individuals see an encounter with difference as a "problem," in Kegan's word, that is a cause for fear and discomfort. A range of attitudes toward difference is possible. One doesn't simply like or dislike a cultural difference.

Psychological Processes for Encountering Diversity: Assimilation Versus Accommodation

Diversity challenges people's habitual, familiar ways of thinking. It can surprise an individual as she or he encounters a different religious view, or moral position, or child-rearing custom, to name a few examples. Individuals have, in a sense, two ways to encounter diversity: assimilation and accommodation. They can *assimilate* it to their current mode—for example, by deciding that what is different is repulsive—or they can *accommodate* it by rethinking their assumptions in light of the new information.

These two notions come from the work of Jean Piaget (e.g., Piaget & Inhelder, 1969). Of the two, assimilation is easier. Psychological assimilation can be defined as *the process of incorporating objects, knowledge or new events into existing schemes that are compatible with what one already knows* (Psychology Glossary, 2012). In assimilation, when individuals are faced with new information, they make sense of this information by referring to information processed and learned previously. Thus, a child may fit all men into the category "Daddy." She or he is trying to fit the new information into the understanding that she or he already has. In sum, assimilation is the viewing of experience through familiar lenses.

Assimilation is adaptive. If, in early summer, a hiker comes across a mother bear with her cubs in the woods, it is adaptive to assimilate quickly with a thought such as, "This is dangerous. I should flee." Humans are hard-wired to assimilate in this way in order to make life predictable at times, especially when encountering situations that might be dangerous.

However, overassimilation, that is, trying to fit all unfamiliar or uncomfortable phenomena into one's current lenses, is maladaptive. This is exemplified by the person who stereotypes as a means of easily identifying "the other." Unexamined prejudice of any kind is a form of overassimilation. Overassimilation may damage relationships, for example, when a father rejects his daughter because she is a lesbian. His old assimilation of what is right and wrong in human sexual expression cannot accommodate the possibility that his daughter's sexual orientation might be a positive, natural expression of her attractions. Diversity is therefore dangerous to him. He has only assimilated the data on his daughter's homosexuality to his current way of knowing. The result of such overassimilation would likely be a rift in the family, increased emotional distancing, and isolation for both her and him.

By contrast, appreciation of diversity might be considered an act of mental *accommodation* to newness. Accommodation can most simply be defined as *the mental process of modifying existing cognitive understandings so that new information can be included.* To make sense of some new information, a person who accommodates actually adjusts the mental schema she or he already has in order to make room for new information. In relation to diversity, accommodation is needed so that individuals can recognize rich differences in human expression and characteristics, even when it is somewhat uncomfortable to do so. Mary Belenky, Blythe Clinchy, Nancy Goldberger, and Jill Tarule (1997), in their landmark study of ways of knowing, found that those who could accommodate diversity were able to pause in their thinking process to weigh the value of a phenomenon before judging it. One aim of the multicultural movement, and of this book, is to encourage such pausing before making assimilations.

This section closes with a personal activity. You are invited to complete Activity 1.3, Attitudes Toward Difference, to help you appreciate a continuum in positions on difference.

Activity 1.3 Attitudes Toward Difference

Below are eight possible responses to cultural difference. Read through each and, in the spaces at the bottom, name a cultural group that is not your own. Then respond to the three questions below.

Repulsion	People who are different in this way are strange and aversive. Anything that will change them to being more normal or part of the mainstream is justifiable.
Pity	People who are different in this way are to be felt sorry for. One should try to make them normal.
Tolerance	Being different in this way is unfortunate, but I can put up with their unfortunate presence.
Acceptance	I need to make accommodations for this difference, since these people's identity is not of the same value as my own.
Support	I would like to act to safeguard the rights of these people, even if I am occasionally uncomfortable myself. I know about the irrational unfairness toward them.
Admiration	I realize that it takes strength to be different in this way. I am working hard on changing my bias.
Appreciation	I value this diversity for what it offers society and I will confront insensitive attitudes.
Nurturance	This group is indispensable to our community. I have genuine affection and delight for this group and I advocate for them.

1. Name a cultural group that is not your own, whether that be an ethnic group, a race, a social class, a gender, a sexual orientation, a religion or nonreligious group, or a disability. _____
_____

2. Name your current attitude toward that group, based on the eight attitudes defined above.
_____

3. What does this exercise tell you? _____

Interpreting the results: This exercise indicates where you and others might have work to do to move toward more positive views of cultural others. The scale is particularly important, as it demonstrates that attitudes toward others are not merely yes/no matters. There are gradations in attitudes. Note that tolerance is in the bottom half of the levels. While the U.S. Constitution and civil rights laws require mere tolerance of some diversities, that is not sufficient for the counselor. The first four of the attitudes imply that there is something inadequate or even wrong with the cultural group. Even the notions of tolerance and acceptance do not require a counselor to fully understand the other from their point of view, to peer inside other cultures with respect, interest, and active engagement. The last four—support, admiration, appreciation, and nurturance—are positive in that they endorse the diversities as important for a well-functioning, growing society, one that is confronted by newness and made stronger for it. The last four imply that you will take active steps to be an ally or activist to oppose prejudice or oppression.

Source: Adapted from Riddle (1994).

THE REQUIREMENTS FOR BEING A CULTURALLY ALERT COUNSELOR

The preceding sections established some evidence for the importance of culture in counseling. You might ask at this point, "What is required to actually do such counseling?" The multicultural counseling competencies are presented here. They guide the readings and activities throughout this book. Specific counseling practices are discussed in Chapters 18 and 19.

The Multicultural Counseling Competencies

The basic competencies required for culturally alert counseling (D. W. Sue, Arredondo, & McDavis, 1992) fall into three categories: awareness, knowledge, and skill. They are enumerated in detail in Appendix A. While you needn't memorize these competencies, a counselor should be familiar with them in an overall way and be able to assess her or his competency in each area.

Broadly speaking, culturally alert counselors must have the following:

- *Awareness of their own cultural values and biases,* that is, cognizance of their own cultures' impacts on their choices, values, biases, manners, and privileges; comfort with cultural differences; recognition of discrimination and stereotyping; acknowledgment of their culturally based limitations; and readiness to seek further training. The readings and exercises in this book, coupled with other life experiences, can increase counselor competency in this area.
- *Knowledge of clients' worldviews,* that is, multicultural literacy, which consists of a reasonable knowledge of many groups and clients' worldviews as seen through the lenses of race, ethnicity, class, gender, sexual orientation, and religion, as well as the counselors' own negative reactions to and stereotypes of other groups. The readings in the subsequent chapters provide a foundation for understanding cultural worldviews.
- *Intervention strategies or skills* to incorporate cultural knowledge into counseling and advocacy

for all members of their populations, including considerations such as clients' language proficiencies, the use of assessment instruments, the ability to refer to indigenous helpers, the capacity to adapt communication styles, commitment to doing advocacy, and sensitivity to trust issues with culturally different clients. Chapters 18 and 19 present the skills needed for culturally alert counseling. Specific strategies are described toward the end of each of the cultural group chapters.

The first competency, cultural self-awareness, is an ongoing task, one that has been initially addressed in the Activities in this chapter. Cultural self-awareness is achieved through personal examination of how one is cultured in every aspect of one's life. Culturally alert counselors strive to gain an understanding of themselves and their work with culturally different clients (Torres-Rivera, Phan, Maddux, Wilbur, & Garrett, 2001). One aim of this book, especially of the Activities in the first few chapters, is to have you discover the cultural discourses that guide your thinking and acting. Two competencies in this area are as follows:

- Culturally skilled counselors are aware of how their own cultural background and experiences, attitudes, and values and biases influence psychological processes.
- Culturally skilled counselors are comfortable with differences that exist between themselves and clients in terms of race, ethnicity, culture, and beliefs. (D. W. Sue et al., 1992, p. 482)

The second competency, multicultural literacy or knowledge, will be tackled in each of the subsequent chapters. The following are two competencies related to knowledge:

- Culturally skilled counselors possess specific knowledge and information about the particular group that they are working with.
- Culturally skilled counselors understand how race, culture, ethnicity, and so forth may affect personality formation, vocational choices, manifestation of psychological disorders, help-seeking behavior, and the appropriateness or inappropriateness of counseling approaches. (D. W. Sue et al., 1992, p. 482)

In light of this broad expectation, a counselor might ask, "How many cultural characteristics and groups must I know about in order to be culturally alert enough?" The question is a legitimate one. Complete knowledge of every important aspect of all cultures is not possible. "Enough," to start, is a solid grasp of the ideas in this book plus some experience in applying it to the groups with whom the counselor is likely to work. In practice, counselors can extend their knowledge and test it in the fire of experience by having an inquisitive and open mind when they are confronted with cultural unknowns.

A reminder of the limits of cultural generalizations is in order at this point. Such generalizations are time-bound because cultures change. Old norms and customs evolve when they encounter each other in an act of mutual acculturation (see Chapter 4). Thus, Anglo-American culture has incorporated many African American elements in the past 40 years, leading to an incorporation of expressions, music, and attitudes about expressing feelings. The same might be said of the Jewish American influence on the dominant American culture through the arts and other public expressions of that culture. And some elements of lesbian and gay culture, as much as one can generalize, have changed since the 1970s in significant ways, while other elements remain stable.

An additional limitation on how much one can know about cultures is the fact that all generalizations must be qualified, as mentioned earlier in this chapter. Even if cultural knowledge were relatively complete and fixed, it would not apply to all individuals at all times. Such overgeneralization would, in fact, be dangerous. Counselors must walk a fine line between assuming that some characteristics are true for members of a cultural group in general and applying them selectively to individual clients.

Thus, instead of questing for perfect cultural know-how, counselors can aim to become relatively multiculturally fluent. They should know basic terms and concepts such as *coming out* (for gay persons), *marianismo* (for some Hispanic people), *the ethic of care/connected knowing* (for many women), and *filial piety* (for some Chinese people). Nevertheless, counselors will inevitably be looking through a glass darkly, in the Christian Apostle Paul's words; that is, they will always have an obscure or imperfect vision of their own and others' cultures.

The third area of multicultural competence, skills, is still the weakest area of multiculturalism (Rodriguez & Walls, 2000). Nevertheless, counselors must be ready to apply culturally alert practice immediately (Cates, Schaefle, Smaby, Maddux, & LeBeauf, 2007). Therefore, skills in applying multicultural awareness and knowledge must be generated, communicated, and enacted. The following are examples of such skills:

- Culturally skilled counselors are able to engage in a variety of verbal and nonverbal helping responses. . . . They are not tied down to only one method or approach to helping but recognize that helping styles and approaches may be culture bound.
- Culturally skilled counselors are able to exercise institutional intervention skills on behalf of their clients. They can help clients determine whether a "problem" stems from racism or bias in others . . . so that clients do not inappropriately blame themselves.(D. W. Sue et al., 1992, p. 483)

Again, these are general. They must be translated into specific practices. Those practices will be described in all of the upcoming culturally specific chapters as well as in Chapters 18 and 19.

SUMMARY

This book represents a challenging, even threatening, excursion into the frontier territory of culture and counseling. Counselors cannot bring all of their old supplies for this expedition into this new world.

The journey into culturally alert counseling takes counselors through three major territories: cultural self-awareness, knowledge of other cultures, and skill at intervening in a culturally alert way. The book will weave these three themes throughout.

This chapter has offered some basic provisions for the journey in the form of foundational definitions, opportunities for self-examination, a description of the changing landscape in the field of counseling, and ways of knowing that can fortify counselors when they are seemingly lost. Much of this material will be new to counselors as they discard the legacy of universalistic individualism and incorporate social construction into their thinking.

But much is unknown and unknowable until the journey begins. Counselors must also pack provisions of openness and humility along with cultural knowledge. Openness enables counselors to tolerate ambiguity, to discover exceptions, and to allow surprises to occur with clients. Humility helps counselors avoid the hubris of overgeneralizing and applying pat methods to solve complex human dilemmas.

Counselors cannot look at this landscape from afar; there is no way to know deeply but through experience. Encountering culture is not just an abstract exercise. Personal contact with cultural others is required, supplemented by reflections on the meaning of those experiences.

And one word of warning for the traveler: The map is not complete. Despite the great progress that has occurred in the field of culture and counseling, all is not settled. As counselors embark on the journey to cultural alertness, they must know that they ought not strive for perfect knowledge of cultures. They can be culturally alert without being completely multiculturally fluent. They must accept that they will always be looking through a glass darkly at their own and others' cultures. Nevertheless, counselors will be well supplied with the basic provisions of an inquiring attitude, great empathy, a "leaning in" to difference, an appreciation of diversity in human expression, and a willingness to examine their own standpoints while inviting those of others. The reader who can begin with those qualities will be capable of beginning the work of culturally alert counseling.

REFERENCES

American Counseling Association. (2005). *ACA code of ethics*. Alexandria, VA: Author.

Aneshensel, C., & Phelan, J. (1999). Preface. In C. Aneshensel & C. Phelan (Eds.), *Handbook of the sociology of mental health* (pp. xi–xiii). New York, NY: Springer-Verlag.

Belenky, M., Clinchy, B., Goldberger, N., & Tarule, J. (1997). *Women's ways of knowing: The development of self, voice, and mind*. New York, NY: Basic Books.

Cates, J. T., Schaefle, S. E., Smaby, M. H., Maddux, C. D., & LeBeauf, I. (2007). Comparing multicultural with general counseling knowledge and skill competency for students who completed counselor training. *Journal of Multicultural Counseling & Development, 35*, 26–39.

D'Andrea, M., & Heckman, E. F. (2008). A 40-year review of multicultural counseling outcome research: Outlining a future research agenda for the multicultural counseling movement. *Journal of Counseling & Development, 86*, 356–363.

Dictionary.com. (2012). *Culture*. Retrieved from http://dictionary.reference.com/browse/culture

Federal Bureau of Investigation. (2010). *Latest hate crimes statistics*. Retrieved from http://www.fbi.gov/news/stories/2010/november/hate_112210/hate_112210/

Freire, P. (2005). *Education for critical consciousness*. New York, NY: Continuum. (Original work published 1974)

Harris Interactive. (2003). *The religious and other beliefs of Americans 2003*. Retrieved from http://www.harrisinteractive.com/vault/Harris-Interactive-Poll-Research-The-Religious-and-Other-Beliefs-of-Americans-2003-2003-02.pdf

Kane, M. N., & Green, D. (2009). Help-seeking from mental health professionals or clergy: Perceptions of university students. *Journal of Spirituality in Mental Health, 1*, 290–311.

Kegan, R. (1998). *In over our heads: The mental demands of modern life*. Cambridge, MA: Harvard University Press.

Kochhar, R., Fry, R., & Taylor, P. (2011). *Wealth gaps rise to record highs between Whites, Blacks and Hispanics*. Retrieved from http://pewresearch.org/pubs/2069/housing-bubble-subprime-mortgages-hispanics-blacks-household-wealth-disparity

Lee, M. A., & Mather, M. (2008). U.S. labor force trends. *Population Bulletin, 63*(2). Retrieved from http://www.prb.org/pdf08/63.2uslabor.pdf

Parisi, D., Lichter, D. T., & Taquino, M. C. (2011). Multiscale residential segregation: Black exceptionalism and America's changing color line. *Social Forces, 89*, 829–852.

Piaget, J., & Inhelder, B. (1969). *The psychology of the child*. New York, NY: Basic Books.

Pinheiro, V. (1990). What is ethnicity? *Revista Farol, 2,* 7.

Psychology Glossary. (2012). *Assimilation.* Retrieved from http://www.psychology-lexicon.com/cms/glossary/glossary-a/assimilation.html

Riddle, D. (1994). *Alone no more: Developing a school support system for gay, lesbian and bisexual youth.* St. Paul: Minnesota Department of Education.

Rivers, I., McPherson, K. E., & Hughes, J. R. (2010). The role of social and professional support seeking in trauma recovery: Lesbian, gay and bisexual experiences of crime and fears for safety. *Psychology & Sexuality, 1,* 145–155.

Rodriguez, R., & Walls, N. (2000). Culturally educated questioning: Toward a skill-based approach in multicultural counselor training. *Applied & Preventive Psychology, 2,* 89–99.

Rushdie, S. (1992). *Imaginary homelands.* London, UK: Granta Books.

Sue, D. W., Arredondo, P., & McDavis, R. J. (1992). Multicultural counseling competencies and standards: A call to the profession. *Journal of Counseling and Development, 70,* 481–483.

Sue, D. W., & Sue, D. (2008). *Counseling the culturally diverse: Theory and practice.* New York, NY: Wiley.

Sue, S., & Lam, A. G. (2002). Cultural and demographic diversity. In J. C. Norcross (Ed.), *Psychotherapy relationships that work: Therapist contributions and responsiveness to patients* (pp. 401–421). New York, NY: Oxford University Press.

Suitts, S. (2010). *A new diverse majority: Students of color in the South's public schools.* Atlanta, GA: Southern Education Foundation. Retrieved from http://www.eric.ed.gov/PDFS/ED524086.pdf

Takaki, R. (1993). *A different mirror: A history of multicultural America.* Boston, MA: Little, Brown.

Torres-Rivera, E., Phan, L. T., Maddux, C., Wilbur, M. P., & Garrett, M. (2001). Process versus content: Integrating personal awareness and counseling skills to meet the multicultural challenge of the twenty-first century. *Counselor Education & Supervision, 41,* 28–40.

Tylor, E. B. (1924). *Primitive culture.* New York, NY: Brentano's. (Original work published 1871)

U.S. Census Bureau. (2010a). *Income, poverty and health insurance in the United States: 2009.* Retrieved from http://www.census.gov/hhes/www/poverty/data/incpovhlth/2009/table4.pdf

U.S. Census Bureau. (2010b). *State and county quickfacts.* Retrieved from http://quickfacts.census.gov/qfd/states/00000.html

U.S. Department of Homeland Security. (2010). *2010 yearbook of immigration statistics.* Washington, DC: Author. Retrieved from http://www.dhs.gov/xlibrary/assets/statistics/yearbook/2010/ois_yb_2010.pdf

Williams, K. (2003). Has the future of marriage arrived? A contemporary examination of gender, marriage, and psychological well-being. *Journal of Health and Social Behavior, 44,* 470–487.

Zinn, H. (2003). *A people's history of the United States.* New York, NY: Harper.

Appendix A

Cross-Cultural Counseling Competencies

A Conceptual Framework

[From D. W. Sue, Arredondo, and McDavis (1992)]

I. COUNSELOR AWARENESS OF OWN ASSUMPTIONS, VALUES, AND BIASES

A. Beliefs and Attitudes

- Culturally skilled counselors have moved from being culturally unaware to being aware and sensitive to their own cultural heritage and to valuing and respecting differences.
- Culturally skilled counselors are aware of how their own cultural background and experiences, attitudes, and values and biases influence psychological processes.
- Culturally skilled counselors are able to recognize the limits of their competencies and expertise.
- Culturally skilled counselors are comfortable with differences that exist between themselves and clients in terms of race, ethnicity, culture, and beliefs.

B. Knowledge

- Culturally skilled counselors have specific knowledge about their own racial and cultural heritage and how it personally and professionally affects their definitions and biases of normality-abnormality and the process of counseling.
- Culturally skilled counselors possess knowledge and understanding about how oppression, racism, discrimination, and stereotyping affect them personally and in their work. This allows them to acknowledge their own racist attitudes, beliefs, and feelings. Although this standard applies to all groups, for white counselors it may mean that they understand how they may have directly or indirectly benefitted from individual, institutional, and cultural racism (white identity development models).

- Culturally skilled counselors possess knowledge about their social impact upon others. They are knowledgeable about communication style differences, how their style may clash or facilitate the counseling process with minority clients, and how to anticipate the impact it may have on others.

C. Skills

- Culturally skilled counselors seek out educational, consultative, and training experiences to enrich their understanding and effectiveness in working with culturally different populations. Being able to recognize the limits of their competencies, they (a) seek consultation, (b) seek further training or education, (c) refer out to more qualified individuals or resources, or (d) engage in a combination of these.
- Culturally skilled counselors are constantly seeking to understand themselves as racial and cultural beings and are actively seeking a non-racist identity.

II. UNDERSTANDING THE WORLDVIEW OF THE CULTURALLY DIFFERENT CLIENT

A. Beliefs and Attitudes

- Culturally skilled counselors are aware of their negative emotional reactions toward other racial and ethnic groups that may prove detrimental to their clients in counseling. They are willing to contrast their own beliefs and attitudes with those of their culturally different clients in a non-judgmental fashion.
- Culturally skilled counselors are aware of their stereotypes and preconceived notions that they may hold toward other racial and ethnic minority groups.

B. Knowledge

- Culturally skilled counselors possess specific knowledge and information about the particular group that they are working with. They are aware of the life experiences, cultural heritage, and historical background of their culturally different clients. This particular competency is strongly linked to the "minority identity development models" available in the literature.
- Culturally skilled counselors understand how race, culture, ethnicity, and so forth may affect personality formation, vocational choices, manifestation of psychological disorders, help-seeking behavior, and the appropriateness or inappropriateness of counseling approaches.
- Culturally skilled counselors understand and have knowledge about sociopolitical influences that impinge upon the life of racial and ethnic minorities. Immigration issues, poverty, racism, stereotyping, and powerlessness all leave major scars that may influence the counseling process.

C. Skills

- Culturally skilled counselors should familiarize themselves with relevant research and the latest findings regarding mental health and mental disorders of various ethnic and racial groups. They should actively seek out educational experiences that enrich their knowledge, understanding, and cross-cultural skills.
- Culturally skilled counselors become actively involved with minority individuals outside the counseling setting (community events, social and political functions, celebrations, friendships, neighborhood groups, and so forth) so that their perspective of minorities is more than an academic or helping exercise.

III. DEVELOPING APPROPRIATE INTERVENTION STRATEGIES AND TECHNIQUES

A. Beliefs and Attitudes

- Culturally skilled counselors respect clients' religious and/or spiritual beliefs and values about physical and mental functioning.
- Culturally skilled counselors respect indigenous helping practices and respect minority intrinsic help-giving networks in the community.
- Culturally skilled counselors value bilingualism and do not view another language as an impediment to counseling (monolingualism may be the culprit).

B. Knowledge

- Culturally skilled counselors have a clear and explicit knowledge and understanding of the generic characteristics of counseling and therapy (culture bound, class bound, and monolingual) and how they may clash with the cultural values of various minority groups.
- Culturally skilled counselors are aware of institutional barriers that prevent minorities from using mental health services.
- Culturally skilled counselors have knowledge of the potential bias in assessment instruments and use procedures and interpret findings keeping in mind the cultural and linguistic characteristics of the clients.
- Culturally skilled counselors have knowledge of minority family structures, hierarchies, values, and beliefs. They are knowledgeable about the community characteristics and the resources in the community as well as the family.
- Culturally skilled counselors should be aware of relevant discriminatory practices at the social and community level that may be affecting the psychological welfare of the population being served.

C. Skills

- Culturally skilled counselors are able to engage in a variety of verbal and nonverbal helping responses. They are able to *send* and *receive* both *verbal* and *nonverbal* messages *accurately* and *appropriately*. They are not tied down to only one method or approach to helping but recognize that helping styles and approaches may be culture bound. When they sense that their helping style is limited and potentially inappropriate, they can anticipate and ameliorate its negative impact.
- Culturally skilled counselors able to exercise institutional intervention skills on behalf of their

clients. They can help clients determine whether a "problem" stems from racism or bias in others (the concept of healthy paranoia) so that clients do not inappropriately blame themselves.

- Culturally skilled counselors are not averse to seeking consultation with traditional healers or religious and spiritual leaders and practitioners in the treatment of culturally different clients when appropriate.

- Culturally skilled counselors take responsibility for interacting in the language requested by the client; this may mean appropriate referral to outside resources. A serious problem arises when the linguistic skills of the counselor do not match the language of the client. This being the case, counselors should (a) seek a translator with cultural knowledge and appropriate professional background or (b) refer to a knowledgeable and competent bilingual counselor.

- Culturally skilled counselors have training and expertise in the use of traditional assessment and testing instruments. They not only understand the technical aspects of the instruments but are also aware of the cultural limitations. This allows them to use test instruments for the welfare of diverse clients.

- Culturally skilled counselors should attend to as well as work to eliminate biases, prejudices, and discriminatory practices. They should be cognizant of sociopolitical contexts in conducting evaluations and providing interventions, and should develop sensitivity to issues of oppression, sexism, and racism.

- Culturally skilled counselors take responsibility in educating their clients to the processes of psychological intervention, such as goals, expectations, legal rights, and the counselor's orientation.

CHAPTER 2

Culture: Clarifications and Complications

Garrett McAuliffe

Old Dominion University

> *I think multiculturalism started out as a very noble effort, teaching people to be aware of other cultures, to be accepting, to be not so harsh in judgments, but it just seemed to me that it has become a kind of a doctrinaire, dogmatic, narrow way of looking at the world.*
>
> Robert Wubbolding, counseling theorist (interviewed by Zalaquett, 2012, para. 8)

Infusing culture into counseling is no simple matter, as perhaps depicted by the opening quote, which represents a debate about infusing culture into counseling. Wubbolding questions any reliance on a single-minded view of multiculturalism. His words must be considered. This chapter tries to present a nuanced, inclusive multiculturalism, one that has no permanent or simplistic answers to the place of culture in counseling. It is hoped that you will leave this chapter with a complex view of culture and its place in counseling. The following vignette represents some of the subtleties involved in culturally alert counseling.

A counselor meets a client, Katie, who looks Asian to him. The counselor then assumes that the client will be hesitant about disclosing negative feelings, obedient to family norms, and rather formal when dealing with someone in "authority," such as a counselor. The counselor, Daryl, proceeds to follow guidelines he learned when studying about counseling Asian clients. For example, he does not encourage Katie to pursue her career dream of being a speech therapist, since her family has suggested that she go into computer consulting. In addition, Daryl doesn't reflect Katie's negative feelings about her parents. At one point, Katie says rather brusquely to him, "This isn't working for me. You seem like you are speaking for my parents instead of for me. I'm not sure you 'get' me." Daryl is surprised to learn that she has been raised since birth by Anglo-American parents to be assertive and autonomous, to think for herself. Katie was adopted from her native Korea as an infant and raised in a New Jersey suburb in a largely European American environment.

The vignette demonstrates the danger of a counselor's taking an overly simple view of culture. To counter that possibility, this chapter helps you appreciate the complexities surrounding culture. In the process, you will gain a nuanced view of culturally alert counseling.

The chapter is divided into three major sections: Important Dimensions of Culture, Individuals' Relationships to Their Cultures, and Culture in Perspective: Potential Misunderstandings.

IMPORTANT DIMENSIONS OF CULTURE

While culture was defined in Chapter 1, you would not be prepared to work with the subtleties of culture without an introduction to additional dimensions of the phenomenon. Toward that end, the first section of this chapter is dedicated to further explaining the nature and impact of culture. Four dimensions of the notion of culture are discussed in this section. Armed with these understandings, it is hoped that the counselor will avoid simplistic applications of culture to counseling. Such was the case in the vignette that opened this chapter.

The four topics that warrant discussion are (1) the distinction between objective and subjective culture, (2) the individualism-collectivism continuum, (3) the invisibility of much culture, and (4) intersectionality.

Objective and Subjective Culture

A distinction can be made between overt, or external, expressions of culture and the mental, or internal, contents of culture. These two manifestations of culture will be clarified through the notions of objective and subjective culture.

Culture that is associated only with visible, concrete expressions, such as languages, art forms, dances, and clothing, is called *objective culture* (Triandis, 1994). This type of culture might also be called *surface* and *folk* culture (see Figure 2.1). Objective culture can be seen at such events as Caribbean Days, a Gay Pride Parade, or a Greek Festival: parades, costumes, and foods. In the area of gender, objective culture is what is most concretely associated with stereotypical men or women: styles of clothing and sex-typed activities.

Such manifestations are not permanent; they are historically and situationally located. In fact, often the visible manifestations of culture are revitalized versions of former, antiquated customs. Thus it might be with German Oktoberfest events and costumes or with old-time Appalachian handicrafts and music. Objective culture can also be quite vital, such as African American worship services, a Hindu temple for a local Asian Indian community, Cajun *fais do-dos* (parties), a Catholic Mass, or the social clubs of Haitian immigrants.

Subjective culture is of special interest to counselors. It is the culture that is internalized by its members. Individuals are thus enculturated to share norms, attitudes, beliefs, and values with fellow cultural group members. See Chapter 4 for a discussion of this concept. Subjective culture is often automatic, unarticulated, and may even be beyond the awareness of the members of a culture themselves. Examples of subjective culture include sexual norms (e.g., the relative restrictions of traditional Chinese, Middle Eastern, and Irish cultures) and emotional expressiveness (e.g., relatively high verbal and emotional expressiveness in Mediterranean and African American cultures). Subjective culture is especially important in the work of counseling because clients operate out of implicit norms and values that affect such crucial aspects of life as relationships, career behavior, aspirations, and support systems. Much of this book is devoted to aspects of subjective culture.

Individualism and Collectivism as Dimensions of Subjective Culture

There is a continuum in how much a culture values the autonomous self or, by contrast, the group. This is the second important topic that might deepen the reader's understanding of culture, namely the notion of individualism and collectivism (Williams,

2003). In some ethnic cultures, the needs and rights of the autonomous self are highly valued (individualism). In others, individual needs are secondary to those of the group (collectivism; McCarthy, 2005). The North American, Australian/New Zealand, and Western European cultures (sometimes summarized as "Western culture") in general value individualism, with an emphasis on rights, freedom, and independence (Hofstede, 2001). By contrast, the Latin American and South Asian cultures are generally collectivist; the individual defers to the group's needs (Hofstede, 2001). Collectivist cultures treat the social networks to which the person belongs and social rules for behavior to be primary. Collectivist cultures are often hierarchical, that is, valuing adherence to authorities, such as elders, husbands, religious figures, and fathers. They are also characterized by *high-context* communication, in which the literal meaning of words is less important than the social message behind them. For example, "Would you like tea?" for some Middle Eastern people is a statement of welcome, one that shouldn't be turned down. In traditional Chinese cultures, an offer of a beverage should first be turned down in order to show humility, and then accepted when offered again. Bargaining while shopping in some cultures is another example of high-context communication, in which a named price is not considered the "real" price.

The Invisibility and Depth of Much Culture

A third, and related, concept for understanding culture is its visibility or invisibility—whether it is *surface* or *deep*. Because much culture is not visible or obvious much of the time, elements of it must be inferred from practices and from disclosures by cultural group members. Figure 2.1 shows how an iceberg metaphor illustrates the levels of awareness that individuals have about their cultures.

Activity 2.1 asks you to name elements of your surface, or visible, cultures and elements of your deep, or invisible, cultures.

Figure 2.1   The Iceberg Concept of Culture

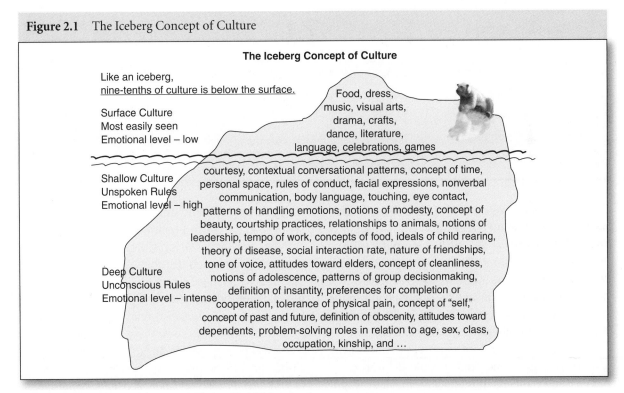

Source: www.homeofbob.com/literature/esl/icebergModelCulture.html.

The tip, or conscious, part of the iceberg consists of those dimensions of cultures that are at least partly known and can be named, such as a group's history, language, and customs. Thus, a Cuban American woman is likely to be aware of some aspects of the homeland, immigration, and life of her people in the United States. So, too, would a woman know something about common women's roles and history.

The undersea, or deep culture, portion of the iceberg contains much that people do not know but that nevertheless influences them. They might consider such invisible elements as merely "the way things are" (and must be): communication styles (e.g., direct/indirect, high/low affect, ironic/earnest), role expectations (e.g., children are to be unquestioning, men are to be strong), nonverbal communication (e.g., a smile indicating disapproval, methods of greeting), order of priorities (e.g., work preceding rest, relationships mattering over achievement), and formality/informality in relationships (e.g., self-disclosure being desirable with all acquaintances, even elders; compliments being required in all relatively new acquaintances). Other elements of deep culture are listed in Figure 2.1.

It might be obvious that deep, invisible culture is important for counselors to know if they are to successfully engage with their clients (Sue, 2004). It is this dimension of culture that will often assist clients to live well or deter them from managing their lives well. Counselors can help clients seek those aspects of culture that are below the surface, especially those assumptions that are maladaptive. For example, for a gay client who has internalized messages from her or his community that same-sex attraction is sick and/or evil, an uncovering and questioning of dominant cultural assumptions would likely be important. One way to do that is to use a narrative approach to counseling, which is discussed in Chapter 19.

Another benefit of counselors knowing about invisible culture is that such knowledge can deflect any superficial assumptions about others based on appearances. Such was the case in the vignette about Katie that opened this chapter. Similarly, an individual who looks "black" cannot be assumed to share all supposed African American cultural assumptions and characteristics. In addition, black persons can be Jamaican, Puerto Rican, Haitian, Nigerian, Brazilian, or Ethiopian, to name just a few groups. Culture is often not visible to the eye.

Intersectionality

Culture is sometimes equated with only ethnicity. Instead, culture can include the many discourses that influence individuals' lives. Individuals see the world, and are seen, through the multiple lenses of ethnicity, race, gender, social class, ability/disability, sexual orientation, and religion. And sometimes an individual belongs to multiple groups that have experienced oppression.

Often being a member of multiple nondominant cultural groups results in several overlapping oppressions, or *compound discrimination*. Oppressions, particularly racism, sexism, classism, and homophobia, can occur simultaneously in any one person. This phenomenon is called *intersectionality*.

The metaphor of a pedestrian at a large intersection illustrates the situation of intersectionality.

Members of multiply burdened groups who are located at these intersections must negotiate the traffic that flows through these intersections in order to obtain the resources for the normal activities of life. This is a particularly dangerous task when the traffic of the dominant social expectations, norms, and opportunities flows simultaneously from many directions. At these crossroads intersectional injuries occur, when disadvantages or conditions interact with preexisting vulnerabilities to create virulent forms of disempowerment. For example, a woman of color who is a lesbian and who is poor must fight through a thicket of social barriers, including attitudes in her own communities, to gain respect and access to the things that matter, like jobs and social approval. Counselors must be empathically supportive of this daily struggle for some clients.

INDIVIDUALS' RELATIONSHIPS TO THEIR CULTURES

This second major section of this chapter on complexities surrounding the notion of culture addresses the varying relationships that individuals have to their cultures. There are three topics under this umbrella. First, individuals can go through phases in their understanding of their cultures (cultural identity development). Second, they may be more or less wedded to cultural norms (culture-centrism and cultural relativism). Finally, individuals may experience membership in a particular cultural group to be relatively important or unimportant (salience).

Cultural Identity Development

Cultural identity development theory can help a counselor understand a client's stance toward her or his, and others', cultures. Cultural identity development theories plot the personal evolution of the experience of culture through phases. Those phases generally show movement from a naïve relationship with one's culture through an integrated or multicultural orientation. It should be noted that those phases are not rigid; people typically exhibit ways of thinking from a number of phases at any one time.

These developmental theories are important tools for counselors because they are both descriptive and prescriptive. As descriptors, they help a counselor understand clients' current attitudes toward themselves, their cultures, and other cultures, including clients' attitudes toward the counselor herself or himself. In particular, these theories can reveal the basis for client self-doubt and mistrust of others or, conversely, cultural pride and openness.

Cultural identity theories are also prescriptive—they can point the way to more adaptive cultural identities. With the characteristics of later phases of cultural identity development in mind, counselors can intervene to help clients expand their cultural identities, if that seems warranted.

Many kinds of cultural identity models have been created, including those for race, ethnicity, women, gay men and lesbians, and minorities in general. Many of those models will be described in the corresponding chapters that follow. Because of the sheer quantity of different models of cultural identity development, a general model, called the Cultural Group Orientation Model, has been developed (see Box 2.1). The phases are here called orientations, to avoid the impression that they are hard, unified states. These orientations should be seen as general tendencies, with individuals being affected by situations as well as showing characteristics of other, proximate orientations. It is recommended that counselors understand the commonalities among the various models of cultural identity, many of which will be presented in subsequent chapters. As practitioners, counselors should know enough about cultural identity development to help themselves and their clients, if warranted, to be challenged toward a more complex cultural identity.

Box 2.1 Cultural Group Orientation Model

Orientation One: Naïve/Accepting

- Accepts the status quo
- Is unaware of own cultural position
- Is unaware of power differentials among social groups (e.g., "What do you mean? What are the assumptions of my cultural group? I'm just a human, like everyone else! We're all the same. I don't think about it. I'm just me.")
- Often characteristic of those who have had little encounter with other groups
- If in the dominant group, likely to think of oneself as "culture-less" (e.g., having no ethnicity, or treating one's gender, social class, sexual orientation, and religion as "the way things are")
- Could have disparaging attitude toward other groups with whom one might have slight contact
- Might have self-deprecating attitude toward own group

Orientation Two: Encountering

- Initial meaningful contact with other group(s) through personal or vicarious experience (e.g., media)
- Beginning awareness that personal history can affect one's assumptions and beliefs
- Beginning awareness of power and status disparities among cultural groups in one's society
- Accepts disparities among groups

Orientation Three: Immersed

- Active exploration of one's cultural identity
- Immersion in cultural activities, reading about the culture, celebration of the group's present or past struggles against injustice; interest in cultural styles and customs (e.g., "I now realize how some assumptions I've made about being a woman are limiting and yet many can be empowering"; "As a male, I realize that I have engaged in many stereotypical behaviors, ones that cause me to miss a lot")
- Often mystification about or denigration of other groups at this stage (Intolerant version: "I don't understand why those people have to talk so loudly. We always keep conversations private"; "I can't believe that they put earrings in children's ears! How weird!"; "Men are so aggressive and self-centered")
- Can become stuck in this phase

Orientation Four: Reflective

- Able to stand back from, or take a perspective on, one's culture (Kegan, 1982)
- Recognizes the constructed story of one's cultural group, therefore is less likely to adhere automatically to cultural prescriptions
- Aware of value and strengths of one's group as well as the limiting elements in the culture (e.g., "There is an anti-intellectual strain in my religious tradition that I do not value")
- Can choose cultural attributes that one wishes to claim, reclaim, or discard
- Consistently faces painful history and/or current oppressions
- Beginning commitment to addressing social inequality, but little action

Orientation Five: Multicultural/Critically Conscious

- Seeks out multiple cultural experiences and perspectives
- Firm commitment to creating a multicultural self by engaging in multicultural experiences
- Dedicated to amelioration of oppressive conditions
- Is empathic, compassionate, and willing to act
- Recognizes effects of oppression on all groups
- Can see dilemmas even for the dominant group
- Interested in instigating dialogue
- Open to one's own rigidities and biases and seeks feedback

Source: Adapted by Garrett McAuliffe, Old Dominion University, from the racial and cultural identity development models of Helms and Cook (1999) and Ivey (1995). It is further based on the cognitive developmental theories of Belenky, Clinchy, Goldberger, and Tarule (1996), Kegan (1982, 1998), and Perry (1970).

A counselor herself or himself should aim to achieve the most developed orientations in each model. At those statuses, greater appreciation of one's own and others' cultures is possible.

Using the descriptions of the five orientations, you are invited to complete Activity 2.2 in order to assess your own cultural identity development in a number of areas.

Activity 2.2 Assessing Your Cultural Group Orientations

Having now familiarized yourself with the *Cultural Group Orientation Model*, complete the boxes below by noting your cultural group memberships, your current orientation to each group, and one influence that membership has in your life. Then reflect on your experience of this activity and on what your tasks ahead might be. Finally, if invited, share your responses with other group members.

Cultural Group Categories	*Names* *A name for your current group membership(s):*	*Orientation* *Your current level of cultural awareness in each category (1 = naïve/accepting; 2 = encountering; 3 = immersed; 4 = reflective; 5 = multicultural/ critically conscious. (see descriptions in Box 2.1)*	*One Influence It Has in Your Life*
Ethnicity			
Race			
Social class, or socioeconomic status (e.g., upper middle class, poor, working class)	Of origin: Current:		
Gender			
Sexual orientation			
Religion	Of origin: Current:		

Comment on the following.

(1) What you noted while doing this activity:

(2) Some goals you might set for yourself based on this assessment:

Culture-Centrism and Cultural Relativism

In Chapter 1, the writer Salman Rushdie (1992) was quoted as saying that he feared the "absolutism of the Pure," as "throughout human history, the apostles of purity, those who have claimed to possess a total explanation, have wrought havoc" (p. 394). In its extreme expression, such "apostles" have engaged in genocide, as has happened in Nazi Germany, the Sudan, and, some would say, the United States in relation to indigenous peoples. In each case, whole groups of people were considered to have an inferior culture and therefore were superfluous. These are extreme versions of what here is called *culture-centrism*. An antidote to such culture-centrism is cultural relativism. This is the second topic in this section on individuals' relationships to their cultures.

It should be noted that all people tend to judge members of other groups from the perspectives of their own groups. Thus, seeing the world through the perceptual lens of culture is unavoidable. Although all individuals are guided by culture, the first three orientations in the previously described Cultural Group Orientation Model (Naïve, Encountering, Immersed) particularly depict individuals who are relatively unaware that their world is culturally constructed.

When judging the world from one cultural view is almost total, it might be called culture-centrism. Culture-centrism is a broad application of the notion of ethnocentrism, which will be discussed in Chapter 4. In psychologists Matsumoto and Juang's (2008) words, culture-centrism is "a tendency to view the world through one's own cultural filters" (p. 376). In its extreme form, culture-centrism results in judging other groups' standards or lifestyles to be inferior. Individuals act in a culture-centric way when they treat their group as the center and all other groups as satellites. Culture-centrism does not refer only to ethnicity. Individuals can also construct their experience through the lenses of gender, social class, religion, ability, age, and sexual orientation.

Some level of culture-centrism cannot be avoided because it is a consequence of enculturation. People learn from birth to make sense through culture, as parents and others demonstrate or instruct individuals in norms, manners, beliefs, and other guidelines. As a consequence, members of all groups share common perceptions about what is good and bad, attractive or unattractive, desirable or undesirable, worth attaining or not. That process helps them adapt to their social and physical environments.

However, such enculturation has a negative dimension. Because cultures communicate what is good and desirable to their members (i.e., the in-group), those members often use their culturally based standards to judge other groups (out-groups). Judgments by in-group members about the ways of out-groups are frequently negative. A danger lies in the fact that such judgments are treated as objective facts. People are frequently oblivious to the ultimate subjectivity of their cultural filters. They do not recognize their ethnicity, sexual orientation, religion, ability, social class, age group, and gender as the source of a "story" that could be different. By contrast, one's culture-centered story can be recognized as one narrative among many about how to live. If instead culture is treated as "the way things are," it might be called *received knowledge* (Belenky et al., 1996), that is, an accepted set of lenses that a person has inherited without questioning it.

A culturally alert counselor would need to go through a process of de-centering from her or his own cultural assumptions in order to have a more multicultural, and therefore less culture-centric, perspective to help clients. De-centering involves the process of taking one's culture as one perspective among many. The more culturally de-centered individuals are, the more aware they are of experiencing others and themselves through their own cultural lenses. With that awareness, the person can try to bracket (mentally set it aside for the moment) her or his cultural filters on the world and consider other perspectives. Matsumoto and Juang (2008) propose a three-step approach to cultural de-centering:

1. *Awareness:* recognizing one's own culture and acknowledging that it is likely to be one's default view

2. *Learning* about other cultures

3. *Vigilance:* making a constant effort to question one's cultural assumptions

Activity 2.3 guides you to examine how you have constructed some of your assumptions—through a culture-centered lens or through a more intentional choice of attitudes, beliefs, values, and behaviors.

Goals: To help individuals authorize their own meanings and standards, with awareness of their enculturation, rather than be ethnocentrically bound to received cultural perspectives.

Walt Whitman, the 19th century American writer, wrote, in his poem *Leaves of Grass*:

> Re-examine all you have been told at school or church [or at home] or in any book, dismiss what insults your own soul, and your very flesh shall be a great poem.

This quote might be interpreted as asking individuals to create a self that can choose the cultural elements it wishes to claim for itself, as much as that is possible. Whitman encourages individuals, in a sense, to have a *self-authorized* (Kegan, 1982) vision of what they believe and value, and how they act, a vision based on careful consideration of what matters to them, a vision that is separate from the supposed "givens" of culture. In this vision of the self-authorizing person, all cultural conventions are treated as social constructions, that is, creations of a community at a particular time and place. Conventions are thus examined for their origins in and use for a particular historical, political, or cultural context. In the process of such examination, we can ask these questions of our assumptions, values, beliefs, and behaviors: Do they still work? Do they help? Whom do they serve? What shall I discard and/or reclaim? What new, more multicultural perspectives might I take?

In order to claim, or reclaim, your cultural givens, and perhaps move closer to self-authorizing them, try this activity. In all, it will take several months of searching, questioning, and reexamining for most of you to engage in more complete self-authorization in all areas. But you can begin here.

1. In the chart below, in Column I, name one belief, "truth," standard, manner, custom, or behavior that you have been taught (e.g., in school, at home, through religion) for each category. Review this list and jot down ideas of your received norms around any of the following: courtesy, personal space, facial expressions, patterns of handling emotions, notions of modesty, concept of beauty, tone of voice, concept of cleanliness, definitions of obscenity, gender roles, attitudes toward expressing sexuality, care for elders, music, food, language, interpersonal behavior, manners, family structures and behaviors, attitudes toward other races or ethnic groups, sexual behavior, alternate sexual orientations, career, patriotism, loyalties, religious notions, the nature of a deity, "true" faith, the good life, material goods, the importance of work versus leisure. Scan this list for specific beliefs and assumptions that you learned from your culture. You can also use the six cultural group memberships of race, ethnicity, gender, social class, sexual orientation, and religion as stimuli for thinking about beliefs and behaviors you have inherited. Take a risk: Name some strong, deeply held beliefs or assumptions (e.g., "Gay and lesbian people are somehow odd and unnatural," "The only courageous stance is to be an atheist") that you hold absolutely about how things should be or about what is true and right. You can also name some lighter, more superficial customs (e.g., "One must always be pleasant," "Everyone should have specific table manners, such as _____").

2. Then, in Column II, write an alternative behavior, custom, or belief, one that challenges the inherited one (e.g., "The gay and lesbian sexual orientation is natural, and I support and appreciate the presence of gay and lesbian people in our community"; "Agnosticism is not the only viable or valuable belief system; belief in God is important for many people and can be a positive force").

3. Next, review each initial inherited belief and each alternative belief, and in Column III, name your current view, which can be different from or the same as your inherited view.

4. In Column IV, name the basis for your current view. That might be simply, "I was raised this way" or "I met people who … and I thought…" or "I experienced … and read …" Remember, you need not necessarily reject cultural customs; you can instead reclaim them in a more intentional way, perhaps more generally as principles, not as rigid rules. Also, more fully reconsidering inherited conventions does not necessarily occur in the short time it takes to do this exercise. Consider this to be the beginning of a self-authorizing way of knowing.

5. In Column V, reflect on doing these activities. What thoughts and feelings come up for you as you consider these experiences and perceptions?

Column I	Column II	Column III	Column IV	Column V
Inherited/learned beliefs/customs	Alternate position (an alternative behavior, custom, or belief, one that is different from and challenges the inherited one)	Current view	Basis for your current view (how you came to it)	Reflections on doing this activity
Race/Ethnicity. What I was taught about race or ethnicity, including particular groups (e.g., characteristics of groups)				
Religion. What I was taught about religion/ spirituality (e.g., divinity, sin, morality, afterlife)				
Sexual Orientation. What I was taught about sexual orientation (e.g., homosexuality, transgender, bisexuality)				
Gender. What I was taught about gender (e.g., roles, rules, parenting, sexual behavior)				

6. Finally, below or on a blank page, write a paragraph on your reactions to doing this activity—your feelings and thoughts.

By contrast to culture-centrism, cultural relativism is the contention that human values are not objective and universal, but fluctuate a great deal based on varying cultural perspectives (Ayton-Shenker, 1995). Cultural relativism challenges counselors to remove their cultural lenses, as much as possible, and to empathically imagine how another culture works for its members in its environment.

The idea of cultural relativism emerged in the first half of the 20th century, especially due to the work of anthropologist Franz Boas (1928), who will be discussed in Chapter 5. It supplanted notions of cultural superiority and ethnocentrism that had in the past dominated both popular thinking and intellectual discourse.

Cultural relativism is a controversial topic. There are extreme views on either side. Some would have it that certain cultures are superior and even more moral than others, based on a supposedly objective standard. Others would propose that there is no noncultural basis for judging cultures. The full argument is not engaged here, as that is an issue for other texts (e.g., Kinnier, Dixon, Barratt, & Moyer, 2008).

The idea of cultural relativism is relatively new. In the recent past, a clear hierarchical arrangement of cultures prevailed. For example, Western society has spent the past two centuries trying to demonstrate the superiority of its culture, applying the very notion of culture or civilization to certain, usually Western, forms of human expression. Claims of superiority have been made, for example, for male, heterosexual, upper-class, and Judeo-Christian cultures. Dominating national cultures have made similar claims of cultural superiority, from the Nazis in Germany to the English in their Empire era. The notion of superiority has led to a form of cruelty toward others who are made to feel ashamed of their language, customs, appearance, accents, expressions, and clothing.

Further questioning of cultural hierarchy has come with the diversity movement because it has opened the fountain of cultural pride for formerly denigrated cultures, such as gay people, people of color, women, and working-class persons. Those groups have claimed their cultures as worthy and as deserving of respect.

Extreme cultural relativism can also be challenged. It is argued that one cannot be purely relativistic in the face of cultural practices that are deemed dehumanizing, demeaning, or cruel. Extreme examples include human and animal sacrifice, female clitorectomy, anti-gay statutes in many places around the world, and women's subservient roles in some cultures. Conversely, some non-Western cultural groups might object to Western norms for the drinking of alcohol, treatment of elders, and explicitness about sexuality.

Cultural relativism, as presented here, is a call for counselors to de-center from their own cultural absolutes and to consider the positive functions of seemingly foreign cultural norms. Perhaps Perry's (1981) notion of relativistic thinking might be a useful framework for considering the value of cultural practices: "I must be wholehearted while tentative, fight for my values yet respect others, believe my deepest values but be ready to learn. I see that I shall be retracing this whole journey over and over" (p. 79). This tolerance of ambiguity, which is part of what Perry calls "relativistic thinking," is a desirable quality in the culturally alert counselor.

Salience

The importance, or salience, of culture varies from person to person, especially in different circumstances and at different times in their lives. This is the third topic in this section on individuals' relationships to their cultures.

In particular, culture is far more important to persons who are in a minority or nondominant group in a community, including immigrants (Jones & McEwen, 2000). Recent immigrants are likely to have high awareness of their ethnicity in all encounters with the dominant culture. For example, the Egyptian taxi driver in Minneapolis might meet white European Americans most of the day. In the process of conversing, he will be aware of his ethnicity in a heightened way. It is similar for many African Americans, who might be the only person of color in a class or a meeting. Their culture becomes more salient in the situation as they note their and others' appearance, language styles, and assumptions.

By contrast, members of the dominant ethnic cultural group commonly pay little attention to the artifacts and expressions of their culture. A group of men at a staff meeting are not likely to be conscious of their maleness on this occasion. They must make a conscious effort to be alert to the gender discourse in the room. Because of their relative obliviousness to their culture, dominant group members are sometimes heard to complain, "Why do (women, persons who are gay, blacks) care so much about their identity? We're all just individuals." This attitude comes from dominant group members' ability to focus exclusively on their individuality because their cultural group membership is relatively invisible.

Culture is also quite salient during early phases of cultural awareness (*encountering* and *immersed* in the Cultural Group Orientation Model) that many individuals go through. These times of intense awareness about culture can be triggered by a person's encounters with bias, discovery of past cultural self-denigration, or other realizations of the presence of culture in one's life. Sometimes this salience is short-lived, as when a member of a dominant culture spends time with members of other cultures. Thus an Anglo-American Protestant couple might become aware of their culture when their offspring marries a Greek Orthodox individual (as happened in the film *My Big Fat Greek Wedding*).

When counselors are working with clients, it is important that they assess cultural salience. Clients who demonstrate low cultural self-esteem (i.e., a view of their culture as inadequate, inferior, or wrong) might need to discover cultural strengths in order to move toward a more positive perspective. Specific methods for helping clients with cultural self-esteem are described in Chapter 19. Counselors can also help members of the dominant culture discover the cultural prescriptions they are subject to and discover which ones are and are not working for them.

More on salience will be presented in Chapter 4.

CULTURE IN PERSPECTIVE: POTENTIAL MISUNDERSTANDINGS

At this point you might wonder what are the dangers and limitations of infusing culture into counseling. Such concerns are what Robert Wubbolding, in this chapter's opening quote, is partly referring to. For the sake of clarifying misunderstandings about the nature of this enterprise, the following topics are discussed in this third major section of the chapter: (1) balancing culture with other explanations of human behavior, (2) stereotyping, (3) exclusive emphasis on "minorities," and (4) language for cultural groups. In addition, at the end of this section, counseling guidelines for flexibility in addressing culture are offered.

Balancing Culture With Other Explanations of Human Behavior

Some counselors might at this point be crying, "Don't forget the individual!" The quick answer is, "Of course not." However, counselors must be wary of overemphasis on the individual, as there is an American cultural bias against acknowledging race, ethnicity, and other cultural attributes (Takaki, 2008). Culture can be a source of tension for Americans, a forbidden topic. One graduate student of counseling recently expressed the dilemma in speaking about race. She declared that she had been taught to see others, without prejudice, as unique individuals, thinking that she should ignore race. These were her words:

Here's my dilemma. . . . In the past, thinking about race and ethnicity was a problem, as they were used against people from minority groups. Then the shift was toward "color-blindness," that is, ignoring race and ethnicity in favor of seeing only the individual. Now we're going back to awareness of race and ethnicity. And now it is considered to be good, rather than a problem. Whew. It seems like a circle in some ways. It's hard to know whether it is good or bad.

It makes sense that this student might be confused, after receiving beliefs from family and community that culture should not be seen or heard. It is also refreshing that students are both puzzled and intrigued by this venture into culture, when so much of their learning has been about the primacy of the individual. There are reasons for that.

The Legacy of Universalistic Individualism

There are thinkers who advocate deemphasizing culture in counseling (e.g., Patterson, 1996; see also Zalaquett, 2012). The critics of the cultural shift in counseling have described the multicultural movement as a distraction from the essential work of knowing and helping the individual by applying universal theories of the ways people grow and change. These authors propose that current individual-oriented counseling models are universally applicable, without significant reference to culture. That perspective is here called *universalistic individualism.*

Historically speaking, the field of counseling ignored culture by assuming that only individual and universal factors mattered in clients' lives. In fact, the great hope of modernist Western psychological science was to reach beyond culture to discover universal laws of behavior. As a result, such universalistic notions as personality and mental disorder have emerged.

To a great extent, the results of the universalistic endeavor have been positive. A more compassionate understanding of mental distress has replaced the moral condemnation of emotional suffering. Depression and other emotional distresses are no longer explained as demonic possession, a lack of will, or any other sign of moral inadequacy. For those reasons, counselors might applaud the good that modern applied psychological science has wrought.

Yet, despite its contributions, this universalistic bias is embedded in an oppressive history, one in which the assumption that all human beings are the same was based on a limited premise, namely, that generalizations for all humans could be made from middle-class, Western, generally male culture. Psychologists and counselors talked to each other and theorized about each other and their culturally similar students. They then called their

theories and findings "universal." Few ventured into conversations with cultural others about their ways of seeing the world. But work in the fields of anthropology and social work, among others, as well as the political changes after the 1960s, challenged this conspiracy of the dominant group in favor of a declaration that all people are cultured and therefore must be included in the conversation.

There are at least three reasons for this shift. First, it is now acknowledged that clients view themselves and others through cultural lenses. Second, it is recognized that cultures are legitimate expressions of adaptation to particular environments (cultural relativism). Finally, it is now more fully recognized that some cultures are privileged and some are oppressed.

As a result of these recognitions, counselors might more easily see that social identities, in the form of race, ethnicity, social class, gender, sexual orientation, and religion, drive both clients' emotional lives and their relative social influence, or the lack thereof. Counselors cannot simply assume a mythical individuality. To do so is inevitably to impose a set of cultural assumptions on clients. Thus, a reliance only on traditional universalistic-individualistic counseling, such as classic psychoanalysis, "pure" humanism, or behaviorism, is inadequate, and unethical, for two reasons. First, some traditional counseling approaches are not helpful for many members of particular cultural groups. This latter point will be delineated in Chapters 18 and 19. Second, universalistic individualism often ignores social inequality. It fails to address the institutional and societal arrangements that contribute to human distress.

Toward a Tripartite Model of Human Experience

What might be an alternative to universalistic individualism? Is culture itself a sufficient explanation for all human behavior? Of course not. People have both a unique individuality and a common humanity. For example, a woman who is experiencing severe doubts about the viability of her marriage might become sad and depressed (universal emotions). She might be prone to depression (an individual factor) because of her temperament or unique past and present life circumstances. Her

Anglo-American, evangelical Christian culture might frown on acknowledging and expressing negative feelings, so she hides the sadness and low mood (cultural factor). Thus, humans are always, in a sense, "in" culture. In the case of this woman, the culturally alert counselor might evoke the concerns over the marriage, probe the client's religious perspective, note the proscription against acknowledging negative feelings while also reflecting them back to her, respectfully ask whether she would like to look at those issues, and perhaps collaborate with a selected clergyperson.

It follows from this example that in place of the universalistic model, a more complex, ethical, and accurate view of human behavior is needed. It is not a question of counselors engaging in either purely individualistic practice or culturally oriented counseling. Instead, it is imperative that counselors acknowledge all dimensions of human influence and meaning-making. Each alone is insufficient. To incorporate all of these dimensions of human experience into counseling, a three-part model of human experience has been proposed by Speight, Myers, Fox, and Highlen (1991; see Figure 2.2). This

model serves to remind the counselor of the sources of human behavior and meaning-making:

1. The *universal* qualities shared by all humans

2. *Individual* temperament, personality, and history

3. *Culture*

Universal human qualities include the common human emotions, such as love, sadness, joy, doubt, and anxiety. Individual dimensions include a particular person's learning styles, talents, and career-related personality styles. (Of course, these notions of individual differences are also culture-bound, rooted as they usually are in Western languages and in limited samples.) Finally, and of greatest interest in this book, are cultural group factors, such as styles of communicating, occasions for shame, expressions of celebration, rules for adherence to group norms, and the structure of social and family groupings and gender roles.

Culture can be addressed without excluding individual and universal explanations for behavior. Here is how one student handles the complexity of including culture in counseling without it becoming another source of stereotyping and without it excluding individual and universal matters:

> I agree that labeling people and stopping there is detrimental. However, one reason that we will probably never be rid of classifying people is that classification is an activity inherent in beings [who are] capable of conceptual thinking. In early times, the ability to classify was vital to survival and it still serves us well today in a number of ways. Ironically, some of the classification activity we perform on other human beings may be the result of earlier classification which resulted in prejudice. For instance, when I was a child in the 1950s, many black people were not admitted to a number of places that white people were. Now when I counsel an African American, I am aware that I *may* be dealing with a person who may have undergone this kind of exclusion or may have been raised and strongly influenced by people who suffered this kind of experience. As I get to know my client better, I will find out whether or not this is true without putting him or her on the spot about it, but it will be helpful if I am aware that this possibility exists and helps

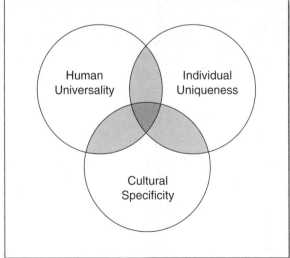

Figure 2.2   The Intersections of Culture, Universality, and Individuality

Human Universality

Individual Uniqueness

Cultural Specificity

Source: Speight et al. (1991).

me understand why this individual may not trust white people. My client may not be aware of how this kind of distrust may color his or her actions, but I will be able to work with my client in exploring this avenue of self-awareness. We should [also] not let classifying that person blind us to the factors that make that person unique. Differences exist within categories as well as between them.

This writer asks counselors to engage in a mental dance among many possibilities—mainly between the cultural and the individual. Such thinking has been called *dialectical* (Basseches, 1984) because it asks the person to entertain two or more seemingly contradictory notions at once. For example, John Bracey, director of African American Studies at the University of Massachusetts, was once asked whether a counselor should think of a person as black first or as an individual first. Bracey paused, and then responded, "Try doing both at the same time." Counselors are challenged to engage in such dialectical thinking (Hanna & Giordano, 1996) and might attempt the delicate task of holding at least two notions at once: the client as a cultural being and as an individual.

Stereotyping

The case for counselors being alert to culture has now been introduced. And the place of culture among other explanations of behavior has been discussed. However, there may still be lingering doubt about infusing culture into counseling. You might be concerned about the danger of paying so much attention to culture. Doesn't discussion of culture invite bias? Doesn't every individual have bias? How might bias be contained? A related question you might ask is: Isn't generalizing about cultures akin to stereotyping? We explore these questions in this section, which is the second potential misunderstanding about culturally alert counseling that must be untangled.

Dealing With Bias

It is expected that counselors, like all people, have some emotional responses when working with diverse individuals (Grant, 2006). It is not reasonable to expect counselors to have an immediately positive reaction to all diversities. As has been discussed before, humans notice differences, such as skin color, body type, religious orientation, mannerisms, sex, and dress. In fact, a basic psychological activity of being human is to classify. Humans resort to quick categorization so that they can be alert to danger. There is even genetic evidence that "outsiders" are perceived by humans as threats (Cottrell & Neuberg, 2005). As social animals, humans identify with their "tribe" and are wary of members of other groups. Thus, counselors need not condemn themselves and others for these initial, automatic human responses to cultural groups.

It is what an individual does with her or his initial response, how she or he acts on that response, that matters. Kegan (1998) proposes an approach for dealing with the immediate reaction to a difference that might be called the *first-five-seconds strategy*. He suggests that individuals not blame themselves for their immediate perceptions, whether those be fear of, distaste for, or attraction to a person from a particular cultural group. Instead, individuals should accept that they will have automatic responses, but then they can take responsibility for the sense they are making after the initial response—that is, after the first five seconds. In his words, "We 'make sense,' but we do not always take responsibility for it as made" (p. 206). Then counselors needn't pretend to be color, or gender, or sexual orientation blind, for example. They can begin to do the work of taking responsibility for the sense that they are making of their and others' cultures, after their initial, somewhat automatic response.

Managing Stereotyping

Bias is a negative predisposition toward a person or another phenomenon. Stereotyping is different from bias, but related. It is different in that it can be positive, neutral, or negative. The term comes from a printing process in which type was set in a solid plate in the 1700s, and it took on the meaning of an image that is perpetuated without change (Harper, 2001–2012). A stereotype is an oversimplified conception, opinion, or image that one has about groups of people, including one's own group. It can be negative or positive (e.g., "the English are unemotional," "women are nurturing," "the French are sexy," "gay men are effeminate," "Evangelical Christians are conservative," "Italians are expressive"). The key dimension of stereotyping is oversimplification. A stereotype may be generally, but not universally, true or it may be totally baseless. Throughout this book, generalizations about cultural groups will be made, based on current knowledge. You might ask: Isn't that an invitation to stereotype?

Counselors can counter the inclination to stereotype by recognizing that generalizations about cultures are always approximations; they are always inadequate attempts to capture some phenomenon with words. That subtlety must not be lost. It asks counselors to recognize the variations among individuals within groups, the limits of any generalization, and the potential ethnocentrism in stereotypes. Thus, culturally alert counselors would be willing to withhold judgment about groups and individuals within groups in favor of remaining open to alternative information. This cognitive complexity might be seen, for example, in the contrast between the following statements:

> *Stereotype:* "Women are _____."

> *Cognitively complex generalization:* "Many women tend to _____ for _____ reasons under _____ conditions. I must continue to experience the individual who is with me, as well as other group members, in an ongoing tentative fashion."

The ability to refrain from stereotyping while recognizing generalizations is a dimension of the aforementioned dialectical thinking.

Exclusive Emphasis on "Minorities"

A third potential misunderstanding about culturally alert counseling is the assumption that it is limited to so-called minority ethnic groups.

Some members of dominant groups, such as white European Americans, men, and heterosexuals, have, in the past, felt left out of the conversation about culture due to their perception that the focus has been on nondominant groups (Scott & Robinson, 2001). This is historically accurate. The past emphasis in the multicultural movement was on nondominant cultural groups. This stress has been a necessary corrective to the dominant cultural stories that have pervaded all aspects of U.S. society. The stories of nondominant groups were, historically, left out or minimized (Takaki, 2008).

Therefore, since much is already known about the dominant groups, intentional effort has been made in the field to present the issues of nondominant cultures and to describe the power differentials among groups. As has been discussed, however, everyone has culture and all cultures matter, not just those of so-called minorities. Counselors will deal with culture with every client, in some form.

Language for Cultural Groups

A fourth misunderstanding about an emphasis on culture lies in confusion about what terms to use for cultural groups. People have been known metaphorically to throw up their hands in confusion about what name to use for different racio-ethnic groups (e.g., black? African American? people of color? Latino? Hispanic?), sexual orientations (e.g., gay? lesbian and gay male? homosexual?), and other cultures. Humans constantly name phenomena. However, names are merely social constructions, that is, expressions of a time and place. Names have no direct link to the phenomena that are labeled (Gergen, 2009). Language is a set of conventions that counselors inherit, and those conventions are not neutral. They are rooted in discourses; there are connotations for all terms. Language carries power. Nondominant groups try to claim power through language by declaring their own terms. Thus, terms for groups change regularly, often in response to nondominant groups' objections to the negative connotations of the words used to describe their groups.

Consider the movement away from once seemingly neutral terms such as *mulatto, colored, girl* (for an adult woman), *Negro, Oriental, queer, retarded,* and *red man.* These terms were created by the dominant group to refer to members of non-dominant groups. They often were accompanied by connotations of being other, exotic, and/or inferior. Today, terms such as *LGBTQ, people of color, gay, developmental disability,* and *brown* are having their day. These, too, will someday pass.

Instead of becoming frustrated with not knowing supposedly correct terms, counselors can be open to the evolving, fluid nature of language. They must recognize that those who are in greater power often label the less powerful with terms that become negative. In practice, counselors can start by asking a client what she or he prefers to use as a cultural label, when and if the matter comes up. Counselors need to work toward using language that is preferred by the group and individual.

This section on potential misunderstandings about culture concludes with some guidelines for avoiding simplistic applications of culture to counseling.

Guidelines for Flexibility in Working With Culture

Consider the following three guidelines for avoiding oversimplified, rigid applications of cultural generalizations:

- *Recognize fluidity in culture.* Do not treat cultural concepts as essences. They are changing social constructions. Members of a particular cultural group create norms for thinking and acting, and members of other groups interpret those norms. And those norms change when conditions change and when cultures encounter each other (see Chapter 4 for a related discussion of acculturation). For example, the customs of immigrant groups change when they encounter other cultures, especially the dominant one. Similarly, men's and women's cultures have changed in the past 40 years and will continue to change. Terms also change over time. For example, the word *queer* has been

reclaimed by many gay and lesbian persons, when once it was a put-down used by many heterosexuals.

- *Make measured, tentative generalizations.* Be wary of treating cultural norms as absolutes. Watch out for tentative generalizations about some people becoming stereotypes about all members of a group (e.g., "Asians always include extended family in their lives," "Anglo-American Protestants don't care about extended family," "Men are all competitive and overly autonomous"). Instead, make reasonable hypotheses. These generalizations can then be treated as probabilities, not certainties, because, in Marger's (2011) words, "we cannot predict the behavior of any single individual or event" (p. 8). For example, men are generally taller than women, but some men are shorter than some women.

- *Adapt traditional counseling theories to cultures, but do so flexibly.* Clemmont Vontress (2003), the noted counselor, educator, and writer, warns about "groupism," that is, the attempt to uniformly match counseling with culture. To paraphrase Vontress, trying to develop a theory for a specific group of people seems like groupism, if not racism. In order to have a people theory, one must agree that people are essentially the same. However, people are forced to adapt to their environments. The environmental adaptation necessarily causes cultural differences. As they move from one environment to another, they must readapt, so to speak. Environmental conditions create cultural change.

Thus, the culturally alert counselor would utilize traditional counseling theories judiciously, adding elements of indigenous healing and other culturally specific approaches as they seem warranted. There is no culturally specific counseling approach that is absolute at this time, nor is there a universal one. More on the topic of culturally alert counseling intervention will be presented in Chapters 18 and 19.

REFERENCES

Ayton-Shenker, D. (1995). *The challenge of human rights and cultural diversity.* Retrieved from http://www.un.org/rights/dpi1627e.htm

Basseches, M. (1984). *Dialectical thinking and adult development*. Norwood, NJ: Ablex.

Belenky, M., Clinchy, B., Goldberger, N., & Tarule, J. (1996). *Women's ways of knowing: The development of self, voice, and mind*. New York, NY: Basic Books.

Boas, F. (1928). *Anthropology and modern life*. New York, NY: W. W. Norton.

Cottrell, C. A., & Neuberg, S. L. (2005). Different emotional reactions to different groups: A sociofunctional threat-based approach to "prejudice." *Journal of Personality & Social Psychology, 88,* 770–789.

Gergen, K. (2009). *An invitation to social construction*. Thousand Oaks, CA: Sage.

Grant, J. (2006). Training counselors to work with complex clients: Enhancing emotional responsiveness through experiential methods. *Counselor Education & Supervision, 45,* 218–230.

Hanna, F. J., & Giordano, F. G. (1996). Theory and experience: Teaching dialectical thinking in counselor education. *Counselor Education & Supervision, 36,* 14–24.

Harper, D. (2001–2012). *Stereotype*. Retrieved from http://www.etymonline.com/index.php?term= stereotype

Helms, J. E., & Cook, D. A. (1999). *Using race and culture in counseling and psychotherapy*. Boston, MA: Allyn & Bacon.

Hofstede, G. (2001). *Culture's consequences: Comparing values, behaviors, institutions, and organizations across nations*. Thousand Oaks, CA: Sage.

Ivey, A. (1995). Psychotherapy as liberation: Toward specific skills and strategies in multicultural counseling and therapy. In J. Ponterotto, J. Casas, L. Suzuki, & C. Alexander (Eds.), *Handbook of multicultural counseling* (pp. 53–72). Thousand Oaks, CA: Sage.

Jones, S. R., & McEwen, M. K. (2000). A conceptual model of multiple dimensions of identity. *Journal of College Student Development, 41,* 405–414.

Kegan, R. (1982). *The evolving self: Problem and process in human development*. Cambridge, MA: Harvard University Press.

Kegan, R. (1998). *In over our heads: The mental demands of modern life*. Cambridge, MA: Harvard University Press.

Kinnier, R. T., Dixon, A. L., Barratt, T. M., & Moyer, E. L. (2008). Should universalism trump cultural relativism in counseling? *Counseling & Values, 52,* 113–124.

Marger, M. N. (2011). *Social inequality: Patterns and processes*. New York, NY: McGraw-Hill.

Matsumoto, D., & Juang, L. (2008). *Culture and psychology*. Belmont, CA: Thomson/Wadsworth.

McCarthy, J. (2005). Individualism and collectivism: What do they have to do with counseling? *Journal of Multicultural Counseling & Development, 33,* 108–117.

Patterson, C. H. (1996). Multicultural counseling: From diversity to universality. *Journal of Counseling and Development, 74,* 227–231.

Perry, W. G. (1970). *Forms of intellectual and ethical development in the college years*. New York, NY: Holt, Rinehart & Winston.

Perry, W. G. (1981). Today's students and their needs. In A. W. Chickering (Ed.), *The modern American college* (pp. 76–116). San Francisco, CA: Jossey-Bass.

Rushdie, S. (1992). *Imaginary homelands*. London, UK: Granta Books.

Scott, D. A., & Robinson, T. L. (2001). White male identity development: The key model. *Journal of Counseling & Development, 79,* 415–421.

Speight, S. L., Myers, J., Fox, D. F., & Highlen, P. S. (1991). A redefinition of multicultural counseling. *Journal of Counseling and Development, 70,* 29–36.

Sue, D. W. (2004). Whiteness and ethnocentric monoculturalism: Making the "invisible" visible. *American Psychologist, 59,* 761–769.

Takaki, R. (2008). *A different mirror: A history of multicultural America*. Boston, MA: Little, Brown.

Triandis, H. C. (1994). *Culture and social behavior*. New York, NY: McGraw-Hill.

Vontress, C. (2003, January 19). Groupism and multicultural counseling. [Message posted to the American University Diversity/Multicultural/ Cross-Cultural Counseling Listserv; no longer available]

Williams, B. (2003). The worldview dimensions of individualism and collectivism: Implications for counseling. *Journal of Counseling & Development, 81,* 370–374.

Zalaquett, C. (2012). *Interview with Robert Wubbolding*. Retrieved from http://www.emicrotraining.com/ resources.php?rPath=1&i Path=14

CHAPTER 3

Equity, Advocacy, and Social Justice

Tim Grothaus, Garrett McAuliffe, Mona Danner, and Lynn Doyle
Old Dominion University

I am a Jew. Hath not a Jew eyes? Hath not a Jew hands, organs, dimensions, senses, affections, passions; fed with the same food, hurt with the same weapons, subject to the same diseases, heal'd by the same means, warm'd and cool'd by the same winter and summer, as a Christian is? If you prick us, do we not bleed? If you tickle us, do we not laugh? If you poison us, do we not die?

William Shakespeare, *The Merchant of Venice*, Act 3, Scene 1, 58–68

T he opening quote is a poignant cry from a member of an oppressed group to be recognized as human. That seems like a simple task. But history is replete with tales of dominance and power, of subtle and obvious discriminations, of privilege, oppression, and persecution. The Irish writer James Joyce called history a "nightmare from which I am trying to awake" in his novel *Ulysses.* However, history also has stories of liberation and compassion. That is the history that can inspire counselors. This chapter is dedicated to the proposition that the future is yet to be written and that counselors have a role to play in its creation. Here is a description of the commitment to the creation of a just and compassionate future modeled by the founder of the counseling field, Frank Parsons:

Frank Parsons (1854–1908), often hailed as "creator" of the counseling field, was a tireless innovator and advocate for all people. In 1908, the year of his death, he founded the Vocational Bureau in a poor immigrant section of Boston. There, the youth of the neighborhood and beyond were counseled and mentored by a fleet of undergraduate volunteers from nearby colleges. Parsons's hope was that no person would be denied her or his dreams because of social class or environmental circumstances.

Less well known is Parsons's broader and lifelong role as a social activist, in which he took on the excesses of large corporations, promoted the ballot for women, and worked for the popular vote for

(Continued)

legislation. For Parsons, counseling was inextricable from societal activism. He used the lectern, the classroom, and the press all of his life to promote the interests of the disempowered. As a consequence, he was ousted from his teaching post at Kansas State University in 1899, although the entire junior class appealed for his reinstatement.

Parsons went on to write 14 books, and in them he called on his colleagues and others to commit themselves to social progress and to do so in practical ways. In his humorous style, Parsons characterized those who didn't work for social improvement as being "not developed much beyond the oyster stage." One of Frank Parsons's last acts was to establish the work of counseling. Advocacy for social justice was thus knitted into the original fabric of the counseling profession.

Over the years, many voices have challenged counselors to move beyond the provision of remedial services in order to attend to the conditions that cause or contribute to mental and social disorder. Frank Parsons was one of those voices. More recently, there has been an abundance of calls for counselors to "return to their roots" (Ratts, 2009, p. 160) by broadening their sense of professional identity and their skill sets to include addressing inequities and social justice concerns. Embracing a commitment to social justice is increasingly cited as an integral component of being culturally competent (Holcomb-McCoy & Chen-Hayes, 2011; Nilsson, Schale, & Khamphakdy-Brown, 2011; Singh, Urbano, Haston, & McMahon, 2010; Sue & Sue, 2008; Wilton, 2010).

This movement to infuse social justice efforts into counseling work also is promoted by professional counseling associations. The American Counseling Association's (ACA, 2005) ethics code revision task force included an emphasis on multiculturalism and social justice when they amended the 1995 code. This emphasis is evident in the current ethical standards (Herlihy & Dufrene, 2011). In addition, ACA and the Association of Counselor Education and Supervision endorsed the advocacy competencies developed by Lewis, Arnold, House, and Toporek (2002). The American School Counselor Association (ASCA, 2005, 2006) included advocacy and systemic change as two of the four themes of their National Model for School Counseling Programs and also published a position statement that advocates for equity for all students. The inclusion of social justice and equity into counseling practice is not meant to be something separate from counseling work. Rather, social justice is clearly connected to counseling efforts (Grothaus, McAuliffe, & Craigen, 2012; Lewis, Toporek, & Ratts, 2010; Ratts, DeKruyf, & Chen-Hayes, 2007).

Counselors' commitment to the field is often grounded in their desire to help others. In many beginning counselors' minds, such helping involves one-to-one or group emotional exploration and individual behavior change. That commitment is admirable. However, without a complementary dedication to social justice action and advocacy, counselors may find themselves to be unwitting accomplices in the preservation of an unjust status quo (Bell, 2012; Chang & Gnilka, 2010; Harley, Alston, & Middleton, 2007; Johnson, 2010; Toporek & Vaughn, 2010). While the clinical interview continues to be a powerful means for helping others, socially just actions that are described throughout this book and in this chapter will be required of counselors in order to ameliorate conditions that lead to client distress (Nilsson et al., 2011). The need for social justice advocacy to create positive and pervasive social change is demonstrated in the following story.

Box 3.1 A Parable About Advocacy

A counselor was walking home from work one day when she heard the mournful cries of an infant child coming from a nearby river. The infant was in peril, placed in a poorly constructed basket that was quickly taking on water. The counselor alertly called 911 and then proceeded to wade into the water to rescue the child. She had just secured the child and reached the riverbank when she heard more distressed cries coming from the chilly waters. She was horrified to see a steady stream of endangered infants floating downstream. A call was issued and additional personnel were recruited as rescue efforts ensued. Shortly thereafter, a temporary clinic was set up to attend to the children's needs. Volunteers were organized and worked in shifts around the clock, lining themselves up across the river to save the babies who were floating downstream with alarming consistency. Despite these efforts, some infants eluded the grasp of the valiant rescuers. One day, when the counselor who first discovered the babies showed up for her shift, she turned and began to walk upstream instead of taking her place in the human chain across the river. As she did, she told her colleagues that she was going to try to address the problem at its source by finding and fixing the factors responsible for the babies landing in the river.

The story illustrates the importance of recognizing that clients' histories, present statuses, and future development are "inextricably embedded in family, neighborhood, school, community, society, and culture and cannot be considered in isolation from these contexts" (Walsh, Galassi, Murphy, & Park-Taylor, 2002, p. 686). Many counselors have experienced this, witnessing someone in their professional care doing well in counseling sessions but struggling to sustain positive gains when they leave the counselor's office and return to living, working, or going to school in unhealthy environments or inequitable institutions.

This chapter examines some of the factors that contribute to inequity and the responsibility of the counselor to address salient social justice concerns. This charge to attend to social justice issues represents a shift in thinking away from the model of counselor as case-by-case responder toward counselor as preventer, activist, and advocate. It moves the conversation from one in which the counselor is to be sealed away in her or his office working with clients in 45-minute increments to one in which the counselor is also in the principal's office, the city council meeting, and the street—that is, anywhere that prevailing social arrangements privilege some and exclude or oppress others (Chang & Gnilka, 2010; Holcomb-McCoy, 2007; Nilsson et al., 2011; Ratts & Wood, 2011; Sue & Sue, 2008; Toporek, Dodge, Trip, & Alarcon, 2010). The social justice impulse stirs counselors to

go beyond an exclusive focus on clients' intrapyschic issues in order to do more than give a client who lives in a dwelling that is flooded with toxic water a weekly supply of "fins and floaties" and wish her or him well. Counselors are instead called to assist in challenging and changing the conditions that cause the client's distress (Martin & Robinson, 2011). As Whalen and colleagues (2004) observe, "Ultimately, counselors must consider the question of whether or how individuals can develop optimally in an oppressive culture. . . . Counseling must help foster an active commitment to actively challenge injustice" (p. 382).

This chapter first features two illustrations of the impact that the sociopolitical context can have on individual lives, followed by descriptions and discussions of key concepts and terms. It then addresses some of the concerns and controversies surrounding the role of social justice in counseling before closing with an overview of the perspectives and skills needed for social justice counseling.

THE IMPACT OF THE SOCIOPOLITICAL CONTEXT ON CLIENTS' LIVES

Two illustrations of social disparity begin this section, one on continuing racism, the other on poverty. Both are important for social justice work in counseling.

Racism

A recent *New York Times*/CBS News poll reported that 50% of registered voters believed that "white and black people have about an equal chance of getting ahead" (*New York Times,* 2012, p. A21). Interestingly, the front page of that same section reported the results of a study which concluded that lawyers, when given information about fictitious couples with identical financial reports, were more likely to recommend a more expensive and burdensome route for bankruptcy to black clients than white clients. The story also noted that, in actual practice, "blacks are about twice as likely as whites to wind up in the more onerous and costly form of consumer bankruptcy" (Bernard, 2012, p. A1).

Along similar lines, recent studies have found that African Americans experience high levels of race-related stress, African American women earn less than two-thirds the wages garnered by white men for similar work, and African American males face discrimination in the job market and in schools (Greer, Laseter, & Asiamah, 2009; McDonald, Lin, & Ao, 2009; W. A. Smith, Hung, & Franklin, 2011). So despite the apparently common perception that racial prejudice is no longer a hindrance to pursuing the American dream, there is documentation of the continuing effects of racism and other inequitable social and environmental conditions (Chen, Androsiglio, & Ng, 2010; Holcomb-McCoy & Mitchell, 2007; Sue, 2010; Trimble, 2012). Indeed, there is a litany of groups who experience discrimination based on their race and/or ethnicity, gender, sexual orientation, social class, ability/disability, and language status. The brief example below sheds some light on another combination of taxing environmental and social conditions experienced by some young clients.

Poverty

With income disparity at levels not seen since 1929, the number of people living in poverty has risen to almost 50 million—approximately one of every six Americans (Barrett, 2012). The consequences of poverty are many. Growing up has a robust link to dropping out of high school and also higher rates of unemployment (Howard & Solberg, 2006).

Not surprisingly, the number of children experiencing homelessness is increasing (Griffin & Farris, 2010). These youth have a higher incidence of academic failure, developmental delays, mental and physical health concerns, school absences, and behavioral issues while also garnering less social support and having fewer close friends than do their peers in stable housing (Gewirtz, Hart-Shegos, & Medhanie, 2008; Grothaus, Lorelle, Anderson, & Knight, 2011; Mansoo, North, Lavesser, Osborne, & Spitznagel, 2008). Many counselors who work with young people have encountered a scene similar to one experienced by the first author. Summoned by an exasperated third-grade teacher who was understandably frustrated with her student falling asleep in class, the school counselor learned that the child had spent much of the previous night on the move with his frightened family. Recognizing the debilitating effect of the context, the desire to blame the victim (or the victim's parents/guardians) evaporated and the need to provide more than a pep talk became readily apparent.

Despite these facts, Americans hear rags-to-riches stories of success from their earliest days. They are told that anyone can succeed, that only hard work breeds success, that "You can do it if you only try," and that "People are poor because they don't want to work or are unwilling to sacrifice." These refrains reinforce an "explanation" that places all responsibility on the person and neglects the impact of pervasive and powerful sociopolitical conditions (Goodman, 2011; Lewis et al., 2010). While individual responsibility is clearly important, the myth of believing that hard work cures all ills, irrespective of the context, falls short when considering the variance in poverty rate over time. In 1959, 18.5% of U.S. families were poor. The number of families in poverty dipped to a low point of 8.7% in 2000. Then in November 2011, the number was up to 16% (Barrett, 2012). These changes cannot be explained merely by individual initiative. It's hard to imagine that hundreds of thousands of individuals simply increased their commitment to work between 1959 and 2000 and then a decade later (2000–2011) so many adults just decided to quit work, thereby throwing their families into poverty. It is therefore impossible to explain shifts in poverty rates as stemming solely from an individual lack of effort. Rather, the sociopolitical context, which in this case includes economic factors, public policy, and social structural shifts, provides the keys to understanding changing poverty rates (Burnes & Manese, 2008; Gallardo, 2012; C. C. Lee & Hipolito-Delgado, 2007; Ratts & Wood, 2011).

SOCIAL DIVERSITY VERSUS SOCIAL JUSTICE

Appreciation of social diversity is itself a revolutionary idea. At other times and in many communities, diversity was often seen as an annoyance, even something to be shunned or punished. Instead, looking alike and thinking alike have been, and are, often valued.

Appreciating diversity is harder work than appreciating uniformity, as it is often uncomfortable. Embracing diversity requires members of a community to encourage all voices, especially formerly silenced and marginalized ones, to be heard. With such openness to diversity, what was once seen as odd and exotic becomes interesting and respected. The aversive becomes curious. Diversity appreciation means experiencing different languages, musical expressions, sexual norms, celebrations, and foods. It revels in variety.

But social diversity, by itself, is a limited notion. It refers only to the recognition of differences in customs, styles, and ways of thinking in a community. It does not refer to differences in power and resources among groups (Goodman, 2011; B. McMahon, 2007). Therefore, simple appreciation of diversity is inadequate for the broader work of counseling without considering the notions of social justice, equity, oppression, privilege, advocacy, and empowerment. These concepts are presented in the rest of this chapter as essential elements in ethical counseling work.

Social Justice

Although *social justice* is a commonly used term, no single universally accepted definition exists. In this chapter, social justice is viewed as both a goal and a process (Chang, Crethar, & Ratts, 2010; Jackson, 2008). It can be described as having three components:

1. addressing issues of equity and power by challenging perceptions, policies, and practices that are associated with inequity, oppression, and discrimination

2. promoting equitable access to the resources needed for each person to live in a safe and healthy environment in order to develop with dignity and to fully participate in society

3. fostering critical thinking and promoting proficiency for engaging in social change (Chang & Gnilka, 2010; Chen-Hayes, Miller, Bailey, Getch, & Erford, 2011; Constantine, Hage, Kindaichi, & Bryant, 2007; Dahir & Stone, 2012; Durham & Barrett, 2009; Goodman, 2011; H. G. McMahon, Paisley, & Molina, 2010; Nieto & Bode, 2008; Odegard & Vereen, 2010; Pinar, 2009; Ratts, 2009; Ratts, Lewis, & Toporek, 2010; Robinson-Wood, 2009; Spitzberg & Changnon, 2009; Toporek & Vaughn, 2010; Watt, 2007)

Each of these components is included in the following discussions of key concepts in social justice.

Social Equality and Equity: Access and Opportunity

Although the terms sound alike, a practical distinction can be made between *equality* and *equity* (Holcomb-McCoy, 2007). Equality refers to the existence of the same treatment for every person in a community or a society, irrespective of her or his social group membership. An example of a rigid application of equal treatment would be a math teacher who divides the 25-minute practice portion of her class by giving exactly 1 minute of assistance to each of the 25 students, regardless of whether they need more or less help to be successful. In contrast, equitable treatment would dictate apportioning time to each student according to her or his need. A mere emphasis on equality that excludes equity ignores the differences in readiness and access to resources needed, as Figure 3.1 illustrates. Espousing only equal treatment would mean giving each of the two youths the exact same amount of time and assistance to climb over the wall and move forward to the next task. They both have access to the wall, but not equitable opportunity.

While Americans cherish the notion of equality, this alone will not achieve the goals of social justice. With the considerable disparities in access, power, and resources that presently exist, to only treat everyone equally would certainly be an improvement over current conditions, but it would likely preserve the unequal status quo.

Simple equality only provides minimal access to an institution. By contrast, equity addresses the disadvantaged positions of some individuals and groups compared to members of the dominant group. Equity goes beyond equal treatment. Equity involves dismantling systemic barriers to success that are present in nearly all aspects of Americans' public lives, such as discriminatory patterns of hiring in workplaces and academic placements in schools, judicial sentencing that differs by race, quality therapeutic and medical services that are more easily accessed by those with money and insurance, preferential financial policies favoring the wealthy along with the predatory practices that affect those with fewer resources. Equity requires that all individuals have fair access to society's resources and the opportunity to use their access in order to be successful (V. V. Lee & Goodnough, 2011; Quijada Cercer, Gutierrez, & Rios, 2010; Wood & D'Agostino, 2010).

Example From Schooling

A good illustration of the difference between equality and equity lies in the public education system. Despite the fact that everyone in the United States has an equal right (access) to receive free, public schooling, not everyone has the same opportunities (equity) for an education that opens doors to a wide variety of desirable postsecondary possibilities leading to an economically successful future (Grothaus & Cole, 2010; Howard & Solberg, 2006). Middle- and upper-class students living in wealthy suburban school districts often attend schools with better educational facilities and programs, more highly qualified teachers, and higher per-pupil expenditures than their lower-class counterparts who live in lower-income districts (Amatea & West-Olatunji, 2007; Dahir & Stone, 2012; Holcomb-McCoy, 2007).

Example From Higher Education

Higher education provides another example of the distinction between equality and equity. Simple equality means allowing underprepared college students to be admitted (access) to universities. However, equity requires further actions to ensure genuine opportunity. Those actions address differential readiness among students. So in addition to working to promote more equitable distribution of educational resources systemically, it may involve providing tutoring and career counseling at the local level. The absence of such services contributes to student attrition. In the words of a common community college expression, "The open door (open admissions) should not be a revolving door."

Other Examples

Counselors in all settings can promote equity through, for example, working with low-income clients, challenging discriminatory policies and practices that preserve advantages for some and erect barriers for others, and providing support for nondominant group members (such as supporting LGBT students in a high school through sponsoring a gay–straight alliance organization). In addition, they can support equitable actions such as civil rights legislation, anti–hate crime laws, affirmative action, women's centers, tutoring programs, financial aid, and disabilities services.

Oppression

The third key concept as it relates to social justice is oppression. Oppression is the condition of being subject to another group's power. Oppression can be very obvious, such as having Jews wear stars to identify themselves in Nazi Germany of the 1930s, or it can be subtle, such as telling heterosexist jokes or using slurs for nondominant groups. Those jokes and slurs have such power only because they are backed up by a larger condition of oppression.

Examples of commonly accepted oppressive beliefs at one time included women's inability to vote or participate in sports and the need to keep persons of different races separated in schools, the armed services, or marriages. Current versions of the way things are or should be could include dominant groups' perspectives about who has a right to marry and also the "normal and acceptable" ways of identifying and expressing one's gender (Wilton, 2010).

Individual Level

On an individual level, oppression may take either active or passive forms. It may be expressed by a person or group actively discriminating against a member of another cultural group. It can also be passive, such as a person hearing a slur based on race, gender, class, or sexual orientation and choosing to say nothing (Holcomb-McCoy, 2007).

Institutional Level

At the institutional level, oppression is apparent in explicit and implicit policies and practices, including those that contribute to the disproportionately low numbers of Latina/o and African American students in honors classes and the disproportionately high percentage of students from wealthy families enrolled at the highest-ranked colleges and universities (Chen-Hayes et al., 2011; Grothaus, Crum, & James, 2010; New American Alliance, 2009; Ponterotto, Utsey, & Pedersen, 2006).

Societal Level

The societal manifestations of oppression are discernible in the dominant norms and values, such as the insistence on the assumption that male standards of communication, language, and competition, are used to represent women and men; and the phenomenon of a particular religion's prayers, traditions, hymns, and holidays being preeminent in public calendars and events (Sue & Sue, 2008; Virginia School Counselor Association [VSCA], 2008).

A look around one's own environment can reveal subtle and not-so-subtle forms of the marginalization of nondominant groups (Pinar, 2009). Who are the janitors, the housekeepers, the landscape workers, the kitchen staff, or the fast-food servers at schools, agencies, colleges, businesses, and hospitals? Do they tend to be members of a particular ethnic group and come from families with fewer economic resources? And who are a disproportionate majority of CEOs, members of congress, dentists, and coaches of professional and major college sports? Oppression exists across cultural identities, and it can be actively or subtly expressed in various forms, such as racism, heterosexism, classism, sexism, and ableism.

Oppressive beliefs and actions are often unintentionally propagated by well-meaning counselors and others who may see themselves as compassionate, caring, and decent people (Love, 2010; Young, 2010). Counselors' failure to challenge oppression is usually not born of an active desire to promulgate these debilitating beliefs, policies, and practices. Counselors often choose to stay comfortable with what they know, which is the worldview promoted in most communities and by the media and educational, religious, and governmental institutions (L. Jackson, 2010). When counselors do this, they choose not to see the oppressions that permeate their institutions and society (Kumashiro, 2009). A counselor's choice not to act or to "rock the boat" is not a neutral act; it is an endorsement of an inequitable status quo (Bell, 2012; Chang & Gnilka, 2010; Harley et al., 2007; Johnson, 2010; Toporek & Vaughn, 2010; VSCA, 2008).

Examples of Oppression for Specific Groups

To assist you in making the invisible oppression visible, illustrations of oppression across a number of cultural groups are provided in Activity 3.1. Most of the oppressive conditions listed are not the result of legal suppression or explicit police force; instead, they are more subtle manifestations of oppressive attitudes and misuse of power. These oppressions contrast to the official U.S. ethic of equal opportunity. Culturally alert counselors can work to ameliorate each element, especially in the settings in which they work.

Are all of the circumstances in Activity 3.1 coincidental? They are obviously not all due to mere chance, which leads to at least two possible conclusions. One is that the disparities are due to a group's inferiority. The other is that they are due to oppression. The inferiority explanation posits that there is some kind of inherent deficient characteristic in groups, either genetic or cultural. Those arguments were attempted by the eugenics movement of the late 19th and early 20th centuries and by the assimilation movement later in the 20th century, as will be discussed in Chapter 5. The genetic explanation has been thoroughly discredited. Instead, the notion of oppression explains disparities among groups.

Oppression can also be internal. Next, the special case of internalized oppression is discussed.

Internalized Oppression

Up to this point, external oppression has been described. Internal oppression must also be accounted for, as it affects clients' hopes and expectations. Given the countless messages, norms, and policies asserting the superiority of the dominant culture, members of nondominant groups can come to assume that they lack power and/or are inferior in relation to a dominant group in some or all domains (Jun, 2010; Ponterotto et al., 2006). Those domains include academic ability, intelligence, language and accents, physical beauty, certain skills, athletic prowess, and customs. Internalized oppression can result in a sense of

hopelessness, a belief that trying against the odds is useless. For example, living with racism can take a personal psychological toll on African Americans as they experience the indignities of subtle and overt discrimination in their daily lives in public spaces, schools, and workplaces (Greer et al., 2009; McDonald et al., 2009; Ratts, 2009; W. A. Smith et al., 2011). Such experience can be internalized. In fact, as early as first grade, children begin to restrict their occupational aspirations based on gender, socioeconomic resources, and race or ethnicity (M. Jackson & Grant, 2004).

Subtle Oppression: Microaggressions

A final oppression-related concept is microaggression. Not all oppression is overt or intentional. In fact, members of nondominant groups regularly experience "microaggressions" (Pierce, Carew, Pierce-Gonzalez, & Wills, 1977; Sue, 2010), that is, daily and disconcerting reminders of being treated differently because of their group membership. Such microaggressions include downplaying the existence of racial bias, seeing a person as being incapable because of gender, assuming an Asian American is foreign-born, pathologizing cultural communication styles (e.g., "Why do blacks have to be so loud?"), and using American Indian mascots and symbols (Sue, 2010). Indeed, counselors' perceptions have been found to be biased, believing members of nondominant groups have less potential than their peers from dominant groups (Auwarter & Aruguete, 2008; Rollins, 2003).

The notion of microaggression also extends to the inability to see the social foundation of inequity. It might consist of seeing oneself as "color-blind" or making the assertion that "It is enough that I treat everyone equally." While they may be well intended, the following claims minimize or deny the experiences of nondominant cultural group members: "I don't see color (or gender or sexual orientation, etc.); I see people" or "I'm not heterosexist; I have a friend who is a lesbian." If made exclusively, they signal an unwillingness to acknowledge one's role in perpetuating an unjust system (Goodman, 2011;

In the table below, read the examples of oppression for six nondominant groups. Then note whether you understand the claim made about oppression, and, after that, decide whether you agree or not or are undecided about these claims. At the end of the activity, write down issues you need to know more about, issues you disagree with, and what you can do to increase your understanding of these specific issues.

Overall Consequence of Oppression	People of Color	Old People	Poor People	Gays and Lesbians	Women	Non-Christians
Isolation	Housing redlining and de facto segregation of schools White flight Understand?____ Agree?____	Being shut-ins Not in traditional workplaces for socialization Understand?____ Agree?____	Gentrification Housing projects No transportation Understand?____ Agree?____	Forced to stay closeted Unsafe in some places Can't easily adopt children Understand?____ Agree?____	Being out alone is seen as dangerous Having responsibility for an inordinate proportion of both family and career responsibilities Understand?____ Agree?____	Experiencing *church* as universal term for religion Hearing only Christian prayers at public events Understand?____ Agree?____
Emotional Abuse	Attributions of lower motivation and intelligence Culture, language devalued Understand?____ Agree?____	Ignored Often ridiculed Talked about in their presence Understand?____ Agree?____	Blamed for poverty Considered universally lazy, prone to crime Understand?____ Agree?____	Seen as sexually perverted Publicly taunted Understand?____ Agree?____	Called pejorative names, especially for body parts Treated as objects Understand?____ Agree?____	Considered heathen and unsaved Understand?____ Agree?____
Sexual Abuse	Do not match the standard idea of beauty Some groups seen as oversexed Understand?____ Agree?____	Seen as unattractive, not able to express sexuality Understand?____ Agree?____	Considered gross and oversexed, untamed Understand?____ Agree?____	Accused of child molestation Ridiculed as not being "real" men and women sexually Understand?____ Agree?____	Rape (including date and marital) Objects in pornography and shows Incest victims Understand?____ Agree?____	Seen as sinful or exotic Understand?____ Agree?____

(Continued)

Economic Abuse	Overt and covert discrimination in hiring and in layoffs. Have to prove selves in job more than others. Understand?___ Agree?___	Victims of fraud schemes. Understand?___ Agree?___	Welfare/workfare regulations renew poverty. Low minimum wage = permanent working poor. Understand?___ Agree?___	Legal discrimination in employment. Often no access to partner benefits or retirement benefits. Understand?___ Agree?___	Low-paying jobs the norm. Paid less than men for same work. Lack of childcare accommodation for career. Understand?___ Agree?___	Can be subject to Christian holiday and celebration prayers and practices. Understand?___ Agree?___
Privilege, Status	Seen as intellectually and socially inferior. Their culture seen as "low". Understand?___ Agree?___	Non-income-producing, therefore seen as nonproductive. Understand?___ Agree?___	Don't live up to middle-class values of dress, manners, etc. Understand?___ Agree?___	Gay expression not as valued as heterosexual expression. Understand?___ Agree?___	Second-class to men. Often seen as subservient. Labeled as too emotional, weak. Understand?___ Agree?___	Holidays not known or recognized. No models of political leaders (e.g., U.S. president). Few corporate or other leaders. Understand?___ Agree?___
Threats, Violence, Intimidation	Racial profiling. Brutality. History of genocide, lynching. Trail of Tears, etc. Understand?___ Agree?___	Threatened by violence. Fear being out at night. Understand?___ Agree?___	Government threatens to take away benefits. No health insurance for care and fewer medical options. Understand?___ Agree?___	Public harassment in schools. Gay bashing. Heterosexism rarely challenged. Understand?___ Agree?___	Battering. Physical intimidation. Understand?___ Agree?___	Swastikas painted on synagogues, harassment of Sikhs and Muslims. Understand?___ Agree?___

After you have completed your responses to each item, complete the following:

1. An issue I need to understand better or know more about: _____

2. An issue I don't understand or don't agree constitutes oppression: _____

3. Specific or general actions I might take to increase my knowledge or understanding of any of these issues: _____

Source: Adapted from Harro (2000).

Miller & Sendrowitz, 2011; Robinson-Wood, 2009; Sue, 2010). Individuals from dominant groups should keep in mind the comment that can be heard at the end of a long day by some clients who are in oppressed groups: "I'm so tired from being [black, or gay, or female, or a person with a disability] all day. It is a lot of work." What is that weariness about? Being looked at because you are different? Being ignored in a classroom or meeting? Being treated as less able, less bright, less moral than others? Being uncertain about whether you were discriminated against in a job, classroom, or housing situation? It could be any of the above for clients from nondominant groups.

All of the above examples are often viewed as "just the way things are and must be" by some members of U.S. society. In each of these cases, the dominant group's values permeate the culture so that nondominant groups' values and views are seen as nonexistent or wrong. What interrupts this hegemony is to contest such assumptions. Counselors can open these topics to discussion and debate.

The related, and somewhat opposite, topic of privilege is discussed next.

Privilege: Invisible and Unearned

Privilege is the condition of a person having distinct advantages by virtue of her or his membership in a dominant cultural group. Such privilege is not asked for, nor is it obvious. It is not earned through individual effort; it is given by group membership. It does not mean that persons with privilege don't work hard to achieve their goals. It does mean that they have unearned advantages of which they are often unaware, including greater access to resources, opportunity, and power (Jun, 2010; Sue, 2010). Privilege is, in a sense, the opposite of oppression (Chang & Gnilka, 2010). While those enjoying the benefits of a privileged status may not recognize this, members of nondominant groups are often acutely aware of their nonprivileged condition.

Invisible privilege is a difficult concept for members of dominant groups to understand (B. McMahon, 2007; Watt, 2007). An apt analogy

might be that a smooth road (privilege) is not easily noticed; a bumpy one, however, is vividly experienced. So it is with everyday privilege—it is taken for granted as the privileged person negotiates the challenges of daily life. As a fish may not be aware of the water that surrounds it, assuming it's just "the way things are," people who have privilege often are unaware of the advantages they enjoy. One example of this may be the advantages accrued by being right-handed. Those of us whose right hand is dominant probably rarely consider the many ways our world is designed for us: desks, notebooks, manual shifts on cars, handshakes, most sports equipment and some sports positions, some musical instruments, and expressions (e.g., being a person's "right-hand" the Latin word for right is *dexter,* so someone who is ambidextrous has two "right" hands; there is the "right" way to do things so you won't be "left" behind). Ask a right-handed person, how often she or he thinks of right-handed privilege and you'll likely get a puzzled look. Someone who is left-handed is probably much more aware of the privileges right-handed folks often take for granted.

Privileges accompany membership in a dominant group. For example, people without a disability that affects their mobility, who are also white, male, native English speakers, upper-middle class, Christian, and heterosexual will enter most schools, businesses, and public places secure in the knowledge that

- they don't have to take many precautions to ensure their safety,
- they won't have to worry whether they will be able to gain access to a building or whether they'll be able to easily use the restrooms,
- the manner of speaking and style of interacting that they use at home will likely be seen as the norm and expected of others,
- they will have easy access to medical care,
- they won't have to decide whether to be "out" when someone asks about their girlfriend or wife,
- they are less likely to be followed around in stores or profiled by law enforcement officials,
- they are less likely to have to take a vacation day to observe a religious holiday, and
- they are less likely to receive negative reactions when they speak their native language.

In other words, their preferred ways of speaking, being, and interacting are seen as normal and, usually, superior; it's assumed that others should strive to be this way too. In each way that a group is privileged and has easier or greater access to resources or power, other groups are disadvantaged. This makes acknowledging privileges hard for those who enjoy them. Most counselors want to believe that they earned what they have without special treatment or advantages. It offends our sense of ourselves as being fair, aware, people who care. McIntosh (1998) proposes that privilege is hidden because those who have privilege have been taught not to see it. Thereby members of the dominant group can maintain a self-serving "feel-good" myth of meritocracy (i.e., that each individual achieves solely on individual merit, without reference to social context) and confirm that democracy is working as it should (H. G. McMahon et al., 2010; Sue, 2010).

It may be the case that some individuals have dominant and privileged statuses for some of their cultural identities (e.g., Christian, native English speaker, middle class) but not others (e.g., female, lesbian, having a disability). It is not unusual for people to either focus mainly on their subordinate statuses or to disavow any sense of privilege by noting that some others have much more than they do (Goodman, 2011). Individuals with privilege may even feel that they are actually at a disadvantage in their struggles to get ahead; they may be able to name numerous incidents in their lives to illustrate this. Meanwhile, they are unaware of or deny the advantages, relatively speaking, that their group membership does bestow. This brings to mind yet another privilege, the ability to ignore one's privileged status.

McIntosh (1998) has conceptualized the notion of a knapsack of invisible privilege. This invisible knapsack carries assets that the privileged individual can regularly draw on to more easily negotiate daily life. Activity 3.2 lists some examples of the privileges possessed by members of dominant groups.

Activity 3.2   Sample Privilege Inventory (adapted from McIntosh, 1998)

Following are some of the invisible privileges that members of various dominant groups carry. Compare your situation with those listed here. Place a check mark next to those that are accurate for you.

- I can go into any home or building because I can be sure that it will be physically accessible to me. (I do not need ramps or lifts or wide doors.)

- When I am told about our national heritage or about "civilization," I am shown that people of my color (or gender) made it what it is. Almost all of our presidents have been my race and gender.

- I can do well in a challenging situation without being called a credit to my race (or gender).

- I can walk on a public path alone and not be afraid that I might be sexually assaulted.

- I can easily buy posters, postcards, picture books, greeting cards, dolls, toys, and children's magazines featuring mostly people of my own race or sexual orientation.

- I can go home from most meetings of organizations to which I belong feeling somewhat connected rather than isolated, out of place, outnumbered, unheard, held at a distance, or feared.

- Most of the time, I can arrange to protect my children from people who might not like them. I did not need to teach my children about racism or heterosexism for their own daily protection.

- If I need medical care, I have a range of facilities and physicians who will accept my insurance.

- If I want to marry someone I love, I can be sure that we are legally entitled to do so anywhere in the United States and that we will have all of the rights and protections afforded to married couples.

- I can worship as I wish and help my faith community build a worship center anywhere we would like without fear or opposition from neighbors.

- Those who have been able to afford the high costs of legal and/or medical training, those who are the CEOs of the largest companies and the presidents of universities, are usually people of my race.

- When it comes to my native language, I can be almost positive people will understand me when I speak, forms and signs will use my language, and people won't question whether I am in the United States legally.

- If I am laughing with friends on a street at night, or talking loudly in a parking lot, it is not assumed that I am dangerous or a member of a gang.

- I live in a home or apartment in a relatively safe neighborhood.

- Poor race relations in the United States are not attributed to my race's criminal behavior, despite a history of race-related breaking of laws by whites over the entire span of Anglo-European life on this continent.

Now comment on what you thought, felt, and noticed as a result of this inventory.

Some readers might understandably be thinking, "But privilege and oppression aren't my fault. I didn't scheme to get privilege." Privilege is not necessarily any individual's fault. In McIntosh's (1998) words, "We did not invent [the inherited systems of overadvantage]" (p. 207). Nor can a person rid herself or himself of all privilege. Randy Cohen (2004) iterates that point in his response to a question about how to avoid participating in oppressive institutions:

Many who sincerely denounce the inequities of our society inevitably profit from them. If you're a man who works at a job where the lack of flex time or on-site day care disadvantages women who do the bulk of childcare, you benefit from sexism. If you're a middle-class white person who attended a decent high school and then applied to college, you had a huge advantage over a poor kid or an African American from an inferior high school. It is impossible to lead an immaculate life in an imperfect world. The task is not merely to insulate yourself from being a beneficiary of injustice—even if that were possible—but to combat injustice. (p. 26)

You are also encouraged to complete Activity 3.3 in order to identify your own possible privileges.

To combat injustice is one of the responsibilities of the counselor. Cohen (2004) suggests that the person with privilege should challenge the rigidity of social arrangements, such as the very existence of whiteness or maleness or heterosexuality as an advantage. Privileged group members can, therefore, act as allies in helping to counter oppressions, instead of participating in continuation of the problem (Collins, 2010; Goodman, 2011; Johnson, 2010).

Oppressive conditions only persist when people allow them to (Dovidio & Gaertner, 1999; Ponterotto et al., 2006). Vigilant voices that have examined and challenged oppression include writers and activists

Review your social group memberships from the Introductory Cultural Self-Awareness activity from Chapter 1 (Activity 1.1).

In which of your seven group memberships do you have invisible privilege? Where that is the case, describe at least one way that you have benefited from this privilege that others who do not have such privilege might not.

1. Ethnicity: _____

2. Race: _____

3. Social Class: _____

4. Gender: _____

5. Sexual Orientation: _____

6. Ability/Disability: _____

7. Religion: _____

such as Jane Addams, the founder of the American community service center for the poor; Jonathan Kozol (1991), who wrote the book *Savage Inequalities*; Carol Gilligan (1982), who wrote *In a Different Voice*; Paulo Freire (1970), author of *Pedagogy of the Oppressed*; and bell hooks (1994), who wrote *Teaching to Transgress*. These socially critical writers have examined such phenomena as tracking in schools, everyday language that excludes, and internalized oppressions or beliefs by members of nondominant groups that they are somehow inferior. Their work is in the tradition of people whose lives have been dedicated to fighting oppression, such as Dr. Martin Luther King Jr.; Sojourner Truth, former slave, abolitionist, and advocate for women's rights; Dorothy Day, of the Catholic Worker movement; Saul Alinsky, community organizer who formed black–white workers' coalitions; Cesar Chavez, leader of Latina/o agricultural workers' rights movement; Marian Wright Edelman, advocate for children; Archbishop Dom Helder Camara, Brazilian Catholic archbishop and champion of oppressed and indigent persons; and Nelson Mandela and Bishop Desmond Tutu, leaders of the South African liberation and reconciliation movements.

Jane Addams, 1860–1935

Marian Wright Edelman, 1939–

These individuals can serve as models for social change action. But counselors might wonder what role they themselves can play in reducing oppressions, especially when such powerful figures as those mentioned above are paraded before them. Lest one believe that change efforts are only doable by larger-than-life figures, Kaufman (2003) reminds counselors,

> ordinary people acting together for common goals have accomplished incredible amounts. There is nothing magical about making social change happen. What is required is a sense of hope that it is possible to make a difference and some understanding of the world that helps orient our choices about what kinds of actions to take. (p. 5)

Kaufman proposes that counselors exhibit relentless hope, hope that is expressed in day-to-day social justice actions. Hope and action. These are watchwords for this chapter. Much of the rest of this chapter reveals the roles that ordinary people can play in increasing social justice and facilitating clients' empowerment. This work is called advocacy.

Advocacy and Empowerment

Advocacy is a crucial skill for challenging privilege and oppression. It is important because privilege and oppression will not disappear of their own accord. *Advocacy comprises attitudes and actions that facilitate the empowerment of individuals or groups by enhancing self-efficacy, removing barriers to needed services, and promoting access to resources and power.* Advocacy occurs when counselors incorporate an activist function into their role as helper.

Counselors cannot close their eyes and minds to the need for advocacy. In effect, business-as-usual counseling supports the inequitable status quo (Bell, 2012; Chang & Gnilka, 2010; Harley et al., 2007; Johnson, 2010; Toporek & Vaughn, 2010). Such counseling is oblivious to oppressive and toxic sociopolitical and economic factors, and it is neither effective nor ethical. Advocacy puts social justice ideals into action (Ratts, 2009). Ideally, advocacy and counseling are clearly connected in counselor training, services, interventions, and also in one's own sense of identity as a counselor (Chen-Hayes et al., 2011; Lewis et al., 2010; Martin & Robinson, 2011).

Box 3.2 provides some examples of everyday situations that call for advocacy.

Asking Questions

Each of the situations in Box 3.2 requires counselors to ask difficult questions and to take risks to address the issues that affect so many in their communities. Advocacy asks counselors to unveil the daily and hidden slights, make the familiar unfamiliar, or question and ameliorate the seemingly certain and fixed oppressive practices. Counselors can begin by asking some of the following socially critical questions about

Box 3.2   Examples of Situations Needing Advocacy

School/agency décor and events that do not represent people of color, LGBT youth, or are not accessible to persons with disabilities

African American males receiving disproportionately harsh sentences and being overrepresented in jails and prisons (as well as the phenomenon of this same group receiving a disproportionate number of discipline referrals and harsher consequences in schools)

Laws, policies, or practices that marginalize members of the community, reducing their access to power or resources (e.g., voting rights, zoning ordinances that "pave" the way for development while displacing less connected community members, English-only policies)

Schools in lower-socioeconomic-status neighborhoods and/or with a higher percentage of people of color having fewer resources, inadequate facilities, and a higher percentage of underqualified teachers

De facto segregation in public school or community activities (e.g., due to the cost of extracurricular materials, access to a computer and private lessons, transportation or childcare issues, or leadership being an exclusive domain of folks from the dominant and privileged culture)

The inability of same-sex partners to marry in many places and also to access all of the benefits given to legally protected partners

Forms at schools, doctor's offices, businesses, and government agencies printed only in English, with no translator available to help access needed services

Women and persons of color receiving lower pay than their white, male counterparts for doing equivalent work; the "glass ceiling" preventing women from being promoted beyond a certain level

Harassment (e.g., sexist comments, anti-gay slurs) without clear and consistently enforced institutional laws or policies prohibiting; lack of prevention programming addressing this issue

Imbalance in academic tracking (e.g., racial imbalance in special education, advanced classes, and gifted and talented programs)

Inequitable access to a safe neighborhood, public services such as police protection and transportation, health care, healthy food, recreational opportunities, and other factors associated with quality of life

Grossly disproportionate accumulation of resources and power by some groups while others are deprived of the resources and power needed to fully participate in the life of the community

African Americans being diagnosed for schizophrenia at twice the rate of whites (and Latinas/Latinos at a 50% greater rate), regardless of income or education levels (Paniagua, 2005).

---

who is served and how they are served by their organizations and by society:

- What are the beliefs, assumptions, and values behind a particular policy, structure, action, or orientation?
- If we act according to the identified beliefs, who prospers? Who loses? Who is disempowered or dehumanized?
- What do the disaggregated data show us in terms of patterns of inclusiveness and/or oppression?
- How can we make a given situation more equitable and democratic?

- How can we encourage a diversity of views and alternatives?
- Who is included in the decision-making process (e.g., hiring, selection, policymaking)?

Advocacy Competencies

Culturally alert counselors need to engage in advocacy when an individual or systemic injustice is present, especially those affecting clients, even when doing so may be uncomfortable or unpopular (Dahir & Stone, 2012; C. C. Lee & Rogers, 2009). Toward that end, counselors have the assistance of

43 advocacy competencies covering six domains: client/student empowerment, client/student advocacy, community collaboration, systems advocacy, public information, and social/political advocacy (Lewis et al., 2002; see Appendix B). It is helpful to note that most of the competencies involve applying skills already commonly used in counseling work (e.g., identifying strengths and resources as well as factors inhibiting healthy development, respectful listening, collaborating to create a plan of action, facilitating self-efficacy and empowerment, assessment, communication). Using these skills, counselors can advocate for changing the systemic policies and practices that contribute to their clients' problems, as opposed to changing the client to adapt to unhealthy or oppressive conditions (Martin & Robinson, 2011).

Empowerment

Advocacy interventions range from assisting individuals to enhance their sense of empowerment (the individual level) to collaborating with allies to effect systemic change (the institutional or societal level). As has been noted, facilitating the empowerment of those with whom counselors work is an essential aspect of advocacy (Dahir & Stone, 2012; Ratts et al., 2007). Empowerment can be seen as "the process by which people or organizations who are oppressed become aware of the power differential in their life, and then learn and exercise the skills necessary to control their lives without oppressing other groups" (Chang & Gnilka, 2010, p. 70). So counselors work both *for* and *with* clients, depending on the need. At times, counselors act on behalf of clients (with a complementary goal of enhancing the clients' self-advocacy skills). At other times, counselors collaborate with clients and allies for individual and/or systemic concerns.

Being an Ally

An ally is a member of a nonoppressed group who endeavors to counter discrimination and oppression, in the belief that this benefits everyone in a society. Allies take a stand against social injustice by speaking and working against oppressive patterns. If counselors are members of a dominant group, they recognize their privileges and take responsibility to learn more about the unearned benefits of this privilege and the contrasting oppressions for members of nondominant groups. They then use their privilege and skills and take actions, even when it's uncomfortable, to change inequity.

Almost everyone can be an ally at some point for those in nondominant groups. An African American male can be an ally for women, a heterosexual woman can be an ally for lesbians and gay men, and an able-bodied Latina/o can be an ally for individuals with disabilities.

The Advocacy Process

These advocacy efforts can involve individual or situational actions, such as confronting jokes and slurs that target people or groups (as opposed to being silent, which appears to signal agreement). Advocacy also involves critically examining institutional policies and practices that discriminate or oppress some groups (e.g., the lack of affordable mental health service options for those with fewer economic resources; the situations listed in Box 3.2) and actively working to change these inequities (e.g., raising awareness via use of data, discussions, and social media; changing policies and accessibility at your workplace; collaborating with those affected by the inequity and other allies; contacting legislators).

There are many models of advocacy steps. The following are key pieces of the process that are included in most models (VSCA, 2008, pp. 105–106):

- clearly identify the problem (supported by data)
- gather collaborators and resources
- choose goal(s) and plan(s) to achieve them (with an aim to empower participants to be successful advocates for themselves)
- act by using your counseling, communication, and collaboration skills

- be persistent and non-defensive, have a plan to deal with resistance
- recognize the need for self-care in this challenging work
- evaluate and celebrate (and/or regroup and retry)

In sum, advocacy, even as seen in some of the small acts named here, requires counselors to be consistently vigilant in examining institutional arrangements that result in inequity. Small and large acts are all important. Thus, counselors can be comforted by knowing that their advocacy contributes in small ways to reducing inequities, even if it doesn't result in major societal changes. The seemingly small acts may be in the spirit of the Hebrew Talmud, which states, "It is not our job to finish the work, but we are not free to walk away from it."

Concerns and Controversies About Social Justice Counseling

As has been noted previously (e.g., with women's suffrage and the integration of schools and other institutions), systems are usually resistant to change (Parsons & Kahn, 2005; Ratts & Wood, 2011). Not surprisingly, within the counseling profession there are varying opinions about the relevance of social justice to the field (S. D. Smith, Reynolds, & Rovnak, 2009; Toporek, Dodge, et al., 2010). Some decry the movement toward social justice in counseling as too difficult, especially for non-university-based practitioners; beholden to a narrow, noninclusive political agenda; and lacking an empirical research foundation (Hunsaker, 2008; King, 2011). Indeed there are varying levels of commitment to social justice among counselors. Even the ethical standard often cited to support social justice activity ambiguously charges counselors to advocate "when appropriate" (ACA, 2005, p. 5). The concerns and issues involved in the movement to infuse social justice in counseling merit at least a brief exploration here.

Challenges

In addition to the difficulties alluded to previously, several authors acknowledge the potential for personal risk being involved. This may include experiencing tension, discomfort, isolation, and possibly even becoming a target for those who disagree with positions or policies for which you are assertively advocating (Bemak & Chung, 2008; Chang & Gnilka, 2010; Holcomb-McCoy, 2007; Singh, 2010; VSCA, 2008). Also, working in a system where third-party reimbursements are primarily geared for remediation efforts, some social justice and advocacy work as a private practitioner may not be remunerated (Toporek & Vaughn, 2010). Moreover, counselors may find that the time involved doing social justice actions may not be accompanied by a reduction in the duties in which they were previously engaged, thereby increasing their workload (Odegard & Vereen, 2010; Singh et al., 2010). Furthermore, there may be challenges in negotiating ethical issues, such as setting relational boundaries and also avoiding imposing one's social justice values on clients as counselors move from the familiar one-on-one talk modality to an array of activities for and with clients (Chang & Gnilka, 2010; C. C. Lee & Hipolito-Delgado, 2007).

Need for Training

In addition, in order to successfully teach, model, and enact these interventions, there is a need for enhanced training in both the concepts and skills of social justice work for students, practitioners, and counselor education faculty (Burnes & Manese, 2008; Holcomb-McCoy, 2007; Miller & Sendrowitz, 2011; Sheely-Moore & Kooyman, 2011; Singh et al., 2010). Many of the established counseling theories and models for helping are seen as either incongruent with the social justice paradigm or guilty of not adequately addressing this topic (Chang & Gnilka, 2010; Ratts et al., 2010).

Single-mindedness

Finally, concerns that the process of promoting social justice sometimes has involved tactics that are either patronizing or intolerant of any dissent have been sounded (Hunsaker, 2008; L. Jackson, 2008; S. D. Smith et al., 2009; Toporek & Vaughn, 2010).

Employing and modeling a fair and respectful process in discussing and promulgating social justice knowledge and skills would appear to be essential (Durham & Barrett, 2009; Love, 2010; Oyler, 2012; Ratts & Wood, 2011). Let us now look at ways of enhancing our knowledge, commitment, and abilities to do this vital work in a fashion that is fair.

Personal Qualities and Skills Needed for Social Justice and Advocacy

A number of personal qualities and skills are needed for advocacy. They include willingness to brook conflict, appreciation of diversity, openness to learning, the ability to engage in social critical thinking, having a critical consciousness, and persistence. Each is discussed in turn.

Conflict and Emotional Readiness

In terms of emotion, the counselor must be ready to engage in difficult dialogues (Oyler, 2012; Sue, 2010). She or he must be willing to take challenging actions, such as approaching administrators, colleagues, and clients with unsettling concerns about inequity (Holcomb-McCoy, 2007). That discomfort has to be embraced because social justice actions will sometimes be met with resistance from colleagues, family members, fellow religious congregants, and community members, to name some examples (Parsons & Kahn, 2005; VSCA, 2008).

Appreciation of Diversity

In order to be more fully effective as advocates, counselors should work on having a well-developed understanding of their own cultural identity before they can advocate for nondominant groups in a fashion that invites empowerment and is not inadvertently condescending or oppressive (Love, 2010; Ponterotto et al., 2006; Sue, 2008). The white person who is resentful of opportunities for people of color is not likely to be an effective ally in race-related matters. The Christian who has a defensive or superior attitude about the standing of her or his religion will probably not be an effective ally for non-Christians. Instead, social justice interest and commitment are positively related to openness to diversity and negatively related to a "color-blind" attitude (Miller & Sendrowitz, 2011).

Openness to Learning

Advocates can also be more effective if they are open to lifelong growth—seeing themselves as learners among learners and equals with their collaborators (Goodman, 2011; L. Jackson, 2008; Toporek & Vaughn, 2010). They must "lean in" to ideas that challenge their current positions and be willing to be confronted about their own behavior and attitudes because they are committed to rectifying inequities. There should not be a one-sided inculcation of any right way to engage in social justice activities.

Flexibility

This lifelong learning works best when the process is not dogmatic or single-minded. There should be room for discussion, instructor reflexivity, and recognition of social progress that has occurred (Holcomb-McCoy, 2007; Ratts & Wood, 2011). There are also some content areas required. For example, any such educational efforts should include the notions of bias, privilege, oppression, and counselors' possible roles in perpetuating an oppressive system (Bell, 2012; Chang & Gnilka, 2010; Love, 2010; Nilsson et al., 2011). In addition, counselors must learn advocacy skills, including the art of persuasion and methods for assisting clients to engage in self-advocacy and in negotiating systems (Herlihy & Dufrene, 2011; Johnson, 2010; Lewis et al., 2002; Odegard & Vereen, 2010). Supervision and mentoring have been found to be effective in aiding this educational and reflective process (Caldwell & Vera, 2010; Parikh, Post, & Flowers, 2011).

Finally, any training for enhanced social justice counseling abilities should include an experiential component involving: community engagement and service, networking and collaborative action, and reflection (Burnes & Singh, 2010; Caldwell &

Vera, 2010; Collins, 2010; Lewis et al., 2010; Nilsson et al., 2011; Oyler, 2012; Sheely-Moore & Kooyman, 2011; Toporek & Vaughn, 2010).

We now turn to the intellectual readiness required to effectively engage in this work, as the concept of critical consciousness is helpful in defining this readiness.

Critical Consciousness

The concept of critical consciousness was developed by Brazilian literacy educator Paulo Freire in his books *Pedagogy of the Oppressed* (1970) and *Education for Critical Consciousness* (1973). Critical consciousness can be defined as the capacity of individuals to consciously reevaluate and reinterpret their relationships with their culture, their sociopolitical world, and their historical age (Mustakova-Possardt, 2003). As seen in this definition, critical consciousness involves the cultural de-centering that was discussed in Chapter 2.

Paulo Freire, 1921–1997

Freire first worked to help poor persons overcome illiteracy in reading and writing. However, he expanded the notion of literacy to include *social illiteracy*. He described social illiteracy as being oblivious to the plight of others and failing to see the hundreds of thousands of people who suffer from homelessness, lack of medical care, and wage slavery (that is, working full-time but not being able to make a living wage). His original educational efforts were with people who saw themselves as victims and who accepted their second-class status in relation to the dominant group of educated, wealthier persons. Freire considered a goal of education to be the development of critical consciousness in oppressed people, so that they might be empowered rather than passive and self-blaming.

Critical consciousness is not just an attitude. It also has a social action dimension. It includes the ability to take steps to diminish the oppressive elements in society. Critical consciousness is difficult to achieve. It requires at least two attributes. First, the critically conscious counselor can consistently see herself or himself as immersed in the political, generational, gender, ethnic, religious, social class, and sexual orientation messages that pervade her or his world. It also requires inquisitiveness about the hidden power relations in a society's daily, pervasive messages.

Mustakova-Possardt's (2003) research revealed critical consciousness to be a cognitive developmental achievement in the Piagetian sense. Such development is usually attained if a person experiences challenges to her or his received ways of thinking about power and stratification. It requires confronting dilemmas and "stretching" one's thinking. And it requires discomfort, the irritation of letting go of familiar ways of knowing.

Thus, to move toward critical consciousness, an individual must meet three conditions. First, she or he must have "disequilibrating" encounters (ones that upset the equilibrium of a current way of knowing) regarding ethnicity, race, gender, ability, social class, religion, and sexual orientation, via in-person experiences, reading, and media. Then she or he must seriously try to understand those phenomena in a new way, especially in terms of power, privilege, and equity. Finally, she or he must be able to accommodate new learning and the reconstruction of cultural identities to reshape her or his perspectives. A person's thinking thus moves from rigid and simplistic characterizations of cultural "others" to flexibility and complexity in thinking about oppressed groups and oneself. The flexibility and complexity of socially critical thinking described above have been associated with greater interest and commitment to social justice and advocacy (Bell, 2012; Caldwell & Vera, 2010; McAuliffe, Grothaus, Jensen, & Michel, 2011; Parikh et al., 2011). This book hopes to provide some of those opportunities for disequilibration.

Persistence

Finally, when engaged in social justice work, one must appreciate the persistence that advocacy requires. Social justice advocates must understand that social change is not a single event but a lifelong process that involves learning from mistakes and trying again. It is essential to have support allies, and to practice self-care (Goodman, 2011; VSCA, 2008).

SUMMARY

Social justice–oriented counseling is an essential dimension of culturally alert counseling. Through promoting social justice, the counseling field returns to its early 20th century roots of advocating for equity for and with underserved and oppressed groups. This work is not easy, nor is the need for it likely to disappear any time soon. As long as there are human beings, unnecessary stratifications and misuses of power are possible. Social justice and advocacy are both attitudes and actions. When counselors are not engaging in social justice advocacy, they are part of the problem. For in not challenging and changing the inequitable status quo, their silence condones and perpetuates it. Each child who experiences schoolyard taunting, each woman who is sexually harassed by a person in power, each immigrant who is discriminated against in a job application, each person with limited economic resources who cannot access needed services, and each gay person who experiences anti-gay policies and practices will need counselors to assist them in engaging in socially critical thinking and self-advocacy as well as counselors who advocate by speaking and acting for and with their clients to achieve equity, access to resources, and justice.

REFERENCES

Amatea, E., & West-Olatunji, C. (2007). Joining the conversation about educating our poorest children: Emerging leadership roles for school counselors in high-poverty schools. *Professional School Counseling, 11*, 81–89.

American Counseling Association. (2005). *ACA code of ethics.* Alexandria, VA: Author.

American School Counselor Association. (2005). *The ASCA national model: A framework for school counseling programs* (2nd ed.). Alexandria, VA: Author.

American School Counselor Association. (2006). *The professional school counselor and equity for all students.* Retrieved from http://www.schoolcounselor.org/files/PS_Equity.pdf

Auwarter, A. E., & Aruguete, M. S. (2008). Counselor perceptions of students who vary in gender and socioeconomic status. *Social Psychology of Education, 11*, 389–395.

Barrett, L. (2012). My fair share. *Notre Dame Magazine, 40*, 39–43.

Bell, L. A. (2012). Introduction. In C. Oyler, *Actions speak louder than words: Community activism as curriculum* (pp. xiii–xiv). New York, NY: Routledge.

Bemak, F., & Chung, R. C. (2008). New professional roles and advocacy strategies for school counselors: A multicultural/social justice perspective to move beyond the nice counselor syndrome. *Journal of Counseling and Development, 86*, 372–382.

Bernard, T. S. (2012, January 21). Blacks face bias in bankruptcy, study suggests. *The New York Times*, pp. A1, B5.

Burnes, T. R., & Manese, J. E. (2008). Social justice in an accredited internship in professional psychology: Answering the call. *Training and Education in Professional Psychology, 2*, 176–181.

Burnes, T. R., & Singh, A. A. (2010). Integrating social justice training into the practicum experience for psychology trainees: Starting earlier. *Training and Education in Professional Psychology, 4*, 153–162.

Caldwell, J. C., & Vera, E. M. (2010). Critical incidents in counseling psychology professionals' and trainees' social justice orientation development. *Training and Education in Professional Psychology, 4,* 163–176.

Chang, C. Y., Crethar, H. C., & Ratts, M. J. (2010). Social justice: A national imperative for counselor education and supervision. *Counselor Education & Supervision, 50,* 82–87.

Chang, C. Y., & Gnilka, P. B. (2010). Social justice counseling. In D. G. Hays & B. T. Erford (Eds.), *Developing multicultural counseling competence: A systems approach* (pp. 53–71). Boston, MA: Pearson.

Chen, E. C., Androsiglio, R., & Ng, V. (2010). Minority stress and health of lesbian, gay, and bisexual individuals. In J. G. Ponterotto, J. M. Casas, L. A. Suzuki, & C. M. Alexander (Eds.), *Handbook of multicultural counseling* (3rd ed., pp. 531–544). Thousand Oaks, CA: Sage.

Chen-Hayes, S. F., Miller, E. M., Bailey, D. F., Getch, Y. Q., & Erford, B. T. (2011). Leadership and achievement advocacy for every student. In B. T. Erford (Ed.), *Transforming the school counseling profession* (3rd ed., pp. 110–128). Boston, MA: Pearson.

Cohen, R. (2004, April 25). The ethicist. *New York Times Magazine,* p. 26.

Collins, P. H. (2010). Toward a new vision: Race, class, and gender. In M. Adams, W. J. Blumenfeld, C. Casteneda, H. W. Hackman, M. L. Peters, & X. Zuniga (Eds.), *Readings for diversity and social justice* (2nd ed., pp. 604–609). New York, NY: Routledge.

Constantine, M. G., Hage, S. M., Kindaichi, M. M., & Bryant, R. M. (2007). Social justice and multicultural issues: Implications for the practice and training of counselors and counseling psychologists. *Journal of Counseling & Development, 85,* 24–29.

Dahir, C. A., & Stone, C. B. (2012). *The transformed school counselor* (2nd ed.). Belmont, CA: Brooks/Cole.

Dovidio, J. F., & Gaertner, S. L. (1999). Reducing prejudice: Combating intergroup biases. *Current Directions in Psychological Science, 8,* 101–105.

Durham, J., & Barrett, K. (2009, October). *From passion to action: Infusing an advocacy, social justice orientation in counselor education and supervision.* Paper presented at the Association for Counselor Education and Supervision biannual conference, San Diego, CA.

Freire, P. (1970). *Pedagogy of the oppressed.* New York, NY: Continuum.

Freire, P. (1973). *Education for critical consciousness.* New York, NY: Seabury Press.

Gallardo, M. E. (2012). Therapists as cultural architects and systemic advocates: Latina/o skills identification stage model. In M. E. Gallardo, C. J. Yeh, J. E. Trimble, & T. A. Parham (Eds.), *Culturally adaptive counseling skills: Demonstrations of evidence-based practices* (pp. 77–112). Thousand Oaks, CA: Sage.

Gewirtz, A., Hart-Shegos, E., & Medhanie, A. (2008). Psychosocial status of homeless children and youth in family supportive housing. *American Behavioral Scientist, 51,* 810–823.

Gilligan, C. (1982). *In a different voice: Psychological theory and women's development.* Cambridge, MA: Harvard University Press.

Goodman, D. J. (2011). *Promoting diversity and social justice: Educating people from privileged groups* (2nd ed.). New York, NY: Routledge.

Greer, T. M., Laseter, A., & Asiamah, D. (2009). Gender as a moderator of the relation between race-related stress and mental health symptoms for African Americans. *Psychology of Women Quarterly, 33,* 295–307.

Griffin, D., & Farris, A. (2010). School counselors and collaboration: Finding resources through community mapping. *Professional School Counseling, 13,* 248–256.

Grothaus, T., & Cole, R. (2010). Meeting the challenges together: School counselors collaborating with students and families with low income. *Journal of School Counseling, 8*(27). Retrieved from http://www.jsc.montana.edu

Grothaus, T., Crum, K. S., & James, A. B. (2010). Effective leadership in a culturally diverse learning environment. *International Journal of Urban Educational Leadership 4,* 111–125.

Grothaus, T., Lorelle, S., Anderson, K., & Knight, J. (2011). Answering the call: Facilitating responsive services for students experiencing homelessness. *Professional School Counseling, 14,* 191–201.

Grothaus, T., McAuliffe, G., & Craigen, L. (2012). Infusing cultural competence and advocacy in strength-based counseling. *Journal of Humanistic Counseling, 51,* 51–65.

Harley, D. A., Alston, R. J., & Middleton, R. A. (2007). Infusing social justice into rehabilitation education: Making a case for curricula refinement. *Rehabilitation Education, 21,* 41–52.

Harro, B. (2000). The cycle of socialization. In M. Adams, W. J. Blumenfeld, R. Casteneda, H. W. Hackman, M. L. Peters, & X. Zuniga (Eds.), *Readings for diversity and social justice: An anthology on racism, sexism, anti-Semitism, heterosexism, ableism, and classism* (pp. 15–20). New York, NY: Routledge.

Hays, D. G., Chang, C. Y., & Decker, S. L. (2007). Initial development and psychometric data for the privilege and oppression inventory. *Measurement and Evaluation in Counseling and Development, 40,* 66–79.

Herlihy, B., & Dufrene, R. L. (2011). Current and emerging ethical issues in counseling: A Delphi study of expert opinions. *Counseling and Values, 56,* 10–24.

Holcomb-McCoy, C. (2007). *School counseling to close the achievement gap: A social justice framework for success.* Thousand Oaks, CA: Corwin.

Holcomb-McCoy, C., & Chen-Hayes, S. F. (2011). Culturally competent school counselors: Affirming diversity by challenging oppression. In B. T. Erford (Ed.), *Transforming the school counseling profession* (3rd ed., pp. 90–109). Boston, MA: Pearson.

Holcomb-McCoy, C., & Mitchell, N. A. (2007). Promoting ethnic/racial equality through empowerment-based counseling. In C. C. Lee (Ed.), *Counseling for social justice* (2nd ed., pp. 137–157). Alexandria, VA: American Counseling Association.

hooks, b. (1994). *Teaching to transgress: Education as the practice of freedom.* New York, NY: Routledge.

Howard, A. S., & Solberg, V. S. H. (2006). School-based social justice: The achieving success identity pathways program. *Professional School Counseling, 9,* 278–287.

Hunsaker, R. (2008, April). Social justice: An inconvenient irony. *Counseling Today,* pp. 21, 43.

Jackson, L. (2008). Dialogic pedagogy for social justice: A critical examination. *Studies in Philosophy and Education, 27,* 137–148.

Jackson, L. (2010). Images of Islam in U.S. media and their educational implications. *Educational Studies, 46,* 3–24.

Jackson, M., & Grant, D. (2004). Equity, access, and career development: Contextual conflicts. In R. Perusse & G. E. Goodnough (Eds.), *Leadership, advocacy, and direct service strategies for professional school counselors* (pp. 125–153). Belmont, CA: Brooks/Cole.

Johnson, A. G. (2010). What can we do? In M. Adams, W. J. Blumenfeld, C. Casteneda, H. W. Hackman, M. L. Peters, & X. Zuniga (Eds.), *Readings for diversity and social justice* (2nd ed., pp. 610–616). New York, NY: Routledge.

Jun, H. (2010). *Social justice, multicultural counseling, and practice: Beyond a conventional approach.* Thousand Oaks, CA: Sage.

Kaufman, C. (2003). *Ideas for action: Relevant theory for radical change.* Cambridge, MA: South End Press.

King, J. H. (2011). Three paradoxes of the counseling social justice movement. *Counseling Today, 54,* 46–47.

Kozol, J. (1991). *Savage inequalities: Children in America's schools.* New York, NY: Crown.

Kumashiro, K. K. (2009). *Against common sense: Teaching and learning toward social justice* (Rev. ed.). New York, NY: Routledge.

Lee, C. C., & Hipolito-Delgado, C. P. (2007). Introduction: Counselors as agents of social justice. In C. C. Lee (Ed.), *Counseling for social justice* (2nd ed., pp. xiii–xxviii). Alexandria, VA: American Counseling Association.

Lee, C. C., & Rogers, R. A. (2009). Counselor advocacy: Affecting systemic change in the public arena. *Journal of Counseling & Development, 87,* 284–287.

Lee, V. V., & Goodnough, G. E. (2011). Systemic, data-driven school counseling practice and programming for equity. In B. T. Erford (Ed.), *Transforming the school counseling profession* (3rd ed., pp. 129–153). Boston, MA: Pearson.

Lewis, J., Arnold, M., House, R., & Toporek, R. (2002). *Advocacy competencies.* Retrieved from http://www.counseling.org/Resources/Competencies/Advocacy_Competencies.pdf

Lewis, J., Toporek, R. L., & Ratts, M. J. (2010). Advocacy and social justice: Entering the mainstream of the counseling profession. In M. J. Ratts, R. L. Toporek, & J. A. Lewis (Eds.), *ACA advocacy competencies: A social justice framework for counselors* (pp. 239–244). Alexandria, VA: American Counseling Association.

Love, B. J. (2010). Developing a liberatory consciousness. In M. Adams, W. J. Blumenfeld, C. Casteneda, H. W. Hackman, M. L. Peters, & X. Zuniga (Eds.),

Readings for diversity and social justice (2nd ed., pp. 599–603). New York, NY: Routledge.

Mansoo, Y., North, C. S., Lavesser, P. D., Osborne, V. A., & Spitznagel, E. L. (2008). Comparison study of psychiatric and behavior disorders and cognitive ability among homeless and housed children. *Community Mental Health Journal, 44,* 1–10.

Martin, P. J., & Robinson, S. G. (2011). Transforming the school counseling profession. In B. T. Erford (Ed.), *Transforming the school counseling profession* (3rd ed., pp. 1–18). Boston, MA: Pearson.

McAuliffe, G., Grothaus, T., Jensen, M., & Michel, R. (2011). Assessing and promoting cultural relativism in students of counseling. *International Journal for the Advancement of Counselling.* Advance online publication. doi:10.1007/s10447-011-9142

McDonald, S., Lin, N., & Ao, D. (2009). Networks of opportunity: Gender, race, and job leads. *Social Problems, 56,* 385–402.

McIntosh, P. (1998). White privilege, color, and crime: A personal account. In C. R. Mann & M. S. Zatz (Eds.), *Images of color, images of crime* (pp. 207–216). Los Angeles, CA: Roxbury.

McMahon, B. (2007). Educational administrators' conceptions of whiteness, anti-racism, and social justice. *Journal of Educational Administration, 45,* 684–696.

McMahon, H. G., Paisley, P. O., & Molina, B. (2010). Individuals and families of European descent. In D. G. Hays & B. T. Erford (Eds.), *Developing multicultural counseling competence: A systems approach* (pp. 333–366). Boston, MA: Pearson.

Miller, M. J., & Sendrowitz, K. (2011). Counseling psychology trainees' social justice interest and commitment. *Journal of Counseling Psychology, 58,* 159–169.

Mustakova-Possardt, E. (2003). *Critical consciousness: A study of morality in global, historical context.* Westport, CT: Praeger.

New American Alliance. (2009). The economic impact of the achievement gap in America's schools. Retrieved from http://mckinseyonsociety.com/downloads/reports/Education/achievement_gap_report.pdf

New York Times/CBS News Poll. (2012, January 21). On race. *The New York Times,* p. A21.

Nieto, S., & Bode, P. (2008). *Affirming diversity: The sociopolitical context of multicultural education* (5th ed.). Boston, MA: Allyn & Bacon.

Nilsson, J. E., Schale, C. L., & Khamphakdy-Brown, S. (2011). Facilitating trainees' multicultural development and social justice advocacy through a refugee/immigrant mental health program. *Journal of Counseling & Development, 89,* 413–422.

Odegard, M. A., & Vereen, L. G. (2010). A grounded theory of counselor educators integrating social justice into their pedagogy. *Counselor Education & Supervision, 50,* 130–149.

Oyler, C. (2012). *Actions speak louder than words: Community activism as curriculum.* New York, NY: Routledge.

Paniagua, F. A. (2005). *Assessing and treating culturally diverse clients: A practical guide.* Thousand Oaks, CA: Sage.

Parikh, S. B., Post, P., & Flowers, C. (2011). Relationship between belief in a just world and social justice advocacy attitudes of school counselors. *Counseling and Values, 56,* 57–72.

Parsons, R. D., & Kahn, W. J. (2005). *The school counselor as consultant.* Belmont, CA: Brooks/Cole.

Pierce, C. M., Carew, J. V., Pierce-Gonzalez, D., & Wills, D. (1977). An experiment in racism: TV commercials. *Education and Urban Society, 10,* 61–87.

Pinar, W. F. (2009). Afterword. In K. K. Kumashiro, *Against common sense: Teaching and learning toward social justice* (Rev. ed., pp. 125–132). New York, NY: Routledge.

Ponterotto, J. G., Utsey, S. O., & Pedersen, P. B. (2006). *Preventing prejudice: A guide for counselors, educators, and parents* (2nd ed.). Thousand Oaks, CA: Sage.

Quijada Cercer, P. D., Gutierrez, L. A., & Rios, F. (2010). Critical multiculturalism: Transformative educational principles and practices. In T. K. Chapman & N. Hobbel (Eds.), *Social justice pedagogy across the curriculum: The practice of freedom* (pp. 144–163). New York, NY: Routledge.

Ratts, M. J. (2009). Social justice counseling: Toward the development of a fifth force among counseling paradigms. *Journal of Humanistic Counseling, Education and Development, 48,* 160–172.

Ratts, M. J., DeKruyf, L., & Chen-Hayes, S. F. (2007). The ACA advocacy competencies: A social justice framework for professional school counselors. *Professional School Counseling, 11,* 90–97.

Ratts, M. J., & Ford, A. (2010). Advocacy competencies self-assessment (ACSA) survey. In M. J. Ratts, R. L. Toporek, & J. A. Lewis (Eds.), *ACA advocacy competencies: A social justice framework for counselors* (pp. 249–251). Alexandria, VA: American Counseling Association.

Ratts, M. J., Lewis, J., & Toporek, R. L. (2010). Advocacy and social justice: A helping paradigm for the 21st century. In M. J. Ratts, R. L. Toporek, & J. A. Lewis (Eds.), *ACA advocacy competencies: A social justice framework for counselors* (pp. 3–10). Alexandria, VA: American Counseling Association.

Ratts, M. J., & Wood, C. (2011). The fierce urgency of now: Diffusion of innovation as mechanism to integrate social justice in counselor education. *Counselor Education & Supervision, 50,* 207–223.

Robinson-Wood, T. L. (2009). *The convergence of race, ethnicity, and gender: Multiple identities in counseling* (3rd ed.). Upper Saddle River, NJ: Merrill.

Rollins, C. P., II. (2003). *High school guidance counselor ratings of success for postsecondary options: A study of socioeconomic, racial and gender bias* (Doctoral dissertation). Available from ProQuest Dissertations and Theses database.

Sheely-Moore, A. I., & Kooyman, L. (2011). Infusing multicultural and social justice competencies within counseling practice: A guide for trainers. *Adultspan Journal, 10,* 102–109.

Singh, A. A. (2010). It takes more than a rainbow sticker! Advocacy on queer issues in counseling. In M. J. Ratts, R. L. Toporek, & J. A. Lewis (Eds.), *ACA advocacy competencies: A social justice framework for counselors* (pp. 29–41). Alexandria, VA: American Counseling Association.

Singh, A. A., Urbano, A., Haston, M., & McMahon, E. (2010). School counselors' strategies for social justice change: A grounded theory of what works in the real world. *Professional School Counseling, 13,* 135–145.

Smith, S. D., Reynolds, C. A., & Rovnak, A. (2009). A critical analysis of the social advocacy movement in counseling. *Journal of Counseling & Development, 87,* 483–491.

Smith, W. A., Hung, M., Franklin, J. D. (2011). Racial battle fatigue and the miseducation of black men: Racial microaggressions, societal problems, and environmental stress. *Journal of Negro Education, 80,* 63–82.

Spitzberg, B. H., & Changnon, G. (2009). Conceptualizing intercultural competence. In D. K. Deardorff (Ed.), *The SAGE handbook of intercultural competence* (pp. 2–52). Thousand Oaks, CA: Sage.

Sue, D. W. (2008). Multicultural organizational consultation: A social justice perspective. *Counseling Psychology Journal: Practice and Research, 60,* 157–169.

Sue, D. W. (2010). *Racial microaggressions in everyday life: Race, gender and sexual orientation.* Hoboken, NJ: Wiley.

Sue, D. W., & Sue, D. (2008). *Counseling the culturally diverse: Theory and practice* (5th ed.). Hoboken, NJ: Wiley.

Toporek, R. L., Dodge, D., Tripp, F., & Alarcon, L. (2010). Social justice and community engagement: Developing relationships beyond the university. In J. G. Ponterotto, J. M. Casas, L. A. Suzuki, & C. M. Alexander (Eds.), *Handbook of multicultural counseling* (3rd ed., pp. 603–617). Thousand Oaks, CA: Sage.

Toporek, R. L., & Vaughn, S. R. (2010). Social justice in the training of professional psychologists: Moving forward. *Training and Education in Professional Psychology, 4,* 177–182.

Trimble, J. E. (2012). Working with North American Indian and Alaska native clients. In M. E. Gallardo, C. J. Yeh, J. E. Trimble, & T. A. Parham (Eds.), *Culturally adaptive counseling skills: Demonstrations of evidence-based practices* (pp. 181–200). Thousand Oaks, CA: Sage.

Virginia School Counselor Association. (2008). *Virginia professional school counseling program manual.* Yorktown, VA: Author.

Walsh, M. E., Galassi, J. P., Murphy, J. A., & Park-Taylor, J. (2002). A conceptual framework for counseling psychologists in schools. *The Counseling Psychologist, 30,* 682–704.

Watt, S. K. (2007). Difficult dialogs and social justice: Uses of the privileged identity exploration (PIE) model in student affairs practice. *College Student Affairs Journal, 26,* 114–125.

West-Olatunji, C. (2010). If not now, when? Advocacy, social justice, and counselor education. *Counseling and Human Development, 42,* 1–12.

Whalen, M., Fowler-Lese, K. P., Barber, J. S., Williams, E. N., Judge, A. B., Nilsson, J. E., & Shikazaki, K. (2004). Counseling practice with feminist-multicultural perspectives. *Journal of Multicultural Counseling and Development, 32,* 379–389.

Wilton, L. (2010). Where do we go from here? In J. G. Ponterotto, J. M. Casas, L. A. Suzuki, & C. M. Alexander (Eds.), *Handbook of multicultural counseling* (3rd ed., pp. 313–323). Thousand Oaks, CA: Sage.

Wood, C., & D'Agostino, J. V. (2010). Assessment in counseling: A tool for social justice work. In M. J. Ratts, R. L. Toporek, & J. A. Lewis (Eds.), *ACA advocacy competencies: A social justice framework for counselors* (pp. 151–159). Alexandria, VA: American Counseling Association.

Young, I. M. (2010). Five faces of oppression. In M. Adams, W. J. Blumenfeld, C. Castaneda, H. W. Hackman, M. L. Peters, & X. Zuniga (Eds.), *Readings for diversity and social justice* (2nd ed., pp. 35–45). New York, NY: Routledge.

Appendix B

Advocacy Competencies (Lewis, Arnold, House, & Toporek, 2002)

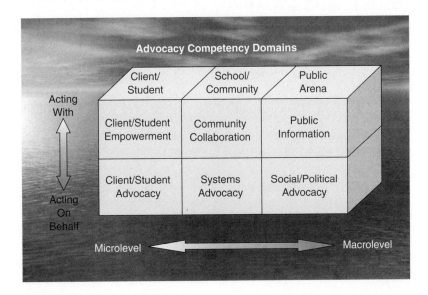

Advocacy Competency Domains

I. Client/Student Empowerment

- An advocacy orientation involves not only systems change interventions but also the implementation of empowerment strategies in direct counseling.
- Advocacy-oriented counselors recognize the impact of social, political, economic, and cultural factors on human development.
- They also help their clients and students understand their own lives in context. This lays the groundwork for self-advocacy.

Empowerment Counselor Competencies

In direct interventions, the counselor is able to:

1. Identify strengths and resources of clients and students.

2. Identify the social, political, economic, and cultural factors that affect the client/student.

3. Recognize the signs indicating that an individual's behaviors and concerns reflect responses to systemic or internalized oppression.

4. At an appropriate development level, help the individual identify the external barriers that affect his or her development.

5. Train students and clients in self-advocacy skills.

6. Help students and clients develop self-advocacy action plans.

7. Assist students and clients in carrying out action plans.

II. Client/Student Advocacy

- When counselors become aware of external factors that act as barriers to an individual's development, they may choose to respond through advocacy.
- The client/student advocate role is especially significant when individuals or vulnerable groups lack access to needed services.

Client/Student Advocacy Counselor Competencies

In environmental interventions on behalf of clients and students, the counselor is able to:

1. Negotiate relevant services and education systems on behalf of clients and students.

2. Help clients and students gain access to needed resources.

3. Identify barriers to the well-being of individuals and vulnerable groups.

4. Develop an initial plan of action for confronting these barriers.

5. Identify potential allies for confronting the barriers.

6. Carry out the plan of action.

III. Community Collaboration

- Their ongoing work with people gives counselors a unique awareness of recurring themes. Counselors are often among the first to become aware of specific difficulties in the environment.
- Advocacy-oriented counselors often choose to respond to such challenges by alerting existing organizations that are already working for change and that might have an interest in the issue at hand.
- In these situations, the counselor's primary role is as an ally. Counselors can also be helpful to organizations by making available to them our particular skills: interpersonal relations, communications, training, and research.

Community Collaboration Counselor Competencies

1. Identify environmental factors that impinge upon students' and clients' development.

2. Alert community or school groups with common concerns related to the issue.

3. Develop alliances with groups working for change.

4. Use effective listening skills to gain understanding of the group's goals.

5. Identify the strengths and resources that the group members bring to the process of systemic change.

6. Communicate recognition of and respect for these strengths and resources.

7. Identify and offer the skills that the counselor can bring to the collaboration.

8. Assess the effect of counselor's interaction with the community.

IV. Systems Advocacy

- When counselors identify systemic factors that act as barriers to their students' or clients' development, they often wish that they could change the environment and prevent some of the problems that they see every day.
- Regardless of the specific target of change, the processes for altering the status quo have common qualities. Change is a process that requires vision, persistence, leadership, collaboration, systems analysis, and strong data. In many situations, a counselor is the right person to take leadership.

Systems Advocacy Counselor Competencies

In exerting systems-change leadership at the school or community level, the advocacy-oriented counselor is able to:

1. Identify environmental factors impinging on students' or clients' development.

2. Provide and interpret data to show the urgency for change.

3. In collaboration with other stakeholders, develop a vision to guide change.

4. Analyze the sources of political power and social influence within the system.

5. Develop a step-by-step plan for implementing the change process.

6. Develop a plan for dealing with probable responses to change.

7. Recognize and deal with resistance.

8. Assess the effect of counselor's advocacy efforts on the system and constituents.

V. Public Information

- Across settings, specialties, and theoretical perspectives, professional counselors share knowledge of human development and expertise in communication.
- These qualities make it possible for advocacy-oriented counselors to awaken the general public to macro-systemic issues regarding human dignity.

Public Information Counselor Competencies

In informing the public about the role of environmental factors in human development, the advocacy-oriented counselor is able to:

1. Recognize the impact of oppression and other barriers to healthy development.

2. Identify environmental factors that are protective of healthy development.

3. Prepare written and multimedia materials that provide clear explanations of the role of specific environmental factors in human development.

4. Communicate information in ways that are ethical and appropriate for the target population.

5. Disseminate information through a variety of media.

6. Identify and collaborate with other professionals who are involved in disseminating public information.

7. Assess the influence of public information efforts undertaken by the counselor.

VI. Social/Political Advocacy

- Counselors regularly act as change agents in the systems that affect their own students and clients most directly. This experience often leads toward the recognition that some of the concerns they have addressed affected people in a much larger arena.
- When this happens, counselors use their skills to carry out social/political advocacy.

Social/Political Advocacy Counselor Competencies

In influencing public policy in a large, public arena, the advocacy-oriented counselor is able to:

1. Distinguish those problems that can best be resolved through social/political action.

2. Identify the appropriate mechanisms and avenues for addressing these problems.

3. Seek out and join with potential allies.

4. Support existing alliances for change.

5. With allies, prepare convincing data and rationales for change.

6. With allies, lobby legislators and other policy makers.

7. Maintain open dialogue with communities and clients to ensure that the social/political advocacy is consistent with the initial goals.

CHAPTER 4

Ethnicity

Garrett McAuliffe
Old Dominion University

Bryan S. K. Kim
University of Hawaii at Hilo

Yong S. Park
University of California, Santa Barbara

The purpose of Chapters 4 and 5 is to provide counselors with an overview of the notions of ethnicity and race, especially in the United States. These two chapters provide a foundation for the succeeding seven chapters on specific ethnic groupings. First, ethnicity and race are disentangled from each other. Then ethnicity is explored for the remainder of the chapter.

ETHNICITY AND RACE: CONFLATED CONCEPTS

Ethnicity and race are not always clearly distinguished from each other in popular usage. It is common to see the combined notion of "race/ethnicity" on public documents such as job or college applications and government forms. These terms have a tangled history.

In the 19th century, race, not ethnicity, was the predominant category used to classify groups of people. Race did all the work of lumping peoples into rigid groups. In fact, the term *ethnic group,* as a referent to people who share culture, was not recorded until the 1940s, under the influence of the relatively new field of anthropology.

It is important to distinguish race from ethnicity. Race is most commonly based on phenotype, that is, physical features. However, in the process of constructing race, a somewhat arbitrary lumping occurs. Distinct ethnic groups, regions, and languages are unfortunately grouped together as one race. In the process, simplistic racial categories such as "black" or "white" are created. These broad racial labels at best merely represent convenient and arbitrary demographic categories, not descriptors of unitary biological communities nor monolithic cultures.

As mentioned earlier, ethnicity, sometimes merely called culture, is a more recent addition to the discourse, coming out of the work of anthropologists of the past century or so. Among social scientists, ethnicity is the preferred concept, over race, for describing group membership. Ethnicity can be recognized as a socially created notion, rather than as a fixed biological entity. Ethnic group can be a useful acknowledgment that groups of people have a shared history, a history in which customs are passed down. As will be shown, however, ethnicity is not a simple concept.

Among social scientists, there are both opponents and proponents of separating the concepts of ethnicity and race. It should be noted that both groups agree that race is an oppressive, nonbiological concept.

Opponents suggest simply discarding the concept of race. Singh (1981) summarizes this perspective: "Distinctions between race and ethnicity . . . are untenable and without empirical support" (p. 2). Thus ethnic groups are misnamed as races, as in "the Jewish race" or "the Japanese race." The opponents of the use of the concept of race recommend that the term *ethnicity* should encompass all aspects of both what has been called race and what is called culture or ethnicity (Phinney, 1996). From this perspective, race is recognized as a still-important social construct, but one that has much oppressive baggage attached to it. In essence, the opponents of the notion of race hope that ethnicity will replace race in the general discourse and in research.

Proponents of keeping the concept of race in the social science discourse refer to the importance of acknowledging it as a public phenomenon, one that carries much social power and therefore must be studied. That position will be represented in this book. Therefore race and racism will be the topic of Chapter 5.

For practical purposes, it is most important that counselors note the contribution of both ethnicity and race to how people think and act. Counselors must especially recognize that there are power differentials among racial and ethnic groups. They should know the distinction between minority (nondominant) groups and majority (dominant) groups in the United States and the impact of those statuses on peoples' opportunities and self-perceptions. First, the fundamental notion of ethnicity is explored.

CONCEPTUALIZING ETHNICITY

This section introduces the notion of ethnicity and explores its importance for counseling work. While ethnicity is often simply called culture, following anthropological practice, the term *culture* will be used in this book more broadly to include shared social group affiliations such as social class, religion, and sexual orientation.

Every person has ethnicity or, more accurately, ethnicities. From the time of their birth, all humans have been enculturated into preferences, manners, behaviors, and values based on the reference groups they are influenced by. Everyone has learned how to dress, how and what to eat, and at least some versions of what is the good life. That enculturation takes place through traditional ethnicity, but also through the cultures of one's region, neighborhood, and religion. Therefore, the ethnicity of the first author might be seen as Irish Catholic American New Yorker. He was enculturated into all of those communities.

Activity 4.1 introduces you to some personal dimensions of your ethnicity.

Activity 4.1 What's in a Name?

Names are one expression of culture. They are always chosen in a social context. To begin your exploration of your own ethnicity, respond to the following questions as best you can.

What is your full name?

Where do your names come from?

Who gave you your names and why?

What do your names literally mean?

What do they mean to you?

What do they mean to other people? (i.e., What do others think of your names? How do they react to your names? What do you make of those reactions?)

What historical, ethnic, regional, or religious trend(s) do your names represent?

How are they different from those of someone from another region of the world or the country?

What experiences of negative bias have you had in relation to your names?

Ethnicity was defined in Chapter 1 as the recognition of common social ties among people due to shared geographic origins, memories of a historical past, cultural heritage, religious affiliation, language and dialect forms, and/or tribal affiliation. Simply put, ethnicity refers to the identity of groups of people who acknowledge their shared origins, geographical location, and customs. The origin may be mythical, for example, in the form of the creation stories of many ethnic groups. The geographical location may have been shared in the past, for example, Jews and the Middle East. The identity may be regional, such as Bostonian or Midwesterner. Ethnic group members perceive themselves as sharing common customs, although they can vary from person to person.

There is no "pure" ethnicity. People have migrated and mixed in the past so that all humans are, in a sense, multiethnic. However, over time there emerge groupings of people who are more or less distinct and who name themselves in contrast to others. It is important, therefore, to treat ethnicity as a social construction, as a story told by and about groups of people, rather than to consider it an objective entity.

Ethnicity represents a set of assumptions that is transmitted within the family and reinforced by social networks (Giordano & Carini-Giordano, 1997). Some of the dimensions of living that are affected by ethnicity include family roles and expectations, parenting, gender roles and expectations, attitudes toward sexuality, manners, directness versus indirectness of communication, attitudes toward alcohol or other mind-altering substances/addictions, perceptions of beauty and body image, and expression of emotion. Ethnicity is expressed in many forms, including in one's sense of self and space (distance, touch, formality), communication and language (directness, gestures, volume), dress and appearance (rules, status, grooming), food and eating habits (restrictions, use of hands and utensils, location, manners), and time consciousness (promptness, pace).

Ethnicity is one window that indicates who a person is. That is why it is important for counseling. Activity 4.2 provides you with an opportunity to look into that window.

Activity 4.2　Ethnic Self-Awareness

You already did some work in this book on your cultural group memberships in Chapter 2. Activity 2.2 asked you to name your ethnicity as well as your relationship to it. If you were Naïve/Accepting in relation to your ethnicity, the following will be more difficult to complete.

Complete the following questions on your ethnicity. As you do, note areas of uncertainty or confusion on your part. What do they say about your ethnic awareness? This activity serves as an alert to work you might do on your ethnicity.

1. What generation(s) in the United States do you represent? (Native Americans can answer "about 11,000 years on the continent" if they wish.) Explain.

2. What is your current identification with your ethnic group(s)? (i.e., How salient, or important, is it to you?)

3. Describe one moment or time (specific or general) when you became aware of your ethnic culture (if you have had that opportunity), such as when you went to college, a religious event, or social event; travelled; stayed with other people; or read something.

4. Identify some of the characteristics of your ethnic culture(s) in at least two of the following categories. (Note: Ethnicity is communicated through the family, community, and sometimes religion.)

Social behaviors (e.g., communication style, expression of different emotions)

     Manners

     Rituals

     Traditions

     Foods

     Celebrations

5. What is the influence of your ethnicity on how you think and act? (Consider the above-named elements and your worldview, how that worldview has been shaped, and how your worldview influences your interactions with others.)

6.

    a. What other ethnic groups and behaviors do members of your group commonly have a negative prejudice against/discriminate against, or have commonly done so in the past? (e.g., How are/were issues of race and ethnicity discussed/addressed in your family?)

    b. From your earliest recollection, what stereotypes, jokes, statements were made about other groups?

    c. Do these sentiments persist today?

7. State something about your ethnic culture that you are

    a. proud of. What customs or values of your culture do you prize the most? (e.g., achievement/work ethic, value placed on relationships, expressions of leisure and celebration, pride in heritage and the group's accomplishments, loyalties)

    b. ambivalent about/unsure of/not attracted to.

8. What might a counselor need to know about your ethnic group in order to be helpful?

PROCESSES THAT AFFECT ETHNICITY

This section delves into six processes by which individuals learn about the notion of ethnicity and how important it is to them. The most fundamental of these processes are enculturation and acculturation. From them follow four possible cultural adaptations: integration or bicultural competence, assimilation, separation, and marginalization.

Enculturation and Acculturation

Enculturation is defined as "the process of learning a culture in all its uniqueness and particularity" (Mead, 1963, p. 187). It is a term coined by anthropologist Melville Herskovits (1948). Through enculturation, a person learns how to live in her or his primary ethnic culture, or cultures, from infancy until death. Everyone is enculturated. The contents of enculturation include learned values, attitudes, and beliefs and corresponding behavior patterns. In the process of learning, a person acquires competence in her or his ethnic culture. It becomes the cognitive map, the term of reference for acting in the world.

While enculturation can occur within one dominant culture, *acculturation*, by contrast, refers to the meeting of at least two different cultures. Acculturation has generally been thought of as the process of an individual's socialization into a different group's ways. It is, therefore, sometimes referred to as second-culture acquisition (Good & Sherrod, 2001). Acculturation has occurred throughout human history as different groups encounter each other. Through acculturation, individuals take on some of the manners, speech patterns, dress, values, and tastes of a culture to which they have been exposed while also maintaining some of their original culture's expressions and norms.

Acculturation is not a one-way process. Over 50 years ago, anthropologists acknowledged the reciprocal exchange that occurs when cultures encounter each other in this classic definition: "Acculturation . . . result(s) when groups of individuals sharing different cultures come into continuous first-hand contact, with subsequent changes in the original culture patterns of either or both groups" (Redfield, Linton, & Herskovits, 1967, p. 182). Thus, for example, European Americans are affected by Hispanic, African American, American Indian, and Asian American ways and vice versa. There are mutual influences in language, music, attitudes, mores, and physical mannerisms. A simple example is the pervasiveness of African American music and verbal expression across the United States and much of the world. Thus, both dominant and nondominant groups potentially change each other as a result of consistent encounters (Casas & Pytluk, 1995).

Acculturation for members of nondominant groups can be particularly stressful because such individuals must become vigilant about customs and daily practices that they take for granted in their group in order to function in the dominant society. Members of nondominant cultures must commonly perform a strenuous balancing act as they simultaneously adjust to the norms of the dominant culture and retain the norms of the indigenous culture. These acculturation issues are especially important for immigrants and refugees. For them, acculturation refers to adjusting or adapting to the new culture while retaining a continuing enculturation in and allegiance to the culture of origin. Those individuals may not know important customs and behaviors that are required for functioning in a new dominant culture (Ponterotto, Utsey, & Pedersen, 2006). Such individuals may experience fear and culture shock in response to the differences that they are not prepared to encounter. That balancing act for immigrants and refugees is called the *acculturation-retaining* tension (Kim & Abreu, 2001), in that such individuals must try to acculturate sufficiently to function within the larger community while retaining their culture of origin.

Four Expressions of Enculturation and Acculturation

Individuals express their enculturation and acculturation in four ways: behavior, values, knowledge, and cultural identity (Kim & Abreu, 2001).

Counselors can assess a client's enculturation and acculturation by observing these phenomena.

The *behavior* dimension refers to such actions as friendship choice, preferences for entertainment and reading, participation in cultural activities, contact with the indigenous culture (e.g., time spent in a country of origin), language use, and food choice. For example, an African American may or may not choose African American friends, a European American may or may not listen to country music, and a first-generation Asian Indian may or may not eat more curried foods than a non-Indian.

The *values* dimension of enculturation and acculturation refers to attitudes and beliefs about social relations, cultural customs, and cultural traditions, along with gender roles and attitudes and ideas about health and illness. For example, an African American might define "family" to include elder friends, aunts and uncles, as well as cousins and siblings; an Arab American might value the authority of the male figures in a household; and a Scandinavian American might value equal gender roles in a family.

The *knowledge* dimension refers to culturally specific information, such as the names of historical figures in the culture of origin and/or the dominant culture, and knowledge of the historical significance of culturally specific activities. For example, a Mexican might honor Cinco de Mayo as the commemoration of a great Mexican battle victory, a Southern white might know much about Robert E. Lee and the Confederacy, and an African American might know the significance of Juneteenth as Emancipation Day.

Finally, the *cultural identity* dimension of enculturation and acculturation refers to a person's level of identification with the culture (e.g., high identification represented by a Chinese American having her name in the Mandarin language) and level of comfort with people of her or his own and other groups. Thus, a Latino man might be comfortable with fellow Latinos, but uncomfortable with Anglos. The cultural identity dimension is further described in the multiethnic identity model in the next section of this chapter.

Four Types of Acculturation/ Enculturation

Acculturation and enculturation are not unitary notions. Instead, an individual can have any of four acculturation statuses (Berry, Trimble, & Olmeda, 1986): integration, assimilation, separation, and marginalization. They explain an individual's level of adaptation to a dominant group's norms and the relative maintenance of her or his indigenous (usually meaning original) group's norms.

Integration/Bicultural Competence

Integration occurs when individuals become proficient in the culture of the dominant group (high acculturation) while retaining proficiency in the indigenous culture (high enculturation). Another term for such integration of the cultures is *bicultural competence* (LaFromboise, Coleman, & Gerton, 1993). Bicultural competence describes the process of a person's successfully meeting the demands of two distinct cultures. Bicultural individuals often perform a balancing act by participating in a dominant culture in one environment (e.g., at work) while fully embracing their original cultural identity in another (e.g., in a religious congregation). Thus, an Asian Indian immigrant might adopt the dominant culture's ways while in work situations, but at home participate in a Hindu community or adhere to traditional gender roles. Such might be the case of an Asian Indian woman who is the supervisor in a workplace, but who chooses to take a more deferential role in the family (Casas & Pytluk, 1995). Activity 4.3 lists the characteristics of bicultural competence.

Assimilation

Assimilation contrasts with integration. In assimilation the individual rejects her or his indigenous culture (low enculturation) while absorbing the culture of the dominant group (high acculturation). Such a process has already happened for many European Americans in the United States as

Think of a person with whom you have come into contact, even from afar through media, who shows some level of bicultural competence. Write the name or initials of that person. (It will likely be someone who is from a nondominant culture, as people from the dominant culture are not often very bicultural.)

_____

Listed below are the capabilities required for bicultural competence. Check off each of the characteristics for the person you named, and then give one example at the bottom.

Knowledge of cultural beliefs and values of both cultures

Positive attitudes toward both groups

Bicultural efficacy, or belief that one can live in a satisfying manner within both cultures without sacrificing one's cultural identity

Communication ability in both cultures

Role repertoire, or the range of culturally appropriate behaviors

A sense of being grounded in both cultures

Which of the above characteristics does this person especially show? _____

Give an example of her or his showing one of the characteristics: _____

they assimilated to the dominant Anglo-American Protestant culture. Thus, for example, the so-called Scotch-Irish, those northern Britons who immigrated to North America in large numbers in the 18th century (Fischer, 1989), and who were seen as a distinct ethnic group at that time, are now virtually indistinguishable from Anglo-Americans. They were similar enough for assimilation to occur.

Sometimes forced assimilation has been attempted in the United States. Many American Indians have ancestral memories of the so-called Indian schools of the early 20th century. Native Americans were sent there to be assimilated to Christian, European ways. In undergoing the assimilation process, they lost their ethnic customs and their pride in tribal ways.

Assimilation is neither desirable nor safe for many groups. For example, many Jews in Germany during the 1920s had assimilated to dominant German cultural ways. However, they were singled out by the dominant group as different (and as undesirable), with catastrophic consequences. In the United States, people of color cannot assimilate to the dominant European American culture, largely due to racialization; that is, those who don't look white generally remain the "other" in relation to the dominant white society.

In recent years, ethnic pride movements have proclaimed the value of embracing one's ethnic group while also being part of a larger nation, that is, *not* assimilating. A client need not give up her or his cultural identity in order to participate in an increasingly multicultural society. She or he can achieve an integrated status. That notion is the basis for the current ethos of multiculturalism in the United States.

Separation

The third acculturation/enculturation status, separation, occurs when an individual is not interested in learning the culture of the dominant group (low acculturation) and wants only to maintain and perpetuate the culture of origin (high enculturation). Individuals with this attitude might reside in ethnic enclaves. For example, an Asian American who works and lives in a Chinatown or a Koreatown in the United States may not have the need to interact with the members of the dominant group. In the past, many first-generation immigrants who arrived in large-enough numbers formed relatively separate communities within the dominant U.S. culture. With such separation, a person may not need to learn the cultural customs of the dominant group or learn to speak English.

Marginalization

The final acculturation status, and a problematic one for individuals, is marginalization. Marginalization represents the situation of a person who has no interest in maintaining or acquiring proficiency in any culture, neither the indigenous one nor the dominant one (low acculturation and enculturation). This can occur when a nondominant group is made peripheral by the larger society. A marginalized individual, or group, is excluded, or devalued, in the economy, in the daily social discourse, and in the customs of the dominant culture. Such exclusion results in the marginalized ethnic group seeming to be functionally useless to a society. Members of marginalized groups have not learned the ways of the dominant culture sufficiently in order to function well within the dominant society and do not feel included in the dominant culture. They also deny their indigenous culture. Thus they are "persons without a country." The devaluing of the nondominant group's language and customs can occur to such an extent that group members become ashamed of their ethnicity. Marginalization has happened to many ethnic groups throughout history. In the United States, it has occurred to many American Indians. Such marginalization occurred at first through the reduction in numbers and loss of homelands. It was further spurred by attempted resocialization of the remaining groups through the aforementioned Indian schools. There, American Indian ways were devalued and replaced with Western language, values, clothing, and other attributes. Other examples of marginalization include American Indians who

leave a reservation to live in an urban area, as they are enculturated into traditional ways that do not help them in that environment. The difficulty for marginalized peoples is that they then suffer from self-depreciation, unless they can "pass" in the dominant culture. Fortunately, ethnic pride movements have countered such marginalization. Marginalized people need to find ways to connect with their indigenous cultures.

Helping Clients With Acculturation

It is important for counselors who work with clients from nondominant groups, especially immigrants, to assess their clients' levels of acculturation and enculturation. Clients who are living in a different culture from their familiar one might have difficulty negotiating the tasks of living in the dominant culture. In counseling, low-acculturated clients might be unfamiliar with the overall norms of Western counseling, such as personal disclosure, expression of emotion, and equality between counselor and client. They might also doubt the helpfulness of a counselor who is from another culture.

Acculturation and enculturation are useful concepts, for they remind counselors to move beyond stereotyping of clients, such as "He is a(n) [name an ethnic group], therefore [name a behavior]." A counselor cannot know an individual's level of acculturation and enculturation by merely being familiar with her or his ethnic label. One must assess how much meaningful contact the person has had with the dominant culture in order to judge acculturation and enculturation.

SALIENCE

It might be clear at this point that ethnicity is not a uniform, static experience. Individuals with the same ethnicity can have very different experiences of their culture's meaning in their lives. That fact was illustrated in the first vignette in Chapter 1. This section discusses the psychological experience of ethnicity, in the form of salience. It parallels the general discussion of salience that was presented in Chapter 2.

Counselors must recognize ethnic salience in order to avoid assuming that ethnicity affects every client in the same way. Here are Marger's (2011) words on salience:

Some [individuals] are very conscious of their ethnic ties and make efforts to sustain them by choosing co-ethnics as friends, neighbors, and marital partners. Others may de-emphasize ethnicity to the point where it is no longer a significant part of their personal identity and affects little of their social life. (p. 280)

Salience is greater for members of nondominant and minority ethnic groups. By contrast, a very dominant group in any society often does not even consider itself to be ethnic. Many European Americans do not recognize their ethnicity as a source of the customs, common ancestry, manners, and artifacts that they value because their ethnicity is so pervasive and dominant. Ethnic salience can become high, however, for dominant group members when they are thrust into foreign contexts, ones in which they become a minority. Thus, for a European American who attends an African American religious service, ethnic salience is momentarily high. In Waters's (2004) words, "It is not until one comes in close contact with many people who are different from oneself that individuals realize the ways in which their backgrounds may influence their individual personalit[ies]" (p. 422).

CATEGORIES AND TERMS USED FOR ETHNICITY

Common terms for ethnicity include the term *nationality* and expressions used to represent specific ethnic groups. The next two sections explore terms used for ethnicity and their meanings.

Nationality

Nationality has often substituted for the term *ethnicity*, especially in the past. However, nationality refers merely to a person's citizenship in a particular state. In fact, there can be many ethnicities within a nation. For that reason, nationality is a less useful concept for explaining a person's socialization than is ethnicity

(Matsumoto & Juang, 2008). A person's current or former nation of citizenship does not explain her or his values and customs as well as does the notion of ethnicity.

On the other hand, nationality can have elements of ethnicity because there are dominant national norms, values, and customs that are shared by most members of a nation across ethnicities. A "national culture" can be spoken of, no matter how elusive and variable it is from person to person. Thus, there is some substance to the notion of "U.S. culture" because people in the United States are generally exposed to shared media, geography, climates, and political institutions. In this book, ethnicities within the overall U.S. nationality will be emphasized.

Labels for Ethnic Groups

When asked, "What are you?", individuals will respond sometimes with a clear ethnic label, a combination of labels, or a confused uncertainty, if they are in the dominant group. There is no official taxonomy of "correct" ethnic terms. As a result, counselors might wonder what terms to use for clients' ethnicity. The simplest recommendation is to ask the client.

Ethnic labels connote different meanings depending on whether the terms have been externally or internally imposed (Comas-Díaz, 2001). In that vein, the term *Hispanic* was created by the U.S. Census Bureau to lump all peoples who are Spanish-speaking or who descend from Spanish-speaking ancestors. Thus, the term *Latino* is preferred by many Latinos, especially those in the eastern United States. It should be noted, however, that many individuals still do refer to themselves as "Hispanic," especially in the southwestern United States. Many Latino people prefer the term that refers to their country of origin, such as *Colombian*, *Cuban*, or *Salvadoran*, with Latino or Hispanic being a secondary description.

The term *Oriental* for Asian Americans has a similar, externally imposed origin, as does *Negro* for African Americans. Each was a term imposed by others. Thus, members of those groups have chosen alternate names for themselves, such as *Asian* or *African American*. Again, there are cases in which some clients might not mind the so-called colonizers' terms, such as *Hispanic* or *Oriental*. Clients may themselves use such terms. That usage might be an indicator of their ethnic identity level and of the possible presence of internalized oppression (Delgado-Romero, 2001). Thus, ethnic terms may vary. Those terms can also have negative, positive, or neutral connotations.

Panethnic Groupings

In order to simplify ethnic categories, ethnicity researchers have created the previously mentioned panethnic or macroethnic groupings for the United States. There are currently five such groupings: Latino/Hispanic, African American, Asian/Pacific Islander American, Native American Indian, and European American (Marger, 2008). In this text, Asian is broken into (a) East and Southeast Asian and (b) South Asian. In addition, there is a separate chapter on Middle Eastern Americans. Those additions reflect broad cultural differences in the subgroups. Such groupings always sacrifice some precision for the sake of simplicity.

It should be noted that those panethnic groupings are slightly different from the U.S. Census Bureau categories for race and ethnicity: American Indian or Alaska Native, Asian, Black or African American, Native Hawaiian or Other Pacific Islander, and White. The U.S. Census Bureau (n.d.) includes two choices on Hispanic origin for all census respondents—"Hispanic or Latino" or "Not Hispanic or Latino"—and declares that Hispanics and Latinos can be of any race. The aforementioned conflation of ethnicity and race is illustrated by these categorizations. It should be noted that individuals can also select one or more races on the census.

Such large ethnic groupings must be seen as convenient constructions, largely useful for government demographic assessment. Those groupings were created from the popular perception that there is enough shared culture, language, and/or geographical origin within these five sets of peoples to call them groups.

People sometimes ask, "What is the purpose of ethnic categorizing?" Panethnic categories do have a function: They help society, especially the government, identify residence patterns, social class discrepancies, and discrimination, which do occur on the panethnic level. The limitation of such groupings, however, is that they gloss over distinct ethnic identities. For example, American Indians often want to be associated with their specific tribe. Similarly, the large grouping of Asian American is problematic because, for example, Japanese, Pakistani, and Thai people are culturally quite different from each other and usually wish to be identified by their particular ethnicity. Similarly, European Americans do not commonly see themselves as such. For example, newly arrived Greeks or Russians will see themselves in those national terms, not as European Americans.

Panethnic groupings also do not include all peoples. For example, where do people from North Africa and the Middle East fit under these panethnic categories? They don't easily fit, although they have been recently included under the general notion of "White" which is defined in the U.S. Census as a person having origins in any of the original peoples of Europe, the Middle East, or North Africa. It should be clear that the panethnic groupings are demographic categories that may be useful for political purposes. They are not as useful for describing culture, however.

Optional or Symbolic Ethnicity

A further complexity in the notion of ethnicity is related to power and status in society. Some ethnic groups have higher status and power. White Anglo-Saxon Protestant has historically been seen as the highest-status ethnicity in the United States. Such is the power of belonging to this group that every U.S. president except for John F. Kennedy and Barack Obama has been what is commonly called white Anglo-Saxon Protestant. By contrast, all other groups have been disparaged at some point, as exemplified by members of those groups often changing their names to Anglo-sounding ones.

In a broader sense, members of European American ethnic groups in general have a certain power that non–European American ethnic groups do not. European Americans can be merely "white" or a hyphenated American, as the situation changes. Thus, ethnicity is mostly symbolic or optional for European Americans. By contrast, it is not optional for people of color (Waters, 2004).

Sociologist Herbert Gans (1979) used the term *symbolic ethnicity* in 1979 to describe an ethnic identification that comes without social cost to the person. Gans proposed that as of the last quarter of the 20th century, European Americans have generally been able to treat ethnicity as a hobby, that is, as a leisure activity. European Americans, unless they are immigrants, are not generally publicly identified in terms of their ethnicity. However, members of other ethnic groups are publicly identified as not white. They are racialized ethnic minorities.

The notion of optional ethnicity is important because European Americans sometimes explain the achievements of their ethnic group as purely individual accomplishments. Many European Americans ignore the added value of being white. They also ignore the mutual assistance that members of white ethnic groups provide to each other. European Americans often claim that their people "made it" despite their ancestors being different from the dominant group. In that vein, European Americans often argue, "Since my ethnic group made it on its own, from poverty and immigration to economic and educational success and acceptance as mainstream Americans, why can't they (people of color) do it too?" Shapiro (2004) describes this phenomenon of laissez faire racism in this way: "[European Americans] view African Americans as individuals just like themselves, . . . rather than as members of a group who were forced to play by rigged rules used historically to ensure their disadvantage and white domination" (p. 101). European American stories of heroic personal effort and family struggle ignore the social benefit that they and their ancestors had, which consisted of being white.

By contrast, racialized ethnic minorities, that is, people of color, cannot choose to have or not have their ethnicity. In Manning Marable's (2000) words, "racialized minorities are fundamentally different from other ethnic groups because they share a common history of oppression, [including] residential segregation, economic subordination, and political disenfranchisement" (p. B34). People of color experience their nonoptional group identity on a daily basis—when they are concerned about job hiring and discrimination, when they are not viewed as middle class, when they don't see many people who look or act like them in visible positions, or when they hear of incidents of ethnic bias in the media.

The nonoptional dimension of ethnicity for some people is captured by the term *people of color*. This is a broad concept that represents all people from nonoptional ethnicities, those who cannot assimilate to whiteness. It is, therefore, a useful term for acknowledging racialized minorities, people whose ethnicity is trumped by their "differentness" from white Americans of European descent.

ETHNICITY AND COUNSELING

Ethnicity can matter in counseling for both clients and counselors. First, ethnic values and customs affect whether clients come to and use counseling at all because of ethnicity-related attitudes toward mental health, feelings about health and health care, and views about use of mental health services. Second, ethnicity also affects clients' expression of psychological distress, including the manifestation of anxiety and depression, eating disorders, and sexual disorders, as well as coping responses, self-esteem, substance abuse, somatization, and adolescent behavior problems. Subsequent chapters will provide specifics on such ethnic factors. Third, ethnic rules can turn into internalized assumptions about communication, sexuality, or career. Ethnic rules can get clients into trouble or, conversely, can help them live well.

It is important to reiterate, in the spirit of strengths-oriented psychology and solution-oriented counseling, that ethnicity can also be a source of strength. In that vein, clients might be asked to do a cultural strengths review, which is illustrated in Chapter 19. In either case, ethnicity is always with a client, for better and for worse. Specific ethnic factors in dealing with mental health issues will be discussed further in subsequent chapters. Two strategies for working with ethnicity are offered in the next sections of this chapter.

Assessing and Incorporating Ethnicity

Counselors are encouraged to assess the place of ethnicity for clients early in the work. Ethnicity is a silent presence in the counseling room, in the form of clients' socially learned attitudes, beliefs, and values. The subtle power of ethnicity is pointed out in the following description of differences between partners in family counseling by family therapists Joe Giordano and Mary Ann Carini-Giordano (1997).

> When Joe, who is Italian-American, first began working with Jewish families, he found it to be exciting. They not only told him what their problem was, but how to solve it. . . . Some had read more Freud than he. . . . But . . . in [some of the] families, an aptitude for seeking out and expounding underlying meaning was effectively used as a "cultural defense" against changing dysfunctional behavior. . . .

> With Irish families, he experienced the opposite. Joe's questions were met with little response and even silence. At other times, these families would be very talkative and humorous, spinning convoluted stories that left him confused as to their meaning. Many [Irish] families had difficulty talking about their feelings or sharing marital conflicts in front of their children.

> When working with families that came from Joe's own Italian-American background, he sometimes would over-identify . . . , thus totally missing . . . necessary interventions. And then there were other families whose behaviors mirrored back to him his own unresolved negative feelings about his Italian-American identity.

> For example, a British [American]-Italian American couple may experience conflict because the British-American takes literally the dramatic expressiveness of the Italian-American, who in turn finds intolerable the British-American's emotional distancing. . . . Thus the British-American husband calls his Italian-American wife "hysterical" and she labels him "unfeeling and rejecting." (p. 4)

These anecdotes illustrate the two-way power of ethnicity in counseling—for client and for counselor.

It is important to note that ethnicity is not the only variable that affects clients' functioning. In that vein, Giordano and Carini-Giordano (1997) reiterate the point made in Chapter 2 about not overgeneralizing across individuals based on culture. In particular, ethnicity might not be as relevant to some clients, although it is always present in every client. Box 4.1 offers guidelines for incorporating ethnicity into counseling.

Box 4.1 Guidelines for Incorporating Ethnicity Into Counseling

Consider the extent to which a client identifies with her or his ethnic background (i.e., salience plus ethnic identity development factors).

Determine whether a client's behaviors reflect ethnic norms, even if ethnicity seems to be unimportant to the client.

Determine how much a client's concerns are related to internal and/or external conflicts in values, as opposed to personality factors. In that regard, Giordano and Carini-Giordano (1997) illustrate the danger of ignoring ethnic values. They say that what may appear as a dysfunctional, enmeshed relationship in an Italian or Puerto Rican family may be perceived by its own members as close and loving, that is, normative. By contrast, for Italian and Puerto Rican families, distance among family members may be a more serious problem than for families who value independence.

Consider other contextual factors, such as social class, educational level, degree of acculturation, and gender, in the client's worldview and expectations.

As a counselor, explore your own cultural attitudes, especially if you are ambivalent about your own ethnicity. The latter is common among upwardly mobile professionals who are trying to cast off their ethnicity in favor of "passing" in the dominant professional culture.

Be an "ethnicity educator" who clarifies the meaning of ethnicity-related (and non-ethnicity-related) behaviors for clients and who promotes the idea that ethnic difference exists and must be negotiated in couples and other relationships.

These guidelines might be new for counselors who are used to considering only individual client factors.

Challenging Problematic Ethnic Rules

Counselors must determine whether internalized ethnic norms are harmful or helpful to clients. Often, clients may be married to rigid ethnic rules that cause distress. When a client reports such a conflict, a counselor can gently probe for the client's allegiances. Such an approach can include a question such as, "How did you come to know that this was the way to be?" Questions like this address the type of relationship that a person has to her or his ethnicity: Is she or he "subject to it," or can the client have a relationship to her or his ethnicity? In the latter case, the client can make choices about what ethnic norms she or he wishes to adhere to. In Chapter 2, Activity 2.3, The Challenge to Culturally Self-Authorize, asked readers to consider their received ethnicity and to consider reclaiming and discarding aspects of it.

The narrative approach to counseling, which will be discussed in Chapter 19, is useful for helping clients separate from problematic allegiances. In that approach, problems are externalized as stories. New, more effective stories can replace them. Similar work can be done with clients for whom received, rigid ethnic rules are causing conflict. Again, not all clients will wish to challenge their ethnic norms, and their readiness to do so must be respected. In many cases, problem solving for living within ethnic norms will be called for.

SUMMARY

Ethnicity is a pervasive presence in all clients' lives. It is sometimes conflated with race. The distinction made here emphasizes the distinction between ethnicity as culture, on the one hand, and race, on the other, as a social construction based on phenotype. Individuals internalize the mores of their ethnic groups. These values affect attitudes toward counseling

and mental health, career, sexuality, hierarchy, and interpersonal relations, to name a few domains. Ethnicity is not equally salient to all individuals. It is especially important to those who are in a minority. Ethnicity has a profound effect on opportunities in society. People of color and immigrants cannot choose whether to pay attention to their ethnicity or not because they are marked in society by their appearance and/or their manners and language. Guidelines for incorporating ethnicity into counseling include educating clients about the ethnic dimension of their behaviors, clarifying how much clients' concerns are related to internalized ethnic values, and knowing when counselors' own ethnic assumptions interfere with understanding clients.

REFERENCES

Berry, J. W., Trimble, J., & Olmeda, E. (1986). The assessment of acculturation. In W. J. Lonner & J. W. Berry (Eds.), *Field methods in cross-cultural research* (pp. 291–324). London, UK: Sage.

Casas, J. M., & Pytluk, S. D. (1995). Hispanic identity development: Implications for research and practice. In J. Ponterotto, J. M. Casas, L. A. Suzuki, & C. M. Alexander (Eds.), *Handbook of multicultural counseling* (pp. 155–180). Thousand Oaks, CA: Sage.

Comas-Díaz, L. (2001). Hispanics, Latinos, or Americanos: The evolution of identity. *Cultural Diversity and Ethnic Minority Psychology, 7,* 115–120.

Delgado-Romero, E. A. (2001). Counseling a Hispanic/Latino client—Mr. X. *Journal of Mental Health Counseling, 23,* 207–221.

Fischer, D. H. (1989). *Albion's seed: Four British folkways in America.* New York, NY: Oxford University Press.

Gans, H. (1979). Symbolic ethnicity: The future of ethnic groups and cultures in America. *Ethnic and Racial Studies, 2,* 1–20.

Giordano, J., & Carini-Giordano, M. (1997). Ethnicity: The hidden dimension in family counseling/therapy. *The Family Digest, 10,* 1, 4.

Good, G. E., & Sherrod, N. B. (2001). Men's problems and effective treatments. In G. R. Brooks & G. E. Good (Eds.), *The new handbook of psychotherapy and counseling with men: A comprehensive guide* to settings, problems, and treatment approaches (pp. 22–40). San Francisco, CA: Jossey-Bass.

Herskovits, M. J. (1948). *Man and his works: The science of cultural anthropology.* New York, NY: Knopf.

Kim, B. S. K., & Abreu, J. M. (2001). Acculturation measurement: Theory, current instruments, and future directions. In J. G. Ponterotto, J. M. Casas, L. A. Suzuki, & C. M. Alexander (Eds.), *Handbook of multicultural counseling* (2nd ed., pp. 394–424). Thousand Oaks, CA: Sage.

LaFromboise, T., Coleman, H. L K., & Gerton, J. (1993). Psychological impact of biculturalism: Evidence and theory. *Psychological Bulletin, 114,* 395–412.

Marable, M. (2000, February 25). We need new and critical study of race and ethnicity. *Chronicle of Higher Education,* p. B34.

Marger, M. N. (2008). *Race and ethnic relations: American and global perspectives.* Belmont, CA: Wadsworth Press.

Marger, M. N. (2011). *Social inequality: Patterns and processes.* Boston, MA: McGraw-Hill.

Matsumoto, D., & Juang, L. (2008). *Culture and psychology.* Belmont, CA: Thomson/Wadsworth.

Mead, M. (1963). Socialization and enculturation. *Current Anthropology, 4,* 187–197.

Phinney, J. S. (1996). When we talk about American ethnic groups, what do we mean? *American Psychologist, 51,* 918–927.

Ponterotto, J. G., Utsey, S. O., & Pedersen, P. B. (2006). *Preventing prejudice: A guide for counselors, educators, and parents* (2nd ed.). Thousand Oaks, CA: Sage.

Redfield, R., Linton, R., & Herskovits, M. J. (1967). Memorandum for the study of acculturation. In P. Bohannan & F. Plog (Eds.), *Beyond the frontier: Social process and cultural change* (pp. 181–186). Garden City, NY: Natural History Press.

Shapiro, T. M. (2004). *The hidden cost of being African American.* New York, NY: Oxford University Press.

Singh, B. (1981). Race, ethnicity and class: Clarifying relationships and continuous muddling through. *Journal of Ethnic Studies, 9*(2), 1–19.

U.S. Census Bureau. (n.d.). *About the Hispanic population of the United States.* Retrieved from http://www.census.gov/population/www/socdemo/hispanic/about.html

Waters, M. C. (2004). Optional ethnicities. In M. L. Andersen & P. H. Collins (Eds.), *Race, class, and gender* (pp. 418–427). Belmont, CA: Wadsworth/Thompson Learning.

CHAPTER 5

Conceptualizing Race and Racism

Garrett McAuliffe, Tim Grothaus, and Edwin Gómez

Old Dominion University

To the extent that race is even a valid concept . . . it does not come in boxes provided by God or Mother Nature. Race is an undifferentiated continuum of gene frequencies that we break into categories. . . . We place markers at various points on that genetic continuum: cross this one and you are Caucasian, cross that one and you are African, cross another and you are Asian. . . . The concept called race is an artifact of the way our minds divvy up and simplify an intricate body of information about human beings. The shape of that artifact is not an idle matter—for better and for worse, the way we conceptualize race makes a difference in the world.

Parker Palmer (1998, pp. 130–131)

A fan threw a banana at black Philadelphia Flyers hockey player Wayne Simmonds during a shootout attempt tonight. Afterwards, Simmonds said, "I don't know if it had anything to do with the fact I'm black. I certainly hope not. When you're black, you kind of expect [racist] things. You learn to deal with it."

James O'Brien, NBC Sports, September 22, 2011

In the first epigram, Palmer (1998) captures the difficulty with the concept of race. It is a confused and contested social construction (Benesh & Henriksen, 2009; Pellegrini, 2005). In fact, it is considered to be the most controversial topic in the social sciences (Marger, 2008). And yet, race is an important social phenomenon, even if it cannot be defined in biological terms. Ask hockey player Wayne Simmonds. Notice his response: "When you're black, you kind of expect [racist] things. You learn to deal with it." So racism is still alive. And it affects all Americans, in subtle and obvious ways. Counselors need to be exquisitely aware of the psychological consequences of the continuing impact of race on clients' lives. This chapter is aimed at pulling apart the murky, but powerful, notion of race so that counselors do not underestimate it, or overestimate it, in their work.

DEFINING A MURKY CONCEPT

Race was defined in Chapter 1 as a group of people of common ancestry, distinguished from others by physical characteristics such as hair type, color of eyes and skin, and stature. The concept of race is "messy"; that is, it is inexact and arbitrary. Sociologist Martin Marger (2011) attempts to describe race thus:

Race crudely describes people who share a set of similar genetic characteristics. . . . Racial categories, however, [are] highly arbitrary. . . . Physical differences between groups are not clear-cut but instead tend to overlap and blend into one . . . forming a continuum, not a set of clearly demarcated types. Within-group differences are actually much stronger than any across-group differences. (pp. 281–282)

An even more nuanced description of race is offered in Box 5.1.

Box 5.1   Race: The Power of an Illusion

Here is a description of the oversimplification of the notion of race, and the negative consequences of doing so, by the producer of the PBS Special "Race: The Power of an Illusion"(California Newsreel, 2003).

What Differences Make a Difference?

by Larry Adelman

In 1851 the Louisiana physician Dr. Samuel Cartwright observed a behavior evident in African Americans but absent in whites. They tended to run away from slave plantations. He attributed this odd behavior to a disease peculiar to Negroes. He even gave the affliction a name, "drapetomania."

Cartwright's "run-away" disease elicits derisive laughter today. So too do all the other 19th and early 20th century exertions to distinguish races by facial angle, skull size, cranial index, length of shin bone and blood type. Our growing knowledge of the genome and human evolutionary history helps us understand why all such efforts to locate the source of innate racial difference were doomed: it doesn't exist. Most geneticists and anthropologists who study human variation agree that humans just don't come bundled into three or four separate groups according to skin color and other physical traits.

We all have ancestors from elsewhere—and if we go back far enough, about 70,000 or so years ago, all our ancestors can be traced back to Africa. But if our idea of race assumes that different groups each share among themselves a different suite of inborn traits, then we have to ask, "What differences make a difference?" There's no question that some gene forms show up more often in some populations than others: alleles that code for blue eyes, or the A, B, O blood groups, and of course, those alleles that influence skin color. . . . But just because some members of a population might carry a specific gene form, doesn't mean all members do. Only a small percentage of Ashkenazi Jews carry the Tay-Sachs allele. When a couple I know were screened upon their pregnancy, the non-Jewish partner was found to be the Tay-Sachs carrier, not the Jewish one.

That's because most human variation falls within, not between populations. About 85% of all genetic variation can, on average, be found within any local population, be they Swedes, Kikuyu, or Hmong. About 94% can be found within any continental population. . . . In fact, there are no characteristics, no traits, not even one gene that turns up in all members of one so-called race yet is absent from others.

Take sickle cell. Doctors were long taught that sickle cell anemia was a genetic disease of Negroes [*sic*], a marker of their race. Yet sickle cell is found among peoples from central and western Africa, but not

---

southern Africa. It is also carried by Turks, Yemenis, Indians, Greeks, and Sicilians. That's because sickle cell arose several thousand years ago as a mutation in one of the genes that codes for hemoglobin. The mutation soon spread to successive populations along the trade routes where malaria was common. It turns out that inheriting one sickle cell allele confers resistance to malaria and thus provides a selective advantage in malarial regions (inheriting sickle cell alleles from both parents causes sickle-cell disease). In other words, sickle cell . . . is a marker not of skin color or race but ancestry, or more precisely, having ancestors from where malaria was common.

Like sickle cell, most traits are influenced by separate genes and inherited independently one from another. . . . Sub-Saharan Africans tend to have dark skin. But so too do Dravidians from India, Aborigines from Australia, and Melanesians from the South Pacific. Large numbers of West Africans are lactose intolerant as are Japanese, but East Africans aren't. German and Papua New Guinean populations have almost exactly the same frequencies of A, B and O blood. At one point on the genome an individual might share a gene form common in Africa, at another site East Asia, and still another, Europe. . . . For each trait we can classify people into "races" by that trait, each giving us different and overlapping races depending on the trait selected.

The reason for all this within-group variation is because, unlike most other species, modern humans, Homo sapiens is young, only about 150,000 years or so old, and we've always moved. As humans migrated around the globe, populations bumped into each other and shared their mates—and genes. Sometimes genes flowed across great distances—through trade, war, slavery, piracy, exile and migration. More often they flowed from village to village to village. Human populations just haven't been isolated from each other long enough to evolve into separate sub-species, or races.

Source: Excerpted from "Race and Gene Studies: What Differences Make a Difference" (http://newsreel.org/guides/race/whatdiff.htm), courtesy of California Newsreel (www.newsreel.org). © 2003 California Newsreel. For more information on the documentary series *Race—The Power of an Illusion*, please visit www.pbs.org/race.

As can be seen, there is no "pure" notion of race. Human beings are "mixed up," to quote Salman Rushdie from the beginning of Chapter 1, due to migration, exploration, invasions, intermarriage, and rape from wars and oppression of minorities (Maglo, 2011). Jorde and Wooding (2004), who are geneticists, declare that there is no pure notion of race, due to migrations and the subsequent movement of genes among different populations (called *gene flow* in biology). Jorde and Wooding further assert that human population groups share most of their genetic variation, and that the danger lies in the public's tendency to create typologies when in fact there are continua. The peoples of current Greece blend into the peoples of Turkey, who blend into Syrians, who blend into Egyptians, who blend into the peoples of Ethiopia, who blend into the peoples of Uganda, and so on. Race as a concept was invented when Europeans encountered sub-Saharan Africans, assuming that there were greater differences, due to the dramatic dissimilarity in superficial appearance. In fact, humans are remarkably alike, despite superficial differences (King, 1981). Of the small amount of total human variation, 85% of the variation in genetics exists within any local population, whether it be Zulu, Laplander, Cambodian, Lakota, or residents of a small, isolated community.

In fact, the notion of race is so crude that DNA tests show that the majority of individuals in a particular study shared genetic markers with people of different skin colors. For example, a high percentage of so-called black persons in the United States have some European genetic ancestry (Parra et al., 1998). Informal studies show that many whites also have varied genetic origins in Asia and Africa (Daly, 2005).

It might be clear from these findings that the concept of race is a contested one. It should be contested. It was inaccurately constructed as an objective notion in the past by scientists and others who promoted the pseudoscientific idea that there are distinct races. That idea has been used as justification to divide and rank different groups of people. Serious harm has resulted from this formulation for many peoples in the United States and elsewhere, including Asians, sub-Saharan Africans, the Irish, Jews, and Mediterranean peoples.

The very notion of seeing physical differences is not in itself problematic. It is, in fact, automatic for human beings (Ponterotto, Utsey, & Pedersen, 2006). People tend to classify by appearance. This act of classifying serves a protective function. Using such physical appearance cues allows humans to determine whether individuals are "one of us" or members of another group, tribe, or nation. What is problematic is the conclusions that are reached after the classifying—conclusions about intellect, sexuality, violence-proneness, and other characteristics that are used to favor one group over another.

You are invited to complete Activities 5.1 and 5.2 in order to assess your own experience of race.

Activity 5.1 Racial Self-Awareness

Complete the following phrases:

I describe myself as a member of the _____ racial group.

I first became aware that my race mattered in this society when

The best thing about being _____ (insert your racial group) is

The worst thing about being _____ (insert your racial group) is

People of my racial group view other racial groups in the following ways

When I am with members of my racial group, the issues, feelings, and thoughts that are not shared in mixed racial company are

The types of influences that these attitudes might have on the counseling interaction are

---

Activity 5.2   Cross-Race Contact

Name a race other than your own, using whatever term is familiar to you.

Describe your experience with people of this group (including how much contact you have with members of this group and how close that contact is).

Name a time when you had a discussion with a member of this racial group about race itself, if ever.

Think of your most recent uncomfortable racial situation in your personal or professional life that left you feeling uneasy and/or confused.

What did you think?

How did you feel?

How did you react (behave)?

What might your mother think, feel, and say to you about this situation?

What might your father think, feel, and say to you about this situation?

Think of a first session you have had, or might have, with clients in terms of their race/ethnicity/culture. With what type of client do you have a tendency to feel the greatest level of comfort and confidence?

What type of client raises your anxiety?

What did you discover from responding to these questions?

Racism

Racism is inevitably tied to the concept of race because race has historically been associated with notions of inferiority and superiority. Racism can most simply be defined as prejudice plus power (Holcomb-McCoy & Chen-Hayes, 2011). In other words, racism consists of (a) the belief that a group of people with characteristics other than those of one's own group are inferior in some way and (b) the ability to act on that belief.

A subtler definition of racism lies in David Wellman's (1977) classic description:

> Racism extends considerably beyond prejudiced beliefs. The essential feature of racism is not hostility or misperception, but rather the defense of a system from which advantage is derived on the basis of race. The manner in which the defense is articulated—either with hostility or subtlety—is not nearly as important as the fact that it insures the continuation of a privileged relationship. (p. 34)

Thus, an individual's supporting of any advantages based on race can be considered racist.

It is important to note that any person or group can be racist, if they have the power to enforce prejudiced beliefs. Thus, racism is not possible only among white people of European descent. However, in U.S. history, so-called white persons have largely had the power to define and enforce the notion of race. For this reason, the term *people of color* has been coined not as a race in itself, but as a description of racialized minorities (Marable, 2000; Takaki, 2008), that is, people who have been colonized and dominated by Europeans and European Americans (Martinez, 2004).

The concepts of race and racism are not unique to the United States, nor are they limited to recent times. Evidence of racism appears in ancient India, China, Egypt, Greece, and Rome (Gossett, 1997). People have set up hierarchies based on various schemes, from skin color to facial features and body types. But these distinctions became especially established with European colonial explorations, for example, as mentioned earlier, in the early 1400s when European explorers encountered sub-Saharan African people who looked different from themselves.

Such stark visual distinctions led Europeans to decide that there were, in fact, distinct races. They failed to acknowledge that there were gradations of peoples who had more or less bred together over centuries. Biologists use the term *populations* to describe this phenomenon.

Categorization of Races

The very number of racial categories has varied over the past two centuries from three to over twenty. Until fairly recently, anthropologists categorized humans into three supposed races: *Mongoloid, Caucasoid,* and *Negroid.*

Caucasoid or *Caucasian,* like the others, is a problematic term. It is based on the German scientist Johann Friedrich Blumenbach's (1752–1840) assumption that white persons are descended from the original humans in the Caucasus region of the present-day nations of Russia and Georgia. His thesis was based partly on the nearness of the Caucasus to the mythical place where Noah's ark of the Hebrew Bible rested, that is, Mount Ararat in eastern Turkey. Modern anthropologists have thoroughly rejected this notion that the first humans came from that region.

It should be noted that the term Caucasian is used in the United States to represent white persons, but in Europe it only represents people from the Caucasus region of the world. Its inexact usage in the United States has led to some racial recategorizing over the years. Before 1923, so-called Caucasians in the U.S. were qualified to become naturalized citizens. However, when several Asian Indians who were, by definition at the time, of the supposed Caucasoid race, successfully petitioned for U.S. citizenship in the 1920s, the U.S. Supreme Court reinterpreted the laws to conclude that only those who were deemed "white" were qualified, forcing these Asian Indians to lose their citizenship. This change in the definition of race from a biological base (in supposed skull shape) to a color base further points to the lack of scientific merit for how these concepts are used. Because of its inaccuracy and racist implications, the term Caucasian is better discarded. In this book "white" will be used to refer to that category. Next is a history of the troubled concept of race in the United States.

The Status of Racism Today

Is racism a story of the past? Is it a nightmare from which we as a nation have awakened, to paraphrase the writer James Joyce? There are strong indications that overt racism is much modified today. Ellis Cose (2011) found there to be greater optimism among blacks about opportunity, accompanied by waning racial bigotry among whites. Increased positive interracial relationships and expanded job opportunities have occurred. Cose notes the movement among many whites across three phases, from (1) general pre–civil rights hostility, to (2) post–civil rights neutrality, to (3) current increases in alliance with blacks. These facts are encouraging, as the days of rage have given way to a hopeful determination among people of color.

However, the situation is complex and confusing. Racism and its legacy persist. Cose notes that two issues persist today: (1) continuing patterns of systemic inequality in jobs, housing, educational achievement, and incarceration, as expressed in hiring practices, law enforcement, and lending practices, and (2) belief by blacks that there is consistent subtle prejudice in their encounters with whites. Only 40% of blacks in 2010 believed that race relations are generally good, whereas 63% of whites did (Condon, 2010). Most important, in the CBS poll that Condon (2010) refers to, twice as many African Americans (57%) as whites (29%) believe that white people have a better chance of getting ahead in today's society. Black people are wary, in Cose's words, as "a people whose history is largely one of dampened, doomed, or shattered expectations" (p. 2). These perceptions matter, and oppression persists.

It is the hope of this book that counselors are vigilant about their own racism (of any kind) and that they are alert to race-related phenomena, including inadequate schooling, the wealth gap between blacks and whites, the need for successful role models, individuals' personal beliefs in racist barriers in jobs and housing, and the concern about daily microaggressions (Smith, Hung, & Franklin, 2011; Sue, 2010). We hope that counselors are part of the solution to counter the continuing disparities and pessimism among blacks. A legacy of hundreds of years of suppression of a people leaves its mark on all. Each of these topics will be discussed in this chapter.

ORIGINS AND HISTORY OF THE CONCEPT OF RACE IN THE UNITED STATES

In the United States, the current notion of race was constructed in the 19th century. The social construction of racial categories in that era is illustrated by Freeman (1998):

> For much of the 19th century . . . the term mulatto was used to indicate a person who had one Black parent and one White parent. This term was essentially abandoned by the end of the century. In the 1900 U.S. Census, the classification quadroon and octoroon were used to denote people who were one-quarter and one-eighth Black, respectively. By the 1920 Census, a Black American was defined as anyone with even one Black ancestor—the "one drop rule." This rule is unique to [the United States] and is the current definition of who is Black. During the last half of the 19th century and well into the 20th century, other groups such as Jews and Irish were also classified as separate races. There is still no international agreement on racial classifications. (p. 220)

It might be clear at this point that the U.S. conception of race is a product of the United States' social and political history (Henriksen & Paladino, 2009a). The following is a brief overview of the sociopolitical trends in the United States that have led to the current race paradigm.

Theories and Movements That Reinforced the Race Paradigm

As mentioned earlier, racial distinctions in the United States are not limited to the black–white differentiation. However, that phenomenon is discussed most extensively in this section because it has arguably had the greatest impact on American life of any social issue. At least four sets of historical foundations have guided the notion of race in the United States: the law, evolutionary theory, genetic inheritance theory, and the assimilationist and melting pot perspectives.

Foundations of Race in Law

The United States was founded on the notion that it was a people held together by common white "blood" and skin color and that only white persons were able to self-govern (Gerstle, 2001). Race theory was not fully articulated at this time. Thomas Jefferson believed that blacks were inferior to whites but declared his uncertainty about the basis for that suspicion (Dain, 2002). Jefferson said, "I advance it as a suspicion only, that the blacks, whether originally a distinct race, or made distinct by time and circumstance, are inferior to whites" (cited in Dain, 2002, p. 30). Despite the absence of a clearly articulated theory of race, the United States was founded as a de facto "white republic," as other peoples were not considered part of the U.S. community. This notion was officially enshrined in the 1790 law that limited naturalization to free white persons. Thus, Africans, Asians, and American Indians were not originally considered to be in the national community (Takaki, 2008).

Foundations of Race in Evolutionary Theory

The notion that blacks and others were inferior to whites was further reinforced by the quasi-sociological view that is called Social Darwinism. This perspective was a misapplication of Charles Darwin's concept of evolution, which was published in his *Origin of Species* in 1859. There, Darwin proposed the idea of biological evolution as an explanation of the emergence and persistence of forms of life. In the later 1800s, English scholar Herbert Spencer translated that notion into the social realm. Social Darwinism explained human differences in terms of survival of the fittest, that is, the notion that some races or peoples are more fit for survival than others and are, therefore, designed by nature to dominate inferior races. His ideas led to the notion that white Protestant Europeans had biologically evolved much further and faster than other "races."

This notion led to an extreme laissez-faire public policy. The Social Darwinist political argument went like this: Since the poor are poor because they lack certain genetic characteristics that would fit them for economic survival, society has no obligation to its poor. To help them would be to allow inferior types to survive and thus interfere with evolution and thereby weaken society. This policy was related to, for example, the British noninterference with the Irish potato famine, resulting in millions of deaths in the 1840s.

Social Darwinism was particularly popular in the United States. It led to the overt and sustained subjugation of African Americans even after slavery was declared illegal. The power of Social Darwinism lasted into the 1920s, with its remnants continuing to surface in the present day in some people's attitudes about racial inferiority and the ineffectiveness of social programs to help some racial groups.

Foundations of Race in Genetic Inheritance Theory

Complementing this application of evolutionary theory was the inheritance theory, which arrived with Gregor Mendel's discovery of genes in the 1860s. It gave birth to the eugenics movement at the end of the 19th century and beginning of the 20th century. Eugenics was a wildly popular notion, adhered to by many thinkers of the age. It was developed in 1883 by Sir Francis Galton, who was a cousin of Charles Darwin. Eugenics refers to the study and use of selective breeding to improve a species over generations. Proponents of eugenics advocated sterilizing whole populations to protect against procreation and mixing the biologically inferior "lower races" with the supposed superior races. The lower races were considered to be any groups who were not from Northern and Western Europe and who were not of the Protestant faith. Evidence of the racial superiority of Northern European Protestants and their American descendants was confirmed by its adherents in the U.S. victory over Spain (considered a Catholic and Latin race at the time) in the Spanish-American War in 1898 and in the hegemony of the British Empire on a worldwide scale.

Through Social Darwinism and its cousin, eugenics, race was inextricably connected to biology and tangentially connected to superiority in ethnicity and religion (with the "lower races," for example, being Mediterranean peoples and Catholics). While the massive extermination of peoples based on "race" did not begin until the Nazi era, it had its origins in the "benign" intentions of the U.S. and British elites who wished to use science to save human beings from themselves (Black, 2003). Eugenics and "race science" were explicitly taught at major universities throughout the United States from the 1880s through the 1920s. A testimony to the popularity of a biological view of racial superiority was a bestseller in 1911, *Heredity in Relation to Eugenics*. The author, Charles Davenport, warned of the biological inferiority of Southern and Eastern Europeans in these words:

> The population of the United States will, on account of the great influx of blood from South-Eastern Europe, rapidly become darker in pigmentation, smaller in stature, more mercurial [i.e., emotional], more attached to music and art [as opposed to science and reason], more given to crimes of larceny, kidnapping, assault, and vagrancy than were the original English settlers. (p. 219)

As a result of this type of pseudoscience, more than 60,000 Americans were actually sterilized and policies were enacted to severely control immigration based on racial and religious attributes (Black, 2003). The influence of eugenics was so pervasive that even Frank Parsons, the social reformer and the founder of the modern notion of counseling, was a believer in it.

These historical and theoretical developments are important for several reasons. First, through them, non-white persons were legally made subordinate, second-class citizens. Second, the "scientific" evolutionary and genetic arguments justified the hegemonic position of Anglo-Protestants in American society. These arguments also laid the foundation for future positions on nature trumping nurture in the inferiority of some races. Biological arguments about race are still put forth (e.g., Herrnstein & Murray, 1996).

Foundations of Race in the Assimilationist and Melting Pot Perspectives

The next major shift that occurred in thinking about race was preceded by the increasing assimilation of European immigrants during the early 20th century in the United States. Recognition of the fact that the supposedly inferior Jewish and Catholic immigrants were able to assimilate into the American mainstream and achieve in the society in great numbers at the highest levels challenged the arguments that Anglo-Protestants were a biologically superior race.

Further challenges to the biological view were presented from social science. For example, psychologists (e.g., Otto Kleinberg of Columbia University) asserted that earlier psychological testing along racial lines was flawed methodologically. Kleinberg demonstrated that environment was the factor in intelligence in his studies of African American migrants to the North in the 1930s. Anthropologists (e.g., Franz Boas; see Box 5.2) were arguing for a separation between culture and biology (Hannaford, 1996).

Box 5.2   Franz Boas, 1858–1942

Franz Boas is a key figure in changing the American conception of race. He played a monumental role in eviscerating the racist worldview that prevailed in 19th and early 20th century American social sciences. Boas stood out among anthropologists as a proponent of cultural explanations of perceived differences among people.

Boas's own experience as a German Jew made him particularly sensitive to the destructiveness of racial bias. When he arrived in America, he noted that anthropology in this country played a central role as apologist for the notion of racial superiority and inferiority. He challenged the dominant eugenic discourse of the day by careful studies of the Eskimos and the Native Americans of British Columbia.

From these and other analyses, he introduced the notion of cultural relativism. Cultural relativism emphasizes differences in peoples to be the results of historical, social, and geographic conditions and that all populations have complete and equally developed culture. In this vein, Boas warned social scientists and others not to judge cultural practices according to one's own cultural ways. The common practice before this time had been to use one's own culture, usually European and European American, as a standard for "civilization" and to find other "races" wanting in comparison. Boas's predecessors had argued that the evolutionary scale led from

(Continued)

savagery to civilization and that Europeans were superior biologically, as evidenced by their version of culture. Boas believed that cultures are too complex to be evaluated according to the broad theorizing characteristic of evolutionary "laws." Instead, Boas sought to understand the development of societies through their particular histories.

Boas worked extensively with black intellectuals, including Booker T. Washington, W. E. B. DuBois, and Zora Neale Hurston. Boas demonstrated that prejudice and racism—not innate inferiority—were black peoples' greatest obstacles in the United States.

Boas's struggle to understand the salience of race in the United States was a foundation for the opening of the topic of race in the 20th century. Just as the work of the early American anthropologists directly influenced the "separate but equal" notion in the *Plessy v. Ferguson* case of 1896, resulting in legal segregation, Boas's work led eventually to the 1954 *Brown v. Board of Education* ruling that made segregation illegal.

The Mind of Primitive Man (1911) was perhaps his most influential book; it demonstrated that there was no such thing as a "pure" race or a superior one. In his words, "If we were to select the most intelligent, imaginative, energetic, and emotionally stable third of mankind, all races would be present." Not surprisingly, his books were banned in Hitler's Germany. Long outspoken against totalitarianism in its many guises, he was a fierce advocate of intellectual freedom, supported many democratic causes, and was the founder of the American Committee for Democracy and Intellectual Freedom. In 1963, the scholar Thomas Gossett wrote, "It is possible that Boas did more to combat race prejudice than any other person in history."

Note: Special thanks to Maura McAuliffe and the Anthropology Department of the College of William and Mary for the information on Franz Boas.

The Assimilationist Perspective

During the 1920s, Robert Park and his students from the Chicago School of Sociology proposed the idea that assimilation was the expected end product of inter-race contact (McKee, 1993). The assimilation idea countered the popular view that non-whites and whites were incompatible. It suggested that (in the past) "lesser" racial groups had been assimilated (culturally and physically) into the mainstream civilization of those who had conquered them, as seemed to be the case with the Roman Empire. Park and his colleagues also noted that assimilation by the dominated group was but one of three possible outcomes to being conquered, the other two being the establishment of a caste system (e.g., India) or having a nation within a nation (e.g., American Indians, Jews in Europe). Significantly, with the assimilationist perspective, the environment, rather than biology, became the dominant explanation for group differences. Some groups happened to be dominated but could mix eventually with the conquerors.

The assimilation notion, however, still perpetuated the idea of a dichotomy between white and "other" in the United States. The common conception of assimilation was still based on a Eurocentric worldview. It posited, in the first place, that the culturally (not necessarily biologically) "lesser" peoples (e.g., Catholic and Jewish European white immigrants) would eventually attain equal status with the Anglo-Protestant whites as the former became more like the latter. But non-white groups were seen as problematic, as they were not so easily assimilated. (It should be noted that these distinctions were not made by Park and his students themselves, but rather by their followers.) As a result of the assimilationist impulse, biological arguments began to wane. Sociologists then began to look at blacks and others as culturally, not biologically, inferior. The view was that it would take major resocialization for them to become more "white" (i.e., advanced). Social policy in the early 20th century followed assimilationist assumptions. For example, American Indians were sent to special schools where their "Indianness" was to be expunged and European American ways taken on. Thus, the basic formulation of cultural superiority-inferiority remained.

However, distinctions among racial groups were made. Blacks were believed to not be able to assimilate into U.S. society. As a result, whites believed that it was natural to have the separate-but-equal segregation policies that followed the *Plessy v. Ferguson* decision. However, this was not a tenable position. The clamor by black people and white allies for full acceptance led to continuing social unrest; for example, the abuses of the Jim Crow system would eventually lead to race riots in the early 1920s.

In mid-century, the notion of race shifted again, this time to a moral problem, with the publication in 1944 of Gunnar Myrdal's *An American Dilemma*. Myrdal chose this title for his voluminous work because he felt that it captured, in McKee's (1993) words, "his sense of the race problem in the United States: a conflict between the highest of American ideals and lower parochial interests and prejudices" (p. 226). In particular, Myrdal noted that it was not so much a black people's problem as it was a white people's problem. Myrdal, however, still supported the assimilationist perspective that the U.S. society was European in its ways and manners and that all others must assimilate to it.

The Melting Pot Perspective

From the 1930s to the 1960s, increased European American assimilation into the mainstream led to the melting pot paradigm. The idea behind the melting pot is that the melding of various cultures makes up one unique America. Unlike assimilation, the melting pot theory, in its ideal formulation, recognized the potential for non-Northern European groups to change the values and customs of the dominant group (Laubeová, 2000), resulting in a transformed, mixed culture. It recognized acculturation as a two-way street, with multiple cultures influencing each other to create one amalgam. No longer was the only acceptable model supposed to be Anglo-Protestant in values and ways of living. However, in practice, the melting pot ideal was translated into the same old assimilation model for people of color. Blacks and Asians were ignored. European ethnic groups were emphasized. Laubeová (2000) has noted,

> ideally the concept of the melting pot should also entail mixing of various "races," not only "cultures." While [nominally] promoting the mixing of cultures, the ultimate result of the American variant of the melting pot happened to be the culture of White Anglo Saxon men, with minimum impact of other minority cultures. (para. 7)

European cultures were still more valued in the melting pot model. European American notions of the "fine" arts, ideals of beauty, communication styles, religious expressions, and music were still held in greater esteem.

The Multicultural Formulation

The current U.S. ethos in thinking about race is multiculturalism. Multiculturalism is defined as the recognition of the coexistence and mutual contribution of multiple cultures to community life within one nation, without there being one standard cultural norm to which all must assimilate.

Four major occurrences have pushed the race paradigm from the melting pot model toward multiculturalism. The first was the civil rights movement of the 1960s. This movement changed how Americans viewed each other in terms of race, religion, gender, disability, and sexual orientation. The second major occurrence was the arrival to the United States of an ever-growing number of new non-European immigrants in the post–civil rights era. Third, the civil rights movement stimulated many non-whites to "get in touch" with their ancestors (e.g., customs, traditions, histories) and prompted ethnic and racial pride and solidarity movements. A fourth occurrence that prompted the multicultural impulse was the existence of relatively self-sufficient ethnic and racial enclaves in U.S. communities. These enclaves of various Asian, Latino, and African-descended peoples demonstrated the persistence of ethnic group identity after migration and immigration, directly threatening the assimilation and melting pot notions. Glazer and Moynihan (1970) were the first to note the persistence of this ethnic group cohesion. They advocated for movement beyond the melting pot model. They suggested that U.S. society could incorporate multiple ethnic and racial groups in all of their distinctiveness.

Multiculturalism has replaced the emphasis on assimilation of all other groups to the dominant Anglo-American ways. The embracing of multiculturalism as a paradigm has led to an explosion of research and other activity in the area of ethnicity. African Americans, Latinos/Hispanics, American Indians, Asian Americans, and non-Anglo European Americans explored their own histories in the 1970s and 1980s. Despite this trend, some voices still challenge multiculturalism, proclaiming that non-European American cultural groups should assimilate to a standard set of so-called Western values, mores, and other expressions.

The rise of multiculturalism has also been accompanied by a decline in the status of race as a scientifically valid construct. Racial terms like *Mongoloid, Caucasian, Red, Negroid,* and *Yellow* are now seen as remnants of an oppressive racist past. Nevertheless, as mentioned at the beginning of Chapter 4, race remains important as long as it is used as a status determiner, as long as bias and social stratification are based on it. The next sections are devoted to the continuing impact of race in U.S. life.

THE CONTEMPORARY STATUS OF RACE AND RACISM

It should again be noted that a large part of this discussion is devoted to two of the so-called races: blacks and whites. That emphasis is due to the fact that the greatest racial divide in the United States is in the area of black–white relations. However, other forms of racism, such as anti–American Indian, anti-Latina/o, or anti-Asian attitudes and practices, continue to exist in American life.

A couple of provisos are in order. First, not all racism is white on black. There can also be racism among and between any of the so-called racial groups. Thus a black person can refuse to hire an Asian, an Asian can deny housing to a Latino, and so on. While there can also be anti-white prejudice, it usually lacks the social power to hurt that bias against people of color does. Second, as mentioned earlier, progress has been made. More whites see themselves as allies with blacks (Cose, 2011), as exemplified by the large number of whites who voted for Barack Obama. Third, despite the continuing existence of racism, many individuals do not act in racist ways, although it should be noted that whites generally benefit from racism in such areas as wealth, housing, and criminal justice.

In order to explore the nature of contemporary racism, and evidence for it, the next sections discuss four topics: the current phenomenon of racism, including contemporary black–white relations; color-blind racism; internalized racism in nondominant groups; and external evidence of contemporary racism, particularly in wealth, housing, criminal justice, and jobs.

Contemporary Black–White Relations

Black–white relations have played a particularly thorny role in American history and society. It is a legacy that Americans live with today because of slavery and massive, officially sanctioned discrimination for almost 400 years. Sociologist Thomas Shapiro's (2005) words iterate the power of the black–white dynamic in the United States: "Recent surveys have shown repeatedly that every social choice that white people make about where they live, what schools their children attend, what careers they pursue, and what policies they endorse is shaped by considerations involving race" (p. 102).

Continuing separation of blacks from other groups is illustrated by speech patterns. Residential segregation and social isolation have caused general black speech styles, regardless of region in the United States, to differ from Standard American English.

> [Black English] evolved independently from Standard American English because Blacks were historically separated from Whites by caste, class, and region. . . . [Black English] has become progressively more uniform across urban areas. Over the past two decades, the Black English vernaculars of Boston, Chicago, Detroit, New York, and Philadelphia have become increasingly similar in their grammatical structure and lexicon, reflecting urban Blacks' common social and economic isolation within urban America. (Massey & Denton, 1998, pp. 162–163)

The existence of a distinct dialect for a people who live in the same country is parallel to the persistence of Yiddish among European Jews up until the mid-20th century. It represents the social isolation of a community.

The ramifications of there being a separate black dialect in the United States are significant. Because black English is uniform and separate and the dominant white culture continues to insist on its use of English, despite the oppressive effects of this ethnocentric bias, it creates barriers to communication between blacks and whites, thereby decreasing social interaction—even in a racially mixed neighborhood. Furthermore, white racist bias concerning the language difference impedes blacks' socioeconomic progress because it is more difficult for black English speakers to find good jobs in the mainstream economy if they do not speak Standard (i.e., white) English well. In this regard, Wilson (1996) noted, "Employers frequently [mention] concerns about [black] applicants' language skills" (p. 116). In fact, language code-switching, that is, alternating between two dialects, is often required for many African Americans who enter into mainstream middle-class American society. Massey and Denton (1998) found that successful blacks "who have grown up in the ghetto literally become bilingual, learning to switch back and forth between black and white dialects depending on the social context" (p. 165). This phenomenon

resembles similar language fluidity in traditional European and Asian immigrant enclaves in the United States, except that, within a generation, many non-blacks adopt Standard English, whereas large numbers of black persons continue to learn and pass on black English.

In addition to race affecting language dialects and subsequent access to jobs, race is also a status determiner in U.S. society. Sociologists Joe Feagin and Karyn McKinney (2005) point to "the preponderance of data showing that a majority of white Americans, including many who are well-educated, harbor antiblack and other racial stereotypes, and that many whites still discriminate against African Americans in such areas as housing and employment" (p. 13). Feagin and McKinney note further that whites benefit greatly from racism—from where they live, to with whom they associate, to comfort in public places, to standards for beauty, to inherited wealth, to continuing social connections that assist career development.

More visible, active racism is also present in U.S. society. In fact, 58% of whites attributed at least one of the following characteristics to blacks: lazy, violent, prefer to live on public assistance, or whining (Bobo, 2001). Fully 78% of blacks believe that racism against blacks is widespread (Jones, 2008), as do a slight majority of whites (51%). The perception of racism by a black person can itself have negative effects on black clients' hopes, aspirations, and interpersonal relations.

Color-Blind Racism

In contrast to "old-fashioned" (overt) racism, modern racism is subtle. It takes the form of the notion that race no longer matters. The term *post-racial society* has been used since the election of Barack Obama, meaning a society in which race is no longer an issue in accessibility and social relations. This "color-blind racism" consists of people denying the lingering effects and continuing presence of racism in the 21st century. It denies the existence of the personal discomfort and aversion on the part of many white people concerning members of nondominant races (Dovidio,

Gaertner, & Kafati, 2000; Lehrman, 2003). That discomfort is commonly expressed in social avoidance rather than intentional aggressiveness, as it often was in the "bad old days." As a result, members of nondominant races do not have access to the mentoring and social connections that play a big part in educational and career opportunities. This type of racial discrimination is, psychologically speaking, traceable to the *similarity effect*: tending to associate with, hire, and accept people who look like oneself.

Box 5.3 illustrates a version of color-blind racism in the form of exclusive social networks that sustain the disparities between races.

Informal and formal associations such as the "good ol' boy" network are where important opportunities get exchanged. They exclude cultural others but are not amenable to affirmative action programs. They are related to human socialization patterns, particularly the tendency for individuals to associate with and favor people like themselves. These tendencies can only be countered by concerted personal effort and advocacy for changed attitudes.

Internalized Racism in Nondominant Groups

As mentioned earlier, internalized racism can also be present within nondominant groups (Telles, 2002). For example, having rounder eyes might be valued in an Asian American community, due to the attempt to look more European. Another example is lighter skin being valued more highly than dark skin in the black community (Hunter, 2002). The so-called paper bag test has been used by some blacks to assess the lightness of a black person's skin. The lighter the color (sometimes called the "café au lait" shade), the more status and access to institutions, such as prestigious churches, a black person might have in her or his community. Henry Louis Gates (2004), the Harvard historian, quoted the old expression, "If you're black, get back; if you're brown, stick around; if you're white [in this case, "light"], you're alright" to describe that phenomenon.

External Evidence of Modern Racism: Wealth, Housing, Criminal Justice, and Jobs

The legacy of racism is especially evident in wealth, housing, criminal justice, and jobs. Each affects the other, resulting in a continuing disadvantage for people of some racial groups.

Wealth

Wealth is defined as the total value of things that people own minus their debts. Wealth accumulation is therefore different from income. Income is the money received during a specific period of time for labor or profit. Thus, income is an immediate source of funds, whereas wealth can be inherited and accumulated by generations. Nevertheless, income is also one factor in wealth.

Wealth is important in any society. It influences access to capital for new businesses, is a source of political and social influence, and provides insurance against fluctuations in labor market income. It affects the quality of housing, neighborhoods, and schools that a family can access, as well as the ability to finance higher education. Wealth is an important "head-start asset," even when it is relatively small. It allows people to borrow from parents to buy new homes, to get by in tough times, to go to college without crushing loans, and to create more wealth through investments (Shapiro, 2005).

In terms of income, African Americans' earnings are approximately 58% of whites' earnings (Christie, 2010). Therefore, one would expect blacks to have less savings. Less savings translates into less wealth. As a result, a high percentage of blacks cannot pass on inherited wealth to their heirs, whereas a high percentage of whites can (Avery & Rendall, 2002; Wolfle, 1987).

The gap in wealth holdings between African Americans and white Americans is even greater than the income gap. The median net worth of black households was $2,200 in 2009, the lowest ever recorded, while the median net worth among white households was $97,900, or 44.5

times that of black households (Allegretto, 2011). Several studies, including those mentioned here, have found large wealth differences even after controlling for differences between blacks and whites in average income and other factors. This gap is due to the American legacy of racism: Blacks have been kept out of important parts of the U.S. economy for generations. As a result, many blacks lack both the knowledge of finances and the personal contacts that assist in wealth accumulation. Such knowledge and contacts affect one's ability to obtain bank loans, awareness of investment opportunities, and investment knowledge (see Box 5.3). The fact that friendships and family ties tend to be within racial groups, such as the previously mentioned "good ol' boy" network, amplifies the race gap in wealth.

Box 5.3   Wealth Gap Between Races

By Ibram Rogers, *The Virginian-Pilot*

February 25, 2005

Financial consultant Vincent D. Carpenter sees a sharp difference in many of his young clients. "For a 25-year-old white kid, you see the signs of transitional wealth," said Carpenter, the president of Chesapeake Financial Services.

"You see grandmothers or grandfathers giving something to them, giving something to the parents. Whereas 25-year-old black kids are starting from ground zero. It's all coming from them—their first house purchase, the down payment is going to come from them."

That's no accident—it's the result of the major, and often overlooked, racial disparities in wealth, said sociologist Thomas M. Shapiro, who [has written a] book, *The Hidden Cost of Being African American: How Wealth Perpetuates Inequality.*

While the income gap between blacks and whites is getting smaller, there is a dime of wealth in the average black household for every dollar of wealth in every white household, said Shapiro, a professor at Brandeis University.

And that wealth gap has widened in recent years, he said.

"Black and white professionals in the same occupation earning the same salary typically move through life with significantly unequal housing, residential, and education prospects, which means that their children are not really on the same playing field," he writes.

Carpenter knows that from personal experience: He left [college] with $12,000 in student loans.

And at his company, he's welcomed black clients who, at age 50 or 60, are making their first investments in the stock market.

"We have more churches in the African American community that have gross receipts in excess of $30,000 a year than we do businesses, and that's an inverse relationship," Carpenter said.

"You'll see this dynamic throughout the country. . . ."

Because Americans believe that equal opportunities lead to equal outcomes, programs like affirmative action were erected. . . .

Carpenter sees the wealth gap as "the final remnants of 300 years of inequality." Only in the past 40 years have black Americans really been able to acquire wealth, he said.

Before then, he said, "we had laws and situations designed to promote ignorance, a spendthrift mentality, and a surviving mode as opposed to a thriving mode, so we're lucky to see these figures."

Significantly unequal residential and educational conditions affect opportunities and hope. It is the responsibility of the counselor to facilitate the empowerment of all individuals, including poor individuals of color, by being proactive in providing such interventions as career counseling, tutoring services, and financial aid information, all resources that most middle-class individuals have in the family and community.

Housing

Housing discrimination is one of the clearest legacies of racism. The good news is that in 2011 blacks were less likely to experience housing discrimination than in 1989 (U.S. Department of Housing and Urban Development, 2011). However, such discrimination still exists at unacceptable levels. In the recent past, Feagin (1999) found that 70%–80% of white Americans will discriminate against black Americans in housing rentals and loans. More recently, black test renters were found to have faced racial discrimination 61%–80% of the time, depending on the city (Feagin & McKinney, 2005). The U.S. Department of Housing and Urban Development (2011) reports that a high percentage of Hispanic and African American home seekers are being told properties are unavailable, when they are still available to whites. In addition, blacks are steered by real estate agents to limited areas. In the area of housing loans, blacks were three times more likely to get a high-interest loan than were whites who had the same credit standing (Nealy, 2008).

Criminal Justice

Bias in the criminal justice system results in a disparity in who gets arrested, convicted, and jailed for the same crimes. A nationwide study prepared by the National Council on Crime and Delinquency (2007) found that at every step of the juvenile justice system, African American and Hispanic youth are treated more harshly than their white peers charged with comparable crimes.

In general, black and Latino felons are 26% more likely to go to prison than white European Americans (Sutton, 2011). In particular, black drug defendants are far more likely to be jailed than white defendants with the same criminal record (Poe-Yamagata & Jones, 2000). In 1996, the National Criminal Justice Commission reported that while blacks account for 13% of all regular illegal drug users, they make up 35% of those arrested, 55% of those convicted, and 74% of those imprisoned (Donziger, 1996).

What are the reasons for such disparities? Socioeconomic factors play a part, in that more affluent offenders, who are more likely to be white, can hire better lawyers and work the system through know-how. Also, poorer people who use drugs are less likely to have private places to do so and thus are more likely to actually be seen engaging in drug-related practices, such as distribution and use.

In addition to the socioeconomic factors, there is likely to be bias, whether conscious or unconscious, at work. The media's (news and entertainment) construction of drug use frequently shows people of color engaged in harmful drug-related practices but usually ignores middle-class white persons' misuse of drugs, especially the use of alcohol.

Bias is also the result of the similarity effect, in which a person is more identified with someone who shares characteristics with herself or himself. Individuals commonly feel greater kinship with those who look and sound like them, even if it is unintentional. Thus, the combination of (a) white judges and lawyers and (b) black defendants is an unfortunate mix for the defendants. Regardless of the races of judges, stereotypes of blacks and criminal behavior might be involved. And finally, explicit, intentional bias lingers. Thus, for many reasons, black clients are more likely than white clients to harbor suspicion about the criminal justice system.

Jobs

Job discrimination is also, unfortunately, a continuing fact, as demonstrated in the study described in Box 5.4.

Box 5.4   Racial Discrimination: Still at Work in the U.S.

By David Wessel, *Wall Street Journal*

Two young high school graduates with similar job histories and demeanors apply in person for jobs as waiters, warehousemen, or other low-skilled positions advertised in a Milwaukee newspaper. One man is White and admits to having served 18 months in prison for possession of cocaine with intent to sell. The other is Black and hasn't any criminal record. Which man is more likely to get called back? It is surprisingly close. In a carefully crafted experiment in which college students posing as job applicants visited 350 employers, the White ex-con was called back 17% of the time and the crime-free Black applicant 14%. The disadvantage carried by a young Black man applying for a job as a dishwasher or a driver is equivalent to forcing a White man to carry an 18-month prison record on his back.

Many White Americans think racial discrimination is no longer much of a problem. Many Blacks think otherwise. In offices populated with college graduates, White men quietly confide to other White men that affirmative action makes it tough for a White guy to get ahead these days. (If that's so, a Black colleague once asked me, how come there aren't more Blacks in the corporate hierarchy?) A recent Gallup poll asked: "Do you feel that racial minorities in this country have equal job opportunities as Whites, or not?" Among Whites, the answer was 55% yes and 43% no; the rest were undecided. Among Blacks, the answer was 17% yes and 81% no. The Milwaukee and other experiments, though plagued by the shortcomings of research that relies on pretense to explain how people behave, offer evidence that discrimination remains a potent factor in the economic lives of Black Americans. "In these low-wage, entry-level markets, race remains a huge barrier. Affirmative-action pressures aren't operating here," says Devah Pager, the sociologist at Northwestern University in Evanston, Ill., who conducted the Milwaukee experiment and recently won the American Sociological Association's prize for the year's best doctoral dissertation. "Employers don't spend a lot of time screening applicants. They want a quick signal whether the applicant seems suitable. Stereotypes among young Black men remain so prevalent and so strong that race continues to serve as a major signal of characteristics of which employers are wary."

In a similar experiment that got some attention last year, economists Marianne Bertrand of the University of Chicago and Sendhil Mullainathan [2004] of the Massachusetts Institute of Technology responded in writing to help-wanted ads in Chicago and Boston, using names likely to be identified by employers as White or African American. Applicants named Greg Kelly or Emily Walsh were 50% more likely to get called for interviews than those named Jamal Jackson or Lakisha Washington, names far more common among African Americans. Putting a White-sounding name on an application, they found, is worth as much as an extra eight years of work experience. These academic experiments gauge the degree of discrimination, not just its existence. Both suggest that a blemish on a Black person's resume does far more harm than it does to a White job seeker and that an embellishment does far less good. In the Milwaukee experiment, Ms. Pager dispatched White and Black men with and without prison records to job interviews. Whites without drug busts on their applications did best; Blacks with drug busts did worst. No surprise there. But this was a surprise: Acknowledging a prison record cut a White man's chances of getting called back by half, while cutting a Black man's already-slimmer chances by a much larger two-thirds. "Employers, already reluctant to hire Blacks, are even more wary of Blacks with proven criminal involvement," Ms. Pager says. "These testers were bright, articulate college students with effective styles of self-presentation. The cursory review of entry-level applicants, however, leaves little room for these qualities to be noticed." This is a big deal given that nearly 17% of all Black American men have

(Continued)

PSYCHOLOGICAL DIMENSIONS OF RACE

For counselors, much of the importance of race lies in its psychological effects. In this section, those effects are explored. In particular, racial identity development for both people of color and for whites is presented.

At least four psychological impacts of racism have been found for blacks. Blacks tend to have lower self-esteem (Kwate, Valdimarsdottir, Guevarra, & Bovbjerg, 2003), they are likely to hide vulnerable emotions like fear and sadness (White & Parham, 1990), they experience greater stress than whites (Utsey, Chae, Brown, & Kelly, 2002), and they have self-limiting beliefs about opportunities (Auerbach, 2002).

One factor in these impacts is blacks' experience of racial microaggressions. Such microaggressions are defined as slight and regular affronts directed at blacks, frequently without thinking (Smith, Yosso, and Solórzano, 2006; Sue, 2010). Three related factors seem to contribute to such stress. Blacks have to live with the tension of determining whether they are merely being tolerated or really accepted, they have to distinguish between the efforts of white allies versus racist white behavior in general, and they have to spend mental energy deciding whether to accommodate or resist oppression (Pierce, 1988). Such microaggressions and uncertainties overwhelmingly predicted stress

in black men who were in traditionally white higher education institutions (Smith et al., 2011).

These psychological impacts are important for counseling. For example, hiding feelings has been a psychological strategy for members of oppressed groups. This Jesse Jackson quote underscores the tactic of masking emotions as a way of dealing with systemic inequalities: "Our strength is measured by absorbing trauma without being embittered" (quoted in Cose, 2011, p. 209). That adaptive attitude can also be a barrier in counseling.

One way to help clients be emotionally open is for the counselor who is of a different race from the client to pay special attention to establishing trust. Even black clients who are confident and emotionally open might nevertheless harbor concerns about being treated fairly in counseling. Counselors who are from the dominant group need to be especially alert to these psychological possibilities when they work with clients from an oppressed group.

Racial Identity Development

A potentially helpful framework for counselors' understanding of the expectations of clients of all races lies in racial identity development models. One of the values of developmental models is that they plot positive movement in individuals' appreciation and understanding of their and others' races. Racial identity developmental models describe increasing flexibility, complexity, and openness in an individual's thinking about race. Racial identity can range from denigration of one's own group, toward pride in one's own group, to a more inclusive perspective about all groups.

Racial identity status affects both clients' and counselors' perceptions of each other. By considering racial identity development factors, counselors can understand a client's mistrust and anger around race or, conversely, relative openness to diversity.

Two sets of such developmental models, one for people of color and one for white persons, are described here.

Identity Development for People of Color

"People of color" can be defined as the racialized ethnic minorities in the United States who share a common history of oppression by whites (Takaki, 2008). It does not mean that these groups of people are ethnically similar in terms of values, lifestyles, and behaviors. Instead, the term describes all peoples who cannot easily assimilate at this time in history into the dominant white culture because of their physical features (Butler, 2001). The concept of people of color holds importance in that it recognizes the commonality in the experience of those who are non–European American. Descendants of white European immigrant groups have assimilated in U.S. society as simply "white" (Ignatiev, 2008). People of color have been generally thought of as "other."

The Racial Identity Development for People of Color (RIDPOC) model represents a synthesis of Helms's (Helms & Cook, 1999), Cross's (1995), and Atkinson, Morten, and Sue's (1998) minority identity development models as well as Slattery's (2004) integration of the three. The model has five statuses, each of which represents an individual's overall tendency at any one time. Cross calls the movement through these statuses a "resocializing experience" (p. 97).

The five statuses in the RIDPOC model for people of color are (1) Conformity, (2) Dissonance and Beginning to Appreciate, (3) Resistance and Immersion, (4) Introspection and Internalization, and (5) Universal Inclusion . Note that these statuses (sometimes called stages) are not rigidly sequential nor unitary. They represent the general tendency; one or two statuses will dominate at any one time in any one person (Helms & Cook, 1999).

While this model has general value, you should note that not all aspects of an individual's thinking can be neatly fit into any stage of a model. For example, a black Haitian who immigrates to the United States may have little direct experience with racial prejudice. She or he will not initially identify as African American, or perhaps even as "black." But within the U.S. context, a good part of her or his identity will nevertheless be subsumed as "black." She or he is likely to often associate with African Americans due to U.S. housing and socialization patterns. However, her or his thinking would not fit the RIDPOC model as easily as a U.S.-born person of color.

The RIDPOC model can give counselors an idea of their client's frame of mind. It can also be prescriptive, in that it can suggest directions for individuals who aim for greater complexity in their thinking. In the latter case, Liberation Counseling, which is described in Chapter 19, can be explicitly applied at each status to assist with such change.

The Racial Identity Development for People of Color Model

Status 1: Conformity

Here, persons of color conform to the dominant, negative cultural view of their race and the dominant race or give little meaning to their race. Individuals in the Conformity status tend to value the physical characteristics, lifestyles, achievements, and manners of the dominant group and denigrate the qualities of people of color (e.g., valuing European-style classical music and seeing jazz as a lower form of art, valuing the physical features of white people more than those of people of color, denigrating the communication style and the dialect of their group).

At the negative extreme in this status, they may feel self-hatred because of their race. However, racial self-denigration is not universal at the Conformity status. Research has shown that some people of color who are in the Conformity status do not necessarily denigrate their race or have low self-esteem (Cross, 1995). Instead, some persons may place little importance on their racial identity (e.g., "I don't know why people make such a fuss about being black"). They are likely to prefer the dominant group's ways while not necessarily feeling negatively about their race.

Counseling Implications

A client in the Conformity status is likely to prefer a white counselor. She or he will likely look up to the white counselor as an authority. The counselor should encourage the client to express her or his negative view of her or his group. The counselor should demonstrate positive attitudes toward racial diversity and particularly toward the client's race.

Status 2: Dissonance and Beginning to Appreciate

At this status, individuals experience confusion, or dissonance, about having a negative view of their own group. They begin to consider their race in a positive light. Such changes are triggered by positive experiences around people of color, for example, through reading, hearing, or seeing an interview with a person of color or having a role model who is proud of her or his racial group. Initial confusion, or dissonance, from this experience gives way to a dawning awareness that members of one's own group are positive in ways that are unexpected by the client. Box 5.5 illustrates the story of one person's discovery of pride in his race.

Box 5.5   Learning About Black Achievers Makes Lessons for a Lifetime

February 24, 2005

By *John L. Horton*

Black History Month is just about over for 2005, but its lessons can reverberate throughout the year—and beyond.

I wasn't aware of the significance of black history until I came of age during the 1960s. Before then, I had spent the first two decades of my life not knowing about the many African American achievers or their achievements.

I was born in 1940 and raised in the colored projects of Chattanooga, Tenn. by a mother who worked as a domestic maid and also received public assistance. My father had deserted my mother and five children when I was 13 years old and in the eighth grade.

During this time, I attended all-black schools in a highly segregated society. My mother taught me to read before I started school. This was quite an accomplishment because she had only two or three years of formal schooling. I became an excellent student, but in the schools of the 1940s and '50s, I learned only about a handful of black heroes and personalities, such as Booker T. Washington, George Washington Carver, Joe Louis, Jesse Owens, and once in a while Harriet Tubman and Sojourner Truth.

But I learned nothing of the likes of more controversial figures such as W. E. B. DuBois, Marcus Garvey, Jack Johnson, or Paul Robeson or of their great dreams and accomplishments.

To boys like me, this lack of information fed into a broader negativity about black people during an era of legal segregation. For example, in the 1940s and '50s in many Southern communities, blacks could not work with whites as policemen, firemen, lawyers, doctors, teachers, pharmacists, contractors, journalists, scientists, economists, and entrepreneurs—no matter how educated or competent they were. As a whole, black people were seen as inferior in terms of abilities and skills.

Meanwhile, things got really tough at home and, in the mid-1950s, I dropped out of 10th grade at age 16. After working at low-paying, go-nowhere jobs, I joined the Marine Corps at 17. It turned out be a good fit because I remained in the Marines for a 30-year career, retiring as a sergeant major in 1988.

I was in the Marines when I read my first textbook about black history. In the early 1960s, one of my white commanding officers had discarded *From Slavery to Freedom,* by John Hope Franklin. The contents opened my eyes! I realized that I and other black people have been great before and could be great again.

For several months, I read *From Slavery to Freedom* cover to cover, time and time again. To this day, I still use this "Black Bible" for knowledge, reference, inspiration, and teaching.

Inspired, I began to intensely read more black history. During this time, I also pushed on to earn my high school GED. This began my journey to other educational milestones while still in the Marine Corps. I received associate's, bachelor's and master's degrees.

Reading all kinds of black history, especially autobiographies and biographies, I discovered how much black people had done, not only in America and Africa, but around the world. I began writing articles and participating in black history and cultural diversity activities inside and outside the military.

In the 1970s, I began teaching black history for Los Angeles Community College while stationed in Okinawa, Japan. Upon returning stateside, I did the same at Cherry Point, N.C., Memphis, Tenn., and Norfolk [Virginia].

I've also worked with troubled teens for about two decades and I've used black history and African culture to motivate and uplift them. I tell them about the trials and tribulations—and triumphs—of those who've gone before. I explain what Jackie Robinson meant by, "A life is unimportant except for the impact it has upon others."

But I continue to see too many African Americans, especially young males, who have given up hope. They simply don't believe in themselves. They don't think they are worthy or deserving of the good life. I have fathered, befriended, cajoled, pushed, pulled, begged—and yes, even threatened them. Too often, I have not been as successful as I would have liked. There have been successes, but it is the failures and crises that keep me awake at night.

But when I feel dejected, I turn to my black history heroes. I draw on their struggles and victories and their countless contributions. This restores my appreciation of where black people have been, where they are now and hopefully where they'll be one day.

I find the strength to reach out again—not just in February but through the year. So, just as learning about black history never ends, always keep in mind that the lessons from our heritage can carry you through a lifetime. It's worked for me.

John L. Horton was a probation officer and is now retired.

Source: © 2005 Virginian-Pilot.

John Horton's story reflects the power of heroes as models for people of color. His journey can be a lesson and a guide for other people of color who wish to progress in their racial identity. Counselors can be catalysts for such racial self-discovery at the Dissonance status.

The person of color at this status discovers that whites have privileges that contribute to their success. What emerges is a mixture of the old cultural self-disparagement with a confusing, emerging cultural self-appreciation. This dawning awareness can be difficult because previous attempts to fit in with the dominant culture all of one's life now encounter the reclaiming of one's race. For example, a Native American Indian might think, "I have taken on the white man's Christianity. We have changed our names to sound Anglo. But my people have many important spiritual traditions that I would like to learn about and honor and a language of our own." A natural consequence of this dissonance and beginning cultural self-appreciation is some mistrust of the dominant culture and a sense of having been "had."

Counseling Implications

Counselors should help clients who are at this status move toward a positive identification with their racial group by introducing and discussing positive cultural symbols, persons, and reading materials (Ivey, Ivey, D'Andrea, & Simek-Morgan, 2008). Counselors will first need significant knowledge of related racial and cultural issues for people of color. Counselors can introduce clients here to the Guided Imagery With Positive Cultural Symbols activity (see Chapter 19) to help clients identify their cultural strengths.

Status 3: Resistance and Immersion

At this status, individuals feel consistently negative about the dominant race's hegemony. Here, individuals are likely to be especially angry about past wrongs done to their group. Persons in this status are immersed in their own racial group's history and culture. They have a beginning sense of pride in their own race for its characteristics and struggles. In fact, they tend to see only positive qualities in their own group and attribute all difficulties to whites. From the Resistance and Immersion frame, individuals begin to idealize their race and are unthinkingly loyal to the group; that is, they are "culture-centric," as discussed in Chapter 2. However, positive feelings about one's own race are not necessarily constant at the Resistance and Immersion status; individuals may continue to have lingering self-deprecating attitudes, especially early in this status.

A type of insularity characterizes Resistance and Immersion. Individuals at this status are now "subject to" the group (Kegan, 1982); they can't step outside of their group's norms and customs to evaluate them. As the word *immersion* implies, awareness of being a person of color here becomes all-consuming.

Late in the experience of this status, individuals of color have a confident identification with people in their own group and a mistrust of whites. They are suspicious of white counselors and see racial slights as pervasive.

Counseling Implications

White counselors who are working with individuals characterized by Resistance and Immersion should expect the client to be suspicious of the counselor as an agent of the oppressive establishment. The client is not as likely to take individual responsibility for choices, but instead will attribute difficulties to group oppression. The client is likely to prefer a counselor who has knowledge of race-related issues and is well-versed about the client's own racial group.

Establishing trust with a white counselor will be difficult. If the counselor is white, she or he should not get defensive about racial issues. The counselor can show knowledge of oppression against people of color and support for efforts to challenge it. If the client is ready, the counselor can help her or him identify her or his autonomous views on issues, rather than the culture-centric view to which she or he is now subject.

Status 4: Introspection and Internalization

Here, individuals become more thoughtful and complex about race. They are introspective rather than being unquestioningly immersed in their own race. A more complex formulation of racial identity is possible.

The initial challenge to the previous Immersed way of thinking may occur through negative encounters with members of one's own group. Individuals here begin to recognize narrow culture-centric thinking in themselves and in others. Culture-centrism doesn't feel true to one's own experiences. Individuals in the Introspection and Internalization status may also have positive encounters with whites in personal or work relationships or through the media, perhaps with white allies who challenge oppression. They thus reconsider their blanket negative assessment of whites.

At Introspection and Internalization, there is a continuing strong sense of pride in and identification with one's own race, its characteristics, and struggles. But from the Introspection and Internalization frame, individuals are better able to step back from automatic assumptions about "us" and "them." They recognize their own ethnocentrism.

There is conflict at the Introspection and Internalization status. Here, individuals experience a dilemma about their strong desire to, on the one hand, attach to their own racial group and, on the other, to discard conformist group-think. They begin to determine the attractive attributes of their own race, rather than have those attributes be dictated by others.

Inclusion of others is now possible. Due to increasing confidence about internalized racial identity, individuals at the Introspection and Internalization status can associate comfortably with white persons. They can also challenge more immersed members of their own group who criticize their increasing contact with the dominant culture.

Counseling Implications

The counselor might help Introspection and Internalization thinkers to solidify their autonomy. The counselor can aid the client in connecting with other complex ideas and thinkers of all races, especially members of her or his racial group who are able to move comfortably among other racial groups.

Status 5: Universal Inclusion

As the term implies, this status involves a multicultural way of thinking. Individuals who think from the Universal Inclusion position clearly value their racial identity. However, they also recognize that there can be oppressions for many groups, including whites. They have moved from the absolute black-and-white view of racial groups toward recognizing the presence of undesirable and desirable dimensions in all cultures. They know the negative legacies of American racism that have led to current attitudes and conditions. They can advocate for social justice for all groups. These persons can integrate aspects of European American culture into their own racial-ethnic culture. Further, they are interested in experiencing all cultures.

Counseling Implications

Clients will be interested in working with any counselor who shares a similarly complex worldview and multicultural awareness. From the Universal Inclusion client perspective, the counselor's race coexists with his or her individuality.

You are encouraged to complete Activity 5.3 at this point in order to connect the RIDPOC statuses to your experience.

Activity 5.3   Applying Racial Identity Development for People of Color

I. Review the description of the racial identity statuses for people of color.

Conformity

Dissonance and Beginning to Appreciate

Resistance and Immersion

Introspection and Internalization

Universal Inclusion

II. If you are a person of color, as U.S. society defines it:

Comment on where you were in the past in terms of any of these statuses.

Comment on your general status now.

Write down actions you might take to move toward the next status.

If you are white, think of a person you have encountered or have seen in the media who seemed to characterize each of these statuses. Write down the status she or he seems to represent and why.

White Racial Identity Development

The notion of white racial identity comes as a surprise to some people. For them, it seems like an empty notion because whites are generally oblivious to the role of race in their lives. However, because race matters, and because differences in white racial identity have been observed, a number of theorists (Hardiman, 1982; Helms, 1990) have described an evolution in white racial identity. Helms's model has been particularly well researched, accompanied as it is by a measure of white racial identity.

White racial identity development models are particularly important at this time in the field of counseling because the vast majority of counselors are white (Middleton, Erguner-Tekinalp, & Petrova, 2005). White counselors who have poor racial identity development might fail to make a commitment to serving people of color, might underplay inequities, might overlook social and political reasons for client difficulties and focus solely on the client's responsibility for current conditions, and might fail to challenge racism in clients.

With higher white racial identity development, white counselors can more effectively work with clients of color, if trust and credibility are established. White counselors must be prepared to respond non-defensively to challenges from clients of color. Such a challenge might take the form of, "What do you know about being (black, Asian, Hispanic/Latina/o, American Indian)?" White counselors who are in the early statuses of white racial identity development would be defensive under such scrutiny as well as insensitive to the racial issues that affect clients' lives.

Knowledge of white racial identity development can alert white counselors who are at the early statuses to the work that they need to do on their own racial awareness. Knowledge of the later statuses can cue white counselors to the importance of engaging in advocacy and racial awareness activities.

What follows is an integration of two of the major white racial identity development models, namely those of Hardiman (1982) and of Helms (1990). There are five statuses in this combined model: (1) Acceptance/Conformity, (2) Dissonance/Disintegration, (3) Immersion, (4) Emersion/Redefinition, and (5) Autonomy/Internalization.

You might notice the general similarity between white racial identity statuses and the previously discussed racial identity statuses for people of color. Like other cultural identity development models, both describe movement from an exclusive and external frame of reference to a more inclusive, self-authorized one. However, the content of the two models does differ, especially at the early positions.

A reminder: Despite the model being laid out in five statuses, movement through them is not strictly linear. Recent research (Middleton et al., 2005) shows that counselors tend to show characteristics of multiple statuses at any one time. For example, a white individual might show elements of Status 2: Dissonance/Disintegration about her or his former acceptance of the dominant view on race in society (e.g., "I am noticing that being a person of color seems to matter regarding clients' opportunities and self-perceptions.") while also wavering between Status 1: Acceptance/Conformity ("I don't think about it a lot. Color is irrelevant.") and Status 3: Immersion (e.g., "I noticed the book *Race Matters* in the bookstore. I browsed through it."). This white person is not likely to show characteristics of the upper statuses (e.g., she or he would not intentionally challenge lack of diversity in a staff or go to an event dominated by people of color).

It should be noted that the implications for each status are directed largely at counselors themselves, since the majority of counselors are white. For white clients, racial identity can be important in their lives and the lives of others, but it may not necessarily affect their lives in obvious ways because they are in the dominant position in society. Of course, it is the socially critical counselor's role to promote a nonracist society, and she or he can use these statuses to instigate challenges to client racism.

Status 1: Acceptance/Conformity

At this status, the individual unquestioningly receives the dominant negative views on people of color. She or he is oblivious to the influence of race on others' lives and one's own life. The Acceptant/Conformist person sees any social differences as evidence of inferiority (genetically or culturally) of non-white groups. This can be a lifelong status.

Counseling Implications

A white counselor at this status can harm clients of color by rejecting or dismissing those who are demonstrating Resistance and Immersion (Status 3) of RIDPOC. Similarly, the counselor in Acceptance/Conformity might pathologize mistrust on the part of clients of color instead of probing for the roots of such mistrust in oppression. The Acceptant/Conformist counselor is also likely to avoid clients of color in general. She or he would also be unaware of their unique issues. She or he will attribute all client struggles to the individual.

Status 2: Dissonance/Disintegration

The white individual here experiences a breakdown in the notion that "race doesn't matter." Dissonance/Disintegration can be initiated by a person learning about racial inequities, perhaps from a course in social and cultural issues in counseling. Such an awakening can also be triggered by media portrayal of racial issues (e.g., a documentary on the civil rights struggle and/or on high-achieving, powerful persons of color) or a friendship with a person of color (e.g., one that happens in the workplace) that challenges previous assumptions. The white individual may be moved to Dissonance/Disintegration by observing clear cases of bias that are disturbing. The person is likely to feel some guilt at this point at her or his past participation in racism.

The white person who thinks largely from this framework is still likely to have negative attitudes about some of the lifestyle expressions of people of color and cross-racial romantic relationships. Dissonance/Disintegration thinkers have little meaningful contact with people of color or their ethnic cultures. Such white individuals are unsure whether acting in a nonracist way is worth it, due to their continuing need for approval from conformist white peers and others. However, Dissonance/Disintegration thinkers can achieve some tolerance of people of color if those people meet white standards (e.g., in the arts, fashion, communication styles). If the person at this status continues to be open to this dissonance, she or he might move toward Status 3 (Immersion) and then to Status 4 (Emersion/Redefinition). Conversely, she or he could stay in Dissonance/Disintegration for life, with continuing dissonance or retreat to the conformity of the Acceptance status. In that case, she or he is likely to retreat to an all-white world and racial biases in order to reduce the discomfort.

Counseling Implications

The white counselor at this status is still likely to ignore racism, even to be defensive about it. She or he may avoid working with or reaching out to clients of color. White counselors at the Dissonance/Disintegration status are likely to associate only with white colleagues in any meaningful way, thereby failing to learn about race.

Status 3: Immersion

This status is characterized by a beginning redefinition of "whiteness." At the early point of this journey, the person is very vigilant about racial issues and highly alert to the topic, perhaps reading, discussing, and viewing videos that evoke race-related themes. Here, the white person actively seeks to understand the nature of racism and of privilege. White individuals in the Immersion status are likely to feel anger at racism. At this status, they are judgmental about their own and other white persons' racism. However, the white person in Immersion continues to only have relatively superficial contact with people of color.

Counseling Implications

The white counselor early in this status might dismiss the non-Immersed client of color as not being racially aware enough. Such a white counselor might ignore the non-race-related dimensions of client concerns that are unique to each individual, such as family distress, mood disorders, and career concerns. The Immersed white counselor could also be overbearing with colleagues who do not share her or his awakening and immersion.

Status 4: Emersion/Redefinition

As the person integrates this awareness, she or he becomes more secure, even calm, in her or his redefinition of "whiteness." At the Emersion/Redefinition status, white individuals consistently challenge their own racism. They acknowledge that being white brings unearned, invisible privilege (see Chapter 3). At this point, individuals feel solidarity with likeminded whites and become more comfortable in and desirous of interacting with people of color.

Counseling Implications

With Emersion and the accompanying Redefinition of whiteness, the counselor is better able to address race issues in counseling rather than hiding from them or denying their impact on the counseling relationship.

Status 5: Autonomy/Internalization

Here, a person has moved toward a nonracist white identity, fully accepting his or her own race without guilt. Race is not a threat to a person in this status. For example, the person can hear people of color speak about racism without experiencing unnecessary personal guilt. At this status, the white person acknowledges her or his role in the continuation of racism.

The white person at the Autonomy/Internalization status seeks out cross-racial experiences and personal contacts. In the area of social action, individuals who think from the Autonomy/Internalization perspective make a commitment to take counter-oppression actions. In particular, they attempt to relinquish unearned privilege from being white or use such privilege as an ally. They are proactive in promoting actions that increase equity (e.g., in organizational decision making, in inclusion of all people and perspectives, in challenging obvious and subtle dominance).

Autonomy/Internalization can be a difficult stance to sustain in a nonsupportive environment, whether it is societal, organizational, or familial.

Counseling Implications

Here, the white counselor is likely to be comfortable working with all clients and able to integrate race issues into counseling. She or he will be able to invite appropriate discussion of race during sessions, free of guilt and avoidance over the topic.

Activity 5.4 offers an opportunity for you to identify white racial identity statuses for yourself or for another.

Activity 5.4   Applying the White Racial Identity Model

I. Review the characteristics of the white identity development statuses.

Acceptance/Conformity

Dissonance/Disintegration

Immersion

Emersion/Redefinition

Autonomy/Internalization

II. If you are a white person:

Note where you were in the past in terms of any of these statuses.

Note your general racial identity status now.

Write down actions you might take to move toward the next status.

If you are a person of color, think of an individual whom you have encountered or have seen in the media who seemed to characterize each of these statuses. Write down the status she or he seems to represent and why.

MULTIRACIAL INDIVIDUALS AND FAMILIES

A simple answer to the common question "What are you?" is challenging for multiracial persons (Henriksen & Paladino, 2009b). This chapter concludes with a discussion of the emerging issue of multiracial identity. The terms *biracial* and *multiracial* are often used interchangeably. *Multiracial* is broader in scope and is the term preferred by many multicultural researchers and scholars (Ponterotto et al., 2006). Wehrly (2005) defines multiracial individuals as persons "whose parents are of different racial heritages" (p. 314). Kenney and Kenney (2009, 2010) expand the range of those included in the multiracial population category to include families who have transracial adoptions (8% of all adoptions) and partners or spouses of different racial heritages (7.4% of all couples—one of the fastest-growing segments).

The number of multiracial individuals and families has increased considerably in the past 40 years, ever since the U.S. Supreme Court struck down the anti-miscegenation laws (banning marriage or sexual unions between persons of different races) that still existed in 14 states (Kenney, 2006). The 2000 census was the first to allow individuals to indicate more than one race to describe their heritage. Almost 7 million individuals did so, roughly 2.4% of the population that was counted. The actual number and percentage of multiracial individuals was probably higher (Choi-Misailidis, 2010; Paniagua, 2005; Ponterotto et al., 2006; Sue & Sue, 2003). Approximately 93% of the multiracial individuals who identified themselves on the census indicated two racial heritages, while the remaining 7% chose three or more (Paniagua, 2005). There has been a significant increase in the number of individuals identifying as multiracial since 2000, a jump from 6.8 million to 9 million in 2010—a 32.4% gain (El Nassar, 2011). There are estimates that 20% of the population will be multiracial by 2050 (Choi-Misailidis, 2010).

The issues to which multiracial individuals are subject include many of the stressors and oppressions outlined previously in this book for members of any nondominant group. For example, in November 2011, a Baptist congregation in Pike county, Kentucky, voted to ban mixed-race couples from becoming members. After an avalanche of criticism, the members soon reversed their decision (Welch, 2011). In addition, individuals with multiracial heritage deal with other distinct issues:

- They are often neglected in the counseling and psychology literature as well as in counselor training programs (Choi-Misailidis, 2010; Kenney & Kenney, 2010; Ponterotto et al., 2006; Wehrly, 2005).
- Multiracial individuals and couples may experience a lack of acceptance by segments of their families and/or of the communities in which they live, work, or go to school (Choi-Misailidis, 2010; Henriksen & Paladino, 2009a; Kenney & Kenney, 2009; Wehrly, 2005).
- The lack of acceptance by others may lead to feelings of marginalization and isolation (Choi-Misailidis, 2010; Henriksen & Paladino, 2009b; Jun, 2010; Root, 1996; Sue & Sue, 2003).
- They are subject to unflattering stereotypes and/or myths (Kenney & Kenney, 2009; Sue & Sue, 2003; Wehrly, 2005).
- They may endure frequent inquiries about their physical features and/or racial heritage (Henriksen & Paladino, 2009b; Kenney, 2006; Ponterotto et al., 2006).
- Multiracial individuals may be pressured to identify with a single racial referent group and to exclude their other racial heritage(s) (Choi-Misailidis, 2010; Kenney, 2006; Wehrly, 2005).

In addition to these difficulties, enculturation may be a more complex process when more than one racial or ethnic heritage is involved. While monoracial or monoethnic individuals are socialized in the ways of their racio-ethnic culture and develop their cognitive map for being and acting in the world, multiracial individuals (and families) are not always mentored in both or all of their salient racial or ethnic cultural identities (Henriksen & Paladino, 2009b). For example, a person who is both African American and European American may be enculturated in African American culture or in European American culture. Thus, parts of her or his heritage and identity are submerged or even dismissed.

Multiracial Identity

Another area of relative neglect involves multiracial identity development. The development of a positive racial identity is considered vital for individuals with multiracial heritage (Choi-Misailidis, 2010; Kenney, 2006; Kenney & Kenney, 2010), yet single-race models of identity development are considered inadequate for use with such individuals (Robinson, 2005; Wehrly, 2005).

Identity development for multiracial individuals is more complex than for single-race persons. In Ponterotto and colleagues' (2006) words, it is "a lifelong process that . . . involves continuing efforts to integrate the many facets that make up one's racial identity" (p. 115). Three models for explaining multiracial identity are outlined next.

Root's Multiracial Identity Model

Maria Root's (1996) model emphasizes the importance of identity for multiracial individuals. Hers is not a stage model. Root outlines four choices that a multiracial individual can make to resolve identity status:

1. Acceptance of the identity that society chooses for the individual (e.g., "Asian" in the case of Asian American and European American)

2. Identification with the racial reference groups of both parents

3. Choosing a racial group identity rather than just accepting the choice assigned (e.g., seeking information on American Indian heritage after having been identified as "white")

4. Identifying with a different group, other persons of multiracial heritage

Each of these choices can both work for individuals and have disadvantages (Ponterotto et al., 2006). Counselors can help clients see which of the choices they have made and which they would like to move toward. Methods include those used to help monoracial individuals move toward appreciation and pride in their identity.

Choi-Misailidis's Multiracial Heritage Awareness and Personal Affiliation Theory

The multiracial heritage awareness and personal affiliation theory was developed by SooJean Choi-Misailidis (2010). She identifies three identity statuses:

1. *Marginal,* in which individuals lack a sense of connection with any racial group, as is the case with marginalized ethnic status in general (see Chapter 3)

2. *Singular,* which is similar to Root's first choice (acceptance of a given identity), in which an individual accepts the designation of the society in which they live

3. *Integrated,* which involves two factors, acceptance and integration of all of the aspects of one's racial heritage and an appreciation for the diversity and commonalities among all racial groups; this status is similar to Status 5 of both of the racial identity models previously discussed

The Integrated identity status was found to be correlated with positive self-esteem and ethnic pride as well as affirmative attitudes toward racial and ethnic diversity. Counselors can help multiracial clients move toward that status.

Henriksen and Paladino's Multiple Heritage Identity Development Model

This model (Henriksen & Paladino, 2009b) consists of six nonlinear phases, called periods.

1. *Neutrality* refers to the time prior to a person being aware that racial or ethnic differences exist

2. *Acceptance* involves individuals first being aware of having a racial/ethnic heritage

3. *Awareness,* a period during which an individual starts to comprehend experiences and factors that accompany being racially different

4. *Experimentation* involves the individual seeking connection by choosing only one part of her or his racial heritage as her or his primary identity

5. *Transition* features the realization that the individual does not fit as a member of any single group

6. *Recognition* often involves individuals choosing to accept who they are racially

While the development and nascent testing phase of these models may be a significant advancement, more research needs to be done to assess their utility and validity (Choi-Misailidis, 2010). In general, the empirical research regarding counseling multiple-heritage individuals, couples, and families consists mainly of qualitative studies, which often contradict each other (Choi-Misailidis, 2010). Recognizing the lack of a broad research foundation, the literature still offers suggestions for work with this population. Many of these recommendations are summarized briefly below.

Implications for Counseling

When working with multiracial individuals, counselors should broach and explore the topics of culture and identity in the context of a trusting working alliance (Day-Vines et al., 2007; Kenney, 2006). Several of the skills discussed in Chapter 19 are also applicable to counseling this population, including counselors being aware of their own biases about multiracial status, having knowledge of each individual's racial group cultures, using a strengths-based focus, involving clients' families of choice, exploring possible internalized oppressions, using bibliotherapy, and advocating for and with multiracial clients and/or families (Harris, 2009; Kenney & Kenney, 2009, 2010; Nettles & Balter, 2012; Sue & Sue, 2003; Wehrly, 2005).

Benesh and Henriksen (2009) support the use of narrative therapy to deconstruct problem stories. When working with families involved in transracial adoptions, exploring the family's choices and questions about integrating aspects of the adoptee's birth culture(s) can be helpful (Baden, Thomas, & Smith, 2009) as can discussions about childrearing practices with a multiple-heritage couple (Kenney & Kenney, 2010). Kenney and Kenney (2010) also recommend seeking specialized training/education for working with this population as well as accessing the growing number of organizations and resources devoted to individuals, couples, and families of multiracial heritage (e.g., the Association of Multiethnic Americans, the Mixed Heritage Center).

SUMMARY

Race is a socially important but biologically problematic concept. Throughout history, race has been used to divide peoples and to enforce hierarchies. In that sense, it cannot be separated from racism. Counselors must understand the power of race in American life and counter its negative effects. This chapter has traced the history of the American notion of race. The continuing presence of racism in attitudes and social institutions also was explored. Racial identity development was described, as was the emerging importance of multiracial identity.

REFERENCES

Adelman, L. (2003). *Race and gene studies: What differences make a difference?* Retrieved from http://www.pbs.org/race/000_About/002_04-background-01-02.htm

Allegretto, S. A. (2011). *The state of working: America's wealth, 2011.* Washington, DC: Economic Policy Institute. Retrieved from http://www.epi.org/publications/entry/the_state_of_working_americas_wealth_2011

Atkinson, D. R., Morten, G., & Sue, D. W. (1998). *Counseling American minorities* (5th ed.). Boston, MA: McGraw-Hill.

Auerbach, S. (2002). "Why do they give the good classes to some and not to others?" Latino parent narratives of struggle in a college access program. *Teachers College Record, 104,* 1369–1392.

Avery, R. B, & Rendall, M. S. (2002). Lifetime inheritances of three generations of whites and blacks. *American Journal of Sociology, 107,* 1300–1346.

Baden, A. L., Thomas, L. A., & Smith, C. (2009). Navigating heritage, culture, identity, and adoption: Counseling transracially adopted individuals and their families. In R. C. Henriksen Jr. & D. A. Paladino

(Eds.), *Counseling multiple heritage individuals, couples, and families* (pp. 125–144). Alexandria, VA: American Counseling Association.

Benesh, A. C., & Henriksen, R. C., Jr. (2009). Intersecting socially constructed identities with multiple heritage identity. In R. C. Henriksen Jr. & D. A. Paladino (Eds.), *Counseling multiple heritage individuals, couples, and families* (pp. 145–155). Alexandria, VA: American Counseling Association.

Bertrand, M., & Mullainathan, S. (2004). Are Emily and Greg more employable than Lakisha and Jamal? A field experiment on labor market discrimination. *American Economic Review, 94,* 991–1013.

Black, E. (2003). *War against the weak: Eugenics and America's campaign to create a master race.* New York, NY: Four Walls Eight Windows.

Bobo, L. (2001, October). *Inequalities that endure? Racial ideology, American politics, and the peculiar role of the social scientists.* Paper presented at The Changing Terrain of Race and Ethnicity, Chicago, IL.

Butler, J. (2001). *Color-line to borderlands: The matrix of American ethnic studies.* Seattle: University of Washington Press.

California Newsreel. (2003). *Race—The power of an illusion.* Retrieved from http://www.pbs.org/race/000_About/002_04-about-04.htm

Choi-Misailidis, S. (2010). Multiracial-Heritage Awareness and Personal Affiliation (M-HAPA): Understanding identity in people of mixed-race descent. In J. G. Ponterotto, J. M. Casas, L. A. Suzuki, & C. M. Alexander (Eds.), *Handbook of multicultural counseling* (3rd ed., pp. 301–312). Thousand Oaks, CA: Sage.

Christie, L. (2010). *Pay gap persists for African-Americans.* Retrieved from http://money.cnn.com/2010/07/30/news/economy/black_pay_gap_persists/index.htm

Condon, S. (2010). *Poll reveals racial divide on opinion of Obama.* Retrieved from http://www.cbsnews.com/8301-503544_162-20020978-503544.html

Cose, E. (2011). *The end of anger: A new generation's take on race and rage.* New York, NY: Ecco/HarperCollins.

Cross, W. E., Jr. (1995). The psychology of nigrescence: Revising the Cross model. In J. Ponterotto, J. M. Casas, L. A. Suzuki, & C. M. Alexander (Eds.), *Handbook of multicultural counseling* (pp. 93–122). Thousand Oaks, CA: Sage.

Dain, B. (2002). *A hideous monster of the mind: American race theory in the early republic.* Cambridge, MA: Harvard University Press.

Daly, E. (2005, April 13). DNA tells students they aren't who they thought. *The New York Times,* p. B8.

Davenport, C. (1911). *Heredity in relation to eugenics.* New York, NY: Holt.

Day-Vines, N., Woods, S., Grothaus, T., Craigen, L., Holman, A., Dotson-Blake, K., & Douglas, M. (2007). Broaching the subjects of race, ethnicity, and culture during the counseling process. *Journal of Counseling and Development, 85,* 401–409.

Donziger, S. R. (1996). *The real war on crime: The report of the National Criminal Justice Commission.* New York, NY: HarperCollins.

Dovidio, J. F., Gaertner, S. L., & Kafati, G. (2000). Group identity and intergroup relations: The Common Ingroup Identity Model. In S. R. Thye, E. Lawler, M. Macy, & H. Walker (Eds.), *Advances in group processes* (Vol. 17, pp. 1–35). Stamford, CT: JAI.

El Nassar, H. (2011, September 30). "Dramatic" jump in claims of black-white heritage. *USA Today,* p. 1A.

Feagin, J. R. (1999). Excluding blacks and others from housing: The foundation of white racism. *Cityscape: A Journal of Policy Development and Research, 4*(3), 79–91.

Feagin, J. R., & McKinney, K. D. (2005). *The many costs of racism.* Lanham, MD: Rowman & Littlefield.

Freeman, H. P. (1998). The meaning of race in science—Considerations for cancer research. *Cancer, 82,* 219–225.

Gates, H. L. (2004, February 2). *America beyond the color line* [Television broadcast]. Arlington, VA: Public Broadcasting System.

Gerstle, G. (2001). *American crucible: Race and nation in the twentieth century.* Princeton, NJ: Princeton University Press.

Glazer, N., & Moynihan, D. P. (1970). *Beyond the melting pot: The Negroes, Puerto Ricans, Jews, Italians, and Irish of New York City.* Cambridge, MA: MIT Press.

Gossett, T. F. (1997). *Race: The history of an idea in America* (New ed.). New York, NY: Oxford University Press.

Hannaford, I. (1996). *Race: The history of an idea in the West.* Baltimore, MD: Johns Hopkins University Press.

Hardiman, R. (1982). White identity development: A process oriented model for describing the racial consciousness of White Americans. *Dissertation Abstracts International, 43,* 104A.

Harris, H. L. (2009). Counseling multiple heritage children. In R. C. Henriksen Jr. & D. A. Paladino (Eds.), *Counseling multiple heritage individuals, couples, and families* (pp. 45–63). Alexandria, VA: American Counseling Association.

Helms, J. E. (1990). *Black and white racial identity: Theory, research and practice.* Westport, CT: Greenwood Press.

Helms, J. E., & Cook, D. A. (1999). *Using race and culture in counseling and psychotherapy.* Boston, MA: Allyn & Bacon.

Henriksen, R. C., Jr., & Paladino, D. A. (2009a). History of racial classification. In R. C. Henriksen Jr. & D. A. Paladino (Eds.), *Counseling multiple heritage individuals, couples, and families* (pp. 1–16). Alexandria, VA: American Counseling Association.

Henriksen, R. C., Jr., & Paladino, D. A. (2009b). Identity development in a multiple heritage world. In R. C. Henriksen Jr. & D. A. Paladino (Eds.), *Counseling multiple heritage individuals, couples, and families* (pp. 25–43). Alexandria, VA: American Counseling Association.

Herrnstein, R. J., & Murray, C. (1996). *The bell curve.* New York, NY: Free Press.

Holcomb-McCoy, C., & Chen-Hayes, S. F. (2011). Culturally competent school counselors: Affirming diversity by challenging oppression. In B. T. Erford (Ed.), *Transforming the school counseling profession* (3rd ed., pp. 90–109). Boston, MA: Pearson.

Hunter, M. L. (2002). If you're light you're alright: Light skin color as social capital for women of color. *Gender & Society, 16,* 175–193.

Ignatiev, N. (2008). *How the Irish became white.* New York, NY: Routledge.

Ivey, A. E., Ivey, M. B., D'Andrea, M., & Simek-Morgan, L. (2008). *Theories of counseling and psychotherapy: A multicultural perspective.* Boston, NY: Allyn & Bacon/Longman.

Jones, J. M. (2008). *Majority of Americans say racism against blacks widespread.* Retrieved from http://www.gallup.com/poll/109258/majority-americans-say-racism-against-blacks-widespread.aspx

Jorde, L. B., & Wooding, S. P. (2004). Genetic variation, classification and "race." *Nature Genetics, 36,* S28–S33. Retrieved from http://www.nature.com/ng

Jun, H. (2010). *Social justice, multicultural counseling, and practice: Beyond a conventional approach.* Thousand Oaks, CA: Sage.

Kegan, R. (1982). *The evolving self.* Cambridge, MA: Harvard University Press.

Kenney, K. R. (2006). Counseling multiracial individuals and families. In C. C. Lee (Ed.), *Multicultural issues in counseling: New approaches to diversity* (3rd ed., pp. 251–266). Alexandria, VA: American Counseling Association.

Kenney, K. R., & Kenney, M. E. (2009). Counseling multiple heritage couples and families. In R. C. Henriksen Jr. & D. A. Paladino (Eds.), *Counseling multiple heritage individuals, couples, and families* (pp. 111–124). Alexandria, VA: American Counseling Association.

Kenney, K. R., & Kenney, M. E. (2010). Advocacy counseling with the multiracial population. In M. J. Ratts, R. L. Toporek, & J. A. Lewis (Eds.), *ACA advocacy competencies: A social justice framework for counselors* (pp. 65–74). Alexandria, VA: American Counseling Association.

King, J. C. (1981). *The biology of race.* Berkeley: University of California Press.

Kwate, N. O., Valdimarsdottir, H. B, Guevarra, J. S., & Bovbjerg, D. H. (2003). Experiences of racist events are associated with negative health consequences for African American women. *Journal of the National Medical Association, 95,* 450–460.

Laubeová, L. (2000). *Melting pot vs. ethnic stew.* Retrieved from http://www.tolerance.cz/courses/texts/melting.htm

Lehrman, S. (2003). *Colorblind racism.* Retrieved from http://www.justicejournalism.org/projects/lehrman_sally/lehrman_colorblind.pdf

Maglo, K. N. (2011). The case against biological realism about race: From Darwin to the post-genomic era. *Perspectives on Science, 19,* 361–390.

Marable, M. (2000, February 25). We need new and critical study of race and ethnicity. *The Chronicle of Higher Education,* p. B34.

Marger, M. N. (2008). *Race and ethnic relations: American and global perspectives.* Belmont, CA: Wadsworth Press.

Marger, M. N. (2011). *Social inequality: Patterns and processes* (3rd ed.). New York, NY: McGraw-Hill.

Martinez, E. (2004). *De Colores means all of us: Latina views for a multi-colored century.* In M. L. Andersen & P. H. Collins (Eds.), *Race, class, and gender* (pp. 111–117). Belmont, CA: Wadsworth/Thomson Learning.

Massey, D. S., & Denton, N. A. (1998). *American apartheid: Segregation and the making of the underclass.* Cambridge, MA: Harvard University Press.

McKee, J. B. (1993). *Sociology and the race problem: The failure of a perspective.* Urbana: University of Illinois Press.

Middleton, R. A., Erguner-Tekinalp, B., & Petrova, E. (2005, October). *Clinical applications of racial identity development: Profile approach to Helms' White Racial Identity Development Model.* Presentation to the meeting of the Association for Counselor Education and Supervision, Pittsburgh, PA.

Myrdal, G. (1944). *An American dilemma: The negro problem and modern democracy.* New York, NY: Harper & Brothers.

National Council on Crime and Delinquency. (2007). *And justice for some: Differential treatment for youth of color in the justice system.* Oakland, CA: Author. Retrieved from http://www.nccd-crc.org/nccd/pubs/2007jan_justice_for_some.pdf

Nealy, M. J. (2008). On the losing end. *Diverse: Issues in Higher Education.* Retrieved from http://diverse-education.com/article/11077/

Nettles, R., & Balter, R. (2012). Preface. In R. Nettles & R. Balter (Eds.), *Multiple minority identities: Applications for practice, research, and training* (pp. xv–xvii). New York, NY: Springer.

O'Brien, J. (2011). *Ontario fan throws banana at Wayne Simmonds in shameful racist display.* Retrieved from http://prohockeytalk.nbcsports.com/2011/09/22/ontario-fans-throw-bananas-at-wayne-simmonds-in-shameful-racist-display/

Palmer, P. J. (1998). *The courage to teach: Exploring the inner landscape of a teacher's life.* San Francisco, CA: Jossey-Bass.

Paniagua, F. A. (2005). *Assessing and treating culturally diverse clients: A practical guide* (3rd ed.). Thousand Oaks, CA: Sage.

Parra, E., Marcini, A., Akey, J., Martinson, J., Batzer, M., Cooper, R., . . . Shriver, M. D. (1998). Estimating African-American admixture proportions by use of population-specific alleles. *American Journal of Human Genetics, 63,* 1839–1851.

Pellegrini, G. M. (2005). Multiracial identity in the post-civil rights era. *Social Identities, 11,* 531–549.

Pierce, C. M. (1988). Stress in the workplace. In A. F. Coner-Edwards & J. Spurlock (Eds.), *Black families in crisis: The middle class* (pp. 27–35). New York, NY: Brunner/Mazel.

Poe-Yamagata, E., & Jones, M. (2000). *And justice for some.* Washington, DC: Building Blocks for Youth.

Ponterotto, J. G., Utsey, S. O., & Pedersen, P. B. (2006). *Preventing prejudice: A guide for counselors, educators, and parents* (2nd ed.). Thousand Oaks, CA: Sage.

Robinson, T. L. (2005). *The convergence of race, ethnicity, and gender: Multiple identities in counseling* (2nd ed.). Upper Saddle River, NJ: Pearson.

Root, M. P. P. (1996). *The multiracial experience: Racial borders as the new frontier.* Thousand Oaks, CA: Sage.

Shapiro, T. M. (2005). *The hidden cost of being African-American: How wealth perpetuates inequality.* New York, NY: Oxford University Press.

Slattery, J. M. (2004). *Counseling diverse clients: Bringing context into therapy.* Belmont, CA: Thomson/Brooks/Cole.

Smith, W. A., Hung, M., & Franklin, J. D. (2011). Racial battle fatigue and the miseducation of black men: Racial microaggressions, societal problems, and environmental stress. *Journal of Negro Education, 80,* 63–82.

Smith, W. A., Yosso, T. J., & Solórzano, D. G. (2006). Challenging racial battle fatigue on historically White campuses: A critical race examination of race-related stress. In C. A. Stanley (Ed.), *Faculty of color teaching in predominantly White colleges and universities* (pp. 299–327). Bolton, MA: Anker.

Sue, D. W. (2010). *Racial microaggressions in everyday life: Race, gender and sexual orientation.* Hoboken, NJ: Wiley.

Sue, D. W., & Sue, S. (2003). *Counseling the culturally diverse: Theory and practice* (4th ed.). New York, NY: Wiley.

Sutton, J. R. (2011). *Structural bias in the sentencing of felony defendants.* Retrieved from http://www.soc.ucsb.edu/faculty/sutton/Design/Assets/scps2000.pdf

Takaki, R. (2008). *A different mirror: A history of multicultural America.* Boston, MA: Little, Brown.

Telles, E. E. (2002). Racial ambiguity among the Brazilian population. *Ethnic and Racial Studies, 25,* 415–441.

U.S. Department of Housing and Urban Development. (2011). *Discrimination in metropolitan housing markets: National results from phase 1, phase 2, and phase 3 of the Housing Discrimination Survey (HDDS).* Retrieved from http://www.huduser.org/portal/publications/hsgfin/hds.html

Utsey, S. O., Chae, M. H., Brown, C. F., & Kelly, D. (2002). Effect of ethnic group membership on ethnic identity, race-related stress and quality of life. *Cultural Diversity & Ethnic Minority Psychology, 8,* 366–377.

Wehrly, B. (2005). *Breaking barriers for multiracial individuals and families.* In F. D. Harper & J. McFadden (Eds.), *Culture and counseling: New approaches* (pp. 313–323). Boston, MA: Allyn & Bacon.

Welch, W. M. (2011, December 5). Ky. church makes room for all believers. *USA Today,* p. 3A.

Wellman, D. (1977). *Portraits of white racism.* New York, NY: Cambridge.

Wessel, D. (2003, September 17). Racial discrimination: Still at work in the U.S. *The Wall Street Journal Online.*

White, J. L., & Parham, T. A. (1990). *The psychology of blacks.* Englewood Cliffs, NJ: Prentice Hall.

Wilson, W. J. (1996). *When work disappears: The world of the new urban poor.* New York, NY: Alfred A. Knopf.

Wolfle, L. M. (1987). High school seniors' reports of parental socioeconomic status: Black-white differences. In P. Cuttance & E. Russell (Eds.), *Structural modeling by example: Applications in educational, sociological, and behavioral research* (pp. 51–64). New York, NY: Cambridge University Press.

PART II

MAJOR ETHNIC GROUPINGS

CHAPTER 6

Culturally Alert Counseling With African Americans

Kathy M. Evans
University of South Carolina

Lift every voice and sing

Till earth and heaven ring

Ring with the harmony of liberty

Let our rejoicing rise

High as the listening skies

Let it resound loud as the rolling sea

Sing a song full of the faith that the dark past has taught us

Sing a song full of the hope that the present has brought us

Facing the rising sun

Of a new day begun

Let us march on till victory is won

—James Weldon Johnson

"Lift Every Voice and Sing," which is quoted throughout this chapter, is also called the Negro National Anthem. It is a powerful evocation of African American strengths and aspirations and of the influence past struggles have had on the present and future of African Americans.

This chapter is devoted to counseling African Americans. It begins by presenting a summary of the African worldview to put the African American experience in historical perspective. The chapter moves on to key notions from the history of the American system of slavery and the evolution of racism and oppression. Two case studies, those of Tamika and Kendra, are presented to assist in describing African American characteristics. They are two very different African American women who share a common ancestry and problems that have similar sociological and psychological origins. The chapter ends with a discussion of counseling practices that build on the strengths of a people.

AMERICANS OF AFRICAN DESCENT: THE PEOPLE AND THEIR HISTORY

In 1964, Malcolm X said, "History is a people's memory, and without a memory, man [*sic*] is demoted to the lower animals" (Spanoudis, 1994–2007). For counselors, understanding the history of a people is important for developing empathy, appreciating present circumstances, and establishing trust with clients of sub-Saharan African heritage. Understanding African Americans begins not only by understanding slavery but also by understanding African culture.

African Heritage

Avid gardeners know the importance of having soil that is nutrient-rich to enable the roots of a particular plant to grow. The roots provide the foundation for the plant's growth and maturation. Africa was such a rich soil for the growth of the human species and the spread of civilizations. Precolonial Africa was a place without strict borders, where African kingdoms shifted with the nutrients of the land. African culture spread also to the Americas, as enslaved Africans created part of the fabric of American society (Cowan, 2004).

African Worldview

Much of the African worldview can be seen in African American culture, although some has been lost due to acculturation. Worldview in general encompasses views of human nature, relationship with nature itself, interrelationships with others, relationship to time, and communication with others. Four distinct elements of the African worldview are human nature, community/family, time, and communication.

The African worldview about human nature is holistic. There is no separation of mind and body. Instead, the whole of the person's experience is considered. People at once think, feel, and sense their lives. They embrace emotions and have a sense of vitality that is apparent in their songs, dances, and language. In the African worldview, there is a belief in the interconnections of all living things, including a connection with God.

The African worldview includes the communitarian notion that the tribe is the defining unit of a person's existence. Individuals and nuclear families exist for the survival and well-being of the tribe.

The perception of time is grounded in the present and the past and measured in terms of life events (e.g., chores, the birth of a child). Time follows the cyclical rhythms of nature (day/night, seasons).

The traditional African way of communicating is call and response—when someone speaks someone else responds to show the speaker she or he has been heard. The spoken word is admired, and oral historians are essential to the life of the tribe (Parham, White, & Ajamu, 1999).

The Impact of Slavery

The American slavery system was designed to strip Africans of their culture and language by never putting individuals from the same tribe together. The effort was only partly successful. Ntloedibe (2006) states, "Neither cultural diversity or linguistic multiplicity [of the different tribes] served as major obstacles to the development of African American cultures in the new world" (p. 402). To think that African Americans lost all vestiges of African culture when they crossed the Atlantic and entered the Americas as slaves is to undermine the strength and resiliency of the captured Africans (Boyd-Franklin, 1989). Many customs, values, traditions, and nuances of language were preserved and passed on through the generations. However, slavery colored the lives of each African who was brought to the Americas and all of his or her descendants.

Slavery

Stormy the road we trod

Bitter the chastening rod

Felt in the days when hope unborn had died

Yet with a steady beat, have not our weary feet

Come to the place for which our fathers sighed

We have come over a way that with tears has been watered,

We have come, treading our path thro' the blood of the slaughtered

Out from the gloomy past, till now we stand at last

Where the white gleam of our bright star is cast.

—James Weldon Johnson

The stanza quoted above from the Negro National Anthem illustrates the significance of slavery in the lives of today's African Americans. Millions of Africans were captured and shackled for sale as part of the trans-Atlantic slave trade that first passed through Cape Coast Castle in what is today Ghana, in West Africa (Phillips, 2004). The voyages were very profitable (J. J. Connor, 2003). From England, various manufactured products—mainly textiles, metal goods, and liquor—were exported to Africa, where they were exchanged for slaves. The transatlantic slave trade moved the people from Ghana through the "door of no return" to a horrifying journey across the Atlantic Ocean (Phillips, 2004). This journey came to be known as the "middle passage" because it was regarded as the middle leg of the triangular trading route. The English slave owners used the proceeds from the sale of slaves in the West Indies to buy sugar, which was shipped back to England, completing the triangle. By the end of the 18th century, this triangular trade route had become a standard feature of the slave traffic (Meier & Rudwick, 1966). In over four centuries of slave trading, researchers estimate that between 30 and 60 million Africans began the journey (Smallwood, 1998). Over 4 million Africans died in the middle passage on the way to slavery in the Americas (Smallwood, 1998). Millions of enslaved Africans were dispersed throughout the African Diaspora to North America, South America, and the Caribbean as well as to Europe. The way slavery was practiced in the United States was dehumanizing and cruel. While this was not the first occurrence of slavery in human history, it was the most extensive and the most widespread based on the color of people's skin.

Table 6.1 summarizes key events and dates in the history of African slavery in America.

Some experts suggest that Western enslavement of Africans is not yet over. Although few traditional forms of colonialism still exist, a version of slavery exists today, in the form of the post-colonial domination of African peoples that continues around the world and in the United States. The descendants of African slaves continue to exist in a social climate that is associated with inferior treatment, economic subjugation, and sociopolitical inequity. What helps to perpetuate the subjugation of individuals of African descent is the racism that was introduced and encouraged during slavery and that continues to this day.

Racism: The Legacy of Slavery

Racism toward African Americans can be directly linked to attitudes that existed at the time of the slave industry. The most powerful misinformation that fueled racist attitudes in the United States was initiated by the Puritans, who identified Africans as inferior on the basis of supposed Christian doctrine (Griffin, 1999). Over the years, Southern slave owners extended that way of thinking, believing that "God had created Black people to be heathen and less than all human beings" (p. 28). This concept was ideal in that it allowed slave owners to continue buying and selling other human beings without guilt. The belief in African inferiority grew in popularity over the centuries and persists in both popular and scientific thinking.

Although the Fourteenth and Fifteenth Amendments to the U.S. Constitution, which were approved during the Lincoln administration in the

Table 6.1 Key Dates of Slaves and Africans in America

Date	Summary
900–1500	The trans-Saharan (from Northern to Southern Africa) slave trade
1502–1600	Slave revolts and Maroon communities in the Spanish and Portuguese colonies of the Caribbean and the Americas
1600–1720	The establishment of French, English, Dutch, and Swedish colonies in the Americas and the Caribbean
1620–1776	English colonial slavery in the New England colonies, Middle colonies, Southern colonies, and the Caribbean
1650–1755	The Native American slave trade, the legalization of slavery, the rise of Slave Codes, and the growth of the African slave population in the English colonies
1710–1776	The British "Triangle of Trade" with colonial America and the growth of the African American slave population in North America
1770–1783	African Americans participate in the American Revolution
1777–1800	The emancipation of slaves in the North and the expansion of slavery in the Southern states and territories of the new American republic
1800	The combined free black and slave population of the United States reaches one million
1808–1865	Slave smuggling in the United States
1865	Major Southern cities destroyed by the end of the Civil War; Southern economy in ruins
1865–1877	Establishment of the Freedmen's Bureau to assist blacks during Reconstruction

1860s, were aimed at having African Americans regain a sense of humanity and dignity, the backlash from former slave owners and other whites was swift and ugly. Whites retaliated by intimidating, terrorizing, and killing African Americans. They accused African American legislators of fraud, and the Ku Klux Klan intimidated African American voters by burning crosses near their homes and lynching African American men who asserted their legal rights. These types of terrorist tactics, along with dwindling support from Northern white Republicans, eventually made it possible for whites to garner enough votes to defeat the Reconstruction reforms (Levine, 1996). By 1871, four Southern states were back in the control of white Democrats. Once back in power, the Southern Democrats proceeded to pass a massive number of laws aimed at "putting blacks in their place." Segregation laws (called Jim Crow laws because of a popular black character in minstrel shows of the time) prohibited blacks and whites from being in contact with one another in all public places. This amounted to having separate toilets, water fountains, and entrances to public places. To circumvent the Fifteenth Amendment, Southern Democratic legislators intentionally excluded blacks from voting by imposing poll taxes and literacy tests on African Americans seeking to vote; whites could get other whites to vouch for them to avoid the poll taxes and literacy tests (Levine, 1996). As a result, African Americans were again excluded from being participants in the democracy and treated cruelly.

In essence, the Jim Crow laws legalized racism. The Supreme Court, rather than striking down these laws, condoned them. In its 1896 decision on *Plessy v. Ferguson*. the court ruled that segregation did not violate the Constitution. For more than 50 years, legal institutional racism made it impossible for African Americans to participate as full citizens in the United States. The Jim Crow laws of segregation kept African Americans in a different kind of slavery well into the 20th century.

Although the 1954 Supreme Court decision in *Brown v. Board of Education* overturned Jim Crow Laws, it was necessary for Congress to pass the Civil Rights Act in 1964 and the Voting Rights Act in 1965 in order to end legal segregation practices. With the passage of these laws and the attendant policies, executive orders, monies, and military support ensuring their enforcement, the lives of African Americans began to change (Levine, 1996). The changes were not without struggle, though. To this day, companies are being sued for violating the civil rights of African Americans. The Voting Rights Act was expanded and renewed in 1970, 1975, and 1982 because unfair practices continued in several states. However, redistricting practices continue to weaken the voting power of African Americans throughout the country.

Given the subtlety of racism, Activity 6.1 can help you determine your attitudes.

Activity 6.1 Do You Have Racial Issues With African Americans?

To find out, place a check mark beside each statement below if it resembles one that you have either thought privately or said aloud.

_____ 1. Black people are racists too.

_____ 2. I don't understand what they expect me to do; I can't do anything about racism. I just know I'm not a racist.

_____ 3. I don't know why African Americans are always bringing up slavery when it has been over for 150 years. Other people have been oppressed, and they don't keep throwing it in our faces.

_____ 4. I (or my relative) didn't get accepted at my first choice of college because of affirmative action.

_____ 5. I don't see Kathy as black; I see her as a person.

_____ 6. I really don't know what to say when I'm around a lot of black people.

_____ 7. I sometimes feel overwhelmed with all the information I have to learn about minorities.

Reasons why these are racist statements:

1. Implies that black bias and prejudices toward whites have a similar effect on whites as white racism has on blacks. Unfortunately, because of the position of power and privilege that many whites are afforded in U.S. society, this is not the case. Except in the case of physical harm, it is rare that black racism will harm whites as much as white racism hurts blacks. Also, this statement assumes that having racist attitudes is acceptable when the targeted group is also guilty of prejudice.

2. Helplessness gives one an excuse not to change the status quo, whether it is one's own behavior or that of others.

3. Indicates a lack of knowledge about the connection between slavery and racism that still exists today. Also, denies the history of a people, which denies the people themselves.

4. Indicates resentment toward African Americans, with a belief that they have unfair advantage. Shows ignorance of white entitlement, insistence that the playing field is level and that whites do not enjoy privilege merely by virtue of being born white.

(Continued)

5. Although intended to be a statement of inclusion, it can be a statement about how much better it is to be white. The speaker might believe that being black is a handicap and that she or he has been able to ignore this deficit as far as Kathy is concerned by denying her racial identity.

6. Indicates discomfort with African Americans and assumes that the speaker will have nothing in common with them.

7. An expression of helplessness and an excuse not to learn or change.

Contemporary Forms of Racism

In the 21st century, the legacy of slavery in the form of racism continues. After strides were made to correct discriminatory practices against people of color during the period following the passage of the Civil Rights Act, there seemed to be a resurgence of negative attitudes toward African Americans beginning in the 1980s. Gains that were made during the administrations of Presidents Lyndon Johnson and Richard Nixon were eroded during the 1980s. That decade brought an era of so-called color-blindness and white resentment of equal opportunity policies (Levine, 1996), sometimes called a backlash. The political climate during the 1980s fostered a trend in which racism was cloaked under the guise of fairness, equality, and "the American Way"—that is, treating individuals purely as individuals, not as connected to social groups. This view was seen as not being racist; it was being American to treat individuals as separate from their opportunity context. However, that assumes that the playing field is level to begin with. These subtler versions of racism have been called *unintentional covert racism* and *color-blind racism* (Dovidio, Kawakami, & Gaertner, 2000; Ridley, 1995). Chapter 5 discussed some of these issues.

The mildest form of contemporary racism is what Ridley (1995) describes as unintentional covert racism, in which the person does not intend to be racist, but her or his behavior results in harm to another. For example, a teacher might unintentionally not call on black children in class as often as others. A similar notion is color-blind racial attitudes (COBRA; Neville, Worthington, & Spanierman, 2001), in which individuals deny the existence of race as a social issue while also wishing to maintain existing white privilege. They blame people of color themselves for their position in American society, and they resist any political efforts to improve conditions for blacks. People with COBRA claim that their own status of entitlement and achievement is due to their own merit and not related to social placement. Chapter 4 describes this phenomenon of optional ethnicity, that is, the claim that individual effort is the sole reason for success and the failure to acknowledge social advantages.

Simply put, remnants of slavery represented by racist attitudes and behaviors have colored the relationships between African Americans and European Americans and impacted the social, emotional, and political lives of all Americans, especially African Americans. Racism and discrimination have permeated the lives of African Americans—their families, education, employment, and psychosocial development—for generations. Those legacies are still alive. However, African Americans have been neither accepting nor passive about the state of affairs. In fact, protests have occurred quite often, both violent and nonviolent. The next section addresses such responses.

The African American Response to Racism

We shall overcome, we shall overcome,

We shall overcome, someday,

Deep in my heart, I do believe

We shall overcome someday.

—Civil Rights Anthem

The legacy of slavery that endures through racism has taken its toll on African Americans. A seminal statement of African American feelings about social conditions was made in 1968 by two African American psychiatrists, William Grier and Price Cobbs, in their book *Black Rage*, when they declared that nothing was more important to know about African Americans than that they were angry. That anger over past and current mistreatment lingers. The scholar Cornel West has been quoted as saying, "We are an unloved people" (Smiley, 2005). If African Americans perceive that they are unloved (or even despised) by non–African Americans, counselors of other racial groups must be especially prepared for client distrust, anger, and hurt.

Chapter 5 discussed the decades of African American struggle against legalized racism and discrimination, or what has been called "American apartheid." African Americans have chosen to combat racism with education, protest, and sometimes violence. Whatever the choice, African Americans have expressed their unhappiness with their treatment as subhumans with limited citizenship. "We Shall Overcome" was the battle cry of the nonviolent civil rights movement of the 1950s and 1960s. It expressed the hope for a brighter future for African Americans. This movement will be discussed next.

The most brutal, visible, effective, and largest civil rights movement by African Americans to date occurred in the 10-year period following the 1954 *Brown v. Board of Education* Supreme Court decision. Although that court ruled that Jim Crow laws were unconstitutional, these laws still existed in many states. As a result of white resistance to equity, the growing anger of African Americans and their supporters led to protests against these laws. They, and many white allies, were hosed down, jailed, and killed, yet they were relentless (C. J. Robinson, 1997). Most of the protests during the 1960s were nonviolent on the part of African Americans, especially those who were under the leadership of the Rev. Dr. Martin Luther King Jr., who was a strong advocate for nonviolence. In 1963, King and the Southern Christian Leadership Conference led over 200,000 people to march peacefully on Washington to raise awareness in the national government of legal oppression in the Southern states.

However, there also were many violent protests during the 1960s in the form of deadly riots, fueled by leaders who stated that African Americans must gain their freedom "by any means necessary," as Malcolm X said, including violence. While the race riots of the 1960s are most memorable, race riots have, in fact, occurred throughout the 20th century whenever African Americans were particularly outraged by a blatantly racist act (C. J. Robinson, 1997; Smallwood, 1998).

Other nonviolent reactions to the oppressive Jim Crow laws included migration back to Africa and movement from the Southern states to the Northern states. In the latter case, African Americans moved north because racism was not as institutionally legalized in the North as it had been in the South, and jobs were more plentiful. However, there was pervasive racism in the North as well. The various responses to racism and oppression are ongoing and have become part of the fabric of the African American subculture.

In conclusion, understanding the history of slavery and its legacy lays an additional foundation for understanding African Americans. In addition to African heritage, this history of oppression has had a direct effect on the culture of African American people. African American survival from oppression is a strength that counselors can call upon when working with African American clients. Using the legacy of the strength of African Americans to fight for their rights can be quite motivating to clients. These are some of the values and worldviews that are discussed next.

AFRICAN AMERICAN VALUES AND CHARACTERISTICS

God of our weary years, God of our silent tears,

Thou who hast brought us thus far on the way

Thou who hast by Thy might

Led us into the light

Keep us forever in the path we pray.

Lest our feet stray from the places, our God, where we met Thee,

Lest our hearts, drunk with the wine of the world we forget they

Shadowed beneath thy hand, May we forever stand

True to our God, True to our native land.

—James Weldon Johnson

This last stanza of the Negro National Anthem is most revealing of African American culture because it indicates the importance of spiritual values to African Americans and their commitment to the United States. In this section, the predominant attributes of the African American people are addressed. The cases of Tamika and Kendra are used to illustrate some of the concepts.

Tamika is a 20-year-old African American woman who recently gave birth to her second child by a man she has yet to marry. He has been in and out of jail for petty crimes over the past few years. Tamika is due to go back to work in 2 weeks but she has been unable to get out of bed for 5 days and her baby cries constantly. Her 5-year-old refuses to pick up after himself, something he had done routinely in the past. Tamika lives with her mother and two siblings (ages 16 and 14). Her mother took a day off from work to take Tamika to the hospital. However, nothing has been found to be physically wrong with Tamika, and the doctor suggested counseling.

Kendra is a 20-year-old African American woman who is a junior at an Ivy League university and an engineering major. She has always excelled in school but is struggling to get Cs this semester. Both of Kendra's parents are professionals. Her father is an engineer and her mother is a math teacher in an inner-city high school. Kendra is attending the university on a scholarship and risks losing it if she does not raise her grades. Her parents are unaware of her academic problems, as she is afraid to tell them. She is sure they will blame her white boyfriend for the problems, which they do about every other problem she reports. After mid-semester grades were posted, Kendra stayed in her room for 3 days and was referred to the counseling center by her boyfriend and the resident director in her dormitory.

African American characteristics cannot be disentangled from the history of oppression. Thus, that history is called on to explain many African American traits in the following discussion. However, many characteristics of African American culture can also be traced to West Africa. The following sections describe 11 dimensions of African American culture:

- relationship with time
- relationships with others
- relationship with nature
- communication
- religion and spirituality
- family and parenting
- racial identity development
- career
- gender
- physical and mental health
- social class

These topics reveal some differences between traditional African American and European American cultures and similarities with African worldviews.

Relationship With Time

African Americans share with many other non-Western cultures the tendency to be "in time" versus "on time." African American culture tends to place less urgency and importance on time and more value on involvement in a specific activity. This characteristic is held in common with the African worldview that time is related to events rather than being measured by a clock. Although African Americans have this view of time, most do adapt to the Western expectations when interacting with white Americans. However, when they are with other African Americans, the Western sense of time is forgotten. For example, on a Saturday morning, Kendra, who is a stickler for being on time for class, may wait comfortably for an hour or more in a black beauty parlor, chatting with the other women, for what was supposed to be a 9:00 A.M. hair appointment.

Relationships With Others

African Americans also differ from the general Anglo-American culture in that they value interdependence over independence, especially in regard to kinship relations. For example, a family counselor who focuses on the nuclear family and who wants Tamika to exert her independence and move from her mother's home will clash with the African American view of family, which includes extended family and even close family friends (T. L. Robinson, 2005; Sue & Sue, 2003). This characteristic is reminiscent of the value of the tribe over the individual, but it also is reflective of the need of the enslaved Africans, having been ripped from their own tribes, to garner kinships with other Africans who have become important in their lives but have no blood relations (Ntloedibe, 2006). This tradition continued throughout slavery when slave owners would sell off the wives, husbands, and children of slaves.

Relationship With Nature

African Americans and other non-European ethnic groups tend to function in harmony with nature rather than be oriented to developing mastery over nature. In other words, they tend to attribute natural phenomena to a higher power rather than to human power. Again, this characteristic is in congruence with an African worldview.

Communication

African Americans have specific styles of communicating that may easily be misinterpreted. The most widely known communication style is the African American Vernacular English (AAVE), also known as Black English or Ebonics. *Ebonics,* a term coined by

Robert Williams in 1975, has been debated over the years. However, there is a consensus today that AAVE is a legitimate language with grammatical rules, semantics, and phonetics (Burling, 1973; Chambers, 1983; Koch, Gross, & Kolts, 2001). An example of AAVE is "There go Susie brother." This statement is grammatically correct in AAVE. However, in Standard English, it would be incorrect because of the omission of an "es" at the end of "go" to indicate the third person present tense and the absence of the possessive "'s" on "Susie."

Even though AAVE is considered a legitimate language by many, others consider it to be simply an incorrect form of communication. Those who speak AAVE exclusively are perceived by many African Americans and whites to be uneducated (Doss & Gross, 1994; Garner & Rubin, 1986). While at least one study has shown that African American college students tend to prefer individuals who speak Standard English, other writers contend that speaking AAVE provides African Americans with a method of bonding with each other and a way of identifying as African American (Garner & Rubin, 1986; Larimer, Beatty, & Broadus, 1988; Naremore, 1980). AAVE distinguishes African Americans and can even intentionally exclude others from the communication. For these reasons, AAVE is accepted and, perhaps, revered by many African Americans.

The existence of AAVE does not mean that African Americans must exclusively use this dialect. AAVE can be honored as a legitimate but not exclusive form of communication. AAVE speakers would do well to code-switch, that is, to use Standard English in some contexts while speaking AAVE among fellow AAVE speakers.

It is very likely that both Kendra and Tamika can code-switch (change from AAVE to Standard English based on their audience). In fact, non-black counselors should not be surprised if clients do not use AAVE in their sessions.

Another aspect of African American communication style that can be problematic for non–African American counselors is that, in social conversation, African Americans are generally animated and speak loudly. They are expressive and emotional in their speech. Among African Americans, language is fluid and colorful, following in the tradition of their

African ancestors. They often use language creatively to tease, assign nicknames, and add new words that become staples in popular vocabulary. Examples of African American words that have made it to general usage over the years include *cool, jazz, chill, dis, rap, bad* (to mean excellent), *hip, yam, gumbo,* and *bogus*. African Americans often engage in a good-natured exchange of insults known as "playing the dozens"— an expression whose roots are in slavery. Playing the dozens has a practical purpose in thickening the skins of African Americans, to prepare them to fight more serious social battles in their lives rather than react to name-calling. Some non–African Americans may interpret such behavior as being aggressive and angry and may be intimidated by it (Sue & Sue, 2003).

Religion and Spirituality

One of the values held dear in African American culture, regardless of socioeconomic status, is spirituality. Spirituality is, in Cook and Wiley's (2000) words, a "foundation of personal and communal life" for African Americans (p. 370). The notion of religion is often synonymous with the Black Church, although there are also other religious affiliations among African Americans. This section will focus on the Black Church because of its power in African American life.

The Black Church is a collective term and encompasses African American churches of all Christian denominations. It is considered to be the first truly American (non–Native American Indian) religious institution (Sanders, 2002) in that it (a) was founded on U.S. soil, (b) is inclusive of several different racial and cultural groups, and (c) has existed in some form since the first Africans were brought to North America in the 1600s. The Black Church is also responsible for maintaining some of the traditions and cultural practices of the Africans who were brought to the Americas. African American worship incorporates African heritage with its rituals, such as ancestor worship, ecstatic ceremonies, holy/ecstatic dancing, drumming, and call-and-response preaching. It also adds Islamic, Judaic, and European American Christian elements (Cook & Wiley, 2000; Sanders, 2002).

The Black Church "is a mixture of Africanism, emotionalism, legalism, ritualism, and theological intellectualism" (Sanders, 2002, p. 77).

Functions of the Black Church

The Black Church provides opportunities for support, leadership, social status, education, cultural affirmation, and political action. After a week of experiencing numerous microaggressions as members of an oppressed nondominant cultural group, African Americans experience the Church as a safe harbor. It is a sanctuary, where at least once per week African Americans can feel empowered. For African American men, the Church offers a way to validate their manhood because those who are relegated to menial jobs in the white world may have a high-status position in the Church (e.g., deacon, trustee). The Black Church is also where African Americans learn their history, understand their political power, and gain not only spiritual but also financial support (Cook & Wiley, 2000).

Churches also teach many African and Christian values. For example, collectivism is not only preached but practiced in the Black Church, where all adults are responsible for training and disciplining the children of the congregation. Children learn responsibility, oral communication, and respect for their elders. It is not uncommon for children to participate monthly in church services—reading scriptures, saying prayers, and serving as ushers. Because of its importance in raising children, the Black Church has been an important part of African American family life.

The Black Church had a critical role in initiating and sustaining the civil rights movement in the 1960s and is still very politically influential today. Once they were freed, many Southern African Americans immediately joined Lincoln's party (the Republican Party), and many more continued to do so in reaction to the rule of the white Southern Democrats, who were called "Dixiecrats." However, during the civil rights movement and afterward, African Americans found more friends among the Northern Democrats than they did among the Republicans. Consequently, Churches were inclined to strongly connect with the Democratic Party and have continued to do so.

Just as the Dixiecrats slowly turned Republican, beginning with the Eisenhower administration and the civil rights movement, party loyalties continue to change (Levine, 1996). The conservative Christianity found in many Black Churches today reflects some conservative Republican beliefs. In fact, some of the credit for recent African American support for U.S. Republican candidates is due to the Black Church's stands against abortion and gay marriage (M. C. Evans, 2004).

The Black Church and Mental Health

The Black Church can be a source of healthy and cathartic experience (Richards & Bergin, 1997). A strong faith was able to sustain African Americans throughout the bitter history of slavery and American apartheid. It may well be a tonic for the challenges of today's African Americans as well. On the other hand, a few individuals may develop an overdependence on the Church, resulting in a reliance on external solutions to problems, dismissing their inner experiences and avoiding conflict.

Historically speaking, the Black Church has eschewed counseling and psychotherapy in favor of prayer and faith. However, in recent years, many denominations have become more receptive to culturally competent counseling (Cook & Wiley, 2000). Counselors would do well to develop their competence in using spirituality in counseling if they work with African Americans (K. M. Evans, 2003; Fukuyama & Sevig, 1999). Chapter 16 of this book expands on that topic of religion in counseling. Studies have overwhelmingly found that religion, spirituality, and/or religiosity are so important and so effective in helping African American clients "get better" that they are an essential element in counseling most African Americans (Ball, Armistead, & Austin, 2003; Bell-Tolliver, Burgess, & Brock, 2009; Jang & Johnson, 2004). In particular, establishing ties with the pastors of Black Churches would create a referral network and complementary resources for clients. Box 6.1 provides some resources that counselors might use to learn about the Black Church.

Box 6.1 Resources on the Black Church

Books

Battle, M. (2006). *The black church in America: African American Christian spirituality*. Malden, MA: Blackwell.

Pinn, A. B. (2002). *The black church in the post-civil rights era*. Maryknoll, NY: Orbis Books.

Websites of the Largest Denominations of Black Churches

National Baptist Convention of America: www.nbcainc.com

National Baptist Convention USA: www.nationalbaptist.com

African Methodist Episcopal Zion Church: www.archaeolink.com/african_methodist_episcopal_zion.htm

African Methodist Episcopal Church: www.ame-church.com

Christian Methodist Episcopal Church: www.c-m-e.org

Progressive National Baptist Convention: www.pnbc.org

Other Helpful Reading

Evans, K. M. (2003). Including spirituality in multicultural counseling: Overcoming counselor resistance. In G. Roysircar, D. S. Sandhu, & V. E. Bibbins (Eds.), *Multicultural competencies: A guidebook of practices* (pp. 161–172). Alexandria, VA: Association for Multicultural Counseling and Development.

Counselors should always explore an African American client's spirituality because it can be a great resource in treatment. If, for example, Kendra has abandoned her religious upbringing during her college years and she and her family were active in the Black Church during her childhood, she may still find comfort in reclaiming some aspects of her spirituality, as would Tamika.

Family and Parenting

The African American family is an institution that has been often misunderstood by the dominant European American society. Prior to the widespread popularity of *The Cosby Show* in the 1980s, the stereotype of an African American family was that of a single female parent, usually on welfare, living in public housing with several children under the age of 10. The only variation on that theme was the notion of a hard-working single mother whose children must look after one another while she works at menial labor to feed her family. In fact, female-headed households living in poverty make up only 18% of African American families. Fully 55% of African American families are headed by two parents (U.S. Census Bureau, 2011).

Those stereotypes have been harmful. For example, researchers have tended to use poor, single female–headed households as their focus and generalized their findings to all African American families (Hill, 1999). While certainly the 26% poverty rate among African Americans is higher than that of almost any other ethnic group, and poverty brings with it a multitude of concerns (Arnold, 2002; U.S. Census Bureau, 2010), generalizing the results from this subpopulation to the whole group is erroneous and misleading.

By contrast, *The Cosby Show* gave the United States sustained exposure to a large, two-parent, middle-class African American family and planted the idea that African American families are very diverse.

Extended Family

As with some aspects of gender roles, African American family traits have been carried over from their roots in West Africa. Today, there continue to be strong consanguineal (blood-related) extended family networks, following the African tradition, primarily among low-income African American families (Sudarkasa, 1988). However, extended family networks also include close friends when family members are not available. Over time, Western influences on African American family structure have become more prominent in middle-class families, with the nuclear family being treated as primary.

Regardless of the familial configuration, African American families assist children in coping with oppression through racial socialization. Getting support from family, especially extended family, is an important part of effective counseling with African Americans (Chadiha, Rafferty, & Pickard, 2003).

Racial Socialization in the Family

To raise a child who has a positive self-concept and high self-esteem, African American parents engage in racial socialization (Greene, 1994; Sanders, 2002; Stevenson, 1994). Racial socialization is the "process of communicating messages and behaviors to children to bolster their sense of identity, given the possibility and reality that their life experiences may include racially hostile encounters" (Stevenson, 1995, p. 51). Many African American parents actively engage their children in learning about their heritage (Bradley, 2002; Peters, 1976). To begin the socialization process, parents often tell their children about the proud history of their people, starting in Africa and continuing with African American leadership and success stories. African American parents also typically teach their children about the realities of racism and bigotry, preparing them for the unfair treatment that they are likely to receive in the larger society and arming them with coping mechanisms for the times that they will be discriminated against. Children are taught the importance of family and spirituality when coping with racism, as well as other forms of coping (Lipford-Sanders, 2002). Stevenson (1995) called these *proactive messages*.

Children also need to hear *corrective messages* that inform them of the untruthful nature of the negative stereotypes about African Americans (Stevenson, 1995). African American children grow up in a society in which some of the strongest and most negative stereotypes are about their own people. In the United States, there is the continued belief that African Americans are intellectually inferior and incapable of achieving on their own merits in anything other than athletics and entertainment. Children who do not receive proactive racial socialization are likely to internalize negative stereotypes about being African American and consequently develop low self-esteem and negative self-concepts (Greene, 1990; Stevenson, 1994). Indeed, such individuals might stay in the pre-encounter stage of racial identity development, which is discussed later in this section. By contrast, children who receive proactive and corrective messages about their race tend to develop a positive sense of self and, in fact, achieve well academically (Bowman & Howard, 1985; Greene, 1990; Hale, 1991). To help children prepare for the rest of their lives in an environment that is likely to be hostile toward them, parenting practices of African Americans may differ from those of other cultures. Box 6.2 lists some of the racial socialization practices of African American families.

Box 6.2 Racial Socialization Practices of African American Families

1. Teaching children about their African and African American ancestors

2. Reinforcing cultural pride

3. Teaching children to be aware of racism and social injustice

4. Using the extended family for emotional support and understanding, especially in instances of racial injustice

5. Providing a spiritual and religious foundation that can be used to cope with adverse racial experiences

6. Using corrective messages that depersonalize racial stereotypes

7. Teaching children how to cope with racism, which includes developing "tough skin"

8. Disciplining children to reduce behaviors that may get them into trouble later with racist law enforcement officers

It would be important for a counselor to explore the messages that Tamika and Kendra received in terms of racial socialization. If middle-class children are better able to access African American role models who defy stereotypes, then Kendra would be more likely than Tamika to have rejected the stereotypes. Counselors should explore each client's racial identity and consequent ability to withstand racism. Counselors can inquire about the client's level of socialization and should consider how such upbringing can be called upon to help the client in her current depression.

Parenting Practices

Within the family, African American parents use a number of disciplinary actions that prepare children to live in a racist environment where unfairness and discrimination are common. The purpose of such practices is to give children the means to survive in that environment (Denby & Alford, 1996). In that vein, respect for authority is typically nonnegotiable in African American families; children who are disrespectful receive the most severe forms of punishment—usually physical (Bradley, 2002).

African American parents have been criticized by some as being overly severe and rigid in their disciplinary practices—especially regarding corporal punishment (Lassiter, 1987; Straus, 1991). This criticism reflects the current democratic, sometimes called "authoritative," disciplinary practices common in the dominant American society. In fact, the overrepresentation of black children among those who have been reported as abused and neglected seems to support this criticism. However, some researchers (Bradley, 2002; Comer & Poussaint, 1992; Peters, 1985) suggest that there are cultural misunderstandings about discipline on the part of social welfare workers, misunderstandings that contribute to the high numbers of child abuse reports. These authors suggest that the strong disciplinary practices of African American parents are preferable to verbal explanation when parents are preparing children to function within the "constraints of oppression" (Bradley, 2002, pp. 32–33). More often than not, democratic discussion is not an option for African Americans in the real world. African American children need to realize that fact early in their lives (Bradley, 2002).

It should be noted that middle-class African American parents are more likely to use explanation of reasons for discipline with their children than are parents from lower socioeconomic classes (Trosper, 2002). However, middle-class African American parents are still more likely than their European American counterparts to use physical discipline where moral misbehavior, such as lying or stealing, is concerned (Pinderhughes, Dodge, & Bates, 2000). Interestingly, Bradley (1998) found that African American parents who applied physical discipline generally did so judiciously, rather than wantonly, with their young children.

Today's African American parents may be conflicted about childrearing practices—especially those who live with extended family members who do not see the need to change from the "old ways" (Arnold, 2002). Regardless of whether physical discipline is appropriate for racial socialization, the fact that the social welfare system has little tolerance for it has had an impact on childrearing practices in the African American community.

In the case of Tamika, the counselor should explore parenting practices because she is currently living with her mother and siblings. It appears that how her children are parented, and by whom, might play into Tamika's current issues of depression. For Kendra, exploring her own current and past experiences of being parented, from the adult child's perspective, is appropriate. Her parents' views are important because she is worried about her parents' disapproval, not only of her academic performance but also of her choice of a boyfriend.

Racial Identity Development

Racial identity development was described in Chapter 5 as a way of plotting positive movement in individuals' appreciation and understanding of their and others' races. The Racial Identity Development for People of Color model was outlined. A more specific model that refers to African Americans is William Cross's (1991) Stages of Nigrescence. Cross describes nigrescence as "the process of becoming black" (p. 157). Cross also calls this model the Negro-to-Black Conversion Experience.

The origins of the model lie in Cross's 1971 publication "The Negro to Black Conversion Experience," in which he articulated the differences among African Americans based on individuals' differential inclinations to identify with their racial reference group (racial identity). Cross found that African Americans develop a positive racial identity by going through specific stages. Since 1971, racial identity theory has evolved. Cross's ideas, as well as those of others, set off an explosion of research and the creation of subsequent models of within-group developmental differences, not only for African Americans but within other groups as well.

As noted in previous chapters of this book, an awareness of racial identity development can be important for counselors because it helps them to empathically understanding their culturally diverse client populations. Also, when they identify their own racial identity attitudes, counselors discover areas of racism and bias that they themselves still need to work on. Since Cross's model is one of the earliest, most researched, and most influential of the development models, it will be the focus here.

The original five stages of the Cross model have been updated and refined over the past 30 years (Vandiver, Fhagen-Smith, Cokley, Cross, & Worrell, 2001). There are now three major stages: Pre-encounter, Immersion-Emersion, and Internalization.

Pre-encounter attitudes generally consist of treating the racial dimension of one's life as insignificant. Cross (1971) names three categories of Pre-encounter: Assimilation, Miseducation, and Self-Hatred. The *Pre-encounter-Assimilated* person is accepting and appreciative of everything about the dominant European American culture. Her or his primary reference group is simply "American" and race is not important. African American individuals with *Pre-encounter-Miseducation* attitudes believe in the negative stereotypes about African Americans. *Pre-encounter-Self-Hatred* attitudes are held by those who identify as being African American but who believe that being black is an intrinsic deficit that is responsible for their negative experiences. Originally, Cross thought that any black person in the Pre-encounter stage would have problems with self-hatred. However, after more than a decade of research on the theory, Cross revised his assessment and proposed that *race salience* (i.e., the importance one places on race, in general) has a greater impact on self-concept than racial identity attitudes alone. An individual who places little importance on race may have a high self-concept even if she or he has Pre-encounter attitudes. The more important race becomes to an individual, the more Pre-encounter attitudes will negatively affect self-concept (Cross, 1991; Sue & Sue, 2003).

The second major stage of Cross's Nigrescence model is *Immersion-Emersion*. Immersion-Emersion attitudes are divided into two categories: Intense Black Involvement and Anti-White. *Immersion-Intense Black Involvement* attitudes occur when the individual begins the journey into his or her blackness and revels in all things black. The *Immersion-Anti-White* attitudes consist of rejecting and denigrating all things European American (Vandiver et al., 2001).

The third stage is *Internalization*. Internalization attitudes are divided into *Afrocentricity,* where individuals develop a long-term commitment to their racial group to the exclusion of all others, and *Multiculturalist Inclusive,* which incorporates both an identity as an African American and an acceptance of other identities (cultures) as well.

The first set of attitudes, that is, Pre-encounter, is more likely to occur early in a person's life, whereas Internalization occurs, if at all, later in adulthood (Parham, 1993, 1999). Even after one has completed her or his racial identity developmental stages, life circumstances (e.g., a new encounter with racism) may cause the individual to recycle through the stages. For example, a person at the Internalization stage may become so discouraged after years of fighting institutional racism that she or he retreats to the Immersion-Intense Black Involvement stage. A line by an African American lawyer on a popular television show, *Law and Order,* illustrates this cycle perfectly: "Stone once asked me if I was a lawyer who just happened to be black or was I a black who just happened to be a lawyer. I thought I was the former and discovered that I was the latter."

Activity 6.2 offers an opportunity to assess racial identity.

Racial identity may be an issue for Kendra, who is dating a European American man. It is likely that she is being rejected not only by her family but by her friends as well. She may feel a combination of guilt, anger, and hurt. She may also be confused about who she is as a racial and cultural being. A counselor would need to help Kendra identify her stage of racial identity and to understand her attitudes about race and her racial identity. The counselor would then help Kendra move toward a greater acceptance of herself by helping her come to her own definition of what it means to be black.

Ascertaining Tamika's racial identity stage will help explain how she is coping with her world. If, for example, part of Tamika's depression is due to a belief that she must be the stereotypical "strong black woman," the counselor would need to work on the cognitive distortions regarding that ideal and encourage her to learn more about African

The statements listed below represent various stages of racial identity development (as described by Cross's new model). Read each one, and identify under which stage or substage that particular statement falls and why you have classified it as such. Discuss your answers with your classmates.

Note: It is not possible to precisely locate an individual in any one stage. Therefore it would be simplistic to provide an answer key here. These items are meant to provoke discussion and understanding on some elements of racial identity.

_____1. Affirmative Action is only needed by people who couldn't get the job in the first place.

_____2. You can never trust white people, so it is better not to tell them anything about your business and minimize your contact with them.

_____3. That counselor just tried to sign me up for the African dance class, and I think she did it just because I'm black. I wonder how many white kids she tried to put in that class. I don't see why they always have to treat us like we're so different. I'm a regular kid just like everyone else.

_____4. I live and work in the black community, and I think it is the perfect way for me to give back to my community and to ensure the future of African Americans in this country.

_____5. It makes me angry when black folks use race as an excuse for their own failures.

_____6. I get a lot of grief for marrying outside my race, but I spend a lot of my time with African American adolescents helping them prepare for their future and support my spouse's efforts in the Latino/Latina community as well.

American female stereotypes. If, on the other hand, Tamika were in the Immersion-Anti-White stage, the counselor might work on helping Tamika explore her stereotypes about whites and encourage her to advocate for herself and others to overcome institutional racism.

Career

Career progress has been slow for African Americans because of the realities of discrimination in U.S. society and because of the legacies of exclusion from jobs (James, 2002). The unemployment rate of African Americans is more than twice that of white Americans (U.S. Census Bureau, 2001).

Factors in the career life of African Americans include continuing discrimination, affirmative action, and the existence of protected occupations. Each of these is discussed next.

Continuing Discrimination

As discussed in Chapter 3, job discrimination continues to exist in the United States. The fact that African Americans are twice as likely to be unemployed and that the incomes for those who are employed fall short of the incomes of white males (U.S. Bureau of Labor Statistics, 2012) speaks volumes in this regard. Because racial discrimination is so intertwined with the structure of U.S. society, African Americans will continue to find occupational achievement difficult (Carter & Cook, 1992). Overcoming discrimination will be a challenge for African Americans because (a) the rules and boundaries of U.S. society continue to control the participation of minority groups in occupations (e.g., in what is possible and appropriate for various ethnic groups, based on career networks and role models or lack of role models); (b) these rules are communicated to African Americans both verbally and nonverbally (i.e., "This career isn't for people like you" might be perceived); (c) these rules and limits are set early in children's lives (e.g., in the overrepresentation of African Americans in special education); and (d) discriminatory practices, such as inadequate funding for urban schools and other services to poor African Americans, result in a continuing restriction of access to higher-level careers. Although Carter and Cook's observations were made in 1992, they are, unfortunately, still relevant today.

Affirmative Action

Another factor in career development for African Americans is affirmative action—the practice of proactively ensuring access to employment and education. Affirmative action was briefly presented in Chapter 3. It has been attacked by dominant group members and others who deny white male privilege and claim that affirmative action is reverse discrimination. This kind of thinking is based on the current popular assumption that affirmative action consists of the arbitrary application of preferential treatment based on race and gender alone, regardless of an individual's qualifications. However, according to Truax, Cordova, and Wood (1998), affirmative action remedies "usually involve goals for hiring and promotion according to sensible timetables. Never are strict quotas allowed, and never should the remedies involve the hiring or retention of unqualified people" (p. 173). Despite its success in providing access, affirmative action can also hurt African Americans: Some people still see affirmative action as a basis for hiring and admitting underqualified people for jobs. Consequently, African Americans and others can be stigmatized once they are on the job or in colleges, thus continuing a perception of inferiority.

Protected Occupations

Affirmative action is not the only route African Americans have used to avoid racial discrimination in the workplace. Another strategy is for African Americans to participate in traditional or "protected" occupations (K. M. Evans & Herr, 1991; Peterson & Gonzalez, 2000). These occupations are referred to as protected because either there is a critical mass of African Americans already employed in them (e.g., social work, service occupations) or they are professions that depend on the African American consumers for survival (e.g., law, medicine, clergy, funeral services).

The Seduction of Athletics and Entertainment

Today, some see these protected occupations as extending to professional sports and entertainment (especially for African American males). Careers in football, basketball, baseball, and hip hop music are high profile and high paying. Many African American boys gravitate to these occupations because they see primarily African American men achieving wealth and status in these professions. In fact, many boys are encouraged to pursue these athletic endeavors if they show even the smallest amount of talent in early childhood. This encouragement can be a trap. Sociologist Harry Edwards (1986) states that, although their athletic abilities have been honed, many of these boys are still educationally challenged, as 25%–35% of African American high school athletes do not meet the academic requirements to play at the college level. Professional sports organizations have gotten around that problem by drafting athletes right out of high school. The larger concern in this situation is that the emphasis on athletics gives young people permission to disregard other, probably more realistic careers, especially those that require lengthy educational programs (Witherspoon, 2005). Because careers in professional athletics are male-dominated, the rejection of college-based careers in favor of an athletic career is more of an issue for African American boys and men than it is for girls and women. Other ethnic groups have entered sports in large numbers before moving on to other professional careers. Counselors must encourage African American boys to look at other options for careers.

Gender

Gender roles in the African American community are rooted in the conditions of slavery.

Slaves were treated as property (or stock); therefore, they were valued for their generic capacity as labor, not as women or as men. After the failures of Reconstruction and the subsequent oppression, including terrorist lynchings, any African American man in the South who dared behave like a "(white) man" was shown his place. This process went on well into the 20th century. Black men were stereotyped in white people's views as angry, dangerous, and so highly sexed that white women had to be protected from them. African Americans, therefore, had to create their own definitions of manhood.

Black women, who were routinely raped by white men during the 250 years of slavery and who bore the children of such violence, were thought of in U.S. society as fitting one of three stereotypes:

- *Jezebel:* Jezebel is a biblical character known as the bad girl, or wicked woman, and/or prostitute. A Jezebel is a promiscuous woman who uses her sexuality to get what she wants no matter whom she hurts.
- *Mammy:* The mammy is one who is "obese, pitch black, . . . and sexually neutered" (Greene, 1994, p. 16). She is seen as motherly, especially in regard to white families.
- *Sapphire:* The Sapphire stereotype depicts a woman who is emasculating to the African American male. She has a big mouth and tells, and tells off, all she knows. She is also laughed at and discounted by black men and is sexually neutered.

With these kinds of stereotypes, an African American woman had no concept of herself as a woman with dignity and pride. That image she has had to create for herself.

Gender Equality in African American Families

African American families have historically promoted egalitarian gender-role socialization. Both boys and girls are trained to be assertive and are usually required to learn all household tasks rather than the tasks being split according to gender (e.g., girls wash dishes, boys take out garbage;

Lewis, 1975). Interestingly, these nonspecific gender roles may be a throwback to African roots (Hill, 1999). In West Africa, "women were expected to be economically productive and had some power and authority in sociopolitical matters" (Hill, 1999, p. 109). This socialization is said to account for the leadership roles of black females, in that they have benefited from developing traditionally "masculine" traits of assertiveness and independence while keeping traditional female traits of nurturing and relationship building. Black males are hurt more for the feminine traits that they acquire, in that U.S. society already values masculine traits more than feminine ones (Carr & Mednick, 1988).

The Dilemmas for Women and Men

Both women and men suffer from the gender consequences of oppression. Those consequences include multiple demands on girls, negative expectations of boys, imbalance in marriage opportunities for women, and dominance of white-based standards of beauty.

According to Chapman (1988), African Americans develop their gender identity at a very early age. There is an old saying, "Black mothers raise their daughters and love [or enable!] their sons." In other words, girls tend to get a strict upbringing and specific information about how to be a good, empowered black woman. For African American boys, on the other hand, independence is not stressed as strongly and they are not as severely disciplined for doing wrong as are girls (Hill, 1999; Staples, 1984). African American girls are taught to be self-sufficient, proud, and strong but caring. They are encouraged to achieve academically, to get a good job, and to be able to take care of their family on their own, if necessary.

Education and Gender

For African American girls and women, education always has been embraced. For boys, the expectation for education has been less clear. In recent years, the dropout rate from secondary school has decreased, but it continues to be an issue for boys and girls. In fact, the dropout rate for African Americans was twice that of whites in 2008, but there was no discernible difference between the rates for males and females. That said, the fact that Kendra is pursuing higher education puts her in good company; more African American women than men were enrolled in college and earned bachelor's degrees in 2007 (Office of Minority Health, 2009). However, because she is getting her degree in a nontraditional career, she may still feel separate not only from her African American friends but also from women of other racial groups. Her parents may have high expectations for her success in college, and she may be feeling that pressure. Her counselor should be careful to have Kendra talk about her family's expectation and the isolation she may be feeling. By contrast, Tamika may or may not have completed high school; she was only 15 years old when her first child was born. It would be worthwhile to explore Tamika's attitudes about education, whether she connects it to her racial identity, and how her socioeconomic status has affected her educational and occupational aspirations.

Negative Expectations for Boys

Boys continuously hear negative statements about black men from a variety of sources—from whites, black women, and other black men. They learn that black men are inferior, that they are unable to obtain and maintain adequate employment or head their households, and that they are unduly hampered by racial attitudes and institutional structures. When this kind of negative input is internalized, it is no wonder that African American men have trouble getting ahead. To an alarming degree, African American men are overrepresented among those incarcerated. In fact, almost half the men in jail today are of African descent (T. L. Robinson, 2005). Incarceration of so many African American men has had a major impact on the African American family and community and on the men themselves.

Black men's masculine development is similar to other men in the United States, complete with a sense of power, control, and privilege common in patriarchal societies (Aymer, 2010). When questioned, black men report socially desirable answers regarding manhood. They publicly define manhood as requiring responsibility, humanism, and self-determination (M. Connor, 2002). However, African American males learn early on that a traditional definition of a "man" is not attainable and these attitudes and beliefs may be the source of many of the physical and psychological problems African American men face (Aymer, 2010).

Standards of Beauty

For all women in the United States, beauty has been a source of social power and privilege. The standard of beauty is based on the Northern European American woman (usually thin, blond, and blue-eyed). Whatever the woman's race, the more closely she resembles the Northern European American standard, the more she is considered beautiful and desirable and the higher is her status. For African American women, meeting that standard is more difficult if their physical attributes resemble those known to be more typical of West Africans—attributes that are devalued and considered unattractive in the dominant American culture.

African American women differ in terms of skin color, hair texture, eye color, body type, and facial features. Both skin color and hair have been sources of emotional pain for African American women. Light-skinned women with "good hair" (needing little or no straightening) often feel rejected by their racial group. Conversely, dark-skinned women with "bad hair" (tightly curled) feel resentment toward the light-skinned women. The tragedy of this situation is that both African Americans and European Americans value light-skinned women more highly than those who are dark-skinned because of their resemblance to the Northern European American standard (Russell, Wilson, & Hall, 1992; Wade & Bielitz, 2005). In fact, research has shown that lighter-skinned women have more education, earn higher salaries, and have husbands with more prestige than do darker-skinned women (Hunter, 2002). While progress was made in the 1960s and 1970s to raise black standards of beauty to the mainstream, the Eurocentric definition still prevails.

Interestingly, study after study of African American women's body image has found that they are positive about their bodies and do not hold the European American ideal body shape to themselves (Jefferson & Stake, 2009). They do, however, perceive the white body type as most attractive. The more the African American woman identifies with African American culture, the less likely she is to accept the white standard of beauty for herself. What this means for counselors is that, even though African American women are aware that they do not meet the white standard of beauty and are hurt by a rejection of their unique kind of beauty by others, if they have a positive racial identity, they are more likely to have positive self-esteem regarding their bodies.

Physical and Mental Health

The issues of physical and mental health have a social and political connection for African Americans that needs to be understood by counseling professionals. For example, although research has found that the mortality rates of African Americans, like other groups, decrease as their socioeconomic status increases, even middle- and upper-class African Americans have higher mortality rates than whites in the same socioeconomic class (Ostrove, Feldman, & Adler, 1999).

While the health of African Americans today is much improved over previous years, they are still more likely than European Americans to be diagnosed with life-threatening diseases such as hypertension, diabetes, obesity, high cholesterol, and cancer (Atkinson, 2004). The infant mortality rate is 2.5 times greater for African Americans than for European Americans; the maternal mortality rate is 4.2 times greater.

The overall death rate for African Americans was 31% higher than it was for whites in 2002. Black males live, on average, 69.7 years; white males live 75.7 years (Office of Minority Health, 2009). Black women live 75.6 years, compared to 80.3 years for white females (Arias, 2004). In 2005, the death rate for African Americans was higher than it was for whites for heart disease, stroke, cancer, asthma, influenza, pneumonia, and diabetes. In general, African American males between the ages of 25 and 55 have double the death rate of white males in the same age group, primarily because they are eight times as likely to be victims of homicide.

As for their mental health, according to the Office of Minority Health (2009) of the U.S. Department of Health and Human Services, African Americans are 30% more likely than European Americans to have psychological distress and less likely to be prescribed antidepressant drugs. However, they are more likely to have severe diagnoses when given a psychiatric diagnosis, and they are more likely to be hospitalized for their mental illness (Snowden & Hu, 1997; Wicker & Brodie, 2003). The prevalence of poverty, low educational levels, and high levels of incarceration may account for the diagnosis of severe mental illness for many African Americans (Atkinson, 2004).

African Americans are diagnosed more frequently with certain illnesses than they are with others. For example, they are more likely to be diagnosed with phobias, somatization complaints (Parham, 2002a; Zhang & Snowden, 1999), and schizophrenia (Adebimpe, 1981; Baker & Bell, 1999; Cornelius, Fabrega, Cornelius, Mezzich, & Maher, 1996; Neighbors & Jackson, 1996). African Americans are also more likely to be underdiagnosed for depression (Cornelius et al., 1996).

The U.S. Department of Health and Human Services suggests that "African Americans may be underrepresented in outpatient services but overrepresented in accessing hospital emergency rooms for mental health concerns" (Parham, 2002c, p. 42). As such, African Americans may be less likely to receive counseling assistance when problems are not severe enough to warrant a complete collapse.

More recently, there may have been an improvement in early intervention for African Americans. In a review of the data from the Medical Expenditure Panel Survey (1996–2006), Chen and Rizzo (2010) discovered that there were no significant differences regarding the use of psychotherapy between African Americans and whites whether or not they were using Medicaid funds. This survey was focused specifically on depression and anxiety disorders.

African Americans are inclined to view mental illness negatively and stigmatize those who are in need of related services (Nickerson, Helms, & Terrell, 1994). In fact, in their study, Leong, Wagner, and Tata (1995) discovered that African Americans preferred to seek assistance from family and friends rather than from mental health professionals. Those professionals are typically white and, therefore, suspect. It seems that this distrust might be warranted because research continues to report bias in diagnosis and treatment by white therapists (Trierweiler et al., 2000). Considering the history of discrimination, psychological abuse, microaggressions, and continued racism in the United States, African Americans have a healthy distrust of European Americans, the government, and its institutions (Atkinson, 2004).

Social Class

This major section on the characteristics and values of African Americans concludes with a discussion of the influence of social class. The topic of social class is presented fully in Chapter 13. Class and race intertwine with culture to create values. Race and class, however, are conflated by many, with race often totally substituting for class as an explanation of ethnic groups' behaviors.

Social class is the dividing line for a great many characteristics within the African American community. Within-group value differences among African Americans tend to be related to social class status. African Americans are alarmingly overrepresented among the poor in the United States, although, as seen in Chapter 3, there are twice as many middle-class blacks now as there were in 1960. Many of the previously discussed values are more likely to be seen in those from the lower economic status groups, as the middle classes of all cultures tend to have values in common with the dominant European American culture (Sue & Sue, 2003). However, core African American values are

likely to be similar across social classes—especially those that are associated with growing up black in the United States. Those include spirituality, interdependence in family and relationships, emotional expressiveness, and ethnic pride.

The Black Middle Class

Middle-class African Americans must often function both in the dominant culture and in their own African American communities. As such, their values may be on a continuum of whiteness to blackness and be applied situationally when they are in those respective settings.

The black middle class is not really parallel to the white middle class, for two reasons. The first is that, more often than not, African Americans would not qualify for middle-class status if it weren't for the presence of two incomes in the household (which is more true than ever for all families, but especially so for African Americans due to lower median household salaries). The second way that the African American middle class can be distinguished from the white middle class in general is that most African Americans do not have the accumulated wealth of whites, as discussed in Chapter 3. In fact, Neville and Walters (2003) state that African Americans' net worth is 1% of the net worth of their European American counterparts.

Black Poverty

One of the reasons that people tend to combine race and class for African Americans is that African Americans are substantially overrepresented among the poor. Approximately 25% of African Americans have incomes below the official poverty line (Office of Minority Health, 2009). Poverty has its own set of behaviors, beliefs, and values (see Chapter 13 for discussions of the culture of poverty). The aforementioned attitude toward time and timeliness is often class related. For example, many poor people (regardless of race) tend to have a casual view of appointment times with professionals, sometimes due to their time not being treated as valuable by the social agencies that serve the poor (Sue & Sue, 2003). It is not uncommon for an agency serving low-income clients to schedule an appointment for one time and not get to the client until many hours later. Also, living in the present is common among poor people. For poor persons, just getting food on the table today is a chore, and planning for some unseen future seems frivolous.

Many poor people, regardless of race, believe in fate more than they do in their own ability to overcome obstacles. Thus, poor people are ambivalent about their own power to affect their lives. However, that tendency should not cause further stereotyping. For example, the stereotype of poor African Americans is the "unwed" mother, living on public assistance with several small children. However, many poor African Americans, like Tamika, work every day, barely making a living wage and living in fear of becoming unemployed.

Other Differences Between the Black Middle and Lower Classes

While they share a common heritage as well as experiences with racism and prejudice, middle-class and lower-class African Americans differ a great deal in how they live. At this time, the biggest chasm between the socioeconomic groups of African Americans is education. Education was traditionally highly valued in the African American community, in part because it was denied to them in slavery and partly because education seemed to be the best way to overcome oppression. Since the civil rights movement and integration, many African Americans have used their educations for upward mobility and as an exit from poverty-ridden neighborhoods. They often have moved to predominantly white suburbs or, more recently, to all-black middle-class suburban enclaves (Cashin, 2000). African Americans who live in the new, predominantly black suburbs are cut off from their lower-income counterparts because they do not have to return to the neighborhood to fulfill their needs for goods or services.

The lack of interaction between the socioeconomic classes may be attributed to the fact that education has lost its appeal to African Americans in lower-income areas (Cole & Omari, 2003). Low-income adolescents now see education as a way of abandoning one's culture and becoming an "Oreo"

(i.e., perceived to be black on the outside and white on the inside). Even some middle-class African American adolescents tend to share this attitude. As discussed in the Career section above, rather than perceiving education as the key to escaping poverty, many African American young people, especially males, gravitate toward careers in sports and entertainment that can maximize their income and minimize their need for education (Hughes, 2005; Witherspoon, 2005).

Note that in the vignettes of Tamika and Kendra, there are differences in the values of each woman based on socioeconomic background. However, many of their core values are similar—especially those associated with growing up black in the United States. For example, a counselor working with Tamika, the 20-year-old mother, or Kendra, the 20-year-old Ivy League college student, would need to ascertain each woman's specific values regarding kinship. It is important to understand the ties that each of them has with her parent(s) and/or other relatives. Care must be taken not to sever these relationships in the name of increasing autonomy. Rather, the counselor may need to call on these relationships as a source of client strength. For Tamika, it may mean actually working with her mother and siblings to help her with her depression. For Kendra, it may mean exploring her commitment to her family and the consequences of disappointing them because of her boyfriend and academic struggles.

CULTURALLY ALERT COUNSELING INTERVENTIONS

Although this section of the chapter discusses counseling interventions with African Americans, the limits of such generalizations must be addressed. African Americans may share a powerfully influential history in the United States, but there is no stereotypical African American; there is no single African American culture. Similarly, there is no single intervention that works for all African Americans. Therefore, this section of the chapter is not a how-to manual. Instead, particular concerns of African Americans are summarized, guidelines for working with African Americans are presented, and two Africentric counseling models are discussed.

Particular Concerns of African American Clients

Some writers in the counseling field have suggested that a unique paradigm is needed for counseling African Americans because of their distinct history and current status in the United States (e.g., Parham, 1999). These writers look to the following five unique issues of African Americans as a basis for the need for a culture-specific model of counseling.

- Why do African American women see skin color and hair texture as so important?
- Why do impoverished, government-assisted African Americans fail to plan for the future?
- Why are many African Americans, when endowed with authority by an institution (e.g., a school), harsher on their own racial group members?
- Why would African American children rather fail than be perceived as acting white and getting good grades?
- Why is it of great importance to African American men to own property and cars?

Other culture-related mental health issues include African American adolescent girls and young women fighting over men and African Americans' distrust of white teachers, counselors, doctors, social workers, and educational institutions. With an Africentric model, which is described in the following sections, these concerns may be most easily addressed.

Counselors using an Africentric approach should have a solid awareness of their own spiritual selves and their ethnic identity. To be successful in counseling African Americans, especially using an Africentric approach, counselors need to develop skills for bonding with their clients, participating in rituals, and assisting a client with reaching his or her goals in an African-centered way. What Africentric counseling approaches have in common is a devotion to spirituality, history, kinship and community, and overcoming oppression.

Guidelines for Counseling African Americans

Chapters 18 and 19 describe counseling skills that the culturally alert counselor must have in order to be competent to perform. Seven guidelines have been adapted from those chapters as they apply to work with African Americans. They are presented in Box 6.3.

Box 6.3 Seven Guidelines for Working With African Americans

1. *Be genuine in verbal and nonverbal communications*. African Americans are high-context communicators, meaning that they are likely to depend less on what a person says than on how it was said and the circumstances surrounding the verbal exchange (Sue & Sue, 2003). Therefore, to be effective with African American clients, it is really important that there be no contradiction between what the counselor says and how she or he feels. Genuineness is important.

2. *Engage in advocacy*. Counselors should probe for any bias that the client may experience or perceive to be related to her or his problem. The counselor should be prepared to intervene on the organizational level as well as the community level. Counselors should also empower clients to work toward eliminating institutional racism by supporting client efforts to document incidents and address them.

3. *Use nonpsychological methods*. Work with the client's spirituality. Encourage the client to speak with her or his pastor.

4. *Have language flexibility*. Not only should counselors understand AAVE, but they should not have any negative reaction to its use. Rather than responding to the client in AAVE, however, the counselor may want to borrow a word or two as a key phrase when talking with clients.

(Continued)

---

5. *Judiciously apply assessment methods.* Standardized testing has been criticized as regards African Americans. It is important for counselors to be knowledgeable and confident about the use of such instruments with the African American population. It may be necessary for the counselor to collect her or his own local data on African Americans if data for this population are not available in the test manual.

6. *Proactively acknowledge societal bias.* Rather than keeping the history of African Americans as interesting information to be stored in the recesses of one's mind, the counselor should use that information to understand the feelings and behaviors of the African American client.

7. *Practice culturally informed consent.* Because of the mistrust that African Americans have for health and mental health institutions, it is imperative that counselors explain their roles, client roles, the process of counseling, and techniques to be used.

Lee's Guidelines for Counseling African Americans

Courtland Lee (1995) offers three guiding ideas for working effectively with African American clients. He first suggests that counselors always inquire about all of the influences in the client's life—not only that part of the client's life that she or he spends in African American culture, but also the time spent in majority culture. Lee also suggests that counselors explore the client's reaction to oppression. Finally, he iterates that counselors should learn about an African American client's family relationships. Lee cautions that none of these areas is mutually exclusive; when a counselor explores one area, she or he is likely to discover information from another area.

Africentric Counseling

An Africentric counseling model is one that is consistent with African values and its people. Such a model would also address the impact of oppression (Parham, 2002b). The two Africentric approaches discussed here are African Centered Psychology and the TRIOS model.

African Centered Psychology

African Centered Psychology (ACP) applies African and African American values such as "ancestor veneration, social collectivity, and the spiritual basis of existence" to counseling (Grills, 2002, p. 15). Counselors who use ACP must have the ability to make the necessary shift from a Western to an African worldview to accommodate the cultural differences that are present when working with African American clients. ACP represents a way of knowing, viewing, and understanding the whole person, particularly the African American client. ACP is considered a spiritual journey of moving toward optimal living.

ACP uses an African perspective to make meaning of life and the world and to define relationships with others and with one's self (Grills, 2002). Before the colonization of Africa, Africans maneuvered through life within an organized system of knowledge that offered a lens through which to understand reality, values, logic, and historical experiences. This system is organized into five fundamental features in ACP: self-definition, spirit, nature, metaphysical interconnectedness, and communal order and self-knowledge.

Self-definition is the ability to define one's self in one's own terms. This is an empowering act. Becoming empowered enough to use your own frame of reference is considered essential in life. *Spirit* is the energy that pervades the essence of all matter (Grills, 2002). *Nature* sets forth the conventions by which humans function, the rhythms of life, and the natural order of things (Grills, 2002). *Metaphysical interconnectedness* is the acknowledgment of higher beings and powers greater than oneself. Finally, there is *communal order and self-knowledge*. People of African descent are relational beings and work from the "we" or community paradigm. Grills (2002) emphasizes knowing oneself through relationships with others.

The TRIOS Model

Another Africentric approach is called TRIOS (Jones, 2003). It is a psychological theory of the African legacy in American culture. It describes African American ways of being that occur automatically. The five themes that counselors who work with African Americans should be aware of are **t**ime, **r**hythm, **i**mprovisation, **o**rality, and **s**pirituality (thus TRIOS). The model describes how the current, residual influences of African culture and the harsh experiences of slavery surface in some African Americans' conceptions of those themes. Following is a brief introduction to the five themes. You would need to study the TRIOS model in greater depth in order to fully understand it.

Time can be seen in at least three ways, depending on culture: In time-oriented societies, time may be saved, wasted, or invested much as any valued resource. That conception represents the general perspective of people of European descent, who have a more linear and rigid relationship with the clock than do people of African descent. By contrast, in some cultures, including African American culture, time has no independent status or value and therefore does not dictate behavior and choice. Instead, activities and relationships do. African Americans are caught between these two conceptions of time.

Rhythm defines a recurring pattern of behavior within specified time frames. Racism often causes disharmonious connections between internal and external states. As a result, African Americans may not live in rhythm if they must deny aspects of themselves when in oppressive or Eurocentric situations. They may find the rhythms more consistent in an African American setting. Such would be the case in the use of AAVE and in expressive communication styles, where the rhythm is different depending on context.

Improvisation is an African-based style of living that emphasizes expressiveness and invention in language, relationships, and action, as opposed to structured, emotionally controlled ways of being. African Americans must play back and forth between these two styles, depending on the environments that they are in. The European American environment values improvisation less than do the African and African American ones.

Orality is a theme that captures the traditions of vocality, drumming, storytelling, praise singing, and naming that are part of African and African American cultures. Orality emphasizes context in expression. Counselors should know that in African American culture, language is a means of control through the use of privileged meanings and neologisms, such as *bad* meaning "good" and *stupid* meaning "smart." Hip hop is a brilliant illustration of orality. It is more than a style of singing and rhyming; it is an assertion of self that is not filtered through the mainstream European American power structure.

Spirituality is defined as the belief in nonmaterial power in human life. African Americans tend to believe that what happens to people is determined, in some measure, by forces that are beyond human control. In African American life, spirituality liberates a person from the dominance of European American cultural expectations and constraints. Instead, the person can make reference to a power greater than the European American norms and rules.

In developing the TRIOS model, Jones (2003) emphasized the importance of passing down family history and African history. The TRIOS model proposes that culture gives credence to the evolution, adaptation, and transformation of people of African descent. Drawing on the human tendency for both self-protection and self-motivation, Jones contends that the TRIOS design assists individuals in coping with racism. As is evident in the summary of the history and characteristics of African Americans in this chapter, many people of African descent employ elements of TRIOS without realizing the legacy on which they are building. See Table 6.2 for a summary of TRIOS domains.

Table 6.2 TRIOS Domains and Assessment

Dimension	Description
Time	Present orientation; living in the now
Rhythm	Interconnection with nature, time, and space; environmental flow
Improvisation	Adaptability; ability to withstand external barriers to success
Orality	Narrative expression of meaning; handing down culture through stories and styles of speech or song
Spirituality	Divine intervention; higher power in daily life

Based on the knowledge that you have gained through reading this chapter, return to the cases of Tamika and Kendra that introduced this chapter and complete Activity 6.3.

Activity 6.3 Follow-Up to the Cases of Tamika and Kendra

1. Please read the cases that were presented previously, and based on the information in this chapter, discuss your original impressions and assumptions about each woman.

   Tamika:

   Kendra:

2. List some questions that you now would have for both of these clients and why you believe it is important to gather this information.

   Tamika:

   Kendra:

SUMMARY

Often, African Americans are asked why they focus so much on slavery when it is "ancient history." The reference to slavery and its legacy is not something African Americans do to garner pity or to make excuses for themselves. Quite the contrary. The fact that their ancestors survived horrific conditions and many were able to thrive is a testament to their strength and tenacity. The discussion of this history in this chapter was meant to emphasize the enormity of the influence of slavery on all Americans and its being a necessary element in any discussion of African American culture. The pervasive nature and legacy of racism, which is the lingering byproduct of slavery, should therefore not be taken lightly. African Americans today are still feeling the effects of slavery and its attendant oppressions in the 21st century. As Cross (2003) stated, "blacks exited slavery with the type of social capital, family attitudes, and positive achievement motivation that could have readily facilitated their rapid acculturation into the mainstream society, had society wanted them" (p. 80). Counselors need to help African Americans discover and build on the strengths of their culture and counter negative models in order to reach their potential as full citizens and human beings.

REFERENCES

Adebimpe, V. R. (1981). White norms and psychiatric diagnosis of black patients. *American Journal of Psychiatry, 138,* 279–285.

Arias, E. (2004). United States life tables, 2002. *National Vital Statistics Report, 53*(6). Retrieved from http://www.cdc.gov/nchs/data/nvsr53/nvsr53_06.pdf

Arnold, M. S. (2002). African American families in the postmodern era. In J. L. Sanders & C. Bradley (Eds.), *Counseling African American families* (pp. 3–16). Alexandria, VA: American Counseling Association.

Atkinson, D. R. (2004). *Counseling American minorities.* Boston, MA: McGraw-Hill.

Aymer, S. R. (2010). Clinical practice with African American men: What to consider and what to do. *Smith College Studies in Social Work, 80,* 20–34.

Baker, F. M., & Bell, C. C. (1999). Issues in the psychiatric treatment of African Americans. *Psychiatric Services, 50,* 362–368.

Ball, J., Armistead, L., & Austin, B. (2003). The relationship between religiosity and adjustment among African-American, female, urban adolescents. *Journal of Adolescence, 26,* 431–446.

Bell-Tolliver, L., Burgess, R., & Brock, L. J. (2009). African American therapists working with African American families: An exploration of the strengths perspective in treatment. *Journal of Marital and Family Therapy, 35,* 293–307.

Bowman, P., & Howard, C. (1985). Race-related socialization, motivation, and academic achievement: A study of black youth in three-generation families. *Journal of the American Academy of Child Psychiatry, 24,* 134–141.

Boyd-Franklin, N. (1989). *Black families in therapy.* New York, NY: Oxford University Press.

Bradley, C. (1998). Child rearing in African American families: A study of disciplinary methods used by African American parents. *Journal of Multicultural Counseling and Development, 26,* 273–281.

Bradley, C. (2002). Parenting: A community responsibility. In J. L. Sanders & C. Bradley (Eds.), *Counseling African American families* (pp. 29–40). Alexandria, VA: American Counseling Association.

Burling, R. (1973). *English in black and white.* New York, NY: Holt, Rinehart & Winston.

Carr, P. G., & Mednick, M. T. (1988). Sex role socialization and the development of achievement motivation in black preschool children. *Sex Roles, 18,* 169–180.

Carter, R. T., & Cook, D. A. (1992). A culturally relevant perspective for understanding the career paths of visible racial/ethnic group people. In H. D. Lea & B. Leibowitz (Eds.), *Adult career development: Concepts, issues and practices* (pp. 192–217). Alexandria, VA: National Career Development Association.

Cashin, S. D. (2000). *Middle-class black suburbs and the state of integration: A post-integrationist vision for metropolitan America* (Georgetown Law and Economics Research Paper No. 241245). Washington, DC: Georgetown University.

Chadiha, L. A., Rafferty, J., & Pickard, J. (2003). The influence of caregiving stressors, social support, and caregiving appraisal on marital functioning among African American wife caregivers. *Journal of Marital and Family Therapy, 29,* 479–490.

Chambers, J. W., Jr. (1983). *Black English: Educational equity and the law.* Ann Arbor, MI: Karoma.

Chapman, A. B. (1988). Male-female relations: How the past affects the present. In H. P. McAdoo (Ed.), *Black families* (pp. 190–200). Newbury Park, CA: Sage.

Chen, J., & Rizzo, J. (2010). Racial and ethnic disparities in use of psychotherapy: Evidence from U.S. National Survey data. *Psychiatric Services, 61,* 364–372.

Cole, E. R., & Omari, S. R. (2003). Race, class and the dilemmas of upward mobility for African Americans. *Journal of Social Issues, 59,* 785–802.

Comer, J. P., & Poussaint, A. F. (1992). *Raising black children.* New York, NY: Penguin.

Connor, J. J. (2003). "The textbooks never said anything about . . .": Adolescents respond to *The Middle Passage: White Ships/Black Cargo. Journal of Adolescent & Adult Literacy, 47,* 240–246.

Connor, M. (2002). Counseling African American fathers. In T. A. Parham (Ed.), *Counseling Persons of African Descent: Raising the Bar of Practitioner Competence* (pp. 119–140). Thousand Oaks, CA: Sage.

Cook, D. A., & Wiley, C. Y. (2000). *Psychotherapy with members of African American churches and spiritual traditions.* In P. S. Richards & A. E. Bergin (Eds.), *Handbook of psychotherapy and religious diversity* (pp. 369–396). Washington, DC: American Psychological Association.

Cornelius, J. R., Fabrega, H., Cornelius, M. D., Mezzich, J., & Maher, P. J. (1996). Racial effects on the clinical presentation of alcoholics at a psychiatric hospital. *Comprehensive Psychiatry, 37,* 102–108.

Cowan, B. A. (2004). African roots/American cultures: Africa in the creation of the Americas. *Journal of African American History, 89,* 82–84.

Cross, W. E. (1971). The negro to black conversion experience: Toward the psychology of black liberation. *Black World, 209,* 13–27.

Cross, W. E. (1991). *Shades of black.* Philadelphia, PA: Temple University Press.

Cross, W. E. (2003). Tracing the historical origins of youth delinquency and violence: Myths and realities about black culture. *Journal of Social Issues, 59,* 67–82.

Denby, R., & Alford, K. (1996). Understanding African American disciplinary styles: Suggestions for effective social work intervention. *Journal of Multicultural Social Work, 4,* 81–98.

Doss, R. C., & Gross, A. M. (1994). The effects of black English and code-switching on intraracial perceptions. *Journal of Black Psychology, 20,* 282–293.

Dovidio, J. F., Kawakami, K., & Gaertner, S. L. (2000). Reducing contemporary prejudice: Combating explicit and implicit bias at the individual and intergroup level. In S. Oskamp (Ed.), *Reducing prejudice and discrimination* (pp. 137–164). Mahwah, NJ: Lawrence Erlbaum.

Edwards, H. (1986). The black "dumb jock": An American sports tragedy. *College Board Review, 131,* 8–13.

Evans, K. M. (2003). Including spirituality in multicultural counseling: Overcoming counselor resistance. In G. Roysircar, S. D. Sandhu, & V. E. Bibbins Sr. (Eds.), *Multicultural competencies: A guidebook of practices* (pp. 161–171). Alexandria, VA: Association for Multicultural Counseling and Development.

Evans, K. M., & Herr, E. L. (1991). The influence of racism and sexism in the career development of African American women. *Journal of Multicultural Counseling and Development, 19,* 173–184.

Evans, M. C. (2004). Gay marriage gained Bush black votes. *Newsday.com.* Retrieved from http://www.edisonresearch.com/homeimg/archives/Newsday11-14-2004.pdf

Fukuyama, M. A., & Sevig, T. D. (1999). *Integrating spirituality into multicultural counseling.* Thousand Oaks, CA: Sage.

Garner, T., & Rubin, D. L. (1986). Middle class blacks' perceptions of dialect and style shifting: The case of southern attorneys. *Journal of Language & Social Psychology, 5,* 33–48.

Greene, B. A. (1990). Sturdy bridges: The role of African American mothers in the socialization of African American children. *Women & Therapy, 10,* 205–225.

Greene, B. A. (1994). African American women. In L. Comas-Diaz & B. A. Green (Eds.), *Women of color* (pp. 10–29). New York, NY: Guilford.

Grier, W. H., & Cobbs, P. M. (1968). *Black rage*. New York, NY: Basic Books.

Griffin, P. R. (1999). *Seeds of racism in the soul of America*. Cleveland, OH: Pilgrim Press.

Grills, C. (2002). African-centered psychology. In T. A. Parham (Ed.), *Counseling persons of African descent: Raising the bar of practitioner competence* (pp. 10–24). Thousand Oaks, CA: Sage.

Hale, J. (1991). The transmission of cultural values to young African American children. *Young Children, 46*, 7–15.

Hill, S. A. (1999). *African American children: Socialization and development in families*. Thousand Oaks, CA: Sage.

Hughes, T. J. (2005). *Factors that influence the career maturity of African American athletes* (Unpublished doctoral dissertation). University of South Carolina, Columbia, SC.

Hunter, M. L. (2002). "If you're light you're alright": Light skin color as social capital for women of color. *Gender & Society, 16*, 175–193.

James, E. H. (2002). Race-related differences in promotions and support: Underlying effects of human and social capital. *Organization Science, 11*, 493–508.

Jang, S. J., & Johnson, B. R. (2004). Explaining religious effects on distress among African Americans. *Journal for the Scientific Study of Religion, 43*, 239–260.

Jefferson, D. L., & Stake, J. E. (2009). Appearance self-attitudes of African American and European American women: Media comparisons and internalization of beauty ideals. *Psychology of Women Quarterly, 33*, 396–409.

Jones, J. M. (2003). TRIOS: A psychological theory of the African legacy in American culture. *Journal of Social Issues, 59*, 217–242.

Koch, L. M., Gross, A. M., & Kolts, R. (2001). Attitudes toward black English and code switching. *Journal of Black Psychology, 27*, 29–42.

Larimer, G. S., Beatty, E. D., & Broadus, A. C. (1988). Indirect assessment of interracial prejudices. *Journal of Black Psychology, 14*, 47–56.

Lassiter, R. J. (1987). Child rearing in black families: Child-abusing discipline. In R. L. Hampton (Ed.), *Violence in the black family: Correlates and consequences* (pp. 39–53). Lexington, MA: Lexington Books.

Lee, C. C. (1995). *Counseling for diversity: A guide for school counselors and related professionals*. Needham Heights, MA: Allyn & Bacon.

Leong, F. T. L., Wagner, N. S., & Tata, S. P. (1995). Racial and ethnic variations in help-seeking attitudes. In J. G. Ponterotto, J. M. Casas, L. A. Suzuki, & C. M. Alexander (Eds.), *Handbook of multicultural counseling* (pp. 415–438). Thousand Oaks, CA: Sage.

Levine, M. L. (1996). *African Americans and civil rights: From 1619 to the present*. Phoenix, AZ: Oryx Press.

Lewis, D. K. (1975). The black family: Socialization and sex roles. *Phylon, 36*, 221–238.

Lipford-Sanders, J. (2002). Racial socialization. In J. L. Sanders & C. Bradley (Eds.), *Counseling African American families* (pp. 41–57). Alexandria, VA: American Counseling Association.

Meier, A., & Rudwick, E. M. (1966). *From plantation to ghetto: An interpretive history of American negroes*. New York, NY: Hill and Wang.

Naremore, R. C. (1980). Language variation in a multicultural society. In T. J. Hixon, L. D. Shrieberg, & J. H. Saxmon (Eds.), *Introduction to communication disorders* (pp. 176–212). Englewood Cliffs, NJ: Prentice Hall.

Neighbors, H. W., & Jackson, J. S. (1996). *Mental health in black America*. Thousand Oaks, CA: Sage.

Neville, H. A., & Walters, J. M. (2003). Contextualizing black Americans' health. In D. Atkinson (Ed.), *Counseling American minorities* (pp. 83–103). Boston, MA: McGraw-Hill.

Neville, H. A., Worthington, R. L., & Spanierman, L. B. (2001). Race, power, and multicultural counseling psychology: Understanding white privilege and color-blind racial attitudes. In J. Ponterotto, J. M. Casas, L. A. Suzuki, & C. M. Alexander (Eds.), *Handbook of multicultural counseling* (pp. 257–288). Thousand Oaks, CA: Sage.

Nickerson, K. J., Helms, J. E., & Terrell, F. (1994). Cultural mistrust, opinions about mental illness, and black students' attitudes toward seeking psychological help from counselors. *Journal of Counseling Psychology, 441*, 59–70.

Ntloedibe, F. (2006). A question of origins: The social and cultural roots of African American cultures. *Journal of African American History, 91*, 401–412.

Office of Minority Health. (2009). *African American profile.* Retrieved from http://minorityhealth.hhs.gov/templates/browse.aspx?lvl=2&lvlID=51

Ostrove, J. M., Feldman, P., & Adler, N. E. (1999). Relations among socioeconomic status indicators and health for African-Americans and whites. *Journal of Health Psychology, 4,* 451–463.

Parham, T. A. (1993). *Psychological storms: The African American struggle for identity.* Chicago, IL: African American Images.

Parham, T. A. (1999). African-centered cultural competencies. In T. A. Parham, J. L. White, & A. Ajamu (Eds.), *The psychology of blacks: An African-centered perspective.* Upper Saddle River, NJ: Prentice Hall.

Parham, T. A. (2002a). Counseling African Americans: The current state of affairs. In T. A. Parham (Ed.), *Counseling persons of African descent: Raising the bar of practitioner competence* (pp. 1–9). Thousand Oaks, CA: Sage.

Parham, T. A. (2002b). Raising the bar for what passes as competence. In T. A. Parham (Ed.), *Counseling persons of African descent: Raising the bar of practitioner competence* (pp. 141–148). Thousand Oaks, CA: Sage.

Parham, T. A. (2002c). Understanding personality and how to measure it. In T. A. Parham (Ed.), *Counseling persons of African descent: Raising the bar of practitioner competence* (pp. 38–51). Thousand Oaks, CA: Sage.

Parham, T. A., & Brown, S. (2003). Therapeutic approaches with African American populations. In F. D. Harper & J. McFadden (Eds.), *Culture and counseling: New approaches* (pp. 81–98). Needham Heights, MA: Allyn & Bacon.

Parham, T. A., White, J. L., & Ajamu, A. (1999). *The psychology of blacks: An African-centered perspective.* Upper Saddle River, NJ: Prentice Hall.

Peters, M. F. (1976). *Nine black families: A study of household management and child rearing in black families with working mothers* (Unpublished doctoral dissertation). Harvard University, Cambridge, MA.

Peters, M. F. (1985). Parenting in black families with young children: A historical perspective. In H. P. McAdoo (Ed.), *Black families* (pp. 228–241). Newbury Park, CA: Sage.

Peterson, N., & Gonzalez, R. C. (2000). *The role of work in people's lives: Applied career counseling and vocational psychology.* Belmont, CA: Brooks/Cole.

Phillips, C. (2004). Restoring a ruptured relationship. *Black Issues in Higher Education, 21,* 31–33.

Pinderhughes, E. E., Dodge, K. A., & Bates, J. E. (2000). Discipline responses: Influences of parents' socio-economic status, ethnicity, beliefs about parenting, stress, and cognitive-emotional processes. *Journal of Family Psychology, 14,* 380–400.

Richards, P. S., & Bergin, A. E. (1997). *A spiritual strategy for counseling and psychotherapy.* Washington, DC: American Psychological Association.

Ridley, C. R. (1995). *Overcoming unintentional racism in counseling and therapy: A practitioner's guide to intentional intervention.* Thousand Oaks, CA: Sage.

Robinson, C. J. (1997). *Black movements in America.* New York, NY: Routledge.

Robinson, T. L. (2005). *The convergence of race, ethnicity, and gender: Multiple identities in counseling.* Upper Saddle River, NJ: Pearson/Merrill Prentice Hall.

Russell, K., Wilson, M., & Hall, R. (1992). *The politics of skin color among African Americans.* New York, NY: Harcourt Brace Jovanovich.

Sanders, R. G. (2002). The black church: Bridge over troubled water. In J. L. Sanders & C. Bradley (Eds.), *Counseling African American families* (pp. 73–84). Alexandria, VA: American Counseling Association.

Smallwood, A. D. (1998). *The atlas of African-American history and politics: From the slave trade to modern times.* Boston, MA: McGraw-Hill.

Smiley, T. (Producer). (2005, February 26). *Smiley presents: State of the black union.* [Television broadcast]. Washington, DC: C-SPAN.

Snowden, L. R., & Hu, T. W. (1997). Ethnic differences in mental health services use among the severely mentally ill. *Journal of Community Psychology, 25,* 235–247.

Spanoudis, S. L. (1994–2007). *Quotations #27: African American expression.* Retrieved from http://www.theotherpages.org/quote/quote-27wx.html

Staples, R. (1984, October). The mother-son relationship in the black family. *Ebony,* pp. 76–78.

Stevenson, H. C. (1994). Racial socialization in African American families: The act of balancing intolerance and survival. *Family Journal: Counseling and Therapy for Couples and Families, 2,* 190–198.

Stevenson, H. C. (1995). Relationship of adolescent perceptions of racial socialization to racial identity. *Journal of Black Psychology, 21,* 49–70.

Straus, M. A. (1991). Discipline and deviance: Physical punishment of children and violence and other crime in adulthood. *Social Problems, 38,* 133–153.

Sudarkasa, N. (1988). Interpreting the African heritage in Afro-American family organization. In H. P. McAdoo (Ed.), *Black families* (pp. 27–43). Newbury Park, CA: Sage.

Sue, D. W., & Sue, D. (2003). *Counseling the culturally diverse.* New York, NY: Wiley.

Trierweiler, S. J., Neighbors, H. W., Munday, C., Thompson, S. E., Binion, V. J., & Gomez, J. P. (2000). Clinician attributions associated with diagnosis of schizophrenia in African Americans and non-American patients. *Journal of Consulting and Clinical Psychology, 68,* 171–175.

Trosper, T. B. (2002). Parenting strategies in the middle class African-American family. *Dissertation Abstracts International Section A: Humanities and Social Sciences, 63(3-A),* 864.

Truax, K., Cordova, D. I., & Wood, A. (1998). Undermined? Affirmative action from the target's point of view. In J. K. Swim & C. Stangor (Eds.), *Prejudice: The target's perspective* (pp. 171–188). San Diego, CA: Academic Press.

U.S. Bureau of Labor Statistics. (2012). *Table A-2. Employment status of the civilian population by race, sex, and age.* Retrieved from http://www.bls.gov/news.release/empsit.t02.htm

U.S. Census Bureau. (2001). *The black population: 2000.* Retrieved from http://www.census.gov/prod/2001pubs/c2kbr01-5.pdf

U.S. Census Bureau. (2010). *Poverty status of the population by sex and age, for black alone and white alone, not Hispanic: 2009.* Retrieved from http://www.census.gov/population/www/socdemo/race/ppl-ba10.html

U.S. Census Bureau. (2011). *Income, poverty, and health insurance coverage in the United States.* Retrieved from http://www.census.gov/prod/2011pubs/p60-239.pdf

Vandiver, B. J., Fhagen-Smith, P. E., Cokley, K. O., Cross, W. E., Jr., & Worrell, F. C. (2001). Cross's nigrescence model: From theory to scale to theory. *Journal of Multicultural Counseling and Development, 29,* 174–200.

Wade, T. J., & Bielitz, S. (2005). The differential effect of skin color on attractiveness, personality evaluations, and perceived life success of African Americans. *Journal of Black Psychology, 31,* 215–236.

Wicker, L. R., & Brodie, R. E. (2003). The physical and mental health needs of African Americans. In D. Atkinson (Ed.), *Counseling American minorities* (pp. 105–113). Boston, MA: McGraw-Hill.

Witherspoon, S. (2005). *The impact of environmental influences on the career choices of African American males: Aspirations of becoming professional athletes* (Unpublished doctoral dissertation). University of South Carolina, Columbia, SC.

Zhang, A., & Snowden, L. (1999). Ethnic characteristics of mental disorders. *Cultural Diversity and Ethnic Minority Psychology, 5,* 134–146.

CHAPTER 7

Culturally Alert Counseling With East and Southeast Asian Americans

Bryan S. K. Kim
University of Hawaii at Hilo

Yong S. Park
Michigan State University

Michael, an 18-year-old sixth-generation Japanese American, is attending a large public university, but he's finding the year difficult. He is anxious about completing his bachelor's degree in mechanical engineering because the classes are not enjoyable. Yet he knows that this field of study is practical and will lead to a high-paying job after college. He is afraid to speak to his parents about this dilemma because they have repeatedly told him that he should become an engineer. Lately, he has had trouble sleeping and does not feel like eating much.

Phuong is a 55-year-old Cambodian American immigrant who works as a clerk in a supermarket at a local shopping mall. Recently, Phuong has noticed that little things irritate her, but she doesn't know why. She says that she doesn't enjoy going to work; she feels lonely without having coworkers who are of the same ethnicity and age range. Phuong has been to her doctor because of recurring gastrointestinal problems, but the doctor can't find anything physically wrong with her. She was advised to take over-the-counter medication for her symptoms.

What kinds of questions might face the counselor of these clients? Michael is a sixth-generation American. What might this mean in terms of his sense of identity as a Japanese American? Michael is struggling with major educational and career issues and is unable to talk to his parents about it. How might a counselor work with him on this issue?

As for Phuong, she is an immigrant. How does this differentiate her from Michael? What about Phuong's Cambodian ethnicity? Does this characteristic suggest some unique historical, social, and political experiences that differentiate her from Michael and other East and Southeast Asian Americans? Phuong seems to be suffering from loneliness, in addition to some physical ailments. How might a counselor try to help her?

The purpose of this chapter is to describe ways in which counselors might become more culturally competent and effective with East and Southeast Asian American clients. Sometimes the simple term *Asian Americans* will be used to refer to East and Southeast Asian Americans. *East Asians* will refer to Chinese, Koreans, and Japanese. *Southeast Asians* will refer to the peoples of the region from Vietnam through Burma. Filipinos will also be included in this chapter, although their geographical status might put them in the cluster of Pacific Islanders. It should be noted that this chapter is not about South Asians, such as Indians, Pakistanis, and Sri Lankans. Chapter 12 addresses the cluster of South Asian cultures.

This chapter begins with a self-assessment of your current knowledge about Asian Americans. This exercise is followed by descriptions of demographic characteristics, the sociopolitical history, cultural systems, and particular mental health issues of East and Southeast Asian Americans. The chapter concludes with a description of intervention strategies that may be useful with these clients. Throughout the chapter, the cases of Michael and Phuong are revisited to illustrate how these descriptions apply to two very different Asian Americans.

To begin, below is a self-assessment about your knowledge of East and Southeast Asian Americans. Please complete it before you read the rest of the chapter, and return to it at the end to see whether your scores have improved. It is our hope that your final score will be 40 points.

East and Southeast Asian American Knowledge Scale

Instructions: Please indicate the extent to which you agree with each statement.

Strongly Disagree	Disagree	Agree	Strongly Agree
1	2	3	4

_____ 1. I have extensive knowledge about the history of East and Southeast Asian Americans in the United States.

_____ 2. I am knowledgeable about the large diversity among East and Southeast Asian Americans in regards to culture, language, and immigration experiences.

_____ 3. I have good knowledge of the cultural norms that may be generalizable to all East and Southeast Asian Americans.

_____ 4. I can provide specific examples of how East and Southeast Asian Americans have been victims of racism in the United States.

_____ 5. East and Southeast Asian Americans represent a wide range in terms of their adaptation to American cultural norms and the retention of traditional Asian cultural norms.

_____ 6. I am familiar with the terms *acculturation* and *enculturation* as they relate to East and Southeast Asian Americans.

_____ 7. I can give examples of cultural values that are salient to East and Southeast Asian Americans.

_____ 8. I am familiar with the model minority myth and how it has negatively affected East and Southeast Asian Americans.

_____ 9. I can offer possible reasons as to why East and Southeast Asian Americans tend to underutilize mental health services.

_____ 10. I can think of specific ways in which counselors can become more culturally relevant and competent with East and Southeast Asian American clients.

Total Score Out of 40:

DEMOGRAPHIC CHARACTERISTICS

The East and Southeast Asian American population represents one of the fastest-growing groups in the United States. As of 2004, the number of East and Southeast Asian Americans (i.e., not counting Asian Indian and Pakistani Americans) stood at nearly 10 million, or 3.5% of the total U.S. population (U.S. Census Bureau, 2007; see Table 7.1). These numbers represent an increase of about 67% since the 1990 census, when the number of East and Southeast Asian Americans stood at 6 million (U.S. Department of Commerce, 1993). It is estimated that by 2050, 1 out of 10 people living in the United States will be able to trace her or his ancestry in part or in full to Asian countries (U.S. Census Bureau, n.d.). This dramatic increase in the number of East and Southeast Asian Americans is largely a result of the huge influx of immigrants from Asia, as nearly 7 out of 10 Asian Americans were born in Asia.

East and Southeast Asian Americans represent a very heterogeneous group that is composed of many ethnic backgrounds, each with distinct cultural norms. Although they are often classified as a single group because of their common geographic origins in the Asian continent, the group includes no fewer than 25 individual ethnic groups, including Cambodians, Chinese, Filipinos, Hmong, Indonesians, Japanese, Laotians, and Vietnamese. These ethnic groups vary significantly in their language, traditions, customs, societal norms, and immigration history.

As for education and socioeconomic status, the proportion of Asian Americans who have a bachelor's or an advanced degree is higher than any other ethnic group. However, paradoxically, the proportion of Asian American (and Pacific Islanders) who have less than a ninth-grade education is also almost twice that for European Americans (Reeves & Bennett, 2003). This contradiction is explained by the fact that, although groups such as Chinese and Japanese tend to have higher rates of educational attainment than European Americans, other Asian American groups, such as Cambodians, Hmong, and Vietnamese, have significantly lower educational achievement than European Americans (Hsia & Peng, 1998).

Table 7.1 Population of the 10 Largest East and Southeast Asian Groups in the United States

Asian Ethnic Group	Number	% of Total
1. Chinese	2,829,627	23%
2. Filipino	2,148,227	18%
3. Vietnamese	1,267,510	11%
4. Korean	1,251,092	10%
5. Japanese	832,039	7%
6. Laotian	226,661	2%
7. Cambodian	195,208	2%
8. Hmong	163,733	1%
9. Thai	130,548	1%
10. Taiwanese	70,771	1%

Source: U.S. Census Bureau (2007).

Note: Population values reflect respondents who reported only one Asian group.

Similarly, there is a significant variation in the amount of earned income for Asian American families. In 2002, 44.2% of Asian American (and Pacific Islander) families earned $75,000 or more per year, whereas 40.1% of European Americans earned this amount (Reeves & Bennett, 2003). However, 14.3% of Asian Americans earned less than $25,000 in the same year, whereas 11.8% of European Americans earned this amount. The figures at the high end of the spectrum must be considered within the context of family size. Family sizes are larger for Asian Americans. In 2002, 19.9% of Asian Americans lived in families with five or more members, compared to 12.1% for European Americans. This difference suggests that the higher-than-average family income may be explained by the fact that more family members work to contribute to earnings in Asian families than in European American families. Corresponding to the income statistics, there is also a significant discrepancy in the percentage of Asian Americans living in poverty in comparison to European Americans. At least 10% of Asian Americans, or 1.3 million, live in poverty, whereas the parallel is 8% for European Americans (Reeves & Bennett, 2003). This group includes a high percentage of the overall Asian elderly population and Southeast Asians (e.g., Cambodians, Vietnamese) in general. Specifically, 22.5% of Cambodians, Hmong, and Laotians live below the poverty line compared to a 10.2% poverty rate for the general Asian American population (Reeves & Bennett, 2004).

SOCIOPOLITICAL HISTORY

The presence of East and Southeast Asian Americans in the United States can be traced back to the mid-1800s with the arrival of migrants from China and Japan, as well as those from India, Korea, and the Philippines in the early 1900s. The first group of Chinese arrived in San Francisco in 1848 to work in the gold fields of California. Twenty years later, in 1868, the Chinese were followed by Japanese migrants. Koreans generally arrived still later, in 1903, followed by the Filipinos in 1906. Most of the Japanese, Korean, and Filipino migrants initially entered Hawaii to work on sugar plantations in the hopes of improving their economic situation (Chan, 1991). As for Asian Indians, they first entered Canada and then moved to the United States in 1907 (Chan, 1991).

Anti-Asian Sentiment

These migrants faced economic exploitation, prejudice, and outright racism. Asian Americans were harassed, beaten, and murdered by other Americans for being Asian (Chan, 1991). This violence against Asian Americans was not limited to the individual or group level, but existed on the structural level as well. Laws forbidding Asian Americans to become citizens, own land, and intermarry were passed by various legislative bodies. Calling Asians "the Yellow Peril," the media soon labeled Asian Americans as "unassimilable aliens" and pushed for legislation banning further Asian immigration into the United States. In fact, such exclusion laws as the Immigration Act of 1924 were passed to bar Asians from even entering the United States. Thus the number of U.S. Asian individuals was kept to about one million for many years.

Although immigration from Asia was severely curtailed by these laws, a small number of Asians (several thousand) nevertheless entered the United States between 1924 and 1965. Most of these individuals were wives of American military soldiers stationed in various Asian countries during World War II (1941–1945) and the Korean War (1950–1953; Chan, 1991). These women tended to fall into two categories: those who married persons from the same ethnic group and those who married European Americans. In the first category, approximately 9,000 Chinese women entered the United States after marrying Chinese American soldiers. By contrast, Japanese, Korean, and Filipina women tended to marry European American soldiers.

However, anti-Asian racism triumphed in a significant way during World War II. Soon after the December 7, 1941, Japanese attack on Pearl Harbor, General John L. DeWitt, commander of the Western Defense Command, under the authority granted him by Executive Order 9066, forcefully interned

112,000 Japanese people who were living on the Pacific Coast, including thousands of U.S.-born citizens, into 10 "relocation centers" (also referred to as concentration camps) in desolate areas of the western and southern United States (Chan, 1991). U.S. political leaders believed that Japanese Americans would be forever loyal to the Emperor of Japan and would support the Japanese war effort by sabotaging important infrastructures in the West Coast, and could not be trusted to be loyal to the United States. None of these beliefs were based on tangible evidence. The Japanese internment contrasted to the absence of any parallel action against other ethnic groups whose ancestors were U.S. enemies, including German and Italian Americans.

The recent dramatic rise in the number of Asian Americans in the United States can be attributed to the following two events: passage of the Immigration Act of 1965 and the end of the war in Southeast Asia in 1975. These two events served to precipitate a large wave of migrants from various Asian countries, especially Cambodia, China, Laos, South Korea, South Vietnam, and Taiwan.

The Immigration Act of 1965

The 1960s were a tumultuous time in U.S. history. The social and political landscape was in a major upheaval, as many Americans, and racial minorities in particular, engaged in a fight for equality and justice. One of the significant outcomes of the civil rights movement was the passage of the Immigration Act of 1965 by the U.S. Congress. This act represented an attempt to improve the international image of the United States as a country committed to freedom, equality, and justice. The severe immigration restrictions imposed by the 1924 Immigration Act had hindered this image.

The 1965 act (and the 1990 extension of that act) had the following two intentions: family reunification and the importation of skilled workers (Ong & Liu, 1994). The goal of reunifying family members was expressed by giving immigration priority to persons who were joining their families already residing in the United States. The goal of importing skilled workers arose out of the country's economic needs.

This intention was expressed by giving immigration priority to persons with special skills judged to be in short supply in the country. Using a preference system based on these principles, the 1965 Act allowed a total of 120,000 migrants from the Eastern Hemisphere (including Asia) to enter the United States per year. By contrast, 170,000 migrants from the Western Hemisphere (including Europe) were allowed to enter. Despite this quota imbalance, Asian countries between 1978 and 1995 were still the leading source of new immigrants to the United States (U.S. Census Bureau, 1997).

The Ending of the War in Southeast Asia

The ending of the U.S. military involvement in Southeast Asia created a different situation for another group of Asian migrants who began to enter the United States next. Beginning in the mid-1950s, the U.S. government provided military and political aid to the governments in South Vietnam, Laos, and Cambodia in an attempt to prevent the spread of Communism to Southeast Asia. When the United States decided to terminate its involvement in this region in 1975, thousands of Southeast Asians who had worked for or were otherwise associated with the U.S. government became fearful of the political persecutions that might be carried out by the Communist forces who were on the verge of victory. As a result, these individuals fled their homelands by boat or on foot. Countless people perished during this escape. In response, the United States, out of moral obligation and humanitarian responsibilities, agreed to receive these refugees and help them settle in the United States. Between 1975 and 1992, more than 650,000 Vietnamese refugees, 230,000 Laotian and Hmong refugees, and 147,000 Cambodian refugees entered the country (Rumbaut, 1995). In addition, 173,000 Vietnamese immigrated, most of them after the establishment of the Orderly Departure Program in 1989 (Rumbaut, 1995). As of 2000, a total of 1.8 million Southeast Asian Americans lived in the United States (Barnes & Bennett, 2002).

Box 7.1 presents a timeline of significant events in the history of Asian Americans.

Box 7.1   Timeline of Asian American Immigration

1848   California Gold Rush.

1882   Chinese Exclusion Act: Chinese migrants were no longer allowed to enter the United States.

1907   Gentlemen's Agreement Act: Immigration of Japanese was restricted to only wives and family members.

1913   Alien Land Act: It became illegal for non-U.S. citizens, including foreign-born Asian Americans, to own land in California.

1924   National Origins Act: All Asian immigration was barred except for Filipinos, who were considered U.S. nationals.

1934   Tydings-McDuffie Act: A timetable for the independence of the Philippines was established. The act also restricted Filipino immigration to 50 persons a year.

1942   Executive Order 9066: President Franklin D. Roosevelt authorized the placement of 110,000 Japanese into 10 internment camps during World War II.

1945   War Brides Act: Spouses and adopted children of U.S. military personnel were allowed to enter the United States.

1965   Immigration and Naturalization Act: Abolished the 1924 National Origins Act and increased the quota to 20,000 immigrants per country, with the total not exceeding 170,000 from the Eastern Hemisphere.

1975   Fall of Saigon: U.S. military troops pulled out of Vietnam. Southeast Asian refugees began entering the United States.

1979   Orderly Departure Program. A system for processing and settling refugees to the United States was founded by the United Nations and the Vietnamese government.

Source: Lee (1998).

Michael is a descendant of the pre-1924 immigrant group. His great-great-great-grandparents emigrated from Japan in 1890 to work in the sugar plantations in Hawaii. After 5 years in the plantations, they moved to California to work in agriculture. Soon, they made enough money to purchase their own small farm, which they did in the name of their U.S.-born 9-year-old eldest son, because the 1913 California Alien Land Law prevented them from owning property permanently in their name. The farm business was successful until 1941, when Michael's family was forced to leave the farm for an internment camp in Colorado. Michael has not had much interest in his Japanese heritage and prefers to consider himself an American. However, Michael recently learned about Japanese American internment while taking a history course in Asian American studies.

Phuong entered the United States as a 20-year-old refugee in 1975, a few weeks after the fall of Phnom Penh to the Khmer Rouge forces. Her parents were both teachers and as a result were killed by the Khmer Rouge; the Khmer Rouge initiated an attempt to form a so-called pure Cambodia by targeting the educated elite and other segments of the population for eradication. On the day that Phuong's parents were taken away, Phuong decided to try to escape to Thailand. On her way there, she witnessed masses of dead bodies that were the result of the Khmer Rouge's genocide of its own population. Even to this day, she sometimes has nightmares about being in the streets of Phnom Penh being chased by the Khmer Rouge. Since arriving in the United States, Phuong has had difficulty adjusting to life here. Because she has not been able to completely grasp the English language, she has not been able to attain a college education. Phuong has worked at various jobs, the latest one being a sales clerk at a grocery store. Although she strongly identifies as a Cambodian American, Phuong seldom has contact with other Cambodian Americans because very few live in her city.

EAST AND SOUTHEAST ASIAN CULTURES

Effective counseling of East and Southeast Asian American clients requires an understanding of the diverse cultural systems in which these persons have been socialized, or enculturated. You must draw on your understanding of the notions of acculturation and enculturation and racial and ethnic identity development from Chapters 4 and 5 in order to avoid treating all Asian American clients as the same. The following sections review these notions as they apply to Asian Americans. After that, cultural values and communication patterns that are salient across East and Southeast Asian cultures are described.

Acculturation and Enculturation

As described above, the grouping that is here called East and Southeast Asian Americans comprises individuals with diverse immigration histories in the United States. This diversity, particularly in terms of length of residence, represents a dramatic range in the degree to which different Asian Americans have adapted to the norms of the mainstream U.S. culture, as well as the extent to which they have retained the norms of the Asian culture. To understand this type of diversity related to differential levels of adaptation, you might recall or review the notions of acculturation and enculturation that were given in Chapter 4.

It makes sense that Asian Americans who are further removed from immigration will adhere to the mainstream U.S. cultural norms more strongly, that is, be more acculturated, than Asian Americans who are recent immigrants (Kim, Atkinson, & Umemoto, 2001). For example, Michael's behaviors, values, knowledge, and cultural identity may be no different from those of other Americans, given that he is several generations removed from immigration. On the other hand, Asian Americans who are closer to immigration will adhere to Asian cultural norms more strongly, that is, they will be more enculturated to those norms, than their counterparts who are many generations removed from immigration. Such is the case with Phuong, whose behaviors, values, knowledge, and cultural identity would be more similar to Cambodian persons who are living in Cambodia, but significantly different from those of other Americans.

The four acculturation statuses of integration, assimilation, separation, and marginalization, as described in Chapter 4, help explain an individual client's adjustment to U.S. culture and her or his mental health. Marginalization is perhaps the most problematic of the four acculturation statuses for Asian Americans. Marginalized people adhere to neither their original nor the dominant cultural systems and tend to reject both sets of norms.

By contrast, the integration, or bicultural competence, status may be the healthiest status for East and Southeast Asian Americans (LaFromboise, Coleman, & Gerton, 1993). While European Americans generally have assimilated to the dominant U.S. culture, that option is not desirable, nor available to people of color, including Asian Americans. Biculturality is desirable because Asian traditions and values are distinct from the dominant U.S. culture and because Asians are physically "marked" by visual cues as "not white." Asians do not have the "optional ethnicity" mentioned in Chapter 4 that European Americans have. An Asian American with bicultural competence is fluent in the differing cultural norms of both the U.S. and Asian cultures and feels good about being a member of both groups. This person may also be fluent in both an Asian language and English. Furthermore, this person is eager to learn the cultural nuances of both cultures as a way to gain expertise in crossing the cultural bridge that exists. LaFromboise et al. (1993) noted that individuals may experience difficulties adjusting to the different and sometimes opposing demands of two cultures, but when they are able to obtain skills in biculturality, they are likely to increase their social and academic functioning as a result of their multicultural fluency.

Racial and Ethnic Identity Development

Racial and ethnic identity can vary from time to time in a person's life. The Racial Identity Development for People of Color (RIDPOC) model that was mentioned in Chapter 5 might be a useful tool to illustrate the variation in how Asian American individuals might see themselves and others. It should be reiterated here that Asian Americans are grouped as "people of color" because, by appearance, they cannot assimilate into the dominant U.S. culture. As a reminder, the five stages of the RIDPOC model are as follows: (1) Conformity, (2) Dissonance and Beginning to Appreciate, (3) Resistance and Immersion, (4) Introspection and Internalization, and (5) Universal Inclusion. They are illustrated with examples of Asian Americans.

Conformity

Asian Americans who are in the Conformity stage will have preference for the dominant European American U.S. cultural values over Asian values. They will have self- and group-depreciating attitudes, while viewing the European American group positively. In addition, because they reject their own status as members of a minority group, Asian Americans at this stage will have discriminatory attitudes toward other people of color, such as Latinos/Latinas and African Americans.

Dissonance and Beginning to Appreciate

Asian Americans who are in the next stage, Dissonance, experience a form of cognitive upheaval that shakes their beliefs and attitudes about their and other people's ethnicities. They may have reached this stage gradually or as a result of a monumental event. An example of a critical event for a Filipino American, for instance, might be learning that, in the past, thousands of Filipinos bravely served in the U.S. Navy but could not become eligible for U.S. citizenship. A Chinese person might learn of the Chinese Exclusion Act and the acts of violence committed against Chinese people in the United States. Asian Americans in this stage will also begin to recognize positive dimensions of their Asian American group (e.g., Confucian wisdom, Asian art forms) as well as negative dimensions of the European American group (e.g., colonialism). As a result of these types of experiences, individuals at this Dissonance stage are now forced to reevaluate their attitudes toward both the Asian and European American groups and to reconcile these dissonant pieces of information. Asian Americans in this stage waver in a state of conflict between depreciating and appreciating attitudes toward themselves and their group. Similarly, they are in a state of conflict over their positive and negative attitudes toward the dominant European American group and toward other minority groups.

Resistance and Immersion

Asian Americans may next move to the Resistance and Immersion stage, which is characterized by a complete endorsement of the Asian group's cultural values and a complete rejection of the mainstream U.S. values. In addition, Asian Americans at this stage experience a growing sense of camaraderie with members of other minority groups as "fellow outsiders." An illustration of an individual in the Resistance and Immersion stage might be the activist who views all European Americans as racists and fights for equal rights for Asian Americans.

Introspection and Internalization

In the next stage, Introspection and Internalization, Asian Americans experience feelings of discontent and discomfort with the strong views that they previously held in the Resistance and Immersion stage. They may begin to have concerns about their overwhelmingly positive view of their Asian American groups and their ethnocentric bias in judging others. They also may begin to recognize the value of many mainstream U.S. cultural elements, such as artistic expressions, but be uncertain about whether to incorporate such elements into their own cultural norms. An example of a person in the Introspection and Internalization stage is someone who seeks to learn about the positive contributions that many European Americans made to the civil rights movement in the 1960s. This person may also question the ethnocentric views of some Asian Americans.

Universal Inclusion

Finally, Asian Americans in the Universal Inclusion stage experience a sense of self-fulfillment with regard to their own identity. According to Atkinson, Kim, and Caldwell (1998), the conflict and discomfort that were experienced during the Introspection and Internalization stage have been reconciled, allowing for greater individual control and flexibility. For example, a person at this stage has more realistic and balanced views about the positive and negative aspects of the dominant European American group and the Asian American group.

Box 7.2 Illustration of Acculturation and Ethnic Identity in the Cases of Michael and Phuong

Michael feels that he has high acculturation to the dominant U.S. culture and low enculturation in his ethnicity of origin, hence placing himself in the Assimilation category of the acculturation levels. He does not consciously endorse any traditional Asian values, particularly values specific to the Japanese culture. He mainly adheres to the mainstream U.S. values, such as individualism, independence, autonomy, and future orientation. Michael feels that, because he is so far removed from immigration, he does not have any ties to his Japanese ancestry. In terms of his identity, Michael feels that he is in the Dissonance stage as a result of recently learning about how thousands of Japanese Americans, including his family, were unjustly placed in internment camps during World War II, while many Japanese Americans also fought courageously for the United States in Europe with the 442nd Regimental Combat Team. He is beginning to have an appreciation for being a Japanese American and wants to learn more about his heritage.

Phuong feels that she has high enculturation but very low acculturation, hence placing herself in the separation category of acculturation. Because she entered the United States as an adult, Phuong retained her proficiency in Cambodian and maintains her traditional values, including collectivism, deference to authority figures, filial piety, and humility. Unfortunately, she has had difficulty fully grasping the English language and adapting to U.S. cultural norms. In terms of her identity, Phuong feels that she is in the Resistance and Immersion stage in that she completely endorses her traditional Cambodian values while rejecting the mainstream U.S. values. Phuong admits that part of the reason she rejects the mainstream U.S. culture is the racist incidents that she has had to endure in her work setting.

Asian Cultural Values

Whatever their level of acculturation and enculturation, or their stage of minority identity development, East and Southeast Asian Americans will usually share particular cultural values (Kitano & Matsushima, 1981; D. W. Sue & Sue, 2003). Fourteen value dimensions of Asian Americans have been identified through focus groups and a nationwide survey (Kim, Atkinson, & Yang, 1999). They are listed in Box 7.3. The first twelve values reflect four related themes from Confucianism and Buddhism: interpersonal harmony, acceptance of one's place in society and the family, obedience, and orientation toward the group (Uba, 1994). Those emphases contrast to current Western values on competition, challenging norms, and autonomy. The last two values are about achievement and achieving inner peace by oneself.

Box 7.3   Common Asian Cultural Values

1. *Avoidance of family shame.* Family reputation is a primary social concern. The worst thing an individual can do is to disgrace her or his family reputation.

2. *Collectivism.* Individuals should feel a strong sense of attachment to the group to which they belong and should think about the welfare of the group before their own welfare. Group interests and goals should be promoted over individual interests and goals.

3. *Conformity to family and social norms and expectations.* Conforming to familial and societal norms is important; one should not deviate from these norms. It is important to follow and conform to the expectations of one's family and the society.

4. *Deference to authority figures.* Authority figures are deserving of respect. Individuals should not question a person who is in a position of authority.

5. *Filial piety.* Children are expected to manifest unquestioning obedience to their parents. Children should never talk back to their parents, go against their parents' wishes, or question their parents' authority.

6. *Importance of family.* Individual family members feel a strong sense of obligation to the family as a whole and a commitment to maintaining family well-being. Honor and duty to one's family are very important, more important than one's own fame and power; personal accomplishment is interpreted as family achievement.

7. *Maintenance of interpersonal harmony.* One should always try to be accommodating and conciliatory and never directly confrontational. One should not say things that may offend another person or that would cause the other person to lose face.

8. *Placing others' needs ahead of one's own.* An individual should consider the needs of others before considering one's own. One should anticipate and be aware of the needs of others and not inconvenience them. Over-asserting one's own needs is a sign of immaturity.

9. *Reciprocity.* An individual should repay another person's favor, that is, repay those people who have helped or provided assistance to the individual. Reciprocity works both ways, and when one does favors for others, he or she should accept favors in return.

10. *Respect for elders and ancestors.* Ancestors and elders should be viewed with reverence and respect; children should honor their elders and ancestors. Elders have more wisdom and deserve more respect than young people.

11. *Self-control and restraint.* One should exercise restraint when experiencing strong emotions. The ability to control emotions is a sign of strength.

12. *Self-effacement.* It is important to minimize or depreciate one's own achievements. One should be humble, modest, and not boastful. It is inappropriate to draw attention to oneself.

13. *Educational and occupational achievement.* Educational and occupational achievement should be an individual's top priorities. Success in life is defined in terms of one's academic and career accomplishments.

14. *Ability to resolve psychological problems.* One should overcome distress by oneself. Asking others for psychological help is a sign of weakness. One should use one's inner resources and willpower to resolve psychological problems.

With any particular individual client, counselors need to weigh the influence of these values in the context of the client's acculturation, enculturation, and minority identity developmental level. The counselor can inquire, using culturally educated questioning, about the importance of any of these values for particular clients. (See Chapter 19 for more on culturally educated questioning.)

Activity 7.1 Values Clarification Exercise Using Asian Values

Reflect for a moment on each of the 14 value dimensions listed in Box 7.3. Next, sort each value dimension based on the following three categories: Agree, Neither Agree nor Disagree, and Disagree. There is no right or wrong way to categorize these value dimensions; we are merely interested in the extent to which you agree or disagree with these values. Finally, answer the follow-up questions for each of the value dimensions that you included in the Agree and Disagree categories.

For each value dimension in the Agree category, please answer the following questions:

How does this value influence your behaviors and relationships?

How did you acquire this value?

How do you feel when you fail to live up to these values?

For each value dimension in the Disagree category, please answer the following questions:

What is a personal value that conflicts with this value?

What are the pros and cons of this value?

What reactions would you have toward an Asian American client who adheres strongly to this value?

Box 7.4   Values in the Cases of Phuong and Michael

Traditional Asian values can be illustrated in the case of Phuong. Since she is an immigrant and is psychologically closer to the Asian cultural norms, Phuong strongly adheres to many of the values. For example, when she interacts with other people, she has a strong tendency to not disagree with what others say, as a way of maintaining interpersonal harmony. She has learned to place the needs of others before her own. She is always respectful, especially to individuals who are older or more educated than she. When someone gives her a gift, regardless of how small, Phuong always reciprocates with a gift of her own. When others praise Phuong for such kindness, she attributes it to her parents for raising her properly. Phuong feels that to behave otherwise would bring shame and dishonor to her family.

It should be noted that Michael also is likely to share many of these values. However, given that he is several generations removed from immigration, he does not adhere to them as strongly as does Phuong.

Variations in Values Among Asian Cultures

These cultural values are commonly observed across a number of Asian American ethnic groups, namely Chinese, Filipino, Japanese, and Korean Americans (Kim, Yang, Atkinson, Wolfe, & Hong, 2001). Generally speaking, the members of these groups perceive and define the values in a similar manner. However, there are also significant differences among the groups on the level of adherence to some of these values (collectivism, conformity to norms, emotional self-control, family recognition through achievement, filial piety, and humility). In particular, Filipino Americans stand out from the other groups, showing (a) less adherence to emotional self-control than the other three Asian American groups, (b) less family recognition of achievement and adherence to filial piety than Japanese and Korean Americans, (c) less adherence to conformity to norms than Chinese and Japanese Americans, and (d) less adherence to collectivism than Japanese Americans. It is clear that Filipino culture has important differences from those other three cultures.

In addition, Japanese Americans have higher adherence to conformity to norms than do Chinese Americans, and Japanese and Korean Americans have higher adherence to family recognition through achievement than did Chinese Americans. These findings are important because they suggest that although these value dimensions are present across the four groups, members of these groups endorse the values in different degrees.

Communication Patterns

In addition to cultural values, effective counseling with East and Southeast Asian American clients requires an understanding of communication norms and behaviors among these clients.

Language

A first consideration is language itself. Given the high number of foreign-born Asian Americans, low levels of English language proficiency are prevalent among many East and Southeast Asian Americans. Based on data from the National Latino and Asian American Study, 16.7% of Asian immigrants reported having poor English language proficiency, and the majority of foreign-born Asians preferred to speak an Asian language rather than English (Gee, Walsemann, & Takeuchi, 2010). This English language difficulty obviously serves as a significant barrier when counselors work with Asian American clients. Language difficulties can contribute to inaccurate exchanges of information, even in the presence of an interpreter. As is the case with other clients for whom English is not a first language, counselors must take care to minimize misunderstandings when they work with clients who have low English proficiency. Chapter 18 has some recommendations in this area.

Context

Beyond literal language are the subtle cues that people communicate with. Every culture uses context for understanding of messages. Thus, in bargaining, sellers in some cultures may proclaim a price, knowing that the context requires bargaining. Asian Americans tend to participate in high-context as opposed to low-context communication. In high-context communication, individuals expect the other person to infer information primarily from the context and knowledge of the communicator. Thus, high-context communication tends to be indirect and implicit. For example, "no" may mean "yes" in some cultures but be a norm for an initial response to an offer. High-context communicators may accurately understand a message among each other without having all of the details spelled out. In contrast, individuals who employ low-context communication assume that the necessary information can be obtained from the explicit transmitted message. Thus, low-context communication tends to be direct and clear (Gudykunst, 2001). Within the purview of the hierarchical social structure predominating in traditional Asian cultures, high-context communication is pervasive.

Consistent with that standard, Asian Americans communicate according to "face." Face, for Asians, consists of having a high status in the eyes of one's peers. Thus it is not culturally appropriate to make fun of another, even in a good-natured way, as it is in other cultures. High-context communication serves the purpose of maintaining and building face. For example, Asians would honor their parent's face by referring to her or him by role, such as "father," rather than "you." Unlike European Americans, who tend to emphasize self-enhancement as a means of building face, Asian Americans are self-effacing and modest. For

example, a European American might be encouraged in career counseling to declare her or his strengths. This would be culturally incongruent for Asian Americans. In addition, while European Americans typically use humor to save face, Asian Americans are usually apologetic.

Pauses and Silence

The importance of face may translate into unique communication patterns when counselors work with East and Southeast Asian American clients. In terms of sequences of vocalizations and pauses, Asian Americans, compared to European Americans, may talk less at any one time (i.e., use fewer words) and have longer silences between vocalizations when communicating with other Asian Americans. On the other hand, when speaking with non-Asians, Asian Americans might feel uncomfortable with silences because they are anxious about the norms and rules for communicating based on the stranger's cultural background.

Politeness and Emotional Expression

Asian Americans also tend to be polite in communication, as they are considerate of others' feelings, foster mutual comfort, and build rapport. The degree to which Asian Americans are polite depends on the relative social position of the communicators. Individuals with higher social statuses are regarded with more politeness (Gudykunst, 2001). In addition, Asian Americans are less likely to express emotion in communication due to the culturally high value placed on stoicism (Gudykunst, 2001).

In sum, the following characterize Asian American communication: being indirect, making inferences about meanings, using apology to maintain and build face, acknowledging hierarchy in social situations, being modest, allowing more silence and fewer words, politeness, and controlling emotional expression (see Table 7.2).

Table 7.2 Significant Differences in Communication Styles Between Asian and European Americans

Communication Style	Definition
European Americans	
Dramatic	Picturesque speech; physically or vocally acting out what a person communicates
Open	Readily revealing personal information about oneself; expressive of one's thoughts and feelings
Precise	Communicating accurate information; trying to cover all possible issues in a discussion
Asian Americans	
Indirect	Communicating ambiguously; expecting others to guess the meaning of one's communication

Sources: Gudykunst (2001); Gudykunst et al. (1996).

MENTAL HEALTH ISSUES FOR ASIAN AMERICANS

In addition to having a good understanding of the cultural systems that have influenced East and Southeast Asian Americans' psychological functioning, it is important to consider the social factors that are related to their mental health. What follows are descriptions of some of these factors that cause East and Southeast Asian Americans to be more vulnerable to mental health problems: racism, the model minority stereotype, and acculturative stress.

This section on mental health issues concludes with a description of cultural expressions of mental distress, called *culture-bound syndromes*.

Racism

From the time of their first arrival in the United States to the present, Asian Americans have experienced and persevered through racism. As defined in Chapter 5, racism refers to (a) the belief that a group of people with characteristics other than those of one's own group are inferior in some way and (b) the ability to act on that belief. Chan (1991) argued that Asian Americans have faced racism in many forms: prejudice, economic discrimination, political disenfranchisement, physical violence, immigration exclusion, social segregation, and incarceration.

History of Anti-Asian Racism

The earliest accounts of racism against Asian Americans go as far back as the 1850s, when Chinese immigrants were denigrated and attacked during the Gold Rush. An atrocious example that illustrates the anti-Asian sentiment during this time period was an incident that occurred in 1871, when 15 Chinese Americans were hanged, 4 shot, and 2 wounded by a white mob in Los Angeles. Such discrimination and violence continued into modern times, exemplified by the 1982 case of Vincent Chin, a Chinese American who was intentionally run down by a car and hit with a baseball bat by an unemployed autoworker who was frustrated by the competition from Japanese auto makers.

Current Anti-Asian Racism

Anti-Asian racism is still present. In 1992, whereas Asians comprised 4% of the Philadelphia population, 20% of the hate crimes involved Asian American victims (Uba, 1994). From 1986 to 1989 in Los Angeles, where Asians comprise 10% of the population, 15.2% of hate crimes involved Asian American victims. Currently, 20% of Chinese Americans report that they have been discriminated against in their lifetime, and 43% of that group said that the discrimination had happened in the past year (Goto, Gee, & Takeuchi, 2002).

Microaggressions

According to Derald Wing Sue, Jennifer Bucceri, Annie Lin, Kevin Nadal, and Gina Torino (2007), acts of overt racism against Asian Americans have transformed into microaggressions, which are defined as "brief and commonplace daily verbal, behavioral indignities, whether intentional or unintentional, that communicate hostile, derogatory or negative racial slights and insults that potentially have harmful or unpleasant psychological impact on the target person or group" (p. 72). Based on focus group responses of Asian American participants, Sue et al. identified the following predominant themes of microaggressions: (a) alien in own land (e.g., perpetual foreigners), (b) ascription of intelligence (e.g., "all Asians are smart in math and science"), (c) denial of racial reality (e.g., invalidation of discriminatory experiences, "Asians are the new whites"), (d) exoticization of Asian American women, (e) invalidation of Asian interethnic differences, (f) pathologizing Asian cultural values/communication styles, (g) second-class citizenship, and (h) invisibility (e.g., being overlooked or left out).

Institutional Racism

In addition to individual acts of racism, institutional racism exists in the current U.S. social structure. For example, the admission rates for Asian Americans who have the same qualifications as their white counterparts are lower at large, prestigious universities in the United States (Uba, 1994; Young & Takeuchi, 1998). Discrimination occurs in the occupational setting as well. With similar educational and work experiences, Asian Americans are less likely than whites to be promoted to managerial positions (Young & Takeuchi, 1998). They also have lower salaries at the same level of work.

Racism and Counseling

Racism can lead to low self-esteem, learned helplessness, and depression (Fernando, 1984).

Counselors should be attentive to these effects on their East and Southeast Asian American clients' mental health. However, counselors should also be reminded that it will be difficult to find out about such effects from many Asian American clients, as they tend to underreport racial discrimination (Umemoto, 2000). Thus it may well be difficult to pinpoint this cause for mental distress in many Asian American clients. Again, culturally educated questioning (see Chapter 19) can be used to uncover these experiences.

The Model Minority Stereotype

One stereotype that has long affected Asian Americans is that of the "model minority." Based on a term first coined by sociologist William Peterson (1966), this notion suggests that Asian Americans embody the modern-day American success story: They are functioning well in society, are somehow immune from cultural conflicts and discrimination, and experience few adjustment difficulties. There is some truth to this general conception, from the perspective that this stereotype represents a central tendency of a number of groups of Asian Americans. Asian cultural values, such as diligence, frugality, emphasis on educational and occupational achievement, ability to hide psychological problems, and maintenance of face, reinforce the stereotype (Crystal, 1989; Kim et al., 1999).

However, the model minority stereotype has other, more troubling implications when these statistics are examined more closely. Two qualifiers are important. First, the model minority notion doesn't apply to all Asian groups. Second, the notion itself creates some mental health difficulties for Asian Americans. These are discussed next.

Model Minority and Diversity Among Asian Americans

The characteristics that go into the model minority notion are not accurate for all Asian groups. As mentioned at the beginning of this chapter, Asian American is a broad, and heterogeneous, ethno-racial category. It includes numerous ethnic groups with different educational, economic, and social characteristics. For example, as mentioned earlier, although Chinese and Japanese Americans tend to have higher rates of educational attainment than European Americans, Cambodians, Hmong, and Vietnamese have significantly lower educational achievement than do European Americans (Hsia & Peng, 1998). Thus, generalization to all Asian American ethnic groups is inaccurate.

Another inaccuracy about the model minority lies in actual income. As mentioned previously in this section, Asian Americans earn significantly less income compared to white people who have the same educational level (Bell, Harrison, & McLaughlin, 1997). A final counter to the universality of the model minority lies in the actual poverty statistics among Asian Americans. As noted earlier, at least 10% of Asian Americans, or 1.3 million, live in poverty, whereas the figure is 8% for European Americans (Reeves & Bennett, 2003).

Model Minority as Stressor

The second major difficulty with the model minority stereotype is that it in itself adds to mental health difficulties for East and Southeast Asian Americans in at least three ways. First, the model minority stereotype alienates Asian Americans from other ethnic minority groups because of the inherent message, "If Asian Americans can succeed, why can't other minority groups?" Intergroup rivalry on this basis was found in one study. Rosenbloom and Way (2004) found that a high number of black and Latino/Latina students in an urban high school consistently physically and verbally harassed Asian American students, due to Asian Americans being seen as favored by teachers.

Another negative mental health consequence of the model minority notion lies in its placing extreme pressure on Asian Americans to conform to high educational, economic, and occupational expectations. Failure to meet the expectations of the stereotype may lead to feelings of failure, underachievement, and inadequacy. In turn, these pressures and stresses may be related to psychological problems and suicide among Asian Americans (Hurh & Kim, 1989). Counselors should be especially alert to this expectation-related distress.

A final mental health consequence of the model minority notion is that the stereotype hinders the allocation of counseling and research resources for Asian American mental health concerns, as the common wisdom erroneously assumes that they tend not to suffer from psychological difficulties.

Acculturative Stress

A final major factor, in addition to racism and the model minority myth, that places East and Southeast Asian Americans at higher vulnerability to mental health problems is acculturative stress. When individuals make contact with the norms of a cultural environment that conflicts with the internalized norms of their indigenous culture, they are likely to experience significant stress. Members of immigrant ethnic minority groups, including Asian Americans, are particularly vulnerable to acculturative stress (Berry & Annis, 1974). For East and Southeast Asian Americans, acculturative stress is particularly pervasive because the dominant European American norms tend to make traditional Asian values and behaviors ineffective in U.S. society. Those contrasting norms include the following important cultural differences: the treatment of parents, assertive behavior, independence, communication, emotional expression, and the meanings of body language. Such acculturative stress is related to depression (e.g., Constantine, Okazaki, & Utsey, 2004). Hence, it is important for counselors to be attentive to the presence of acculturative stress among East and Southeast Asian Americans.

You are invited to try Activity 7.2 in order to increase your empathy in the area of acculturative stress.

Culture-Bound Syndromes

The cultural background of clients influences how they experience, interpret, and manifest their psychological distress. The American Psychiatric Association (2000) developed a list of psychological disorders that are unique to various cultural groups and labeled them *culture-bound syndromes*. Below are examples of syndromes specific to East and Southeast Asian cultures. (Such syndromes are further explored in Chapter 19.)

Hwa-byung's literal translation in Korean is "anger-syndrome." It is a rather broadly inclusive category for the experience of long-term and suppressed anger. Symptoms include insomnia, fatigue, panic attacks, fear of impending death, dysphoria (a state of feeling unwell or unhappy), indigestion, anorexia, dyspnea (breathing discomfort or significant breathlessness), palpitations, generalized aches and pains, and a feeling of a mass in the epigastrium (the part of the abdominal wall above the belly button) due to anger suppression.

Koro is an episode of sudden and intense anxiety over the belief that the penis in males, and the vulva and nipples in females, will recede into the abdomen and cause them to die. This anxiety is based on the folk tale that ghosts with missing sexual organs will steal them from the living. Cases of *koro* have been reported mainly in China and Thailand.

Taijin Kyofusho is a culture-bound syndrome in Japan that refers to an intense fear that one's body may displease, embarrass, or be offensive to another person. Within the Japanese nosology for mental disorders, *Taijin Kyofusho* refers to the fears of blushing, a deformed body, eye contact, and having foul body odor.

Shenjing shauriruo consists of the following symptoms: physical and mental fatigue, dizziness, headaches, other pains, concentration difficulties, sleep disturbance, memory loss, gastrointestinal problems, sexual dysfunction, irritability, excitability, and disturbance of the autonomic nervous system. This syndrome has been documented in China, and it is highly similar to a mood or anxiety disorder.

INTERVENTION ISSUES AND STRATEGIES

Box 7.5   Mental Distress and the Cases of Michael and Phuong

Michael feels that his current difficulties regarding career choice may have a lot to do with the model minority myth that he has internalized for himself. Although he realizes that part of the pressure to obtain a degree in electrical engineering comes from his parents and their values of academic and career achievement, he also feels that he can't see himself change his major to one that might be perceived by others as being less prestigious. In addition, his difficulties with mathematics make him feel ashamed that he is a less-than-good student; he feels that he should be good in math regardless of whether he likes it. As a result, he is struggling to stay in a major that he does not enjoy and is trying to cope with its psychological consequences.

Phuong reports that her ailments could be related mainly to the stresses from her job. She describes acts of prejudice and racism from her coworkers and customers that she has had to endure. For instance, Phuong recalls several incidents in which she was called a name (e.g., "dumb Jap") by customers who were angry because Phuong couldn't understand what they wanted. In addition, most recently, Phuong was bypassed for a night manager position in favor of a European American worker who had less experience than she. When Phuong inquired about why she was not selected, the general manager told her that she may have difficulties managing the other workers because she is so "different." Even when Phuong is not working, she feels like an "outsider," although she has been in the United States for 35 years. Because she is in a predominantly European American community with very few Cambodian Americans, she has no sources of ethnic support (e.g., Cambodian Mutual Association). The nearest Cambodian enclave ("Little Phnom Penh") is in a city that is 200 miles away, and it is not easy for her to go there. She notes that she has tried not to think about these problems as a way of coping with them.

The previous sections presented the historical, sociopolitical, and cultural characteristics of East and Southeast Asian Americans and described issues related to their mental health. Attention is now turned to culturally relevant, effective counseling with this population. The following section describes treatment issues to be aware of when working with East and Southeast Asian Americans and offers strategies that may be effective with these individuals. The following topics will be addressed: (a) attitudes toward seeking mental health services, (b) psychological assessment, (c) indigenous healing methods, (d) conventional approaches to psychological treatment, (e) modification of conventional counseling, (f) five factors for working with Asian Americans, and (g) additional sources of mental health support.

Attitudes Toward Seeking Mental Health Services

Client attitudes toward counseling are primary, as these attitudes will influence whether individuals even seek counseling services and how long they will persist in counseling. In that vein, Asian attitudes are significant. Asian Americans tend not seek psychological services, and even if they enter treatment, they tend to terminate prematurely (e.g., Snowden & Cheung, 1990). More recently, a qualitative interview study found that Asian Americans would see a counselor only as the last resort, with friends and family being first sources of help (Kim, Brenner, Liang, & Asay, 2003). At first glance, one might interpret these findings as showing that Asian Americans experience mental health problems at a lower rate than other racial groups. In addition, they may suggest that, when Asian Americans seek psychological services, the problems tend to be minor in nature, thereby causing clients to not return for subsequent sessions. However, these possibilities have been challenged by thinkers who argue that there are no particular reasons why Asian Americans, in comparison to other cultural groups, should have a lower rate of incidence for psychological problems (e.g., Atkinson et al., 1998). In fact, given the experiences of oppression that Asian Americans face, as described earlier, it seems reasonable to expect that the need for mental health services among this group would be greater than it is for European Americans.

A number of factors within and outside the Asian American group limit Asian Americans' uses of psychological services. First, within Asian American communities, there may be preexisting and readily available therapeutic systems. These systems may include a network of family members, respected elders, and practitioners of indigenous healing methods, who may be perceived as more credible sources of help than Western-based psychological services (Atkinson et al., 1998; D. W. Sue & Sue, 2003). Consistent with these alternate sources of help, Chu, Hsieh, and Tokars (2011) found that Asian Americans struggling with suicidal ideation preferred seeking help from nonprofessionals than from professionals.

In terms of the outside factors, mainstream psychological service providers may be seen as lacking cultural relevance and competency, which may discourage Asian Americans from seeking help (Atkinson et al., 1998; D. W. Sue & Sue, 2003). Asian Americans who are not acculturated to the dominant U.S. culture might perceive conventional psychological services to be "foreign" or even threatening (Atkinson et al., 1998; D. W. Sue & Sue, 2003). Less acculturated Asian Americans are most likely to exhibit this uncertainty (Atkinson & Gim, 1989). This finding supports the idea that Asian Americans' underutilization of psychological services is related to their lack of familiarity with Western norms and lack of belief that counseling can be helpful.

Even if they were more familiar with counseling norms, Asian Americans who are strongly enculturated to their Asian culture may feel ashamed about having mental health problems and hesitate to reveal their problems to individuals outside of their family, such as professional counselors (Atkinson et al., 1998). High adherence to Asian cultural values is associated with both less positive attitudes toward seeking psychological help and less willingness to see a counselor (Kim & Omizo, 2003). Hence, underutilization of psychological services among Asian Americans is related to Asian cultural norms.

Counseling Implications of Attitudes Toward Professional Help

These findings suggest several counseling implications. First, given the lack of positive attitudes toward seeking professional psychological help by many East and Southeast Asian Americans, particularly those who are strongly enculturated or not acculturated, counselors should consider *conducting more outreach* services in their schools, colleges, agencies, and private practices. It may be helpful to disseminate educational materials describing the potential benefits of psychological services. Second, mental health agencies should consider *hiring Asian American counselors* so that they can serve to attract Asian American clientele. This suggestion is especially appropriate if the agencies are located in communities with a large proportion of East and Southeast Asian Americans. Third, when working with Asian American clients who are strongly enculturated, low acculturated, or both, counselors can *use culturally educated questioning* (see Chapter 19) to evoke the issues of shame and embarrassment about seeking help. If the clients are embarrassed about their need for counseling, counselors can help them strategize effective ways to cope with these feelings. Fourth, a useful strategy might be to *assign clients to an ethnically similar counselor*. Having a counselor with a similar ethnic background may lead the client to have a greater appreciation for the normality and the benefits of the help-seeking endeavor. On the other hand, however, it should be noted that some Asian American clients who are assigned to an ethnically similar counselor might feel an increased sense of shame and embarrassment because they may be sensitive to the fact that an in-group person will be learning about their mental health problems.

Psychological Assessment

Four approaches to assessment can facilitate useful assessment with Asian clients. The first relates to dealing with the general reluctance among many East and Southeast Asian Americans to seek professional help. When they in fact do enter counseling, Asian clients may have a great deal of skepticism and culture-related concerns. If those uncertainties about counseling are unattended to, the client might prematurely terminate from counseling. Hence, it is important for counselors to *broach the question of clients' attitudes and concerns about counseling* itself at the beginning of the counseling relationship.

As with any clients, counselors should assess the nature, severity, and duration of the presenting issue, and the ways in which the problem was addressed in the past. In addition, it is very important for counselors to obtain information about the factors that are related to clients' cultural background, which could lead to more relevant and helpful counseling relationships and interventions. Finally, counselors should explicitly assess culture-related factors, including (a) levels of acculturation, enculturation, and racial and ethnic identity statuses; (b) attitudes about counseling; (c) experiences with oppression; (d) possible presence of culture-specific psychological disorders; and (e) availability of other sources of support.

Indigenous Healing Methods

Based on the results of a psychological assessment, counselors might consider taking one of two routes of treatment: (1) conventional counseling that integrates culturally relevant and sensitive interventions and/or (b) referral to practitioners of indigenous healing methods. If traditional Asian American clients (i.e., those who are highly enculturated) might not do well with conventional forms of counseling, even with the augmentation of culturally relevant and sensitive interventions, counselors could consider referring the clients to practitioners of indigenous healing practices. Some of these practices are presented in Chapter 19.

One type of indigenous healing method for many East and Southeast Asians, especially Chinese persons, is *ta'i chi ch'uan*, which involves an exercise whose purpose is to induce relaxation and meditation (Sandlund & Norlander, 2000). It involves a complex pattern of slow movements in the arms and legs. Research suggests that ta'i chi ch'uan enhances overall psychological well-being and mood (Sandlund & Norlander, 2000).

Another type of indigenous healing method is acupuncture. Acupuncture treatments are based on principles of Chinese medicine in which health and illness are viewed in terms of a balance between the *yin* and the *yang* forces (Meng, Luo, & Halbreich, 2002). Acupuncture involves inserting small pins on specific points on the body to improve the proper circulation of energy, which may be associated with psychological difficulties. Acupuncture has been used successfully to treat depression, anxiety disorders, alcoholism, and substance abuse (Meng et al., 2002).

Conventional Approaches to Psychological Treatment

It seems paradoxical that Asian American clients who have high adherence to Asian cultural values tend to perceive counselors more positively than the clients who are low in adherence to Asian values (Kim, Li, & Liang, 2002; Kim, Ng, & Ahn, 2005). This is especially true if the counselors also are Asian Americans (Kim & Atkinson, 2002). This phenomenon may be due to Asian respect for professionals and authorities. A counselor may be seen as a physician would be. Thus, with highly enculturated East and Southeast Asian American clients, counselors may be able to gain quickly the necessary credibility as helpers and then move onto addressing the presenting problems, especially if the counselors are also Asian Americans. However, with low enculturated East and Southeast Asian American clients, counselors may need to spend as much time as they would with other clients to gain the necessary credibility as a helper.

Some Western counseling approaches are likely to be problematic with many Asian American clients. A match or mismatch among a client's cultural values, a counselor's cultural values, and the values inherent in the counseling interventions can influence the counseling process and, ultimately, the counseling outcome (Atkinson et al., 1998; D. W. Sue & Sue, 2003). Potential problems can particularly occur in encouraging emotional expression, doing depth exploration, evoking self-affirmation activities, and promoting an egalitarian relationship. For example, Gestalt Theory posits the notion that emotional expression is beneficial and even curative for clients' problems. However, for Asian American clients who adhere to traditional Asian values and believe that stoicism and reticence are signs of psychological strengths, being forced to express their emotions might leave them feeling embarrassed and out of control. Regarding depth exploration, psychodynamic theories posit the importance of exploring the underlying unconscious dynamics causing clients' problems, which often include unresolved issues with family members or other significant figures in one's early life. For traditional Asian Americans who value avoiding family shame, such exploration may be threatening and leave them feeling disloyal to their family. In the area of self-affirmation, as mentioned before, for clients who adhere to Asian values of self-effacement, the cognitive and career counseling interventions of having clients openly describe their achievements and accomplishments, perhaps as a way to dispute their negative self-concepts, may

be counterproductive and leave clients feeling arrogant. Finally, egalitarian approaches to counseling, such as person-centered approaches, may also run counter to traditional Asian American deference to authority figures. Such clients may look to counselors to provide guidance and possible solutions to the problems. Being forced to treat the counselor in an egalitarian manner may lead clients to feel uncomfortable in the relationship.

There may also be positive potentials for combining conventional counseling approaches and traditional Asian cultural values. For example, the value of interpersonal harmony may lead clients to work just as hard as counselors to form a good working alliance, a key ingredient in humanistic counseling theories.

Modification of Conventional Counseling

If assessment shows that clients can benefit from conventional forms of counseling, care must be taken to augment the treatment with culturally relevant and sensitive strategies. There have been a number of research studies on counselor types and counseling interventions that may be effective with Asian American clients (for a review, see Kim et al., 2005).

Five Factors for Working With Asian Americans

Five factors have been found to be important for working with Asian American clients: (1) the person of the counselor, (2) counselor cultural sensitivity, (3) counselor self-disclosure, (4) counseling style, and (5) solution focus. The notion of gift-giving is also potentially important in working with Asian American clients. These generalizations must of course be made tentatively, keeping acculturation/enculturation and other individual differences in mind. Table 7.3 summarizes these factors.

Person of the Counselor

Research results suggest that Asian American clients favor ethnically similar counselors over

Table 7.3 Five Factors in Working With Asian Americans

Factor	Counseling Process
Person of the Counselor	Clients prefer counselors who are ethnically similar, have similar attitudes, are more educated, are older in age, and have similar personality.
Counselor Cultural Sensitivity	Clients view culturally knowledgeable counselors as being more credible and culturally competent.
Counselor Self-Disclosure	Clients prefer counselors who disclose personal information about successful strategies.
Counseling Style	Clients favor a logical, rational, directive, and authoritative counseling style.
Solution Focus	Clients prefer the goal of looking for immediate resolution of the problem.

ethnically dissimilar counselors. They also favor counselors who are older in age, with similar attitudes, more education, and similar personality. In the area of similar attitudes, for example, Asian American clients prefer counselors who try to match the client's worldview in terms of a possible cause of the client's problem than counselors who do not match the worldview (Kim et al., 2005). Other examples of worldview match are having similar beliefs about values, religion, and human nature as well as similar levels of gender identity and maturity. Also, bicultural Asian Americans, in comparison to their Western-identified counterparts, perceive counselors as being more attractive than do monocultural clients (Atkinson & Matsushita, 1991). To illustrate with the case of Phuong, she may feel threatened by a non-Asian counselor because of her experiences with racism. She may instead connect better with an Asian American counselor because she may perceive her or him to have had similar experiences. Also, Phuong may find an older counselor to be more credible than a younger one, given emphasis on older age.

Counselor Cultural Sensitivity

Asian American clients view culturally sensitive counselors as being more credible and culturally competent than less sensitive counselors (Gim, Atkinson, & Kim, 1991; Zhang & Dixon, 2001). Michael, who is entering the Resistance and Immersion stage, may be more open to a counselor who is sensitive and knowledgeable about Asian-related issues because Michael's attention is becoming more focused on his Asian ethnicity and culture.

Counselor Self-Disclosure

Asian American clients perceive counselors who disclose personal information about successful strategies they themselves used in similar situations to be more helpful than counselors who disclosed other types of personal information (Kim, Hill, et al., 2003). To illustrate, in many Asian American families, parent–child conflict regarding career choice is not an uncommon occurrence. Thus, a counselor may do well to self-disclose about how she or he resolved conflicts, if any, with her or his parents in regards to entering the counseling profession.

Counseling Style

Asian American clients favor a logical, rational, and directive counseling style to a reflective, affective, and nondirective one (Atkinson, Maruyama, & Matsui, 1978; Li & Kim, 2004), especially if the counselor is an Asian American (Atkinson & Matsushita, 1991). Also, in the area of style, acculturated Asian international student clients view authoritative/somewhat directive peer counselors as being more credible than collaborative peer counselors (Merta, Ponterotto, & Brown, 1992). With the case of Phuong, for example, a counselor may teach and direct her to create a plan for negotiating a promotion at her current job as a way of offering more logical, rational, and directive counseling.

Solution Focus

In general, Asian American clients, especially those who are less acculturated to the dominant American culture, favor the goal of looking for immediate resolution of the problem, rather than the goal of exploring the problem to gain insight about its source (Kim, Li, & Liang, 2002). For example, a counselor can conceptualize the anxiety that an Asian American client suffers as a "problem" that can be "fixed." The counselor would then immediately prescribe relaxation and desensitization techniques to reduce the anxiety before or in lieu of further exploration of related issues.

Immediate Benefit as Gift-Giving

An additional notion that might be helpful is that of gift giving. The metaphor of gift can be translated into counselors helping clients gain some immediate benefits from counseling. For counselors to be perceived as culturally responsive and to reduce clients' premature termination, counselors can focus on such gift-giving, in this case helping clients experience immediate and concrete benefits of counseling in the initial sessions. Examples of gifts are, in general, resolution of a presenting problem and, in particular, anxiety reduction, depression relief, cognitive clarity, normalization, and skills acquisition. Such gifts can be expressed through counseling skills such as information-giving, advice, directives, pointing out logical consequences, interpretation, positive reframing, role playing, and making a complementary referral to a physician or psychiatrist. Stanley Sue and Nolan Zane (1987) pointed out that ethnic minorities in general and Asian Americans in particular have the need to attain some type of meaningful gains early in counseling because they tend to be more skeptical of the long-term benefits of talk therapy.

Additional Sources of Mental Health Support

Counselors might consider referring Asian American clients for adjunctive support services to organizations that serve Asian Americans. One inherent benefit of utilizing existing sources of support found within any ethnic community is that service providers may be able to speak the native languages of the clients. Another is familiarity and trust. Such additional sources include religious and fraternal associations. For example, it has been well documented that Korean Americans and Filipino Americans are highly represented in Christian churches in comparison to other Asian ethnic groups. They therefore tend to seek support from clergy and other parishioners (Park, 1989). Hence, when working with a traditional Korean American client who is Christian, counselors may do well to help establish a connection between the client and a local Korean church in the community. Similarly, counselors might refer traditional Vietnamese American Buddhist clients to temples in which priests can provide supportive services. As for Asian American college students, there are Asian organizations that may offer support for culturally related concerns, such as the Association for Chinese Students, Kababayan for Filipino students, and Hapa for multiracial Asian students. Also, Asian Americans from the community can be connected to other coethnics for support through organizations such as the Japanese American Citizens League and Korean American Coalition. There also may be more specific Asian American organizations within communities across the United States.

A proviso should be offered to a counselor using culture-based sources of support: Care should be taken so that the clients will not experience shame and embarrassment when they seek help from members of their own ethnic group. As mentioned previously, when Asian Americans experience psychological problems, it is seen as a source of embarrassment and shame not only for the individuals but their families. Hence, if other members of the community learn that these individuals suffer from psychological difficulties, it could lead to a great deal of discomfort on the part of these persons. To avoid such situations, counselors should work closely with their clients to identify support sources with which the clients feel comfortable.

Box 7.6 Applying Culturally Alert Interventions With Michael and Phuong

What follows are descriptions of counseling work with Michael and Phuong. They describe different counseling approaches that attend to each person's particular situation, both of which are based on culturally alert conceptualizations. As you read these vignettes, please consider what other culturally alert approaches you might use with these clients.

During the first session with Michael, you learn that he has no qualms about coming in for counseling. In fact, he reports to you that this is his second time seeing a counselor. As you further assess Michael, you discover that he is highly acculturated to U.S. culture but low enculturated in his ethnic group of origin, which then allows you to turn to conventional counseling methods. In addition, because you are aware of the beneficial effects of gift-giving, even for a highly acculturated Asian American, you work with Michael during this session to come up with some concrete ideas on how he might be able to communicate with his parents about his career uncertainty. At the end of the session, Michael has a number of strategies in mind to help him communicate effectively with his parents, including pointing out to his parents that other majors could still lead Michael to a well-paying job and prestige. For future sessions, Michael agrees to work with you to further explore his other problem regarding his view that he has to be a model minority.

During the first session with Phuong, you learn that she is quite nervous about coming in for counseling and feels ashamed that she couldn't resolve her problems by herself. Hence, you spend time in the beginning addressing this issue and helping her cope with these feelings of embarrassment. As you further assess Phuong, you learn that she is highly enculturated but low acculturated, which then allows you to determine that you could either refer her to an indigenous healer or modify conventional counseling methods to address the fact that she operates largely based on traditional Asian norms. Because there are no Cambodian healers nearby, you decide to modify your service. After further assessment, you determine that Phuong's problem has a more external origin (i.e., racism). The goal therefore becomes to remediate her current problem (i.e., being bypassed for the managerial position). Hence, you decide to take the advocate role, in which you contact (with Phuong's permission) officials in the local Civil Rights office to see how the racism that Phuong experienced can be most effectively confronted. In addition, you contact the nearest Cambodian Mutual Association to find out how Phuong might be able to access its support network. Furthermore, you work to provide support to Phuong as she engages in this process of healing.

These scenarios in Box 7.6 illustrate the importance of counselors taking a culturally alert stance when working with East and Southeast Asian Americans. For example, they show the importance of conducting a culturally alert assessment, including examining the levels of client acculturation and enculturation. In addition, they point out the importance of attending to cultural factors such as feelings of embarrassment about seeing a counselor, as in Phuong's case.

SUMMARY

From their first immigration phase in the mid-1800s to the large influx that came after the passing of the 1965 Immigration Act, Asian Americans have become visible members of U.S. society. Moreover, by 2050, they are projected to comprise approximately 10% of the U.S. population. In the adaptation, adjustment, and maintenance of their communities, Asian Americans face distinct challenges such as acculturative stress (Uba, 1994), discrimination and racism (Young & Takeuchi, 1998), and identity issues (Atkinson et al., 1998), all of which are related to mental health problems. However, despite these mental health risk factors, Asian Americans tend not to use counseling services because they may be culturally incongruent. Thus, it is important for the mental health community to gain the appropriate knowledge of Asian American cultural systems in order to provide culturally congruent services to this population. When working with Asian American clients, it is important to first assess their acculturation and enculturation levels, strength of ethnic identity, experiences with racism, and other concerns discussed in this chapter before implementing interventions. Through the discussion of Asian culture and counseling strategies, counselors are encouraged to begin reflecting on how they can infuse these cultural considerations with their current therapeutic approach in order to craft a culturally alert way of effectively helping Asian American clients.

REFERENCES

American Psychiatric Association. (2000). *Diagnostic and statistical manual of mental disorders* (4th ed., Text. rev.). Washington, DC: Author.

Atkinson, D. R., & Gim, R. H. (1989). Asian-American cultural identity and attitudes toward mental health services. *Journal of Counseling Psychology, 36*, 209–212.

Atkinson, D. R., Kim, B. S. K., & Caldwell, R. (1998). Ratings of helper roles by multicultural psychologists and Asian American students: Initial support for the three-dimensional model of multicultural counseling. *Journal of Counseling Psychology, 45*, 414–423.

Atkinson, D. R., Maruyama, M., & Matsui, S. (1978). The effects of counselor race and counseling approach on Asian Americans' perceptions of counselor credibility and utility. *Journal of Counseling Psychology, 25*, 76–83.

Atkinson, D. R., & Matsushita, Y. J. (1991). Japanese-American acculturation, counseling style, counselor ethnicity, and perceived counselor credibility. *Journal of Counseling Psychology, 38*, 473–478.

Barnes, J. S., & Bennett, C. E. (2002). *The Asian population: 2000.* Retrieved from http://www.census.gov/prod/2002pubs/c2kbr01-16.pdf

Bell, M. P., Harrison, D. A., & McLaughlin, M. E. (1997). Asian American attitudes toward affirmative action in employment: Implications for the model minority myth. *Journal of Applied Behavioral Science, 33*, 356–377.

Berry, J. W., & Annis, R. C. (1974). Acculturative stress: The role of ecology, culture and differentiation. *Journal of Cross-Cultural Psychology, 5*, 382–406.

Chan, S. (1991). *Asian Americans: An interpretative history.* Boston, MA: Twayne.

Chu, J. P., Hsieh, K-Y., & Tokars, D. A. (2011). Help-seeking tendencies in Asian Americans with suicidal ideation and attempts. *Asian American Journal of Psychology, 2*, 25–38.

Constantine, M. G., Okazaki, S., & Utsey, S. O. (2004). Self-concealment, social self-efficacy, acculturative stress, and depression in African, Asian, and Latin American international college students. *American Journal of Orthopsychiatry, 74*, 230–241.

Crystal, D. (1989). Asian Americans and the myth of the model minority. *Social Casework, 70*, 405–413.

Fernando, S. (1984). Racism as a cause of depression. *International Journal of Social Psychiatry, 30*, 41–49.

Gee, G. C., Walsemann, D. M., & Takeuchi, D. T. (2010). English proficiency and language preference: Testing the equivalence of two measures. *American Journal of Public Health, 100*, 563–569.

Gim, R. H., Atkinson, D. R., & Kim, S. J. (1991). Asian-American acculturation, counselor ethnicity and cultural sensitivity, and ratings of counselors. *Journal of Counseling Psychology, 38*, 57–62.

Goto, S. G., Gee G. C., & Takeuchi, D. T. (2002). Strangers still? The experiences of discrimination among Chinese Americans. *Journal of Community Psychology, 30*, 211–224.

Gudykunst, W. B. (2001). *Asian American ethnicity and communication.* Thousand Oaks, CA: Sage.

Gudykunst, W. B., Matsumoto, Y., Ting-Toomey, S., Nishida, T., Kim, K., & Heyman, S. (1996). The influence of cultural individualism-collectivism, self-construals, and individual values on communication styles across cultures. *Human Communication Research, 22*, 510–543.

Hsia, J., & Peng, S. S. (1998). Academic achievement and performance. In L. C. Lee & N. W. S. Zane (Eds.), *Handbook of Asian American psychology* (pp. 325–358). Thousand Oaks, CA: Sage.

Hurh, W. M., & Kim, K. C. (1989). The "success" image of Asian Americans: Its validity, and its practical and theoretical implications. *Ethnic and Racial Studies, 12,* 512–538.

Kim, B. S. K., & Atkinson, D. R. (2002). Asian American client adherence to Asian cultural values, counselor expression of cultural values, counselor ethnicity, and career counseling process. *Journal of Counseling Psychology, 49,* 3–13.

Kim, B. S. K., Atkinson, D. R., & Umemoto, D. (2001). Asian cultural values and the counseling process: Current knowledge and directions for future research. *The Counseling Psychologist, 29,* 570–603.

Kim, B. S. K., Atkinson, D. R., & Yang, P. H. (1999). The Asian values scale: Development, factor analysis, validation, and reliability. *Journal of Counseling Psychology, 46,* 342–352.

Kim, B. S. K., Brenner, B. R., Liang, C. T. H., & Asay, P. A. (2003). A qualitative study of adaptation experiences of 1.5-generation Asian Americans. *Cultural Diversity and Ethnic Minority Psychology, 9,* 156–170.

Kim, B. S. K., Hill, C. E., Gelso, C. J., Goates, M. K., Asay, P. A., & Harbin, J. M. (2003). Counselor self-disclosure, East Asian American client adherence to Asian cultural values, and counseling process. *Journal of Counseling Psychology, 50,* 324–332.

Kim, B. S. K., Li, L. C., & Liang, C. T. H. (2002). Effects of Asian American client adherence to Asian cultural values, session goal, and counselor emphasis of client expression on career counseling process. *Journal of Counseling Psychology, 49,* 342–354.

Kim, B. S. K., Ng, G. F., & Ahn, A. J. (2005). Effects of client expectation for counseling success, client-counselor worldview match, and client adherence to Asian and European American cultural values on counseling process with Asian Americans. *Journal of Counseling Psychology, 52,* 67–76.

Kim, B. S. K., & Omizo, M. M. (2003). Asian cultural values, attitudes toward seeking professional psychological help, and willingness to see a counselor. *The Counseling Psychologist, 31,* 343–361.

Kim, B. S. K., Yang, P. H., Atkinson, D. R., Wolfe, M. M., & Hong, S. (2001). Cultural value similarities and differences among Asian American ethnic groups. *Cultural Diversity and Ethnic Minority Psychology, 7,* 343–361.

Kitano, H. H. L., & Matsushima, N. (1981). Counseling Asian Americans. In P. B. Pedersen, J. G. Draguns, W. J. Lonner, & J. E. Trimble (Eds.), *Counseling across cultures* (2nd ed., pp. 163–180). Honolulu: University of Hawaii Press.

LaFromboise, T., Coleman, H. L. K., & Gerton, J. (1993). Psychological impact of biculturalism: Evidence and theory. *Psychological Bulletin, 114,* 395–412.

Lee, L. C. (1998). An overview. In L. C. Lee & N. W. S. Zane (Eds.), *Handbook of Asian American psychology* (pp. 1–19). Thousand Oaks, CA: Sage.

Li, L. C., & Kim, B. S. K. (2004). Effects of counseling style and client Adherence to Asian cultural values on counseling process with Asian American college students. *Journal of Counseling Psychology, 51,* 158–167.

Meng, F., Luo, H., & Halbreich, U. (2002). Concepts, techniques, and clinical applications of acupuncture. *Psychiatric Annals, 32,* 45–49.

Merta, R. J., Ponterotto, J. G., & Brown, R. D. (1992). Comparing the effectiveness of two directive styles in the academic counseling of foreign students. *Journal of Counseling Psychology, 39,* 214–218.

Ong, P., & Liu, J. M. (1994). U.S. immigration policies and Asian migration. In P. Ong, E. Bonacich, & L. Cheng (Eds.), *The new Asian immigration in Los Angeles and global restructuring* (pp. 45–73). Philadelphia, PA: Temple University Press.

Park, K. (1989). "Born Again": What does it mean to Korean-Americans in New York City? *Journal of Ritual Studies, 3,* 287–301.

Peterson, W. (1966, January 9). Success story: Japanese American style. *The New York Times Magazine,* pp. VI–20.

Reeves, T., & Bennett, C. (2003). *The Asian and Pacific Islander population in the United States: March 2002.* Retrieved from http://www.census.gov/prod/2003pubs/p20-540.pdf

Reeves, T. J., & Bennett, C. E. (2004). *We the people: Asians in the United States.* Retrieved from http://www.census.gov/prod/2004pubs/censr-17.pdf

Rosenbloom, S. R., & Way, N. (2004). Experiences of discrimination among African American, Asian American, and Latino Adolescents in an urban high school. *Youth & Society, 35,* 420–451.

Rumbaut, R. G. (1995). Vietnamese, Laotian, and Cambodian Americans. In P. G. Min (Ed.), *Asian Americans: Contemporary trends and issues* (pp. 232–270). Thousand Oaks, CA: Sage.

Sandlund, E. S., & Norlander, T. (2000). The effects of Tai Chi Chuan relaxation and exercise on stress responses and well-being: An overview of research. *International Journal of Stress Management, 17,* 139–149.

Snowden, L. R., & Cheung, F. H. (1990). Use of inpatient mental health services by members of ethnic minority groups. *American Psychologist, 45,* 347–355.

Sue, D. W., Bucceri, J., Lin, A. I., Nadal, K. L., & Torino, G. C. (2007). Racial microaggressions and the Asian American experience. *Cultural Diversity and Ethnic Minority Psychology, 13,* 72–81.

Sue, D. W., & Sue, D. (2003). *Counseling the culturally different: Theory and practice* (4th ed.). New York, NY: Wiley.

Sue, S., & Zane, N. (1987). The role of culture and cultural techniques in psychotherapy: A critique and reformulation. *American Psychologist, 42,* 37–45.

Uba, L. (1994). *Asian Americans: Personality patterns, identity and mental health.* New York, NY: Guilford Press.

Umemoto, K. (2000). From Vincent Chin to Joseph Ileto: Asian Pacific Americans and hate crime policy. In P. M. Ong (Ed.), *The state of Asian Pacific America: Transforming race relations* (pp. 243–278). Los Angeles, CA: LEAP Asian Pacific American Public Policy Institute and the UCLA Asian American Studies Center.

U.S. Bureau of the Census. (2007). *The American community—Asians: 2004.* Retrieved from http://www.census.gov/prod/2007pubs/acs-05.pdf

U.S. Census Bureau. (1997). *Statistical abstract of the United States: 1997* (117th ed.). Washington, DC: U.S. Government Printing Office.

U.S. Census Bureau. (n.d.). *U.S. interim projections by age, sex, race, and Hispanic origin: 2000–2050.* Retrieved from http://www.census.gov/population/www/projections/usinterimproj/

U.S. Department of Commerce. (1993). *We the Americans: Asians.* Retrieved from http://www.census.gov/apsd/wepeople/we-3.pdf

Young, K., & Takeuchi, D. T. (1998). Racism. In L. C. Lee & N. W. S. Zane (Eds.), *Handbook of Asian American psychology* (pp. 401–432). Thousand Oaks, CA: Sage.

Zhang, N., & Dixon, D. N. (2001). Multiculturally responsive counseling: Effects on Asian students' ratings of counselors. *Journal of Multicultural Counseling and Development, 29,* 253–262.

CHAPTER 8

Culturally Alert Counseling With Native Americans

Michael Tlanusta Garrett
Eastern Band of the Cherokee Nation
University of West Georgia

J. T. Garrett
Eastern Band of the Cherokee Nation
Carteret County Health Director

Lisa Grayshield
Washoe Nation
New Mexico State University

Cyrus Williams
Regent University

Tarrell Awe Agahe Portman
White River Cherokee
University of Iowa

Edil Torres Rivera
University of Florida

Gloria King
Navajo Nation
Navajo Regional Behavioral Health Center

Tami Ogletree, Mark Parrish, Barbara Kawulich
University of West Georgia

Old Indian Trick

hide your thoughts with words

like white girls

so blood, crushed bone, burned flesh

terrify only as ghosts

of brown women's lives

Indian silence

leaves no room to hide

except in dreams

visions of light and spirit

to wipe terror away.

—Rayna Green, Western Cherokee
Nation (excerpt from "Old Indian
Trick," in Velie, 1991)

Native people existed on this continent long before the arrival of any other groups. The history and stories of their lives are often portrayed in the media, playing on age-old stereotypes held about this population. But there are often untold stories of pain and persistence that have carried over from generation to generation as the people continue to survive beyond what is portrayed in books and movies. The poem that opens this chapter evokes that pain and the clash of cultures that continues to be part of the Native American experience on the North American continent. It also refers to contrasting communication styles between two cultures (white use of "words" versus "Indian silence").

Native scholars have written extensively about the ongoing effects of generational and intergenerational trauma on indigenous people, their families, and their tribal communities for decades (Deloria, 1994; Duran & Duran, 1995; M. T. Garrett & Garrett, in press; M. T. Garrett & Portman, 2011; Gone, 2009). These scholars have consistently described the challenges that Native Americans encounter as they navigate a world that is drastically different from that of their own indigenous/tribal cultures.

If professionals hope to impact this population of people, they must understand that it is simply not enough to know about Indians, be part Indian, go to a sweat lodge meeting, take a class on Native Americans, or have an insatiable curiosity about them. Before anyone can begin to apply conventional psychological principles and theories to an ethno-cultural group, she or he must first understand its unique life ways and thought ways (M. T. Garrett & Portman, 2011; Trimble & Gonzalez, 2008).

There are, however, some generalizations that can be drawn from the collective experiences of Native Americans as social-political groups and as individuals from unique tribal/indigenous backgrounds. It is a salient thought to know that Native American people as unique tribal/cultural groups and individuals do still exist, many within the boundaries of their own homelands. It is also important to note that many tribal/indigenous people vehemently continue to protect their cultural ways through efforts to promote and revitalize their traditions, spiritual practices, and unique tribal languages despite numerous attempts to assimilate them into the dominant value system.

The real lives of real people are what counselors must understand in order to best assist Native clients who may come to them with words, ghosts, dreams, and visions of their own. The purpose of this chapter is to offer a comprehensive overview and understanding of Native Americans in contemporary society for the purpose of generating culturally congruent counseling practices with them. Specific sections of this chapter address the following:

- terms and definitions of what group membership means for Native Americans
- an overview of the people, with particular discussion of demographics, indigenous ways of knowing, acculturation, tribal and cultural identity, and the meaning of family
- the historical context of cultural genocide, assimilation efforts, and historical trauma
- current and ongoing social, economic, and political issues
- Native American cultural values and worldview

- various elements of Native American communication style
- Native American strengths and challenges in context
- implications for practice with Native American clients using contemporary counseling interventions and treatment modalities
- practical, tribally specific interventions
- a social justice and advocacy counseling perspective
- a call for culturally relevant research for and by Native peoples

First, let us consider a few case scenarios that might help you apply the concepts that are discussed throughout this chapter.

CASE SCENARIOS

The following scenarios are based on actual cases and intended to stimulate thoughtful consideration of how to best work with Native clients with a variety of presenting issues and from a variety of backgrounds.

Cheryl

Cheryl is a Navajo woman in her mid-50s who lives in an urban setting. She is divorced. She has two children from that marriage whom she has raised as a single mom while pursuing a career in finance. Cheryl is very talkative and doesn't hesitate to describe her experience in Indian boarding school until age 11 or her participation in Indian activist groups during the 1970s. She proudly expresses that she has been sober now for over 9 years, after a long period of drinking heavily. She recently has begun to work closely with Native youth as a mentor in the local urban Indian center where her two children are active participants. Cheryl says she was not involved much in cultural matters when she was young, but she has found that her talent and involvement as a respected shawl dancer on the local powwow circuit has helped her maintain her sobriety. With the recent death of her mother, however, with whom she was very close, she has been questioning what she should do next.

You are invited to respond to the questions in Activity 8.1 regarding the case of Cheryl.

Activity 8.1 Responding to the Case of Cheryl

1. How would you earn Cheryl's trust?

2. Furthermore, what would you choose to address first with her?

3. How would you approach it in a way that would be culturally responsive to her?

4. Where does Cheryl seem to be on the acculturation continuum?

5. How might that impact your approach to counseling with her?

6. How are you similar to or different from Cheryl based on your life experiences and worldview, given what you know about her right now?

7. What would it mean to work from a social justice and advocacy perspective with Cheryl? (See Chapter 3 for reminders.)

Rodney

Rodney is a Seminole sixth grader who attends public school just off the reservation. He is very bright, but reserved, and frequently gets either shunned or made fun of by other kids because of being overweight. Recently, his grades have begun to drop significantly, and he has been getting into fights with other kids. His family has expressed concern over Rodney's lack of friends in the school, and they are thinking about pulling him out of the school to enroll him instead in the reservation school system. Prior to now, Rodney had talked about his hopes of being the first in his family to attend college and wanting to study either fine art or business. Lately, he has said that he just wants to "go home."

You are invited to respond to the questions in Activity 8.2 regarding the case of Rodney.

Activity 8.2   Responding to the Case of Rodney

1. How would you develop rapport with Rodney in order to provide effective therapeutic intervention?

2. How might you include and draw upon Rodney's family as both a personal and cultural resource for him?

3. Would you consider conducting a suicide assessment with Rodney, and if so, how might you go about doing that in a way that would be culturally responsive?

4. How would you characterize Rodney's cultural identity and level of acculturation at this point, and what could you do to help him develop positive cultural identity that would help him meet his goals?

5. What would it mean to work from a social justice and advocacy perspective with Rodney?

The case scenarios provided above are based on real people and thus designed to stimulate deeper consideration of what the collective Native American experience encompasses. It is important that further awareness, knowledge, and skills for addressing issues endemic to this population be fostered in counseling training programs in order to facilitate relevant and multiculturally competent counseling practices.

GROUP MEMBERSHIP AND TERMS

Terminology used to describe Native people has posed some challenges. It is not uncommon for a Native person to be asked by non-Natives, "How much Indian are you?" This question refers to *blood quantum*, also known as *degree of Indian blood*, and *certificate of Indian blood* (CIB). However, many Native Americans are not enrolled members of federally recognized tribes, or are unable to trace their degree of blood in a specific tribe to satisfy the blood quantum requirement. Blood quantum requirements are hot topics on reservations due to intermarriage with non-tribal members or the existence of those who are not considered enrolled members. While populations on reservations are growing, especially among the younger generations, tribal membership is vastly declining on many reservations. Issues of blood quantum pose numerous challenges in forming healthy identities for Native American people. Nonetheless, this concept remains the primary identifying modality in determining who is an Indian. As such, it is critical that this discussion of what it means to be Native American begins by clarifying some definitions and concepts around group membership.

The term *Native American* is often used to describe indigenous peoples of the Western Hemisphere. The U.S. Bureau of Indian Affairs (2012) legally defines *Native American* (or *American Indian/Alaska Native*) as

> someone who has blood degree from and is recognized as such by a federally recognized tribe or village (as an enrolled tribal member) and/or the United States. Of course, blood quantum (the degree of American Indian or Alaska Native blood from a federally recognized tribe or village that a person possesses) is not the only means by which a person is considered to be an American Indian or Alaska Native. Other factors, such as a person's knowledge of his or her tribe's culture, history, language, religion, familial kinships, and how strongly a person identifies himself or herself as American Indian or Alaska Native, are also important. In fact, there is no single federal or tribal criterion or standard that establishes a person's identity as American Indian or Alaska Native. ("Who Is an American Indian or Alaska Native?", para. 1)

Blood quantum is not literally a measure of "degree of blood" as it implies. Instead it refers to the percentage of ancestry that can be traced to people from a specific tribe or nation. Most tribes/nations require 1/4 blood quantum for membership (Russell, 2004), while others set alternative criteria to address differing sociopolitical issues. For example, the Cherokee Nation of Oklahoma enrolls members with blood quantum as little as 1/512, while the Ute Nation of Utah requires a minimum blood quantum of 5/8 for tribal membership. However, the U.S. Census Bureau (2011) relies on self-identification to determine who is a Native person, thus allowing numerous individuals who may not necessarily be members of any tribe to profess their Native American heritage. However, Oswalt (1988) points out that

> if a person is considered an Indian by other individuals in the community, she or he is legally an Indian . . . [in other words], if an individual is on the roll of a federally recognized Indian group, then she or he is an Indian; the degree of Indian blood is of no real consequence, although usually she or he has at least some Indian blood. (p. 5)

Nonetheless, issues of blood quantum have posed some unique social and psychological challenges for Native people with respect to having children with someone other than a registered member of one's tribe. Numerous issues have arisen in current generations of Native children whose cultural and tribal identities have been questioned as a result of "not being enough Indian." It is important to be aware of the conflicting messages that may play a role in a Native person's identity as a member of a specific tribal group as she or he navigates her or his way in various social and political structures within the dominant system.

Some of the terms used historically or currently to refer to Native people are *American Indian, Alaskan Native, Native people, Indian, First American, Amerindian, Amerind, First Nations people, Aboriginal people,* and *indigenous people.* The terms *Native American* and *Native people* (and sometimes, *Indian*) are used here to refer generally to those people who are indigenous to the United States, who self-identify as Native American, and who maintain cultural identification as so-called Native persons through membership in a specific Native American tribe that may or may not be recognized by the state or federal government or through other tribal affiliation and community recognition. The term *indigenous* will also be used in a general sense to refer to Native Americans as the most original people to have settled in specific localities. This term contrasts to non-indigenous people who call a specific locale their "Native" homelands but who are not necessarily from the original people groups that were there previously. Now that there is a better understanding of some of the definitions and terms involved with group membership among Native Americans, it is necessary to discuss more in depth what it means to be Native American in contemporary society.

NATIVE AMERICANS TODAY

In order to understand the contemporary experience of Native Americans, we begin by taking a look at current demographic information. Then, we move to a contextualized discussion of IWOK (Indigenous Ways of Knowing) followed by a description of issues related to acculturation, tribal and cultural identity, and the meaning of family.

Demographics

Native Americans today have a steadily growing population of more than 2.8 million people, according to the most recent U.S. Census data (U.S. Census Bureau, 2011). Approximately 1.2 million of that total are identified as enrolled members of federally recognized nations. In addition, 1.6 million people, or 0.6%, reported American Indian or Alaskan Native and one or more other races. These census numbers also indicate that the Native American population is steadily growing. Although the population total for Native Americans represents only 1% of the total population of the United States, Native people have been described as representing "fifty percent of the diversity" of ethnic groups in the United States due to the vast array of unique differences in languages, traditions, and culture that exist across tribal groups (Hodgkinson, 1990, p. 1, as cited in M. T. Garrett & Portman, 2011).

Across the United States, there are more than 565 federally recognized tribes (228 of which exist in Alaska) and more than 50 state-recognized tribes, with several hundred in various stages of petitioning the federal government for recognition (M. T. Garrett & Garrett, in press; M. T. Garrett & Portman, 2011; Russell, 2004). Given the wide-ranging diversity within this population, it is important to understand that the term *Native American* encompasses multiple individual tribal traditions that are represented by hundreds of Indian nations that exist across the country, such as Navajo, Catawba, Shoshone, Lumbee, Cheyenne, Cherokee, Apache, Lakota, Seminole, Comanche, Pequot, Cree, Tuscarora, Paiute, Creek, Pueblo,

Shawnee, Hopi, Osage, Mohawk, Nez Perce, and Seneca. These are only a handful. Furthermore, according to recent U.S. Census Bureau (2011) estimates, a little over one-third of the 2,786,652 Native Americans in the United States live in three states: 413,382 in California, 294,137 in Arizona, and 279,559 in Oklahoma. As of the most recent census numbers, the largest tribes in the United States by population were Navajo, Cherokee, Choctaw, Sioux, Chippewa, Apache, Blackfeet, Iroquois, and Pueblo.

The wide-ranging diversity of Native Americans is illustrated by the approximately 150 different languages still spoken today, though this number is expected to decrease drastically in coming years (M. T. Garrett & Garrett, in press; M. T. Garrett & Portman, 2011; Russell, 2004). Although acculturation to the dominant American culture plays a major role in the current Native American worldview, there still tends to be a high degree of psychological homogeneity in the form of a certain degree of shared cultural standards and meanings, based on common core values that exist for traditional Native Americans across tribal groups (M. T. Garrett, 1999b; M. T. Garrett & Portman, 2011; McLeigh, 2010). For example, Cherokees and Navajos are both Native Americans, but their regional cultures, climatic adaptations, and languages differ greatly. However, part of what they share in common is a strong sense of tradition based on fundamental cultural values and worldview. However, worldview and degree of commitment to traditional culture varies among individuals and within groups among Native people.

It is important to understand that, contrary to the stereotypical image that Native Americans only live on reservations and rarely exist in contemporary mainstream society, approximately 78% of the Native American population resides in urban areas, while only 22% live on reservations or other typically rural areas. Native Americans come from different tribal groups with different customs, traditions, and beliefs; they live in a variety of settings, including rural, urban, and reservation (M. T. Garrett & Garrett, in press; Garrett & Pichette, 2000). In spite of this obvious diversity of tribal identities, a prevailing sense of indigeneity or "Indianness" based on common worldview and common history in what Grayshield and Mihecoby (2010) refer to as *indigenous ways of knowing* seems to bind Native Americans together as a people of many peoples (M. T. Garrett & Pichette, 2000; M. T. Garrett & Portman, 2011). The next section describes such ways of knowing.

Indigenous Ways of Knowing

It is important that the counselor understand the multifaceted experiences of Native people in contemporary society in terms of the impact of culture and identity from an individual, community, and spiritual perspective across time/generations and geographic space. To apply theories and models of counseling without consideration of cultural constructs would be counterproductive in promoting optimal well-being for Native American people. Counselors should not, however, make any assumptions regarding their clients' tribal/indigenous identities and experiences, as the variables involved in producing an adequate assessment are far too numerous.

First of all, anyone working in Native American communities must be aware of a deep sense of cultural loss that has resulted from a collective experience of colonization. That negative experience does not preclude the strengths of Native cultures. Cultural sources of strength exist within tribal/communal/familial entities as valuable resources in Native Americans' understanding of how to navigate one's life journey. Moreover, an indigenous epistemology in our understanding of health and well-being may promote counseling processes that are more sustainable and respectful in numerous venues for all individuals. What is it about an indigenous view of the world that is unique and important to understand? For thousands of years, the subsistence of indigenous people has largely relied on the relationship of these groups with their natural surrounding environment without widespread destruction. It is reasonable to conclude that the attitudes, values, and beliefs (epistemology) of this worldview and experience would have something to teach other Americans about balance and

harmony in today's world. Indigenous knowledge forms have allowed tribal groups to maintain their existence in specific geographic locations over time. They have done so through the combined paradigms of their epistemologies, ontologies, and cosmologies that construct ways of being and experiencing in relationship to their physical surroundings (Grayshield & Mihecoby, 2010). In essence, indigenous peoples have found ways historically to live in harmony with the environment, not only as an essential means of survival, but more fully as a way of allowing deeper spiritual truths to emerge in the daily lived experience of human beings.

Indigenous ways of knowing (IWOK) can be defined as "a multidimensional body of lived experiences that informs and sustains people who make their homes in a local area and always takes into account the current socio-political colonial power dimensions of the Western world" (Grayshield & Mihecoby, 2010, p. 6). In other words, it is, in a sense, an approach to life that strives for harmony and balance among all things. According to Grayshield and Mihecoby (2010), there are three central features of indigenous knowledge that have implications for practice related to the means by which indigenous/tribal cultures

- related harmoniously to their environment,
- experienced colonization, and
- provided an alternative perspective on human experience that differed from Western empirical science.

According to Vine Deloria Jr. (cited in Grayshield & Mihecoby, 2010), indigenous forms of knowledge are "the result of keen observations in the experience of daily life and in the interpretive messages received from spirits in ceremonies, visions and dreams" that coincide with a reality for tribal people based on "the experience of the moment coupled with the interpretive scheme that had been woven together over the generations" (p. 5).

From the perspective of IWOK, the true purpose of the helping process would be to promote engagement in activities that increase one's awareness of nature as a basic and fundamental construct of health and being well. Grayshield and Mihecoby

(2010) contend that the philosophical foundations of IWOK applied to the methodological constructs of academic disciplines have the potential to bring about transformative and sustainable change in human behavior. They conclude that

> the field of [counseling] would do well to yield its cognitive behavioral science to one that addresses the needs of the masses at a level of consciousness. The helping profession can become one that is relevant to worldwide global peace, unity and solidarity for generations to come. (p. 15)

Current Socioeconomic Status: The Good Red Road?

The "good red road" is a phrase used by some Native people referring to walking a path that is respectful and replete with spiritual truth and contributing to community, environmental, and universal harmony and balance. In context of the historical perspective, past American policies of assimilating nondominant cultural groups have had a pervasive impact on Native peoples and their way of life. Historical factors and experiences, the outcome of which has been referred to as "historical grief and trauma," have affected Native Americans psychologically, economically, and socially for generations and have challenged the integrity of Native spiritual traditions in this country. The following information based on U.S. Census Bureau (2011) data helps provide a better understanding of the current socioeconomic status of Native people by looking at age, families, education, income, poverty, employment, and several other pertinent statistics.

Age

A total of 33.9 % of the Native American population is under the age of 18. The next largest age group is 30.9% between 25 and 44 years of age. Only 5.6% of Native Americans are over the age of 65.

Families

Native American families are distinct in that they tend to be intergenerational and include nonblood (fictive) kinship ties; they also have a history of cultural adoptions. More than half of Native American grandparents are responsible for grandchildren for longer than a 5-year period. That is a high percentage. It is due to necessity in some instances as well as cultural norms. Over 8% of American Indian and Alaska Native grandparents live with their grandchildren.

Educational Attainment

Native Americans have a 70.9% high school graduation rate. Native Americans receive bachelor's degrees at a rate of 11.3%, which is below the national average. Achievement of advanced degrees (3.9%) is far below that of the general population in the United States.

Income and Poverty Rate

The recent average median income for Native Americans has been reported at around $33,000. Native Americans have a reported poverty level of 25.7%, compared to 12.4% of the total U.S. population living in poverty. American Indians and Alaska Natives have the lowest monthly expenses for their households, with a median of $879.

Employment

Most American Indians and Alaska Natives who are employed reported occupations in the management, professional, and related occupations (24.3%) and sales and office occupations (24%). The service category held the next highest percentage, with 20.6%. In terms of income and occupational data, 75% of the Native workforce earns less than $7,000 per year. The average unemployment rate for Native people is 45%; however, on some reservations the unemployment rate is as high as 90%.

Other Current Demographic Statistics

Native Americans have been described as a group of persons facing enormous problems. This includes unemployment rates 3 to 11 times greater than that of the general population, a median income half that of the majority population, high school dropout rates exceeding 60% in many areas, arrest rates 3 times those for African Americans, and a rate of alcoholism double that of the general population. In terms of health concerns, Fetal Alcohol Syndrome rates for Native people are 33 times higher than for non-Native people. Alcohol mortality is 6 times the rate for all other ethnic groups. Tuberculosis is 7.4 times greater than for non-Indians. Diabetes is 6.8 times greater than for the general population. In terms of mental health concerns, one in six Native adolescents has attempted suicide, a rate 4 times that of all other groups. Regarding living conditions, 46% have no electricity, 54% have no indoor plumbing, and 82% live without a telephone. Some of the challenges that Native people face in life and bring with them to the counseling process are evident and must be taken into account in the therapeutic process as needed; however, the resiliency of Native people both as individuals and as a population should also be understood and capitalized upon as well.

ACCULTURATION

Like other groups, Native peoples' relationship with their cultural heritage and ethnicity varies from person to person. Individuals vary with regard to acceptance and commitment to specific tribal values, beliefs, and traditional practices (J. T. Garrett & Garrett, 1996; M. T. Garrett & Portman, 2011; Garrett, Torres-Rivera, Dixon, & Myers, 2009). Those differences are related to variations in (a) level of acculturation, (b) geographic setting (urban, rural, or reservation), and (c) socioeconomic status, of which the latter two aspects impact the former (Choney, Berryhill-Paapke, & Robbins, 1995; M. T. Garrett & Pichette, 2000; Herring, 1999; LaFromboise, 1993; LaFromboise, Coleman, & Gerton, 1993; LaFromboise & Rowe, 1983; LaFromboise, Trimble, & Mohatt, 1990; Scholl, 2006).

Acculturation is generally defined as the process of being in a dominant culture and adopting the behavior patterns of that surrounding culture. Garcia and Ahler (1992) add a two-way dimension to acculturation in their definition: "The cultural

change that occurs when two or more cultures are in persistent contact" (p. 24). Michael Garrett and Eugene Pichette (2000), drawing on the work of Garcia and Ahler, define five levels of acculturation for Native peoples from their research:

1. *Traditional*—They may or may not speak English, but generally speak and think in their native language; they hold only traditional values and beliefs and practice only traditional tribal customs and methods of worship.

2. *Marginal*—They may speak both the native language and English; however, they may not fully accept the cultural heritage and practices of their tribal group nor fully identify with mainstream cultural values and behaviors.

3. *Bicultural*—They are generally accepted by dominant society and tribal society/nation; they are simultaneously able to know, accept, and practice both mainstream values and behaviors and the traditional values and beliefs of their cultural heritage.

4. *Assimilated*—They are accepted by dominant society; they embrace only mainstream cultural values, behaviors, and expectations.

5. *Pantraditional*—They are assimilated Native Americans who have made a conscious choice to return to the "old ways." They are generally accepted by dominant society, but seek to embrace previously lost traditional cultural values, beliefs, and practices of their tribal heritage. Therefore, they may speak both English and their native tribal language. (M. T. Garrett & Pichette, 2000; LaFromboise et al., 1993)

These five levels represent a continuum along which any given Native American individual may fall. Regardless of blood quantum, the most popular but most deceiving means of determining a person's "Indianness" and degree of traditionalism comes not only from heritage, but also from life experiences and self-identity. Thus the degree of traditionalism versus the degree of acculturation to mainstream American values and cultural standards for behavior is not universal (M. T. Garrett & Pichette, 2000; M. T. Garrett & Portman, 2011;

Scholl, 2006). For example, urban living can impact the sense of traditionalism and access to community from which a person's cultural and community traditions originate. Regardless of what level of acculturation one lives, the most salient concept to grasp is that not all Indians are alike.

CULTURAL IDENTITY AND THE TRIBAL NATION

For most Native people, cultural identity is rooted in tribal membership, community, and culture rather than in personal achievements, social or financial status, or acquired possessions. Social structure and hierarchy of power can vary from nation to nation. Many Native nations, such as the Cherokee, are considered to be matriarchal/matrilineal or matriarchal/patrilineal, which means that children trace their heritage through the mother or grandmother, and the social structure of the tribe may place more emphasis on power held by women. Other tribes, however, have taken on values that were imposed on them through processes of colonization (assimilation) by dominant value structures of church and state. Even so, the extended family (at least three generations) and tribal group take precedence over all other affiliations.

The tribe is an interdependent system of people who perceive themselves to be part of the greater whole (i.e., the tribe/nation) rather than to be a whole consisting of individual parts (Kawulich, 2008). Moreover, many nations maintain a deep sense of cultural pride in tribal ancestral heritage being intricately interconnected with the surrounding natural environment. Thus, indigenous thought and identity have been defined by the interconnectedness of relationships on numerous levels—human, animal and plant, environment, and spirit all intertwined. This principle is expressed through traditional Native people's judging themselves and their actions according to whether they are benefiting their respective communities' harmonious functioning. By contrast, in mainstream American society, worth and status are based on "what you do" or "what you have achieved." For Native Americans, "who you are is where you come from." Native Americans essentially believe that "if you know my family, clan, or tribe, then you know me." As a result, traditional Native people might be likely to describe some aspect of their family or tribal heritage when asked to talk about themselves.

Family

It has been said that "about the most unfavorable moral judgment an Indian can pass on another person is to say 'He acts as if he didn't have any relatives'" (DuBray, 1985, p. 36). As mentioned previously, in contrast to the popular conversational question in majority culture when two people meet for the first time, "What do you do?", many Native people may ask, "Where do you come from? Who's your family? To whom do you belong? Who are your people?" The speaker's intent is to find out where she or he stands in relation to this new person and what commonality exists. In fact, this is a simple way of building bridges—or recognizing bridges that already exist, but that are as yet unknown. Family may or may not consist of blood relatives. It is common practice in the Indian way, for instance, to claim a non-blood-related person as a relative, thereby welcoming him or her as a real family member. From that point on, that person is a relative, and that is that. After all, family can be a matter of both blood and spirit.

In the traditional way, the prevalence of cooperation and sharing in the spirit of community is essential for harmony and balance. It is not unusual for a Native child to be raised in several different households over time. This is generally not due to a lack of caring or responsibility, but because it is both an obligation and a pleasure to share in raising and caring for the children in one's family (Harper, 2011; Hunter & Sawyer, 2006). Grandparents, aunts, uncles, and other members of the community are all responsible for the raising of children, and they take this responsibility very seriously (BigFoot & Funderburk, 2011).

Wisdom Keepers

Native elders are the keepers of the sacred ways. They are protectors, mentors, teachers, and support givers. Native communities honor their elders as the "Keepers of the Wisdom," for their lifetime's worth of knowledge and experience. Elders have always played an important part in the continuance of the tribal community by functioning in the role of parent, teacher, community leader, and spiritual guide (M. T. Garrett & Garrett, 1997; Harper, 2011). To refer to an elder as Grandmother, Grandfather, Uncle, Aunt, Old Woman, or Old Man is to refer to a very special relationship that exists with that elder, characterized by deep respect and admiration.

There is a very special kind of relationship based on mutual respect and caring between Indian elders and Indian children as one moves through the Life Circle, from birth to old age, from being cared for to caring for, as Red Horse (1997) puts it. With increase in age comes an increase in the sacred obligation to family, clan, and tribe. Native American elders pass on to the children the notion that their own life-force carries the spirits of their ancestors (Hunter & Sawyer, 2006). With such an emphasis on connectedness, Native traditions revere children, not only as ones who will carry on the wisdom and traditions, but also as "little people" who are still very close to the spirit world and from whom we have much to learn. The following anecdote from Brendtro, Brokenleg, and Van Bockern (1990) illustrates the importance of being a caretaker within Native culture as a manifestation of family:

> In a conversation with his aging grandfather, a young Indian man asked, "Grandfather, what is the purpose of life?" After a long time in thought, the old man looked up and said, "Grandson, children are the purpose of life. We were once children and someone cared for us, and now it is our time to care." (p. 45)

SURVIVING "HISTORY": A STORY OF HEALING FROM INTERGENERATIONAL GRIEF AND TRAUMA

A true understanding of what it means to be Native today involves the influence of the historical context from which Native individuals and their families come. As such, it is important to consider the powerful influence of what many Native people refer to as *generational grief and trauma,* or what Brave Heart has simply termed *historical trauma,* and the effect this aspect of the Native experience has had on Native worldview and life. Deloria (1988) recounts, "When questioned by an anthropologist about what the Indians called America before the White man came, an Indian said simply, 'Ours'" (p. 166).

Throughout U.S. history, there have been deliberate attempts to destroy the Native American institutions of family, clan, and tribal structure; religious belief systems and practices; customs; and traditional way of life. This was done by mainstream American institutions such as government agencies, schools, and churches (Deloria, 1988; Heinrich, Corbine, & Thomas, 1990; Locust, 1988; Reyhner & Eder, 1992). The dominant culture has a long history of opposition to Native cultures and attempts to assimilate Native people, all of which has had a long-lasting effect on the cultures and Native peoples' ways of life (Brave Heart, 2005; Deloria, 1988, 2002, 2006; Duran, 2006; Duran, Firehammer, & Gonzalez, 2008; Gone, 2009; Locust, 1988; Turner & Pope, 2009).

It is generally understood that there are five stages of U.S. government policy leading to the current state of tribal sovereignty experienced by Native tribes (Deloria, 1988, 2002, 2006; Duran, 2006; M. T. Garrett, 1996b; Oswalt, 2009): (1) the removal period (1600s to 1840s) characterized by the saying "the only good Indian is a dead Indian"; (2) the reservation period (1860 to 1920s) characterized by the saying "kill the Indian, but save the man"; (3) the reorganization period (1930s to 1950s) with schools allowed on reservations; (4) the termination period (1950s to 1960s) with Relocation Programs intended to achieve sociocultural integration in order to end dependence on the federal government (which resulted in the sale of huge acres of Native lands and increased poverty); and (5) the self-determination period (1975 to the present), with increased tribal sovereignty following a period of Native activism, referred to as Red Power.

Efforts by the United States to destroy or assimilate Native peoples in this country are abundant. By the end of the 18th century, the once extensive population of Native peoples had been reduced to 10% of its original size (Oswalt, 1988). Policies of extermination and seizure of lands were common in the history of the United States' interaction with Native American tribes. Even today, the depiction of President Andrew Jackson on the U.S. $20 bill reminds many Native Americans in the U.S. Southeast and West of the betrayal by the government in 1838. At that time Jackson defied the Supreme Court by signing off on an act that forced the removal of over 16,000 Cherokees and members of other tribes from parts of North Carolina, South Carolina, Tennessee, and Georgia to the Oklahoma territory (M. T. Garrett, 1998; Oswalt, 2009). This forced movement of people is known as the Trail of Tears.

Even after being forced onto reservation lands, many Indian families experienced disruption of their cultural traditions. Many Native American children were deliberately taken from their homes and forced to attend boarding schools where they were not allowed to speak their native language or practice their traditions. The children usually spent a minimum of eight continuous years away from their families and communities (Brave Heart, 2005; Deloria, 1988, 2002, 2006; Duran, 2006; M. T. Garrett & Portman, 2011; Herring, 1999). It was not until 1924 that the U.S. government recognized the citizenship of Native Americans—when they were no longer a threat to national expansion—through passage of the Citizenship Act (Deloria, 1988; M. T. Garrett & Garrett, in press). Native Americans were not granted religious freedom until 1978, when the American Indian Religious Freedom Act was passed. This act overturned the Indian Religious Crimes Code of 1889 and guaranteed Native people the constitutional right to exercise their traditional religious practices for the first time in a century (Deloria, 1988; Loftin, 1989; Oswalt, 2009). In more recent times, massive efforts to "civilize" Native people through the aforementioned government-supported, religiously run boarding schools and the Relocation Programs of the 1950s added to the generational trauma and cultural discontinuity

(M. T. Garrett & Portman, 2011; Gone, 2009; Hirschfelder & Kreipe de Montano, 1993; Oswalt, 2009). These events have affected Native Americans psychologically, economically, and socially for generations. From both a historical and contemporary perspective, oppression is and continues to be a very real experience for Native people.

Brave Heart (2000) and other scholars have identified three aspects of the pertinent historical experience as being critically important in creating trauma: colonization, the boarding school experience, and forced assimilation. According to McLeigh (2010), colonization is an apt description for the entire experience of Native peoples being subjugated through European conquest, including the impact of infectious diseases, the introduction of alcohol (which had not been part of indigenous cultures), and other major traumatic events such as massacres and forced migration that had and continue to have long-lasting repercussions.

Contemporary Native scholars such as Brave Heart and others have coined the term *historical trauma* (HT) as a way of naming the cumulative emotional and psychological wounding, over the lifespan and across generations, emanating from massive group trauma experiences (Brave Heart, 2000, 2003, 2005; Brave Heart & DeBruyn, 1998; Crazy Thunder & Brave Heart, 2005; Grayshield & Mihecoby, 2010). As such, the *historical trauma response* (HTR) is the constellation of features in reaction to this trauma that may include substance abuse, as a vehicle for attempting to numb the pain associated with trauma, and often includes other types of self-destructive behavior, suicidal thoughts and gestures, depression, anxiety, low self-esteem, anger, and difficulty recognizing and expressing emotions (Brave Heart, 2003). Associated with HTR, according to Brave Heart, is *historical unresolved grief* that accompanies the trauma; this grief may be considered impaired, delayed, fixated, and/or disenfranchised (Brave Heart & DeBruyn, 1998).

To help illustrate, in the following excerpt a Navajo elder relates her first experience at age seven in boarding school over 40 years ago. She was unable to speak any English and had always lived on the reservation until being taken away:

It was the first time I've seen a brick building that was not a trading post. The ceilings were so high, and the rooms so big and empty. It was so cold. There was no warmth. Not as far as "Brrr, I'm cold," but in a sense of emotional cold. Kind of an emptiness, when you're hanging onto your mom's skirt and trying hard not to cry. Then when you get up to your turn, she [the teacher] thumbprints the paper and she leaves and you watch her go out the big metal doors. The whole thing was cold. The doors were metal and they even had this big window with wires running through it. You watch your mama go down the sidewalk, actually it's the first time I seen a sidewalk, and you see her get into the truck and the truck starts moving and all the home smell goes with it. You see it all leaving.

Then the woman takes you by the hand and takes you inside and the first thing they do is take down your bun. The first thing they do is cut off your hair, and you been told your whole life that you never cut your hair recklessly because that is your life. And that's the first thing them women does is cut off your hair. And you see that long, black hair drop, and it's like they take out your heart and they give you this cold thing that beats inside. And now you're gonna be just like them. You're gonna be cold. You're never gonna be happy or have that warm feeling and attitude towards life anymore. That's what it feels like, like taking your heart out and putting in a cold river pebble.

When you go into the shower, you leave your squaw skirt and blouse right there at the shower door. When you come out, it's gone. You don't see it again. They cut your hair, now they take your squaw skirt. They take from the beginning. When you first walk in there, they take everything that you're about. They jerk it away from you. They don't ask how you feel about it. They never tell you anything. They never say what they're gonna do, why they're doing it. They barely speak to you. They take everything away from you. Then you think, mama must be whackers. She wants me to be like them? Every time you don't know what they're doing, they laugh at you. They yell at you. They jerk you around. It was never what I wanted to be. I never wanted to be like them. But my mom wanted me to be like them. As I got older, I found out that you don't have to be like them. You can have a nice world and have everything that mama wanted, but you don't have to be cold. (McLaughlin, 1994, pp. 47–48)

For this elder, the boarding school experience she underwent in childhood is still very real and very vivid in her memory, carrying forward in ways that might be hard to understand. Yet her narrative represents a vivid illustration of cultural genocide and a reminder of the soul wound that many Native clients might carry (Duran, 2006; Duran et al., 2008). Across Native populations in the United States and throughout the world, boarding schools were consistently an element of the policy of forced assimilation through removal from, and denigration of, traditional culture. McLeigh (2010) enumerates the transgenerational effects of the residential schools that resulted from disruption of families and communities; confusion of parenting with punitive institutional practices; impaired emotional response (a reflection of the lack of warmth and intimacy in childhood); repetition of physical and sexual abuse; loss of knowledge, language, and tradition; and systematic devaluing of native identity.

By way of example of these effects, Grayshield and Mihecoby (2010) share their perspective of the generational impact of the boarding school experience on their own family:

> The majority of my relatives, my father's age and older, were recipients of the government boarding schools' assimilation agendas. They were subject to personal, cultural and familial cruelty. However, the vast majority of them did not strike me as angry. While the atrocities that occurred in the process of colonizing were unfounded, it appeared that the anger increased with successive generations. (p. 13)

In fact, post-colonial stress disorder (PCSD) can be seen as a form of posttraumatic stress disorder (PTSD; Duran & Duran, 1995). PCSD is a way of describing the generationally cumulative effects of the Native American experience. PCSD is a "form of ongoing trauma" resulting from forced acculturation whereby indigenous/tribal people are "constantly under extreme pressure to assimilate the lifeworld of the perpetrators of the Holocaust" (Duran & Duran, 1995, p. 32). Historical trauma, such as the impact of the boarding school experience, captures the "collective emotional and psychological injury (both over the life span and across generations) that is the product of a cataclysmic history of genocide" (McLeigh, 2010, p. 178). Accordingly, counselors must recognize and address historical trauma. Such alertness provides a starting point for the design of ethnically specific preventive and therapeutic interventions, ones that take into account the historical experience of colonization and the current social and political issues facing any given tribal community.

CURRENT SOCIAL, ECONOMIC, AND POLITICAL ISSUES

Native people continue to address a number of social and political issues that pose challenges for them as they strive to maintain their unique traditional/tribal identities while simultaneously living in the world of the dominant culture. One Native scholar stated it this way:

> We also have to exist in the non-Native world. A place where we have to dress in a certain way, go by clock time, and always are serious at work, a place where money is all that counts along with how much we earn and how we earn it. . . . I walk a fine line and keep one foot in each world. That is how it is for me. (Bonnet, 2003, p. 36)

This section offers an overall context to many of the struggles of Native people by examining issues of identity, tribal resources, treaty rights, religious freedom, mascots, gaming, and cultural preservation.

Identity

Among some of the long-term ramifications for Native people on the issue of identity are the continuing dilution of blood quantum and the survival of urban Indians. The assessment of blood quantum to determine Indian ethnicity causes much division in Indian communities. Although some tribes have modified their enrollment criteria to incorporate members who possess heritage from more than one tribe, no tribe allows enrollment in more than one tribe. The unfortunate but unavoidable reality is that some people are going to be excluded who should be included, and some people will be included who should be excluded.

Like some other ethnic groups, inclusion, via indicators of identity and traditionalism, can be the degree to which one speaks her or his native language or practices her or his cultural teachings and spirituality. In terms of language, for a scant few Native peoples English is a second language. Indigenous languages are disappearing. Thus it is well understood that indigenous language speakers are valuable resources in maintaining the cultural integrity of the tribe. The Native American Indigenous Languages Act of 1990 was enacted to allow for the continuation of indigenous languages because the rate at which they are disappearing is alarming.

Names may also say something about a Native person's identity, whether the names are anglicized or not. For some, there may be two names, one mainstream and one traditional, often based somehow on a traditional family surname or ceremonial rites of passage depending on the nation. Given the historical context in which many Native people of an older generation exist, both adoption and/or the boarding school experience may have had long-lasting effects on identity, where among many things, a Native person's original name could have been changed altogether at an early age.

Self-Determination and Sovereignty

In the United States, as mentioned previously, there are more than 565 federally recognized tribal governments that possess the right to form their own government, enforce laws (both civil and criminal), tax members, establish requirements for membership, license and regulate activities, zone areas, and exclude persons from tribal territories. Existing limitations on tribal powers of self-government include the same limitations applicable to states; for example, neither tribes nor states have the power to make war, engage in foreign relations, or coin money (including paper currency). The sovereignty that exists for Native American nations is the result of the Indian Self-Determination and Education Assistance Act passed in 1975, marking the culmination of 15 years of policy changes at that time. An outcome of Indian activism and the Red Power movement, the civil rights movement, and community development aspects of social programs of the 1960s, the act recognized the need of Native Americans for self-determination. It marked the U.S. government's movement away from the policy of termination; the U.S. government encouraged Native Americans' efforts at self-government and determining their futures that continues to this day in a variety of forms.

For most tribal communities, self-determination means they have governments that administer services like firefighting, natural resource management, law enforcement, and court systems, often reflecting various forms of moral and social authority vested in traditional affiliations within the community, to adjudicate matters related to local ordinances. In addition, to address the housing needs of Native Americans, Congress passed the Native American Housing and Self Determination Act in 1996 directed toward Indian Housing Authorities with a block grant program intended to replace earlier public housing programs dating back to 1937. These are all examples of sovereignty practiced by Native American tribes as distinct nations possessing their own governments and systems of functioning.

Federal and State Recognition

Federal recognition of American Indians and Alaska Natives is based on historical and governmental relationships involving treaties and contracts made in the past with certain tribes. Under federal laws (such as the Indian Civil Rights Act of 1968 and related federal acts and amendments), the tribes are considered sovereign, with the federal government having a trust responsibility over them.

Some tribal nations have been unable to establish their heritage and obtain federal recognition. These include many of the smaller Eastern tribes that have been applying to gain official recognition of their tribal status. This recognition brings with it some benefits, including the right to label arts and crafts as Native American and permission to apply for grants that are specifically reserved for Native Americans. However, gaining recognition as a tribe is extremely difficult and includes the requirement to submit extensive genealogical proof of tribal descent as well as continuous existence as a tribe since 1900.

In addition to the 565 federally recognized nations, there are a number of tribes that are recognized by individual states but not by the federal government. The rights and benefits associated with state recognition vary from state to state. State recognition is based on tribal organizations located within specific state boundaries, which is based on historical and mutual relationships established by state legislatures or executive actions by state governors. For example, North Carolina has established the North Carolina Indian Commission, with representation from the state and federally recognized tribes within its jurisdiction. Other states, such as Maine, South Carolina, and Georgia, have recognized tribes within their jurisdiction with commissions or staff in the governor's office or another administrative office to deal with Native concerns.

Indian Education Policy and the Achievement Gap

The impact that the American education system has had on Native American people, their families, and their tribal communities has had devastating effects. The original goal of Indian education was summed up best by Henry Pratt, who established the most famous government boarding school, called Carlisle Indian School, in 1879. Pratt's motto was "Kill the Indian, save the man" (M. T. Garrett & Pichette, 2000).

Research regarding the formal education of Native American students suggests that the traditional value orientation of these students remains in constant conflict with the value orientation upon which U.S. school systems function (Capriccioso, 2005; Charleston, 1994; Garcia & Ahler, 1992;

M. T. Garrett & Portman, 2011; Grande, 2004; Little Soldier, 1992; Marsiglia, Cross, & Mitchell, 1998; Shutiva, 2001; Simmons & Barrineau, 1994). Thus, these students often experience poor academic achievement, poor self-concept, low self-esteem, and higher rates of educational attrition (Brandt, 1992; Colodarci, 1983; Deyhle, 1992; M. T. Garrett & Portman, 2011; M. T. Garrett et al., 2009; Hornett, 1990; Marsiglia et al, 1998; Mitchum, 1989; Radda, Iwamoto, & Patrick, 1998; Swisher, Hoisch, & Pavel, 1991). Native American students have dropout rates twice the national average—the highest rate of any U.S. ethnic or racial group (Capriccioso, 2005; M. T. Garrett & Portman, 2011; Radda et al., 1998). Boredom in school and difficulty with teacher and peer relationships are among a few of the reasons for Native American high school students dropping out before graduation (Brandt, 1992; Capriccioso, 2005; Colodarci, 1983; Deyhle, 1992; M. T. Garrett et al., 2009). These statistics suggest that both the quality of relational interactions in schools and the content and presentation of curricula play important roles in the degree of cultural conflict experienced by Native American students.

Overcoming generations of historical trauma due to the boarding school experience and government oversight with the tribal school experience, many tribes are making specific efforts to incorporate culturally based learning such as language immersion, tribal cultural arts and crafts, storytelling traditions, and mentoring by elders into regular classrooms and into the overall curriculum with successful results. Overall, it has become increasingly clear that if policymakers do not pay specific attention to cultural and traditional ways of teaching Native American students, the achievement gap will continue to widen, with serious implications for the well-being of Native communities throughout the United States.

BARRIERS TO ECONOMIC DEVELOPMENT

According to a 2007 survey by the U.S. Small Business Administration, only 1% of Native Americans own and operate a business. Native Americans rank at the bottom of nearly every social statistic: highest teen suicide rate of all minorities, highest teen pregnancy rate, highest high school dropout rate at around 54%, lowest per capita income, and unemployment rates between 50% to 90%. Today, these numbers are very telling when it comes to understanding that many tribes struggle economically, except for tribes that have managed to successfully develop and run casinos. It should be noted that some tribes have had success with gaming as a means of economic development. However, only 40% of the 562 federally recognized tribes operate casinos. The reality is that Native Americans are the most impoverished of all ethnic groups. Among some of the economic barriers that exist on Native American reservations are the following:

- lack of access to capital
- lack of human capital (education, skills, technical expertise) and the means to develop it
- lack of effective planning
- reservation lands poor in natural resources
- reservations with natural resources, but tribes often lacking sufficient control over those resources
- reservations being disadvantaged by their distance from markets and the high costs of transportation
- tribes not being able to persuade investors to locate on reservations because of intense competition from non-Native communities
- entrepreneurial skills and experience as well as programs to foster these skills and experience often being scarce

In spite of the barriers that exist, many tribes have focused energy and resources on social and cultural preservation programs, such as language immersion schools and cultural arts programs, that also include elements of economic growth and development as well as educational opportunities for the younger generations.

Gaming

Native American gaming operations in the form of casinos and/or bingo halls create a stream of revenue that those communities have been using as leverage to build diversified economies. Although the gaming industry has become a major source of income and economic development for many Native American nations as well as controversy and scandal for some, the challenge for many tribes at this point is how to maintain positive revenue streams, and plan for the future so that the growth continues in a positive way, to benefit the people beyond a limited number of extremely successful tribes that have chosen to participate in gaming. Unfortunately, the vast majority of tribal casinos are not very financially successful, particularly those in the Midwest and Great Plains. Many tribes have viewed this limited financial success as being tempered by slight decreases in reservation unemployment and poverty rates, although other socioeconomic deficits have persisted. Overall, many tribal governments have seen substantial improvements in their ability to provide public services to their members due to new or increased revenues that result in the ability to build schools, create community-based programs, improve infrastructure, and fund various social programs such as efforts aimed at cultural preservation.

Tribal Resources

When considering tribal resources, it is first important to understand what is the most important environmental and spiritual resource from a Native perspective—the land. Although most of the Native population resides in urban areas, reservations, which are lands set aside by the federal government at various points in history for tribes based on treaty agreements, continue to be the primary center of Native traditionalism and cultural preservation. There are over 311 federally recognized reservations in the United States, totaling approximately 55 million acres. However, 11 million acres (20%) within reservation boundaries are owned by non-Indians. Despite some gains, many tribes are locked in heated legal battles with the government and private interests to maintain and protect treaty-based rights to their homelands and sacred sites that are continually being encroached upon by outside interests.

Treaty Rights

As mentioned previously, another current issue faced by many tribes/nations is that of protecting treaty rights. One controversial example is the fishing rights of Native people in both the Pacific Northwest and the Great Lakes area of Michigan, Minnesota, and Wisconsin. In both instances, tribes have resorted to "fish-ins" that defy state law but that are in accordance with Indian treaty rights with the U.S. government. One of the most controversial topics to hit the media in recent times is the whaling rights of tribes in the Pacific Northwest. Strong opposition has come from state agencies, non-Native fisherman, conservationists, and environmentalists and has only added to the strain already placed on tribes by an increased influx of people, more industry, and more recreation in many of those areas.

Religious Freedom

Passage of the American Indian Religious Freedom Act of 1978 guaranteed religious freedom for Native people in this country for the first time in a century. Symbolic of this religious freedom is another key piece of legislation, the "eagle feather law" (Title 50 Part 22 of the Code of Federal Regulations), which stipulates that only individuals of certifiable Native American ancestry enrolled in a federally recognized tribe are legally authorized to obtain eagle feathers for religious or spiritual use.

Sacred Sites

Traditional Native practices are inseparably bound to the land and natural formations that exist in whatever geographic location a tribe occupies. Native people have sacred places and go to these sacred places to pray, fast, seek visions, conduct ceremonies, receive guidance from spirit guides, and teach youth the traditional ways. Unfortunately, many of the sacred sites revered by Native people do not exist under their control, but instead are under the control of federal agencies intent on using the land for the purpose of tourism development, clear-cutting, and uranium mining. Many legal efforts are being undertaken by tribes across the country to protect and preserve not only the sacred sites on which their culture is based, but also their very way of life from generations past.

Repatriation and Reburial

Among the many sacred sites disturbed or destroyed by such things as erosion and flooding, plowing, urban development, road building, land clearing, logging, and vandalism have been the ancient graves of Native people. Perhaps worst of all has been the desecration of Native graves by pothunters and vandals seeking to loot those graves for objects that are valued in national and international markets. Native people have persevered through the passage of critical legislation that now protects Native gravesites from looting and provides Native people with legal means for reclaiming both remains and sacred objects. Many of these remains and objects have been ceremonially returned to their original sites when possible under the careful guidance and blessing of tribal elders and Medicine people.

Mascot Issues

As many tribes/nations continue to move toward increased sovereignty and consequent pride in their ethnicity, land and natural resources are only part of the concern. A constant source of controversy between Native and non-Native peoples in both the United States and Canada has been sports mascots depicting Native people in a derogatory manner. Americans have a long history of "playing Indian" that dates back to at least the 18th century and has tended to be based on stereotypical, romanticized images of the heroic Native American warrior. For the most part, Native mascot images fall into one of two categories: the hostile, warlike Indian or the dopey, clown-like figure with headdress, big nose, red skin, and big lips, among other stereotypical features. As such, many Native Americans and human rights groups think that the use of Indian mascots is both offensive and demeaning. The question remains, in a day and age where social mores and laws exist to protect the dignity and basic human rights of all groups of peoples, why is it still acceptable to exploit images of Native people in this way?

Professional, college, and high school sports teams across the country have been challenged to do away with stereotypical, racist images of Native people as mascots. Prominent examples include baseball's Atlanta Braves and Cleveland Indians, football's Washington Redskins, and college sports' Florida State University Seminoles. While many universities (e.g., North Dakota Fighting Sioux of University of North Dakota) and professional sports teams (e.g., Chief Wahoo of Cleveland Indians) no longer use such images without consultation with Native American nations, some lower level schools' sports teams continue to do so. Native people and Native American rights advocates in many places have become increasingly outspoken, demanding the same respect, both socially and legally, that is paid to other cultural and racial groups in the United States.

Cultural Preservation

Increased sovereignty for many Native nations also means increased control over the way that cultural resources are maintained and preserved. In many Native nations and communities across the country, huge efforts are being made to preserve culture by developing programs both in and outside of the schools to teach Native youth such things as traditional arts and crafts, the language, ceremonies and prayers, songs and chants, as well as dance. This cultural appreciation impulse lies in distinct contrast to the previously accepted mainstream notion of only one or two generations ago that "civilizing" Indians was essential. That "civilizing" was done through mandated largely Christian, government-supported Indian boarding schools whose primary objective was to strip Native youth of any cultural Indian foundation. While many issues remain regarding how federal and state governments relate with Native Americans, tribes are preserving their cultural heritage, traditions, and language in many ways through family and community programs. Almost every tribe has some type of program in education, health, community, and religious activities to encourage pride in and preservation of their tribal traditions.

LIVING NATIVE WAYS: CULTURAL VALUES

Although acculturation plays a major role in the Native American worldview, there tends to be a high degree of psychological homogeneity, a certain degree of shared cultural standards and meanings, based on common core values that exist for traditional Native Americans across tribal groups.

Common core values that characterize Native traditionalism are the importance of community contribution, sharing, acceptance, cooperation, harmony and balance, noninterference, extended family, attention to nature, immediacy of time, awareness of the relationship, and a deep respect for elders (Dufrene, 1990; J. T. Garrett, 2001; J. T. Garrett & Garrett, 1996; M. T. Garrett 1996a, 1998, 1999b; M. T. Garrett & Garrett, 2003; Heinrich et al., 1990; Herring, 1999; Hunter & Sawyer, 2006; Kawulich, 2008; Little Soldier, 1992; Plank, 1994; Red Horse, 1997; Rybak, Eastin, & Robbins, 2004). These traditional values reveal the importance of honoring, through harmony and balance, what Native people believe to be a very sacred connection with the energy of life and the whole of biodiversity; this is the basis for a traditional Native worldview and spirituality across tribal nations (see Table 8.1). Several of the dominant Native values—humility, generosity, patience, time, being, spirituality, and the sacredness of the eagle feather—are highlighted in the following sections.

Humility

Boasting of one's accomplishments and loud behavior that attracts attention to oneself are discouraged in the traditional way. In the traditional value system, self-absorption and self-importance are seen as bringing disharmony upon oneself and one's family. In the life circle, the group must take precedence over the individual. And, as discussed earlier, the wisdom of age takes precedence over youth, although age does not make anyone better or more worthy than anyone else. Many times, a traditional Native person may drop her or his head and eyes or at least be careful not to look into the eyes of another as a sign of respect for any elder or other honored person. No one is worthy of staring into the eyes of an elder or looking into the spirit of that honored person. This deferential behavior is also an act that signifies that a person does not view herself or himself as better than anyone else.

Generosity

Traditional Native views concerning property accentuate the underlying belief that whatever belongs to the individual also belongs to the group and vice versa. It should come as no surprise to see Native people sharing and/or giving "their possessions" away to others in certain circumstances such as giveaway ceremonies practiced by many nations. Generosity is considered a sign of wisdom and humility.

Patience

In the Native worldview, everything has its place. Very often, it is simply a matter of time before one recognizes where and how things fit together. In Native traditions, there is a sacred design to the world in which humans live, a design to the process of life itself. And, very often, it is not a matter of whether "things" fall into place, but whether humans' capacity for *awareness and understanding of "things"* falls into place. It is therefore important to be able to learn through careful observation, listening, and patience as well as to ask questions or think things through. Everything offers humans a valuable lesson, from all of one's surroundings to each of one's experiences. It takes time and a special kind of willingness or openness to receive all of the lessons that are offered throughout life. Many Native elders will share with younger people how important it is to talk less so you can hear more, for example.

Table 8.1 Comparison of Cultural Values and Expectations

Traditional Native American	Contemporary Mainstream American
Harmony with nature	Power over nature
Cooperation	Competition
Group needs more important than individual needs	Personal goals considered important
Privacy and noninterference; try to control self, not others	Need to control and affect others
Self-discipline both in body and in mind	Self-expression and self-disclosure
Participation after observation (only when certain of ability)	Trial-and-error learning; new skills practiced until they are mastered
Explanation according to nature	Scientific explanation for everything
Reliance on extended family	Reliance on experts
Emotional relationships valued	Concerned mostly with facts
Patience encouraged (allow others to go first)	Aggressive and competitive
Humility	Fame and recognition; winning
Win once, let others win also	Win first prize all of the time
Follow the old ways	Climb the ladder of success; importance of progress and change
Discipline distributed among many; no one person takes blame	Blame one person at cost to others
Physical punishment rare	Physical punishment accepted
Present-time focus	Future-time focus
Time is always with us, things happen in their own time	Clock-watching
Present goals considered important; future accepted as it comes	Plan for future and how to get ahead
Encourage sharing freely and keeping only enough to satisfy present needs	Private property; encourage acquisition of material comfort and saving for the future
Speak softly, at a slower rate	Speak louder and faster
Avoid singling out the listener	Address listener directly (by name)
Interject less	Interrupt frequently
Use fewer "encouraging signs"	Use verbal encouragement (*uh-huh*, head nodding)
Delayed response to auditory messages	Immediate response
Nonverbal communication	Verbal skills highly prized

Source: Adapted from M. T. Garrett & Pichette (2000).

Time

In the traditional Indian view, humans do not always have to live by the clock. Mother Earth has her own unique rhythms that signal the beginnings and endings of things. One need only observe and listen quietly to know when it is time. So-called Indian time says that things begin when they are ready and things end when they are finished. For example, a ceremony or gathering might be set to begin at sunrise, per se, rather than a specific "clock time," and end whenever sufficient time has been spent to complete what needed to be done. In that sense, the American Indian view of time is similar to that of all rural people over the world, where tasks and natural rhythms dictate time.

Being

Native tradition ("the Medicine Way") emphasizes a unique sense of "being" that allows one to live in accord with the natural flow of life-energy. The notion of being communicates, "It's enough just to be; our purpose in life is to develop the inner self in relation to everything around us." Being receives much of its power from connectedness. Belonging and connectedness lie at the very heart of where Indian people came from, who they are, and to whom they belong. True being requires that individuals know and experience their connections and that they honor their relations with all their heart. So for many traditional Native people, the relationship with someone is much more important than any personal accomplishment, and as a result, the strength of a person's inner peace and presence in the here and now would say more to a traditional Native person than anything else.

Spirituality

As a result of the historical context, in which Christianity has had so much influence on Native communities and nations, it should come as no surprise that Native people may ascribe to and practice Christianity and any number of religious belief systems, in place of or even along with traditional tribal systems. Overall, however, it is important to understand traditional Native spirituality as a basic frame of reference (Hunter & Sawyer, 2006; Rybak et al., 2004).

The spiritual beliefs of any individual Native American depend on a number of factors, including her or his level of acculturation (traditional, marginal, bicultural, assimilated, pantraditional), geographic region, family structure, religious influences, and tribally specific traditions (M. T. Garrett & Pichette, 2000; M. T. Garrett & Portman, 2011; M. T. Garrett et al., 2009; LaFromboise et al., 1993). However, it is possible to generalize, to some extent, about a number of basic beliefs characterizing Native American traditionalism and spirituality across tribal nations.

In order to better understand more generally what it means to "walk in step," that is to live a life that respects and focuses on harmony and balance with oneself, one's family and community, one's natural surroundings, and one's universal circle, according to Native American spirituality, it is important to discuss four basic cultural elements: medicine, harmony, relation, and vision (M. T. Garrett & Wilbur, 1999).

Medicine: Everything Is Alive

In many Native American tribal languages there is no word for religion because spiritual practices are an integral part of every aspect of daily life, which is necessary for the harmony and balance, or wellness, of individual, family, clan, and community (M. T. Garrett & Garrett, 2002; M. T. Garrett, Garrett, & Brotherton, 2001; M. T. Garrett, Torres-Rivera, et al., 2011). Healing and worship are considered as one and the same. For Native American people, the concept of health and wellness is not only a physical state, but a spiritual one as well. Medicine, as a Native concept, implies the very essence of our being, or the life force that exists in all creatures on Mother Earth (Deloria, 2006; J. T. Garrett & Garrett, 1996; M. T. Garrett & Garrett, in press; M. T. Garrett, Torres Rivera, et al., 2011; Hunter & Sawyer, 2006; Rybak et al., 2004). In the traditional way, Medicine can consist of physical remedies such as herbs, teas, and poultices for physical ailments, but Medicine is simultaneously something much more than a pill taken to cure illness, get rid of pain, or correct a physiological malfunction. Medicine is everywhere. It is that which gives inner power.

Harmony: Everything Has Purpose

Every living organism has a reason for being. Traditional Native Americans look upon life as a gift from the Creator. As such, it is to be treated with the utmost care out of respect for the giver. This means living in a humble way and giving thanks for all of the gifts that one receives every day, no matter how big or small. Harmony is also represented by numbers. Native American spirituality often places great emphasis on the numbers four and seven. The number four represents the spirit of each of the directions—east, south, west, and north—usually depicted in a circle. The number seven represents the same four directions as well as the upper world (Sky), lower world (Earth), and center (often referring to the heart, or sacred fire) to symbolize universal harmony and balance (visualized as a sphere). In the traditional way, Native people seek to understand what lessons are offered to them by giving thanks to each of the four directions for the wisdom, guidance, strength, and clarity that they receive. Not every tribe practices the directions in this way, but almost all tribes have some representation of the four directions as a circular symbol of the harmony and balance of mind, body, and spirit with the natural environment (and spirit world; see Figure 8.1).

Relation: All Things Are Connected

Central to Native American spiritual traditions is the importance of *relation* as a total way of existing in the world. The concept of family extends to brothers and sisters in the animal world, the plant world, the mineral world, Mother Earth, and Father Sky, to name some examples. Respect for Medicine also means practicing respect for the interconnection that humans share. Across tribal nations, certain natural or social laws must be observed out of respect for relation. These often point to

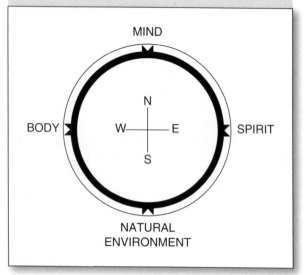

Figure 8.1 Medicine Circle Representing the Four Directions

restrictions on personal conduct in relation to such things as death, incest, the female menstrual cycle, witchcraft, certain animals, certain natural phenomena, certain foods, marrying into one's own clan, and strict observance of ceremonial protocol (Deloria, 2006; M. T. Garrett & Portman, 2011; Locust, 1988). A general rule of thumb in Native tradition is that you (a) never take more than you need, (b) give thanks for what you have or what you receive, (c) take great care to use all of what you do have, and (d) give away what you do not need (or what someone else may need more than you do). An example of this tradition is put into practice when a spiritual person searches for particular herbs or medicines in the natural environment and must do so following these basic tenets and with the right intent in order to be successful.

Vision: Embrace the Medicine of Every Living Being

Across tribal nations, many different ceremonies are used for healing, giving thanks, celebrating, clearing the way, and blessing (Lake, 1991). Among the various ceremonies are the sweat lodge, vision quest, clearing-way ceremony, blessing-way ceremony, pipe ceremony, sunrise ceremony, and sundance (Deloria, 2006; M. T. Garrett, Torres-Rivera, et al., 2011; Heinrich et al., 1990; Lake, 1991; Rybak et al., 2004). One of the functions of ceremonial practice is to reaffirm one's sense of connection with that which is sacred. By contrast, a major tenet of American mainstream ideology is that the purpose of life consists of "life, liberty, and the pursuit of happiness." From a traditional Native perspective, a corollary would be "life, love, and the pursuit of harmony." Understanding one's vision is understanding the direction of one's path as a caretaker moving to the rhythm of the sacred heartbeat. As Black Elk, Oglala Lakota Medicine Man, put it in referring to the many trials and tribulations of his life-journey, "The good road and the road of difficulties, you have made me cross; and where they cross, the place is holy" (quoted in M. T. Garrett, 1998, p. 85).

The following, adapted from Locust (1988, pp. 317–318), lists a number of basic Native American spiritual and traditional beliefs. It is by no means a comprehensive list. It does, however, provide insight into some of the assumptions that may be held by a "traditional" Native client.

1. There is a single higher power known as Creator, Great Creator, Great Spirit, or Great One, among other names (this being is sometimes referred to in gender form, but does not necessarily exist as one particular gender or another). There are also lesser beings known as "spirit beings" or "spirit helpers."

2. Plants and animals, like humans, are part of the spirit world. The spirit world exists side by side with, and intermingles with, the physical world. Moreover, the spirit existed in the spirit world before it came into a physical body and will exist after the body dies.

3. Human beings are made up of a spirit, mind, and body, all of which are interconnected; therefore, illness affects the mind and spirit as well as the body.

4. Wellness is harmony in body, mind, and spirit; unwellness is disharmony in body, mind, and spirit.

5. Natural unwellness is caused by the violation of a sacred social or natural law of Creation (e.g.,

participating in a sacred ceremony while under the influence of alcohol or drugs, or having had sex within 4 days of the ceremony).

6. Unnatural unwellness is caused by conjuring (witchcraft) from those with destructive intentions.

7. Each of us is responsible for our own wellness by keeping ourselves attuned to self, relations, environment, and universe.

Eagle Feathers and Eagle Medicine

Eagle feathers are considered to be infinitely sacred among Native Americans. These feathers are used for a variety of purposes, including ceremonial healing and purification. Native traditionalists refer to Eagle Medicine, which represents a state of being achieved through diligence, understanding, awareness, and completion of tests of initiation such as the vision quest or other demanding life experiences (Deloria, 2006; M. T. Garrett & Garrett, in press; M. T. Garrett & Osborne, 1995; M. T. Garrett, Torres-Rivera, et al., 2011; Rybak et al., 2004). Highly respected elder status is associated with Eagle Medicine and the power of connectedness and truth. It is through experience and patience that this Medicine is earned over a lifetime. And it is through understanding and choice that it is honored. There is an old anecdote that probably best illustrates the lessons of the eagle feather by reminding us about the power of perspective: "Once while acting as a guide for a hunting expedition, an Indian had lost the way home. One of the men with him said, 'You're lost, chief.' The Indian guide replied, 'I'm not lost, my tipi is lost.'"

The Eagle feather represents duality in existence. It tells the story of life by symbolizing harmony and balance through which life has been able to persist. It tells of the many dualities or opposites that exist in the Circle of Life, such as light and dark, male and female, substance and shadow, summer and winter, life and death, peace and war (M. T. Garrett & Myers, 1996; M. T. Garrett & Portman, 2011).

The Eagle feather has both light and dark colors, dualities and opposites. Though one can make a choice to argue which of the colors is most beautiful or most valuable, the truth is that both colors come from the same feather, both are true, both are connected, and it takes both to fly (J. T. Garrett & Garrett, 1996; M. T. Garrett & Portman, 2011). The colors are opposite, but they are part of the same truth. The importance of the feather lies not in which color is most beautiful, but in finding out and accepting what the purpose of the feather as a whole may be. In other words, there is no such thing as keeping the mountains and getting rid of the valleys; they are one and the same, and they exist because of one another. As one elder puts it:

> The Eagle feather teaches about the Rule of Opposites, about everything being divided into two ways. The more one is caught up in the physical, or the West, then the more one has to go in the opposite direction, the East, or the spiritual, to get balance. And it works the other way too—you can't just focus on the spiritual to the exclusion of the physical. You need harmony in all Four Directions. (J. T. Garrett, 1991, p. 173)

COMMUNICATION STYLE

Native interaction style emphasizes nonverbal communication over verbal communication. Moderation in speech and avoidance of direct eye contact are nonverbal communicators of respect for the listener, especially if it is a respected elder or anyone in a position of authority (M. T. Garrett, 1996a; M. T. Garrett & Portman, 2011). Careful listening and observation are exercised to understand more of what is meant and less of what is actually said. Storytelling is commonly used to express feelings, beliefs, and the importance of experience (Deloria, 2006; M. T. Garrett & Garrett, 1997). Oral recitation is common. It is a time when listeners are expected to be silent, patient, and reflective.

In an attempt to be respectful of harmony, traditional Native people practice self-discipline through silence, modesty, and patience. Direct confrontation is avoided as it disrupts the harmony and balance that are essential in keeping good relations. There are believed to be more effective ways to deal with discrepancies and dissatisfaction. Cooperation and sharing, as a reflection of harmony, are an important part of interacting with others. By contrast, individuals in the dominant American culture are rewarded for being outgoing and assertive. Such behaviors as asking questions, interrupting, speaking for others, telling others what to do, or arguing are fairly common in mainstream society. These behaviors severely contradict what traditional Native people have been taught are respectful and appropriate ways of interacting with others (BigFoot & Funderburk, 2011; M. T. Garrett, 1995).

Indian Humor

Contrary to the stereotypical belief that Native people are solemn, stoic figures posed against a backdrop of tepees, tomahawks, and headdresses, the fact is that Native Americans, generally and culturally speaking, love to laugh (J. T. Garrett & Garrett, 1994; M. T. Garrett, Garrett, Wilbur, Roberts-Wilbur, & Torres-Rivera, 2005; Maples et al., 2001). Indeed, humor is a critical part of the culture, especially around mealtime. A transformation occurs when Native Americans come together around food—everyone is laughing, cutting up, sharing side-splitting stories, and teasing each other. Many tribal oral traditions emphasize important life lessons through the subtle humor expressed in the stories. Laughter plays a very important role in the continued survival of the tribal communities. After all, laughter relieves stress and creates an atmosphere of sharing and connectedness.

MENTAL HEALTH ISSUES AND COUNSELING NATIVE AMERICANS

Now that the nature of traditional forms of everyday Native communication and interaction have been explored, we turn to a discussion of contemporary interventions and treatment modalities involved in culturally alert counseling with this population.

Native Strengths and Challenges

Although Native Americans face obstacles, this population also possesses many strengths that have helped them survive overwhelming adversity over generations. Natives have been the target of racism, forced relocation, and genocide (Brave Heart & DeBruyn, 1998). Today, this population is not just surviving, but thriving in many areas (see Table 8.2) as evidenced by statistics that indicate nearly 55% of all Native Americans own their own home, over 70% age 25 and older have at least a high school diploma, and over 11% have a bachelor's degree (Goodluck, 2002). In fact, 42 specific strengths of Native Americans have been named across three categories: extended family, spirituality, and social connections (Goodluck, 2002). These are significant to acknowledge in an entire body of literature about Native people that tends to focus on implicit struggles and obstacles rather than cultural strength and resilience.

The struggles that Native adults endure continue, and the need for appropriate, effective, culturally responsive help is pervasive. Much of the literature on Native Americans emphasizes the high-risk behaviors of many individuals in this population and the negative consequences that these behaviors have on physical and mental health. Likewise, counselors and social workers who work with this population often focus on "fixing" the maladaptive behaviors their Native clients struggle to overcome rather than considering a more holistic perspective that might include cultural, environmental, and historical influences. It is suggested that new theories and perspectives be adopted to facilitate a shift from addressing the negative aspects of Native Americans in the direction of counseling theory that is consistent with this population's traditions and has a more hopeful viewpoint (Neumann, Mason, Chase, & Albaugh, 1991).

Native American health care needs from U.S. government statistics indicate that high mortality rates due to alcoholism, accidents, suicide, and homicide are greater than for the overall U.S. population (Indian Health Service, 1997). Mental health issues are the fourth leading cause of hospitalization among American Indians 15 to 44 years of age and the fifth leading cause for ambulatory visits for indigenous peoples 25 to 44 years of age (Provan & Carson, 2000).

Originally, the federal government established a program to provide health services to Native American peoples through a treaty. However, today these Indian Health Service (IHS) facilities are located primarily near recognized Native American Indian communities in states with large Native American populations. Prevention, treatment, and rehabilitation services are offered, including mental health and referral services (Pfefferbaum, Pfefferbaum, Rhoades, & Strickland, 1997).

Contemporary Counseling Interventions for Native Americans

The tension between cultural and individual understandings of clients must be reiterated here. In order to work most effectively with members of this population, it is important to understand the nature of the cultural experience from which they come, but also to remember how important it is to see the uniqueness of each and every client. The cultural dimension, which is emphasized here, allows the counselor to better conceptualize current issues in a cultural context and select methods of approaching that client and issue(s) so that cultural values, beliefs, practices, and experiences are used as strengths and valuable resources for the client.

In working with most Native American clients, counselors should attend to two early-assessment factors: (1) assessing the extent to which the process of acculturation has affected the client's cultural identity and (2) understanding the influence of oppression on her or his experience and current presenting issues (Robinson-Wood, 2009).

Table 8.2 Summary of Information on Native Americans

Demographics	Strengths	Challenges	Recommendations
Total population • Approximately 2.8 million self-identified Native Americans (1.7 million enrolled tribal members; 770,000 nonenrolled people) • Represents roughly 1% of the total U.S. population	Extended family • Group belonging • Relational focus • Personal relationships • Honoring and caring for elders • Sense of community and common history	Health, education, and economic disparities • Alcoholism rate two times that of general population • 52% finish high school • 75% of the Native American work force earns less than $7,000 per year	Develop new theories • Literature tends to emphasize high-risk behaviors and negative consequences on physical and mental health • Practitioners often focus on "fixing" maladaptive behaviors rather than considering more holistic perspective, including cultural, environmental, and historical influences • New theories can be adopted to shift from negative aspects to perspective consistent with Native culture and traditions
Nations • More than 565 federally recognized tribes/nations • 228 of these are located in Alaska • Several hundred state-recognized tribes/nations	Social connections • Helping each other • Artistic behaviors and valuing of creative expression • Sharing work • Caring for each other	Intergenerational grief and trauma • United States did not recognize citizenship of Native Americans until 1924 • Native Americans were not granted religious freedom until 1978 through the American Indian Religious Freedom Act • Government-supported, religiously run boarding schools and relocation programs of 1950s	Understand help-seeking behaviors • Studies have revealed perception of help-seeking outside of the Native communities as a sign of weakness • Many Native Americans seek help through traditional healing practices if available • Acculturation and tribal affiliation must be understood as context; more insight into acculturation is needed when considering Native Americans living in rural, urban, or suburban geographic contexts

Demographics	Strengths	Challenges	Recommendations
Location/language • 78% of total Native population lives in urban areas • 22% lives in rural areas or on any of the 314 federally recognized reservations and 46 state-recognized reservations • Approximately 252 different languages	Spirituality • Emphasis on harmony and balance • Tribal affiliation • Kinship • Tribal identity • Traditions	Current social and political issues • Identity/blood quantum • Natural resources/treaty rights • Religious freedom • Mascot issues and cultural perception • Gaming • Cultural/language preservation	Explore systemic, environmental, and other contextual factors • Historical factors • Isolation • Generational splits • Sociodemographics • Physiology and health • Social facilitation • Coping mechanisms • Noninterference and respect

Identity, Family, and Acculturation

A first step in the counseling relationship, and a sign of respect, lies in the counselor's finding out from which tribe the client comes, and possibly whether that person is directly affiliated with that tribe (federal, state, and/or community recognition). It is not the job of the counselor to pass judgment on who is Indian and who is not. Thus a counselor should not ask a Native client "how much Indian" she or he is or relate personal stories of Indian heritage in her or his family as a way of connecting with that client. That is often a quick way to lose a Native person's receptivity and trust. If a client says that she or he is Native, then a counselor must assume that it is so. This acceptance of client's self-report is a way to understand her or him without having to get into the painful (and sometimes irrelevant) politics of categorization. More important, it gives the counselor insight into that person's perception of her or his experience and place in the world.

When working with a Native client, it is important to get a sense of that person's level of acculturation. This sense can be gotten by the counselor's informally assessing the client's (a) values (traditional, marginal, bicultural, assimilated, pantraditional), (b) geographic origin/residence (reservation, rural, urban), and (c) tribal affiliation (tribal structure, customs, beliefs); for further

discussion of formal and informal assessment of Native American acculturation, see M. T. Garrett & Pichette (2000).

Both verbal and nonverbal cues will give counselors a good sense of a Native American client's level of acculturation (J. T. Garrett & Garrett, 1994; M. T. Garrett & Pichette, 2000; Scholl, 2006). If questions remain, it is important to pose them in a respectful, unobtrusive way. Following are some examples of general leads intended to respectfully elicit important culturally relevant information:

• Where do you come from?
• Tell me about your family, clan, and/or community.
• What tribe/nation are you? Tell me a little bit about that.
• Tell me about you as a person, culturally and spiritually.
• Tell me how you identify yourself culturally.
• Tell me how your culture/spirituality plays into how you live your life.
• Tell me about your life as you see it, past, present, or future.

To further determine acculturation and subsequent worldview, the counselor should gather information on the family history and structure, as well as on community of origin versus community of choice. As mentioned earlier, one cannot assume because a person "looks Indian" that she or he is traditional in her or his cultural and spiritual ways, or that because a person "does not look Indian" she or he is not culturally traditional. Instead, it is important to explore the meaning of the core values and beliefs that characterize what it means to be Native for any given client.

Healing From Historical Trauma and the Impact of Oppression

The second assessment issue that a counselor should attend to is the influence of oppression on the client. Given the historical and current context of social and political issues facing Native people, a major underlying, and ongoing, issue in counseling for most Native clients is trust versus mistrust, as it is with many oppressed peoples (Grayshield & Mihecoby, 2010). The question that the counselor must ask herself or himself is, "What can I do to create and maintain trust with a Native client?" Chapter 18 presents ways of establishing trust when cultural differences exist.

It may be time well spent to ask the client to relate experiences that have had an impact on her or his life for better or for worse. Counselors can ask where the client is from and, likewise, where her or his family is from as well. Counselors might further ask what are some of the experiences across generations that have impacted the client and helped to shape how she or he sees the world. Specifically, counselors should inquire as to what ways might family and intergenerational history be playing into what has brought the client in for services.

One model useful in both prevention and intervention programs is the Historical Trauma and Unresolved Grief Intervention (HTUG), which addresses risk and protective factors for substance abuse through group trauma and psychoeducational interventions that seek to restore attachment to traditional values (Brave Heart, 2000, 2003, 2005; Brave Heart & DeBruyn, 1998; Crazy Thunder & Brave Heart, 2005). Intervention goals are congruent with PTSD treatment in which a sense of mastery and control are transmitted (Brave Heart, 2003) in a traditional retreat-like setting, providing a safe, affectively containing milieu. Participants in the HTUG model are exposed to content, through audiovisual materials, that stimulates historically traumatic memories; this is done to provide opportunities for cognitive integration of the trauma as well as affective cathartic working through, which is necessary for healing (Brave Heart, 2003). Small- and large-group processing provide occasions for increasing capacity to tolerate and regulate emotions, trauma mastery, and at least short-term amelioration of HTR. Traditional prayer and ceremonies, incorporated throughout the intervention as feasible, afford emotional containment and increased connection to indigenous values and a pretraumatic tribal past. Purification ceremonies have been observed as having a curative effect in PTSD treatment (Brave Heart, 2003, 2005).

Preliminary research on the HTUG model and on its integration into parenting sessions indicated that there was (a) a beginning trauma and grief resolution, including a decrease in hopelessness as well as an increase in joy; (b) an increase in positive tribal identity; (c) an increase in protective factors and a decrease in risk factors for substance abuse; (d) perceived improved parental relationships with children and family relationships across generations; and (e) perceived improvement in parenting skills, family connections, and sensitivity to one's children (Brave Heart, 2000). By educating themselves about the history of tribes from which Native clients come and cutting-edge treatment modalities such as HTUG, counselors can better understand the impact of institutional racism and acculturation as well as the meaning of the Native American experience for any given client, and they can begin the process of healing in a way that incorporates culture as a central focus.

Drawing on Traditions

In contrast to many of the traditional Native values and beliefs discussed herein, mainstream American values tend to emphasize self-promotion, saving for the future, domination of others, accomplishment, competition, individualism and the nuclear family, mastery over nature, a time orientation toward living for the future, a preference for scientific explanations, time-consciousness, winning, and reverence for youth (M. T. Garrett, 1995, 1999a, 1999b; M. T. Garrett & Garrett, in press; Hunter & Sawyer, 2006; Kawulich, 2008; Rybak et al., 2004). Each of these values contrasts to Native ones. For Native people, there is great potential for cultural conflict due to a clash of values with those of the larger society. Therefore, exploration of cultural conflicts itself may be an important goal for counseling.

Native clients can be encouraged to talk about the meaning of family, clan, or tribe as a way of exploring worldview, especially in light of intergenerational differences or the effects of oppression or presenting issues. Once again, as mentioned previously, counselors must ask themselves, "What can I do to create and maintain trust with a Native client and create a deeper understanding of her or his individual needs?" Counselors should think about some of the traditional Native values, beliefs, experiences, and traditions related so far in this chapter. They should ask themselves which of these their client holds and in what ways they are played out in her or his life. Further, counselors should consider how to build on their knowledge of these values, beliefs, experiences, and traditions in order to show understanding, develop rapport, and match interventions.

Integrating Spirituality

A counselor must recognize the vast diversity of spiritual traditions and customs that can be tribally specific, ones that may also be influenced by or replaced by forms of Christianity or other belief systems. It may be important to let the client describe what she or he needs in terms of spiritual support or ceremony and how that might be best achieved within the context of counseling. As stated, Native spirituality manifests itself in many different forms, such as traditional tribal ways, Christian traditions, or the Native American Church. With a client who seems to have more traditional values and beliefs, it may be particularly helpful to suggest that family or a Medicine person participate in the process to support the client as she or he moves through important personal transitions and subsequent personal cleansing. It should be noted that having a general understanding of Native American spirituality does not prepare counselors to participate in or conduct Native ceremonies as part of the counseling process (M. T. Garrett, Torres-Rivera, et al., 2011; Matheson, 1996). That is the responsibility of those who are trained as Native Medicine persons and who also can serve as an important resource to counselors working with Native clients.

VALUES: USING THE RULE OF OPPOSITES AND SEEKING BALANCE

An understanding of the Rule of Opposites, or contrary way, is essential for working with Native American clients who may be experiencing dissonance in their lives (Herring, 1994). A traditional Native client might perceive dissonance in a much different way than might be expected within the majority culture by seeking ways to embrace the apparent dissonance in order to discover valuable healing and learning, possibly intended by spirit "helpers" and the Creator. From an indigenous-centered view, it is important to ask the right questions from the perspective of harmony and balance rather than from the perspective of separation and categorization. Just as important for non-Native counselors is being open to interpretations of experiences as spiritual processes, and the perceived impact of influences (helpful or harmful) from a spiritual perspective. Remembering all of these will help bridge the gap between what counselors see and what exists underneath perceived facades. Given the understanding that, from the Native worldview, everything has meaning and purpose, one goal of counseling becomes that of helping Native clients discover their purpose, examine their assumptions, seek an awareness of universal and personal truths, and make choices that allow them to exist in a state of harmony and balance within the Circle of Life. Talking with the client about her or his powerful cultural symbols, such as the Eagle feather, and what they represent to that particular client may help facilitate an opening to a dialogue that will give much insight into current issues, internal and external resources, and needed approaches. They provide insight into potential therapeutic goals for achieving harmony and balance among the four directions—mind, body, spirit, and natural environment.

Communication

Once the counselor has some general information concerning the client's cultural identity, experiences, spiritual ways, and specific needs, she or he will have a better understanding of what may or may not be considered appropriate with and for the client. The following recommendations (M. T. Garrett, 1999b; M. T. Garrett & Pichette, 2000; M. T. Garrett & Portman, 2011) are intended as culturally alert ways for working with a traditional Native client:

1. *Greeting.* For traditional Native Americans, a gentle handshake is the proper way of greeting. Sometimes just a word of greeting or head nod is sufficient. To use a firm handshake can be interpreted as an aggressive show of power and a personal insult. It may be important to follow, rather than lead, the client in manner of greeting.

2. *Hospitality.* Given the traditional emphasis on generosity, kindness, and gifting as a way of honoring the relation, hospitality is an important part of Native American life. Therefore, it is helpful to be able to offer the Native client a beverage or snack as a sign of good relation. In the traditional way, to not offer hospitality to a visitor or guest is to bring shame on oneself and one's family.

3. *Silence.* In the traditional way, when two people meet, very little may be said between them during the initial moments of the encounter. Quiet time at the beginning of a session is an appropriate way of transitioning into the therapeutic process by giving both counselor and client a chance to orient themselves to the situation,

get in touch with themselves, and experience the presence of the other person. This brief time (perhaps a couple of minutes or so) can be nonverbal, noninteractive time that allows the client to be at ease. This is an important show of respect, understanding, and patience.

4. *Space.* Taking care to respect physical space is an extension of the principle that one need not always fill relational space with words. In Native tradition, both the physical form and the space between the physical is sacred. In counseling, it is important to respect the physical space of the client by not sitting too close and not sitting directly across from the client, which allows scrutiny of the other. A more comfortable arrangement, traditionally, is sitting together more side by side in two different chairs at an off angle. The burning of sage, cedar, or sweetgrass (a method of spatial cleansing known as *smudging*) is customary but should only be done at the request or with permission of the Native client.

5. *Eye contact.* Native American clients with traditional values (and possibly those who are marginal or bicultural) may tend to avert their eyes as a sign of respect. To subtly match this level of eye contact is respectful and shows an understanding of the client's way of being. The eyes are considered to be the pathway to the spirit; therefore to consistently look someone in the eye is to show a level of entitlement or aggression. It is good to glance at someone every once in a while, but listening, in the traditional way, is something that happens with the ears and the heart.

6. *Intention.* One of the biggest issues with many Indian clients in the counseling relationship is trust. This should come as no surprise given the history of broken promises and exploitation experienced by all tribal nations. Typically, an Indian client will read the counselor's nonverbals fairly quickly to determine whether the counselor is someone to be trusted. Therefore, counselors can focus on honoring the mental space between counselor and client by seeking to offer respect and humility in the counseling process. Acceptance by the counselor means not trying to control or influence the client, which is considered "bad Medicine."

7. *Collaboration.* In counseling, more traditional Native clients may welcome (or even expect) the counselor to offer helpful suggestions or alternatives. From a traditional perspective, respect for choice is important, but healing is a collaborative process. Therefore, the counselor should offer suggestions without offering directions. There is a difference between encouraging and pushing. With traditional Native American clients, actions will always speak louder than words.

Humor

While humor is one of the important Native coping mechanisms, it should only be used if the client invites it, meaning that the client trusts the counselor enough to connect on that level. What in one situation can be humor between two people, in another can be interpreted as ridicule or wearing a mask. Counselors therefore have to be sensitive to using humor in a way that doesn't reinforce various means of oppression that the client has endured probably for all of her or his life.

However, on the opposite side of this issue lies the opportunity to connect with the client on her or his ground and share a powerful trust through humor that seems appropriate following the client's verbal and nonverbal cues. In sum, although counselors working with Native clients should exercise caution when using humor, they definitely should not overlook it as a powerful therapeutic technique. Indian humor serves the purpose of reaffirming and enhancing the sense of connectedness as part of family, clan, and tribe. To the extent that it can serve that purpose in the counseling relationship, it is all the better.

PRACTICAL INTERVENTIONS

Having discussed some important overall counseling interventions and treatment modalities, this section now explores ways for incorporating tribally specific interventions to meet the cultural, spiritual, personal, and/or career needs of specific Native clients. The following (M. T. Garrett & Carroll, 2000; M. T. Garrett & Portman, 2011) are offered as practical recommendations:

- *Foster cultural connections:* Native clients can reconnect with a sense of purpose by participating in community programs and cultural activities intended to combat the high rates of unemployment, inadequate housing, low educational levels, poverty-level incomes, and isolated living conditions. Participation in community-wide volunteer programs to help those in need has proved to be a successful part of healing for many Indian people. Also, in the past 10 years or so, powwows and other pantraditional events have become more and more popular around Native communities for whom that event is not indigenous as well as those for whom it is.

- *Encourage physical health:* Native people should be encouraged to get regular physical check-ups and blood tests (e.g., blood sugar) as a preventive measure in dealing with the high incidence of diabetes and other conditions prevalent among Native populations.

- *Examine/teach the historical context:* A critical component of counseling could include facilitating a psychoeducational experience or dialogue about Native experience in the United States. The counselor can discuss or lead the Native client to resources such as those listed at the end of this chapter to help create critical consciousness about the exploitation of Native people through discrimination, assimilation through boarding schools and Relocation Programs, and disruption of traditional cultural and familial patterns. Discussions of this nature might be helpful to Native clients in exploring their own level of cultural identity development.

- *Promote positive cultural identity:* Native clients can be assisted with exploration of their cultural identities and career issues by focusing on the positive cultural themes of belonging, mastery, independence, and generosity (Brendtro et al., 1990; M. T. Garrett & Portman, 2011). Counselors can use the following general questions to generate strengths and positive dimensions of clients' lives: (a) Where do you belong? (belonging); (b) What are you good at? What do you enjoy doing? (mastery); (c) What are your sources of strength? What limits you? (independence); (d) What do you have to offer/contribute?

(generosity). These provide an entry into useful dialogue and any number of therapeutic interventions that could be useful for clients based on a variety of issues. In addition, counselors can help the client learn about the expectations and ways of the dominant culture so that the client is prepared to engage in mainstream activities, if she or he wishes.

- *Reduce isolation/enhance social connections:* Participation in social events allows Native clients to experience social cohesion and social interaction in their communities. Some Native clients can benefit thereby from a sense of reconnection with community and traditional roles. This has been accomplished through the revival of tribal ceremonies and practices (e.g., talking circles, sweat lodges, powwows, peyote meetings). These revivals can reestablish a sense of belonging and communal meaningfulness for Native people "returning to the old ways" as an integral part of modern life.

- *Reduce generational splits:* Native clients of all ages can benefit from acting as (or learning from) elders by serving as role models and teachers for young people. This, too, has become more commonly practiced by tribal nations across the country in therapeutic programs and schools.

- *Enhance coping mechanisms:* Native clients can learn better methods of dealing with stress, boredom, powerlessness, and the sense of emptiness associated with acculturation and identity confusion. Consultation with or participation of a Medicine person (i.e., traditional Native healer) may prove very helpful.

- *Work with the noninterference principle:* The principle of noninterference has been identified as a value of traditional Native culture and is based on a common cultural practice of showing respect among one's relations (M. T. Garrett, 1999b; M. T. Garrett & Portman, 2011; M. T. Garrett et al., 2009). Noninterference means that a person is not to interfere with the choices of another, as it would be considered disrespectful and insulting. However, in certain situations noninterference can also be seen as avoidance behavior of family and community members with regard to persons who may be in need of help. This potential avoidance behavior can be challenged with Native clients, as well as with family and community members, to the extent that it may be destructive.

Carol Attneave's (1969, 1985) Network Therapy has been very effective with Native clients by extending family therapy to include the social network of the identified client. As such, Network Therapy consists of working with an individual in the family and community context whereby family and community members are incorporated into the counseling process, often through the use of group interventions that complement the cultural context.

WORKING FROM A SOCIAL JUSTICE AND ADVOCACY COUNSELING PERSPECTIVE

Native American people today are faced with the daunting task of attempting linguistic and cultural revitalization of their respective tribal traditions and customs as well as addressing the numerous challenges resulting from current and historical oppression (Grande, 2004, Turner & Pope, 2009). Native American people have a deep and profound understanding of the dichotomous relationship between the two worlds they find themselves a part of. One is the competitive, economically driven, technological metropolis of the Western European paradigm that has grown up around them. The other is their own earth-based spiritual perception of life's journey that has sustained their peoples' harmonious existence for hundreds and thousands of years.

Counselors must appreciate how socioeconomic status, oppression, and institutional and sociopolitical policies affect Native American clients and their respective communities' ability to change and grow. Overall, counselors working from a social justice and advocacy perspective must have a clear understanding that oppression occurs on many levels (ethno-racial, gender, worldview, national origin, socioeconomic status); therefore it is vital that counselors advocate for clients at the individual, community, and national levels. Thus, counselors can focus on three main levels of practice from an advocacy and social justice counseling perspective: (1) client and student advocacy, (2) school and community advocacy, and (3) public arena advocacy (Choudhuri, Santiago-Rivera, & Garrett, 2012).

In the first case, *client and student advocacy*, the helping professional implements direct counseling strategies based on understanding the social, political, economic, and cultural contexts in which clients live. The counselor also facilitates self-advocacy on the part of the client. For instance, a helping professional might join an organization offering counseling services to returning Native American veterans and their families. Furthermore, the counselor may directly address external barriers that impede the client's development. The client herself or himself may be unable to address these barriers due to lack of resources, access, or power. For example, a school counselor might intervene directly with a health education teacher who has failed a student for turning in a paper on indigenous healing methods.

The second level for advocacy practice is *school and community advocacy*. Here the helping professional might get involved in assisting community organizations that are working for change, such as developing a cultural sensitivity training program for volunteers at a food bank. Furthermore, counselors might get involved by going to a larger stage to maintain a direction for change that will have an impact on macro levels of access and resources. An example of this may be to join ongoing lobbying efforts to maintain funding and services for Native American–based ex-offender employment and rehabilitation programs.

Finally, in *public arena advocacy*, counselors might get involved in disseminating information widely to raise social consciousness that assists in deepening understanding. So helping professionals might write an article for the local newspaper on Native American mental health concerns, increasing public awareness of ongoing discrimination. Furthermore, counselors might get involved with working on large social issues that will then indirectly trickle into impacting the experience of Native Americans, such as advocating for Native American–owned businesses, purchasing Native American–made products in conjunction with the Indian Arts and Crafts Act of 1990, challenging inaccurate or exploitative information about Native Americans in the media, and creating critical consciousness about current issues around treaty rights.

It is additionally important that non-tribally affiliated service providers maintain an awareness of a long history of mistrust that has developed between agency-affiliated persons and tribal people. Numerous government and church agencies have historically abused the relationships that were established with the intention of "helping" Native people live in a system that is drastically different than the one they were taught to value. Thus, social justice and advocacy efforts should be engaged in with the intention of promoting the programs and processes that were previously established by the specific tribal nations themselves. Many tribes and tribal communities have formed advocacy groups to address the numerous challenges they face, such as cultural and linguistic revitalization, health and nutrition, economic and environmental stewardship, education and vocation advancement, and a whole host of other social and political interests. This may mean the counselor's attending community meetings, educating the general population, and organizing activities to highlight the needs of Native Americans.

Another strategy that may assist counselors in promoting Native communities' participation in advocacy is to identify the strengths of Native individuals and use those assets in their strategies. For example, one of the strengths of Native Americans is their proficiency in storytelling. Counselors can impress upon the individuals in the communities that storytelling is the foundation of enacting change. If these stories are communicated well, they can influence local, state, and federal politicians, resulting in more resources and attention to the needs of their community.

STORIES REVISITED

Through culturally alert counseling, counselors can practice in a way that is more congruent with traditional Native worldviews, experiences, and needs. The culturally alert counselor would be aware of some of the life-stories of Native elders, adults, and youngsters alike. The following quote from a Native elder is illustrative of the power of tradition and community to many American Indians. He was asked to describe who he was as a Native person:

Well, I think the stories probably gave me a sense of connection with the Indian side more than anything else. What I remember most of all is everything that my grandfather ever said because to me, he must have been the tallest man in the world. I was such a little boy, and I'd look up at him, and he was tall, tall and slender. Boy, I thought he was such a fine man. The first thing he'd say every time I'd see him was "Ceo Tsayoga," in other words, hello there little bird, how you doing. The first thing he would always do is he'd put me up on his shoulders, I remember that, and take me down to the creek bank. He'd say, "Come on, let's go to the creek bank . . . gonna do some fishin." I never fished. I never got a chance to fish. I don't know that he ever fished. It's like if he had a chance to take me fishing, that was a chance to tell me stories, teach me values. And one that I do remember very much was when we'd look in the water because I really enjoyed as a little kid just looking at the little minnows, seeing the fish in the water. And he'd let me look for hours, and I don't know whether he was fishing or not, I think he was. We never brought home any fish. I think he would always put the fish back, even if he caught one. (J. T. Garrett, Eastern Band of Cherokee, quoted in M. T. Garrett, 1996a, p. 12)

SUMMARY

Stories carry the words, ghosts, dreams, and spirit of Native life. With the knowledge, awareness, and skills that have been discussed in this chapter, counselors might have a better sense of where Native people have come from and where they are going. Counselors also begin to understand the importance of attending to the stories—the meanings, language, experiences, images, and themes—of Native clients. And they begin to learn, as it has traditionally been taught by so many Native elders, that learning is a life-long process, just as a story unfolds and offers the gift of its life to us.

REFERENCES

Appleton, V. E., & Dykeman, C. (1996). Using art in group counseling with Native American youth. *Journal for Specialists in Group Work, 24,* 224–231.

Ashby, M. R., Gilchrist, L. D., & Miramontez, A. (1987). Group treatment for sexually abused American Indian adolescents. *Social Work With Groups, 10,* 21–32.

Attneave, C. L. (1969). Therapy in tribal settings and urban network intervention. *Family Process, 8,* 192–210.

Attneave, C. L. (1985). Practical counseling with American Indian and Alaska Native clients. In P. Pedersen (Ed.), *Handbook of cross-cultural counseling and therapy* (pp. 135–140). Westport, CT: Greenwood.

BigFoot, D. S., & Funderburk, B. W. (2011). Honoring children, making relatives: The cultural translation of parent-child interaction therapy for American Indian and Alaska Native families. *Journal of Psychoactive Drugs, 43,* 309–318.

Bonnet, M. B. (2003). Blood flowing in two worlds. In M. Moore (Ed.), *Genocide of the mind: New Native American writing* (pp. 13–20). New York, NY: Thunder's Mouth Press/Nation Books.

Brandt, E. A. (1992). The Navajo area student dropout study: Findings and implications. *Journal of American Indian Education, 31,* 48–63.

Brave Heart, M. Y. H. (2000). Wakiksuyapi: Carrying the historical trauma of the Lakota. *Tulane Studies in Social Welfare, 21–22,* 245–266.

Brave Heart, M. Y. H. (2003). The historical trauma response among Natives and its relationship with substance abuse: A Lakota illustration. *Journal of Psychoactive Drugs, 35,* 7–13.

Brave Heart, M. Y. H. (2005). *Substance abuse, co-occurring mental health disorders, and the historical trauma response among American Indians/Alaska Natives.* Washington, DC: Bureau of Indian Affairs, DASAP.

Brave Heart, M. Y. H., & DeBruyn, L. M. (1998). The American Indian holocausts: Healing historical unresolved grief. *American Indian and Alaska Native Mental Health Research, 8*(2), 55–78.

Brendtro, L. K., Brokenleg, M., & Van Bockern, S. (1990). *Reclaiming youth at risk: Our hope for the future.* Bloomington, IN: National Education Service.

Capriccioso, R. (2005). *Native American education under the microscope.* Retrieved from http://sparkaction.org/content/native-american-education-under-microscope

Charleston, G. M. (1994). Toward true Native education: A treaty of 1992 final report of the Indian nations at risk task force, draft 3. *Journal of American Indian Education, 33*, 1–56.

Choney, S. K., Berryhill-Paapke, E., & Robbins, R. R. (1995). The acculturation of American Indians: Developing frameworks for research and practice. In J. G. Ponterotto, J. M. Casas, L. A. Suzuki, & C. M. Alexander (Eds.), *Handbook of multicultural counseling* (pp. 73–92). Thousand Oaks, CA: Sage.

Choudhuri, D. D., Santiago-Rivera, A. L., & Garrett, M. T. (2012). *Counseling and diversity: Central concepts and themes for competent practice.* Boston, MA: Cengage/Lahaska Press.

Colmant, S. A., & Merta, R. J. (1999). Using the sweat lodge ceremony as group therapy for Navajo youth. *Journal for Specialists in Group Work, 24*, 55–73.

Colodarci, T. (1983). High school dropout among Native Americans. *Journal of American Indian Education, 23*, 15–22.

Crazy Thunder, D., & Brave Heart, M. Y. H. (2005). *Cumulative trauma among tribal law enforcement officers: Search, rescue, and recovery at Ground Zero and on the reservation.* Washington, DC: Bureau of Indian Affairs, DASAP.

Deloria, V., Jr. (1988). *Custer died for your sins: An Indian manifesto.* Norman: University of Oklahoma Press.

Deloria, V., Jr. (1994). *God is red.* Golden, CO: Fulcrum.

Deloria, V., Jr. (2002). *Evolution, creationism, and other modern myths.* Golden, CO: Fulcrum.

Deloria, V., Jr. (2006). *The world we used to live in: Remembering the powers of the medicine men.* Golden, CO: Fulcrum.

Deyhle, D. (1992). Constructing failure and maintaining cultural identity: Navajo and Ute school leavers. *Journal of American Indian Education, 31*, 24–47.

DuBray, W. H. (1985). American Indian values: Critical factor in casework. *Social Casework, 66*, 30–37.

Dufrene, P. M. (1990). Exploring Native American symbolism. *Journal of Multicultural and Cross-Cultural Research in Art Education, 8*, 38–50.

Duran, E. (2006). *Healing the soul wound: Counseling with American Indians and other native peoples.* New York, NY: Teachers College Press.

Duran, E., & Duran, B. (1995). *Native American postcolonial psychology.* Albany: State University of New York Press.

Duran, E., Firehammer, J., & Gonzalez, J. (2008). Liberation psychology as the path toward healing cultural soul wounds. *Journal of Counseling & Development, 86*, 288–295.

Four Worlds Development Project. (1984). *The sacred tree: Reflections on Native American spirituality.* Wilmot, WI: Lotus Light.

Garcia, R. L., & Ahler, J. G. (1992). Indian education: Assumptions, ideologies, strategies. In J. Reyhner (Ed.), *Teaching American Indian students* (pp. 13–32). Norman: University of Oklahoma Press.

Garrett, J. T. (1991). Where the medicine wheel meets medical science. In S. McFadden (Ed.), *Profiles in wisdom: Native elders speak about the earth* (pp. 167–179). Santa Fe, NM: Bear.

Garrett, J. T. (2001). *Meditations with the Cherokee: Prayers, songs, and stories of healing and harmony.* Rochester, VT: Bear.

Garrett, J. T., & Garrett, M. T. (1994). The path of good medicine: Understanding and counseling Native Americans. *Journal of Multicultural Counseling and Development, 22*, 134–144.

Garrett, J. T., & Garrett, M. T. (1996). *Medicine of the Cherokee: The way of right relationship.* Santa Fe, NM: Bear.

Garrett, M. T. (1995). Between two worlds: Cultural discontinuity in the dropout of Native American youth. *The School Counselor, 42*, 186–195.

Garrett, M. T. (1996a). Reflection by the riverside: The traditional education of Native American children. *Journal of Humanistic Education and Development, 35*, 12–28.

Garrett, M. T. (1996b). "Two people": An American Indian narrative of bicultural identity. *Journal of American Indian Education, 36*, 1–21.

Garrett, M. T. (1998). *Walking on the wind: Cherokee teachings for harmony and balance.* Santa Fe, NM: Bear.

Garrett, M. T. (1999a). Soaring on the wings of the eagle: Wellness of Native American high school students. *Professional School Counseling, 3*, 57–64.

Garrett, M. T. (1999b). Understanding the "Medicine" of Native American traditional values: An integrative review. *Counseling and Values, 43*, 84–98.

Garrett, M. T., & Carroll, J. (2000). Mending the broken circle: Treatment and prevention of substance abuse among Native Americans. *Journal of Counseling and Development, 78,* 379–388.

Garrett, M. T., & Crutchfield, L. B. (1997). Moving full circle: A unity model of group work with children. *Journal for Specialists in Group Work, 22,* 175–188.

Garrett, M. T., & Garrett, J. T. (1997). Counseling Native American elders. *Directions in Rehabilitation Counseling: Therapeutic Strategies With the Older Adult, 3,* 3–18.

Garrett, M. T., & Garrett, J. T. (2002). Ayeli: Centering technique based on Cherokee spiritual traditions. *Counseling and Values, 46,* 149–158.

Garrett, M. T., & Garrett, J. T. (2003). *Native American faith in America.* New York, NY: Facts on File.

Garrett, M. T., & Garrett, J. T. (in press). *Native American faith in America* (2nd ed.). New York, NY: Facts on File.

Garrett, M. T., Garrett, J. T., & Brotherton, D. (2001). Inner circle/outer circle: Native American group technique. *Journal for Specialists in Group Work, 26,* 17–30.

Garrett, M. T., Garrett, J. T., Wilbur, M., Roberts-Wilbur, J., & Torres-Rivera, E. (2005). Native American humor as spiritual tradition: Implications for counseling. *Journal of Multicultural Counseling and Development, 33,* 194–204.

Garrett, M. T., & Myers, J. E. (1996). The rule of opposites: A paradigm for counseling Native Americans. *Journal of Multicultural Counseling and Development, 24,* 89–104.

Garrett, M. T., & Osborne, W. L. (1995). The Native American sweat lodge as metaphor for group work. *Journal for Specialists in Group Work, 20,* 33–39.

Garrett, M. T., & Pichette, E. F. (2000). Red as an apple: Native American acculturation and counseling with or without reservation. *Journal of Counseling and Development, 78,* 3–13.

Garrett, M. T., & Portman, T. A. A. (2011). *Counseling and diversity: Counseling Native Americans.* Boston, MA: Cengage/Lahaska Press.

Garrett, M. T., Torres-Rivera, E., Brubaker, M., Portman, T. A. A., Brotherton, D., West-Olatunji, C., . . . Grayshield, L. (2011). Crying for a vision: The Native American sweat lodge ceremony as therapeutic intervention. *Journal of Counseling and Development, 89,* 318–325.

Garrett, M. T., Torres-Rivera, E., Dixon, A. L., & Myers, J. E. (2009). Acculturation and wellness of Native American adolescents in the United States of North America. *Perspectivas Socials/Social Perspectives, 11,* 39–64.

Garrett, M. T., & Wilbur, M. P. (1999). Does the worm live in the ground? Reflections on Native American spirituality. *Journal of Multicultural Counseling and Development, 27,* 193–206.

Gone, J. P. (2009). A community-based treatment for Native American historical trauma: Prospects for evidence-based practice. *Journal of Consulting and Clinical Psychology, 77,* 751–762.

Goodluck, C. (2002). *Native American children and youth well-being indicators: A strengths perspective.* Portland, OR: National Indian Child Welfare Association. Retrieved from http://www.nicwa.org/research/03.Well-Being02.Rpt.pdf

Grande, S. (2004). *Red pedagogy: Native American social and political thought.* Lanham, MD: Rowman & Littlefield.

Grayshield, L., & Mihecoby, A. (2010). Indigenous ways of knowing as a philosophical base for the promotion of peace and justice in counseling education and psychology. *Journal for Social Action in Counseling and Psychology, 2,* 1–16.

Harper, F. G. (2011). With all my relations: Counseling American Indians and Alaska Natives within a familial context. *Family Journal, 19,* 434–439.

Heinrich, R. K., Corbine, J. L., & Thomas, K. R. (1990). Counseling Native Americans. *Journal of Counseling and Development, 69,* 128–133.

Herring, R. D. (1994). The clown or contrary figure as a counseling intervention strategy with Native American Indian clients. *Journal of Multicultural Counseling and Development, 22,* 153–164.

Herring, R. D. (1996). Synergetic counseling and Native American Indian students. *Journal of Counseling and Development, 74,* 542–547.

Herring, R. D. (1999). *Counseling with Native American Indians and Alaska Natives: Strategies for helping professionals.* Thousand Oaks, CA: Sage.

Hirschfelder, A., & Kreipe de Montano, M. (1993). *The Native American almanac: A portrait of Native America today.* New York, NY: Macmillan.

Hodgkinson, H. L. (1990). *The demographics of American Indians: One percent of the people; fifty percent of the diversity.* Washington, DC: Institute for Educational Leadership.

Hornett, D. (1990). Elementary-age tasks, cultural identity, and the academic performance of young American Indian children. *Action in Teacher Education, 12,* 43–49.

Hunter, D., & Sawyer, C. (2006). Blending Native American spirituality with individual psychology in work with children. *Journal of Individual Psychology, 62,* 234–250.

Indian Health Service. (1997). *Trends in Indian health 1997; General mortality statistics.* Retrieved from http://www.ihs.gov/publicinfo/publications/trends97/tds97pt3.pdf

Kawulich, B. B. (2008). Giving back to the community through leadership. *Advancing Women in Leadership, 28.* Retrieved from http://advancingwomen.com/awl/awl_wordpress

LaFromboise T. D. (1993). American Indian mental health policy. In D. R. Atkinson, A. Morten, & D. W. Sue (Eds.), *Counseling American Indian minorities* (p.123–144). New York, NY: Wiley.

LaFromboise, T. D., Coleman, H. L. K., & Gerton, J. (1993). Psychological impact of biculturalism: Evidence and theory. *Psychological Bulletin, 114,* 395–412.

LaFromboise, T. D., & Rowe, W. (1983). Skills training for bicultural competence: Rationale and application. *Journal of Counseling Psychology, 30,* 589–595.

LaFromboise, T. D., Trimble, J. E., & Mohatt, G. V. (1990). Counseling intervention and American Indian tradition: An integrative approach. *The Counseling Psychologist, 18,* 628–654.

Lake, M. G. (1991). *Native healer: Initiation into an ancient art.* Wheaton, IL: Quest Books.

Little Soldier, L. (1992). Building optimum learning environments for Navajo students. *Childhood Education, 68,* 145–148.

Locust, C. (1988). Wounding the spirit: Discrimination and traditional American Indian belief systems. *Harvard Educational Review, 58,* 315–330.

Loftin, J. D. (1989). Anglo-American jurisprudence and the Native American tribal quest for religious freedom. *American Indian Culture and Research Journal, 13,* 1–52.

Maples, M. F., Dupey, P., Torres-Rivera, E., Phan, L. T., Vereen, L., & Garrett, M. T. (2001). Ethnic diversity and the use of humor in counseling: Appropriate or inappropriate? *Journal of Counseling and Development, 79,* 53–60.

Marsiglia, F. F., Cross, S., & Mitchell, V. (1998). Culturally grounded group work with adolescent American Indian students. *Social Work With Groups, 21,* 89–102.

Matheson, L. (1996). Valuing spirituality among Native American populations. *Counseling and Values, 41,* 51–58.

McLaughlin, D. (1994). Critical literacy for Navajo and other American Indian learners. *Journal of American Indian Education, 33,* 47–59.

McLeigh, J. D. (2010). What are the policy issues related to the mental health of Native Americans? *American Journal of Orthopsychiatry, 80,* 177–182.

Mitchum, N. T. (1989). Increasing self-esteem in Native American children. *Elementary School Guidance and Counseling, 23,* 266–271.

Neumann, A. K., Mason, V., Chase, E., & Albaugh, B. (1991). Factors associated with success among southern Cheyenne and Arapaho Indians. *Journal of Community Health, 16,* 103–115.

Oswalt, W. H. (1988). *This land was theirs: A study of North American Indians* (4th ed.). Mountain View, CA: Mayfield.

Oswalt, W. H. (2009). *This land was theirs: A study of North American Indians* (9th ed.). New York, NY: Oxford University.

Pfefferbaum, R. L., Pfefferbaum, B., Rhoades, E. R., & Strickland, R. J. (1997). Providing for the health care needs of Native Americans: Policy, programs, procedures, and practices. *American Indian Law Review, 21,* 211–258.

Plank, G. A. (1994). What silence means for educators of American Indian children. *Journal of American Indian Education, 34,* 3–19.

Portman, T. (2001). American Indian women sex role attributions. *Journal of Mental Health Counseling, 23,* 72–84.

Portman, T., & Garrett, M. T. (2005). Beloved women: Nurturing leadership from an American Indian perspective. *Journal of Counseling and Development, 83,* 284–291.

Portman, T. A., & Herring, R. D. (2001). Debunking the Pocahontas paradox: The need for a humanistic perspective. *Journal of Humanistic Counseling, Education and Development, 40,* 185–199.

Provan, K. G., & Carson, L. M. P. (2000). Behavioral health funding for Native Americans in Arizona: Policy implications for states and tribes. *Journal of Behavioral Health Services & Research, 27,* 17–28.

Radda, H. T., Iwamoto, D., & Patrick, C. (1998). Collaboration, research and change: Motivational influences on American Indian students. *Journal of American Indian Education, 37*(2). Retrieved from http://jaie.asu.edu

Red Horse, J. G. (1997). Traditional American Indian family systems. *Families, Systems, & Health, 15,* 243–250.

Reyhner, J., & Eder, J. (1992). A history of Indian education. In J. Reyhner (Ed.), *Teaching American Indian students* (pp. 33–58). Norman: University of Oklahoma Press.

Roberts-Wilbur, J., Wilbur, M., Garrett, M. T., & Yuhas, M. (2001). Talking circles: Listen or your tongue will make you deaf. *Journal for Specialists in Group Work, 26,* 368–384.

Robinson-Wood, T. L. (2009). *The convergence of race, ethnicity, and gender: Multiple identities in counseling* (3rd ed.). Upper Saddle River, NJ: Merrill.

Russell, G. (2004). *American Indian facts of life: A profile of today's tribes and reservations.* Phoenix, AZ: Native Data Network.

Rybak, C. J., Eastin, C. L., & Robbins, I. (2004). Native American healing practices and counseling. *Journal of Humanistic Counseling, Education & Development, 43,* 25–32.

Scholl, M. B. (2006). Native American identity development and counseling preferences: A study of Lumbee undergraduates. *Journal of College Counseling, 9,* 47–59.

Shutiva, C. L. (2001). *Career and academic guidance for American Indian and Alaska Native youth.* Charleston, WV: ERIC Clearinghouse on Rural Education and Small Schools. (ERIC Document Reproduction Service No. ED458062)

Simmons, G., & Barrineau, P. (1994). Learning style and the Native American. *Journal of Psychological Type, 29,* 3–10.

Swisher, K., Hoisch, M., & Pavel, D. M. (1991). *American Indian/Alaskan Native dropout study, 1991.* Washington, DC: National Education Association.

Thomason, T. C. (1991). Counseling Native Americans: An introduction for non-Native American counselors. *Journal of Counseling and Development, 69,* 321–327.

Trimble, J. E., & Gonzalez, J. (2008). Cultural considerations and perspectives for providing psychological counseling for Native American Indians. In P. Pedersen, J. Draguns, W. Lonner, & J. Trimble (Eds.), *Counseling across cultures* (6th ed., pp. 93–111). Thousand Oaks, CA: Sage.

Turner, S. L., & Pope, M. (2009). North America's native peoples: A social justice and trauma counseling approach. *Journal of Multicultural Counseling & Development, 37,* 194–205.

U.S. Bureau of Indian Affairs. (2012). *Frequently asked questions.* Retrieved from http://www.bia.gov/FAQs/index.htm

U.S. Census Bureau. (2011). *2010 census counts of American Indians, Eskimos, or Aleuts and American Indian and Alaska Native areas.* Washington, DC: Author.

Velie, A. R. (Ed.). (1991). *American Indian literature: An anthology.* Norman: University of Oklahoma Press.

Vick, R. D., Sr., Smith, L. M., & Iron Rope Herrera, C. (1998). The healing circle: An alternative path to alcoholism recovery. *Counseling and Values, 42,* 132–141.

Appendix C

Additional Resources—Further Reading and Exploration

Experiential Activities

Following are but a few suggestions for individual and group experiential activities to increase knowledge, awareness, and skills for working with Native American clients.

INDIVIDUAL ACTIVITIES

- Read novels, poetry, short stories, historical accounts, biographies of Native people or written by Native authors (see www.nativeauthors.com for examples).
- Investigate sources listed in this text for further information on particular issues or interventions (e.g., Appleton & Dykeman, 1996; Ashby, Gilchrist, & Miramontez, 1987; BigFoot & Funderburk, 2011; Brave Heart, 2000, 2003, 2005; Brave Heart & DeBruyn, 1998; Brendtro, Brokenleg, and Van Bockern, 1990; Colmant & Merta, 1999; Crazy Thunder & Brave Heart, 2005; Duran, 2006; Duran, Firehammer, & Gonzalez, 2008; Four Worlds Development Project, 1984; J. T. Garrett, 2001; J. T. Garrett & Garrett, 1996; M. T. Garrett, 1998; M. T. Garrett & Carroll, 2000; Garrett & Crutchfield, 1997; M. T. Garrett & Garrett, 2003; M. T. Garrett, Garrett, & Brotherton, 2001; M. T. Garrett, Garrett, Wilbur, Roberts-Wilbur, & Torres-Rivera, 2005; M. T. Garrett & Osborne, 1995; M. T. Garrett, Torres-Rivera, et al., 2011; Gone, 2009; Grayshield & Mihecoby, 2010; Harper, 2011; Heinrich, Corbine, & Thomas, 1990; Herring, 1994, 1996, 1999; Hunter & Sawyer, 2006; Kawulich, 2008; LaFromboise & Rowe, 1983; LaFromboise, Trimble, & Mohatt, 1990; Lake, 1991; Portman, 2001; Portman & Garrett, 2005; Portman & Herring, 2001; Roberts-Wilbur, Wilbur, Garrett, & Yuhas, 2001; Thomason, 1991; Turner & Pope, 2009; Vick, Smith, & Iron Rope Herrera, 1998).
- Read current professional journal articles dealing with Native issues.
- Read current Native periodicals and other sources of news such as *Native Peoples Magazine* (www.nativepeoples.com), Indian Country Today (http://indiancountrytodaymedianetwork.com), *Whispering Wind Magazine, The Indian Trader, News From Indian Country, Arizona Native Scene,* Four Winds Trading Company, National Museum of the American Indian (http://nmai.si.edu/home), *Native American Times* (www.nativetimes.com), or tribally specific periodicals (i.e. newspapers, magazines, or any other material published by a particular tribe).
- Listen to Native music: powwow, traditional chant, flute, contemporary, rock, rap, chicken scratch, blues, or country (www.nativeamericanmusic.com, www.silverwave.com).
- Watch movies dealing with Native issues, especially those directed by, produced by, or starring Native people.
- Check out current informational Native websites (e.g., www.nativepeoples.com, www.nativeweb.org) as well as websites for any specific tribe.
- Learn more about Native social, economic, educational, and political organizations such as the American Indian Movement, First Nations Development Institute, Morningstar Institute, American Indian College Fund, American Indian Science and Engineering Society, Native American Public Broadcasting Consortium, and Native American Rights Fund (www.narf.org).
- Research and learn more about current legal issues facing specific tribes.
- Research and learn more about current health issues facing Native people.

GROUP ACTIVITIES

- Attend powwows, cultural demonstrations, art exhibits, or other Native gatherings or festivities as appropriate and available.
- Attend the museums and/or arts and crafts cooperatives of particular tribes, or find information about these online.

- Find out about local Native organizations or resources, and meet with them.
- Meet and talk with willing Native people of any age.

SOURCES FOR FURTHER READING AND REFERENCE

American Psychological Association (articles)

www.apa.org/monitor/mar00/listening.html

www.apa.org/monitor/jun03/indian.html

www.apa.org/monitor/jan04/indian.html

www.apa.org/monitor/oct04/services.html

Other Articles & Papers

www.med.upenn.edu/cmhpsr/documents/NativeAmericanLitReview.PDF

www.aisc.ucla.edu/rsrch/uaichildren.htm

Educational Program Targeting Counseling to American Indian Populations

www.uark.edu/depts/rehabres/AmIndian/AImain.htm

Agency Resource Pages

www.bia.gov/

www.ihs.gov/

www.nicoa.org/

www.aisc.ucla.edu/rsrch/uaichildren.htm

www.umass.edu/native/nasss/proginf.html

North American Indian & Indigenous People's Organizations and Associations

www.yvwiiusdinvnohii.net/assoc.html

HONOR (Honor Our Neighbors' Origins and Rights): http://honoradvocacy.org

International Indigenous Youth Conference: http://iiyc.resist.ca/

Native American Rights Fund: www.narf.org/pubs/index.html

Native Voter (non-partisan political information for Native community) AZ Native Voter, NM Native Voter, WI Native Voter, MN Native Voter To sign up visit: http://www.ccp.org/resources/lists.html

Turning Point: www.turning-point.ca/

Wordcraft Circle: www.wordcraftcircle.org/

Native American Journals

American Anthropologist (American Anthropological Association): www.jstor.org/journals/00027294.html

American Antiquity (Society for American Archaeology): www.saa.org/AbouttheSociety/Publications/AmericanAntiquity/tabid/124/Default.aspx

American Ethnologist: www.americanethnologist.org/

American Indian and Alaska Native Mental Health Research: The Journal of the National Center: www.ucdenver.edu/academics/colleges/PublicHealth/research/centers/CAIANH/journal/Pages/journal.aspx

American Indian Culture & Resource Journal (UCLA American Indian Studies Center Publications Unit): www.books.aisc.ucla.edu/cat-aicrj.asp

American Indian Law Review: (University of Oklahoma): www.law.ou.edu/content/american-indian-law-review

American Indian Report: www.americanindianreport.com/

American Indian Review: www.users.globalnet.co.uk/~tlt2auro/

American Indian Quarterly (University of Nebraska Press): www.jstor.org/journals/0095182X.html

American Journal of Archaeology: www.ajaonline.org/

Archaeology of Eastern North America (Eastern States Archaeological Federation): www.esaf-archeology.org/publications.html

Arctic Anthropology (University of Wisconsin Press): www.wisc.edu/wisconsinpress/journals/journals/aa.html

Arctic: Journal of the Arctic Institute of North America (University of Calgary): www.arctic.ucalgary.ca/publications/arctic-journal

Ayaangwaamizin: The International Journal of Indigenous Philosophy: www.cep.unt.edu/lakehead/

Canadian Journal of Native Education (Spring/summer issue compiled at First Nations House of Learning at the University of British Columbia; fall/winter edition compiled by First Nations Graduate Education Program at the University of Alberta): www.lights.com/sifc/cjne.htm

Canadian Journal of Native Studies (Canadian Indian/Native Studies Association): www2.brandonu.ca/library/cjns/

Cultural Survival Quarterly: www.culturalsurvival.org/publications/cultural-survival-quarterly

Estudios de Cultura Nahuatl: www.ejournal.unam.mx/cuadros2.php?r=9

Ethnohistory: www.dukeupress.edu/ethnohistory/

Etudes Inuit Studies (Université Laval): www.fss.ulaval.ca/etudes-inuit-studies/

Gohweli: A Journal of American Indian Literature: www.uwm.edu/~michael/journal/

Indigenous Policy Journal (American Indian Studies Program, Michigan State University): www.indigenouspolicy.org/

International Journal of Cultural Property (Cambridge University Press): http://journals.cambridge.org/action/displayJournal?jid=JCP

Journal of American Indian Education (Center for Indian Education, College of Education, Arizona State University): http://jaie.asu.edu/

Journal of Indigenous Nations Studies (University of Kansas): http://kuscholarworks.ku.edu/dspace/handle/1808/5725

Journal of Indigenous Studies: www.metismuseum.ca/browse/index.php?id=882

Journal of Native Health: www2.brandonu.ca/Native/JNH.html

Journal of World Anthropology (University at Buffalo): http://wings.buffalo.edu/research/anthrogis/JWA/

Latin American Antiquity (Society for American Archaeology): www.saa.org/AbouttheSociety/Publications/LatinAmericanAntiquity/tabid/127/Default.aspx

Midcontinental Journal of Archaeology (Midwest Archaeological Conference): www.midwestarchaeology.org/mcja/

Native Peoples: www.nativepeoples.com/

Native Studies Review (Native Studies Department, University of Saskatchewan): http://publications.usask.ca/nativestudiesreview/

News From Native California: www.heydaybooks.com/news/

North American Archaeologist (Baywood Publishing): www.baywood.com/journals/previewjournals.asp?id=0197-6931

Pacific Health Dialog: www.pacifichealthdialog.org.fj/

Pacific Northwest Quarterly (University of Washington): www.washington.edu/uwired/outreach/cspn/Website/PNQ/PNQ%20Main.html

Plains Anthropologist: www.ou.edu/cas/archsur/plainsanth/pa/pa.htm

The Raven Chronicles: http://ravenchronicles.org/

Red Ink Online (American Indian Studies Program, University of Arizona): www.redinkmagazine.com/

Redwire: www.redwiremag.com/site/redwire/redwire-magazine

Serving Native American Students: New Directions in Student Services (Issue 109, Spring 2005): www.wiley.com/WileyCDA/WileyTitle/productCd-0787979716.html

Seventh Native American Generation (SNAG) Magazine: www.snagmagazine.com/

Southeastern Archaeology (Southeastern Archaeological Conference): www.southeasternarchaeology.org/journal.html

Standards: An International Journal of Multicultural Studies (University of Colorado, Boulder): www.dustjacketpress.com/standards/index2.html

Studies in American Indian Literature: https://facultystaff.richmond.edu/~rnelson/asail/sailhp.html

Tribal Arts Magazine: www.tribalartmagazine.com/a_la_une.php

Tribal College Journal: www.tribalcollegejournal.org/

Wicazo Sa Review (University of Minnesota Press): http://muse.jhu.edu/journals/wic/ or www.upress.umn.edu/journals/wsr/default.html

Winds of Change: www.wocmag.org/

Indigenous Electronic Mailing Lists

http://groups.yahoo.com/group/Indian_education/

http://groups.yahoo.com/group/indigenousmedia/

https://lists.resist.ca/cgi-bin/mailman/listinfo/redwire

https://lists.resist.ca/cgi-bin/mailman/listinfo/iiyc2

https://lists.resist.ca/cgi-bin/mailman/listinfo/indigenousyouth

urbanvoice@mac.com

http://groups.yahoo.com/group/worlds-indigenous-people/

Native American History and Culture Books

- *Bury My Heart at Wounded Knee: An Indian History of the American West:* Western historian Dee Brown's seminal 1971 book, famous for presenting the Native American side of the "Indian Wars" to the general public for the first time. Carefully researched, compellingly written, still important 40 years later.
- *Lakota Woman:* Mary Brave Bird (Crow Dog)'s autobiographical history of the American Indian Movement. A civil rights must-read.

- *Atlas of the North American Indian:* Excellent, detailed maps showing the pre-columbian, colonial, and current locations of hundreds of native tribes and nations. A great classroom reference.
- *Encyclopedia of Native American Tribes:* Past and present information about the culture groups of native North America. Outstanding presentation. This reference book is easy enough to read that it works as a children's resource, but it doesn't "dumb down" or get lost in silly romanticizing. We could recommend this to anyone with an interest.
- *A Native American Encyclopedia:* Another good resource book offering specific historical and demographic information about each tribal group of North America, explaining the differences between the diverse cultures clearly and precisely. This would make a good classroom reference for older kids.
- *Encyclopedia of North American Indians: Native American History, Culture, and Life:* Another good resource book presenting different ancient and modern Indian cultures respectfully and fairly. Sometimes it rambles a little. *Encyclopedia of Native American Tribes* is more clearly and uniformly written. But *Encyclopedia of North American Indians* has more pieces by native authors. Having both volumes together would be ideal.
- *500 Nations: An Illustrated History of North American Indians:* This history of Native America reads a little like a textbook but is very thorough. Recommended for history buffs, maybe not for casual or younger readers.
- *Of Earth and Elders: Visions and Voices from Native America:* Fascinating mosaic of interviews, essays, poems, and other musings from dozens of contemporary Indians.
- *Encyclopedia of American Indian Costume:* A good overview of the different clothing styles and regalia in hundreds of tribes and nations. Disappointingly few pictures, but the ones that are there are interesting.
- *Powwow:* Beautiful photography of contemporary Indian powwow regalia, interspersed with interesting interviews about the powwow.
- *Wolf That I Am:* This is an interesting book about how not to do anthropological studies of indigenous people.

- *Indian Metropolis: Native Americans in Chicago, 1945–75*: An interesting book about Indian urbanization.
- *Charcoal's World*: Interesting historical examination of a Blackfoot man's clash with white culture and the law.
- *The Vinland Sagas*: Viking account of their early attempts to colonize America and their interactions with the natives.
- *Cheyenne Again; My Name Is Sepeetza; Out of the Depths*: Books about the Indian residential schools. The first one is a lovely illustrated book for children, capturing the trauma of the boarding school experience without getting into the more adult issues (such as child molestation). The second is a harsher autobiography still suitable for kids. The third one, also autobiographical, is the most powerful, most difficult reading. This is not an easy subject, and these three books treat it well.
- *The Native American Sweat Lodge*: History of the sweat lodge by Abenaki author Joseph Bruchac.
- *Keepers of the Children*: An interesting book by the wife of a Pascua Yaqui man about applying Native American parenting techniques to non-Indian life.
- *Prison Writings: My Life is My Sun Dance; In the Spirit of Crazy Horse; Trial of Leonard Peltier*: Books about American Indian Movement activist and political prisoner Leonard Peltier. *Prison Writings* is by Leonard himself, and he makes his own case eloquently. *In the Spirit of Crazy Horse* is famous for the FBI's bizarre attempts to stop its publication (the courts didn't let them). We have not read the third one.
- *Life and Death of Anna Mae Acquash*: Book about slain AIM activist Anna Mae Aquash.
- *Where White Men Fear to Tread*: Controversial Lakota activist Russell Means's autobiography and history of the American Indian Movement.
- *Strange Empire: Narrative of the Northwest; Loyal Till Death*: Good books about the Cree and Metis people and Canada's Northwest Rebellion.
- *War Under Heaven; Pontiac and the Indian Uprising; Haughty Conquerors; The Conspiracy of Pontiac*: Good books about Chief Pontiac and the Pontiac Rebellion.
- *Massacre at Sand Creek; Sand Creek Massacre; From Sand Creek*: Good books about the Sand Creek Massacre.
- *Killing Custer: The Battle of Little Bighorn and the Fate of the Plains Indians*: Good book about the Battle of Little Bighorn and its aftermath.
- *Black Hawk*: Autobiography of 19th century Sauk Chief Black Hawk. This was narrated through a string of translators, so it's not 100% authentic as an autobiography, but Black Hawk's story is still compelling.
- *Grey Owl: The Mystery of Archie Belaney*: Poetic biography of the Canadian environmentalist married to a Cree woman, by Ojibwe author Armand Garnet Ruffo.

Native American Dictionaries and Language Books

- *The Languages of Native North America*: Comprehensive linguistic reference by Marianne Mithun. If you're interested in more than one Indian language, this is your first stop. Brief profiles of each and every language, linguistic information about unusual features of some of the languages, and the bibliography is priceless.
- *Western Abnaki Dictionary; Western Apache-English Dictionary; Blackfoot Dictionary of Stems, Roots, and Affixes; Alberta Elders' Cree Dictionary; A Dictionary of Creek/Muskogee; Delaware-English/English-Delaware Dictionary; Hopi Dictionary; Lakota Dictionary; Kolusuwakonol: Philips S. Lesourd's English and Passamaquoddy-Maliseet Dictionary; English-Micmac Dictionary; One Thousand Useful Mohawk Words; An Analytical Dictionary of Nahuatl: A Concise Dictionary of Minnesota Ojibwe; Lushotseed Dictionary; Sm'Algyax: A Reference Dictionary and Grammar for the Coast Tsimshian Language*: Native American language dictionaries for sale.
- *Apache; Introduction to Cherokee; Let's Talk Cheyenne; Introduction to Chickasaw; Spoken Cree: Level One; Passamaquoddy/Maliseet Reference Book; Let's Speak Mohawk; Ojibwe; Introduction to Shoshoni Language*: Native American language learning books and audiobooks for sale.
- Abnaki-Penobscot (www.native-languages.org/abna.htm#materials); Algonquin (www.native-languages.org/algonquin.htm#materials); Arapaho (www.native-languages.org/arapaho

.htm#materials); Atikamekw (www.native-languages.org/atikamekw.htm#materials); Blackfoot (www.native-languages.org/black-foot.htm#materials); Cheyenne (www.native-languages.org/cheyenne.htm#materials); Cree (www.native-languages.org/cree.htm#materials); Montaignais (www.native-languages.org/montagnais.htm#materials); Kickapoo (www.native-languages.org/kickapoo.htm#materials); Lenape (www.native-languages.org/lenape.htm#materials); Maliseet-Passamaquoddy (www.native-languages.org/lenape.htm#materials); Menominee (www.native-languages.org/menominee.htm#materials); Miami-Illinois (www.native-languages.org/miami-illinois.htm#materials); Michif (www.native-languages.org/michif.htm#materials); Mi'kmaq (www.native-languages.org/michif.htm#materials); Ojibway (www.native-languages.org/chippewa.htm#materials); Wiyot (www.native-languages.org/wiyot.htm#materials): More materials about individual Indian languages.

Native American Literature

- *House Made of Dawn*; *Way to Rainy Mountain*; *The Ancient Child*; *In the Presence of the Sun*; *The Man Made of Words*; *The Names*; *Conversations With N. Scott Momaday*: Novels, stories, poems, and memoirs by Pulitzer Prize–winning Kiowa author N. Scott Momaday.

- *Smoke Signals*; *The Lone Ranger and Tonto Fistfight in Heaven*; *Reservation Blues*; *Ten Little Indians*; *First Indian on the Moon*; *The Business of Fancydancing*; *Indian Killer*; *Toughest Indian in the World*: Screenplay, stories, and poems by acclaimed Spokane/Coeur d'Alene writer Sherman Alexie.

- *Custer Died For Your Sins*; *Spirit and Reason*; *Red Earth, White Lies*; *Behind the Trail of Broken Treaties*: Essays and criticism by Standing Rock Lakota thinker Vine Deloria Jr.

- *Fools Crow*; *The Heartsong of Charging Elk*; *Winter in the Blood*; *The Indian Lawyer*; *The Death of Jim Loney*; *Riding the Earthboy 40*: Novels and poems by Blackfoot/Gros Ventre writer James Welch.

- *Love Medicine*; *Last Report on the Miracles at Little No Horse*; *Original Fire*; *Baptism of Desire*; *The Blue Jay's Dance*; *A Birth Year*; *The Birchbark House*; *Tracks*; *The Beet Queen*; *The Bingo Palace*; *Tales of Burning Love*; *The Antelope Wife*: Novels, poetry, and stories by Turtle Mountain Chippewa writer Louise Erdrich.

- *The Hiawatha*; *Little*: Novels by Leech Lake Ojibwe writer David Treuer.

- *Walking the Rez Road*; *Rez Road Follies*: Stories by Fond du Lac Ojibwe writer Jim Northrup.

- *Black Eagle Child: The Facepaint Narratives*; *Remnants of the First Earth*; *The Invisible Musician*; *The Rock Island Hiking Club*; *Winter of the Salamander*: Poetry and stories by Meskwaki author Ray A. Young Bear.

- *We Are the Dreamers*: Recent and early poetry by Mi'kmaq poet Rita Joe.

- *Indian Singing*: Poems by Onondaga-Micmac writer Gail Tremblay.

- *Absentee Indians and Other Poems*; *Trailing You*: Poems by White Earth Ojibwe writer Kimberly Blaeser.

- *Briefcase Warriors*; *Survivor's Medicine*: Stories and plays by Fond du Lac Ojibwe writer E. Donald Two-Rivers.

- *The Surrounded*; *Wind From an Enemy Sky*; *Runner in the Sun*; *The Hawk Is Hungry*: Books on Indian life by prominent Cree author D'Arcy McNickle.

- *The Rez Sisters*; *Dry Lips Oughta Move to Kapuskasing*; *Kiss of the Fur Queen*: Contemporary plays and a novel by Cree author Tomson Highway.

- *In Search of April Raintree*; *Spirit of the White Bison*; *Unusual Friendships*; *In the Shadow of Evil*: Novels and stories by Canadian Metis author Beatrice Mosionier.

- *Sojourners and Sundogs*; *Bent Box*; *Daughters Are Forever*; *Ravensong*: Stories, poems, and novels by Metis author Lee Maracle.

- *Only Drunks and Children Tell the Truth*; *The Baby Blue Bootlegger Blues*; *Buz'Gem Blues*: Plays and essays from Curve Lake Ojibwe writer Drew Hayden Taylor.

- *Fugitive Colors*; *Not Vanishing*; *Dream On*; *Fire Power*: Poetry from mixed-blood lesbian poet Chrystos.

- *Halfbreed*: Wrenching autobiography of Metis writer Maria Campbell.

- *Dirt Road Home*: Poems by Abenaki writer Cheryl Savageau.

- *Molly Molasses and Me*: Stories by Penobscot author Ssipsis.

American Indian Legends and Folklore

- *American Indian Myths and Legends*: Well-attributed collection of many diverse traditional stories of Native America. Like any other body of mythology, some of the stories involve adultery, rape, or sexual situations, so be sensible about which ones you share with young children.
- *On the Trail of Elder Brother: Glous'gap Stories of the Micmac Indians*: Collection of traditional stories retold by a Mi'kmaq author and illustrator.
- *American Indian Genesis*: Creation myths explored by a Blackfoot author.
- *The Manitous: The Spiritual World of the Ojibway*; *Ojibway Ceremonies*; *Tales the Elders Told*; *Mermaids and Medicine Women: Native Myths and Legends*; *Ojibway Heritage*; *Ojibway Tales*; *The Star-Man and Other Tales*; *Tales of the Anishinaubaek*; *The Bear-Walker*; *Dancing With a Ghost*: Books on Ojibway mythology, folklore, and spirituality by Ojibway writer Basil Johnston.
- *Full Moon Stories*: Thirteen Arapaho legends from an Arapaho writer/illustrator.
- *Sacred Stories of the Sweet Grass Cree*: Collection of Cree traditional stories and legends.

Native American Genealogy Books

- *Student's Guide to Native American Genealogy*: Step-by-step guide through beginner's genealogy and the process of tracing your American Indian ancestry.
- *Cherokee Proud*: How-to book about Cherokee genealogy.

Native American Art Books

- *Native North American Art*: American Indian art history from ancient times to today.
- *North American Indian Art*: Book by a Cree scholar on contemporary First Nations art.
- *Beauty, Honor, and Tradition: The Legacy of Plains Indian Shirts*: Showcasing Plains Indian beadwork, quillwork, clothing, and culture.
- *Southwestern Pottery*: Overview of Southwest Indian pottery, with photographs and advice for collectors.
- *The Fetish Carvers of Zuni*: Overview of fetish carvings, their forms, and meaning.
- *Looking at Indian Art of the Northwest Coast*: An overview of Northwestern Indian art, designs, and symbolism.
- *Inuit Art*: Photographs and history of Inuit carving and other traditional arts.

Native American Children's Books

- *Weaving a California Tradition* (Mono); *Ininatig's Gift of Sugar* (Chippewa); *Clambake* (Wampanoag); *Songs From The Loom* (Navajo); *A Story to Tell* (Tlingit); *Fort Chipewyan Homecoming* (Dene/Metis); *Four Seasons of Corn* (Winnebago); *Kinaalda* (Navajo); *The Sacred Harvest* (Ojibway); *Shannon, Ojibway Dancer* (Ojibway); *Children of Clay* (Pueblo); *Drumbeat, Heartbeat* (Assiniboine): The charming "We Are Still Here" photoessays on Indian life, featuring contemporary young protagonists and their families.
- *Children's Literature by Bruchac*: Children's books by Abenaki author Joseph Bruchac.
- *Crossing the Starlight Bridge*: A 9-year-old Penobscot girl struggles to keep her culture after her parents' divorce forces her to leave the reservation.
- *Night of the Full Moon*: Historical fiction about two girls (one Potawatomi, one white) trying to escape from a forced relocation westward.
- *Jim Thorpe: 20th-Century Jock*: Good biography of the celebrated athlete; deals with the complexity of his racial status as well as his athletics.
- *Forest Warrior*: Kids' biography of Ottawa Chief Pontiac.
- *Maria Tallchief*: Biography of Maria Tallchief, the Osage ballerina.
- *People of the Buffalo*: Book about the Plains Indians, written by a Metis (mixed-blood Cree) author.
- *Dreamcatcher*; *Powwow Summer*; *Jingle Dancer*; *Coyote in Love With a Star*; *Sky Dogs*; *Star Boy*; *Cheyenne Again*; *Death of the Iron Horse*; *Shingebiss: An Ojibwe Legend*; *Northwoods Cradle Song*: Picture books for young children about American Indian life.

American Indian Music and Other Audio

- *Up Where We Belong; Illuminations; Moonshot; She Used to Wanna Be a Ballerina*: Music by Cree folksinger Buffy Sainte-Marie.
- *Black Lodge Singers; Tribute to the Elders; People Dance; Powwow People; Kids' Pow-Wow Songs*: Music by the popular Blackfoot drum group Black Lodge Singers.
- *Dance Hard; Showtime; Here to Stay; Honor Eagle Feather; Come and Dance; Songs of Caddo*: Music from popular powwow band Northern Cree Singers.
- *Mawio'mi; Tomegan Gospem*: Music from Indian fusion-rock band Medicine Dream.
- *Echoes of the Night*: Audio recordings of Abenaki storyteller Tsonakwa.
- *Gluskabe Stories*: Audio recording of Abenaki storytelling by Joseph Bruchac.
- *Band of Wild Indians; Fingermonkey; Circle*: Music by Ojibwe musician Keith Secola.
- *My Ojibway Experience*: Music by Ojibway blues guitarist Billy Joe Green.

American Indian Movies and Other Videos

- *Bury My Heart at Wounded Knee* (HBO)
- *The Business of Fancydancing* (Wellspring)
- *Dance Me Outside* (A-Pix). Canadian movie tells a coming-of-age story set on an Ontario reserve. Native cast.
- *Dreamkeeper* (Hallmark)
- *Edge of America* (Showtime)
- *Four Sheets to the Wind* (First Look)
- *Grand Avenue* (HBO)
- *How the West Was Lost I & II* (Discovery)
- *Incident at Oglala: The Leonard Peltier Story*. Robert Redford documentary about American Indian Movement activist and political prisoner Leonard Peltier.
- *Lakota Woman* (New Line). The story of the American Indian Movement, based on Mary Crow Dog's autobiography.
- *The Magdalene Sisters* (Miramax)
- *Medicine River* (UAV)
- *Pow Wow Highway* (Anchor Bay)
- *Running Brave* (Tapeworm)
- *Skins* (First Look)
- *Skinwalkers* (Warner)
- *Smoke Signals* (Miramax). Sundance feature about a friendship between two Coeur d'Alene men, written by Sherman Alexie. Native cast, director, and writer, shot on site at the Coeur d'Alene reservation.
- *Thunderheart* (Columbia Tristar)
- *We're Still Here: Native Americans in America* (PBS)
- *Windtalkers* (MGM). War movie revolving around the Navajo code-talkers of World War II.

CHAPTER 9

Culturally Alert Counseling With European Americans

Lee J. Richmond
Loyola College Maryland

Mary H. Guindon
Johns Hopkins University

Most cross-cultural counseling texts do not include a chapter on counseling European American clients, although recent research supports the notion that the time has come for counselors to pay attention to this varied group (Sue, 2011; Todd & Abrams, 2011). It is commonly assumed that all a counselor needs to know in order to counsel European Americans is Western worldview–based counseling theory and some familiarity with the specific individual issue or issues that caused them to seek help. Yet culture for European Americans, as for all other humans, is a mediating factor in how issues or problems are both perceived and resolved.

In the vignettes that follow, Tom, Ellen, and Tony are all European Americans. However, they not only have different emotional and interpersonal concerns, they come from different ethnic and socioeconomic groups. Their backgrounds have influenced what they do and how they see the world, just as in any ethnic group.

In this chapter, European Americans are defined as so-called white people who reside in the United States and whose family origins are anywhere on the continent of Europe. They may have immigrated to America anytime from the colonial period to the present day and may vary in native language, religion, education, occupation, and socioeconomic status. Regardless of time of immigration, all European immigrants have shared common cultural characteristics, with the exception of those who have been shattered by the trauma of the fairly recent wars in Eastern Europe.

White people as a whole are viewed by others, and sometimes by themselves, as monolithic, as having been in America for a long time, and as the dominant group in American society, therefore as privileged. It should be noted that European Americans may not call themselves by that label, as dominant groups usually do not have such labels for themselves. But for the most part, white people of European descent share values and customs as a group, with many variations based on subgroup and regional identity. And as with all statements about ethnic characteristics, the statements here are generalizations, to be modified by individual differences, enculturation, and acculturation.

Tom, 52, manages a department of 10 employees responsible for computer training in a large state government agency. He earned a college degree on the G.I Bill after serving 6 years in the Navy. He received his initial computer training as a young seaman and then acquired on-the-job training through the government agency where he has worked since. Originally from northeast Pennsylvania and of Scotch Irish and German parents, Tom grew up in an economically depressed area. Some Polish and Italian families lived in the area, but Tom's parents looked down on "those Catholics" and didn't want him associating with them. His family, Protestants and older white Americans, thought of themselves as "the real Americans" and considered themselves better than these others. The family originally worked on a small farm and were "dirt poor," but in two generations they had saved enough money to buy a small general store where they sold clothing and notions to the miners. However, they lost everything during the Great Depression. Then Tom's family started working in the coal mines. Tom could have been a miner too, but the military saved him from that difficult occupation.

The father of three college-age daughters, he has been separated from his stay-at-home wife for 6 months and has temporarily moved in with his older sister and her husband. This living arrangement is not common in his culture and is a source of tension. Tom considers himself to be a self-made man. He is proud of his independence, a trait that he acquired from his Scotch Irish father's side. He is emotionally restrained, but he sees himself as pleasant and friendly. These qualities, he feels certain, come from his mother's side. His mother called this calm cheerfulness, or gemutlichkeit. Tom admired her "gentility"—her warm yet restrained style.

Tom has been turned down for two promotions in the last 3 years, although he was fully qualified for both jobs and has had outstanding performance evaluations. In each case, Tom believes that the individuals chosen—a 40-year-old African American woman and a 34-year-old Dominican man with "a strong accent"—were less qualified in years of service and amount of training. He expresses anger and resentment toward them and toward the government policies that he feels gave them preferential treatment.

He has been referred to the Employee Assistance Program (EAP) for counseling because he has been experiencing symptoms of anxiety and stress. He is angry and depressed and has been drinking nightly at the roadside tavern.

Ellen, 35, earns $240,000 a year as a vice president of a paint manufacturing company. She works long hours and travels frequently to several locations. In addition to her job, Ellen, a PhD-level chemist, has two children—a boy, 3, and a girl, 6. Ellen's husband Steve is also a PhD-level chemist, but unlike his wife he remains a bench chemist. Steve, Ellen, and their children are Reform Jews who practice their religion. The children attend Hebrew school one afternoon a week and on Sunday. During the week they attend both private school and afterschool day care.

There are several problems in the household. Although Steve is proud of Ellen's success at work, his salary is only a third of hers. He resents the amount of housework and childcare that he has to do when she travels. Furthermore, Ellen's mother, an Orthodox Jew, dislikes the fact that Ellen became Reform, which is a liberal movement in Judaism, when she married. Becoming Reform was a compromise for the couple, as Steve had had little contact with religious Judaism. His mother was a nonpracticing Jew by birth, and his father was not Jewish. By contrast, Ellen had grown up in a household where the Sabbath and the Jewish dietary laws were strictly observed. Her grandmother and grandfather used to converse in Yiddish, a language that her mother had learned but that Ellen did not learn. There are times when Ellen's grandparents still speak Yiddish around her. She thinks that they do so only when they are talking about their displeasure with her marriage to Steve.

Ellen thought she would please her mother by becoming a respected professional and a good home-maker. Instead, it seems that Ellen is never able to do enough. She doesn't really know what her mother expects of her. Furthermore, when her mother is angry about something, she involves the children, saying things to them like "You should come to my house, and have a real Shabbos [Sabbath] dinner with candles and wine, not like your other grandmother who would serve you bacon if she could."

Ellen's mother often remarks directly to Ellen that if Steve were a better provider, Ellen wouldn't have to work so hard and be away from the children so much. Ellen loves her work but wonders if life would be much simpler if she should return to being a bench chemist, earn what Steve earns, and place the children in public school. Recently the live-in maid quit. Feeling overwhelmed, Ellen decides to seek counseling.

Tony, a high school senior, works in his father's Italian delicatessen and grocery store, where he has worked afternoons after school since he was in the eighth grade. His father told Tony that, upon graduation, he could earn a real salary in the business and soon start doing some of the buying. It is obvious to Tony that his father is very proud to be the owner of a store that was started as a pushcart by his immigrant great-grandfather and passed down from generation to generation. It is also obvious to Tony that his father intends for him to own the business in the future. The problem is that Tony is not interested in doing so and does not know how to tell his father.

Although Tony plays on the school football team, and enjoys it, sports are not his main interest either. Ever since Mrs. Garner, his English teacher, praised him for his latest composition, Tony has toyed with his real love: writing. He has always secretly enjoyed writing stories and poetry, which he has kept hidden in a secret place under the loose floorboards in his room. He never expected to go to college, but when Mrs. Garner told him that he might qualify for a scholarship at the state university, the thought of college began to take concrete form. He fears his father's disappointment because his father considers college impractical. What seems really strange to Tony is that his sister, Mary Louise, has the real head for business and his father doesn't see it. She could run the store, but if his father has his way, that will never be.

Mrs. Garner thinks he should begin preparations to apply to colleges. When he told her that he will have to go into the family business even though he doesn't want to, she suggested that he talk to his school counselor. No one in his family has ever talked to a counselor as far as he knows, although every now and then his mother goes to talk to Father Leo, the local parish priest. If his dad has problems he would never let anyone know it. Tony does not know what to do. Perhaps he will speak with Mrs. Garner again. Maybe seeing the school counselor will help, but Tony sure doesn't know how.

Tom, Ellen, and Tony are all European Americans, although their worldviews are quite different from each other. Activity 9.1 challenges you to think about how you would counsel each of these clients.

Imagine that Tom, Ellen, and Tony are your clients.

1. What do you see as each person's issues?

   - Tom:

   - Ellen:

   - Tony:

2. What approach to counseling would you use in working with each of them?

   - Tom:

   - Ellen:

   - Tony:

3. What do you think you need to know about European American cultures and history to work effectively with each of them?

   - Tom:

   - Ellen:

   - Tony:

After you read this chapter, your answers to these questions may change.

To establish a baseline of knowledge, you are invited to complete Activity 9.2.

Activity 9.2   Knowledge About European Americans

This self-assessment activity helps you determine how much you know about the history of Europeans in America and about their worldviews. It might provide a guide, and a motivation, for what is contained in this chapter. When you have finished reading the chapter, you may come back to these questions and answer them again. See if you are more confident in your answers the second time.

In the blank after each statement below, place a T if you think the statement is true, F if you think it is false, or DN if you do not know. The answers appear at the end of the activity.

1. People of English, Dutch, French, and Spanish origin were the only Europeans in the original 13 colonies._____

2. Georgia was the only English settlement established as a Catholic colony._____

3. Reason and nature, rather than revelation from the Bible, demonstrated the existence of God in the articulated philosophy of the people who shaped the United States as a nation._____

4. After the French and Indian War, it was clear that Britain stood triumphant in America._____

5. The founders of the United States strove for liberty and justice for all people who lived here._____

6. The wave of immigration that brought Eastern and Mediterranean European immigrants to America occurred largely in the late 19th century._____

7. Like the explorers who originally "discovered" America, the Eastern Europeans came to bring new wealth back to the countries that they had left._____

8. There is little difference between the cultures of Mediterranean people and Northern Europeans._____

9. The accomplishments that European Americans made during the 19th and early 20th centuries gave them a feeling of superiority, even though other peoples had assisted in these achievements._____

10. White females have historically shared in the achievements accorded to white males._____

11. By the end of the 21st century, European Americans will not comprise the majority of the American population._____

12. Racism affects those who hold racist views as well as those who are victims of those views._____

13. Diversity pertains to European Americans as well as to other groups of people._____

14. It was not until after the Civil War that Jewish men, like black men, were considered citizens and allowed to vote._____

15. The "Old Irish," or Scotch Irish, Protestants welcomed Irish Catholics to America because they knew that many suffered greatly from the potato famine in Ireland._____

Answers: Of the 15 statements above, 3, 6, 9, 11, 12, and 13 are true. The rest are false.

If you scored 15 or 14 correct, you know some basic facts about European American history and characteristics. If you scored 12 or 13, you are on the right track. If you scored less than 12, you have much to learn about how Americans, whatever their race or ethnic culture, became who they are today.

HISTORICAL ORIGINS OF EUROPEAN AMERICA

Modern North America has roots in the worldwide European search for wealth in the late 15th century. England, Holland, Spain, and France each explored and seized parts of what came to be called America from its native inhabitants (Gutman, 1989). Many immigrants followed, seeking wealth, adventure, release from indenture, and freedom to practice their religion.

It was only logical that each European nation's settlements in America would occur in the geographic areas where its early explorers traveled. English colonies were first established in Jamestown, Virginia, and in Plymouth, Massachusetts. These colonies were followed by other English settlements up and down the East Coast. The Dutch paid an Englishman, Henry Hudson, to explore the area around what is now known as the Hudson River and claimed that territory for Holland. The Dutch named it New Amsterdam and held it until the second Anglo-Dutch war in 1664. It was then claimed by England and was renamed New York.

Table 9.1   European American Nationality/Ethnic Groups and Immigration Patterns

Historical Origins	Nationality/Ethnic Group	Major Geographic Settlement Areas
Early settlers/Old Europeans (late 16th–early 18th century)		
Original settlers	English	Virginia, Massachusetts, other colonies
	Dutch	New York, Delaware River Valley*
	French	(Canada), New England
	Spanish	Florida, American West
		Jews: through Holland to Delaware River Valley,* New Mexico
	German	Delaware River Valley,* Virginia
	Swedish	Delaware River Valley*
Old Europeans/North Britons	"Scotch Irish": Northern Irish, Northern English, Lowland Scots	13 Colonies, Appalachians**
First wave of "Hyphenated Americans" (mid-18th century)	Irish Catholics	Cities/slums in New England, New York, other areas
	German Lutherans, German Catholics	Small towns in Delaware Valley, Midwest
	German Jews	American West
	Scandinavians: Swedish, Norwegian	Minnesota, Upper Midwest
Mediterranean and Eastern Europeans (late 19th century)	Italian, Greek	Industrialized cities: Northern/middle East Coast, Chicago, St. Louis, San Francisco, New Orleans
	Non-Jews: Polish, Hungarian, Lithuanian, Czech, Russian	East Coast port cities, then throughout United States
	Jews: Polish, Russian	East Coast port cities, then throughout United States

*Eastern Pennsylvania, Delaware, Southern New Jersey

**Tennessee, Kentucky, eastern Midwest

By the end of the 17th century, three-fourths of North America was actually claimed as New France. However, France was not as successful at settling its territories as was England. Over the years and after several wars, almost all French lands were lost to England. Most of the rest of the lands in the Americas were Spanish. Following Christopher Columbus's lead, Ponce de Leon, Hernando de Soto, and Francesco Vasquez de Coronado continued Spanish exploration of the New World. St. Augustine, Florida, was actually the first permanent European settlement in what is now the United States, as it had become a Spanish fort in 1565. However, most Spanish settlements north of Mexico were in the American West, in places such as Santa Fe (1609) and Taos (1615). What are now Southern California, Texas, and parts of Oklahoma were also explored and settled as part of New Spain.

The English, Dutch, French, and Spanish were not the only European peoples to settle in the Americas during this period. Some Swedes also came to settle in the Delaware River Valley. Many Germans, known as Old Germans, came to the colonies in the 1700s. They soon mixed with the Anglo inhabitants, due to their predominantly Protestant and cultural similarities. Tom, from this chapter's first vignette, proudly traces some of his paternal ancestors back to these original Old German settlers in Northeast Pennsylvania. Jewish families, fleeing the Spanish Inquisition, migrated to Holland and from there to New Amsterdam. Other Jews journeyed to Mexico in the 1600s and from there to Santa Fe and Taos, where their ancestors still live (Tobias, 1992). From the second vignette, Ellen's husband, Steve, can count these immigrants among his earliest American ancestors and still has cousins in that area.

Over a hundred years after the original English settlements, Northern Irish, Northern English, and Lowland Scottish Protestants—the North Britons (Fischer, 1989), who later called themselves Scotch Irish or Scots Irish—came in waves in the 1700s to the English colonies. Since the fertile flat lands were already taken, the Scotch Irish largely settled in the mountainous country west of the coast. Tom's maternal ancestors, who settled in the mountains of western Pennsylvania and northern West Virginia, were among these immigrants. They experienced significant bias, being seen as uneducated and violent people, in contrast to the more pastoral and mercantile English and Germans. The Scotch Irish were a very individualistic and pioneering people and settled the backwoods. Many of them, like Daniel Boone, struck out to cross the Appalachians into what is today Kentucky and Tennessee and points further west. These Scotch Irish produced many American writers (e.g., Poe, Irving), military leaders (e.g., Grant, McClellan), captains of American business (e.g., Rockefeller), and no fewer than 13 U.S. presidents, including Jackson, Wilson, and Clinton (Leyburn, 1962; Webb, 2004).

The Nation's Founders: Their Principles and Practices

The founders of the United States were, for the most part, of English descent and lived throughout the original 13 colonies. In a literal sense, every person who had a part in the formation of the United States might be called a founder (Cousins, 1958), including African American, American Indian, and European American men and women, all of whom played parts. However, in time the term *founder* has come to be used more selectively. It is applied to the largely Anglo-American men who drew up the Declaration of Independence, instigated the war against England, created the Constitution, and with some struggle, united the states.

The early Americans of English ancestry lived throughout the 13 colonies. There were different regions in these colonies, which affected their cultures. In the flatter lands of the Southern colonies, many people lived on farms, tobacco plantations, and, farther south, cotton plantations. In the more mercantile North, many European Americans lived in cities or on small farms that the family worked. It is ironic that the founding fathers, who spoke so glowingly of freedom and equality, applied neither concept to slaves, nor to American Indian peoples, nor to white women, who were literally owned by their husbands.

Much of America's vitality lay in the articulated Enlightenment philosophy of Western Europe. One notion that Enlightenment philosophers stressed was freedom of religion, including freedom *from* religion. Many of the early settlers came for freedom to practice their own faith (e.g., the Pilgrims in Plymouth, the Quakers in Pennsylvania, the Catholics in Maryland, the Congregationalists in Connecticut and Rhode Island). While many colonists called themselves Christians and were versed in scripture, others among the founders were naturalists, rationalists, or Unitarians (Cousins, 1958), believing in divine creation but not a divine trinity nor revelation nor the power of a deity to influence human affairs. Reason and nature, rather than scripture, demonstrated the existence of a God for many of the founders. The "brotherhood of man" and the belief in his ability to govern himself in a just society free from domination by any Church was their creed, and it remains an important belief of the American people to this day.

Old and New European Americans and a New Kind of Struggle

The New World was seen as an opportunity to get away from the old world of class issues, religious strife, and the competitiveness of European nations. This impulse, coupled with the common cause of liberty and justice for all (white) men, inspired the new republic and bound together those who had lived in the former British colonies. The philosophy of the day was that of amalgamation. Just as various metals can combine to make one amalgam, stronger than any of the metals alone, so the pervasive ethic was that the various groups of largely Northern European American people who lived in America could combine and make one strong American people. Differences were ignored. Thus, a Jew named Chaim Soloman, friend of George Washington and financier of the Revolutionary War, Alexander Hamilton, son of a Huguenot and first secretary of the Treasury, and John Carroll, a Catholic from Maryland and signer of the Declaration of Independence, all became part of the amalgam that was the United States. Yet these Americans were not prepared to amalgamate the influx of European immigrants that was yet to come in the next century. These immigrants would bring worldviews that differed significantly from those of the early citizens of the United States and from each other. They had to acclimate themselves to a nation whose inhabitants were not entirely open to accepting them.

The Second Wave of Immigration

A large wave of European immigration took place starting in the mid-1800s, long after the settlements of the Eastern Seaboard had become colonies and after the colonies had become states (Boorstin, 1974). The Western Europeans who came to America in the mid-1800s formed the vanguard of what came to be known as the *hyphenated Americans* (Boorstin, 1974), that is, German-Americans, Irish-Americans, Scandinavian-Americans, and so forth. These immigrant groups left their countries of origin because those places could no longer economically support them (Boorstin, 1974).

This group of immigrants was similar in some ways to the earlier dominant European immigrant groups, as they were also largely from Western Europe, but they experienced significant bias from the earlier European groups. For some of them, their religion was different. For others, their language was. The Irish Catholics constituted the largest group, followed by the new Germans. After the potato famine of 1847 and beyond, droves of people left Ireland in order to survive. They generally settled in cities, in slums and shanty towns. These "Low Irish," as they were called, were not welcomed by the more refined "Old Irish" Anglo Protestants who had long before settled with the English in Boston and other cities. Nor were they welcomed by the Scotch Irish, who immediately identified themselves as separate by assuming that new name. The Irish Catholics huddled together and did the hard labor that a country building railroads, bridges, canals, and buildings needed. Women worked as maids in houses and hotels, and many of the men served as soldiers in the Civil War.

Great waves of German immigration also occurred in the 19th century. They followed an early immigration of Germans who had fled Germany in the 1700s for political and religious reasons. The early Germans were already living in New York State, Pennsylvania, and the Shenandoah Valley in Virginia. By the 1800s most of the earlier German immigrants were English speaking. The old Germans did not at first welcome the influx of new Germans, who set up little German-speaking towns within cities. In a short while, however, the new immigrants became bankers, brewers, machinists, and tailors. Tom, from the opening scenario, counted many of his paternal ancestors among this group. Most of the mid-19th century immigrants from Germany were Lutherans or Catholics. However, with them came 250,000 German-speaking Jews, who were by and large Reform Jews, meaning that they had progressive and secular ideas on politics, religion, and social behavior (Richmond, 1999, 2003). They spoke German in their temples and behaved in other ways very much like their Christian countrymen. It was from this group of immigrants that Ellen's husband Steve's immediate family descended, although the German language was replaced by English by the time of his grandfather's generation. In fact, his mother was not reared in the religion at all, and thus marrying a non-Jew was not an issue in her family.

Another major group of peoples who immigrated to the United States throughout the 1800s was the Scandinavians, primarily Norwegians and Swedes. Population increase, mandatory military training, and oppression drove them out of their countries. In 1858, in Sweden the State Lutheran Church became the official religion, and people who practiced otherwise were fined, jailed, or exiled. America looked like a place of escape for many. In Minnesota, government treaties with the American Indians made much inexpensive land available, and the Homestead Act of 1862 offered land to settlers who promised to live on it for 5 years (Zinn, 2005). Minnesota had become a state in 1858 and had a climate similar to that of Norway and Sweden. Swedes and Norwegians saw both freedom and opportunity in the American Midwest, and they settled it.

The Late 19th Century Waves of European Immigration

The immigrants thus far discussed were all Northern and Western Europeans. More difficult to assimilate were the Mediterranean and Eastern European peoples who came during the latter half of the 19th century. Italians constituted the largest group of Mediterranean immigrants, although Greeks also came in significant numbers. During the latter half of the 19th century, many Italians migrated to America with the intent to earn money and return to their homeland. Heavy taxes, antiquated agricultural methods, and lack of industrial opportunities caused men to leave Italy and seek their fortunes in the United States. For the most part, the Italian immigrants were poorly educated, unskilled, and illiterate. They found low-paying jobs in a burgeoning industrial America. Instead of returning home, however, most eventually brought their families over to the new country. In the third vignette, both Tony's paternal and maternal ancestors were among this immigrant group. His great-grandfather immigrated first, then worked and saved his money to bring over his soon-to-be bride. The largely Catholic Italian immigrants, like the Irish Catholics before them, were not easily socially integrated into the American society. They met with much negative prejudice, even from fellow Catholics. The Italian immigrants built their own small communities where they lived, often managed grocery stores, and developed a community life of their own. This was the case with Tony's family, and his parents expected him to continue the family tradition. The Italian population grew fast and spread rapidly throughout East Coast cities and other urban areas such as Chicago, St. Louis, San Francisco, and New Orleans. By 1900 there were over 20,000 Italians living in Philadelphia alone.

Greeks came to America at approximately the same time as Italians and for similar reasons (Killian & Agathangelou, 2005). Most stayed and then brought their families to America. Despite the fact that Greeks and Italians differed in religion and language, many Anglo-Americans, who were not very familiar with either group, lumped Italians and Greeks together as Mediterranean people hitherto unknown and, at first, unwelcomed.

While the Irish, Germans, Scandinavians, Italians, and Greeks continued to arrive through the turn of the 20th century, another wave of European peoples immigrated to the United States in the late 19th century, this time from Eastern Europe. Half of the Eastern European immigrants were Jews, predominantly from Poland but also from Russia. Non-Jewish Poles, Hungarians, Lithuanians, and Czechs and other Eastern Europeans had various reasons for leaving their country of origin; most came to escape conscription in the army or starvation at home, and almost all were poor. Most of these people had great difficulty with the English language. It was hard for the nation to assimilate them, and many did not wish to be assimilated.

The Jewish immigrants did not share the dominant religion of most Americans, yet they were largely European. Some were Orthodox. Ellen's mother descended from this group. Others whose families had once been Orthodox were secular. These new Jewish immigrants had experienced only totalitarianism. To the assimilated Reform Jews who had come to America in the early to mid-1800s from Berlin and its suburbs, the Orthodox Jews from tiny towns and ghettoes, like Ellen's grandparents, were backward strangers engaging in religious practices that had been abandoned by Reform Jews, who liked to call themselves Americanized Jews (Shapiro, 1992).

Also strange and sometimes an embarrassment to Americanized Jewry were the secular Eastern European Jewish immigrants who were tired of waiting for God or a Messiah to redeem them from the oppression that they had suffered under the Czars, and who often became radicals, particularly Marxists. Because Marx believed that people and societies produced their own material lives and were responsible for their own betterment and that of society (Nerlich, 1989), some secular Jews who espoused that philosophy became part of the workers movement. *The Jewish Daily Forward*, a Yiddish-language newspaper, was founded in 1897 by the Jewish Socialist Press. It helped immigrant Jews define what it meant to be a Jew in America, fostered the American labor movement, and became the most widely read foreign language newspaper in the nation. Ellen's grandparents and her mother continued to read Yiddish, occasionally speak it in their home, and identified closely with their Eastern European origins.

However, Jews were not the only late 19th century immigrants who struggled in adapting to the dominant American culture. Language was a problem for most of them and was an immediate identifier of difference. These Southern and Eastern European immigrants were unfamiliar with the grammar, syntax, and intonation of the English language. With little help coming from the culture at large, each new ethnic group had to struggle to adapt to the culture of the Anglo-American majority and be accepted by them. Additionally, the various immigrant groups were not always friendly to each other.

From European Immigrants to European Americans

Each new European group that came to America became the brunt of stereotype and suspicion. Cartoons and Vaudeville shows caricatured the Germans, Irish, Italians, and Jews who had recently arrived. Gradually, however, even if not liked by all, each was absorbed into 20th century America. By the end of the first quarter of the 20th century, European immigration had slowed. Eventually, as described in Chapter 4, European Americans of all ethnicities were lumped as so-called Caucasians and came to be regarded as a monolithic majority culture, different from so-called Negro, Hispanic, Native, and Asian American minorities. In truth, however, European Americans have never become such an amalgam. Customs and religions continue to distinguish groups of European Americans from each other in important ways. The most basic distinction among the groups has been between Northern European Protestant Americans and other European Americans.

Most recently, immigrants from Kosovo arrived as victims of the 1998–1999 war. The migration that peaked during the late 1990s and early 2000s brought traumatized adults and children through Western Europe to the shores of the United States. Being disaster victims, many arrived needing financial and mental health support. Furthermore, exposure to terrorism, whether direct or indirect, required post-exposure intervention (Slone & Shoshani, 2008). The need for treatment, including normalizing fears and teaching basic stress management techniques, makes this group, like Middle Eastern victims of violence (see Chapter 10), different from other European immigrants.

However, instead of being viewed as a multiplicity of groups with distinct ethnic origins, all whites have tended to be perceived as a monolithic majority and thought to share common culture and social privilege. There is some validity to the notion that European Americans have been subsumed under the racial category of "white." However, throughout much of American history, Anglo-American Protestants dominated the political, economic, and cultural scene. As a result, other European Americans have had to try to assimilate to the Anglo standard, for example, masking their identities by Anglicizing their names in order to have opportunities (Reed, 1997).

RETHINKING THE TRADITIONAL EUROPEAN AMERICAN WORLDVIEW: ITS BENEFITS AND LIMITATIONS

A description of the roots of Western thought and philosophy from which the dominant European American culture sprang is beyond the scope of this chapter. However, most readers are likely to be aware of the general beliefs that have emerged from these roots. Fundamental American values include individualism and autonomy, faith in problem solving that is action oriented, the desirability of competitiveness and achievement, and materialism. These, along with an orientation toward the future, the maintenance of rigid time schedules, and a strict work ethic in which hard work results in both monetary and intrinsic worth, were all used to build a nation. Trust in rationalism and empiricism (i.e.,

the belief that reality is knowable and measurable through reason and observation), the imperative of self-discipline and self-monitoring, a belief in utilitarianism (i.e., what is useful is good and is morally superior), and the importance of thoughts and actions over feelings were all a part of the making of America.

The political and commercial accomplishments that were achieved during the 19th and early 20th centuries in the United States were accompanied by European American feelings of superiority. It was as though white Anglo-American males were masters of a universe that their own ingenuity had created. They wrote about it, sang songs about it, sculpted it, and painted pictures of it. Then, by means of a new art form called "movies" (an industry that was actually largely run by Jewish men, but which nevertheless produced films that portrayed the values of the dominant Anglo-American Protestant culture), they mythologized it and eventually worshipped it to such a degree that their version of the dominant worldview became the only one acceptable for many. This myth shaped the belief that to be an Anglo-American white male was superior to being anyone else.

The white Northern European Protestant American culture held the worldview that was responsible for scientific experimentation and led to many accomplishments. Freedom, individual rights, geographic mobility, the nuclear family, individual achievement, and free market competition became the dominant ways of thinking in the United States. This worldview was seen in both Western Europe and in the United States as the only possible "civilized" view. Anglo-American Protestant culture treated other manners and worldviews as unfamiliar, ignorable, or discountable.

There are many positive elements inherent in the European American worldview, but there are also limitations to it. However much women and minority Americans may have played a part in the achievements of the age, little mention was made of it. The white male was seen as the sole creator of this world of invention, of goods beyond belief, of the marvels of mass communication, and of the tools of mass communication. He, who had just recently freed his black slaves and still held power over his wife, believed that he was rightfully the privileged of the earth, and he continued to instigate and uphold laws that reinforced that view, even in all children who read his textbooks. Non-whites, be they Native peoples, Asians, Latinos/Latinas, or African Americans, were seen as racially inferior (Gutman, 1989). Non-whites were seen as people to be used for the good of the dominant culture, not as valuable human beings in their own right. This privilege that was gifted only to white Americans was legally protected throughout the first half of the 20th century. In a large part of the nation, black Americans were excluded from the front seats of trolleys and trains, forced to use separate lavatories and drink from separate water fountains. In most American cities they could not try on clothing in department stores, nor sleep in hotels that were not designated for them alone. Black children could not eat in the very restaurants where their mothers might work as cooks or cleaners. Minorities, for the most part, could acquire only menial jobs that whites either did not want or could not do. Thus, contradictions to the Western European values of freedom and equality caused much injustice to large groups of people. The ethos was the aforementioned denigration of any non-Anglo-Americans.

In the last half of the 20th century, Americans rethought the messages of Anglo-American and European American superiority that they may have learned from earlier, less tolerant generations, at home and in school. There was a trend to recognize that multiple worldviews exist and are equally valid.

As mentioned in Chapter 5, cultural pluralism, rather than amalgamation or assimilation, has become the model as European Americans reclaim pride in their ethnic heritages and as America becomes the home of increasing numbers of non-European immigrants (Portes & Rimbaut, 2001; Reed, 1997).

Nevertheless, significant elements of the European American worldview predominate in the nation's values, customs, and norms. That is especially true of the chief assumption of the dominant European worldview that success is within

the control of the individual. Consistent with that view is that people have a duty to act in their own behalf and thereby determine their own futures. In fact, that belief, and an opportunity to enact it, remains one of the main reasons that people from all nations continue to this day to immigrate to the United States.

Roots of the Counseling Profession in the European American Worldview

What has evolved to be the contemporary counseling profession was founded on the premise of the Western, dominant-culture worldview. Counseling is a fusion of many influences (Belkin, 1988). It is also often called a uniquely American profession. It incorporates the scientific orientation of psychology and psychiatry through the influences of seminal European thinkers such as Sigmund Freud and Anton Pavlov, the testing movement through the works of European Americans such as G. Stanley Hall and James Cattell, and the pragmatism of the social reform and vocational guidance movements of the late 19th and early 20th century United States through the work of those such as Jane Addams and Frank Parsons. Later, the precepts of Carl Rogers and others melded these influences into the profession of counseling. Inherent in the practice of counseling is the view that people can realize who they are, change, and find personal meaning and mission in life.

The counseling profession was founded on the scientific assumption that all phenomena are knowable and that all problems are solvable through observation, analysis, and reason. The founding European American researchers and thinkers did not question this worldview. They assumed it had universality, applying to all people regardless of race, gender, country of origin, religion, or ethnicity. They also would have assumed that their worldview was superior to others. They did not know, nor could they have known, how the sociocultural, socioeconomic, and linguistic differences among the diverse groups that settled in the United States would need to be accounted for to meet each group's educational and mental health needs.

Constructivist thinking, which is presented in Chapter 1, led to a change in counseling orientation. Indeed, the development of the social constructionist movement is seen by many to have significant ethical implications for counselors (Guterman, 2008). A relevant approach is Yamagishi's (2011) concept of a *niche construction approach*. Culture can be conceived of as a social institution (or niche) of specific constraints and incentives, not a universally applicable set of assumptions. In this approach, individuals connect "culturally shared beliefs and culture-specific behaviors" (Yamagishi, 2011, p. 251) in pursuit of goals that also anticipate the actions of others. For example, a theory of career personality types is applicable to occupations in the United States but is not applicable in many other cultures where the social structure of work is different. (For a good grounding in the history of the psychological constructionist approach, see Gendron, 2009.) Embracing constructivism, the "Fourth Force"

developed multicultural and cross-cultural counseling methods and, more recently, led to a "Fifth Force," one that recognizes the importance of social justice and advocacy.

MENTAL HEALTH ISSUES FOR EUROPEAN AMERICANS

Four significant and related contributors to mental health problems for European Americans are (1) social privilege or entitlement, (2) isolation, (3) intolerance, and (4) gender roles. Each is addressed in turn. Those four issues have also influenced the career development and mental health of European American people. In particular, the tendencies toward individualism and self-sufficiency that are typical of Northern European Americans exacerbate career- and family-related mental health problems. They are especially exaggerated when monetary problems exist and entitlement is challenged. The vignette of Tom illustrates this issue. See Activity 9.3 for an opportunity to apply these ideas to his case.

Activity 9.3   Working With Tom

In the vignette at the beginning of this chapter, Tom expects to succeed at work and feels anger and resentment that this has not happened. He suggests that the African American woman and the Dominican man who were successful were less qualified than he is. There is an implication that he deserved the job and that those who received it did so only because they were minorities. Such is commonly the case for European Americans when unexpected barriers to goals present themselves. Some European Americans, like Tom, react in emotionally problematic ways, using denial, resentment, and anger as coping mechanisms. As Tom's counselor, answer the following:

1. What part do you think privilege plays in Tom's thinking?

2. If you were Tom's counselor, how would you deal with his notion of privilege?

3. If you were Tom's counselor, how would you work with his anger?

Issues Associated With Entitlement

The idea of privilege, sometimes called entitlement, may be attractive. However, it can create problems, not only for those who lack it, but also for those to whom it is attributed.

European Americans generally have invisible privileges, as described in Chapter 3. They do not experience the kinds of barriers in work and life that are routinely encountered by others. However, they are not aware of the psychological dangers of their privileged status. Because of the high expectancy levels of many whites, coupled with a lack of social support, setbacks such as loss of an expected promotion or being denied access to a professional or social club might cause difficulties that would be hard for less privileged people to comprehend. Tom's feelings in response to not being promoted illustrate this concept. Tom is distraught about being turned down for two jobs. He belongs to a group of Anglo-Americans who believe that they are entitled to get what they want based on effort and qualifications, as if social conditions should never get in the way. He is particularly upset because members of groups who were not as qualified, according to him, were given the opportunities that he thought that he deserved. While it is natural to feel disappointed when one does not get what one wants, Tom's reaction was one of bitterness and resentment along with anger and depression. He was not only upset because of losing two job opportunities, he was also resentful because those opportunities were given to people of the "wrong type," people whom he believed were inherently not as capable. Members of nondominant groups frequently experience denial of opportunity. This bias may similarly cause depression and anger in non-European Americans. Thus privilege causes anger and sadness in both the haves and the have nots, in a sense.

Individualism and Isolation

The individualism of the mythic American hero can be a mental health hazard. The mythic American hero is frequently thought of as one who leaves family and friends to go forth and bring about some good as a result of his or, in very few cases, her journey (Fiedler, 1966).

It has been suggested that Northern European Americans frequently live more isolated lives than do most Mediterranean and Eastern Europeans, Latinos/Latinas, or African Americans (McGill & Pearce, 2005). In the second vignette that opened this chapter, Ellen follows an individualistic pattern that results in both gains and losses for her. She leaves the Orthodox religion of her childhood. When she does this, she loses some closeness with her family of origin. She feels fragmented because she does much with very little help and few people to turn to. She seeks a counselor to assist her with her concerns partly in order to connect with someone who she believes will be helpful.

The simple fact that most European Americans live in nuclear rather than extended families keeps them from having the kind of supportive sharing that is typical of multigenerational households. Because courage and lonely individualism are characteristics of the American hero, some young people may actually be attracted to an "ideal of aloneness rather than togetherness" (Bellah, Madsen, Sullivan, Swindler, & Tipton, 1996, p. 146). Despite this romantic notion of freedom, there is a danger in a person being hyperindividualistic with little regard for community. According to Bellah et al. (1996), radical individualism prevents European Americans from understanding their connectedness to each other. They propose that European Americans seek community especially in religion because of this isolation.

The Consequences of Intolerance

Intolerance can be described as "the state of being unwilling or unable to endure or accept the beliefs, perspectives, or practices of others. It also involves a lack of recognition and respect for the fundamental rights and choices of others" (Guindon, Green, & Hanna, 2003, p. 168). Many writers have described the social and psychological problems that result from intolerance in the form of racism, sexism, or homophobia (Davidson, 1999; DuBois, 1903/ 1961; Fanon, 1969; Hanna, Talley, & Guindon, 2000; Kleg, 1993; Miller, 1986; Robinson & Ginter, 1999; Sue, 1981).

European Americans are, of course, not alone in being intolerant toward others who are not like them. However, because they are members of the dominant culture and, de facto, have been in a position of power, they are more likely to be oppressor than oppressed.

As part of their social privilege, some European Americans learn to maintain social distance from those who are perceived to be different from them. Many are fearful and less trusting of the ethnic or racial "others"—strangers who are not like them in race, ethnicity, or social class. Some of this discomfort is due to lack of contact. Many European Americans, unlike members of other ethnic groups, generally do not have to spend a lot of time with ethnic others, due to housing and social patterns. Especially with regard to African Americans, some European Americans experience fear when they are in situations where they themselves are not in the majority. As a result, European Americans are denied the richness of contact with the cultures of people of color.

Furthermore, those who do not tolerate diverse others, culturally or interpersonally, can not only do harm to these diverse others, but also cause pain for themselves and their societies, even if unknowingly (Guindon et al., 2003). Racism and sexism, where they exist, are seen by many as forms of oppression, thus all members of society are its victims (Pettigrew, 1981).

European American Gender Issues

The fourth and final mental health–related issue for European Americans is gender. Prior to the impact of the women's movement and the advent of feminist therapy, white women seeking career roles outside of the home were looked upon as having psychological problems. In the 1960s and 1970s, as a result of federal grants and initiatives, many married women were able to go to college without as much social stigma as in the past in order to retool after having experienced a break in their education. The first author of this chapter (Richmond, 1972) studied these so-called returning women and the special programs that community colleges, colleges, and universities provided to ease their way. She found that, frequently, returning women would tell their college counselors that their private therapists urged them not to come to school, but rather deal with their intrapsychic conflicts in order to quell their high achievement needs outside of the home (Richmond, 1972).

Although this may sound extreme in the present day, Blustein (2006) reports research that documents that women still "face various forms of sexism in their schooling, preparation for careers, and in the occupational context" (p. 168). Power, according to Blustein, remains at the root of many inequities. It is important that counselors, both male and female, are aware of the many gender issues that continue to face women. (See Chapter 14 for a fuller treatment of gender.)

In the area of family roles for European Americans, there is great conflict due to gender differences. Men, rich and poor, have problems adjusting to the changing roles of males within the family (Waite & Nielsen, 2002). The revolution in the roles of today's dual-earner family has caused many men to be confused about the roles that they play as husbands and fathers, compared to the roles that they grew up expecting to play. What is thought of as acceptable male and female roles influences what is viewed as acceptable sexual behavior, as well as issues such as who diapers, cooks the dinner, and earns the higher salary. In the case of Ellen, there is a reversal of traditional sex roles. Ellen earns more; she travels for work. And Steve, her husband, resents that he is left with childcare and housework. The next sections explore the European American gender dilemmas further.

Activity 9.4   Gender and European Americans

The role reversal between Ellen and Steve is becoming more common among European Americans.

1. As a counselor, how might you help Steve?

2. Think about all of the gender issues in Ellen and Steve's story. List them. How would you address each of them?

3. In what ways is the gender gap between white women and white men narrowing?

4. In what ways is it widening?

European American Men

It is commonly held that European American men have been taught to show only limited emotional expression. When hurt, for example, most are taught not to cry. As a result of this emotional containment, men may feel isolated or alienated during difficult times. They may be guarded about revealing family problems and acknowledging personal problems. Sports and alcohol may substitute for intimacy. Even today, many European American men have a difficult time turning to counselors for help in resolving their problems. Stress reactions associated with lack of achievement are a common result of the dominant-culture worldview that emphasizes performance and achievement over affiliation and relationships.

European American Women

Because the dominant culture favors the European American male, European American women are in a paradoxical social situation, as they are both members and nonmembers of the dominant culture. Their struggle for gender equality was long fought, and gains were hard won. For example, women's right to vote, including European American women, was not granted until 1920. Another 52 years went by before the U.S. Congress passed the Equal Rights Amendment that granted women legal rights to equal education and equal pay for equal work. Although the major legal battles are over, the war is not yet won. Since many European American men "live to work," many men still expect women to keep a home and care for children while those women are also working outside the home to help support the family. As a result, European American women (and some men) struggle to balance work and family responsibilities as do Ellen and Steve.

Women need more family-friendly, relational, and employee-driven workplaces in the place of the traditional, individual- and employer-driven ones in which work and family are completely separate (Moen & Han, 2001). Whether she is an administrative assistant to the boss or the boss herself, today's woman, regardless of race or ethnicity, is still less privileged in a largely male-dominated American workplace. A vast body of literature describes the inequities that continue to adversely impact women's lives in the workplace. The traditionally male-dominated culture has encouraged, for example, some women in poverty to use their sexuality as a commodity, and equal pay for equal work is still not a reality for most women (Blustein, 2006). The National Partnership for Women & Families and the American Association of University Women show that the wage gap costs America's working women hundreds of billions of dollars in critical income each year. The Institute for Women's Policy Research shows women earning less than men in 107 of 111 occupations, regardless of levels of education (National Committee on Pay Equity, 2012).

In the area of beauty and sex appeal, women particularly struggle. Many popular magazines publish photographic advertisements showing European American women that esteem and influence often depend more on body build than on brains and more on youth than on wisdom. Women tend to introject this cultural view. European American women are especially prone to believing that perfection in body, especially as defined by an unrealistic level of thinness, is an achievable and desirable goal. Hence, a large number of European American women and teens suffer from eating disorders in their attempt to copy fashion's model of beauty.

Social class intersects with gender also. As discussed in Chapter 13, many upper-middle- and upper-class European American women frequently feel inferior to and dependent on men for status. It is in these areas that counselors can be of great help, not only by hearing client stories, but also by challenging women's maladaptive beliefs about body shape, family duties, and care for self.

CHARACTERISTICS OF SPECIFIC EUROPEAN AMERICAN ETHNIC GROUPS

The generalizations made in this chapter about the mega-ethnic group called European Americans must be modified by a more precise description of specific ethnic groups. What follows, although also generalized, is a description of some specific issues for particular European American ethnic groups. Included in this discussion are counseling issues and adaptations of counseling strategies that might match members of each of these groups.

Newer counseling strategies recognize and adapt to the fact that European American groups, to varying degrees, have been acculturated into the dominant Anglo-American culture. They have also, to a lesser extent, affected that culture. How much acculturation has occurred depends on recency of immigration to the United States, the desire to maintain ethnic practices, and the increasing prevalence of multiethnicity due to ethnic intermarriage, especially within the three dominant religious groups of European Americans, namely Catholics, Jews, and Protestants (Shapiro, 1992). The section that follows focuses on five somewhat arbitrary groupings of European Americans: Northern European Protestants, Irish Catholics, Mediterranean peoples, Jews (as an ethnic group), and non-Jewish Eastern Europeans. Not every European American ethnic group is included, not because they do not deserve to be discussed, but because they are relatively small in number in the context of the entire population of the United States. For example, French Canadian Americans, Portuguese Americans, and Louisiana Cajuns, although all are deeply rooted in American history and important to its culture, are not included in this section. You are encouraged to supplement this review with other readings for those groups. Table 9.2 summarizes characteristics of and counseling considerations for each of the subgroups discussed.

Northern European Protestants

Northern European Protestants, variously called Anglo-American, White Anglo Saxon Protestants, and British Americans, comprise the Northern European group that is the prototype for the dominant U.S. culture. Their culture is not often discussed in a multicultural context because it is so pervasive and therefore less obviously visible

Table 9.2 Counseling Considerations for Specific European American Ethnic Groups

Ethnic Group	Characteristics/Issues	Counseling Considerations
Northern European Protestants	Prototype dominant U.S. culture "Privileged" Respect for work Well-defined nuclear family *Value:* autonomy, achievement, punctuality, emotional restraint	Traditional counseling techniques are useful. Employ empathy and genuineness. Structure sessions. Begin with formal then move toward informal relationships.
Regional Variation for Northern European Protestants		
Southern Whites	*Value:* hierarchy, religiosity (including fundamentalism), indirect communication, gentility, and good manners	Begin with formality and show of manners. Address conformance and perfectionistic tendencies. Be aware of rules of behavior and sensitive issues of religion and sexuality.
Scotch Irish	*Value:* independence, religiosity (including evangelism and individual salvation), arguing, discipline and strength, pride in self and community	Prepare for difficulty in opening up and guarded emotionality. Exercise patience. Understand and be prepared to discuss sin and salvation. Consider family in addition to individual counseling.
Scandinavians	*Value:* independence, heartiness, tolerance for isolation, peace and nonviolence, emotional control, democracy, egalitarianism, orderliness, nonexhibitionism	Counseling is undertaken only for critical issues. Use client-centered approach to build trust. Avoid appearance of leading or authoritarian session structure. Work toward helping clients with emotional expression without shame.
Irish Catholics	Paradoxical-pessimistic worldview, yet fun-loving and capacity to enjoy life Resilient, yet high alcohol consumption Emotionally expressive and gregarious High tolerance for nonrealistic thinking *Value:* humor, fantasy, large gatherings, raucous behavior, strong mother role and restricted father role, church and Catholicism, strict rules of sexual behavior and marital fidelity	Denial of health and mental or emotional problems is common. Reliance on alcohol can be problematic. Be aware of difficulty in dealing directly with conflict. Expect sarcasm, anger, inability to share or communicate deep feelings. Keep friendly distance to avoid shame. Use humor, but remain businesslike. Work toward understanding underlying issues masked by humor and denial. Remain sensitive to anxiety. Introduce nontraditional roles for both genders.

Ethnic Group	Characteristics/Issues	Counseling Considerations
Mediterranean Peoples: Greeks	Sense of alienation from and stigmatization by dominant cultural groups *Value:* extended family, Greek Orthodox Church, Greek language, Greek neighborhoods, arranged marriages, rigidly defined gender roles, men's male social life, strict child-rearing practice in which sons exceed fathers and daughters remain submissive	Recognize key cultural importance of family, including dominance of familial over individual needs. Develop relationship of acceptance and understanding of client's needs and culture. Normalize counseling, and minimize idea of pathology. Restructure client problem as health/stress related. Use psychoeducational behavioral approach.
Mediterranean Peoples: Italians	Differences in Italian subcultures, locations, and/or generations Most are Roman Catholic *Value:* celebrations; Catholic Church, including pageantry; family interests over education (first and second generation); education and upward mobility (later generation); authoritarian male head of household; revered, powerful mother; sanctity of marriage (no divorce); sexual fidelity in women; infidelity in men expected; large families	Issues vary by generation. Many cause intergenerational conflict. Counseling viewed with suspicion; there is a belief that problems should be kept within the family. Family enmeshment can cause problems. Understand individual's need to stay connected yet separate from family of origin. Younger generations differ from older generations on issues such as interfaith marriage, acceptable clothing, and traditional roles. Older Italians may be dealing with effects of early anti-Italianism and discrimination.
Ethnic Jews	Common bond despite lack of homogeneity in religion, social group, or European national roots Commonality of history of oppression and persecution and Diaspora *Value:* communal life, intellectual pursuits, social causes, equality, high achievement, discussion/debate of ideas, direct communication, children's welfare and expression of opinion	There is familiarity with and acceptance of counseling and psychotherapy. Clients will seek counseling readily. Permeable boundaries between parent and child may be problematic. Be aware of easy expression of feelings, including negative affect (anger). Inquire about influence of Jewish religion on life and level of client's religious observances.
Non-Jewish Eastern Europeans: Polish, Hungarian, Lithuanian, Czech, Armenian, Romanian, etc.	Characteristics vary widely. Individual ethnic groups formed own communities, including use of ethnic language and traditions. Some remain so; others are fully integrated into the dominant American culture. *Value:* traditional roles in extended families; ethnic music, food, language; religion (Catholicism); obedience in children; stoicism; conservatism about sex and marriage	They experience shame when seeking counseling. Be aware of clients' experience of perpetuated bigotry. Alcoholism can be a problem. The need for relationship is not easily expressed. Clients are reticent in discussing nontraditional views of sex and marriage or less traditional gender roles. Intergenerational conflict may be an issue.

as an ethnicity. This is the group that historically has been privileged. McGoldrick (2005) declares that Anglo-Americans, like all other people, are ethnic in that they are shaped by the culture from which they come. For this discussion, Protestant Dutch, German, Scotch Irish, Southern whites, and Scandinavians are included here, as they share many characteristics of the other subgroups in this category. Small sections are devoted to a discussion of the latter three subgroups, as they retain some distinct characteristics and ethnic identity.

The Northern European Protestant group provides the prototype for both counselor and client. It is the group from which the majority of counselors themselves come and for whom most theories of counseling have been developed.

Northern European Protestant culture is characterized by restraint, thoroughness, respect for work and a job well done, and a well-defined nuclear family. Such values as autonomy, achievement, punctuality, and emotional restraint characterize not only Anglo-American culture, but indeed, the idealized American culture itself.

Counseling Considerations

Anglo-Americans tend to be responsible about counseling and take it seriously. Materials found in general counseling texts will probably be useful with this population. Sessions, whether group or individual, should be well structured and begin and end on time. Anglo-Americans will generally react positively to empathic responding and genuineness. Structure is important to Northern European Protestants, although after the beginning sessions the relationship generally can become less formal. You are invited to complete Activity 9.5 to get a better handle on this group.

Activity 9.5   Tom and Northern European Protestant Assumptions

The case of Tom from the vignette at the beginning of this chapter illustrates aspects of Northern European culture.

1. What Northern European traits do you see in Tom?

2. How do you think his inherited family characteristics will affect the counseling process?

3. How would you respond to Tom's resentment and anger?

4. How might what you know about the phases of white racial identity help in understanding and helping Tom?

5. Would you or would you not introduce the concept of white privilege with him?

Southern Whites

There are regional variations within the Northern European Protestant group, most notably in the American South. Three distinct characteristics of Southern white culture are hierarchy, indirectness in communication, and religiosity (Batson, 1993; O'Connor, n.d.). A way of life that honors the appearance of gentility and the practice of good manners is traditional in the South. Being humble, courteous, well behaved, friendly, and modest; never forgetting to say "please" and "thank you"; referring to women as "ladies"; addressing them as "ma'am" and addressing men as "sir" are all Southern traditions (Cardwell, n.d.). Along with courtesy, graciousness, and manners, church attendance has always been particularly important to many Southern whites. Religion in general, religious fundamentalism, and revivalism are more common there than in other regions of the United States. These tendencies have significant mental health implications.

Counseling Considerations

A counselor working with Southern whites, especially those from the middle class, should expect an outward show of manners and formality and be prepared to respond in kind. Counselors should recognize and be prepared to discuss any perfectionist tendencies that their clients may harbor about being socially proper and conforming to social codes. It is wise and appropriate for the counselor to ask the client about Southern traditions that may seem different from those of the counselor. Counselors should be aware that counseling issues are frequently embedded in all of the issues that affect Southern living, including both religion and sexuality. Both are sensitive issues and are related, as both are often guided by rules for behavior.

The Scotch Irish

This group was discussed in detail earlier in the chapter along with other Northern Europeans. While here the group is treated separately, it should be noted that the Scotch Irish have mixed with other Northern European Protestant groups. There are places, like southern Appalachia, where their culture is more distinct and dominant. They also comprise a good percentage of those who migrated across Kentucky to Texas, Oklahoma, and the central Midwest and beyond during the 19th century. Independence is a traditional characteristic of the Scotch Irish, who are also known as canny, notoriously argumentative, proud, strong, and disciplined (Webb, 2004). The strictness that marked the Scotch Irish Presbyterian Church in early America has continued (Leyburn, 1962). They are a strong element in the evangelistic religious tradition in the United States, in which individual salvation rather than communal social action is emphasized.

Counseling Considerations

Counselors should be aware that, in spite of the stalwart appearance and genuine fortitude of the Scotch Irish client, a need for help may be present. It may be difficult for the Scotch Irish client to be emotionally open and to receive counseling assistance. This is particularly true of men, but women are also likely to be guarded emotionally. Therefore the counselor should be patient in waiting for client disclosure and emotional expression. The counselor should also be prepared to converse about sin and salvation if the client chooses to do so and brings up the topic during a session. The counselor should also be aware that Scotch Irish parents may not express demonstrative caring. Family counseling as well as individual counseling may be an important component of treatment.

Tom is of Scotch Irish decent. Significantly, in his vignette little is said about the nature of his relationships with others. Tom's tale illustrates the independence and aloneness that can be problematic for people of Scotch Irish descent.

Scandinavians

Like the Scotch Irish, Scandinavians are Northern Europeans and largely Protestant. The Scandinavian population in the United States primarily comprises Norwegians and Swedes, with a strong presence of Danes. Finns, while not technically Scandinavians, also arrived in large numbers in the 19th century and live in larger numbers in the upper Midwest.

Because of the harshness of the climate in their countries of origin, most Scandinavians are hearty, independent, and share a tolerance for isolation (Christianson, 1992). According to Erickson (2005), Scandinavians also tend to be reflective, honest, and very practical. Not pushy, they tend to value peace and nonviolence. Scandinavians tend to keep emotions inside, emphasizing positive feelings over hurt and sadness. Emotional control extends to affection. An old joke has the Scandinavian husband saying to his wife on their wedding day, "I'll say I love you now. That should do for the rest of our marriage. If anything changes, I'll tell you."

Scandinavians have high regard for democracy and egalitarianism, prefer orderliness, and downplay exhibitionism. As a rule, they do not call attention to themselves, and they try not to display emotion in public and tend to disapprove of those who do.

Counseling Considerations

The counselor should know that when a Scandinavian client comes for counseling, the issues are possibly critical. Because Scandinavians are suspicious of authority, the counselor cannot pose as a leader who has power over the client or over the client's situation. Erickson (2005) suggests that counselors who work with Scandinavians must know how to lead without being obvious, and keep order in sessions without being authoritarian. Client-centered counseling is consistent with Scandinavian culture. Erickson also suggests that counselors should know how to help clients express appropriate emotions without shame and "gently help families speak the unspeakable" (pp. 650–651).

Irish Catholics

Irish Catholics are the descendants of the waves of poor peasants who came to America between the mid-19th and early 20th century, many directly or indirectly as a result of the massive potato famine of the late 1840s. Although they were Northern European and largely English speaking, the Catholic Irish nevertheless were seen as a group that was distinct from other Northern Europeans.

Because they were originally maligned by the Northern European Protestants, life in America frequently was difficult for the Catholic Irish. As a result they acquired a mixture of humor and pessimism. McGoldrick (2005) put it this way:

> The Irish are a people of many paradoxes. While having a tremendous flair for bravado, they may inwardly assume that anything that goes wrong is the result of their sins. . . . They love a good time, . . . yet are drawn to tragedy. (p. 595)

Among the distinctive characteristics that counselors might see in Irish Americans is a remarkable resiliency and the ability to enjoy life even when circumstances are far less than ideal. Humor is used to mask feelings of conflict and pain. They are inclined to celebrate even loss expressively and heartily. They value large gatherings and raucous behavior, which may occur even in time of mourning. However, this hearty gregariousness can mask emotional denial of negative feelings. Drinking alcohol is common, and like the church, the bar has been a communal meeting place for Irish Americans. On the one hand, alcohol consumption can be a benign social convention for them. On the other hand, alcoholism is a problematic issue for Irish Catholics.

In Irish Catholic families, fathers have historically been "shadowy or absent figures" (McGoldrick, 2005, p. 602) who deal with their wives and with their family problems largely by distancing from them rather than confronting them. The Irish mother is legendary in the sense that she is sentimentalized as strong and all powerful. However, she is also a very vulnerable person.

The Catholic Church has been a dominant force in Irish American life, and it has traditionally maintained very strict rules of sexual behavior. The straightness of Irish step-dancers is characteristic of the rigidity of Irish views toward sex, which is traditionally considered a sin outside of marriage. Hence, expressing their sexuality remains a thorny issue for many Irish Catholics.

In sum, three particular issues might be sources of emotional difficulty for Irish Catholic clients, namely alcoholism, repressed sexuality, and lack of emotional expression disguised as humor.

Counseling Considerations

Counselors should be aware that the Irish have a high tolerance for nonrealistic thinking. They value fantasy. They have difficulty in dealing directly with conflicts and frequently use sarcasm, outbursts of anger, and interpersonal cutoffs in order to avoid them (McGoldrick, 2005). Not inclined to share deep emotions, the family as a whole suffers for the inability of its members to communicate feelings.

Prone to denial, the Irish are also disinclined to acknowledge health problems. Counselors must therefore be alert to the possibility that their Irish Catholic clients may be concealing physical as well as social and family problems.

When Irish Catholics seek counseling, they are likely to see it as "similar to confession" (McGoldrick, 2005, p. 608). The Catholic Irish endure suffering for as long as possible, then turn to their priest in the secrecy of the confessional and recite that which is believed to be a wrong thought or deed. McGoldrick (2005) suggests that when working with Irish Catholics it is helpful for counselors to keep a friendly distance, not unlike the curtain on the confessional, so as to avoid shame. It is important to be serious and businesslike while maintaining a sense of humor. Because the client may be given to humor in order to disguise a problem, or fantasize in order to deny it, the counselor will have to read between the lines to determine what is really at the root of the client's issues. It is important that the counselor not use techniques that will increase the anxiety that normally runs high in this population. McGoldrick suggests that a good strategy with which to help Irish Catholic clients is to limit guilt and suffering by restricting them to particular time intervals.

Because of the traditional nature of Irish Catholic culture, it may be important to introduce the traditional Irish Catholic woman to some non-traditional roles that she might play in addition to motherhood. It may also be important for counselors to help men learn to be emotional supports to their mates.

Mediterranean Peoples (Greeks and Italians)

Italians and Greeks, while distinct ethnic groups, share some general characteristics. Both traditionally have strong paternal authority in families, allow for much expression of emotion, and value practical and hands-on work. Though both groups are Mediterranean, they are discussed separately here. (Spaniards, although also Mediterranean Europeans, share cultural characteristics discussed in Chapter 11.)

Greeks

Greeks immigrated to the United States in two major waves. The "old immigrants" came between 1890 and 1920, and new immigrants arrived after the immigration act of 1965 (Killian & Agathangelou, 2005). The former came to America for economic reasons; many were men who made money and later brought their families here. The latter came not only for economic reasons but also because their country was devastated by civil war, poverty, and political upheaval. *They* came as families, and most had the skills required for business or trades. Many intended to educate their children in America and then return to Greece. The Anglo culture was quite strange to them. They were also, in turn, strange to non-Greek Americans. The Greek language used a different alphabet, Greek foods were largely unknown, and the Greek Orthodox religion, although Christian, was unfamiliar to non-Greeks. The Greek immigrants who endured the alienation from the dominant culture and remained in America took two different paths. Some gave up their Greek ways as quickly as possible, learned English, and identified as Americans rather than as Greek Americans. Those who did not adopt Anglo ways used both the Greek Orthodox Church and Greek-language publications to help them very gradually adjust to their new land. These Greek immigrants remained in "Greek Towns" and found solace in their neighborhoods, priests, and families.

Counseling Considerations

Counselors should recognize that family is a very important element of Greek culture. Its needs are put before the needs of the individual. It is typical of Greeks who are in need to turn to the extended family for support. In traditional Greek family life, marriages are frequently arranged, and husband and wife roles are rigidly defined (Killian & Agathangelou, 2005). Childrearing is strict: Sons are expected to exceed their fathers, daughters are supposed to be well educated but submissive. The Greek Orthodox Church reinforces this structure. If counseling is needed, it is likely that the Greek mother, not the father, will seek it. Fathers often maintain a distance from their children and their wives, spending much of their social life with male friends. Children often go to parochial school, where they learn English and therefore often serve as interpreters for their parents. Counselors need to be sensitive to the English capabilities of Greek clients. Because Greeks have been stigmatized by Anglo culture, it is important that the counselor develop a relationship in which the client feels well regarded and understood. Because therapy carries a negative connotation to many Greeks, who assume that it is primarily for persons who have severe psychological problems, a counselor can reduce his or her client's discomfort by restructuring or reframing the client's presenting problem as related to health or stress. A counselor might also use a psychoeducational behavioral approach to trigger client change. This will serve to minimize the notion of pathology and normalize the counseling experience.

It should also be noted that in times of crisis Greeks will often turn to the Orthodox priest as a resource for support before they would consider seeking the help of a counselor.

Italians

Italians do not necessarily have a common culture. Northern and Southern Italians are quite different, and the difference is rooted in geography and economics as well as history. Northern Italy benefited from industrialization and has much in common with Germany and Switzerland. Southern Italy is poorer. Many of its inhabitants are farmers, and much of the soil is not fertile. What Americans consider typically Italian is largely Southern Italian. Many Southern Italians, like Greeks, came to America with the intention of making money and then going home. Those who stayed in America brought their families overseas as soon as they could. Most Italian immigrants came to America as peasants and settled in "little Italies," from which the first two generations rarely ventured forth (Giordano, McGoldrick, & Klages, 2005). Italians are, for the most part, Roman Catholic by religion and tradition. They are celebratory and enjoy the familiarity and pageantry of the church.

To first- and second-generation Italians, education is secondary to family interests. It is not unusual for the children of first- and second-generation Italian immigrants to have been asked by their parents to stop going to school and work in the family business or trade. To the present generation, however, education is more valued, and many children of Italian families are upwardly mobile.

The traditional head of the Italian household is the father, and he can be quite authoritarian. The Italian mother is the heart of the family. She is honored, frequently revered, and as such is powerful. Italians love their families, which are generally quite large. Women traditionally have stayed at home and cared for their children. They are expected to be sexually faithful to their husbands. However, the Italian male has been given far greater latitude in sexual and career matters (Giordano et al., 2005).

Counseling Considerations

Italians, like Greeks, have regarded counseling with suspicion. It is assumed that all problems are to be handled within the family. If a family can't handle its problems it is considered shameful. A priest might be consulted, because he is supposed to be learned and also bound to secrecy.

Separation from family can be traumatic and can cause major disruptions in life. On the other hand, enmeshment is typical of many Italian families, and it can also cause serious problems. This is particularly true for Italian young people who may love their families but want to avoid becoming swallowed up by them. Counselors should understand a client's need both to be close to family and to get away from it. This was seen in the vignette about Tony, who wanted to be his own person. However, he did not want to displease his parents, particularly his father.

Counseling issues vary with the generations. Italian grandparents may remember the stories that their parents told them about discrimination in America against them. It is difficult for young Italians Americans to imagine the serious anti-Italianism that existed in the United States before and during World War II (Candeloro, 1992). Some older Italians may enjoy the strong role the Catholic Church has played in helping them feel at home here, while their offspring may resent the restrictions that it imposes. Young adults may seek counseling concerning interfaith marriage, abortion, or the use of birth control, all of which are inconsistent with traditional religious beliefs. Many Italian women through generations have disliked the double standard for sexual behavior. Younger people are most likely to disregard it or seek counseling with regard to it. While previous generations had little use for education (Candeloro, 1992), today's young adults are socially mobile and they know that they need education in order to succeed in many occupations. Many of these issues of generational conflict are present in Tony's story; see Activity 9.6.

Activity 9.6   Working With Tony and His Culture

Review the case of Tony from the vignette at the beginning of the chapter, and respond to the following questions.

1. Why do you think Tony is so confused?

2. What class-related work ethic does his father represent?

3. Why do you think Tony feels that his father does not see Mary Louise as a potential store owner?

4. What role does Tony's mother possibly play in this vignette and in life?

5. What is the role of Father Leo and the Church within the community?

6. What might/should Tony do?

Jews

Nearly half of world Jewry lives in the United States (Rosen & Weltman, 2005). Over time many changes have taken place in the Jewish community as Jews from everywhere in the Diaspora migrated to America. It is somewhat amazing that Jews, who lived in dispersion throughout all parts of the world, were able to form a common bond, since Jews are not a homogeneous religious or social group, nor is there a central authority for all Jewish people.

Judaism is both a religion and an ethnic group. Jews may be agnostic or atheist and still identify as Jewish. The common experience of most, although not all, Jews, according to Rosen and Weltman (2005), is the history of oppression found at one time or another in many Jewish settlements throughout the world. The tenuousness of their lives in lands in which they were strangers and the persecution that took place in many communities are important explanations for the unity of the Jewish people.

Jewish communal life in America is strong. Community was solidified in the past in the United States by a common history and the use of a common language, Yiddish. Now virtually a dead language, Yiddish was spoken by the entire community at one time. However, the majority of the descendants of turn-of-the-20th-century Jewish immigrants are today assimilated into American culture. It was not always that way. Prior to World War II, there was so much prejudice against Jews in the United States that Jewish communities built their own hospitals and educational institutions. For example, the existence of Brandeis University is testimony to the exclusionary practices of prestigious universities toward the admission of talented Jewish youth.

Although most Jewish immigrants from Eastern Europe were poor, lacking citizenship in the countries that they left behind, many became affluent citizens in their new home. They sponsored liberal causes and excelled in intellectual pursuits. Jews, a tiny minority (less than 1% of the American population), are seen in every walk of American life. Since their beginnings in America, Jews have distinguished themselves in many fields, including medicine (e.g., Jonas Salk), law (e.g., Lewis Brandeis, Alan Dershowitz), music (e.g., Irving Berlin, Leonard Bernstein), and communications (e.g., Louis B. Meyer, Jack Warner, David Sarnoff; Lipset & Raab, 1995; Shapiro 1992).

Counseling Considerations

Most American Jews are familiar with counseling and psychotherapy and are quite amenable to it. Freud, Adler, Frankl, Ellis, Beck, and many other notable counseling theorists and practitioners were of Jewish extraction. As a rule, most Jews are highly verbal.

Jewish culture values high achievement (Rosen & Weltman, 2005). Jewish parents place high value on their children's welfare and opinions, and are likely to seek help for them whenever and wherever it is needed. Children are generally encouraged to speak their mind. Boundaries between parents and children are permeable. Equality is valued and authority is questioned in Jewish culture. Among both young people and adults, there exists a tradition of discussion and debate about ideas. Even religious and ethical issues are seen as not settled and in need of discussion and debate.

Most Jews express their feelings readily. What may be taken by outsiders as anger could simply be a response to disagreement and may well be understood within the group as an expression of affection. Communication is generally quite direct and can seem even aggressive to those from other cultures. Jews are likely to seek counseling for just about any problem when they think that counseling will benefit them. Counselors of Jewish clients should not feel shy about asking their clients about the relative influence of Jewish religious observances on their lives. The case of Ellen illustrates these themes. Note the reference to dietary laws and Sabbath practice in the vignette and in Activity 9.7.

Activity 9.7   Working With Ellen and Her Culture

Review the case of Ellen from the beginning of this chapter, and respond to the following questions.

1. What do you think is behind the conflict between Ellen and her mother?

   - Are such conflicts universal?

   - Do you see any ethnic characteristics in the family relationships in this vignette?

2. Do you think family therapy or couples counseling is warranted?

3. In what ways does religion play into Ellen's life script?

4. What do you think Ellen's mother means when she says, "serve you bacon if she could"? Is it about only religious practices and food, or is something else going on here?

5. How much do you think Ellen's counselor needs to understand about Jewish dietary laws and Sabbath practices to work with Ellen?

6. How much do you now know about religious difference among Jewish groups?

Eastern Europeans

Many people from Eastern European countries such as Poland, Lithuania, Armenia, Hungary, and Romania came to America at the turn of the 20th century as peasants and unskilled workers. Each group banded together in its own community and worshipped mainly in Catholic churches that were frequently flavored with the language and traditions of the lands that they had left behind. The immigrants often found work as laborers and brought with them ethnic music, food, and language. Many lived out traditional roles in extended families, which were their major source of psychological support. In time, many of their children became educated; intermarried, usually with Catholic European American spouses of other ethnicities (sometimes not with the blessing of parents on either side); and became fully integrated into the mainstream of European American life.

A newer wave of Eastern Europeans, including Russians, resulted from the collapse of the Communist system in 1991. These immigrant populations in many ways are unlike their earlier counterparts. Some had no religious beliefs or affiliations, while others maintained underground Christian Orthodox communities throughout the Communist era. Many are skilled or more educated than their predecessors but with credentials that go unrecognized in America. Consider the case of Svetlana and her mother.

Svetlana Koslev, known to her classmates as Lana Kay, is a 15-year-old high school student who was brought to a counselor by her mother, Raesa. Raesa expresses concern that Svetlana does not listen to her, likes to talk on the phone, and plays the radio too often. She says Svetlana is disrespectful, continually begs for new clothing, and comes home at the last possible minute. Raesa does not understand why her daughter is not more eager to excel in school, cannot be satisfied with the three skirts and sweaters that she owns, and does not help more in the apartment.

Raesa works hard cleaning other people's homes to support herself and her daughter. She worked as a respected senior administrative assistant in Lithuania, but since she emigrated 3 years ago, she has not been facile enough with English to continue that line of work. Occasionally, Raesa receives some financial help from a friend, Boris, who works as a truck driver. Raesa claims that Svetlana neither likes nor listens to Boris. Raesa sees this as disrespectful and seeks counseling for her daughter in the hope that the counselor will talk sense into her and make her behave. She tells the counselor that this is what therapists do back home.

For her part, Svetlana views her mother as too strict and unlike the parents of her American classmates. She admits that in her native village, the three skirts and sweaters that her mother purchased at Goodwill would have been more than sufficient clothing for school, but now she wants to keep up with her friends. She thinks their clothing is much more fashionable. Furthermore, her classmates all have iPods, and the only way she can keep up with the music that they talk about is by listening to the radio at night. She thinks that the 10 minutes on the phone that her mother allows her each evening is not enough. Svetlana does not understand how her mother, who is divorced from her Russian father, can talk to Boris on the phone for "hours" while she is allowed only minutes. She also worries that her mother and Boris drink too much when they go out. She is unhappy that her mother is interested only in schoolwork and does not care if Svetlana has friends. She thinks that her mother wants to keep her separated from the ways of American teens. She does not like that she was forced to stay home when her girlfriend's father drove her friend and two other girls to a concert. She has thought about running away and is very frustrated with how she lives. Svetlana worries that the other kids see her as very different. Every time she tries to talk about this to Raesa, she is told that when she becomes an adult she can make her own choices, but for now she needs to obey without question and concentrate only on school. In reality, Svetlana does better-than-average work in school and, unlike her mother, speaks English quite well. Her one desire is to fit in and be like the other kids.

Counseling Considerations

Eastern Europeans are likely to experience shame if and when they need counseling. They are aware of the bigotry that has been applied to them and to other Slavic families, for example, in the form of the jokes that call them "dumb." Counselors need to know that, while many Eastern European immigrants were poor, some were political refugees, professionals and intellectuals, and even former nobility (Folwarski & Smolinski, 2005).

Alcoholism is a problem that affects many Eastern European Americans and causes interruptions in smooth family relations. It is also a cause of shame.

Eastern Europeans are primarily Catholic in religion, and the goal in childrearing is obedience. Conservative in matters of marriage and sex, many Eastern Europeans are likely to avoid discussions that negate traditional gender roles. Among Poles and other Eastern Europeans, stoicism is valued, and a need for relationship and connectedness is not easily expressed. However, in younger generations, Slavic Americans, like other European American ethnic groups, are relaxing the rules, and counselors need to be aware of generational conflicts that may arise as a result.

Counseling Resolutions in the Vignettes

Four very different European American clients have been presented. Each came into counseling without an awareness that her or his issues might be culture specific. In Tom's case, his EAP counselor addressed his frustrations and anger, using cognitive behavioral processes and techniques. He worked with him on his inappropriate use of alcohol to relieve his anxiety and stress. Tom learned to channel his stress into the healthier outlets of running and family activities. Although Tom did not gain appreciable insight into his prejudice or an understanding of his position of "white privilege," he was able to come to terms with how his use of alcohol might have contributed to his lack of promotions. He learned to live life with less anger, and he exercised his need for "white male superiority" by working as a volunteer in a local men's social club.

Ellen's counselor, working with her individually, was nevertheless well versed in family therapy, particularly Bowenian and structural theory and techniques. She helped Ellen realize that her primary allegiance needed to be to her husband, rather than to her mother. Eventually Ellen and Steve entered couples counseling, where they were able to resolve their problems and learned to live in greater harmony, each realizing how

their different understanding of "being Jewish" had contributed to their discord. They vowed to raise their children in a different way than either of them had been raised.

Tony's school counselor initially empathized with Tony using Rogerian, client-centered processes, then moved to using techniques from solution-focused counseling and assertiveness training. These approaches helped Tony gain insight into his family situation. He was able to articulate to his counselor what his own desires and goals were. He rehearsed how he might express his desires to his father while still honoring his father's traditional Italian values. When he finally did so, his father was more accepting than Tony had anticipated. Tony's prior talk with his mother, and her subsequent talk with Father Leo, had added to his father's understanding. Tony also talked to his sister about her telling their parents about her interest in business. Tony planned to attend community college for his first year of college so he could continue to work in the family store and train his sister to take his place. He applied for a scholarship to the state university under a delayed entry program.

Svetlana's school counselor helped her and Raesa understand how difficult it was for both of them to straddle two different worlds—that of Raesa's past and that of Svetalana's present and future. She helped them hold an honest dialogue so that they each better understood the reality of the other's world. Svetlana came to see that her education was critical to her mother because she herself had so many opportunities denied her since immigrating to the United States. Raesa accepted that her daughter needed to adapt to the culture in which she now lived. Through solution-focused approaches, both learned to compromise and accommodate what was most important to each of them. Svetlana became more respectful of her mother's wishes, and Raesa allowed Svetlana time to socialize with her friends.

Now that you have read most of the chapter, respond to the questions in Activity 9.8.

Activity 9.8   Review: Counseling European Americans

Having now read about various European American ethnic groups, answer the following questions.

1. Describe the changes that have occurred in the European American population from the inception of the United States to the present day.

2. Which of the European American groups described in this chapter would it be easiest for you to work with? Most difficult for you to work with? Explain.

3. What topic covered in this chapter would you like to know more about in order to be a culturally alert practitioner?

4. Now that you have read this chapter, go back to the quiz in Activity 9.2 and answer those questions once more.

SUMMARY

The Europeans who immigrated to the United States are not a homogeneous group. They formerly lived in different national and social environments. They came to America from different countries at different times and for different reasons. They settled in various parts of America and by so doing changed both themselves and the United States.

Professionals who counsel European Americans need to understand their clients' unique cultural worldviews in order to be helpful in ways that clients can understand and accept. Counselors need to think about what framework can best be applied when working with clients from any of the European American groups. Interventions should not be limited to a "one size fits all" model.

It is also important to know that privilege is not equally distributed among all European Americans. Ethnic origin, gender, social class, and sexual orientation have much to do with privilege and with worldview. Counselors need to be further reminded that European Americans are not necessarily Anglo. Not all are privileged in the same way. Those who have enjoyed social privilege often have struggles and issues nevertheless.

Finally, it is important that counselors not overgeneralize. European Americans, along with all other Americans, will continue to change and continue to develop themselves, this nation, and our field.

REFERENCES

Batson, A. B. (1993). *Having it, y'all.* Nashville, TN: Rutledge Hill Press.

Belkin, G. S. (1988). *Introduction to counseling* (3rd ed.). Dubuque, IA: William C. Brown.

Bellah, R. N., Madsen, R., Sullivan, W. M., Swindler, A., & Tipton, S. M. (1996). *Habits of the heart: Individualism and commitment in American life* (Updated ed.). Berkeley: University of California Press.

Blustein, D. L. (2006). *The psychology of working*. Mahwah, NJ: Lawrence Erlbaum.

Boorstin, D. J. (1974). *The Americans: The democratic experience*. New York, NY: Vantage Press.

Candeloro, D. (1992). Italian Americans. In J. D. Buenker & L.A. Ratner (Eds.), *Multiculturalism in the United States* (pp. 233–255). New York, NY: Greenwood.

Cardwell, T. C. (n.d.). *Proper Southern manners*. Retrieved http://tcc230.tripod.com/SManners.htm

Christianson, J. R. (1992). Scandinavian Americans. In J. D. Buenker & L.A. Ratner (Eds.), *Multiculturalism in the United States* (pp. 343–372). New York, NY: Greenwood.

Cousins, N. (1958). *In God we trust*. New York, NY: Harper and Brothers.

Davidson, M. G. (1999). Religion and spirituality. In R. M. Perez & K. A. DeBord (Eds.), *Handbook of counseling and psychotherapy with lesbian, gay, and bisexual clients* (pp. 409–433). Washington, DC: American Psychological Association.

DuBois, W. E. B. (1961). *The souls of black folks*. Greenwich, CT: Fawcett. (Original work published 1903)

Erickson, B. M (2005). Scandinavian families: Plain and simple. In M. McGoldrick, J. Giordano, & N. Garcia-Preto (Eds.), *Ethnicity and family therapy* (3rd ed., pp. 641–653). New York, NY: Guilford Press.

Fanon, F. (1969). *The wretched of the earth*. (C. Farrington, Trans.). New York, NY: Grove Press.

Fiedler, L. A. (1966). *Love and death in the American novel*. New York, NY: Stein and Day.

Fischer, D. H. (1989). *Albion's seed: Four British folkways in America*. New York, NY: Oxford University Press.

Folwarski, J., & Smolinski, J. (2005). Polish families. In M. McGoldrick, J. Giordano, & N. Garcia-Preto (Eds.), *Ethnicity and family therapy* (3rd ed., pp. 711–723). New York, NY: Guilford Press.

Gendron, M. (2009). Reconstructing the past: A century of ideas about emotion in psychology. *Emotion Review, 1,* 316–339.

Giordano, J., McGoldrick, M., & Klages, J. G. (2005). Italian families. In M. McGoldrick, J. Giordano, & N. Garcia-Preto (Eds.), *Ethnicity and family therapy* (3rd ed., pp. 616–628). New York, NY: Guilford Press.

Guindon, M. H., Green, A. G., & Hanna, F. J. (2003). Intolerance and psychopathology: Toward a general diagnosis for racism, sexism, and homophobia. *American Journal of Orthopsychiatry, 73,* 167–173.

Guterman, J. T. (2008). Social constructionism and ethics: Implications for counseling. *Counseling and Values, 52,* 136–144.

Gutman, H. G. (1989). *Who built America?* (American Social History Project, Vol.1). New York, NY: Pantheon Books.

Hanna, F. J., Talley, W. B., & Guindon, M. H. (2000). The power of perception: Toward a model of cultural oppression and liberation. *Journal of Counseling & Development, 78,* 430–441.

Killian, K. D., & Agathangelou, A. M. (2005). Greek families. In M. McGoldrick, J. Giordano, & N. Garcia-Preto (Eds.), *Ethnicity and family therapy* (3rd ed., pp. 573–585). New York, NY: Guilford Press.

Kleg, M. (1993). *Hate, prejudice, and racism*. Albany: State University of New York Press.

Leyburn, J. G. (1962). *The Scotch Irish*. Chapel Hill: University of North Carolina Press.

Lipset, S. M., & Raab, E. (1995). *Jews and the new American scene*. Cambridge, MA: Harvard University Press.

McGill, D. W., & Pearce, J. K. (2005). American families with English ancestors from the colonial era: Anglo Americans. In M. McGoldrick, J. Giordano, & N. Garcia-Preto (Eds.), *Ethnicity and family therapy* (3rd ed., pp. 520–533). New York, NY: Guilford Press.

McGoldrick, M. (2005). Irish families. In M. McGoldrick, J. Giordano, & N. Garcia-Preto (Eds.), *Ethnicity and family therapy* (3rd ed., pp. 595–615). New York, NY: Guilford Press.

Miller, J. B. (1986). *Toward a new psychology of women*. Boston, MA: Beacon Press.

Moen, P., & Han, S. K. (2001). Gendered careers: A life-course perspective. In A. Hertz & N. Marshall (Eds.), *Working Families* (pp. 42–57). Berkeley: University of California Press.

National Committee on Pay Equity. (2012). Wage gap statistically unchanged. Retrieved from http://www.pay-equity.org/

Nerlich, G. (1989). *Values and valuing*. New York, NY: Oxford University Press.

O'Connor, F. (n.d.). *A good man is hard to find.* Retrieved from http://pegasus.cc.ucf.edu/~surette/goodman.html

Pettigrew, T. (1981). The mental health impact. In B. P. Browser & R. G. Hunt (Eds.), *Impact of racism on white Americans* (pp. 88–96). Newbury Park, CA: Sage.

Portes, A., & Rimbaut, R. G. (2001). *Legacies: The story of the immigrant second generation.* Berkeley: University of California Press.

Reed, I. (1997). *A multi America.* New York, NY: Viking.

Richmond, L. J. (1972). A comparison of returning women and regular college age women at a community college (Doctoral dissertation, University of Maryland, College Park). DAI-A 33/03.1028

Richmond, L. J. (1999). Transcultural counseling and European Americans. In J. McFadden (Ed.), *Transcultural counseling* (2nd ed., pp. 297–314). Alexandria, VA: American Counseling Association.

Richmond, L. J. (2003). Counseling European Americans. In F. Harper & J. McFadden (Eds.), *Culture and counseling: New approaches* (pp. 133–146). Boston, MA: Allyn & Bacon.

Robinson, T. L., & Ginter, E. J. (Eds.). (1999). Racism: Healing its effects [Special issue]. *Journal of Counseling & Development, 77*(1).

Rosen, E. J., & Weltman, S. F. (2005). Jewish families: An overview. In M. McGoldrick, J. Giordano, & N. Garcia-Preto (Eds.), *Ethnicity and family therapy* (3rd ed., pp. 667–679). New York, NY: Guilford Press.

Shapiro, E. (1992). Jewish Americans. In J. Buenker & L. Ratner (Eds.), *Multiculturalism in the United States* (pp. 257–280). New York, NY: Greenwood.

Slone, M., & Shoshani, A. (2008). Indirect victimization from terrorism: A proposed intervention. *Journal of Mental Health Counseling, 30,* 255–265.

Sue, D. W. (1981). *Counseling the culturally different: Theory and practice.* New York, NY: Wiley.

Sue, D. W. (2011). The challenge of white dialectics: Making the "invisible" visible. *The Counseling Psychologist, 39,* 415–422.

Tobias, H. J. (1992). *A history of the Jews in New Mexico.* Albuquerque: University of New Mexico Press.

Todd, N. R., & Abrams, E. M. (2011). White dialectics: A new framework for theory, research and practice with white students. *The Counseling Psychologist, 39,* 351–395.

Waite, L. J., & Nielsen, M. (2002). The rise of the dual-worker family, 1963–1997. In F. R. Herts & N. L. Marshall (Eds.), *Working families: The transformation of the American home* (pp. 23–41). Berkeley: University of California Press.

Webb, J. H. (2004). *Born fighting: How the Scots-Irish shaped America.* New York, NY: Broadway Books.

Yamagishi, T. (2011). Micro-macro dynamics of the cultural construction of reality: A niche construction approach to culture. In M. J. Glefand, C. Chiu, & Y. Hong (Eds.), *Advances in culture and psychology* (pp. 251–308). New York, NY: Oxford University Press.

Zinn, H. (2005). *A people's history of the United States.* New York, NY: Harper Perennial Modern Classics.

CHAPTER 10

Culturally Alert Counseling With Middle Eastern Americans

Julie Hakim-Larson
University of Windsor

Sylvia Nassar-McMillan
North Carolina State University

Ashley D. Paterson
University of Windsor

Nadia is an attractive 15-year-old daughter of Muslim Arab American parents. Her mother is an immigrant and her father was born in the United States. Nadia resents the freedoms afforded her brothers as well as her brothers' surveillance of her activities. A school counselor heard her exclaim while crying at school, "I wish I were dead!" This incident occurred after Nadia had an argument at school with one of her brothers. Nadia's mother supports her sons' behaviors. She also feels that Nadia is disrespectful. For instance, Nadia has been seen to remove the traditional headcovering (hijab) while attending services in the mosque, although neither mother nor daughter typically wears the hijab while outside of the mosque. While trying to board a plane, Nadia's father was mistakenly identified as someone else, detained, and not allowed to board his flight. He has suffered emotional turmoil and shame as a result. A counselor first saw Nadia and each of her parents individually before they attended family therapy sessions.

(Adapted from Nassar-McMillan, Hakim-Larson, & Amen-Bryan, 2008)

Elias is a 35-year-old Iraqi male refugee in the United States. He is single and unemployed. He worked in the field of communications in Iraq before he was imprisoned and tortured. After his release, he fled to another Middle Eastern country before arriving in the United States. His symptoms included anxiety attacks, suicidal behavior, hallucinations, nightmares, and flashbacks. Another refugee referred him for services. His case manager referred him to community social service agencies and a crisis phone line.

(Continued)

He has received individual psychotherapy, psychiatric evaluations, and medication management, which has resulted in symptom reduction and improved self-esteem. With ongoing treatment and continued medication management, Elias is expected to continue to remain stable and make gains in his ability to cope and contribute to American society as a productive citizen.

(Adapted from Jamil, Farrag, et al., 2007)

Youssef was born in the United States. He is the 18-year-old son of immigrants from the Middle East. He is in his senior year of high school and was recently arrested for drug possession. Only his family's native language is spoken at home. Thus his parents rely on him to interpret and explain any communication that occurs in English. As a child, he was overindulged and was raised permissively, with few rules and restrictions placed on his behavior. Youssef learned English as a second language and performed poorly throughout school, although he managed to pass. His teachers told his parents that they thought he had attention deficit hyperactivity disorder and that he should see a psychologist for testing and a psychiatrist for evaluation because he might need medication. In high school, he belonged to one of a number of competing local gangs. After his court appearance for the drug possession, he minimized the severity of his situation by mistranslating the proceedings to his parents.

This chapter provides counselors with some ways in which they can increase their understanding of people like Nadia and her parents, Elias, Youssef, and others. It explores the varied cultures and peoples of the Middle East. It consequently offers counselors a framework for enhancing their delivery of mental health services to Middle Eastern Americans.

In spite of the differences in age, ethnic background, and life experiences, Nadia and her parents, Elias, and Youssef each have family histories that involve immigration to North America from a country located in the Middle East.

Nadia is struggling with trying to reconcile her ethnic identity and relationship with her mother and brothers with her identity as a young American woman. Her more acculturated father has to contend with feelings of being the recent target of discrimination and profiling. Culturally sensitive family therapy, with the involvement of the protective brothers at some point, appears to be warranted.

Elias has experienced the extreme traumatic memories of having been the survivor and witness of political imprisonment and torture. As a young man with employable skills in the field of communication, his comprehensive treatment program holds promise in promoting his continued progress.

Youssef's symptoms of poor attention, impulsivity, and hyperactivity have been further exacerbated by already difficult acculturation problems and have extended into his life at school and in the community.

It is important that counselors consider their attitudes and knowledge about Middle Easterners. Counselors might note their reactions to Nadia, who is attempting to establish her identity; to Elias, who may be seen as a victim or survivor of extreme trauma and torture; and to Youssef, who fits the pattern of a rebellious teen with a possible disability. It is especially important for counselors to consider whether ethnicity plays a dominant role in their own initial reactions and thoughts.

You are invited to examine your current state of knowledge about this population by completing Activity 10.1.

You are invited also to reflect on personal experiences with Middle Eastern Americans in Activity 10.2 and to increase your personal experiences with Middle Eastern individuals and cultures in Activity 10.3.

POPULAR VIEWS OF MIDDLE EASTERNERS

What images do the often interchangeably used terms *Middle Easterner* and *Arab* conjure? These two terms should be distinguished from each other. As is defined further in the next section of this chapter, the term *Middle Eastern* refers to people located in a broader geographical region, many of whom speak different languages (e.g., Arabic, Hebrew, Turkish, Farsi), while the term *Arab* refers to people who speak Arabic and originate from one of the 22 League of Arab states. Arabs are Middle Easterners, but not all Middle Easterners are Arabs. For many people brought up in the West, at least some of their perceptual images of Middle Easterners and Arabs come from Hollywood and likely include pervasive and stereotypically negative visual images such as camel-riding villains, ill-mannered and ill-meaning powerful sheiks, enslaved maidens or harem girls, terrorists, and Egyptian caricatures (Shaheen, 2001). As noted in Shaheen's (2001) research on the portrayal of Arabs, particularly in films,

Arab evil-doers are seen in every sort of film imaginable: sword and sandal soap [operas], Foreign Legion and terrorist shoot 'em ups, camel-operas, musical comedies, magic-carpet fantasies, historical tales, movie serials, and even contemporary dramas and farces that have absolutely nothing to do with Arabs. (p. 13)

Comic strips (Shaheen, 1991) and even computer games (Wingfield & Karaman, 1995) have also portrayed negative images of Middle Easterners. In fact, Shaheen (2001) discovered that over 900 Hollywood feature films project Arabs as villains. As he suggests,

when you come across rigid and repetitive movies brandishing stereotypical slurs and images, keep in mind not all negative images are alike: there are distinctions and nuances. Some Arab portraits are dangerous and detestable and should be taken seriously; others are less offensive. And pay special attention to those Arabs you *do not see* on movie screens. Missing from the vast majority of scenarios are images of ordinary Arab men, women, and children, living ordinary lives. Movies fail to project exchanges between friends, social and family events. (p. 13)

The Turner Classic Movies network has featured films depicting Arabs hosted by Jack Shaheen and Robert Osborne for the Race & Hollywood film series (see Table 10.1).

You are invited to complete Activities 10.4 and 10.5 in order to discover the media portrayals of Arabs and other Middle Easterners.

Activity 10.4 Responding to Arabs in Films

Watch two or more films from Table 10.1, each from different categories.

- Compare and contrast the images of Arabs that are portrayed.

- What assumptions are being made about Arabs in the films?

- Are the assumptions ever questioned, and if so, by whom?

- In the films that you have chosen, are the characteristics of Arabs stereotypical and overgeneralized, or are the Arab characters treated fairly as unique individuals even though they belong to a specific group?

Activity 10.5 Analyzing Media Coverage of Middle Eastern Issues

Select a recent political issue or conflict between the United States and some region or country in the Middle East (e.g., Afghanistan, Iraq, Palestinian/Arab-Israeli conflict). Listen to or watch media coverage of the issue/conflict/event. This can be done with different students or subgroups assigned to different media sources. Respond to the following questions:

- How has the media influenced your views of conflicts with the Middle East and its countries?

- Has your view changed through your experience in this activity (as researcher/participant, as moderator, as observer)? If so, how?

Table 10.1   Films in Turner Classic Movies' Race and Hollywood: Arab Images on Film Series

Early Images	Arab Maidens
The Sheik (1921)	*Chandu the Magician* (1932)
The Sea Hawk (1924)	*Kismet* (1944)
The Thief of Bagdad (1924)	*Caesar and Cleopatra* (1945)
Tarzan the Fearless (1933)	*Dream Wife* (1953)
The Lost Patrol (1934)	*The Desert Song* (1955)
Arabs as Villains	**Arabs as Sheiks**
Adventure in Iraq (1943)	*Son of the Sheik* (1926)
Action in Arabia (1944)	*Drums of Africa* (1963)
Sinbad the Sailor (1947)	*Harum Scarum* (1965)
Sirocco (1951)	*The Wind and the Lion* (1975)
	Jewel of the Nile (1985)
Epics	**Even-Handed Portrayals**
The Four Feathers (1939)	*Bataan* (1943)
Lawrence of Arabia (1962)	*Five Graves to Cairo* (1943)
Young Winston (1972)	*Sahara* (1943)
Lion of the Desert (1981)	*King Richard and the Crusaders* (1954)
	The Black Tent (1956)
	Three Kings (1999)
Arabs as a Subject of Ridicule	**Images From Outside Hollywood**
Arabian Tights (1933)	*Princess Tam Tam* (1935)
Ali Baba Goes to Town (1937)	*Battle of Algiers* (1966)
Popeye the Sailor Meets Ali Baba and the Forty Thieves (1937)	*Taste of Cherry* (1997)
Road to Morocco (1942)	*Rana's Wedding* (2003)
Mummy's Dummies (1948)	*The Band's Visit* (2007)
Abbott and Costello Meet the Mummy (1955)	
Bowery to Baghdad (1955)	
Sahara Hare (1955)	
The Sad Sack (1957)	
Little Beau Porky (1964)	
Hare-Abian Nights (1966)	

Source: Reclaiming Our Identity, Dismantling Arab Stereotypes (2011).

For a number of reasons, images of the people of the Middle East pervade the media—newspapers and magazines, television, radio, and the Internet—as well as the movies. In addition to wars in the Middle East over the past century (Lewis, 1995) and the sociopolitical instability of the region, there is evidence of discrimination, fear of backlash, and psychological distress among Arab, Muslim, and Middle Eastern Americans since September 11, 2001 (e.g., Nassar-McMillan, Lambert, & Hakim-Larson, 2011; Padela & Heisler, 2010). Arab, Muslim, and Middle Eastern Americans continue to be under public scrutiny and the topic of feature reports in the media.

The information on and interpretations of world events that people receive help to shape their attitudes and ultimately their biases toward those from the Middle East. Increasingly, however, mental health researchers have called for challenging the pervasive stereotypes of Middle Easterners (e.g., Nassar-McMillan, 2003b; Nassar-McMillan, 2007; Nassar-McMillan, 2010). Additionally, what is needed is addressing the mental health needs of Americans of Middle Eastern ancestry with the same compassion and empathy afforded other ethnic groups, through the use of empirical data. Engage in Activity 10.6 to gain additional perspectives on portrayals of Middle Easterners.

Activity 10.6   Exploring Middle Eastern Websites

Several websites are relevant to contemporary Middle Eastern Americans, such as those of the Arab American Institute (www.aaiusa.org) and the Arab Community Center for Economic and Social Services (ACCESS; www.accesscommunity.org). International resources, such as Al Jazeera in English (www. aljazeera.com) may be referenced for this activity. Explore at least one of these sites, and write two to three sentences on what you found and what additional perspective you gained.

Researchers have begun to publish their findings on the mental health issues of people from the Middle East. What has emerged are frameworks for professionals to understand the assessment, diagnoses, and treatment of this population, many of whom have settled outside of their countries of origin in North America in search of a better life (e.g., Abudabbeh, 1996; Erickson & Al-Timimi, 2001; Nassar-McMillan & Hakim-Larson, 2003; Nobles & Sciarra, 2000).

This chapter begins by putting into context the complexities of Middle Eastern ethnic identity and then presenting an overview of characteristics of peoples from the Middle East. Many first-, second-, and third-generation Americans with a Middle Eastern ethnic background have complex identity issues based on their gender, country of origin (e.g., Afghanistan, Egypt, Iraq, Jordan, Kuwait, Lebanon, Morocco, Palestine), religion (e.g., Melkite, Greek Orthodox, Sunni Muslim, Druze, Shiite Muslim, Jewish, Maronite Catholic), level of education, and socioeconomic status. The second part of the chapter summarizes the mental health literature on diagnoses, presents treatment strategies and techniques that have been used with Americans of Middle Eastern descent, and provides a short conclusion. The multicultural activities that appear in this chapter will help counselors learn more about the people of the Middle East and how they can best position themselves to promote the mental health of those who seek their services.

DEFINING THE IDENTITY OF MIDDLE EASTERNERS

The peoples of the Middle East generally have inhabited portions of northern Africa, southwestern Asia, and Europe.[1] They include the peoples of the 22 Arab League states as well as some of the non-Arab peoples from the surrounding geographical region, such as Afghanis, Kurds, Persians (from Iran), Turks, and Israelis (Farag, 2000). Nonetheless, and in spite of this geographic expanse, Middle Easterners are often automatically viewed by mainstream Americans as representing one homogenous group. However, if Americans were asked to explicitly define Middle Eastern,

---

[1] *Middle East* is a Western European term designating the lands to the east that were a moderate distance from Western Europe; China and other lands even farther east were termed the Far East. The term Near East was applied to Eastern Europe.

they might be hard pressed to articulate their conceptualizations. For example, in the aftermath of the attacks of September 11, 2001, on the United States, the image of "Middle Eastern" spanned Arab Americans, Muslim Americans, and Sikhs as well as non-Arab Middle Easterners such as Afghanis and Iranians, and even further, including those who might not fall into any typical definitions of Middle Eastern, such as Pakistanis and Bangladeshis. For example, one study on immigration conducted on behalf of the U.S. Census Bureau defined Middle Eastern immigration to the United States as representing countries ranging from Pakistan to Morocco (Camarota, 2002). Camarota created the perception of immigration problems, including those related to national security, for peoples from a region of origin far more vast than the typical definition of the Middle East. Civil liberties advocates attribute such misperceptions to the domestic political agenda intended to cast a wide net for scapegoats of terrorism and other alleged threats to national security. Given this lack of clarity among mainstream North American populations about exactly how to define Middle Eastern, it comes as no surprise that individuals of Arab descent may, themselves, suffer from confusion in relation to self-identity (Nassar-McMillan, 2003b).

Those people of Middle Eastern descent who reside in the United States are primarily Arab American. The Arab Middle East is comprised primarily of countries that belong to the League of Arab States, speak Arabic as a national language, or can be otherwise defined as Arab. Other non-Arabic-speaking Middle Eastern groups, such as Iranians, Afghanis, and Turks, also represent sizable populations in the United States, particularly in certain states. To complicate the matter, even within the Arab American population significant subcultural differences exist, for example, among peoples from the Gulf States (i.e., Saudi Arabia, Kuwait, Qatar, Bahrain, United Arab Emirates, and Oman) versus those from Greater Syria (which includes both modern-day Syria and Lebanon) versus those from the Meghreb, or North African countries.

Over the course of U.S. immigration history, the definition of Middle Easterner has been fluid.

In the last hundred or so years, Middle Easterners have been variously defined by the federal government as being from "Turkey in Asia," "Colored," "Asiatic," and "White" (Samhan, 1999). In contemporary U.S. society, individuals of Middle Eastern descent may not themselves have a clear or well-defined ethnic identity. Like their counterparts from other ethnic groups, they may identify as more or less American, depending on their levels of acculturation and ethnic identity development (Jackson & Nassar-McMillan, 2005). In an age of heightened threats to civil liberties, discrimination and profiling may particularly inhibit the identity development of many Middle Eastern Americans, especially those who fit Middle Eastern–looking or –sounding demographic profiles; indeed, these Middle Eastern Americans may altogether hide or minimize their ethnic identities. On the other hand, Arab American and other Middle Eastern ethnic groups in the United States have increased ethnic pride and awareness in recent years by organizing to establish a unified voice for advocacy, cultural preservation, and education about Middle Easterners. This collective ethnic pride may well serve to foster improved ethnic identity development and pride in younger generations.

The terms *Arab American*, *Muslim*, and *Middle Eastern* are often used indiscriminately and interchangeably. Although some people may belong to all three groups, most in fact do not. Some people belong to only one or two of the categories (Salari, 2002). For example, a Persian (Iranian) Christian would only fit the Middle Eastern grouping. All Arab Americans can be thought of as being of Middle Eastern descent, but not all Arab Americans are Muslim. In fact, currently, most Arab Americans are Christian. Many Muslims are neither Arabic speaking nor Middle Eastern in their heritage (e.g., they may have ancestors from Indonesia or Bosnia). Finally, some people from the Middle East are not considered Arab because they do not speak Arabic (e.g., Turks speak Turkish, Iraqi Chaldeans speak Aramaic, Israeli Jews speak Hebrew, Iranians speak Farsi).

The complexity in the identity of Middle Easterners underscores the necessity for counselors to think of each person who seeks mental health services as having a unique history, based on her or his family's country of origin, native language(s) and dialect, religion, gender, socioeconomic status, and history of immigration (see, e.g., Amer & Hovey, 2007; Nassar-McMillan, 2003a; Samhan, n.d.). When the person immigrated (e.g., after a war or famine) and the person's current age are related to the types of stresses she or he is likely to endure in adapting to Western life, with older adults requiring some different considerations by counselors than younger ones (e.g., Wrobel, Farrag, & Hymes, 2009).

Given that most information available today on Americans of Middle Eastern descent concerns Arab Americans, there is heavy emphasis on this group in this chapter. However, where relevant literature is available on other groups, that literature too is reviewed.

IMMIGRATION FROM THE MIDDLE EAST

Immigration from the Middle East to North America has occurred in several waves since the late 1800s. Most Arab Americans today actually represent the third or fourth generation in North America. That is due to a migration that occurred around the turn of the 20th century, when many poor, predominantly Christian, uneducated laborers and merchants immigrated from Greater Syria in search of better economic opportunities and to escape the Ottoman Empire. These Arab American Christians (e.g., Orthodox, Eastern Rite, Maronite Catholic) are descendants of this group.

The later waves of Middle Eastern immigration have been occurring from the late 20th century to now. They have included more educated people, more Muslims, and a greater diversity of ethnic backgrounds (e.g., Palestinians, Egyptians, Jordanians, Yemenis, Iraqis). Of great significance is the fact that many of the immigrants from the Middle East entering the United States in the last few decades are refugees, and many have histories of direct or vicarious exposure to wars, including the civil war in Lebanon, the Palestinian-Israeli conflict, the Iran-Iraq war, the war in Afghanistan with the Soviet Union, and the Persian Gulf Wars in Iraq (see, e.g., U.S. Committee for Refugees and Immigrants, 2012).

Based on statistics from the Arab American Institute approximately 3.5 million Americans are of Arab descent, with the top six metropolitan concentrations being in Los Angeles, Detroit, New York, Chicago, Washington, D.C., and Northeastern New Jersey. In descending order of frequency reported, the National Arab sub-ancestry is as follows: Lebanese, Arab/other Arab, Egyptian, Syrian, Palestinian, Moroccan, Iraqi, and Jordanian (Arab American Institute, 2009–2012). Note that this report does not include the demographics for other Middle Eastern countries that are not considered Arab, such as Turkey and Iran. Thus, the estimated number of Middle Eastern Americans would be more than 3.5 million.

CHARACTERISTICS OF MIDDLE EASTERN CULTURES

As is the case for other major cultures, Middle Eastern cultures can best be understood by first considering the core values embedded in the customs, language, and roles that the older generation attempts to transfer to the younger one. In this section, the core values of Middle Eastern cultures are highlighted and discussed in connection with acculturation to American life, family and parenting roles, gender roles, religion and social support, communication styles, and school and career aspirations. In addition, descriptions of traditional clothing, the cultural arts, and general community health issues are provided.

Core Values

Although many religions other than Islam have coexisted in the Middle East, Islam is the predominant religion across the region. As a result, Islam has strongly influenced Middle Eastern cultural values throughout history (Lewis, 1995).

The core values include two particular ones, namely *collectivism*, as represented in strong family cohesion and loyalty, and *paternalism*, as represented in dominant male authority (Nassar-McMillan, 2003a, 2003b; Nassar-McMillan & Hakim-Larson, 2003). Paternalism is described further later in this section in the broader discussion of family roles and parenting.

Collectivism

Individuals from Middle Eastern cultures, particularly those of Arab and/or Muslim background, have been described as more collectivistic, rather than individualistic, in their identity (Sayed, Collins, & Takahashi, 1998; Triandis, 1994). Collectivistic Middle Easterners value interdependence among members of their specific nationality and religious group (Sayed, Collins, & Takahashi, 1998). Hence, there is an expectation that the goals of the individual will reflect those of the group. Sayed et al. (1998) cite an Arab proverb that demonstrates the importance of collective responsibility for others: "The believer is for his brother—like connecting building blocks supporting each other; if one part falls ill, the whole body crumbles of fever and sleeplessness" (p. 444). Another proverb similarly emphasizes group validation and belongingness: "We rise together, we fall together" (p. 444). By contrast, in individualistic cultures, the identity of the individual is often linked with an autonomous sense of self and the self's own needs and achievements.

Socio-emotional stratification and individuation in the Arab subcultures is viewed as unhealthy by traditional Middle Easterners. They see those phenomena as leading to fragmentation, social disintegration, and feelings of isolation and loneliness. On the other hand, however, the downside to a strong collectivistic identity may at times include overintrusiveness in individuals' lives and inadequate boundaries among people (Abi-Hashem, 2008).

Cultural norms are evolving. Although collectivism is associated with Eastern cultures and individualism is associated with Western cultures, the intermixing of cultural values is occurring in much of the world, including the Middle East. That intermixing is not new. Judeo-Christian and Western influences on Middle Eastern culture have been pervasive throughout history and are continuing to influence the peoples from that region.

Regardless of ethnic background, individuals can now have both collectivistic and individualistic views to varying degrees, with few falling at the extreme ends of the spectrum. Thus, Middle Eastern Americans may vary widely in whether they favor the dominant traditional collectivistic stance or a more Western individualistic one. Counselors need to be cautious not to overgeneralize research findings on cultural influences about any supposed ethnic group.

Tables 10.2 and 10.3 are provided as summaries of two sets of key values for many Middle Eastern Americans.

Table 10.2   Definitions of Individualism and Collectivism

Individualism	Collectivism
• The views, needs, and goals of self are most important. • The pleasure principle and personal profit-loss form the basis of behavior. • Individual beliefs are autonomous and viewed as independent of the group. • There is emotional detachment from the collective group and independent social behaviors.	• The views, needs, and goals of the collective group are most important. • The norms and duties determined by the collective form the basis of behavior. • Shared beliefs emphasize what the individual and collective have in common. • There are cooperative, dependent, self-sacrificing in-group social behaviors and indifference or hostility to out-group social behaviors.

Source: Triandis (1994).

Table 10.3   Definitions of Paternalism and Maternalism

Paternalism	Maternalism
• Men should have more power than women. • Men should protect women who are dependent on them and provide for them. • Chivalrous protection and affection toward women who hold conventional roles coexists with hostility toward women who try to gain power.	• Men need to be cared for physically and emotionally. • Men need women's help in domestic matters. • Women may feel ambivalence and resentment concerning men's greater power but hold a benevolent maternalistic attitude toward them nonetheless

Source: Feather (2004); Glick & Fiske (2001).

You might probe your experience of the values listed in Table 10.3 by completing Activity 10.7.

Activity 10.7   Clarifying Values: Individualism and Collectivism, Paternalism, and Maternalism

Consider these two dichotomous sets of terms, as discussed in this chapter:

- individualistic and collectivistic
- paternalistic and maternalistic

1. Examine your own value systems according to those two spectrums, identifying the ways in which you subscribe to each of the terms (e.g., who makes the decisions in your family?).

2. What is the communication pattern in your family or support network?

3. What are some examples of collectivistic approaches you take to your life? Individualistic ones?

4. Examine your thoughts, emotions, and behaviors (verbal and nonverbal) with respect to each of the terms. How might you increase your empathy for clients with differing worldviews (i.e., who operate on different ends of the spectrum) based on your increased self-awareness in this arena?

5. What challenges can you foresee in such situations?

Acculturation and Middle Eastern American Families

Because most early, turn-of-the-20th-century immigrants from the Middle East (largely Syria/Lebanon) were Christian, they shared a version of the dominant faith in American society (Samhan, n.d.). Many of these early immigrants came to America in search of better economic opportunities, which led to their getting jobs in city factories ("The Lure of the Automobile," 2001). The similarity of these early immigrants to other immigrants of the time, along with their Christian background, facilitated their acculturation and absorption into American society through intermarriage, a process that has taken place over the last few generations (Abudabbeh, 1996; Samhan, n.d.).

Later waves of immigrants from the Middle East have often been more educated than the earlier ones. As mentioned earlier, these later immigrants have come from all over the Arab world (Abudabbeh, 1996). They have included a greater percentage of Muslims, whose religious traditions and customs are more different, thereby increasing the potential for a clash of norms and values with the predominantly Christian American society. As a result, the normal difficulties associated with the acculturation process may be exacerbated for Middle Eastern Muslims. Samhan (n.d.) illustrates these differences:

> The beliefs of Islam place importance on modesty, spurn inter-faith marriage, and disapprove of American standards of dating or gender integration. Religious practices that direct personal behavior—including the five-times-daily prayers, the month-long fast at Ramadan, beards for men, and the wearing of the *hijab* (. . . headcover)—and that require special accommodation in such places as work, schools, and the military, make Muslims more visible than most religious minorities and often vulnerable to bigotry. (p. 1)

Although Middle Eastern Muslims may have a more difficult time assimilating than their Christian counterparts, high religious involvement and a high level of education may also play a role in the ease or difficulty of assimilation into American society (Jackson & Nassar-McMillan, 2005). Maintaining heritage traditions shared within a family may serve a protective function. For example, in one study, Muslim university students who shared an appreciation for their culture that matched that held by their family members had fewer depressive symptoms (Asvat & Malcarne, 2008).

Ongoing tensions in the Middle East likely play a significant role in the adaptation of more recent immigrants because discrimination may act as a barrier to acculturation. After the tragic events of September 11, 2001, Arab Americans, who had been historically considered "white" and not people of color, were subjected to levels of discrimination, hate, and intolerance in the United States unparalleled in the 100 years in which they had participated in and contributed to American life in economic, political, and popular entertainment domains (Cainkar, 2002). In Awad's (2010) sample of Arab/Middle Eastern Americans, 77% reported being subjected to offensive comments because of their race and 52% indicated that they had been presumed to be dangerous or violent because of their ethnicity. Coping with the backlash in the post-9/11 era may be especially difficult for elderly Arab Americans, Muslims, and other immigrants from the Middle East who may be worried about their own safety in public and the future of their children and grandchildren as potential targets of discrimination (Salari, 2002). In particular, Muslims and those with stronger Arab/Middle Eastern ethnic identities perceive greater discrimination as compared to Christian Arabs (Awad, 2010).

Several recent studies have examined acculturation and mental health. Arab American Muslim youth who were moderately bicultural experienced greater acculturative stress compared to both youth with strong bicultural identities and youth with strong Arab cultural values (Britto & Amer, 2007). Arab American Christians were more likely to endorse assimilative and integrative acculturation orientations, whereas Muslims were more likely to report separated acculturation orientations (Amer & Hovey, 2007). Regardless, however, no difference was found in family functioning, levels of depression, and acculturative stress. Instead, religiosity was most predictive of positive family functioning and lower levels of depression. Amer and Hovey (2007) suggest that Christian and Muslim Arabs experience unique processes of acculturation.

In addition to acculturation issues, the roles of family members and parenting strategies influence the overall adaptation of Middle Eastern Americans. These are discussed next.

Family Roles and Parenting

As occurs with families of all ethnic backgrounds, the family roles and the rules for parenting in Middle Eastern families vary in some predictable ways both by ethnicity as well as by specific family. Because such a large percentage of the Arab world and the Middle East practices Islam, Muslim traditions and values have historically had an influence on both Christian and Muslim Arab family roles and parenting (Abudabbeh, 1996). For example, as mentioned earlier, many Middle Easterners share the collectivistic emphasis on placing the family's needs before the wishes of the self and maintaining strong parent-child relationships (Abi-Hashem, 2006, Alkhateeb, 2010). This section addresses family roles and parenting issues via the following topics: collectivism and families, paternalism, women's issues, marriage and divorce, family structure, and parental discipline.

Collectivism and Families

Collectivism plays out in multiple ways in Middle Eastern communities and families. In typical Middle Eastern families, it is not uncommon for several generations of family members to reside in the same household and play active roles in the structure and dynamics of the family household. It is more common for elderly and aging parents to reside with younger generations than to be in retirement or nursing home communities, even if additional health and physical care are needed. Extended family members are likely to live near each other. Many families, dating back to initial immigration patterns, have settled into close-knit Middle Eastern enclaves, by specific country. Within these communities, there is a collective altruistic perspective for taking care of those who are less fortunate. These communities consist of large kinship networks that are connected by blood and origin (i.e., specific city or village in the old country). Such social networking in everyday life situations "is also the bridge that links the family to the larger society" (Abi-Hashem, 2006, p. 130). However, in addition to the sense of connectedness and well-being that may result, sometimes clannish factions develop that compete with each other (Nassar-McMillan & Hakim-Larson, 2003; Shryock, 2000). Regardless of the resulting tension and potential for family feuds, the close connection within families meets many psychological needs (Abi-Hashem, 2006).

Paternalism

As noted earlier, paternalism is a strong current running through the structure of Middle Eastern families. Middle Easterners have traditionally shared a patriarchal, patrilineal, and hierarchical view of the extended family, with fathers and other male members of the family exerting the greatest authority (e.g., Shryock, 2000). Paternalism refers to the family hierarchy being passed intergenerationally through the males of the family unit. This does not grant males the ultimate authority in the family; rather, it demarcates the decision-making voice for affairs external to the family as being the male elder's responsibility. By contrast, affairs within the family fall into the elder female's domain. Typically, in contemporary Middle Eastern American societies, such decisions are made by both partners in marital partnerships, even though the father or male elder might still serve as the family spokesperson. In the absence of a father figure, an elder uncle or even elder son may serve such a role. In refugee populations, this "typical" family structure can be upset, in that there may be no elder male to serve in such a role. In such cases, the mother or female elder might play such a role. Thus the family dynamics and structure need to be renegotiated within the refugee status (Nassar-McMillan & Hakim-Larson, 2003).

Women's Issues

The Arab daughter in American life, or *bint Arab*, does not fit the stereotype of the oppressed and degraded female as historically depicted in the media, whether she is an immigrant or a descendant of immigrants. Shakir (1997) notes that, while Arab American women have had their share of difficulties in negotiating between American values and ideals and those of their Middle Eastern heritage, they have been resilient and resourceful in developing individualized solutions to conflicts about issues such as modesty in clothing, dating, chastity, and rebellion against husband or spousal authority. For example, some Middle Eastern women have developed strategies to flexibly adapt their clothing and social behavior according to the social situation, as was the case with Nadia's mother in the opening vignette. Some also maintain a high motivation to assimilate to North American life by voluntarily participating in community organizations and by adopting American cultural traditions. They perceive fewer restrictions on their freedom if they are successful in doing so.

Marriage and Divorce

Norms and traditions involving marriage and the spousal relationship vary considerably by religion and nationality. Some subgroups of Muslim immigrants may come from countries where practices such as endogamy (marriage between cousins) is the norm or where polygamy or divorce is permitted, subject to certain restrictions (Abudabbeh, 1996; Jalali, 1996), whereas such may not be the case for other specific subgroups. For example, Simon (1996), summarizing studies conducted in Australia among Lebanese immigrants, found that divorce was rare or denied as a viable option for both Muslims and Christians.

Family Structure

Even though there is much variation by religion and nationality, the nuclear family structure, and especially the mother's relationship with her children, is of utmost importance in Middle Eastern cultures. For example, mothers may focus more on their relationship with their children, even as adults, than on their relationship with their spouses, and may spend more time and attention on their children than they do on their spouses (Simon, 1996). Even so, the divorce rate is lower than that of average Americans (Abraham, 1995). For Arab Americans, in particular, such familial and marital satisfaction can be attributed to the role of both nuclear and extended family members in collectively meeting the needs of individual spouses. The pressure in mainstream U.S. society for spouses to solely meet their partners' needs, then, is lessened in this traditional Middle Eastern family model.

However, with acculturation comes conflict between the older and younger generations that challenges the status quo of the family structure in traditional Middle Eastern communities. According to past convention, when children, particularly boys, came of age within the family, they would join with the mother and help maintain her power position in the family. As children jockey for increased individual power and autonomy within the context of contemporary North American culture, the traditional family power structure and mother-child bonds have been somewhat derailed (Meleis, 1991). Moreover, in recent immigrant families, the children often take on the role of English translator for parents who may be lacking in English language skills, thus resulting in a role reversal of power in the family structure. Some families who had moderate views in their homeland become increasingly traditional after immigrating to the United States in the effort to preserve traditions (Abi-Hashem, 2006).

Parental Discipline

Children are expected to respect their parents and other elders; thus, obedience is highly valued. Parental discipline is enforced via overtly expressed parental anger and punishment. Children have a subservient role (Abudabbeh, 1996). In a Canadian sample, Egyptian Canadian parents reported greater anger in hypothetical parental discipline situations and higher authoritarianism than their Anglo-Canadian counterparts (Rudy & Grusec, 2001).

Consistent with these findings, Arab American teens have been found to complain about the lack of privacy in their ethnic community. Because everyone seems to know everyone, community gossip is prevalent (Abi-Hashem, 2006), and parents can thus use this threat of stigma and potential shame as a means of socially controlling their children (Ajrouch, 2000). Such social constraints are often heightened for girls and young women of Middle Eastern backgrounds due to traditional gender roles.

Counselors working with Arab American families should first join with the family and support their shame-based discipline, and then encourage positive reinforcement as a means of training alternative and adaptive behaviors (Haboush, 2007). In Arab families, an inconsistent parenting style has been associated with mental health disorders and lower social connectedness as compared to more controlling or flexible parenting styles (Dwairy, Achoui, Abouserie, & Farah, 2006). Thus, evidence does not necessarily appear to support detrimental effects of a shame-based approach to discipline among Arab American families.

Degree, frequency, and severity of use of this shame-based approach are likely to be important considerations for the counselor working with Middle Eastern families. For instance, high parental control, which may incorporate the use of shame-based techniques, has shown a strong negative relation with well-being (Henry, Stiles, Biran, & Hinkle, 2008). It is even stronger among Arab American youth who perceive their parents to be closed to the American culture or as working toward preserving their Arab culture. What is important to note is that, in working with families of Middle Eastern cultures, one must assess parenting and other family dynamics in a culturally appropriate context (Nassar-McMillan, 2010).

Gender Roles

The role of the males in the family structure as ultimately being responsible for the family finances, and of the females, as being responsible for family relationships, is reflected in early socialization processes. Upon reaching adolescence, boys are given more social autonomy, which is seen as fostering the skills and connections that they will need to pursue financially lucrative careers. Because girls are not expected to have those same skills, there is often not a compelling need for them to socialize outside the family and community structure (Ajrouch, 2000).

At the onset of early adolescence, children begin conforming to traditional gender roles, and this then especially becomes the focus of parents' childrearing practices (Meleis, 1991). Gender segregation in the public domain is the norm throughout much of the Middle East. This custom clashes with the dominant American practice. Thus newly arrived immigrants from the Middle East must contend with the extensive cross-sex socializing and other gender role flexibility that is permitted and even encouraged in the United States as normal and healthy in American high schools (Shryock, 2000).

The gender double standard is upheld, with virginity, modesty, and fidelity emphasized for girls and women. Although premarital and extramarital sex is taboo for females, it is criticized but tolerated for males (Jalali, 1996; Simon, 1996). In traditional families, dating itself is taboo, and if it is found to occur, it is expected that a marriage proposal will follow. Family conflicts and even violence can result when parents, who are trying to maintain old-country traditions, discover that their daughters are secretly dating boys and are out in public in mixed company. Traditional Middle Eastern families may also arrange marriages.

The experience of pressure to hold onto old-country traditions varies for daughters and sons. First-generation immigrant parents from the Middle East try to hold onto their ethnic identity through their daughters by attempting to put anti-assimilation pressure on them and by carefully monitoring their social activities (Ajrouch, 1999). By contrast, parents may attempt to attain the American dream through their sons, who are afforded more opportunities for assimilation into mainstream American life. The resulting permissiveness for boys can potentially be problematic (as in the case of Youssef introduced at the beginning of the chapter) when a child's individual needs require more structured adult monitoring. When such problems do arise in the family, recent immigrants are more likely to go for help to their religious institution than to a public agency.

Having read about Middle Eastern families, you are invited to do some reflection on different family styles in Activity 10.8.

Activity 10.8   Descriptive Evaluation of Family Characteristics

To gain an appreciation for the family roles and parenting issues that are important to their clients, it helps if counselors come to an understanding of these issues in their own family networks. This activity asks you to examine your family characteristics and their implications for working with others.

- Generate a list of adjectives that describe your family network (e.g., permissive, controlling, secretive, warm, autonomous, disengaged, sarcastic, ironic, expressive). Evaluate each of these characteristics on a scale of 1 to 10, based on how much (or how little) you like each one.

- Generate a list of characteristics with which you are less familiar (perhaps some that you have observed but that are not commonly practiced in your own family network). Evaluate these based on the same scale of 1 to 10.

- Describe how these lists and scaled self-evaluations differ between the characteristic adjectives from your family network as compared to those observed outside your family network.

- Describe whether your self-evaluations are comparable to where you would like to be.

- Finally, assess/discuss what it would be like for you to work with clients who may exhibit characteristics different from your own. How might those characteristics serve as facilitative or inhibitive factors in developing relationships with clients or in working toward client goals?

Religion and Social Support

Based on U.S. Census 2000 data, the Arab American Institute (2004) reports that 24% of Arab Americans declare themselves to be Muslim (Sunni, Shiite, and Druze). Thus the majority of American Arabs are non-Muslim, mostly Christian. Of Arab Christians, 35% are Catholic (Roman Catholic, Maronite, Melkite/Greek Catholic), 20% Orthodox (Antiochian, Syrian, Greek, Egyptian Coptic), 11% Protestant, and the remaining are other denominations or have no affiliation.

The religion and ethnicity picture is even more complex. For example, some Iraqi Chaldeans and Assyrians are Christians from northern Iraq and do not consider themselves Arabs, since their language is Aramaic (Schopmeyer, 2000). Lebanese Maronite Christians are Catholics who have maintained some early Christian traditions and are under the jurisdiction of the Pope in Rome; they maintain a long and rich history of ties and allegiance to the Roman Catholic church. Their religious norms and values appear quite similar to those of European ethnic groups of Catholics in the United States (e.g., Greek, Irish, Polish, Italian).

For Muslim Middle Eastern families, religious affiliation is strongly related to their social identity and meets many psychological needs (Abi-Hashem, 2006). Expressing one's faith is a way of life, and people often refer to their religious beliefs in their daily routines (Abi-Hashem, 2006). The mosque (or *masjid* in Arabic) provides avenues for fellowship, education, cultural events, and the like (Council on Islamic Education, 1995).

Both Muslims and Christian Middle Easterners utilize their mosques or churches as centers for community support and fellowship. For both groups, religious traditions are highly salient and valued (Arab American Institute, 2004). Church or mosque attendance and adherence to holiday and other religious traditions are typical behaviors within Middle Eastern communities. For example, many Islamic centers and Catholic churches in Arab American enclaves have begun teaching Arabic language classes to the community's youth. Their imams (i.e., clerics) in the Muslim faith and priests or pastors in the Christian faiths often serve in counseling roles on matters of marriage and family decisions. Despite this pattern, however, counselors who work with Arab Americans have noted that it is important to not automatically assume that a client maintains her or his family's religious beliefs and traditions, or even assume that she or he believes in God (Nassar-McMillan & Hakim-Larson, 2003).

Communication Styles

Individuals of Middle Eastern descent, like many individuals of non-Western heritage, often use nonverbal expression to communicate how they feel (Jackson & Nassar-McMillan, 2005). Such nonverbal behaviors may include a high volume during intense emotion and gesticulation while speaking. In addition, to make a point, individuals often repeat the same phrase several times, each time increasing the volume (Via, Callahan, Barry, Jackson, & Gerber, 1997). Metaphors are often used in verbal exchanges to express emotions (Abi-Hashem, 2006).

Power dynamics within relationships may influence both verbal and nonverbal communication as well as interaction styles between individuals. For example, based on the familial hierarchies addressed previously, a husband or father would express anger to a spouse or child. A mother would, in turn, express anger to a child, and also perhaps to her spouse, but in private. In terms of physical

space, same-gender individuals often speak to one another while standing very closely together and often use touch, such as holding hands or kissing one another on the cheek—once, twice, or even three times, depending on country or subculture of origin, by way of greeting or parting gesture.

Love and attachment are communicated through Arabic metaphors and terms of endearment, passed down from one generation to the next. *Yahabooboo* expresses the idea of "darling." Love is also communicated through physical gestures of affection and endearment toward loved ones, especially children (Simon, 1996).

Highly valued in Middle Eastern culture are sociability, hospitality, and frequent connectedness to significant others (Abi-Hashem, 2006; Shryock, 2000). Unplanned drop-in visits from the extended kinship network of family and friends are frequent. Loud, animated conversations may occur over the noise of TV and stereos, which typically remain on even with guests in the home. Shyrock (2000) notes that this pattern of frequent contact (e.g., by telephone) within Arab American kinship networks may extend into the workplace as well, and that local employers in large Arab American enclaves may make accommodations for that practice.

School and Career

Collectivism as a value may affect the quality of school and career aspirations for Middle Easterners, although further research evidence is needed to clarify just how that is playing out. For example, in a study carried out in Israel, Palestinian Arab high school students had high scores on collectivistic test items that emphasized their own social group. They tended to value such items as "solidarity with the poor in my country" more than did Israeli Jewish high school students, who scored higher on more individualistic items such as "freedom of opinion." It should be noted, however, that similarities between the two groups were greater than differences, as both groups of students overall tended to be collectivistic (Sagy, Orr, Bar-On, & Awwad, 2001). For Arab Americans, such collectivistic in-group values may also affect the social life of the school-age child.

Children in American schools are often taught more individualistic values, which places emotional stress on less acculturated parents (e.g., first-generation immigrants), who may fear losing control over their children (Laffrey, Meleis, Lipson, Solomon, & Omidian, 1989). As a result, some Arab Muslims in the United States prefer to send their children to private Islamic schools because they want their children to retain the customs, learn Arabic, and read the Qur'an (Koran; Samhan, n.d.).

Respecting authorities is of importance in Middle Eastern families, which has implications for children in classroom settings. Arab youth are taught to respect authority by suppressing their opinions and avoiding disagreements. They value and accept the teacher's opinion without debate, possibly because their learning style does not emphasize debate or critical thinking in the same ways that classrooms in North America do (Haboush, 2007). As such, they may appear passive or uninterested in a classroom setting that encourages debate (Amer, 2002; Haboush, 2007). Children may also be at risk for academic failure because of the discrepancies between school systems in North America and in the Arab world. Academic learning is typically based on rote memory skills in Arab countries, whereas in North America, critical

thinking is central to learning (Haboush, 2007). School counselors in particular need to maintain an awareness of such cultural consideration in working with Arab American immigrant youth (Nassar-McMillan, Gonzalez, & Mohamed, 2010).

Regardless of socioeconomic status, academic achievement is highly valued among many Middle Eastern cultures (Arab American Institute, 2009–2012). Both girls and boys are expected to excel in school as well as in their later career endeavors. For Arab Americans, in particular, both educational and income levels tend to be higher than the norm for average Americans (Arab American Institute, 2009–2012). Career paths mirror those of mainstream North American cultures, with the exceptions that Middle Easterners tend to choose more entrepreneurial and fewer governmental careers. Alkhateeb (2010) examined self-concepts among samples of Arab American and Lebanese youth 11 to 13 years old. Results suggest that Arab American students have access to a greater number of resources to aid in their academic undertakings partly because of their bicultural identity.

Activity 10.9 suggests that you meet a counselor who might give you a description of her or his firsthand experience with Middle Eastern American youth.

Activity 10.9   Consultation With a School Counselor

Speak with a school counselor about her or his experiences with students of Middle Eastern ethnicity. Has she or he ever noted obvious differences between these youth and their peers that may have prompted discriminatory attitudes and peer rejection? How can such differences be addressed constructively within the school setting?

Traditional Clothing

Another characteristic of Middle Eastern culture is the Muslim convention that upholds modesty for both men and women. For devout Muslims, such modesty means wearing opaque, loose-fitting clothing. As noted in the opening vignette with Nadia and her mother, some Muslim women may

wear a headcovering, or *hijab*, over their heads. In addition, some women may wear the black *abaya*, which is a traditional robe-like cloak (e.g., Abraham, 2000; Walbridge & Aziz, 2000). The cultural meaning of the *hijab* and *abaya* varies. For Muslim women who are proponents of wearing traditional clothing, veiling is seen as protecting them from sexual advances and affording them greater respect from men in the public domain while at school or work. By contrast, for Muslim women who oppose the necessity of wearing traditional clothing, the veil is viewed as an outdated way to socially control women. They feel that they can be good Muslim believers without it (Read & Bartkowski, 2000).

For non-Muslim Middle Easterners, dress is almost as variable as it is in Western cultures, although for people from more recently immigrated groups, the Muslim emphasis on modesty in clothing may still represent the norm.

Cultural Arts and Contributions to American Life

National agencies such as the Naim Foundation and the Arab American Institute, in Washington, D.C., currently exist to facilitate the dissemination of cultural information and to provide social services (Abudabbeh, 1996). Another agency, TAMKEEN: The Center for Arab American Empowerment, is located in Brooklyn, New York, and was founded to address the needs of Arab American New Yorkers in the post-9/11 era. One of the largest, most densely populated geographic concentrations of people from the Middle East is in the metropolitan Detroit area, located in southeastern Michigan, where early immigrants settled at the turn of the 20th century and made a living as shopkeepers and peddlers, until the Industrial Revolution and auto industry boom afforded the opportunity for factory work (Shryock & Abraham, 2000). To locally serve their needs, the Arab American and Chaldean Council and the Arab Community Center for Economic and Social Services (ACCESS) were developed (Abudabbeh, 1996).

As more immigrants were drawn from the Middle East into the Detroit area over the last century, more Arab/Chaldean-owned businesses emerged, including Middle Eastern bakeries and restaurants, grocery stores, and specialty clothing stores, many of which are adorned with bilingual neon signs in Arabic script and English. Cultural products such as food, music, clothing, and artwork are produced locally or imported from the Middle East and sold in these stores, and represent

one way that Middle Easterners attempt to preserve their heritage. Some Middle Eastern dishes (e.g., chick pea dip, or hummus; parsley salad, or tabouli; lamb or beef shish kebab) have now been assimilated into many grocery stores and restaurant menus in some parts of North America.

Arab Americans have a rich history of playing musical instruments (e.g., *nay,* or flute; *'oud,* or round-bellied lute; violin; *darabukkah,* or vase-shaped drum; *riqq,* or tambourine) at their parties, which are called *haflah* or *hafle;* variations of line dancing (*dabkah* or *dubke*) and informal individual, couple, or group "belly" dancing commonly occurs at weddings and other formal and informal celebrations (Rasmussen, 2000). Traditional folk arts include embroidery, Arabic calligraphy, making musical instruments, making dolls, and henna design applications to the hands and feet of young women (Howell, 2000).

Dearborn, Michigan, is home to the annual Arab ethnic festival and the first Arab American National Museum sponsored by ACCESS. The museum documents the cultural contributions of many Arab Americans in the literary world (e.g., the poet Khalil Gibran), the medical and scientific world (e.g., renowned surgeon Dr. Michael DeBakey, NASA scientist Dr. Farouk el-Baz, Antarctic explorer Dr. George Doumani), the political arena (e.g., presidential candidate Ralph Nader), the sports world (e.g., automobile racer Bobby Rahal), the musical world, and the visual arts, including television and movie actors.

Community Health Issues

The literature on the health of Arab Americans indicates that they suffer disproportionately from cardiovascular problems, such as hypertension and high cholesterol, and from diabetes (Hassoun, 1999). While the traditional Middle Eastern diet is thought to be healthy (e.g., high in vegetables, fruits, grains), the ready availability of foods in the United States that were historically eaten only occasionally, such as red meat and sugar-laden desserts, has contributed to obesity in Arab Americans, consistent with the general American trend. Diet and obesity are also predisposing factors for Type 2 diabetes, which has been found to be extremely high in Arab Americans (Jaber et al., 2003). Smoking (cigarettes, cigars, or the traditional Turkish water pipe, or *nargile*) is a predisposing factor for cancer and for cardiovascular disease. Smoking has been found to occur at high rates in studies of both Arab American adults (Hammad & Kysia, 1996; Jamil, Hammad, Jamil, Stevens, & Pass, 2001; Rice & Kulwicki, 1992) and teenagers (Kulwicki & Rice, 2003; Rice, Templin, & Kulwicki, 2003).

ACCESS conducted a health needs assessment survey in 1996 with a randomly selected sample of its mostly Lebanese, Iraqi, and Yemeni low-income clients in Michigan (Hammad & Kysia, 1996). This survey identified the main barriers to primary health care as lack of transportation to doctors' offices, language, cultural practices, and lack of insurance or financial limitations. To help address these needs, ACCESS has since sponsored Biennial National Conferences on Health Issues in the Arab American Community. At these conferences, mental health issues such as posttraumatic stress disorder in refugees as well as issues involving cardiovascular disease, cancer, diabetes, and maternal and childcare have figured prominently in presentations, and researchers continue to implement many of the recommendations for further research.

MENTAL HEALTH ISSUES FOR MIDDLE EASTERN AMERICANS

This section covers the various mental health issues and diagnostic disorders that particularly affect the lives of Middle Eastern Americans who seek or are referred for mental health treatment. First, risks, stressors, and diagnosed mental disorders are discussed. Then ethnic identity and adjustment issues are presented.

The focus here is on immigrant families, who have special risk factors that are associated with their pre- and postmigration experiences and adaptation to their new culture. Such immigrant families and other Middle Eastern Americans also confront the same psychosocial risks and stresses that are common for most Americans in daily life

(e.g., family conflicts). Learning and applying the language, laws, and traditions of their new culture, as well as learning about practical resources such as transportation, add to the emotional burden of the transition for recent immigrants. It is important to note, however, that counseling interventions should pay attention to both client struggles and strengths.

Risks, Stressors, and Diagnosed Mental Disorders

Immigrants from the Middle East are a population that is particularly at risk for anxiety, depression, and trauma-related disorders. Males are at risk for personality, behavioral, and addictive disorders, whereas females are at greater risk for affective and somatic disturbances (Abi-Hashem, 2006). It should be noted that mental health disorders may be somaticized, with the client citing medical complaints rather than emotional ones.

Stressors

The risk for disorders can be attributed to four factors: immigration-related traumas, cultural differences with North American life, loss of the extended family support system when only some family members immigrate, and limited knowledge of American legal and health care systems (e.g., Laffrey et al., 1989). Hattar-Pollara and Meleis (1995) conducted a study that illustrates the everyday stresses encountered by a sample of female immigrants and their means of coping. They found that Jordanian women who had settled in the greater Los Angeles area had to balance feelings of isolation and unease with the practical requirements of daily life, which included ensuring that the family had a steady income, getting the children enrolled in school, and setting up their homes. These women attempted to accomplish all of this while trying to overcome the language barrier and feelings of loneliness due to the loss of social support and status in the community that they had left behind. Adding to this acculturative stress, many of these women also felt a need to protect their ethnic identity and preserve the values of their culture. Conforming to those traditions was seen as bringing honor to the family, whereas violating them by taking on American ways brought shame. One method of coping was to re-create familiar religious and social activities within their Eastern Rite Melkite church parish.

Children and Elderly With Special Needs

At this time, little is known about the potential impact of cultural context on specific age-related risks and disabilities. We do know that Middle Eastern American families may be hesitant to identify a child with a special need because of the shame and dishonor that it may bring to the family. Instead, they may choose to educate the child at home (Haboush, 2007). Counselors can take the approach of reframing disabilities within the context of religious and cultural values in which kindness toward those with disabilities is emphasized (Haboush, 2007). A complicating factor is that some Middle Eastern families continue to encourage marriage among cousins, which increases the chances of having a child with special needs (Haboush, 2007).

In addition to children with special needs, the elderly require special consideration. More recent immigration is associated with greater acculturative stress and depression in older Arab American adults who may have had to immigrate involuntarily because of war and conflict in their homeland; such stress is linked to the country of origin, with more acculturative stress and depression in the Iraqi elderly than in the Palestinian or Lebanese elderly (Wrobel et al., 2009).

Domestic Violence

Domestic violence can be a problem in the Middle Eastern American community. Protecting family honor and avoiding shame, combined with inadequate knowledge of Western legal standards, may contribute to a risk for domestic violence in some Middle Eastern immigrant families (Kulwicki & Miller, 1999). Among the risk factors for domestic violence are patriarchal attitudes, family history of physical abuse, use of corporal punishment, poverty, and social isolation. These have been the focus of education, prevention, and intervention efforts by researchers and community social service agencies.

Reporting child or elder abuse in Middle Eastern families involves sensitive care. This is because such reports may shame families and retraumatize the victims if their family rejects them (Haboush, 2007). Abu-Baker and Dwairy (2003) outline a procedure for reporting abuse among Arab families that involves seeking support within the community, identifying an advocate, engaging in a ceremony in which the family punishes the abuser, and therapeutic interventions at the individual and family levels.

Trauma

In addition to the stresses that occur once an immigrant has resettled, the aforementioned extreme premigration stressors such as war trauma, torture, and persecution in her or his country of origin also add to the risk of the possible development of adjustment disorders or more serious forms of psychopathology (e.g., Keyes, 2000). For instance, the people of Afghanistan have suffered more than two decades of war and conflict and years of drought, and many have experienced a series of displacements as refugees. It is thus not surprising that a national survey in Afghanistan itself found high rates of depression, anxiety, and PTSD in adolescents and adults (Cardozo et al., 2004). Wartime traumas are perhaps the most extreme psychosocial risk factor affecting Middle Eastern Americans who entered the United States as refugees.

In contrast to the early Middle Eastern immigrants who in the early 20th century left their country of origin voluntarily and under relatively stable conditions, more recently there are many who left in a state of crisis during or after wars as refugees. Of note is the finding in one study that most Iranian immigrants with psychiatric problems met the criteria for adjustment disorder with depressed or anxious mood (Bagheri, 1992). Their diagnosed adjustment disorder was related to the stresses of adapting to Western life and learning a new language. However, some had experienced severe trauma and torture in their homeland and also met the criteria for PTSD.

Both physical and mental health symptoms have been noted in Iraqi Americans (Jamil, Farrag, et al., 2007; Kira et al., 2006). As with the case of Elias described at the beginning of the chapter, many Middle Eastern refugees have suffered years of extreme trauma and emotional suffering before finally receiving treatment. This scenario is especially the case for refugees from Iraq who immigrated to the United States after the Persian Gulf War of the early 1990s. Broken family ties, shame, and fears related to their history of trauma and torture have led some to develop serious symptoms of depression and anxiety that often supersede the diagnostic criteria for PTSD. Several studies have been conducted on the mental health and well-being of refugees from Iraq, who represent a large proportion of late 20th and early 21st century immigrants from the Middle East (e.g., Jamil et al., 2002; Jamil, Nassar-McMillan, & Lambert, 2004; Via et al., 1997). Some Iraqi refugees have witnessed the death and torture of loved ones or have personally experienced torture (Kira 2001, 2002; Kira et al., 2006). Some have experienced malnutrition and inadequate water supplies, multiple relocations, and temporary settlement in refugee camps (Kira, 2001). Such multiple traumas and serious losses accumulate over time and thus lead to complex trauma. In counseling, it is then necessary to address the social trauma and collective grief experienced by the targeted community (Abi-Hashem, 2006).

Somatization

To add to the difficulties, somatization of symptoms, such as headaches and stomachaches, has been found to occur often in such samples of Middle Easterners and others with ethnic origins in the Arabic-speaking world, due to the cultural stigma associated with mental illness (e.g., Nassar-McMillan & Hakim-Larson, 2003).

Because mental health problems are often somaticized, many Middle Easterners may initially visit a physician or take their complaints to a medical facility before they are referred for mental health treatment (e.g., Hakim-Larson, Kamoo, Nassar-McMillan, & Porcerelli, 2007). The medical personnel and counselors who work with Middle Eastern American clients frequently need to address acculturation difficulties, marital and family conflicts, and school and educational problems in family members.

Other Common Disorders

Commonly diagnosed disorders include major depression, bipolar disorder, anxiety disorders such as PTSD, and schizophrenia as well as behavioral problems and developmental disabilities in children such as attention deficit hyperactivity disorder (Hakim-Larson, Kamoo, & Voelker, 1998). Counselors need to be aware of a number of key issues related to these disorders. For example, upon immigration, the extended family network and kinship ties are broken and thus there is an upheaval in basic family dynamics and relationships. Depression, anxiety, and PTSD have been found to be quite prevalent in Iraqi refugees of both non-Kurdish (Farrag, 1999; Gorman, 2001; Jamil et al., 2002; Takeda, 2000) and Kurdish background who have sought mental health treatment (Gorst-Unsworth & Goldenberg, 1998). Although treatment outcome studies are lacking, some retrospective data from medical charts suggest that most Arab American immigrants and refugees who have sought mental health treatment have a partial or full remission of their symptoms after treatment (e.g., Jamil et al., 2002).

A similar pattern of symptoms has been found in refugees from Afghanistan to the United States, although the physical and psychological effects vary by specific subgroup. Both depression and PTSD were found in two groups of young Afghan refugees who immigrated to the United States in the 1990s after the war with the Soviet Union and the takeover of the country by the Taliban (Mghir & Raskin, 1999).

Addictions: Substance Abuse and Gambling

Another arena of mental health concern for Middle Eastern Americans is that of addictions such as substance abuse and gambling. Although substance use is prohibited for Muslims and alcohol abuse is generally rare in Middle Eastern American communities (Abudabbeh & Hamid, 2001), substance abuse has emerged as enough of a problem since 1992 for the first bilingual Arabic-English Alcoholics Anonymous program to be formed as a result of increasing problems with drunk driving arrests, domestic violence, and other illicit drug abuses (Berry, 2003a, 2003b; Jamil, Ajo, & Jamil, 2000). Typically, Middle Eastern clients who present with alcohol or drug abuse are also more likely to be English speaking, more educated, and more Westernized (Abudabbeh & Hamid, 2001).

In the area of potential chemical dependence, some counselors who work in the Arab American community have also been concerned about the cultural practice of using the stimulant khat (also spelled kat or qat) by pregnant women and children (Hakim-Larson, 2001). Khat is defined as "a shrub (*Catha edulis*) cultivated by the Arabs for its leaves that act as a stimulant narcotic when chewed or used as a tea" (Merriam-Webster, 2012).

Ethnic Identity and Adjustment Issues

The psychological adjustment of Middle Easterners, especially immigrants, can be understood as the balancing of one's ethnic identity derived from the heritage culture with one's civic identity in the host culture and country of residence. Middle Eastern ethnic identity issues are important across the spectrum of age, gender, and background, but especially so in youth because identity development is a critical developmental task. The challenge is for the adolescent or adult of Middle Eastern heritage to successfully negotiate an integrated identity that includes the various facets of the self (Hakim-Larson & Nassar-McMillan, 2006). However, an assimilation bias occurs when members of the ethnic group negatively evaluate others in their own or another subgroup who assimilate too completely and too quickly to the dominant host culture, or not enough (Nassar-McMillan & Hakim-Larson, 2003).

The relative balance or imbalance in degree of assimilation to the dominant culture and degree of ethnic preservation appear to have implications for identity development. In research with Arab American teens, more recent "old-fashioned" immigrants are sometimes labeled "Boaters" (i.e., just off the boat), while very acculturated Middle Eastern Americans are known as "whites" (Ajrouch, 2000; Shryock & Abraham, 2000). Both positive and negative aspects are attributed to each group (Ajrouch, 2000). A Boater is not yet acculturated and has not assimilated to the dominant culture, as evidenced by her or his speech and dress. She or he is generally considered inferior among teens to those who are somewhat more Americanized. Nevertheless, the teens in Ajrouch's (2000) study also clearly appreciated the benefits of living in a close, ethnic community with shared values and close family relations where everyone helps each other. On the other hand, the more acculturated or white person was seen to have greater status and prestige, and better access to education, power, and wealth; however, the white person was also viewed as being too free and lacking in a sense of responsibility or obligation to family and friends. It is interesting to note that Arabs of Syrian and Lebanese backgrounds are more likely to identify as white as compared to Arabs of Yemeni and Iraqi descent (Ajrouch & Jamal, 2007). This difference is related to historical differences in immigration patterns and efforts toward economic stability in America.

COUNSELING INTERVENTIONS

Because the concept of a God-determined fate has been traditionally used to explain life crises and problems by people from the Middle East (Nobles & Sciarra, 2000), many functions provided by counselors have in the past been performed by physicians, priests, or imams (Loza, 2001) or by fortune tellers, magicians, or healers (Al-Krenawi

& Graham, 2000). However, with outreach efforts by community mental health centers and increased media advertisement of mental health services, many more individuals from the Middle East in need of treatment are getting appropriate interventions. This section includes a description of the positive cultural protective factors and resources that are useful in supporting intervention efforts, and the various counseling modalities and clinical issues that can arise during interventions.

Protective Factors in Middle Eastern Americans

Two salient protective factors for Middle Eastern Americans are family connections and the ethnic community. Both the family and the community can help to alleviate mental health problems by using some culturally sanctioned remedies while also helping new immigrants fully utilize mental health therapeutic options such as counseling and medication. For example, counselors who work with the Arab American community have described the following example of a cultural practice involving social support as a coping strategy: When an Arab woman is depressed, many of her female friends and family members may encourage her to dance with them, with the exercise and camaraderie thus helping to alleviate and lift her depressed mood (Hakim-Larson, 2001). Coming together in social gatherings and sharing food also meets some therapeutic needs (Abi-Hashem, 2006).

In addition, community centers provide arts and crafts programs; social programs; and legal, medical, and career advice. Such social support is often viewed as a critical part of a treatment plan for those with compromised mental health. Since the 1990s, Arab American community agencies such as ACCESS have had outreach programs via radio, television, and the Internet to help community members seek and use mental health intervention programs and join support groups offered in their community (e.g., Abudabbeh, 1996). This effort has helped individuals overcome the stigma associated with mental health diagnoses and treatment.

Family and Community Involvement in Individuals' Lives

In developing a treatment plan for a Middle Eastern American client, family members and the local community are important considerations (Nassar-McMillan & Hakim-Larson, 2003). For example, children are taught to seek guidance from the family when making decisions and problem solving. Developing individual coping strategies is not emphasized (Al-Krenawi & Graham, 2000). For some identified clients, family members will get involved at some point in the treatment process. This may be the case whether or not the clinician feels it is therapeutically indicated. For instance, a woman who needs individual counseling may want her husband and children to be present in sessions. Due to patriarchal traditions, a husband may want to attend some sessions with his wife before feeling comfortable that he can trust the counselor enough so that she might come on her own. In line with that tradition, a husband/father may resent any perceived challenges to his role as the authority figure in a family, may engage in denial about a family problem, and may then refuse to cooperate in the treatment of his wife or child when his participation is needed (Abudabbeh & Aseel, 1999).

If the counselor belongs to the same ethnic enclave as the client and speaks the same language and dialect, issues of privacy, confidentiality, and trust may arise. If the counselor is not from the same ethnic community, the client who is accustomed to the open dissemination of information in the community (i.e., gossip) may have difficulty trusting that the counselor will keep the information confidential. The issue of shame may also play a role, since less educated clients may be particularly reluctant to disclose shameful behaviors that would reflect upon the whole family (Abudabbeh & Aseel, 1999).

Activity 10.10, which was adapted from Ibrahim and Dykeman (2011), offers an opportunity to obtain personal contact with a Middle Eastern American.

Conduct an informational interview of someone who has immigrated from the Middle East. Ask the following questions.

- Where is the person from?

- Where was she or he born?

- How long has the family been in the United States?

- Does the individual/family identify as Middle Eastern (generally or by country of origin)?

- Does the individual/family speak Arabic or another Middle Eastern language in the home?

- Is the person/family Muslim/Christian/some other religion?

- What are some of the key current issues in terms of U.S. domestic and foreign policy with which the person identifies?

- What are/were some of your reactions to the interview? To the interviewee?

- What stereotypes did you have that were addressed in the interview?

- In what way were they addressed?

- In what way has this interview changed your view of Middle Easterners?

- What are the implications for your clinical practice, broadly speaking?

Assessment and Recommended Counseling Modalities: Structured and Relational

The assessment of Middle Eastern clients needs to take into consideration a variety of factors such as the person's cultural and spiritual values, level of acculturation, migration issues, languages spoken and/or written, occupation and educational status both in the culture of origin (if the person is an immigrant) and in the host culture, family composition, and social supports (Ibrahim & Dykeman, 2011). Middle Eastern clients have been noted to be more oriented toward survival and solving their immediate, concrete problems than they are toward gaining insight into their own past or that of their family. They are generally passive in the counselor-client relationship and view the counselor as the benevolent authority who will tell them what to do so that they can be cured (Al-Krenawi & Graham,

2000). Obtaining informed consent must be done with care because disagreeing with authority figures is looked upon poorly (Haboush, 2007).

Thus, counselors who have worked with Middle Easterners recommend the use of clear, direct instructions; behavioral or cognitive-behavioral interventions rather than psychodynamic ones; and interventions that are more relationship oriented (Haboush, 2007; Nassar-McMillan, 2003a, 2003b). Counseling approaches that are more structured, short-term, and directive have been cited as being more useful in working with recent Middle Eastern immigrants (Abudabbeh & Aseel, 1999; Al-Krenawi & Graham, 2000).

Choice of treatment techniques and modality is likely to be influenced by the client's degree of acculturation and educational level as well, in that more educated and acculturated individuals may be better able to complete and follow through on outside homework assignments that involve self-monitoring and documentation for the next session. Also, the degree of acculturation will likely inform the therapeutic approach. For example, more acculturated families may benefit from interventions that focus on individual accomplishments, whereas more traditional families will benefit from interventions addressing more traditional values such as collectivism (Haboush, 2007). Assessing religious beliefs may help implement culturally sensitive interventions (Haboush, 2007).

Counselor Self-Awareness

Counseling Middle Eastern Americans with counselor self-awareness means that the counselor has reflected upon her or his own history of beliefs and attitudes regarding the various ethnic groups that make up this heterogeneous classification (Roysircar, 2004). In her review, Roysircar (2004) notes that such awareness is crucial for effective therapeutic work with clients from different ethnic backgrounds from one's own. Being open-minded and clarifying both common ground and regions of difference appear to be important considerations in this analysis.

By critically reflecting on the similarities and differences of background experiences and discussing these with peers, supervisors, and, as appropriate, with the clients, the counselor is in a better position to feel genuine empathy. Improving multicultural competency in clinical work with Middle Eastern Americans first involves an assessment of personal biases and stereotypes, values, and the match of one's own theoretical orientations and preferred treatment modalities with that of the client's needs (Roysircar, 2004).

Counselor Advocacy and Other Roles

Beyond the critical aspects of examining one's own attitudes and beliefs toward Middle Eastern culture, along with recognizing the impacts of multicultural sensitivity and responsiveness in personal as well as clinical practice, the American Psychological Association suggests additional guidelines as well (Nassar-McMillan, 2007). The need for promoting accurate education and research is great, particularly about the Middle East and people of Middle Eastern descent. Inaccuracies lead to not only continued cyclical and self-fulfilling prophecies, but inadequate and detrimental counseling and mental health interventions for individuals of Middle Eastern descent. Finally, counselors today need to be open to playing the role of change agents—in both organization and policy. With Middle Eastern populations, in particular, it is critical to be aware of current legislation that continues to profile and discriminate against these individuals and communities. It is equally critical to stand ready to combat this legislation at both micro and macro levels. For more information on the promotion of change, visit the website of the Arab American Institute, www.aaiusa.org.

SUMMARY

Middle Eastern Americans have a rich and varied history that spans over a century of experiences in North America. Country of origin, religion, socioeconomic status, and length of time in North America since immigration are all likely influences on overall adaptation and adjustment. Potential risks for Middle Eastern Americans include anxiety, depression, and trauma-related disorders, especially for recent immigrants who have premigration war experiences. Family and community social support in Middle Eastern Americans can serve as potential protective factors and resources for treatment planning. Recommended treatments for Middle Eastern Americans include the use of structured, cognitive-behavioral interventions and relationship-oriented approaches. Refugees from the Middle East who have experienced cumulative complex trauma and torture may require a multidisciplinary comprehensive approach to adequately address their mental health needs. Issues of discrimination and backlash continue to be of concern to Middle Eastern Americans as we proceed into the second decade of the 21st century.

REFERENCES

Abi-Hashem, N. (2006). *The agony, silent grief, and deep frustration of many communities in the Middle East: Challenges for coping and survival.* Dallas, TX: Spring.

Abi-Hashem, N. (2008). Arab Americans: Understanding their challenges, needs, and struggles. In A. Marsella, J. Johnson, P. Watson, & J. Gryczynski (Eds.), *Ethnocultural perspectives on disaster and trauma* (pp. 115–173). New York, NY: Springer.

Abraham, N. (1995). Arab Americans. In R. J. Vecoli, J. Galens, A. Sheets, & R. V. Young (Eds.), *Gale encyclopedia of multicultural America* (Vol. 1., pp. 84–98). New York, NY: Gale Research.

Abraham, N. (2000). Arab Detroit's "American" mosque. In N. Abraham & A. Shryock (Eds.), *Arab Detroit: From margin to mainstream* (pp. 279–309). Detroit, MI: Wayne State University Press.

Abu-Baker, K., & Dwairy, M. (2003). Cultural norms versus state law in treating incest: A suggested model for Arab families. *Child Abuse & Neglect, 27,* 109–123.

Abudabbeh, N. (1996). Arab families. In M. McGoldrick, J. Giordano, & J. K. Pearce (Eds.), *Ethnicity and family therapy* (pp. 333–346). New York, NY: Guilford.

Abudabbeh, N., & Aseel, H. A. (1999). Transcultural counseling and Arab Americans. In J. McFadden (Ed.), *Transcultural counseling* (pp. 283–296). Alexandria, VA: American Counseling Association.

Abudabbeh, N., & Hamid, A. (2001). Substance use among Arabs and Arab Americans. In S. L. A. Straussner (Ed.), *Ethnocultural factors in substance abuse treatment* (pp. 275–290). New York, NY: Guilford.

Ajrouch, K. J. (1999). Family and ethnic identity in an Arab-American community. In M. Suleiman (Ed.), *Arabs in America: Building a new future* (pp. 129–139). Philadelphia, PA: Temple University Press.

Ajrouch, K. J. (2000). Place, age, and culture: Community living and ethnic identity among Lebanese American adolescents. *Small Group Research, 31,* 447–469.

Ajrouch, K. J., & Jamal, A. (2007). Assimilating to a White identity: The case of Arab Americans. *International Migration Review, 41,* 860–879.

Alkhateeb, H. M. (2010). Self-concept in Lebanese and Arab-American pre-adolescents. *Psychological Reports, 106,* 435–447.

Al-Krenawi, A., & Graham, J. R. (2000). Culturally sensitive social work practice with Arab clients in mental health settings. *Health and Social Work, 25,* 9–22.

Amer, M. (2002). *Evaluation of measures of acculturation and mental health for second generation and early immigrant Arab Americans* (Unpublished master's thesis). University of Toledo, Toledo, OH.

Amer, M. M., & Hovey, J. D. (2007). Socio-demographic differences in acculturation and mental health for a sample of second generation/early immigrant Arab Americans. *Journal of Immigrant and Minority Health, 9,* 335–347.

Arab American Institute. (2004). *Demographics.* Document available from the Arab American Institute, 1600 K Street, NW, Suite 601, Washington, DC 20006.

Arab American Institute. (2009–2012). *Demographics.* Retrieved from http://www.aaiusa.org/pages/demographics/

Asvat, Y., & Malcarne, V. L. (2008). Acculturation and depressive symptoms in Muslim university students: Personal-family acculturation match. *International Journal of Psychology, 43,*114–124.

Awad, G. H. (2010). The impact of acculturation and religious identification on perceived discrimination for Arab/Middle Eastern Americans. *Cultural Diversity and Ethnic Minority Psychology, 16,* 59–67.

Bagheri, A. (1992). Psychiatric problems among Iranian immigrants in Canada. *Canadian Journal of Psychiatry, 37,* 7–11.

Berry, A. (2003a, October). *The dynamics of addiction.* Paper presented at the Third Biennial National Conference on Health Issues in the Arab American Community, Dearborn, MI.

Berry, A. (2003b, October). *The dynamics of recovery from alcoholism/addiction.* Paper presented at the Third Biennial National Conference on Health Issues in the Arab American Community, Dearborn, MI.

Britto, P. R., & Amer, M. M. (2007). An exploration of cultural identity patterns and the family context among Arab Muslim young adults in America. *Applied Developmental Science, 11,* 137–150.

Cainkar, L. (2002). *Arabs, Muslims, and race in America* (Middle East Report 224). Washington, DC: Middle East Research and Information Project.

Camarota, S. A. (2002). *Immigrants from the Middle East: A profile of the foreign-born population from Pakistan to Morocco.* Washington, DC: Center for Immigration Studies.

Cardozo, B. L., Bilukha, O. O., Crawford, C. A. G., Shaikh, I., Wolfe, M. J., Gerber, M. L., & Anderson,

M. (2004). Mental health, social functioning, and disability in postwar Afghanistan. *Journal of the American Medical Association, 292,* 575–584.

Council on Islamic Education. (1995). *Teaching about Islam and Muslims in the public school classroom* (3rd ed.). Fountain Valley, CA: Author.

Dwairy, M., Achoui, M., Abouserie, R., & Farah, A. (2006). Parenting styles, individuation, and mental health of Arab adolescents. *Journal of Cross-Cultural Psychology, 37,* 262–272.

Erickson, C. D., & Al-Timimi, N. R. (2001). Providing mental health services to Arab Americans: Recommendations and considerations. *Cultural Diversity and Ethnic Minority Psychology, 7,* 306–327.

Farag, S. (2000). Arab states: Egypt and the Arab states. In A. E. Kazdin (Ed.), *Encyclopedia of psychology* (Vol. 1, pp. 224–228). Washington, DC: American Psychological Association.

Farrag, M. F. (1999, April). *Mental health issues in the Arab American community.* Paper presented at the First National Conference on Health Issues in the Arab American Community, Southfield, MI.

Feather, N. T. (2004). Value correlates of ambivalent attitudes toward gender relations. *Personality and Social Psychology Bulletin, 30,* 3–12.

Glick, P., & Fiske, S. T. (2001). An ambivalent alliance: Hostile and benevolent sexism as complementary justifications for gender inequality. *American Psychologist, 56,* 109–118.

Gorman, W. (2001). Refugee survivors of torture: Trauma and treatment. *Professional Psychology: Research and Practice, 32,* 443–451.

Gorst-Unsworth, C., & Goldenberg, E. (1998). Psychological sequelae of torture and organised violence suffered by refugees from Iraq: Trauma-related factors compared with social factors in exile. *British Journal of Psychiatry, 172,* 90–94.

Haboush, K. L. (2007). Working with Arab American families: Culturally competent practice for school psychologists. *Psychology in the Schools, 44,* 183–198.

Hakim-Larson, J. (Ed.). (2001, May). *Summary of conference proceedings: Mental health and behavioral issues session.* Dearborn, MI: Arab Community Center for Economic and Social Services.

Hakim-Larson, J., Kamoo, R., Nassar-McMillan, S., & Porcerelli, J. H. (2007). Counseling Arab and Chaldean American families. *Journal of Mental Health Counseling, 29,* 301–321.

Hakim-Larson, J., Kamoo, R., & Voelker, S. (1998, July). *Mental health services and families of Arab ethnic origin.* Poster presented at the Family Research Consortium II 5th Annual Summer Institute, Blaine, WA.

Hakim-Larson, J., & Nassar-McMillan, S. (2006, April). *Identity development in Arab American youth: Implications for practice and research.* Education Session presented at the Annual Convention of the American Counseling Association/Canadian Counseling Association, Montreal, Quebec, Canada.

Hammad, A., & Kysia, R. (1996). *ACCESS Arab American primary care and health needs assessment survey.* Unpublished manuscript.

Hassoun, R. (1999). Arab-American health and the process of coming to America: Lessons from the metropolitan Detroit area. In M. Suleiman (Ed.), *Arabs in America: Building a new future* (pp. 157–176). Philadelphia, PA: Temple University Press.

Hattar-Pollara, M., & Meleis, A. I. (1995). The stress of immigration and the daily lived experiences of Jordanian immigrant women in the United States. *Western Journal of Nursing Research, 17,* 521–539.

Henry, H. M., Stiles, W. B., Biran, M. W., & Hinkle, S. (2008). Perceived parental acculturation behaviors and control as predictors of subjective well-being in Arab American college students. *Family Journal: Counseling and Therapy for Couples and Families, 16,* 28–34.

Howell, S. (2000). The art and artistry of Arab Detroit. In N. Abraham & A. Shryock (Eds.), *Arab Detroit: From margin to mainstream* (pp. 487–513). Detroit, MI: Wayne State University Press.

Ibrahim, F., & Dykeman, C. (2011). Counseling Muslim Americans: Cultural and spiritual assessments. *Journal of Counseling & Development, 89,* 387–396.

Jaber, L. A., Brown, M. B., Hammad, A., Nowak, S., Zhu, Q., Ghafoor, A., & Herman, W. H. (2003). Epidemiology of diabetes among Arab Americans. *Diabetes Care, 26,* 308–313.

Jackson, M. L., & Nassar-McMillan, S. (2005). Counseling Arab Americans. In C. C. Lee (Ed.), *Multicultural issues in counseling: New approaches to diversity* (3rd ed., pp. 235–248). Alexandria, VA: American Counseling Association.

Jalali, B. (1996). Iranian families. In M. McGoldrick, J. Giordano, & J. K. Pearce (Eds.), *Ethnicity and Family Counseling* (pp. 347–363). New York, NY: Guilford.

Jamil, H., Ajo, S. M., & Jamil, L. H. (2000, October–November). *Cultural differences in substance abuse between Iraqi and Caucasians in a mental health clinic, USA.* Paper presented at the International Congress on Environmental Health Issues in Primary Health Care, Cairo, Egypt.

Jamil, H., Farrag, M., Hakim-Larson, J., Kafaji, T., Abdulkhaleq, H., & Hammad, A. (2007). Mental health symptoms in Iraqi refugees: Postraumatic stress disorder, anxiety, and depression. *Journal of Cultural Diversity, 14,* 19–25.

Jamil, H., Hakim-Larson, J., Farrag, M., Kafaji, T., Duqum, I., & Jamil, L. (2002). A retrospective study of Arab American mental health clients: Trauma and the Iraqi refugees. *American Journal of Orthopsychiatry, 72,* 355–361.

Jamil, H., Hammad, A., Jamil, L., Stevens, T., & Pass, H. (2001, May). *Characteristics of Arab and Chaldean smokers residing in South-East Michigan 1999–2000.* Paper presented at the Second Biennial Conference on Health Issues in the Arab American Community, Dearborn, MI.

Jamil, H., Nassar-McMillan, S. C., & Lambert, R. (2004). Aftermath of the Gulf War: Mental health issues among Iraqi Gulf War veteran refugees in the United States. *Journal of Mental Health Counseling, 26,* 295–308.

Keyes, E. F. (2000). Mental health status in refugees: An integrative review of current research. *Issues in Mental Health Nursing, 21,* 397–410.

Kira. I. A. (2001). Taxonomy of trauma and trauma assessment. *Traumatology, 7,* 73–86.

Kira, I. A. (2002). Torture assessment and treatment: The wraparound approach. *Traumatology, 8,* 23–51.

Kira, I., Templin, T., Lewandowski, L., Clifford, D., Wiencek, E., Hammad, A., . . . & Mohanesh, J. (2006). The effects of torture: Two community studies. *Peace and Conflict, 12,* 205–228.

Kulwicki, A. D., & Miller, J. (1999). Domestic violence in the Arab American population: Transforming environmental conditions through community education. *Issues in Mental Health Nursing, 20,* 199–215.

Kulwicki, A., & Rice, V. H. (2003). Arab American adolescent perceptions and experiences with smoking. *Public Health Nursing, 20,* 177–183.

Laffrey, S. C., Meleis, A. I., Lipson, J. G., Solomon, M., & Omidian, P. A. (1989). Assessing Arab-American health care needs. *Social Science Medicine, 29,* 877–883.

Lewis, B. (1995). *The Middle East: A brief history of the last 2,000 years.* New York, NY: Scribner.

Loza, N. (2001, May). *Insanity on the Nile: The history of psychiatry in Pharaonic Egypt.* Paper presented at the Second Biennial National Conference on Arab American Health Issues, Dearborn, MI.

The lure of the automobile. (2001, January–February). *Arabica,* pp. 32–35.

Meleis, A. I. (1991). Between two cultures: Identity, roles, and health. *Health Care for Women International, 12,* 365–377.

Merriam-Webster. (2012). *Kat.* Retrieved from http://unabridged.merriam-webster.com/cgi-bin/unabridged?va=Khat+&x=0&y=0

Mghir, R., & Raskin, A. (1999). The psychological effects of the war in Afghanistan on young Afghan refugees from different ethnic backgrounds. *International Journal of Social Psychiatry, 45,* 29–36.

Nassar-McMillan, S. C. (2003a). Arab Americans. In N. A. Vacc, S. B. DeVaney, & J. Brendel (Eds.), *Counseling multicultural and diverse populations* (4th ed., pp. 117–139). New York, NY: Brunner-Routledge.

Nassar-McMillan, S. C. (2003b). *Counseling Arab-Americans: Counselors' call for advocacy and social justice.* Denver, CO: Love.

Nassar-McMillan, S. C. (2007). Arab American populations. In M. G. Constantine (Ed.), *Clinical practice with people of color: A guide to becoming multiculturally competent* (pp. 85–103). New York, NY: Teachers College Press.

Nassar-McMillan, S. C. (2010). *Counseling Arab Americans.* Pacific Grove, CA: Brooks-Cole/Cengage.

Nassar-McMillan, S. C., Gonzalez, L. M., & Mohamed, R. H. (2010). Individuals and families of Arab descent. In D. Hays & B. Erford (Eds.), *Developing multicultural counseling competence: A systems approach* (pp. 216–245). Boston, MA: Pearson.

Nassar-McMillan, S. C., & Hakim-Larson, J. (2003). Counseling considerations among Arab Americans. *Journal of Counseling and Development, 81,* 150–159.

Nassar-McMillan, S., Hakim-Larson, J., & Amen-Bryan, S. (2008). *Counseling Arab Americans II: Clinical vignettes* [DVD]. United States: Microtraining Associates.

Nassar-McMillan, S. C., Lambert, R. G., & Hakim-Larson, J. (2011). Discrimination history, backlash fear, and ethnic identity among Arab Americans: Post 9/11 snapshots. *Journal of Multicultural Counseling and Development, 39,* 38–47.

Nobles, A., & Sciarra, D. (2000). Cultural determinants in the treatment of Arab Americans: A primer for mainstream counselors. *American Journal of Orthopsychiatry, 70,* 182–191.

Padela, A. I., & Heisler, M. (2010). The association of perceived abuse and discrimination after Sept. 11, 2001, with psychological distress, level of happiness, and health status among Arab Americans. *Research and Practice, 100,* 284–291.

Rasmussen, A. (2000). *The sound of culture, the structure of tradition.* In N. Abraham & A. Shryock (Eds.), *Arab Detroit: From margin to mainstream* (pp. 551–572). Detroit, MI: Wayne State University Press.

Read, J. G., & Bartkowski, J. P. (2000). To veil or not to veil? A case study of identity negotiation among Muslim women in Austin, Texas. *Gender & Society, 14,* 395–417.

Reclaiming our identity, dismantling Arab stereotypes. (2011). *Turner Classic Movies Presents "Arab Images on Film."* Retrieved from http://arabstereotypes .org/blog/201105/25-389

Rice, V. H., & Kulwicki, A. (1992). Cigarette use among Arab Americans in the Detroit metropolitan area. *Public Health Reports, 107,* 589–594.

Rice, V. H., Templin, T., & Kulwicki, A. (2003). Arab-American adolescent tobacco use: Four pilot studies. *Preventive Medicine, 37,* 492–498.

Roysircar, G. (2004). Cultural self-awareness assessment: Practice examples from psychology training. *Professional Psychology: Research and Practice, 35,* 658–666.

Rudy, D., & Grusec, J. E. (2001). Correlates of authoritarian parenting in individualistic and collectivistic cultures and implications for understanding the transmission of values. *Journal of Cross-Cultural Psychology, 32,* 202–212.

Sagy, S., Orr, E., Bar-On, D., & Awwad, E. (2001). Individualism and collectivism in two conflicted societies: Comparing Israeli-Jewish and Palestinian-Arab high school students. *Youth & Society, 33,* 3–30.

Salari, S. (2002). Invisible in aging research: Arab-Americans, Middle Eastern immigrants, and Muslims in the United States. *The Gerontologist, 42,* 580–588.

Samhan, H. (1999). Not quite white: Race classification and the Arab American experience. In M. Suleiman (Ed.), *Arabs in America: Building a new future* (pp. 209–226). Philadelphia, PA: Temple University Press.

Samhan, H. H. (n.d.). *Who are Arab Americans?* Retrieved from http://aai.3cdn.net/21b02cde94d4307c47_ jsnmvy5dd.pdf

Sayed, M., Collins, D. T., & Takahashi, T. (1998). West meets East: Cross-cultural issues in inpatient treatment. *Bulletin of the Menninger Clinic, 62,* 439–454.

Schopmeyer, K. (2000). A demographic portrait of Arab Detroit. In N. Abraham & A. Shryock (Eds.), *Arab Detroit: From margin to mainstream* (pp. 61–92). Detroit, MI: Wayne State University Press.

Shaheen, J. (1991). The comic book Arab. *The Link, 24,* 1–11.

Shaheen, J. G. (2001). *Reel bad Arabs: How Hollywood vilifies a people.* Brooklyn, NY: Interlink.

Shakir, E. (1997). *Bint Arab: Arab and Arab American women in the United States.* Westport, CT: Praeger.

Shryock, A. (2000). Family resemblances: Kinship and community in Arab Detroit. In N. Abraham & A. Shryock (Eds.), *Arab Detroit: From margin to mainstream* (pp. 573–610). Detroit, MI: Wayne State University Press.

Shryock, A., & Abraham, N. (2000). On margins and mainstreams. In N. Abraham & A. Shryock (Eds.), *Arab Detroit: From margin to mainstream* (pp. 15–35). Detroit, MI: Wayne State University Press.

Simon, J. P. (1996). Lebanese families. In M. McGoldrick, J. Giordano, & J. K. Pearce (Eds.), *Ethnicity and family counseling* (pp. 364–375). New York, NY: Guilford.

Takeda, J. (2000). Psychological and economic adaptation of Iraqi male refugees: Implications for social work practice. *Journal of Social Work Practice, 26,* 1–21.

Triandis, H. C. (1994). Major cultural syndromes and emotion. In S. Kitayama & H. R. Markus (Eds.), *Emotion and culture: Empirical studies of mutual influence* (pp. 285–306). Washington, DC: American Psychological Association.

U.S. Committee for Refugees and Immigrants. (2012). Available from www.refugees.org

Via, T., Callahan, S., Barry, K., Jackson, C., & Gerber, D. E. (1997). Middle East meets Midwest: The new health care challenge. *Journal of Multicultural Nursing and Health, 3,* 35–39.

Walbridge, L. S., & Aziz, T. M. (2000). After Karbala: Iraqi refugees in Detroit. In N. Abraham & A. Shryock (Eds.), *Arab Detroit: From margin to mainstream* (pp. 321–342). Detroit, MI: Wayne State University Press.

Wingfield, M., & Karaman, B. (1995, March–April). Arab stereotypes and American educators. *Social Studies and the Young Learner, 7*(4), 7–10.

Wrobel, N. H., Farrag, M., & Hymes, R. (2009). Acculturative stress and depression in an elderly Arabic sample. *Journal of Cross Cultural Gerontology, 24,* 273–290.

CHAPTER 11

Culturally Alert Counseling With Latino/Latina Americans

Edward A. Delgado-Romero, Bailey J. Nevels, Cristalis Capielo
University of Georgia

Nallely Galván
University of Illinois, Urbana-Champaign

Vasti Torres
Indiana University, Bloomington

Activity 11.1   Self-Reflection

Before you start reading this chapter, answer this question: What comes to mind when you think of Latinos/Latinas or Hispanics?

What are some stereotypes that people have about Latinos/Latinas or Hispanics?

What are your preconceptions of what counseling will be like with a Latino/Latina or Hispanic client?

José is a 13-year-old student referred to his school counselor, Jillian, by his math teacher, Mr. Justice. Mr. Justice reports that José appears disinterested in his class assignments and fails to complete his homework assignments. Mr. Justice recognizes that it is only midway through the semester and that José can raise his grade to passing. However, Mr. Justice notes that José often has a worried expression on his face. Additionally, he observes that José does not talk to his classmates. While it is not uncommon for a student to be shy, Mr. Justice had José as a math student last year and remembered him as an outgoing boy who frequently participated in class and earned an A for his final grade. Realizing this change of behavior and attitude, Mr. Justice has attempted to check in on José to see how he is doing and whether he could provide math tutoring for him after school. José denies that anything is wrong with him and says that he does not want to stay after school for tutoring. Jillian reads through José's file and discovers that he and his younger sister were born in the United States. She notices that there is very little information about José's parents in the file other than that they both work for a local orchard. She confirms that José has earned As and Bs ever since Kindergarten.

When Jillian meets with José for the first time, he is reluctant to open up to her. He acknowledges that his school performance has decreased, but at this point will not share why he has been unable to focus on school and has lost interest in socializing with his peers. Jillian ends the first session feeling confused. She makes a second appointment with him for next week. She decides to consult with a counselor in the community who works with Latino/Latina clients, hoping that this counselor might give Jillian suggestions for building rapport with José. This counselor informs Jillian that José may be experiencing anxiety due to rumors that Immigration and Customs Enforcement is cracking down on undocumented workers in the local orchard. José may feel uncertain about his family's future and may feel that the public school system, funded by the government, is an unsafe place to discuss his family's situation. This counselor encourages Jillian to continue building rapport with José and to not discount the importance of the sociopolitical context of his experience. The next week Jillian has three individual sessions with José, working to establish the therapeutic alliance so that he may open up to her about his anxiety.

Carmen, a 28-year-old Puerto Rican female graduate student in a southeastern U.S. university, came into the university counseling center because she was experiencing feelings of loneliness and depression. During the initial interview, Carmen asked for help setting boundaries with family and friends because she was experiencing a lot of guilt about her relationships. Her grades had begun to suffer, and she was afraid she might be placed on academic probation. As the interview continued, the counselor learned that Carmen had recently moved to the mainland United States to attend graduate school and she had no family here. Although she had gone on a couple of dates, she was single. She received constant pressure from her new friends to date more and enjoy singlehood. On the other hand, whenever she called home, Carmen was bombarded by her mother about meeting someone and settling down, but her mother warned her about becoming "muy gringa" (too Americanized) and independent.

In counseling, Carmen and her counselor worked on how she could cope with feelings of isolation and also on assertiveness training. Assertiveness, her counselor recognized, was important to work on while acknowledging the context of values such as respeto and familismo. It was also significant to explore the process and the impact of acculturation in her life and in her family's life. It was pivotal for Carmen's counselor to be cognizant of how her own enculturation into a mainly individualistic society might impact the therapeutic process. Similarly, it was important for Carmen's counselor to be aware of unique differences between Puerto Ricans and other groups of Latinos/Latinas in order to best help Carmen negotiate issues of ethno-cultural identity and social well-being. Addressing Carmen's concerns from a collectivistic perspective and accounting for her unique acculturative experience led to a trusting and respectful relationship between Carmen and her counselor, which helped facilitate Carmen's successful adjustment into graduate school.

In the first vignette, when Jillian met with José, she assumed that he would automatically feel comfortable opening up to her about his anxiety. Jillian had to do research on the sociopolitical climate for Latinos/Latinas who may feel anxious about whether they, their family members, and/or members of their community may be able to stay in the United States. Consultation provided Jillian with context for José's reluctance in counseling. Similarly, in the second vignette, the counselor remained culturally alert by keeping in mind the potential similarities and differences between herself and Carmen regarding acculturation and enculturation, which might create conflict in their working relationship.

INTRODUCTION

Due the dramatic increase in the U.S. Latino/Latina population over the last 20 years, it has become vitally important for counselors to be prepared to work with Latino/Latina clients. Both of this chapter's vignettes present some of the counseling issues (e.g., language, family values, culture, acculturation, gender roles) that counselors will encounter when working with Latinos/Latinas. This chapter explores these issues and their influence on the counseling relationship with Latino/Latina clients. It begins by discussing the terms used to identify members of this large panethnic group and then discusses demographic information that could be useful in understanding Latinos/as' needs and living conditions. From there, other salient variables needed for understanding Latino/a clients and implications for counseling will be discussed.

HISPANIC OR LATINO/ LATINA: WHAT'S IN A NAME?

A name is often the introduction to identity for an individual person or group of people. For Hispanic/Latino/Latina people, many names have been used to describe them (e.g., Hispanic; Latino; Chicano; Raza; Spanish American; specific country names like Mexican, Cuban, and Puerto Rican).

Counselors need to be aware that the terms *Hispanic* and *Latino/Latina* have different political implications and origins. Some people argue that these terms reflect a legacy of colonialism in the Americas (i.e., they define a group of people by the names of the empires—Spanish [Hispanic] and Roman [Latino]—that historically colonized and oppressed them). In this section we discuss these controversial terms.

Hispanic is the official U.S. government term (Office of Management & Budget, 1997) for people of Mexican, Puerto Rican, Cuban, and Central and South American origin. It is also an English word, one that is thought to emphasize the white European (Spanish and Portuguese) colonial heritage while excluding the indigenous, slave, mixed (mestizo), and non-European and non-Spanish-speaking heritages. For example, a Peruvian of Mayan Indian descent may feel the term Hispanic does not reflect who she or he is. Many scholars also find the term Hispanic to be an undesirable panethnic term that can gloss over vital differences among many people (e.g., Senices, 2005). This misleading homogenization of ethnic diversity denies the cultural and racial variations within this population (Rinderle & Montoya, 2008; Senices, 2005).

The term *Latino*, or the feminine form *Latina*, has been thought of as a more inclusive and politically progressive term (Santiago-Rivera, Arredondo, & Gallardo-Cooper, 2002) and has in many areas become a more preferable term than Hispanic. Latino/Latina is considered more inclusive because (a) it is gender specific, (b) it refers to all people from Latin American, (c) it explicitly includes Brazilians (i.e., in contrast to the rest of South America, Brazil was colonized by the Portuguese and is therefore not Hispanic), and (d) it prevents the inaccurate labeling of European Spaniards as an ethnic minority in the United States (Comas-Díaz, 2001).

However, what is often missing from the discussion of terminology is what this diverse group of peoples would call themselves. As Comas-Díaz (2001) points out, the power to name oneself represents liberation over colonization. In this chapter the general term Latino/Latina is used (unless U.S.

government products such as the census are mentioned, which requires use of the term Hispanic). We recognize that, for some people, national (e.g., Mexican, Mexican-American), regional (e.g., Nuyorican, Caribeño/Caribeña), political (e.g., Chicano/Chicana), panethnic (e.g., Raza), or racial (e.g., LatiNegro/LatiNegra) terms may be preferred. As the first author (Delgado-Romero, 2001) advised in a case study focused on Latino/Latina issues, it is important for the counselor to assess how Latino/Latina clients identify themselves, both collectively and individually (e.g., the pronunciation and language of their name). The way in which clients choose to define their names and identities may reflect the importance of ethnic, racial, and cultural identity and political consciousness (or lack thereof). This aspect of self-definition may change throughout the course of counseling as issues related to culture are addressed.

LATINO/LATINA DEMOGRAPHICS

It is important for counselors to understand how representative of the United States' overall population Latinos/Latinas are and the circumstances in which many of them live. Their living situations may influence their ability to access medical and mental health services and may give an indication of their mobility in academic and social environments. Culturally competent counselors need to understand the existing interplay between a group's demographic characteristics and mental health disparities in U.S. society. For example, although it is generally true that counselors need to know about clients' financial situations regardless of their ethnicity or race, this issue becomes more salient in cases where the individual might be undocumented and/or uninsured. Having an awareness of Latino/Latina clients' financial positions and living circumstances will aid the counselor in better serving their needs. This section provides descriptions of Latino/Latina clients' demographic characteristics, historical background, and other contextual factors regarding race and ethnicity.

General Demographic, Historical, and Contextual Descriptors

Although there has always been a Latino/Latina presence since the inception of the United States, there has recently been an increasing awareness of the growing numbers of Latinos/Latinas in the United States. This section addresses the demographics of the U.S. population.

The U.S. Census reports that the United States has recently seen a dramatic increase in the Latino/Latina population, from 35.3 million in 2000 to nearly 50.5 million in 2010, a 43.1% increase (Ennis, Rios-Vargas, & Albert, 2011). This growth accounted for more than half of the total population increase in the United States. Thanks to this significant population increase, Hispanics are the largest-growing minority ethnic group in the United States. Among U.S. Hispanics, 63% are of Mexican origin, 9.2% are of Puerto Rican origin, 3.5% are of Cuban origin, and 24.3% are "other Hispanics." More than 12 million fall into this "other" category, which includes six million Hispanics whom the census has problems classifying (see Guzmán & McConnell, 2002; McConnell & Delgado-Romero, 2004); approximately 7.9% are from Central America, 5.5% from South America, and 2.8% from the Dominican Republic. Contrary to popular misconceptions, the growth of the Latino/Latina population can be greatly attributed to high fertility rates rather than solely due to immigration.

Latinos/Latinas tend to be younger that the rest of the U.S. population. Their median age is 27 years, compared to 41 years for non-Hispanic whites (Pew Hispanic Center, 2009). Those of Mexican origin have the highest numbers of people under the age of 18 (37.1%). Cubans tend to be older, with a median age of 40, compared to the U.S. population and other Hispanics with median ages of 36 and 27, respectively (Dockterman, 2011).

The household size of Latinos/Latinas tends to be larger than that of non-Hispanic whites. Latinos/Latinas are also more likely to live in poverty and to be unemployed (U.S. Census Bureau, n.d.). Differences exist among Latinos/Latinas, with Puerto Ricans (24%) having higher rates of poverty than Mexicans (22.9%) and Cubans (14.2%; Collazo, Ryan, & Bauman, 2010). Thirty-eight percent of Latinos/Latinas over the age of 25 lack a high school diploma, with the two largest groups, Mexicans and Puerto Ricans, being the least likely to have a high school diploma (U.S. Census Bureau, n.d.).

Access to counseling is a problem for many Latinos/Latinas. Age and education affect their access to some kinds of counseling. Younger adults are less likely than older adults to be insured. Health insurance is a key to accessing health care. Thirty-one percent of Latinos/Latinas are uninsured, compared with 13.3% of whites and 18.1% of African Americans (U.S. Census Bureau, n.d.). Mental health use is significantly higher among Puerto Ricans, for example, 1 out of 5, compared to 1 of 10 Mexicans, will use mental health services (and this number is lower for immigrants) compared with 1 of 2.75 whites (Alegría et al., 2007; Alexandre, Martins, & Richard, 2009). Even more dramatic is the fact that only 1 in 20 Hispanic American immigrants uses mental health services, and only 1 in 10 uses general health care services (U.S. Department of Health and Human Services, 1999). The health disparities among Latinos/Latinas have an impact on their access to mental health services and on their overall physical and mental well-being.

Along with demographic descriptors, historical and contextual factors are important in understanding Latino/Latina clients, especially the circumstances of immigration and related attitudes toward the country of origin and the United States. For example, a Cuban family that immigrated to the United States to escape Communism in the first wave of Cuban immigration (and was received in the United States with official resettlement programs) might have a reason to feel differently about the United States and their homeland than would a Puerto Rican family that is allowed to travel freely between the two countries. In our opening vignettes we saw that circumstances of immigration are important, as José feared deportation and Carmen, despite being a U.S. citizen by virtue of being born in Puerto Rico, faced serious acculturation issues in the mainland United States.

Latino/Latina clients differ in their racial or cultural identity (e.g., cultural pride versus shame) depending on the circumstances that brought them to the United States and where they choose to live. The circumstances of their immigration may also affect attitudes toward counseling, other minority groups, and the importance of retaining the Spanish language and/or Latino/Latina culture. The rest of this section looks in greater detail at the important and often-overlooked issue of Latino/Latina ethnicity and race.

Latino/Latina Ethnicity and Race

According to the U.S. government, Hispanics are the only "official" ethnicity in the country. Therefore, U.S. Census takers expect Hispanics to choose both an ethnicity (Hispanic/non-Hispanic) and a race (white, black, Asian Pacific Islander, Native American). However, it is not clear that all U.S. Latinos/Latinas endorse this particular parsing of identity. Many endorse national (e.g., Puerto Rican) or panethnic terms (e.g., Hispanic) instead of a race or a country of origin (Campbell & Rogalin, 2006). This panethnic response represents a growing identity for Latinos/Latinas. However, as with any other group in the United States, race has historically played a complicated role in the Latino/Latina population and continues to do so. For example, Logan (2003) analyzed census data by race and found three main racial groups of Hispanics: white Hispanics, black Hispanics, and what he termed *Hispanic Hispanics* (i.e., those who chose Hispanic as their racial designation). He found that success and educational attainment fell out along racial lines, with white Hispanics being more successful than Hispanic Hispanics and black Hispanics. Because the number of Hispanic Hispanics (now more than 16 million) is growing more rapidly than other Hispanic groups, it is even more important to be aware of the distinctiveness of Hispanics who identify neither as black nor as white.

Racial and ethnic issues are not limited to self-identification. It is important to remember that clients also face daily interactions with others who want to classify them into categories. For example those Latinos/Latinas with strong Spanish accents or who outwardly (skin and eye color, hair color and texture) represent what Latinos/Latinas are expected to look like may find that they are strongly identified as Latino/Latina by others (Vaquera & Kao, 2006). Conversely, light-skinned Latinos/Latinas without accents may struggle to be seen as legitimately Latino/Latina (Delgado-Romero, 2004), and dark-skinned Latinos/Latinas may face additional racial challenges when identified as black or African American by others (Comas-Díaz, 1994). Counselors should be aware that racial and ethnic identity issues may be important to address with clients. This can be done in terms of simple self-identification, or it can refer to potential discrimination or invalidation related to race and ethnicity that a client may encounter in society.

Although the growing panethnic identity of many U.S. Latinos/Latinas can be seen as a positive development in terms of political unity for this population, an imposed panethnic identity may also be distressing to a client who has a strong nationalistic or regional identity. It should be noted that, upon entry into the United States, many Latinos/Latinas experience a transformation of identity as they enter the binary (black/white) racial and ethnic categorization system of the United States. Previously they may have defined themselves nationally or regionally and along a continuum of racial descriptors found in Latin American countries (Duany & Silver, 2010).

However, once in the United States, they may have a new ethnicity (Hispanic or Latino/Latina) and race. This transformation can be confusing and disorienting. For example, in the second vignette, Carmen is a Puerto Rican who identifies herself as an Isleña (i.e., someone from the island of Puerto Rico as opposed to a Puerto Rican who was born in the United States; see Soto-Carlo, Delgado-Romero, & Galván, 2005) and Tiana (a reference to the indigenous people of Puerto Rico). However, she is now identified in the United States as simply Hispanic and/or black. This new identification can cause an identity crisis and marginalization. In response to an imposed categorical system, several Latinos/Latinas have chosen racialized terms to describe themselves, such as *La Raza* which means "the people" or "the race," to claim a place in the racial hierarchy of the United States (Márquez & Espino, 2010). Counselors might find it helpful to explore how their Latino/Latina clients are impacted by their racial and ethnic identities and the issues that surface during counseling.

Stereotypes, Racism, and Prejudice

Categorizations of race and ethnicity also are accompanied by stereotypes, racism, and prejudice. In the United States, Latinos/Latinas have to face several stereotypes that have been perpetuated in the media. You are invited to complete Activity 11.2 to consider this issue.

Activity 11.2   Self-Reflection

What negative stereotypes of Latinos/Latinas have been perpetuated in the media?

What are the stereotypical roles for men versus women in the Latino/Latina community?

What are some stereotypes of Latinos/Latinas that you consider to be positive?

Negative stereotypes include the idea that all Latino men are dedicated to their family yet are domineering and that men are the abusive macho or machista Latino. Latina women, by contrast, are seen as self-sacrificing and unassertive (a phenomenon called *marianismo*, which is discussed later). Other common stereotypes include portraying Latino/Latina people as lazy, overly emotional, unreliable, illegally in the United States, speaking broken English, and criminal. There are also specific stereotypes according to country; for example, Cubans are sometimes portrayed as the "model" Latino/Latina population, and Colombians are often portrayed as drug traders. Counselors should be aware of the power and pervasiveness of stereotypes because these stereotypes not only affect clients' self-perceptions, they also affect the counselor's worldview. The general issue of the relationship between (a) stereotypical expectations, both internal and external, and (b) a decreased sense of competence and self-defeating behavior that may result for Latino/Latina clients is something counselors should be aware of.

Latinos/Latinas do not face oppression and stereotypes only from outside their community. Racismo—discrimination—also exists within and between the Latino/Latina groups (Lavariega Monforti & Sanchez, 2010). Latino/Latina people may internalize stereotypes about other Latino/Latina groups (e.g., Mexican Americans as "lazy"), learn to devalue certain racial groups (e.g., Latinos/Latinas who are also black or indigenous), or have long-standing rivalries or conflict with other national groups (e.g., between Colombians and Venezuelans). Therefore a Latino/Latina client may resent being "lumped" into a generic racial or ethnic category with other groups or may have strong negative opinions of other Latino/Latina groups. In sum, it is important for counselors to realize that Latinos/Latinas may face multiple oppressions from at least three sources: the majority culture, other minority cultures, and the Latino/Latina community.

Despite pervasively negative stereotypes, it is important for counselors to focus on and work with strengths in Latino/Latina culture. For example, there is evidence for Cuban Americans in particular that family plays a positive role in the psychosocial development of Cuban American children, in that family pride and cohesion act as buffers for acculturative stress (Ayón, Marsiglia, & Bermudez-Parsai, 2010). Similarly, in the case of Carmen (in the second vignette that opened this chapter), developing and practicing assertiveness skills in the context of her family values is important. This recognition of family context helped her believe that she was respecting her family; therefore they could continue to count on each other for support (thus lessening her feelings of guilt). Consequently, counselors need to see Latino/Latina families as a potential source of support and a buffer for clients, rather than solely endorsing individualistic notions of independence and individuation (family relationships are described more fully later in this chapter).

LATINO/LATINA CULTURES

The use of one term, Latino/Latina, for a grouping of peoples creates the impression that all Latinos/Latinas are a monolithic racial or ethnic group and that they share a common culture. But this population is widely diverse. The term is used to represent millions of people from the different countries in Central and South America and the Caribbean. Further, those peoples who are grouped together as Latino/Latina simultaneously represent indigenous, African, European, and Asian influences and speak an array of languages (including Spanish, Portuguese, English, and Amerindian languages). Each country and region of origin reflects a unique political, economic, social, religious, and cultural constellation. In addition, each has a unique history relative to the United States (e.g., Puerto Rico has been a commonwealth of the United States since the Spanish-American War, in contrast to Mexico, which lost a border war to the United States, has free trade agreements, and shares a common border). Each also has unique immigration issues that influence how each group is perceived within the United States (V. Torres, 2004).

Commonalities Among Latino/Latina Peoples

Although there is considerable within-group diversity among the U.S. Latino/Latina population, some general similarities define Latino/Latina people. Such similarities include a shared history of conquest and oppression, the struggle for liberation, domination by white European immigrants, and destruction of indigenous cultures, religions, and people (Acosta-Belén & Santiago, 2006; Garcia-Preto, 1996).

Latino/Latina people share a history of ethnic mixing that is a product of Central and South American participation in slavery. That history has resulted in mestizo (racially mixed) people. This indicates, as Garcia-Preto (1996) acknowledges, that "Latinos are descendants of [both] the oppressors and the oppressed" (p. 143).

The following are also important similarities among Latino/Latina people: the widespread use of the Spanish language (with regional variations), the influence of Roman Catholicism, and an ambivalent relationship with U.S. foreign policies and political intervention in the history of Caribbean and Central and South American countries (Delgado-Romero & Rojas, 2004).

In addition, at least five overall value orientations have been attributed to the Latino/Latina people (Altarriba & Bauer, 1998): *personalismo* (a preference for close personal relationships), *respeto* (respect for elders and authority, which is maintained by all family members), *familismo* (an emphasis on the family, including the extended family and friends), *simpatia* (a need for behaviors that promote pleasant and nonconflicting social relationships), and allocentrism (high levels of conformity, mutual empathy, willingness to sacrifice for the welfare of the group, and personal interdependence; Marín & Marín, 1991). Clients will vary in the degree to which they endorse these value orientations.

Regional Differences

In addition to cultural differences originating in the country of origin, the region of the United States in which Latino/Latina people live can also contribute to similarity (or dissimilarity). Latinos/Latinas are increasingly found throughout the country, but they are still concentrated in several areas and states. According to the 2010 census, 41% live in the West and 36% live in the South. Figure 11.1 shows the distribution of the Latino/Latina population in the United States.

Mexican Americans are mostly found in California, Texas, Illinois, and Arizona; Puerto Ricans in New York, Florida, New Jersey, and Pennsylvania; and two-thirds of all Cubans live in Florida (U.S. Census Bureau, n.d.). The general point here is that in each region there is a dominant Latino/Latina culture that may differ significantly from the Latino/Latina culture in other regions. Consequently, a regional identity may be more important than national origin to some clients. For example, a Latino/Latina born and raised in Miami, Florida, may encounter culture shock when visiting Mexican American communities in Houston or Puerto Rican communities in New York City. Thus it is important to consider the Latino/Latina client's relationship to both the dominant (e.g., white) culture and the dominant regional Latino/Latina culture. In this chapter's vignettes, for example, the regions of the United States in which José and Carmen live might be key to understanding them as well as what resources may be available to them. It may be the case that Carmen's family is concerned that she is becoming less Puerto Rican and more like her Mexican or Cuban peers. Her family may be distressed to hear Carmen speaking Spanish with a different accent. The next section deals with the issues of language.

Language: Spanish, English, and Spanglish

Like Latino/Latina cultures, the Spanish language itself is not unitary. As with English, Spanish has national and regional variations and slang forms. Some U.S. Latinos/Latinas have combined English and Spanish into an idiosyncratic form of communication often referred to as "Spanglish." According to Stavans (2000),

Figure 11.1 Distribution of the Latino/Latina Population by State: 2010 (in %)

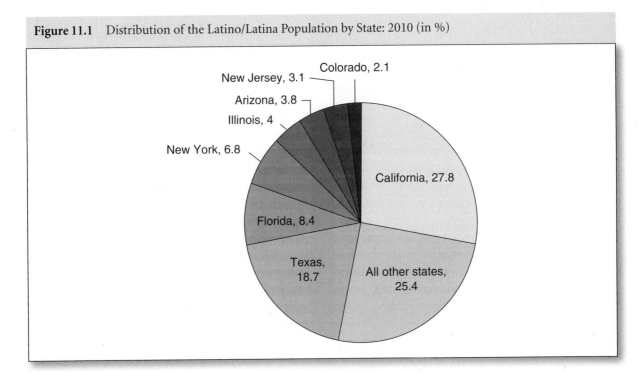

New Jersey, 3.1
Colorado, 2.1
Arizona, 3.8
Illinois, 4
New York, 6.8
California, 27.8
Florida, 8.4
Texas, 18.7
All other states, 25.4

Source: U.S. Census Bureau (n.d.).

It is commonly assumed that Spanglish is a bastard jargon: part Spanish and part English, with neither gravitas nor a clear identity. It is spoken (or broken) by many of the approximately 35 million people of Hispanic descent in the United States, who, no longer fluent in the language of Cervantes, have not yet mastered that of Shakespeare. (p. B7)

Consequently, due to the variations in the Spanish language, even counselors trained in technical Spanish may not be able to effectively communicate with Spanish-speaking clients (for examples, see Rivas, Delgado-Romero, & Ozambela, 2004). In cases in which communication is compromised, the use of trained interpreters may be necessary (American Psychological Association, 2003). However, the use of untrained interpreters, who may not understand counseling or the profession of interpretation, is ethically inappropriate and potentially harmful.

It should be noted that most (75%) U.S. Latinos/Latinas who speak Spanish also report that they speak English. Thus choosing which language to speak in counseling might be a decision that is based on necessity (e.g., if the client does not speak English) or choice (e.g., if the client prefers to speak Spanish). For example, in the first vignette, José preferred to speak Spanish although he could speak English. In the area of language, it is important to note that Latino/Latina clients do not need to be seen in counseling by bilingual Latino/Latina counselors, nor are Latino/Latina counselors automatically "experts" on all Hispanic clients. All counselors should strive to be culturally competent (American Psychological Association, 2003; S. Sue, 2006). Indeed, counselors from any racial or ethnic background can become competent to work with Latino/Latina clients, with the proper training.

There are three language-related problem domains central to working with Latino/Latina clients: language choice, resources, and attitude (Rivas et al., 2004).The first domain, language choice, includes issues such as the meaning behind a client's choice of language (e.g., which one she or he chooses at which points in the session and for how long), the implications of a counselor's choosing to address (or not) language use, the power dynamics involved with language, the effect that these factors have on the therapeutic relationship, and the extent to which language and related dynamics interfere with or deepen the counseling process.

The second domain refers to the resources available for bilingual counselors. For example, bilingual counselors face inadequate supervision because clinical supervisors might not be proficient in Spanish. Lack of accreditation criteria and lack of resources available to bilingual counselors (e.g., appropriately validated assessment tools and therapeutic instruments) are additional concerns for bilingual counselors. Moreover, the scarcity of bilingual counselors may lead to large caseloads and burnout.

The third domain, attitude, includes issues such as the comfort level of a counselor with her or his culture, the level of comfort with language proficiency (including reading, writing, speaking, and comprehending/communicating), and the counselor's own ethnic identity and acculturation status. Of equal importance to the previously discussed issues of race/ethnicity, region, identity, and language is the centrality of the Latino/Latina family. The next section explores this important issue.

La Familia: Family Relationships in Latino/Latina Culture

The strong familial relationships that presented such a paradox in the cases of José and Carmen are central to Latino/Latina culture. Latinos/Latinas should be conceptualized in the context of *La Familia*, that is, the whole family rather, than only as individuals (Santiago-Rivera et al., 2002). However the notion of family is not the stereotypical nuclear family. Latinos/Latinas often extend their notion of family to include relatives and close friends.

The family is a source of both identity and potential conflict for Latinos/Latinas. Many Latinos/Latinas define themselves in the collectivist context of their families (Delgado-Romero, 2001). For example, Dr. Melba Vasquez (2001) described her own family circle this way:

I grew up in a small central Texas town during the 1950s. I was the first of seven children born to first-born parents. . . . In other words, I had the privilege of a considerable amount of attention, adoration, and regards from my parents, large extended family (including 16 aunts and uncles and all four grandparents plus great uncles and aunts, second cousins, and so on!). (p. 65)

While traditional Latin notions of family are important, it is critical to understand that the concept of the Latino/Latina family is not static. It is something that is in transition and is variable because of the acculturation process (described later in this chapter), migration experience, language, race, nationality, and socioeconomic background of each family (Santiago-Rivera et al., 2002).

Four types of family structures are important in working with Latinos/Latinas (Santiago-Rivera et al., 2002). The first is the intact familia, which consists of parents who continue to live together. This configuration may include grandparents or other members of the extended family. This family structure is likely to be patriarchal, and the parents may take on specific gender roles. This is what is thought of as the "traditional" Latino/Latina family. The second is the single-parent familia, which is most commonly headed by Latina single mothers. High rates of poverty and teen pregnancy in Latino/Latina communities contribute to the existence of this structure. It should be noted that single Latina mothers are at a high risk for depression. The third is the bicultural familia. There are two types of bicultural familias: acculturated (in which a Latino/Latina family has some level of acculturation to the dominant culture) and cross-cultural (i.e., those produced by intercultural marriage). The fourth is the immigrant familia. Migration is a significant event in the life of a family. It can bring several forms of transformation to the family structure, such as new gender roles or increased responsibility for children. Some families migrate in stages, and separation and reunions are important events.

There are counseling implications for each one of these family types (Santiago-Rivera et al., 2002). One implication lies in the distinction between an intact family and other types of families. The issues that an intact familia will deal with in counseling can be very different from the issues faced by a single mother. Similarly, the intact familia will differ from a family who is separated either by geography (i.e., members having different times of immigration) or by cultural conflicts. Counselors should take care to assess the familial context of the client in order to understand the particular dynamics that each individual faces. In the next section, traditional (and changing) gender roles that often have their origin in the traditional Latino/Latina family structure are addressed.

Latino/Latina Gender Issues

A common struggle for all ethnic minority family groups in the United States is the conflict between culturally and historically traditional gender roles and the roles in the majority culture. Gender role ideologies commonly influence Latino/Latina family dynamics. But they are not monolithic. The perceptions that men and women have about their gender role and their role in the family are dependent upon their socialization, their own economic and social status, acculturation, and historical events (Parra-Cardona, Córdova, Holtrop, Villarruel, & Wieling, 2008).

It would be to the counselor's advantage to be alert to how gender role ideologies may impact relationships, the decisions clients make, and the reasons they make those decisions. As stated earlier, many Latinos/Latinas define themselves in the context of their families (Delgado-Romero, 2001). Thus, understanding the role of gender within the family context becomes crucial. In the second vignette, Carmen experienced a conflict with her family related to her independence and relationship history. This conflict was no doubt rooted in differing gender role expectations.

The following paragraphs provide an overview of Latinos/Latinas' gender role ideologies and the traditional gender role characteristics of males (machismo) and females (marianismo). The influence of acculturation and economic status on machismo and marianismo are also discussed, as are other possible ways in which gender role conflict may play out on Latinos/Latinas' personal and career decisions.

Although Latinos/Latinas are a very diverse group, they share a history of European (particularly Spanish) influence on their religion and culture, which in turn has dictated what it means to be a man or a woman (Arredondo, 2002). In Latino/Latina culture, gender roles can provide clear and rigid expectations for men and women. Arciniega, Anderson, Tovar-Blank, and Tracey (2008) described two different types or factors of machismo. For example, machismo can sometimes be characterized by male dominance, aggression, promiscuous behavior, excessive use of alcohol, and restricted emotions. These negative characteristics are together called traditional machismo (Arciniega et al., 2008). However, machismo can also include positive characteristics, called *caballerismo*, such as pride, *nobleza* (nobility), honor, responsibility as a provider for one's loved ones, and assertive behavior (Arciniega et al., 2008; Parra-Cardona et al., 2008).

In the case of Latinas, marianismo has been associated with a number of stereotypical attributes (self-sacrificing, submissive, unassertive behavior). These attributes have been shaped by the images of the Madonna, or Virgin Mary, which indicates that women put their needs last, be married, not be independent-minded, and not want change (see Arredondo, 2002). However, there are also strengths inherent in female gender roles as well, such as having a family orientation and being a keeper of tradition. Counselors should not rush to view all traditional Latino/Latina gender roles as entirely negative.

As Latino men and Latina women integrate or identify with multiple cultures (e.g., their culture of origin and the dominant culture), they are likely to challenge negative, more rigid, and traditional attributes that have characterized their ethnically prescribed gender roles. Latino/Latina individuals who challenge and negotiate gender roles can experience great stress, particularly in the context of the family and community.

This was the case for Carmen. She reported being criticized by her family for being too independent and for not acting on her duties (e.g., cooking for husband) as a woman. She had begun to acculturate to U.S. female gender roles and was negotiating her role as woman in the community and in her family. However, her family members did not appear to share her enthusiasm for changing or expanding her gender role and were demanding that she act in a traditional manner.

Carmen's experience is a common conflict, as not all members of a family will acculturate or integrate into the new culture at the same rate or on the same issues. For example, younger individuals tend to learn the language of the new culture faster and will face the demands of acculturation coupled with internalized and externalized prejudice. Latinos/Latinas facing these challenges may feel a lack of support or understanding from their families or communities, which might be pressuring them to adhere to the more traditional gender roles. Conflict from the inability to challenge traditional Latino/Latina views of gender roles can manifest itself as psychological stress, depression, and/or anxiety (Liang, Salcedo, & Miller, 2011).

Counselors can help Latinos/Latinas reduce their emotional stress by incorporating in their intervention an understanding of Latino/Latina gender role expectations, acknowledging positive attributes of machismo and marianismo, and considering cultural values of respeto and familismo. Returning to the vignette of Carmen, the counselor first acknowledged respeto, familismo, and gender roles before helping Carmen improve her assertiveness skills. As Falicov (1998) has explained, although Latinas are becoming independent (e.g., seeking equal pay or access to institutions), for many of them their family and their commitment to their culture remain a top priority. By contrast, a counselor's emphasizing independence from family can alienate Latino/Latina clients from participating in counseling because they may feel that their values are not shared or understood by the counselor.

Gender roles cannot be understood in isolation (Gloria, 2001). Race/ethnicity should also be incorporated as gender roles, family, and career values can vary depending on the person's racial/ethnic background. Ignoring the impact of race/ethnicity on Latinos/Latinas' experiences when this is important to them will minimize discount their cultural realities and their status as ethnic minority women or men in this country (Gloria, 2001; Liang et al., 2011). The next section deals directly with acculturation.

Acculturation

As Chapter 4 pointed out, acculturation can be defined as the process by which a group adapts to the norms of a dominant culture, although it was also noted that acculturation is a two-way process, as groups inevitably influence each other in some ways. Chapter 4 also refers to enculturation, which is the process by which the norms of a person's indigenous culture are learned and retained.

The issue of acculturation is important because it indicates a person's facility with the dominant way of living. Acculturation is a controversial issue in the mental health treatment of Latinos/Latinas. As presented in Chapter 4, acculturation was formerly framed in the United States in terms of cultural assimilation, guided by the experiences of European immigrants. Within this notion of a "melting pot," it was expected that immigrants' racial, national, and ethnic differences would be replaced in successive generations by the values of the dominant culture. Because of the lingering ethos of the melting pot, groups that choose to retain aspects of their indigenous culture (e.g., use of the Spanish language) face intense pressure to conform to mainstream norms. Specifically, Latino/Latina youth may be marginalized and face discrimination because of their immigration status (Edwards & Romero, 2008).

The psychological stress of having to choose between cultures is referred to as acculturative stress (Smart & Smart, 1995). It can be expressed in familial discord, intergenerational conflict, and racial/ethnic identity conflict and thus may be a topic for counseling sessions. Acculturative stress has also been demonstrated to be associated with negative psychological outcomes. Specifically, Arbona et al. (2010) found that undocumented Latino immigrants were more likely than others to experience stress related to "employment, communication, discrimination, and legal status" (p. 376). Given the stricter changes in immigration laws, one might expect this stress to be exacerbated.

Acculturation as a process has implications for Latino/Latina identity and identity development, as the next section reveals.

UNDERSTANDING CLIENT ETHNIC IDENTITY

Individual differences among Latino/Latina clients must be assessed so that overgeneralizations do not occur in counseling. Ethnic identity is one such individual difference that is both fluid and contextual. For example, counselor Luis Rivas (2004) remarked on the identity shift he experienced when he left Latino/Latina-dominant Puerto Rico to attend college in the midwestern United States:

> When I became a "minority" I certainly did not have a say over what that meant for me and how others were or were not to perceive me. Yet it affected, and still affects, my everyday life. No matter how many professional degrees I attain or how much good I may do in the world, people will still judge my character and me by the preconceived notions they have of others who are like me. (p. 87)

Like Rivas (2004), Latino/Latina clients may experience struggles with their ethnic identities. A number of models can help counselors recognize their own and their individual clients' ethnic identity characteristics. As seen in the cultural identity development models described in previous chapters, such models map how individuals evolve in their relationship to their and others' race and ethnicity. The majority of the work on racial identity development has been devoted to comparing black and white groups (e.g., Cross, 1971; Hardiman, 1982; Helms, 1990). More often than not Latinos/Latinas have been either ignored or fitted into generic minority models, such as the Racial Identity

Development for People of Color model described in Chapter 4, the Minority Identity Development Model (Atkinson, Morten, & Sue, 1989), the Racial/Cultural Identity Model (D. W. Sue & Sue, 1999), and the Adolescent Ethnic Identity Development (Phinney, 1993). These generic models, however, may gloss over factors specific to the Latino/Latina experience as well as differences between national groups. Ethnic identity is important to examine when a counselor seeks to effectively counsel Latinos/Latinas, because an increased awareness and attachment to ethnic identity has been shown to be a coping strategy for Latino/Latinas who are dealing with discrimination, particularly for youth (Edwards & Romero, 2008).

Two models of identity that are particularly useful for counselors are reviewed next: the Chicano/Latino Model of Ethnic Identity (Ruiz, 1990) and the Bicultural Orientation Model (V. Torres, 1999). Interested readers are directed to the Latino Dimensions of Family and Personal Identity (Santiago-Rivera et al., 2002) for another study.

The Chicano/Latino Model of Ethnic Identity

The Chicano/Latino Model of Ethnic Identity (Ruiz, 1990) describes the development, transformation, and resolution of ethnic identity conflicts for Latino/Latinas. It particularly incorporates enculturation and acculturation factors. It is based on case histories with Mexican American and other Latino/Latina university students. Ruiz (1990) based the model on four related assumptions:

1. Marginality (see Chapter 4) correlates highly with maladjustment.

2. Negative experiences of forced assimilation are destructive to the individual.

3. Pride in one's ethnic identity is positively correlated with mental health.

4. Pride in one's ethnic identity results in freedom to choose, especially in the acculturation process.

Ruiz posited the following five stages of ethnic identity for Latinos/Latinas. The four assumptions are incorporated into the stages.

1. *Causal stage.* Messages from the environment and important others ignore, negate, or denigrate Latino/Latina heritage. The person may experience humiliating and traumatic experiences related to being Latino/Latina and fail to identify with Latino/Latina culture. In this stage counselors may find individuals who believe the negative stereotypes about Latinos/Latinas and therefore believe they cannot overcome these negative traits.

2. *Cognitive stage.* Three erroneous belief systems are incorporated as a result of negative or distorted messages: (1) group membership as a Latino/Latina is associated with poverty and prejudice; (2) assimilation into dominant (white) society is seen as the only viable means of escape; and (3) one-way assimilation (into the dominant culture) is the only road to success. At this stage counselors may see that an individual is more focused on how to cope or remove herself or himself from the negative stereotypes rather than analyzing the content of the negative message.

3. *Consequence stage.* The fragmentation of Latino/Latina identity intensifies, especially when the person experiences bias, and the individual may actively reject his or her Chicano/Latino heritage. Individuals in this stage may seek counseling because they are not being successful in their desire to reject their culture or because of their intense desire to conform to mainstream norms. This stage can be especially difficult for Latinos/Latinas who either look (skin color) or sound (accent) different than mainstream peers.

4. *Working through stage.* This stage begins the integration of a healthier Chicano/Latino identity. In this stage the individual is no longer able to cope with ethnic dissonance and realizes that an alien ethnic identity is not acceptable. This stage is characterized by an increase in ethnic consciousness and reclaiming, reintegrating, and reconnecting with an ethnic identity and community. Counselors may encounter individuals in this stage

as they attempt to reconstruct negative images into positive images. This process requires the introduction of alternative messages about Latino/Latina identity that are not negative and allow the individual to consider the merit of the alternative messages.

5. *Successful resolutions stage.* This stage is characterized by the individual's greater acceptance of self, Latino/Latina culture, and ethnicity; improved self-esteem; and a belief that a Latino/Latina identity is positive and promotes success. It is at this stage that counselors may feel comfortable not having the individual in counseling. At this point the resolution of the ethnic identity crisis has been resolved, and a more positive image is at the core of the individual's beliefs.

The Chicano/Latino Model of Ethnic Identity describes a process by which Latino/Latina clients could achieve a healthy identity. Ruiz provides culturally sensitive and stage-appropriate strategies for counselors to facilitate this growth. For example, individuals in the first three stages need positive alternative information to consider. At this point counselors can provide evidence that there are positive dimensions of Latino/Latina culture. In the fourth stage counselors can assist the individual in making sense of the messages and helping the individual make meaning of her or his previous beliefs in the context of newly found information.

The Bicultural Orientation Model

The Bicultural Orientation Model (V. Torres, 1999) is helpful for understanding the choices Latinos/Latinas make between their culture of origin and the majority white (Anglo) culture in the United States. The model was validated with Latino/Latina college students in majority white areas of the country and also in areas where Latinos/Latinas have a critical mass within the greater societal structures. The model assesses both acculturation to the majority Anglo culture and ethnic identity with the culture of origin. The outcome of these measures places an individual according to her or his cultural orientation (high to low on each of the scales). Notably, the model's four orientations are parallel to the four acculturation statuses discussed in Chapter 4. Latinos/Latinas were found to have four possible orientations: Bicultural, Latino, Anglo, and Marginal.

It is important to note that higher levels of adaptability to the majority culture do not necessarily correspond with a loss of ethnic identity. The Bicultural orientation includes both acculturation and strong ethnic identity. Although individuals in areas where there were few Latinos/Latinas had higher levels of acculturation, they still could have high ethnic identity (V. Torres, Winston, & Cooper, 2003). Counselors can help clients become more bicultural, if they wish. They can help those with an Anglo orientation increase pride in their culture of origin by using Liberation Counseling, for example, which is described in Chapter 19.

PARTICULAR SUBGROUPS OF LATINOS/LATINAS

Like the term Latino/Latina itself, much of the research on Latinos/Latinas is overly general and glosses over subgroups with distinct mental health needs and risk factors. This section highlights some of the relevant subgroups that will need attention from counselors in the future. They include less well-known Latino/Latina ethnic groups, sexual minorities, Latino/Latina professionals and students, and the elderly.

National Groups Outside of the "Big Three"

Because the majority of Latinos/Latinas in the United States are from Mexico, Puerto Rico, or Cuba, these groups rightfully receive the most attention in the counseling literature. However, much needs to be learned about the approximately 10 million Latinos/Latinas who are not from the "Big Three" countries. For example, Central Americans, including Dominicans, comprise 7.9% of the U.S. Latino/Latina population, yet very little

has been written about the needs of this group (Delgado-Romero & Rojas, 2004; U.S. Census Bureau, n.d.). Another significant group, South Americans, comprise 5.5% of the U.S. Latino/Latina population (U.S. Census Bureau, n.d.). The experiences of these two groupings are virtually untouched in the counseling literature, yet counselors should become familiar with the experiences of Central and South Americans. For example, Guatemalans, who often arrive from small villages and only speak indigenous dialects, have to learn Spanish in addition to English as a way to adapt to their communities in the United States. Another example of an important but neglected group is Colombians, who are the largest South American group in the United States. They may be traumatized by a civil war that has raged in Colombia for over 40 years (Delgado-Romero & Rojas, 2004).

One helpful resource for counselors who are seeking greater familiarity with the needs of Latinos/Latinas with national origins outside of the Big Three are clinical case studies such as those of counseling with a Dominican (Spanakis, 2004) or a Colombian (Wilczak, 2003) client. However, much work still needs to be done in understanding the needs of Latinos/Latinas outside of the Big Three.

LGBT Latinos/Latinas

Traditional Latino/Latina culture, steeped in a history of Roman Catholicism, does not openly support lesbian, gay, bisexual, or transgendered (LGBT) people. In general, Latino/Latina families do not support open admission of homosexuality or "coming out." Such an admission may lead to isolation, excommunication from the family, or even violence.

However, it should be noted that there is a gender difference in these attitudes. Sexual behavior for males is not extremely restricted, compared to women. Traditional conceptualizations of sexual behavior in Latin American countries view the male sex drive as overwhelming. Therefore less concern is placed on whom a man has sex with. Consequently, a man can have sex with other men, and yet not be thought of as homosexual as long as he continues to function in a gender role consistent with other phases of life. In fact, a recent study demonstrated that gay Mexican American men conceptualize gender consistently with Arciniega and colleagues' (2008) two-factor model of machismo (traditional machismo and caballerismo), which is described earlier in this chapter (Estrada, Rigali-Oiler, Arciniega, & Tracey, 2011). Conversely, the sexuality of Latinas is supposed to be confined to marriage and procreation. Sexual behavior outside of these confines is seen as sinful for women. Consequently, the Latina lesbian faces a dual stigma of both being sexually active outside of marriage and doing so with another woman.

When a Latino/Latina's LGBT sexual behavior and orientation intersects with other oppressive conditions, the combination can prove to be a powerfully negative force in her or his life. For example, the combination of poverty, racism, and homophobia produce a high risk of HIV for gay male Latinos (Diaz, Ayala, & Bein, 2004). Other problems can arise when LGBT Latinos/Latinas who live in the majority white LGBT community experience racism, oppression, and dehumanization (e.g., being sought out by others for their "exotic" qualities). Counselors need to be aware of the multiple oppressions that LGBT Latinos/Latinas may face in their lives.

Latino/Latina Professionals and Students

Latinos/Latinas who have successfully acquired or are acquiring an education often, in Comas-Díaz's (1997) words, "represent a source of pride and joy for their families and communities," and "frequently they are identified as role models" (p. 143). Successful Latinos/Latinas are expected to return to and give back to their families and communities. Latino/Latina professionals face tremendous pressure to balance the often-conflicting demands and values of the mainstream workplace (e.g., in predominantly white institutions of higher education) while maintaining ties to their culture.

Often Latino/Latina professionals may feel that they are victims of their own success. Acculturation to the dominant culture, which is seen as a prerequisite for success, may lead to a sense of disconnection with the family and generational conflict. Therefore, Latino/Latina professionals may not feel connected with or understood by their families as they struggle to achieve.

The relatively small number of Latino/Latina professionals in U.S. public life makes the disconnect even greater. Illustrations of this alienation lie in personal narratives by Delgado-Romero, Flores, Gloria, Arredondo, and Castellanos (2003) and by Niemann (1999). They describe the challenges that Latino/Latina psychology faculty face as they try to advance in higher education. Being a role model can be a very lonely existence (Delgado-Romero, 2001). Another deficit in the lack of status and power for Latinos/Latinas in U.S. higher education is that they are thus precluded from being positive role models for Latino/Latina students (Verdugo, 1995). That is, because there are fewer Latino/Latinas in positions of high status and power in higher education institutions, Latino/Latina students have fewer mentors that can lead by example or inspire Latina/Latino students to pursue such high-status positions. This situation often places Latino/Latina faculty in a no-win situation. Counselors should encourage Latino/Latina professionals and college students to reconnect with the family and help such clients find other support (Comas-Díaz, 1997; Gloria & Rodriguez, 2000; Ruiz, 1990). Counselors themselves will need to challenge their own stereotypes of Latinos/Latinas. For example, counselors might associate Latinos/Latinas with poverty or a lack of education. These stereotypes will be challenged when counselors are to work with Latino/Latina professionals. In sum, counselors should take care to be alert to the possible discrimination and family conflicts that professionals may face as well as to their own biases.

The Elderly

It is often emphasized that, as a whole, Latinos/Latinas are the youngest population in the United States. Thus, much attention is paid to Latino/Latina adolescents. What is lost in that trend is attention to older people. For example, Cubans have the oldest mean age of Latino/Latina subgroups. Consequently, counselors who work with Cuban Americans may be more likely to deal with an older population. There is little guidance for counselors in this area. The issues that Cuban elderly face can be instructive for counselors as the overall Latino/Latina population begins to age. In the early and mid-1990s, Gonzalez (1995) studied the challenges facing the Cuban elderly. Cuban American elderly tend to view the "Americanization" of their children and grandchildren in the United States with ambivalence. They are likely to have pride in the success of their family, but also resent younger generations losing cultural connection and/or intermarrying with non-Cubans. Thus there is a benefit and a cost for acculturation. For the Cuban elderly, acculturation brings with it social and economic mobility, but it consequently erodes available support and potential caregivers, as children may not care for their parents or grandparents in the traditional way (Gonzalez, 1995).

In general, generational conflict, acculturative stress, medical decision making, and decisions on when to institutionalize Latino/Latina elderly (even when medically indicated) are challenges that face Latino/Latina families in dealing with elderly family members (Santiago-Rivera et al., 2002). These issues will intensify in the future as the Latino/Latina population ages. Counselors should be aware that generational conflicts may come into sharp focus as topics such as retirement and living arrangements for the elderly become issues for a Latino/Latina family.

Other Vulnerable Subgroups

As the U.S. Latino/Latina population grows, the awareness of subgroups within the population will come to the attention of counselors. A few vulnerable groups that are likely to have counseling needs are veterans, prisoners, and children. Considering the overrepresentation of Latinos/Latinas in the military and the recent wars conducted by the United States, counselors must keep in mind the possible need for mental health services for current and future Latino/Latina war veterans and their families. According to Hannold, Freytes, and Uphold (2011), Puerto Rican veterans of Operation Enduring Freedom and Operation

Iraqi Freedom have struggled with mental health problems such as depression and symptoms of posttraumatic stress disorder.

Unfortunately, there are many Latinos/Latinas who are incarcerated. Members of this group have been found to have higher rates of mental health disorders when compared to community residents (U.S. Department of Health and Human Services, 2001). In addition, many incarcerated Latinos/Latinas may struggle with violence, substance abuse, and other health problems (e.g., HIV), which can complicate their mental health status.

Finally, Latino/Latina children in the U.S. school system are at risk. More research needs to be done about the issues of Latino/Latina schoolchildren who are dropping out of the U.S. educational system at all levels and experiencing emotional, behavioral, and mental health problems from childhood to adolescence.

COUNSELING LATINOS/LATINAS

This chapter has tried to provide you with some ideas to consider when working with Latino/Latina clients. As has been emphasized throughout this book, individual clients will present unique problems. However, there will likely be some consistent themes (e.g., language, acculturation, family, cultural values), as has been demonstrated in the cases of José and Carmen. These cultural themes will take precedence over simple universal application of counseling theory if counselors want to practice culturally alert counseling. Next, four general guidelines for working with Latinos/Latinas are presented, followed by suggestions regarding acknowledging racism, adapting language, and providing access to Latino/Latina clients. These points reflect the key practice guidelines in Chapters 18 and 19 as they particularly apply to this specific population.

Four Guidelines

Because of the general tendency to group Latinos/Latinas together in one overly generalized group, there is limited guidance for counselors on the process of counseling with individual Latinos/Latinas. Four general recommendations for working with these clients can be made, based on the literature. In working with most Latinos/Latinas, counselors should

- be present-oriented
- focus on problem solving
- consider and incorporate the family hierarchy, and
- involve the family in counseling. (Bernal & Shapiro, 1996)

In the first case, traditional Latino/Latina culture tends to focus on the present rather than on the past or the future. Therefore, traditional Latino/Latina clients would expect a counselor to focus on the present concerns rather than explore the past. Regarding the second guideline, traditional Latinos/Latinas expect the counselor to focus on problem solving. Thus they may not respond well to nondirective counseling. In the case of family, traditional Latino/Latina family hierarchy should be respected. Finally, the family should be involved in counseling. Each of these four guidelines is especially true for traditional Latino/Latina clients and families, whereas acculturated (to majority norms) Latino/Latina families may not differ much from white clients and families.

In the area of family relations, counselors should have skills in addressing intergenerational conflict with Latino/Latina immigrant families, especially relative to acculturation and assimilation (Gonzalez, 1991). Such conflict is more likely because some Latino/Latina families immigrate in stages and, given the tendency for acculturation to happen at different paces in a family, the youngest members often acculturate and learn English first.

Acknowledging Racism and Prejudice

As was mentioned in Chapter 3, external oppressions, in the form of racism and prejudice, must be addressed to the extent that these issues are problems for the client. Not every Latino/Latina client will struggle with racism or prejudice. However, counselors should be open to processing these issues (see Delgado-Romero, 2001). Simply said, counselors should not engage in denial, avoidance, or intellectualization in the face of racism.

Language

Language is often a main barrier to obtaining counseling for Latino/Latina clients who do not speak English (Preciado & Henry, 1997). Language has traditionally been neglected as a counseling variable in the professional literature (Rivas et al., 2004). Thus the role that language choice plays in the counseling process has yet to be definitively examined. Yet recall the case of José, in which language choice was an issue. In general, counselors should not underestimate the power of language differences in counseling.

Access

Language alone is not the only barrier to counseling services. Barriers to Latino/Latina use of counseling are largely around access. Such access includes lack of (a) physical access to services, (b) affordability, (c) awareness of treatment options, and (d) the presence of Latino/Latina and/or culturally competent and/or bilingual counselors and support staff. In addition to these barriers, in traditional Latino/Latina culture, people are socialized to not openly share problems with non-family members. This reticence to share problems can be compounded when the client is undocumented and fears deportation by government officials. Counselors may not think of themselves as government officials, but they often have governmental ties (e.g., work for governmental agencies, receive federal funding, attend state universities) that may scare a potential client. Therefore, access and trust-building should exist in the ways described in Chapter 18.

SUMMARY

To ensure social justice in their work with Latino/Latina clients, counselors are called to do many things: gain knowledge and specialized training in working with these clients, participate in and learn about Latino/a communities, recognize and reinforce the strengths of Latino/Latina clients, and, most important, recognize and work through their own biases and assumptions. By doing so, counselors will be armed with an open attitude for work with a dynamically evolving Latino/Latina culture in the United States.

Counselors must realize that when a client participates in counseling, she or he is taking a personal risk, and when that client is part of a group that has been historically oppressed and marginalized, that risk is even greater. Consequently, counselors must respond by taking risks of their own (e.g., stepping outside of the office, participating in the community, learning some Spanish or at least learning to pronounce Spanish names, becoming an advocate for Latino/Latina issues) as ways to demonstrate to clients that they are culturally committed and alert.

The call to be culturally alert is complicated by the fact that Latino/Latina culture in the United States is dynamic and constantly changing. It is not uncommon to see culture interpreted differently between Latinos/Latinas from the same country or even within the same family. The counselor has the daunting task of being aware of both general cultural themes (e.g., importance of family, acculturation conflicts, the meaning of independence, gender roles) and at the same time needing to understand how these cultural themes are interpreted and lived by a Latino/Latina individual and her or his family. Given estimates that by the year 2050 one in four people in the United States will be Latino/Latina, and that this group will have an ever-expanding influence on the future of the United States, counselors must do their best to be culturally alert in their work with Latinos/Latinas.

REFERENCES

Acosta-Belén, A. C. E., & Santiago, E. (2006). *Puerto Ricans in the United States: A contemporary portrait*. Boulder, CO: Lynne Rienner.

Alegría, M., Mulvaney-Day, N., Woo, M., Torres, M., Gao, S., & Oddo, V. (2007). Correlates of past-year mental health service use among Latinos: Results from the National Latino and Asian American Study. *American Journal of Public Health, 97*, 76–83.

Alexandre, P. K., Martins, S. S., & Richard, P. (2009). Disparities in adequate mental health care for past-year major depressive episodes among Caucasian and Hispanic youths. *Psychiatric Services, 60*, 1365–1371.

Altarriba, J., & Bauer, L. M. (1998). Counseling the Hispanic client: Cuban Americans, Mexican Americans and Puerto Ricans. *Journal of Counseling and Development, 76*, 389–396.

American Psychological Association. (2003). Guidelines on multicultural education, training, research, practice and organizational change for psychologists. *American Psychologist, 58*, 377–402.

Arbona, C., Olvera, N., Rodriguez, N., Hagan, J., Linares, A., & Wiesner, M. (2010). Acculturative stress among documented and undocumented Latino immigrants in the United States. *Hispanic Journal of Behavioral Sciences, 32*, 362–384.

Arciniega, G. M., Anderson, T. C., Tovar-Blank, Z. G., & Tracey, T. J. G. (2008). Toward a fuller conception of machismo: Development of a traditional machismo and caballerismo scale. *Journal of Counseling Psychology, 55*, 19–33.

Arredondo, P. (2002). Mujeres Latinas—Santas y marquesas. *Cultural Diversity and Ethnic Minority Psychology, 8*, 308–319.

Atkinson, D. R., Morten, G., & Sue, D. W. (1989). A minority identity development model. In D. R. Atkinson, G. Morten, & D. W. Sue (Eds.), *Counseling American minorities* (pp. 35–52). Dubuque, IA: W. C. Brown.

Ayón, C., Marsiglia, F. F., & Bermudez-Parsai, M. (2010). Latino family mental health: Exploring the role of discrimination and familismo. *Journal of Community Psychology, 38*, 742–756.

Bernal, G., & Shapiro, E. (1996). Cuban families. In M. McGoldrick, J. Giordano, & J. K. Pearce (Eds.), *Ethnicity and family counseling* (2nd ed., pp. 155–168). New York, NY: Guilford Press.

Campbell, M. E., & Rogalin, C. L. (2006). Categorical imperatives: The interaction of Latino and racial identification. *Social Science Quarterly, 87*, 1030–1052.

Collazo, S. G., Ryan, C. L., & Bauman, K. J. (2010). *Profile of the Puerto Rican population in United States and Puerto Rico: 2008*. Paper presented at the

Annual Meeting of the Population Association of America, Dallas, TX.

Comas-Díaz, L. (1994). LatiNegra: Mental health issues of African Latinas. *Journal of Feminist Family Counseling, 5,* 35–74.

Comas-Díaz, L. (1997). Mental health needs of Latinos with professional status. In J. G. García & M. C. Zea (Eds.), *Psychological interventions and research with Latino populations* (pp. 142–165). Boston, MA: Allyn & Bacon.

Comas-Díaz, L. (2001). Hispanics, Latinos, or Americanos: The evolution of identity. *Cultural Diversity and Ethnic Minority Psychology, 7,* 115–120.

Cross, W. E., Jr. (1971, July). The Negro-to-black conversion experience. *Black World,* pp. 13–27.

Díaz, R. M., Ayala, G., & Bein, E. (2004). Sexual risk as an outcome of social oppression: Data from a probability sample of Latino gay men in three U.S. cities. *Cultural Diversity and Ethnic Minority Psychology, 10,* 255–267.

Delgado-Romero, E. A. (2001). Counseling a Hispanic/Latino client—Mr. X. *Journal of Mental Health Counseling, 23,* 207–221.

Delgado-Romero, E. A. (2004). *No parece:* The privilege and prejudice inherent in being a light-skinned Latino with no accent. In S. K. Anderson & V. A. Middleton (Eds.), *Explorations in privilege, oppression, and diversity* (pp. 119–126). Belmont, CA: Brooks/Cole.

Delgado-Romero, E. A., Flores, L., Gloria, A., Arredondo, P., & Castellanos, J. (2003). The majority in the minority: Developmental career challenges for Latino and Latina psychology faculty. In L. Jones & J. Castellanos (Eds.), *The majority in the minority: Retaining Latina/o faculty, administrators, and students in the 21st century* (pp. 257–283). Sterling, VA: Stylus Books.

Delgado-Romero, E. A., & Rojas, A. (2004). Other Latinos: Counseling Cuban, Central and South American clients. In C. Negy (Ed.), *Cross-cultural psychotherapy: Toward a critical understanding of diverse client populations* (pp. 139–162). Reno, NV: Bent Tree Press.

Dockterman, D. (2011). *Hispanics of Cuban origin in the United States, 2009.* Washington, DC: Pew Hispanic Center. Retrieved from http://pewhispanic.org/files/factsheets/73.pdf

Duany, A. P., & Silver, J. D. (2010). The "Puerto Ricanization" of Florida: Historical background and current status. *CENTRO Journal, 22*(1), 4–31.

Edwards, L. M., & Romero, A. J. (2008). Coping with discrimination among Mexican descent adolescents. *Hispanic Journal of Behavioral Sciences, 30,* 24–39.

Ennis, S. R., Rios-Vargas, M., & Albert, N. G. (2011). *The Hispanic population: 2010.* Washington, DC: U.S. Census Bureau. Retrieved from http://www.census.gov/prod/cen2010/briefs/c2010br-04.pdf

Estrada, F., Rigali-Oiler, M., Arciniega, M., & Tracey, T. J. G. (2011). Machismo and Mexican American men: An empirical understanding using a gay sample. *Journal of Counseling Psychology, 58,* 358–367.

Falicov, C. J. (1998). *Latino families in counseling: A guide to multicultural practice.* New York, NY: Guilford Press.

Garcia-Preto, N. (1996). Latino families: An overview. In M. McGoldrick, J. Giordano, & J. K. Pearce (Eds.), *Ethnicity and family counseling* (2nd ed., pp. 141–154). New York, NY: Guilford Press.

Gloria, A. M. (2001). The cultural construction of Latinas: Practice implications of multiple realities and identities. In D. B. Pope-Davis & H. L. K. Coleman (Eds.), *The intersection of race, class, and gender in multicultural counseling* (pp. 3–24). Thousand Oaks, CA: Sage.

Gloria, A. M., & Rodriguez, E. R. (2000). Counseling Latino university students: Psychosociocultural issues for consideration. *Journal of Counseling and Development, 78,* 145–154.

Gonzalez, G. M. (1991). Cuban Americans: Counseling and human development issues, problems, and approaches. In C. C. Lee & B. L. Richardson (Eds.), *Multicultural issues in counseling: New approaches to diversity* (pp. 157–169). Alexandria, VA: American Association for Counseling and Development.

Gonzalez, G. M. (1995). Cuban-Americans. In N. A. Vacc, S. B. DeVaney, & J. Wittmer (Eds.), *Experiencing and counseling multicultural and diverse populations* (pp. 293–316). Bristol, PA: Accelerated Development.

Guzmán, B., & McConnell, E. D. (2002). The Hispanic population: 1990–2000 growth and change. *Population Research and Policy Review, 21,* 109–128.

Hannold, E. M., Freytes, M., & Uphold, C. R. (2011). Unmet health services needs experienced by Puerto Rican OEF/OIF veterans and families post deployment. *Military Medicine, 176,* 381–388.

Hardiman, R. (1982). *White identity development: A process oriented model for describing the racial consciousness of white Americans* (Unpublished doctoral dissertation). University of Massachusetts, Amherst, MA.

Helms, J. E. (1990). *Black and white racial identity: Theory, research and practice.* Westport, CT: Praeger.

Lavariega Monforti, J., & Sanchez, J. (2010). The politics of perception: An investigation of the presence and sources of perceptions of internal discrimination among Latinos. *Social Science Quarterly, 91,* 245–265.

Liang, C. T. H., Salcedo, J., & Miller, H. A. (2011). Perceived racism, masculinity ideologies, and gender role conflict among Latino men. *Psychology of Men & Masculinity, 12,* 201–215.

Logan, J. R. (2003). *How race counts for Hispanic Americans.* Albany, NY: University at Albany, Lewis Mumford Center for Comparative Urban and Regional Research.

Marín, G., & Marín, B. V. (1991). *Research with Hispanic populations.* Newbury Park, CA: Sage.

Márquez, A. R., & Espino, B. (2010). Mexican American support for third parties: The case of La Raza Unida. *Ethnic and Racial Studies 33,* 290–312.

McConnell, E. D., & Delgado-Romero, E. A. (2004). Panethnic options and Latinos: Reality or methodological construction? *Sociological Focus, 4,* 297–312.

Niemann, Y. F. (1999). The making of a token: A case study of stereotype threat, stigma, racism, and tokenism in academe. *Frontiers: A Journal of Women Studies, 20,* 11–34.

Office of Management and Budget. (1997). Revisions to the standards for the classification of federal data on race and ethnicity. *Federal Register, 62*(210), 58782–58790.

Parra-Cardona, J. R., Córdova, D., Jr., Holtrop, K., Villarruel, F., & Wieling, E. (2008). Shared ancestry, evolving stories: Similar and contrasting life experiences described by foreign born and U.S. born Latino parents. *Family Process, 47,* 157–172.

Pew Hispanic Center. (2009). *Statistical portrait of Hispanics in the United States, 2009.* Retrieved from http://pewhispanic.org/files/factsheets/hispanics2009/Table%209.pdf

Phinney, J. S. (1993). A three-stage model of ethnic identity development in adolescence. In M. E. Bernal & G. P. Knight (Eds.), *Ethnic identity: Formation and transmission among Hispanics and other minorities* (pp. 61–79). Albany: State University of New York Press.

Preciado, J., & Henry, M. (1997). Linguistic barriers in health education and services. In J. G. García & M. C. Zea (Eds.), *Psychological interventions and research with Latino populations* (pp. 235–254). Boston, MA: Allyn & Bacon.

Rinderle, A. D., & Montoya, S. R. (2008). Hispanic/Latino identity labels: An examination of cultural values and personal experiences. *Howard Journal of Communications, 19,* 144–164.

Rivas, L. A. (2004). Visible and invisible minority: Double-whammy or double blessing? In G. S. Howard & E. A. Delgado-Romero (Eds.), *When things begin to go bad: Narrative explorations of difficult issues* (pp. 85–92). Dallas, TX: Hamilton Books.

Rivas, L., Delgado-Romero, E. A., & Ozambela, K. R. (2004). Our stories: Convergence of the language, professional, and personal identities of three Latino counselors. In M. Rastogi & L. Wieling (Eds.), *Voices of color: First-person accounts of ethnic minority counselors* (pp. 23–41). Thousand Oaks, CA: Sage.

Ruiz, A. S. (1990). Ethnic identity: Crisis and resolution. *Journal of Multicultural Counseling and Development, 18,* 29–40.

Santiago-Rivera, A. L., Arredondo, P. A., & Gallardo-Cooper, M. (2002). *Counseling Latinos and la familia: A practical guide.* Thousand Oaks, CA: Sage.

Senices, J. (2005). The complexity behind the Hispanic identity. *Journal of Applied Rehabilitation Counseling, 36*(2), 20–24.

Smart, J. F., & Smart, D. W. (1995). Acculturative stress of Hispanics: Loss and challenge. *Journal of Counseling and Development, 73,* 390–396.

Soto-Carlo, A., Delgado-Romero, E. A., & Galván, N. (2005). Challenges of Puerto Rican Islander students in the US. *Latino Studies Journal, 3,* 288–294.

Spanakis, N. C. (2004). Difficult dialogues: Interviewer, white inner voice, and Latina interviewee. *Journal of Multicultural Counseling and Development, 32,* 249–254.

Stavans, I. (2000, October 13). The gravitas of Spanglish. *The Chronicle Review,* p. B7.

Sue, D. W., & Sue, D. (1999). Counseling the culturally different: Theory and practice (3rd ed.). New York, NY: Wiley.

Sue, S. (2006). Cultural competency: From philosophy to research and practice. *Journal of Community Psychology, 34,* 237–245.

Torres, V. (1999). Validation of a bicultural orientation model for Hispanic college students. *Journal of College Student Development, 40,* 285–299.

Torres, V. (2004). The diversity among us: Puerto Ricans, Cubans, Caribbean, Central and South Americans. In A. M. Ortiz (Ed.), *Addressing the unique needs of Latino/a American students* (pp. 5–16). San Francisco, CA: Jossey-Bass.

Torres, V., Winston, R. B., Jr., & Cooper, D. L. (2003). The effect of geographic location, institutional type, and stress on Hispanic students' cultural orientation. *NASPA Journal, 40*(2), 10.

U.S. Census Bureau. (n.d.). *Census 2010 Summary File 1.* Retrieved from http://2010.census.gov/news/press-kits/summary-file-1.html

U.S. Department of Health and Human Services (1999). *Mental health: A report of the Surgeon General.* Rockville, MD: Author.

Vaquera, A. G., & Kao, E. (2006). The implications of choosing "no race" on the salience of Hispanic identity: How racial and ethnic backgrounds intersect among Hispanic adolescents. *Sociological Quarterly, 47,* 375–396.

Vasquez, M. J. T. (2001). Reflections on unearned advantages, unearned disadvantages and empowering experiences. In J. Ponterotto, J. M. Casas, L. A. Suzuki, & C. M. Alexander (Eds.), *Handbook of multicultural counseling* (pp. 64–77). Thousand Oaks, CA: Sage.

Verdugo, R. R. (1995). Racial stratification and the use of Hispanic faculty as role models: Theory, policy, and practice. *Journal of Higher Education, 66,* 669–685.

Wilczak, C. (2003). A counselor trainee's conversations with a Colombian immigrant woman. In G. Roysircar, P. Arredondo, J. N. Fuertes, J. G. Ponterotto, & R. L. Toporek (Eds.), *Multicultural counseling competencies 2003: Association for Multicultural Counseling and Development* (pp. 89–101). Alexandria, VA: Association for Multicultural Counseling and Development.

CHAPTER 12

Culturally Alert Counseling With South Asian Americans

Daya Singh Sandhu
University of Louisville

Jayamala Madathil
Sonoma State University

Anita is a 23-year-old international student from India. She comes from a middle-class family in South India. Anita has just completed her first semester in a social sciences program at a mid-sized university in the southern United States. She lives alone and finds herself in tears a lot. She is the first member of her family to come to the United States for higher studies. Her parents and her cousins helped to pay for her application fees and other expenses, such as an airplane ticket to the United States. The only reason she was able to attend the university was that she was offered a full scholarship with tuition waiver.

Since her arrival at the university, Anita has found that she feels very lonely. She is not sure to whom she can talk. She happened to mention her crying to one of her fellow American students in passing. The student suggested that Anita use the university counseling center. The concept of counseling is somewhat foreign to Anita. Because she has no one to talk to, she has decided to make a visit to the counseling center. She is very apprehensive about talking to a stranger about her problem. In addition, she is also afraid that the American counselor may not understand her concerns. Anita is even afraid that communication, due to language and different accents, might be a problem. During her first meeting with her counselor, who is a European American male, Anita is asked to share personal information about her relationships and whether she is sexually active. Anita finds these questions to be very inappropriate and is somewhat offended and embarrassed by them.

(Continued)

(Continued)

Sameer is a 45-year-old businessman living in the Northeast. He immigrated to the United States 5 years ago from Bangladesh. Sameer was mandated to attend counseling sessions by the judge in a case of suspected domestic violence. He has been informed that attending counseling is not optional for him and that he would be in violation of the judge's orders if he did not attend the counseling sessions, which could result in him being imprisoned. The judge gave Sameer the option of choosing his therapist for the individual counseling sessions. However, he was also required to attend the 8-week domestic violence offender group offered by Mandy, a therapist who is well established and has an excellent reputation and respect in the community. Sameer started attending the groups. However, he did his best to distance himself from the other four members of the group, John, David, Jason, and Richard. He kept insisting that he was not an "offender" and that he did not need to be in the counseling group. He also proceeded to inform the therapist that the only reason he was in the group was because of the judge's orders. Sameer was not willing to share anything in the group, nor was he responsive to receiving feedback from the therapist or the other group members.

Sameer informed the therapist that his wife, Nasreen, was getting to be "too smart and too Americanized" and that he needed to show her who was the boss in the house. For that reason, he hit her when she "talked back" to him. He had done this in their garage when the garage door was open. A neighbor across the street had seen Sameer hitting his wife and pulling her inside by her hair. The neighbor called the police. When the police arrived, there were marks on Nasreen's body. At first, Sameer's wife was hesitant and informed the police that nothing was wrong. However, after the officers talked with Nasreen for several minutes, she admitted that he had been beating her on a regular basis. On that particular day, she had not finished cleaning up the garage as ordered by Sameer, and he had punished her by beating her with a rolling pin. While Sameer was inattentive in the group, he made every effort to communicate to Mandy that he was a good man and that he provided well for his wife. He also insisted that as a husband he had the right to discipline his wife. Working with Sameer was a challenge for Mandy. She was quite concerned with Sameer's attitude toward beating his wife. She was further concerned about his justification of his action and the lack of remorse.

Nooran Khan was brought to see a counselor in the San Francisco area by her daughter, Sophia. The Khans immigrated from Pakistan 25 years ago and moved to the United States when Mr. Khan's eldest brother sponsored them. They have lived in the San Francisco Bay Area ever since. The couple runs a small convenience store. Their only child, Sophia recently completed her residency in family medicine and is in the process of establishing a practice in the area. Mr. Khan passed away unexpectedly about 6 months ago.

Sophia suspects that Mrs. Khan is depressed. Mrs. Khan has never been to a therapist and is very confused about why her daughter brought her to see the counselor. She is also afraid that her daughter and the other members of her community will think that she is "crazy." Meanwhile, Sophia has already talked with the therapist. She has communicated her guilt about not being able to help her mother as much as she should have during this emotionally difficult time. Sophia is struggling to establish her medical practice, and she admits that the past few months have been extremely difficult for her mother because of Sophia's "benign neglect" of her.

This chapter focuses on the experiences of individuals such as Anita, Sameer, and Mrs. Khan. It provides an introduction to South Asian cultures, especially ways in which counselors can help individuals from these cultures. It also attempts to provide mental health professionals with the means to become culturally sensitive and effective service providers to South Asian Americans. Before reading further, you are encouraged to assess your knowledge of important issues for working with this population by completing Activity 12.1.

Activity 12.1   Self-Assessment on South Asian American Culture and Issues

The purpose of this exercise is to help you become aware of your assumptions about South Asian Americans and to increase your cultural awareness regarding this group.

1. I can identify the South Asian countries on a world map: Yes/No

2. I know what the term *collectivist cultures* means: Yes/No

3. I agree with the media portrayal of South Asians: Yes/No

4. I am familiar with the mate selection process followed by the majority of South Asians: Yes/No

5. I can name three of the major religions widely practiced by South Asians: Yes/No

6. I have an accurate understanding of the variations in arranged marriages: Yes/No

7. I can name three different cultural/religious holidays observed by individuals from South Asian cultures: Yes/No

8. I have a clear understanding of how South Asian cultures regard the elderly individuals in their community: Yes/No

9. I can identify some of the struggles faced by South Asians in the United States: Yes/No

10. I can list cultural competencies that a mental health professional might need in order to work effectively with individuals from South Asian cultures: Yes/No

Give one point for each "Yes" response, and add up your total. Calculate your knowledge by using the scale below.

Total Score out of 10: _____

Scoring Rubric:

	1 2 3 4	5 6 7	8 9 10
Your Knowledge About	_____	_____	_____
South Asians	Poor	Average	Superior

This activity is meant to help you think further about your understanding of South Asian cultures. As described in Chapters 1, 2, and 3, having an understanding of specific ethnic cultures helps mental health professionals see key issues that they might otherwise miss or misinterpret (e.g., the South Asian client's experience of arranged marriage, views on care of the elderly). In addition, an increased awareness of these cultural factors helps counselors become better advocates for these minority groups at the social and political levels.

DEMOGRAPHIC CHARACTERISTICS OF SOUTH ASIANS

First, South Asian cultures must be distinguished from other Asian cultures. It is important for mental health professionals to be careful not to lump all Asians into the Asians/Pacific Islanders category. South Asians are a distinct cultural grouping, one that is different in significant ways from the East and Southeast Asian grouping that includes people from countries such as Cambodia, China, the Philippines, Indonesia, and Japan. Those cultural groups were described in Chapter 7.

It is particularly important that counselors, while being culturally sensitive and aware of different cultural norms and expectations, do not use these similarities among South Asians to stereotype their clients. This is something that counselors have to be intentional about and must remind themselves about.

Who are South Asians as a group? What are some of the similarities among individuals from the South Asian cultures? What are some cultural factors that a mental health professional would need to remember while trying to help an individual from these cultures? These questions will be addressed in the next section.

South Asians, as defined here, are people who come from the seven nations of Bangladesh, Bhutan, India, Maldives, Nepal, Pakistan, and Sri Lanka. Afghanistan, located in the center of Asia, also forms a part of South Asia, in addition to some of its parts in Central Asia and Western Asia. A map of South Asia is presented in Figure 12.1.

Figure 12.1   Map of South Asia

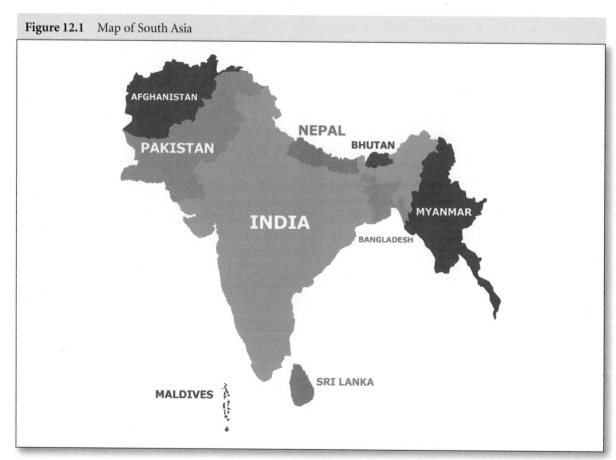

Source: Speight et al. (1991).

There is a great diversity within this population with regard to religious affiliation, language ability, immigration history, socioeconomic status, education, and acculturation level (Inman & Tewari, 2003; Madathil, 2011; Sandhu, 1999; Sue & Sue, 2008). Despite all these differences, South Asians are presented here as a single group because of their common geographic origin. While it is not a homogenous group, South Asian cultures, in general, have some common characteristics that set them apart as a group from other major cultural and ethnic groups. These include customs, values, individual and family expectations, and beliefs about mental health problems (Maker, Mittal, & Rastogi, 2005; Sandhu, 1997).

Historically, these countries constituted one great nation called Bharat. Pakistan and Bangladesh were carved out of India as separate countries, when the British left India in 1947. South Asia is notably diverse in religious traditions. Hinduism, Buddhism, Jainism, Sikhism, Zoroastrianism, Islam, Judaism, tribal religions, and almost all denominations of Christianity are represented. South Asia is also known for a number of diverse languages. There are 22 official languages in India alone. The total number of languages listed for India is 428, of which 13 are considered extinct.

IMMIGRATION PATTERNS AND EXPERIENCES OF SOUTH ASIANS

South Asians are one of the fastest-growing populations in the United States. South Asians' migration to the United States took place in three major waves. The first wave of immigration from the Indian subcontinent took place from 1897 to 1924. As is true with other immigrants, South Asians saw the United States as a land of opportunity and liberty. Most of the immigrants who arrived from South Asian countries during the 1800s were farmers and ship workers (Sheth, 1995). However, these immigrants were not allowed to own land, nor were they allowed to bring their spouses and other family members to the United States. Although these South Asians were invited as laborers, they were not seen by the host culture as worthy of citizenship because of their racial and cultural differences (Takaki, 1989).

The Immigration and Naturalization Act of 1965 marked the beginning of the second wave of immigration. It also ended the racial discrimination against South Asians and other so-called tawny races of Asia. Entry into the United States was no longer determined by race but by the knowledge and skills of the potential immigrants, in terms of what they could offer to the United States (Prathikanti, 1997). Consequently, a large percentage of South Asians in the second wave were highly educated professionals. For instance, in a sample of 46,000 Asian Indian immigrants, Doshi (1975) found that at least 50% of them were working as medical doctors, scientists, and engineers. These newly arrived South Asian immigrants generally achieved financial success and obtained U.S. citizenship. They were also allowed to bring their spouses and children with them.

A significant demographic shift took place during the 1980s, as many second-wave and well-established South Asian Americans started sponsoring their family members through the Family Reunification Act. Many of these immigrants were less educated and less fluent in English than their predecessors. Most of these new arrivals are now working as taxi drivers, convenience store clerks, and small motel operators. Also, some of them own small businesses (McMahon, 1995). Because this group is demographically and culturally quite different from the second wave of South Asian immigrants, they are classified as the third wave (Prathikanti, 1997; Sandhu & Malik, 2001).

According to the 2010 U.S. Census data, there are 3.4 million South Asian Americans living in the United States. Various groups among South Asians increased remarkably in the decade between 2000 and 2010. The South Asian community as a whole, comprising Indians, Bangladeshis, Pakistanis, and Sri Lankans, increased 78% during that time.

Also according to the 2010 census, the population of the United States was reported as 308,745,538, a 9.7% increase from the 2000 census. A demographic snapshot of South Asians carved out from the 2010 census data reveals that the

Indian American population in the United States (including multiple ethnicities) grew 68% from 2000 to 2010, from 1.9 million to 3.19 million. That made Indian Americans the third largest Asian American group (16% of the total Asian population) after Chinese Americans (3.79 million) and Filipino Americans (3.42 million), but with a much faster growth rate. According to data released by the Asian American Foundation and South Asian Americans Leading Together (2012), an organization devoted to strengthening South Asian communities in America, the voting-age population of Indian Americans (those who are U.S. citizens) has now exceeded 1 million. It grew 100% from 2000, when it was 576,000, to 1.15 million in 2010.

People who identified themselves as of Indian origin comprise the largest segment of the 3.4 million South Asian Americans, making up over 80% of the total, followed by Pakistanis, Bangladeshis, Sri Lankans, Nepalis, and Bhutanese.

The Bangladeshi community experienced the most significant growth, jumping 212% to 147,300 in 2010. The combined Bhutanese and Nepali populations grew by at least 155%.

The growth of the South Asian population in the United States is presented in Table 12.1.

Table 12.1 Changes in South Asian American Population, 2000 to 2010

	Single Ethnicity Reported			Single and Multiple Ethnicities Reported		
	2000	2010	% Change	2000	2010	% Change
Bangladeshi	41,280	128,792	212	57,412	147,300	157
Bhutanese	N/A	15,290	N/A	N/A	19,439	N/A
Indian	1,678,765	2,843,391	69	1,899,599	3,183,063	68
Nepali	N/A	51,907	N/A	N/A	59,490	N/A
Pakistani	153,533	363,699	137	204,309	409,163	100
Sri Lankan	20,145	38,596	92	24,587	45,381	85
Total South Asians	N/A	3,441,675	N/A			
Total for Four Census Groups (Bangladeshi, Indian, Pakistani, Sri Lankan)	1,893,723	3,374,478	78			

The South Asian population grew more in some cities than in others. Five notable states in which the South Asian population became the largest compared to other states were California, New York, New Jersey, Texas, and Illinois. It is interesting to note that different metropolitan areas became more attractive to different South Asian groups. For instance, the largest number of all South Asian groups settled in New York, except Bhutanese, who chose Dallas as their first choice for their domicile.

Detailed information about preferred metropolitan areas is presented in Table 12.2.

Individuals vary in their levels of education, age, income, religious beliefs, and length of stay in the United States. It is important to remember that there could be a considerable difference between the first-generation immigrants who have arrived in the United States recently and second- or third-generation individuals who were born and raised in this country.

Table 12.2 Top Five U.S. Metropolitan Areas for Selected South Asian Groups, 2010

Bangladeshi	Bhutanese	Indian	Nepali	Pakistani	Sri Lankan
1. New York	1. Dallas	1. New York	1. New York	1. New York	1. New York
2. Washington, DC	2. Atlanta	2. Chicago	2. Washington, DC	2. Houston	2. Los Angeles
3. Detroit	3. Houston	3. Washington, DC	3. Dallas	3. Chicago	3. Washington, DC
4. Los Angeles	4. Seattle	4. Los Angeles	4. Boston	4. Washington, DC	4. San Francisco
5. Philadelphia	5. Phoenix	5. San Francisco	5. San Francisco	5. Dallas	5. Dallas

CULTURAL VALUES AND CHARACTERISTICS OF SOUTH ASIAN AMERICANS

One definition of culture is

> a set of guidelines, both explicit and implicit, which individuals inherit as members of a particular society, and which tells them how to view the world, how to experience it emotionally, and how to behave in it in relation to other people. (Helman, 1990, pp. 2–3)

Such guidelines vary as groups adapt to their environments. Of special importance to South Asian Americans are five major values: patriarchy, filial piety, reticence, collectivism, and religion and spirituality. These values are briefly explained below.

Patriarchy

South Asian families are traditionally patriarchal. The father or the eldest male in the extended family is generally the head of the household and is responsible for taking care of the financial and emotional needs of all family members (Madathil, 2011; Sandhu, 1997). Patriarchy is related to the value of collectivism, which was presented in previous chapters in this book and is discussed later in this section. In collectivism, the individual wishes of a person are sacrificed for the collective welfare of the family; what is best for the family is best

for the individual (Chandras, 1997; Das & Kemp, 1997). For this reason, family members defer to the authority figures, who, it is assumed, can ensure the collective welfare.

The preferred method of solving individual problems is to defer to the authority figure in the family. Family members are discouraged from discussing personal concerns with strangers, including mental health professionals. South Asians consider the head of the household to have the prerogative to make final decisions (Abrahams & Salazar, 2005). Family members are expected to accept this person's decisions willingly.

Many other South Asian values can be described as extensions or corollaries of patriarchal values. Such values include nonconfrontation with older siblings and respect and reverence for the elderly. Wisdom gained through real-life experience is valued more than book knowledge.

Filial Piety

South Asian cultural values include filial piety, which is considered to be one of the greatest virtues in Asian cultures. It means taking care of one's parents; not being rebellious; showing love, respect, and support. It also includes accepting the advice of one's parents, concealing their mistakes, displaying sorrow for their sickness and death, and carrying out sacrifices in their names after their death. The shortcomings of parents are overlooked. Ancestors and parents are worshipped, and they are appreciated as role models for generations to come.

Reticence

Silence is considered another virtue in South Asian culture. South Asian parents admonish their children to talk less and think more. "Only an empty vessel makes a lot of noise" is an age-old popular adage among South Asians. Children should be seen but not heard around the parents. In addition, South Asians are taught at an early age to restrain themselves from strong emotional expressions. Thus verbal and behavioral expressiveness are discouraged in South Asian populations (Atkinson, 2004). South Asian parents emphasize and value *self-control* more than *self-expression*. Some of these characteristics are similar to those of East and Southeast Asians.

In addition, open expression of sexual feelings is considered "cheap" and a sign of emotional immaturity. Modesty about sexual matters is encouraged. Public demonstration of sexual affection is considered offensive and characteristic of low or loose moral character. In South Asian cultures, even married couples refrain from holding hands, embracing, and kissing in public.

Collectivism

As opposed to the glorification of the individual, *collectivism* is the premiere cultural value of South Asians. Collectivism requires individual members to sacrifice their interests for the good of the family. Their personal interests and aspirations are less important. Generally speaking, in collectivist societies, authority and communication flow from top to bottom. Relationships are rigidly structured, and obedience from the young members toward their elders is expected and enforced.

Individuals' accomplishments are celebrated by the entire family, and a person's failure is considered to be the failure of the entire family. Therefore, all family members are expected to solve their problems within their familial context. One's duties to the family are of utmost importance, while one's individual rights are not emphasized (Das & Kemp, 1997; Sodowsky, Kwan, & Pannu, 1995).

Religion and Spirituality

In South Asian communities, importance is attached to preserving and practicing the original religion of one's ancestors. In addition to Hindu temples, Muslim mosques, and Sikh Gurudwaras, a special and sacred place is kept in many South Asian homes for daily worship and prayers. During family or personal crises or on the occasions of celebrations, South Asians hold special prayers to seek help and blessings from their beloved deities. While they are frequently fatalistic and believe in predestination, South Asians also believe that a sincere prayer from the heart can avert tragedies and change the course of their lives for the better. Here lies a contrast with Western counseling strategies. While South Asians strongly believe in spiritual solutions to their problems, the Western psychological strategies remain in the physical and mental realms of existence and often minimize or ignore the spiritual perspectives (Yeh & Kwong, 2009).

Summary and Implications of South Asian Values

Patriarchy, filial piety, reticence, collectivism, and religion and spirituality significantly affect the psychological make-up of South Asians. Specific values include formality in interpersonal relationships, inhibition of strong feelings, obedience to the authority of elders, primary allegiance to the family, and deep respect for religion (Atkinson, 2004). It is also important for counselors to note that some of these values could be in direct conflict with the values and expectations of the majority European American culture, which emphasizes independence, individualism, and autonomy. Counselors particularly need to be aware of differences in values so that they do not inappropriately label South Asian clients' behaviors as dysfunctional.

These traditional values of South Asian Americans have significant implications for counseling. The values affect the manifestation of psychological problems, the expression of emotions, and help-seeking behaviors (Sue & Sue, 2008). In

South Asian cultures, family hierarchy, avoidance of shame, emotional restraint, and saving face are highly prized. For this reason, South Asian people are expected to take problems to their significant others if they are unable to resolve themselves. If this approach does not work, only then do they turn to temples, mosques, churches, and Gurudwaras or consult their elders. Seeking professional psychological help is generally considered a violation of family hierarchy and shameful. It brings disgrace to the person and his or her family (Shea & Yeh, 2008).

Also, as mentioned in previous chapters, the generation since immigration to the United States is important. First-generation South Asian Americans might adhere to these values more than second- or third-generation South Asian Americans (Kim, Atkinson, & Umemoto, 2001). Box 12.1 illustrates some of the important values issues in terms of the vignettes that began this chapter.

Box 12.1 The Three Vignettes and the Cultural Values of South Asians

Patriarchy, filial piety, reticence, collectivism, and religion and spirituality have been identified as some of the notable cultural values of South Asian people. It is important for mental health professionals to examine the role and impact of their clients' values on their psychological problems before some viable and effective solutions are explored.

This discussion focuses on the three vignettes presented at the beginning of this chapter to demonstrate the role of the cultural values of South Asian Americans. For brevity's sake, only the South Asian value of patriarchy is discussed here, with some specific information from each vignette.

As stated in the first vignette, Anita migrated to the United States from India, apparently from a patriarchal family. She felt terribly lonely and lost. She did not know who she should talk to or what she should do. She was also very apprehensive about talking with strangers. Most likely, her father, as the head of the household, had been handling her problems as part of his patriarchal responsibilities, and Anita never had to learn how to take care of her problems on her own.

In the second vignette, Sameer's domestic violence incident is directly related to his perceived patriarchal responsibilities to maintain discipline in the house as the head of the family. He kept insisting that he was not an offender. On the contrary, he felt that as a husband he had the right to discipline his wife. South Asian patriarchal responsibilities are not limited to the children; they also extend to all members of the household who are living together, including the wife and even brothers and sisters if they are members of the extended family.

The third vignette is quite interesting. After the death of her father and due to her advanced level of education, Sophia assumed patriarchal obligations in the Khan family. Since Mrs. Khan is unable to take care of her problems, her daughter became a surrogate guardian of her mother and took her to a counselor for her depression-related problems.

ACCULTURATION CHALLENGES AND STRATEGIES FOR SOUTH ASIAN AMERICANS

For immigrants, adaptation to the cultural norms, behaviors, and values of the dominant group generally causes unavoidable psychological distress (Sandhu, Portes, & McPhee, 1996). This section of the chapter addresses acculturation stress and acculturation strategies as they relate to South Asian Americans. It concludes with a reminder for counselors to assess levels of acculturation in their clients.

Acculturation Strategies

Acculturation strategies are methods that individuals use in responding to stress-inducing cultural contexts (Bhatia & Ram, 2004). As presented in previous chapters, these strategies can be classified into four categories (Berry & Sam, 1997). The first is an *assimilation* strategy, which occurs when individuals decide not to maintain their own cultural identity and seek extensive contact with the dominant group in their daily interactions. The second strategy, *separation,* refers to individuals holding on to their original culture and seeking no contact with the dominant group. A third strategy, *integration,* is characterized by individuals expressing an interest in maintaining strong ties with their own ethnic group and with the dominant group. The fourth strategy, *marginalization,* happens when individuals lose contact with both their traditional culture and the larger society.

The acculturation level linked with the most positive outcome is integration, and the one associated with the most negative outcome is marginalization. Separation and assimilation strategies fall somewhere in between as far as effectiveness is concerned (Berry & Sam, 1997). It can be concluded that South Asian immigrants would use these strategies to deal with acculturation stress as well. Therefore, helpers working with this population must be trained to recognize the different levels of acculturation and adaptation strategies. Box 12.2 illustrates some of the stages of acculturation for the individuals in the vignettes that opened this chapter.

Box 12.2   Acculturative Processes and Levels in the Three Vignettes

In reviewing the three vignettes presented at the beginning of the chapter, it is interesting to note that some of the acculturative stages and processes are represented. For instance, it is safe to assume that Anita is still at separation. She has just completed a semester and has not been residing in the United States very long. Apparently she is still holding on to her original culture and has not made any appreciable efforts to contact people from the dominant European American culture. She is even apprehensive about speaking with the white male counselor about her problems. However, it is important to note that her separation is not a deliberate effort to avoid the dominant culture; it seems to be caused by her lack of awareness and knowledge about the new culture.

In contrast, Sameer, in the second vignette, has deliberately resisted assimilation into the dominant culture. Like Anita, Sameer could be classified as in the separation category of acculturation. For example, he told the counselor that he would not like to participate in the group sessions as required by the judge. He was not interested in sharing nor in receiving any feedback from the other group members. He also tried his best to distance himself from the other four group members, who presumably belonged to other ethnic groups. Sameer's rejection of the dominant culture became even more evident when he justified striking his wife Nasreen for becoming "too smart and too Americanized." Sameer also insisted that he was a good husband who provided well for his wife and that as a husband he had the right to discipline her. It is interesting to note that even after living in the United States for 5 years, Sameer behaved as if he were still in Bangladesh. However, a significant difference remains in the acculturating process of Sameer and Anita. Anita's acculturating difficulties might be attributed to her innocence or ignorance about the new culture, while Sameer's resistance to acculturation is caused by his outright rejection of some American values.

The third vignette affords an opportunity to compare and contrast the acculturating process of a mother, Mrs. Khan, with that of her daughter, Sophia. It seems that Mrs. Khan is beginning the integration stage of acculturation, maintaining strong ties with her native culture of Pakistan while also taking on some of the dominant culture through the counseling process. Despite the fact that Mrs. Khan has been living in the United States for 25 years, she had no prior knowledge of counseling and mental health services and had never been to a therapist. Most likely, according to South Asian values, her late husband would have taken care of her psychological needs and provided her with necessary emotional support.

On the other hand, Sophia seems to be fully immersed in American culture. She has been raised and educated in the United States. Apparently, she is well informed about counseling services. She contacted a therapist and discussed her mother's depression-related problems with her. Sophia clearly has extensive contacts, daily interactions, and experiences with persons from the dominant culture. Consequently, Sophia is in the assimilation stage of acculturation.

It should be noted that acculturation seems to be facilitated more by the attitudes and proactive efforts of the immigrants rather than by mere length of time residing in a culture. Education, work, and other social opportunities that afford immigrants a chance to mingle with others are ways to help newly arrived immigrants participate in and become an integral part of the multicultural society of the United States.

Acculturative Stress

The process of acculturation takes place when individuals from different cultures come into contact with a mainstream dominant group through sojourning, foreign study programs, and voluntary or involuntary migrations. Whatever the circumstances, individuals from different cultures experience inevitable psychological changes when they interact with one another (Furnham & Bochner, 1986; Sandhu et al., 1996). As with other groups, South Asians, as a minority group, experience a wide variety of psychological stressors relating to the acculturation process when they attempt to adapt to the cultural values, norms, and behaviors and the political, social, and economic systems of the United States. Those acculturation-related stressors include culture shock, experiences of prejudice, changes in ethnic identity, shifting gender roles, family conflict, sense of inferiority, sense of uncertainty, communication problems, loss of support systems, nostalgia or homesickness, and feelings of guilt (Madathil, 2011; Sandhu et al., 1996). Each of these stressors is described in the next sections.

Culture Shock

Culture shock is a term coined by anthropologists to describe the anxiety and other negative feelings experienced when a person is introduced to a radically new environment. Culture shock is produced when immigrants encounter new expectations and social norms over a period of time while they strive to establish relationships with a host culture (Ozbay, 1994). The cumulative differences in climate, food, mannerisms, lifestyles, marriage customs, and religious practices contribute to culture shock. It is safe to assume that, like many individuals from other migrating groups, South Asian persons experience culture shock when they enter the United States. Counselors need to be alert to culture shock as an explanation for anxiety and depression in South Asian immigrant clients.

Experiences of Prejudice or Perceived Prejudice

Acculturation stressors also include perceptions and actual experiences of prejudice and discrimination (Lay & Nguyen, 1998). Perceived discrimination and expectations of future discrimination are related to increased levels of depression and lower levels of self-esteem (Rumbaut, 1994). Therefore, mental health professionals who provide services to acculturating individuals must pay attention to clients' concerns about prejudice (Rahman & Rollock, 2004).

There are several differences in perceived prejudice among South Asian subgroups, based on their religious affiliations. In an empirical study, Sodowsky and Plake (1992) reported that Muslims perceived prejudice more significantly than South Asians of other religious backgrounds. These differences might be a reflection of the contemporary sociopolitical climate in the United States as well as long-standing prejudices and stereotypes. Sodowsky and Plake also pointed out that South Asians who belonged to non-Western religions perceived more prejudice, were less acculturated, and used English less than did

South Asians who were affiliated with traditional Western religious groups.

There have been numerous incidents of racism, prejudice, and hate crimes against South Asian Americans. Dotbusters (referring to the dot on the forehead of Indian women), a group of hatemongers from New Jersey who are against Asian Indian women, is one example of prejudice. Since the tragedy of September 11, 2001, hate crimes against South Asian immigrants, especially against the Sikhs, have increased significantly. For example, in Mesa, Arizona, Balbir Singh Sodhi was shot to death by a man who mistook him for a follower of Osama Bin Laden. South Asian Americans Leading Together, a national nonprofit organization, documented 645 incidents of backlash in the first week after the September 11 terrorist attacks.

Experiences of prejudice might not be limited to the adults in the South Asian community. It is also likely that the children of South Asian immigrants will experience prejudice in their educational and social environments, such as in schools and on the playgrounds. Children of South Asian immigrants are socialized into two cultures: the culture of their own family and the culture of the larger American society. In the family, most parents try to inculcate ethnic pride and awareness of their cultural heritage into their children. Children are also encouraged to practice their own religions, such as Hinduism, Islam, Jainism, and Sikhism.

For young school-age children, acculturation into the larger society sometimes poses a difficult problem. These children stand out as distinctly different from the dominant community because of their physical appearance. For that reason, they are often teased or rejected by other children. Most young children lack the ability that adults have to deal with such hostility by basing positive self-esteem on their own ethnic heritage (Das & Kemp, 1997).

This issue of prejudice is an important one that mental health practitioners might have to directly address with their clients. Since it is possible that a client might not discuss this topic with the helper for fear of being further judged, a counselor might want to bring up this topic herself or himself.

Changes in Ethnic Identity

Another source of acculturation stress is the transformation of ethnic identity. Immigrants and first-generation South Asians typically have a strong ethnic identity wherever they are in the world and are aware of the differences between them and the host culture. They do not feel that they have to deny such differences because their ethnic pride is extremely strong. While acculturating to American society, most South Asians also start acquiring a partially American identity; they become South Asian Americans. In short, now their self-identity is transformed from a single intact identity to a hyphenated or hybrid identity (Sandhu, 1999).

Most of these immigrants are able to function with a dual identity or develop a fused identity as Asian Indian Americans or Pakistani Americans, to name just two examples (Das & Kemp, 1997). For example, most South Asian men seem to adopt the Western mode of dress, etiquette, and manners used in the workplace or in formal social contacts with other Americans. However, they generally hold on to their cultural food preferences, family ideology and values, and religious beliefs and practices at home or in their private lives (Sodowsky & Carey, 1988). As with other groups, although the desire to maintain a distinct ethnic and cultural identity remains strong in the first generation, with every successive generation born and raised in the United States, the offspring becomes more and more acculturated and an integral part of the mainstream culture.

The acculturation of subsequent generations is affected by their experiences in the United States more than by their country of origin. Those experiences include racist encounters and discrimination, the culture of an inner-city area, the presence of other immigrant ethnic communities, and the South Asian community's emphasis on preservation of its home culture (Bhatia & Ram, 2004).

A mental health professional should attempt to assess the ethnic identity of the South Asian client early in the counseling process. A client's worldview, based on her or his cultural heritage, self-concept, and ethnic identity, shapes her or his values, beliefs, and behaviors (Grieger & Ponterotto, 1995). To understand and resolve clients' problems, it is important that counselors understand their clients' worldviews and their ethnic identity development. Box 12.3 provides some questions that counselors might ask regarding ethnic identity.

Box 12.3   Assessing Ethnic Identity

Here are some questions that counselors may find helpful in determining their clients' ethnic identity:

- How do you identify your cultural heritage?
- What language(s) do you speak at home?
- What language(s) do you teach your children? (if the client has children)
- With whom do you associate during your leisure time?
- What are some customs and practices that you value highly?
- What (if any) aspects of the majority culture do you value?
- What (if any) aspects of your own culture do you value?

Shifting Gender Roles

Another acculturation issue pertains to gender role and hierarchy. Gender attitudes of South Asian Americans vary with generation in the United States, educational level, social class, and economic stability. For example, the immigrant generation is more likely to adhere to traditional gender roles. The gender hierarchy among South Asians can range from extremely patriarchal to egalitarian. On the patriarchal extreme, the family of South Asian immigrants would expect men to act dominant in public in order to show the other cultural groups that the men are in control of their family. However, it should be noted that, in actuality, the power and control in the family resides with the oldest person, regardless of gender, even when the oldest person in the family lives 10,000 miles away in India, Pakistan, or Sri Lanka (Ibrahim, Ohnishi, & Sandhu, 1997).

The role of women in South Asian American families must be addressed carefully. South Asian women are generally considered to be the primary family caregivers. However, that role can become complicated as immigrant women struggle to find their new place in American society (Madathil, 2011; Sandhu, 1997).

Men are traditionally identified with the higher-status roles of breadwinner and caretaker of the family (Inman & Tewari, 2003). For this reason, in traditional South Asian families, boys are preferred to girls. As a result, in many of the South Asian subcultures, mothers of male children are respected more than are mothers of only female children.

It should also be noted that even though men are generally considered to be the head of the household in South Asian families, the exact gender roles within a family vary depending on social class, educational level, and economic status. There may be many South Asian families in which the family relationships are more egalitarian. However, it is rare that a woman would become the head of the household when the husband is still living.

South Asian American women experience intersectionality (see Chapter 1) in that as "brown" minority women, they face racial discrimination and prejudice from the larger American society, and at the same time, they also have to deal with gendered oppression within their own communities (Bhatia & Ram, 2004; Patel, 2007). While European American women are now socialized to be confident, assertive, and self-possessed, in a direct contrast South Asian American women are seen in their communities as passive, submissive, subservient, and exotic (Dasgupta, 1998; Pyke & Johnson, 2003). Given this framework, South Asian American women are left to either comply with an objectified stereotypical version of South Asian womanhood or constantly prove that they are "not like the others" and risk being perceived as "acting white. "In fact, female children are sometimes seen as a liability because of ancient dowry customs in South Asian cultures that require parents to pay large sums of money, jewelry, or property to the daughter's in-laws.

The acculturation process and identity formation of many South Asian American first- and second-generation immigrant women has been a painful, difficult, and complex process. Many South Asian parents become particularly concerned and experience high levels of anxiety as their daughters mature and are ready for marriage. Out-of-group and especially interracial marriages are discouraged. Dating is not an accepted phenomenon in South Asian cultures. Many South Asian American youth instead engage in secret dating (Inman & Sandhu, 2002; Inman & Tewari, 2003). Premarital sex is strictly prohibited. Under some extremely unfortunate circumstances, pregnant South Asian girls have been the victims of "honor" killings at the hands of their fathers or brothers, who believed they were saving the face, name, and honor of their family.

Both arranged marriages and love marriages, with the consent of the parents, are norms in many South Asian families at this time. Most South Asian American parents try their best to maintain their religious and cultural traditions by encouraging their children to marry individuals from families and subgroups that are similar or compatible with their own cultural or ethnic groups. In South Asian cultures, marriage is considered a religious and sacred duty to the family, community, and lineage. Marriage in these cultures is expected to be a lifelong commitment (Madathil & Sandhu, 2008). South Asian children who don't heed this advice commonly cause a significant amount of acculturative distress to their parents.

Family Conflicts

As mentioned earlier in regard to South Asian values, South Asian families place a high priority on the needs of the family as a unit, rather than on the individual or on specific needs of each family member (Inman & Tewari, 2003; Madathil, 2011; Sodowsky et al., 1995). The family-first concept plays a pivotal role in maintaining and promoting stability and cohesiveness among all the family members (Sandhu, 1997). However, the obligation to attach more importance to family needs above one's own personal desires can become a source of psychological affliction for acculturating South Asian families. Dramatic and painful value conflicts occur when South Asian children, born and raised in individualistic American society, reject and defy their parents' ways of living (Sandhu, 1997).

Sense of Inferiority

In the process of acculturation, many South Asian immigrants are subject to downward mobility. South Asians might have been very successful in many ways in their native lands, such as in education, business, and high-status jobs. However, they often suffer from status loss upon arrival in the United States when they have to start all over with low-paying and low-status jobs. This downward mobility often occurs when the degrees, diplomas, and professional credentials earned from their native countries are not recognized in their new country. It is not uncommon for newly arrived Indian, Pakistani, or Bangladeshi doctors, engineers, scientists, and educators to drive cabs or work as store clerks for their economic survival. Suddenly becoming vulnerable in this way can result in a deep sense of inferiority (Das & Kemp, 1997; Madathil, 2011; Sandhu, 1997; Sandhu & Malik, 2001).

Sense of Uncertainty

South Asian immigrants worry about their future in the newly adopted country and also lament the uncertainty about when they will see their loved ones who were left behind in their native country. This uncertainty produces a deep sense of guilt and the psychological pain of homesickness for many South Asian immigrants (Sandhu, 1997; Sandhu & Asrabadi, 1994, 1998).

Communication Problems

Not all South Asian immigrants are proficient or fluent in writing and speaking English. This lack of facility with the English language becomes a major obstacle for these immigrants when participating in social, cultural, and political processes in the United States. Consequently, many South Asian Americans are deprived of professional and economic opportunities. To exacerbate these problems, language barriers could also keep them from seeking professional help (Maker et al., 2005; Sandhu, 1995).

Loss of Support Systems

Separation from familiar economic, political, social, and cultural support systems, including abrupt separation from extended family members, is a major psychological stressor that is directly associated with the migration experience of South Asian Americans. This loss of support systems has been called the uprooting disorder, one that causes disorientation, alienation, feelings of isolation, and powerlessness for immigrants (Zwingman, 1978).

Nostalgia or Homesickness

Being separated from close friends and extended family members in a distant, strange land for an uncertain period of time can cause a profound sense of loss. After migration, South Asian immigrants' contacts with their long-term acquaintances and familiar surroundings in their home countries end abruptly. This psychological void is never completely filled and generally becomes a painful source of nostalgia or homesickness for newly arrived immigrants and their first-generation offspring (Sandhu, 1997; Sandhu, Kaur, & Tewari, 1999).

Feelings of Guilt

A final expression of acculturative stress is guilt. Most South Asian people migrate for economic reasons, at the cost of their close relationships with parents and other family members. South Asians migrate from the most populous countries. For instance, India has a population of more than 1 billion people; Pakistan, more than 180 million; and Bangladesh, 145 million people. They rank number two, six, and seven, respectively, when compared with populations of other nations of the world. The natural and other economic resources have been depleted in these countries due to overpopulation, invasion, and colonization. Living comfortably in the United States while leaving loved ones behind in misery and wrenching poverty causes feelings of guilt for many South Asian immigrants (Sandhu, 1997; Sandhu & Asrabadi, 1998).

Assessing Acculturation

Given the presence of these sources of acculturation stress in the life of many clients, one of the most important requirements for counselors who work with South Asian Americans is to recognize their clients' acculturation levels. These acculturation levels guide the initiation and termination of counseling relationships, the making of the necessary referrals, and recommendations for group therapy sessions. Box 12.4 illustrates acculturative stress in three of the individuals from the vignettes that began this chapter.

MENTAL HEALTH AND SOUTH ASIAN AMERICANS

South Asians, like all other human beings, experience emotional distress and personal disruption. A primary purpose of this section is to make counselors aware of the special needs, concerns, and issues of South Asian Americans. In the process, the "model minority" myth as it is applied to South Asian Americans will be debunked. However, you must continue to keep in mind the message of

Box 12.4 Acculturation Stress in the Three Vignettes

Acculturative stress is one of the most difficult problems that afflicts South Asian immigrants. As discussed previously, several contributing factors are responsible for causing this distress. Of course, not all these factors are applicable to each individual case. Some specific acculturative stress factors for each vignette are identified here:

Anita, the International Student

Anita is obviously experiencing a debilitating level of acculturative stress. It is impairing her ability to function effectively in her studies. This acculturative stress can be attributed to several factors, including nostalgia or homesickness, loneliness, loss of social support systems, and culture shock. Loneliness and nostalgia are clearly the salient factors that cause Anita to "find herself in tears a lot." After leaving India, she was abruptly cut off from her social support system of family and friends. For this reason, "she is not sure to whom she can talk."

Anita's acculturative stress is also caused by her lack of fluency in English. She is quite aware of it and "even afraid that communication, due to language and different accents, might be a problem." Anita experienced immediate culture shock when her counselor asked her "to share personal information about her relationships and whether she is sexually active." She was offended and embarrassed to answer such questions, which she considered culturally quite inappropriate, especially when asked by a male counselor.

Sameer, the Businessman

Sameer, who has been living in the United States for the past 5 years, might have experienced acculturative stress due to all of the factors, including nostalgia, loneliness, and language problems, that were mentioned in Anita's case. However, with time in the United States, during which he has achieved a higher acculturation level, he seems to have been able to cope with those acculturative stress factors.

Sameer's current acculturative stress seems to be caused by the mandatory participation in group therapy because of domestic violence. This acculturative stress is also caused by culture shock because Sameer did not expect that in America he would be punished for hitting his own wife. He still insists that he is not "an offender" because he did not do anything wrong by disciplining his wife, who was getting "too smart and too Americanized." Sameer fails to understand the new expectations and social norms of American society. He still wants to prove to his wife that he is the boss and he can hit her when she "talked back to him."

As mentioned earlier, gender roles are changed, and even reversed, when South Asian immigrants arrive in the United States. But even after migration, some South Asian immigrant men act dominant in public to prove that they have power and control over their wives and children. This attitude causes problems with the law. Sameer seems to fit into that category. By hitting his wife, Sameer unfortunately caused a lot of acculturative stress for her and himself.

Mrs. Khan, the Depressed Widow

The third vignette brings up the acculturative stress issues of Mrs. Khan. After the unexpected death of her husband 6 months ago, naturally Mrs. Khan would feel depression to some degree.

It is interesting to note that even after residing in the United States for 25 years, Mrs. Khan does not know why her daughter brought her to see a counselor. As noted elsewhere, many South Asians lack awareness of available counseling services and question their appropriateness and usefulness. In addition, South Asian Americans have cultural prohibitions against revealing personal problems to strangers, including mental health professionals. They also consider disclosing mental health problems to bring stigma and shame to the whole family. No wonder that Mrs. Khan is "afraid that her daughter and the other members of her community will think that she is 'crazy.'"

The main factors that contribute to Mrs. Khan's acculturative stress are her sense of uncertainty about working on her depression through a counseling process; communication problems; loss of support system, with the exception of some help from her daughter (who also acknowledges "not being able to help her mother as much as she should have during this emotionally difficult time"); and a profound sense of loss after the death of her husband.

Chapter 2: The individual and universal dimensions of human life must also be factored into the work.

This section is divided into four parts. First, reasons for the lack of information on mental health and South Asian Americans are presented. Then, misconceptions about South Asians and issues that are known to be especially relevant to South Asian mental health are discussed. Third, presenting problems of this client group are discussed. Finally, specific mental health concerns of South Asian are presented.

The Absence of Information on Mental Health and South Asian Americans

Objective, research-based information on significant aspects of the experience of South Asian Americans in the United States is lacking (Herrick & Brown, 1999). Unlike other Asian American groups, South Asian immigrants have not been studied by social scientists to any appreciable degree (Das & Kemp, 1997; Madathil, 2011; Maker et al., 2005; Myers, Madathil, & Tingle, 2005; Rastogi, 2002; Sandhu, 1999). For example, not much is known about the quality of their lives, the stresses and strains of their day-to-day life, their mental health needs, and the degree to which they use mental health services. Two reasons for the neglect or oversight of South Asian Americans' adjustment and mental health problems are their image as a model minority and their infrequent use of mental health services.

Asian Americans as a Model Minority

The term *model minority,* mentioned in Chapter 7, manifests here as the view that Asian Americans in general function well in society and experience few adjustment difficulties. The author of the term, William Peterson (1966), compared the success of Asian Americans and Jewish Americans and described them as highly successful model minorities in contrast with other so-called problem minorities.

The term was also applied to the second wave of South Asians who immigrated to the United States under the Immigration and Naturalization Act of 1965, also known as the McCarran-Walter Immigration Act. This elite group of South Asian immigrants was highly educated and showed great promise for upward economic mobility. For instance, in a sample of 46,000 Asian Indian immigrants, Doshi (1975) found that at least 50% were working as medical doctors, scientists, and engineers.

This second wave of professional immigrants exhibited very little criminal activity and earned a higher income than many European Americans. Their children were also higher scholastic achievers and did not demonstrate juvenile delinquency.

Due to the model minority myth, a common perception among mental health service providers is that members of *South* Asian communities do not suffer from mental health problems and that any problems they might have are easily resolved within their families and communities (Johnson & Nadirshaw, 2002). Their strong family ties, stability, and structure are cited as the contributing factors to South Asians' success on all fronts of life (Bell, 1996), including the mental health arena.

Model Minority Myth Debunked

The common perception of South Asian Americans as a model minority must be challenged. This label is problematic in that it has been overgeneralized. It fails to acknowledge the psychological, social, and academic problems that exist for many members of this group In fact, the model minority myth is especially less appropriate in recent years. Many of the more recent South Asian immigrants are less educated and lack English language skills. As mentioned earlier, they generally work as taxi or truck drivers, convenience store clerks, and small motel operators or small business owners (Inman & Tewari, 2003; Sandhu & Malik, 2001). Due to their low economic status and low educational background, but greater acculturation difficulties, South Asian Americans now are at more serious risk of psychological problems than ever before.

It is therefore important that mental health professionals not buy into the popular model minority myth in order to adequately address the serious concerns of this generally overlooked population (Sandhu et al., 1999). In an interview with Morrissey (1997), Sandhu highlighted the mental health issues that are hidden by the model minority myth:

> The myth of Asians as a model minority, based on the success image of a few elite individuals, has a very negative and debilitating effect on the general population of Asian Americans. Several mental health concerns and psychological afflictions, such as threats to cultural identity, powerlessness, feelings of marginality, loneliness, hostility, and perceived alienation, and discrimination remain unaddressed and hidden under the veneer of the model minority myth. (pp. 21–22)

Failure to Seek Professional Help

Another reason South Asians do not show up in the mental health literature is that they infrequently use mental health services (Beliappa, 1991; Leong, 1986; Sue & Sue, 2008). This phenomenon may be attributed to lack of awareness of available services, lack of confidence in the effectiveness and appropriateness of counseling, concerns about cultural and language barriers, and fear that confidentiality will not be preserved. Other reasons for infrequent use of counseling services include a cultural emphasis on restraining strong feelings, strict parental control of offspring, and cultural prohibitions against revealing family or personal problems to anyone outside the family. In South Asian families, disclosing mental problems or mental illness is viewed as bringing great shame and stigma to the whole family (Atkinson, 2004).

In particular, matters relating to sex are considered too personal to be discussed with others. Sex is a taboo subject in South Asian cultures because it is considered a strictly private matter. Discussing personal sexual matters with someone other than one's life partner is considered to be immature or a sign of looseness in character that invites embarrassment, shame, and insult to the self and the family. Thus, South Asian clients are extremely reticent to address their sex-related concerns such as sexual orientation or any episodes of sexual abuse.

Misconceptions About Mental Health and South Asian Americans

Through an extensive review of the available literature about South Asians residing in Britain, Johnson and Nadirshaw (2002) identified several misconceptions that might also have relevance for South Asians in the United States. Some are positive; some are negative. All are inaccurate and dangerous because counselors might be susceptible to them and therefore not respond appropriately to South Asians. The misconceptions are followed by challenges to them.

1. South Asians are psychologically more robust than the indigenous populations of the countries to which they immigrate, and they do not need to use available therapeutic services.

Actually, the low rate of reported mental health problems among South Asian Americans is attributed to their fear of stigmatization, lack of awareness of available mental health services, and cultural and language barriers, but definitely not due to an absence of mental health problems. As a matter of fact, Beliappa (1991) reported an alarmingly high rate of emotional distress among South Asians, with no outlet to express it.

2. South Asian culture is dominated exclusively by men; women play a dependent, submissive role. Therefore there is no role confusion.

This perception might be more true in the native cultures and countries of origin. However, due to the Western emphasis on individualism, including economic independence, women are forced to reexamine their traditional passive gender roles in their newly adopted mainstream American culture (Sandhu, 1997). With more educational and economic opportunities available to women in Western countries, especially in the United States, women's traditional docile and passive roles are transformed to egalitarian and even dominant roles when the women join the cadres of highly educated professionals.

3. South Asians are obsessed with religion.

As discussed previously, this perception is misleading. It is fair to say that after immigration, South Asians are more concerned about earning money and meeting their financial obligations than with their religion. They are not just meditating or practicing yoga.

4. South Asians have arranged marriages, and arranged marriages are not happy.

The practice of arranged marriages often becomes unacceptable to first- and second-generation South Asian offspring in the United States. The number of South Asian American children who have arranged marriages is relatively insignificant. South Asian parents strongly believe in arranged marriages and consider them to be more satisfying. One view of love in arranged marriage is that it "grows" rather than it is "found," as in Western relationships.

On the contrary, one of the major concerns for South Asian parents, and a root cause of family discord, is their children's interethnic and interracial marital relationships, as well as dating in general. In extreme cases, South Asian parents cut off financial and emotional relations with their children if they marry someone who is from a non–South Asian cultural background and ancestry (Inman & Tewari, 2003). In general, intimate relationships and dating can be a source of intergenerational family conflicts for many South Asian American parents.

5. South Asian culture is stifling and denies freedom to the individual.

For first- and second-generation South Asian Americans, South Asian culture is not stifling. While South Asians may sacrifice their personal freedom for the sake of their extended family in their native countries, this changes when they arrive in the Western world. In their newly adopted land, more emphasis is placed on the rights and glorification of the individual than on the demands of the family. A family member's personal needs become more salient than the needs of her or his family of origin.

6. Asians look after their own within extended family networks.

This misconception implies that South Asian Americans do not require any professional counseling services. As mentioned previously, members of this ethnic group are seen as either psychologically so robust and sound that they simply don't have any problems or having strong family networks that are capable of solving all their problems. In reality, both assumptions are wrong. South Asian Americans have their fair share of psychological problems (Beliappa, 1991), and their extended networks are usually disrupted after their migration to the United States.

Most of the perceptions about immigrant South Asians are accurate when viewed in the context of their original cultures and native countries. However, these stereotypes are either overgeneralizations or just mistaken beliefs about second- or third-generation South Asian Americans as acculturation occurs.

While counseling South Asian clients, mental health professionals must remember that, as with all other immigrants, acculturation is central. When South Asian immigrants enter the United States, their cultural transformation is immediately instantiated in new local settings. This transformation shakes up their identities, resulting in significant changes in their values, priorities, and behaviors (Sandhu et al., 1999; Weisner, 1993; Whiting & Edwards, 1988). They are now neither South Asians nor Americans, but South Asian Americans. Some of the stereotypes identified by Johnson and Nadirshaw (2002) might be very important for newly arrived South Asians but might have very little relevance to first-, second-, and third-generation South Asian Americans.

Presenting Psychological Problems of South Asians

Now that myths and misconceptions have been discussed, we turn to trends in how South Asian Americans' mental health issues are expressed. South Asian Americans are likely to present their problems in a different way from mainstream American clients (Ananth & Ananth, 1996; Dasgupta, 1986; Jayakar, 1994; Prathikanti, 1997; Sandhu, 1999). They are likely to emphasize physical complaints, make external attributions, avoid exploring childhood experience, spiritualize emotional difficulties, and emphasize academic or career difficulties. Each is discussed in turn.

Physical Complaints

South Asians' clinical presentations often consist of multiple somatic complaints, such as headaches, stomachaches, and bodily fatigue. As Asians generally view the body and mind as unitary rather than separate, clients tend to focus more on physical problems rather than on emotional afflictions, thus leading to a high number of expressions of somatic complaints for Asians (Lin & Cheung, 1999). These complaints may take them to medical doctors rather than to counselors (Prathikanti, 1997). Counselors should be keenly aware of the somatization of South Asian Americans' emotional problems and look beyond their physical ailments. In a sense, frequent headaches might signal frequent heartaches.

External Attributions

South Asians may also externalize emotional concerns by attributing their problems to supernatural forces, including black magic; the casting of evil eyes from people who are jealous of their successes; angry spirits of dead ancestors; and bad karmic deeds from their previous lives (Jayakar, 1994; Prathikanti, 1997). Many South Asian clients with such psychic distress often seek help from indigenous healers, including palmists, herbalists, sorcerers, and a variety of shamans, whose therapeutic efforts include classical astrology, alchemy, and magic (Jain & Sandhu, in press; Kumar, Bhugra, & Singh, 2005; Yeh & Kwong, 2009).

Avoiding Early Childhood Exploration

Out of deep respect for their parents and due to the aforementioned filial piety, South Asian clients rarely discuss problematic childhood experiences that might be contributing to their presenting problems. Children must show love and respect to parents and their ancestors and take care of them in their old age (Ikels, 2004). Children are also expected to conceal their parents' mistakes and avoid dishonoring them. In addition, deceased parents and ancestors are worshipped in many South Asian families and are considered living members of the family. Related to filial piety is the concept of shame. Children must not bring shame to the family through inappropriate behaviors that might tarnish the family's reputation and prestige in the community (Schoen, 2005). Thus, a counselor's probing for childhood experiences will be resisted by most South Asians. However, since family is a central theme in South Asians' lives, it should be addressed in a respectful way, through culturally educated inquiring, as discussed in Chapters 18 and 19.

Spiritualizing Emotional Difficulties

Many South Asian clients tend to present their problems as a manifestation of disturbance in body, mind, and soul, or lack of the fulfillment of social and religious duties, called *dharma* (Obeyesekere, 1977; Prathikanti, 1997; Sandhu, Leung, & Tang, 2003). Religion and spirituality play major roles in the daily lives of many Asian Indian and Nepalese Americans, especially those who profess their faith in Hinduism and Sikhism. For many South Asian Americans, the spiritual dimension is generally presented as integrated or intertwined with their emotional concerns.

Career Concerns

Generally speaking, concerns about career or academic matters are the major presenting problems for which South Asian Americans might seek professional counseling. Both academic and career success are paramount for South Asians and their families and are a source of pride or shame. There is much pressure to do well in those areas. Career uncertainty, career failure, or family disapproval of career choice are all potential presenting problems of South Asian Americans. These are also "safer" topics, ones that might cover other concerns. As mentioned, South Asian Americans rarely discuss personal and emotional problems that may bring shame to the family. It is well known that South Asian Americans tend to underutilize mental health counseling, but they generally overuse career counseling services (Baruth & Manning, 2012; Leong, Lee, & Chang, 2008).

Specific Mental Health Concerns of South Asians

Although little is known about South Asians' mental health issues at this time, a few topics have been studied. Two particular, and related, sets of problems are highlighted here: youth-related issues around substance abuse and domestic violence and conflict between parents and offspring.

Problems of South Asian American Youth

South Asian American youth now have serious problems related to substance abuse and domestic violence. In addition, according to Scalia (1997), criminal activity is much more serious among the Asian American juvenile population than would be expected. However, due to model minority myths and the other erroneous assumptions that were mentioned previously, adolescent and young adult South Asian clients' mental health needs remain either unaddressed, overlooked, or handled inadequately.

South Asian American Parents' Concerns About Their Children

Another set of concerns lies in parent–child conflict. South Asian young adults are challenging parental authority in general by marrying outside the ethnic group. Most South Asian American parents worry about their children becoming too Americanized, especially when the children express their strong feelings through acting out or talking back to their parents. As discussed earlier, South Asian families are patriarchal, and the father is authoritarian. Communication flows vertically from father downward to children. Any talking back to the father is considered insulting and unacceptable.

The previously mentioned disapproval of dating and interethnic relationships is a cause for conflict between offspring and parents. In fact, most of the dissatisfaction in South Asian American families is due to two main reasons: not getting married within one's own culture or not having a prestigious job that parents may approve.

Additional Concerns

In addition to the issues mentioned previously, recent research found three particular concerns that affect nonimmigrant South Asian Americans (Das & Kemp, 1997):

- Minority status might predispose people to feelings of social isolation and heightened stress.
- Young school-age children of immigrants may become the target of negative stereotyping and social rejection.
- Second-generation South Asian Americans may find it offensive to be seen as foreigners.

As mentioned previously, second-generation South Asian Americans in particular may experience tension between mainstream American values and their ethnic cultural values. For example, a young second-generation girl who finds her social life unduly restricted by traditional parents may find it irksome and begin to rebel.

With these manifestations and conflicts in mind, counselors are better prepared to work with this population. The chapter now turns to guidelines for practice with South Asian Americans.

COUNSELING AND PSYCHOTHERAPY WITH SOUTH ASIAN AMERICANS

The counseling needs of South Asian Americans must be met within their cultural context (Sandhu et al., 2003; Tewari, Inman, & Sandhu, 2003). Thus, the applicability and effectiveness of Western models of treatment with South Asians who have different worldviews, values, and cultural systems must be examined (Maker et al., 2005). For this reason, the following sections provide (1) themes and guidelines for working with South Asian Americans, (2) applications for three stages of counseling, (3) and four culturally specific helping methods.

Special Guidelines

The following 10 themes should be considered when working with South Asian clients, especially those who are less acculturated to the dominant American culture. This list serves partly as a reiteration and summary of some of the themes that were discussed earlier in this chapter.

Counselor Self-Examination

Counselors must examine their own unintentional biases toward South Asian clients and avoid stereotypes, including the model minority myth. This is a guideline for all culturally alert counseling.

Consultation With Healers in the South Asian Community

Consultation with *hakims* (wise men), *matas* (female priests), *yogis* (those who are expert in the practice of yoga), and *gurus* (teachers in Sikhism, Hinduism, and Buddhism) can prove quite helpful to South Asian clients (Johnson & Nadirshaw, 2002). These figures are acquainted with longstanding treatment modalities, such as yogic, tantric (i.e., concerned with powerful ritual acts of body, speech, and mind), and Ayurvedic (a set of ancient and contemporary medicine practices) methods. Counselors themselves are not likely to be acquainted with these indigenous helpers, but they can always encourage their clients to seek such help. Counselors working with South Asians would also benefit from acquainting themselves with some Asian psychotherapies (Walsh, 2000), possibly using them in conjunction with Western models.

The Role of Religion and Spirituality in Counseling

Religion and spirituality are extremely important for understanding and treating the mental health problems of South Asians (Hussain & Cochrane, 2002). South Asian clients may view their mental health problems not only as psychological or emotional, but also as spiritual and religious in nature. They might find it difficult to untangle them.

South Asians believe that if properly understood, all human problems, in the final analysis, are really spiritual problems (Sandhu, 2006). Counselors working with South Asian Americans must be prepared to answer their clients' religious or spiritual questions as they relate to their psychological problems.

The Family-First Concept

Counselors should recognize the power of familism in South Asian life (Paniagua, 2005). Familism is the notion that family is central for all life events and decisions. Since South Asians come from collectivist societies, an individual's problem is considered to be a family's problem (Triandis, 1994). For example, many South Asian clients first discuss their personal or economic problems with their parents or extended family members before seeking professional help. Some family members or friends may even accompany the client to see the counselor. Counselors should consider their client not only as an individual but also in relationship to the whole family.

As is true in most other collectivist societies, a South Asian father, as the head of the household, is responsible for taking care of all family members' problems. Thus, it is not uncommon that a father might receive counseling for his son, daughter, or even wife. This type of indirectness is generally more prevalent in collectivist societies than it is in individualistic societies like the United States (Vontress, 1991).

South Asians as Targets of Prejudice and Discrimination

Counselors must be aware that because they are physically different, politically powerless, and socially isolated from the dominant culture, South Asians may feel alienated and disconnected. Incidents of racism, discrimination, and hate crimes, including physical violence, are not unfamiliar to these ethnic groups (Sandhu, 1997). In that vein, counselors and other mental health professionals must acknowledge how power relationships between them and their clients might affect the therapeutic process (Johnson & Nadirshaw, 2002).

South Asians and Internalized Racism

Like many other nondominant ethnic groups, South Asian clients generally suffer from internalized racism, that is, the acceptance of negative and demeaning verbal and nonverbal messages from the dominant culture (Sharma, 2005). Self-devaluation, rejection of ancestral culture, hopelessness, and helplessness are some of the common characteristics of internalized racism that affect many South Asian Americans (Jones, 2000).

Level of Acculturation

It is important that counselors understand a South Asian client's level of acculturation before initiating any counseling or therapeutic interventions. Such knowledge for the counselor is critical to the success of the counseling process (Ibrahim et al., 1997). One tool that can be used to assess South Asian American clients' acculturation levels is the Cultural Adaptation Pain Scale (Sandhu et al., 1996). Generally speaking, higher levels of acculturation indicate that clients will be more receptive and able to benefit from counseling services (Vontress, Johnson, & Epp, 1999).

Generation Gap Issues of South Asian Immigrants and Their Children

Immigrants often face chronic difficulties specific to the acculturation experience, including conflicts with family members, members of their own ethnic group, and members of other ethnic groups (Lay & Nguyen, 1998). Children of immigrants may experience different acculturative stressors from their parents, such as conflicts between the children and parents regarding culturally acceptable behaviors. The offspring of immigrants report more in-group conflicts and marginally lower self-esteem than do immigrants (Abouguendia & Noels, 2001). The offspring of immigrants also experience conflict between parents' traditional cultural values and the contrasting values of the dominant culture (Lay & Nguyen, 1998). These results emphasize the need for considering the acculturation issues of the first-generation South Asian Americans as being different from that of the second- and third-generation members of the community.

Using a Relational Style of Counseling

A highly relational style, characterized by warmth and disclosure, should be used while counseling South Asian clients (Ibrahim, 1993). Both counselor and client should be willing to share their experiences and values. This exchange will likely increase trust and rapport with the client. A silent counselor who expects a South Asian client to reveal her or his deepest fears and anxieties is likely to fail. It is important to note that South Asian American clients often exhibit much greater respect for their counselors than do European Americans clients.

Dealing With Sex-Related Concerns

As mentioned previously, discussion about sexual matters, especially with the opposite sex and with younger clients, is still taboo in the South Asian population. Counselors should refrain from abruptly asking questions or initiating conversation about sex, unless the clients themselves initiate the discussion of their sexual concerns.

Incorporating Strategies Into Three Main Stages of Counseling

One model for counseling South Asian American clients can be conceptualized as incorporating particular elements into three main stages of counseling (Sandhu et al., 2003): exploration, insight, and action. The relational dimension of counseling is emphasized in each of these stages.

First Stage: Exploration

As mentioned earlier, South Asian clients are generally reluctant to discuss their concerns with strangers. For this reason, it is important that a counselor develop a special relationship with the South Asian client. Instead of being perceived only as an expert professional, an effective counselor would become personal and familiar, like a friend or another family member. Rogers's (1957) three facilitating conditions—empathy, respect, and genuineness—can prove quite helpful for building good rapport with

South Asian clients. A professionally distant, neutral stance with these clients might be detrimental to therapeutic efforts because they most likely would withdraw prematurely from counseling sessions.

Second Stage: Insight

In the second stage, the client increases awareness of her or his motivations and behaviors. Such insight is usually thought of in individual terms. However, with South Asian American clients, such awareness should account for family, not only individual, needs. At this stage, counselors should keep in mind the aforementioned concept of family first, or familism. South Asian Americans are generally willing to sacrifice their own interests for the sake of family members. They may prefer to suffer silently than to disrupt family harmony and peace. Thus, South Asian American clients might disagree with counselors' reflections and interpretations if they believe that those observations conflict with their desire to maintain family harmony and interpersonal relationships. Counselors can complement this concern by helping their South Asian American clients gain insight into how the counseling process ultimately can help their entire family.

Third Stage: Action

During this third and final stage, the aim of counseling is for a client to think, behave, and feel differently. Methods for such change can be wide-ranging. It has been suggested that Asian American clients prefer a directive style of counseling and respond more favorably to problem-solving and cognitively oriented interventions (Sue & Sue, 2008). Such assertions have also been questioned (Sandhu et al., 2003). Culturally alert counselors must possess a full repertoire of intervention strategies and use them as needed to resolve their clients' problems in the context of their cultural and family backgrounds. This repertoire should include ecological, spiritual, behavioral, and cognitive dimensions and approaches such as network therapy, narrative therapy, and feminist models (Ibrahim et al., 1997). Each of these is described elsewhere in this book.

Four Strategies for Working With South Asian Clients

Four specific types of interventions can be particularly useful for counseling South Asian Americans: cultural genograms, narratives and stories, bibliotherapy and psychoeducation, and group counseling (Inman & Tewari, 2003).

Cultural Genograms

Since family is an important source of support for South Asians, mental health providers need to address client issues in the familial context. A cultural genogram can help clients identify and understand the immigration history, family structure, and alliances in the extended family. The use of such a genogram can also help counselors assess the levels of acculturation of South Asian clients and their religious affiliations and ethnic identification. The making of a cultural genogram will be described in Chapter 13.

In Mrs. Khan's situation (from this chapter's third vignette), a cultural genogram could be used to identify the role of women in the family, especially after the death of a spouse. It could also help her daughter see the familial expectations and responsibilities that are placed on children after the death of a parent.

After Mrs. Kahn draws such a genogram, the counselor can explore the following with her: Which aspects of your culture or values make you proud? Which ones might make you afraid or guilty? Which parts of your cultural or familial expectations have you exceeded, and which ones have you compromised? What are the messages that are passed on from generation to generation regarding widowhood? How did this experience affect the lives of the women in your family? How did the other women in the family face it? What roles did their children play in these situations? What were their sources of support? What were the religious and cultural beliefs?

Information gathered from these questions could be helpful for Mrs. Khan and her daughter to understand their emotions and reactions in their cultural context. In addition, the information could also help them recognize the strengths of the women in their family and how the women in their culture dealt with difficult times.

Narratives and Stories

Because of the possibility that South Asians might be more comfortable sharing their experiences through stories, as opposed to directly disclosing emotions, counselors can encourage South Asian families to share their experiences and struggles related to immigration and acculturation by using stories and narratives (Inman & Tewari, 2003). Stories and narratives can also serve as powerful tools for exploring parents' expectations and relationship with their children.

To illustrate, narratives could be used to help Anita, the international student who was presented in the first vignette. She could be encouraged to narrate the story of her life, in which she is the heroine. The counselor could help Anita tell her story in such a way that she could perhaps see the themes in her life. She might identify the rewards and the obligations she has chosen and received and then develop ways to address those topics in counseling. This may provide her with the means to explore the expectations placed on her and to make helpful choices.

Bibliotherapy and Psychoeducation

Bibliotherapy and psychoeducation can be safer ways to help South Asians, as they provide some distance from the personal issues. Reading about related phenomena and other people's experiences can normalize situations and feelings that otherwise are considered stigmatizing and shameful to clients and their families. For example, in the case of spousal abuse in the second vignette, the counselor could suggest to Sameer a reading on anger or a workshop on spousal abuse at a local Hindu temple. Sameer might be encouraged to read literature from his own culture that focuses on taking care of one's spouse and treating the person with respect. That may make the message less foreign, less threatening, and less personal for him.

Group Counseling

Due to its cost effectiveness and practical efficacy, group counseling is a popular modality. Group counseling could be especially useful for South Asian clients, if the focus of the group is specifically on South Asian issues (Tewari et al., 2003). However, group counseling with South Asians can be a great challenge because their cultural values are diametrically opposed to the processes and dynamics of group counseling (Baruth & Manning, 2012; Mann & Duan, 2002; Merta, 1995). Group counseling requires directness, open expression of feelings, self-disclosure, and active participation. By contrast, South Asians are generally reluctant to express strong feelings in the presence of other group members, they lack verbal expressiveness, and they generally don't like to share personal or family problems with strangers. It can be helpful to have other South Asian clients in the group in order to encourage trust in the process. Thus, Sameer might find the group experience more beneficial if he were placed in a group with other individuals from similar cultural backgrounds. Perhaps, then, he might be more open and willing to share and be challenged by the other group members.

Another barrier to traditional group counseling for South Asian Americans is their expectation that a group leader will be an authority figure (DeLucia-Waack, 1996). Even when a challenge could be beneficial to all group members, South Asian clients are not likely to question or challenge the group leader (Gladding, 2012). Because a group leader is considered an expert, South Asian group members commonly would expect some concrete advice or solutions from the leader for solving their problems, not just the exploration of their feelings in the presence of others (Baruth & Manning, 2012).

With those provisos in mind, counselors should first explain the goals, structure, and dynamics of group counseling before asking South Asians to join such groups. Careful screening, selection, explanation, and preparation can help South Asian clients benefit from group counseling like all other clients. It is also important that mental health professionals first provide some individual counseling sessions with South Asian American clients, before starting group counseling sessions with them.

SUMMARY

This chapter introduced readers to South Asian Americans as a rapidly increasing distinct ethnic minority group with unique characteristics, cultural values, special counseling needs, and mental health concerns. Several myths, misconceptions, and mistaken beliefs about this generally overlooked group were discussed. Acculturative experiences, threats to ethnic identity, barriers to seeking counseling, clinical presentations of mental health problems, and special recommendations for counseling were presented as special topics as they apply to South Asian American clients. In addition, various counseling considerations and strategies were presented to enhance counseling effectiveness with this group. Three case examples illustrated South Asian issues and counseling strategies that might be effective with South Asian American clients.

Now that you have completed this chapter, respond to the questions in Activity 12.2 to assess your understanding of South Asian Americans and counseling.

Activity 12.2   Discussion Questions About South Asian Americans

1. Who are South Asian Americans? Describe their demographic characteristics.

2. Discuss some of the cultural values of South Asian Americans. How do these values contribute to the acculturative stress of South Asian Americans?

3. Generally, South Asian Americans have been recognized as a model minority. Do you agree or disagree with this characterization? Please provide a rationale to support your answer.

---

4. Identify some common mental health problems of South Asian Americans. What are some beliefs and assumptions regarding these mental health problems?

5. Discuss intervention strategies that are culturally relevant and effective for helping South Asian Americans.

6. How would you incorporate counseling strategies into three stages—exploration, insight, and action—while counseling South Asian Americans?

7. What are some of the major acculturative issues of South Asian Americans?

8. How would you help your South Asian American clients cope with acculturative stress?

9. Discuss the role of women in South Asian American families.

REFERENCES

Abouguendia, M., & Noels, K. A. (2001). General and acculturation-related daily hassles and psychological adjustment in first- and second-generation South Asian immigrants to Canada. *International Journal of Psychology, 36,* 163–173.

Abrahams, S., & Salazar, C. F. (2005). Potential conflicts between cultural values and the role of confidentiality when counseling South Asian clients: Implications for ethical practice. In G. R. Walz & R. Yep (Eds.), *Vistas: Compelling perspectives on counseling 2005* (pp. 145–148). Alexandria, VA: American Counseling Association.

Ananth, J., & Ananth, K. (1996). *East Indian immigrants to the United States: Life cycle issues and adjustment.* East Meadow, NY: Indo-American Psychiatric Association.

Asian American Federation & South Asian Americans Leading Together. (2012). *A demographic snapshot of South Asians in the United States.* Retrieved from http://www.saalt.org/pages/Reports%7B47%7DPublications.html

Atkinson, D. R. (2004). *Counseling American minorities* (6th ed.). New York, NY: McGraw-Hill.

Baruth, L. G., & Manning, L. (2012). *Multicultural counseling and psychotherapy: A lifespan approach.* Boston, MA: Pearson.

Beliappa, J. (1991). *Illness or distress? Alternative models of mental health.* London, UK: Confederation of Indian Organizations.

Bell, D. A. (1996). America's greatest success story: The triumph of Asian-Americans. In R. C. Monk (Ed.), *Taking sides: Clashing views on controversial issues in race and ethnicity* (2nd ed., pp. 30–40). Guilford, CT: Dushkin.

Berry, J. W., & Sam, D. L. (1997). Acculturation and adaptation. In J. W. Berry, M. H. Segall, & C. Kagitcibasi (Eds.), *Handbook of cross-cultural psychology, Volume 3: Social behavior and applications* (2nd ed., pp. 291–326). Boston, MA: Allyn & Bacon.

Bhatia, S., & Ram, A. (2004). Culture, hybridity, and the dialogical self: Cases from the South Asian diaspora. *Mind, Culture and Activity, 11,* 224–240.

Chandras, V. K. (1997). Training multiculturally competent counselors to work with Asian Indian Americans. *Counselor Education and Supervision, 37,* 50–59.

Das, A. K., & Kemp, S. F. (1997). Between two worlds: Counseling South Asian Americans. *Journal of Multicultural Counseling & Development, 25,* 23–34.

Dasgupta, S. D. (1986). Marching to a different drummer? Sex roles of Asian Indian women in the United States. *Women and Therapy, 5,* 297–311.

DeLucia-Waack, J. L. (1996). Multiculturalism is inherent in all group work. *Journal for Specialists in Group Work, 21,* 218–223.

Doshi, M. (1975). *Who is who among Indian immigrants in North America.* New York, NY: B. K. Verma.

Furnham, A., & Bochner, S. (1986). *Culture shock: Psychological reactions to unfamiliar environments.* London, UK: Methuen.

Gladding, S. (2012). *Groups: A counseling specialty* (6th ed.). Upper Saddle River, NJ: Pearson Education.

Grieger, I., & Ponterotto, J. G. (1995). A framework for assessment in multicultural counseling. In J. G. Ponterotto, J. M. Casas, L. A. Suzuki, & C. M. Alexander (Eds.), *Handbook of multicultural counseling* (pp. 357–374). Thousand Oaks, CA: Sage.

Helman, C. G. (1990). *Culture, health, and illness: An introduction for health professionals* (3rd ed.). Boston, MA: Wright.

Herrick, C., & Brown, H. N. (1999). Mental disorders and syndromes found among Asians residing in the United States. *Issues in Mental Health Nursing, 20,* 275–296.

Hussain, F. A., & Cochrane, R. (2002). Depression in South Asian women: Asian women's beliefs on causes and cures. *Mental Health, Religion, and Culture, 5,* 285–311.

Ibrahim, F. A. (1993). Existential worldview theory: Transcultural counseling. In J. McFadden (Ed.), *Transcultural counseling* (pp. 23–57). Alexandria, VA: American Counseling Association.

Ibrahim, F. A., Ohnishi, I., & Sandhu, D. S. (1997). Asian American identity development: A culture-specific model for South Asian Americans. *Journal of Multicultural Counseling & Development, 25,* 34–51.

Ikels, C. (Ed.). (2004). *Filial piety: Practice and discourse in contemporary East Asia.* Stanford, CA: Stanford University Press.

Inman, A. G., & Sandhu, D. S. (2002). Cross-cultural perspectives on love and sex. In L. D. Burlew & D. Capuzzi (Eds.), *Sexuality counseling* (pp. 41–62). Huntington, NY: Nova Science.

Inman, A. G., & Tewari, N. (2003). The power of context: Counseling South Asians within a family context. In G. Roysircar, D. S. Sandhu, & V. E. Bibbins Sr. (Eds.), *Multicultural competencies: A guidebook of practices* (pp. 97–107). Alexandria, VA: Association for Multicultural Counseling and Development.

Jain, S., & Sandhu, D. S. (in press). Counseling in India. In T. Hohenshil, N. Amundson, & S. Niles (Eds.), *International counseling.* Alexandria, VA: American Counseling Association.

Jayakar, K. (1994). Women of the Indian subcontinent. In L. Comas-Diaz & B. Greene (Eds.), *Women of color: Integrating ethnic and gender identities in psychotherapy* (pp. 161–181). New York, NY: Guilford Press.

Johnson, A. W., & Nadirshaw, Z. (2002). Good practice in transcultural counseling: An Asian perspective. In S. Palmer (Ed.), *Multicultural counseling: A reader* (pp. 119–128). Thousand Oaks, CA: Sage.

Jones, C. P. (2000). Levels of racism: A theoretical framework and a gardener's tale. *American Journal of Public Health, 90,* 1212–1215.

Kim, B. S. K., Atkinson, D. R., & Umemoto, D. (2001). Asian cultural values and counseling process: Current knowledge and directions for future research. *The Counseling Psychologist, 29,* 570–603.

Kumar, M., Bhugra, D., & Singh, J. (2005). South Asian (Indian) traditional healing. In R. Moodley & W. West (Eds.), *Integrating traditional healing practices into counseling and psychotherapy* (pp. 112–121). Thousand Oaks, CA: Sage.

Lay, C., & Nguyen, T. (1998). The role of acculturation-related and acculturation non-specific daily hassles: Vietnamese-Canadian students and psychological distress. *Canadian Journal of Behavioral Science, 30,* 172–181.

Leong, F. T. L. (1986). Counseling and psychotherapy with Asian Americans: Review of the literature. *Journal of Counseling Psychology, 33,* 196–206.

Leong, F. T. L., Lee, S. H., & Chang, D. (2008). Counseling Asian Americans: Client and therapist variables. In P. B. Pederson, J. G. Draguns, W. J. Lonner, & J. E. Trimble (Eds.), *Counseling across cultures* (6th ed., pp. 113–128). Thousand Oaks, CA: Sage.

Lin, K., & Cheung, F. (1999). Mental health issues for Asian Americans. *Psychiatric Services, 50,* 774–780.

Madathil, M. (2011). Working with Asian immigrant families, part II: South Asia. In A. Zagelbaum & J. Carlson (Eds.), *Working with immigrant families: A practical guide for counselors* (pp. 137–149). New York, NY: Routledge/Taylor & Francis.

Madathil, M., & Sandhu, D. S. (2008). The practice of marriage and family counseling and Hinduism. In J. D. Onedera (Ed.), *The role of religion in marriage and family counseling.* New York, NY: Taylor & Francis.

Maker, A. H., Mittal, M., & Rastogi, M. (2005). South Asians in the United States: Developing a systematic and empirically based mental health assessment model. In M. Rastogi & E. Wieling (Eds.), *Voices of color: The first person accounts of ethnic minority therapists* (pp. 233–254). Thousand Oaks, CA: Sage.

Mann, M., & Duan, C. (2002). Multicultural group counseling. In J. Trusty, E. J. Looby, & D. S. Sandhu (Eds.), *Multicultural counseling: Context, theory and practice, and competence* (pp. 247–259). Huntington, NY: Nova Science.

McMahon, S. (1995). *Overview of the South Asian diaspora.* Retrieved from http://www.lib.berkeley.edu/SSEAL/SouthAsia/overview.html

Merta, R. J. (1995). Group work: Multicultural perspectives. In J. G. Ponterotto, J. M. Casas, L. A. Suzuki, & C. M. Alexander (Eds.), *Handbook of multicultural counseling* (pp. 567–585). Thousand Oaks, CA: Sage.

Morrissey, M. (1997). The invisible minority: Counseling Asian Americans. *Counseling Today, 40*(4), 1, 21–22.

Myers, J. E., Madathil, J., & Tingle, L. R. (2005). Marriage satisfaction and wellness in India and the U.S.: A preliminary comparison of arranged marriages and marriages of choice. *Journal of Counseling and Development, 83,* 183–190.

Obeyesekere, G. (1977). The theory and practice of psychological medicine in the Ayurvedic tradition. *Culture, Medicine and Psychiatry, 1,* 155.

Ozbay, Y. (1994). An investigation of the relationship between adaptational coping process and self-perceived negative feelings of international students. *Dissertation Abstracts International, 54,* 2958A.

Paniagua, F. A. (2005). *Assessing and treating culturally diverse clients: A practical guide.* Thousand Oaks, CA: Sage.

Patel, N. R. (2007). The construction of South-Asian American womanhood: Implications for counseling and psychotherapy. *Women & Therapy, 30*(3–4), 51–61.

Peterson, W. (1966, January 9). Success story: Japanese American style. *The New York Times,* pp. VI–20.

Prathikanti, S. (1997). East Indian American families. In E. Lee (Ed.), *Working with Asian Americans: A guide for clinicians* (pp. 79–100). New York, NY: Guilford Press.

Pyke, K. D., & Johnson, D. L. (2003). Asian American women and racialized femininities: "Doing" gender across cultural worlds. *Gender and Society, 1,* 33–53.

Rahman, O., & Rollock, D. (2004). Acculturation, competence, and mental health among South Asian students in the United States. *Journal of Multicultural Counseling and Development, 32,* 130–142.

Rastogi, M. (2002). Mother-adult daughter questionnaire (MAD): Developing a culturally sensitive instrument. *Family Journal, 10,* 145–155.

Rogers, C. R. (1957). The necessary and sufficient conditions of therapeutic personality change. *Journal of Consulting Psychology, 21,* 95–103.

Rumbaut, R. G. (1994). Origins and destinies: Immigration to the United States since World War II. *Sociological Forum, 9,* 583–621.

Sandhu, D. S. (1995). An examination of the psychological needs of the international students: Implications for counselling and psychotherapy. *International Journal for the Advancement of Counselling, 17,* 229–239.

Sandhu, D. S. (1997). Psychocultural profiles of Asian and Pacific Islander Americans: Implications for counseling and psychotherapy. *Journal of Multicultural Counseling and Development, 25,* 7–22.

Sandhu, D. S. (Ed.). (1999). *Asian and Pacific Islander Americans: Issues and concerns for counseling and psychotherapy.* Commack, NY: Nova Science.

Sandhu, D. S. (2006). Seven stages of spiritual development: A framework to solve psycho-spiritual problems. In O. J. Morgan (Ed.), *Counseling and spirituality: Views from the profession* (pp. 64–92). Boston, MA: Lahaska & Houghton Mifflin.

Sandhu, D. S., & Asrabadi, B. R. (1994). Development of an acculturative stress scale for international students: Preliminary findings. *Psychological Reports, 75,* 435–448.

Sandhu, D. S., & Asrabadi, B. R. (1998). An acculturative stress scale for international students: A practical approach to stress measurement. In C. P. Zalaquett & R. J. Wood (Eds.), *Evaluating stress: A book of resources* (Vol. 2, pp. 1–33). Lanham, MD: Scarecrow Press.

Sandhu, D. S., Kaur, K. P., & Tewari, N. (1999). Acculturative experiences of Asian and Pacific Islander Americans: Considerations for counseling and psychotherapy. In D. S. Sandhu (Ed.), *Asian and Pacific Islander Americans: Issues and concerns for counseling and psychotherapy.* Commack, NY: Nova Science.

Sandhu, D. S., Leung, S. L., & Tang, M. (2003). Counseling approaches with Asian Americans and Pacific

Islander Americans. In F. D. Harper & J. McFadden (Eds.), *Culture and counseling: New approaches* (pp. 99–114). Boston, MA: Allyn & Bacon.

Sandhu, D. S., & Malik, R. (2001). Ethnocultural background and substance abuse treatment of Asian Indian Americans. In S. L. A. Straussner (Ed.), *Ethnocultural factors in substance abuse treatment* (pp. 368–392). New York, NY: Guilford Press.

Sandhu, D. S., Portes, P. R., & McPhee, S. (1996). Assessing cultural adaptation: Psychometric properties of the cultural adaptation pain scale. *Journal of Multicultural Counseling and Development, 24,* 15–25.

Scalia, J. (1997). *Juvenile delinquents in the federal criminal justice system. Special report.* Washington, DC: U.S. Department of Justice, Bureau of Justice Statistics.

Schoen, A. A. (2005). Culturally sensitive counseling for Asian Americans/Pacific Islanders. *Journal of Instructional Psychology, 32,* 253–258.

Sharma, M. (2005). Emerging identity: An Asian Indian female psychologist's perspective. In M. Rastogi & E. Wieling (Eds.), *Voices of color: First-person accounts of ethnic minority therapists* (pp. 13–22). Thousand Oaks, CA: Sage.

Shea, M., & Yeh, C. J. (2008). Asian American students' cultural values, stigma, and relational self-construal: Correlates of attitudes toward professional help seeking. *Journal of Mental Health Counseling, 30,* 157–172.

Sheth, M. (1995). Asian Indian Americans. In P. G. Min (Ed.), *Asian Americans: Contemporary trends and issues* (pp. 169–198). Thousand Oaks, CA: Sage.

Sodowsky, G. R., & Carey, J. C. (1988). Relationship between acculturation-related demographics and cultural attitudes of an Asian-Indian immigrant group. *Journal of Multicultural Counseling and Development, 16,* 117–136.

Sodowsky, G. R., Kwan, K. K., & Pannu, R. (1995). Ethnic identity of Asians in the United States. In J. G. Ponterotto, J. M. Casas, L. A. Suzuki, & C. M. Alexander (Eds.), *Handbook of multicultural counseling* (pp. 123–154). Thousand Oaks, CA: Sage.

Sodowsky, G. R., & Plake, B. S. (1992). A study of acculturation differences among international people and suggestions for sensitivity to within-group differences. *Journal of Counseling and Development, 71,* 53–60.

Sue, D. W., & Sue, D. (2008). *Counseling the culturally diverse: Theory and practice* (5th ed.). Hoboken, NJ: John Wiley & Sons.

Takaki, R. (1989). *Strangers from a different shore.* Boston, MA: Little, Brown.

Tewari, N., Inman, A. G., & Sandhu, D. S. (2003). South Asian Americans: Culture, concerns, and therapeutic strategies. In J. S. Mio & G. Y. Iwamasa (Eds.), *Culturally diverse mental health: The challenges of research and resistance* (pp. 191–209). New York, NY: Brunner-Routledge.

Triandis, H. C. (1994). *Culture and social behavior.* New York, NY: McGraw-Hill.

Vontress, C. E. (1991). Traditional healing in Africa: Implications for cross-cultural counseling. *Journal of Counseling and Development, 70,* 242–249.

Vontress, C. E., Johnson, J. A., & Epp, L. R. (1999). *Cross-cultural counseling: A casebook.* Alexandria, VA: American Counseling Association.

Walsh, R. (2000). Asian psychotherapies. In R. J. Corsini & D. Wedding (Eds.), *Current psychotherapies* (6th ed., pp. 407–444). Itasca, IL: F. E. Peacock.

Weisner, T. S. (1993). Overview: Sibling similarity and differences in different cultures. In C. W. Nuckolls (Ed.), *Siblings in South Asia: Brothers and sisters in cultural context* (pp. 1–17). New York, NY: Guilford Press.

Whiting, B., & Edwards, C. (1988). *Children of different worlds: The formation of social behavior.* Cambridge, MA: Harvard University Press.

Yeh, C. J., & Kwong, A. (2009). Asian American indigenous healing and coping. In N. Tewari & A. N. Alvarez (Eds.), *Asian American psychology: Current perspectives* (pp. 559–574). New York, NY: Taylor & Francis.

Zwingman, C. A. A. (1978). *Uprooting and related phenomena: A descriptive bibliotherapy* (Doc. No. MNH/78.23). Geneva, Switzerland: World Health Organization.

PART III

SOCIAL GROUPS

CHAPTER 13

Social Class

Patricia Goodspeed-Grant
College at Brockport, State University of New York

Karen L. Mackie
University of Rochester

"We are what we know." We are, however, also what we do not know. If what we know about ourselves—our history, our culture, our national identity—is deformed by absences, denials, and incompleteness, then our identity—both as individuals and as Americans—is fractured. . . . Such a self lacks access both to itself and to the world.

William Pinar, educator (1993, pp. 4–5)

Pinar's quote is particularly apt for the topic of social class in the United States. Americans know little about social class—their own and that of others. It is one of the purposes of this chapter to fill in some of the "absences" and acknowledge some of the American denial about social class, so that counselors have "access," in Pinar's words, to themselves and to the world of their clients. The following three vignettes highlight the impact of social class.

The Bryants live in a middle-class neighborhood. Melvin is an executive for a large corporation, while Tracy is a successful attorney. They typically enjoy yearly family vacations and are active in their children's schools and in community organizations. Antonia, their daughter, and William, one of their sons, have always been top students. Antonia has just obtained her master's degree, and William is attending law school. The youngest, Michael, is considered by his family to be "different." He is socially awkward and doesn't seem to be as smart as his older siblings. However, with extra help from a tutor, he passed most of his classes in high school. Michael is pursuing a degree in automotive mechanics at the local community college. While Tracy and Melvin brag about Antonia and William to their friends, Michael is a source of some embarrassment for them, and they are reluctant to talk about his educational achievements.

(Continued)

(Continued)

Annie, a working-class 34-year-old married European American mother of two, has a bachelor's degree in business from the local state college. Her husband, a high school dropout, worked his way up to a $40,000-a-year factory job in a manufacturing company. After staying home to raise her family and then engaging in a fruitless 4-year search for a job in her field, Annie is now turning to her former college's career office for help. She is tearful, angry, and discouraged because so far she cannot find the secure job that she believes she "deserves," one in which she can use her education. The staff at the career office does not believe that she currently has the attitudes, skills, or appearance that would make her employable in the corporate world.

Louise is a 52-year-old woman from an affluent and prominent family. Her husband recently left her for another woman. She had maintained their expensive home and entertained his colleagues for 22 years. She had been an active volunteer, working around her husband's schedule and commitments. Behind her facade of perfection, however, lay her misery that resulted from her husband's periodic physical assaults (sometimes resulting in bone fractures) and verbal assaults ("You're fat, ugly, you have no skills and no brains"). She has told no one of her problems, not even her best friend. Because the violence was well concealed, and her husband's power and standing in the community so strong, she thinks that no one will believe her about the abuse, including a judge. She is frightened to be on her own because she must support herself for the first time in her life. Other than being a good hostess in the home, Louise believes she has no occupational skills.

The Bryant family exemplifies the American Dream of the middle class. They are successful. The two older children attended "good" universities, they are on their way to successful careers, and their parents are very proud of them. However, when Michael began to exhibit difficulties in school, and to aspire to a working-class vocation rather than to a professional career, his family was disappointed.

If middle-class aspirations and lifestyles are considered normal and desirable, non-middle-class values give rise to subtle feelings of embarrassment, inadequacy, and shame. Such is the case for Annie, the working class woman in the second vignette. Her disappointment that her college degree didn't result in the American Dream of a middle-class life is one such class story. The attitudes, appearance, and behaviors that were valued in her parents' working-class world turned out to be barriers to finding the career she hoped for. Others, such as the staff at the career office, have labeled Annie as deficient when she is merely behaving in a manner consistent with her family's values. Those are subjective elements of class. External class factors also play a part in a person's class story. Unlike the Bryant children, Annie had to pay her own way through college with ever-dwindling needs-based grants, student loans, and part-time work to pay her expenses. She struggled academically, barely making it through her degree. She had particular difficulty with writing assignments, because her instructors seemed to require a different "language" than she was used to using. She believed that by working hard and sticking it out, though, she would raise her status to become "more respectable."

While Annie may believe that being a member of the upper class equates with being worry free, individuals in this class are more isolated than those in other classes. Note that in the third vignette, Louise hid her husband's abuse for years. People in her class feel pressure to maintain status. She bore her burden alone because she was too ashamed to admit to anyone that she had problems.

The experiences and dilemmas of each of these individuals are rooted in social class. Class-related attitudes, values, and behaviors are treated in this chapter as narratives that people tell about what they hope for, expect, and know. You are asked to reflect on your own class story, and its relationship to your experience of social life, as you read through this chapter.

DEFINITIONS AND IMPLICATIONS OF CLASS

This sections presents some of the many ways in which social class is defined in the literature and experienced by individuals. It begins with (1) criteria for determining class, then presents (2) the subjective dimension of class, and (3) discusses the contextual nature of class. When considering these characteristics, it is important to remember that social class is not a fixed entity, but a dynamic, evolving construct. It is only one aspect of a person's identity and is part of a larger context in which each individual is socially positioned as to privilege or lack thereof.

Definitions: Criteria for Determining Class

Socioeconomic Status

Socioeconomic status (SES) is an objective notion (Marger, 1999; Zweig, 2000). It can be defined as

> a multifaceted construct that is rooted in both objective features of material wealth and access to resources (income, education) as well as in conceptions of socioeconomic status (SES) rank vis-à-vis others in society. These facets of social class all reflect real, material conditions that shape the lives and identities of upper and lower class individuals. (Piff, Kraus, Cote, Cheng, & Keltner, 2010, p. 772)

In other words, SES represents the discrepant power and life chances among groups of people. SES is usually measured by household income, education, and/or occupation (Marger, 1999; Zweig, 2000).

Social Class

The term *social class* has a subjective quality: It is people's perceptions about which social class group they and others belong to (Liu, Ali, et al., 2004). SES is structural; that is, there are categories of income, occupations, and education into which an individual can fall that are not necessarily conscious to the individual. Social class, on the other hand, has a personal cultural dimension. Social class is full of assumptions, rules, and hidden meanings that are shared among those of a similar class. It is the "underwater" part of the Iceberg Concept of Culture described in Chapter 2. For example, if an individual grew up in a middle-class family, she or he may find the Bryant family to be "normal" regarding their expectations about pursuing a postgraduate education and a professional career. The fact that Michael wants to become an automobile mechanic has a very different meaning for a middle-class family than for a working-class or poor family, who might be proud that their child aspired to such a skilled occupation.

Objective Dimensions of Class

Based on income, level of education, and occupation (Hollingshead & Redlich, 1958; Zweig, 2000), social class groups can be roughly divided into rankings that may include upper class, upper middle class, lower middle class, working class, the working poor, and the underclass (Marger, 1999). While such categorizing simplifies the task of describing SES for research purposes, there are no distinctive markers that distinguish one class from another. To further complicate matters, these classifications are not static, but are, in fact, dynamic and fluid as people move in and out of labor market sectors (Shin, 2007), pursue higher education, or experience rises or declines in income as a result of economic recessions (Abramowitz & Teixeira, 2009).

There has been a dramatic shift in the class structure spanning many decades. The period of the 1940s to the 1970s saw rises in educational levels and an increase in income. For example, in 1940, approximately 75% of adults were high school dropouts, and 5% had a college degree. By 2007, 14% were high school dropouts and 29% had bachelor's degrees. In 1940, approximately 32% of workers held white collar jobs, compared to 60% in 2007. In 1947, the median family income (in 2007 dollars) was around $22,000; by 2005, it was $56,000 (Abramowitz & Teixeira, 2009). While this translates into a less-than-perfect categorization of a family's social class category, the trends are evident.

In contrast to this apparent increase in education and income, after about the 1970s, the United States began to also experience a growing disparity between the richest and poorest families (Boushey & Fremstad, 2008; Fischer & Mattson, 2009; U.S. Census Bureau, 2012). The percentage of those in wealth and in the upper-middle classes has increased precipitously, while the percentage and wealth of those in the middle have declined (Boushey & Fremstad, 2008), a trend that has worsened since the Great Recession of 2008 (Kneebone & Garr, 2011). For example, whereas the total mean median income in the United States between 1975 and 2010 rose from $12,000 to $49,000—a 308% increase—the total compensation of the 500 largest corporations rose 1200%, from $1 million to $13 million (Ferguson, 2012).

There has also been a shift toward an increase in the number of low-wage, low-skill service jobs.

This has resulted in a large class category known as the working poor (Boushey & Fremstad, 2008), who now constitute some 20% of the population (Ehrenreich, 2009). The working poor are those who work at one or more jobs, but whose wages are insufficient to meet basic needs. This is more fully discussed later in the chapter.

Table 13.1, represents an attempt at objective approximations by social scientists. However, like all social phenomena, social class is more complex than such categories can allow. It is presented here for the purpose of painting a clear picture of general class descriptions.

Objective Descriptions of Classes

Following are some brief descriptions of class, based primarily on Marger's (1999) categories, followed by some descriptions of class differences in family and lifestyles. Note that while the highest and lowest classes are quite distinct from one

Table 13.1   Marger's (1999) Categories of Socioeconomic Status

Household	% of Population	Annual Income	Education	Examples of Occupations
Upper	< 1	> $1 million	Prestigious prep schools, colleges	Corporate executives with enormous ownership shares in companies
Upper middle	18–20	$75,000–$1 million	College, postgraduate training	Physicians, attorneys, engineers, scientists, professors
Lower middle*	20–30	$35,000–$75,000	High school, some college degrees	Middle managers, nurses, skilled technicians, craftspersons, retail sales workers, police, firefighters, public school teachers, small business owners
Working*	25–30	$25,000–$40,000	High school, some college	Skilled and semiskilled factory workers, bank tellers, truck drivers, routine computer programmers, postal workers
Working poor	12–15	$12,000–$15,000	Jobs require least education	Housekeepers, waiters and waitresses
Underclass	9–10	< $12,000	Varies, but usually low	Unemployed, work "under the table"

*These two are combined in some of the discussion below, due to shared values and lifestyles.

another, the broad categories around "middle class" are much less so.

The Upper Classes

Individuals in the upper classes at the current time are predominantly Anglo-American Protestants who were born into their positions (Kliman & Madsen, 1999; Marger, 1999). In the upper class, according to Marger (1999), income is largely derived from inherited wealth, investments, and/or real estate rather than from wages. Such individuals are likely to hold major shares in large corporations. The occupations they hold are highly esteemed in society. Individuals in this class have significant authority and make important societal decisions, such as creating corporate or public policy and making large-scale financial deals. These are the "blue blood" families in society. Past President George W. Bush, for example, was born into an upper-class family.

The Upper Middle Classes

Upper-middle-class occupations include the professions and upper management positions that command a high degree of respect, such as physicians, attorneys, college professors, and corporate CEOs. This segment of the middle class generally has greater income, occupational prestige, and social power than do those in the classes below it. The number of individuals who occupy this class is steadily rising (Abramowitz & Teixeira, 2009). Small business owners, defined as those who employ 100–500 employees, may also fall into this category (Zweig, 2000).

The Lower Middle and Working Classes

Unlike some sociologists, Marger (1999) does not designate a middle middle class. However, throughout the world, individuals who are not at either of the extremes of wealth tend to place themselves in a middle category (M. D. R. Evans & Kelley, 2004).

The lower middle and working classes are the least clearly definable and most diverse (Gorman, 1998). While many have attended some college, the percentage of college graduates in this group is far below that of the upper middle class. The working class may include a broad range of occupations of both blue and white collar workers. Jobs tend to be relatively routine and procedure driven, with little opportunity for creativity or innovation and little authority. Working-class occupations include licensed practical nurse, receptionist, trash collector, plumber, police officer, customer service representative, and technical help desk personnel. Incomes are generally below society's median. Most lower-middle- and working-class individuals are paid an hourly wage rather than an annual or monthly salary.

The Poor: Working Poor and Underclass

The poor, or lower class, are defined as individuals or families whose income or assets fall either below the official U.S. government poverty line or slightly above it. There are two categories of poor people: the working poor and the underclass. These groups are disproportionately female, less educated, and with children (Brady, Fullerton, & Cross, 2010; Kalleberg, 2007; U.S. Department of Labor, 2007).

The Working Poor

While the poor may include those who depend on social or other services for their existence, the working poor are those who are poor but who work at jobs. Working poor families are those who receive inadequate income despite long and irregular work hours (Newman & Chin, 2003). Their jobs require the least education, are the least desirable, and are the least skilled. Sample jobs include restaurant servers and day laborers. While poor and working poor families are often lumped together, there are four times more working poor than poor families (Brady et al., 2010; Caputo, 2007; Newman & Chin, 2003). The working poor may be less visible in society, and they have historically been concentrated in inner cities and rural areas. A more recent trend, however, indicates that more than one-quarter of all families in this category reside in suburban neighborhoods (Kneebone & Garr, 2011). Working poverty is a particularly American problem. The United States has much higher rates of working poverty (more than 2.7 standard deviations higher) than 18 affluent societies (Brady et al., 2010).

The Poor or Underclass

Members of the underclass primarily derive their income from social services. They may also operate on the margins of the mainstream economy, for example, working "under the table" or doing odd jobs. Economic security is tenuous and temporary, as it may be partly derived from illegal work activities (Kliman, 1998). Although all ethnicities are represented, the highest absolute number of those in the underclass are white. However, African Americans living in urban areas are disproportionately represented in the underclass, given their total numbers in the population (Marger, 1999).

These categories describe approximate descriptions of access to material resources. They can also be thought of as labels that tell us very little about the daily lives of individuals or their families (Liu, Soleck, et al., 2004). Life stories are molded by one's earnings, type of job, amount and type of education, when one works, options for retirement, what one pays for or does for oneself, and who cares for elderly or infirm family members. These circumstances represent the contextual nature, or environmental influences, of class that are discussed in the upcoming section of this chapter.

Before continuing, complete Activity 13.1. Your instructor may ask you to discuss your responses in small groups. The activity will be more useful if it is begun outside of class time.

Activity 13.1   Identifying Your Social Class of Origin

Begin by drawing a genogram on a large piece of paper. A genogram is a family tree in which you graphically identify members of your family. Individuals are represented by symbols: circles for women, squares for men.

Go back as far as you can. For each person in your family, identify the following information and place it next to the person's symbol:

Education level attained

Occupation

Income

Source(s) of income (e.g., jobs, investments, social service, financially dependent on others)

At what age did each person retire? (Or did they retire?)

Next, review your genogram and respond in writing to the following questions:

Which class grouping best describes your family of origin?

Does your family fit into more than one category?

Did your grandparents, parents, or other family members grow up in a different class from your parents?

If so, which best describes their class position(s)?

As you may have noticed during the genogram activity, identifying your family's class is not as simple as it first appears. Different family members may fall into different classes; the entire family may have changed class positions over one or more generations, or one or more family members may have changed their class by attaining higher, or lower, education levels than others in the family. In the latter case, it is not uncommon for individuals to have strained relationships with the family due to changes in income or their values, although individual families experience these issues differently.

One's place in the objective class structure described above shapes lives in many ways, including what people expect out of life, the timing of life course events, what values they embrace (or not), the lifestyle choices they make, and how they feel about themselves (Lawler, 2005). The second major topic in this section describes the subjective experience of class and its implications.

The Subjective Dimensions of Class

This refers to the internalized notion of what class one belongs to as well as the adoption of class-related values. Sometimes choices are related to access to resources and money (such as attending college), while others are related to peer influence (such as choice of leisure activities; Kliman & Madsen, 1999; Pinderhughes, Dodge, Bates, Pettit, & Zelli, 2000). Peer influence is important because it is human nature to want to be respected by those we value and with whom we associate. Fundamentally, social class, in experience terms, is about value judgments. Individuals judge behavior, possessions, or cultural practices based on some valuation of what is respectable or desirable. Values are class-related because what appears to be respectable to one group of people may be dismissed by another group as something to be ashamed of (Edensor & Millington, 2009). For example, lawn decorations or styles of clothing valued by those in one class may seem gaudy to someone in another class. When one does not feel respected or respectable relative to such

values, a sense of shame ensues. This situation may occur when someone from a lower-class position, through education, occupation, or financial success, crosses class lines to a higher-class position and now moves into new social circles. That person may become ashamed of her or his families of origin or former neighborhoods. This situation is discussed in the upcoming section on changing class status.

Class in Context

Context refers to the setting for an event, idea, or experience from which it can be understood. The contextual dimensions of class are subjective and cultural; that is, attitudes, values, goals, and practices of everyday existence are shared by people who occupy the same social space. These values are transmitted from generation to generation. When referring to social class, context includes access to resources, working conditions, and other pressures that lend meaning to life events. This section first presents a discussion of the multiple identities that comprise the context of clients' lives. That is followed by discussions of some of the cultural dimensions of class, where experiences of marriage; childhood and parenting; and education, career, and work life are experienced differently by those who occupy different class positions.

The Context of Multiple Identities

Individuals have multiple social memberships out of which they internalize a personal and cultural identity. Social class is interwoven into other identities, such as race, age, and gender, that comprise social membership and cannot be understood, except stereotypically, by reference to any one of these identities by itself. For example, equally educated men and women of different races have different chances of getting a mortgage, living to old age, or earning a living wage. These facts have to do with differential access to bank loans, health care, and education. In the area of gender, responsibility for an ailing elder parent may fall to adult children of either gender, but statistically it most often falls to women as daughters, daughters-in-law, or wives. Further, class does not determine the caregiving alone, and gender alone is not an explanation of opportunities and attitudes. Whereas a middle- or upper-class woman may be able to hire someone to help with care, a working-class or poor woman may not have that opportunity. That means the working-class or poor woman must take time off from work, resulting in lower earnings or increased work–family conflict (Ammons & Kelly, 2008). She would experience more stress and fatigue because she would need to both work and take care of relatives during her off-work hours. Thus a woman's experience of the burden of care for family members is experienced differently in families with and without economic means. Another example of the intersection of identities is the way in which race and ethnicity interact with social class. There is common wisdom about a shared endorsement of the Protestant work ethic for the middle and working classes (Bellah, Madsen, Sullivan, Swidler, & Tipton, 1996) that does not necessarily hold true for black men. Contextually, a plausible explanation lies in the fact that while white men have historically experienced a strong positive relationship between working hard and achieving success, the life experiences of black men have typically included racism and discrimination. Hard work has not generally led to the same rewards.

Cultural Patterns and Lifestyle Perspectives in the Context of Class

Counselors need to understand the subjective and cultural dimensions of individuals from all class backgrounds in order to fully appreciate the norms, expectations, sources of stress, and aspirations they are facing. Attitudes, values, and behaviors relating to family life, education, career, and work life are also embedded in the context of class. There are two important points to consider, however, in attempting to classify class-embedded values, lifestyles, and behaviors. The first is that the literature has not always looked at people on their own terms, from their own perspectives, to depict how their actions reflect meaningful behaviors in their own context. Instead, it has been fraught with prior assumptions and potential bias on the part of the researchers that middle-class or upper-middle-class ways are judged to be better. In that regard, some recent qualitative inquiries have emerged that suggest that the meanings and values of such institutions as marriage, parenting, children's experiences, and attitudes toward education are not as dissimilar as once thought (Luthar & Latendresse, 2005). How they are played out in everyday life, however, becomes part of the class story.

The second factor to consider when thinking about purported class differences is that classed perspectives are constantly evolving as individuals negotiate the dynamics of ever-changing social, cultural, and economic conditions. What is presented here may change with time as social conditions and attitudes shift. With this in mind, we offer the following summaries of what the literature has reported on class-based cultural patterns and lifestyles, perspectives on family life, childhood and parenting, education, and career development and work life issues. It is important to emphasize that, while there may be some shared and common experiences and meanings, a family's experiences, values, and decisions may be lived out in very different ways. What is presented here is the most recent literature describing class-based perspectives on marriage and family life, parenting, children's experiences, and orientation toward education and careers.

FAMILY LIFE IN THE CONTEXT OF CLASS

This section presents what is currently known about values, attitudes, and expectations associated with family life, education, work, and career.

Marriage in the Context of Class

Attitudes toward and experiences within marriage are affected by class. It stands to reason that there would be different stresses on a family that falls below the poverty line than on one that is concerned with maintaining generations of inherited wealth. On the lower end of the scale, working-class and poor women rely on marriage or domestic partnerships for economic survival (Wells & Zinn, 2004). Yet women in lower classes are half as likely to be married, twice as likely to be divorced if married, and several times more likely to raise children outside of marriage. Single parents struggle financially, and those in the lower classes, particularly women and families of color, have been disproportionately affected by the economic recession that began in 2008 (Conger, Conger, & Martin, 2010). Because of their lower marriage rates, earlier research had incorrectly assumed that those in lower and working classes didn't value marriage and that they lacked skills to resolve marital disputes. However, it is now known that marriages are more threatened not by a lack of conflict resolution skills, but by the degree of stress a couple may experience. Couples of any class have difficulty using conflict resolution skills in the presence of high stress generated by outside demands.

Because disposable income is typically lower than for those in the middle and upper classes, working-class parents often sacrifice their own wants and needs to provide for their children (Shelvin, Zandy, & Smith, 1999). They may also find themselves caring for an elderly parent, since they do not often have the financial resources to hire help. This puts further strain on the working class and poor, particularly women, because they must both work to earn a living and care for family members (Gerstel, 2011). They develop a mutual dependence on friends and relatives to help them with these issues. A positive aspect of this situation is that those in the poor and working class often develop deep social relationships that the wealthy do not generally experience (Luthar & Latendresse, 2002).

Middle-class families are certainly not immune to economic downturns, but they may be less affected than the poor. Many families have accumulated sufficient reserves, so they can continue to choose to live in family-friendly neighborhoods with access to good schools and other neighborhood resources. However, as numbers of families in the middle class continue to shrink, these families may also begin to find themselves struggling financially (Abramowitz & Teixeira, 2009). Middle-class marriages endorse more egalitarian ideals than those in working-class (Stillson, O'Neil, & Owen, 1991) or upper-class families (Wolfe & Fodor, 1996). Women may work in careers that allow them some degree of financial independence. This may lead to other stresses, a topic that is discussed in the section on careers and work life.

It is important for upper-class families to ensure that their image is congruent with their status in society. Upper-class marriages operate to manage their existing wealth and status. These marriages are reported to be quite patriarchal. The husband has greater business, government, social, and marital power and may control the wife's access to money and require her to account for her expenditures. The division of labor tends to be rather rigid. Men are responsible for managing the family's fortunes, and women maintain a high public profile, often through charity work. The wife is also expected to manage the household and the children, arrange their social and home life, accompany her husband on business or social trips, and entertain lavishly (Luthar & Latendresse, 2005; Wolfe & Fodor, 1996). All of these activities are oriented toward maintaining the family's position, and husband and wife have different roles in this endeavor.

Parenting Styles in the Context of Class

A second aspect of family life in the context of class culture is related to raising children. Parents in different classes are reported to have contrasting parenting styles. In the area of discipline, working-class and poor parents are more authoritarian; that is, they tend to use directives rather than reasoning, use physical punishment, and restrict the actions of their children. Children in these families typically do not argue with parents. These behaviors ostensibly prepare working-class children to succeed in subordinate adult work roles (Luster, Rhoades, & Haas, 1989; Minton, Shell, & Solomon, 2004).

Middle-class parents, by contrast, generally value their children being curious and self-directed, and want them to demonstrate self-control, responsibility, competence, and achievement (Luster et al., 1989; Minton, Shell, & Solomon, 2004). To achieve these objectives, they are more likely to have discussions with their children rather than demand obedience. They teach their children to be assertive, and children are free to argue or disagree with parents. These characteristics prepare them to succeed in management and professional occupations.

Recent investigations have begun to question some of these long-held assumptions about differences in childrearing practices. Disciplinary practices were found to be more similar than different when parent behavior was directly observed by the researcher rather than characterized based on parents' self-report. While it might appear that middle-class parents negotiate rules with their children, they actually use subtle coercion to encourage them to make specific choices that encourage talents and skills. Conversely, contrary to being authoritarian, working-class parents actually give their children a great deal of autonomy in specific areas, such as in their leisure activities. Being aware of the subtleties of childrearing practices can help counselors understand the complexity of childrearing value systems and thereby avoid value judgments that may arise from assuming that middle-class childrearing practices are superior.

Experience of Childhood and Adolescence in the Context of Class

Children have different experiences in the family, depending on the family's social class. How children spend their time, contributions they are expected to make to the family, and behavioral issues developed from within the context of class are presented next.

Lower-class children spend much more time than middle-class children in leisurely, spontaneous, informal activities—hanging out with friends and relatives, watching television, and playing unorganized games. Middle-class children, on the other hand, tend to have very hectic schedules and spend much more time in organized activities that are related to performance and skill building (Lareau, 2002). Affluent adolescents are often left home alone for several hours each week, with many parents believing that this promotes self-sufficiency (Luthar & Latendresse, 2005). This sometimes results in feelings of loneliness for these teens, feelings that are linked with problem behaviors, which is discussed below.

Class affects young persons' work responsibilities. In the working and poor classes, older children often carry responsibilities for housework and for younger siblings. This is necessary because parental wages are so low that childcare is unaffordable, or because the family's cultural background presumes the involvement of older siblings and extended kin (aunts, uncles, cousins) in the care of dependent children and elders. Lower-middle- and working-class teens often work to pay for expenses through high school (Kliman & Madsen, 1999). They may even contribute financially to the family.

By contrast, upper-middle- and middle-class adolescents are relatively free of serious family or work obligations, although they may work for luxuries. One key characteristic of the upper class is that youth are supported primarily by trust funds rather than through parental wages. Thus, children may have little concern about earning a wage income or learning daily money management or domestic skills. However, financial support may be coupled with family expectations and obligations, and children can be threatened with disinheritance for not carrying out parents' choices of schools, careers, or marriage partners (Wolfe & Fodor, 1996).

Children and youth from all classes sometimes exhibit problems. Children in financially stressed families are said to experience greater psychological and behavioral problems, which further impact the functioning of the adults in the household. Poor and minority children get more serious consequences for behavioral disruptions in school than their more affluent peers (Boroughs, Massey, & Armstrong (2005).

Affluent adolescents are not immune to emotional and behavioral problems. They demonstrate significantly higher instances of self-injury (Yates, Tracey, & Luthar, 2008), drug and alcohol use, depression, anxiety, and eating disorders when compared to the general population (Luthar & Latendresse, 2005). The link is particularly strong when adolescents believe that their parents value their accomplishments more than their personal character or when children's needs for emotional closeness suffer when professional parents' careers displace quality family time (Luthar & Latendresse, 2005).

Adolescents at both socioeconomic extremes admire classmates who openly flout authority. The consequences, however, are different for poor and affluent youth who engage in potentially destructive behaviors. Wealthy youth have sufficient safety nets that are derived from their socially privileged position; drug use or delinquency does not end up compromising their life prospects (Luthar & Latendresse, 2005). This would not be true for poor and working-class youth, whose relative lack of social privilege may combine with racism to create damaging outcomes for similar behavior.

Transition to Adulthood

How long and when children stay in the family home is also related to class. Poor youth frequently live with extended family to pool resources while they transition to adulthood. Members of the lower social classes are likely to make a transition directly from secondary school to work or to entering the military (Blustein et al., 2002). Poor and working-class children are considered adults when they marry and/or get full-time employment, which could come as early as age 16 (Kliman & Madsen, 1999). Parents with limited resources may look forward to relieving their financial load. Thus, the sooner a working-class young person can start to earn a living, the fewer financial stresses there will be on the family. This trend is changing, however, with recent changes in the economy. Young adults in both working-class and middle-class families are living with extended family for longer periods of time in order to save enough money to be independent. Middle-class children typically leave home to attend college, whereas children in upper-class families may leave home for boarding school or for travel.

Education in the Context of Class

Continuing the theme of the contextual implications of class, attitudes toward and experiences with education can be radically different among the social classes. The poor sometimes have difficult relationships with educational institutions. This may be due to external or internal barriers that keep them from becoming involved, attitudes and biases of educators toward lower-class individuals, or values differences between the culture of school and the culture of the home. Some external barriers to being involved in children's schooling are very basic. Low-income parents often lack transportation and have inflexible work schedules, making it difficult to meet with teachers (Heymann, 2000; Newman & Chin, 2003) or attend school functions. They may lose wages or be threatened with termination if they miss work to attend a school meeting.

There are also internal barriers to schooling. Working-class and poor parents may have had their own difficulties with school. These parents often feel excluded from and resentful of schools and academic learning (Diamond & Gomez, 2004; McNeely, Nonnemaker, & Blum, 2002). Sometimes formal education is not valued, since abstract school subjects might be considered irrelevant because they do not relate to getting along in life. The experiences and worldviews of poor families are frequently at odds with the middle-class culture of schools. As a result, some families feel misunderstood and believe that their children are perceived as inferior by teachers. Consequently, poor and working-class parents may become confrontational with school personnel in order to protect their children from such perceptions or to assert the value of their own local knowledge. Unless school personnel are class-alert, reproduction of class-based exclusion of such parents may occur.

Those in the lower middle and working class have historically valued basic education as a means to achieving a good job more than as a source of personal fulfillment. Working-class parents are more interested in their children blending in with others and staying out of trouble (Gillies, 2011). Given their realistic and pragmatic orientation, too much education may even be looked down on in working-class families (Gorman, 1998; Shelvin et al., 1999). Because some lower-middle- and working-class families resist class mobility (Gorman, 1998), attending college can become a source of family tension, as it introduces fear of leaving family behind in favor of moving toward new opportunities and nonshared knowledges. On the other hand, many working-class and poor families do value education and believe in nurturing their children's talents. However, they may lack the financial resources to provide their children with expensive extracurricular activities or academic enrichment (Chin & Phillips, 2004). Middle-class parents, regardless of ethnicity, value reading and literacy (Bialostok, 2002; Haynes, 2000) and are actively involved in their children's schooling (Diamond, & Gomez, 2004; Gillies, 2005; McNeely et al., 2002). In their interactions with teachers, middle-class parents stress their children's uniqueness and individuality. They expect their children to attend college and assist them in meeting competitive standards for college admissions. In that vein, if the children are having academic difficulties, middle-class parents call on their social and cultural resources to give their children special help, such as tutoring or enrichment.

Upper-class children are expected to attend the best private schools and universities. Admission to such institutions is often guaranteed through family name and connections rather than only through academic achievement (Wolfe & Fodor, 1996).

Trends in education regarding class may be changing, with the working and middle classes converging. With more competition in the labor market, increasing numbers of working-class youth are out of necessity pursuing higher education, financing themselves through loans (Kliman & Madsen, 1999). For example, working-class Annie, in the second vignette, sought upward class mobility. Her family did not know how to help her, nor

did they have the financial resources or the cultural capital to do so. Therefore, she paid her own way at the local state 4-year college and incurred considerable debt. Working- and middle-class families alike are being affected by the prohibitive costs of higher education in relation to job earnings potential in a depressed economy (Barton, 2008; Whitaker & Zenker, 2011). Families are considering the cost-benefit ratio of a 4-year liberal arts education versus career-focused preparation at community colleges with transfer options to reduce financial burdens.

Career Development and Work–Life Issues in the Context of Class

It is important that counselors understand how occupation and work are both affected by, and affect, social class experiences, as these issues are likely to present themselves often in counseling.

Career Choices

Occupational security and predictability predominate over self-fulfillment for the working class and working poor (Chaves et al., 2004). They may therefore take whatever jobs are open and available rather than plan a career. This perspective fits with the nature of jobs that poor persons see around them and can be reflected psychologically in a learned fatalism (e.g., the belief that control is external rather internal to the self). For working-class individuals, work may be more of a means to an end than a statement of identity. They have high respect for nonprofessional businesses or trades, including the tools and the skills it takes to maintain these properly (Shelvin et al., 1999).

Career choices for the middle class tend to be based on criteria of self-fulfillment, good pay, and career progression (Lapour & Heppner, 2009). Work provides a sense of identity and is an expression of interests and values, which is not necessarily the case for those in lower classes. A middle-class individual may value a professional occupation rather than a trade. Young middle-class women are expected to pursue careers and to be financially independent (Dickerson, 2004).

Work–Family Issues

Women in all classes remain primarily responsible for maintaining children and the family. Counselors may encounter issues with women who experience role conflict and divided loyalties. When women work, they find themselves attending to both responsibilities. Middle-class, working-class, and poor mothers, however, have very different experiences around these issues.

Out of economic necessity, both parents in intact working-class and poor families are usually employed even though they would prefer to be home with their children (Hennessy, 2009a; Wells & Zinn, 2004). Poor black women generally expect to have to work to support themselves due to the effects of institutional racism on the employment and longevity chances of poor black men (Wells & Zinn, 2004). When women work out of necessity at jobs that are not particularly interesting, they tend to value work for the friendships and relationships they form rather than for the intrinsic value of the work itself (James, 2008). Working-class and poor women with young children are more likely to sacrifice work time when there are family problems to attend to (Ammons & Kelly, 2008).

Middle-class women are more likely to work in a professional career. In contrast to poorer women, they prefer to direct more time and energy toward their careers than toward family issues (Hennessy, 2009a, 2009b; James, 2008) and are more likely to sacrifice family time to tend to work matters (Ammons & Kelly, 2008). There may be some disadvantages to this arrangement for them, however. Despite more egalitarian gender roles in middle-class families, much of the responsibility for home life continues to fall upon women. When they struggle to meet all these demands, they experience conflict as they try to balance work and family roles (Ammons & Kelly, 2008; Dickerson, 2004; James, 2008).

Culturally alert counselors should become familiar with career orientation and related stresses associated with all classes, as these issues are likely to arise when working with clients, students, and parents in all counseling settings.

CHANGE IN CLASS STATUS

Upward class mobility is a value in American culture. It is common (although by no means universal) for parents to want their children to raise themselves to a higher class than they themselves have attained. Class mobility is achieved ostensibly through the hard work that leads to higher education and career success. Yet even those who have worked hard, obtained a degree, and otherwise looked forward to the future have found themselves falling further behind.

One problem with the ideology of upward mobility lies with the ethos of individualism, which declares that if one works hard, one can achieve upward social class mobility. There are at least two overall reasons for questioning the assumptions surrounding mobility: (1) the nature of the labor market and (2) inequity in opportunity. Mobility is not due solely to individual characteristics, but rather to a number of factors, including the structure of the labor market (Shin, 2007). If one were to look at the U.S. Bureau of Labor Statistics (2012) list of the 30 projected largest-growing occupations into the year 2020, only 8 require education above an associate's degree, with 22 requiring only on-the-job training. The latter are also the lowest-paid occupations. While there may be occupations requiring college degrees that are growing at a faster rate, in many cases these are the occupations with the fewest number of workers. Thus, the actual number of available jobs are overwhelmingly located in the lowest-paid sectors.

A second problem with the individualist ethos lies in the fact that the chances for upward mobility are not equal. Because the effects of social class and other statuses intersect, African Americans, immigrants, and other minority groups, regardless of class, do not have equal opportunities to become mobile (Hardaway & McLoyd, 2009; Nelson, Englar-Carlson, Tierney, & Hau, 2006; Pais, 2011; Wagmiller, Kuang, Aber, Lennon, &

Alberti, 2006). In particular, racism affects the context in which children develop, which in turn affects the quality and quantity of education, mentorship, and other cultural resources. This in turn affects the attitudes needed for achievement in schooling. Factors such as these contribute to a lesser chance of upward mobility (Cole & Omari, 2003; Hardaway & McLoyd, 2009). Further barriers include the disproportionate costs for those in the lower social classes to attend college (Bloom, 2007), both in economic and in emotional terms (Cole & Omari, 2003; Hardaway & McLoyd, 2009; Lehmann, 2009). For many in the lower and working classes, it is safer to pursue the aspirations and lifestyles that are familiar than to risk the costs, particularly when they don't believe that it will lead to better outcomes.

Costs of Upward Mobility

The subjective dimension of class is especially important for counselors, as it is infused with a person's identity, values, aspirations, and expectations. Core values common in the working class include a strong work ethic, provider orientation (for men), the dignity of all work and workers, and humility (Lucas, 2011). Because individual values and worldviews are learned from within one's class of origin, it can be difficult for those who cross class lines successfully to ever fully unlearn the set of values and perspectives with which they were raised (Liu, Soleck, et al., 2004; Tingle, 2004). In other words, it is possible for an individual to have the subjective values of one class (class of origin), yet, by virtue of income, education, or occupation, to fall into another class (current class). This juxtaposition is particularly true for those who change class positions in adulthood, as many class-related values persist, regardless of changes in income. For example, a janitor with a high school education who grew up in a working-class family and who wins the lottery would probably not feel comfortable at the upper-middle-class country club, despite being able to now afford its yearly membership fees. Conversely, an unemployed engineer who currently works as a clerk at the local hardware store is not likely to change her or his leisure interests and social network merely because of a new economic class position.

Those who cross class lines sometimes exist in a state between two worlds, where they often feel different from the group they have adopted, harbor secret doubts about belonging, feel ashamed, and hide their class background in order to manage a new, tenuous identity (Granfield, 1991). This dissonance may be a particular problem for those who are the first in their families to attend college. They may find themselves at a disadvantage because they have not grown up with middle-class values, yet they find they must learn them in order to succeed and fit in (Jetten, Iyer, Tsivrikos, & Young, 2008). This disjuncture between existing values and new class position can produce tensions and conflicts, both intrapsychically and within families. Counselors might find, for example, that family members might consider a male family member lazy if he was unemployed for an extensive length of time, or that a professional woman carries a sense of shame about her working-class background, resulting in her not feeling comfortable socializing with her new workmates. All of these are examples of some of the problems associated with upward mobility.

Downward Social Mobility

One fact that cannot be ignored is the effects of the global recession of 2008 and the lingering high unemployment rates as of this writing. Families who are newly in the middle class are disproportionately affected by long-term unemployment, because they have accumulated less wealth than those who have been solidly middle or upper middle class for generations. This is particularly true for African Americans, who are more financially vulnerable (Hardaway & McLoyd, 2009) than their white counterparts. More middle-class families are experiencing financial strain, which impacts their quality of life.

This discussion regarding the contextual dimensions of class perceptions, experiences, values, and attitudes forms the basis for the next major section, which is a discussion of classism. Fundamentally, class is about value judgments, where the values and attitudes of the middle and upper classes are presumed to be better, while those of the poor and working classes are problematic. Before reading the next section, complete Activity 13.2 to gain a sense of your family's class-based stories.

Activity 13.2   The Class Genogram

The first genogram activity (Activity 13.1) served as a graphic way to locate you and your family within the patterned social class structure. Yet class identity is more than what people in your family did for a living or how much money they earned; it is also how they communicated who you were and where you belonged in the social picture. You can continue to explore your family's class context by reflecting on the stories that have come down to you and what values you have internalized. Looking back at your genogram, answer the following questions. Once you have jotted down some answers, discuss what you learned in small groups.

What occupations are respected in your family? Why?

What occupations are not respected? Why?

Did anyone ever hold a job that was not respected? If so, what was the family's "story" about that person?

How did people talk about the contribution of their work, or how work fit in with the greater good of society?

What did your family believe constituted a "good" education? Were there different views among members of your family?

How were the elderly or chronically ill members of the family taken care of?

What were moments when social class awareness was heightened in your family? (For example, were there any instances of changed circumstances, marrying up or down, a family member attaining an educational level different from the family norm, being unemployed or underemployed?)

How did family members react?

Relate what you have discovered from the above questions with what you have just read in the text. How has social class become a lived experience, full of tensions, contradictions, and stories that change over time?

CLASSISM

Now that the definitions and descriptions of class have been discussed, we present the topic of classism. The misuse of hierarchy and power were discussed in Chapter 3, under the topic of oppression. Classism is one version of oppression. Classism can take three forms: (1) external, in the form of a person's attitudes and behaviors toward another who is of a different class; (2) internalized; and (3) institutionalized. This section begins with a discussion of external classism and then moves on to descriptions and examples of internalized and institutional classism. Before reading further, complete Activity 13.3.

Activity 13.3   What Is Your Response to This Story?

Read the following scenario. Notice your reactions, perhaps relating it to a similar situation that you might have encountered.

Laura is a 34-year-old single mother of three school-age children. She is participating in a support group for women who are adult survivors of sexual abuse. She is the only woman in the group who is receiving welfare benefits. The other participants either work outside the home or have partners who provide financially for the family. Laura mentioned that she would not be attending the next group session because she was taking her children on a beach vacation before school starts again. Two of the other women clearly resented the fact that Laura was able to plan a vacation trip. They considered themselves to be self-sufficient. As they saw it, they had worked hard, put themselves through graduate school, and were paying off student loans. They couldn't currently afford such luxuries. You, as a counseling intern, have been working as the facilitator of this group for 4 months and have in fact not been able to afford to treat yourself to a movie and dinner out for quite some time, and you are also paying off your student loans. You are exhausted from putting in internship hours while also working at a job that pays very little. Your resentment starts to interfere with your ability to provide Laura with the support, respect, and positive regard she needs. One woman said exactly what you were thinking: "I can never afford such extravagance."

1. What was your initial reaction to Laura's statement that she planned to go on vacation?

2. Did you feel somewhat critical of her decision to use her economic resources in this way?

3. Have there been times when you've been unable to offer support for and respect to others because of the decisions they have made? Please describe.

4. What alternative explanations would change the significance of this story for you?

External Classism

External classism refers to negative prejudice and discrimination on the part of an individual from one class toward one of another class. It occurs when one holds negative stereotypes and discriminates against those of lower social classes. It may include making jokes at the expense of the poor or assuming that workers in low-status jobs are stupid, uneducated, unworthy of respect, irresponsible, hostile, or illogical (Lott & Saxon, 2002). All of these perceptions have their basis in stereotypes and can have serious negative social implications in schools, the workplace, and society in general.

Classism in America is related to the American ethos of individualism, which accounts for success in mostly individual terms, rather than acknowledging the social dimension of class status. Americans in general expect upward social mobility (Bellah et al., 1996). The characteristics that are assumed to contribute to moving up, such as having a focus on the future, delayed gratification, abstract reasoning, doing well in school, and getting a college degree, are classist. People who believe strongly in merit have little sympathy for other people's failures. Yet individuals in the middle or upper classes are more likely to have privilege in the form of sufficient material and cultural (and therefore internalized) resources to enable them to reap these rewards. If someone doesn't succeed, it is assumed that she or he is lazy or deficient in some way rather than affected by systematic social structural factors. These factors include access to jobs, education, and informal groups that are set up to favor members of one group over the other in different ways, as discussed in Chapters 3 and 5. Those attitudes in turn affect social policy, such as having or not having compensatory financial aid and academic assistance programs in schools and colleges.

Internalized Classism

Internalized classism refers to the process by which individuals come to believe negative attributes about their class and themselves as members of that class. It occurs when dominant class groups present the models for "normal" human relationships and presume other class-related lifestyles and attitudes have less value. Members of subordinate class groups subsequently find it difficult to believe in their own abilities (Liu, Ali, et al., 2004).

Internalized classism influences self-concept and relationships with others. For example, children come to believe in their own abilities through classroom experiences. When educational values between parents and teachers differ, teachers see children as less competent, treat them accordingly (Hauser-Cram, Sirin, & Stipek, 2003), and hold lower expectations for academic success (Alexander, Entwisle, & Thompson, 1987). These lower expectations become internalized. Poor and working-class children then expect less from themselves and perform to those expectations, resulting in a self-fulfilling prophecy.

Institutional Classism

The class dominance that becomes embedded in the social structure and perpetuates class inequality is called institutional classism. Upper- and middle-class groups make the most of the policy decisions relative to the distribution of resources. These policies and the rationales that justify them systematically provide advantages to the upper and middle classes over working-class and poor persons. An example of a rationale is when corporate executives justify receiving millions in compensation in the face of their firm's financial collapse by reasoning that they somehow represent superior talent that deserves such high pay.

Institutional Classism in Public Policy

Public policies and funding decisions, which are partly based on individual voters' and politicians' attitudes, are set up to systematically favor those in higher classes and thereby disproportionately affect the poor and working class in a negative way. Examples of institutional classism in government can be found when governments provide poorer municipal services to low-income neighborhoods, resulting in greater physical deterioration (G. Evans, 2004). Or it can be as simple as building private beachfront property with no public access, so that poorer persons are excluded from those facilities. Classism is also present when tax codes favor unearned income or when government watchdogs target Medicaid recipients for fraud but do not do so equally for the service providers who file false claims. Another instance of classism occurs when middle-class families can legally transfer assets while remaining eligible for Medicaid funding in nursing homes, yet basic health services for the poor are reduced (Wegner & Yuan, 2004).

Institutional Classism in Education

Examples of institutional classism can be found in schools and colleges. Due to disparities in school funding, school districts attended by poor and minority children receive far less money than the districts that serve mostly white and more affluent children (Education Trust, 2005). Poor schools are staffed by fewer well-qualified teachers. For example, 27% of high school math teachers in low-income school districts majored in mathematics in college, compared with 43% of those in more affluent school districts (Ingersoll, 1999).

There is a similar trend for colleges, which increasingly award financial aid to more affluent students. From 1995 to 2003, college grants to students with family incomes of more than $100,000 increased at a faster rate than to students with family incomes of less than $20,000. When colleges succumb to pressure to inflate their average SAT scores and *U.S. News & World Report* rankings, they make admission decisions that favor the very best students, most of whom are from highly educated, affluent households, at the expense of low-income peers (Hancock, 2006; Nichol, 2003).

Class position wends its way into all aspects of a person's life, including experiences of mental health or distress. Thus class has profound implications for counselors. The following sections review some class differences in the prevalence, prognosis, and symptoms of mental disorders and some possible explanations for these observations.

MENTAL HEALTH AND CLASS DIFFERENCES

Social class and mental health are related. Some disorders are found to be more prevalent in the lower classes, and sometimes the symptoms of the same disorders are experienced differently by those in different classes. This section presents the prevalence of disorders by class as well as some of the explanations for the differences in the experience of those disorders.

Prevalence of Disorders

Strong associations between socioeconomic position, illness, and mortality have been observed dating back to ancient Greece and Egypt (Krieger, Williams, & Moss, 1997). This observation remains true today. Virtually all indicators of physical and mental health favor persons of higher socioeconomic status. Blue-collar workers experience more psychological distress than do white-collar workers (Belek, 2000). Poorer persons get sicker more often, for longer periods, and with more serious consequences than do people with means (Demakakos, Nazroo, Breeze, & Marmot, 2008; Green & Benzeval, 2011; Lund et al., 2010; Ozawa & Yeo, 2008; Tucker & Dixon, 2009). Further, such effects are cumulative, with the greatest risk occurring for those who have experienced hardship over a sustained period of time (G. Evans, 2004).

Counselors should be aware of the relationship between social class and health so that they can understand the class-related hardships faced by some of their clients. For example, counselors in all settings should be aware that adults and children in lower social classes experience higher rates of depression, anxiety, substance abuse, and antisocial behavior. They are also more likely to have problems in at least three areas: severe disorders requiring hospitalization, higher injury rates, and higher rates of school absences due to ear or respiratory infections (Chen, Matthews, & Boyce, 2002). Table 13.2 presents a summary of some correlations between various disorders and social class.

Table 13.2 Social Class and Mental Disorders

Major Findings	Authors	Variables
Low income and low SES are associated with high rates of mental disorder, chronic diseases, depression, anxiety, and diabetes.	Demakakos, Nazroo, Breeze, & Marmot, 2008; Everson, Maty, Lynch, & Kaplan, 2002; Green & Benzeval, 2011; Lewis et al., 2003; Norman, 2004; Ozawa & Yeo, 2008; Tucker & Dixon, 2009	Depression, anxiety, chronic diseases, and SES
Alcohol regulates feelings of anxiety and depression, substance abuse is influenced by culture and class.	Nichter, 2003; Wiles et al., 2007	Substance use in lower classes
50% of upper-middle- and upper-class adults are frequent drinkers, compared to 30% of general population; affluent children engage in high substance use.	Luthar & Latendresse, 2002; Priory Group, 2004	Substance use in upper classes
Anxiety, depression, antisocial disorder, and attention deficit disorder each has a unique relationship with SES.	Miech, Caspi, Moffitt, & Wright, 1999	Depression, antisocial disorder, attention deficit disorder
Obesity is inversely related to social class; lower-class women are more obese than upper-class women; black women are more obese than white women and all men; white men are more obese than white women.	Broom & Warin, 2011; Smith & Holm, 2010; Wardle, Waller, & Jarvis, 2002; Williams, Germov, & Young, 2011	Obesity
Upper-class girls tend to diet, count calories, binge, and engage in vigorous physical exercise, whereas boys and women of color do not.	Drewnowski, Kurth, & Krahn, 1993; Ogden & Thomas, 1999	Dieting behavior and race, class
Serious and chronic anorexia is higher in middle classes.	Darmon, 2009; McClelland & Crisp, 2001	Anorexia nervosa
There is a higher rate of antisocial behavior in lower classes.	Dishion, French, & Patterson, 1995	Antisocial behavior
There are higher suicide rates in males of lower classes.	Kposowa, 2001	Suicide

It can be seen from Table 13.2 that body weight, body image, and eating disorders are related to class, age, race and ethnicity, and gender. Lower-class individuals are generally heavier than those in upper classes. This is significant because severe obesity is thought to cause or aggravate depression (Dixon, Dixon, & O'Brien, 1993; Faith et al., 2011) and can lead to other health problems such as diabetes.

Persons in the upper classes experience many of the same problems as others, which contradicts stereotypes that the wealthy have few difficulties. They can even be disadvantaged in some ways. For example, middle- and upper-class individuals diagnosed with schizophrenia experience more depression and hopelessness when coping with career losses than do lower-class persons. Since they have higher career aspirations (Lewine, 2005), they regret the loss of their potential to a greater extent. Another example of wealth being a disadvantage lies in the case of affluent women with histories of child abuse and domestic violence who feel ashamed to seek help for those problems (Louise, in Vignette 3, experienced this issue). They may instead present with chronic pain syndromes and other psychosomatic complaints (Kendall-Tackett, Marshall, & Ness, 2003) that are less shameful.

Reasons for Class Differences in Mental Health

Several explanations for social class differences in health have been offered. Three common influences of social class are discussed here: the effects of the environment, class-related values, and research and diagnostic bias.

Effects of the Environment

Aversive environments have both direct and indirect effects on health. Those who live in poverty are exposed to more crime, violence, and aggressive peers (Aneshensel & Sucoff, 1996; Evans, 2004). Thus they are at greater risk for physical and psychological problems due to the quality of these environments (Pilisuk, 1998). The more threatening the neighborhood, the more common are symptoms of depression, anxiety, oppositional defiant disorder, and conduct disorder (Aneshensel & Sucoff, 1996).

The environment affects physical health directly when poor children live in substandard housing. For example, they are more likely to ingest paint chips contaminated with lead. Lead is a known toxin that has adverse effects on intellectual, neurological, and behavioral development. Poor and working-class families are also more likely to live near industrial sites, where industrial pollution and hazardous waste have a direct negative impact on physical and mental health (Downey & van Willigen, 2005).

Environments also have indirect effects on health through increased vulnerability to the effects of stress (Hudson, 2005). And such stress is class-related. Lower-class individuals struggle with inadequate resources and difficulties of daily living. This stress can cause tension and frustration, which in turn affect health (Adler, Epel, Castellazzo, & Ickovics, 2000).

Class-Related Values

Class-related values can contribute to emotional distress in any class. For example, in the upper middle class, excessive pressures to achieve and adolescents' isolation from parents, as noted earlier, may contribute to depression and substance abuse (Luthar & Latendresse, 2005). Similarly, upper-middle-class family values and wider social pressures to achieve play a part in the development of disorders such as anorexia nervosa (McClelland & Crisp, 2001).

Research and Diagnostic Bias

Sometimes class differences in mental health can be accounted for by looking at the counselor. In conceptualizing the nature and extent of a client's problem, a counselor can be biased in either a positive or negative way due to social class. For example, the classist assumption that more material wealth is better may lead the counselor to wrongly assume that those from higher classes are in good mental health (Csikszentmihalyi, 1999; Leeder, 1996; Robinson, 1999). Therefore, there may be a tendency to underdiagnose upper-class clients and to overdiagnose those in lower classes. Negative stereotypes held by counselors toward lower-class clients may lead to pathologizing attitudes and behaviors that may be perfectly functional in a classist environment.

In summary, the prevalence, definitions, and symptoms of disorders are infused with cultural meaning and interpreted through the lens of social class. Having depression, diabetes, or schizophrenia, and getting help for these conditions, is a very different experience for wealthy persons than it is for poor persons. In order to counteract classism, counselors must uncover their class-based assumptions and values, beginning with excavating their own class identifications—whether they were raised in the upper, middle, working, or poor class. The next section discusses how these concepts play out in the practice of counseling.

CLASS BIAS IN COUNSELING PRACTICE

Social class is a psychological and social phenomenon that powerfully shapes clients' and counselors' experiences (Constantine, 2002; Kliman, 1998). Until now, the counseling profession has failed to substantively focus on the disparity between counselors' own middle-class/professional culture and the varied class cultures of their clients. This, in turn, has led to at least five middle-class assumptions, or potential biases, that must be accounted for when working with non-middle-class clients: (1) the research that informs counseling theory and practice is objective and unbiased, (2) all mental health issues are intrapsychic, (3) humans are largely self-determining, (4) communication should be extensively verbal, and (5) vulnerability and self-disclosure must be promoted. The nature of these assumptions, as they apply to clients and the counselling process, are reviewed next.

Class-Biased Assumptions

Early literature tended to label lower-class persons as deficient, poorly adjusted, and in need of change. Poor clients were blamed for not following through in counseling, for lacking insight, and for preferring advice and immediate solutions (Baum & Felzer, 1964; Brill & Storrow, 1960). The poor have also been characterized as having intellectual limitations, low creativity, restricted capacity for emotional depth, and lack of impulse control (Lott & Saxon, 2002; Shen & Murray, 1981). These broad generalizations about poor persons ignored the realities of living in stressful environments or experiencing chronic and persistent lack of resources. For example, the poor who drop out of counseling are more likely to lack insurance coverage for mental health treatment (Edlund et al., 2002). The above pronouncements reveal a lack of understanding about daily living in poverty and blame victims for their own problems.

The second class-biased assumption in counseling is that all individual problems are intrapsychic and are rooted in childhood and the family. This presumption can be classist in the sense that responsibility, or sometimes blame, is assigned completely to individuals for problems that may arise from the social context. Consider a father who is a factory worker who works 10-hour days and whose boss is extremely demanding and critical. Upon arrival home after a difficult day at work, he is withdrawn and relaxes in front of the TV rather than playing with his children. A counselor might view him as an uninvolved father who should spend more "quality" time with his children. From his perspective, he is fulfilling his role as a father and financial provider. But he is so stressed and exhausted from hard physical labor and ill treatment at work that he has no physical or emotional resources left to give to his family. A counselor who sees this family or the children would need empathy about the father's plight. With that empathy, the counselor can generate solutions for all members of the family rather than villainize the father.

The third assumption of traditional middle class–based counseling is that people have relatively free choices to determine their lives. This view assumes that clients can and should fully control their lives and their environments, that they should have a goal orientation, and that they need to take action to solve their problems (Katz, 1985). Working-class and poor clients are more likely than others to believe that forces outside themselves control their lives—a phenomenon sometimes called fatalism. Acceptance is countercultural to the American middle-class ethos. However, acceptance, rather than striving, is one functional coping mechanism for working-class and poor persons. Fatalism is often based on generations of very real experiences in which people have had few choices in their lives in areas of work, housing, or public policies that affect them. Counselors must acknowledge that more fatalistic worldview while discussing the notion of relative choice in clients' lives.

The fourth middle-class assumption is that communication must emphasize verbal processing, accompanied by counselor reflective listening. Such a style is more relevant for the dominant white middle class. As noted, those in the lower and working classes are more likely to take a direct, pragmatic approach to communication. Working-class and poor clients usually seek counseling because of extreme emotional distress resulting from a crisis in their lives that needs immediate attention (Chalifoux, 1996; Leeder, 1996). When such urgency is present, clients look for a problem-solving approach that will help them manage their lives rather than seek personal growth or insight into emotional patterns (Chalifoux, 1996; Leeder, 1996).

The fifth assumption of middle-class counseling is that self-disclosure is valuable, even necessary, for problems to be solved. However, the poor are not as likely as the middle class to reveal their vulnerabilities. In fact, it may even be unsafe for some clients to do so. Consider an unmarried mother who is trying to survive with only social service assistance. She would face very real consequences—losing her social service benefits—should she reveal that the father of her children is living with her, providing emotional and financial support. While she may feel guilty about lying to the authorities, this is one of the moral compromises that she must make in order to get her material and emotional needs met at the same time.

Class Bias in the Counseling Relationship

Class differences can affect the ways in which counselors and clients work together. Some of these differences are related to power, and others to class-related values and life experiences. This section presents how some of these differences affect the counseling relationship in a general sense, and then discusses how they may affect counselors specifically in school and mental health settings.

Power

Clients usually enter into counseling in a vulnerable state, and lower-class clients, especially, find themselves in a position where they may feel exposed. Counselors, by default, have greater power in the relationship. For lower-class clients, that power difference is a barrier to engaging with the counselor (Chalifoux, 1996; Schore, 1990). Low-income clients are often embarrassed about seeing a mental health provider (Edlund et al., 2002; Smith, 2008). Seeing a counselor implies that they are deficient in some way, that they are not doing something "right." It can invoke a sense of shame rather than support and contribute to further feelings of disempowerment.

Compromises and Values

Class-alert counselors would recognize the compromises that poor clients must make to survive. For example, a working-class or poor woman may choose to stay in an unhappy marriage to ensure that her children get what they need financially. While a middle-class counselor may earn sufficient income to provide for a family on her or his own, a poor client may not earn enough, even with two incomes, to provide even a basic standard of living. Clients may want confirmation from their counselors of the value of their choices, which are grounded in economic realities. One of these realities may include depending on the assistance of others (Balmforth, 2009; Leeder, 1996).

Shame

Upper-class clients are not immune from the effects of class bias. Similar to the problem of stigma for lower-class clients, problems are often hidden in upper-class families. Because of the upper-class (combined often with Anglo-Protestant) cultural imperative of not making problems public, they are not likely to initiate conversations with either friends or counselors. This might lead counselors to underestimate upper-class clients' difficulties (Wolfe & Fodor, 1996). In addition, counselors who come from middle- or working-class backgrounds may have negative preconceived notions about those in the upper classes, which may affect their ability to provide support. Louise, in this chapter's third vignette, presented herself in counseling as aloof, which might have been interpreted by a class-unaware counselor as a superior attitude rather than as shame or extreme fear of disclosure. In Louise's case, a class-alert assessment revealed severe depression, anxiety, and feelings of worthlessness. This awareness led to Louise getting the help she needed.

The next section addresses some of these issues as they may occur in school and mental health counseling settings.

Class Bias in Schools and School Counseling

Schools sometimes perpetuate classism through pervasive, sometimes subtle, class bias in favor of middle-class norms. This may occur when school counselors selectively attend to middle-class concerns by solely focusing on helping students with the college selection process. For those students who don't have college aspirations, assistance is usually limited to ensuring that graduation requirements have been met, ignoring vocational selection issues altogether. By becoming familiar with options for transition to the world of work,

counselors can consider the vocational aspirations of all students.

In some cases, school personnel make biased, incorrect assumptions about the motivations of lower-class students and their parents. This happens when poor children do not seem motivated to do school work or when parents don't attend school functions. In many cases, survival needs precede education needs. For example, it is difficult for a child to concentrate on school work if she or he is hungry or experiencing domestic violence at home. Even the definition of intelligence itself reflects a class bias. Individuals from lower socioeconomic classes often hold a practical view of intelligence, viewing with suspicion those who are "book smart" but who cannot get by in the everyday world using practical resourcefulness (Leeder, 1996). Counselors would be wise to honor the adaptive intelligence of lower-class persons.

Box 13.1 demonstrates a case in which class differences between school staff and a poor family almost resulted in an inappropriate referral, which could have led to a negative outcome for the entire family had a class-alert counselor not intervened.

Box 13.1 A Class-Conscious School Counseling Intervention

A classic example of class-related problems with basic needs is Alice, a 13-year-old girl whose teachers brought her to the attention of the counselor because she was friendless. She was ostracized because she wore the same dirty outfits day after day, never seemed to wash or comb her hair, and exhibited body odor. Alice's teachers had also referred her to the health office, hoping that if she knew how to practice personal hygiene, including combing her hair, she would be less offensive to her peers and she could then develop a support network. From a middle-class perspective, a regular shower is normative and thus is the standard from which judgments about those living in poverty are made.

School personnel concluded that the parents had neglected their children. School staff pressured them to change their attitudes and behavior, threatening to report the parents to Child Protective Services when no changes were forthcoming.

Fortunately, the school counselor was sensitive to class circumstances and able to understand the child's experiences. It turned out that the family lived in a rented trailer and had no washing machine and no hot water. Alice had been showering at a friend's house, but she didn't feel comfortable imposing on them any more often than once a week.

(Continued)

During a home visit, the counselor learned that the parents were loving toward their children. However, they didn't always have enough money to pay their rent in a timely manner and the landlord had neglected, in turn, to repair the hot water heater. Thus the family had lived without hot water for several months. Alice didn't want to risk alienating one of the few friends she had by asking her to use her shower too often.

Reporting the family for neglect would have been an abuse of the reporting system and insensitive to the needs of the family. The counselor arranged for Alice to use the school's gym shower as an additional resource. She also volunteered to help Alice learn to style her hair without being condescending. Counseling sessions were utilized to practice hair styling, thus providing a creative activity that was focused on something other than problems.

Class Bias in Mental Health Counseling

In addition to the classism previously discussed in the section on mental disorders, a prominent class-related problem in community and mental health counseling is lack of access to services for poor persons. Mental health services are not easily available for poorer persons (Leeder, 1996; Schore, 1990). Such lack of access for this group of people lies in stark contrast to the need. One class bias factor in access is cost. Community service boards and other agencies are charged largely with serving the poorest clients. Because poverty is associated with greater prevalence and severity of problems, the need for services is greater than available resources. Because social service agencies operate with limited funding that is frequently subject to budget cuts, they can provide mental health services only for the most extreme problems, leaving many issues like anxiety, career distress, and most versions of depression unattended to.

Another cost issue for lower-class clients may include their strong resentment about the cost of counseling in private practice or other settings (Leeder, 1996), that is, being charged what they see as high fees for "only" talking with someone. Even for those who have insurance, a $50 co-pay may well represent a substantial percentage of a week's take-home pay for a working-class or poor single parent. Thus, more direct interventions, a solution focus, self-help resources, and sliding scales are more class-sensitive when clients are concerned with finances.

CLASS-ALERT COUNSELING: ASSESSMENT AND INTERVENTION

Now that class-related characteristics and bias have been discussed, positive strategies for class-alert counseling are presented: (1) considering class factors, (2) doing class-alert client assessments, and (3) engaging in class-alert interventions.

Considering Class Factors: Counselor Self-Assessment

Counselors need to ask themselves whether, from a middle-class perspective, they see client issues as evidence of pathology rather than as arising from contextual factors related to social class or other contextual experiences. They also need to inquire about how clients perceive the relationship between themselves and the problem-in-context. Class-alert counselors can then use these understandings to engage in class-sensitive interventions. Such culturally alert counselor behavior honors the local knowledge of clients about their situations rather than basing the assessment or intervention on the counselor's interpretation of what the difficulty is. In other words, the client should be an equal participant. Class-alert counselors therefore ask clients about the meaning and nature of the cultural dimensions of their lives. Areas to explore include the importance or salience of culture, any experiences of oppression, and the cultural values that guide a person's life.

When working with clients who have different class backgrounds from their own, counselors might use the questions in Box 13.2 during the counseling interview. Some of these questions focus on the counselor's awareness of self, while others help the counselor hear more clearly the submerged or undervoiced class-related information contained in the presentations of the problem. In the first set of questions, some are asked directly of the client, while others are learned as a result of hearing and reflecting on the client's story.

Box 13.2   Class Factors to Consider During Assessment

Questions oriented toward the client's experience of the presenting issues

1. What is the client's description of the issue or problem?
2. What sense is being made of it?
3. Is the way the problem is framed self-defeating or self-enhancing for the client?
4. Given that the client is the expert in her or his own context, what would she or he know about the problem she or he is having that I don't know?
5. What have others who are important to the client said about the problem or issue?
6. What would the client like me to know about her or his (class-related) experience?
7. What is my client most proud of in her or his life, family, culture, or community unrelated to current challenges or struggles?
8. What has sustained my client in rough times in the past?

Questions for counselor reflection and case conceptualization

9. What is my own class positioning and/or class privilege relative to my client?
10. What understandings about myself and others do I carry forward from my own social background or current social context?
11. What values, expectations, and life experiences do I demonstrate when I am in the position of being "the professional" with my client?
12. Do I have a negative label or story about my client based on different class values?
13. Do I perceive that any resistance in therapy sessions might be connected to shame or to other unvoiced class experiences that are difficult to put into words?
14. When I listen to my client's story, can I detect dimensions of class, race, gender, and other similar contextual factors in what she or he is telling me about the problem?
15. Do my client's behaviors or symptom patterns represent extremes inside her or his race, class, or gender group?
16. Might my client and I perceive the power dynamics or effectiveness of our relationship differently as a result of class influences?
17. Do I have a conception of class-related strengths, that is, how clients also thrive within the context of their social class experiences?

Source: Adapted from the frameworks of Arthur & Collins (2005), Madsen (2007), Mehl-Madrona (2010) an Parry & Doan (1994)

The questions in Box 13.2 represent a switching of perspectives, from one that assumes a common middle-class worldview and circumstance to one that sees unique values and cultural environments that affect members of different classes. The counselor's challenge is to think about context: All behaviors and symptoms occur within a social and relational context. If counselors understand the context, they can frame the issues differently. With working-class or poor clients, counselors can assume that at least part of a client's difficulties can properly be attributed to socially oppressive practices that complicate, if not actually create, life challenges. The following sections discuss class-alert assessments and interventions that honor class-related experiences.

Assessing for Class Context

Class-alert intentional inquiry about the experiences and meanings of clients' lives can help the counselor understand the meaning that individuals give to their class-related experiences. Three notions can guide culturally alert assessment: questioning and assessing the problem through the client's lens, helping the client identify issues of classism, and using the client's strengths to develop new strategies. First, through culturally educated questioning, as described in Chapter 19, the counselor uses her or his prior knowledge of class issues to inquire about the client's own experience. For example, the counselor can help the client recognize the impact of class-related experiences of oppression on family relationships. In the process, the counselor can assess the impact of classism on a client's hopes and self-perception. Then the counselor can assist the client in recognizing class-related strengths and developing new strategies (see Chapter 19). The following case illustrates how a culturally alert assessment process can be used to incorporate social class factors into client assessment.

The Case of Jean

Jean is a 55-year-old white, divorced home health aide who was referred to the mental health agency because she was feeling anxious and depressed and was having difficulty sleeping. She has been told she will be evicted from her apartment in 2 weeks, and she has no place to go. She is very agitated and confrontational, shouting, "I don't need someone to talk about my feelings. I know how I feel. I need help NOW!" According to the intake form, she has a record of driving while under the influence and her license has been suspended.

During the first few minutes of the interview, the counselor, Tanya, observes Jean's agitation. Her speech is demanding and blunt, and she is uncooperative. Jean is angry because she gets the "run-around" when she tries to contact the social services office to apply for housing assistance. She can never get through to a staff person, and they have never returned any of her voicemails. Imagine that you are Jean's counselor as you complete Activity 13.4.

Activity 13.4   Initial Mental Status Examination

Respond in writing to the following questions:

1. From the information provided, what are your initial impressions of Jean?

2. What thoughts, feelings, or reactions does she elicit in you?

3. Based on this limited observation, what is your initial assessment of Jean?

4. As you think about your responses, what are some of the assumptions you might be making about Jean?

5. What else would you like to know about Jean to help you with your assessment?

It would be easy to have an initial defensive reaction to Jean, given her demanding presentation. With patience and persistence, however, and by using Questions 1–4 in Box 13.2, Tanya is able to elicit Jean's understanding of her presenting issues. Jean has been eking out a living but is having increasing difficulty paying her bills. Several of her home health aide assignments have, in her words, "not worked out" because of "personality conflicts" and tardiness, and the agency has been calling her less often for assignments. She is often late for work because she has to rely on public transportation, which is not always convenient to her and her clients' places of residence. Jean believes she is trying as hard as she can, but she is extremely frustrated because she can't get any help, and she doesn't know what else to do. Now complete Activity 13.5.

Activity 13.5   Further Assessment

1. Given this new information, does your impression of Jean change in any way? If so, how?

2. Which of the questions for counselor reflection in Box 13.2 (Questions 9–16) would be useful to you in thinking about Jean?

3. What other information would help you understand this client?

By using information learned from Questions 7 and 8 in Box 13.2, Tanya learns that 7 years prior, Jean was laid off from her job as a computer programmer at a large manufacturing company. She had held that job for 20 years. When Tanya inquires about the DWI, Jean acknowledges that she couldn't afford a lawyer to help her. She believes that she was "tricked" by the prosecutor into pleading guilty to the DWI. She reports that she was very confused at the time and can't remember any of the details. This resulted in the loss of her driver's license. Now respond to the questions in Activity 13.6.

Activity 13.6   Case Conceptualization Reflections

1. Does learning any of this information in any way alter your thinking about Jean or her difficulties?

2. How are race, class, and/or gender dimensions entering into your thinking?

There are many chances for a counselor to experience class-biased misperceptions and to engage in clinical misjudgments. Tanya initially wonders whether chemical dependency might be the source of many of Jean's personal, financial, and work-related problems. However, due to Jean's agitation, it is difficult to gather sufficient information to formulate a diagnosis. Next we share a class-alert assessment of Jean.

Class-Alert Assessment of Jean

A class-alert assessment begins with basic counseling skills. These include active listening so that Tanya really hears what Jean is trying to say. During the first session, Tanya pauses a moment to collect her thoughts so as to not react defensively to Jean. She then continues to validate Jean's experience and pay attention to her context. Guided by the questions in Box 13.2 and through the use of empathic responses (a basic counseling response that elicits client thoughts and/or feelings and connects them to particular experiences and behaviors), Tanya learns that, because Jean has no money and no work assignments on the horizon (experience), she is terrified (feeling) that she will soon be living in the streets (experience). Further, Tanya learns that Jean's mother died just 3 months ago (experience). This event precipitated a personal and financial crisis, as her mother had been Jean's primary source of support since her job loss. Jean now feels alone and afraid (feeling), and she is extremely sad because she misses her mother (feeling). Her demanding and abrupt demeanor (behavior) is a way to appear tough and to cover up her fears, and it represents her attempt to gain some control over her situation.

By correctly identifying the pain and fear that lie underneath Jean's hard exterior shell, Tanya gains some empathic insight into Jean's dilemma. She is obviously grieving for her mother. Not only has she lost her only source of financial and other tangible support, but she also misses her best and only friend. At this point, Tanya turns to Question 7. When she invites Jean to tell her about a time when things were going well, Jean starts to beam as she talks about her previous job as a computer programmer. She loved that job, felt competent and secure, earned adequate income, and had good benefits. Because she had been a good employee for 20 years, she didn't see the layoff coming. The impact was emotionally and financially devastating, as she had never been able to find comparable work, no matter how hard she tried. She was beginning to feel desperate because her unemployment had ended. Home health aide jobs were readily available and the agency was within walking distance of her home, so she could begin to work again. The job, however, just wasn't what she had hoped for because it didn't provide the security and benefits of her old job.

Jean's class-related context is beginning to emerge. Although her job was terminated 7 years earlier, Jean is experiencing difficulty adjusting to her employment situation. Jean managed to get by with her mother's help and support. With her mother gone, she felt scared, lonely, and lost, which led her to seek help. With the client's view in mind, the counselor's initial diagnostic considerations expanded to include other contextual considerations. For example, working-class and poor clients often seek counseling when they are in crisis (Chalifoux, 1996; Leeder, 1996). Tanya now considers that Jean might be showing signs of an adjustment disorder with mixed symptoms of anxiety and depression precipitated by the loss of her mother.

Class-Alert Intervention With Jean

The following discussion focuses on interventions that take into account the hidden dynamics of class as experienced specifically by Jean. As you read through the case, see if you can identify the questions noted above that were embedded in the dialogue. It is important to remember that because class is invisible in our society, class-related issues are not always obvious.

Paying Immediate Attention to Survival Needs

One pressing problem for Jean lies in the urgency of her survival needs. With financial, legal, housing, and food problems bearing down on her, Jean feels desperate and afraid that she will have no place to live or anything to eat. Therefore, her immediate needs are to obtain housing and food.

Addressing Structural Issues

Another class-related contextual issue that may not necessarily be visible to Jean, but is important for the counselor to know, is the current structure of the labor market. Based on Table 13.1, it can be seen that low-level computer programming is a working-class occupation characterized by little autonomy and requires little formal education beyond high school. With the new service economy, low-level computer programming jobs have disappeared. Jean was unaware that the now-prevalent low-wage service jobs would not allow her to earn enough money to meet her basic survival needs (Boushey & Fremstad, 2008; Gatta, Boushey, & Appelbaum, 2009; Sheely, 2010). Had Tanya not considered Jean's prior stable work history, she would not have recognized that Jean's crisis response was triggered by her working-class expectations that she would have job security so long as she was a loyal employee who did her job satisfactorily. The problem for Jean is that she wasn't aware that these "rules" had changed. Further, Jean never had contact with any social service system in the past, so she has no idea how to navigate the complex networks that have been established in order to discourage oversubscription and fraud. She feels intimidated, frustrated, and ashamed that she is in the position of needing social service assistance.

Being Alert to Class-Related Communication Style

The direct and blunt manner in which Jean expresses her needs is normative in her working-class culture. A counselor who is accustomed to polite clients who talk about their feelings could easily view Jean as having a disorder rather than as an individual under stress who is also underresourced. Jean rightly believes that a counselor's sympathetic listening is not going to solve her immediate problem of finding a place to live. Her communication style and her demands are consistent with the scope and intensity of her presenting problems.

Pathologizing Grief

Tanya could interpret Jean's symptoms of agitation and worry as symptoms of an anxiety disorder, depression, or other pathology. Yet given her life circumstances, these symptoms may not fit the criteria for a clinical disorder in that they are based on a very real concern for her survival and her recent experience of multiple losses. Tanya must investigate Jean's symptoms within the context of her life events before making a final diagnosis, as they could be considered normal and expected, given her life circumstances.

The Class-Alert Counselor's Actions

Fortunately, Jean's counselor is class-alert. First, Tanya pays attention to trust and rapport building, using reflection and self-disclosure. To attend to the differences in power in the relationship, Tanya self-discloses by appropriately mentioning the loss of her own mother a few years ago. She also offers empathic responses to communicate understanding of Jean's desire to be soothed, which led Jean to use alcohol. All too often, counselor suggestions of alcohol abuse are heard as judgmental accusations. Tanya acknowledges both Jean's anxiety and her strengths, as well as her negative emotions and difficulties.

An additional consideration in this case involves Tanya's knowledge of career counseling. It is important for counselors to understand work–life issues and how they become interwoven with other life problems. Tanya hears that Jean felt very happy and competent as a computer programmer, but she is having difficulty being successful as a home health aide. Armed with a basic understanding of career theories, Tanya knows that Jean is exhibiting a mismatch between her interests, the job skills previously required of her, and the ones needed for her current job. Home health aides are among the largest-growing occupations projected by the Bureau of Labor Statistics, which accounts for the relative ease with which Jean found employment. Because this type of work is associated with women, it pays very little (Boushey & Fremstad,

2008; Gatta et al., 2009). The nature of this job requires Jean to attend to those with acute physical and emotional needs. As Jean is experiencing such a high degree of emotional distress herself, it is extremely difficult for her to provide support to others in distress. The "personality conflicts" Jean described during her intake interview could just as likely be due to a poor person–environment fit, and the extraordinary emotional energy required of a paid caregiver, than to Jean's individual failure. As a computer programmer, she had not been called upon to use very many people skills.

Guided by Question 8 above, Tanya validates Jean's strengths in (1) being able to survive the loss of her mother when she had no other source of support, (2) being able to keep her previous job for 20 years, and (3) having completed many home health aide assignments despite not having a driver's license.

By eliciting Jean's employment history and by being aware of current labor market trends and work–life issues, Tanya can prioritize Jean's needs in a class-consistent way and provide the direct assistance that Jean needed. She gives Jean a direct contact for social services so that Jean can avoid the automated voice messaging system that frustrated her.

Once the food and shelter needs are addressed, Tanya helps Jean understand the broader issues associated with a service economy. By locating the employment problem within the economic context rather than blaming Jean for her situation, Tanya could then turn her attention to Jean's career needs. Realizing that Jean's finances were limited, Tanya could either help Jean work on her career issues herself or refer her to a career counseling service that is free or based on a sliding scale. Being able to pursue a career or identify retraining opportunities would be far more useful to Jean at this point than only exploring her emotions and meanings.

Class-Alert Practice

A class-alert counselor needs to be capable of asking about class socialization and oppression, as that subject matter is largely unvoiced, both by clients and by society in general. That means having a full understanding of the dynamics of privilege and classism that lead to systematic oppression of those in the lower classes.

At times, counselors may need to be a "culture broker." In that role, they help clients make connections to resources, educate them about how systems operate, and otherwise bridge the cultural gap. Tanya performed this role for Jean by connecting her with housing assistance and helping her obtain help with her career issues. The counselor can also serve as an activist-advocate, one who addresses organizational and institutional inequities. Such actions represent simultaneously empowering the client and culture-brokering.

Counselors must engage in class-alert activities when working with clients of all classes. Knowledge about class issues and the ability to fully understand the class experiences of someone of a class different from one's own is critical. With awareness of these trends, alert counselors will know that they should assess for social class context, with its hidden assumptions, attitudes, aspirations, and experiences of oppression and how they may appear in clients' stories.

SUMMARY

This chapter has explored the major groupings of social class, contextual dimensions of class, and their implications for counseling. Helping professionals are not immune to class bias, and counseling research and practice has been slow to recognize classism. There has been a tendency to blame clients for their own problems and for not engaging in the counseling process when, in fact, it is the helpers who have not understood the class experiences of their clients. Some specific suggestions for class-sensitive counseling assessment and interventions were offered.

Counselors must not only learn about class, they must develop greater consciousness of their own class identities. In gaining a perspective on their own class narrative, middle-class counselors can learn that not all clients share the same class-related values, aspirations, or life goals as themselves. When a client's perspective and needs conflict with the middle-class value system of

counseling, it is the counselor's responsibility to bridge the class gap (Lott, 2002) and to co-create solutions congruent with the client's social class background and values. Counselors can help clients reinterpret their life stories to see strength, possibility, and resilience in the face of classism rather than deficits and pathology.

REFERENCES

Abramowitz, A., & Teixeira, R. (2009). The decline of the white working class and the rise of a mass upper-middle class. *Political Science Quarterly, 124,* 391–422.

Adler, N. E., Epel, E. S., Castellazzo, G., & Ickovics, J. R. (2000). Relationship of subjective and objective social status with psychological and physiological functioning: Preliminary data in healthy white women. *Health Psychology, 19,* 586–592.

Alexander, K. L., Entwisle, D. R., & Thompson, M. (1987). School performance, status relations, and the structure of sentiment: Bringing the teacher back in. *American Sociological Review, 52,* 665–682.

Ammons, S. K., & Kelly, E. L. (2008). Social class and the experience of work-family conflict during the transition to adulthood. *New Directions for Child and Adolescent Development, 119,* 71–84.

Aneshensel, C. S., & Sucoff, C. A. (1996). The neighborhood context of adolescent mental health. *Journal of Health & Social Behavior, 37,* 293–310.

Arthur, N., & Collins, S. (2005). *Culture-infused counseling: Assessment in multicultural counseling. Celebrating the Canadian mosaic.* Calgary, Alberta, Canada: Counselling Concepts.

Barton, P. E. (2008, January/February). How many college graduates does the labor force really need? *Change,* pp. 16–21.

Baum, O. E., & Felzer, S. B. (1964). Activity in initial interviews with lower-class patients. *Archives of General Psychiatry, 10,* 345–353.

Belek, I. (2000). Social class, income, education, area of residence and psychological distress: Does social class have an independent effect on psychological distress in Antalya, Turkey? *Social Psychiatry and Psychiatric Epidemiology, 35,* 94–101.

Bellah, R. N., Madsen, R., Sullivan, W. M., Swidler, A., & Tipton, S. (1996). *Habits of the heart: Individualism and commitment in American life.* Berkeley: University of California Press.

Bialostok, S. (2002). Metaphors for literacy: A cultural model of white, middle-class parents. *Linguistics & Education, 13,* 347–371.

Bloom, J. (2007). (Mis)reading social class in the journey towards college: Youth development in urban America. *Teachers College Record, 109,* 343–368.

Blustein, D. L., Chaves, A. P., Diemer, M. A., Gallagher, L. A., Marshall, K. G., Sirin, S., & Bhati, K. S. (2002). Voices of the forgotten half: The hole of social class in the school-to-work transition. *Journal of Counseling Psychology, 49,* 311–323.

Boroughs, M., Massey, O. T., & Armstrong, K. H. (2005). Socioeconomic status and behavior problems: Addressing the context for school safety. *Journal of School Violence, 4*(4), 31–46.

Boushey, H., & Fremstad, S. (2008). The wages of exclusion: Low-wage work and inequality. *New Labor Forum, 17,* 8–19.

Brady, D., Fullerton, A. S., & Cross, J. M. (2010). More than just nickels and dimes: A cross-national analysis of working poverty in affluent democracies. *Social Problems, 57,* 559–585.

Brill, N. Q., & Storrow, H. A. (1960). Social class and psychiatric treatment. *Archives of General Psychiatry, 3,* 340–344.

Broom, D. H., & Warin, M. (2011). Gendered and class relations of obesity: Confusing findings, deficient explanations. *Australian Feminist Studies, 26,* 453–467.

Caputo, R. K. (2007). Working and poor: A panel study of maturing adults in the U.S. *Families in Society, 88,* 351–359.

Chalifoux, B. (1996). Speaking up: White, working class women in therapy. *Women and Therapy, 18,* 25–34.

Chaves, A. P., Diemer, M. A., Blustein, D. L., Gallagher, L. A., DeVoy, J. E., Casares, M. T., & Perry, J. C. (2004). Conceptions of work: The view from urban youth. *Journal of Counseling Psychology, 51,* 275–285.

Chen, E., Matthews, K. A., & Boyce, W. T. (2002). Socioeconomic differences in children's' health: How and why do these relationships change with age? *Psychological Bulletin, 128,* 295–329.

Chin, T., & Phillips, M. (2004). Social reproduction and child-rearing practices: Social class, children's

agency, and the summer activity gap. *Sociology of Education, 77,* 185–210.

Cole, E. R., & Omari, S. R. (2003). Race, class and the dilemmas of upward mobility for African Americans. *Journal of Social Issues, 59,* 785–802.

Constantine, M. G. (2002). The intersection of race, ethnicity, gender, and social class in counseling: Examining selves in cultural contexts. *Journal of Multicultural Counseling and Development, 30,* 210–215.

Csikszentmihalyi, M. (1999). If we are so rich, why aren't we happy? *American Psychologist, 54,* 820–827.

Darmon, M. (2009). The fifth element: Social class and the sociology of anorexia. *Sociology, 43,* 717–733.

Demakakos, P., Nazroo, J. Breeze, E., & Marmot, M. (2008). Socioeconomic status and health: The role of subjective social status. *Social Science & Medicine, 67,* 330–340.

Diamond, J. B., & Gomez, K. (2004). African American parents' educational orientations. *Education & Urban Society, 36,* 383–427.

Dickerson, V. C. (2004). Young women struggling for an identity. *Family Processes, 43,* 337–348.

Dishion, T. J., French, D. C., & Patterson, G. R. (1995). The development and ecology of antisocial behavior. In D. Cicchetti & D. J. Cohen (Eds.), *Developmental psychopathology: Vol. 2. Risk, disorder, and adaptation* (pp. 421–471). New York, NY: Wiley.

Dixon, J. B., Dixon, M. E., & O'Brien, P. E. (2003). Depression in association with severe obesity: Changes with weight loss. *Archives of Internal Medicine, 163,* 2058–2065.

Downey, L., & van Willigen, M. (2005). Environmental stressors: The mental health impacts of living near industrial activity. *Journal of Health & Social Behavior, 46,* 289–305.

Drewnowski, A., Kurth, C. L., & Krahn, D. D. (1993). Body weight and dieting in adolescence: Impact of socioeconomic status. *International Journal of Eating Disorders, 16,* 61–65.

Edensor, T., & Millington, S. (2009). Illuminations, class identities and the contested landscapes of Christmas. *Sociology, 43,* 103–121.

Edlund, M., Wang, P. S., Berglund, P. A., Katz, S. J., Lin, E., & Kessler, R. C. (2002). Dropping out of mental health treatment: Patterns and predictors among epidemiological survey respondents in the United States and Ontario. *American Journal of Psychiatry, 159,* 845–851.

Education Trust. (2005). *The funding gap 2005: Low-income and minority students shortchanged by most states.* Retrieved from http://www.edtrust .org/sites/edtrust.org/files/publications/files/ FundingGap2005.pdf

Ehrenreich, B. (2009, June 14). Too poor to make the news. *The New York Times,* p. 10.

Evans, G. (2004). The environment of childhood poverty. *American Psychologist, 59,* 77–92.

Evans, M. D. R., & Kelley, J. (2004). Subjective social location: Data from 21 nations. *International Journal of Public Opinion Research, 16,* 3–39

Everson, S. A., Maty, S. C., Lynch, J. W., & Kaplan, G. A. (2002). Epidemiologic evidence for the relation between socioeconomic status and depression, obesity and diabetes. *Journal of Psychosomatic Research, 53,* 891–895.

Faith, M. S., Butryn, M. M., Wadden, T. A., Fabricatore, A. A., Nguyen, A. M., & Heymsfield, S. B. (2011). Evidence for prospective associations among depression and obesity in population-based studies. *Obesity Reviews, 12,* 438–453.

Ferguson, N. (2012). Rich America, poor America. *Newsweek, 159*(4), 42–47.

Fischer, C. S., & Mattson, G. (2009). Is America fragmenting? *Annual Review of Sociology, 35,* 435–455.

Gatta, M., Boushey, H., & Appelbaum, E. (2009). High-touch and here-to-stay: Future skills demands in low-wage service occupations. *Sociology, 43,* 968–989.

Gerstel, N. (2011). Rethinking families and community: The color class, and centrality of extended kin ties. *Sociological Forum, 26,* 1–20.

Gorman, T. (1998). Social class and parental attitudes toward education: Resistance and conformity to schooling in the family. *Journal of Contemporary Ethnography, 27,* 10–44.

Granfield, R. (1991). Making it by faking it: Working-class students in an elite academic environment. *Journal of Contemporary Ethnography, 20,* 331–351.

Green, M. J., & Benzeval, M. (2011). Ageing, social class, and common mental disorders: Longitudinal evidence from three cohorts in the West of Scotland. *Psychological Medicine, 41,* 565–574.

Hancock, K. (2006). *Promise abandoned: How policy changes and institutional practices restrict college opportunities.* Retrieved from http://www.edtrust.org/ sites/edtrust.org/files/publications/files/Promise AbandonedHigherEd.pdf

Hardaway, C., & McLoyd, V. (2009). Escaping poverty and securing middle class status: How race and socioeconomic status shape mobility prospects for African Americans during the transition to adulthood. *Journal of Youth & Adolescence, 38,* 242–256.

Hauser-Cram, P., Sirin, S. R., & Stipek, D. (2003). When teachers' and parents' values differ: Teachers' ratings of academic competence in children from low-income families. *Journal of Educational Psychology, 95,* 813–820.

Haynes, F. E. (2000). Gender and family ideals: An exploratory study of black middle-class Americans. *Journal of Family Issues, 21,* 811–837.

Hennessy, J. (2009a). Choosing work and family: Poor and Low-income mothers' work-family commitments. *Journal of Poverty, 13,* 152–172.

Hennessy, J. (2009b). Morality and work-family conflict in the lives of poor and low-income women. *Sociological Quarterly, 50,* 557–580.

Heymann, J. (2000). What happens during and after school: Conditions faced by working parents living in poverty and their school-aged children. *Journal of Children & Poverty, 6,* 5–20.

Hollingshead, A. B., & Redlich, F. C. (1958). *Social class and mental illness.* New York, NY: Wiley.

Hudson, C. G. (2005). Socioeconomic status and mental illness: Tests of the social causation and selection hypothesis. *American Journal of Orthopsychiatry, 75,* 3–18.

Ingersoll, R. (1999). The problem of under qualified teachers in American secondary schools. *Educational Researcher, 28,* 26–37.

James, L. (2008). United by gender or divided by class? Women's work orientations and labor market behavior. *Gender, Work and Organization, 15,* 394–412.

Jetten, J., Iyer, A., Tsivrikos, D., & Young, B. (2008). When is individual mobility costly? The role of economic and social identity factors. *European Journal of Social Psychology, 38,* 866–879.

Kalleberg, A. L. (2007). *The Mismatched Worker.* New York, NY: Norton.

Katz, J. H. (1985). The sociopolitical nature of counseling. *The Counseling Psychologist, 13,* 615–624.

Kendall-Tackett, K., Marshall, R., & Ness, K. (2003). Chronic pain syndromes and violence against women. *Women & Therapy, 26,* 45–66.

Kliman, J. (1998). Social class as a relationship: Implications for family therapy. In M. McGoldrick (Ed.), *Re-visioning family therapy: Race, culture, and gender in clinical practice* (pp. 50–61). New York, NY: Guilford Press.

Kliman, J., & Madsen, W. (1999). Social class and the family life cycle. In B. Carter & M. McGoldrick (Eds.), *The expanded family life cycle: Individual, family and social perspectives* (pp. 88–105). Boston, MA: Allyn & Bacon.

Kneebone, E., & Garr, E. (2011). *The suburbanization of poverty: Trends in metropolitan America.* Washington, DC: Brookings Institution. Retrieved from http://www.brookings.edu/~/media/research/files/papers/2010/1/20%20poverty%20kneebone/0120_poverty_paper.pdf

Kposowa, A. J. (2001). Unemployment and suicide: A cohort analysis of social factors predicting suicide in the US National Longitudinal Mortality Study. *Psychological Medicine, 31,* 127–138.

Krieger, N., Williams, D. R., & Moss, N. E. (1997). Measuring social class in US public health research. *Annual Review of Public Health, 18,* 341–378.

Lapour, A. S., & Heppner, M. J. (2009). Social class privilege and adolescent women's perceived career options. *Journal of Counseling Psychology, 56,* 477–494.

Lareau, A. (2002). Invisible inequality: Social class and childrearing in black families and white families. *American Sociological Review, 67,* 747–776.

Lawler, S. (2005). Introduction: Class, culture and identity. *Sociology, 39,* 797–806.

Leeder, E. (1996). Speaking rich people's words: Implications of a feminist class analysis and psychotherapy. *Women & Therapy, 18,* 45–57.

Lehmann, W. (2009). Becoming middle class: How working-class university students draw and transgress moral class boundaries. *Sociology, 43,* 631–647.

Lewine, R. R. J. (2005). Social class of origin, lost potential, and hopelessness in schizophrenia. *Schizophrenia Research, 76,* 329–335.

Lewis, G., Pebbington, P., Brugha, T., Farrell, M., Gill, B., Jenkins, R., & Meltzer, H. (2003). Socio-economic status, standard of living, and neurotic disorder. *International Review of Psychiatry, 15,* 91–96.

Liu, W. M., Ali, S. R., Soleck, G., Hopps, J., Dunston, K., & Pickett, T., Jr. (2004). Using social class in counseling psychology research. *Journal of Counseling Psychology, 51,* 3–18.

Liu, W. M., Soleck, G., Hopps, J., Dunston, K., & Pickett, T., Jr. (2004). A new framework to understand social class in counseling: The social class worldview model and modern classism theory. *Journal of Multicultural Counseling and Development, 32,* 95–122.

Lott, B. (2002). Cognitive and behavioral distancing from the poor. *American Psychologist, 57,* 100–110.

Lott, B., & Saxon, S. (2002). The influence of ethnicity, class, and social context on judgments about U.S. women. *Journal of Social Psychology, 142,* 481–499.

Lund, C., Breen, A., Flisher, A. J., Kakuma. R., Corrigall, J., Joska, J. A., . . . & Patel, V. (2010). Poverty and common mental disorders in low and middle income countries: A systematic review. *Social Science & Medicine, 71,* 517–528.

Luster, T., Rhoades, K., & Haas, B. (1989). The relations between parental values and parenting behaviors: A test of the Kohn hypothesis. *Journal of Marriage and the Family, 51,* 139–147.

Luthar, S. S., & Latendresse, S. J. (2002). Adolescent risk: The costs of affluence. *New Directions for Youth Development 2002, 95,* 101–122.

Luthar, S. S., & Latendresse, S. J. (2005). Children of the affluent. *Current Directions in Psychological Science, 14,* 49–53.

Madsen, W. (2007). *Collaborative therapy with multistressed families* (2nd ed.). New York, NY: Guilford.

Marger, M. (1999). *Social inequality: Patterns and processes.* Mountain View, CA: Mayfield.

McClelland, L., & Crisp, A. (2001). Anorexia nervosa and social class. *International Journal of Eating Disorders, 29,* 150–156.

McNeely, C. A., Nonnemaker, J., & Blum, R. W. (2002). Promoting school connectedness: Evidence from the National Longitudinal Study of Adolescent Health. *Journal of School Health, 72,* 138–146.

Mehl-Madrona, L. (2010). *Healing the mind through the power of story.* Rochester, VT: Bear.

Miech, R. A., Caspi, A., Moffitt, T. E., & Wright, B. R. E. (1999). Low socioeconomic status and mental disorders: A longitudinal study of selection and causation during young adulthood. *American Journal of Sociology, 104*, 1096–1139.

Minton, J., Shell, J., & Solomon, L. Z. (2004). A comparative study of values and attitudes of inner-city and middle-class postpartum women. *Psychological Reports, 95*, 235–249.

Nelson, M. L., Englar-Carlson, M., Tierney, S. C., & Hau, J. M. (2006). Class jumping into academia: Multiple identities for counseling academics. *Journal of Counseling Psychology, 53*, 1–14.

Newman, K. S., & Chin, M. M. (2003). High stakes: Time poverty, testing, and the children of the working poor. *Qualitative Sociology, 26*, 3–34.

Nichol, G. (2003, October 13). Educating for privilege. *The Nation*, p. 22.

Nichter, M. (2003). Smoking: What does culture have to do with it? *Addiction, 98*, 139–145.

Norman, J. (2004). Gender bias in the diagnosis and treatment of depression. *International Journal of Mental Health, 33*, 32–43.

Ogden, J., & Thomas, D. (1999). The role of familial values in understanding the impact of social class on weight concern. *International Journal of Eating Disorders, 25*, 273–279.

Ozawa, M. N., & Yeo, Y. H. (2008). Race/ethnicity and socioeconomic class as correlates of disability in old age. *Journal of Gerontological Social Work, 51*, 337–365.

Pais, J. (2011). Socioeconomic background and racial earnings inequality: A propensity score analysis. *Social Science Research, 40*, 37–49.

Parry, A., & Doan, R. E. (1994). *Story re-visions: Narrative therapy in a postmodern world.* New York, NY: Guilford Press.

Piff, P. K., Kraus, M. W., Cote, S., Cheng, B. H., & Keltner, D. (2010). Having less, giving more: The influence of social class on prosocial behavior. *Journal of Personality and Social Psychology, 99*, 771–784.

Pilisuk, M. (1998). The hidden structure of contemporary violence. *Journal of Peace Psychology, 43*, 197–216.

Pinar, W. (1993). Notes on understanding curriculum as a racial text. In C. McCarthy & W. Crichlow (Eds.), *Race identity and representation in education* (p. 60–70). New York, NY: Routledge.

Pinderhughes, E. E., Dodge, K. A., Bates, J. A., Pettit, G. S., & Zelli, A. (2000). Discipline responses: Influence of parents' socioeconomic status, ethnicity, beliefs about parenting, stress and cognitive-emotional processes. *Journal of Family Psychology, 14*, 380–400.

Priory Group. (2004). Alcohol for the soul. *Counselling & Psychotherapy Journal, 15*, 10.

Robinson, T. (1999). The intersections of dominant discourses across race, gender, and other identities. *Journal of Counseling & Development, 77*, 73–79.

Schore, L. (1990). Issues of work, workers, and therapy. *New Directions for Mental Health Services, 46*, 93–100.

Sheely, A. (2010). Work characteristics and family routines in low-wage families. *Journal of Sociology & Social Welfare, 37*(3), 59–77.

Shelvin, D., Zandy, J., & Smith, L. R. (1999). *Writing work: Writers on working-class writing.* Huron, OH: Bottom Dog Press.

Shen, J., & Murray, J. (1981). Psychotherapy with the disadvantaged. *American Journal of Psychotherapy, 35*, 268–275.

Shin, T. J. (2007). The impact of structural dynamics on job mobility rates in the United States. *Social Science Research, 36*, 1301–1327.

Smith, L. (2008). Positioning classism within counseling psychology's social justice agenda. *The Counseling Psychologist, 36*, 895–924.

Smith, L. H., & Holm, L. (2010). Social class and body management. A qualitative exploration of differences in perceptions and practices related to health and personal body weight. *Appetite, 55*, 311–318.

Stillson, R. W., O'Neil, J. M., & Owen, S. V. (1991). Predictors of adult men's gender-role conflict: Race, class, unemployment, age, instrumentality-expressiveness, and personal strain. *Journal of Counseling Psychology, 38*, 458–464.

Tingle, N. (2004). The vexation of class. *College English, 67*, 222–230.

Tucker, C., & Dixon, A. L. (2009). Low-income African American male youth with ADHD symptoms in the United States: Recommendations for clinical mental health counselors. *Journal of Mental Health Counseling, 31*, 309–322.

U.S. Bureau of Labor Statistics. (2012). *EP tables.* Retrieved from http://www.bls.gov/emp/#tables

U.S. Census Bureau. (2012). *Income, expenditures, poverty, and wealth.* Retrieved from http://www.census.gov/compendia/statab/cats/income_expenditures_poverty_wealth.html

U.S. Department of Labor, Bureau of Labor Statistics. (2007). *A profile of the working poor, 2005.* Retrieved from http://www.bls.gov/cps/cpswp2005.pdf

Wagmiller, R. L., Jr., Kuang, L., Aber, J. L., Lennon, M. C., & Alberti, P. M. (2006). The dynamics of economic disadvantage and children's life chances. *American Sociological Review, 71,* 847–866.

Wardle, J., Waller, J., & Jarvis, M. J. (2002). Sex differences in the association of socioeconomic status with obesity. *American Journal of Public Health, 92,* 1299–1305.

Wegner, E. L., & Yuan, S. C. (2004). Legal welfare fraud among middle-class families. *American Behavioral Scientist, 47,* 1406–1418.

Wells, B., & Zinn, M. (2004). The benefits of marriage reconsidered. *Journal of Sociology and Social Welfare, 3,* 59–80.

Whitaker, S., & Zenker, M. (2011). *Are underemployed graduates displacing nongraduates?* Retrieved from http://www.clevelandfed.org/research/trends/2011/0711/01labmar.cfm

Wiles, N. J., Lingford-Hughes, A., Daniel, J., Hickman, M., Farrell, M., Macleod, J., . . . & Lewis, G. (2007). Socio-economic status in childhood and later alcohol use: A systematic review. *Addiction, 102,* 1546–1563.

Williams, L., Germov, J., & Young, A. (2011). The effect of social class on mid-age women's weight control practices and weight gain. *Appetite, 56,* 719–725.

Wolfe, J. L., & Fodor, I. G. (1996). The poverty of privilege: Therapy with women of the "upper" classes. *Women & Therapy, 18,* 73–90.

Yates, T. M., Tracey, A. J., & Luthar, S. S. (2008). Nonsuicidal self-injury among "privileged" youths: Longitudinal and cross-sectional approaches to developmental process. *Journal of Consulting and Clinical Psychology, 76,* 52–62.

Zweig, M. (2000). *The working class majority: America's best kept secret.* Ithaca, NY: Cornell University Press.

CHAPTER 14

Counseling Men and Women: Considering Gender and Sex

Heather C. Trepal
University of Texas at San Antonio

Kelly L. Wester, Lori Notestine
University of North Carolina at Greensboro

Chris Leeth
University of Texas at San Antonio

The scene is a birthing room, with the mother in the late stages of delivery, the excited father recording it all with his video camera, and the doctor ready to receive the newborn infant. "You have a beautiful baby . . ." The doctor's voice trails off. "A beautiful baby what?" demands the father. "I don't know," the doctor responds, "I can't tell." Subsequent tests reveal that the baby is chromosomally male; however, it would be easier medically to perform surgery to give him female genitalia (more extensive surgery would be needed for male genitalia, which could not be "fully functional" in adulthood). (Glick & Fiske, 1999, p. 365)

A new client comes in seeking counseling to deal with feelings of depression and helplessness related to a career transition. The transition includes resigning from a lucrative position in the corporate world at a Fortune 500 company to stay at home with three young children. The client mentions wanting to stay home with the children, yet reports frustration over leaving a rewarding career at a company that has offered a pay raise in order to entice the client to stay and wasting so many years in college attempting to achieve this career. The client reports having many hobbies and interests, including cooking, sports, spending time with friends and family (including a spouse and three kids), and gardening, yet reports recently not having a desire to partake in any of them. The client has no history of depression, nor does the client's family of origin. When asked about family of origin, the client mentions that they are all healthy, alive, and living close to home. The client's mother was a full-time homemaker and the father worked as a corporate lawyer to support the family.

The first vignette describes a scene from a dramatic television series (Glick & Fiske, 1999). This illustration of ambiguous biological sex demonstrates the importance of biological sex. Classifying people by sex is an automatic response that has been found to develop within the first few years of life (Beal, 1994), earlier than other classifications, such as skin color. When an individual encounters another person, she or he is typically categorized as male or female within seconds, and it is usually done unconsciously. Indeed, some readers may have found the second vignette, chosen to illustrate and stimulate thinking on topics covered in this chapter, frustrating to read because the vignette does not specify a biological sex of the client—or maybe you unconsciously assigned a sex while reading the vignette. Before reading the rest of this chapter, answer the questions in Activity 14.1.

Activity 14.1   Beginning to Examine Gender

Take a moment to write down your thoughts on the following questions related to the second vignette. Other activities in this chapter provide additional opportunities to explore your thinking about this client's situation.

1. Although more information is needed, what might a provisional diagnosis for this client be?

2. What do you think the prognosis is for this client? Explain your thoughts.

3. What are the strengths of the client?

4. What are some weaknesses that might hinder the client's prognosis?

5. What are a few goals that you would select to work on with this client?

6. What did you approximate the client's age to be?

7. The client's race?

8. The client's biological sex?

9. Explain your reasoning about how you came to the answers regarding the demographics of the client.

10. What aspects of the vignette caused you to come to these conclusions?

Sex classification is important because it helps people determine how to interact with each other and identify expectations of the other person. Have you ever been unsure of someone's sex? If so, what was your response to this person? Did you know how to interact? Did you find yourself attempting to figure out whether the person was female or male throughout the entire interaction? Were you uncomfortable? Activity 14.2 illustrates the power of sex classification in our experience of the world.

Activity 14.2   Communication Without Identifiers

At home or in class: Have a 3-minute conversation with a person in which you describe something you did this weekend with a friend, family member, or partner. However, do *not* mention that person's name and do *not* reveal that person's sex through any identifiers. After the conversation, comment on the following:

What did you observe about yourself?

Was the conversation easy or difficult?

How much thought did you have to put into not mentioning the individual's biological sex?

Did you succeed in this conversation?

What did you observe about the listener?

Now switch roles in this activity, and for 3 minutes, listen to someone else tell you about an activity that she or he did this weekend with someone, but, again, without revealing the biological sex.

What was it like for you to listen to a conversation without knowing someone's biological sex?

Did you have difficulty listening to the conversation?

Did you attempt to figure out the biological sex of the person she or he was talking about?

Were you able to listen to the content of the conversation, or were you too involved in attempting to figure out the sex of the person?

In this chapter, the nature of gender and socialization is presented, followed by specific issues related to counseling women and men.

GENDER: HISTORY, SOCIALIZATION, THEORY

Gender and sex are often confused. A review of the history of these distinctions will help you appreciate the socialization that creates gender roles. That appreciation can then be brought to the counseling session, where gender role conflict can be explored and client options can be discussed.

Sex Versus Gender

Margaret Fuller (1845/1999), whose work profoundly influenced the 19th century women's rights movement, once wrote, "Male and female represent the two sides of the great radical dualism. But in fact they are perpetually passing into one another. . . . There is no wholly masculine man, no purely feminine woman" (p. 103). But societal gender roles often mask that subtlety because biological sex and gender are often seen as interchangeable (although they are not).

In Western and other societies, people usually attribute characteristics, features, and traits to a person's biological sex. However, this assignment of traits and characteristics is more accurately referred to as *gender*. In Simone de Beauvoir's words, "one is not born, but rather becomes a woman [or man]" (cited in Gilbert & Scher, 1999, p. 3).

Many people tend to use the terms *sex* and *gender* synonymously, even though these terms do not mean the same thing. Sex refers to "whether one is born biologically female or male" (Gilbert & Scher, 1999, p. 3). Gender, by contrast, is what is assumed of an individual who is born into a particular sex, that is, "the psychological, social, and cultural features and characteristics that have become strongly associated with the biological categories of male or female" (p. 3). Biological sex roles for a female and a male differ in any society or culture (unless the person is intersexed) due to the distinct male and female sex and reproduction organs. By contrast,

a person's gender role consists of the actions and behaviors that are seen as acceptable and appropriate for a female or male to engage in within a culture. For example, in Western society, it is more acceptable for a female to wear a skirt or makeup than it is for a male, while it is more appropriate for a male to show aggressive or angry behaviors. Now, take a moment to consider the second vignette, the one in which the client has left a corporate position. What biological sex did you assign to the client? Does the biological sex you assigned appear to align itself with the characteristic gender roles from your culture or society for males or females?

Despite these societal gender–sex constraints, however, men and women cross society's gender lines. For example, female athletes rate themselves as more traditionally masculine (i.e., assertive, independent, and goal-oriented) than nonathletes are (J. L. Miller & Levy, 1996). Similarly, a man who stays home to raise children may score low on masculine characteristics and high on feminine characteristics, according to Western society.

As a general rule, however, male and female gender roles are distinct from each other, based on the culture in which one is socialized. And not all societies have the same norms. For example, in the Wodaabe tribe in northern Nigeria, men, rather than women, are considered to be beautiful and physically attractive.

> At annual gerewol festivals, hundreds of people gather, and the young men spend hours painting their faces and ornamenting their bodies. The men also dance vigorously for seven full nights, showing off their health and endurance. Towards the end of the week-long ceremony, the men line up and display their beauty and charm to the young women. Each woman invites the man she finds most attractive for a sexual encounter. Wodaabe women usually prefer the tallest men with the whitest teeth, the largest eyes, the straightest nose, the most elaborate body-painting, and the most creative ornamentation. (G. Miller, 2001, pp. 276–277)

Thus, gender is not innately related to an individual's biological sex, but is constructed socially, within the family and society.

GENDER ROLE DEVELOPMENT AND SOCIALIZATION

As discussed, sex and gender are not synonymous, although they are inappropriately used interchangeably. In Pearson's (1996) words, "by using 'gender' as a synonym for 'sex,' we confuse the language and perpetuate the myth that biology is destiny" (p. 329). It has been a difficult endeavor to separate gender from sex. This effort and current socialization practices are briefly discussed here.

In the 1970s, feminist theorists made a distinction between sex and gender (Connell, 1999). This distinction was considered to be a breakthrough because it no longer suggested that differences between men and women could be totally ascribed to biology. Instead, the distinction suggested that people could choose the gender they wished to adhere to. Specifically, that it is possible, and common, for men and women to vary in the degree to which they adopt, endorse, and are affected by gender roles (Mintz & O'Neil, 1990).

Although feminist theory has suggested that men and women can choose their gender, gender roles still have strong association with biological sex in the United States and elsewhere. Men and women are typically socialized to have differing characteristics (e.g., Gilbert & Scher, 1999; Mintz & O'Neil, 1990; Prentice & Carranza, 2002) and to be viewed as opposites based on their biological sex. Gilbert and Scher (1999) depicted these differences as the Traditional Model of "Opposite" Sex (Gender) Identity. This model, which pits men and women against each other as opposites in every respect, portrays the dominant U.S. gender formulation. In that model, males and females are conceptualized differently in various aspects of life (e.g., biological sex, life roles, personality, sexual partner), and one's gender identity is prescribed directly according to one's biological sex.

Gender identity is the gender with which a person identifies. For example, one person can be a biological male (i.e., sex) but identify more with the typical gendered characteristics of females, such as a desire to be more intimate in relationships, focus on fashion and styles, and get one's nails done at a salon. Based on this definition of gender identity, therefore, there is no one *true, direct* connection between sex and gender because one's gender identity can diverge from one's biological sex. Gender may be affected by a variety of social structures, including a person's ethnicity, employment status, religion or absence of religion, and family.

The Traditional Model, which treats men and women as opposites when considering their sex and gender, results in the gender stereotypes of Western society. Based on these gender stereotypes, biological males should avoid all things seen as feminine, such as expressing emotions other than anger or caring for children. They should also be more competitive, act tough and aggressive, and have women as sexual partners. Additionally, the traditional male gender role emphasizes career, competition, violence, risk-taking, and power over women (Mahalik, Good, & Englar-Carlson, 2003). On the other hand, women should try hard to make relationships work, be emotional and expressive, be the caretaker of a family, make children a priority, and have men as sexual partners (Gilbert, 1987; Gilbert & Scher, 1999; Kaplan, 1979).

As mentioned previously, and contrary to the Traditional Model, gender is not directly related to biological sex. Gender is a social construction that occurs within a cultural environment. That process creates what is appropriate and acceptable for women and men in a particular society (Deaux & LaFrance, 1998). The process also helps people fit within society based on these social constructions. It is a process that starts with birth, when the doctor says, "It's a girl (or boy)"—or even before birth when ultrasound tests are done—and the socialization continues until death.

These prescribed gender roles are revealed early to children. Most children indicate at a young age that they have clearly learned gender roles (Beal, 1994; Etaugh & Liss, 1992) and have a sense of their own gender identity by 24 to 36 months of age (Powlishta, Sen, Serbin, Poulin-Dubois, & Eichstedt, 2001). Beal (1994) suggested that in the United States, boys are expected to dress in pants, play outdoors, be active, get dirty, and hold their tears back when they are frightened, while girls are expected to stay clean, play close to home, be pretty, and be nice to other children. Thus, awareness of gender roles can be an important aspect of childhood development.

It should be noted that gender roles might not be as rigid now as they were in the past. Nevertheless, subtle differences still exist and traditional role restrictions remain in effect. For example, in many current popular songs, the artists sing of a culture in which women are valued as sexual objects and men as monetary providers. Another traditional gender role assumption is made when one drives up to the take-out window at a fast-food outlet and orders a child's special meal with a toy in it. The customer will be asked, "Boy or girl?" to determine which toy to give to the child. In this case, boys are usually given superheroes or cars—more action-oriented toys—while girls are given little dolls or ponies.

Historical Shifts in Gender Assumptions

Throughout the years, ideas and stereotypes of gender roles have changed in Western society in many ways (Beal, 1994). For example, before 1920, women were denied the right to vote in the U.S. because men were supposed to make all the decisions for women. Males were considered to be more rational and, therefore, to know what was in the community's best interest. Most women did not work outside the home, although it should be noted that working-class women have always supplemented the family income by having such jobs as taking in wash and taking care of other people's children. The exception occurred during the two World Wars, when women had to take on physical, low-wage factory jobs. It was rare for men to be the stay-at-home parent (Rochlen, Suizzo, McKelley, & Scaringi, 2008).

Obviously, times have changed. Women can now vote and run for government office, and they commonly work outside the home. Moreover, due to high divorce rates, women are often the major breadwinners of a family. However, women continue to earn a lower average wage than men

(Longley, 2004), and they continue to be the primary caregivers or assume the majority of the managerial responsibility for things related to the family (Zappert, 2001).

In more recent years, men have stayed at home more often. Specifically, in 2010 an estimated 154,000 dads stayed home to care for their children and remained out of the workforce for at least 1 year to care for children under the age of 15 (Lofquist, Lugaila, O'Connell, & Feliz, 2010). Many of these stay-at-home dads have been found to be more active in their family relationships, especially with children. However, many men who stay at home experience feelings of isolation and gender role conflict. Both are possible consequences to not conforming to the pre-established gender role. These phenomena (for both men and women) may be related to traditionally prescribed gender roles in some cases, but in other cases may be related to the occupational choices that are made.

Although it appears that the idea of males and females being opposites has disappeared through the centuries and that gender role socialization has become more flexible, the Traditional Model still has much power. Over four decades ago, Broverman and her colleagues found that both college students and counselors described different desirable traits for men and women (Broverman, Broverman, Clarkson, Rosenkrantz, & Vogel, 1970). Men's desirable traits reflected "competency," including attributes such as being independent, objective, active, competitive, and logical. Mental health workers identified these masculine traits as the characteristics of a healthy adult. However, these same participants reported that desirable traits for men, and healthy adults, were not the same as the desirable traits for women. Traits desirable for women included warmth and expressiveness as well as being less independent, less rational, and less ambitious. These were not seen as key characteristics of a healthy adult. Similar findings have been reported more recently (e.g., Prentice & Carranza, 2002; Wester & Trepal, 2004). Traditional gender prescriptions persevere, with women being seen as more relational relative to societal standards, yet also more dependent and weak in nature. Men are seen as more aggressive and independent, which, in turn, has been viewed as being more competent overall.

Suffice to say, gender is a powerful and organizing variable in society. However, not all of the characteristics associated with gender differences are negative. The differences in gender roles, for each sex, are important and add to the diversity of human experiences and interactions.

The Power of Socialization

As described in Chapter 2, humans learn how to think and act through the process of socialization. The socialization that creates gender occurs through families' expectations and modeling as well as through the media and other environments (such as schools). Parents in the recent past described their newborn children differently by gender within 24 hours after birth, portraying their daughters as more delicate and their sons as hardier and more coordinated (Rubin, Provenzano, & Luria, 1974). Parents continue to describe their children in much the same way as their children get older, believing that boys are more competent, are better able to take care of themselves, and can accomplish tasks earlier than girls. Parents also describe girls as needing more protection because they are more fragile and physically vulnerable (Beal, 1994). That latter belief is contradicted in at least one area by the fact that boys are more vulnerable to infectious diseases than are girls when they are first born (Robinson & Howard-Hamilton, 2000).

Children are socialized—ortrained—to adhere to gender-appropriate behavior both at home and at school. Many families begin training their children about gender-appropriate behavior through both subtle and overt communications about how to behave, speak, and dress according to the social norm (Philpot, Brooks, Lusterman, & Nutt, 1997). Parents also train for gender by modeling behavior, rewards, and consequences. Such socialization also occurs outside the home. Some parents report attempts to raise their children at home in "gender-neutral" ways. However, when the children go to school they begin to alter their behavior to become more "gender appropriate" (Gilbert & Scher, 1999). Teachers and children in schools promote conformity to gender-appropriate behavior through direct instruction, encouragement, exclusion in play, and teasing (Martin, 1998; Thorne, 1993). Consider the "perfect mom," a person who provides unconditional love and care for others and her family—a cultural perspective that females are expected to mature into caregivers (Simmons, 2002). On the other hand, boys are taught the "boy code" in terms of a gender role (Blazina, 2004). This code teaches boys the expectation to be strong, stoic, and in control, and this code is carried into adulthood for men (Watts & Borders, 2005).

Activity 14.3 provides you with an opportunity to examine the role of socialization in gender.

Activity 14.3   Checking in on Socialization

Look again at your responses to questions about this chapter's second vignette in Activity 14.1.

1. How were the client's parental roles related to the biological sex that you assigned to the client? (Did you assign "male" to the client because the client had worked in the corporate world, as had the client's father? Or did you deem the client "female" because the client had a desire to stay home, regardless of a rewarding career?)

(Continued)

---

2. What were the characteristics that drove you to select the biological sex of the client in the vignette? For example, what did you select as the strengths of the client?

3. Were the strengths more caring and family oriented, or were they more ambitious and career oriented?

4. Are these strengths, along with the biological sex you assigned to the client, associated with how you were socialized (regardless of whether your socialization is through Western society, family values, or cultural messages)?

5. What was it like to grow up in your family?

6. What chores were you responsible for as a child/adolescent?

7. What were your brothers and sisters responsible for, if you had any?

8. Were the chores assigned on the basis of biological sex differences, or were they assigned based on skills?

Fill in the blanks:

9. As a boy/girl I was encouraged to _____
   and from this I learned that boys/girls should _____.

10. As a girl/boy I was discouraged from _____
    and from this I learned that girls/boys should not _____.

11. During traditional holiday meals, women and men performed certain roles, which were _____
    _____.

12. The women and men I was closest to as a child modeled that women and men _____
_____.

13. Now describe what your family's expectations were for men and women—thinking of both immediate and extended family.

14. Were there any gender-related patterns in the above questions between the men and women in your family? (e.g., Were men given specific chores related to outdoor activities or strength-based tasks? Were women given more homemaker type chores? Was individuality stressed more than gender-stereotyped activities, behaviors, or expectations?)

15. What messages might these patterns have given you?

16. How do the gender messages you received in your family play a role in your beliefs about men and women today?

THEORIES OF GENDER DEVELOPMENT

Over the years, there have been a number of theories of gender development. A common thread running through some of the theories is the "nature versus nurture" debate. This debate revolves around the relative influence of biology (nature) and socialization (nurture) on gender. Although a discussion of all theories is beyond the scope of this chapter, the two emphases are briefly described here (see Table 14.1 for a summary).

Although discussion of the impact of gender socialization is emphasized in this chapter, counselors need to understand the biological dimension of gender, which is commonly called sex, as mentioned earlier. Biology has been found to play a role in some differences between men and women. In fact, one extreme view posits that biology is primarily responsible for creating and structuring gender identity. This view places importance on the impact of genes and hormones on the mind and the body. The next two sections present the extreme views on nature versus nurture. There is room for a nuanced understanding of the interaction of the two and the individual differences that affect gender assumptions and behavior.

Emphasis on Nature in Gender Development

Evolutionary psychologists explain the foundation for gender differences to be rooted in biology, or nature. Evidence for the nature dimension includes the significant physical differences between the sexes that can affect behavior. For example, women and men respond differently to

Table 14.1 Summary of the Biological and Social Gender Development Themes

Theory	Explanation of Male Behavior	Explanation of Female Behavior	Explanation of Differences	Conclusion
Biological (Nature)	XY chromosomes	XX chromosomes	Attributed to having different genes and hormones; having a different biology explains the differences	Males and females look, act, and respond differently based on their different biological make-up.
Social (Nurture)	Imitate males they encounter in society	Imitate females they encounter in society	Attributed to social learning (rewards and punishments) from others based on societal standards of masculine and feminine behavior	Culture transforms the male or female.

medication; they require different dosages for the same body weight. Nature-oriented theorists also cite as evidence of a biological difference the fact that women are more likely to experience depression and anxiety than are men (Padgett, 1997), which has been suggested to be caused by differences in hormone secretion (Moreau, 1996). In addition to depression, women have been found to have more physical and psychological illnesses than men, regardless of country or context, with possible causes being explored, including menstrual cycles, postpartum, and menopause—all biological aspects of being a female (Chandra et al., 2009).

Other biology-oriented writers have pointed to brain composition and chemistry as playing a role in gender differences and behavior (Quartz & Sejnowski, 2002). Brain tissue has been found to be different between men and women, with females seeming to have the capability to use both sides (left and right hemispheres) of the brain for language and speech, while males' language seems to be associated more with the left side of the brain (Sax, 2005).

Additional biological differences have been found between women and men. For example, males hear less well than females do. Thus, a male student who does not seem to be paying attention or is gazing out into space in a classroom setting may not have attention deficit disorder (ADD) but instead may be unable to hear the teacher at the front of the room (Sax, 2005). In addition, from birth, boys are more interested in action-oriented items than in relational items. For example, in a study of 102 infants, males were more interested in a mobile than in a woman's face, while the female babies were more likely to look at the person's face than at the mobile (Sax, 2005). Thus, researchers are suggesting that sex differences in social interest may be biological in origin. Girls have also been found to be better at tasks that involve object discrimination, thus answering the question of "what is it" versus "where is it," while boys are better at object location (Sax, 2005). Even shopping behavior has been attributed to biology, with women "gathering" and men "hunting" (*"Men Buy, Women Shop,"* 2007).

Interestingly, it has been found that at birth and in the first few months after, males tend to be more emotionally expressive than female infants (Mejia, 2005). That fact is ironic in the sense that women tend to be socialized in Western society to exhibit a wide array of emotions. Male infant expressiveness may be related to men's tendency to be more physically aggressive. By age 5, very few boys are likely to express feelings other than anger (Pollack, 1998), which can at least partly be explained by the nurture dimension.

Nature-oriented explanations also explain attractiveness in biological terms, with facial symmetry, thinness, and an hourglass figure for women and a muscular triangle shape for men indicating fertility and therefore desirability (Swami & Furnham, 2008).

Emphasis on Nurture in Gender Development

Theories that emphasize nurture propose that gender differences largely stem from socialization. In these views, gender is an invisible societal structure that organizes the world into masculine and feminine. These gender categories are conceptualized as polar opposites, and men and women are seen as being rewarded for assimilating their behavior to the socially "correct" pole and penalized if aligning to the other pole. For example, women in Western cultures are socialized to dress and look attractive and sexy, which is typically defined as being thin (e.g., Sneddon, 2003). When women do not "achieve" this physical appearance, people tend to have a lower opinion of them; they actually view such women as less intelligent. Such women tend to be more depressed and less satisfied with their body image. They may punish themselves in other ways in order to fit this gender stereotype (Davis & Scott-Robertson, 2000).

Similarly, men may feel pressure to conform to a masculine appearance (Robinson, 2005). Men may strive to have a muscular body or a body with much definition. These men who strive for a more mesomorphic body type may do so to feel and appear more masculine, to avoid appearing weak, or to be seen as more attractive. In any case, societal pressure has dictated the importance of appearance in men. According to the nurture perspective, these behaviors, desires, and actions are not biologically driven, but tend to be socialized and accepted through social learning.

Pulling apart the nature/nurture factors in gender behavior is not the task of this chapter. For counselors, it is important to know how and when gender stereotypes and rules limit client adjustment. Therefore, the next section addresses gender stereotypes.

GENDER STEREOTYPES

Gender stereotyping is one of the ways in which people structure, organize, and categorize the world around them (Scher & Good, 1990; Stevens-Smith, 1995). Such stereotyping can be useful in organizing social discourse, and it can seriously limit human potential.

The Function of Gender Stereotypes

Indeed, as noted in Chapter 2, categorizing is an act of assimilation that can be functional. Categorizing is a cognitive label-saving device (Glick & Fiske, 1999, p. 368) that allows humans to determine quickly how to treat people without having to take in unique individual aspects and the surrounding context for every individual (Glick & Fiske, 1999). Gender stereotypes guide a person's behavior so that she or he fits into predictable roles. Such assimilation can act as an organizer that structures society in terms of behaviors, expectations, and personalities. For children, gender acts as "a powerful tool" that helps them "make sense of their social world. . . . In other words, gender becomes an 'organizing principle' for children, helping them understand and interpret the behavior of those around them" (Beal, 1994, p. 92). Gender stereotypes thus help shape children's development, leading children to master the skills they will require as adults as well as assisting in socializing them so that they fit into their culture in terms of what society believes is a well-functioning adult (Beal, 1994).

Drawbacks of Gender Stereotypes

Although gender stereotypes can be functional, they can also have serious drawbacks, both for society in general and for counseling specifically. Gender development theories (e.g., biological, psychodynamic, external-cultural), whether fundamentally based on biological, social, or psychological assumptions, are still rooted in the men-versus-women paradigm. Thus, although at times they can be helpful, stereotypes can exaggerate the notion of men and women as opposites, suggesting that behavior, activities, dress, and other traits are directly a result of biological sex

(Beal, 1994). When individuals adhere rigidly to the restrictions of gender stereotypes, they constrain their own experiences and abilities and may possibly inhibit or judge others. In the counseling arena, a counselor's gender stereotypes can impact how she or he assesses men and women, leading to overpathologizing, often by overusing certain diagnoses for a particular sex (Owen, Wong, & Rodolfa, 2009).

Gender stereotypes may have consequences for clients. A client expecting herself or himself to adhere firmly to a gender stereotype might take away opportunities to experiment with other behaviors, often leading to feelings of depression, loneliness, or anger. For example, a woman who adheres strictly to the Traditional Model might give up her career to be a stay-at-home mother and raise her children while her husband goes to work to advance his career and be the breadwinner in the family. That situation might occur for her even if her goal in life was to advance in her career and be the CEO of a Fortune 500 company. In another example, a gay male who adheres to gender stereotypes might marry a woman out of social gender stereotype pressure and possibly have children with her. In both of these examples, the individuals are adhering to the Traditional Model of gender, or what they have identified as appropriate expectations for someone of their biological sex. However, placing themselves into the rigid box of a gender stereotype may ultimately lead them into a counselor's office due to depression and disappointment.

Another salient aspect of not conforming to traditional gender roles is gender role conflict (GRC; Wester & Vogel, 2002). GRC is the anxiety a person feels when her or his thoughts, feelings, or actions do not match those prescribed to the traditional gender role (Wester & Vogel, 2002). For example, for men this anxiety can stem from not feeling as masculine as other men appear (i.e., comparing oneself to peers, actors, or athletes).

Besides gender stereotyping affecting oneself, expecting others to adhere to a strict gender stereotype may guide interactions with others. Although one can seemingly choose the level at which one adheres to stereotypic gender roles (Connell, 1999; Mintz & O'Neil, 1990), violations of gender stereotypes are met with forms of societal punishment, devaluation, and exclusion (Fiske, Bersoff, Borgida, Deaux, & Heilman, 1991; Rudman & Glick, 1999). Those who deviate from the traditional, expected gender stereotype tend to pay a price (e.g., being teased, being excluded from groups, being less likely to make friends, having a difficult time establishing intimate relationships, becoming a victim of violence). For example, O'Neil (1982) noted that the terms *sissy* for boys and *tomboy* for girls who deviate from gender role expectations are pejorative and inhibiting.

Often these stereotypes are expressed in microaggressions. Microaggressions have been described in the literature as brief, everyday occurrences and exchanges that send condescending messages to people of a specific group, such as people of color, LGBT individuals, and women (Sue & Capodilupo, 2008). Although microaggressions can be intentional, typically these incidents are often subtle. In terms of gender, microaggressions can be covert and subtle expressions of sexism. Microaggressions are worth attending to, as formerly overt forms of sexism have become more disguised, resulting in hidden prejudice based on stereotypical perceptions of both women and men (Glick & Fiske, 2001). Examples of such microaggressions include men who are emotionally sensitive being labeled as weak (Philpot et al., 1997) and boys who play with dolls being ostracized by their peers (Bailey, 2003). In a similar vein, women who identify excessively with masculine gender stereotypes tend to be characterized as overly aggressive. Box 14.1 looks at the relationship between gender and microaggressions.

It should be noted that men who deviate from masculine stereotypes often pay a greater societal price than women who deviate from feminine stereotypes. For men, shame can be an influential reason to conform to masculine norms (Brooks, 2001). Being teased by peers, ridiculed by family, and socially ostracized are all motivators to avoid violations of the traditional masculine gender role.

Box 14.1 Gender and Microaggressions

The potentially detrimental effect of microaggressions on the therapeutic relationship has begun to gain increased interest in the past few years. When considering the detrimental effects of gender microaggressions, counselors should consider the ways in which microaggressions can affect the therapeutic process and alliance (Sue & Capodilupo, 2008). This can occur when counselors unknowingly condone sexist attitudes and practices while purporting to support gender equality (Swim & Cohen, 1997). This process can devalue individuals based on biased gender stereotypes, which in turn can have a significant impact on the therapeutic alliance (Owen, Tao, & Rodolfa, 2010). In a recent study of microaggressions in counseling, researchers noted that women who experienced some form of microaggression from their counselor also reported a decreased therapeutic alliance and counseling outcomes (Owen et al., 2010).

Counselors would do well to try to empathize with nontraditional men in order to reduce feelings of shame (Brooks, 2001).

In sum, gender stereotypes can be functional. However, when adhered to inflexibly, stereotypes can be damaging. It is important, therefore, for counselors to keep in mind that in actuality, women and men have many characteristics that overlap, leading to the concept of *fluid gender*. Gender is fluid in that, for example, both sexes experience sexual desire and similar feelings and emotional reactions (e.g., sadness, happiness, frustration, anger, pain). In addition, both sexes can perform many of the same occupations and roles within a family (homemaker, breadwinner, parent). Gender stereotyping thus can be a constriction on human potential, and gender fluidity can be freeing.

GENDER AND COUNSELING

Gender, like all expressions of culture, is a two-way street in counseling because it is present in both the client and the counselor. All humans are embedded in the gender discourse of their society. All have gender-constructed experiences. It is these experiences that can impact counselors' work with clients. Thus, since the counseling process mirrors the societal context, gender roles influence session content (Mintz & O'Neil, 1990).

There are several important topics to consider regarding gender in counseling. First, the typical experiences of men and women in counseling are presented. Then, the impact of gender stereotypes in counseling are discussed. Finally, the influence of the four combinations of sex dyads in counseling, namely (a) male to male, (b) female to male, (c) male to female, and (d) female to female, are discussed.

Men and Women in Counseling

According to the Traditional Model of "Opposite" Sex (Gender) Identity discussed earlier, more men in Western society are generally inclined, partly through socialization and partly due to biology, to be more emotionally controlled, independent, assertive, powerful, heterosexual (i.e., attracted to women), and to be providers (Gilbert & Scher, 1999). It follows, then, that men do not often seek counseling because requesting help goes against the bias to be autonomous, strong, and unemotional. In fact, men adhering to the masculine gender role may actually perceive seeking help as a threat (Addis & Mahalik, 2003). When men do go into counseling, their typical entrance pathway is forced (i.e., by spouse, employer, court system, or involuntary commitments; Rondon, 2009), with a small percentage of men coming into counseling of their own volition. On the other hand, women tend to enter counseling voluntarily or through referrals from a primary care physician (Rondon, 2009). This fact may be related to the socialization for women to express more emotions, disclose vulnerabilities, and rely on others for assistance (Owen et al., 2009).

Lest gender stereotypes be promoted in the following sections, it should be noted that not all clients fit into the Traditional Model. Also, it should be reiterated that some genuine biologically based sex differences exist between men and women.

Counseling Men

In counseling, some men may tend to show avoidant behaviors, such as fidgeting or averting eye contact as a result of fear (Mintz & O'Neil, 1990). As mentioned previously, seeking help is discontinuous with many men's self-concepts and socialization (J. Allen & Laird, 1991; Wilcox & Forrest, 1992). Men who seek counseling tend to be viewed more negatively by society (Pederson & Vogel, 2007). In fact, only one in seven men seeks counseling (McCarthy & Holliday, 2004), and men that seek counseling tend to be more likely to withdraw after the initial intake (Cottone, Drucker, & Javier, 2002). This discrepancy in the counseling rates of men is cause for concern, as men are much more likely to commit suicide (Rochlen & Hoyer, 2005), engage in substance use (Brooks, 2001), and take part in violent or risky behavior (Courtenay, 1998) than women. Many of these behaviors result from threats to their masculinity or because seeking help violates the masculine norm (Sabo, 2000). To engage in counseling, men must step out of their "typical" roles of being autonomous, aggressive, and in control. By contrast, as counseling clients, males move into a position of vulnerability, one in which they are challenged to acknowledge emotional pain (Pederson & Vogel, 2007; Robinson & Howard-Hamilton, 2000). Thus it may be helpful to use or describe alternative methods of counseling for males (e.g., classes, workshops, video, seminars) rather than just one-on-one talk that is focused on emotions (Pederson & Vogel, 2007).

When men are in counseling, they tend to present certain main issues. Four of those issues are (1) the lack of ability to express emotions (Gilbert & Scher, 1999; Goodman, Koss, & Russo, 1993), (2) violent behavior (Goodman et al., 1993), (3) lack of intimacy and a desire to connect interpersonally (Gilbert & Scher 1999), and (4) career- and work-related stress (Gilbert & Scher 1999; Mintz & O'Neil, 1990).

In the case of expressing emotions, men will typically depend on women to express the emotions in a couples counseling session (Pleck, 1981). For example, instead of crying or stating that he is sad, a male may expect or wait for his partner or wife to mention and/or exhibit these emotions so that he doesn't have to. This lack of emotional expression may especially occur in the male client–male counselor dyad (Gilbert & Scher, 1999; Scher, 2001) because men sometimes have an increased difficulty expressing emotions in front of other men.

Two possible explanations for the lack of emotional communication in men are (1) a phenomenon called *alexithymia* and (2) disturbances in emotional processing. Alexithymia merely means "the inability to put emotions into words" (*a* = "not," *lex* = "word"; Levant et al., 2003, p. 92). Though not a sign of other pathology, alexithymia may be an explanation for why a male client may seem uncommunicative or resistant to counseling. Thus, instead of being unwilling to participate in counseling, he may actually be experiencing difficulty in identifying or articulating his feelings. The second explanation entails disruptions at various points in emotional processing. Wong and Rochlen (2005) suggest a model of recognizing and processing feelings in men. The components of this model range from processing the physiological feelings associated with an emotion (i.e., increased heart rate) to deciding on the contextual appropriateness of displaying emotions (e.g., gauging whether it would be all right to cry in this particular situation). The final two stages of this model involve determining whether the emotion violates the masculine gender role (e.g., would the client feel "weak" if he were to cry) and then whether it is appropriate to show or discuss the emotion (Wong & Rochlen, 2005).

Counseling Women

More than 60% of counseling clients are women (McCarthy & Holliday, 2004). Women tend to enter counseling more often than men, and one reason is that there is less of a personal and social penalty for women regarding sharing their feelings. Women are seen as relationship oriented, expressive, and verbal. All of those qualities are consistent with counseling.

Women's presenting concerns, and their ideas about where these concerns stem from, are diverse. When women come into counseling, they are more likely than men to present with relationship problems, such as fear of upsetting a partner, frustrations with nonexpressive male partners, or problems in general with relationships (Gilbert & Scher, 1999; Mintz & O'Neil, 1990). Women also tend to present issues of low self-confidence, even though that may not be consistent with their actual academic or work performance; feeling marginalized at work; feeling overwhelmed due to responsibilities and multiple roles and role conflict; dissatisfaction with physical appearance and body image; and sexual harassment or abuse (Gilbert & Scher, 1999). When asked, women will typically suggest that their emotional difficulties stem from social relationships, early sexual experiences, intimate partner violence, or other adverse social experiences (Rondon, 2009). In general, women will be more expressive and show more emotions and affect in counseling than will men.

Although women are more likely to seek counseling, they tend to feel powerless and sense a lack of safety in the mental health system, feeling out of control in terms of what happens to them or how they are treated. Thus it may be helpful, in general, to provide women with choices in therapy and inform them about what counseling is about and what will ensue throughout the process.

The Power of Gender Stereotypes and Biases in Counseling

Counselors need to be acutely aware of how their own gender socialization and beliefs affect what they consider to be appropriate behavior for others, including clients who may or may not fit within the Traditional Model. Thus, it is imperative that counselors examine the stereotypes and biases that they bring into the counseling session.

Most clients and many counselors are unaware of the role that gender plays in their lives. In particular, highly educated counselors often consider themselves to be immune to the influence of gender stereotypes (Philpot et al., 1997). These biases play a role in clinical judgment, diagnoses, competence, and other aspects of counseling.

Counselors' own gender role socialization is a powerful determinant of how they work with clients (Daniluk, Stein, & Bockus, 1995). Counselors form impressions of their clients very quickly (Sandifer, Horden, & Green, 1970; Vogel, Epting, & Wester, 2003), often resulting in inaccurate assumptions and decisions based on easily identifiable information. For example, biological sex is easily identifiable. People are unconsciously classified by biological sex within seconds (Beal, 1994; Glick & Fiske, 1999). Thus, a counselor's initial understanding of a client tends to be based on supposed biological sex (e.g., Deaux, 1976; Knudson-Martin, 1997; Knudson-Martin & Mahoney, 1996; Stabb, Cox, & Harber, 1997) or, in actuality, on the assumptions of expected gendered traits of a client's biological sex. This has resulted in overdiagnosis of disorders such as depression and anxiety, histrionic or borderline personality disorder, eating disorders, and self-harm behavior for women, and antisocial personality, alcohol and drug abuse, and attention deficit disorder for men (e.g., Owen et al., 2009; Rondon, 2009). The fifth edition of the *Diagnostic and Statistical Manual of Mental Disorders* is slated for publication in the spring of 2013. Until then, we won't know the precise changes involved, but given that diagnostic categories and rates of diagnosis for men and women change over time, we can expect to see some changes in these data.

In the next sections, the influence of the various gender dyads is presented. Then the effects of counselor biases in counseling are presented. In addition, bias in relation to sexual orientation is briefly discussed, although that topic is addressed more fully in Chapter 15. Activity 14.4 asks you to examine assumptions that might influence counseling.

The Effects of Sex Combinations in Counseling

There are four typical biological sex combinations that can occur in counseling: female counselor–female client, female counselor–male client, male counselor–female client, and male counselor–male client (see Table 14.2). (Of course, with transgendered individuals, these categories don't hold.) Each of these combinations is accompanied by some likely counseling dynamics.

It should be noted that one combination is not necessarily worse or better than another. The different sex combinations are here offered so that counselors can be alert to possible problematic dynamics and intentionally guard against them.

Gender competence is an important aspect of counseling. While a "female counselor effect," which refers to clients (both male and female) believing that female counselors have a better ability to form therapeutic alliance, has historically been discussed since the 1970s (e.g., Jones & Zoppel, 1982; Kirshner, Genack, & Hauser, 1978),

more recent research has found that both male and female counselors can and do form effective therapeutic alliances with their clients (Cottone et al., 2002; Owen et al., 2009). Specifically, therapeutic alliance is not about the makeup of the counselor–client dyads, but effectiveness is more about the counselor's gender competence. Gender competence is the degree to which counselors can work effectively with both men and women. Owen and colleagues (2009) found that not all counselors could effectively work with male and female clients and that some could work better with one sex versus another. Therefore, it is most important for counselors to understand the cultural and familial factors in gender among their clients and to have a clear understanding of their own gendered assumptions and experiences, rather than being focused solely on the client's sex.

Table 14.2 presents a summary of some common issues that can occur for various sex dyads in counseling. Awareness of them can alert the counselor to counter them if they are countertherapeutic.

Table 14.2   Possible Counselor Biases and Counseling Issues Based on Sex Dyads

Traditional Male Gender Attributes	Traditional Female Gender Attributes
Independence	Caretaking
Competitiveness	Relationally oriented
Aggressiveness	More verbal
Male Client–Male Counselor	**Female Client–Male Counselor**
Possible counseling dynamics:	**Possible counseling dynamics:**
Competition	Power issues
Difficulties with empathy	Sexuality issues
Difficulties sharing emotions	Client may be tentative about revealing presenting concerns
Male Client–Female Counselor	**Female Client–Female Counselor**
Possible counseling dynamics:	**Possible counseling dynamics:**
Client discomfort	Questioning counselor's capabilities
Power issues	Emotionally intense
Client may be more open	

Male Client–Male Counselor

A male–male counseling dyad, or pairing, may be characterized by competitiveness, lack of emotion and/or empathy, and possibly homophobia. Due to the traditional male gender role being typified by independence, competitiveness, and aggressiveness, male counselor–client dyads can sometimes also become competitive, particularly when the client questions the counselor's judgment (Gilbert & Scher, 1999; Scher, 2001). In addition, male counselors who have identified with the Traditional Model may find it difficult to show warmth, concern, or caring to male clients because this would go against their established male gender role. Conversely, male clients may have difficulty with a male counselor who *is* empathic (Heppner & Gonzalez, 1987). Such male clients may have difficulty expressing emotions and may feel shame and embarrassment about seeking or needing help from another male because such behaviors are stereotypically viewed as weak. One study that examined male counselor–client dyads found that when confronted with a male client who did not quite fit the male counselor's gender stereotype, the counselor felt less empathic, was less comfortable with the client, and had less willingness to see the client (Wisch & Mahalik, 1999).

Female Counselor–Male Client

Female counselor–male client dyads may exhibit power struggles and sexuality issues. Regarding power, it may be difficult for some male clients to cede power to a female counselor (Mintz & O'Neil, 1990). On the positive side, male clients may reveal more emotions with a female counselor than with a male counselor because females are stereotypically seen as empathic, nurturing, and good listeners. Consistent with that finding, male clients exhibiting anxiety concerns who were paired with female counselors experienced greater improvement after counseling than any other counseling dyad (Cottone et al., 2002). On the negative side, since female counselors have been found to focus primarily on emotional content, more so than male counselors or male clients (Vogel et al., 2003), male clients may feel threatened, which may lead them to withdraw early from counseling (Cottone et al., 2002). Further, in the female counselor–male client dyad, if they are heterosexual, male clients may view female counselors as sex objects (Gilbert & Scher,

1999) and, as a consequence, may not take them as seriously in their professional role.

Male Counselor–Female Client

Echoing the dynamic in the previous dyad, in the male counselor–female client dyad, if they are heterosexual, male counselors may view female clients as sex objects (Gilbert & Scher, 1999). In one research study, female clients who dressed up to look physically attractive received more supportive comments from male counselors than female clients who were not seen as physically attractive (Schwartz & Abramowitz, 1978). That dynamic is based on the traditional view of females as sexual objects. The result in counseling can be that the client's goal is not adequately worked on, due to at least four reasons: (1) the counselor's discomfort in the relationship, (2) his inability to focus, (3) his incorrectly judging the female client's behavior and nonverbals, and/or (4) his abandoning the client by terminating counseling or referring her. Heterosexual male counselors must make an effort to manage such "sexual tension" in their work by treating all clients respectfully.

Male counselors may also adopt a power position (i.e., be more directive and authoritarian) in a session with female clients (Heatherington & Allen, 1984; Robinson & Howard-Hamilton, 2000). In turn, female clients may automatically assume a subordinate role in this dyad (Kaplan, 1979), which may relate to feeling powerless in the mental health system. Indeed, it has been reported that male counselors are more annoyed with female clients than with males when females question the counselor's judgment (Gilbert & Scher, 1999). Male counselors see themselves as less open and more self-critical than do female counselors working with female clients (Robinson & Howard-Hamilton, 2000).

Female Counselor–Female Client

When the counseling dyad is female–female, clients were found in the past to question the competence of the female counselor regarding her training, experience, and competence (Kaplan, 1979). While this may be less so today, it is worth being alert to. Such doubt about the counselor's competence can result in limited therapeutic gain.

In a contrasting dynamic, it has also been found that the female counselor–female client dyad tends to be the most emotionally intense therapeutic pairing. This dyad has been shown commonly to result in full exploration of presenting concerns, childhood experiences, and interpersonal relationship problems, as well as to have more expression of affect in the session (Jones, Krupnick, & Kerig, 1987; Jones & Zoppel, 1982). It should be noted, however, that aggression and anger are still less accepted by all counselors from female clients (Kaplan, 1987; Robinson & Howard-Hamilton, 2000).

While this dyad has the ability to be emotionally intense and can be therapeutically helpful, it can also be problematic and shaming. For example, it can be problematic if the female counselor who holds a traditional view of womanhood (i.e., stereotyped view of female overdedication to family, appearance, and submission) works with a female client who is a less traditional woman (i.e., strong/independent; more stoic and nonexpressive; or has masculine qualities such as competitiveness, violence issues, or risk-taking behavior). The result may be the counselor shaming the client for not being "feminine" enough, trying to sway the client to take on more caretaking roles or express more emotions, or perceiving that the client is resistant in counseling. Thus this female counselor may blame the client for her own problems or symptoms.

Being Alert to Gender Bias: Overall Issues

Regardless of the dyad combination, counselor gender bias must be attended to. Bias occurs when counselors consciously or unconsciously influence clients to be in only conventional or traditional gendered roles (e.g., men must be breadwinners or must be stoic, women must be caretakers and put family first or must be emotional). Thus, regardless of sex (of the client or the counselor), counselors must be wary of encouraging traditional gender roles or outwardly discouraging them. Counselors need to consider clients' cultural factors, norms, values, and beliefs before determining how to work with a particular client or even before assessing and diagnosing a client—as gendered behavior and gender assumptions play a role in all aspects of counseling.

In the case of male clients, counselors must be wary of unconsciously or nonverbally encouraging men to be emotionally distant. Counselors must also avoid automatically discouraging males from taking responsibility in their relationships or in caretaking for children. Such bias can limit the male client's choices to rigid career-driven and stoic gender roles.

On the other hand, counselors should not tend toward the other extreme, forcing the male client to immediately disclose emotions. This is likely to push a male client outside of his comfort zone and cause him to retreat from counseling early. Instead, counselors should assess male (and female) clients' gendered beliefs and behaviors or, for some men, the possible presence of alexithymia. Of course, counselors should not automatically accept a man's inclination to disregard family and make career a priority. Instead, it is simply important that counselors be aware of their immediate reactions toward a client and help clients be alert to their own gendered lenses. A fuller discussion of how to enact such alertness is presented in the later section on feminist theory.

Counselors might see women as being emotional, dependent, and oriented toward relationships. In that vein, both counselors and clients tend to view women as being better able than men to make relationships work. However, counselors also fault women more than men if there are problems in a relationship (Fitzgerald & Nutt, 1986; Hare-Mustin, 1983). Counselor bias may also support and communicate the stereotypical view that it is more important for a woman to make sacrifices and/or quit her career in order to take care of the children because she is more nurturing.

The next sections discuss gender bias against both men and women in the areas of client assessment, career issues, and family and couples counseling.

COUNSELOR BIAS IN ASSESSMENT AND DIAGNOSIS

In addition to potential bias in general, bias can affect clinicians' judgments of psychological disturbances due to predispositions about gender and gender role (Biaggo, Roades, Staffelbach, Cardinali, & Duffy, 2000; Broverman et al., 1970; Rondon, 2009; Vogel et al., 2003). As noted earlier, mental health professionals have in the past equated the characteristics of a healthy adult with those of a healthy man (Broverman et al., 1970). By contrast, healthy women were characterized as less aggressive, more submissive, more excitable, and less competitive—characteristics associated more with less well or more pathological adults.

Similar results have been found more recently. For example, in a survey of 99 mental health professionals, including licensed social workers, psychologists, and counselors, female clients were seen as less competent than male clients, regardless of age (Danzinger & Welfel, 2000). Counselors tend to describe male and female clients in gender stereotypical terms (O'Malley & Richardson, 1985; Vogel et al., 2003). When clients do not conform to the gender roles represented in the Traditional Model of "Opposite" Sex (Gender) Identity (Gilbert & Scher, 1999), counselors tend to view them as pathological (Robertson & Fitzgerald, 1990). This perception can lead to gender bias in the form of diagnoses and treatment recommendations (Cook, Warnke, & Dupuy, 1993; Rondon, 2009; Vogel et al., 2003). Take, for example, a counselor working with a woman who is not particularly emotional or articulate with her feelings. Counselors who hold very stringent gender role expectations may erroneously attribute this lack of emotion to pathology. Conversely, if that same counselor worked with a man who happened to be very "in touch" and expressive with his feelings, she or he may label that man as overly emotional (i.e., histrionic).

Males and females with identical symptomology may earn different diagnoses (Hamilton, Rothbart, & Dawes, 1986). For example, in one study, clinicians rated females as significantly more histrionic than males who exhibited the identical symptoms (Hamilton et al., 1986). In general, women have been found to be diagnosed more frequently with depression, anxiety, eating disorders, and borderline personality disorder, while males are more commonly diagnosed with alcohol and drug problems, antisocial personality disorder, hypo-emotional disorders, and being out of touch (Owen et al., 2009; Rondon, 2009).

The *Diagnostic and Statistical Manual of Mental Disorders* (DSM; American Psychiatric Association, 2000) itself has elements of gender bias. According to Cook et al. (1993), disorders in the DSM have a great deal of overlap with stereotypes of men and women in Western society. Most of the diagnoses that men are given include behaviors that are considered to be "acting out," such as antisocial behavior, oppositional defiant disorder, conduct disorder, and attention deficit disorder, while diagnoses bestowed on women tend to include more "acting in" behaviors, such as major depressive disorder, dysthymia, and posttraumatic stress disorder.

Gender-Neutral Assessment

In order to avoid errors in diagnosis based on gender stereotypes, a counselor should assess a client's beliefs about gender roles and stereotypes, experiences as a man or woman, and current stressors. The counselor should begin to formulate her or his assessment of client issues based on the client's beliefs about her or his role as a member of a particular sex, especially the gendered characteristics to which she or he adheres. See the section on feminist theory later in this chapter for assessment methods. The counselor would then examine the possible interaction among demographic factors (e.g., race, ethnicity, age, social class), the client's biological sex, and gender identity to provide a more reliable assessment of mental health (Kastrup & Niaz, 2009). After taking demographic interactions into account, the counselor would look at the presenting concern (e.g., in the vignette at the beginning of the chapter, depression) and consider the possible life events and subsequent stressors related to gender (e.g., the client's beliefs about her or his current professional role and her or his competing aspirations to take a larger childrearing role). Collection and examination of this information throughout the intake process will help the counselor determine useful diagnoses and intervention plans. You are encouraged to complete Activity 14.5 in order to examine gender issues in diagnosis.

Activity 14.5   Diagnostic Assessment

Respond to the following questions:

When thinking about the depressed homemaker in the vignette at the beginning of the chapter, what was your provisional diagnosis?

Did your diagnoses tend to relate to the "acting-in" or "acting-out" diagnoses as suggested by Cook et al. (1993), or did the severity increase and the prognosis decrease if the diagnosis crossed typical gender lines? For example, if the client was male, was he not diagnosed with depression and instead considered to have more of an adjustment disorder? Or if he was diagnosed with a depressive disorder, was it considered to be more severe in terms of the level of depression or to have a poorer prognosis?

Comment on how the client's sex interacts with other demographic variables. Think of other chapters on ethnicities, race, social class, and religion in this book to determine what stereotypes might exist for men and women from different groupings.

Finally, how might current life events affect the client's depression? Keep in mind that society's expectations of gender cannot be removed from this vignette. Thus, if the client is a woman, how might expectations to be a mother and homemaker versus being a career woman affect her decision and feelings? Or, conversely, how might these expectations play a role in the desire of a man to stay home with his children, and how might the expectations of his company, friends, and society impact his emotions and decisions?

COUNSELOR BIAS IN CAREER-RELATED COUNSELING

Career is an area in which gender bias plays an important role; both women and men experience gender-related career and job pressures. This is a confusing topic for both genders, especially around the balance between paid work and other responsibilities. Men and women have been socialized to value different types of work (e.g., historically a particular emphasis on paid work for men vs. unpaid work, such as cooking, buying, and childcare, for women).

Men and Career

For men, work can dominate their identity and therefore their lives. Common terms include *manning the desk* (instead of *staffing the desk*) and *chairman* (instead of *chairperson*). In most cultures, men are usually expected to be the primary breadwinner (Meth, Pasick, Gordon, Feldman, & Gordo, 1990). Men commonly feel societal pressure to bring in more income than women. Thus work can become a single-minded pursuit at the expense of other things. They justify this socialized assumption by rationalizing that they are providing better for their families. But this bias about being the main monetary provider may backfire because overwork can lead to marital and familial dissatisfaction on the part of the man, his partner, or his family (Meth et al., 1990). Adding to the distress, employment may be harder to come by for a male who has decided to stay home to take care of children, thus entering back into the workforce may be harder for a male than for a female. Additionally, the sense of being a success or failure as a person based on one's work role can be oppressive for men and those around them.

Women and Career

For women, the world of work can be complex. Women have been found to sacrifice in the area of career to care for their families, and attempt to combine career with shouldering the responsibility for managing the family (e.g., determining who will cook or watch the children; Zappert, 2001). Counselors need to consider all of the factors in a woman's life when discussing career aspirations and stressors. In addition to aspirations and multiple familial roles, the workplace itself can play a role for women. The effects of gender on the economy can translate into lower-wage employment, silent discrimination against working mothers (e.g., being passed over for a promotion or chance to advance based on the assumption that having children means less interest in work), and possible harassment (Moghadam, 1999). Although wage discrimination is sometimes treated as a thing of the past, in 2004, female employees won the right to launch a class action lawsuit against Wal-Mart—the largest sex discrimination lawsuit of its kind in history. On behalf of 1.6 million current and former female employees, the lawsuit alleged gender discrimination in pay and promotions (Equal Rights Advocates, 2004).

Helping Women and Men in Career

In the area of career and gender, counselors should pay attention to the gendered context of career choice and the work environment, particularly when people are preparing for career transitions (Cook, 1993). Gender-related issues include childcare, employment gaps, and the culture of the work environment.

Regarding women who are returning to the workplace, several issues should be considered. First, some work environments might tend to employ recent graduates. This may be problematic for a woman who is returning to the workforce after raising children. Second, the absence of accessible childcare may be a factor for women and sometimes for men (Farmer, 1997). Finally, the culture of the work environment itself can be problematic. In professional work, long hours, weekend work, and frequent travel may be the norm for an organization. A male client who is interested in spending more time with his family might have to evaluate the fit of such a career opportunity. Working-class and poor workers may face additional burdens regarding childcare.

In light of these gender-related career factors, clients should be encouraged to do gender role analysis (Enns, 2000), that is, to explore and challenge the gendered context of their career aspirations, choices, and workplace experiences. Gender role analysis is explained later in this chapter, in the Gender-Fair Counseling section. Clients should be encouraged to examine their values and expectations regarding their career choices so that they can feel positively about them. It is important to consider that there may not be much support for clients' nontraditional gender career choices in society.

COUNSELOR BIAS IN COUPLES AND FAMILY COUNSELING

Relationships and family are another area in which gender bias may exist in counseling. Although there are many different types of relationships (e.g., dating, partnered, married, heterosexual, homosexual), the focus in this section is on heterosexual relationships because another chapter in this text focuses on lesbian, gay, bisexual, and transgender issues and counseling.

With respect to heterosexual couples, paying attention to gendered relations has been acknowledged as central to the practice of family counseling (Zak-Hunter et al., 2010). Gender may create challenges in problem solving and intimacy (Knudson-Martin & Mahoney, 1999). Many couples (and counselors) re-create gender-learned patterns from their own development in their relationships. For example, when searching for solutions, women may be more exploratory while men may be more problem solving; regarding intimacy, women may tend toward verbal expression while men may tend toward physical expression. Although partners may rely on each other in a relationship to meet each other's physical and emotional needs, they may define and express problem solving and intimacy in different ways (Hook, Gerstein, Detterich, & Gridley, 2003).

Men and Relating

In the traditional masculine gender role, men do not express emotions that can make them seem vulnerable in an outward way, thus creating potential difficulties in intimacy with a partner. Often, men have not learned how to emote or relate intimately. While love relationships and intimacy mean a great deal to men, they often do not know how to foster or nurture intimacy (M. Allen & Robinson, 1993). Women typically show intimacy through emotional and physical closeness, while men tend to show intimacy through actions, such as making time to do activities with their partner, giving up friends, and performing romantic acts (e.g., making dinner, lighting a candle; M. Allen & Robinson, 1993). One problem for the couple lies in the tendency for men to do most of these actions in the earlier stages of dating. Thus, by doing so much in the beginning of the relationship, men can either lose part of who they are (e.g., giving up friends) or be unable to decide what they want emotionally because they often allow their partners to take the lead in intimacy. In a sense, once they "catch" a partner, men tend to reduce their efforts at intimacy. They then are surprised when a woman wants more than money, sex, or time (M. Allen & Robinson, 1993). Thus, later in the relationship, when their female partners are looking for emotional intimacy, men may still be relying on action-oriented expression, which is not always perceived as intimate by their partner.

Patterns of Relating for Women

Women are expected to be the emotional caretakers. When traditional gender roles are dominant in heterosexual relationships, it is often the woman who does the larger share of the emotional/relational work in the relationship (Knudson-Martin, 2003). The assumption that women should be responsible for intimacy and connectedness in a relationship, or that a man is not responsible for or capable of emotional expression and intimacy in heterosexual relationships, is a bias that may present in counseling—on the part of the client *or* the counselor. For example, if a man and woman who are lacking intimacy in their relationship come in for couples counseling, the counselor may suggest that the female partner enhance the relationship by increasing her sexual engagement with her male partner in order for the couple to become closer, rather than asking the male to increase his emotional overtures. This role of the emotional caretaker also extends to the family. There may be an assumption on the part of the client, family, and/or counselor that the woman does the lion's share of the emotional work in the family system (e.g., responding to feelings, establishing social connections for the family).

Summary: Consequences of Gender Bias for Counseling

Assumptions made by counselors, consciously or unconsciously, based on biological sex and gender stereotypes can harm a client (Tsui & Shultz, 1988) and impact gender competence, which affects counseling outcomes (Owen et al., 2009). Because of gender bias, the client may receive inappropriate or inadequate treatment in counseling, incorrect diagnoses may be given, or restrictive notions may be applied to the roles that men and women should assume, thereby limiting behaviors available to the client because the client is not encouraged to "step outside of the gendered box."

It needs to be noted, however, that if a client is comfortable within the Traditional Model, and this model is not causing distress, then it is not a counselor's role to convince the client otherwise. Gender differences can be respected, if each member of the couple shows flexibility and choice in gender roles and throughout the relationship. For example, division of labor is not, in itself, a problem in couples, but when problems arise, the refusal to adapt because of inflexibility in gender roles can become a problem.

IMPLICATIONS FOR PRACTICE

Every client who comes in for counseling is a gendered being. As discussed earlier, it is imperative that counselors be aware of the impact of their gendered selves as well as the impact that clients, as gendered beings, have on the counseling process. Therefore, a brief overview and discussion of the implications and expectations for counseling men and women is provided, as well as a discussion of how to develop a process of gender-fair counseling. The topics to be discussed are women and men in counseling, feminist theory, and gender-fair counseling.

Women and Men in Counseling

Women tend to seek out counseling services more readily than men do (Fisher & Turner, 1970; McCarthy & Holliday, 2004). As stated before, only one in seven men seeks counseling. Thus, when men seek out counseling services, they are more likely to be in a crisis (Neukrug, 2003) or be externally forced (Mejia, 2005) by a spouse, partner, or system (e.g., work, court). Men are also less likely to talk, share feelings, or collaborate with the counselor. This reticence may be due to the socialized masculine gender role in Western society, which encourages men to be strong, independent, and competitive—not collaborative, self-revealing, and weak. As mentioned earlier, men tend to reveal emotions, especially intimacy, with action-oriented behaviors—not necessarily through talk. Thus, methods other than talk (e.g., creative modalities such as expressive arts and physical activities) may need to be considered by the counselor to help men learn to share feelings. Counselors should note that because men tend to defer recognition of certain feelings, they are also at an increased risk of experiencing a crisis, having overwhelming feelings, attempting or committing suicide, and having a shorter life expectancy than women (Neukrug, 2003).

Women have a tendency to seek counseling more than men; this may be related to their relational and communicative orientation. Most women will open up and discuss presenting concerns and feelings to a counselor fairly easily. However, their valuing relationships more also can make them feel responsible for a relationship that is failing—regardless of the reasons. In addition, given the effects of gender socialization, women may have difficulty establishing and maintaining self-boundaries (Collier, 1982). Women may think of others' needs to the exclusion of their own. As we have considered different aspects regarding men and women in the counseling relationship, we will also consider how counselors can best work with both. Two approaches that can be helpful in working with gender issues in counseling are feminist theory and gender-fair counseling. Both are briefly discussed below.

Feminist Theory

Broadly speaking, feminist theory is an approach to counseling, for men and women, that considers gender roles. More of an overall philosophy than a set of specific techniques, feminist theory can specifically address the impact of gender in clients' lives. According to Trepal and Duffey (2011),

> feminist theory is often described as an approach, or lens, through which counselors view themselves, clients, client concerns, and the world. Through this lens, much attention is paid to issues of adherence to gender roles, issues of power and privilege, and to the role of advocacy. Inherent in this approach is the use of personal power. (p. 107)

While a full discussion of this theory and its resulting applications in counseling are beyond the scope of this chapter, and while it is certainly not the only approach to use with clients that focuses on gender, this theoretical lens can be particularly powerful.

Gender-Fair Counseling

In light of the trends discussed earlier, counselors need to make an effort to implement gender-fair counseling (Van Buren et al., 1989). Gender-fair counseling aims at facilitating the development of full client potential based on an individual's unique characteristics, regardless of her or his gender.

Van Buren (1992) proposed four steps for gender-fair counseling: (1) examining values and beliefs of both the counselor and the client, (2) confronting biases that may exist in the counselor or client that may limit client options, (3) taking action toward gender-fair goals, and (4) evaluating

the outcomes. These steps are discussed next in some depth.

Examining the Values and Beliefs of Counselor and Client

As has been emphasized throughout this chapter, it is imperative that counselors examine their own and their clients' gender identities and socialization. According to the ethical standards of the American Counseling Association (2005), counselors must be "aware of their own values, attitudes, beliefs, and behaviors and avoid imposing values that are inconsistent with counseling goals" (§ A.4.b). Given these ethical guidelines, counselors must recognize their own beliefs about gender. These beliefs may not be in their conscious awareness because sex classification, along with beliefs about gender, tends to occur instantaneously.

Along with exploring their own gender identity and beliefs, counselors must in turn proactively help clients examine their own gender identities and beliefs. Specifically, a counselor should inquire about the history of the client's gender roles and behaviors with questions such as these: How have others, for example, your friends and family, reacted to your choice to quit your job and stay home with your kids? What about your coworkers or your boss? How has this choice affected you, your spouse, your family, or your lifestyle? These types of questions are discussed further in Chapter 19 as culturally educated questions, in the sense that the counselor uses knowledge of the cultural trends to frame probing culture-related questions.

These questions can be asked of both women and men. Counselors should also not just ask these types of questions when a client steps out of the Traditional Model—that would not be gender-fair counseling. Question 10 in Activity 14.3 ("As a girl/boy I was discouraged from _____ and from this I learned that girls/boys should not _____") is a good example of how a counselor might do a gender analysis by exploring a client's history, background, and socialization of gender. For the client in the second vignette that began this chapter, a counselor might ask how the client's parental roles of homemaker and corporate lawyer had an impact on her or his career choice and on the struggle with leaving her or his career and staying at home. In addition, the client might be asked what were the messages about life, career, and family that the client received from her or his parents and how did these messages align or conflict with society's messages.

The counselor's in this part of gender analysis is to make patterns and assumptions about gender in the client's life visible and help the client see that there are options for making changes in her or his life (Knudson-Martin, 2003). For example, the counselor might say, "I notice that you always seem to take on the responsibility in your relationships without handing any of that accountability over to your partner," or ask, "Based on what you are telling me, have you ever expressed your desire to stay home with your kids instead of working? What might be your partner's reactions to this desire?" By pointing out these patterns and assumptions, the counselor is able to help the client examine them and their role in her or his life.

Also, as part of examining gendered values and beliefs, it is helpful to encourage clients to process how developmental aspects of their manhood or womanhood have changed over time (Meth et al., 1990). For example, a female's assumptions of gender, ideas about gender roles, and her own gender identity might change when she becomes a mother, or a man's might change when he becomes a father. A counselor might ask, "What are your expectations of your partner? Have these expectations changed now that your son is born?" or "What changed when you moved out of your childhood home? Did your gender identity and roles change?" A counselor should not judge a client's responses as right or wrong, but instead simply listen to and validate them while continuing to search for the patterns and themes in the client's life.

Links between the client's gender identity, expectations, and presenting concerns may begin to arise during this examination. However, the counselor's role is not to push a client to pick up a gendered role or expectation that she or he does not want, or is not ready for, based on the counselor's own expectations or agenda. Instead, simple statements identifying the client's pattern can be made in order to bring these gendered blueprints into awareness. Activity 14.6 can be used with clients to evoke gender socialization and assumptions.

Activity 14.6   Gender Lens Activity

Each of us has her or his own personal experiences, including educational, ethnic, familial, and religious experiences. These make up our Gender Lens.

For example, think about your past educational, ethnic, familial, and religious experiences, and try to think of an example of a gendered message or perception you heard or experienced. Then, think of an image, word, phrase, or color that might represent these experiences or messages. Then, take a few minutes to make a drawing that reflects your own set of gendered experiences.

Awareness of your Gender Lens is the first step in understanding your socialization, culture, and judgments or biases toward gender and/or sex.

This activity can be done with clients.

Source: © Wester & Trepal (2003).

Confronting Client Gender Biases

The second step in gender-fair counseling is for counselors to help clients discover the ways in which gender biases take effect in their lives and explore and challenge old gendered patterns (Knudson-Martin, 2003). These biases can be covert (implicit) or overt. In this vein, counselors can reframe gender differences, which may or may not be influenced by nature, as choices. This type of discourse leaves open the possibility of change.

Counselors should assume that clients can achieve flexible gender behaviors and that they can be developed by both sexes (Knudson-Martin, 2003). For example, as indicated previously, with heterosexual couples it is important to assume that both men and women are capable of developing skills that are stereotypically associated with the other sex (e.g., men can be emotional and women can be aggressive). Instead of viewing one gender role or the other as correct or right, counselors can focus on the strengths of all potential roles and behaviors, ones that can be used by both genders (Heesacker & Prichard, 1992).

Counselors can also confront clients' gender biases. Consider the following example. A female client says that she cannot become more assertive because for her whole life people have been telling her that she is kind. Thus she doesn't see any other way of acting as appropriate. The client has a gender bias—thinking that she can only act a certain way, based on her history. In this situation, the counselor may choose to confront the client's bias by helping her uncover some exceptions (e.g., surely there was a time, however minute, when she was mildly assertive) or find opportunities to experiment with a new behavior. The goal is to help the client expand her choices, both in behaviors and in attitudes (Collier, 1982).

Taking Action Toward Gender-Fair Goals

The third step in gender-fair counseling is to present gender-fair strategies that should be used within and outside the counseling setting to make gender fairness a reality in U.S. society (Knudson-Martin & Mahoney, 1999; Van Buren, 1992). These

strategies can include actively encouraging clients to be gender fair to themselves and others as well as "going public" by presenting and writing about gender-fair counseling and treatment. Such actions include confronting gender bias when it appears.

It should be noted, in setting gender-fair goals, that it is difficult for counselors to be neutral while also being ethical regarding gender. On the one hand, counselors are trained to take a neutral stance and not to impose their own values and beliefs on clients. In addition, they are trained to conceptualize clients and enact related subsequent treatments by the symptoms they present and their diagnosis (M. Allen & Robinson, 1993). However, on the other hand, gender cannot be treated as a neutral factor. It is fraught with power and equity issues. Therefore, counselors need to be socially critical (see Chapter 3) with regard to social and political issues (e.g., current issues that are related to gender) in order to accurately conceptualize the gendered context of counseling (Van Buren, 1992). In helping to set gender-fair goals, counselors must ask, "What degree of a client's concern is due to mostly internal struggle or is a problem stemming from societal pressure (e.g., to conform when one is not conforming and/or when one does not want to conform)?" The answer to each will determine the goals.

Counselors must keep in mind that some clients may not be ready to actively engage in gender-fair behaviors or discussions within a counseling session, let alone outside a counseling session. Thus, the first step should always be threefold: (1) validating the client's feelings and presenting concerns, regardless of what they are; (2) validating the client's gender identity; and (3) exploring patterns and/or desire to alter some gender roles—or, conversely, understanding that the client does not yearn to change gender roles or alter her or his expectations. If a client wants to alter her or his behaviors or perceptions, counselors need to realize that this may be a slow process, depending on how aware the client is about her or his gendered expectations and socialization.

Evaluating Outcomes

The final step in gender-fair counseling is continuing evaluation. Once the client makes a change, the counselor and the client need to examine that change. How is the client doing with the change? Does she or he like it? Does the change seem to "fit" with her or him? Do other people in the client's life (e.g., family, friends) agree with and support the change? Is there any conflict? Do any additional changes need to occur? For example, suppose that a female client is trying to become more assertive. She may have a history of not being assertive, and consequently there may be some uncomfortable moments, both for the client and for others in her life, when she attempts to change long-standing patterns that can have gendered messages (e.g., women are not rewarded for being assertive). The counselor should evaluate by asking the client about the change that she has made and follow up by exploring the effects of the new behavior in her life.

SUMMARY

As demonstrated in this chapter, there are several ways in which gender emerges in counseling, including simple differences in how each sex tends to think, feel, and act regarding stereotypes that both the counselor and the client might have. Gender tendencies can be beneficial, as they help people feel comfortable in the world. However, when adhered to inflexibly, stereotypes can serve to limit clients' options. It is important to keep in mind that in actuality, men and women have many characteristics that overlap, leading to the concept of fluid gender. It is imperative that counselors take a critical look at their own gendered lives, as well as those of their clients, in order to establish culturally alert practice.

REFERENCES

Addis, M. E., & Mahalik, J. R. (2003). Men, masculinity, and the contexts of help-seeking. *American Psychologist, 58,* 5–14.

Allen, J., & Laird, J. (1991). *Feminist approaches for men in family therapy.* New York, NY: Harrington Park Press.

Allen, M., & Robinson, J. (1993). *In the company of men: A new approach to healing for husbands, fathers, and friends.* New York, NY: Random House.

American Counseling Association. (2005). *Code of ethics.* Alexandria, VA: Author.

American Psychiatric Association. (2000). *Diagnostic and statistical manual of mental disorders* (4th ed., text rev.). Washington, DC: Author.

Bailey, J. M. (2003). *The man who would be queen: The science of gender-bending and transexualism.* Washington, DC: Joseph Henry Press.

Beal, C. R. (1994). *Boys and girls: The development of gender roles.* New York, NY: McGraw-Hill.

Biaggo, M., Roades, L., Staffelbach, D., Cardinali, J., & Duffy, R. (2000). Clinical evaluations: Impact of sexual orientation, gender, and gender role. *Journal of Applied Social Psychology, 30,* 1657–1669.

Blazina, C. (2004). Gender role conflict and the disidentification process: Two case studies on fragile masculine self. *Journal of Men's Studies, 12,* 151–161.

Brooks, G. R. (2001). Masculinity and men's mental health. *Journal of American College Health, 49,* 285–297.

Broverman, I. K., Broverman, D. M., Clarkson, F. E., Rosenkrantz, P. S., & Vogel, S. R. (1970). Sex-role stereotypes and clinical judgments of mental health. *Journal of Counseling and Clinical Psychology, 34,* 1–7.

Chandra, P. S., Herman, H., Fisher, J., Kastrup, M., Niaz, U., Rondon, M. B., & Okasha, A. (2009). *Contemporary topics in women's mental health: Global perspectives in a changing society.* Oxford, UK: Wiley-Blackwell.

Collier, H. V. (1982). *Counseling women: A guide for therapists.* New York, NY: Free Press.

Connell, R. W. (1999). Making gendered people: Bodies, identities, sexuality. In M. M. Ferree, J. Lorber, & B. B. Hess (Eds.), *Revisioning gender* (pp. 449–471). Thousand Oaks, CA: Sage.

Cook, E. P. (1993). The gendered context of life: Implications for women's and men's career-life plans. *Career Development Quarterly, 41,* 227–237.

Cook, E. P., Warnke, M., & Dupuy, P. (1993). Gender bias and the DSM-III-R. *Counselor Education and Supervision, 32,* 311–322.

Cottone, J. G., Drucker, P., & Javier, R. A. (2002). Gender differences in psychotherapy dyads: Changes in psychological symptoms and responsiveness to treatment during 3 months of therapy. *Psychotherapy: Theory, Research, Practice, Training, 39,* 297–308.

Courtenay, W. H. (1998). College men's health: An overview and a call to action. *Journal of American College Health, 46,* 279–290.

Daniluk, J. D., Stein, M., & Bockus, D. (1995). The ethics of inclusion: Gender as a critical component of counselor training. *Counselor Education and Supervision, 34,* 294–307.

Danzinger, P. R., & Welfel, E. R. (2000). Age, gender and health bias in counselors: An empirical analysis. *Journal of Mental Health Counseling, 22,* 135–149.

Davis, C., & Scott-Robertson, L. (2000). A psychological comparison of females with anorexia nervosa and competitive male bodybuilders: Body shape ideals in the extreme. *Eating Behaviors, 1,* 33–46.

Deaux, K. (1976). Sex: A perspective on the attitudinal process. In J. H. Harvey, W. J. Ickes, & R. F. Kidd (Eds.), *New directions in attribution research* (Vol. 1, pp. 335–352). Hillsdale, NJ: Lawrence Erlbaum.

Deaux, K., & LaFrance, M. (1998). Gender. In D. Gilbert, S. Fiske, & G. Lindzey (Eds.), *Handbook of social psychology* (pp. 788–827). New York, NY: McGraw-Hill.

Enns, C. Z. (2000). Gender issues in counseling. In S. D. Brown & R. W. Lent (Eds.), *Handbook of counseling psychology* (3rd ed., pp. 601–638). New York, NY: Wiley.

Equal Rights Advocates. (2004). *Federal judge orders Wal-mart Stores, Inc., the nation's largest private employers, to stand trial for company-wide sex discrimination.* Retrieved from http://www.equalrights.org/media/walmart062204.asp

Etaugh, C., & Liss, M. B. (1992). Home, school, and playroom: Training grounds for adult gender roles. *Sex Roles, 26,* 129–147.

Farmer, H. S. (1997). Future directions for research in women's career development. In H. S. Farmer (Ed.), *Diversity and women's career development:*

From adolescence to adulthood (pp. 293–306). Thousand Oaks, CA: Sage.

Fisher, E. H., & Turner, I. (1970). Orientation to seeking professional psychological help: Development and research utility of an attitude scale. *Journal of Consulting and Clinical Psychology, 35,* 79–90.

Fiske, S. T., Bersoff, D. N., Borgida, E., Deaux, K., & Heilman, M. E. (1991). Social science research on trial: Use of sex stereotyping research in Price Waterhouse v. Hopkins. *American Psychologist, 46,* 1049–1060.

Fitzgerald, L. F., & Nutt, R. L. (1986). The Division 17 principles concerning the counseling/psychotherapy of women: Rationale and implementation. *The Counseling Psychologist, 14,* 180–216.

Fuller, M. (1999). *Woman in the nineteenth century.* New York, NY: Dover. (Original work published 1845)

Gilbert, L. A. (1987). Female and male emotional dependency and its implication for the therapist-client relationship. *Professional Psychology: Theory, Research, and Practice, 18,* 555–561.

Gilbert, L. A., & Scher, M. (1999). *Gender and sex in counseling and psychotherapy.* Needham Heights, MA: Allyn & Bacon.

Glick, P., & Fiske, S. T. (1999). Gender, power dynamics, and social interaction. In M. M. Ferree, J. Lorber, & B. B. Hess (Eds.), *Revisioning gender* (pp. 365–398). Thousand Oaks, CA: Sage.

Glick, P., & Fiske, S. T. (2001). An ambivalent alliance: Hostile and benevolent sexism as complementary justifications for gender inequality. *American Psychologist, 56,* 109–118.

Goodman, L. A., Koss, M. P., & Russo, N. F. (1993). Violence against women: Physical and mental health effects. Part I: Research findings. *Applied and Preventative Psychology, 2,* 79–89.

Hamilton, S., Rothbart, M., & Dawes, R. M. (1986). Sex bias, diagnosis, and DSM-III. *Sex Roles, 15,* 269–274.

Hare-Mustin, R. T. (1983). An appraisal of the relationship between women and psychotherapy: 80 years after the case of Dora. *American Psychologist, 32,* 889–890.

Heatherington, L., & Allen, G. J. (1984). Sex and relational communication patterns in counseling. *Journal of Counseling Psychology, 3,* 287–294.

Heesacker, M., & Prichard, S. (1992). In a different voice revisited: Men, women and emotion. *Journal of Mental Health Counseling, 14,* 274–290.

Heppner, P. P., & Gonzalez, D. S. (1987). Men counseling men. In M. Scher, M. Stevens, G. Good, & G. A. Eichenfield (Eds.), *Handbook of counseling and psychotherapy with men* (pp. 30–38). Newbury Park, CA: Sage.

Hook, M. K., Gerstein, L. H., Detterich, L., & Gridley, B. (2003). How close are we? Measuring intimacy and examining gender differences. *Journal of Counseling and Development, 81,* 462–472.

Jones, E. E., Krupnick, J. L., & Kerig, P. K. (1987). Some gender effects in brief psychotherapy. *Psychotherapy, 24,* 336–352.

Jones, E. E., & Zoppel, C. L. (1982). Impact of client and counselor gender on psychotherapy process and outcome. *Journal of Consulting and Clinical Psychology, 50,* 259–272.

Kaplan, A. G. (1979). Toward an analysis of sex-role related issues in the therapeutic process. *Psychiatry, 43,* 112–120.

Kaplan, A. G. (1987). Reflections on gender and psychotherapy. In M. Braude (Ed.), *Women and counseling* (pp. 11–24). New York, NY: Haworth Press.

Kastrup, M., & Niaz, U. (2009). The impact of culture on women's mental health. In P. S. Chandra, H. Herman, J. Fisher, M. Kastrup, U. Niaz, M. B. Rondon, & A. Okasha (Eds.), *Contemporary topics in women's mental health: Global perspectives in a changing society* (pp. 463–484). Oxford, UK: Wiley-Blackwell.

Kirshner, L. A., Genack, A., & Hauser, S. T. (1978). Effects of gender on short-term psychotherapy. *Psychotherapy: Theory, Research and Practice, 15,* 158–167.

Knudson-Martin, C. (1997). The politics of gender in family therapy. *Journal of Marital and Family Therapy, 23,* 421–437.

Knudson-Martin, C. (2003). Gender and biology: A recursive framework for clinical practice. *Journal of Feminist Family Therapy, 15,* 1–21.

Knudson-Martin, C., & Mahoney, A. R. (1996). Gender dilemmas and the myth in the construction of marital bargains: Issues for marital therapy. *Family Process, 35,* 137–153.

Knudson-Martin, C., & Mahoney, A. R. (1999). Beyond different worlds: A "postgender" approach to relational development. *Family Process, 38,* 325–335.

Levant, R. F., Richmond, K., Majors, R. G., Inclan, J. E., Rossello, J. M., Heesacker, M., . . . & Sellers, A. (2003). A multicultural investigation of masculinity ideology and alexithymia. *Psychology of Men & Masculinity, 4,* 91–99.

Lofquist, D., Lugaila, T., O'Connell, M., & Feliz, S. (2010). *Households and families: 2010.* Washington, DC: U.S. Census Bureau. Retrieved from http:// www.census.gov/prod/cen2010/briefs/c2010br-14 .pdf

Longley, R. (2004). *Gender wage gap widening, census data shows.* Retrieved from http://usgovinfo.about .com/od/censusandstatistics/a/paygapgrows.htm

Mahalik, J. R., Good, G. E., & Englar-Carlson, M. (2003). Masculinity scripts, presenting concerns, and help seeking: Implications for practice and training. *Professional Psychology: Research & Practice, 34,* 123–131.

Martin, K. A. (1998). Becoming a gendered body: Practices of preschools. *American Sociological Review, 63,* 494–511.

McCarthy, J., & Holliday, E. L. (2004). Help-seeking and counseling within a traditional male gender role: An examination from a multicultural perspective. *Journal of Counseling & Development, 82,* 25–30.

Mejia, X. E. (2005). Gender matters: Working with adult male survivors of trauma. *Journal of Counseling and Development, 83,* 29–39.

"Men buy, women shop": The sexes have different priorities when walking down the aisles. (2007). Retrieved from http://knowledge.wharton.upenn.edu/article.cfm?articleid=1848

Meth, R. L., Pasick, R. S., Gordon, B. A., Feldman, J., & Gordon, L. B. (1990). *Men in therapy, The challenge of change.* New York, NY: Guilford Press.

Miller, G. (2001). *The mating mind: How sexual choice shaped the evolution of human nature.* New York, NY: Anchor.

Miller, J. L., & Levy, G. D. (1996). Gender role conflict, gender-typed characteristics, self-concepts, and sport socialization in female athletes and non-athletes. *Sex Roles, 35,* 111–122.

Mintz, L. B., & O'Neil, J. M. (1990). Gender roles, sex, and the process of psychotherapy: Many questions and few answers. *Journal of Counseling and Development, 68,* 381–387.

Moghadam, V. M. (1999). Gender and the global economy. In M. M. Ferree, J. Lorber, & B. B. Hess (Eds.), *Revisioning gender* (pp. 129–160). Thousand Oaks, CA: Sage.

Moreau, D. (1996). Depression in the young. In J. A. Sechzer, S. M. Pfafflin, F. L. Denmark, A. Griffin, & S. J. Blumenthal (Eds.), *Women and mental health* (pp. 31–44). New York, NY: New York Academy of Sciences.

Neukrug, E. S. (2003). *The world of the counselor: An introduction to the counseling profession* (2nd ed.). Pacific Grove, CA: Brooks/Cole.

O'Malley, L. M., & Richardson, S. S. (1985). Sex bias in counseling: Have things changed? *Journal of Counseling and Development, 63,* 294–299.

O'Neil, L. M. (1982). Therapist bias in rating level of pathology as a function of client gender and role disturbance. *Dissertation Abstracts International: Section B, 43*(4-B), 1262–1263.

Owen, J., Tao, K., & Rodolfa, E. (2010). Microaggressions and women in short-term psychotherapy: Initial evidence. *The Counseling Psychologist, 38,* 923–945.

Owen, J., Wong, Y. J., & Rodolfa, E. (2009). Empirical search for psychotherapists' gender competence in psychotherapy. *Psychotherapy: Theory, Research, Practice, Training, 46,* 448–458.

Padgett, D. (1997). Women's mental health: Some directions for research. *American Journal of Orthopsychiatry, 67,* 522–534.

Pearson, G. A. (1996). Of sex and gender. *Science, 274,* 328–329.

Pederson, E. L., & Vogel, D. V. (2007). Male gender role conflict and willingness to seek counseling: Testing a mediation model on college-aged men. *Journal of Counseling Psychology, 54,* 373–384.

Philpot, C. L., Brooks, G. R., Lusterman, D., & Nutt, R. L. (1997). *Bridging separate gender worlds: Why men and women clash and how counselors can bring them together.* Washington, DC: American Psychological Association.

Pleck, J. H. (1981). *The myth of masculinity.* Cambridge, MA: MIT Press.

Pollack, W. (1998). *Real boys: Rescuing our sons from the myths of boyhood.* New York, NY: Random House.

Powlishta, K. K., Sen, M. G., Serbin, L. A., Poulin-Dubois, D., & Eichstedt, J. A. (2001). From infancy through middle childhood: The role of cognitive and social factors in becoming gendered. In R. K. Unger (Ed.), *Handbook of the psychology of women and gender* (pp. 116–132). New York, NY: Wiley.

Prentice, D. A., & Carranza, E. (2002). What women should be, shouldn't be, are allowed to be, and don't have to be: The contacts of prescriptive gender stereotypes. *Psychology of Women Quarterly, 26,* 269–281.

Quartz, S., & Sejnowski, T. (2002). *Liars, lovers, and heroes: What the new brain science reveals about how we become who we are.* New York, NY: HarperCollins.

Robertson, J. M., & Fitzgerald, L. F. (1990). The (mis)treatment of men: Effects of client gender role and life-style on diagnosis and attribution of pathology. *Journal of Counseling Psychology, 37,* 3–9.

Robinson, T. L. (2005). *The convergence of race, ethnicity, and gender: Multiple identities in counseling.* Upper Saddle River, NJ: Pearson Education.

Robinson, T. L., & Howard-Hamilton, M. F. (2000). *The convergence of race, ethnicity and gender.* Upper Saddle River, NJ: Merrill.

Rochlen, A. B., & Hoyer, W. D. (2005). Marketing mental health to men: Theoretical and practical considerations. *Journal of Clinical Psychology, 61,* 675–684.

Rochlen, A. B., Suizzo, M., McKelley, A., & Scaringi, V. (2008). "I'm just providing for my family": A qualitative study of stay-at-home fathers. *Psychology of Men & Masculinity, 9,* 193–206.

Rondon, M. B. (2009). Gender sensitive care for adult women. In P. S. Chandra, H. Herman, J. Fisher, M. Kastrup, U. Niaz, M. B. Rondon, & A. Okasha (Eds.), *Contemporary topics in women's mental health: Global perspectives in a changing society* (pp. 323–336). Oxford, UK: Wiley-Blackwell.

Rubin, J. Z., Provenzano, F. J., & Luria, Z. (1974). The eye of the beholder: Parents' views on sex of newborns. *American Journal of Orthopsychiatry, 44,* 512–519.

Rudman, L. A., & Glick, P. (1999). Prescriptive gender stereotypes and backlash toward agentic women. *Journal of Social Issues, 57,* 743–762.

Sabo, D. (2000). Men's health studies: Origins and trends. *Journal of American College Health, 49,* 133–142.

Sandifer, M., Horden, A., & Green, L. (1970). The psychiatric interview: The impact of the first three minutes. *American Journal of Psychiatry, 126,* 968–973.

Sax, L. (2005). *Why gender matters: What parents and teachers need to know about the emerging science of sex differences.* New York, NY: Random House.

Scher, M. (2001). Male therapist, male client: Reflections on critical dynamics. In G. R. Brooks & G. E. Good (Eds.), *The new handbook of psychotherapy and counseling with men* (Vol. 2, pp. 719–734). San Francisco, CA: Jossey-Bass.

Scher, M., & Good, G. E. (1990). Gender and counseling in the twenty-first century: What does the future hold? *Journal of Counseling and Development, 126,* 388–391.

Schwartz, J. M., & Abramowitz, S. I. (1978). Effects of female client physical attractiveness on clinical judgment. *Psychotherapy: Theory, Research and Practice, 15,* 251–257.

Simmons, R. (2002). *Odd girl out: The hidden culture of aggression in girls.* Orlando, FL: Harcourt.

Sneddon, A. (2003). Naturalistic study of culture. *Culture & Psychology, 9,* 5–29.

Stabb, S. D., Cox, D. L., & Harber, J. L. (1997). Gender-related counselor attributions in couples therapy: A preliminary multiple case study. *Journal of Marital and Family Therapy, 23,* 335–346.

Stevens-Smith, P. (1995). Gender issues in counselor education: Current status and challenges. *Counselor Education and Supervision, 34,* 283–293.

Sue, D. W., & Capodilupo, C. M. (2008). Racial, gender, and sexual orientation microaggressions: Implications for counseling and psychotherapy. In D. W. Sue & D. Sue (Eds.), *Counseling the culturally diverse: Theory and practice* (5th ed., pp. 105–130). Hoboken, NJ: Wiley.

Swami, V., & Furnham, A. (2008). *The psychology of physical attraction.* London, UK: Routledge.

Swim, J. K., & Cohen, L. L. (1997). Overt, covert, and subtle sexism. *Psychology of Women Quarterly, 21,* 103–118.

Thorne, B. (1993). *Gender play: Girls and boys in school.* New Brunswick, NJ: Rutgers University Press.

Trepal, H., & Duffey, T. (2011). Feminist theory. In S. Degges-White & N. Davis (Eds.), *Bringing the arts to the science of counseling* (pp. 107–116). New York, NY: Springer.

Tsui, P., & Shultz, G. L. (1988). Ethnic factors in group process: Cultural dynamics in multi-ethnic counseling groups. *American Journal of Orthopsychiatry, 58,* 136–142.

Van Buren, J. (1992). Gender-fair counseling. *Counseling and Human Development, 24,* 1–12.

Van Buren, J. B., Miller, K. L., Deason, M. G., Gipson, R. A., Goldstein, A. E., Patton, D. M., & Scher, M. K. (1989). *A model for gender-fair counseling: Viewer's guide.* Indianapolis: Indiana Common Vocational and Technical Education.

Vogel, D. L., Epting, F., & Wester, S. R. (2003). Counselors' perceptions of female and male clients. *Journal of Counseling and Development, 81,* 131–141.

Watts, R. H., Jr., & Borders, L. D. (2005). Boys' perceptions of the male role: Understanding gender role conflict in adolescent males. *Journal of Men's Studies, 13,* 267–280.

Wester, K. L., & Trepal, H. C. (2003). *Gender lens activity.* Unpublished manuscript.

Wester, K. L., & Trepal, H. C. (2004). *Identifying and working through our gendered stereotypes.* Athens, GA: Southern Association for Counselor Education and Supervision.

Wester, S. R., & Vogel, D. L. (2002). Working with the masculine mystique: Male gender role conflict, counseling self-efficacy, and the training of male psychologists. *Professional Psychology: Research & Practice, 4,* 370–376.

Wilcox, D. W., & Forrest, L. (1992). The problems of men and counseling: Gender bias or gender truth? *Journal of Mental Health Counseling, 14,* 291–304.

Wisch, A. F., & Mahalik, J. R. (1999). Male therapists' clinical bias: Influence of client gender roles and therapist gender role conflict. *Journal of Counseling Psychology, 46,* 51–60.

Wong, Y. J., & Rochlen, A. B. (2005). Demystifying men's emotional behavior: New directions and implications for counseling and research. *Psychology of Men & Masculinity, 6,* 62–72.

Zak-Hunter, L., Marshall, L., Arnold, A. L., Consiglio, S., Gale, J., Liddy, C., & Magwitz-Greyson, D. (2010). Finding our voices in the face of dominant discourse: A closer look at gender roles' impact on student clinicians. *Journal of Feminist Family Therapy, 22,* 187–202.

Zappert, L. T. (2001). *Getting it right: How working mothers successfully take up the challenge of life, family and career.* New York, NY: Touchstone.

CHAPTER 15

Counseling Lesbian, Gay, Bisexual, and Transgendered Clients

Dawn M. Szymanski

University of Tennessee

Roger is a junior in high school. He is doing well academically and is a star quarterback on the school's football team. College scouting agents are beginning to watch him play and offer sports scholarships. He is also dating one of the most popular and prettiest girls in the school. From an outsider's perspective, Roger seems to have everything going for him, yet he presents to his high school counselor with feelings of loneliness and feeling different from the other guys on the football team, confusion concerning his lack of romantic interest in his girlfriend, and an unspoken speculation that he might be gay. He wonders what all of this might mean for him and his football career, particularly given all the "fag" jokes and anti-gay remarks that he hears in the locker room. He has barely begun to consider what it would mean in his family if they found out he might be gay.

June was at a lesbian bar hanging out with a group of friends. Because she had to work early in the morning, she drank only two beers and left at 11:30 P.M. It was a crowded night at the club and her truck was parked about three blocks away. As she left the bar, a group of guys drove by her in a blue car, laughing and screaming out, "Dyke! You f___ing lezzie! I'll show you what you need." June ignored their bantering and quickened her pace. When she arrived at her truck, two of the men from the blue car were there to meet her. June turned around to run but one of the men grabbed her by the arm and attempted to sexually assault her. Thankfully, some other bar patrons were passing by and were able to scare off the two men. June enters counseling two weeks after this incident complaining of difficulty sleeping, disturbing memories of the attempted assault, anxiety, feeling emotionally numb, and being hyper-alert.

In her song "Silent Legacy," Melissa Etheridge (1993) sings about her own struggle with sexual orientation. She describes the pain of individuals concealing who they are despite their powerful attractions, ones that are automatic and natural. She describes the shame that comes from societal rejection and its transformation into anger. Her lyrics touch on people's lack of accurate information about sexual orientation issues, the negative attitudes and myths about lesbian, gay, bisexual, and transgendered (LGBT) persons that exist in U.S. society; and the pain and isolation that many LGBT persons experience in their coming-out process. If you have access to the song, you might listen to it and try to identify some of the feelings and experiences that may be associated with the coming-out process, so that you have a feel for what it might be like to be LGBT. These lyrics also evoke the power of heterosexism, that is, the privileging of heterosexual forms of relating while concurrently devaluing nonheterosexual forms of relating. Heterosexism can negatively affect the psychological well-being of LGBT persons. Etheridge's song lyrics also relate to this chapter's two vignettes, that is, to Roger's grappling with his own sexual identity and to June's traumatic experience of heterosexism.

Chapter 2 described the overall competencies associated with culturally alert counseling (Roysircar, Arredondo, Fuertes, Ponterotto, & Toporek, 2003). In those competencies, there are three overarching steps to becoming a multiculturally competent counselor that can be applied to sexual minorities: (1) becoming more *aware* of one's own attitudes and biases toward sexual-minority persons, (2) increasing one's *knowledge* about sexual orientation and gender identity issues, and (3) learning *skills* to provide culturally sensitive practice with sexual minority persons. Thus, this chapter is organized along these lines—self-awareness, knowledge, and skills—as it describes the ways in which counselors can become more culturally competent clinicians when working with LGBT clients.

Before beginning, it is worth mentioning that I had much difficulty in writing this chapter because lesbian, gay male, bisexual, and transgendered issues are here lumped together, yet these groups have unique differences. Most of the research and theoretical writings have focused predominantly on gay male, followed by lesbian, then bisexual, then transgender issues. Furthermore, lesbian, gay, and bisexual (LGB) issues fall under the category

of sexual orientation (i.e., attraction to someone of the same and/or different sex), while transgender issues usually fall under the category of gender identity (one's internal or self-identification as a gender or one's psychological sense of being male or female; American Psychological Association [APA], 2004).

Thus, one's sexual attraction to an individual, or sexual orientation, should not be confused with one's gender identity. For example, many transgender persons have heterosexual identities but, since they are discriminated against in similar ways that LGB persons are discriminated against, they often work together with LGB persons to advocate for those who challenge the dominant societal conceptions of sex, gender, attraction, and behavior, ones that are considered outside the heterosexual norm (Sausa, 2002).

This chapter discusses all of these issues, but distinguishes sexual orientation from gender identity. What follows focuses primarily on LGB sexual orientation issues, with attention given to similarities and differences among lesbians, gay men, and bisexual women and men. Then a section is devoted to addressing the unique issues of transgender persons. In addition, it is important for counselors to be familiar with the acronym LGBTQQI, which stands for lesbian, gay, bisexual, transgender, queer, questioning, and intersex.

SELF-AWARENESS

Self-awareness reflects a process of becoming aware of and challenging one's own values, biases, and personal limitations with regard to working with LGB clients. This section focuses on providing general information concerning attitudes toward LGB persons and demonstrates how these attitudes can impact counselors' therapeutic work with LGB clients.

One of the first steps in this process is to assess one's own attitudes and beliefs about homosexuality, bisexuality, and transgenderism. You are invited to complete Activity 15.1 to measure some of your own attitudes, knowledge, and experiences with LGBT persons.

Activity 15.1 Self-Assessment Regarding LGBT Persons

Instructions: Please indicate your agreement or disagreement with each of the following statements by writing in the appropriate number from the scale below.

Strongly Disagree	Disagree	Neither Agree Nor Disagree	Agree	Strongly Agree
1	2	3	4	5

_____ 1. I believe homosexuality is a sin.

_____ 2. I would feel disappointed if I learned that my child was lesbian, gay, bisexual or transgendered (LGBT).

_____ 3. Same-sex couples should be allowed to marry.

_____ 4. Children should be taught that being gay is a normal and healthy way for people to be.

_____ 5. If a member of my sex asked me out for a date, I would feel flattered.

_____ 6. Most lesbians hate men.

_____ 7. Lesbianism is the result of traumatic relationships with men.

_____ 8. Gay men are more likely than heterosexual men to be pedophiles.

_____ 9. Most men who display effeminate traits are gay.

_____ 10. Bisexual men and women are really "closeted" gay men and lesbians.

_____ 11. I have LGBT friends.

_____ 12. Someone has "come out" to me in the past 2 years.

_____ 13. I am familiar with religious groups that welcome and affirm LGBT persons.

_____ 14. I know someone who has been beaten up or murdered because of their sexual orientation.

_____ 15. I have attended LGBT establishments and events, such as a gay bar or a gay pride festival.

_____ 16. I understand the costs of coming out that LGBT persons face.

_____ 17. I am knowledgeable about a variety of reactions a parent might have after learning that her or his child is LGBT.

_____ 18. I am familiar with the community resources in my area for LGBT persons (e.g., bookstores, hotlines, support groups, bars).

_____ 19. I understand the significance of the Stonewall riots to the LGBT community.

_____ 20. I am knowledgeable about the conditions of "triple jeopardy" that affect lesbians and bisexual women of color.

Scoring: Reverse score (that is, 1 = 5, 2 = 4, 3 = 3, 4 = 2, 5 = 1) the following items: 1, 2, 6, 7, 8, 9, and 10. Then add up all the items for a total score. Scores can range from 20 to 100. Items 1–5 reflect attitudes toward LGBT persons, Items 6–10 reflect commonly held myths about LGBT persons, and Items 11–20 reflect knowledge about and experiences with LGBT persons and communities. Higher scores reflect positive attitudes and more knowledge and experiences with LGBT persons and communities. Lower scores reflect negative attitudes and limited knowledge and experiences with LGBT persons and communities.

Again, the focus here is on LGB, with a later discussion of transgender, for simplicity's sake. However, the attitudes mentioned also are directed at transgender persons.

Attitudes toward LGBT persons range on a continuum from condemnation to acceptance to affirmation. At the most negative end of the continuum is viewing same-sex attraction and behavior as crimes against nature. Persons with these attitudes believe that LGBT persons are immoral, sick, and inferior. They believe that anything, including hospitalization, prison, and electric shock therapy, is justified to change LGBT persons. Those with more accepting attitudes tend to view sexual-minority individuals as no different than heterosexual persons, believe in equal rights for sexual-minority persons, and accept a person's sexuality as long as sexual-minority persons don't "flaunt it." At the most positive end of the continuum is affirming same-sex attraction as a natural expression of human sexuality. Such individuals appreciate, validate, and affirm LGBT individuals and communities and believe that LGBT persons are indispensable to a society. They are willing to reject and confront negative stereotypes and discriminatory practices. They actively work to eradicate oppression and improve the lives of LGBT persons (Herek, 1994, 1995; *Riddle Homophobia Scale*, n.d.).

Over the past three decades, attitudes toward same-sex sexuality have become more tolerant; however, many heterosexuals still hold negative attitudes toward lesbians and gay men (Herek, 1994; Jones, 2009). For example, a fairly recent Gallup poll revealed that 44% of Americans believe that same-sex relations should be illegal, 57% do not support gay marriage, 46% do not support adoption rights for gay couples, and 28% believe that gays and lesbians should not be hired as elementary school teachers (Jones, 2009). In addition, 51% of Americans in 2006 believed that homosexuality is morally wrong (Saad, 2006).

Consistent with national samples, research on heterosexual college students' negative behaviors toward lesbians and gay men indicates an intolerant climate. For example, Franklin (2000) found that 24% of her sample reported calling lesbians or gay men insulting names and 10% reported physically assaulting or threatening lesbians or gay men. Of the 66% of students who denied committing verbal or physical harassment of lesbians or gay men, 23% reported witnessing such incidents. Remarkably, in a more recent study, similar results were found: 43% of students reported yelling insulting comments at gay men, 43% had told an anti-gay joke, 32% spread negative talk about gay men, and 11% warned gay men to stay away from them (Jewell & Morrison, 2010).

Perhaps as you took the self-assessment in Activity 15.1, you noticed that you hold some of these negative attitudes and believe some of the myths about LGBT persons. You also may have noticed that you lack information about sexual-minority persons. Keep your current attitudes in mind as you work through this chapter. Be open to the data presented here, even if such data counter your current views.

Correlates of Heterosexuals' Attitudes and Behaviors Toward LGB Persons

Attitudes toward LGBT persons tend to be related to a variety of factors. For example, negative attitudes toward lesbians and gay men are associated with being male, being older, having a low educational level, belonging to a conservative religious denomination, engaging in more religious behavior, being politically conservative, holding various forms of sexist attitudes (e.g., benevolent sexism, hostile sexism, negative attitudes about equal rights for women, adherence to and promotion of traditional gender roles attitudes), and lacking interpersonal contact with lesbians and gay men. In contrast, positive attitudes toward lesbians and gay men are associated with being female, being younger, reporting a high educational level, not being religious or belonging to a liberal religious denomination, being politically liberal or moderate, accepting egalitarian and nontraditional gender roles for women and men, and having positive interpersonal experiences with lesbians and gay men (Baunach, Burgess, & Muse, 2010; Goodman & Moradi, 2008; Herek, 1994; Jones, 2009; Kilianski, 2003; Morrison & Morrison, 2002). Consistent with these findings, positive attitudes regarding bisexuality among heterosexuals are related to more positive attitudes toward lesbians and gay men, lack of or infrequent religious attendance, more liberal political ideology, and prior contact with LGBT persons (Mohr & Rochlen, 1999).

Attitudes are related to behavior. Anti-lesbian and anti-gay behaviors, including perpetration of sexual orientation–based hate crimes, are influenced first, and obviously, by those anti-lesbian and anti-gay attitudes mentioned previously. Anti-LGBT behaviors are also related to gender, with males committing more violent anti-lesbian and anti-gay behaviors than females, peer dynamics (e.g., gaining social approval from friends, proving heterosexuality and toughness to friends), supposed self-defense (e.g., retaliating against perceived aggression or flirtation from a sexual-minority person), the need to alleviate feelings of discomfort experienced when encountering gay men, and thrill seeking (e.g., alleviating boredom, having fun; Franklin, 1998, 2000; Goodman & Moradi, 2008; Jewell & Morrison, 2010; Morrison & Morrison, 2002). Other research suggests that heterosexual men may react more negatively to gay men when feelings of attraction to other men create anxiety for them (Adams, Wright, & Lohr, 1996) and/or when they feel less masculine (Gramzow, 2002). Taken together, anti-LGBT behaviors appear to be largely a developmental means through which males in particular visibly assert their masculinity and heterosexuality (Franklin, 1998, 2000).

Information concerning correlates of anti-LGBT attitudes and behaviors gives counselors a sense of how to work toward eradicating heterosexism and anti-LGBT prejudice and discrimination. For example, increasing heterosexual persons' positive contacts with LGBT persons, using interventions targeting traditional gender role attitudes, targeting demographic groups holding more negative LGBT attitudes, facilitating education and training to increase awareness and knowledge about LGBT issues and heterosexism, increasing empathy toward victims of LGBT prejudice, influencing and strengthening prosocial and LGBT-affirmative norms in peer networks and communities—all of these seem to be important in reducing heterosexism (for a full discussion of interventions designed to address perpetrators and victims of heterosexism, see Szymanski & Moffitt, 2012). These also help counselors know the context of the lives of LGBT persons who are making decisions about coming out to others and/or dealing with heterosexism in their lives.

Counselors' Attitudes Toward LGB Persons

Counselors tend to be more open-minded about sexual-minority identities than people in general. The majority of counselors have lower levels of heterosexism than do members of the general public. Counselors generally do not view same-sex attraction as psychopathology, and they are by and large supportive of LGB clients who are coming to terms with their sexual identity (Bieschke, McClanahan, Tozer, Grzegorek, & Park, 2000). Despite these overarching positive trends, negative attitudes toward LGBT clients still persist in the counseling profession. A fairly recent survey of 1,328 mental health professionals found that 17% of respondents had assisted at least one client in trying to change her or his same-sex orientation (Bartlett, Smith, & King, 2009). In addition, experiences of heterosexist bias in the training of counseling and psychology students and such bias within the profession itself have been well documented (c.f., Burkard, Knox, Hess, & Schultz, 2009; Croteau, Lark, Lidderdale, & Chung, 2005; Pilkington & Cantor, 1996).

Similar to research on heterosexuals' attitudes toward LGBT persons, negative attitudes toward lesbians and gay men among counselors are associated with being older, frequency of religious attendance, not having a gay or lesbian friend or personal acquaintance, being a member of the Republican Party, not having participated in training about LGBT issues in the past year, and not having worked with a gay or lesbian client (Satcher & Leggett, 2007; Satcher & Schumacker, 2009). You might consider how you can be an advocate for LGBT persons in those and other settings.

The Impact of Heterosexist Biases in Counseling Work

It is clear that heterosexist counselor attitudes, behaviors, and language negatively affect LGBT clients (Dorland & Fischer, 2001). Even among counselors who reported low levels of heterosexism in themselves, negative views of homosexuality were found (Barrett & McWhirter, 2002; Gelso, Fassinger, Gomez, & Latts, 1995; Hayes & Erkis, 2000; Hayes & Gelso, 1993). In addition, Liddle (1996) found that client-reported heterosexist behaviors and attitudes were positively related with the risk of the client terminating after one session. It makes sense, therefore, that most lesbian and gay clients prescreened their counselors for LGBT affirmativeness (Liddle, 1997). This screening was linked to greater client satisfaction with counseling.

Examining the power of language in counseling, Dorland and Fischer (2001) found that LGBT participants who were exposed to a counseling vignette that was free from heterosexist language bias were more likely to return to see the counselor, to perceive the counselor as more credible, to indicate greater willingness to disclose personal information in counseling, and to express greater comfort in disclosing her or his sexual orientation to the counselor than participants exposed to a similar counseling vignette that contained heterosexist language. That is important for counselors to know, as engaging in heterosexist bias such as making assumptions that a client is heterosexual can result in the client not fully engaging in the therapeutic process or, worse yet, not returning to therapy. Relatedly, non-LGBT-affirming supervision negatively affects not only LGBT supervisees and the supervision relationship but also client outcomes (Burkard et al., 2009).

Types of Problematic Counselor Heterosexist Responses

Sexual-minority clients might encounter four types of heterosexist counselor responses (Falco,

1991). You might consider which one, if any, would typify your current tendency.

The first one is "You're Not Really an LGBT Person." This type of response can vary from the extreme of counselors telling clients that they are outright liars to counselors suggesting that clients are going through a phase or that they don't really know what they want. The effects of this type of response are to silence clients and convey to them that they are not able to trust their own perceptions.

The second type of heterosexist counselor reaction is "The Inadequate Response," whereby the counselor either automatically assumes a client is heterosexual or treats sexual identity issues with avoidance. Thus, when a client tells the counselor that she or he is LGBT, the counselor ignores the relevance and importance of this social identity to the client, refuses to discuss this topic in any depth, and often changes the subject when the client brings it up.

The third response is "The Liberal Response," whereby the counselor seems open to sexual-minority identities, but tries to treat LGBT clients just the same as if they were heterosexual. This type of response denies all of the unique dynamics and stressors, such as experiences of external and internalized heterosexism, that sexual-minority clients experience and bypasses very important counseling material.

The fourth heterosexist counselor behavior is "The Lecture," in which the counselor provides an unfounded description of sexual-minority persons as immature, developmentally arrested, acting out, unhealthy, or pathological. An extreme form of this type of heterosexist bias can be seen in proponents of "conversion" or "reparative" therapies, ones that aim to assist clients in changing their sexual orientation. These types of therapies assert that same-sex feelings are unacceptable and pathological and need to be "cured." Conversion therapies are based on misleading, oppressive, and unsupported hypotheses. They have been shown to cause considerable damage, such as increased self-hate, psychological distress, and suicidality, to those who undergo them (Beckstead & Morrow, 2004; Morrow & Beckstead, 2004; Shidlo & Schroeder, 2002). In addition, they violate many principles of both the American Counseling Association's and the American Psychological

Association's ethical codes, including respect for people's rights and dignity, competence, integrity, and social responsibility (Tozer & McClanahan, 1999).

Identifying and Challenging Heterosexism

Although there has been some positive change, North American culture is still predominantly heterosexist and homophobic, conveying negative messages about LGBT identities, persons, and communities. Future counselors are likely to have internalized these messages to some degree or another. For some counselors these attitudes and beliefs are overt and conscious (e.g., believing that homosexuality is a sin), and for others they are covert and unconscious (e.g., assuming that a

client is heterosexual). So the question is not "Am I heterosexist?" but "How am I heterosexist, and how might that affect my work with LGBT as well as heterosexual clients?" (Morrow, 2000).

Counselor self-awareness about LGB issues is a continual process of self-examination, of identifying and challenging one's values, beliefs, attitudes, biases, and personal limitations in working with LGBT clients. Counselors must examine their own sexual orientation and how it has affected their own development and identity. From there they have to study their own heterosexist socialization and identify specific attitudes and beliefs from their upbringing that indicate both respect and a lack of respect for LGBT persons. In other words, counselors must look at how their personal feelings influence their interactions with their LGBT clients (see Activities 15.2 and 15.3).

Activity 15.2   Examining Messages Learned About Sexual Orientation

As a part of becoming more self-aware concerning sexual orientation issues, it is important for you to examine both the overt and subtle messages that you learned about heterosexuals, lesbians, gay men, and bisexual women and men. In doing so, you might consider the following questions:

1. What are your earliest memories related to hearing others speak about sexual orientation?

2. How did you learn about heterosexuality, homosexuality, and bisexuality as a child, adolescent, and adult?

3. What messages did you hear from the government, media, school, religious institutions, colleagues, acquaintances, friends, and family of origin about heterosexuality, homosexuality, and bisexuality?

4. What stereotypes exist in the general culture (e.g., dominant U.S.) about lesbians, gay men, and bisexual persons? What impact do you think these stereotypes might have on both heterosexuals and sexual-minority clients?

5. When was the first time, or a significant time, if ever, that you were forced to rethink or were challenged about your attitudes concerning sexual orientation?

6. How have your attitudes about sexual orientation issues developed over time?

7. How do you feel about interacting with and counseling others whose sexual orientation is the same as yours?

8. How do you feel about interacting with and counseling others whose sexual orientation is different from yours?

You are encouraged to complete Activity 15.3 in order to be more alert to the oppressive factors in the lives of LGBT persons.

Activity 15.3   Becoming Aware of Heterosexual Privilege

Heterosexual privilege refers to unearned benefits and social advantages that are enjoyed by heterosexual people but not by sexual-minority people. Many heterosexuals are likely to consider these privileges to be "natural." They frequently go unarticulated and unexamined by those who benefit from them. Examples of heterosexual privilege include showing affection to your romantic partner in public without fear of retaliation, having the tax benefits associated with marriage, and talking openly to a coworker about the vacation you had with your romantic partner.

This activity is based on Peggy McIntosh's work on white privilege (see Chapter 3). It was written by a number of straight-identified students at Earlham College who got together to look at some examples of straight privilege. These dynamics are but a few examples of the privilege that straight people have. Lesbian, gay, bisexual, and queer-identified folks have a range of different experiences but cannot count on most of these conditions in their lives. Respond with *yes* or *no*.

On a daily basis:

1. I can be pretty sure that my roommate, classmates, neighbors, and/or coworkers will be comfortable with my sexual orientation.

2. If I pick up a magazine, watch TV, or play music, I can be certain my sexual orientation will be represented.

3. When I talk about my sexuality (e.g., in a joke, talking about my relationships), I will not be accused of pushing my sexual orientation onto others.

4. I do not have to fear that if my family or friends find out about my sexual orientation there will be economic, emotional, physical, or psychological consequences.

5. I did not grow up with games that attack my sexual orientation (e.g., "fag tag," "smear the queer").

6. I am not accused of being abused, warped, or psychologically confused because of my sexual orientation.

7. I can go home from most meetings, classes, and conversations without feeling excluded, fearful, attacked, isolated, outnumbered, unheard, held at a distance, stereotyped, or feared because of my sexual orientation.

8. I am never asked to speak for everyone who is of my sexual orientation.

9. People don't ask why I made my choice of sexual orientation.

10. People don't ask why I made my choice to be public about my sexual orientation.

11. I do not have to fear revealing my sexual orientation to friends or family. It's assumed.

12. My sexual orientation was never associated with a closet.

13. People of my gender do not try to convince me to change my sexual orientation.

14. I don't have to defend my sexuality.

15. I can easily find a religious community that will not exclude me for my sexual orientation.

16. I can count on finding a counselor or doctor willing and able to talk about my sexuality.

17. I am guaranteed to find sex education literature for couples with my sexual orientation.

18. Because of my sexual orientation, I do not need to worry that people will harass me.

19. I have no need to qualify my sexual identity.

20. My masculinity/femininity is not challenged because of my sexual orientation.

21. I am not identified by my sexual orientation.

22. I can be sure that if I need legal or medical help my sexual orientation will not work against me.

23. If my day, week, or year is going badly, I need not ask of each negative episode or situation whether it has sexual orientation overtones.

24. Whether I rent a movie or go to a theater, I can be sure I will not have trouble finding my sexual orientation represented.

25. I am guaranteed to find people of my sexual orientation represented in my workplace or school.

26. I can walk in public with my significant other and not have people double-take or stare.

27. I can choose to not think politically about my sexual orientation.

28. I do not have to worry about telling my roommate or coworkers about my sexuality.

29. I can remain oblivious of the language and culture of LGBTQ folk without feeling in my culture any penalty for such oblivion.

30. I can go for months without being identified by my sexual orientation.

31. I'm not grouped because of my sexual orientation.

32. My individual behavior does not reflect on people who identify with my sexual orientation.

33. In everyday conversation, the language my friends and I use generally assumes my sexual orientation. For example, *sex* referring to only heterosexual sex or *family* meaning heterosexual relationships with kids.

34. People do not assume I am experienced in sex (or that I even have it!) merely because of my sexual orientation.

35. I can kiss a person of the opposite gender on the street or in the cafeteria without being watched and stared at.

36. Nobody names my sexual orientation with maliciousness.

37. People can use terms that describe my sexual orientation and mean positive things, instead of demeaning terms (e.g., "ewww, that's gay," being "queer").

(Continued)

KNOWLEDGE ABOUT SEXUAL ORIENTATION

As mentioned earlier, part of the process of becoming a culturally alert counselor involves increasing your knowledge of historical, social, and psychological issues pertaining to LGBT persons and communities. This section addresses "Why?" and "How much?" questions in relation to sexual orientation in five areas: (1) sexual orientation as a continuum; (2) the pervasiveness of same-sex attraction; (3) the causes of sexual orientation; (4) the social and psychological dimensions of minority sexual orientation; and (5) the unique issues of bisexuals, transgender persons, sexual-minority women, and LGB persons of color.

Sexual Orientation as a Continuum

Sexual orientation refers to the direction of emotional, romantic, and sexual feelings or behavior. Those directions can be toward people of the opposite sex (heterosexuality), people of the same sex (homosexuality), and people of both sexes (bisexuality). Rather than these being discrete categories, Kinsey, Pomeroy, and Martin (1948) found that romantic and sexual attraction and behavior could be categorized on a 7-point continuum: (1) exclusively heterosexual, (2) predominantly heterosexual with incidental homosexuality, (3) predominantly heterosexual with more than incidental homosexuality, (4) equal amounts of heterosexual and homosexual activity, (5) predominantly homosexual with more than incidental heterosexuality, (6) predominantly homosexual with incidental heterosexuality, and (7) exclusively homosexual.

Same-Sex Attraction

Same-sex attraction and sexual behavior are forms of sexuality that occur consistently in humans as well as in other species of the animal world. Same-sex sexual behavior has been documented in almost every animal species, including cats, cows, dogs, fish, frogs, lions, and rabbits (Roughgarden, 2004; Weinrich, 1982). For example, observations of bird species, such as Western gulls, provide examples of two animals of the same sex engaging in committed, long-term attachments (Hunt & Hunt, 1977). In humans, same-sex romantic attraction and relationships have occurred in both Western and non-Western societies, from ancient Greece to modern times (Bohan, 1996). Reactions ranging from affirmation and celebration on the one hand to persecution on the other hand toward sexual-minority persons have differed across time and cultures (Bohan, 1996; Weinrich & Williams, 1991). For example, same-sex marriage was permitted among many Native American tribes but neither same-sex marriage nor civil unions is allowed in 35 of the 50 U.S. states as of this writing. By contrast, Canada and most European countries allow some kind of registered partnership (Michaels, 2003).

Estimates of how many LGBT persons exist range dramatically, depending on definitions (e.g., engaging in same-sex sexual behaviors versus self-identifying as LGBT) and sampling methods (e.g., random versus convenience samples) used. Findings from the National Survey of Sexual Health and Behavior (2010), the largest nationally representative study of sexual and sexual-health behaviors ever fielded, revealed that about 8% of adult men and 7% of adult women identify as gay, lesbian, or bisexual, but the proportion of individuals in the United States who have had same-sex sexual interactions at some point in their lives is higher. LGBT persons come from all ethnic backgrounds, socioeconomic levels, educational levels, religions, personality styles, career paths, and life philosophies (Bell & Weinberg, 1978). LGBT persons are demographically as diverse as their heterosexual counterparts and therefore cannot be described as a unitary group. However, as is discussed later in this chapter, certain stressors associated with being a sexual-minority person are unique to LGBT persons and can have an effect on psychological well-being and interactions with counselors (Meyer, 2003).

Causes of Sexual Orientation

The third knowledge area important for counselors to understand is causes of sexual orientation. Sexual orientation is shaped through a complex interaction of biological, cognitive, and environmental factors. Overall, sexual attraction typically emerges in early adolescence without any prior sexual experience (American Psychological Association, 2004). Although how a particular sexual orientation develops is not well understood by scientists, there is considerable evidence suggesting the important role of hereditary or genetic factors in determining sexual orientation.

Hereditary and genetic investigations of sexual orientation consist of family pedigree studies, twin studies, adoption studies, and DNA linkage analysis. A pedigree analysis is founded on the principle that, if a trait—in this case, homosexuality—is genetically influenced, it will tend to aggregate in families. Thus, by studying the degree and patterns of familial aggregation, inferences can be made concerning the possible number of genes involved in the expression of a trait and how these genes may act (Pillard, Poumadere, & Carretta, 1981). Family studies indicate that homosexual participants have more homosexual siblings and relatives than do heterosexual participants and more than would be expected, given population frequencies (Pattatucci & Hamer, 1995; Pillard et al., 1981; Pillard & Bailey, 1998).

Twin and adoptee studies investigate the comparison of concordance between monozygotic/identical twins (those developed from the splitting of a single fertilized egg), dizygotic/fraternal twins (those developed from the fertilization of two separate eggs by two separate sperm), and adopted siblings (biologically unrelated individuals) reared together. If the influence of genes is paramount, monozygotic twins will frequently be concordant, whereas dizygotic twins will have the same concordance as non-twin biological siblings. It is significant that adopted siblings, sharing the family's environment but not their genes, will share the trait no more often than an average sample of the population (Pillard & Bailey, 1998). This points to a biological factor in sexual orientation. In addition, reviews of the twin studies indicate that the rate of adult homosexuality is higher among monozygotic than dizygotic twins, and that twin, sibling, and adoptee concordance rates are compatible with the hypothesis that genes may account for half of the variance in sexual orientation (Pillard et al., 1981; Pillard & Bailey, 1998).

There is more specific evidence of biological bases of sexual orientation emerging. DNA linkage studies of families in which the homosexuality trait appears to be genetically segregating are done by chromosomal mapping of the loci of the relevant DNA sequences. Those studies have revealed statistically significant correlations between the inheritance of genetic markers on chromosomal region Xq28 of the sex chromosome in male, but not female, sexual orientation (Hu et al., 1996). Evidence for the relative contribution of biology and environment to sexual orientation is still accumulating.

The Social and Psychological Dimensions of Minority Sexual Orientation

The fourth topic related to knowledge about LGBT issues is the social and psychological factors associated with sexual orientation minority identity. These dimensions are discussed in terms of (1) the history of the LGBT rights movement, (2) the impact of heterosexism, (3) internalized heterosexism, and (4) the coming-out process.

A Brief History of the LGBT Rights Movement

Societal attitudes toward LGBT persons have evolved over time. In her historical review, Esther Rothblum (2000) described three key events or factors contributing to the evolution of the LGB rights movement and the current increased

understanding of LGB mental health. The first factor in social change for gays and lesbians was the Stonewall riots that occurred in New York City's Greenwich Village during late June and early July of 1969 and their aftermath. The uprising occurred in a working-class gay and lesbian bar called the Stonewall Inn. It was a response to a routine police raid that was typical at that time of harassing actions against gay bars. Unexpectedly, the patrons resisted and the incident escalated into a riot that continued for several days. Most people view this event as the beginning of the modern LGBT rights movement, and most U.S. cities hold a gay pride celebration each June to commemorate the Stonewall riots.

The second factor was the influence of psychological and sex-related research. Most notable was research conducted by Alfred Kinsey and Evelyn Hooker (Hooker, 1957; Kinsey et al., 1948; Kinsey, Pomeroy, Martin, & Geebhard, 1953). Kinsey's research indicated that (a) sexual orientation could be measured on a continuum; (b) same-sex sexual attraction, fantasies, and behavior occurred among individuals who were married or otherwise conventional; and (c) homosexuality and bisexuality were normative, that is, common and pervasive across all populations and historical eras. Hooker's research indicated that gay men were as psychologically well adjusted as heterosexual men. In contrast to previous pathology-based studies of gay men who were either prisoners or psychiatric clients, Hooker's study was the first to examine "normal" gay men. Her landmark study set the stage for future psychological research that would indicate that LGB individuals are as well adjusted as heterosexuals.

The third factor consisted of changes that were made to the *Diagnostic and Statistical Manual of Mental Disorders*. Most notable was the removal of homosexuality from the list of mental disorders by the American Psychiatric Association in 1973. This change led to more affirmative stances on minority sexual orientation by the counseling and psychology professions (Rothblum, 2000).

Heterosexism and Its Relationship to LGBT Mental Health

Heterosexism refers to attitudes and behaviors that deny, devalue, or stigmatize any non-heterosexual form of community, relationship, identity, or behavior. It can manifest itself on individual, familial, institutional, political, and cultural levels (Herek, 1995). Sometimes it is obvious and overt, sometimes less intentional and subtle. Examples of heterosexism include anti-gay jokes; LGB harassment and violence; rejection by family due to sexual orientation; sexual orientation–based school bullying; religious condemnation of homosexuality; sexual orientation–based discrimination in housing and employment; loss of child custody due to being a sexual-minority parent; failure of the federal government to grant the more than 1,000 federal rights, benefits, and protections associated with marriage (e.g., inheritance rights, tax benefits) to lesbian and gay couples; and infrequent or negative portrayals of LGBT persons in the media.

Heterosexism is sometimes subtle and passive, but it is also too often overt and aggressive. Two examples of its most violent expressions are the following. (It should be noted that they would not likely happen without a pervasive anti-gay sentiment in society.) On October 6, 1998, a student from the University of Wyoming named Matthew Shepard was brutally tortured, was tied to a fence, fell into a coma, and ultimately died. The abduction, beating, and burning were due solely to the fact that he was an openly gay man. On February 2, 2006, a teenager armed with a hatchet and a handgun opened fire inside a gay bar in New Bedford, Massachusetts, wounding at least three people, after asking whether it was a gay bar. The police deemed it to be a hate crime. See Box 15.1 for personal experiences of violent heterosexism.

Box 15.1   Personal Experiences of Violent Heterosexism

In Knoxville, Tennessee, where I work, there were recent shootings resulting in death at the gay-affirmative Unitarian Universalist Church and the burning down of a lesbian couple's home. The editor of this book, Garrett McAuliffe, recalled two additional incidents. While he was living in the Roanoke, Virginia, area a gay man named Danny Overstreet was killed after a man named Ronald Gay opened fire in the Backstreet Cafe after seeing Overstreet and John Collins hug one another. Earlier that evening, Gay had asked for directions to a gay bar and said he was hunting homosexuals. In a second incident, Garrett was staying at a rural bed-and-breakfast inn when his and others' car windows were smashed in the parking lot overnight. A group of lesbian women had been vacationing at the inn and had gathered at a local bar-restaurant the evening before, where they were noticed by the local crowd.

Unfortunately, the incidents described in Box 15.1 are not rare; anti-gay violence occurs in all regions of the United States. In 1999, a large study found that approximately 20% of sexual-minority women and 25% of sexual-minority men had been victims of a sexual orientation–based hate crime or attempted hate crime, such as physical assault, sexual assault, robbery, and vandalism (Herek, Gillis, & Cogan, 1999). In a related study, the same researchers asked participants about their hate crime victimization experiences. Here is one example in which a man describes having his house fire-bombed and his car windows smashed:

> I was asleep on the front porch and a Molotov cocktail was lobbed up onto the second-story front porch where I was at. . . . And it immediately ignited the porch. I was asleep in that porch. As the building was burning I could hear the windows being broken out of the cars. And the people doing it laughing and screaming "Faggot" at the top of their lungs. . . . There was a note attached to the windshield of my car: "The faggot that lives here will be dead within a week." (Herek, Cogan, & Gillis, 2002, p. 326)

In addition to hate crime victimization, many LGBT persons have experienced other types of anti-gay harassment and discrimination. For example, approximately 50% of LGBT persons have experienced sexual orientation–based verbal harassment, and more than 10% reported having experienced sexual orientation–based housing or employment discrimination (Herek, 2009). Similarly, a 2001 population-based study by Vickie Mays and Susan Cochran revealed that LGBT adults reported more discrimination and victimization experiences than their heterosexual peers. In addition, they found pervasive anti-gay discrimination, with more than 50% of LGBT participants reporting lifetime experiences of sexual orientation–based discrimination, including not being hired for a job, being fired from a job, being prevented from renting or buying a home, being hassled by the police, and being denied or given inferior services. Other studies using primarily convenience samples of LGB persons have found that sexual orientation–based prejudice, rejection, harassment, discrimination, and violence are widespread and common (c.f., Berrill, 1992; Rankin, 2003; Szymanski, 2009).

Similar results have been found in U.S. high schools. For example, in 2007, the Gay, Lesbian and Straight Education Network (GLSEN) conducted a national survey of 6,209 students between the ages of 13 and 21 years old, with 54% identifying as lesbian or gay. The survey revealed that 86% of LGBT students were verbally harassed at school in the previous year,

44% were physically harassed, and 61% believed that because of their sexual orientation, they were not safe at school. In addition, GLSEN found that over 60% of these students who were victimized did not report it to their teachers or other school staff members because they believed either it would make it worse or nothing would be done. In another study, Grossman and D'Augelli (2006) found that transgender youth reported that attending school was the most traumatic aspect of growing up.

Like the case of June presented at the beginning of this chapter, studies also indicate that the victims of anti-gay violence experience poor mental health. For example, LGB survivors of sexual orientation–based hate crimes manifest greater anger, anxiety, depression, and posttraumatic stress than do LGB survivors of non-sexual-orientation-based crime victimization and LGB nonvictims (Herek et al., 1999). Additional studies have confirmed further that experiences of heterosexist stressors such as anti-LGB prejudice, rejection, harassment, and discrimination; workplace-specific heterosexism; and anti-LGB policies, legislation, and initiatives (e.g., Defense of Marriage Amendment movements) are related to poorer mental and physical health, negative job-related outcomes, and poorer academic performance (for a review, see Szymanski & Moffitt, 2012). The price paid by LGB individuals in the United States is high and is experienced daily. Activity 15.4 provides you with an opportunity to see the consequences of heterosexism.

Activity 15.4   Experiencing Heterosexism

One way for counselors to begin to understand what it is like to live with heterosexism on a daily basis is to engage in experiential exercises that provide a feeling for heterosexism. A good way to do this is to watch the 2000 HBO movie *If These Walls Could Talk 2*.

1. Watch the first segment, in which Vanessa Redgrave plays an elderly woman whose lesbian partner of 50 years dies. Vanessa's character finds herself unprotected and alone as she deals with her in-laws.

2. After viewing the video segment,

   a. Note your own feelings and your reactions to what transpired.

   b. Identify the ways in which heterosexism operated and affected the lesbian characters' lives and psychological well-being.

Internalized Heterosexism and Its Relationship to LGBT Mental Health

In addition to experiencing external oppression, LGBT persons frequently internalize the negative attitudes toward and images about homosexuality and bisexuality that permeate a culture. This is a psychological consequence of heterosexism.

Internalized heterosexism is the presence of negative attitudes about one's own same-sex attractions in LGBT persons. It also includes anti-gay religious and moral attitudes in LGBT persons, resulting in their isolation from the LGBT community, attempts to "pass" and live a lie, subsequent fear of discovery concerning their LGBT identity, and their own negative attitudes toward other LGBT persons (Szymanski & Chung, 2001).

Internalized heterosexism can be both overt (e.g., "There have been times when I've felt so awful about being LGB that I wanted to be dead; if I could take a pill to become heterosexual, I would") and subtle (e.g., "I get nervous when people around me talk about homosexuality; I act as if my same-sex lovers are merely friends"; Mayfield, 2001; Shidlo, 1994; Szymanski & Chung, 2001).

Internalized heterosexism is typically greatest and most overt during the early phases of sexual identity development, which are discussed in the next section. However, it often continues in more covert and subtle ways even in LGBT persons who hold positive sexual identity attitudes. My colleagues and I (Szymanski, Kashubeck-West, & Meyer, 2008) reviewed the empirical literature and found that internalized heterosexism is related to a variety of psychosocial and relational difficulties in LGBT persons at any age. These difficulties pertain to the coming-out process, low self-esteem, loneliness, depression, psychological distress, lower levels of social support, more avoidant coping, and less relationship quality and sexual satisfaction. In addition, internalized heterosexism is related to lower levels of openness, responsibility, and motivation for the counseling process and appears to impede clients' discussion of sexual identity issues.

The Coming-Out Process

Counselors can facilitate positive sexual identity development. It is a critical dimension of gay-affirmative counseling. Sexual identity development models serve as a guide for the counselor and client (McCarn & Fassinger, 1996). The coming-out process is described here in the context of LGB identity development.

Sexual Identity Development Models

Several models of sexual identity development have been proposed in the literature. The first and most widely cited was developed by Vivian Cass in 1979. Several more models followed her lead (e.g., Coleman, 1982; Lewis, 1984; Sophie, 1982). Those models are combined here in the form of four phases that seem to be similar across each of the models, although differences do exist.

The first phase, which was illustrated in the case of Roger at the beginning of this chapter, is called *Being Different* by Lewis (1984) and *Identity Confusion* by Cass (1979). It typically involves a general feeling of being distinctive, feelings of confusion, and an initial wondering if one is lesbian or gay. The second phase, called *Coming Out to Self* by Sophie (1982) and *Identity Comparison* by Cass, involves acknowledging that one is lesbian or gay, working toward self-acceptance of one's sexual identity, and reducing internalized heterosexism.

The third phase, called *Coming Out to Others* by Sophie (1982), involves making decisions about disclosing one's sexual identity to others. Many LGB persons first come out to others who are LGB supportive. Individuals typically come out to other LGB people first, which helps them decrease feelings of isolation and shame and increase their social support network. During this phase, LGBT individuals are likely to become immersed in gay culture, for example, attending LGBT organizations and gay pride events. Coming out to heterosexuals is often the next step in this phase. It is more difficult for many LGBT persons because it increases the chances of their encountering heterosexism, rejection, discrimination, and violence. The decision to come out to others needs to be weighed against the possible negative consequences that may follow (Falco, 1991). However, research supports the notion that hiding one's sexual identity is costly in terms of psychological health (Jordan & Deluty, 1998; Morris, Waldo, & Rothblum, 2001). See Activity 15.5 for a vivid illustration of the coming-out process.

Activity 15.5 An Illustration of Coming Out and Family Members' Reactions

An illustration of coming out and family members' reactions to an LGB person's self-disclosure of her or his sexual identity can be found in the 2001 Starlight Signature Series/Hearst Entertainment movie *The Truth About Jane*, starring Stockard Channing and Ellen Muth. Watch the movie, and then answer the following questions:

1. How does heterosexism manifest itself in Jane's and her family's life? Discuss specific examples.

2. What did you see in the video that is illustrative of each of the four phases of sexual identity development described in this chapter?

3.
   a. How do Jane's teacher and mother's friend help Jane accept her sexuality?

   b. If their response to her had not been so positive, how might this have affected Jane?

4.
   a. Discuss the reactions of family members (mother, father, brother) to Jane's disclosure of her sexual orientation.

   b. How do these reactions fit or not fit with the typical reactions of family members to an LGB person's disclosure discussed earlier in this chapter?

5. Stop the movie right after Jane's teacher confronts Jane's mother and father about their behavior and her daughter's suicidal ideation (about 70 minutes into the movie). If Jane and her family were to come see you for counseling at this time to help them in their "coming-out process" struggles, what goals and strategies would you implement?

6. Create a culturally focused case conceptualization and treatment plan for Jane and her family. The goals of case conceptualization are to provide a clear, theoretical explanation for what the client is like as well as theoretical hypotheses for why the client is like this. Based on this conceptualization, the clinician develops a treatment plan that will help the client change. The focus of your case conceptualization should be on how cultural issues and the sociopolitical context are influencing the client's current struggles and should integrate research and theoretical literature related to the client's problem and cultural identity. In addition to course readings and lectures, use at least one outside reference in developing your case conceptualization and treatment plan. The treatment plan should flow from the case conceptualization, include both long- and short-term goals, provide specific and useful suggestions for constructive change, and take advantage of the client's strengths and values.

Cass (1979) adds three more phases at this point: *Identity Tolerance, Identity Pride, and Identity Acceptance.* However, for simplification purposes, those are omitted from this description.

The fourth phase, called *Identity Synthesis* by Cass (1979), involves a feeling of pride concerning one's lesbian/gay identity and an integration of one's sexual identity into other aspects of the self. This phase also involves confronting heterosexism.

These sexual-minority identity models provide a useful framework to guide counselors who work with LGB clients. However, such models have at least four limitations. First, there is much variation in how a person establishes a sexual-minority identity. Many LGB persons do not follow the steps outlined in the aforementioned models (Garnets & Peplau, 2001). For example, a lesbian who views sexual orientation as a private matter may be less likely to disclose her sexual orientation to others, yet still feel pride about herself as a lesbian. Similarly, a Latino gay man may feel good about himself as a gay man but choose not to disclose his sexual orientation in his ethnic community in order to maintain respect in his community and to avoid ridicule and outcast status (Greene, 1997).

Second, gender differences exist in the coming-out process for sexual-minority women and men. These differences parallel gender-related trends in the general heterosexual population. For example, lesbians are more likely than gay men to come out in the context of an emotionally connected same-sex romantic relationship and to emphasize affectional rather than sexual experiences (McCarn & Fassinger, 1996).

A third limitation of sexual-minority identity development models is that many such models confound *individual* sexual identity development (i.e., the process of recognizing and accepting one's own same-sex attraction and lifestyle preferences) with *group* membership identity development (i.e., the process involving the acceptance of one's status as a member of an oppressed group and the confrontation of societal oppression as a member of that group; Fassinger & Miller, 1996; McCarn & Fassinger, 1996).

A final limitation of the developmental models is that many phase models fail to acknowledge the existence of multiple factors, such as bisexuality and transgenderism, and the impact of multiple identities (e.g., race, ethnicity, class) on sexual identity development (Garnets & Peplau, 2001).

The Reactions of Family Members to Coming Out

LGBT clients are confronted with the unique dilemma of having to decide whether to come out to family members. Because openness, honesty, and congruence are important in establishing intimate relationships, many LGBT persons decide to come out to family members (Brown, 1989). Family members' responses can range from negative to neutral to positive. The session with Vanessa on the video *Working With Gay and Lesbian Youth: A Multi-ethnic Demonstration* (McAuliffe, 2012) demonstrates a counseling session focused on such coming out.

There are several typical family reactions to a family member's self-disclosure of her or his same-sex attraction. They generally follow Kubler-Ross's (1969) formulation of the grieving and acceptance process. Therefore, a typical early reaction to a family member's disclosure of her or his sexual identity is *denial* (Matthews & Lease, 2000). Frequently, family members will suggest that the LGBT person is simply "going through a phase" and does not really know what she or he wants. At other times, family members may be overtly rejecting, even trying to change or "cure" their family member's sexual orientation or disown her or him.

Anger toward the LGBT person is another reaction that often stems from family members' beliefs that the LGBT person's sexual orientation is a rejection of them and their values. Another possible response is *depression*, which often manifests itself in family members' worries about what a sexual identity status means for their LGBT family member and for themselves. *Guilt* feelings may also surface, and family members may question if they have done something wrong

to cause this to happen. Another common reaction is *grief*. This may take the form of grieving for the child or sibling they thought they had and a loss of dreams associated with a traditional heterosexual lifestyle.

Whatever the initial reaction, family members must face the negative cultural stereotypes and myths that they have learned about LGBT persons, as they confront those negative images in light of their daughter, son, sibling, grandchild, niece, or nephew. Family members must begin to re-evaluate and challenge these heterosexist messages (Matthews & Lease, 2000).

Family members of LGBT persons often find it helpful to engage in bibliotherapy, that is, reading gay-affirmative materials (Fairchild & Hayward, 1998). Another helpful activity is to connect with formal support systems, such as Parents and Friends of Lesbians and Gays (P-FLAG). These activities can help family members accept and affirm their daughter, son, or sibling's sexual orientation and help in their own "coming out" as the parent or sibling of an LGBT family member (Brown, 1989).

Unique Issues of Bisexual Persons

Bisexual persons deal with many of the same issues, such as heterosexism and internalized heterosexism, that lesbians and gay men contend with; however, they also face unique issues. This section provides information about these unique issues, which include the myths about bisexuality, coming-out issues, and biphobia.

Myths

At least five myths in U.S. culture about bisexuality can negatively influence both a bisexual person's self-acceptance of her or his sexual identity and a counselor's work with bisexual clients. These myths include that bisexuals (a) are "closeted" lesbians and gay men who are in denial of their homosexual identity, (b) are stuck in the transition phase from heterosexuality to homosexuality, (c) are indecisive and ambivalent "fence sitters," (d) are incapable of monogamy and unable to make relationship commitments, and (e) need concurrent relationships with both genders for personal satisfaction (Dworkin, 2001; Firestein, 1996; Guidry, 1999). These myths arise in part out of socially constructed assumptions that sexual orientation is dichotomous and fixed rather than continuous and fluid (Morrow, 2000). None of them are true. If that surprises you, read them again.

Coming-Out Issues

Bisexual women and men face various issues in the coming-out process that frequently make it a difficult transition. These include fear of isolation, alienation, and rejection. In particular, a bisexual individual can be considered an outsider by a previously identified heterosexual or gay group. Bisexual individuals also experience lack of community social support and feeling marginalized. They often have identity confusion. Finally, they usually have to deal with a lack of social confirmation for their bisexual identity (Dworkin, 2001; Fox, 2000; Guidry, 1999).

Although there are similarities in the coming-out process among bisexuals, lesbians, and gay men, there are also distinct differences for bisexual clients. Lesbians and gay men only need to acknowledge and affirm their same-sex attractions and relationships in order to achieve positive and integrated sexual identities. By contrast, bisexuals need to acknowledge and affirm both the homosexual and heterosexual components of their identities (Fox, 2000). Such a dual acknowledgment and affirmation process for bisexuals can be confusing and challenging, especially given the dichotomous and often categorical view of sexuality in the larger U.S. culture and the fluidity of sexuality, especially for women (Diamond, 2005, 2008). That is, research suggests that women's sexual attractions, behavior, and identity are often fluid, nonexclusive, and variable (Diamond, 2005); there are both stable and fluid subtypes of lesbian and bisexual women (Diamond, 2005); and the difference between

lesbian and bisexual is one of degree rather than type (Diamond, 2005, 2008).

Particularly notable in this area is Lisa Diamond's (2005, 2008) longitudinal study following lesbian, bisexual, and "unlabeled" women from late adolescence to young adulthood. Diamond (2005) compared patterns of attraction and behavior among three groups of sexual-minority women: (a) stable lesbians, or those who consistently maintained a lesbian identification during an 8-year period; (b) fluid lesbians, or those who alternated between lesbian and non-lesbian labels; and (c) stable non-lesbians, or those who never adopted a lesbian label but had same-sex attractions and engaged in same-sex sexual behaviors. She found that fluid lesbians reported more same-sex sexual physical attractions (80%) and sexual behavior (70%) with women than stable non-lesbians (who reported 45% and 32%, respectively) but less than stable lesbians (who reported 93% and 92%, respectively). In addition, she found that fluid and stable non-lesbians reported more absolute fluctuations in their emotional and physical attractions for women from assessment to assessment than stable lesbians during the 8-year period. Finally, Diamond (2008) found that bisexuality can be a third type of sexual orientation characterized by stable attractions to both women and men as well as a strong form of all women's capacity for flexibility in sexual response. In contrast, she found no support for the long-standing myth that female bisexuality is just an experimental phase in which heterosexual women try out same-sex sexual behaviors or a transitional stage to a lesbian identity.

Biphobia

Bisexual women and men must also deal with biphobia and internalized biphobia in addition to dealing with heterosexism and internalized heterosexism (Dworkin, 2001; Fox, 2000; Guidry, 1999; Ochs, 1996). Biphobia is defined as a fear or dislike of those who do not identify as either heterosexual or lesbian/gay (Dworkin, 2001). Biphobia manifests itself in the denial of the very existence of bisexual people and in the double discrimination that many bisexual women and men experience. They often suffer rejection both by some members of the lesbian and gay community, who criticize them for possessing a degree of heterosexual privilege, and by some members of the heterosexual community, who view them as amoral hedonistic spreaders of disease and disrupters of families (Ochs, 1996).

As a result of biphobia, bisexual women and men often struggle to have their sexual orientation recognized as legitimate. For example, if a bisexual person is in a relationship with a person of the same sex, she or he often struggles to be recognized as bisexual rather than being immediately perceived as lesbian or gay. Similarly, if a bisexual person is in a relationship with a person of the opposite sex, she or he often struggles to be seen as legitimately bisexual. Thus, the sexual identities of bisexual women and men are often rendered invisible because of simplistic portrayals of sexual orientation as defined by the sex of one's romantic partner (Bieschke, Croteau, Lark, & Vandiver, 2005).

Internalized biphobia refers to the internalization of both negative messages about bisexuality and experiences of rejection. Those encounters result in self-hatred, self-doubt, and low self-esteem (Guidry, 1999). Internalized biphobia can be overpowering. The experience of isolation, illegitimacy, shame, and confusion felt by many bisexuals can be debilitating (Guidry, 1999; Ochs, 1996). Internalized biphobia is characterized by feelings of conflict and shame concerning one's bisexuality. These feelings often result from a person feeling like she or he does not fully fit into either lesbian/gay or heterosexual worlds. They also stem from a sense of betraying one's identity group, if that is dichotomously hetero- or homosexual at one time. When a bisexual person ends a relationship with a member of the same sex and later gets involved with a member of the opposite sex (Ochs, 1996), she or he might feel guilty about reinforcing negative stereotypes about bisexuals in general.

Unique Issues of Transgender Persons

Transgender refers to "a range of behaviors, expressions, and identifications that challenge the pervasive bipolar gender system in a given culture" (Carroll, Gilroy, & Ryan, 2002, p. 139). A vast range of often-unrelated identity categories, such as transgenderists, transsexuals, intersex, transvestites, drag queens, and drag kings, fall under the classification of transgender behaviors (Carroll et al., 2002; Gainor, 2000). Each is defined here.

The term *transgenderist* refers to an individual, such as a cross-dresser or nonsurgical transsexual, who has chosen to live life as the other gender on a continuous basis but does not wish to have sex reassignment surgery (Gainor, 2000). The term *transsexual* refers to individuals whose gender identity is different from their anatomical sex, who frequently seek sex hormones and/or sex reassignment surgery, and who desire to permanently live their lives as members of the other gender. The terms *intersex* or *hermaphrodite* refer to individuals who are born with some mixture of ambiguous genitalia (Carroll et al., 2002). The term *transvestite* refers to individuals who wear clothing of the opposite gender for emotional satisfaction and/or sexual stimulation (Gainor, 2000), but who are not necessarily sexually attracted to members of the same sex. The terms *drag queen* and *drag king* refer to individuals who identify themselves as gay or lesbian and who cross-dress for entertainment purposes in lesbian and gay clubs (Carroll et al., 2002).

Due to the diversity of identity categories within this population, self-definition is a complicated process for many transgender persons. This process is often made more difficult due to the marginalization of transgender persons in U.S. society (Carroll et al., 2002; Gainor, 2000). In addition, the dichotomist models of gender identity in U.S. culture often invalidate the experiences of gender fluidity and multiplicity for many transgender individuals (Diamond & Butterworth, 2008). These cultural and societal pressures also create or exacerbate issues that transgender persons might present in counseling, such as anxiety, depression, low self-esteem, substance abuse, hate crime victimization, and physical and emotional abuse (Carroll et al., 2002; Gainor, 2000).

Transgender clients are often skeptical about the counseling and medical communities. They have usually had experiences of discrimination with service providers. That is especially relevant because health professionals serve the role of gatekeeper; that is, counselors and physicians can make decisions about who can and cannot go through the gender transition process (Carroll et al., 2002; Gainor, 2000). It is therefore important that counselors, when working with transgender clients, avoid medical and psychiatric perspectives that pathologize transgenderism. They should also use correct terminology to identify or label such clients. In addition, helpers need to be aware that feminine and masculine behaviors are generally the creation of cultural standards and not of biological specification. They should use approaches that give transgender clients a voice to tell their story and help them overcome negative feelings of powerlessness, such as client-centered, feminist, and constructivist therapies (Butler, 1990; Carroll et al., 2002). Counselors may also be called upon to help transgender clients struggling with gender dysphoria to find congruence between their psychological sense of gender and their physical appearance and behavior, and to navigate the host of options available to align these two parts of themselves (e.g., choosing how to dress, changing one's name, hormone therapy, genital surgery; Denny, 2004, 2007).

Intersections of Oppression for Sexual-Minority Women and Persons of Color

This chapter so far has focused on heterosexism as a main form of oppression faced by LGBT persons. As mentioned in Chapter 2 under the notion of intersectionality, other nondominant statuses may intersect in one individual's life. Many LGBT persons have multiple identities and may experience oppression based on other minority statuses (e.g., gender, race/ethnicity, socioeconomic status, ability level, religious affiliation). The intersection of minority sexual orientation and gender and race/ethnicity are discussed next.

The Intersection of Heterosexism and Sexism

Lesbian and bisexual females must deal not only with heterosexism, but also with sexism

(Szymanski, 2005b). Research has demonstrated that many lesbian and bisexual women have experienced sexist stressors such as sexual abuse as a child, sexual assault, gender discrimination, and hearing degrading sexual jokes about women. These experiences themselves are associated with poorer mental health (Bradford, Ryan, & Rothblum, 1994; Descamps, Rothblum, Bradford, & Ryan, 2000; Szymanski, 2005b). In addition, research has demonstrated that women who experience both heterosexist and sexist stressors report more psychological distress than women who report experiencing only one form of oppression (either heterosexism or sexism; Descamps et al., 2000; Szymanski, 2005b; Szymanski & Owens, 2009). These research findings indicate that the experience of multiple forms of oppression can have a profound impact on psychological health.

Bias Against LGBT Persons of Color

Racism intersects with sexual-minority status for LGBT people of color. Lesbian and bisexual women of color have to deal with what Beverly Greene (1994) called *triple jeopardy*, the interactive influences of racism, heterosexism, and sexism. Research has demonstrated that many persons of color have experienced racial discrimination, such as being treated unfairly by employers, being accused of stealing or breaking the law, and being called a racist name. These experiences are related to adverse psychological and health outcomes. For example, Landrine and Klonoff (1996) found that 98% of African Americans reported experiencing some type of racial discrimination in the past year. They also found that more experiences of racial discrimination were related to greater psychological distress and, interestingly, to increased cigarette smoking.

In addition to the negative effects of racism on LGBT persons of color, it is important for counselors to recognize that LGBT persons of color also experience a minority racial identity formation process regarding their culture that has many parallels to the minority sexual identity development process. It can be a challenge to effectively maintain the two minority identities, for example, as a Latino or an African American, and as a gay or lesbian person. This may be especially difficult for LGBT persons who come from ethnic communities that are less accepting of nonheterosexual identities. In that sense, LGBT persons of color can be considered to have conflicting dual identities.

In addition to one's ethnic group rejecting LGBT status, conversely, some LGBT communities may not be easily accessible to persons of color. For example, Chung and Katayama (1998) asserted that the intensity of heterosexism is much stronger in Asian cultures than in the dominant U.S. culture because Asian cultures tend to maintain traditional gender roles for men and women and tolerate less openness about sexuality. Thus, an Asian gay man's disclosure of his sexual-minority status may be seen as a rejection of his appropriate roles within the culture and as a threat to the continuation of the family line. In racial/ethnic communities where heterosexism is rampant, LGBT members may experience more anxiety during the coming-out process. They

may also choose not to disclose their sexual minority identity to members of their family and racial/ethnic community. Supporting this notion, experiences of heterosexism in communities of color was a unique predictor, along with internalized heterosexism, race-related dating problems, and less "outness" to the world, in predicting psychological distress among Asian American sexual-minority persons (Szymanski & Sung, 2010).

A double oppression can confront many LGBT people of color because they may find it difficult to connect with mainstream LGBT communities. Their race may prove to be a barrier to finding support. They may be subject to shunning, stereotyping, outright rejection, or blatant racism for their racial/ethnic minority identity. Thus, counselors need to understand that the combined effects of heterosexism, racism, and sexism can create especially intense stressors for racial and ethnic minority LGBT persons (Greene, 1997).

This section on knowledge of LGBT cultures and issues concludes by inviting you to complete Activity 15.6 to learn more.

Activity 15.6   Learning About LGBT Identities and Cultures

To increase your knowledge of LGBT identities and cultures, you might consider:

1. reading an LGBT novel or magazine

2. watching television shows and movies with LGBT themes and characters (e.g., *Will and Grace, Queer as Folk, The L Word, Boys Don't Cry, Desert Hearts, Philadelphia, The Birdcage, Latter Days, Doing Time on Maple Drive, Two Mothers for Zachary, Serving in Silence, Tales of the City, For the Bible Tells Me So*)

3. attending LGBT community events, such as a gay pride festival or a gay comedy or music performance

Note: Many of the movies and shows mentioned in this chapter can be found at video stores, through www.wolfevideo.com or www.amazon .com, or at gay bookstores.

SKILLS

The final step in becoming a culturally alert counselor involves practicing relevant and sensitive counseling interventions when working with LGBT clients. Such interventions are described next under

the following nine rubrics: (1) avoiding heterosexist assumptions, bias, and language; (2) responding appropriately to clients' disclosures of their sexual identities; (3) conceptualizing the role of sexual orientation in the counseling process; (4) facilitating sexual identity development and the coming-out process; (5) attending to external oppression; (6) identifying and challenging internalized heterosexism and biphobia; (7) exploring multiple identities of LGBT clients; (8) addressing the issue of whether and how the counselor's sexual orientation should be disclosed; and (9) supporting the elimination of homophobia and heterosexist bias in institutions and among colleagues/peers.

Using Nonheterosexist, Gender-Neutral Inclusive Language

Counselors need to remain current with the LGBT literature and monitor their own use of language, stereotypes, and bias. Terms that describe individuals who are in nondominant or minority groups require particular sensitivity, because they have the power to hurt and can be backed up by oppressive action. That is the case with sexual minorities.

As described in Chapter 2, terms for nondominant cultural groups are fluid; they are products of a time and a consciousness. The counselor needs to be flexible in determining what terms to use with sexual minorities. Asking clients for the terms they prefer for themselves is, of course, recommended.

The term *homosexuality* is currently acceptable as a description of the overall phenomenon of same-sex attraction. However, in reference to an individual, the terms *lesbian* or *gay man* are preferred to the term *homosexual,* for at least three reasons. *Homosexual* has been used in the past with negative, stereotypical connotations. It has also been used to label lesbian and gay identity as a psychological disorder. Finally, it emphasizes the sexual aspect of LGBT experience rather than the multifaceted nature of LGBT identity and community (APA, 2001; Bohan, 1996).

The currently preferred terms for referring to people who have same-sex attraction are *lesbians, gay men, sexual minorities,* and *LGBT persons* (APA, 2001). The terms *gay* and *gay persons* generally refer to all LGB persons. However, those terms have their origins in reference only to gay men, leaving lesbians in a subordinate position, and thus replicating societal sexism.

Finally, counselors should make language inclusive. They should avoid language that assumes universal heterosexuality. Instead, they might use nonheterosexist language with all clients. For example, a counselor working with a client might ask, "Do you have a partner?" or "Are you involved in a romantic relationship?" rather than "Are you married?" or "Do you have a boyfriend/husband/girlfriend/wife?" Furthermore, it is important for counselors not to assume that current romantic partners are the same sex as past partners. In a similar vein, the heterosexist use of marital status (single, married, divorced, widowed) on a counseling intake form ignores LGBT relationships, thereby rendering them invisible. The word *partnered* might be added to counselors' vocabulary and to intake forms.

Responding to Clients' Disclosures of Their Sexual Identities

At some point in the counseling relationship, many sexual-minority clients will make the decision to disclose their sexual identity to their counselor. For clients who have been "out" for a long period of time and are accepting of their sexual identity, disclosing their orientation may feel very comfortable and be "no big deal." It is important for counselors to respond to such disclosures with acceptance and acknowledgment of the realistic obstacles of being a sexual-minority client in a heterosexist society. Thus a counselor might respond to client disclosure by saying, "I'm glad that you felt comfortable enough to come out to me. I know that coming out can be a difficult process. What has your experience been like?" In addition, counselors might ask clients to tell them about their coming-out story, paying particular attention to whom the client has disclosed to, how others have reacted to the disclosures, and how much support the client has from LGBT persons and heterosexual allies.

For clients who are in the early phases of the sexual-minority development process, coming out to a counselor may feel threatening. Such a self-disclosure is apt to be of great significance to the client, even though it may be obscured by how the client chooses to disclose her or his sexual identity. For example, a client may indicate that she or he has something to talk about, but be unable to state what it is. In that case, the counselor should honor the client's hesitance and not push disclosure. Such is the case in the aforementioned demonstration video in the case of Joseph (McAuliffe, 2012). The counselor there doesn't push Joseph to declare himself gay, even though there are strong indications that that is the case.

In other cases, a client may disclose her or his sexual-minority status indirectly. For example, the client may refer to a "partner" or provide hints of her or his LGBT status without directly disclosing sexual orientation. Or the client may do so defiantly, as in, "I'm gay. I hope you are not a homophobe." Finally, the client may disclose covertly, for example, in a written note to the counselor. In each case, the client may then wait for the counselor's reaction before deciding if it is safe to continue on this topic (Sophie, 1987).

However the client chooses to disclose, it is important that the counselor realize how difficult such a disclosure might be. The counselor's non-judgmental acceptance is crucial. Examples of counselors' responses to such disclosures include "Thanks for coming out to me. That took a lot of courage. How long have you known you were gay?" and "I feel honored that you came out to me. How are you feeling about sharing this part of yourself with me?"

Conceptualizing the Role of Sexual Orientation in the Counseling Process

One of the tasks for counselors who work with sexual-minority clients is to determine what role, if any, sexual orientation plays in a client's clinical issues and in the counseling process. The importance of sexual-minority orientation can range from being central to a person's life to being relatively inconsequential, depending on the environment in which she or he exists and her or his identity development phase.

For some clients, sexual orientation issues will be central in the counseling process. For example, it is likely to be a core counseling issue for a client who is in the early phases of coming out. She or he is likely to be struggling to overcome internalized heterosexism and is possibly dealing with sexual orientation–based family rejection. In these cases, the counselor should explore the meaning of being lesbian, gay, or bisexual and check on the implications for family and religion. Finally, the counselor can share gay resources, such as literature and support groups. This can help the early-phase client move toward a positive gay identity. Two learning resources that demonstrate sessions with LGBT clients are the training videos *Lesbian, Bisexual, Gay and Transgendered Counseling* (Chen-Hayes & Banez, 2001) and *Working With Gay and Lesbian Youth: A Multi-ethnic Demonstration* (McAuliffe, 2012).

For other clients, sexual orientation issues may be relevant but not central to their issues and counseling process. For example, sexual orientation issues might not be central to a client who is dealing with grief issues over a parent's death. However, they still might be relevant (e.g., if the client is experiencing additional loss associated with losing an LGBT-affirmative parent). Finally, in the case of an LGBT person who has achieved an integrated sexual identity (e.g., Cass's Identity Synthesis), a counseling issue may barely touch on sexual-minority matters. However, it should be noted that all LGBT persons experience "gay stressors," that is, the strains of living in an oppressed status in a heterosexist society.

Facilitating Sexual Identity Development and the Coming-Out Process

Counselor responses should vary with client readiness. The phases described previously can serve as a general guide to counselor behavior. The next sections outline desirable counselor responses at each identity phase.

Responding to the Early Identity Phases

When clients such as Roger (from the vignette at the beginning of this chapter) are in the early phases of the sexual identity development process, they often are not ready to declare themselves to be LGBT. They only wonder if they *might* be LGBT. Counselors working with clients in these early phases need to help them explore their feelings and thoughts free from evaluation or labeling by using unconditional positive regard and responding empathically.

As clients' recognition of same-sex attraction begins to emerge, counselors should affirmatively provide support and complete acceptance of their clients' same-sex feelings as well as their worries and doubts about these feelings. For example, a counselor could validate Roger's feelings of confusion about whether he is really gay or not and his feelings of worry about what being gay might mean for him in his future while also supporting his attraction to other men at the same time. At this early phase, counselors should discourage clients from adopting an LGBT label as long as that identity has a primarily negative meaning for them (Sophie, 1987). In addition, many sexual-minority persons, especially those with nonexclusive attractions (i.e., bisexual orientations), often change the labels they use to describe their sexual identity over time in response to specific interpersonal and social contexts (Diamond, 2005). Because of this fluidity, the important focus in this phase should be on acceptance of same-sex sexuality rather than adoption of a particular sexual identity label. As mentioned above, it is also important for counselors to identify, explore, and challenge the client's negative stereotypes and maladaptive beliefs about LGBT persons.

Responding to Coming-Out Issues

Once clients who are in the early phases of sexual-minority identity development have worked through some of their internalized heterosexism and have developed positive feelings about being LGB, it is useful to help them with the decision to come out to others such as family, friends, and coworkers (Brown, 1989; Padesky, 1988; Sophie, 1987). One of the first steps in this process is to help the client explore some of the reasons for deciding to come out or not to come out to a particular person. Expressions of why a client might want to come out to a parent include "I'm sick of silence in my family" and "I won't have to come up with excuses for not visiting anymore." Expressions of why a client might not want to come out to a parent include "My support system isn't strong enough right now" and "I'm afraid my father might get violent."

In addition to helping clients explore the risks and benefits associated with coming out to each important individual in their lives, counselors might facilitate clients' awareness of the costs of hiding and denying one's sexuality (Brown, 1989; Gartrell, 1984; Neisen, 1993). Once clients have decided to self-disclose their sexual identity, counselors can work collaboratively with them to develop a sequence from high- to low-priority persons to whom they will come out (Gartrell, 1984). In the process, counselors might help clients explore their fears, hopes, and expectations about coming out to others. Subsequently, they might help clients select an appropriate time and setting in which to do so (Gartrell, 1984; Sophie, 1987).

In order to prepare clients for the coming-out disclosure, counselors might model various ways that clients can present their sexual-minority identity in an affirmative, proud, and direct manner (Gartrell, 1984). "Empty chair" role-plays, in which the client plays both parts of a conversation, are particularly useful for rehearsing a self-disclosure. This technique can serve at least three purposes. First, it helps the client anticipate what reactions she or he might expect and possibly fear from the target person. Second, it can provide information about the client's relationship with the target person and that person's assumptions about sexual minorities. Third, such experiential activities can help the client appreciate the difficulties of the target person's role. The role-plays can be amplified by discussing best- and worst-case scenarios (Sophie, 1987).

Beyond role-playing coming out, the counselor might also educate the client about common initial reactions of family and friends to a disclosure (e.g., shock, hurt, anger, guilt, possible rejection).

The counselor can remind the client that the family member, friend, or coworker may go through her or his own developmental process of coming to accept the client's sexual-minority identity. The counselor can therefore encourage the client to provide interested family members and friends with articles and books that contain accurate information about LGBT issues and inform the client about support groups and LGBT-affirmative counselors who can help the target person come to terms with the client's disclosure if needed (Brown, 1989; Gartrell, 1984; Padesky, 1988).

After each disclosure has been achieved, the counselor might facilitate the client's expression of her or his feelings about both positive and negative responses received from others (Falco, 1991). If the client experiences a rejection from an important person as a result of the disclosure, the counselor's task is to help the client deal with these negative reactions without permanent damage to her or his own positive self-identity (Padesky, 1988). Clients who have experienced rejections that are particularly meaningful often internalize these rejections and deny their feelings of anger and hurt. In that case, counselors can help them express their feelings by using experiential methods. This visceral experience can frequently move clients to a more comfortable resolution of the loss, or perhaps lead them to try a different approach with the person who rejected them (Falco, 1991). Additionally, by role-play and discussion of others' possible reactions, counselors might find out what meaning these negative reactions have for clients. For example, some clients might believe that they can't trust anyone and therefore might be inclined to stay in the closet. Counselors then might facilitate the mourning process that accompanies the loss of trust or relationship. On the other hand, they might help clients see where their conclusions might be distorted (Padesky, 1988).

Beyond Coming Out

Beyond the major challenges of initial disclosure to family and friends, LGBT persons must continue to make choices about being out as LGBT every day of their lives. The development of a positive LGBT identity does not protect an individual from the additional pressures that LGBT persons face. For example, an LGBT person will face whether, where, when, and how to express affection toward a same-sex partner in public (Gartrell, 1984). Having to hide a relationship can be a constant source of tension. Other special pressures include the common situations in which gay or lesbian couples have to deal with financial and legal constraints on their partnership and feel family pressures to appear at holidays without their partners (Padesky, 1988). In addition, there are important career considerations, especially for jobs with high public profiles, such as politicians, sports stars, physicians, and movie stars, that may make the decision to come out more difficult and place added pressures on LGB individuals and their families.

Counselors can assist clients in dealing with these situations by employing four strategies: (1) helping them clarify their values and what is important to them, (2) assisting them in evaluating the disadvantages and advantages of varying responses to the situations, (3) assisting with ongoing development of social support networks, and (4) facilitating the perspective that being a sexual minority is only one, albeit a central one, of the many aspects of their life (Gartrell, 1984, Padesky, 1988; Sophie, 1987).

The next two sections offer specific strategies for working with external and internal oppression.

External Oppression: Attending to the Heterosexist Context of Clients' Lives

The continuing heterosexist context of LGBT clients' lives must be accounted for in the work of counseling these clients. This can be done in two phases: (1) assessing the impact of heterosexism and (2) incorporating the heterosexist dimension of LGBT clients' lives in the ongoing counseling.

Counselors should first assess the negative impact of heterosexist experiences on sexual-minority clients. Counselors can proactively ask

LGB clients about their experiences of prejudice, discrimination, harassment, violence, rejection, and invisibility. Questions at this phase might include "What has it been like for you living as a gay man/lesbian/bisexual woman/man in a heterosexist society?" and "Have you had incidents where you thought you were treated unfairly because you are a sexual-minority person?"

The second phase of this process involves explicitly conceptualizing clinical issues in a heterosexist context. The counselor here tries to note the ways that heterosexism may be influencing a client's presenting problems and psychological well-being. For example, a counselor working with an LGBT client who is struggling with anxiety might include minority stress and heterosexist experiences in her or his client conceptualizations, along with other LGBT-related factors that may be contributing to anxiety issues (e.g., parental criticism and overly high expectations, suppression of feelings, anxious self-talk, high-stress lifestyle). In a similar vein, a counselor can incorporate the heterosexist context with a gay client who is struggling with whether to come out to a work colleague. The counselor might help her or him see how heterosexism in the workplace, the absence of sexual orientation–based nondiscrimination workplace policies, and the client's previous experiences of rejection after such self-disclosures might be contributing to her or his indecision.

Internalized Oppression: Identifying and Challenging Internalized Heterosexism

In addition to acknowledging external pressures on LGBT clients, counselors should be able to assess and address their LGBT clients' levels of internalized heterosexism or biphobia. This process might be conceptualized in several phases. First is assessment. The counselor should determine the extent to which these internalized negative messages are influencing the client's presenting concerns. In many cases, the counselor will need to help the client explore the impact of internalized heterosexism or biphobia on her or his life and continually challenge various aspects of the client's

internalized heterosexism or biphobia (Brown, 1989; Gartrell, 1984; Szymanski, 2005a).

To facilitate clients' awareness and expression of these internalized negative beliefs, counselors might ask them about attitudes and stereotypes about LGBT people that they have heard while growing up. Counselors might then explore what impact these stereotypes might have on clients and their levels of self-acceptance of their sexual-minority identity. In a related vein, counselors might ask clients about times when they felt ashamed or embarrassed about their sexual orientation and, conversely, about times when they felt proud about their sexual orientation.

Once internalized negative messages have been identified, counselors can use several methods to challenge those internalizations. Simple instruction and bibliotherapy can be useful, as the counselor might provide factual information or affirmative readings about homosexuality or bisexuality. In addition, the counselor might use cognitive methods to help the client evaluate the validity of these beliefs. Finally, the counselor can encourage contact with other LGBT persons (Gartrell, 1984; Sophie, 1987; Szymanski, Balsam, & Chung, 2001), which, in turn, can provide affirmation, role models, and self-acceptance.

Counselors might assist clients in seeing how their internalized heterosexism or biphobia may be related to any of their current struggles (Szymanski, 2005a). For example, a counselor working with a gay male couple might help them explore ways in which internalized negative beliefs that "gay men are not capable of monogamy" and "gay male relationships don't last" might be contributing to their relationship problems.

Exploring Multiple Identities of LGBT Clients

Another dimension of counseling LGBT persons is attending to the intersections of oppression for clients who have more than one minority status. Counselors can use the feminist model of an Integrated Analysis of Oppression (IAO) in such a situation. An IAO consists of (1) increasing LGBT clients' awareness of their other relevant nondominant social identities (e.g., gender, race, physical abilities, class), (2) facilitating identity development within these identities, and (3) promoting an awareness of how clients' multiple identities influence both external and internalized heterosexism and psychosocial difficulties (Szymanski, 2005a; Worell & Remer, 2003). An IAO can be illustrated in the case of a counselor encountering an African American lesbian client who has heard racist messages in the LGBT community and, conversely, heterosexist messages from her family and racial/ethnic community. In the latter case, she is accused of betraying her people as a black lesbian, since lesbianism is seen by her community as a "white problem." A counselor can intervene by helping this client explore how racism in the LGBT community is contributing to her feelings of alienation and distress, and how heterosexism in her racial/ethnic community is compounding her experiences of external and internalized heterosexism (Szymanski, 2005a). In addition, the counselor might help the client discuss the impact of racism on herself and other African Americans, identify beliefs about gay persons in the African American community, explore the client's realistic fears of rejection from other African Americans if she comes out as a lesbian, and provide her with readings about the issues confronting African American lesbians (cf. Greene, 1994).

Counselors' Self-Disclosure of Their Sexual Orientation

One of the challenges that counselors face when working with sexual-minority clients is whether, and how, the counselor's sexual orientation should be disclosed. Both nondisclosure and disclosure of one's sexual identity can convey important messages to the client. For example, by not disclosing her or his sexual identity, a counselor might be colluding with the larger culture in perpetuating the norm of secrecy. This might, in turn, make it more difficult for a client to disclose her or his sexual identity to others (Morrow, 2000). Likewise, by the counselor disclosing her or his sexual-minority identity, she or he might convey an affirmation of LGBT identities and serve as a positive role model for clients. Alternatively, there

may be good reasons not to disclose one's own sexual orientation to a client. For example, a gay client might ask you directly not to disclose personal information about yourself so that she or he can find her or his own strength and healing.

Whatever their sexual orientation, counselors should explore with clients what the counselor's own sexual identity might mean for the client. For example, a counselor might ask LGBT clients what it would mean to them if she or he were lesbian, gay, bisexual, or heterosexual and how this might affect their relationship with her or him. A client might, or might not, indicate that she or he is more comfortable talking with a sexual-minority counselor about certain issues.

A client might ask the counselor directly about her or his sexual orientation. Sophie (1987) asserts that counselors finding themselves in such a situation should be aware that refusal to self-disclose in response to a direct request for this information is likely to lead to distrust, which can negatively affect the counseling relationship. An important question for the counselor to consider is what this information would mean to the client. If the client's motivation is to find out whether an LGBT counselor has or has not gone through the coming-out process, it is a legitimate concern and should be acknowledged with an honest response. The counselor may then wish to explore the meaning of this response to the client. If, on the other hand, the client's motivation is based on stereotyped and homophobic assumptions, or on distorted thought processes due to severe disturbance, it is probably advisable to risk some distrust by refraining from responding to her or his question until further work has occurred. It might be clear at this point that the issue of counselors' self-disclosure is complex and should be evaluated on a case-by-case basis (Sophie, 1987).

For counselors who themselves are sexual minorities, it is important to have worked through some of their own internalized heterosexism and biphobia. They should be comfortable with their own sexual orientation before they decide to come out to a client.

For counselors who are heterosexual, it is important for them to have worked through some of their own heterosexism, biphobia, and heterosexual privilege. It is also important for them to be aware that offhanded self-disclosures of their heterosexual identity, such as casual references to a spouse or children, may be interpreted by the client as an expression of discomfort with the client's sexuality or pressure toward a heterosexual orientation (Sophie, 1987).

Engaging in Activism Toward the Eradication of Heterosexism

As part of their professional responsibility, counselors need to actively work to eradicate heterosexism and other forms of oppression. As Coretta Scott King said at the 1996 Atlanta Gay Pride Celebration,

> Gay bashers and church burners drink from the same poisonous well. The civil rights movement I support believes in unity and inclusion, not division and exclusion. I will continue to support elimination in this country of all forms of bigotry— of racism, of sexism, of homophobia.

Counselors can work in various ways as advocates and activists to make the world a better and safer place for LGBT persons. They can discourage heterosexist behavior by, for example, refusing to laugh at jokes about LGBT persons and by confronting others' stereotypes about homosexuality and bisexuality. Counselors can model nonheterosexist behaviors, such as being equally affectionate with women and men, not teasing someone for nontraditional gender behaviors, avoiding "heterosexual credentializing" (i.e., making a point of one's heterosexuality), and using gender-neutral language, such as using *partner* rather than *wife* or *husband*.

In their own offices or agencies, counselors can provide a welcoming place for LGB clients by placing something LGBT-related such as a rainbow flag sticker, LGBT books, and an affirmative brochure on sexual orientation in an easily viewable place. Counselors might also recruit LGBT employees to their workplaces and advocate for sexual orientation to be included in their agency's nondiscrimination policies. They also can analyze their agency's counseling materials for heterosexist bias and make the needed changes (Szymanski, 2005a). For example, instead of offering *marriage* and family counseling, counselors might change the term to *couples* and family counseling.

Outside their offices, counselors should be familiar with community resources for LGBT persons in their areas, such as bookstores, hotlines, support groups, clubs, and religious groups. They can provide LGBT affirmative outreach programs as part of their work in schools, agencies, or colleges. Finally, they can become actively involved in an LGB organization in the community or in the counseling profession. Even if a counselor is not LGBT, she or he can proudly be an ally of LGBT persons by engaging in the activities enumerated above.

Activity 15.7   Activist Reflections

Part of becoming a social change agent is being able to make a commitment to specific ways that you can work toward the eradication of heterosexism. To help you reflect on your experiences of injustice, address the following questions. First write responses alone, then discuss in pairs or small groups.

1. Describe a time when you felt angry about heterosexism or biphobia in society.

2. Describe a time when you felt helpless as an individual to create change regarding heterosexism or biphobia in society.

3. Describe a time when you decided to actively resist heterosexism or biphobia.

4. Make a list of three ways that you will actively resist heterosexism and biphobia in both your personal and professional lives over the next few weeks.

Skills: Case Example

Jason is a 21-year-old white gay male. He is a senior majoring in biology. He has a 3.6 GPA and is president of the Biology Club, research assistant for the Biology Department chair, and mentor for new students majoring in biology. However, he still fears failure and feels that he should be getting all As and doing more biology-related activities. In the past he was told he would never amount to anything by his father because he was gay. This increases his fear of failure. He describes himself as a perfectionist and is very hard on himself. Jason is also dealing with stress about multiple responsibilities, both at school and at home. He decides to enter counseling because he is feeling overwhelmed and is experiencing symptoms of anxiety such as difficulty sleeping, shallow breathing, and racing thoughts.

As he enters the university counseling center, Jason is feeling very anxious and unsure of what his experience will be like, particularly since he had a bad experience with a homophobic counselor in the past. While waiting for his counselor, he sees a pamphlet on coming-out issues and a couple of LGBT magazines on the table in the lobby. His counselor, a white female, comes out to greet him and leads him to her office. As they enter her office, Jason sees a Safe Zone sticker on her door and several LGBT books in her bookcase, and this begins to put him at ease.

During the initial intake interview, the counselor asks Jason about his previous counseling experience. He states that he saw a counselor in high school for about three sessions when he was dealing with coming out as a gay man but stopped going to that counselor when he suggested that Jason's homosexuality was caused by having an "overbearing and smothering" mother. Jason's counselor responds to his past therapy experience with shock and states that she is sorry that Jason had to deal with such an uninformed and biased counselor. She made it clear to Jason that she did not believe that his being gay was caused by his mother, and she normalized homosexuality as a natural form of emotional/sexual attraction. At this point, Jason asks his counselor what her sexual orientation is. She states that she is a heterosexual woman and asks what her sexual orientation means to him and how he feels about working with her given that she is both heterosexual and a woman. Jason responds that he feels comfortable working with her and was just curious because she seemed so gay-friendly.

The counselor proceeds to ask Jason about his coming-out experience and his experiences of being a gay man in a heterosexist society. Jason states that he had difficulty in high school accepting being gay but that he feels good about himself now as a gay man. He states that he is out to his family and some heterosexual and LGBT friends. He reports that reactions to his self-disclosures of his sexual orientation have been good, except for his father's response, which was very negative. Jason states that his father, a successful businessman, and he have a conflictual, distant relationship and that when they do talk his father is very critical of him, believes he needs to be doing more to be successful in his career, and frequently says derogatory comments about his being gay. After further exploration, Jason admits that he has internalized some of his father's heterosexist comments about gay men not being successful in work and not feeling good enough at times because he is gay. Jason also states that he is not out as a gay man at school because he believes it could ruin his career. He doesn't believe it is safe because he has heard his department chair make heterosexist comments.

The counselor continues with the clinical interview finding out more information about Jason's family history, medical history, alcohol and drug use, and educational, interpersonal, and vocational histories. She also checks for any suicidal and homicidal ideation/attempts and checks for a history of abuse, rape, and assault. At the end of the session, she checks in with Jason to see how he is feeling about their first session. Jason states that he feels good and would like to continue their work together.

After Jason leaves, the counselor reviews the session and feels she has a good beginning case conceptualization and some ideas for counseling. She believes that Jason's presenting issues of stress and anxiety are fueled and maintained by several sources. First, she identities two subpersonalities, the Critic and the Perfectionist (see Bourne, 2005, for a full discussion of these subpersonalities), that tend to be prominent in people who are prone to anxiety. She believes that it might be helpful to assist Jason in identifying when he is engaging in these negative self-talks (e.g., "I should be more involved in biology-related activities"), demonstrate how they are contributing to his anxiety issues, illustrate how they may be connected with his family-of-origin issues (e.g., growing up in a family that set excessively high standards and was overly critical), help him replace his negative self-talk with more positive self-talk (e.g., "It's important to have a balance in my life, and it's okay to take care of my personal needs"), and teach him self-nurturing skills. In addition, she would like to explore Jason's fears related to failing and not feeling good enough, even though he is at the top of his class. She would like to challenge some of his catastrophizing thoughts that are not reality-based using cognitive therapy.

The counselor also believes that Jason's high-stress lifestyle, juggling multiple responsibilities, and lack of personal time for himself are contributing to his anxiety. She would like to discuss ways that Jason might achieve more of a balance between his school demands and personal time. Also, she might discuss other stress management techniques such as exercising, deep breathing, progressive muscle relaxation, and listening to music to help him decrease his stress level.

The counselor would also like to further discuss Jason's feeling that he needs to be the best at everything and an overachiever. She would like to make connections to how this relates to both external (e.g., heterosexist behaviors from father and department chair) and internalized heterosexism (e.g., "gay men are not successful at work," "to be gay is to be not good enough"). She would like to explore and challenge Jason's s internalized heterosexism using cognitive and feminist methods, using bibliotherapy, and encouraging his making connections with gay men who are successful in their careers. She also wonders if Jason has unfinished business with his father. In that vein, she would like to further discuss their relationship, his father's rejection of his being gay, and his feelings of anger and hurt toward his father. She thinks it also might be helpful to further explore his school situation and decision not to come out at school, noting both the pros and cons of staying closeted in this area. At some point in therapy, she would also like to discuss more fully Jason's experiences of heterosexism and ways he dealt with these behaviors. Finally, she may want to discuss and role-play ways Jason might confront and deal with other people's heterosexist beliefs and behaviors.

Skills: Activities

You are invited to engage in Activities 15.8 and 15.9 in order to gain deeper knowledge of LGBT issues through personal contact and practice in providing counseling responses to LGBT-related situations.

Activity 15.8   Interviewing an LGBT Person

Locate an LGBT person who is willing to be interviewed, for example, through a local college LGBT organization, a gay-friendly religious organization, or a local P-FLAG chapter. Conduct a personal interview with that person, and ask her or him about her or his coming-out experiences, how she or he handled the disclosure or nondisclosure of her or his sexual identity, reactions of others to the self-disclosures, experiences with external and internalized heterosexism, and challenges and coping strategies for living in a heterosexist environment. Green (1996) provides additional structured and detailed questions you might ask concerning families of origin, lesbian and gay couple relationships, parenting issues, and families of choice. When conducting this interview, be sure to implement some of the LGBT-affirmative counseling skills you learned in this chapter.

SUMMARY

Heterosexist bias, prejudice, and discrimination often go unchallenged in U.S. culture and are often tolerated and accepted. As demonstrated in this chapter, these oppressive conditions can make managing a sexual-minority identity complex, challenging, and difficult. Even within the counseling profession, LGBT issues are often marginalized, even in the area of multicultural counseling itself. Thus, it is imperative for counselors to engage in growth-producing dialogues about LGBT issues and move sexual orientation issues from the margin to the center of counseling discourses.

REFERENCES

Adams, H. E., Wright, L. W., & Lohr, B. A. (1996). Is homophobia associated with homosexual arousal? *Journal of Abnormal Psychology, 105,* 440–445.

American Psychological Association. (2001). *Publication manual of the American Psychological Association.* Washington, DC: Author.

American Psychological Association. (2004). *Answers to your questions for a better understanding of sexual orientation and homosexuality.* Retrieved from http://www.apa.org/pubinfo/answers.html

Barrett, K. A., & McWhirter, B. T. (2002). Counselor trainees' perceptions of clients based on client sexual orientation. *Counselor Education and Supervision, 41,* 219–232.

Bartlett, A., Smith, G., & King, M. (2009). The response of mental health professionals to clients seeking help to change or redirect same-sex sexual orientation. *BMC Psychiatry, 9*(11), 1–8.

Baunach, D. M., Burgess, E. O., & Muse, C. S. (2010). Southern (dis)comfort: Sexual prejudice and contact with gay men and lesbians in the South. *Sociological Spectrum, 30,* 20–64.

Beckstead, A. L., & Morrow, S. L. (2004). Mormon clients' experiences of conversion therapy: The need for a new treatment approach. *The Counseling Psychologist, 32,* 651–690.

Bell, A. P., & Weinberg, M. S. (1978). *Homosexualities: A study of diversity among men and women.* New York, NY: Touchstone.

Berrill, K. T. (1992). Antigay violence and victimization in the United States: An overview. In G. M. Herek & K. T. Berrill (Eds.), *Hate crimes: Confronting violence against lesbians and gay men* (pp. 19–45). Newbury Park, CA: Sage.

Bieschke, K. J., Croteau, J. M., Lark, J. S., & Vandiver, B. J. (2005). Toward a discourse of sexual orientation equity in the counseling professions. In J. M. Croteau, J. S. Lark, M. A. Lidderdale, & Y. B. Chung (Eds.), *Deconstructing heterosexism in the counseling professions: A narrative approach* (pp. 189–228). Thousand Oaks, CA: Sage.

Bieschke, K. J., McClananhan, M., Tozer, E., Grzegorek, J. L., & Park, J. (2000). Programmatic research on the treatment of lesbian, gay and bisexual clients: The past, the present, and the course for the future. In

R. M. Perez, K. A. DeBord, & K. J. Bieschke (Eds.), *Handbook of counseling and psychotherapy with lesbian, gay, and bisexual clients* (pp. 309–335). Washington, DC: American Psychological Association.

Bohan, J. (1996). *Psychology and sexual orientation.* New York, NY: Routledge.

Bourne, E. J. (2005). *The anxiety and phobia workbook.* Oakland, CA: New Harbinger.

Bradford, J., Ryan, C., & Rothblum, E. D. (1994). National Lesbian Health Care Survey: Implications for mental health care. *Journal of Consulting and Clinical Psychology, 62,* 228–242.

Brown, L. (1989). Lesbians, gay men and their families: Common clinical issues. *Journal of Gay and Lesbian Psychotherapy, 1,* 65–77.

Burkard, A. W., Knox, S., Hess, S. A., & Schultz, J. (2009). Lesbian, gay, and bisexual supervisees' experiences of LGB-affirmative and nonaffirmative supervision. *Journal of Counseling Psychology, 56,* 176–188.

Butler, J. (1990). *Gender trouble: Feminism and the subversion of identity.* New York, NY: Routledge.

Carroll, L., Gilroy, P. J., & Ryan, J. (2002). Counseling transgendered, transsexual, and gender-variant clients. *Journal of Counseling & Development, 80,* 131–139.

Cass, V. C. (1979). Homosexual identity formation: A theoretical model. *Journal of Homosexuality, 4,* 219–235.

Chen-Hayes, S., & Banez, L. (2001). *Lesbian, bisexual, gay and transgendered counseling.* Framingham, MA: Microtraining Associates.

Chung, Y. B., & Katayama, M. (1998). Ethnic and sexual identity development of Asian-American lesbian and gay adolescents. *Professional School Counseling, 1,* 21–25.

Coleman, E. (1982). Developmental phases of the coming out process. *Journal of Homosexuality, 7,* 31–43.

Croteau, J. M., Lark, J. S., Lidderdale, M. A., & Chung, Y. B. (2005). *Deconstructing heterosexism in the counseling professions: A narrative approach.* Thousand Oaks, CA: Sage.

Denny, D. (2004). Changing models of transsexualism. *Journal of Gay and Lesbian Psychotherapy, 8,* 25–40.

Denny, D. (2007). Transgender identities and bisexual expression: Implications for counselors. In B. A. Firestein (Ed.), *Becoming visible: Counseling bisexuals across the lifespan* (pp. 268–284). New York, NY: Columbia University Press.

Descamps, M. J., Rothblum, E., Bradford, J., & Ryan, C. (2000). Mental health impact of child sexual abuse, rape, intimate partner violence, and hate crimes in the National Lesbian Health Care Survey. *Journal of Gay and Lesbian Social Services, 11,* 27–55.

Diamond, L. M. (2005). A new view of lesbian subtypes: Stable versus fluid identity trajectories over an 8-year period. *Psychology of Women Quarterly, 29,* 119–128.

Diamond, L. M. (2008). Female bisexuality from adolescence to adulthood: Results from a 10-year longitudinal study. *Developmental Psychology, 44,* 5–14.

Diamond, L. M., & Butterworth, M. (2008). Questioning gender and sexual identity: Dynamic links over time. *Sex Roles, 59,* 365–376.

Dorland, J. M., & Fischer, A. R. (2001). Gay, lesbian, and bisexual individuals' perceptions: An analogue study. *The Counseling Psychologist, 29,* 532–547.

Dworkin, S. H. (2001). Treating the bisexual client. *JCLP/In Session: Psychotherapy in Practice, 57,* 671–680.

Etheridge, M. (1993). Silent legacy. *Yes, I Am.* New York, NY: Island Records.

Fairchild, B., & Hayward, N. (1998). *Now that you know: What every parent should know about homosexuality.* San Diego, CA: Harcourt Brace Jovanovich.

Falco, K. L. (1991). *Psychotherapy with lesbian clients: Theory into practice.* New York, NY: Brunner/Mazel.

Fassinger, R. E., & Miller, B. A. (1996). Validation of an inclusive model of sexual minority identity formation on a sample of gay men. *Journal of Homosexuality, 32,* 53–78.

Firestein, B. A. (1996). Bisexuality as paradigm shift: Transforming our disciplines. In B. A. Firestein (Ed.), *Bisexuality: The psychology and politics of an invisible minority* (pp. 263–291). Thousand Oaks, CA: Sage.

Fox, R. C. (2000). Bisexuality in perspective: A review of theory and research. In B. Greene & G. L. Croom

(Eds.), *Psychological perspectives on lesbian and gay issues: Vol. 5. Education, research, and practice in lesbian, gay, bisexual, and transgendered psychology* (pp. 161–206). Thousand Oaks, CA: Sage.

Franklin, K. (1998). Unassuming motivations: Contextualizing the narratives of antigay assailants. In G. M. Herek (Ed.), *Stigma and sexual orientation: Understanding prejudice against lesbians, gay men, and bisexuals* (pp. 1–23). Thousand Oaks, CA: Sage.

Franklin, K. (2000). Antigay behaviors among young adults: Prevalence, patterns, and motivators in a noncriminal population. *Journal of Interpersonal Violence, 15*, 339–362.

Gainor, K. A. (2000). Including transgender issues in lesbian, gay and bisexual psychology: Implications for clinical practice and training. In B. Greene & G. L. Croom (Eds.), *Psychological perspectives on lesbian and gay issues: Vol. 5. Education, research, and practice in lesbian, gay, bisexual, and transgendered psychology* (pp. 131–160). Thousand Oaks, CA: Sage.

Garnets, L. D., & Peplau, L. A. (2001). A new paradigm for women's sexual orientation: Implications for therapy. *Women & Therapy, 24*, 111–121.

Gartrell, N. (1984). Combating homophobia in the psychotherapy of lesbians. *Women & Therapy, 3*, 13–29.

Gay, Lesbian and Straight Education Network. (2007). *The 2007 National School Climate Survey.* New York, NY: Author.

Gelso, C. J., Fassinger, R., Gomez, M. J., & Latts, M. G. (1995). Countertransference reactions to lesbian clients: The role of homophobia, counselor gender, and countertransference management. *Journal of Counseling Psychology, 42*, 356–364.

Goodman, M. B., & Moradi, B. (2008). Attitudes and behaviors toward lesbian and gay persons: Critical correlates and mediated relations. *Journal of Counseling Psychology, 55*, 371–384.

Gramzow, R. H. (2002, February). *Self and social attitudes: Predicting and manipulating attitudes toward homosexuals.* Paper presented at the annual meeting of the Society for Personality and Social Psychology, Savannah, GA.

Green, R. (1996). Lesbians, gays, and family psychology. Resources for teaching and practice. In B. Greene &

G. L. Croom (Eds.), *Psychological perspectives on lesbian and gay issues: Vol. 5. Education, research, and practice in lesbian, gay, bisexual, and transgendered psychology.* Thousand Oaks, CA: Sage.

Greene, B. (1994). Lesbian women of color: Triple jeopardy. In L. Comas-Díaz & B. Greene (Eds.), *Women of color: Integrating ethnic and gender identities in psychotherapy* (pp. 389–427). New York, NY: Guilford Press.

Greene, B. (1997). Ethnic minority lesbians and gay men: Mental health and treatment issues. In B. Greene (Ed.), *Psychological perspectives on lesbian and gay issues: Vol. 3. Ethnic and cultural diversity among lesbians and gay men.* Thousand Oaks, CA: Sage.

Grossman, A. H., & D'Augelli, A. R. (2006). Transgender youth: Invisible and vulnerable. *Journal of Homosexuality, 51*, 111–128.

Guidry, L. L. (1999). Clinical intervention with bisexuals: A contextualized understanding. *Professional Psychology: Research and Practice, 30*, 22–26.

Hayes, J. A., & Erkis, A. J. (2000). Counselor homophobia, client sexual orientation, and source of client HIV infection as predictors of counselor reactions to clients with HIV. *Journal of Counseling Psychology, 47*, 71–78.

Hayes, J. A., & Gelso, C. J. (1993). Male counselors' discomfort with gay and HIV-infected clients. *Journal of Counseling Psychology, 40*, 86–93.

Herek, G. M. (1994). Assessing heterosexuals' attitudes toward lesbians and gay men: A review of empirical research with the ATLG Scale. In B. Greene & G. M. Herek (Eds.), *Lesbian and gay psychology: Theory, research and clinical application* (pp. 206–228). Thousand Oaks, CA: Sage.

Herek, G. (1995). Psychological heterosexism in the United States. In A. D'Augelli & C. Patterson (Eds.), *Lesbian, gay, and bisexual identities over the lifespan: Psychological perspectives* (pp. 321–346). New York, NY: Oxford University Press.

Herek, G. M. (2009). Hate crimes and stigma-related experiences among sexual minority adults in the United States: Prevalence estimates from a national probability sample. *Journal of Interpersonal Violence, 24*, 54–74.

Herek, G. M., Cogan, J. C., & Gillis, J. R. (2002). Victim experiences in hate crimes based on sexual orientation. *Journal of Social Issues, 58*, 319–339.

Herek, G. M., Gillis, J. R., & Cogan, J. C. (1999). Psychological sequelae of hate crime victimization among lesbian, gay, and bisexual adults. *Journal of Consulting and Clinical Psychology, 67,* 945–951.

Hooker, E. (1957). The adjustment of the male overt homosexual. *Journal of Projective Techniques, 21,* 18–31.

Hu, S., Pattatucci, A. M., Patterson, C., Li, L. Fulker, D. W., Cherny, S. S., . . . & Hamer, D. H. (1996). Linkage between sexual orientation and chromosome Xq28 in males but not in females. *Nature Genetics, 11,* 248–256.

Hunt, G. L., & Hunt, M. W. (1977). Female-female paring in western gulls in southern California. *Science, 196,* 1466–1467.

Jewell, L. M., & Morrison, M. A. (2010). "But there's a million jokes about everybody . . . ": Prevalence of, and reasons for, directing negative behaviors toward gay men on a Canadian university campus. *Journal of Interpersonal Violence, 25,* 2094–2112.

Jones, J. M. (2009). *Majority of Americans continue to oppose gay marriage.* Retrieved from http://www .gallup.com/poll/118378/Majority-Americans-Continue-Oppose-Gay-Marriage.aspx

Jordan, K. M., & Deluty, R. H. (1998). Coming out for lesbian women: Its relationship to anxiety, positive affectivity, self-esteem, and social support. *Journal of Homosexuality, 35,* 41–63.

Kilianski, S. E. (2003). Explaining heterosexual men's attitudes toward women and gay men: The theory of exclusively masculine identity. *Psychology of Men and Masculinity, 4,* 37–56.

Kinsey, A. C., Pomeroy, W. B., & Martin, C. E. (1948). *Sexual behavior in the human male.* Philadelphia, PA: W. B. Saunders.

Kinsey, A. C., Pomeroy, W. B., Martin, C. E., & Geebhard, P. H. (1953). *Sexual behavior in the human female.* Philadelphia, PA: W. B. Saunders.

Kubler-Ross, E. (1969). *On death and dying.* New York, NY: Macmillan.

Landrine, H., & Klonoff, E. A. (1996). The Schedule of Racist Events: A measure of racial discrimination and a study of its negative physical and mental health consequences. *Journal of Black Psychology, 22,* 144–168.

Lewis, L. A. (1984). The coming out process for lesbians: Integrating a stable identity. *Social Work, 29,* 464–469.

Liddle, B. J. (1996). Counselor sexual orientation, gender, and counseling practices as they relate to ratings of helpfulness by gay and lesbian clients. *Journal of Counseling Psychology, 43,* 394–401.

Liddle, B. J. (1997). Gay and lesbian clients' selection of counselors and utilization of therapy. *Psychotherapy, 34,* 11–18.

Matthews, C., & Lease, S. H. (2000). Focus on lesbian, gay, and bisexual families. In R. M. Perez, K. A. DeBord, & K. J. Bieschke (Eds.), *Handbook of counseling and psychotherapy with lesbian, gay, and bisexual clients* (pp. 249–273). Washington, DC: American Psychological Association.

Mayfield, W. (2001). The development of an internalized homonegativity inventory for gay men. *Journal of Homosexuality, 41,* 53–76.

Mays, V. M., & Cochran, S. D. (2001). Mental health correlates of perceived discrimination among lesbian, gay, and bisexual adults in the United States. *American Journal of Public Health, 91,* 1869–1876.

McAuliffe, G. J. (2012). *Working with gay and lesbian youth: A multi-ethnic demonstration.* Alexandria, VA: Microtraining/Alexander Street Press. Available from http://www.emicrotraining.com/product_info.php?products_id=151

McCarn, S. R., & Fassinger, R. E. (1996). Revisioning sexual minority identity formation: A new model of lesbian identity and its implications for counseling and research. *The Counseling Psychologist, 24,* 508–534.

Meyer, I. H. (2003). Prejudice, social stress, and mental health in lesbian, gay, and bisexual populations: Conceptual issues and research evidence. *Psychological Bulletin, 129,* 674–697.

Michaels, R. (2003). *Same-sex marriage: Canada, Europe and the United States.* Retrieved from http://www .asil.org/insigh111.cfm

Mohr, J. J., & Rochlen, A. B. (1999). Measuring attitudes regarding bisexuality in lesbian, gay male and heterosexual populations. *Journal of Counseling Psychology, 46,* 353–369.

Morris, J. F., Waldo, C. R., & Rothblum, E. D. (2001). A model of predictors and outcomes of outness among lesbian and bisexual women. *American Journal of Orthopsychiatry, 71,* 61–71.

Morrison, M. A., & Morrison, T. G. (2002). Development and validation of a scale measuring modern prejudice toward gay men and lesbian women. *Journal of Homosexuality, 43*(2), 15–37.

Morrow, S. L. (2000). First do no harm: Therapist issues in psychotherapy with lesbian, gay, and bisexual clients. In R. M. Perez, K. A. DeBord, & K. J. Bieschke (Eds.), *Handbook of counseling and psychotherapy with lesbian, gay, and bisexual clients* (pp. 137–156). Washington, DC: American Psychological Association.

Morrow, S. L., & Beckstead, A. L. (2004). Conversion therapies for same-sex attracted clients in religious conflict: Context, predisposing factors, experiences, and implications for therapy. *The Counseling Psychologist, 32,* 641–650.

National Survey of Sexual Health and Behavior. (2010). Retrieved from http://www.nationalsexstudy.indiana.edu

Neisen, J. H. (1993). Healing from cultural victimization: Recovery from shame due to heterosexism. *Journal of Gay & Lesbian Psychotherapy, 2,* 49–63.

Ochs, R. (1996). Biphobia: It goes more than two ways. In B. A. Firestein (Ed.), *Bisexuality: The psychology and politics of an invisible minority* (pp. 3–50). Thousand Oaks, CA: Sage.

Padesky, C. A. (1988). Attaining and maintaining positive lesbian self-identity: A cognitive therapy approach. *Women & Therapy, 8*(1/2), 145–156.

Pattatucci, A. M. L., & Hamer, D. H. (1995). Development and familiarity of sexual orientation in females. *Behavior Genetics, 25,* 407–420.

Pilkington, N. W., & Cantor, J. M. (1996). Perceptions of heterosexual bias in professional psychology programs: A survey of graduate students. *Professional Psychology: Research and Practice, 27,* 604–612.

Pillard, R. C., & Bailey, J. M. (1998). Human sexual orientation has a heritable component. *Human Biology, 70,* 347–365.

Pillard, R. C., Poumadere, J., & Carretta, R. A. (1981). Is homosexuality familial? A review, some data, and a suggestion. *Archives of Sexual Behavior, 10,* 465–475.

Rankin, S. R. (2003). *Campus climate for gay, lesbian, bisexual, and transgender people: A national perspective.* Retrieved from http://www.thetaskforce.org/reports_and_research/campus_climate

Riddle homophobia scale. (n.d.). Retrieved from http://www.bgsu.edu/downloads/sa/file14270.pdf

Rothblum, E. D. (2000). "Somewhere in Des Moines or San Antonio": Historical perspectives on lesbian, gay, and bisexual mental health. In R. M. Perez, K. A. DeBord, & K. J. Bieschke (Eds.), *Handbook of counseling and psychotherapy with lesbian, gay, and bisexual clients* (pp. 137–156). Washington, DC: American Psychological Association.

Roughgarden, J. (2004). *Evolution's rainbow: Diversity, gender, and sexuality in nature and people.* Berkeley: University of California Press.

Roysircar, G., Arredondo, P., Fuertes, J. N., Ponterotto, J. G., & Toporek, R. L. (2003). *Multicultural counseling competencies.* Alexandria, VA: American Counseling Association.

Saad, L. (2006). *Americans at odds over gay rights.* Retrieved from http://www.gallup.com/poll/23140/Americans-Odds-Over-Gay-Rights.aspx

Satcher, J., & Leggett, M. (2007). Homonegativity among professional school counselors: An exploratory study. *Professional School Counseling, 11*(1), 10–16.

Satcher, J., & Schumacker, R. (2009). Predictors of modern homonegativity among professional counselors. *Journal of LGBT Issues in Counseling, 3,* 21–36.

Sausa, L. A. (2002). Updating college and university campus policies: Meeting the needs of trans students, staff, and faculty. *Journal of Lesbian Studies, 6,* 43–55.

Shidlo, A. (1994). Internalized homophobia: Conceptual and empirical issues in measurement. In B. Greene & G. M. Herek (Eds.), *Lesbian and gay psychology: Theory, research and clinical application* (pp. 176–205). Thousand Oaks, CA: Sage.

Shidlo, A., & Schroeder, M. (2002). Changing sexual orientation: A consumers' report. *Professional Psychology: Research and Practice, 33,* 249–259.

Sophie, J. (1982). Counseling lesbians. *Personnel and Guidance Journal, 60,* 341–345.

Sophie, J. (1987). Internalized homophobia and lesbian identity. *Journal of Homosexuality, 14,* 53–65.

Szymanski, D. M. (2005a). A feminist approach to working with internalized heterosexism in lesbians. *Journal of College Counseling, 8,* 74–85.

Szymanski, D. M. (2005b). Heterosexism and sexism as correlates of psychological distress in lesbians. *Journal of Counseling & Development, 83,* 355–360.

Szymanski, D. M. (2009). Examining potential moderators of the link between heterosexist events and gay and bisexual men's psychological distress. *Journal of Counseling Psychology, 56,* 142–151.

Szymanski, D. M., & Chung, Y. B. (2001). The Lesbian Internalized Homophobia Scale: A rational/theoretical approach. *Journal of Homosexuality, 41,* 37–52.

Szymanski, D. M., Kashubeck-West, S., & Meyer, J. (2008). Internalized heterosexism: Measurement, psychosocial correlates, and research directions. *The Counseling Psychologist, 36,* 525–574.

Szymanski, D. M., & Moffitt, L. B. (2012). Sexism and heterosexism. In N. A. Fouad (Ed.), *Handbook of counseling psychology: Vol. 2. Theories, practice, training, and policy.* Washington, DC: American Psychological Association.

Szymanski, D. M., & Owens, G. P. (2009). Group-level coping as a moderator between heterosexism and sexism and psychological distress in sexual minority women. *Psychology of Women Quarterly, 33,* 197–205.

Szymanski, D. M., & Sung, M. R. (2010). Minority stress and psychological distress among Asian American sexual minority persons. *The Counseling Psychologist, 38,* 848–872.

Tozer, E. E., & McClanahan, M. K. (1999). Treating the purple menace: Ethical considerations of conversion therapy and affirmative alternatives. *The Counseling Psychologist, 27,* 722–742.

Weinrich, J. D. (1982). Is homosexuality biologically natural? In W. Paul, J. D. Weinrich, J. C. Weinrich, W. L. & Williams, (1991). *Strange customs, familiar lives: Homosexuality in other cultures.* (pp. 44–59). Newbury Park, CA: Sage.

Worell, J., & Remer, P. (2003). *Feminist perspectives in therapy: Empowering diverse women* (2nd ed.). Hoboken, NJ: Wiley.

CHAPTER 16

Religion and Spirituality

Karen Eriksen
Eriksen Institute

Shelley A. Jackson
Texas Woman's University

Chet Weld
Counselor Renewal Centers

Susan Lester
Old Dominion University

Brittany is a single 34-year-old Evangelical Christian. She attends a small Evangelical Baptist church in her rural town. Recently she has been struggling with not being married because being married and raising a family are the desires of her heart. She has been wondering why God has waited so long to bring a partner into her life, why He has not answered her prayers. Although she lives in a small town and attends a small church, there are a number of eligible men her age both in her town and in nearby towns. Most of these men are Christian. However, it seems that those whom she is interested in are not interested in her, and those interested in her, she is not interested in. She has been questioning whether she is faithful enough for God to answer her prayers. She is also questioning whether there is something wrong with her that keeps her from forming successful relationships with men. She consults with a counselor because she has been feeling depressed about her life situation.

Geoff is a 19-year-old Orthodox Jewish American undergraduate student majoring in pre-med at a large metropolitan university. He grew up in a relatively small city in another part of the state. He recently began attending a relationship support group at the campus counseling center because he is feeling depressed and isolated from friends and family. During the third session, Geoff shares with the group that he has found himself developing a phone relationship with the campus late-night male DJ. The phone calls have led to Geoff's masturbating to sexual fantasies about the DJ. Geoff's understanding of the Torah is that both homosexuality and masturbation are sins, so he feels that he can't go to the rabbi with

(Continued)

(Continued)

his struggle. But he wonders if masturbation is really wrong. He feels torn between, on the one hand, his and his family and temple's orthodox commitments and, on the other, his attraction to this man. The struggle creates a sense of isolation as he wonders whom he can talk with—his faith community doesn't seem to offer support or answers, while the secular perspectives challenge the faith and community that have supported him since birth.

Joseph is a 65-year-old man who has faithfully practiced Christian Science for 30 years. He now finds himself ill. His doctors say that he is dying from cancer. Because Christian Science is a healing faith that involves praying for people when they are ill and eschewing most medical services, and because he has not been healed despite many years of his own and healers' prayers, he and his family find themselves in a quandary. His parents are not believers in Christian Science, his wife is somewhat less committed to Christian Science, and his children left the faith years ago. So Joseph is experiencing extreme pressure to do "what most people would do"—that is, to see a doctor and undergo medical counseling. He is now doubting his faith because it seems to be deserting him at a critical moment in his life. He thinks that, after all, if God is not healing him now, perhaps there is no heaven and God will not greet him when he dies. He comes into family counseling with his wife and three adult children.

Religion has been at the heart of some of the best and some of the worst impulses and events in U.S. history. For example, it has played a part in the events of 9/11 and the subsequent wars, the Salem witch trials of 1692, the pro-life and pro-choice debates, the evolution and intelligent design controversies, and the debate over legalizing gay marriage (Kosmin, Mayer, & Keysar, 2001). For better and for worse, throughout history, people have considered spiritual or religious[1] beliefs to be fundamental to who they are. Some authors have proposed that spirituality and religion are universal impulses in human beings. For instance, more than 45 years ago, biblical commentator Merrill Unger (1966) stated, "There is that in a [human being's] nature which prompts him [sic] to some sort of faith and worship . . . he [sic] requires the satisfaction and consolation and guidance, which comes from faith in the unseen and the eternal" (p. 916). More recently, psychologist Paul Wong (1998) agreed, attributing the power of religion to its rootedness in a deep human need for connection, identity, and certainty.

Some people, such as agnostics and atheists, would disagree with the universality of those statements. But religiosity is a major facet of many, if not most, Americans' lives. According to Gallup (2012), approximately 55% of Americans said that religion is very important, and 81% very to somewhat important. More than 75% of Americans identified themselves as Christian, at least by birth. Even those without a belief in a higher power may consider it important to decide on a relationship with the ultimate—to find some ultimate meaning in their lives (Fowler, 1981).

THE CASE FOR INCLUDING RELIGION AND SPIRITUALITY IN COUNSELING

Because the quest for the sacred is so common among people, including those seeking counseling, many mental health professionals believe that spiritual concerns should be addressed in counseling (Wade & Worthington, 2003). Genia (2000)

---

[1] These are distinct but related concepts and sometimes are used interchangeably in the chapter.

advocated that even secular counselors become more empathic and competent in treating religious individuals. Miranti and Burke (1995) have noted that clients sometimes identify spirituality as a "sustaining core or essence" (p. 5) that enables them to survive otherwise untenable experiences and suggest counselors must become adept in addressing spiritual issues.

Counselors' observing the importance of spiritual concern to clients has resulted in ethical and professional mandates related to counseling and spirituality. In particular, the American Counseling Association (ACA; 2005) *Code of Ethics* indicates that ACA "members recognize diversity and embrace a cross-cultural approach in support of the worth, dignity, potential, and uniqueness of people within their social and cultural contexts" (Preamble, p. 3). Counselors are expected to try to understand their own and their clients' cultural identities and explore their effect on counseling practice; these cultural identities include religion and spirituality. In addition, the standards of the Council for the Accreditation of Counseling and Related Educational Programs (2001) specifically include sensitivity to "spiritual values" as a required goal in preparation of counselors (Standard K.2).

Ignoring faith issues can, at a minimum, be considered "passively prejudicial" (Esau, 1998, p. 32). At worst, counselors can do harm if they fail to grasp the significance of a client's organizing belief system, a system that, for religious people, may be based on their traditions and interpretation of scriptural teachings (Johnson & Johnson, 1997). Further, harm may occur if, when speaking of faith, counselors fail to intervene in a way that is appropriate to the person's faith development stage (Fowler, 1981).

Thus, if counselors are to remain within the bounds of ethical standards when counseling spiritual or religious clients, they must understand the beliefs and values of these clients (Bishop, 1992; Genia, 2000; Ridley, 1985). These beliefs and values may take direction from religion, from a central sense of meaning, or from something ultimate that gives clients' lives direction and substance (Fowler, 1981).

Beyond ethical considerations for competence in addressing religion in counseling are practical matters. Clients have limited choices in selecting a counselor. Most people's counseling choices are currently restricted by the limits of managed care. Therefore clients may not have the luxury of receiving counseling from someone who shares their faith. Therefore, if a counselor fails to understand and respect their belief system, clients may reject necessary counseling services, particularly if they are religiously conservative (Post & Wade, 2009). Because many counselors feel unprepared to work competently with religious material (Shafranske, 1996; Shafranske & Malony, 1990), such clients may find it difficult to get their mental health needs met.

Consider the vignettes at the beginning of this chapter. Each clearly includes religious challenges and requires a degree of competence on the part of the counselor concerning religious issues. Brittany, who is a single Evangelical Christian, is questioning whether there is something wrong with her that keeps her from forming successful relationships with men. Geoff, an Orthodox Jewish American, wonders if masturbation and homosexuality are sins. He is depressed and torn between his family's orthodox beliefs and those of a secular society. Joseph, a Christian Scientist, is sick, perhaps dying, and is being pressured by his family to receive traditional medical treatment for his cancer despite the conflict with his beliefs. Counseling each of these clients requires the counselor to have spiritual competencies such as those developed by the Association for Spiritual, Ethical, and Religious Values in Counseling (ASERVIC; see Table 16.1).

This chapter addresses each of the ASERVIC competencies and is organized under the following major headings: (1) Definitions of Religion and Spirituality, (2) Cultural Dimensions of Religion and Spirituality, (3) Psychological Dimensions of Religion and Spirituality, (4) Encouraging Development Toward Reflective Faith, (5) Religion and Counseling, (6) Beliefs of Major Religious Groups in the United States and Implications for Counseling, (7) General Interventions That Are Alert to Religion and Spirituality, and (8) Applying Religiously Alert Interventions to the Vignettes.

Table 16.1   Summary of Competencies for Addressing Spiritual and Religious Issues in Counseling

Culture and Worldview	Describe similarities and differences and relationship between spirituality and religion, including basic beliefs and practices of various spiritual and religious systems, and recognize clients' beliefs as central to their worldviews.
Counselor Self-Awareness	Explore one's own attitudes, beliefs, and values about spirituality and/or religion; evaluate the influence of these on the client and the counseling process; identify one's limits in understanding the client's perspective; and know religious and spiritual resources and leaders.
Human and Spiritual Development	Describe and apply various models of spiritual and/or religious development.
Communication	Recognize and respond to religious and spiritual content in client communication, address said content when therapeutically relevant, and use concepts during counseling that are consistent with the client's faith perspectives and are acceptable to the client.
Assessment	Understand the client's spiritual and/or religious perspectives through intake and assessment processes.
Diagnosis and Counseling	Recognize the client's spiritual and/or religious perspectives as contributing to well-being or problems, set therapy goals that are consistent with the client's faith perspectives, modify therapeutic techniques, and use spiritual and/or religious practices as techniques when acceptable to client and in ways that are supported by theory and current research.

Source: ASERVIC (2009).

DEFINITIONS OF RELIGION AND SPIRITUALITY

Religion and spirituality need to be distinguished from one another. Religion usually has a group element and a prescribed set of beliefs or principles. Spirituality is an individual experience that is creedless.

Defining Religion

Most definitions of religion include belief in a personal deity or some supernatural entity. Unfortunately, those definitions exclude faith communities that do not necessarily require belief in a deity, such as Buddhism and Unitarian Universalism (Stifoss-Hanssen, 1999). Post and Wade (2009) offer a more inclusive definition of religion, using the terms *ultimate* and *sacred* to identify the focus of religious belief. The English word *religion* may derive from the Latin word *religio,* which means "good faith" or "ritual." It may also be related to the Latin *religāre,* which means

"to bind back or to tie fast," as in *ligament* (Stifoss-Hanssen, 1999). From these origins comes the idea of religion as an element that ties people together in a faith commitment. This chapter uses the broad definition of religion that was given in Chapter 1: *The organized set of beliefs that encode a person's or group's attitudes toward, and understanding of, the essence or nature of reality.*

Religion is generally communal. It brings people together in a group to share their spirituality and to ponder the meanings of life. This chapter discusses some of the main belief systems found in the United States: Christianity, Islam, Judaism, Hinduism, Buddhism, Paganism, Unitariani Universalism, agnosticism, humanism, and atheism.

Defining Spirituality

The term *spirituality* derives from the Latin root word *spirare,* which means "to breathe." In that sense, spirituality is a means for people to stay consciously connected with a life force, like the air they breathe or the universe around them.

Spirituality variously connects individuals with their inner self, with other people, with universal elements such as a divine force (Richards & Bergin, 1999), or with what is ultimate and what gives their life meaning (Fowler, 1981). Myers (1990) defined spirituality broadly as "a continuing search for meaning and purpose in life; an appreciation for the depth of life, the expanse of the universe, and natural forces which operate" (p. 11; see also Hartz, 2005). In the traditional religious literature, spirituality is defined as (a) values and beliefs connected to a formal religion; (b) metaphysical, mystical, or transcendent experiences; or (c) a sense of connectedness with or love of another person or persons, nature, and/or God (Hartz, 2005; Jankowski, 2002; Post & Wade, 2009). For the purpose of this chapter, spirituality is defined, as it was in Chapter 1, as *a mindfulness about the existential qualities of life, especially the relationships among self, other, and the world.*

Comparing Religion and Spirituality

Religion and spirituality are often conflated. However, Richards and Bergin (1999) find three major differences between them. First, spirituality has no doctrines, while religion relies on principles or rules. Second, religion is primarily external, while spirituality is fundamentally internal. Finally, religion is exclusive, while spirituality is usually inclusive. Each of these distinctions is discussed in turn.

Doctrine

Spirituality is doctrine-less. It places its primary emphasis on individual experiences of the divine, what is ultimate, or what gives life meaning. There is no "creed" in spirituality. Instead, each person brings something different to her or his relationship with and perceptions of spirit. By contrast, religion has the aforementioned group dimension. Religion ties people together with common principles, doctrines, and rules. The doctrines vary from religion to religion and from denomination to denomination within each religion.

This distinction between religion and spirituality can be confusing when both meet in one individual (Goud, 1990). For example, Roman Catholic teaching indicates that a human being's highest authority is her or his individual conscience while the Church concurrently endorses the notion of a just war. A Catholic might decide, after sincerely searching her or his conscience, that she or he takes a pacifist position on war, and as a result may struggle to find a way for her or his spiritual stance to stand alongside that of the Catholic Church.

Spirituality, then, makes each person responsible for her or his own relationship with the sacred. While spiritual guides may recommend practices that have helped others in their spiritual journeys, each person has to do her or his own spiritual "work." Spirituality embraces intangibles, gray areas, and paradoxes, which may make it unattractive to those who are more comfortable with certainties, including those at earlier faith development stages (Fowler, 1981). It might be said that religions, with some exceptions, are systems of answers, whereas spirituality is about questions.

External Versus Internal

The second distinction between religion and spirituality is that religion has an external dimension, while spirituality is primarily internal. External expressions of religion include rituals, requirements, and practices, such as accepting Jesus as Savior and studying the Bible (Protestant Christianity), going to confession and Mass (Roman Catholic Christianity), adhering to the rules of the Talmud and Torah (Judaism), praying five times daily and making a pilgrimage to Mecca (Islam), or meeting as a community to raise questions through readings and discussion (Unitarian Universalism).

By contrast, spirituality, as an internal proposition, encourages humans to pursue personal communion with a force more pervasive, powerful, and ultimate than themselves, to pursue a sense of meaning in life (Fowler, 1981). Spirituality stresses integration with the divine and all of creation by bringing a personal relationship with the divine into all other relationships. In spirituality, such integration is largely achieved through meditation, prayer, and contemplation rather than through external, group rituals (Goud, 1990).

Exclusivity Versus Inclusivity

The final distinction between religion and spirituality is the exclusivity of religion versus the inclusivity of spirituality (Goud, 1990). In most cases, only those who agree with the prescribed beliefs and follow the prescribed principles and rules may become part of a religious group. Those who belong have usually been brought into the group by initiation rituals, such as baptism, or formally agreeing to a creed. Failing to comply with the principles or rules may mean that one cannot be part of the group. This exclusiveness offers an identity and a sense of community solidarity for members of a religion. Positive feelings are often attached to being part of the "right" group, or even to becoming "saved" by accepting the tenets of the group. Members may feel supported by religion in their life's journeys. They may feel free from the stress of challenges by outsiders because outsiders are not allowed in, or, if they are already in, they are removed, excommunicated, or disciplined. Members may thus gain a sense of comfort from knowing that everyone in their group generally thinks or behaves the way they do. In this sense, the exclusivity of religion may provide a kind of safety in comparison with the often uncertain and individual journey of spirituality, a safety that is necessary in early stages of development (Fowler, 1981).

The Limits of the Distinction Between Religion and Spirituality

In some ways, distinctions between religion and spirituality may be a bit arbitrary and somewhat artificial. Some people are spiritual without participating in a religion, and some religious people lack spirituality. Conversely, individuals' spirituality is often supported by the rituals and communal experiences of religion. And many people find their religion empowered and enlivened by spirit. Therefore, as noted previously, the terms are sometimes used interchangeably in this chapter.

In reflecting on the cases that began this chapter, it seems apparent that each client's religious beliefs have been challenged by their recent life experiences. In the long run, they may resolve the conflicts that they are currently experiencing with guidance from their religions as they currently understand them, or may grow spiritually or cognitively and increase the complexity of their thinking about those religions. Counselors who assist them in the journey will need to be able to articulate an understanding of their own spirituality and its development throughout their lives (Frame, 2003). Activity 16.1 helps counselors toward this end.

Activity 16.1   Assessing One's Own Spirituality and Religion

A. Read the following descriptions and statements made by thinkers and theologians about the nature of spirituality. Use these definitions to help yourself develop a better understanding of the spiritual dimension in your life and work. Write down which statements resonate with your views.

Spirituality is. . .

- the search for harmony and wholeness in the universe (Cervantes & Ramirez, 1992).

- that which is related to one's ultimate concern and is the meaning-giving dimension of culture (Tillich, 1959).

- an appreciation for the sacredness of life; a balanced appreciation of material values, altruism toward others, a desire for the betterment of the world, and an awareness of life's tragic side (Elkins, Hedstrom, & Hughes, 1988).

- "any experience of transcendence of one's former frame of reference that results in greater knowledge and love" (Chandler, Holden, & Kolander, 1992, p. 170), new meanings, and growth (Hinterkopf, 1994).

- "less a method than an attitude, a posture of one's very being that allows seeing not different things but everything differently" (Holifield, 1983, p. 88).

- "an inner-generated, thoughtful and sometimes skeptical search for universal connections, with no quid pro quo from a higher power sought or intended" (Winarsky, 1991, p. 186).

B. Briefly write your own personal definition of spirituality.

C. Now ask another person who has significantly different religious beliefs from your own to read the quotes above and give you her or his definition of spirituality.

D. Ask yourself and that person the following questions and record the responses:

- Where do your beliefs come from (e.g., parents, church, synagogue, temple)?

- Briefly describe your religious beliefs (may be different from describing spiritual beliefs).

- What sources of authority, if any, do you use for your religious beliefs (e.g., Torah, Bible, Qur'an, philosophy, other sources)?

- Does your belief system encourage reasoning and questioning or urge you to accept established beliefs?

- Why have you chosen your belief system over all others? Why do you consider it the best choice?

CULTURAL DIMENSIONS OF RELIGION AND SPIRITUALITY

A religion, through its beliefs, rituals, and moral codes, as well as its emotional and communal components, can be considered a culture (Saroglou, 2002). Traditionally, the religion that people participate in affects most aspects of their lifestyle and community. In fact, religion is identified in a number of fields as an inextricable aspect of ethnicity. Even in the United States, where separation of religion and state is institutionalized, reference to religion is found on the currency, in the Pledge of Allegiance, and in the Declaration of Independence. Religion can also have an explicit relationship with an ethnicity, as seen in the designations Polish Catholic, Greek Orthodox, Anglo-Protestant, and Arab Muslim. While the overlap is not universal, ethnic groups often claim an identity that includes

spiritual beliefs and codes for living (Smith, Faris, Denton, & Regnerus, 2003).

The Culture of Religion in the United States

Religion is a particularly powerful force in U.S. life. Religion or spirituality is regarded by many people in the United States as the deepest source of meaning and belonging in life. The impact of religion goes beyond worship and family life. It also shapes and reinforces the political and social views of vast numbers of citizens.

Varieties of Religion in the United States

The United States has moved beyond the largely Protestant pluralism of its early history and the Protestant, Catholic, and Jewish triumvirate of the 20th century to a diversity that includes almost every religious expression in the world, including agnosticism, atheism, and claiming no religious affiliation (Newport, 2010).

Religious groups' beliefs vary not only in content but in intensity as well. Sometimes the most profound religious and cultural differences are not between traditional denominations or religious groups, but between liberals and conservatives within denominations. In American Protestantism, for example, conservatives are sometimes criticized by liberals for being overly strict on moral issues, closed-minded, intolerant of other religious views, fanatical about their beliefs, too harsh, overly focused on guilt or sin, too concerned about their own salvation, and unreasonably rigid and simplistic. Liberals are sometimes faulted by conservatives for substituting social concerns for the "true gospel," compromising with "the world," being morally loose, having a shallow knowledge of the scriptures, and being too heavily influenced by secular humanism (Hoge, 1996).

Results of research on the intensity of belief are inconsistent. The Center for the Study of Religion at Princeton University (Wuthnow, 2004) found that one in four people in the United States is devoutly religious, one in four is secular, and the remaining two are moderately interested in religion. Other national polls report that 9 out of 10 Americans believe in God and consider religion to be an important part of their lives (Elkins, 1999). Both Bergin and Jensen (1990) and the Gallup Poll Daily tracking program (Newport, 2009b) found religious beliefs to be important to an estimated two-thirds of the U.S. population.

The inconsistency of the research results may be explained by the influence of historical events on religious practices at the time the data were gathered (Silk, 2005). For instance, there was a surge in religious observation after the terrorist attacks on New York City and Washington in 2001. Some religious leaders predicted that the phenomenon would be short-lived. Others saw it as the start of a major revival in the United States. It appears that the increase lasted only about 2 months. By November 2001, attendance at religious services had returned to usual levels (Gallup, 2012). Measuring intensity of faith before, during, or after this event (or others) might, therefore, explain inconsistent research results.

Inconsistencies may also result from difficulties in collecting religious data. Naming and identifying religious groups is itself difficult (Silk, 2005), a problem that is compounded by the lack of government data on religion. The U.S. Census Bureau feels proscribed by the First Amendment from including religious affiliation questions on either the census or the Current Population Survey (CPS; Petersen, 2003). A national census of religious bodies was last conducted in 1936, and the CPS has not asked about religion since 1957 (Mueller & Lane, 1972). Therefore, authoritative and detailed statistics on religion are in short supply (Silk, 2005).

However, the American Religious Identification Survey (ARIS) was conducted by Kosmin and Keysar in 2008 and published in 2009. Christianity, including its many subcategories, was claimed by 76% of the persons surveyed. Those identifying with no religion are not only the second-largest group, at 15% of the population, but are also the fastest growing, having more than doubled in number since 1991. Non-Catholic Christians have grown by only 10% in the same period. Table 16.2 lists the most identified religious and denominational affiliations in the United States in 2008.

Religions are not distributed uniformly across the United States. Particular faiths tend to be concentrated within regions. For example, Catholicism is the largest single group in the New England, Middle Atlantic, East North Central, Mountain, and Pacific regions. Southern Baptists form the single largest group in the West North Central, South Atlantic, East South Central, and West South Central regions (Guiso, Sapienza, & Zingales, 2003). Southern U.S. culture, in general, embraces religion more substantially than other regions in the United States (Smith et al., 2003). In particular, Baptist adults and youth in the South have the highest levels of church participation of any group (Smith et al., 2003). Table 16.3 shows areas of concentration for the country's largest religious groups.

Table 16.2   Self-Identification of U.S. Adults by Religious Tradition, 2008

Religion	Estimated Adult Population	Percentage of U.S. Population
Catholic	**57,199,000**	**25.1**
Baptist	**36,148,000**	**15.8**
Mainline Christian	**29,375,000**	**12.9**
• Methodist	11,366,000	5.0
• Lutheran	8,674,000	3.8
• Presbyterian	4,723,000	2.1
• Episcopalian/Anglican	2,405,000	1.1
• United Church of Christ	736,000	0.3
Christian Generic	**32,441,000**	**14.2**
• Unspecified	16,834,000	7.4
• Nondenominational	8,032,000	3.5
• Protestant unspecified	5,187,000	2.3
• Evangelical/born again	2,154,000	0.9
Pentecostal/Charismatic	**7,948,000**	**3.5**
• Pentecostal unspecified	5,416,000	2.4
• Assemblies of God	810,000	0.4
• Church of God	663,000	0.3
Protestant Denominations	**7,131,000**	**3.1**
• Churches of Christ	1,921,000	0.8
• Jehovah's Witness	1,914,000	0.8
• Seventh Day Adventist	938,000	0.4
Mormon/Latter Day Saints	**3,158,000**	**1.4**
Jewish	**2,680,000**	**1.2**
Eastern Religions[1]	**1,961,000**	**1.2**
• Buddhist	1,189,000	0.9
Muslim	**1,349,000**	**0.6**
New Religious Movements & Other Religions[2]	**2,804,000**	**1.2**
None/No religion[3]	**34,169,000**	**15.0**
• Agnostic	1,985,000	0.9
• Atheist	1,621,000	0.7
Don't Know/Refused	**11,815,000**	**5.2**

Source: Kosmin & Keysar (2009).

[1] Buddhist, Hindu, Taoist, Baha'i, Shintoist, Zoroastrian, and Sikh.

[2] Scientologist, New Age, Eckankar, Spiritualist, Unitarian Universalist, Deist, Wiccan, Pagan, Druid, Indian Religion, Santeria, and Rastafarian.

[3] None, No religion, Humanistic, Ethical Culture, Agnostic, Atheist, and Secular.

Guiding Ethic of Religious Tolerance

One striking aspect of the culture of religion in the United States is the ethic of religious tolerance. The United States has managed to avoid major religious strife, in contrast with other nations' experience. The choice not to participate in a religion is also part of the U.S. ethos.

In contrast, worldwide, more people died because of their religious convictions during the 20th century than in any previous century, more

Table 16.3 Regional Concentrations of Religious Identification in the United States

Non-Catholic Christian	More than 70% of the population in Tennessee, West Virginia, North Carolina, South Carolina, Kentucky, Oklahoma, Alabama, Georgia, Arkansas, and Mississippi
Catholic	More than 40% of the population in Massachusetts, Connecticut, Rhode Island, and New Jersey
Jewish	7% of the population in New York (greatest concentration in New York City); over 3% in Washington, DC, New Jersey, Massachusetts, Florida, Maryland, Rhode Island, California, and Connecticut
Mormon	Over 60% of the population of Utah, and 5%–20% in bordering states
No religion	More than 20% of the population in Oregon, Vermont, Washington, Alaska, New Hampshire, Hawaii, and Maine

Source: Newport (2009a).

than two-thirds of the wars in the 1990s were attributed to religious or ethnic differences (Hoge, 1996), and religiously inspired conflict is no longer limited by geographical borders (Barker & Muck, 2004). For example, serious outbreaks of religious and ethnic bigotry and division have occurred in Eastern Europe despite tremendous advances in democracy there. Tensions between Muslims and Christians have resulted in violence in Bosnia, Azerbaijan, Armenia, Nigeria, Egypt, and elsewhere. Hindus and Muslims have clashed in India. Anti-Semitism has dramatically risen throughout Eastern Europe (Hoge, 1996). Religiously inspired conflict has been visible during the 21st century not only in Ireland, Palestine, Iraq, and Indonesia, but also in the international efforts to defeat Al Qaeda and the Taliban.

By contrast, the United States, one of the most intensely religious nations and *the* most religiously diverse nation in the world, has managed to avoid the "holy wars" so prevalent throughout history and throughout the world. This remarkable achievement may be traced directly to the religious liberty clauses of the First Amendment (Gaustad & Dishno, 2000). The founding fathers, especially Thomas Jefferson, were adamant that no religion would be favored by government. In spite of outbreaks of religious bigotry, religious tolerance has generally held.

The Intersection of Religion and Ethnicity

The relationship between ethnicity and religion varies. As mentioned previously, for some groups religion and ethnicity are integrally connected. Sixty-four percent of Latino congregations and half of African American congregations consider their churches to be a primary means of preserving cultural heritage (Kosmin et al., 2001). About one-third of white congregations tend to link ethnic traditions with the religious community, as in Italian Catholic or Scandinavian Lutheran churches. Although religious identifications may be shared across racial and ethnic distinctions, Sunday morning religious hours have been considered the most racially segregated hours in the United States (Kosmin et al., 2001).

Religion has played a particularly central role in the political and social history of African Americans from the Colonial period to the present. Indeed, black Christian churches provided much of the moral and political leadership of the civil rights movement. Among African Americans, Baptist denominations dominate, with 45% professing Baptist affiliation (Kosmin & Keysar, 2009).

Among Hispanic Americans, 59% identify as Catholics. Among non-Hispanic white Americans, 62% identify with non-Catholic Christian traditions and 21% with the Catholic faith; 16% claim no religious tradition (Kosmin & Keysar, 2009). Asian Americans report the greatest variety of religious affiliations (most Muslims and members of Eastern religions are of Asian heritage) and also the largest percentage of nonreligious people and people who decline to claim a religion (Kosmin & Keysar, 2009).

PSYCHOLOGICAL DIMENSIONS OF RELIGION AND SPIRITUALITY

Beyond the cultural dimensions of religion, the psychological aspects of religion and spirituality play powerful roles in individual lives. They are therefore important knowledge for counselors. Four such psychological aspects of religion and spirituality warrant discussion here: (1) their contribution to a sense of meaning in life, (2) their place in people's experience of support and community (Saroglou, 2002), (3) the ways people choose a religion, and (4) how religious identity develops.

Meaning

Religion can satisfy a fundamental human need to find meaning in life, to feel in control, to find connection or belonging, to cope with trouble and death, and to forgive others (Baumeister, 1992). Humans, aided by an enormously imaginative brain, have for thousands of years sought to connect with a higher power that will protect and provide for them and make sense of natural events (Baumeister, 1992).

Many of the promises of religion have helped adherents handle life's misfortunes and deal with their fear of death. Religion evokes hope in troubling situations (Yahne & Miller, 1999) and creates serenity despite difficulties (Connors, Toscova, & Tonigan, 1999). Religious experience may also help members find acceptance and forgiveness and a subsequent sense of relief (Sanderson & Linehan, 1999). Pargament (2002) and Fowler (1981) have found that faith that is internalized and that provides meaning in life fosters a sense of well-being. The payoffs of religion are so attractive and comforting, in fact, that participants in a religion may find questions about their faith or religion to be extremely threatening (Baumeister, 1992).

Support and Community

A second psychological dimension of religion is the sense of belonging and social support that it provides, which accrue many other positive results.

For instance, many studies find that religious affiliation, when accompanied by frequent attendance and prayer, is associated with positive mental health and a decreased likelihood of mental illness (Ellison, 1991; Koenig, George, & Peterson, 1998; Levin & Chatters, 1998; Levin & Taylor, 1998). Although earlier studies consistently showed differences based on demographics, numbers from the Gallup-Healthways Wellbeing Index survey in 2010 showed a clearly significant correlation between religiosity and well-being in all six subindexes and across 50 states and all demographic parameters (Newport, Witters, & Agrawal, 2010). The social aspect of religious involvement is a likely mediator of this well-being (Bradley, 1995; Ellison & George, 1994; Ellison, 1991; Idler, 1995; Newport et al., 2010).

Particular benefit from religion has been found in three subgroups: socially marginalized groups, more religiously committed people, and those experiencing very stressful situations like chronic illness, disability, or death (Chibon, 1992; Landis, 1996; Larson, Wood, & Larson, 1993; Nathanson, 1995; Nino, 1997). Benefits may result from a search for spiritual meaning and from congregations providing an array of instrumental (e.g., food, money, transportations), informational, emotional, and spiritual support. Even the most controversial and sometimes seemingly damaging religions seem to have psychological benefits (Pargament, 2002). For instance, religious fundamentalism correlates both with greater prejudice toward those who are different from oneself and with increases in well-being.

The case of Geoff at the chapter's beginning, for example, illustrates both the strengths and difficulties of belonging to a religious tradition. Geoff has found support in his Orthodox Jewish faith since birth. It has provided him with a sense of safety, support, belonging, and answers to life's big questions. However, when he experienced challenges to its orthodoxy, he experienced a true loss and great confusion. He no longer felt he could approach his rabbi with his struggle about masturbation, and yet his longstanding Orthodox commitments prevented him from believing that other answers could be justified. The struggle created a sense of isolation as he wondered about whom he could talk to. His faith community didn't seem to offer support or answers, but secular answers challenged a faith and community that had supported him for a long time.

Religion of Choice and Religion of Origin: Developmental Considerations

People in the United States and in most of the world are usually enculturated into a religion, which is then considered their *religion of origin*. The enculturation process is powerful. A strong religious upbringing is a leading indicator of adult religious participation and religious identity (Bartz, Richards, Smith, & Fischer, 2010; Kluegel, 1980). For some, the religion chosen by their parents and community continues as a life practice. For others, an inherited religion may become a more conscious choice, or a person may deliberately choose a religion distinct from that of the parents or community. This latter phenomenon can be referred to as *religion of choice*.

Religious Identity Development

Whether or not people practice an inherited religion is strongly related to their faith development and maturity. That is, those who progress from more received ways of knowing to more self-authorized ways of knowing (Kegan, 1982, 1998), as described in the first chapters in this book, also tend to move from practicing a religion of origin to practicing a religion of choice. They claim, or reclaim, their religious stance on their terms. Such developmental change, as explained by a neo-Piagetian model of cognitive development (e.g., Fowler, 1981, 1991, 2004; Kegan, 1982, 1998; Kohlberg, 1981; Loevinger, 1976; Perry, 1970), requires that an individual experience internal conflict about an old way of knowing accompanied by support and challenge that leads to a new way of knowing. An overview of James Fowler's Stages of Faith Development is offered here to clarify the

development of faith and its impact on the degree to which clients choose their religion. Fowler's stages of faith parallel the stages of other structural developmentalists, as can be seen in Table 16.4. Fowler indicates that these developmental *processes* or progressions in faith occur regardless of the *content* of a person's faith, that is, whether she or he is Christian, Jewish, Buddhist, or atheist.

Stage 1. Intuitive-Projective Faith—Ages 3–7

Children's thinking at this stage is fluid, magical, and concrete rather than logical. They respond to and create stories and fairy tales that incorporate ideas of God, "the good," and the sacred. These are particularly important as they try to organize their communities' ideas about death, sex, and taboos. Their images are absolute and harsh, and are powerfully influenced by the examples, mood, and actions of important adults in their lives. Thus, these adults have tremendous responsibility for creating a helpful environment with quality stories and freedom of self-expression.

Stage 2. Mythic-Literal Faith—Ages 7–12

Mythic-literal faith is ushered in by the cognitive accomplishment of concrete operations, and the advent of perceiving a more orderly, literal, and dependable world. Children now want to discover "truth" and literalism rather than depending solely on imagination. Relationally, children in this stage have the ability to understand that others, including God, may have perspectives that differ from their own, but their imagination is limited to perspectives from their *own* culture, parents, or experiences.

In Stage 2, people can conceive of reciprocity and fairness in God's dealing with humans. They understand that someone who breaks the law will be punished and believe conscience ought to direct a person to do the right thing. However, their sense of right and wrong is rather absolute and rigid, and they may find the need to separate themselves from others who are different, and whom they may perceive as "sinners." Fowler holds that some people

Table 16.4 Stages of Faith Development - Comparisons and Characteristics

Fowler's Stage	Form of logic (Piaget)	Perspective taking (Selman)	Form of moral judgment (Kohlberg)	Bounds of social awareness	Locus of authority	Form of world coherence	Symbolic function
1. Intuitive Projective	Preoperational	Rudimentary (egocentric)	Punishment-reward	Family, primal others	Attachment/ dependence relationships; size, power, visible symbols of authority	Episodic	Magical-numinous
2. Mythic-Literal	Concrete operational	Simple perspective taking	Instrumental hedonism (reciprocal fairness)	"Those like us" (in familial, ethnic, racial, class, and religious terms)	Incumbents of authority roles, salience increased by personal relatedness	Narrative-dramatic	One-dimensional
3. Synthetic-Conventional	Early formal operations	Mutual interpersonal	Interpersonal expectations and concordance	Composite of groups in which one has interpersonal relationships	Consensus of valued groups and in personally worthy representatives of belief-value traditions	Tacit system, felt meanings symbolically mediated, globally held	Symbols multidimensional; evocative in symbol
4. Individuative-Reflective	Formal operations (dichotomizing)	Mutual, with self-selected group or class (societal)	Societal perspective, reflective relativism or class-biased universalism	Ideologically compatible communities with congruence to self-chosen norms and insights	One's own judgment as informed by a self-ratified ideological perspective; authorities and norms must be congruent with this	Explicit system, conceptually mediated, clarity about boundaries and inner connections of system	Symbols separated from symbolized, translated (reduced) to ideations; evocative power inheres in meaning conveyed by symbols

(Continued)

Table 16.4 (Continued)

Fowler's Stage	Form of logic (Piaget)	Perspective taking (Selman)	Form of moral judgment (Kohlberg)	Bounds of social awareness	Locus of authority	Form of world coherence	Symbolic function
5. Conjunctive	Formal operations (dialectical)	Mutual with groups, classes, and traditions "other" than one's own	Prior to society, principled higher law (universal and critical)	Extends beyond class norms and interests; disciplined ideological vulnerability to "truths" and "claims" of out-groups and their traditions	Dialectical joining of judgment-experience with reflective claims of others and of various expressions of cumulative human wisdom	Multisystemic symbolic and conceptual mediation	Postcritical rejoining of irreducible symbolic power and ideational meaning; evocative power inherent in the reality in and beyond symbol and in the power of unconscious processes in the self
6. Universalizing	Formal operations (synthetic)	Mutual, with the commonwealth of being	Loyalty to being	Identification with the species; trans-narcissistic love of being	In a personal judgment informed by the experiences and truths of previous stages, purified of egoic striving and linked by disciplined intuition to the principle of being	Unitive actuality felt and participated unity of "one beyond the many"	Evocative power of symbols actualized through unification of reality mediated by symbols and the self

Source: Adapted from Fowler (1981).

end their faith development in Stage 2, and adults characterized by Stage 2 may be ideologically rigid, may adopt very conservative religious perspectives, will need the guidance of very clear rules of right and wrong, and will avoid and possibly condemn those who operate from different perspectives. Counselors may encounter these adults when their rigidity threatens their marriage, relationships with their children, or relationships with church members who maintain different perspectives.

Stage 3. Synthetic-Conventional Faith—Ages 13 and Older

Synthetic-conventional faith requires formal operational thinking, or the ability to reflect on one's thinking and appraise a situation or problem. As people enter adolescence and develop the ability to take another's perspective, their peers' perspectives become very important and trigger their own reflection and questions. They then hunger for a God (and peers) who know and accept and confirm their "self" as it develops.

While their relationship with God becomes very personal, however, synthetic-conventional thinkers remain strongly influenced by significant authority figures (school, church, etc.), and the conventions of the surrounding community or church are treated as the ultimate source of knowing. These believers conform to the group that surrounds them, and adhere loyally to their religion of origin, "the way I was brought up" or "the way it has always been done." They experience great stress when they are required to think beyond their religion's rules, when something about their religion isn't working for them, or when they must deal intimately with people whose values and beliefs differ from their own.

In the vignettes at the beginning of this chapter, Brittany, Geoff, and Joseph demonstrate characteristics of Stage 3 faith. Brittany's received knowing is challenged by questions about whether her faith has the answers she needs: "Will God answer my prayers?" or "Is there something wrong with me that I can't form relationships with men?" Geoff also finds his conventional faith challenged by his attractions and his encounters with alternative sexual perspectives, while Joseph's conventional faith is challenged by his impending death, which raises seemingly unanswerable questions for both him and his family.

In both adults and children, conventional faith is a tacit system, an unexamined grouping of values. Counselors may encounter conventional clients when they are surprised by marital or parent–child relationships that are not working, when the rules by which their lives have always been run seem to be failing them. These clients may feel powerless to make changes and may become depressed. They cannot say how they know about their faith, reflect on their values, or identify social factors that may be limiting their lives. The mere process of counselors asking them questions about their faith or the reasons they choose to live in certain ways may trigger the reflection and self-appraisal necessary to move their faith development ahead.

Stage 4. Individuative-Reflective Faith

Individuative-reflective faith is characteristic of young adults who have left home and their defining peer groups, moved beyond reliance on external sources of authority, and developed the ability to choose and to take responsibility for their choices. They may keep parts of their inherited faith by using a self-determined method of weighing alternatives and generating evidence. They have gained the capacity for critical reflection about themselves and their ideology, and their faith becomes a religion of choice.

Stage 4 individuals are self-authorizing and can stand back from their relationships, roles, rules, spiritual leaders, and religious denomination and evaluate objectively or individually what they will claim for themselves. Their positions do not rely ultimately on whether others agree, and they define their own identities. They are self-initiating, self-correcting, and self-evaluating. They take responsibility for what happens to them, and their thinking becomes less rigid, exclusive, simplistic, and dogmatic to be more flexible, open, complex, and tolerant of differences. Research indicates that only about 20% of adults achieve individuative-reflective faith in a consistent way (Allison, 1988; Alvarez, 1985; Bar-Yam, 1991; Beukema, 1990; Binner, 1991; Dixon, 1986; Goodman, 1983; Greenwald, 1991; Jacobs, 1984; Lahey, 1986; Roy, 1993; Sonnenschein, 1990).

Individuative-reflective faith is desirable in counselors as they work with faith-related issues in counseling. More complex ways of knowing are associated with higher empathy levels, a fundamental element of good counseling (Benack, 1988; Bowman & Reeves, 1987; Lovell, 1999; McAuliffe & Lovell, 2006), an internal locus of control, and open-mindedness (Neukrug & McAuliffe, 1993). They are also associated with the abilities to tolerate ambiguity, be reflective, focus on client process rather than only on content, use evidence for choices, and demonstrate insight into clients' issues (McAuliffe & Lovell, 2006). Individuative-reflective knowing is important if counselors are to avoid imposing their values on clients and are to help clients move toward claiming a religion of choice (Brendel, Kolbert, & Foster, 2002).

Stage 5. Conjunctive Faith

While people in Stage 4 use logic that reflects choice between opposing ideas, people who see themselves, their world, and their faith from a conjunctive position see many sides of an issue simultaneously, understand that perspectives are organically related to each other, tune into the interrelatedness in things, and try to avoid force-fitting things into their own prior mind-set. Conjunctive faith depends on a self-certainty and trust that allows people to handle uncertainties and to engage in "I-thou" relationships about faith and other issues. People operating from this stage know that their own perspectives on faith are partial, and they embrace encounters with other traditions as opportunities to enhance their own understandings and grow in their faith. They recognize that their current understandings are limited due to their experiences within their culture of origin. Rarely do people reach Stage 5 thinking before midlife.

Stage 6. Universalizing Faith

"The self at Stage 6 engages in spending and being spent for the transformation of present reality in the direction of a transcendent actuality" (Fowler, 1981, p. 200). People with a universalizing faith are future oriented, heedless of self-preservation, devoted to universalizing compassion and a higher vision, and freed from concerns with survival, security, and significance. They frequently become martyrs. Their faith spreads to the people and systems around them and transforms the world as they refuse to accept things as they are. They commit to combating destructive forces with their whole beings, relinquishing ego attachments in favor of divine intentions "to redeem, restore, and fulfill all being" (p. 210). They seem able to form important relationships with people from all other stages and faith traditions. Such names as Gandhi, Mother Teresa, and Martin Luther King come to mind.

ENCOURAGING DEVELOPMENT TOWARD REFLECTIVE FAITH

Counselors can help clients move away from more limiting faith toward more transformative faith. They are most likely to encounter people troubled by the failures of their conventional faith when a dilemma has triggered the awareness that the old rules of their religion of origin don't work in every situation, as with Brittany and Geoff. They may be discovering their sexuality in new ways or finding their old ways of believing less than satisfactory, or they may find themselves trapped by rigid gender roles.

In order to assist such clients, counselors must optimally *match* (support) and *mismatch* (challenge) clients' current way of knowing. Matching implies relating to clients from within their currently dominant way of knowing, and mismatching means relating to clients from the next potential way of knowing (McAuliffe & Eriksen, 1999). Clients operating from received or conventional-synthetic ways of knowing need an authority-based experience, and to match or support such clients, counselors give clear direction and a lot of structure, particularly using the authority of the client's religious precepts (Kegan, 1982, 1998). In order to mismatch or challenge people toward a religion of choice, counselors urge clients to think about why they are doing what they are doing, to examine their inner urges, and to establish a separateness from others' definitions. Counselors might ask clients to investigate inconsistencies in religious texts, to pray about how to resolve them, and to come to a religiously grounded and justifiable decision about beliefs that might be more helpful. Counselors, teachers, and other leaders might also create ambiguous values discussions (e.g., ethical dilemma discussions) so as to challenge the more rigid received or conventional-synthetic knowing toward individuative-reflective faith (Kegan, 1982, 1998) or employ exercises such as Activities 16.2 and 16.3.

Activity 16.2   Religious De-centering

This activity is a variation on the cultural de-centering activity from Chapter 2. Here the focus is on faith. Describe your past and current ways of religious knowing by using the descriptions in this text of *religion of origin* and *religion of choice* to make a list of those characteristics that fit you, and give examples.

1. Characteristics of my religion of origin (in the past or present; e.g., treating the conventions of your community as the ultimate source of knowing, adhering loyally to your religion of origin, being a follower of a religion based on peer or authority influence)

2. Characteristics of a self-authorized knowledge of a religion of choice (if you have at least partially engaged in such thinking up to this point; e.g., not being automatically bound by the faith that you may have inherited, being able to choose a spiritual or religious direction by using a relatively autonomous method of weighing alternatives and self-generated evidence)

Activity 16.3   Experiencing Alternate Religious Perspectives

In an effort to promote your own spiritual development, take a "plunge" into another religious experience, meet the people, and experience the rituals. Afterward, ask yourself the following questions:

1. How did it feel to be with people who believe differently?

2. Do you see your group as dominant (e.g., generally in a position of greater power and/or favor at the current time and place) or as nondominant in comparison with the group you visited? How might this affect your perceptions of them?

3. What rituals or procedures were different from your own? Similar?

4. What was it like to experience their rituals? How did the experience differ from those of your own faith?

5. What does your faith say about other faith experiences? What do you think about that?

6. How might this experience assist you with clients whose faith is different from your own?

Many people seeking counseling may be doing so as a result of conflicts that have the potential to be resolved by movement to a more complex way of knowing. However, such movement is not without risks. For instance, transitions between stages are fraught with feelings of "being out at sea but not in sight of any shore." This experience can be quite stressful. Further, movement from religion of origin to religion of choice may put clients at odds with their families and their religious communities. If the religious community encompasses a client's whole cultural or social group, as sometimes occurs in more traditional societies, clients may find themselves ostracized and without a people. Geoff, for example, believed that he would be cut off by his religious community and family.

Counselors, therefore, must carefully consider the risks as well as the benefits of encouraging development and use informed consent procedures to help clients carefully weigh the benefits and risks of moving beyond traditionalism. During a move to individuative-reflective religious choice, individuals will need "bridge people," that is, others like themselves who share their journey. Counselors might, for instance, help such clients find a supportive group of peers who are exploring new religious or spiritual meanings.

RELIGION AND COUNSELING

Historically speaking, the mental health professions have had a contentious relationship with religion, frequently considering it to be part of clients' pathology and preferring to leave spirituality to spiritual leaders (Wiggins-Frame, 2005). Some of the struggle evolved from the different philosophical underpinnings of science and religion (Wiggins-Frame, 2005). Mental health professionals have endeavored to understand the psychological and behavioral aspects of human life and have used scientific method as one basis for determining validity of ideas (Patterson, Hayworth, Turner, & Raskin, 2000), while religion has usually focused on the spiritual dimension and the influence of a supreme being on human behavior and used belief as a basis (Richards & Bergin, 2005). This counseling-related

section of the chapter presents, in this order, the differing philosophical foundations of counseling and religion, trends in integrating the two, the dangers of harmful faith, guidelines for assessing clients' relationship to faith, and the risks of religious countertransference.

Differential Foundations of Counseling and Religion

The historical conflicts between counseling and religion come from the differing philosophical foundations of psychology and religion. Bergin (1980) identifies two primary philosophical underpinnings of counseling: *clinical pragmatism,* which embodies predominant cultural values on what works to improve clients' lives, and *humanistic idealism,* which embraces positive values such as human dignity and self-actualization but manifests "a relative indifference to God" (p. 98). Bergin proposes that a third view, *theistic realism,* might become an underpinning for the work of mental health professionals. Theistic realism posits that God exists, that human beings are creations of God, and that there are unseen spiritual processes by which the link between God and humanity is maintained. Fowler (1981), in a more integrative fashion, finds links between the two disciplines in their commitments to helping clients find meaning in life or develop a relationship with what is ultimate in life; these aims have relevance for many people, regardless of faith perspective.

The Rapprochement Between Counseling and Religion

Since the 1980s, when most religiously conservative clients sought counseling only with religious leaders, separations between counseling and religion have begun to diminish (Richards & Bergin, 2005; Worthington & Aten, 2009). The ongoing rapprochement between counseling and religion is evidenced by a growing eclecticism of models of counseling, including transpersonal counseling, recognition of the importance of values in counseling, and the articulation of spiritual views by mental health professionals (Elkins, 1995; Richards & Bergin, 2005; Worthington & Aten, 2009). Specialty fields and "religiously accommodative" therapy approaches (Worthington & Aten, 2009, p. 125) have evolved that make it possible for clients to seek out counselors who have skill in addressing spiritual issues in counseling (Genia, 2000).

More evidence of the growing inclusion of religious or spiritual issues in the framework of psychological thought is the addition of "Religious or Spiritual Problem" to the *Diagnostic and Statistical Manual of Mental Disorders* (American Psychiatric Association, 1994, 2000). Similarly, the increasing number of studies being conducted to evaluate the links among people's spirituality, their mental health, and effective counseling (e.g., Gordon et al., 2002; Wade & Worthington, 2003) indicates that counseling professionals are taking a more amiable posture toward religion, and vice versa, than has previously been seen.

The multicultural counseling movement has also spurred more inclusion of religion and spirituality in counseling practice, an inclusion that is encouraged by ethical counseling standards (ACA, 2005; American Psychological Association, 2010). It is now better understood that knowledge about spiritual issues encourages counselors to attend to the benefits of faith, which, in turn, helps counselors more easily maintain the therapeutic alliance with religious or spiritual clients (Genia, 2000). For counselors who do not share their clients' faith or religious experiences, the therapeutic alliance may be enhanced when counselors focus with clients on what gives their life meaning and on what is of central importance in their lives.

Many counselors themselves also demonstrate a high degree of personal spiritual commitment. The majority of mental health practitioners claim some type of religious affiliation, believe that spirituality is personally relevant, and value personal prayer (Basham & O'Connor, 2005; Bergin & Jensen, 1990; Frame, 2003; Hagedorn, 2005; Shafranske & Malony, 1990). In particular, marriage and family counselors incorporate religion into their personal and professional lives more than

other mental health professionals. Ninety-five percent of marriage and family counselors believe that there is a relationship between spiritual and mental health, 94% believe that spirituality is an important aspect of their personal lives, 82% report regularly spending time getting in touch with their spirituality, and 71% report praying regularly (Carlson, Kirkpatrick, Hecker, & Killmer, 2002).

Despite the high regard given to spiritual issues by mental health providers, not all believe that spirituality should be integrated into counseling. Only 62% of marriage and family counselors believe that a spiritual dimension should be included in clinical practice, and only 47% believe that it is necessary to address a client's spirituality in order to help her or him (Carlson et al., 2002). In one study, only 29% of clinical psychologists, psychiatrists, clinical social workers, and marriage and family counselors "expressed a belief . . . that religious matters are important for counseling efforts with all or many of their clients" (Bergen & Jensen, 1990, p. 6). Carlson et al. (2002) attribute the disparity between beliefs in the importance of spirituality and the integration of spirituality in counseling to (a) a lack of education on how to integrate spirituality and counseling and (b) spirituality coming into counseling rhetoric only recently (p. 167). Wiggins-Frame (2005) attributes the disparity to counselors' own unresolved religious/spiritual issues.

Harmful Faith

In the past, many counselors maintained that religion itself was psychologically limiting, even harmful, and that it often contributed to or expressed some clients' psychopathology. Although more recent evidence, cited above, counters this perspective, it is certainly true that in some cases, clients with mental health problems may act out their problems in religious ways.

For instance, faith may become religious addiction. The religiously addicted hold onto elements of religion that may cause harm in order to avoid facing challenging realities (Arterburn & Felton, 1992, p. 114). An uninformed counselor might unintentionally reinforce compulsive prayer by including prayer as a part of the counseling process (Taylor, 2002). When a religiously addicted and authoritarian spouse engages in physical abuse when the other partner violates a dogmatic rule, including spirituality in counseling might inadvertently reinforce the controlling behavior and cause further damage (Taylor, 2002). Box 16.1 lists specific indications of religious pathology.

Box 16.1   Indications of Religious Pathology

The following are 10 indications of probable religious pathology:

- self-oriented or narcissistic displays
- religion used to gain rewards from a divine power
- scrupulosity in avoiding sin or error
- relinquishing responsibility for problematic behavior to the devil or other evil forces
- ecstatic frenzy or intense emotionality
- persistent church/temple/mosque-shopping
- inappropriate sharing of one's religious experiences
- religiously inspired "love" that causes pain or confusion
- using the scriptures to answer "ordinary questions about daily living"
- reports of possession by evil spirits or the devil

Source: Lovinger (1996, pp. 348–349).

Ethical counselors remain alert to both the harms and benefits that may accrue from religious faith. Alertness may be enhanced by conducting ongoing assessment, especially early in counseling, of the client's understandings and uses of faith. In that vein, counselors might assess four issues: (1) the role of faith in a client's life, (2) the ways in which the client expresses her or his faith, (3) the client's expectations about the role of spirituality in the counseling sessions, and (4) the most helpful uses of faith in intervening with this particular client (Magaletta & Brawer, 1998). Such a four-part assessment enables counselors to investigate the potential interactions among religious behavior or beliefs and the client's presenting problems (Spero, 1982; Yarhouse, 1999). The counselor can then exercise caution in using spiritual interventions that might collude with or exacerbate the client's problems (Richards & Potts, 1995; Spero, 1982).

Countertransference

Countertransference regarding religious and spiritual issues occurs because of their social significance and inherent personal meaning to counselors as well as to clients. To avoid countertransference and to interact positively with a client's faith system requires a great deal of self-awareness on the part of counselors. Those without religious identity who work with religious clients and religious counselors who work with nonreligious clients must engage in self-reflective work in order to counsel both ethical and technical soundness in their practice (Spero, 1982). Activity 16.4 offers the opportunity to examine your relationships with religion.

Activity 16.4   Integrating Counseling With Religion and Spirituality

You are encouraged to answer the following questions in order to become more aware of how you are (or are not) integrating your beliefs about counseling with religion and/or spirituality.

1. What is your overall worldview, and how does it relate to your religious and spiritual beliefs?

2. What are your worldview's implications for counseling practice?

3. Consider the core conditions for effective counseling (empathy, unconditional positive regard, genuineness). What are the spiritual and religious dimensions of these concepts?

4. What theories of counseling and therapy appeal to you? From what approach do you personally plan to practice? What influence do your own spiritual and religious beliefs have on your choice?

5. How would clients from different religious backgrounds respond to your favored approaches?

6. How does your personal religious and spiritual developmental history, as influenced by your family and culture, affect your answers to the above questions.

7. How will you continue to reflect on the influence of your personal history and your present religious and spiritual beliefs on your performance as a counselor? For instance:

   • Are you participating in your own counseling?

   • What is a developmental goal of yours for personal growth?

Counselors may find their self-awareness in relation to religion hampered by unresolved issues that were developed in response to damaging experiences with or without religion. Countertransference may emerge in both religious and secular counselors. Box 16.2 summarizes types of religious countertransference.

Box 16.2   Types of Religious Countertransference

Below are six types of countertransference, as they relate to religious issues, that counselors might exhibit.

1. The Sibling Complex is characterized by excessive agreement or loose interpersonal boundaries with the client because of commonalities such as similar values and similar expectations from one's religious community.

2. The Missionary counselor uses the therapeutic relationship to proselytize clients.

3. The Spiritualizer views all client issues as requiring a spiritual intervention when many other legitimate interventions may be appropriate, a view that may be encouraged by the client's misinformed expectations about a counselor's role.

4. The Reactionary counselor experiences aggressive feelings against the (religious) group or unresolved rebelliousness that can result in inappropriately avoiding religious interventions or acting in defiance of the client's religious traditions, behaviors, or spiritual statements.

5. The Window Shopper exhibits excessive curiosity about the client to gratify her or his own needs (e.g., asking clients to divulge all of their sexual secrets perhaps due to the counselor's restrictive religious beliefs regarding sexuality).

6. My Way is Yahweh counselors pose as the experts in spiritual matters, instead of recognizing that many different and valid opinions and interpretations exist about specific spiritual issues, some of which may be held by the client.

Source: "Potential Sources of Countertransference Among Religious Counselors," by P.W. Case, 1997, *Counseling and Values, 41,* pp. 97–106. Copyright 1997 by American Counseling Association. Reprinted with permission.

In order to appropriately manage any countertransference that becomes apparent, counselors should pursue their own counseling or supervision (Agass, 2002; Astor, 2000; Wolitzky, 1995). Self-examination encourages counselors to scrutinize their religious attitudes to determine whether their perspectives are useful or dysfunctional, mature or immature. Ethical counselors are those who counter their own anxiety, anger, and frustration when working with clients who are religiously different from themselves. They must be tolerant of the client's need for emotional, even if not always rational, belief (Spero, 1982).

At times, when countertransference is too difficult to manage, referral is in order. Genia (2000) and the ACA (2005) *Code of Ethics* advocate making appropriate referrals to other counselors who share a worldview with the client or to spiritual advisors who are trained to address spiritual issues.

Instead of referring, counselors might also consider working with the parallels between counseling and some definitions of faith. Culturally Alert Counseling DVD Working With Conservative Religious Clients (McAuliffe, 2009) for a demonstration of working with a client's faith. For instance, both counseling and faith engage questions of values and meaning and what some would call positive mental health. Fowler (1981), for instance, calls faith "a generic feature of the human struggle to find and maintain meaning" (p. 91); of the experience of self, others, and world; of how to face the ultimate conditions of existence; of how to live with character, values, and power. Faith can be broadly defined as what a person commits herself or himself to, sets her or his heart on, or holds dear (Smith et al., 2003). Faith asks the universal questions:

- What are you spending and being spent for? What commands and receives your best time, your best energy?
- What causes, dreams, goals, or institutions are you pouring out your life for?
- As you live your life, what power or powers do you fear or dread? What power or powers do you rely on and trust?
- To what or whom are you committed in life? In death?
- With whom or what group do you share your most sacred and private hopes for your life and for the lives of those you love?
- What are those most sacred hopes, those most compelling goals and purposes in your life? (Fowler, 1981, p. 3)

Clearly, counselors should find all of these characteristics of faith consonant with their profession's aims to assist people to find internal peace, integrity in life's pursuits, harmony in relationships, and recovery from all manner of psychological ills.

With these definitions of faith, it is easy to see that although the *content* of one's faith might differ from that of other people, the *processes* of her or his faith (as indicated in the actions and orientations above) may very well hold commonalities. Much of this chapter focuses on the content of different faiths, the *what*, and counselors' roles in becoming knowledgeable about that content so as to be ethical and effective with clients of different spiritual and religious orientations. However, during the counseling experience, counselors frequently focus on the process of faith, that is, on meaning-making and purpose in life, and urge clients to discover and take action on what they want, what they most care about, how they want to spend their time, what careers or majors they want to pursue, how they will find hope in the midst of the despair of a chemical imbalance or a serious life struggle, and how they will aspire to what is optimal in communication skills, values and character, and human relationships. Engaging in discovery and acting on fundamental meanings

and values is a process that Fowler would call faith, or an orientation toward the ultimate, or discovering life's meaning and direction. Few counselors would argue about the relevance or benefits of such faith, regardless of their personal position on particular religious experiences or mandates.

BELIEFS OF THE MAJOR RELIGIOUS GROUPS IN THE UNITED STATES AND IMPLICATIONS FOR COUNSELING

This section briefly explores some beliefs of the following major religions in the United States: Christianity, Islam, Judaism, Hinduism, and Buddhism. In addition, paganism, agnosticism, and humanism, although not usually considered religions, are discussed at the end of this section. Each segment offers a brief history, a table indicating any religious practices and customs that might manifest in the counseling room, and recommendations for practice.

Christianity

The religion based on the life and teachings of Jesus, or Yehoshua in Hebrew, is called Christianity (Keller, 1999). Jesus was also named the "Christ" ("the Anointed One" in Greek), thus leading to the common name Jesus Christ. About one-third of the world's population is considered Christian and can be divided into three main branches: (1) Roman Catholic (the largest coherent group, representing over one billion baptized members), (2) Orthodox Christianity (including Eastern Orthodoxy and Oriental Orthodoxy), and (3) Protestant (comprising many denominations and schools of thought, including Anglican, Reformed, Presbyterian, Lutheran, Methodist, Evangelical, Baptist, and Pentecostal). Christians believe that because of humanity's fall from God's grace through sin, people were separated from God. Christ's death on the cross was necessary to pay for or atone for that sin so that people could regain a relationship with God. Christians maintain their relationship with God in various ways. Therefore, the denomination to which a person belongs tends to determine how that relationship is expressed. Prayer, reading the Bible, and meeting in congregations for worship, confession, and celebration of communion are examples of common Christian practices.

Roman Catholicism

The Catholic Church is the Westernmost of two churches that were created by the East/West split of Christianity in 1054 CE. The term *catholic*, at its root, comes from the Latin *catholicus*, which means "universal." Catholicism's headquarters are in Rome at the Vatican. Its leader is the Pope, who occupies the top point of a hierarchy that begins at the lower end with the laity and the priests and extends up through bishops, archbishops, and cardinals. Catholics emphasize the importance of the Church's teaching authority and the sacraments. The central act of worship is the Mass, which is the complex of prayers and ceremonies that make up the service of the Eucharist. The Eucharist is a ceremony of giving thanks that parallels what Jesus did with His disciples at the last supper before his death. Holy Communion is part of the Mass also, at which time congregants partake of the consecrated bread and wine as a means of receiving grace (Hoge, 1996).

Table 16.5 outlines some of the traditional Catholic beliefs that may intersect with counseling concerns. Great variance exists among Catholics in terms of the influence of religion and spirituality on their lives; however, the table outlines some general reminders for counseling with Catholic people.

Table 16.5   Catholic Beliefs and Counseling

Marriage and Divorce	Family is viewed as holy, permanent, and monogamous. The marriage ceremony is a sacrament. The family's holy role is to cooperate with God by procreating children, who are destined to be the adopted children of God, and to instruct them for His kingdom. The absence of offspring as a result of artificial devices (birth control) is thus considered immoral. The Roman Catholic Church regards marriage as permanent and indissoluble, except after the death of a spouse. However, the church can in some circumstances issue an annulment. That document, in effect, states that a valid marriage never existed. This allows Catholics to remarry in the church.
Sexuality	Premarital, homosexual, and extramarital sexual behaviors are considered sinful.
Abortion and Birth Control	Abortion and artificial birth control are considered sinful.
View of Counseling	Catholics may prefer a counselor whose faith is consistent with their own, but there is a wide degree of variance in opinions among Catholics about the importance of the faith of the counselor. Catholics are open to the use of medication.
Spiritual Practices and Healing Traditions	There are many sacraments that are part of ritual worship, including anointing the sick, use of holy water, prayer, and devotion.
Potential Religious-Clinical Issues	Conflicts about the relationship to authority, sexuality, interfaith marriage, divorce, abortion, suicide, artificial insemination, genetic engineering, and euthanasia.
Counseling Recommendations	Be aware of Church teachings about suffering, death, resurrection, confession, and reconciliation. Explicitly integrate religious resources. Consult with clergy.

Source: Adapted from Richards & Bergin (1999).

Protestant Christianity

The Christian Protestant churches originated during the Reformation in the 16th century when many European Christians broke away from the Catholic Church—that is, they "protested." The German Martin Luther is considered the founder of Protestantism; his followers became Lutherans. The Frenchman John Calvin (born Chauvin) was influential in Protestantism as well, and his followers became Calvinists, who later, in the United States under the influence of the Scotsman John Knox, became Presbyterians. The Englishman John Wesley's followers became Methodists. From Switzerland came the followers of Ulrich Zwingli, who were called Anabaptists; they later became the Baptists and Mennonites. In the beginning, few Protestant denominations existed. Later, however, Protestantism experienced many divisions. As a result, numerous Protestant denominations now exist in the United States.

Mainline Protestant Christianity

Mainline Protestants are generally characterized by a progressive theology and an openness both to other churches and, at times, even to other religions. Historically speaking, mainline Protestants have practiced a "social gospel," which strongly emphasizes activism to address social problems as a primary outward expression of a faithful life. For instance, mainline Protestants have often been in the forefront of movements such as the abolition of slavery, prison reform, orphanage establishment, hospital building, and founding educational institutions. Today, this activism is also expressed in literacy training, adoption agencies, food banks, and daycare centers for children (Esau, 1998). Some of the groups that are considered mainline Protestants are the United Church of Christ (historically known as Congregationalists), the American Baptist Church (Northern Baptists), the Episcopal Church, the Presbyterian Church, the United Methodist Church, the Evangelical Lutheran Church, and the Disciples of Christ. Table 16.6 lists some of the mainline Protestant beliefs that may intersect with counseling concerns and offers counseling recommendations.

Evangelical and Fundamentalist Protestant Christianity

Evangelical and/or fundamentalist Christian denominations generally emerged in the United States as a reaction against the perception that mainline denominations, in emphasizing the social gospel, were "falling away" from God and scripture. Evangelicals desired to practice faith more explicitly as they saw it described in the New Testament.

Commentators and historians have described four distinctive characteristics of evangelicals (Bebbington, 1989). The first is an emphasis on the conversion experience. The conversion is also called being "saved" or being "born again" (*Holy Bible*, 1983, John 3:3). Evangelicals are sometimes referred to as "born-again Christians" because of this emphasis. The second is the use of the Bible as the primary source of God's revelation to people and, therefore, the ultimate religious authority. That is why the term *fundamentalist* is sometimes used to describe this type of belief—because of an allegiance to the fundamental inerrancy of the Bible. The third is evangelism, which is the act of sharing one's beliefs with others, either in organized missionary work or through personal evangelism, so that others, too, may be "saved." The fourth characteristic is a central focus on Christ's redeeming work on the cross, especially as the means for salvation and the forgiveness of sins (Esau, 1998).

Evangelicals try to follow the biblical injunction to be *in* the world yet not *of* the world (*Holy Bible*, 1983, John 17:14–18), which means to make a difference in the world while not adopting the world's "ungodly" ways. Evangelicals primarily engage with those who believe similarly to themselves or with those whom they are evangelizing. As a result, evangelicals may not be open to secular counseling, feeling safe only with a counselor of their own faith. During such counseling, spiritual interventions such as forgiveness, prayer, examining distorted religious beliefs, and consultation with clergy may be expected and therefore necessary (Esau, 1998).

Evangelicals are also very active in conservative social causes, often taking action against abortion, same-sex marriage, pornography, abstinence

Table 16.6 Mainline Protestant Beliefs and Counseling

Marriage and Divorce	Marriage is considered a union blessed by God. Divorce, single-parent families, and remarriage are tolerated though not encouraged.
Sexuality	Many Protestant religions advocate responsible sexual behavior, understood as sexual expression that matches the seriousness and permanence of the relationship. Teenage and extramarital sex are seen as morally unacceptable in most cases. No clear positions are stated on masturbation. In some mainline Protestant religions, homosexuality is morally acceptable, but many denominations will not conduct same-sex unions or ordain homosexual ministers.
Abortion and Birth Control	Mainline Protestants acknowledge legitimate diversity of opinion related to abortion. Abortion may be acceptable under circumstances of rape or incest, physical or mental deformity of the fetus, or threats to the physical or mental well-being of the mother. Most oppose its use as a method of birth control and acknowledge that the state has at least a limited interest in regulating abortion, but they believe in safe and affordable access to abortions in acceptable situations. Contraceptive use is acceptable in most Protestant religions.
View of Counseling	Protestants tend to have a positive view of counseling. Sometimes clients might fear that counselors will not include or accept their religious beliefs.
Spiritual Practices and Healing Traditions	Worship services, prayer, meditation, Bible reading, teachings about grace and forgiveness.
Potential Religious-Clinical Issues	Sexuality, divorce, substance abuse, abortion, euthanasia.
Counseling Recommendations	Mainline Protestants are usually comfortable with secular approaches to counseling. Use forgiveness as a therapeutic tool. Collaborate with pastoral care in using spiritual interventions.

Source: Adapted from Richards & Bergin (1999).

education in schools, and school prayer. Within Protestantism there is often a political dichotomy, with the mainline denominations and the evangelicals often both actively lobbying in Washington, but on opposite sides of the same issues (Hannon, Howie, & Keener, 1994). Table 16.7 lists some of the traditional evangelical and fundamentalist Protestant beliefs that may intersect with counseling concerns. It also offers recommendations for counseling practice.

In the cases presented at the beginning of the chapter, Brittany would be considered an evangelical Christian. She struggles with how to date and find a mate while remaining godly. A counselor would need to remember that "secular" dating behaviors would probably be considered "of the world" and therefore ungodly in her eyes. Eriksen, Marston, and Korte (2002) provide a guide to counseling conservative Christians on such issues.

Islam

Islam was founded by Mohammed (570–632). Orphaned at the age of 6, he worked as a shepherd and camel driver. Muslims believe that when Mohammed was 40 years old and married, he was visited in Mecca by the Angel Gabriel. Subsequently, he believed himself to be a prophet and began converting people to his new religion. At first he faced stiff opposition. However, through military activity and political negotiation, he eventually became a powerful leader, firmly establishing Islam in the Middle East as the dominant faith and as the second

Table 16.7 Evangelical and Fundamentalist Protestant Beliefs and Counseling

Marriage and Divorce	Evangelicals oppose divorce and remarriage except in cases of a spouse's infidelity.
Sexuality	They oppose premarital, homosexual, and extramarital sex.
Abortion and Birth Control	Evangelicals oppose abortion as a means of birth control or a means of eliminating unwanted pregnancies. Contraception is acceptable.
View of Counseling	Evangelicals often have a positive view of counseling as long as the counselor shares her or his faith. They often prefer the "biblical" counseling offered by nonprofessional "called" members of their church.
Spiritual Practices and Healing Traditions	Social support is gained through the church and congregation, through prayer, Bible study, and participation in services and activities.
Potential Religious-Clinical Issues	Fear of authority figures and of emotional conflict, repression of negative feelings, group dependency, perfectionism, excessive guilt and shame, low self-esteem, dogmatism, sexual addiction.
Counseling Recommendations	Use forgiveness, prayer, and relevant scriptures. Challenge distorted religious beliefs. Consult with religious leaders.

Source: Adapted from Richards & Bergin (1999).

largest religion in the world (Council on American-Islamic Relations, 2012).

The Arabic word *Islam* means "submission" or "peace," referring to the peace experienced by the person who completely submits herself or himself to God, or Allah. A person who follows Islam is called a Muslim. The Qur'an is the holy book of Islam, believed to be the literal and final word of God in Arabic as it was revealed to Mohammed. Also important to Muslims is the Sharia, or the Islamic law, also known as the Law of Allah. Classic Islam draws no distinction between religious and secular life. Hence, Sharia covers not only religious rituals but many aspects of day-to-day life, politics, economics, banking, business or contract law, and social issues (Council on American-Islamic Relations, 2012). Table 16.8 lists some of the traditional Muslim beliefs that may intersect with counseling concerns.

Judaism

According to the Exodus story, the Jews originally settled on a thin strip of land at the eastern end of the Mediterranean Sea, probably sometime in the 13th century BCE. Their subsequent history is one of dispersion throughout the world (called the Diaspora). As a result of expulsion from non-Jewish communities, Jews established their own communities throughout much of the world. The centers of Jewish life moved during the last two millennia from Judea to Babylonia to Spain to Poland to the United States and finally back to Israel. During the Middle Ages, Jews divided into distinct regional groups. These groupings are the Ashkenazi (Northern and Eastern European Jews) and Sephardic (Spanish, Mediterranean, and Middle Eastern Jews).

Two major organizing events of contemporary Judaism are the Holocaust and the defense of Israel's statehood. In the Holocaust, the Nazis killed over six million Jews and rendered hundreds of thousands homeless. The Holocaust spurred the creation of the nation of Israel in 1948. The country was immediately besieged by armies from several Arab countries. After weeks of fighting, Israel remained, holding more territory than it had originally claimed. At this point, Jews sent out a call for all Jews to return to Israel. And Jews came, often being airlifted out of Arab countries just ahead of

Table 16.8 Muslim Beliefs and Counseling

Marriage and Divorce	Marriage and children are encouraged. Polygamy is permitted, but rarely practiced in the United States. Romantic love is not a prerequisite to marriage. Divorce is discouraged but is permitted and is easier for men to obtain than for women.
Sexuality	All sexual relationships outside of marriage are forbidden. Homosexual behavior is forbidden.
Abortion and Birth Control	Abortion is discouraged but permitted under certain circumstances. Contraception is permitted.
View of Counseling	Muslims commonly view counseling with suspicion.
Spiritual Practices and Healing Traditions	Ritual prayers, fasting, pilgrimage, visiting mosque, reading or listening to the Qur'an, participating in holidays.
Potential Religious-Clinical Issues	Conflicts with mainstream secular culture and values, depression, somatization of problems, suicidal ideation.
Counseling Recommendations	Gain knowledge about Muslim religion and cultural values, involve the family, and consult with members of the Muslim community.

Source: Adapted from Richards & Bergin (1999).

persecution. They also came from the European countries where they had often been outcasts. The support of Israel and the defense of its borders has captured a great deal of Jewish energy since Israel first became a country (Heilman & Cohen, 1989).

There are three general strands in Judaism: Reform, Conservative, and Orthodox. The *Reform Jews* comprise the most liberal strand. Beliefs vary among Reform Jews and include nonbelief or questioning of belief. They generally see scripture as a cultural product to be interpreted as an ethical guide and in historical terms. Reform Jews generally do not believe in original sin or hell. *Conservative Judaism* affirms belief in God and in the divine inspiration of the Torah; however, it also affirms the legitimacy of multiple interpretations of these. The term *conservative* signifies that Jews should attempt to conserve Jewish tradition, rather than reform or abandon it; it does not mean that the movement's adherents are politically conservative. *Orthodox Judaism* adheres to a strict interpretation and application of written and oral laws and ethics. All branches of Judaism encourage asking questions about how to live ethically.

Not all Jews are religious. The American Jewish Identity Survey of 2000 (Kosmin et al., 2001)

concluded that there are 5.5 million ethnic Jews in the United States. Of these, about 3 million, or 51% of ethnic Jews, are religious. Jews also vary in their degree of orthodoxy. Table 16.9 lists some of the traditional Jewish beliefs that may intersect with counseling concerns and offers counseling recommendations.

Geoff, one of the clients presented at the beginning of the chapter, is a religious Jew from an Orthodox sect. It would seem that his small-town upbringing and his orthodoxy, rather than his Jewishness, are the factors leading to his emotional distress at this time. These factors would make it difficult for him to integrate or relate to the vast array of beliefs present in a large city or on a metropolitan college campus.

Hinduism

Hinduism is the dominant religion of the Indian subcontinent and the third-largest religion in the world, after Christianity and Islam. Established over 3,000 years ago, Hinduism is based on ancient scriptures known collectively as the Vedas. Although the Vedas serve as a foundation for Hinduism, many modifications have

Table 16.9   Jewish Beliefs and Counseling

Marriage and Divorce	Marriage and children are highly valued. Divorce is permitted and remarriage is encouraged.
Sexuality	Conservative and Reform Jews allow premarital sex as a matter of personal choice but view adultery and incest as sinful. Male homosexual behavior is viewed as more unfavorable than female homosexual behavior. Some Orthodox Jews view premarital, homosexual, and extramarital sex as sinful.
Abortion and Birth Control	Orthodox Jews view abortion as a sin, except if the mother's life is in danger or when a rabbi sanctions it. For the Orthodox Jew, contraception is discouraged and usually only permitted for medical reasons. Conservative and Reform Jews allow abortion when the life or health of the mother is threatened. For them, contraception is acceptable.
View of Counseling	There are various views of counseling. Some may be reluctant to seek counseling for fear it will undermine or conflict with their values. Psychoanalysis, however, has been especially attractive.
Spiritual Practices and Healing Traditions	Study of the Torah, Mishna, and Talmud. Prayer and worship, holidays, and ceremonies.
Potential Religious-Clinical Issues	Depression, identity conflicts, intellectualization, guilt, interfaith marriage, family enmeshment, marital discord, sexual problems, homosexuality, masturbation, feelings of spiritual inadequacy.
Counseling Recommendations	Psychodynamic and cognitive approaches may be more acceptable. Debate, discussion, and argument may be appropriate. Consult with rabbis.

Source: Adapted from Richards & Bergin (1999).

been made over the years, resulting in a religion characterized by a multitude of often-conflicting ideologies and practices. Hindus believe in a supreme spiritual force called Brahman, with which an individual will become one after cleansing their Karma through a cycle of birth, death, and rebirth (reincarnation). Karma represents the total of all that an individual has done, is currently doing, and will do. In life, Hindus follow the laws of dharma, or the doctrine of the rights and duties of each individual. Hinduism's salient characteristics include an ancient mythology, an absence of a specific recorded origin or founder, a cyclical notion of time, a pantheism that infuses divinity into the world around, a relationship between people and divinity, a priestly class, and a tolerance of diverse paths to the Ultimate. Its sacral language is Sanskrit, which came to India about 5,000 years ago with a tribe called the Aryans, from Central Asia (Kumar, Bhugra, & Singh, 2005). Table 16.10 presents some of the traditional Hindu beliefs that may intersect with counseling concerns and offers counseling recommendations.

Buddhism*

For centuries, Buddhism has been the dominant religion of the Eastern world. Today, it remains the predominant religion in China, Japan, and much of Southeast Asia and is one of the largest religions in the world. With the rise of the Asian population in the United States, Buddhism has expanded tremendously in this country (Das & Kemp, 1997). A growing number of native-born Americans are also practicing Buddhism, with nearly three out of four Buddhists in the United States describing themselves as converts (Pew Forum on Religion & Public Life, 2008).

---

*Note: Special thanks go to Dr. Allen Sandler, Buddhist scholar, for editing and adding to this section.

Table 16.10   Hindu Beliefs and Counseling

Marriage and Divorce	Marriage and childrearing are highly valued. Arranged marriages are common. Divorce is discouraged but allowed in certain circumstances.
Sexuality	Premarital and extramarital sex are discouraged. Homosexuality is tolerated. Chastity is valued.
Abortion and Birth Control	Abortion and contraception are acceptable.
View of Counseling	Counseling may be viewed with skepticism. Importance is placed on families taking care of their own.
Spiritual Practices and Healing Traditions	Meditation, yoga, religious devotions and prayers, rituals, festivals and pilgrimages.
Potential Religious-Clinical Issues	Acculturation and value conflicts, family and marital problems, dating and marriage concerns, domestic violence, incest.
Counseling Recommendations	Use the concept of Karma. Explore contradictions. Learn more about the Hindu religion.

Source: Adapted from Richards & Bergin (1999).

Buddhism began in India as an offshoot of Hinduism. Siddhartha Gautama, the founder of Buddhism, was born in approximately 560 BCE in northern India. Deeply distressed by the suffering he saw around him, he began a quest to find an answer to the problem of human suffering. Gautama eventually turned to a life of meditation. While deep in meditation, he experienced the highest degree of God-consciousness, called Nirvana. Subsequently, he became known as the Buddha, or the "enlightened one." As he began his teaching ministry, he gained an audience with the people of India because many had become disillusioned with Hinduism. By the time of Gautama's death at age 80, Buddhism had become a major force in India. Three centuries later, Buddhism had spread to all of Asia (Muramoto, 2002).

The basic teachings of Buddhism are found in the Four Noble Truths and the Eightfold Path. The First Noble Truth is that there is suffering and that the nature of this suffering can be understood. The Second Noble Truth relates to the cause of suffering. There are many potential causes of suffering, but primary among them is desire—the desire for wealth, sex, fame, power, or simply for things to be other than they are. The Third Noble Truth is that there is a way out of suffering, or, stated in a more positive way, well-being is possible. The Fourth Noble Truth is the path that leads from suffering toward well-being— the Eightfold Path (Hanh, 1999). The Eightfold Path consists of eight "right practices" (right thinking, right speech, right livelihood, right mindfulness, etc.) that lead to healing and an end to suffering (Hanh, 1999).

Three important concepts in Buddhism are Karma, Samsara, and Nirvana. Karma, as in Hinduism, refers to the law of cause and effect in a person's life—reaping what one has sown. Samsara holds that everything is in a birth and rebirth cycle and that every person must go through a process of birth and rebirth until she or he reaches the state of Nirvana. Nirvana is not a place like heaven, but rather a state of being in which there is no suffering and there are no desires. Buddha taught that the existence of an individual self or ego is an illusion; therefore, Nirvana is also the state in which individual consciousness ends. Buddhists believe that through self-effort one can attain the state of peace called Nirvana (Richards & Bergin, 2005). In general, Buddhists are pantheistic in their view of God. Many view God as an impersonal force composed of all living things that holds the universe together. Buddhism is a moral philosophy, an ethical way of life (Muramoto, 2002).

Table 16.11 lists some of the traditional Buddhist beliefs that may intersect with counseling concerns and offers treatment recommendations.

Table 16.11   Buddhist Beliefs and Counseling

Marriage and Divorce	No specific Buddhist teachings exist about marriage and divorce or childrearing.
Sexuality	Buddhists believe that sex before marriage is not immoral if there is love and consent between the two parties involved. As long as the act of sex does not cause harm, it is permissible. Homosexuality is accepted.
Abortion and Birth Control	Respect for all life is important. Abortion is unethical. Contraception is acceptable.
View of Counseling	A range of attitudes exist among Buddhists.
Spiritual Practices and Healing Traditions	Meditation, being one's own spiritual teacher, daily worship, prayers, holy days, festivals, studying Buddhist teachings.
Potential Religious-Clinical Issues	Self-contempt, addictions, pathological selfishness.
Counseling Recommendations	Be supportive of and encourage meditative practices. Consult with Buddhist teachers. Use insight-oriented approaches. Relate the repetition of chanting to cognitive-behavioral strategies of self-help.

Source: Adapted from Richards & Bergin (1999).

Earth-Based Religions/Paganism

Paganism, which since the 1960s has been referred to as Neo-Paganism, is a set of spiritual paths and traditions in which reverence for the Earth and all of its creatures is celebrated. Pagans generally believe that all life is interconnected and try to experience this interconnectivity as part of their religious practices. Some may do this by taking care of the space they inhabit, while others try to deal with the problems that are harming the earth on a wider scale. These earth-based religions focus on connection to divinity through nature. Pagan religions are characterized by personal autonomy, polytheism, and immanent divinity. Immanent divinity is the belief that there is a single divinity, a life force of the universe who is immanent in the world. Pagans value diversity, good works, living lightly on the Earth, individual freedom, personal responsibility, community service, gender equity, and spiritual development (Seymour, 2005). Table 16.12 lists some of the pagan beliefs that may intersect with counseling concerns and offers counseling recommendations.

Agnosticism/Humanism/Unitarian Universalism

Agnosticism is the philosophical and theological view that the existence of God, gods, or deities is either unknown or inherently unknowable, but that to deny the existence of God is also untenable. The term is used to describe those who are unconvinced or noncommittal about the existence of deities as well as other matters of religion. The word *agnostic* comes from the Greek *a* (no) and *gnosis* (knowledge), or "not knowing" (*Agnosticism,* 2006).

Humanism, though not a religion in a full sense, is an influential and important belief system. Humanism is oriented toward the satisfaction of human needs, both material and spiritual, and the fulfillment of human potential, in the here and now. Humanists, therefore, lack interest in the supernatural and theological or in an afterlife. Religious and secular humanists hold in common the belief that nothing should be accepted on faith. Rather, there must always be good evidence for beliefs, religious or otherwise. This is the most fundamental tenet of rationalism. Nothing specific to humanism precludes belief in God. In the humanist view, the controversy over the existence of God is far less relevant to ethical living than is ordinarily held by believers in God (Firth, 1996).

Humanism has two core beliefs:

1. People should think for themselves, rather than blindly accepting what they are told by authorities. Authority figures too often have agendas

Table 16.12 Pagan Beliefs and Counseling

Marriage and Divorce	"Handfasting" is practiced. It represents making a 1-year trial marriage commitment, after which time the couple can stay together or "handpart," that is, choose to separate. Both the male and the female are considered essential to the creation of new life, and therefore, neither should be subordinate to the other.
Sexuality	Pagans have no set rules against homosexuality, nudity, or premarital sex. Sex is viewed positively as the generative force in nature and is seen by most pagans as something utterly sacred. The physical act of love is to be approached with great respect and responsibility.
Abortion and Birth Control	The majority of modern pagans favor safe and legal access to abortions.
View of Counseling	Pagans may view counselors with distrust and apprehension, fearing that their faith will be misunderstood.
Spiritual Practices and Healing Traditions	Diverse kinds of divination, altered states of consciousness or trances, magic spells and incantations, special rites for seasonal holy days.
Potential Religious-Clinical Issues	Prior prejudices about the word *pagan*. The frequent, inaccurate association between paganism and evils such as satanic abuse.
Counseling Recommendations	Recognize that paganism is a nature religion in which self-realization is a central tenet. Acknowledge spirituality, and respect indigenous traditions.

Source: Adapted from Seymour (2005).

of their own, frequently for the enhancement of their own wealth or power, or may be uninformed or confused.

2. Values are based in the human person. In order to know whether a given course of conduct is meaningful or right, an individual can ask herself or himself whether it promotes the maintenance or development of the normal capabilities of human beings, such as thinking, feeling, and physical health. (Firth, 1996)

It is worth noting that many Unitarian Universalists consider themselves to be humanists. Unitarian Universalism is a nondoctrinal religion that is guided by seven principles:

- the inherent worth and dignity of every person
- justice, equity, and compassion in human relations
- acceptance of one another and encouragement to spiritual growth in our congregations
- a free and responsible search for truth and meaning
- the right of conscience and the use of the democratic process within congregations and in society at large

- the goal of world community with peace, liberty, and justice for all
- respect for the interdependent web of all existence of which we are a part (Unitarian Universalist Association of Congregations, 1996–2012b)

Table 16.13 displays some of the traditional Agnostic/Humanist issues that may intersect with counseling concerns.

GENERAL INTERVENTIONS THAT ARE ALERT TO RELIGION AND SPIRITUALITY

This section is divided into awareness, knowledge, and skills, in accordance with the three overall multicultural competencies that are discussed in Chapter 2. Overall, counselors' basic respect for humanity and the mandates of the profession require counselors to respect clients' religious perspectives. In fact, both religious and secular counselors need to seriously reflect on these mandates;

Table 16.13   Agnostic/Humanist Beliefs and Counseling

Abortion	The American Humanist Association endorses elective abortion and Unitarian Universalists, many of whom are humanists, "believe in the right of every woman to safe and affordable abortion services, including federally funded abortion counseling and abortion provision, and [have] called for governmental protection for abortion providers and women who receive abortions" (Unitarian Universalist Association of Congregations, 1996–2012a).
Other Contemporary Issues	Agnostics, humanists, and atheists generally support equality for lesbian, gay, bisexual, and transgendered people; gender equality; a secular approach to divorce and remarriage; working to end poverty; promoting peace and nonviolence; and protecting the environment.
View of Counseling	Views of counseling are positive.
Spiritual Practices and Healing Traditions	No specific practices, but open to many.
Potential Religious Clinical Issues	May overemphasize personal responsibility, intellectualize as a defensive strategy, and fear appearing dependent or weak.
Counseling Recommendations	Be open to exploring beliefs, but do not make assumptions. Be inclusive in language.

Source: Adapted from Richards & Bergin (1999).

religious counselors run the risk of believing that all encounters are spiritual and may be inclined to impose spiritual interventions on clients, while secular counselors may resist incorporation of any spirituality in the counseling process.

Awareness

As mentioned earlier, spiritual self-awareness consists of two competencies: (a) awareness of one's own faith and faith development, including how one's faith has been or might be beneficial and how one's faith experiences may have been harmful, and (b) awareness of countertransference issues that may hinder one's work with religious or spiritual clients.

Regarding their own faith, counselors need to be able to comfortably think and talk about their personal beliefs and practices in order to help others in those areas (Hagedorn, 2005, p. 69). Counselors may take the same assessments that they might use with clients in order to understand their own faith, or they may ask themselves the questions posed in Activities 16.1 and 16.2. Such activities can help counselors gain clarity on their spiritual history and development and on the benefits or problems that they have experienced as a result of their faith or as a result of their nonbelieving. Counselors should be able to respond to the following faith-related questions: "Where did I come from?" "Where am I going?" "What does life mean [for me]?" "What is worth living for?" (Helminiak, 2001, p. 163).

To become comfortable with their own spirituality, counselors need to consider in their and others' lives questions of sacredness, transcendence, pain and trouble, faith, death, eternity, right and wrong, and a higher power (Hagedorn, 2005). Counselors need to reflect on spiritual themes that permeate their lives or set the tone of life; on spiritual influences; and on life lessons that may be useful to pass along to others (Faiver & Ingersoll, 2005); they must also ask and answer questions about how they will integrate their value/faith system with the counseling process. Finally, they need to assess how comfortable they are with exploring such issues with clients.

Benefits of Spiritual Self-Assessment

Participation in spiritual or religious self-exploration may promote counselors' development toward what Fowler would call individuative-reflective or conjunctive faith, and away from the religious or antireligious dogmatism and countertransference that could harm the therapeutic relationship. Self-assessment can also help religion-skeptical counselors consider the benefits of faith for clients, particularly if a client's worldviews differ from counselor worldviews (Hagedorn, 2005).

Overcoming Bias

Should counselors discover, during self-assessment, any religious biases that might hinder their responsiveness to clients, they will need to find help for overcoming these biases. Supervision, of course, may assist in this process (ACA, 2005). Other means of overcoming bias include building meaningful relationships with people who differ in faith perspectives (Bishop, 1992), gaining knowledge about other faiths, and educating themselves through reading. Knowledge about others may increase the sense of competence enough to reduce counselor uncertainty about meeting clients of different faiths.

Knowledge

Along with developing self-awareness, counselors need to be competent in the second area of multicultural competence: knowledge about different religious groups, especially as seen through the eyes of clients. This chapter has offered a very brief overview of different faiths, but adequate understanding requires more substantive reading, as well as "plunges" into the activities and rituals of different faiths (Bishop, 1992), especially the faiths practiced by the clients in the counselor's practice.

Counselors must be knowledgeable in four domains, each of which has been introduced in this chapter. Counselors should (1) be able to define and understand the differences between spirituality and religion; (2) have a general understanding of the tenets of the major world religions and familiarity with helping resources within various spiritual and religious traditions; (3) understand the interactions between professional ethical standards and spiritual and religious issues (especially where they clash); and (4) be able to differentiate between positive and negative spiritual and religious beliefs, that is, between those attitudes and practices that support awareness, growth, and flexibility and those that do not (Miller, 1999).

Knowing the Benefits of Spiritual Practices

Nonreligious counselors might familiarize themselves with research on the benefits of various spiritual practices in order to appreciate the healthy potentialities of religious involvement (Genia, 2000). They might further strive to understand how faith practices and beliefs can be integrated with psychological theory and counseling practice (Bishop, 1995). At a minimum, counselors should be sensitive to the world's mainline religions, including Hinduism, Buddhism, Islam, Judaism, and Christianity (Kelly, 1995).

Knowing Harmful Practices

In addition to knowing the benefits of various faiths, counselors also need to understand the ways in which people's misinterpretation of faith principles could lead to harm and how the idiosyncrasies of particular faiths may serve as pitfalls for well-intentioned counselors (Eriksen et al., 2002). For instance, the Bible asks Christians to be in the world but not of the world (*Holy Bible*, 1983, John 17:14–18) and indicates that it would be better if one plucked out one's eye or cut off one's hand rather than have these body parts cause one to sin (*Holy Bible*, 1983, Matthew 5:29). Healthy Christians do not interpret these scriptures to mean that they should live in complete isolation or do themselves bodily harm, although believers with psychological problems might. Harmful faith was more clearly articulated earlier in this chapter.

The Risks of Being Misinformed

Counselors who are unfamiliar with idiosyncrasies of particular faiths can hinder the work of counseling. For instance, one cannot talk glibly about a marriage of equals to all conservative Christian clients because many believe strongly in the Bible's mandate that husbands are to be the head of the family (*Holy Bible*, 1983, Ephesians 5:22–24). Similarly, counselors should probably not ask abused conservative Christian wives why they are staying with their husbands because the wives may then believe the counselor is advocating for divorce, which, from their perspective, would probably be considered a sin (*Holy Bible*, 1983, Matthew 5:31–32). In fact, the client might not return for counseling if the counselor were to simplistically push such issues. Counselors should be aware not only of such idiosyncrasies, but of how people within particular faith traditions address complexities that arise because of the idiosyncrasies. Should these complexities be too difficult for the counselor to ferret out, she or he should refer to or consult with clergy who can help with alternative interpretations of teachings.

Skills

Counselors need specific skills in four areas when incorporating religious dimensions into counseling: informed consent, assessment, intervention, and networking.

Informed Consent

Religious clients' sensitivities about faith issues and about including spiritual interventions in counseling require counselors to inform clients about the nature of counseling and about the presence or absence of an explicit religious dimension in the counselor's practice. Clients should also have the opportunity to participate in the decisions about how spiritual interventions might be incorporated into the counseling process (ACA, 2005, A.2). Success in both of these areas requires counselors to develop a straightforward language with which to communicate about religious values (Bishop, 1995), to initiate a discussion about values, and to discuss their own perspectives on religion or spirituality.

Assessment

Counselors can assess clients' spirituality in order to fully understand what interventions might be appropriate, inappropriate, or helpful. Richards and Potts (1995) advise counselors to learn about clients' unique religious understandings, even when they identify with the same or similar religions. In assessing clients' religious and spiritual perspectives, counselors might use the following informal or formal assessment procedures.

Informal Religious Assessment Strategies

Four approaches to informally inquiring about a client's religious or spiritual beliefs are possible. First, and most simply, the counselor might ask the following questions

- Do you have a religious preference?
- Do you currently attend religious services?
- What are your reasons for attending services?
- How important are your religious beliefs to you? (Griffith & Griggs, 2001, p. 22)

A second, more complex exploration may include the following five questions that evoke conversation about spirituality (Pargament, 2002):

- How does your faith give your life meaning?
- What are the advantages and disadvantages of your faith?
- Does your faith help you with some situations more than with others?
- Who supports you so that you grow in your faith in helpful ways?
- Might there be a solution to your problems that includes other personal strengths besides your faith?

A third informal assessment of religious meaning involves the counselor asking the following questions to explicitly integrate a client's issues with religious themes while assessing the client's general religious orientation and meaning-making (Hartz, 2005):

- How does your spirituality contribute to your understanding of the problem or solutions?
- How did you chose your religious community, and how helpful is this community in supporting you with the current problems?

- What spiritual practices do you engage in, and how are these helpful in addressing the current problems?
- What is your relationship with God like, and how has this changed over the years?

By assessing clients' current religious practices and thoughts, counselors may also ask how clients find their faith to be helpful in coping with difficult situations (McCullough & Larson, 1999).

A fourth and deeper assessment of client religiosity consists of the counselor taking a thorough spiritual history in order to fully understand the client's religious upbringing, feelings, beliefs, and practices, particularly tuning in to the stage of faith the client may have reached (Fowler, 1981).

Regardless of the method of assessment, counselors need to include clients in the decision-making process about the place of religion in counseling by asking, "In what ways do you want to include spirituality in our counseling sessions?" With any of the above-suggested questions, the counselor, during the initial interviews, gains important information and conveys to the client the notion that religious material is a legitimate topic in counseling.

Formal Religious Assessment Strategies

More formal assessment might include use of available religious assessment instruments or strategies. First, the Religious Background and Behaviors Questionnaire (Hartz, 2005) offers a formal way of asking the questions listed in the previous section.

Second, the Spiritual Surrender Assessment Scales (Cole & Pargament, 1999) measures the degree to which clients defer, plead, self-direct, collaborate, or surrender to a higher power in very difficult situations. On this instrument, it is considered better for one's mental health to surrender in situations over which one has no control.

Other quantitative instruments are presented and evaluated by Harper and Gill (2005). These may include assessments of values, beliefs, lifestyle, and spiritual experiences. More qualitative approaches may include a values assessment, a sentence completion task, a spiritual autobiography, or a spiritual genogram (Harper & Gill, 2005).

Intervention

The third area of multicultural competency includes skills or interventions. How might counselors best respect and/or integrate spirituality and/or religion in their work with clients, should they choose to do so or should the client need them to do so? Two ways—*implicit* integration and *explicit* integration—are possible (Tan, 1996b).

Implicit Integration

In implicit integration, counselors respectfully and sensitively respond to religious themes as they emerge or as the client brings them up during the counseling process. Counselors do not, however, initiate the discussion of religious or spiritual issues or directly use spiritual resources like prayer and sacred texts in counseling (Tan, 1996b). For instance, counselors might validate helpful facets of religion, reinterpret religious meanings into psychological terms, or challenge maladaptive religious beliefs.

Validating Positive Aspects of Religion

Most simply, the counselor might use reflection and affirmation to show appreciation for a client's religious understandings and their helpfulness in her or his life. Such encouragement is consistent with findings of the psychology of religion that religious belief can facilitate psychological healing and personal integration (Bergin, 1980, 1991; Bergin, Payne, & Richards, 1996; Ellis, 1980; Hood, Spilka, Hunsberger, & Gorsuch, 1996; Jones, 1994; Moberg & Brused, 1978; Wulff, 1997). A counselor might, therefore, appreciate and encourage the client's belief in a loving and caring God; the need to make some sense of life's happenings; a commitment to honesty, compassion, and goodwill; the faith's approaches to repentance and forgiveness; the client's membership in a supportive community; participation in reassuring rituals; practice of private devotions and meditative exercises; and opportunities for transcendence beyond day-to-day existence.

Reinterpreting Religious Meanings

It may be helpful to reinterpret or reframe in psychological terms some aspects of a client's religion. Certain facets of a client's spirituality may hinder authentic growth and may therefore need to be adjusted. For example, people may pray, expecting a miracle. For them, God may still fit the childhood fantasy of the "Great Magician in the Sky" (Woodward, 1997), consistent with Fowler's (1981) earlier stages. It can be maladaptive to build one's life around the expectation of external miracles, especially when neglecting personal efforts that could contribute to a needed counseling outcome. Therefore, without taking a theological stand on the validity of such a practice, the counselor can both (a) understand the psychological significance of the belief for the person and express empathic understanding about how such a practice can sustain hope and trust (Bergin et al., 1996), while (b) at the same time urging the client to take other helpful actions. The counselor is thus able to deal with matters of the human spirit without being explicitly religious or theological herself or himself.

Other psychological reinterpretation strategies might also help clients bridge their religious and psychological experiences (Prest & Keller, 1993):

1. The counselor might discover that some of a client's spiritual solutions are no longer working and then help the client explore alternative spiritually grounded solutions. For example, if a client accepts her or his suffering from depression because of a belief that suffering ensures entrance into an afterlife, the counselor might help the client get into a religious group that encourages participants to adopt more positive ways of coping with mental distress.

2. The counselor can elicit fundamental beliefs and offer alternative meanings for metaphors. For example, the "rod" metaphor in the Bible (*Holy Bible*, 1983, Proverbs 13:24) that is used to justify corporal punishment might be reframed to include time-outs or other noncorporal punishments.

3. The counselor can initiate a discussion about "incongruent spiritual maps" (Prest & Keller, 1993, p. 143). For example, with a husband whose "spiritual map" tells him to be the spiritual authority of the home, the counselor can suggest that spiritual authority can be manifested in sacrificial love and that this would also contribute to the effectiveness of the "head" of the household. Ways to demonstrate sacrificial love may then become a topic of discussion.

Overall, reinterpretation asks counselors first to validate the client's valuing of a doctrine, next to challenge interpretations that are harmful, and finally to offer an alternative interpretation (Lovinger, 1996; Spinney, 1991). An alternative interpretation might emerge from reading the verses in context, exploring other translations and the historical context of the writing, or examining the alternative interpretations offered by experts. Reinterpretation clearly involves a good deal of religious education or consultation with spiritual experts on the counselor's part.

Challenging Clients' Beliefs

Counselors may, in some cases, actually confront the legitimacy of the client's spiritual and religious beliefs (Helminiak, 2001). Such confrontation requires a great deal of client–counselor trust, accompanied by the client's sense that the counselor does not reject the religion outright. Counselors need to understand the client's need for and valuing of a belief; however, some beliefs are antithetical to psychological healing and wholesome growth (Helminiak, 2001). For example, the client's protest that "evil forces made me do it" poses some challenges for the culturally alert counselor. Some individuals with collectivistic values may actually get better when problems are attributed to outside forces. However, other clients may be abdicating their responsibilities. Therefore, the counselor would not reject this belief without exploring its meaning for the client. Other harmful religious practices were discussed previously.

Explicit Interventions

In explicit interventions, both spiritual and nonreligious counselors directly integrate spiritual approaches, such as prayer or discussion and interpretation of sacred writings, with traditional therapeutic methods (Richards & Bergin, 2005). For instance, counselors can attempt to enter client worldviews with vocabulary and imagery that are congruent with clients' faith experiences (Ingersoll, 1995). However, in many cases, explicitly incorporating religion requires religious training beyond what is provided in most counselor education programs (Richards & Bergin, 2005; Shafranske & Malony, 1996). Box 16.3 suggests some explicit religion-based interventions.

Box 16.3   Religious and Spiritual Counseling Interventions

- Use religious images during guided imagery (Worthington, 1978; Yarhouse, 1999), including images that decrease anxiety or increase a sense of comfort (Tan & Johnson, 2005).
- Offer scriptural passages or other religious textual materials that correspond to therapeutic prescriptions (Eriksen et al., 2002).
- Use prayer as a means to shift cognitions (McCullough & Larson, 1999).
- Introduce religious texts to dispute cognitions that are not working (Tan & Johnson, 2005).
- Ask clients to journal about beliefs and values, how they developed, and how they might help in the current situation (Basham & O'Connor, 2005).
- Suggest books related to spiritual issues (O'Connor, 2002).
- Use liberation, transformation, or celebration rituals from different religious traditions (Basham & O'Connor, 2005).
- Incorporate "inner healing" to help heal unresolved developmental issues or childhood traumas (Tan, 1987; see Tan, 1996a, for a seven-step model for inner healing prayer).
- Use religious perspectives that help the client move toward the ideal (e.g., from a Christian perspective it would be becoming more Christ-like, in the Buddhist tradition it would be getting closer to one's Buddha nature).
- Stress the healing power of God's spirit (Tan, 1987).
- Join the resistance when clients express doubt by indicating that there is no faith without doubt (Lovinger, 1979).
- Consider God a member of the family, or place God in an empty chair, therefore bringing God directly into the counseling process (Hannon et al., 1994).
- Consider the clients' experiences of God to be "similar to their experiences of other significant psychological *objects*" (italics added; Shafranske, 2005, p. 110).
- Self-disclose one's own spiritual journeys to encourage change. For example, the counselor could speak of the times that she or he thought that God answered prayer and other times that she or he wondered whether God existed.

Each of the specific strategies in Box 16.3 reflects the old adage: "You need to get into someone's house before you can help them rearrange the furniture." As a condition of encouraging a client to change, counselors need to demonstrate respect for clients by speaking in language that reflects an understanding and acceptance of clients' faith. Both Miller (1999) and Sperry and Shafranske

(2005) discuss a range of ideas from a variety of theoretical perspectives about how one might integrate spirituality into clinical practice.

Network, Referral, Consultation, and Partnership With Indigenous Healers

The fourth set of religiously alert skills accesses the help of other faith experts. Counselors who do not share their client's faith need to develop a cadre of experts with whom to consult. Counselors can engage and network with religious leaders; become familiar with community resources, such as churches, synagogues, prayer groups, 12-step programs, and lay religious counselors; and develop a referral network that is composed of religious professionals from a variety of faiths (Yarhouse, 1999).

Consultation and partnership can be important when religion is explicitly brought into counseling. As will be discussed in Chapter 19, counselors might further consult with the client's other "healers," such as clergy, when questions arise about how to intervene (Ingersoll, 1995; Tan, 1987). Counselors might coordinate care with the client's pastor (with the client's permission; Johnson & Johnson, 1997). Counselors can also partner with local religious groups to gain their support when developing programs and services (Johnson & Johnson, 1997). If the various suggested strategies are not working, counselors need to know when and how to refer clients to other professionals who might be more facile with those clients' religions.

APPLYING RELIGIOUSLY ALERT INTERVENTIONS TO THE VIGNETTES

Further understanding of this chapter's content can be facilitated by applying the multicultural counseling competencies of religious self-awareness, knowledge, and intervention to the clients presented in vignettes at the beginning of the chapter: Brittany, a single 34-year-old Evangelical Christian; Geoff, a 19-year-old Orthodox Jewish American undergraduate student; and Joseph, a 65-year-old man who has faithfully practiced Christian Science for 30 years. Some of the multicultural competencies may be applied similarly to all three clients, while other interventions might be more appropriate to particular clients.

Applying Universal Competencies to the Cases

For each case, counselors need to begin with self-awareness, that is, awareness of their own attitudes and beliefs about spirituality and religion and a sense of their preconceived notions about their clients' religious perspectives. Strategies for increasing such awareness were delineated in a previous section. Counselors also need to know or learn about the faiths practiced by each of these clients: Evangelical Christianity, Orthodox Judaism, and Christian Science.

Counselors also need to fully assess each client's spiritual or religious experiences, beliefs, and development, including the salience of the religion for the client and the level of enculturation into it. Counselors need to acknowledge both the centrality of faith to the clients' lives and the strong connections between religious issues and the presenting problems.

As part of the informed consent process in each case, counselors need to openly negotiate the desired role of spirituality/religion in the counseling process with clients. Further, because of the importance of religion to Brittany, Geoff, and Joseph, their counselors need to respond to religious themes as they arise in counseling, as part of implicit integration of religion into counseling. Counselors could (1) acknowledge the positive impact of faith on these clients' lives, (2) use the resources provided by the clients' faith communities, (3) network with consultants who could offer information about the particular faiths, and (4) be alert to when or if client beliefs became psychologically harmful.

Applying Countertransference Awareness to the Cases

In one or more of the vignettes, counselors might find their countertransference to be aroused by the strength or dogmatism of the client's faith experiences and beliefs. Even counselors who are open to integrating spirituality into all counseling with all clients may find that the orthodoxy, evangelicalism, conservatism, and powerful faith commitments of these particular clients are difficult hurdles to overcome. Clients with such powerful faith commitments nearly always demand that mental health professionals explicitly integrate religion into the helping process, and this demand would tax many providers' competence, or counselors may find themselves feeling put off by the intensity of their clients' commitments.

In the case of Joseph, the Christian Scientist, counselors might experience countertransference as difficulty not "siding" with Joseph's family in insisting that Joseph receive standard Western medical care. How does one not label Joseph "crazy" for refusing medical care when he is in such dire straits? Might one feel ethically challenged by someone who is seeming to harm himself in this way?

Counselors might also experience surprise, and perhaps bias, should they ask Brittany during assessment about her prior and current sexual relationships. Her conservative beliefs probably preclude sexual activity prior to marriage and may also forbid activities that are sexually arousing (even without actual intercourse). She may, therefore, be shocked or embarrassed to even be asked questions about her sexuality, and the very asking of the questions might damage the therapeutic alliance.

In both Joseph's and Brittany's cases, counselors need to know enough about each of these clients' faiths to appreciate and work with the positive aspects and, when confronted with problems related to the faith, to find alternative answers from *within* the faith. They need to consult with experts from each faith to discover ways in which those from that particular faith live differently than the general population, in order to avoid surprises or at least to prevent expressions of dismay when the clients first introduce very-different-from-the-mainstream beliefs. Counselors need to be sufficiently aware of their own beliefs, faith development, and biases to distinguish between, on the one hand, negative reactions that cue them to an area that the client might need to change and, on the other hand, negative reactions that are countertransferential and require the counselors themselves to examine problematic attitudes, perhaps through supervision.

One way for counselors to reframe countertransference is to view dogmatism from a developmental perspective (i.e., synthetic-conventional faith). They might then intervene by matching and mismatching clients' developmental levels in order to help clients become more flexible and open. Fowler (1981, 2004) suggests that such developmental change is movement not away from faith, but toward a more mature faith.

Applying Explicit Interventions to the Cases

This section presents examples of explicit interventions for each of the cases presented in the beginning of this chapter. Such explicit interventions may require a level of religious knowledge not common to all counselors. These interventions need to be grounded in the client's faith position and the counselor's theory. Accurate and relevant decisions about such interventions would require greater information about the clients than has thus far been presented in the vignettes. However, a number of possibilities are presented below as examples. Initially, a number of expected cultural phenomena within these cases are discussed, followed by ways in which the clients may demonstrate psychological difficulties no differently than other clients. Finally, theoretically grounded and spiritually sensitive interventions are offered.

Intervening in the Case of Brittany

Brittany has clearly remained single beyond what is typical in rural and conservative Christian communities. In rural communities, early marriage and childbearing is correlated with less education, fewer opportunities for women, and traditional values that place women in the home, bearing and caring for children. In conservative Christian communities, early marriage seems to be related to the requirement for sexual abstinence before marriage. Early childbearing seems grounded in strong beliefs about the value of family. Brittany would be unlikely to value any life vocation or occupation more than marriage and raising a family. Within Christian communities, because others have usually married in their early 20s, unmarried folks beyond their 20s often feel left behind, as though all of the "good" partners have been taken and as though God is not being faithful to them in providing a life partner. In some cases, clients like Brittany may wonder what "sin" God wants them to discover and repent of in order to be ready for the sacrament of marriage.

Brittany's own individual struggles may be further exacerbated by her church community's belief that she should be married and raising children and that she is failing in God's purpose for her life by not "getting on with it." They may "encourage" her with prayer and by bringing men to her doorstep, expecting her to respond with gratitude to their assistance. She may instead feel pressured to accept others' answers when her own heart is not in agreement.

Brittany may also struggle with her faith's demands for premarital sexual abstinence and for being "equally yoked," that is, partnered only with a Christian. Men who are her age may be less patient with her belief in abstinence, which may generate conflict as relationships become more emotionally intimate, and thus relationships may end before they can flower. And Brittany may, as a result of her dissatisfaction with the available Christian men, find her gaze wandering outside of her faith. However, her guilt and those men's struggle with the conservativeness of her faith may also end relationships before they can begin.

During assessment counselors would clearly need to be knowledgeable about these possibilities, which differ from mainstream culture, and add questions related to these possibilities to the more typical questions for assessing the reasons for Brittany's continuing singleness. Spiritually sensitive assessment would thus include asking Brittany about her feelings and beliefs about being single; her beliefs, hopes, or images about her life at this age; the messages she is currently receiving from her family and community about this issue; her experiences with relationships to this point; how she currently experiences God's will in her life since she is without the desired husband and children; and how her relationships with friends her age and with her church community may have been affected by her remaining single. Assessment goals would include determining possible reasons for Brittany's singleness and the degree to which faith and/or interpersonal issues might contribute to her difficulties in finding a marital partner. Treatment goals would include either making peace with singleness or resolving spiritual, interpersonal, cultural, or geographical hindrances to marriage.

Spiritually alert counseling might operate from a range of different theoretical perspectives. If the counselor operates from a family counseling or systems perspective, she or he might observe the here-and-now process between Brittany and herself or himself as illustrative of the ways in which Brittany relates to men and perhaps to God. If the counselor observed any problematic ways of being, she or he could then make Brittany aware of her or his observations and could assist her in relating in more helpful ways. But the counselor would need to exercise caution to ensure that these "more helpful ways" were congruent with conservative Biblical understandings. In pursuit of understanding Biblical perspectives, the counselor might ask Brittany what the Bible would say or advise given her or his observations. The counselor might ask Brittany to consult and pray with her spiritual mentors about these observations and to solicit their perspectives. The counselor might also consult with a minister from a conservative Christian church before proposing possible solutions.

The counselor who prefers a Gestalt perspective might ask Brittany to place God in a chair and have a conversation with God about her disappointment. Or the counselor might teach Brittany deep relaxation and walk her through guided imagery related to singleness and marriage. Both interventions would serve to bring to Brittany's awareness all of her feelings about, and historical needs related to, this situation. The counselor might ask Brittany to journal about her feelings related to this issue or to write a letter to God. Full catharsis of these feelings and congruence in expression might be the therapeutic goals and the means toward insight. However, once all of the feelings were "out" verbally or on paper, the counselor might go beyond "human" insight to suggest that Brittany pray about everything she has thus far discovered so as to obtain God's guidance. The counselor would also need to know whether Brittany would find experiencing and expressing such emotions to be contradictory to Biblical injunctions about "the greatest of these" being "peace, love, and joy" (*Holy Bible,* 1983, I Corinthians 13:13) or to focus on others rather than herself. Again, Brittany's homework might include consulting and praying with prayer partners, spiritual elders, or her pastor. The counselor might also consult with Brittany's pastor (with Brittany's permission) to safeguard against potential landmines and to determine the best of the possible interventions.

Intervening in the Case of Geoff

Geoff finds himself on the cusp of a great number of developmental opportunities. He has moved from a small city to a large metropolitan area, which entails exposure to a wide variety of possibilities and life choices that he never previously imagined. He finds himself, as many college students do, comparing the values, choices, faith, and lifestyles that he inherited with a vast array of new possibilities presented by his peers. But he most likely lacks the capacities yet to carefully weigh which of the old ways that he wishes to reject, and which of the new he wants to adopt. He finds himself attracted to a man, which may undermine all he has ever believed about marriage and family life. He may, as a result of each of these challenges, feel as though he straddles a great chasm between his previous life and some new life that he has yet to

create or discover or know. This chasm threatens to engulf him and does not allow him to easily move backward or forward. He may feel as though it is an either/or choice, and that to choose to move forward is to reject all that he has previously valued, that is, to reject his family and his religion. So it is no surprise that Geoff finds himself depressed, torn, isolated, and having difficulty making decisions among the myriad of choices that confront him.

Geoff may find it very difficult to consult any rabbi or family member, but may find it equally difficult to have complete faith in those who differ from his family or religion. And it may be that the orthodoxy of his faith (or his family's faith) increases the challenge, as orthodoxy's message may be rather "all or nothing," "in or out," "with God or without God." Or he may be overinterpreting the Torah's messages due to his small-town and possibly more traditional upbringing. That is, the Torah offers a faith that comes with many traditions, but rarely requires Jewish people to follow all of them. Deciding which traditions to preserve is often left up to individual conscience. Assessment would need to more fully explore these areas and hypotheses.

Treatment goals would include helping Geoff recognize the potential of a developmental process and to gain the supports he needs in the journey. As a means to normalize his experience, he may be helped by information about internalized homophobia and about the stages of the coming-out process. He may be helped by a constructive developmental perspective that conceptualizes his experience as an understandable and normal response to the situations in which he finds himself. That is, his experience is fairly common for those moving out of a received, traditional, or conventional way of knowing toward a more self-authorized or autonomous way of knowing (Kegan, 1982, 1998; see previous developmental discussion). He may benefit from knowing that developmental progression doesn't have to mean rejecting all that has come before. In fact, in the best of cases, it means incorporating or reconstructing the old into some new way of knowing and being.

Further, he may be ideally situated—because of an available college counseling center—for receiving developmental counseling, since college counselors and student affairs practitioners are usually the only specialty of counselors who are cognizant of constructive developmental theory.

These counselors may be able to structure his counseling and other college experiences so as to support Geoff firmly at each point along the bridge (Eriksen, 2006) between the two developmental stages. Support would mean having him talk about his traditions and how they have worked for him and for his family and friends, and then reflecting, appreciating, and honoring these traditions. It might also mean finding "authorities" from his faith community to respond to his questions. Challenge might mean focusing on the value that the Jewish faith places on asking questions, posing different and opposing views, and asking people to struggle with, discuss, and reflect upon possibilities, and then asking him to use that value and the skills he has thus developed within his tradition to consider and make decisions about all of the differing perspectives that he is facing.

Geoff may find himself in over his head (Kegan, 1998) if a counselor from outside his faith attempts to promote development, as he may fear that the counselor could lead him away from God as he has understood him. Therefore, Geoff may be supported in his developmental progression by *bridge people*. That is, he may benefit by meeting with a support group of Jewish gay men who are struggling to integrate their faith with their sexual orientation. This may both honor his faith and make him more comfortable with knowing that he doesn't have to abandon his faith in order to make sense of his sexual feelings. Bibliocounseling might serve as a bridge by introducing Geoff to scholars of the Torah who have written about homosexuality and masturbation from both sides of the debate (e.g., Heilman & Cohen, 1989; Schneer, 2002). Clearly, the counselor would need connections in the Jewish community in order to assist in finding such books and to either connect Geoff with a support group or develop one herself or himself. Geoff might also find a bridge in connecting with

an orthodox Jewish man (or men) from a metropolitan area or who is a transplant like himself, but who has already moved beyond his developmental struggle. Again, careful networking would be necessary so as not to introduce Geoff to someone who would stand in judgment of him at a time when he would need the space to explore more freely.

Intervening in the Case of Joseph

Joseph is most likely feeling scared and alone with his illness at this point. Christian Science believes strongly in the healing power of prayer, and unless bones are broken, people of this faith do not typically pursue traditional medicine or visit medical practitioners. The religion instead offers healers who pray with the person for healing. Clearly if Joseph has visited doctors, it must be because the healing rituals have not worked. And those same doctors must be recommending treatment for the cancer, which he is probably not taking advantage of. Herein lies his individual struggle—God is not healing him through prayer alone for some reason. The doctors indicate that he is dying.

Joseph wonders, "Why is God not healing me?" Will he betray his faith and his God if he pursues more traditional medical treatment? Can he really believe God's promises about salvation and an afterlife if God is not "following through" with the promised healing? Added to these spiritual concerns is the fact that in waiting this long, Joseph may have reduced the chances that traditional medicine will prove curative. Further traditional cancer treatment is far from universally successful even in the best of circumstances. Joseph may find himself questioning himself and his God about whether he should now pursue traditional medical treatment or should have pursued it long ago. He is also probably wondering if this is "his time," that is, wondering whether it is time to make peace with death and move on.

Joseph's family may find themselves in a different sort of quandary. His parents, wife, and children do not want to lose him prematurely to cancer. The typical end-of-life questions about the right time to make peace and let go may be complicated by their worries about his mental health, given his persistent belief in faith healing despite evidence of its ineffectiveness in this situation. They may find themselves angry at God for not healing Joseph or angry at Joseph for adhering so strongly to something they themselves have at least partially rejected. They may find that his end-of-life issues trigger their own fears about death, particularly given their having rejected or not fully participated in their faith.

During assessment, the counselor will need to attend fully to this range of possibilities of beliefs, feelings, thoughts, and challenges to relationships. The assessment goals would be discovering what is realistic regarding Joseph's treatment and chances for recovery so as to aid in his and his family's end-of-life decisions; what the condition of family relationships have been historically and are currently, and what relationship issues might need to be resolved regardless of Joseph's treatment choices; and how the family members' spiritual lives may hinder or help the current dilemma in which they find themselves.

Treatment goals could include making clear decisions about whether to stop pursuing healing options or to keep hoping, and for how long; improving family relationships so that the family can be fully functional as they make very important life decisions, perhaps using this situation to resolve past pains; and helping each family member grow spiritually, perhaps developing spiritual relationships with one another, and make peace with God as they understand the deity.

Clearly God will be "in the room" when counseling this family, whether or not the counselor chooses to acknowledge it, so it is probably better to recognize God's presence explicitly. This might be done in a variety of ways. An empty chair could be placed in the family circle (or outside of it if the nonbelieving family members would prefer it) and could be named "God's chair." As in Brittany's case, the family members might be encouraged to voice their struggles directly to God or could merely use the chair to remain aware of God's involvement with the family's struggle. Family members might be instructed to journal or write a letter to God about this situation and then might share their letter with other family members. And the counselor could include God as a key part of any interpretation or observation of family process. The usual family counseling or end-of-life interventions would include assisting all family members in talking openly with one another about their thoughts, feelings, needs, and beliefs about the illness, impending death, faith, and medical treatment; helping them address conflicts in these areas and negotiate ways to be at peace with each other and with each other's decisions, despite differences; discovering in the process inadequacies in the ways that the family functions, and creating change strategies to shift to healthier functioning; and acknowledging family strengths, including their spirituality, and building on these to address the presenting dilemma. In all of these efforts, their faith may be helpful in finding and offering forgiveness and in moving from a past position of "sinfulness" or failures to a place of understanding and acceptance.

SUMMARY

Many of the colonies that became the United States were born out of religious persecution and the desires of their foreparents to practice their religions freely. Americans seem to have persisted in their passion for spiritual and religious involvement throughout the years, being more intent on practicing their faiths than people in many other countries. The United States has continued to be a refuge for those fleeing religious persecution. Further, constitutional mandates for free practice of one's religion seem to have allowed those of differing faiths to live relatively harmoniously next door to one another, in comparison with people in some other countries. During the past 20 years, the mental health professions seem to have caught up with these initial and continuing popular culture impulses. It is now acknowledged that competence with spiritual or religious clients is necessary for ethically mandated multicultural competence. This chapter has provided a place for counselors to begin their journey toward such competence. We hope that such beginnings will draw your attention to the spiritual issues affecting your work and your clients and will whet your appetite for pursuing more in-depth and comprehensive competence at the intersections of counseling and spirituality.

REFERENCES

Agass, D. (2002). Countertransference, supervision, and the reflection process. *Journal of Social Work Practice, 16,* 125–133.

Agnosticism. (2006). Retrieved from http://en.wikipedia.org/w/index.php?title=Agnosticism&oldid=55354656

Allison, S. (1988). *Meaning-making in marriage: An exploratory study* (Unpublished doctoral dissertation). Massachusetts School of Professional Psychology, Boston, MA.

Alvarez, M. (1985). *The construing of friendship in adulthood: A structural-developmental approach* (Unpublished doctoral dissertation). Massachusetts School of Professional Psychology, Boston, MA.

American Counseling Association. (2005). *Code of ethics and standards of practice.* Alexandria, VA: Author.

American Psychiatric Association. (1994). *Diagnostic and statistical manual of mental disorders* (4th ed.). Washington, DC: Author.

American Psychiatric Association. (2000). *Diagnostic and statistical manual of mental disorders* (4th ed., Text rev.). Washington, DC: Author.

American Psychological Association. (2010). *Ethical principles of psychologists and code of conduct.* Retrieved from http://www.apa.org/ethics/code/index.aspx

Arterburn, S., & Felton, J. (1992). *Faith that hurts, faith that heals.* Nashville, TN: Thomas Nelson.

Association for Spiritual, Ethical, and Religious Values in Counseling. (2009). *Competencies for addressing spiritual and religious issues in counseling.* Retrieved from http://www.aservic.org/resources/spiritual-competencies

Astor, J. (2000). Some reflections on empathy and reciprocity in the use of countertransference between supervisor and supervisee. *Journal of Analytical Psychology, 45,* 367–383.

Barker, P. W., & Muck, W. J. (2004, April). *Holy war for the 21st century: Globalization, U.S. foreign policy, and the development of Islamic identity.* Paper presented at the annual meeting of the Midwest Political Science Association, Chicago, IL. Retrieved from http://citation.allacademic.com/meta/p_mla_apa_research_citation/0/8/4/3/2/pages84324/p84324-1.php

Bartz, J. D., Richards, P. S., Smith, T. B., & Fischer, L. (2010). A 17-year longitudinal study of religion and mental health in a Mormon sample. *Mental Health, Religion & Culture, 13,* 683–695.

Bar-Yam, M. (1991). Do women and men speak in different voices? A comparative study of self-evolvement. *International Journal of Aging and Human Development, 32,* 247–259.

Basham, A., & O'Connor, M. (2005). Use of spiritual and religious beliefs in pursuit of clients' goals. In C. S. Cashwell & J. S. Young (Eds.), *Integrating spirituality and religion into counseling* (pp. 143–167). Alexandria, VA: American Counseling Association.

Baumeister, R. F. (1992). *Meanings of life.* New York, NY: Guilford Press.

Bebbington, D. (1989). *Evangelicalism in modern Britain: A history from the 1730s to the 1980s.* London, UK: Unwin Hyman.

Benack, S. (1988). Relativistic thought: A cognitive basis for empathy in counseling. *Counselor Education and Supervision, 27,* 216–232.

Bergin, A. E. (1980). Counseling and religious values. *Journal of Counseling and Clinical Psychology, 48,* 95–105.

Bergin, A. E. (1991). Values and religious issues in counseling and mental health. *American Psychologist, 46,* 394–403.

Bergin, A., & Jensen, J. (1990). Religiosity of psychocounselors: A national survey. *Counseling, 27,* 3–7.

Bergin, A. E., Payne, I. N., & Richards, P. S. (1996). Values in counseling. In E. P. Shafranske (Ed.), *Religion and the clinical practice of psychology* (pp. 297–325). Washington, DC: American Psychological Association.

Beukema, S. (1990). *Women's best friendships: Their meaning and meaningfulness* (Unpublished doctoral dissertation). Harvard Graduate School of Education, Cambridge, MA.

Binner, V. F. (1991). *A study of Minnesota entrepreneurship: Balancing personal, business, and community demands* (Unpublished doctoral dissertation). Graduate School of the Union Institute, Cincinnati, OH.

Bishop, D. R. (1992). Religious values as cross-cultural issues in counseling. *Counseling and Values, 36,* 179–191.

Bishop, D. R. (1995). Religious values as cross-cultural issues in counseling. In M. T. Burke & J. G. Miranti (Eds.), *Counseling: The spiritual dimension* (pp. 59–71). Alexandria, VA: American Counseling Association.

Bowman, J. T., & Reeves, T. G. (1987). Moral development and empathy in counseling. *Counselor Education and Supervision, 26,* 293–298.

Bradley, D. E. (1995). Religious involvement and social resources: Evidence from the Americans' changing lives data. *Journal for the Scientific Study of Religion, 34,* 259–267.

Brendel, J. M., Kolbert, J. B., & Foster, V. A. (2002). Promoting student cognitive development. *Journal of Adult Development, 3,* 217–227.

Carlson, T. D., Kirkpatrick, D., Hecker, L., & Killmer, M. (2002). Religion, spirituality, and marriage and family counseling: A study of family counselors' beliefs about the appropriateness of addressing religious and spiritual issues in counseling. *American Journal of Family Counseling, 30,* 157–171.

Case, P. W. (1997). Potential sources of countertransference among religious counselors. *Counseling and Values, 41,* 97–107.

Cervantes, J. M., & Ramirez, O. (1992). Spirituality and family dynamics in counseling with Latino children. In L. A. Vargas & J. D. Koss-Chioino (Eds.), *Working with culture: Psychotherapeutic interventions with ethnic minority children and adolescents* (pp. 103–128). San Francisco, CA: Jossey-Bass.

Chandler, H. C., Holden, J. M., & Kolander, C. (1992). Counseling for spiritual wellness: Theory and practice. *Journal of Counseling and Development, 71,* 168–175.

Chibon, J. (1992). Healing and spirituality. *Pastoral Psychology, 40,* 235–245.

Cole, B. S., & Pargament, K. I. (1999). Spiritual surrender: A paradoxical path to control. In W. R. Miller (Ed.), *Integrating spirituality into treatment: Resources for practitioners* (pp. 179–198). Washington, DC: American Psychological Association.

Connors, G. J., Toscova, R. T., & Tonigan, J. S. (1999). Serenity. In W. R. Miller (Ed.), *Integrating spirituality into treatment: Resources for practitioners* (pp. 234–250). Washington, DC: American Psychological Association.

Council for the Accreditation of Counseling and Related Educational Programs. (2001). *CACREP accreditation standards and procedures manual.* Alexandria, VA: Author.

Council on American-Islamic Relations. (2012). *About Islam and American Muslims.* Retrieved from http://www.cair.com/AboutIslam/IslamBasics.aspx

Das, A. K., & Kemp, S. F. (1997). Between two worlds: Counseling South Asian Americans. *Journal of Multicultural Counseling & Development, 25,* 23–33.

Dixon, J. W. (1986). *The relation of social perspective stages to Kegan's stages of ego development* (Unpublished doctoral dissertation). University of Toledo, Toledo, OH.

Elkins, D. N. (1995). Psychotherapy and spirituality: Toward a theory of the soul. *Journal of Humanistic Psychology, 35,* 78–99.

Elkins, D. N. (1999). Spirituality. *Psychology Today, 32,* 45.

Elkins, D. N., Hedstrom, L., & Hughes, L. (1988). Toward a humanistic-phenomenological spirituality: Definition, description, and measurement. *Journal of Humanistic Psychology, 28,* 5–18.

Ellis, A. (1980). Counseling and atheistic values: A response to A. E. Bergin's "Counseling and religious values." *Journal of Counseling and Clinical Psychology, 48,* 635–639.

Ellison, C. (1991). Religious involvement and subjective well-being. *Journal of Health and Social Behavior, 32,* 80–99.

Ellison, C., & George, L. (1994). Religious involvement, social ties, and social support in a southeastern community. *Journal for the Scientific Study of Religion, 33,* 46–61.

Eriksen, K. (2006). Robert Kegan, Ph.D.: Subject-object theory and family counseling. *The Family Journal, 14*(3), 1–9.

Eriksen, K., Marston, G., & Korte, T. (2002). Working with God: Managing conservative Christian beliefs that may interfere with counseling. *Counseling and Values, 47,* 48–72.

Esau, T. G. (1998). The evangelical Christian in counseling. *American Journal of Counseling, 52,* 28–36.

Faiver, C., & Ingersoll, R. E. (2005). Knowing one's limits. In C. S. Cashwell & J. S. Young (Eds.), *Integrating spirituality and religion into counseling* (pp. 169–183). Alexandria, VA: American Counseling Association.

Firth, R. (1996). *Religion: A humanist interpretation.* London, UK: Routledge.

Fowler, J. W. (1981). *Stages of faith: The psychology of human development and the quest for meaning.* San Francisco, CA: Harper & Row.

Fowler, J. W. (1991). Stages in faith consciousness. *New Directions for Child Development, 52,* 27–45.

Fowler, J. W. (2004). Stages of faith and identity: Birth to teens. *Child and Adolescent Clinics of North America, 13,* 17–33.

Frame, M. W. (2003). *Integrating religion and spirituality into counseling.* Pacific Grove, CA: Brooks/Cole.

Gallup. (2012). Religion. Retrieved from http://www.gallup.com/poll/1690/religion.aspx

Gaustad, P. L., & Dishno, R. W. (2000). *New historical atlas of religion in America.* New York, NY: Oxford University Press.

Genia, V. (2000). Religious issues in secularly based counseling. *Counseling and Values, 44,* 213–222.

Goodman, R. (1983). *A developmental and systems analysis of marital and family communication in clinic and non-clinic families* (Unpublished doctoral dissertation). Harvard University, Cambridge, MA.

Gordon, P. A., Feldman, D., Crose, R., Schoen, E., Griffing, G., & Shankar, J. (2002). The role of religious beliefs in coping with chronic illness. *Counseling and Values, 46,* 162–174.

Goud, N. (1990). Spiritual and ethical beliefs of humanists in the counseling profession. *Counseling and Values, 68,* 571–574.

Greenwald, J. M. (1991). *Environmental attitudes: A structural developmental model* (Unpublished doctoral dissertation). University of Massachusetts, Amherst, MA.

Griffith, B. A., & Griggs, J. C. (2001). Religious identity status as a model to understand, assess, and interact with client spirituality. *Counseling and Values, 46,* 14–25.

Guiso, L., Sapienza, P., & Zingales, L. (2003). People's opium? Religion and economic attitudes. *Journal of Monetary Economics, 50,* 225–282.

Hagedorn, W. B. (2005). Counselor self-awareness and self-exploration of religious and spiritual beliefs: Know thyself. In C. S. Cashwell & J. S. Young (Eds.), *Integrating spirituality and religion into counseling* (pp. 63–84). Alexandria, VA: American Counseling Association.

Hanh, N. (1999). *The heart of the Buddha's teaching: Transforming suffering into peace, joy, and liberation.* New York, NY: Broadway.

Hannon, J. W., Howie, C. C., & Keener, R. J. (1994). Counseling conservative and fundamentalist Christians: Issues and implications for the counselor. *Journal of Humanistic Education and Development, 32,* 121–132.

Harper, M. C., & Gill, C. S. (2005). Assessing the client's spiritual domain. In C. S. Cashwell & J. S. Young (Eds.), *Integrating spirituality and religion into counseling* (pp. 31–62). Alexandria, VA: American Counseling Association.

Hartz, G. W. (2005). *Spirituality and mental health.* New York, NY: Haworth Pastoral Press.

Heilman, S. C., & Cohen, S. M. (1989). *Cosmopolitans and parochials: Modern Orthodox Jews in America.* Chicago, IL: University of Chicago Press.

Helminiak, D. A. (2001). Treating spiritual issues in secular counseling. *Counseling and Values, 45,* 163–189.

Hinterkopf, E. (1994). Integrating spiritual experiences in counseling. *Counseling and Values, 38,* 165–175.

Hoge, D. (1996). Religion in America: The demographics of belief and affiliation. In E. Shafranske (Ed.), *Religion and the clinical practice of psychology* (pp. 21–41). Washington, DC: American Psychological Association.

Holifield, E. B. (1983). *A history of pastoral care in America: From salvation to self-realization.* Nashville, TN: Abingdon.

Holy Bible. (1983). Grand Rapids, MI: Zondervan.

Hood, R. W., Spilka, B., Hunsberger, B., & Gorsuch, R. (1996). *The psychology of religion: An empirical approach* (2nd ed.). New York, NY: Guilford Press.

Idler, E. L. (1995). Religion, health, and nonphysical senses of self. *Social Forces, 74,* 683–704.

Ingersoll, R. E. (1995). Spirituality, religion, and counseling: Dimensions and relationships. In M. T. Burke & J. G. Miranti (Eds.), *Counseling: The spiritual dimension* (pp. 5–18). Alexandria, VA: American Counseling Association.

Jacobs, J. (1984). *Holding environment and developmental stages: A study of marriage* (Unpublished doctoral dissertation). Harvard University, Cambridge, MA.

Jankowski, P. J. (2002). Postmodern spirituality: Implications for promoting change. *Counseling and Values, 46,* 69–79.

Johnson, W. B., & Johnson, W. L. (1997). Counseling conservatively religious fathers: Salient treatment issues. *Journal of Psychology and Christianity, 16,* 36–50.

Jones, S. (1994). A constructive relationship for religion with the science and profession of psychology: Perhaps the boldest model yet. *American Psychologist, 49,* 184–199.

Kegan, R. (1982). *The evolving self.* Cambridge, MA: Harvard University Press.

Kegan, R. (1998). *In over our heads.* Cambridge, MA: Harvard University Press.

Keller, R. R. (1999). Religious diversity in North America. In P. S. Richards & A. E. Bergin (Eds.), *Handbook of counseling and religious diversity* (pp. 27–55). Washington, DC: American Psychological Association.

Kelly, E. W., Jr. (1995). *Spirituality and religion in counseling and psychotherapy: Diversity in theory and practice.* Alexandria, VA: American Counseling Association.

Kluegel, J. R. (1980). Denominational mobility: Current patterns and recent trends. *Journal for the Scientific Study of Religion, 19,* 26–40.

Koenig, H. G., George, L. K., & Peterson, B. L. (1998). Religiosity and remission from depression in medically ill older patients. *American Journal of Psychiatry, 155,* 536–542.

Kohlberg, L. (1981). *The philosophy of moral development.* San Francisco, CA: Harper & Row.

Kosmin, B. A., & Keysar, A. (2009). *American religious identification survey [ARIS 2008]: Summary report.* Retrieved from http://commons.trincoll.edu/aris/files/2011/08/ARIS_Report_2008.pdf

Kosmin, B. A., Mayer, E., & Keysar, A. (2001). *American religious identification survey, 2001.* New York: City University of New York, Graduate Center.

Kumar, M., Bhugra, D., & Singh. J. (2005). South Asian (Indian) traditional healing: Ayurvedic, Shamanic, and Sahaja counseling. In R. Moodley & W. West (Eds.), *Integrating traditional healing practices into counseling and psychotherapy* (pp. 112–121). Thousand Oaks, CA: Sage.

Lahey, L. (1986). *Males' and females' construction of conflict in work and love* (Unpublished doctoral dissertation). Harvard University, Cambridge, MA.

Landis, B. (1996). Uncertainty, spiritual well-being, and psychosocial adjustment to chronic illness. *Issues in Mental Health Nursing, 17,* 217–231.

Larson, D., Wood, G., & Larson, S. (1993). A paradigm shift in medicine toward spirituality. *ADVANCE: The Journal of Mind-Body Health, 9,* 39–49.

Levin, J. S., & Chatters, L. M. (1998). Religion, health, and psychological well-being in older adults. *Journal of Aging and Health, 10,* 504–531.

Levin, J. S., & Taylor, R. J. (1998). Panel analyses of religious involvement and well-being in African Americans: Contemporaneous vs. longitudinal effects. *Journal for the Scientific Study of Religion, 37,* 695–709.

Loevinger, J. (1976). *Ego development.* San Francisco, CA: Jossey-Bass.

Lovell, C. W. (1999). Empathic-cognitive development in students of counseling. *Journal of Adult Development, 6,* 195–203.

Lovinger, R. J. (1979). Therapeutic strategies with "religious" resistances. *Counseling: Theory, Research, and Practice, 16,* 419–427.

Lovinger, R. J. (1996). Considering the religious dimension in assessment and counseling. In E. P. Shafranske (Ed.), *Religion and the clinical practice of psychology* (pp. 327–364). Washington, DC: American Psychological Association.

Magaletta, P. R., & Brawer, P. A. (1998). Prayer in counseling: A model for its use, ethical considerations, and guidelines for practice. *Journal of Psychology and Theology, 26,* 322–330.

McAuliffe, G. J. (2009). *Culturally alert counseling DVD: Working with religiously conservative clients.* Thousand Oaks, CA: Sage.

McAuliffe, G. J., & Eriksen, K. P. (1999). Toward a constructivist and developmental identity for the counseling profession: The context-phase-stage-style model. *Journal of Counseling and Development, 77,* 267–280.

McAuliffe, G. J., & Lovell, C. W. (2006). The influence of counselor epistemology on the helping interview: A qualitative study. *Journal of Counseling and Development, 84,* 308–317.

McCullough, M. E., & Larson, D. B. (1999). Prayer. In W. R. Miller (Ed.), *Integrating spirituality into counseling: Resources for practitioners* (pp. 85–110). Washington, DC: American Psychological Association.

Miller, W. R. (Ed.). (1999). *Integrating spirituality into counseling: Resources for practitioners.* Washington, DC: American Psychological Association.

Miranti, J., & Burke, M. T. (1995). Spirituality: An integral component of the counseling process. In M. T. Burke & J. G. Miranti (Eds.), *Counseling: The spiritual dimension* (pp. 5-18). Alexandria, VA: American Counseling Association.

Moberg, D. O., & Brused, P. M. (1978). Spiritual well-being: A neglected subject in quality of life research. *Social Indicators Research, 5,* 303–323.

Mueller, S. A., & Lane, A. V. (1972). Tabulations from the 1957 Current Population Survey of Religion: A contribution to the demography of American religion. *Journal for the Scientific Study of Religion, 11,* 76–98.

Muramoto, S. (2002). Buddhism, religion and counseling in the world today. In P. Young-Eisendrath (Ed.), *Awakening and insight: Zen Buddhism and counseling* (pp. 15–29). New York, NY: Brunner-Routledge.

Myers, J. E. (1990). Wellness through the lifespan. *Guidepost, 32,* 11.

Nathanson, I. (1995). Divorce and women's spirituality. *Journal of Divorce and Remarriage, 22,* 179–188.

Neukrug, E. S., & McAuliffe, G. (1993). Cognitive development and human services education. *Human Services Education, 13,* 13–26.

Newport, F. (2009a). *Religious identity: States differ widely.* Retrieved from http://www.gallup.com/poll/122075/Religious-Identity-States-Differ-Widely.aspx

Newport, F. (2009b). *State of the states: Importance of religion.* Retrieved from http://www.gallup.com/poll/114022/state-states-importance-religion.aspx

Newport, F. (2010). *In U.S., increasing number have no religious identity.* Retrieved from http://www.gallup.com/poll/128276/increasing-number-no-religious-identity.aspx

Newport, F., Witters, D., Agrawal, S. (2010). *Religious Americans enjoy higher wellbeing.* Retrieved from http://www.gallup.com/poll/152723/Religious-Americans-Enjoy-Higher-Wellbeing.aspx

Nino, A. (1997). Assessment of spiritual quests in clinical practice. *International Journal of Counseling, 2,* 193–212.

O'Connor, M. (2002). Spiritual dark night and psychological depression: Some comparisons and contrasts. *Counseling and Values, 46,* 137–149.

Pargament, K. I. (2002). The bitter and the sweet: An evaluation of the costs and benefits of religiousness. *Psychological Inquiry, 13,* 168–181.

Patterson, J., Hayworth, M., Turner, C., & Raskin, M. (2000). Spiritual issues in family counseling: A graduate-level course. *Journal of Marital and Family Counseling, 26,* 199–210.

Perry, W. G. (1970). *Forms of intellectual and ethical development in the college years: A scheme.* New York, NY: Holt, Rinehart & Winston.

Petersen, W. (2003). Social consequences of religion. *Society, 40,* 53–57.

Pew Forum on Religion & Public Life. (2008). U.S. religious landscape survey Report 1: Religious affiliation. Retrieved from http://religions.pewforum.org/reports

Post, B. C., & Wade, N. G. (2009). Religion and spirituality in psychotherapy: A practice-friendly review of research. *Journal of Clinical Psychology, 65,* 131–146.

Prest, L. A., & Keller, J. F. (1993). Spirituality and family counseling: Spiritual beliefs, myths, and metaphors. *Journal of Marital and Family Counseling, 19,* 132–148.

Richards, P. S., & Bergin, A. E. (1999). Toward religious and spiritual competency for mental health professionals. In P. S. Richards & A. E. Bergin (Eds.), *Handbook of counseling and religious diversity* (pp. 3–26). Washington, DC: American Psychological Association.

Richards, P. S., & Bergin, A. E. (2005). Western and Eastern spiritual worldviews. In P. S. Richards & A. E. Bergin (Eds.), *A spiritual strategy for counseling and psychotherapy* (pp. 49–74). Washington, DC: American Psychological Association.

Richards, P. S., & Potts, R. W. (1995). Using spiritual interventions in counseling: Practices, successes, failures, and ethical concerns of Mormon psychocounselors. *Professional Psychology: Research and Practice, 26,* 163–170.

Ridley, C. R. (1985). Imperatives for ethnic and cultural relevance in psychology training programs. *Professional Psychology: Research and Practice, 16,* 611–622.

Roy, N. S. (1993). *Toward an understanding of family functioning: An analysis of the relationship between family and individual organizing principles* (Unpublished doctoral dissertation). Harvard Graduate School of Education, Cambridge, MA.

Sanderson, C., & Linehan, M. M. (1999). Acceptance and forgiveness. In W. R. Miller (Ed.), *Integrating spirituality into counseling: Resources for practitioners* (pp. 199–216). Washington, DC: American Psychological Association.

Saroglou, V. (2002). Religion and the five factors of personality: A meta-analytic review. *Personality and Individual Differences, 32,* 15–25.

Schneer, D. (2002). *Queer Jews.* New York, NY: Routledge.

Seymour, E. (2005). Pagan approaches to healing. In R. Moodley (Ed.), *Integrating traditional healing practices into* counseling *and psychotherapy* (pp. 233–245). Thousand Oaks, CA: Sage.

Shafranske, E. (1996). Religious beliefs, affiliations, and practices of clinical psychologists. In E. Shafranske (Ed.), *Religion and the clinical practice of psychology* (pp. 149–162). Washington, DC: American Psychological Association.

Shafranske, E. P. (2005). A psychoanalytic approach to spiritually oriented counseling. In L. Sperry & E. P. Shafranske (Eds.), *Spiritually oriented counseling* (pp. 105–130). Washington, DC: American Psychological Association.

Shafranske, E., & Malony, H. (1990). Clinical psychologists' religious and spiritual orientations and their practice of counseling. *Counseling, 27,* 72–78.

Shafranske, E., & Malony, H. (1996). Religion and the clinical practice of psychology: A case for inclusion. In E. Shafranske (Ed.), *Religion and the clinical*

practice of psychology (pp. 561–586). Washington, DC: American Psychological Association.

Silk, M. (2005). Religion and region in American public life. *Journal for the Scientific Study of Religion, 44,* 265–270.

Smith, C., Faris, R., Denton, M. L., & Regnerus, M. (2003). Mapping American adolescent subjective religiosity and attitudes of alienation toward religion: A research report. *Sociology of Religion, 64,* 111–123.

Sonnenschein, P. C. (1990). *The development of mutually satisfying relationships between adult daughters and their mothers* (Unpublished doctoral dissertation). Harvard Graduate School of Education, Cambridge, MA.

Spero, M. H. (1982). Countertransference in religious counselors of religious patients. *American Journal of Counseling, 35,* 565–575.

Sperry, L., & Shafranske, E. P. (Eds.). (2005). *Spiritually oriented counseling.* Washington, DC: American Psychological Association.

Spinney, D. H. (1991). How do fundamental Christians deal with depression? *Counseling and Values, 35,* 114–128.

Stifoss-Hanssen, H. (1999). Religion and spirituality: What a European ear hears. *International Journal for the Psychology of Religion, 9,* 25–33.

Tan, S. Y. (1987). Cognitive-behavior counseling: A biblical approach and critique. *Journal of Psychology and Theology, 15,* 103–112.

Tan, S. Y. (1996a). Practicing the presence of God: The work of Richard J. Foster and its applications to psychotherapeutic practice. *Journal of Psychology and Christianity, 15,* 17–28.

Tan, S. Y. (1996b). Religion in clinical practice: Implicit and explicit integration. In E. Shafranske (Ed.), *Religion and the clinical practice of psychology* (pp. 365–387). Washington, DC: American Psychological Association.

Tan, S. Y., & Johnson, W. B. (2005). Spiritually oriented cognitive-behavioral counseling. In L. Sperry & E. P. Shafranske (Eds.), *Spiritually oriented counseling* (pp. 77–103). Washington, DC: American Psychological Association.

Taylor, C. Z. (2002). Religious addiction: Obsession with spirituality. *Pastoral Psychology, 50,* 291–315.

Tillich, P. (1959). *Theology of culture.* New York, NY: Oxford University Press.

Unger, M. F. (1966). *Unger's Bible dictionary* (3rd ed.). Chicago, IL: Moody Press.

Unitarian Universalist Association of Congregations. (1996–2012a). *Abortion: Right to choose.* Retrieved from http://www.uua.org/statements/statements/20271.shtml

Unitarian Universalist Association of Congregations. (1996–2012b). *Our Unitarian Universalist principles.* Retrieved from http://www.uua.org/beliefs/principles

Wade, N. G., & Worthington, E. L., Jr. (2003). *Religious and spiritual interventions in counseling: An effectiveness study of Christian counseling* (Unpublished manuscript). Iowa State University and Virginia Commonwealth University.

Wiggins-Frame, M. (2005). Spirituality and religion: Similarities and differences. In C. S. Cashwell & J. S. Young (Eds.), *Integrating spirituality and religion into counseling* (pp. 11–29). Alexandria, VA: American Counseling Association.

Winarsky, M. (1991). *AIDS-related counseling.* New York, NY: Pergamon.

Wolitzky, D. L. (1995). The theory and practice of traditional psychoanalytic counseling. In A. S. Gurman & S. B. Messer (Eds.), *Essential psychotherapies: Theory and practice* (pp. 12–54). New York, NY: Guilford Press.

Wong, P. T. (1998). Spirituality, meaning, and successful aging. In P. T. Wong & P. S. Fry (Eds.), *The human quest for meaning: A handbook of psychological research and clinical applications* (pp. 359–394). Mahwah, NJ: Lawrence Erlbaum.

Woodward, K. L. (1997, March 31). Is God listening? *Newsweek,* pp. 56–64.

Worthington, E. (1978). The effects of imagery content, choice of imagery content, and self-verbalization on the self-control of pain. *Cognitive Counseling and Research, 2,* 225–240.

Worthington, E. L., Jr., & Aten, J. D. (2009). Psychotherapy with religious and spiritual clients: An introduction. *Journal of Clinical Psychology, 65,* 123–130.

Wulff, D. (1997). *Psychology of religion: Classic and contemporary* (2nd ed.). New York, NY: Wiley.

Wuthnow, R. (2004). *Saving America? Faith-based services and the future of civil society.* Princeton, NJ: Princeton University Press.

Yahne, C. E., & Miller, W. R. (1999). Evoking hope. In W. R. Miller (Ed.), *Integrating spirituality into counseling: Resources for practitioners* (pp. 217–233). Washington, DC: American Psychological Association.

Yarhouse, M. A. (1999). When psychologists work with religious clients: Applications of the general principles of ethical conduct. *Professional Psychology: Research and Practice, 30,* 557–562.

CHAPTER 17

Counseling Individuals With Disabilities

Yvette Q. Getch
University of Georgia

Adrianne L. Johnson
State University of New York at Oswego

Paul is a white 19-year-old male who is about to graduate, but he will not be receiving a regular high school diploma. He is described by teachers as responsible, friendly, polite, and a hard worker. Paul has excellent social skills and gets along well with others. He has difficulty calculating math problems beyond addition and subtraction, and he reads at a second-grade level. However, he is an avid sports fan who can tell you all kinds of interesting facts and stats in regard to his favorite baseball team. Paul is able to make people laugh, and people genuinely seem to enjoy his company. However, Paul has difficulty with more than three-step directions and becomes frustrated when presented with difficult problems to solve. He is enthusiastic about becoming a doctor like his mom and dad. Paul has refused to look at other options even when his parents and school counselor explained how his reading and math skills were not at the level to be successful in college. Paul would counter that he would just work hard and improve these skills.

Paul's school counselor is concerned about how to approach Paul in regard to his career aspirations. After the counselor met with Paul and his parents, it became obvious that although Paul's parents have tried to get Paul to look at different career options, he is still adamant that he wants to be a doctor. The school counselor doesn't want to crush his ambitious nature and enthusiasm, but Paul has a significant intellectual disability and will not be receiving a regular high school diploma. The school counselor has been working with Paul's vocational rehabilitation counselor so that they can empower Paul to make career decisions that will fit for him. Paul's parents are encouraging and supportive but also are unsure about how to approach the issue of career choice with Paul.

You are invited to think about counseling in the case of Paul by responding to Activity 17.1.

Activity 17.1 The Case of Paul

1. What are some of the questions the counselor might have when preparing to work with Paul?

2. What counseling approaches might be best?

3. What things need to be taken into consideration regarding Paul's intellectual disability?

4. What are several strategies that could be used to assist Paul in the career exploration and decision-making process?

INTRODUCTION

This chapter is an exploration of disability and the issues that arise when counseling individuals with disabilities and their families. The chapter is organized in the following fashion. First is an overview of disability, including descriptions of different disabilities, common barriers faced by individuals with disabilities, and legislation that has been passed to protect the civil and employment rights of individuals with disabilities. After these basics have been presented, explanations and examples of key concepts, including ableism, spread, interaction strain, self-determination, empowerment, bias in counseling, bias in assessment, and the importance of language use, are addressed. Once these have been covered, implications for counseling practice and the need for social justice advocacy are presented.

Perhaps the most neglected, misunderstood, and marginalized group of individuals with whom counselors work is individuals with disabilities. While on the surface this may seem to be a bold statement, the mere fact that so little is included in counseling texts about individuals with disabilities gives credence to this statement. More than 49 million Americans age 5 and older have a disability, making persons with disabilities the largest group of traditionally marginalized people other than women (Center for the Critical Analysis of Social Difference, 2008; Lahmann, 2009; Waldrop & Stern, 2003).

Disability happens to people. Anyone can become a part of this marginalized and oppressed group at any time during her or his life. People are injured, become ill, or become disabled as a result of hereditary conditions or trauma at or after birth. Disability does not discriminate. That point is made dramatically by these words: "People with disabilities constitute our nation's largest minority group, which is simultaneously the most inclusive and the most diverse. Everyone is represented: of all genders, all ages, all religions, all socioeconomic levels and all ethnic backgrounds" (The ARC, 2012, para. 2).

While disability is not a culture in a traditional sense, individuals with disabilities experience similar barriers, prejudices, oppression, and marginalization. Counselors have an ethical responsibility to acquire the knowledge needed to work with individuals with varying abilities, needs, and desires (ACA [2005] *Code of Ethics*, A.1; American Psychological Association, 2010a). If counselors are truly social justice advocates, then they must educate themselves about the needs, issues, career goals, life goals, and barriers faced by individuals with disabilities.

This chapter provides a basis for counselors to understand, first, the issues faced by individuals with disabilities and, second, the attitudes, knowledge, and skills that counselors must acquire to work successfully with persons with disabilities. To begin this process, you are invited to assess your current beliefs about disabilities by completing Activity 17.2.

Activity 17.2   Self-Assessment of Counselor Beliefs About Disabilities

Choose your level of agreement with each of the following statements by writing in the corresponding number from the scale below.

Strongly Disagree	Disagree	Neither Agree Nor Disagree	Agree	Strongly Agree
1	2	3	4	5

_____ 1. People with disabilities are limited in their choices of careers.

_____ 2. Individuals with visual disabilities are not likely to become effective counselors because they are unable to see the nonverbal behaviors of the persons they will serve.

_____ 3. People with intellectual disabilities are not able to learn complicated information.

_____ 4. People who experience paralysis are not able to enjoy sexual activities.

_____ 5. People with disabilities can live full and meaningful lives.

_____ 6. I would feel comfortable in a romantic/physical relationship with an individual with a physical disability.

_____ 7. People with disabilities must overcome their disability.

_____ 8. Successful people with disabilities are courageous.

_____ 9. People with cerebral palsy who have speech impairments also have intellectual disabilities.

_____ 10. All people with Down syndrome are friendly and happy.

_____ 11. Employment opportunities for people with intellectual disabilities are limited to jobs like busing tables, custodial positions, stocking positions, and greeter positions.

_____ 12. People with disabilities often seek counseling to adjust to their disability.

(Continued)

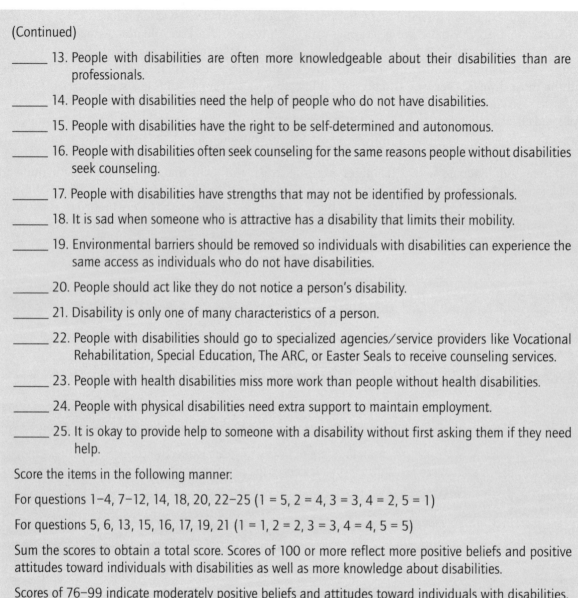

(Continued)

_____ 13. People with disabilities are often more knowledgeable about their disabilities than are professionals.

_____ 14. People with disabilities need the help of people who do not have disabilities.

_____ 15. People with disabilities have the right to be self-determined and autonomous.

_____ 16. People with disabilities often seek counseling for the same reasons people without disabilities seek counseling.

_____ 17. People with disabilities have strengths that may not be identified by professionals.

_____ 18. It is sad when someone who is attractive has a disability that limits their mobility.

_____ 19. Environmental barriers should be removed so individuals with disabilities can experience the same access as individuals who do not have disabilities.

_____ 20. People should act like they do not notice a person's disability.

_____ 21. Disability is only one of many characteristics of a person.

_____ 22. People with disabilities should go to specialized agencies/service providers like Vocational Rehabilitation, Special Education, The ARC, or Easter Seals to receive counseling services.

_____ 23. People with health disabilities miss more work than people without health disabilities.

_____ 24. People with physical disabilities need extra support to maintain employment.

_____ 25. It is okay to provide help to someone with a disability without first asking them if they need help.

Score the items in the following manner:

For questions 1–4, 7–12, 14, 18, 20, 22–25 (1 = 5, 2 = 4, 3 = 3, 4 = 2, 5 = 1)

For questions 5, 6, 13, 15, 16, 17, 19, 21 (1 = 1, 2 = 2, 3 = 3, 4 = 4, 5 = 5)

Sum the scores to obtain a total score. Scores of 100 or more reflect more positive beliefs and positive attitudes toward individuals with disabilities as well as more knowledge about disabilities.

Scores of 76–99 indicate moderately positive beliefs and attitudes toward individuals with disabilities.

Scores of 26–75 indicate slightly negative beliefs and attitudes toward individuals with disabilities as well as less knowledge about disabilities.

Scores of 25 or less indicate negative beliefs and attitudes toward individuals with disabilities and limited knowledge of disabilities.

Many barriers faced by individuals with disabilities are attitudinally or environmentally imposed, rather than physical or internal (The ARC, 2012; Gray, Gould, & Bickenbach, 2003; Miller, Chen, Glover-Graf, & Kranz, 2009; North Carolina Department of Health and Human Services, 2012; Pivik, McComas, Laflamme, 2002; Van der Klift & Kunc, 1994; Ware, Hopper, Tugenberg, Dickey,

& Fisher, 2007). For example, a meeting where chairs are placed so close together that it makes it difficult for individuals with mobility disabilities to navigate the space creates a physical/environmental barrier. Inadequate space sends the message that the space is not for persons with mobility difficulties. In other words, "We did not expect you, and you are not welcome."

A less noticeable attitudinal barrier occurs when people offer someone too much help. Too much help or help that is forced upon someone is disempowering and disrespectful (Van der Klift & Kunc, 1994). An example of too much help is when a person with a disability is denied the opportunity to finish a task. This often happens because someone who does not have a disability feels the need to finish the task for the person who has a disability. The person who does not have the disability finishes the task without first asking if help is needed or wanted. Indeed, success or failure, as well as completion or incompletion of tasks, often has little to do with the individual's capabilities but instead has much to do with how society limits the potential of individuals with disabilities (Pivik et al., 2002; Van der Klift & Kunc, 1994; Ware et al., 2007).

THE CAPABILITIES APPROACH

This chapter introduces the Capabilities Approach (Ware et al., 2007), which takes into account what individuals can do and what they can be in everyday life. Such capacity is called the *degree of human agency*. A person's capabilities are in large part dependent on the opportunities provided. In other words, situations must offer chances for the individual to develop and practice skills (Ware et al., 2007). Without the opportunity to develop or practice skills, individuals are unlikely to exercise the very skills that are necessary to fully participate in their community. Check your own attitudes by responding to the questions in Activity 17.3.

Activity 17.3 Attitudes and Disability in the Case of Paul

Go back and review the case of Paul. After reading the case again, ask yourself the following questions:

1. What are your biases and assumptions as you ponder Paul's career dilemma?

2. What tools would you use from your toolbox, and how would you use them?

3. What are your initial thoughts and ideas regarding how you would approach career counseling with Paul?

4. Be honest, what do you think Paul can do for a career?

5. Write down your feelings about working with Paul. Do you have the knowledge and skills needed to empower him?

Many times full participation in society is thwarted by the attitudes, biases, and stereotypes that professionals hold (The ARC, 2012; Henderson & Bryan, 2011; Special Olympics, 2003; Van der Klift & Kunc, 1994; Ware et al., 2007). The story in Box 17.1 illustrates how professionals can limit the full participation of individuals with disabilities by assuming they have limitations based on their disability. The assumption of limitations can itself create barriers to participation.

Box 17.1   Knowledge Is Power

Several years ago a researcher initiated a self-advocacy program to assist a group of students who were deaf and attending public schools. The program provided students with instruction on how to direct their own Individualized Educational Program (IEP) meetings, information about their educational rights, and instruction on how to manage an interpreter. IEP meetings are typically attended by teachers, professionals, parents, and the child with a disability to develop an individualized plan to support children with disabilities in their academic progress. All of the program participants were deaf and used American Sign Language as their primary form of communication. Thus, an interpreter was needed to translate information from spoken English into the visual language of American Sign Language.

At the beginning of the fall semester, the group leader called the researcher. She was excited because a middle school student had, in her words, "put into practice" what he had learned. The group leader explained that the student, Don, received his class schedule for the fall semester and noticed that he had art for an elective. Don did not like art and wanted to take music. He approached his advisor and said that he wanted music instead of art. His advisor proceeded to tell him that he could not take music. When he inquired as to why he could not sign up for music the advisor replied, "Because you are deaf." Don then asked if other students were able to choose their electives and the advisor said, "Yes." Don then said, "If other students get to choose their elective, then I have a right to choose mine. I choose music." Needless to say, Don was able to take music. However, he did not stop there. A friend of his who was also deaf was registered for art. Don asked his friend if he wanted to take art and his friend said, "No, I want to take music." Then Don replied, "Remember what we learned this summer. It is your right; you can take music." Both students took music.

The story in Box 17.1 is an example of what can happen when counselors and other professionals provide information to students and help them learn skills to successfully advocate on their own behalf. It is also an example of how counselors may limit the choices and experiences of students with disabilities based on the counselor's own prejudices, biases, and limited knowledge. Being deaf or hard of hearing does not preclude someone from enjoying music or playing a musical instrument. People's biases, prejudices, limited knowledge, and attitudes can limit individuals from fully participating in opportunities that others freely enjoy.

You are invited to complete Activity 17.4 to assess your experience of the issues around disability.

Counselors are in a unique position to advocate on behalf of and with individuals with disabilities. To be social justice advocates, counselors must understand the issues and barriers encountered by persons with disabilities. Understanding disability includes being aware of the social context whereby individuals with disabilities experience marginalization and oppression (Mackelprang & Salsgiver, 2009).

The next section provides the federal definitions of disability as well as descriptions of specific disabilities.

Part of learning to become a social justice advocate (see Chapter 3) is learning to recognize injustice when you encounter or witness it. When working with individuals with disabilities, it is important that counselors have an understanding of the discrimination, microaggressions, prejudices, and stereotypes faced by individuals with disabilities. To help you begin to identify the discrimination, stereotypes, and barriers to access that individuals with disabilities encounter, you need to begin to reflect on times when you may have witnessed or experienced injustice. First, write your responses to each of the following questions. After you have explored each of these questions alone and have written your responses, discuss your responses in pairs or in small groups.

1. Describe a time when you witnessed someone who was using a wheelchair having difficulty getting to a location due to the terrain, absence of ramps, absence of curb cuts, crowded spaces that did not provide enough space for a wheelchair, or other physical barriers.

2. Describe an event that you attended where closed captioning was not provided or where an interpreter for the deaf was not provided.

3. Describe a time when you interacted with a person with a physical disability and felt uncomfortable.

4. Describe a time when you witnessed someone making jokes about people with disabilities or using language in a way that degrades a person with a disability.

DEFINITIONS OF DISABILITY

To work effectively with individuals with disabilities, counselors need to have working definitions of disability-related concepts. This section provides such definitions of disability and describes major categories of disabling conditions. First, a legal definition of disability is provided, followed by organizational definitions of disability, and then descriptions of specific categories of disabling conditions.

Both Section 504 of the Rehabilitation Act (1973) and the 1990 Americans with Disabilities Act (ADA) consider a disability to be an impairment that substantially limits a major life activity. Major life activities are functions such as caring for oneself, performing manual tasks, walking, seeing, hearing, speaking, breathing, learning, and working (ADA, Part 104). To be "qualified" as having a disability, a person must have a physical or mental impairment that substantially limits one or more major life activities, have a record of such impairment, or be regarded as having such an impairment (Rehabilitation Act, 761a(i)(1)).

To assist you in understanding what disabilities are and how they may be substantially limiting, a description of the broad categories of disabilities is included below. Five major categories of disability are discussed: mobility and physical disabilities, sensory disabilities, health disabilities, psychological disabilities, and intellectual disabilities. In addition to these five major categories, two sub-categories (learning disabilities and disorders of attention) are also described.

Mobility and Physical Disabilities

Physical disabilities include those related to mobility, upper and/or lower limb disability, manual dexterity disability, or any disability that involves coordination with any of the body's organs (*Definition of Disabilities*, 2012). Additionally, physical disabilities are usually considered to be "either neurological or musculoskeletal in nature" (Bowe, 2000, p. 7). Examples of physical and mobility disabilities include spinal cord injuries, amputations, muscular dystrophy, restriction of limb movement due to stroke or disease, or spasticity or rigidness of muscles due to conditions such as cerebral palsy.

Sensory Disabilities

Major categories of sensory disabilities include vision and hearing disabilities. Visual impairment is considered along a continuum of loss of sight, including blindness. Blindness is often designated when the primary method of learning involves methods other than sight. Persons with low vision are considered to be able to still primarily learn information through sight (Farrell, 2011).

More specific definitions of blindness and low vision are as follows. In Bowe's (2000) words, "blindness is 20/200 vision or tunnel vision where the central vision subtends at an angle of 20% or less as measured with corrective lenses" (p. 254). Next on the scale is low vision, which is somewhere between 20/70 vision to 20/200 vision as measured with corrective lenses. Bowe explains that "the more useful question in education is whether the individual has enough residual vision (functional vision) to be able to use the eyes to learn or whether other senses (notably the ears and the fingers) must be used" (p. 255).

Individuals with hearing impairments can be classified as being either hard of hearing or deaf. In the first case, individuals who have mild/moderate hearing loss, that is, who are hard of hearing, can usually hear and understand speech but need the assistance of amplification (hearing aids) or speech reading. By contrast, individuals who are classified as deaf have a severe or profound hearing loss and are usually unable to hear and understand speech through the ear even with amplification (Bowe, 2000). A working definition of deafness is the "inability to hear and understand speech through the ear alone" (Schein, 1987, p. 5). This definition implies that the person cannot use hearing to understand speech. It acknowledges that a person who is deaf may indeed be able to hear speech but is not able to understand it. A person who is deaf understands speech by using additional means, including speech reading, context, sign language, visual cues, and perhaps other avenues as well (Schein, 1987).

Health Disabilities

Health disabilities or health impairments are often considered to be impairments that limit endurance or may be life threatening (Bowe, 2000). For a school-age child to be considered protected under the "Other Health Impaired" category, the child must have a chronic or acute health condition that limits her or his strength, vitality, or alertness (Hardman, Drew, & Egan, 1996). Examples of health impairments are asthma, sickle-cell disease, cancer, kidney disease, and cystic fibrosis. Additionally, attention deficit hyperactivity disorder (ADHD) is also often included under this category. The key is to remember that these conditions significantly impact a person's endurance, vitality, strength, alertness, or life activities in other ways (Bowe, 2000; Hardman et al., 1996).

Psychological Disabilities

Although the *Diagnostic and Statistical Manual of Mental Disorders* (American Psychiatric Association, 2000) provides a definition for *mental disability* that may be interchangeable with the more positive term *psychological disability*, a functional definition for psychological disabilities has been provided by Kanfer and Goldstein (1991). Generally speaking, individuals with psychological disabilities experience problems in their relations with others, in their perceptions of the world, or in their perceptions and attitudes toward the self. A more specific and workable definition of a psychological disability is a condition in which an individual (a) experiences fears, worries, and/or discomfort that are not easily resolved by themselves; (b) displays behavioral deficits or overly engages in behaviors that interfere with functioning; and (c) engages in behaviors that are considered deviant and result in severe consequences for self or others (Kanfer & Goldstein, 1991). This definition is useful because counselors can identify the behaviors and problems that are not easily resolved by the individual. Examples of psychological disabilities include anxiety disorders, depression, bipolar disorder, schizophrenia, and eating disorders (American Psychiatric Association, 2000).

It is important for counselors to note that the classification of psychological disorders classifies disorders, not people. For example, a person has schizophrenia. The person should not be referred to as a schizophrenic (American Psychiatric Association, 2000). This is *person-first* language. Person-first language is thoroughly discussed later in the chapter under the heading Language and Disability.

Intellectual Disabilities

Disabilities that affect the way individuals learn, perceive, and process information are often categorized as intellectual or cognitive disabilities. For counselors and other professionals, it is important to remember that the term *mental retardation* is outdated and has been increasingly replaced by the term *intellectual disability* (Schalock et al., 2007).

Major categories here include cognitive/intellectual disabilities, learning disabilities, and disorders of attention. These are discussed in the order presented. It is important to note that intellectual disabilities is a broad category and some professionals disagree about which disabilities should be included in it. For the purposes of this chapter, learning disabilities and disorders of attention (ADHD) are discussed as separate categories rather than being subsumed under intellectual disabilities.

An intellectual disability is a disability that originates before the age of 18 and is characterized by significant limitations in both intellectual functioning and adaptive behavior. These limitations are evident in everyday social and practical skills (American Association on Intellectual and Developmental Disabilities [AAIDD], 2012). An intellectual disability takes into account both intellectual and adaptive functioning. Intellectual functioning (intelligence) includes general mental capacity such as general reasoning, problem solving, and learning. Adaptive skills include conceptual skills (i.e., learning, calculation, language expression and acquisition, self-direction), social skills (i.e., understanding relationships, interpersonal skills, and social cues), and practical skills (i.e., activities of daily living, routines, healthcare, safety skills). The person's individual strengths and weaknesses as well as the community context must also be considered (AAIDD, 2012; Schalock et. al., 2007).

Learning Disabilities

Learning disabilities are generally described as those that affect a person's processing of information.

This broad definition is necessary because of the diverse characteristics that are present among individuals with learning disabilities. There are at least seven domains of learning disabilities: motor problems, perceptual deficits, attention deficits, memory disorders, language disorders, social perceptual disorders (difficulty in reading and understanding social cues or nonverbal cues in communication), and emotional overlay (emotional difficulties resulting from dealing with the learning disability, such as feelings of anger, isolation, low self-esteem, frustration; McNamara, 2007).

Although the category of learning disabilities has been described as "the most heterogeneous special education classification" (McNamara, 2007, p. 3), there are specific legal and diagnostic criteria for someone to qualify as having a learning disability. The current definition used to identify children for special education services is provided by the Individuals with Disabilities Education Improvement Act of 2004:

> Specific learning disability means a disorder in one or more of the basic psychological processes involved in understanding or in using language, spoken or written, that may manifest itself in the imperfect ability to listen, think, speak, read, write, spell, or to do mathematical calculations, including conditions such as perceptual disabilities, brain injury, minimal brain dysfunction, dyslexia, and developmental aphasia. (Section 300.8)

Counselors should keep in mind that the definition of learning disabilities includes the assumption that individuals have at least average intellectual capacities and exhibit a discrepancy between their potential and their achievement. Furthermore, the deficit is caused by dysfunctions in the central nervous system, and the deficits cannot be the result of another condition such as a visual or hearing disability or an economic or educational disadvantage (McNamara, 2007). The reauthorization of the Individuals with Disabilities Education Act also specifies what the definition of learning disabilities does not include: "Specific learning disability does not include learning problems that are primarily the result of visual, hearing, or motor disabilities, of mental retardation [*sic*], of emotional disturbance, or of environmental, cultural, or economic disadvantage" (Section 300.8).

Any individual who meets the criteria for learning disabilities may have deficits in linguistic, attention, and/or perceptual skills (American Psychiatric Association, 2000). However, counselors must keep in mind that these deficits cannot be due to another condition, and the individual must have at least average intellectual capabilities (McNamara, 2007).

As mentioned at the beginning of this section, the fundamental characteristic of learning disabilities is that such individuals have one or two overall characteristics: (1) problems processing information correctly (Levinson & Ohler, 1998; McNamara, 2007) and, in many cases, (2) the brain having difficulty handling the phonology or sounds of the language (Bowe, 2000; McNamara, 2007).

As a result of the deficits in processing, perception, and linguistics, many persons with learning disabilities find it difficult to learn information, organize information, plan their time, or remember things (Kavale & Forness, 1996; Learning Disabilities Association of America, 2005–2011). In addition, individuals with learning disabilities may have particular deficits in math reasoning skills, written expression, reading, and social skills (Kavale & Forness, 1996; Learning Disabilities Association of America, 2005–2011). It is also important to note that they may have consequent difficulty in self-assessing their own abilities, deficits, interests, and values, that is, they don't know what they don't know (Vogel & Adelman, 1992).

Unfortunately, persons with learning disabilities may attribute their difficulties to "not being smart" instead of to the specific learning disability. Counselors can facilitate positive self-regard by assisting these individuals in gaining knowledge about the learning disability and its impact on their performance. Assisting individuals in the self-management of their disability using cognitive-behavioral approaches and solution-based approaches is likely to facilitate positive integration of the disability as a characteristic of the self that does not totally define who they are as individuals.

Disorders of Attention

ADHD is a developmental disorder that consists of problems with self-control, attention span, impulse control, and level of activity. People with ADHD experience a wide variety of problems, including disorganization, poor time management, and difficulty paying attention for extended periods of time (Barkley, 2000; National Institute of Mental Health [NIMH], 2008). Children and adults with ADHD often have difficulty starting tasks, completing tasks, and meeting deadlines. Additionally, they tend to make impulsive decisions or act impulsively without adequate attention to details or consequences (NIMH, 2012).

Now that definitions of disability have been given, the chapter turns to the evolution of legislation protecting and supporting individuals with disabilities. The next section provides an overview of relevant legislation, the Disability Rights Movement, and the Independent Living Movement.

EARLY DISABILITY LEGISLATION AND DISABILITY MOVEMENTS

Understanding disability from a historical perspective will provide you with an appreciation of the importance of legislation as well as the grassroots efforts of individuals with disabilities striving to receive the same access and opportunities afforded to their fellow citizens. Toward that end, this section first provides a historical backdrop to disability and early legislation. Then the Disability and Independent Living Movements are introduced, followed by a discussion of recent legislation.

Historical Perspective

War and injured soldiers returning from war have repeatedly been precursors to federal assistance for persons with disabilities. One of the first federal acts providing assistance to veterans who had become disabled during World War I was the Soldier Rehabilitation Act of 1918. This act authorized the provision of vocational rehabilitation services for veterans who had become disabled. Just 2 short years later, in 1920, the Smith-Fess Act was passed. This act extended the provision of vocational services to civilians with physical disabilities.

Individuals with disabilities would have to wait 23 more years before any other significant legislation was passed. In 1943, during World War II, the Barden-Lafollette Act was passed. Although this act was not directly related to the needs of veterans with disabilities, it was passed during wartime when the needs for goods and services to support the war effort increased. The Barden-Lafollette Act extended rehabilitation services to individuals with mental illness, mental retardation, and also provided support to individuals who were blind by establishing the state–federal program for persons who are blind (Jenkins, Patterson, & Szymanski, 1998).

Each of the previously mentioned pieces of legislation was instrumental in laying the foundation for the Disability Rights Movement and future legislation.

The Disability Rights Movement

The Disability Rights Movement began in the 1960s, sparked by the examples of the African American civil rights and women's rights movements (Frum, 2001). The Disability Rights Movement is aimed at securing equal opportunities and equal rights for people with disabilities. The three specific goals and demands of the movement were, and are, (1) accessibility and safety in transportation, architecture, and the physical environment; (2) equal opportunities in independent living, employment, education, and housing; and (3) freedom from abuse, neglect, and violations of patients' rights (Bagenstos, 2009).

One of the most important developments of the Disability Rights Movement was the growth of the Independent Living Movement, which emerged in California in the 1960s through the efforts of Edward Roberts and John Hessler, who were the first students with severe spinal cord injuries to live on the University of California at Berkeley campus. The Independent Living Movement, a subset of the Disability Rights Movement, emphasizes that people with disabilities are the best experts on their own needs, and therefore they must take the initiative, individually and collectively, in designing and promoting better solutions and must organize themselves for political power (Bagenstos, 2009; Varela, 1983). For example, advocates for the rights of people with mental illnesses focus mainly on self-determination and an individual's ability to live independently (Barnartt & Scotch, 2001).

The Disability Rights Movement and the Independent Living Movement represent the collective efforts of many individuals with disabilities. As a result of these efforts, legislation came to focus on nondiscrimination and the rights of individuals with disabilities.

The Rehabilitation Act of 1973

The Rehabilitation Act of 1973 serves as an umbrella of important disability legislation consisting of a variety of regulations. Section 504 of the act, which went into effect in 1977, prohibits discrimination based on disability in all institutions that receive federal funds. Buildings constructed or altered after June 3, 1977, were required to comply with the relevant accessibility code mandated by Section 504, which states, "No otherwise qualified individual in the United States shall, solely by reason of disability, be excluded from participation in, be denied the benefits of, or be subjected to discrimination under any program or activity receiving federal financial assistance." Thus Section 504, as well as Sections 501 and 503, of this law prohibit discrimination in federal programs and services and all other programs or services receiving federal funds (Regents of the University of California, 2008).

This was the first civil rights law guaranteeing equal opportunity for people with disabilities. However, in 1977, Joseph Califano, U.S. Secretary of Health, Education and Welfare, refused to sign meaningful regulations for Section 504. After an ultimatum and deadline, demonstrations took place in 10 U.S. cities on April 5 of that year. The demonstration at the San Francisco Office of the U.S. Department of Health, Education and Welfare,

led by Judith Heumann, became the longest sit-in at a federal building to date. More than 150 demonstrators refused to disband, and this action prompted Califano to sign the regulations on April 28. This protest was significant not only because its goal was achieved, but also because it was the foremost concerted effort among people of different disabilities coming together in support of legislation that affected the overall disability population, rather than only specific groups (Fleischer, 2001; Varela, 1983).

Individuals with Disabilities Education Act

In 1975, the Education for All Handicapped Children Act (EAHCA) was enacted to meet the needs of children who were not receiving the education necessary for them to be successful in society (Murdick, Gartin, & Crabtree, 2007). The act was created to meet the educational needs of all children with disabilities (Murdick et al., 2007). This piece of legislation is credited with mandating "free and appropriate education" for all children with disabilities and ensuring the rights of children with disabilities and their parents. The act later became known as the Individuals with Disabilities Education Act of 1990 (IDEA). This change incorporated the use of person-first language and extended services to children with disabilities through age 21. IDEA also extended services to include transition services, assistive technology, rehabilitation counseling, and social work services. Additionally, services were expanded to include traumatic brain injury and autism (Murdick et al., 2007). IDEA uses concepts including *least restrictive environment* and IEPs to ensure that students with disabilities receive education appropriate for their individual needs.

The Americans With Disabilities Act

Further legislation, in the form of the Americans with Disabilities Act (ADA), was signed into law in 1990. This act provided comprehensive civil rights protection for people with disabilities and was considered one of the most comprehensive acts since the passage of EAHCA in 1975. It extended the mandate for nondiscrimination on the basis of disability to the private sector and the nonfederal public sector (i.e., state and local governments). The ADA was closely modeled after the Civil Rights Act of 1964 and the previously mentioned Section 504 of the Rehabilitation Act. It was the most sweeping disability rights legislation in American history (Murdick et al., 2007).

Four areas of the ADA were particularly important. First, it mandated that local, state, and federal governments and programs be accessible. Second, it stated that employers with more than 15 employees make "reasonable accommodations" for workers with disabilities and not discriminate against otherwise qualified workers with disabilities. Third, it required that public accommodations such as restaurants and stores not discriminate against people with disabilities and that they make "reasonable modifications" to ensure access for these members of the public. Fourth, it mandated access in public transportation, communication, and other areas of public life (Fleischer, 2001). This groundbreaking piece of legislation brought to the forefront barriers that are commonly placed in the way of individuals with disabilities.

The ADA used the definition of disability that was put into place by the Rehabilitation Act of 1973. Someone is considered to be a person with a disability if she or he (a) has a disability that substantially limits at least one major life activity, (b) has a record of the disability, or (c) is regarded as having a disability. The ADA is considered thus far to be the most significant disability legislation for mandating that all public programs, regardless of funding, provide reasonable accommodations for individuals with disabilities (Schriner & Scotch, 2001). According to the ADA, all public services, including restaurants, libraries, hotels, employment, transportation, and stores, are to be accessible for individuals with disabilities. Thus, disability is now perceived as a discriminatory factor such as race, gender, and religion (Schriner & Scotch, 2001).

Figure 17.1

"I WOULDN'T BE TARDY IF THE SCHOOL HAD WHEELCHAIR ACCESS."

© Norman Jung

New Rules for the Americans with Disabilities Act

On March 15, 2011, the new rules for the ADA came into effect. These rules expanded accessibility requirements for recreational facilities and, perhaps most important, incorporated the rules from the 2010 ADA Standards for Accessible Design (Department of Justice, 2010). The accessibility requirements now include public venues such as swimming pools, golf courses, exercise clubs, and boating facilities. These rules also set standards for the use of power wheelchairs and other mobility devices, including Segways (two-wheeled transports that are self-balancing), golf carts, and all-terrain vehicles in public spaces. Further, these rules changed the standards for things such as having wheelchair-accessible seating at public sporting events and guaranteeing accessible hotel rooms.

The new rules also clearly defined a "service animal" as any dog that is specifically trained to perform tasks that will directly benefit an individual with a disability (U.S. Department of Justice, 2010). Defining a service animal is important because it legitimizes the critical services provided by animals to individuals with disabilities. This portion of the law also clarified that the services provided by the service animal must be directly related to the person's disability. Furthermore, dogs that provide crime deterrence or merely emotional support cannot be defined as service animals (*New ADA Rules Go Into Effect*, n.d.).

Now that the evolution of disability definitions and rights has been discussed, several key concepts related to disability are presented.

KEY CONCEPTS

This section introduces eight key concepts: ableism, spread, interaction strain, bias in counseling, language and disability, self-determination, empowerment, and bias in assessment. These concepts are important for counselors to understand and recognize because these notions often impact services provided to individuals with disabilities. Additionally, the concepts also undergird some of the attitudes that are held by professionals and members of society toward individuals with disabilities.

Ableism

Rauscher and McClintock (1997) define *ableism* as "a pervasive system of discrimination and exclusion that oppresses people who have mental, emotional, and physical disabilities" (p. 198). Ableism operates on multiple levels, namely individual, institutional, and societal. Similar to racism and sexism, ableism is a form of oppression. No one term can capture the wide range of oppressive experiences encountered by individuals with disabilities. However, ableism can be coined "disability oppression" because it reflects the attitude that people with disabilities are somehow deficient and unable to meet social and economic roles (Rauscher & McClintock, 1997). Ableism results in individuals having reduced expectations of people with disabilities and limiting their opportunities (Zascavage & Keefe, 2004). In the process, ableism can be internalized, resulting in lower self-esteem and reduced self-efficacy of persons with disabilities. Such beliefs, including the belief that persons with disabilities need assistance in all areas, or that physical disabilities imply intellectual limitations, are potentially devastating (Lynch & Gussel, 1996; Pivik et al., 2002).

Examples of ableism include the assumption that individuals with disabilities cannot perform or engage in certain hobbies or kinds of work. The example in Box 17.2 illustrates the lowered expectations and limiting attitudes many people hold about individuals with visual disabilities.

Box 17.2 A Case of Ableism

One of my (Yvette's) friends loves woodworking and is quite a skilled craftsman. People are often astonished to learn that he is blind. When asked why they are astonished, they often make comments such as these: "He can't see what he is doing." "Isn't it dangerous for him to be using saws and such when he can't see?" "It must have taken him years of instruction to learn to do that!" Perhaps one of the most disturbing comments I have heard was "I don't understand why he does that because he can't even see how beautiful it is anyway." The underlying attitude is ableism. Ableism assumes that surely only individuals who have the ability to see can craft and appreciate beautiful pieces of woodwork, when in fact sight has little to do with the hobby at all. The skills involved include knowledge of wood, measurement, carpentry, and equipment safety.

As illustrated in Box 17.2, ableism is evident in the comments people make about individuals with disabilities. That example also leads one to ask, "How many individuals have been steered away from or denied opportunities because of ableism?" and "How are peoples' views distorted regarding the capabilities of persons with disabilities?" To assist you in more fully understanding ableism, you are invited to complete Activity 17.5 to explore your own reactions to the situations presented.

Activity 17.5   Everyday Events in the Lives of Persons With Disabilities

Many individuals have ideas about what certain groups of people can and cannot do. People have biases and stereotypes that impact people with disabilities by limiting their participation or creating environments that contain attitudinal or physical barriers. In this exercise, read each scenario and then honestly evaluate how you feel about it. Then write your reactions to the scenario. If counselors are going to challenge biases and stereotypes, they must first recognize the biases and stereotypes that they hold.

1. You overhear the following comment in a heated conversation at a basketball game. "Can you believe they let that deaf kid play in such an important game? He may have just cost us the championship by missing that pass. Anyone knows you have to be able to hear to play basketball at this level."

   What are your thoughts about this situation?

2. A person in an expensive sports car parks in a designated accessible parking space reserved for individuals with disabilities immediately before a play begins at a local theater. The person becomes enraged later when he realizes his car has been towed. He yells at the manager of the theater. His argument is that no persons with disabilities had used the parking space and he was in a hurry so he would not miss the beginning of the performance. The manager explained that, indeed, a person with a disability had needed the space a few minutes after he had parked there. The man replied with this statement, "Well you know all those crippled people expect to get parking right at the entrance, so they don't mind waiting till the last minute to show up. I think that if they are not using the space at least 15 minutes before a performance, then anyone should be able to use the space. It's not fair that those people can show up late and still get a prime parking spot!" Just at that moment, the person who parked in the accessible parking spot walks to the car. The enraged man yells, "I bet that cane you're using is a prop just so you can get a parking spot while the rest of us get our cars towed when we park there!" As the car pulls away, the license plate was clearly marked as one for persons with disabilities.

   What is your reaction to this scenario?

(Continued)

How do you think you would respond if you were the manager?

How would you respond if you were a bystander and witnessed the situation?

3. Your agency is setting up a series of informational sessions about teen pregnancy and the services and programs that are available in your county. An administrator from a local agency that serves individuals with intellectual disabilities asks if she can provide transportation to a large number of individuals from their programs on a particular night so that interested persons would have transportation. The number that the administrator mentions means that the majority of the seats will be filled with individuals with intellectual disabilities from this community agency.

What are your thoughts about having such a large number of individuals with intellectual disabilities attending community teen pregnancy prevention sessions?

What would your response be to the administrator of the agency?

Spread

Spread is the tendency for people without disabilities to act as if the individual's disability has a more pervasive impact than it does (Wright, 1983). These assumptions often result from stereotypes that have been formed about persons with disabilities (Henderson & Bryan, 2011; Van der Klift & Kunc, 1994; Wright, 1983). Two examples of spread are in order. First, a common myth or assumption is that all individuals with Down syndrome are happy and friendly (Van der Klift & Kunc, 1994).

Second, when an individual uses a cane because she or he has a visual disability, it is not uncommon to find that people raise their voices and talk slower to the person as if the individual also has a hearing disability and/or an intellectual disability. In the second example, the fact that the individual has a visual disability likely has no bearing on her or his hearing status or cognitive capabilities. Spread is an important concept for counselors to keep in mind because they need to be cognizant of their own biases as well as the impact spread has on individuals with disabilities in all aspects of their lives,

Alexa came home from school and asked her mom if she could invite a new friend to her birthday party. Alexa's mom said, "Tell me a little about your new friend." Alexa excitedly explained, "Danielle is a new girl in my class. She just moved here from Colorado. It's so cool because she used to get to go snow skiing all the time and you know how much I love to ski. We have so much in common. She's so funny and she likes almost all the same things I do. I just know she is going to become one of my best friends." Her mom replied, "That sounds great. Of course you can invite her." Alexa then said, "Oh, by the way, her mom will have to bring her to the bowling alley because our van is not wheelchair accessible." Alexa's mom replied, "Gosh, that's too bad that she can't ride with us, that means she'll miss some of the conversation. Do you think Danielle would like for all of us to ride with her?" Alexa replied, "I'm sure she'd like that, but let me call and ask her first." Then Alexa's mom said, "If Danielle wants us to ride with her, let me know so I can call her mom and work out the details. That way Danielle won't miss a minute of the fun."

including relationships, education, and career. The vignette in Box 17.3 is a positive example of the absence of spread and demonstrates how disability is only one characteristic of an individual.

In the situation in Box 17.3, the disability was not mentioned until it was necessary because of the need for an accessible form of transportation. Additionally, the need for an accessible van was discussed in much the same way as asking a friend to transport children to a birthday party because their vehicle is larger and holds more people. The focus was on the need for accessible transportation, not on the disability. As this vignette demonstrates, language often sets the tone for how others will react to situations and to persons with disabilities. Alexa described Danielle to her mom. The disability was not mentioned in her initial description because it was not one of the characteristics that was at the forefront of Alexa's mind.

Individuals with disabilities are individuals first. The most salient characteristics of who they are often does not include their disability. In the vignette above, Alexa and Danielle shared common interests and were developing a friendship based on their commonalities. The fact that Danielle has a mobility disability is just a small part of who Danielle is as a person. While her disability may need to be accommodated in some way, it does not determine her hobbies, personality, or other characteristics.

Interaction Strain

Interaction strain occurs when individuals without disabilities interact with persons with disabilities and experience anxiety as a result of not being confident in how they should interact (Siller, 1976; Wright, 1983). Sometimes these interactions become awkward because of the lack of exposure and knowledge that persons without disabilities have regarding varying disabling conditions. For example, an interaction might become strained when someone says "Let's go for a walk" to a person who uses a wheelchair. Once the word *walk* is used, the anxiety level of the person without a disability often increases. Counselors need to be aware that words such as *see, walk,* and *hear* are common expressions and are not taken literally by individuals with disabilities during the course of a conversation. When people become uncomfortable they usually apologize, saying things like "I'm sorry, I didn't really mean go for a walk, I meant let's go for a . . . uhhhmmm . . . uhhmmm. . . ." Often, the individual with a mobility disability will step in and say, "It's okay to use the word *walk*. It doesn't offend me."

Bias in Counseling

Bias in counseling includes counselors' using their very first impressions of a client with a disability. These impressions can result in bias when they are not changed even when there is evidence that contradicts the original conclusion drawn (Rosenthal & Kosciulek, 1996). Therefore, it is important for counselors to be aware of their own propensity toward bias.

On a positive note, researchers have found that health care professionals in certain fields have positive attitudes toward persons with disabilities. Such attitudes among occupational therapists, for example, were found to be due to the profession's holistic philosophy, its educational curriculum, and the personal characteristics of those who choose to pursue a career in these fields. However, that is not the case among counselors. Instead, negative biases were found among rehabilitation professionals and mental health counselors (Chubon, 1982; Cook, Kunce, & Getsinger, 1976; Holmes & Karst, 1990; Rosenthal, Chan, & Livneh, 2006; Sullivan et al., 2011). The counseling profession can learn from the health care fields.

Box 17.4 illustrates counselor bias at work. The story also shows how a counselor can be open to feedback from persons with disabilities.

Box 17.4   Two Illustrations of Counselor Bias

When I (Yvette) was a young counselor educator, I was quite taken aback to hear a group of counselor educators discuss their thoughts regarding the improbability of an individual who was blind becoming a counselor. Discussions focused on transportation issues, the difficulty of the individual being able to access records and other information, and their ideas about how the person could possibly be as effective as others because she could not see the body language of the persons that she would be counseling. The entire conversation focused on the barriers and perceived inabilities of the individual based on the disability itself.

The lack of knowledge many counselors and counselor educators have regarding disabilities perpetuates stereotypes and limits career and life opportunities for the very individuals whom counselors and counselor educators are supposed to serve and advocate with and for in many instances.

On the other hand, one of the most valuable learning experiences I encountered was during one of my practicum experiences at a center serving individuals with visual disabilities. Most of my experience had been counseling individuals who were deaf, and I was accustomed to being physically present by using facial expressions and appropriate body language. When I met with a man in his mid-50s who was blind, I started off getting to know him and was listening intensely to his story. After a few minutes, the man stopped and asked, "Are you still here?" I realized in a very profound way that I had not used even one verbal minimal encourager! All of the skills I had used were skills that someone with a visual disability might not be able to access. I had not used one vocal indication that I was listening. This was a profound learning experience for me. The man with whom I was working had quite a laugh when I explained that I had been head nodding and leaning forward and using other physical cues that he could not see. We continued our session and developed excellent rapport. He often took the opportunity to joke with me about my obvious oversight during our first session. I took valuable lessons away from this experience. Although I had the knowledge about how to demonstrate basic attending skills, in the moment I was using the skills I had developed while working with individuals who were deaf or hard of hearing. Knowledge without proper application is of little use.

Language and Disability

Although the *Diagnostic and Statistical Manual of Mental Disorders* (American Psychiatric Association, 2000), the American Psychological Association (2010a) code of ethics, the American Counseling Association (2009) code of ethics, and the American Psychological Association (2010b) *Publication Manual* address the issue of person-first language, the prevalence of disability-first language in society and in everyday conversation is high. It is not uncommon to hear phrases like "that blind woman," "those poor disabled kids," "special needs kids," "that's retarded," "he rides the short bus," or "the cripple." The ARC (2012) explains the power of such language: "Our words and the meanings we attach to them create attitudes, drive social policies and laws, influence our feelings and decisions, and affect people's daily lives and more. How we use them makes a difference" (para. 5).

Language conveys attitudes, positions of power, and prejudices, as well as how accepting one is regarding persons with disabilities. Person-first language is just that: putting the individual first (Blaska, 1993; National Youth Leadership Network & Kids as Self Advocates, 2006; The ARC, 2012). By contrast, using a diagnosis to define a person perpetuates stereotypes and prejudice and "also robs the person of the opportunity to define him/herself" (The ARC, 2012, para. 5). Not only are counselors ethically bound to use person-first language (American Psychological Association, 2010a), but as social justice advocates counselors should demand and ensure that person-first language is used.

As counselors, they must be aware of the language they use while educating themselves and others regarding the power of language, particularly in the therapeutic environment. Activity 17.6 provides you with an opportunity to reflect on language that is used to describe individuals with disabilities. Take a few minutes to complete the activity. To get the most benefit, it is helpful to be honest and to write down the first thing that comes into your mind. It is also helpful if you are able to discuss your answers with others.

Activity 17.6   The Power of Language

Take a moment to read each term in the list below. After you read the word, jot down the first thing that pops into your head.

1. Retard

2. Cripple

3. Quadriplegic

4. Deaf and dumb

5. Special needs kids

6. Confined to a wheelchair

7. Spastic

Now that you have written down the first thoughts that popped into your head, discuss your responses with a peer. (Students could also write a short reflection about their responses.)

(Continued)

(Continued)

After you have finished the section above, take a moment to read the descriptions in the list below. After you read each one, jot down the first thought that pops into your mind.

1. A person with an intellectual disability

2. A person who uses a cane

3. A person with a spinal cord injury

4. A person who is deaf

5. Kids with developmental disabilities

6. A person who uses a wheelchair

7. A child who experiences uncontrolled muscle movements

After you have written down the first thoughts that popped into your mind, discuss your responses with a peer. (Students could also write a short reflection about their responses.)

What do you notice about the effects of each set of words?

A counselor's use of language and willingness to address how a person feels and reacts to the language used to describe disability is of utmost importance. If counselors are uncomfortable discussing disability terminology or they ignore the way language can disempower and hurt persons, then counselors are contributing to the marginalization of individuals with disabilities. Thereby, counselors are perhaps unintentionally creating a "them" and "us" dichotomy.

This dichotomy has been referred to as *othering* (Goffman, 1963). Othering occurs when one distinguishes oneself or one's group from a traditionally marginalized group of individuals. For example, reference to a group as "those" people is never an inclusive term. "Those" implies separation, lack of acceptance, and lack of inclusion. Rather than saying "those disabled children," instead say "children with disabilities." Better yet, do not even refer to the disability unless it is central to what is happening or to the situation (Blaska, 1993; National Youth Leadership Network & Kids as Self Advocates, 2006). People should be addressed by their name and not by their disability (National Youth Leadership Network & Kids as Self Advocates, 2006). Perhaps

Mark Twain explained the importance of language best. In his letter to George Bainton, Twain wrote, "The difference between the right word and the almost right word is a large matter—it's the difference between the lightening bug and lightening." Language is how individuals communicate the very essence of who they are as human beings. Our language can include or exclude, unite or separate, disempower or empower. Table 17.1 provides examples of empowering and disempowering language. It would be good for you to learn these terms.

Self-Determination

Self-determination is the basic human right of having full control over one's own life. Self-determination incorporates the concepts of choice, freedom, independence, personal agency, autonomy, self-direction, and personal responsibility (UIC National Research and Training Center on Psychiatric Disability & UIC NRTC Self-determination Knowledge Development Workshop, 2002). Self-determination has been defined as "a combination of skills, knowledge,

Table 17.1 Empowering and Disempowering Language

Disability	Outdated Language	Respectful Language
Blind or visual impairment	Invalid, dumb	Person who is blind, person who is visually impaired, person who has a visual disability
Deaf or hearing impairment	Deaf and dumb, deaf and mute	Deaf, person who is deaf, person who is hard of hearing
Speech/communication disability	Dumb, one who talks badly	Person with a speech or communication disability
Learning disability	Retarded, slow, brain-damaged, special ed.	Person with a learning disability, person with a cognitive disability
Intellectual/cognitive disability	Retarded, slow, brain-damaged, special ed., "special"	Person with an intellectual disability, person with a cognitive disability, person with a developmental disability
Mental health disability	Psycho, nuts, crazy, wacko, schizo, manic-depressive, bipolar	Person with a psychiatric disability, person with a mental health disability, person with a psychological disability
Physical or mobility disability	Wheelchair-bound, confined to a chair, gimp, lame, crippled, handicapped, spastic, physically challenged, spaz	Person who uses a wheelchair, person who has a physical disability, person with a mobility disability
Emotional disability	Emotionally disturbed	Person with an emotional disability
Health disability	Victim, stricken with a disability (e.g., cancer, HIV)	Survivor, someone living with a disability (e.g., someone living with cystic fibrosis)
Short stature	Dwarf, midget	Someone of short stature, little person

Source: Adapted from National Youth Leadership Network & Kids as Self Advocates (2006).

and beliefs that enable a person to engage in goal-directed, self-regulated, autonomous behavior" (Field, Martin, Miller, Ward, & Wehmeyer, 1998, p. 2). Self-determination asserts that one has an understanding of one's own strengths and weaknesses. Additionally, when one enacts these skills and attitudes, the person is able to exercise power over her or his own life (Field et al., 1998).

To be empowered, individuals need self-determination skills as well as an environment that is free of restrictions. Self-determination implies that an individual both possesses a skill set and enacts behaviors that are independent, self-realizing, autonomous, and goal-oriented (Bremer, Kachgal, & Schoeller, 2003; Karvonene,

Test, Wood, Browder, & Algozzine, 2004; Palmer & Wehmeyer, 1998; Stancliffe, Abery, Springborg, & Elkin, 2000; Wehmeyer, Field, Doren, & Mason, 2004; Wehmeyer, Kelchner, & Richards, 1996).

Empowerment

Empowerment can be defined as a social process that is multidimensional and facilitates one's ability to gain control over one's own life. This process fosters power. When power is fostered, individuals are able exercise and execute decisions regarding their own life. In addition, when people are able to exercise power, they are able to decide what issues they want to act on in their own lives and in their communities (Page & Czuba, 1999).

To be empowered, an individual needs an environment that offers options such as deciding where to live, work, or go to school. Further, individuals need the freedom to use their own authority to choose options that are most appropriate from their point of view (Rapp & Goscha, 2006; Ware et al., 2007). For example, a college student who has a disability may choose not to disclose her or his disability in some classes and to some professors while deciding to disclose this disability in other classes. Not surprisingly, it is strongly suggested in the counseling field that the more options actually available to a person (meaning the person has the freedom to choose) and the more times the person makes independent choices, the greater is the contribution to that person's empowerment (Ware et al., 2007).

Empowerment is also affected by the subjective reality of the person. A person may have many options, but her or his perception of the options may be much more limited. In the previous example of the college student, the student must perceive that she or he has the option to disclose or not disclose the disability. In addition, the student must understand that she or he has the option to disclose the disability to one professor and not to another. Recognizing the available options allows the student to choose not to disclose the disability at all, to disclose the disability to one or more professors, or to disclose the disability to all the professors.

A model frequently used to increase empowerment is a *strengths model*. Such a model emphasizes options, personal authority to choose from those options, confidence in the self, and the personal agency to take action (Rapp & Goscha, 2006). An illustration of a strengths model in action is provided by referring back to the case of Paul at the beginning of the chapter. Look briefly at his case, and then read Box 17.5, where the use of a strengths-based model is presented. After reading Box 17.5, respond to the question in Activity 17.7.

Box 17.5 Strengths-Based Model in Career Counseling

In the case of Paul, the counselor fortunately had extensive experience working with young adults with significant intellectual disabilities. She expanded her toolbox of counseling skills based on the fact that Paul had fairly significant cognitive limitations. Paul had a group of individuals on his side who were invested in him and his future and who believed in empowering him; they also chose not to limit Paul to careers that have been traditionally picked for individuals with significant cognitive limitations. While they all recognized that it was unrealistic for Paul to become a physician or a surgeon, they used their entire toolbox as they walked through the career counseling process with Paul.

When working with people with disabilities, it is important to lay aside your biases and assumptions. The vocational rehabilitation counselor approached Paul's career dilemma much like she would anyone else's. She started with Paul's desire to become a doctor. They talked about his strengths and his weaknesses and also about the reasons Paul wanted to become a physician. The counselor was careful to note all the reasons Paul wanted to be a doctor. Approaching him without automatically focusing on the fact that he did not have the cognitive ability to become a physician allowed the counselor to "listen" to what Paul was seeking in a career. They listed Paul's strengths, talked about his values, and discussed the type of work environment that he was interested in.

After meeting with Paul and building rapport, the counselor came up with a list of Paul's desires for a career:

1. Paul wanted to work in an environment where he was respected.

2. Paul wanted to have an important job that included a name badge and a pager.

3. Paul wanted to work in the hospital. He knew people there and knew every inch of the hospital.

4. Paul wanted to wear a white hospital lab coat.

5. Paul wanted to be able to help people.

6. Paul wanted to earn an income that allowed him to do the things he enjoyed.

7. Paul wanted to be near his family. He wanted a career that would keep him in the same city.

The counselor also used a strengths-based approach and came up with a list of strengths that matched Paul's desires for a career.

1. Paul was friendly and had excellent social skills.

2. Paul remembered facts and also had extensive knowledge of the people and the layout of the hospital where his mom and dad worked.

3. Paul was able to keep a schedule and show up for work on time.

4. Paul could read and write at approximately a beginning third-grade level.

5. Paul's verbal communication skills were good.

6. Paul was a hard worker who enjoyed working with others.

Activity 17.7   Thinking of Working With Paul

Now that you have information regarding Paul's career aspirations as well as some of his strengths and weaknesses, how would you approach him? What direction would you go in regard to his career search?

Bias in Assessment

Another key concept for counselors in their work with persons with disabilities is bias in assessment. Such bias includes errors in judgment based on inferred rather than factual information (Morrow & Deidan, 1992). Inferred or stereotypical information about groups of individuals can lead to inappropriate selection and use of instruments.

Counselors need to recognize and systematically work to eliminate such bias because assessment occurs at all system levels, from the individual and personal to the institutional and societal (Mackelprang & Salsgiver, 2009). Additionally, assessment provides a foundation for contracting, goal setting, and interventions. Therefore, accurate assessments are necessary to select appropriate interventions that are effective, multidimensional, and purposeful (Hepworth,

Rooney, Rooney, Strom-Gottfried, & Larson, 2010; Mackelprang & Salsgiver, 2009).

While the counseling profession generally recognizes the importance of encouraging individual strengths and using a holistic framework in practice with persons with disabilities, many assessment instruments and methods currently lack a holistic dimension. Language, culture, acculturation, trauma, and previous experiences make it impossible to be entirely certain that the results of any standardized assessment are unbiased and nondiscriminatory (Fraine & McDade, 2009).

Although it generally is understood that people live in complex social milieus that dramatically affect them, assessment rarely takes into account larger social variables. Instead, problem-based (rather than strengths-based) assessments are often used during counseling sessions. These problem-based assessments measure individual rather than social-environmental explanations of human problems (Condeluci, 1995). Attempting to solve problems without taking into account the greater environment will often result in less valid results or inaccurate conceptualization of the issues for which the individual is seeking counseling services.

The alternative to problem- and individual-based assessments lies in using systems and social ecology models, which address environmental contributions to the presenting issues of persons with disabilities (Condeluci, 1995; Mackelprang & Salsgiver, 2009). These systems account for the myriad of contributing variables in the lives of individuals with and without disabilities. For example, transportation is often an issue for many individuals with disabilities (e.g., visual disabilities, traumatic brain injury, intellectual disabilities, epilepsy). The stressors associated with depending on public transportation or others (friends or coworkers) are important for counselors to understand. Planning for disruptions in transportation, assisting individuals in identifying backup transportation means, and understanding the time-consuming processing of securing transportation are important factors to consider when working with individuals where transportation is an issue.

When using assessment tools to assist persons with disabilities, counselors must do a dance: They need to consider the person's strengths and also gather enough information about the disability to present a variety of resources, supports, and opportunities that may be available to the individual. These resources may include individual or group counseling, support groups, vocational rehabilitation services, community resources, educational opportunities, assistive technology, and health-related resources. Limiting resources to those specified for individuals with disabilities limits options and perpetuates stereotypes, thereby infusing biases in the assessment process.

IMPLICATIONS FOR PRACTICE

This section first addresses the unique challenges faced by counselors in working with individuals with disabilities. After that, specific strategies, supports, interventions, and examples for working with individuals with disabilities are provided.

Understanding the Challenges Associated With Disability

Individuals who have a disability or chronic illness face challenges at different points in their lives. These challenges may include increasing demands, changing technology, secondary disabilities, transitions, and shifting roles (Power & Dell Orto, 2003; Sullivan et al., 2011). Some of these demands could be a change in job duties or accepting a new position that requires one to move to a different city. Other challenges include entering college or becoming a parent. There is also the possibility of development of secondary disabilities (e.g., visual disabilities or amputation as a complication of diabetes).

However, counselors must also consider that acquiring a disability does not mean an individual will have psychological or adjustment issues. Many individuals have a wide variety of resources (internal and external) that assist them in coping with life experiences including disability (Mackelprang & Salsgiver, 2009). Just as counselors working with people without disabilities consider the context of a person's stress, counselors should consider the context of the stress or problems expressed by individuals with disabilities. The stress may stem from others' reactions to the disability rather than the person's adjustment or acceptance of her or his disability (Mackelprang & Salsgiver, 2009).

In addition to the situations that persons with disabilities encounter, their significant others are also impacted by these challenges. Significant others have their own reactions, worldviews, outlooks, needs, and expectations for what will happen and how to react to the disability and life events (Power & Dell Orto, 2003). While some of the events are experienced by many individuals, disability or chronic illness often adds additional variables that must be considered. For example, a change in insurance may drastically impact persons with disabilities and their families. When insurance changes, co-pays, deductibles, and coverage of supplies, durable equipment, therapies, and medications may or may not be the same as with previous insurance.

Prerequisite: Counselor Knowledge of Disabilities

A starting place for working with clients with disabilities is knowledge. Counselors must gain knowledge about specific disabilities if they are to work effectively with individuals with disabilities. Although there is considerable variation among persons with similar disabilities, counselors' understanding of common misperceptions, barriers, and possible functional limitations may greatly enhance outcomes. It is also helpful if counselors understand some of the basics regarding counseling individuals with disabilities. Box 17.6 provides helpful tips in this regard.

Box 17.6   Counseling Tips

Three guidelines should be kept in mind when you are working with clients with disabilities. First, it is important for counselors to remember that individuals with disabilities are individuals first. Second, many of the skills needed to work with individuals with disabilities are skills that counselors use on a daily basis, including basic attending, listening, and responding skills. Third, effective counseling relationships are developed when counselors demonstrate respect and acceptance of individual differences (Henderson & Bryan, 2011). Below are general things to keep in mind when working with individuals with disabilities.

General Tips

1. Counselors need to make the environment welcoming by including posters, pictures, or other items that include individuals with disabilities in empowered situations.

2. Counselors should use all the relevant tools in their toolbox when counseling individuals with disabilities. Eliminating tools based on perceptions of disabilities limits counselor effectiveness.

3. Counselors should always work from a strengths-based approach. Focus on the individual's capabilities.

4. Do not assume that the person is seeking counseling regarding issues related to her or his disability. People with disabilities often seek counseling for the same reasons as people without disabilities. Keep in mind the environmental and attitudinal barriers that may accompany the problem or that may need to be considered when planning or problem solving.

Although the above tips generally apply to all individuals with disabilities, the tips listed below are useful to keep in mind when counseling or interacting with persons with specific disabilities.

Tips for Working With Specific Disabilities

1. A wheelchair is considered part of one's personal space. Do not lean on it, sit on it, hold it, or push it without first asking the person's permission.

2. Ensure that your counseling office, agency, or any space that you use for services is physically accessible for individuals with physical/mobility disabilities.

3. Ensure that furniture is physically accessible so that persons can transfer from their wheelchair to another seat if they so choose.

(Continued)

(Continued)

4. Ensure that walkways, hallways, and other spaces are free of clutter or things that may cause someone with a mobility or visual disability to trip or to have difficulty moving in the environment.

5. Ask individuals with visual disabilities if they need a well-lit room, large print, or other assistance with reading materials.

6. Always ask permission before touching or distracting a service dog.

7. When giving directions, be explicit. For example, "The chair is 3 feet ahead to your left" rather than "The chair is over there."

8. When you are counseling individuals with visual disabilities, make sure that you use verbal minimal encouragers and statements of interest rather than nonverbal minimal encouragers or gestures.

9. When counseling individuals who are deaf or who have visual disabilities, do not talk slowly, exaggerate your speech, or talk too loudly. Speak at the same rate and loudness as you do on a regular basis.

10. Do not assume that a person who is deaf uses an interpreter. However, if using an interpreter, talk to the individual, not to the interpreter. The interpreter is there to translate communication and for no other purpose.

11. Dim lighting often makes it more difficult for persons who are deaf or hard of hearing to speech read and read gestures. Offices with dimmer switches are preferable because the lighting can be adjusted easily.

12. If you have difficulty understanding the person, ask her or him to repeat what was said. If you still have difficulty, try another form of communication, such as writing, using a computer, or using other communication aids.

13. Adjust your level of vocabulary to that of the individual you are counseling. Do not assume the person has a decreased vocabulary based on her or his disability. Check for understanding just as you would for individuals who do not have disabilities.

Source: Adapted from *People With Disabilities in the Federal Government: An Employment Guide* (n.d.).

The tips in Box 17.6 are not all-inclusive, but they are helpful reminders of things to consider when working with individuals with disabilities.

The following section presents counseling strategies for working with individuals with disabilities. It should be noted that no specific theory or set of interventions is effective for all individuals with disabilities, nor should counselors expect it to be.

ADOPTING A PERSON-CENTERED APPROACH

Counselors should have as a foundation an overall person-centered approach to their interactions with

individuals with disabilities. This approach incorporates five basic counselor qualities as established by Rogers (1957): (1) respect for the client; (2) genuineness; (3) empathic understanding; (4) communication of empathy, respect, and genuineness to the client; and (5) structuring. These qualities are necessary for effective counseling relationships and are the facilitative factor in all interpersonal relationships (Patterson, 2004). Because this approach takes into account the client's worldview, it is likely that the therapeutic relationship will facilitate the identification of barriers that are problematic for individuals with disabilities. The person-centered approach also conveys respect and encourages autonomy and self-determination. When counselors foster self-determination, they are likely to choose interventions and tools that reflect attention to the counseling issue at hand rather than select tools based on the person's disability.

STRENGTHS-BASED APPROACHES

In addition to the grounding in a person-centered approach, specific strategies can be used with individuals with disabilities. These strategies include strengths-based approaches as well as systems- and social ecology-based interventions.

A strengths-based approach consists of identifying strengths, discussing these strengths with the individual, and using these strengths to achieve the individual's goals. Counselors who use strengths- and capabilities-based approaches are much more likely to utilize their entire toolbox of counseling skills because they are focusing on abilities and possibilities rather than disabilities and limitations (Mackelprang & Salsgiver, 2009).

Seeing ability rather than disability opens doors of opportunity (Mackelprang & Salsgiver, 2009).

For example, a person with paraplegia can explore becoming a rancher if the counselor working with the person sees the abilities of the individual rather than assuming the disability precludes the person from becoming a rancher. Essential job functions of a rancher are feeding cattle, mending fences, and moving cattle from one location to another. The rancher with paraplegia can operate a cattle feeding system from the truck bed by using technology incorporated in the truck cab. The rancher can use an all-terrain vehicle to reach fences that need mending and to assist in moving cattle from one location to another (North Carolina Department of Health and Human Services, 2012). How the tasks are accomplished may be different when compared to a person who does not have a disability, but the essential functions of the job can be fulfilled.

Reflect again on the vignette about Paul presented at the beginning of the chapter. Then read Box 17.7 to find out how a strengths-based approach was used to continue to assist Paul in his career development journey. After reading this material, respond to the questions in Activity 17.8.

Box 17.7   Empowerment and Strengths in the Case of Paul

Paul's counselor spoke with the local hospital and was able to develop a relationship with several people in different departments. She found out that one of the issues facing the hospital was getting lab specimens and other important documents (X-rays, etc.) from one part of the hospital to another. Thinking about Paul's strengths and his career aspirations, the counselor helped to carve out a job specifically for Paul that met a true need at the hospital. Paul had the requisite skills to perform the job and he could learn other skills that might be required.

The job created was a specialized courier position that entailed other duties as well. Paul's position was seen as important because it filled a true gap in services at the hospital. Listed below are some of Paul's initial duties, although the position expanded as the hospital's needs changed.

1. Paul wore a pager and was given a work cell phone. He was called or paged when items needed to be taken from one part of the hospital to another. Paul's strength was that he knew the hospital layout and knew people in each department.

2. A hospital name badge with his position clearly communicated that Paul was responsible for sensitive information at times.

(Continued)

(Continued)

3. Paul sometimes assisted in transporting patients from their rooms to other areas of the hospital.

4. Paul was also paged if small construction items, supplies, or equipment needed to be moved from one area of the hospital to another.

5. Paul helped set up rooms for conferences and learned to set up basic equipment, including projectors and portable white boards.

6. Paul helped set up for important meetings that included lunches for hospital administrators.

7. Paul's pleasant demeanor, excellent social skills, rapport with the hospital staff, and desire to do a good job matched the demands of the position.

8. Paul's reading and writing skills were adequate for the job. Most of the instructions included simple directions regarding delivery and setup.

Activity 17.8   Critiquing the Work With Paul

Ponder what occurred in Paul's career dilemma. What do you think about the counselor's approach?

How did a strengths-based approach and using all the tools in the toolbox assist the counselor in securing a job that matched Paul's career aspirations?

A specific strengths-based approach is Solution-Focused Brief Therapy (SFBT). SFBT helps individuals, including individuals with intellectual disabilities, focus on solutions rather than on the problem (Roden, Bannink, Maaskant, & Curfs, 2009). You are encouraged to review SFBT in order to be ready to work with clients with disabilities such as Paul.

IMPLEMENTING THE SOCIAL/ MINORITY MODEL

The Social/Minority Model posits that disability is just a variation of the human condition. It is a part of

how human beings differ. As such, this model asserts that the problems that individuals with disabilities encounter are a result of the social construction of disability (Mackelprang & Salsgiver, 2009). People with disabilities have not been allowed to achieve in many instances; they have been denied access, denied education, and denied the basic human right of free choice (Bagenstos, 2009; Field et al., 1998; Page & Czuba, 1999; Varela, 1983). The Social/Minority Model focuses on strengths and capabilities, empowerment, and the idea that social change needs to occur if individuals with disabilities are to fully participate in society (Mackelprang & Salsgiver, 2009).

One of the many ways to incorporate a Social/Minority Model into counseling practice is to choose theoretical approaches that provide a framework for disability as a social construct rather than something that is inherently deficient and must be changed at an individual level. Constructivist or narrative approaches can be used to assist individuals in constructing and reconstructing their lives. The narrative approach is briefly presented here as it applies to working with disabilities.

The Use of Narrative Approaches

Narrative approaches allow individuals to tell all the details of their story from their own personal lens. (An application of narrative counseling is presented in Chapter 19.) Counselors can assist in this process and at the same time gather important information regarding the nature of the issues at hand and whether there are social, attitudinal, or environmental barriers that are hampering the person's opportunity to resolve issues. Narrative approaches are transformative, meaning individuals can learn how to use narrative therapy to identify problem stories, brainstorm different stories, and then seek supports from others to help sustain changes they have made. Box 17.8 demonstrates the use of a narrative approach with an individual with a disability.

Box 17.8   The Case of Andrew and the Narrative Approach

Using narrative approaches can be very helpful when counseling individuals who are adjusting to or coping with the challenges of a newly acquired disability. Take for example the case of Andrew, a 54-year-old male with a PhD in genetics. Andrew fell and sustained a traumatic brain injury (TBI). After spending 2 months in the hospital and 6 months in a comprehensive rehabilitation center, Andrew returned home with the hope of returning to his job as a geneticist. Although the firm he worked for had held his job, they expressed concerns about Andrew's ability to return to work given the nature of his injury. Andrew had residual issues including aphasia (difficulty remembering or recalling specific words), and he struggled with depression. After months of conversations with his boss, Andrew suddenly found that both his boss (who had been a close friend) and his coworkers began avoiding him and not returning calls.

At the urging of his wife, Andrew sought counseling. The counselor chose a narrative approach. He first listened to Andrew's story, and as he listened, he began to note several recurring themes. Andrew recalled many times since his injury that people had rewritten his reports, finished his sentences, walked away from conversations, or simply indicated they felt sorry for him. In summary, Andrew said to his counselor, "People think I'm stupid. They see me as brain damaged. They don't believe I can do my job."

The counselor worked with Andrew to identify the barriers and the themes that were present. Then they set to work on dismantling and deconstructing the story. The focus was on Andrew's perception of how others viewed him after his TBI. The counselor asked several key questions: "What do you think others know about aphasia?" "What do you think others' fears might be?" "How does having difficulty finding the right word impact the quality of your written work?" "How does the aphasia impact your communication with others?" Andrew and the counselor spent time examining the limiting aspects of viewing others as thinking he was stupid. They were able to separate out the aphasia and his looking different than he did before the accident from who he is as an intelligent, educated, hard-working individual.

(Continued)

(Continued)

Once they had (1) identified the problem stories and (2) separated the problem from Andrew as a person, the counselor assisted Andrew in creating new stories ("re-storying"). Re-storying was accomplished by getting Andrew to talk about how he wanted his life (work and interpersonal relationships) to be. He discovered that at the center of his wants was the desire to be respected at work, but he also discovered that at the heart of some of his negative feelings was the stress he felt when constantly interacting with others verbally. The counselor then asked a key question: "Andrew, what would you like your job to consist of on a daily basis?" Andrew told the counselor that he felt he was a much stronger writer than a conversationalist, and if his job consisted of genetic research and then writing the reports rather than giving verbal reports or interacting with others verbally, he would feel less stressed and the quality of his work would speak for itself.

This discovery led Andrew on a quest to find different employment that entailed more independent research and writing. The counselor then worked with Andrew to sustain the change. This was done by eliciting the help of Andrew's wife. They all became partners on the journey to find employment that would lend itself to Andrew's strong analytical and writing skills while limiting the amount of verbal communication that contributed to Andrew's feelings of "not being smart."

After months of searching, Andrew secured a job with a research company. He was able to conduct genetic research and write reports, thereby limiting his verbal reports. He worked independently and sent most of his reports to a team who, in return, often communicated via e-mail rather than by voice. Andrew's self-confidence soared. He began sharing how his new boss now sent him other people's reports to review for errors. Andrew's wife shared that when Andrew realized that he could do something slightly different (more writing and less verbal communication), his stress level went down and he began focusing on completing excellent written work. Although it took Andrew longer to complete his reports than it did before he acquired his TBI, the quality of his work was praised by his new employer.

Andrew periodically complained of the time it took for him to complete a report because he couldn't immediately think of the precise word he wanted to use. He also shared that he had become comfortable with using assistive technologies and felt comfortable asking others when he could not recall the precise term. The counselor suggested that Andrew make a list of commonly used terms and include the definition as well as synonyms for the terms. That way Andrew could use this as a cheat sheet to save time and frustration. Andrew incorporated the cheat sheet and discovered it was a useful tool.

Additionally, Andrew began to apply narrative approaches to other problems he encountered. These approaches facilitate the identification of problem stories and allow counselors to help individuals create alternative stories to achieve their goals. In the case of Andrew, the counselor's use of a narrative approach helped Andrew discover barriers to his success. The residual aphasia made impromptu conversation difficult and frustrating and often led to his feeling humiliated and unintelligent. The deconstruction and re-storying process allowed Andrew to focus on his strengths of research and writing. This led to the decision to find a new position that required less verbal communication and more written communication. In the end, Andrew rediscovered his confident work identity.

Now read in Box 17.9 the story of what happened with Paul.

Box 17.9 Summary of Paul's Career Development Journey

Paul's job eventually grew and encompassed many more responsibilities. Paul learned simple computer skills that allowed him to assist with inventory, and he eventually became the point person for setting up rooms for important training sessions and meetings. He was seen as a vital part of the hospital staff because he delivered important information, equipment, and supplies to different employees in all parts of the hospital. His friendly personality and his desire to do a great job meant that Paul followed through and delivered items in a timely manner. He also was eager to help and would step in when needed in other departments.

Although part of his job was eventually phased out due to technology (lab reports and digital X-rays could be sent electronically), Paul had become such an important part of the staff that people had come to depend on his ability to deliver equipment, supplies, and important signature documents when needed. The fact that the hospital provided training to him in regard to room and equipment setup was vital in allowing Paul to keep his position when technological advances made several of his initial duties obsolete.

Paul tells people he loves his job. His job is important and his coworkers and supervisors often say they know when he is out sick because things just do not get done.

The use of strengths-based and Social/Minority approaches was evident in the case of Paul. First, the counselor listened to what Paul wanted and affirmed his desire to work in a hospital. The counselor gathered information from Paul and also used information provided by his teachers and parents to help him identify his strengths. Instead of focusing on Paul's deficits and what he could not do, the counselor focused on his capabilities and strengths. In doing so, the counselor was able to determine that Paul had a marketable skill set. He was personable, could follow multistep directions, could read basic instructions and directions, had good memory skills, was enthusiastic and a hard worker, and knew the layout of the local hospital. After identifying Paul's strengths, the counselor worked with Paul, his family, and the community to find a job that might match Paul's skill set, values, personality, and interests. Using the Social/Minority Model, the counselor recognized that many people might try to limit Paul's job opportunities. Because the counselor was thinking outside the box, she saw an opportunity to create a job that

incorporated Paul's career aspirations and to use his skill set as a strength. In essence, a social change occurred because a new position was developed and Paul was not pigeon-holed into a "traditional" job. Additionally, Paul's job incorporated opportunities for him to practice new skills by building on his strengths. These opportunities for practice proved crucial as some of Paul's initial job duties were phased out due to technology. The hospital administration kept Paul on and expanded his job duties rather than phasing out his job. He was given the opportunity to achieve because the counselor used approaches that focused on strengths.

The counselor also advocated with and on behalf of Paul to help create a position that provided him with the opportunity to build his career. It was also evident that some social change occurred within the hospital administration because they offered Paul training to acquire new skills. Perhaps their social construction of intellectual disabilities was changed due to their interaction with Paul and their realization that he was a valuable employee who possessed many strengths.

SUMMARY

Disability is an equal opportunity minority. It includes persons regardless of their race, creed, sex, national origin, economics, or age. It is also the group that anyone can unexpectedly join at any given time and in which membership is often determined by circumstance (The ARC, 2012; Henderson & Bryan, 2011). To competently serve individuals with disabilities, counselors must have sufficient knowledge about specific disabilities (Sullivan et al., 2011) as well as general knowledge related to myths, barriers, and societal attitudes. Counselors must also become familiar with legislation protecting individuals with disabilities.

While working with clients with disabilities, counselors must account for their own biases and stereotypes that may be a result of ableism. In particular, challenging one's own perceptions of the abilities of others is crucial when working with individuals with disabilities. Thus, counselors must be careful not to use assessments that focus on a person's deficits compared to some overall norm while ignoring the societal and environmental obstacles that actually create barriers to productivity. Additionally, counselors must be aware of the attitudinal, societal, systems, and institutional barriers encountered by individuals with disabilities. Finally, counselors must recognize the injustices faced by persons with disabilities and strive to facilitate the removal of attitudinal, systemic, and societal barriers.

REFERENCES

American Association on Intellectual and Developmental Disabilities. (2012). *Definition of intellectual disability.* Retrieved from http://www.aamr.org/content_100.cfm?navID=21

American Counseling Association (2005). *ACA code of ethics.* Retrieved from http://www.counseling.org/resources/codeofethics/TP/home/ct2.aspx

American Psychiatric Association. (2000). *Diagnostic and statistical manual of mental disorders* (4th ed., Text. rev.). Washington, DC: Author.

American Psychological Association. (2010a). *Ethical principles of psychologists and code of conduct.* Retrieved from http://www.apa.org/ethics/code/index.aspx

American Psychological Association. (2010b). *Publication manual of the American Psychological Association* (6th ed.). Washington, DC: Author.

Americans with Disabilities Act, 42 U.S.C. § 12101 *et seq.* (1990).

The ARC. (2012). *What is people first language.* Retrieved from http://www.thearc.org/page.aspx?pid=2523

Bagenstos, S. (2009). *Law and the contradictions of the disability rights movement.* New Haven, CT: Yale University Press.

Barkley, R. A. (2000). *Taking charge of ADHD: The complete, authoritative guide for parents.* (Rev. ed.). New York, NY: Guilford Press.

Barnartt, S. N., & Scotch, R. (2001). *Disability protests: Contentious politics 1970–1999.* Washington, DC: Gallaudet University Press.

Blaska, J. (1993). The power of language: Speak and write using "person first." In M. Nagler (Ed.), *Perspectives on disability* (2nd ed., pp. 25–32). Palo Alto, CA: Health Markets Research.

Bowe, F. (2000). *Physical, sensory, and health disabilities: An introduction.* Upper Saddle River, NJ: Merrill/Prentice-Hall.

Bremer, C. D., Kachgal, M., & Schoeller, K. (2003). Self-determination: Supporting successful transition. *NCSET Research to Practice Brief, 2*(1). Retrieved from http://www.ncset.org/publications/viewdesc.asp?id=962

Center for the Critical Analysis of Social Difference. (2008). *The future of disability studies.* Retrieved from http://www.socialdifference.org/projects/future-disability-studies

Chubon, R. (1982). An analysis of research dealing with the attitudes of professionals toward disability. *Journal of Rehabilitation, 48*(1), 25–30.

Condeluci, A. (1995). *Interdependence: The route to community* (2nd ed.). Winter Park, FL: GR Press.

Cook, D., Kunce, J., & Getsinger, S. (1976). Perceptions of the disabled and counseling effectiveness. *Rehabilitation Counseling Bulletin, 19*, 470–475.

Definition of disabilities. (2012). Retrieved from http://www.disabled-world.com/disability/types/

Department of Justice. (2010). *2010 ADA standards for accessible design.* Retrieved from http://www.ada.gov/regs2010/2010ADAStandards/2010ADAStandards.pdf

Education for All Handicapped Children Act, 20 U.S.C. § 1400 *et seq.* (1975).

Farrell, M. (2011). *The effective teacher's guide to sensory and physical impairments* (2nd ed.). New York, NY: Routledge.

Field, S., Martin, J., Miller, R., Ward, M., & Wehmeyer, M. (1998). *A practical guide for teaching self-determination.* Reston, VA: Council for Exceptional Children.

Fleischer, D. (2001). *The disability rights movement.* Philadelphia, PA: Temple University Press.

Fraine, N., & McDade, R. (2009). Reducing bias in psychometric assessment of culturally and linguistically diverse students from refugee backgrounds in Australian schools: A process approach. *Australian Psychologist, 44*, 16–26.

Frum, D. (2001). *How they got here: The 70s.* New York, NY: Basic Books.

Goffman, E. (1963). *Stigma: Notes on the management of spoiled identity.* New York, NY: Simon & Schuster.

Gray, D. B., Gould, M. & Bickenbach, J. E. (2003). Environmental barriers and disability. *Journal of Architectural and Planning Research, 20*, 29–37.

Hardman, M. I., Drew, C. J., & Egan, M. W. (1996). *Human exceptionality: Society, school, and family.* Needham Heights, MA: Allyn & Bacon.

Henderson, G., & Bryan, W. V. (2011). *Psychosocial aspects of disabilities.* Springfield, IL: Charles C. Thomas.

Hepworth, D. H., Rooney, R. H., Rooney, D. G., Strom-Gottfried, K., & Larson, J. (2010). *Direct social work practice: Theory and skills* (8th ed.). Belmont, CA: Brooks/Cole.

Holmes, G., & Karst, R. (1990). The institutionalization of disability myths: Impact on vocational rehabilitation services. *Journal of Rehabilitation, 56*(1), 20–27.

Individuals with Disabilities Education Act, 20 U.S.C. §1400 *et seq.* (1990).

Individuals with Disabilities Education Improvement Act of 2004, Pub. L. No. 108-446, § 601 *et seq.*, 118 Stat. 2647 (2005).

Jenkins, W. M., Patterson, J. B., & Szymanski, E. M. (1998). Philosophical, historical, and legislative aspects of the rehabilitation counseling profession. In R. M. Parker & E. M. Szymanski (Eds.), *Rehabilitation counseling basics and beyond* (3rd ed., pp. 1–40). Austin, TX: Pro-ed.

Kanfer, F. H., & Goldstein, A. P. (1991). Introduction. In F. H. Kanfer & A. P. Goldstein (Eds.), *Helping people change: A textbook of methods* (pp. 1–19). New York, NY: Pergamon.

Karvonene, M., Test, D., Wood, W., Browder, D., & Algozzine, B. (2004). Putting self-determination into practice. *Exceptional Children, 71*, 23–41.

Kavale, K. A., & Forness, S. R. (1996). Social skill deficits and learning disabilities: A meta-analysis. *Journal of Learning Disabilities, 29*, 226–237.

Lahmann, S. (2009, July 6). Disability 101—Disabled: Our largest minority. *Summit Daily.* Retrieved from http://www.summitdaily.com

Learning Disabilities Association of America. (2005–2011). *Types of learning disabilities*. Retrieved from http://www.ldanatl.org/aboutld/teachers/understanding/types.asp

Levinson, E. M., & Ohler, D. L. (1998). Transition from high school to college for students with learning disabilities: Needs, assessment, and services. *High School Journal, 82*(1), 62–69.

Lynch, R. T., & Gussel, L. (1996). Disclosure and self-advocacy regarding disability-related needs: Strategies to maximize integration in post-secondary education. *Journal of Counseling & Development, 74*, 352–357.

Mackelprang, R. W., & Salsgiver, R. O. (2009). *Disability: A diversity model approach in human service practice* (2nd ed.). Chicago, IL: Lyceum Books.

McNamara, B. E. (2007). *Learning disabilities: Bridging the gap between research and classroom practice*. Upper Saddle River, NJ: Merrill/Prentice Hall.

Miller, E., Chen, R., Glover-Graf, N., & Kranz, P. (2009). Willingness to engage in personal relationships with persons with disabilities: Examining category and severity of disability. *Rehabilitation Counseling Bulletin, 52*, 211–224.

Morrow, K. A., & Deidan, C. T. (1992). Bias in the counseling process: How to recognize and avoid it. *Journal of Counseling & Development, 70*, 571–577.

Murdick, N. L., Gartin, B. C., & Crabtree, T. (2007). *Special education law* (2nd ed.). Upper Saddle River, NJ: Merrill/Prentice Hall.

National Institute of Mental Health. (2008). *What is attention deficit hyperactivity disorder?* (NIH Publication No. 08-3572). Retrieved from http://www.nimh.nih.gov/health/publications/attention-deficit-hyperactivity-disorder/adhd_booklet.pdf

National Youth Leadership Network & Kids as Self Advocates. (2006). *Respectful disability language: Where's what's up!* Retrieved from http://www.disabilitylawcenter.org/publications/Language%20Doc.pdf

New ADA rules go into effect. (n.d.). Retrieved from http://www.abilitymagazine.com/New-ADA-Rules-Go-Into-Effect.html

North Carolina Department of Health and Human Services. (2012). *Attitudinal barriers*. Retrieved from http://www.ncdhhs.gov/dvrs/newspubs/pubs/Attitudinal_Barriers.pdf

Page, N., & Czuba, C. E. (1999). Empowerment: What is it? *Journal of Extension, 37*(5). Retrieved from http://www.joe.org

Palmer, S., & Wehmeyer, M. (1998). Students' expectations of the future: Hopelessness as a barrier to self-determination. *Mental Retardation, 36*, 128–136.

Patterson, C. H. (2004). Do they need multicultural competencies? *Journal of Mental Health Counseling, 26*, 67–73.

People with disabilities in the federal government: An employment guide. (n.d.). Retrieved from http://www.opm.gov/disability/text_files/Employment_Guide.PDF

Pivik, J., McComas, J., & Laflamme, M. (2002). Barriers and facilitators to inclusive education. *Exceptional Children, 69*(1), 97–107.

Power, P. W., & Dell Orto, A. (2003). *The resilient family: Living with your child's illness or disability*. Notre Dame, IN: Sorin Books.

Rapp, C. A., & Goscha, R. J. (2006). *The strengths model: Case management with people with psychiatric disabilities* (2nd ed.). New York, NY: Oxford University Press.

Rauscher, L., & McClintock, M. (1997). Ableism curriculum design. In M. Adams, L. A. Bell, & P. Griffin (Eds.), *Teaching for diversity and social justice* (pp. 198–225). New York, NY: Routledge.

The Regents of the University of California. (2008). *The Disability rights and independent living movement*. Berkeley: University of California, Berkeley.

Rehabilitation Act, 29 U.S.C. § 794 *et seq*. (1973).

Roden, J. M., Bannink, F. P., Maaskant, M. A., & Curfs, L. M. G. (2009). Solution-focused brief therapy with persons with intellectual disabilities. *Journal of Policy and Practice in Intellectual Disabilities, 6*, 253–259.

Rogers, C. R. (1957). The necessary and sufficient conditions of therapeutic personality change. *Journal of Consulting Psychology, 21*, 95–103.

Rosenthal, D. A., Chan, F., & Livneh, H. (2006). Rehabilitation students' attitudes toward persons with disabilities in high- and low-stakes social context: A conjoint analysis. *Disability and Rehabilitation, 28*, 1517–1527.

Rosenthal, D. A., & Kosciulek, J. F. (1996). Clinical judgment and bias due to client race or ethnicity:

An overview with implications for rehabilitation counselors. *Journal of Applied Rehabilitation Counseling, 27*(3), 30–36.

Schalock, R. L., Luckasson, R. A., Shogren, K. A., Borthwick-Duffy, S., Bradley, V., Buntinx, H. E., . . . & Yeager, M. H. (2007). Perspectives: The renaming of mental retardation: Understanding the change to the term intellectual disability. *American Journal on Intellectual and Developmental Disabilities, 45*, 116–124.

Schein, J. D. (1987). The demography of deafness. In P. C. Higgins & J. E. Nash (Eds.), *Understanding deafness socially.* Springfield, IL: Charles C. Thomas.

Schriner, K., & Scotch, R. K. (2001). Disability and institutional change: A human variation perspective on overcoming oppression. *Journal of Disability Policy Studies, 12*, 100–106.

Section 504 of the Rehabilitation Act, 34 C.F.R. § 104.35(b). (1977).

Siller, J. (1976). Attitudes toward disability. In W. S. Neff (Ed.), *Contemporary vocational rehabilitation* (pp. 67–69). New York, NY: New York University Press.

Soldier Rehabilitation Act of 1918, 40 Stat. 617.

Special Olympics. (2003). *Multinational study of attitudes toward individuals with intellectual disabilities.* Retrieved from http://www.specialolympics .org/research_multinational_attitudes.aspx

Stancliffe, R., Abery, B., Springborg, H., & Elkin, S. (2000). Substitute decision-making and personal control: Implications for self-determination. *Mental Retardation, 38*, 407–421.

Sullivan, W. F., Berg, J. M., Bradley, E. Cheetham, T., Denten, R., Heng, J., . . . & McMillan, S. (2011). Primary care of adults with developmental disabilities: Canadian consensus guidelines. *Canadian Family Physician, 57*, 541–553.

UIC National Research and Training Center on Psychiatric Disability & UIC NRTC Self-determination Knowledge Development Workshop. (2002). *Self-determination framework for people with psychiatric disabilities.* Chicago, IL: Author.

U.S. Department of Justice. (2011). *ADA 2010 revised requirements: Service animals.* Retrieved from http://www.ada.gov/service_animals_2010.htm

Van der Klift, E., & Kunc, N. (1994). Hell-bent on helping: Benevolence, friendship, and the politics of help. In J. Thousand, R. Villa, & A. Nevin (Eds.), *Creativity and collaborative learning: A practical guide to empowering students and teachers.* Baltimore: Paul H. Brookes.

Varela, R. A. (1983). Changing social attitudes and legislation regarding disability. In N. Crewe & I. K. Zola (Eds.), *Independent living for physically disabled people* (pp. 28–48). San Francisco, CA: Jossey-Bass.

Vocational Rehabilitation of Persons Disabled in Industry Act of 1920 (Smith-Fess Act), 41 Stat. 735.

Vogel, S. A., & Adelman, P. B. (1992). The success of college students with learning disabilities: Factors related to educational attainment. *Journal of Learning Disabilities, 25*, 430–441.

Waldrop, J., & Stern, S. M. (2003). *Disability status: 2000.* Retrieved from http://www.census.gov/ prod/2003pubs/c2kbr-17.pdf

Ware, N. C., Hopper, K., Tugenberg, T., Dickey, B., & Fisher, D. (2007). Connectedness and citizenship: Redefining social integration. *Psychiatric Services, 58*, 469–474.

Wehmeyer, M., Field, S., Doren, B., & Mason, C. (2004). Self-determination and student involvement in standards-based reform. *Exceptional Children, 70*, 413–425.

Wehmeyer, M., Kelchner, K., & Richards, S. (1996). Essential characteristics of self-determined behavior of individuals with mental retardation. *American Journal on Mental Retardation, 100*, 632–642.

Wright, B. (1983). *Physical disability: A psychosocial approach* (2nd ed.). New York, NY: Harper & Row.

Zascavage, V. T., & Keefe C. H. (2004). Students with severe speech and physical impairments: Opportunity barriers to literacy. *Focus on Autism and Other Developmental Disabilities, 19*, 223–234.

PART IV

IMPLICATIONS FOR PRACTICE

CHAPTER 18

The Practice of Culturally Alert Counseling: Part One

Garrett McAuliffe

Old Dominion University

Mario is a 17-year-old biracial young man of Puerto Rican and Italian heritage who has just moved to suburban Denver, Colorado. He is originally from a multiethnic community in Queens, New York. He speaks English and Spanish fluently. He was raised as a Roman Catholic and had, until recently, attended Catholic schools in Queens. Those schools had many Latino/Latina students from various countries. Mario had experienced little or no negative bias from his peers or others in his school there. His family's move to Colorado was due to his father's being transferred by the airline for which he works as a mechanic. The family members already miss their close extended family in the New York area, especially the father's mother, who lived next door and helped to raise Mario and his younger sister. There are only a handful of Latino/Latina students in Mario's new school, and Mario is not accepted by these students, who are mostly Mexican children of farm workers. He is ignored by most of the European American students, being seen by them as "not like us," especially given his Latin, New York accent. Most of the other students are white and Protestant, with a large segment being evangelical Christians. Mario has been unsuccessful in meeting girls as well. He is isolated and shows very low mood. The school counselor is alerted to his situation by an attentive English teacher who read a paper that Mario wrote called "I Am No One." The counselor, a middle-class European American woman from Minnesota of German and Norwegian descent, calls Mario into her office to check on his situation.

Mario's story is infused with important cultural issues. He has experienced cultural displacement in a number of ways. He is disconnected from his culture of origin. His accent and communication style are different from those of his peers. He looks different from the dominant group. He feels inadequate to meet the dominant standard for appearance, language, and religion. He is also in an important developmental phase as an adolescent, one in which peers are central to his sense of identity. These and other issues play parts in Mario's distress. This chapter is dedicated to helping counselors know what to do with

543

clients like Mario. The counselor who is working with Mario must bring culture to the foreground, at least part of the time, to help Mario trust the process, to incorporate specific ethnic dimensions (e.g., language, the nature of family, communication style), and to help him find strength from his heritage. Every client's world is constructed by cultural factors such as ethnicity, race, gender, social class, sexual orientation, age/generation, abilities/disabilities, and religion/spirituality. This chapter and the next chapter introduce practical strategies for counseling in a culturally alert fashion. You are invited to complete Activity 18.1, which will trigger your thinking on what to do as a counselor.

Activity 18.1   How Might a Counselor Help Mario?

In the case of Mario, what combination of the following should a counselor do? Check off the items that you believe would be important in this case:

Establish rapport by sharing aspects of herself as an adolescent who had also moved to a new school. _____

Show warmth and caring by attending to Mario with a concerned facial expression and some casual physical touching on the shoulder. _____

Assess depression and suicide by asking where he is on a 10-point scale of sadness. _____

Help him identify the strengths of his heritage by reading and talking to others of similar heritage in the community. _____

Form a group in the school for the 10 or so students who share Latino/Hispanic heritage. _____

Talk to the teachers and the principal about the situation so that it is addressed in a school assembly, for example, through a film presentation and discussion on diversity. _____

Bring in Mario's parents to explore the situation and their experiences. _____

Initiate or participate in efforts to reach out to the larger Hispanic community, which is composed mostly of Central American agricultural workers. _____

Go to his classes and open up the discussion of bias. _____

Refer Mario to a psychotherapist for his adjustment difficulties. _____

All of these interventions are actually worthy of consideration. They range from simple empathy and rapport, to parental involvement, to group psychoeducation, to community activities. The consequences of the counselor's action, or inaction, in such culturally infused situations can be enormous. In particular, clients from less dominant or marginalized groups are especially at risk, as can be seen in counseling attrition rates for clients of color, suicide rates for gay and lesbian youth, and rates of violence against women. For clients from dominant groups, culture is less a source of externally imposed distress. However, like in all cultures, it can still be a source of internal conflict as well as of strength.

OVERVIEW OF THE CHAPTER

This chapter first provides readers with general guidelines for culturally alert practice. It then gets more specific. It presents strategies for the first major grouping of culturally alert skills; accessibility.

The importance of this and the next chapter lies in their presenting the third group of multicultural counseling competencies: skills

(Sue, Arredondo, & McDavis, 1992). This topic is important because of its scarcity in the literature. Multicultural counseling skills are the least developed of the three multicultural competencies (i.e., awareness, knowledge, and skills; Alberta & Wood, 2009). To remedy that insufficiency, a literature review of multicultural counseling skills was done (McAuliffe, Grothaus, & Mendoza, 2011). Thus these two chapters are an attempt to present the best multicultural counseling practices that are available at this time. It should be noted that, for the sake of convenience, the term *practices* is used interchangeably with *skills* to describe these specific interventions.

This chapter is divided into two major parts. In the first section, complexities and controversies related to culturally alert counseling practice are presented. Then the three categories of culturally alert counseling practice are introduced; accessibility, assessment, and intervention. Skills for increasing accessibility are then discussed in more depth. The following chapter presents assessment and intervention in more detail.

A couple of provisos are in order. First, previous chapters already described a number of practices focused on working with specific populations. Therefore, these last two chapters complement those ideas. Second, remember that all counseling is multicultural counseling in that gender, race, ethnicity, social class, religion, sexual orientation, and ability/disability are always to be accounted for. Thus, for example, building rapport and evoking the influence of family systems are good practices for all counseling work. However, some of these skills, such as the more directive and behavioral approaches that are discussed in Chapter 19, are particularly relevant for work with members of specific cultural groups. Others, such as trust building and broaching, are crucial for encounters in which the client and counselor are from very different cultural groups.

CULTURALLY ALERT INTERVENTION: AN INEXACT ART

No single counseling theory, construct, or tradition adequately suits all of the cultural groups in the United States (Corey, 1996; Fuertes & Gretchen, 2001). The following statement captures the nature of culturally alert practice.

> Multicultural counseling is neither a theoretical orientation on its own nor is it an outgrowth of any one traditional orientation. [It consists of] using awareness of culture during counseling.... [It is] an added dimension to the therapy process, much like relationship building and other core conditions of counseling. (Kincade & Evans, 1996, p. 90)

Therefore, it is unrealistic to expect there to be a prescription for culture-specific interventions. Instead, culturally alert counseling consists of counselor vigilance about the impact of culture on people accompanied by a set of some culturally alert practices. In fact, many existing counseling approaches can be used, but in a culturally intentional way.

Culture and Counseling Methods: Current Status and Debates

The whole domain of culturally alert counseling intervention is new and emergent. Until about 20 years ago, the great psychodynamic, humanistic, and behavioral counseling meta-theories competed with each other to explain human nature and to suggest related helping strategies. Their proponents shared the modernist ambition to find and spread comprehensive, universal truths about humans. Each vied for dominance, and proponents sought arguments to prove their cases. Of course, many voices also spoke for an intelligently eclectic and integrated approach to counseling.

Counselors who enter the field now are participating in a humbler, more complex endeavor. The cultural construction of all counseling approaches, including supposed universal theories, is recognized. This so-called postmodern perspective posits that people tell stories based on their assumptions in order to explain the world. In that vein, counselors must recognize that counseling theories are stories themselves, each relatively useful or not in particular cultural contexts.

Today, therefore, counselors are challenged to know three types of stories: their own cultural stories, the story behind their counseling theories, and their clients' stories. The great Western counseling theories must be used judiciously by counselors who recognize that these theories are not universal solutions to universal human problems. They may be quite useful, but the theories, the counselors who use them, and their clients are always in a cultural discourse, as described in Chapter 1. This recognition of culture as a counseling factor has resulted in culturally alert counseling being called the emerging *fourth force* (after psychodynamic, humanistic, and behaviorist) in the field (Pedersen, 2001).

But there is a catch: Knowledge about culturally oriented counseling skills is emerging, being built as we speak from new research and theorizing. Rodriguez and Walls (2000) describe the state of the field in this way: "Current multicultural training efforts are 'top-heavy': understandably preoccupied with the development of multicultural awareness and with the dissemination of culture-specific facts and trends but neglectful of the skill-driven mechanisms by which such knowledge is translated into effective interventions" (p. 90). Of course, cultural self-awareness and knowledge of other cultures, which are the first two multicultural counseling competencies, are important foundations for any culturally alert practices (Hunt, Matthews, Milsom, & Lammel, 2006; Pedersen, 2004; Sciarra, Chang, McLean, & Wong, 2005). In that vein, Ponterotto, Utsey, and Pedersen (2006) note, "the first step for counselors . . . is to work through their own ethnocentrism" (p. 151).

While the skills domain of multicultural competency is still relatively new and evolving, there have been some promising research results, particularly in the area of trust and the therapeutic alliance. Studies have linked culturally alert counseling practice with enhanced perception of the counselor's credibility, trustworthiness, and effectiveness (Ancis, 2004; Zang & Dixon, 2001). Clients experiencing culturally alert practice report feeling "more understood and respected" (Smith, Richards, Granley, & Obiakor, 2004, p. 5). Given the acknowledged importance of the therapeutic relationship (Murphy, 1997), a culturally alert stance is a significant advantage.

The Particularist–Universalist Debate

The current discussion about how to practice multicultural counseling revolves around the tension between emphasizing *particulars* or universals. The extreme particularist view would prescribe specific (particular) culturally matched practices for each cultural group. Examples of particular practices include practicing healing methods and using very structured, directive methods for traditional members of certain ethnic groups. By contrast, as mentioned in Chapter 2, the universalist approach emphasizes the general application of Western counseling theories to individuals, regardless of culture. Counselors need not embrace either extreme position.

There is little empirical evidence to support the strict particularist matching of specific culturally based counseling methods with corresponding clients from those cultures (Atkinson & Israel, 2003). Attempts at matching a specific practice with members of a cultural group must always be qualified by the existence of individual client differences. Individual clients vary in levels of enculturation, acculturation, temperament, personal history, and the convergence of multiple cultural identities (e.g., gender, class, multiple ethnicities) in one person (Ancis, 2004; Robinson, 2005). Particularism is also limited by the fact that culture is not a total explanation for human behavior. While culture is always present in clients' lives, it may not be salient for their concerns at any one time. Instead, individual personality, situational, and universal human condition issues may be more prominent.

The universalist stance alone is also inadequate. A universalist view of applying a counseling theory to all clients without regard for culture is a form of cultural imperialism. Draguns (2002) refers to the folly of applying humanism, for example, as a cure-all for all clients:

Opportunities for misunderstanding . . . are prodigious. For example, a therapist's encouraging the client to search for his or her own solutions [i.e., in the person-centered tradition] can be misconstrued as indifference or even incompetence. . . . [Further,] what a therapist may intend as . . . egalitarianism may be interpreted by the client as a lack of respect and violation of dignity and decorum. (p. 43)

The Culturally Alert Alternative

Given the limitations of relying solely on either universalism or particularism, counselors need an alternative path to culturally alert counseling. Draguns (2002) provides a balance: "[Counseling], wherever it is applied, constitutes a blend of universally effective and culturally specific components" (p. 29).

It follows, then, that counselors can use traditional Western methods while being aware of culture, but do so selectively. They can also apply some culturally specific strategies, such as varying structure and directiveness, emotionality, and the use of silence and pause time. However, counselors must simultaneously remind themselves of the limits of generalizations: As stated earlier, individuals within groups vary greatly in their levels of acculturation, enculturation, and cultural identity, as well as other characteristics (Matsumoto & Juang, 2004). Thus, all generalizations must be qualified.

Illustration of Culturally Alert Counseling

What follows is an illustration of how the universal, the individual, and the cultural are integrated in one case. In this example, one of the counselor's intentions is to establish trust in the context of a cultural factor, namely gender. Another counselor intention is to explore the client's concerns and to educate the client, if that is warranted, about the gender dimensions of her situation.

In this interchange, empathic listening is mixed with six particular counseling skills, all of which are discussed in this and the next chapter:

1. Broaching cultural differences
2. Culturally oriented questioning
3. Intentional self-disclosure
4. Instruction and information-giving
5. More directive leads
6. Advocacy

In the process of responding to the client, the counselor must consider all three previously mentioned dimensions that affect lives:

1. The cultural *particulars* of gender and other factors
2. The *individual's* situation, history, personality, and temperament
3. The *universal* human emotions and dilemmas of living

The client, Andrea, is discussing her male partner's emotional unavailability and lack of involvement in their children's upbringing. He is sometimes verbally abusive to her and to the children, especially when he is under the influence of alcohol. She is very unhappy with him and is thinking of separating. This segment picks up in the middle of the session.

Client: I don't know if you can understand my need to make sure that my children are okay and also my fear of being left without a partner who can provide for them and keep me from being alone.

Counselor: It seems that you're uncertain that I, as a male, can appreciate your dedication to your children's welfare and, perhaps, recognize your financial worries. Is that correct? How does it feel to work with me on these issues?

[COUNSELOR INTENTIONALLY BROACHES THE GENDER DIFFERENCE TO SEE IF IT NEEDS TO BE EXPLORED.]

Client: Well, I don't know. You seem okay. I guess we'll have to see. A lot of men seem to forget that children need much, almost constant care. My husband stays away both physically and mentally from us and leaves their total caretaking to me. And I feel very alone. I don't have family in the area, so I need his emotional support and involvement.

Counselor: I hear some anger about his not doing his part, which is made worse by your aloneness.

[EMPATHIC RESPONSE WITH EMPHASIS ON TWO FEELINGS]

Client: Yes. But I feel stuck. He says he has to be gone most of the time to make money for the family. But I think he does it for himself. He says he can't stand kids most of the time. However, I'd still rather have him around more and have less money. Plus, if it were about money, I could even add some income by working for pay myself. But I can't put in many hours of work outside of family duties, with the children to care for and all.

Counselor: That is an issue for many women—being torn between their commitments to family, work, and a partner. I sense that you are clear that the children are your current top priority and that you want help in raising them. Your dedication to your children is clear. I can sense the strong nurturing you give them. The other side of your dedication is what might be called "caretaking exhaustion," which many women experience—taking care of others and not leaving room for themselves.

[COUNSELOR EMPOWERS BY (1) INFORMING THE CLIENT OF SOME GENDER PATTERNS AND (2) POINTING OUT CLIENT STRENGTHS. ADDITIONALLY, COUNSELOR (3) NOTES MIXED FEELINGS/DILEMMA BETWEEN DEDICATION AND EXHAUSTION.]

Client: Yes! But what am I supposed to do? The three kids are all under 6 years old!

Counselor: [Pause] Tell me what you learned in your religious tradition and from your family about women's and men's roles.

[COUNSELOR PROBES RELIGIOUS, ETHNIC, AND SOCIAL CLASS CULTURAL MESSAGES ABOUT GENDER.]

[SEGMENT DELETED, INCLUDING PORTIONS ON CULTURAL MESSAGES AND ASSESSMENT OF ANY PHYSICAL ABUSE, OF WHICH THERE HAS BEEN NONE.]

[TEN MINUTES LATER]

Counselor: How would you like things to be in the ideal?

Client: I'd like my husband to be around, to treat us right, and to bring in the income we need.

Counselor: Let's look at all of these wishes plus your needs for self-care. It is not uncommon for men to believe that they have to prove themselves in the world at the expense of family and relationships. Sometimes I even have to catch myself when I get buried in reading the newspaper after work while my kids need care and attention. Your husband hasn't caught himself, it seems.

[COUNSELOR POINTS OUT MALE PATTERN AND SELF-DISCLOSES.]

Client: That's for sure, to say the least! He justifies it. And he expects sex after all that! It feels like there is nothing left between us. I should end the marriage. But I never thought I would be without a man. I do try to please him so he'll stay. But I'm at the end of my rope.

Counselor: You mentioned previously your anxiety about "being alone" and your panic attacks when you were a child. Could you tell me more about that?

[SEGMENT DELETED]

[LATER IN THE SESSION]

Counselor: Your husband seems to you to be one more person to take care of. In fact, *you* want some emotional care taken of you too, by him. Your needs get lost in the process. And I hear that you don't want to do that anymore but can't figure out how. I know that you said that you were raised to believe that the man is both the provider and authority at all times. Let's hold that aside for a moment and talk about your needs.

[MATERIAL DELETED IN WHICH COUNSELOR AND CLIENT EXPLORE SUPPORT GROUPS, INCLUDING RELIGIOUS COMMUNITIES, FOR HER TO CONNECT WITH]

[TOWARD THE END OF THE SESSION]

Counselor: Our time is nearly up. We have done a lot of work today, it seems to me. I'd like to ask you two things: What did you think of our session today? And what might you want to ask me, about anything? I see us as working together to help you get your own needs met while continuing to nurture those you love.

[COUNSELOR GIVES CLIENT A CHANCE TO SHARE PERCEPTIONS, TO PARTICIPATE IN THE HELPING PROCESS.]

Activity 18.2 asks you to think critically about the cultural dimensions in Andrea's situation and the interaction between Andrea and her counselor.

Activity 18.2   Thinking About the Case of Andrea

1. Identify at least one each of the cultural, individual, and universal elements in the case of Andrea:

   Cultural:

   Individual:

   Universal:

2. What, in your view, might the counselor do differently or add to the counseling work as it proceeds in the future?

In this scenario, the male counselor attempted to gain the trust of the female client by responding empathetically, self-disclosing, acknowledging the gender difference, showing awareness of distinct behavior patterns for men and for women, directing the client to resources, affirming strengths, and using the term *us* to show his alliance with her. He also checked in with the client on how the session was working for her.

Overall, the counselor acknowledged the cultural *particulars* of gender, religion, ethnicity, and social class as well as the *individual's* unique life circumstances and temperament, all the while knowing that such phenomena as fear, longing, loneliness, intimacy, and security are *universal* human needs.

The counselor had many additional choices. One was to suggest outside supportive resources, such as a women's group, books that provide relevant information and support for her situation, and referral to financial counseling and/or social services guidance so that she might have a financial plan. Another issue that could have been addressed in this session was the client's and her husband's ethnic communities and their influence on each of their expectations for family life. All of the above can be held in the counselor's mind as possibilities.

Now that these general issues have been discussed, this chapter turns to the first set of culturally alert counseling practices—those that enhance accessibility and connection between counselors and clients.

SKILLS THEME ONE: ACCESSIBILITY

Counseling can be daunting for members of many ethnic and religious groups. For example, many clients of color might see counseling as a largely European American enterprise, from the nature of its origins to the ethnicity of most of its current practitioners. Similarly, working class clients often doubt the value of paying money for "just talking." Actually, in any cross-cultural counseling encounter, a client often wonders, for example, "Can this Latino counselor understand me?" (from the perspective of a European American client), "Does this male 'get' women's issues?" "Does that heterosexual counselor resonate with the concerns of gay people like me?"

Because of this uncertainty, people do prefer to see counselors who are like themselves. But that is not possible at all times, nor does it guarantee successful work. In order to counter these culturally related doubts that clients bring, counselors must be accessible. To paraphrase the previously-mentioned expression: "You have to get in the door before you can rearrange the furniture." In that vein, counselors cannot assume that clients can find them, afford them, understand them, or trust them. Three ways for counselors to be accessible are described below: being approachable, adapting language, and showing trustworthiness.

Accessibility by Being Approachable

Being approachable begins with counselors making services physically accessible to clients. In our literature review, we found four ways to make counseling and counselors more approachable: place and time, atmosphere, cost, and outreach. These aim at welcoming all cultural groups to the counseling enterprise.

Place and Time

Many clients do not engage in counseling because of logistics, which include the location, the times services are offered, and/or difficulties with issues such as childcare or transportation. As noted in Chapter 13, for example, low-income working parents often have little choice about jobs, working conditions, and hours, and they cannot take time off from work to attend counseling or school events without the risk of losing pay or even their jobs. Therefore, accessible programs make place and time convenient for clients.

Regarding place, approachable programs have central or satellite locations that are easily reached and accessible to people with disabilities. Accessibility by time is represented, for example, by counselors being available when clients are.

For example, school counselors and mental health agencies might be available on some evenings and late afternoons or on some weekends. They can also make home visits (Kim, 2005).

Atmosphere

A second way for counselors to be approachable is to create an inviting atmosphere for diverse clients. The physical counseling setting should be inclusive and welcoming, with culturally diverse décor, evidence of commitments to social justice (but perhaps not explicit factional political allegiances), and hospitable front-line staff (Neukrug, 2002). No matter how neutral we think décor is, it is always saying something about some dimensions of culture, whether they be class, sexual orientation, race, or gender. Decorating one's office with diversity-attuned posters and other artifacts (e.g., gay-supportive symbols, multiethnic artifacts, multiple religious symbols) shows some clients that the counselor is aware of all cultures and all groups' struggles.

In the specific area of physical atmosphere and disabilities, given that people with disabilities are the biggest minority group in the United States (Hanjorgiris & O'Neill, 2006), accommodations for disabilities must be made. Examples of such accommodations include having materials for people with visual impairments (Hunt et al., 2006), such as large-print, braille, and/or audio versions of consent forms, and counselors being familiar with various assistive technologies that might be needed by persons with disabilities (Olkin, 2004). Finally, there should be multicultural training for all in the office, including support staff (Paniagua, 2005).

Cost

The third factor in approachability is cost. It is a simple fact that clients with fewer financial resources cannot often see private practitioners because most counselors do not accept Medicaid (see Chapter 13). Even with insurance, co-payments are daunting to people with low income. This is particularly important, as persons of lower socioeconomic status have higher rates of certain mental disorders, such as depression. Individuals who have low incomes include many college students and young adults, who are in a life phase in which money is scarce. One form of demonstrating cost approachability is to offer some pro bono (lower-cost or free) counseling services and sliding fee scales based on client income.

Outreach

If potential clients do not know of counseling services, or assume that they are for others, the conditions of place and time, atmosphere, and cost might be for naught. The fourth and last way that culturally alert counselors can be approachable is by reaching out to potential clients who might not come to counseling before a crisis occurs. Counselors need to anticipate the concerns of particular populations and be creative in reaching them (Rayle, 2005). Such outreach can be planned if counselors are active in and aware of the needs of the communities in which their clients live (Sue et al., 1992; Vera, Buhin, & Shin, 2006). For example, a school counselor can arrange for transportation to evening school assemblies for low-income parents who lack transportation. One recommended means of planning and accomplishing outreach is to collaborate with leaders and/or indigenous healers in the community (Simcox, Nuijens, & Lee, 2006; Wallace, 2006). Thus, for example, the school counselor might link with local religious organizations to create space for afterschool tutoring programs.

A particular expression of doing outreach is prevention. Counselors can balance the more common reactive work with the provision of preventive activities in the communities they serve (D'Andrea, 2006; Ponterotto et al., 2006; Vera et al., 2006). For example, school counselors might run career planning groups for undecided high school juniors and seniors. Other prevention efforts include conducting study skills and test-taking workshops for lower-achieving college students; providing support groups for lesbian, gay, and bisexual clients; reaching out to unemployed men and women;

offering groups for immigrant students and adults; facilitating community forums about issues of concern (Wallace, 2006); and providing culturally sensitive life skills training (D'Andrea, 2006).

Accessibility by Adapting Language

The second major category in the literature on culturally alert counseling skills under the accessibility theme is the use of language in counseling. There are two ways that language can be used in a culturally alert way. One is understanding the literal language of the client. The other is related to slang, jargon, and terms for cultural groups.

Using a Translator

Language is obviously a basic issue in communication, whether it is auditory or sign language. The most basic concern is whether the counselor and client speak the same tongue; that is not assured in the United States. According to data from the 2000 U.S. Census, 11 million people in the United States indicated that they speak English "not well" or "not at all" (cited in Paniagua, 2005, p. 28). The *Multicultural Counseling Competencies* provide guidance in this regard:

> Culturally skilled counselors take responsibility for interacting in the language requested by the client and, if not feasible, make appropriate referral. A serious problem arises when the linguistic skills of a counselor do not match the language of the client. This being the case, counselors should (a) seek a translator with cultural knowledge and appropriate professional background and (b) refer to a knowledgeable and competent bilingual counselor. This guideline is basic but too often ignored, resulting in miscommunication, frustration, and loss of trust. (Sue et al., 1992, p. 483)

Language is particularly important in diagnosis, as diagnosis tends to be less accurate when clients are not allowed to use their language of preference (Paniagua, 2005).

When a client does not speak English, or speak it well, a translator can be used. In the case of translators, the following guidelines should be considered:

- The translator should have training in mental health and culturally related mental disorders/syndromes.
- It is preferable for the translator to share the client's racial and ethnic background and dialect, and there should not be a major difference in their levels of acculturation.
- Early in the process, the counselor should allow the client and translator to have some time together (without the counselor) in order to discuss common interests.
- Plan ahead for extra time, as translated exchanges are likely to take longer.
- Avoid using a friend or relative (especially the client's child) as a translator. (Paniagua, 2005, pp. 16–17)

There is some controversy in the field about whether translators should be used at all. Paniagua (2005) points out two problems with the use of translators:

> First, the translator introduces a third person into the psychotherapy process, and this can lead to distortion and misrepresentation of the client's verbalizations. Omissions, additions, and substitutions are examples of common distortions or errors associated with the process of translation in the practice of psychotherapy. . . . Second, the client may find communicating through a translator to be a disagreeable experience. (p. 15)

Obviously, there is a tradeoff in using a translator. However, having a translator shows interest in and respect for the language differences, and it provides a means of communication when there may be no other.

Being Alert to Jargon, Inclusive Language, and Terms

The second aspect of language that makes a counselor more or less approachable lies in how she or he uses language.

Jargon

First, counselors must watch jargon. Many clients are already intimidated by the jargon of the professional counseling and education fields. Clients can be daunted merely be entering a school or agency building to meet with a "professional." One way to be accessible is for counselors to speak in commonly understood language in order to avoid jargon. For example, acronyms for programs and diagnoses, such as IEP, OCD, and ADHD, should be explained in clear terms.

Inclusive Language

Second, the culturally alert counselor would use inclusive language. A counselor must be sensitive to the connotations of dominant terms, how they serve to marginalize nondominant persons, and the unearned power they promote. For example, counselors can be inclusive by saying "her or him" when speaking generically instead of only "him," "humankind" instead of "mankind," "staffing" instead of "manning," "partner" instead of "husband/wife" or "boyfriend/girlfriend," and "place of worship" instead of the Christian term "church." Counselors should scan their intake forms and other paperwork for inclusive language, or lack thereof (Miville & Ferguson, 2006).

Terms

A related notion around approachability in language is using clients' preferred terms for their groups. Using culturally preferable terms is a subtle undertaking, as terms change in different eras, variously taking on negative and positive connotations. For example, the formerly neutral term *retarded*, which simply denotes "delayed," took on a derogatory connotation over time. As a result, the more recent term *intellectual disability*, which denotes the same phenomenon, came into use. A similar evolution has occurred with terms such as *girl* (for an adult woman), *Negro*, *Oriental*, and *homosexual*. Each of these terms was once considered acceptable for members of these nondominant groups. But members of these groups recognized that those names had been given by the dominant group.

Instead, many members of nondominant groups often wished to claim their own names for themselves. The counselor should make an effort to learn and use language that is preferred by members of a cultural group. Culturally alert counselors should be ready to use preferred terms such as *woman* for an adult (as opposed to *girl*), *African American*, *Asian*, *lesbian*, and *gay man*. There is no guarantee, however, that particular members of any group would agree on such terms. The counselor can simply ask the client what term she or he prefers.

It should be noted, paradoxically, that formerly negative terms can reverse their meanings when nondominant groups reclaim them as positive labels, as some gay men and lesbians have done with *queer*, some Appalachian people have done with *hillbilly*, and some activist women's groups have done with *girl*.

Accessibility by Showing Trustworthiness

The third, and most critical, dimension of cultural accessibility is the client believing that the counselor is trustworthy. Trust in the counselor's competence and in her or his concern are needed if the client is to hear the counselor. It is also a precondition for clients to feel safe in revealing themselves.

Establishing trust is an early task of all counseling relationships. It is most easily established when the counselor and client share similar cultures. In cross-cultural encounters, rapport must be explicitly attended to. Trust is particularly important if the counselor is a member of the dominant group and the client is not. Kincade and Evans (1996) describe the reasons for this uncertainty:

> Many clients from cultural . . . groups that have historically been at the bottom of the class structure . . . have developed coping mechanisms that may make it difficult for them to trust counselors but [those coping mechanisms] are appropriate within the context of their lives. (p. 104)

Thus clients who are gay, working class, black, Latino, Asian, or American Indian, for example, must overcome their wariness in order to trust a counselor from the dominant group. In that vein, Pedersen (2003) proposes that the counseling context must be an especially "safe space"; he reminds counselors that in counseling, "dangerous questions" must be asked (p. 29). These include questions related to sensitive gender and racial differences and attitudes or a particular social group's negative social stigma, as is still often the case for homosexuality, poverty, and disability. As Lewis (2003) says, "Creating safety and trust while having difficult dialogues is central to multiculturalism, as is creating an environment in which clients from oppressed groups feel secure enough to engage in the counseling process" (p. 262).

Overall, ways to increase trust are for the counselor to show warmth, engage in small talk, and make self-disclosures. For example, counselors can share something of themselves at some point in the early part of the relationship (Wehrly, 1995). Such revelation can increase the shared bond by helping clients see the counselor as an authentic person with a "real life" (Davies & Neal, 2003). In fact, counselor self-disclosure has been found to often be a prerequisite to client disclosure with people from communitarian cultures, such as many Native American Indians and Asian Americans (Sue & Sue, 2008). Simple disclosures about interests, relatives, and family can be valuable. Of course, such disclosure should be brief, relevant, true, and followed by a quick return to the client's concerns.

There is at least one situation in which trust is usually easier to establish. That is when a client is in significant distress or crisis (Kopta, Howard, Lowry, & Beutler, 1994). Thus, a culturally different client who has urgent emotional needs will likely disclose more openly even if trust issues have not been dealt with extensively.

Five specific ways of increasing trust are presented next: (1) sharing commonalities with clients who are culturally different from you; (2) providing informed consent; (3) proactively "leaning in" to client mistrust and anger; (4) demonstrating knowledge of clients' cultures; and (5) broaching cultural differences, especially if they seem to be a concern. Of course, the two previously described practices of being approachable (through place and time, atmosphere, and outreach) and adapting language of course contribute to trust-building.

Sharing Commonalities

Trust is increased when counselors and clients recognize shared worldviews or other commonalities, despite having sometimes seemingly great cultural differences between them. Clients often wonder if counselors can "get" them if the counselors are of a different gender, race, ethnicity, sexual orientation, ability, social class, or religion. To counter that emphasis on difference, counselors can share commonalities with clients. As Ibrahim (2003) declares, "The key to establishing a trusting and respectful relationship [is] . . . being able to find common ground or creating a shared worldview in an emotionally warm environment" (p. 198). This can be done by selective self-disclosure about parallel life experiences. But finding such commonalities is not always possible and, of course, not enough in itself. For example, a black working-class client might more easily trust a white counselor when he learns that the counselor has also come from the working class. Of course, such self-disclosure should not be made in an artificial or overdone fashion, but should flow naturally out of the conversation.

Providing Informed Consent

Another way to increase rapport that is related to self-disclosure is to provide culturally informed consent (Davidson, Yakushka, & Sanford-Martens, 2004). This type of informed consent is especially important for members of nondominant ethnic groups and persons with low incomes, for whom counseling might seem like a mysterious middle-class, foreign practice. Many members of such groups have had little exposure to the culture and norms of counseling work. In that regard, the *Multicultural Counseling Competencies* urge counselors to "educat[e] their clients to the processes of psychological intervention, such as goals, expectations, legal rights, and the counselor's orientation" (Sue et al., 1992, p. 483; see Appendix A). This statement urges counselors to create an open, transparent counseling environment, including sharing diagnoses, notes, the counselor's background, awareness of a client's culture, the general methods of counseling, and aspects of medications.

"Leaning In" and Being Empathic

Another way of establishing trust is to demonstrate an especially proactive form of empathy called "leaning in" (McGoldrick, 1998). Leaning in is especially important when counselors are confronted with ideas and customs that are foreign, even distasteful, to them. There are legitimate grounds for counselors to have an initial negative reaction to some client disclosures, manners, and attitudes. For example, a client may make an ethnically prejudicial remark or advocate a custom, such as corporal punishment of children, that is distasteful or even morally questionable to the counselor.

As mentioned in Chapter 1, it is easier to psychologically assimilate, that is, to take in what is familiar and therefore comfortable, than to accommodate. For this reason, when a counselor meets a "foreign" idea or custom, she or he is likely to have at least momentary difficulty with it. However, culturally alert counseling requires the ability to pause, reflect, and consider alternative responses. Leaning in allows that counselor to accommodate unsettling newness and contradiction.

Leaning in consists of actively hearing the legitimacy of customs and ideas that are initially irritating to the counselor. McGoldrick (1998) proposes that counselors do so to counter their prejudices and other cultural blinders when they are confronted with unfamiliar or difficult cultural differences. McGoldrick has the following recommendation for the counselor who is feeling resistant: "Just listen. Try to take in the pain of what [the other] is saying, instead of thinking of the exceptions" (p. 225). She offers the example of having to lean in to appreciate men's dilemmas when she was initially immersed in feminism. At first, she couldn't hear that men had gender-related dilemmas also. Leaning in helped her let go of her bias and hear the new perspective.

McGoldrick (1998) proposes that leaning in is especially important when there are power differences and cultural controversies. Leaning in might be especially important for the agnostic who is working with the evangelical Christian, and vice versa, or the feminist counselor who is working with the woman client who adheres to strict gender roles. Cultural empathy and leaning in are especially important for dominant group members when they are confronted with client claims of oppression. Dominant group members might be inclined to think, regarding oppression, "Everyone has equal opportunity. Let's drop the subject and move on." Leaning in requires pausing and working hard to enter another's framework. It is an important attitude for any counselor who thinks "I just don't get it" about a value or cultural dimension.

Demonstrating Cultural Knowledge

Trust is also engendered by the counselor's demonstrating specific knowledge of clients' cultures and their experiences of oppression (Pieterse & Collins, 2004). The counselor should not have to ask the client to completely educate the counselor on the client's cultures (Davies & Neal, 2003). Empathy and questioning are not substitutes for cultural knowledge. For example, in East and Southeast Asian cultures, as described in Chapter 7, gifts are part of relationship acknowledgment. The counselor who knows about gift giving might give a "gift" to the client in the form of sharing a problem-solving strategy, a tentative diagnosis, or a reframe early in the process (Paniagua, 2005; Wehrly, 1995).

In this area of having and using cultural knowledge, there are at least two general cultural issues that counselors should know about: communication styles and cultural phenomena. In the first area, culturally alert counselors should be able to engage appropriately in a variety of verbal and nonverbal helping responses. They should not be tied down to only one counseling approach but should recognize that helping styles may be culture-bound. When they sense that their helping style is limited and potentially inappropriate, counselors can adjust it or raise a question about its usefulness.

Knowledge of cultural communication styles would include, for example, being oriented to the importance of the relationship for more collectivist, status-oriented, and uncertainty-avoidant cultures (Matsumoto, 1991). In those cases, counselors might need to regularly acknowledge the relationship with the client and with family members, using compliments and statements of appreciation. They might also learn to be less confrontational and more indirect when challenging client thinking, due to the collectivist emphasis on preserving harmonious relationships. Another example of a cultural communication style to be aware of lies in head nodding among Japanese people. For many Japanese people, vigorous head nodding is not necessarily a sign of agreement, but instead shows attentive listening.

Other cultural phenomena that a counselor should be familiar with are artistic expressions, verbal expressions, values about health and family, and core beliefs. Counselors could know about such phenomena as the meaning of Afrocentric hair styles; gay "chosen families"; hip-hop music; salsa dancing; sickle-cell anemia; women's career–family conflicts; working-class values; the Rule of Opposites for Native American Indians; the central place of family involvement in the counseling process for Middle Eastern clients; and fundamental Islamic, Jewish, Christian, pagan, and other tenets.

A qualification about how much cultural knowledge a counselor can expect to have is in order. Counselors cannot be expected to know everything about clients' cultures. In cases where counselors are unaware of aspects of a client's culture, they can ask (Wehrly, 1995). (See the Doing Culturally Oriented Questioning section in Chapter 19.)

In sum, to be able to demonstrate cultural knowledge, counselors should have a solid working understanding of each of the cultural groups that are discussed in this book. Further, to educate themselves counselors can participate in cultural events, read, watch, and consult with cultural informants.

Broaching Cultural Differences

At times, the counselor will sense a tension in the room that might be related to trust. As mentioned earlier, clients generally prefer to work with counselors of the same race, gender, sexual orientation, and ethnicity as themselves. Ambivalence about working with a counselor of a different culture can be forthrightly dealt with by the counselor acknowledging the presence of cultural differences, sometimes called *cultural immediacy*.

The counselor initiates such immediacy through what Day-Vines et al. (2007) call *broaching*. Broaching consists of the counselor bringing up the subject of cultural differences. Following are some questions that a counselor might use to broach culture:

> People have different perspectives based on their experiences and cultures. You and I are from different cultures. How do you feel about working with me, a [fill in race/ethnicity/sexual orientation], on your concerns?
>
> How do you feel about working with a [fill in the cultural group] counselor?
>
> What is this experience like for you as a(n) [fill in race/ethnicity/sexual orientation, etc.] man/woman?

The counselor can then follow the client's response to these questions by saying, "If at any time you have any questions about my ability to understand you and your situation, please tell me."

Thus, the elephant in the room is acknowledged. Culture may or may not be seen as a salient issue at that point. Either way, the client is now more likely to feel comfortable bringing up the topic if it becomes a concern. If it is an issue, it can be explored. The client feels invited to ask the counselor questions about herself or himself and to share any doubts about the counselor's ability to assist the client. The result of such conversations is likely to be increased trust between counselor and client

REFERENCES

Alberta, A. J., & Wood, A. H. (2009). A practical skills model for effectively engaging clients in multicultural settings. *The Counseling Psychologist, 37,* 564–579.

Ancis, J. R. (2004). Culturally responsive practice. In J. R. Ancis (Ed.), *Culturally responsive interventions: Innovative approaches to working with diverse populations* (pp. 3–21). New York: Brunner-Routledge.

Atkinson, D., & Israel, T. (2003). The future of multicultural counseling competence. In D. B. Pope-Davis, H. L. K. Coleman, W. M. Liu, & R. L. Toporek (Eds.), *Handbook of multicultural competencies in counseling and psychology* (pp. 591–606). Thousand Oaks, CA: Sage.

Corey, G. (1996). Theoretical implications of MCT theory. In D. W. Sue, A. E. Ivey, & P. B. Pedersen (Eds.), *A theory of multicultural counseling and therapy* (pp. 99–111). Pacific Grove, CA: Brooks/Cole.

D'Andrea, M. (2006). In liberty and justice for all: A comprehensive approach to ameliorating the complex problems of white racism and white superiority in the United States. In M. G. Constantine & D. W. Sue (Eds.), *Addressing racism: Facilitating cultural competence in mental health and educational settings* (pp. 251–270). Hoboken, NJ: Wiley.

Davidson, M. M., Yakushka, O. F., & Sanford-Martens, T. C. (2004). Racial and ethnic minority clients' utilization of a university counseling center: An archival study. *Journal of Multicultural Counseling and Development, 32,* 259–271.

Davies, D., & Neal, C. (2003). *Pink therapy: A guide for counselors and therapists working with lesbian, gay, and bisexual clients.* Philadelphia, PA: Open University Press.

Day-Vines, N. L., Wood, S. M., Grothaus, T., Craigen, L., Holman, A., Dotson-Blake, K., & Douglas, M. J. (2007). Broaching the subjects of race, ethnicity, and culture during the counseling process. *Journal of Counseling and Development, 85,* 401–409.

Draguns, J. G. (2002). Universal and cultural aspects of counseling and psychotherapy. In P. Pedersen, J. Draguns, W. Lonner, & J. E. Trimble (Eds.), *Counseling across cultures* (5th ed., pp. 29–50). Thousand Oaks, CA: Sage.

Fuertes, J. N., & Gretchen, D. (2001). Emerging theories of multicultural counseling. In J. G. Ponterotto, J. M. Casas, L. A. Suzuki, & C. M. Alexander (Eds.), *Handbook of multicultural counseling* (2nd ed., pp. 509–541). Thousand Oaks, CA: Sage.

Hanjorgiris, W. F., & O'Neill, J. H. (2006). Counseling people with disabilities: A sociocultural minority perspective. In C. C. Lee (Ed.), *Multicultural issues in counseling: New approaches to diversity* (3rd ed., pp. 321–342). Alexandria, VA: American Counseling Association.

Hunt, B., Matthews, C., Milsom, A., & Lammel, J. A. (2006). Lesbians with physical disabilities: A qualitative study of their experiences with counseling. *Journal of Counseling and Development, 84,* 163–173.

Ibrahim, F. A. (2003). Existential worldview counseling theory: Inception to applications. In F. D. Harper & J. McFadden (Eds.), *Cultural and counseling: New approaches* (pp. 196–208). Boston, MA: Allyn & Bacon.

Kim, Y. S. E. (2005). Guidelines and strategies for cross-cultural counseling with Korean American clients. *Journal of Multicultural Counseling and Development, 33,* 217–231.

Kincade, E. A., & Evans, K. M. (1996). Counseling theories, process, and interventions within a multicultural framework. In J. L. DeLucia-Waak (Ed.), *Multicultural counseling competencies: Implications for training and practice* (pp. 89–113). Alexandria, VA: Association for Counselor Education and Supervision.

Kopta, S. M., Howard, K. I., Lowry, J. L., & Beutler, L. E. (1994). Patterns of symptomatic recovery in psychotherapy. *Journal of Consulting and Clinical Psychology, 62,* 1009–1016.

Lewis, J. (2003). The competent practice of multicultural counseling: Making it happen. In G. Roysircar, D. S. Sandhu, & V. E. Bibbins (Eds.), *Multicultural competencies: A guidebook of practices* (pp. 261–267). Alexandria, VA: Association for Multicultural Counseling and Development.

Matsumoto, D. (1991). Cultural influences on facial expressions of emotion. *Southern Communication Journal, 56,* 128–137.

Matsumoto, D., & Juang, L. (2004). *Culture and psychology* (3rd ed.). Belmont, CA: Wadsworth/Thompson Learning.

McAuliffe, G. J., Grothaus, T., & Mendoza, K. (2011). *Content analysis of the multicultural counseling intervention literature.* Unpublished manuscript, Old Dominion University, Norfolk, VA.

McGoldrick, M. (1998). Belonging and liberation: Finding a place called home. In M. McGoldrick (Ed.), *Re-visioning family therapy: Race, culture, and gender in clinical practice* (pp. 215–228). New York, NY: Guilford Press.

Miville, M. L., & Ferguson, A. D. (2006). Intersections of sexism and heterosexism with racism: Therapeutic implications. In M. G. Constantine & D. W. Sue (Eds.), *Addressing racism: Facilitating cultural competence in mental health and educational settings* (pp. 87–103). Hoboken, NJ: Wiley.

Murphy, J. J. (1997). *Solution-focused counseling in middle and high schools.* Alexandria, VA: American Counseling Association.

Neukrug, E. (2002). *Skills and techniques for human service professionals: Counseling environment, helping skills, treatment issues.* Pacific Grove, CA.: Brooks/Cole.

Olkin, R. (2004). Making research accessible to participants with disabilities. *Journal of Multicultural Counseling and Development, 32,* 332–343.

Paniagua, F. A. (2005). *Assessing and treating culturally diverse clients: A practical guide* (3rd ed.). Thousand Oaks, CA: Sage.

Pedersen, P. B. (2001). Multiculturalism as a generic approach to counseling. *Journal of Counseling and Development, 70,* 6–12.

Pedersen, P. B. (2003). "Walking the talk": Simulations in multicultural training. In G. Roysircar, D. S. Sandhu, & V. E. Bibbins (Eds.), *Multicultural competencies: A guidebook of practices* (pp. 29–38). Alexandria, VA: Association for Multicultural Counseling and Development.

Pedersen, P. B. (2004). The multicultural context of mental health. In T. B. Smith (Ed.), *Practicing multiculturalism: Affirming diversity in counseling and psychology* (pp. 17–32). Boston, MA: Pearson.

Pieterse, A. L., & Collins, N. M. (2004, February). *Active multicultural awareness and counselor training: A critique and extension of current approaches to competence.* Paper presented at the 21st Annual Winter Roundtable on Cultural Psychology and Education, New York, NY.

Ponterotto, J. G., Utsey, S. O., Pedersen, P. B. (2006). *Preventing prejudice: A guide for counselors, educators, and parents* (2nd ed.). Thousand Oaks, CA: Sage.

Rayle, A. D. (2005). Cross-gender interactions in middle school counselor-student working alliances: Challenges and recommendations. *Professional School Counseling, 9,* 152–155.

Robinson, T. L. (2005). *The convergence of race, ethnicity, and gender: Multiple identities in counseling* (2nd ed.). Upper Saddle River, NJ: Pearson.

Rodriguez, R. R., & Walls, N. E. (2000). Culturally educated questioning: Toward a skills-based approach in multicultural counselor training. *Applied & Preventive Psychology, 9,* 89–99.

Sciarra, D., Chang, T., McLean, R., & Wong, D. (2005). White racial identity and attitudes towards people with disabilities. *Journal of Multicultural Counseling and Development, 33,* 232–242.

Simcox, A. G., Nuijens, K. L., & Lee, C. C. (2006). School counselors and school psychologists: Collaborative partners in promoting culturally competent schools. *Professional School Counselor, 9,* 272–277.

Smith, T. B., Richards, P. S., Granley, H. M., & Obiakor, F. (2004). Practicing multiculturalism: An introduction. In T. B. Smith (Ed.), *Practicing multiculturalism: Affirming diversity in counseling and psychology* (pp. 3–16). Boston, MA: Pearson.

Sue, D. W., Arredondo, P., & McDavis, R. J. (1992). Multicultural counseling competencies and standards: A call to the profession. *Journal of Counseling and Development, 70,* 477–486.

Sue, D. W., & Sue, D. (2008). *Counseling the culturally diverse.* New York, NY: Wiley.

Vera, E. M., Buhin, L. & Shin, R. Q. (2006). The pursuit of social justice and the elimination of racism. In M. G. Constantine & D. W. Sue (Eds.), *Addressing racism: Facilitating cultural competence in mental health and educational* (pp. 271–287). Hoboken, NJ: Wiley.

Wallace, B. C. (2006). Healing collective wounds from racism: The community forum model. In M. G. Constantine & D. W. Sue (Eds.), *Addressing racism: Facilitating cultural competence in mental health and educational settings* (pp. 105–123). Hoboken, NJ: Wiley.

Wehrly, B. (1995). *Pathways to multicultural counseling competence: A developmental journey.* Pacific Grove, CA: Brooks/Cole.

Zang, N., & Dixon, D. N. (2001). Multiculturally responsive counseling: Effect on Asian students' rating of counselors. *Journal of Multicultural Counseling and Development, 29,* 253–262.

CHAPTER 19

The Practice of Culturally Alert Counseling: Part Two

Garrett McAuliffe, Tim Grothaus
Old Dominion University

David Paré
University of Ottawa

Ali Kyle Wolf
University of North Carolina at Greensboro

This chapter describes two categories of culturally alert counseling skills: assessment and intervention. These are practical strategies that the counselor might use every day in order to do culturally alert counseling. These skills range from simple culturally educated questioning to recognition of indigenous healing practices.

SKILLS THEME TWO: ASSESSMENT

Counselors know that there is no counseling without ongoing assessment of the client, for counseling is a dialogical process. The process of assessment occurs throughout counseling. Counselors continually assess the client's mental status, assets, and other characteristics. Assessment may even precede the initial client–counselor meeting. For example, before a first session counselors might have referral information or records to preview. When the client arrives, counselors also assess by using their observational skills to evaluate the client's functioning through her or his verbal and nonverbal behavior.

Assessment is powerful because it influences the course of counseling. That is especially why assessment must account for culture. In Ancis's (2004b) words, "Understanding the client's cultural and sociopolitical context is essential for accurate assessment, interpretation, and treatment" (p. 8).

Unfortunately, instances of cultural ignorance and bias in assessment have occurred. For example, African American clients score lower on intelligence tests administered by European American evaluators than they do on the same tests when evaluated by African American evaluators (Paniagua, 2005). The test-takers' self-beliefs seem to be affected by the test giver, especially in tests that require interactions.

Diagnosis is a specific form of assessment. It can be affected by skin color and dialect. For example, Paniagua (2005) notes that "when clinicians are not aware of a client's racial/ethnic identity, they tend to arrive at the correct diagnosis, whereas when they know the racial/ethnic identity of a non-Anglo client, their diagnoses tend to be more severe" (p. 134). In addition, Hays, Chang, and Dean (2007) found that some counselors resented wealthy clients and assessed them as having few serious problems when that was not the case.

Culturally alert assessment asks the counselor to have a "third ear" open for cultural dimensions that help to explain a client's situation. In order to know the client better, counselors must find out about the client's world. That includes the always-present cultural dimension (Pedersen, 2004). Such assessment comes in three forms: culturally oriented questioning in the interview, culturally sensitive diagnosis, and culturally sensitive use of tests. In each of these cases, the client should be a participant. She or he should know the nature and foundations of the questions or instrument used and be part of the meaning-making that results from the assessment activity.

Four types of culturally alert assessment are discussed here: simple client observation, culturally oriented questioning, diagnosis, and testing.

Culturally Alert Observation of Clients

Counselors must be especially alert to client emotion by observing tone of voice, gestures, and facial expressions. These nonverbals include looking away, body shifting, jiggling legs, and gestures such as closing one's arms, nose touching, or lint picking (Ivey, Ivey, & Zalaquett, 2010). These behaviors can indicate discomfort, conflict, or some kind of avoidance. However, they may have different meanings according to culture.

In cases where culture may affect the interpretation of such behaviors, the counselor can inquire about these behaviors or, if trust has been established, point them out and possibly interpret them. For example, in one case a counselor said,

"When I asked about how you felt about your father, you crossed your arms and were silent." The client was a Chinese young adult who believed that he should never criticize a father's authority. Thus the counselor's inquiry caused conflict for the client, who would not publicly acknowledge his feelings toward his father. The counselor in this case followed with, "It is not all right to think negatively of your father, is it?" Then the counselor, showing respect for the cultural norm, let the client choose whether he wanted to disclose his feelings.

Previous chapters presented specific cultural norms around verbal and nonverbal expression. Some of those, as they affect client observation, are American Indians' tendency to restrain facial expression, African Americans' norm of showing such expression, southern European Americans and Latinos being more likely to touch than northern European Americans, smiling being a sign of awkwardness in traditional Japanese culture, and European Americans expecting listeners to look at the speaker. Counselors can be alert but not absolute in their observations of clients.

Doing Culturally Oriented Questioning

Culturally oriented questioning refers to the practice of intentionally asking clients about the meaning and nature of the cultural dimensions of their lives. The importance of asking for clients' cultural stories is emphasized by Rodriguez and Walls (2000): "Client self-report is the most reliable source of information regarding the relevance of cultural factors. [It] always supercedes the counselor's textbook knowledge of that culture" (p. 93). Even when counselors know much about a client's culture, checking how it plays out for that particular client is essential. By inquiring, counselors can avoid making incorrect assumptions about the nature and impact of clients' cultures. These inquires will especially help counselors assess clients' enculturation and acculturation (see Chapter 4). The asking of such questions is actually common in everyday life: People who find themselves with a culturally different person frequently ask questions about the other's culture to reduce the uncertainty of the situation and increase predictability.

Counselors can inquire about at least three topics: (1) the importance, or salience, of culture for a client; (2) the values and customs of the client's culture; and (3) the experiences of oppression for members of nondominant groups. Box 19.1 has examples of culturally oriented questions that a counselor might ask.

Box 19.1   Suggestions for Culturally Oriented Questions

Following are some suggested questions, organized by general intent, that bring the cultural dimension into the work.

Overall Importance of Culture

What place did a gender [and/or social class] script play in your career [or relationship] choices?

Help me understand what you are going through as a(n) [fill in ethnicity/race/sexual orientation] woman/man.

In what way has your ethnicity influenced your life?

Different people have different perspectives based on their experiences. In our [school/community/agency], we have a wide range of cultures. How do you feel that your culture affects your relationship with others?

How do you think people perceive you as a result of your ethnicity [disability, sexual orientation, upbringing, etc.]? What is that like for you?

Norms in a Client's Culture

What would you like me to know about your experience in your culture?

The Client's Experience With Cultural Others, Including Experiences of Bias

What was your first experience with someone different from you?

What has been your experience with other races (ethnic groups, etc.)?

What has your experience as a(n) [fill in ethnicity/race/sexual orientation] woman/man been at this [school/college/workplace/other institution]?

Ironically, with such questioning counselors can avoid overemphasizing culture. After all, they might assume that culture wields more power in some clients' lives than it actually does. In fact, the importance of culture will vary from person to person. Merely knowing a person's gender, sexual orientation, ethnicity, religion, or social class does not indicate the power of those factors in her or his worldview. If clients are in a nondominant group or are immigrants, culture will likely be central. If clients are in stages of cultural identity development in which their culture has become prominent for them, it will also probably be very important.

Practicing Culturally Sensitive Diagnosis

The third topic under culturally alert assessment is diagnosis. Diagnosis is an attempt to succinctly capture key characteristics of a person's mental state. It can be a reminder that there is more than meets the eye when it comes to clients. In fact, diagnosis may especially help counselors who, due to their developmental and humanistic tradition, might underestimate the seriousness of clients' disorders. Diagnosis was not popular with counselors in the past because it seemed to interfere with an egalitarian, authentic relationship between counselor and client. It was also seen as objectifying clients instead of treating them as whole persons.

Positive Aspects of Diagnosis

There are many positive dimensions to diagnosis, when done carefully and tentatively. When diagnosis is used judiciously and not treated as an absolute, it can help counselors raise hypotheses about the client's dynamics. In turn, diagnosis, at its best, can also help counselors plan actions that correspond to the nature and severity of a client's distress and avoid imposing arbitrary, unethical interventions.

Diagnosis can help clients themselves. A clear set of terms and explanations for emotional distress can transform self-blame into self-acceptance of a known phenomenon. Thus, clinical depression and generalized anxiety, to name two examples, can be framed as expressions of a combination of biological and psychological concomitants, none of which are the "fault" of the individual. In its best sense, therefore, diagnosis can be a humanizing and comforting phenomenon. It can counteract the historical tendency to blame individuals for mental distress, which was common in pre-psychological Western societies. It can be concluded, therefore, that when used carefully, diagnosis can be a complement to good interviewing and ongoing assessment.

Potential Negative Aspects of Diagnosis

Diagnosis also has well-known risks. A counselor might view a diagnostic category as an essential characteristic of an individual. A diagnostic category is a socially constructed generalization that fits more or less with a person's experience. A diagnostic category is the result of a professional community's agreement. Such categorizations are approximations, fluid notions that cannot capture any one individual's experience. The diagnostic category captures common elements across individuals. However, the idiosyncratic dimension must be accounted for by the counselor. Therefore, there are as many individual expressions of, for example, generalized anxiety disorder as there are persons, in terms of the frequency, internal experience, and triggers for what is called anxiety. Therefore, diagnosis must always be done tentatively, with the recognition of individual and cultural variation in how disorders are experienced and expressed.

Culture and Diagnosis

Like all psychological constructions, diagnosis is an expression of culture. The accepted guide in much of the world for such diagnosis is the *Diagnostic and Statistical Manual of Mental Disorders*. The latest version as of this writing is the 4th edition, Text Revision (*DSM-IV-TR*; American Psychiatric Association, 2000); the 5th edition will be available in 2013. The *DSM* is a U.S. product and is therefore particularly situated in a U.S. context. While the *DSM* is an attempt to objectify observations about people, those observations are always made within a language and a culture. That, in itself, does not discount the value of diagnosis. In fact, the same basic patterns of mental disorders have been found around the world (Westermeyer, 1987). However, how these disorders are expressed and interpreted is influenced by culture, including how a community treats those who experience them. Therefore, it is important for the culturally alert counselor to consider diagnostic categories as social constructions, not entities. They have been assembled through a process of consensus by Western psychiatrists, social workers, and psychologists.

Guide to Culturally Alert Use of the DSM

Following is a three-step guide to culturally alert diagnosis: (1) assessing client cultural identities and salience before diagnosing, (2) considering local descriptions of mental distress, and (3) working through the *DSM-IV-TR* in an Axis IV-III-I-II order. Each of the three steps is discussed next. Additional information on cultural factors in diagnosis can be found in three places in the *DSM-IV-TR*: on p. xxxiv, in Appendix I, and in the descriptions of some disorders throughout the manual.

Assessing Enculturation, Cultural Identity, and Salience

Before doing a *DSM-IV-TR* diagnosis, a counselor should, early in the relationship, assess the client's experience of her or his culture. Three dimensions can be assessed: level of enculturation ("What was it like where you grew up?" "What did you learn about [e.g., sexuality, spirituality, achievement, gender roles, emotional expression]?"), cultural identity development ("How do you feel about being [e.g., Muslim, gay, female, working class]?"), and the salience of her or his culture (e.g., "How important is being [e.g., Jewish, Puerto Rican, from the rural Midwest] to you?"). The culturally oriented questioning that was discussed earlier in this chapter should precede a diagnosis. Of course, enculturation, cultural identity, and salience can also be assessed by listening to the client and watching her or him. By such assessment of cultural dimensions, the counselor might discover, for example, that a client is mainly experiencing an acculturation problem, which is described in the Other Conditions (i.e., not official mental disorders) section of the *DSM-IV-TR*. For example, a young immigrant may find that her young adult identity problem around career or relationships is exacerbated by her acculturation difficulties, including her language and appearance, and is inseparable from them. Culture can also play a significant role in religious, academic, and occupational problems, none of which are themselves mental disorders. A cultural explanation of the client's distress should be considered early in the client assessment, especially for members of nondominant groups.

Recognition of Cultural Terms for Mental Distress

A second step in culturally alert diagnosis is to consider the "local" cultural description of a client's symptoms. For example, many European and African Americans describe a family member or coworker who has become unable to function well as having had a "nervous breakdown." That culture-bound designation was the Western folk term from the 1930s through the 1970s for a host of possible conditions, mostly major depression, and it is still used by some. But there is no "nervous breakdown" in the *DSM*. Past Western terms for such a syndrome were *melancholia* and, later, *neurasthenia*. Other common Western cultural descriptions of mental disorders include "having the blues" and "a case of nerves." Each comes with a corresponding explanation and sometimes treatment suggestions. The *DSM-IV-TR* now terms such notions *folk categories,* although, curiously, it leaves out the preceding Western folk terms. *DSM-IV-TR* folk categories include such notions as *zar,* a term used in parts of North Africa and the Middle East to describe dissociative episodes ascribed to being possessed by a spirit; *ataque de nervios,* a Hispanic term for a sense of being out of control, often as a result of a stressful event; and *hwa byung,* which translates literally from Korean as "anger syndrome" and includes a host of symptoms that are related to the suppression of anger, such as insomnia, fatigue, dysphoria, indigestion, and palpitations. The culturally alert counselor should know, or learn about, such categories when working with specific populations. Then the counselor can complement that understanding with the Western diagnostic descriptions of those symptoms and explain those to the client, if warranted.

Using the DSM-IV-TR With Cultural Alertness

Counselors can do culturally alert diagnosis by considering the *DSM* in this order: Axis IV, III, I, and II. First, counselors can consider the Psychosocial and Environmental Problems, or Axis IV. Many emotional difficulties can be culturally related, such as inadequate social support, discrimination, disruption of family, illiteracy, unemployment, inadequate housing, insufficient finances, inadequate health care services, lack of transportation, or exposure to disasters and war. Each of those problems is delineated in Axis IV.

In line with looking at Axis IV psychosocial or environmental problems, counselors should consider culturally related problems that can cause distress, such as religious or spiritual problems, acculturation problems, or identity problems. For example, the children of immigrants from collectivist cultures are often caught between a Western emphasis on (1) autonomy or separation from family and (2) an ethnic expectation to have ultimate loyalty to the group. These concerns are listed under Other Conditions in the *DSM-IV-TR*.

Next, culturally alert counselors should weigh the medical conditions (Axis III) that might contribute to, trigger, or be the source of distress. In some cultures, medical conditions are commonly hidden from oneself and from others, and it may take some effort for the client to even know of or acknowledge physical pain (McGoldrick, 2005).

Clinical disorders or other conditions that may be a focus of clinical attention (Axis I) can next be considered. Here, cultural considerations are also warranted. Some seeming disorders are actually acceptable cultural expressions, such as talking to spirits or hearing direction from a deity. Knowing those cultural phenomena should not, of course, rule out more serious mental disorders.

Finally, Axis II, which includes personality disorders, must be addressed with special care. Culture particularly affects personality. For example, what is seen as aggressive in midwestern U.S. culture might be seen as merely direct and involved by New Yorkers (Tannen, 1990). Similarly, what is avoidant in one culture can be merely respectful in another. However, it should be reiterated that cultural elements do not preclude serious disorder in the area of personality. Counselors can use the filter of culture to distinguish the merely culturally acceptable, but perhaps contextually inappropriate, from the consistent pattern of dysfunction that is a personality disorder.

Using Tests in a Culturally Alert Fashion

A fourth and final dimension of culturally alert client assessment lies in the use of formal psychological testing. Tests can be helpful for the counseling process. When they are used well, psychological tests such as career interest inventories and personality tests can help clients decide on a course of career action, recognize psychological issues (such as depression) that need to be confronted, optimize strengths, and manage weaknesses, as in the case of learning style and personality assessment.

However, when formal tests are used, they must be put in cultural context. Tests can masquerade as universal when they are in fact culture bound. Two dimensions of testing call for cultural alertness. One is the validity of tests themselves and the other is their use.

Cross-Cultural Validity

Two important factors in the cross-cultural fairness of tests are their content and their norming.

Content

The content of tests is inevitably constructed from material that is more or less culture bound. For example, a mental status examination commonly asks, "Who is the president of the United States?" or "What are the four seasons?" Each of those questions relies on local knowledge. For example, in tropical climates, there are often only rainy and dry seasons. Thus, a first requirement for a psychological test is that its content acknowledge the culture of the client if the counselor is to make generalizations about the client's mental status.

If items on a test seem to be particularly culture bound, counselors should go over the specific items with clients instead of relying on simple summary scores. For example, a recent immigrant from the Middle East who is taking *The Self-Directed Search* (Holland, Powell, & Fritzsche, 2011) might not know items such as "a Human Relations course," "income tax forms," or even "the Red Cross."

Norming

A second concern about the cultural validity of tests is their standardization on particular populations. A counselor should note the group on which a test was normed. If tests are used to make predictions about the future (e.g., how well a person will perform on a job), they must show that they predict accurately for all groups.

The Use of Tests

In addition to determining the validity of tests, it is also important for counselors to monitor the use of test results. Interpretations and other uses can affect educational and career opportunities for clients. For example, aptitude and achievement tests have been used to strictly assign students into lower and higher academic tracks in school. This assignment early in life can have long-term consequences for students of color and for students of lower socioeconomic status. A classic statement of this "cumulative deficit problem" is the following:

> At the very outset of their educational careers, on the basis of low test results, these students are placed in classes for poor performers; when they fail to make progress, which is again measured in terms of tests not geared for them, they fall further and further behind their white [and middle-class] peers. (Deutsch, 1967, as quoted by Samuda, 1998, p. 9)

When counselors see members of one ethnic group disproportionately placed in lower-level tracks, they must raise questions about such tracking, including "What are the reasons for such disparities?" and "How can I as a counselor promote adequate academic preparation for members of all groups?"

Guidelines for Culturally Alert Testing

Counselors might apply a "test for culturally valid tests" (Paniagua, 2005, p. 126) by asking these questions:

Content Equivalence

Are the items relevant for the cultures being tested? Items featuring dominant culture customs, games, or history may be less meaningful or unknown to members of nondominant cultures.

Semantic Equivalence

Is the meaning of each item the same in all cultures that are being tested? Some terms have different connotations or meanings across cultural lines; for example, in Ireland and Britain, the word *bonnet* refers to the part of a car that covers the engine.

Technical Equivalence

Is the method of assessment comparable across cultures? Sole reliance on verbal questioning may disadvantage individuals from nondominant cultures who rely more heavily on nonverbal communication.

Criterion Equivalence

Would the interpretation of variables remain the same when compared with the norms for all cultures studied? Desired levels of measured variables, such as autonomy or masculinity, may be specific to the dominant culture. Their values may not be shared by nondominant cultures.

Conceptual Equivalence

Does the test measure the same theoretical construct across cultures? A construct such as self-esteem in an individual from a culture that reinforces modesty and collective identity may result in inaccurate interpretation of the results.

Paniagua (2005) asserts that in fact no existing psychological test meets all five criteria. Counselors should use the least-biased instrument available. They should also complement such tests with culture-specific assessments, including assessing socioeconomic factors in test performance and asking culturally appropriate questions—all in the client's preferred language (Paniagua, 2005; Pedersen, 2004).

THEME THREE: COUNSELING INTERVENTIONS

Intervention is of course the heart of the work of the counselor. Interventions, whether they be interpretations, cognitive disputing, narrative reconstruction, or person-centered responding, are meant to trigger more helpful ways of thinking, feeling, and acting in clients. Therefore, in addition to the first two criteria for culturally alert counseling, namely being accessible and doing culturally sensitive assessment, counselors must have culturally alert intervention skills.

This major section of the chapter is organized around five groupings of culturally alert strategies. The first grouping targets internalized oppression through evoking cultural strengths and doing liberation counseling. The second consists of applications of common counseling interventions to cultural diversity. The third is applying the narrative approach in a culturally alert way. The fourth is advocacy, which is mentioned here but discussed fully in Chapter 3. The fifth is using or referring to indigenous healing practices.

Intervention Strategy One: Challenging Internalized Oppressions

A primary task of the culturally alert counselor is to help all clients free themselves from self-limiting attitudes based on cultural membership. People from dominant and nondominant groups can suffer from limiting internalized cultural assumptions. Examples of such inaccurate negative self-perceptions include believing that membership in one's group indicates less competence, less attractiveness, or other inferiority. For example, a working-class Latina might think that she should not aspire to higher education, because that is for others. In the case of a dominant group member, a male might be captive of a rigid gender role, believing that he has to be stoical and authoritarian, leaving no room for emotional expression and nurturance of others. Each of these represents internalized oppression.

What to Do

Counselors can evoke and challenge such self-limiting internalized oppressions. Two means of challenging internalized oppression are presented here. The first is strengths-oriented counseling. The second is applying liberation counseling.

Emphasizing Cultural Strengths

Not all clients know or believe in the strengths of their cultures. In fact, the hegemony of European American, Christian, heterosexual, male, and middle-class standards in the United States results in other cultural groups being seen as substandard.

The terms *internalized colonization* (Said, 1994) and *autocolonialism* (Utsey, Bolden, & Brown, 2001) have been used to describe oppressed peoples' acceptance of the dominant culture's ideology. Such internalized colonization is expressed in oppressed peoples' embarrassment at languages, accents, physical appearances, clothing, and names, to mention a few examples. For example, due to European colonization, lighter-colored skin is seen as prettier in many countries in Africa, the Middle East, and Asia. In those places, paler women are believed to be more educated and more desirable (Samhita, 2006).

Counselors can counter oppression by explicitly helping clients discover their cultural strengths (Ancis, 2004a; Constantine, 2006; Miville & Ferguson, 2006). Such strengths exist in every culture. For example, an overarching strength of nondominant cultures is their resilience in the face of regular oppression and discrimination. Nondominant cultures have thrived despite such oppression through such adaptations as religious gatherings and traditions, code languages, musical expressions, resistance, and mutual support,

In previous chapters, cultural strengths of each group are mentioned. For example, in Chapter 6, the African American cultural strengths of resilience, flexibility, persistence, extended family, religiosity, and forgiveness are named. In Chapter 8, American Indian cultural strengths such as belonging, generosity, and tradition are evoked. In Chapter 10, on Middle Eastern Americans, strengths that were presented include extended family support and expression through dance.

The counselor can evoke cultural strengths also with members of dominant cultures. For example, the men's movement has attempted to reclaim aspects of men's culture. Members of Northern European American ethnic groups can similarly find strength in such values as individualism and the work ethic. White Southerners can identify with white Southern civil rights activists, rather than with the oppressors. Thus, counselors can help any client find and build on cultural strengths.

The counselor might bring out such strengths in at least two ways, namely, the asset search and the guided imagery activity. First, a simple positive cultural asset search might suffice to bring out cultural strengths. This search technique is illustrated in the videos that are available as complements to this text (McAuliffe, 2007).

The Asset Search

An asset search can be done by simply asking the client, "What positive qualities do you see in your ethnic group, gender, social class, sexual orientation, or religion?" The counselor can also suggest some strengths based on her or his knowledge of the client's life and cultures. Activity 19.1 is a cultural strengths self-assessment, which suggests cues that the counselor can use to evoke strengths in others.

Activity 19.1   Cultural Strengths Search: Self-Assessment

In order to help clients find strengths, it is helpful for the counselor to have discovered her or his own cultural assets. Consider your ethnic or regional culture(s). Think about the values, humor, habits, norms, and other cultural expressions. List as many positive assets of your culture(s) as you can. This exercise is best completed after you have had a chance to read and think about your culture, perhaps through an ethnicity self-awareness project.

Some of the strengths of my culture:

In work:_____

In humor: _____

In interpersonal support (e.g., family, networks): _____

In leisure/recreation: _____

In arts: _____

In the community/neighborhood: _____

In cultural artifacts, places, or symbols that can evoke pride and strength:_____

In activities: _____

Other areas of strength: _____

Guided Imagery

A more sensory way of evoking cultural strengths is to use with clients the Guided Imagery With Positive Cultural Symbols activity in Box 19.2 (Ivey, D'Andrea, Ivey, & Simek-Morgan, 2002). In this activity, clients imagine a positive cultural symbol, such as a stained glass window, a revered ethnic figure, or a sacred place, with their eyes closed. Later, outside the session, they are directed to mentally access that symbol when they experience culturally related doubts and difficulties. It is also demonstrated in the video that accompanies this book (McAuliffe, 2007).

Box 19.2   Guided Imagery With Positive Cultural Symbols

This exercise is designed to help clients recognize and use strengths from their cultural background. When employed carefully, using concrete language, the exercise also can be effective with children.

Inform your client about your process and intent. Rather than surprise the client, tell her or him what is about to happen and why it is potentially helpful.

Generate an image. Ask your client to relax and then to generate a positive image that can be used as a resource. Suggest that the image be related to cultural background. A black person might imagine a picture of an African or African American hero, a Navajo person a mountain or religious symbol, an Egyptian the pyramids, a Chinese person Confucius, and so on.

Focus on the image. Ask the client to see the image in her or his mind. What does she or he see, hear, feel? Ask the client to locate the positive feelings in the body. Then identify that image and feeling as a positive resource that is always available to the client.

Take the image to the problem. Using relaxation and free association techniques, guide the client to the problem that has previously been discussed or to any problem the client chooses. Suggest to the client that he or she use the positive resource image to help work with the problem. It is important to stress to the client that the image may or may not solve the problem. If the problem seems too large, the image should be used to work on a small part of the problem rather than to solve it.

Source: Adapted from Ivey et al. (2002).

Liberation Counseling

In addition to challenging clients' internalized oppressions by means of cultural strengths searched, counselors can apply what Ivey (1995) calls *psychotherapy as liberation*. This approach is here called *liberation counseling* (LC). This model directly helps clients challenge both internal and external limitations. In Ivey's words, liberation counseling aims at helping clients "see how their difficulties are the logical result of social history" (p. 54). With that knowledge, clients might be able to consider what relationship they wish to have with their cultures of origin and what aspect of their difficulty is due to external oppression. In a sense, liberation counseling is a way of helping clients have more choices about their relationships to their cultures.

Liberation counseling strategies are explicitly tailored to a client's current cultural identity level, or stage. In fact, LC aims at promoting clients' cultural identity development to a higher level, when that seems appropriate. Ivey (1995) describes five client cultural identity levels (or stages) that guide the counselor. These stages parallel those of the Cultural Group Orientation Model (CGOM) from Chapter 2 and other cultural identity development models. To simplify the model, we have presented four stages by combining the first two stages (Naïve/Accepting). Each stage is accompanied by suggested counselor actions that might move the client along in her or his development. It should be noted that a person is never fully *in* a stage of cultural identity. Instead, a person uses thinking from a number of stages, likely centered on one way of thinking (Middleton, Erguner-Tekinalp, & Petrova, 2005).

In order to illustrate LC at each stage, the case of a woman who has been living in an abusive situation with her husband and two children is presented.

Naïveté/Acceptance

Clients who are Naïve or Accepting are unaware of their culture and its effects on their opportunities and limitations. In the case of Tiffinee, who was in an abusive partnership, she at first merely accepted that she, as a woman, was powerless due to financial dependence and internalized notions that a woman needs to be married. She did not consider the gender factor in her experience or think about how to empower herself.

With a client at the Naïve/Accepting stage, the counselor would *encourage her to first describe her experience in concrete terms*, thereby transforming her story from inchoate physical expressions, such as stomach disorders, anxiety, and anger, into a story that is partially outside her sensory experience. The counselor can then *point out discrepancies as well as the cultural dimension:* "You say that he treats you well much of the time, but you are angry when he puts you down and raises his voice. Women sometimes get caught up in taking such abuse because of financial needs. Is that possibly what is going on for you?" Here, the gender issue is intentionally raised through culturally oriented questioning. The client is prepared to challenge any internalized oppressions, which might take the forms of self-blame, automatic receipt of a problematic status quo, and a sense of hopelessness.

Naming and Resistance

A counselor might meet a client at the Naming and Resistance stage (equivalent to Encountering in the CGOM). At this stage, a client has at least acknowledged that she has learned some behaviors as part of enculturation and is beginning to be aware that they might affect her life situation. With a client who is at the Naming and Resistance stage, a counselor would help her *explicitly name the contradictions between herself and society* through discussion in the session or via out-of-session reading or support groups.

The counselor would then *encourage the client to gather resources* so that she might have alternatives to her previous acceptant stance. Tiffinee might read a book on gender roles, contact a lawyer who specializes in women's issues, meet with an advocate for women who have endured domestic violence, and see a financial counselor. By venturing down this road, she will be taking the first steps toward separating herself from the automatic thinking of the Naïve/Accepting stage—that women must depend on men, that women cannot work on their own finances, that women must accept verbal and even physical abuse. The counselor can also help Tiffinee gather resources by helping her discover strong women role models and confirming the assets of women's culture.

Redefinition and Reflection

Through those beginning awareness activities, the client can move toward Redefinition and Reflection (Immersed and Reflective in the CGOM). Conversely, a client might already show characteristics of this stage. At Redefinition and Reflection, the client is becoming aware of her internal responsibility to reconsider socially prescribed roles that are no longer acceptable. She is beginning to take a perspective on her culture, that is, to de-center rather than being unthinkingly wedded to its social roles and internal prescriptions for thinking and acting in certain ways.

The counselor might then *affirm the growth* by saying to Tiffinee, "I hear a strong voice in you that is saying, 'I'm not going to play out a powerless script as a woman. I can stand up for myself and for my children at the same time.'" At this stage the counselor might hear Tiffinee declare, "I called the women's advocate at the shelter and got great support and advice. I've hired a lawyer. I've learned a lot in a short time about finances. I've gotten support from friends. I'm not going to be a victim. The children and I can live well in this house without him, without his abusing us with his financial and physical power. I have met a group of women through the local college women's center who help each other be strong and assertive."

Multiperspective Integration

At the stage of Multiperspective Integration (Multicultural/Critically Conscious in the CGOM), the client is engaged in continually creating her cultural identity and is actively seeking multicultural experiences, including understanding men's issues. She can now move back and forth from reflection, to anger, to taking action, to taking some responsibility for her choices, to recognizing external barriers.

At this point, the counselor can *help the client take action for herself and others.* The counselor (or the client) can also *affirm progress* with a statement such as "You have been advocating for other women by speaking with them about similar situations to the one you were in, and by speaking to men also. You recognize the trap that women can fall into—being caregivers to others while not taking care of themselves. You also realize that men are caught up in this gender discourse too, as they scramble to prove themselves by being breadwinners and being strong at the expense of being nurturing and relationship oriented. But you know that is no excuse for abuse." The counselor can now help Tiffinee make difficult but more intentional choices about career, family, and housing. She might now help others who are abused.

This example has emphasized the internal transformation of one woman. The counselor can also work to change external oppressions, a topic that was discussed in Chapter 3 and is addressed later in this chapter.

A proviso is in order as we close this section. It is not the counselor's job to "force" changes in cultural identity on clients. In fact, in some contexts, so-called liberation might increase frustration and disconnection from the client's community. For some clients, it is difficult to return "home" after certain liberating experiences (Montgomery, Marbley, Contreras, & Kurtines, 2000). For example, the first author of this chapter once worked with a woman from a conservative Islamic culture who was an international student in the United States. Her increasing awareness of Western feminism led to frustration. She recognized that when she returned to her country, she might be ostracized for taking on a more equal role with men. In this case, the counselor helped her weigh her behavioral options, rather than merely encouraging her to forge a public feminist identity in her country. The decision to engage in liberation work must therefore be made in consultation with the client, based on her or his needs and cultural context.

Activity 19.2 asks you to apply liberation counseling strategies to a particular case.

Activity 19.2 Applying Liberation Counseling to a Case

Here is the case of Ronaldo. Read it, and imagine him evolving through each of Ivey's (1995) cultural identity stages. Look back at the text on liberation counseling, and then write suggestions for counselor or client activity at each stage.

Ronaldo is a working-class Mexican American man from rural western Texas who was heard to say, "I've never seriously considered going back to school in the field I'd love, school teaching. I've always just assumed, somehow, that was something out of my reach as a farm worker's son. I've never had high career aspirations. That's why I've always followed my friends, first into the Navy and now back here as a stockman in this department store. I just have to make a living. Plus, I don't know any Mexican Americans who have college degrees. And I have an accent. I don't think I would be hired as a teacher."

Cultural Identity Stage Counselor and/or Client Activities That Might Promote Growth

Naïve/Accepting

Naming and Resistance

Redefinition and Reflection

Multiperspective Integration

Intervention Strategy Two: Adapting Common Counseling Approaches to Culture

In addition to encouraging clients to find strength in their cultures, culturally alert counselors also can practice the classic Western methods for counseling. However, counselors can adapt common counseling approaches to specific cultures, as is described in this section.

In a review of the multicultural counseling literature, nine counseling practices emerged that can be adapted to members of particular cultural groups: (1) authority and directiveness, (2) the use of groups, (3) expression and emotion, (4) career counseling, (5) the use of insight, (6) cognitive behavioral approaches, (7) use of humor, (8) positive reframing, and (9) bibliotherapy. Each is discussed in turn.

Authority and Directiveness

Authority, directiveness, and solution focus in counseling are likely to suit members of more hierarchical cultures. Many cultures do not value self-exploration and emotional expression. The literature suggests that counselors be more solution focused and more directive in general with persons of lower socioeconomic status and traditional Asians, Middle Easterners, and Latinos, as described in the chapters in this book that deal with those specific populations. For example, Chapter 7 proposes that counselors are likely to be more successful if they selectively give directives and advice with traditional Asians. With many persons from low socioeconomic status, a practical and advisory role is often similarly effective, more so than immediate exploration of inner psychological states.

Communicating one's expertness is also recommended when working with clients from hierarchical cultures. The counselor can help clients gain confidence in her or his capability early in the counseling relationship by mentioning previous successes with similar clients or displaying degrees and certifications earned (see Chapter 7). Such strategies can appeal to those cultures' valuing of hierarchical relationships and expertise in authorities.

It is also recommended that counselors help traditional clients from these groups see some immediate, concrete benefits early in the counseling relationship (Sue & Zane, 1987). In that vein, the solution-focused approach, which addresses immediate concerns in concrete fashion, would suit many members of those cultural groups.

The Use of Groups

Group work has cultural implications. Groups help clients connect with others; groups are communities themselves. Groups can be particularly important for individuals who feel isolated from family and others. In that vein, European Americans, who often lack connections via extended family and community support, can benefit from the mutuality of groups.

With people from more communitarian cultures, groups can reflect the existing community. For example, bringing the family—as defined by the client—into the work for Asian Americans and others, either for discussion or in sessions, is recommended (Ancis, 2004a; Kim, 2005; Vera, Buhin, & Shin, 2006; Wehrly, 2003).

Nondominant group members might benefit from support groups in general because they can experience solidarity in such settings and reduction in feelings of isolation and powerlessness in the larger society (Day-Vines, Patton, & Baytops, 2003; Holcomb-McCoy, 2005).

Finally, groups can be used to promote understanding of diverse cultures and to teach culturally sensitive interpersonal skills. For example, Simcox, Nuijens, and Lee (2006) suggest students from diverse cultural backgrounds can participate in a psychoeducational group at school, which can be called a Friendship Group. A goal for group members in the Friendship Group is to learn about and practice using social skills that are appropriate for different cultures. The results could include the acquisition of positive social skills for all students, such as basic friendship-building tools, as well as enhanced openness to diversity and prevention of bullying and related social problems, such as ostra-cizing and teasing students from minority groups at the school.

Expression and Emotion

Physical and emotional expression varies according to ethnic group norms. In more emotion-ally restricted cultures, such as Northern European American cultures (McGoldrick, Giordano, & Garcia-Preto, 2005) and male culture in general, expressive approaches such as music, art, dance, or guided imagery can be liberating. They would bal-ance those cultures' emphasis on rationalism and emotional control. Of course, expressive counsel-ing methods would have to be introduced care-fully, with clear trust established in the counseling relationship, or they might scare those clients away.

Expressive counseling approaches are particu-larly inappropriate for cultures in which stoicism and reticence are seen as signs of psychological strength, such as in East Asian cultures, and should be avoided. See Chapter 7 for more on that topic.

Career Counseling

Career counseling strategies need to vary with culture. First, members of nondominant groups should not be discouraged from striving for non-traditional occupations.

Career is an especially complex area for women. Their career patterns can be quite varied during the lifespan as they balance multiple commitments. The lack of support for childcare in U.S. society makes many women's career lives stressful and disappointing. That pattern is reinforced by the stereotypes of males as breadwinners and high achievers. The existing gender ethos also discour-ages men from making nontraditional choices, such as childrearing and less lucrative occupations.

Another side of career life is balancing work and other dimensions of life. It can be important to introduce the idea of balancing work, family, and leisure for European Americans, many of whom may be caught up in an achievement ethic, some-times called the Protestant work ethic, that drives them at the expense of family and leisure.

Finally, some career counseling methods may need to be modified for traditional members of some ethnic groups. For example, naming achieve-ments and skills is common practice in career counseling (Bolles, 2011). That practice can be counter-cultural for traditional Asian clients, who are likely to value self-effacement.

The Use of Insight

A fifth issue in adapting counseling to par-ticular cultural groups is the use of psycho-logical insight. Some insight-oriented counseling approaches, such as gestalt, person-centered, and psychodynamic approaches, might not be help-ful with particular groups. For example, insight-oriented counseling might be counter-cultural for many traditional Asians. Such methods often chal-lenge the client to explore unresolved issues with family members or other significant figures in her or his early life. For traditional Asian Americans, who value avoiding family shame, such exploration might leave them feeling disloyal to their family.

Similarly, in the area of social class, a pure person-centered, insight-oriented approach might not be effective for many poor clients. Persons in the lower and working class often take a more direct and pragmatic approach to communication, whereas verbal communication and self-disclosure are highly valued in counseling work. It should be noted, however, that elements of person-centered counseling can still be very valuable in establishing rapport and helping the client hear what she or he has said.

Cognitive Behavioral Approaches

What is a counselor to do if insight-oriented approaches are not as useful with many members of some cultural groups? Some voices in the profes-sional literature suggest that behavioral or cogni-tive behavioral therapies (CBT) show promise for working with people who have non-Western cul-tural backgrounds (Ancis, 2004a; Harper & Stone, 2003; Paniagua, 2005; Pedersen, 2004; Ponterotto, Utsey, & Pedersen, 2006).

Changing thinking patterns not only holds promise for ameliorating negative or undesired behavior, it also can be used to combat autocolonialism, that is, the internalization of oppression by the subjects of oppressive systems. Ponterotto et al. (2006) propose that helping clients restructure their cognitions "is a powerful tool in the fight against prejudice and racism" (p. 157). In Paniagua's (2005) words,

> Many culturally diverse clinicians and researchers believe that behavioral approaches are probably the most effective strategies for the assessment and treatment of clients from the four [non-European] cultural groups. . . . This is because these strategies are authoritative and concrete, and they emphasize learning focused on the immediate problem—all characteristics of treatment that members of these groups generally prefer. (p. 7)

Replacing negative, or dysfunctional, thoughts with positive, more functional ones can help clients access their inner strengths and their outer community and family resources. They can use these new ways of thinking to take action toward a culturally congruent positive change.

There is a danger in exclusively using CBT with clients from nondominant groups. A counselor who only addresses individual psychological issues leaves out the social dimension that affects clients' lives. In that vein, D'Andrea (2006) observes that CBT is "often less effective when used among persons of color who are adversely impacted by white racism" (p. 259). He proposes that any individually oriented counseling theory be complemented by advocacy, possibly involving interventions in the community, as described later in this chapter.

Use of Humor

Humor in the counseling process may increase trust and a sense of connectedness in the counseling relationship, lessen anxiety and discomfort, relieve stress, help clients cope with painful and/or oppressive situations, and assist clients in gaining a new perspective on their concerns or situation (M. T. Garrett, Garrett, Torres-Rivera, Wilbur, & Roberts-Wilbur,

2005; Rayle, Chee, & Sand, 2006; Vereen, Butler, Williams, Darg, & Downing, 2006). Humor is esteemed by all cultures and can sometimes offer insight into a culture's perspective and values.

In general, humor is most appropriately utilized in the context of a trusting and respectful counseling relationship (Stone & Dahir, 2006). Four caveats for the use of humor are needed. First, a counselor who is not a member of the client's cultural group should exercise caution in using humor about painful historical or current oppressive situations. What may be appropriate for members of one cultural group to joke about may be considered offensive coming from an "outsider." Second, the counselor should also be wary about sending a message that she or he is not taking the client's concerns seriously. Third, humor has the potential to mask issues that might be helpful for clients to explore. Fourth, humor can also be ill timed, seen as disrespectful, or irrelevant to the process at hand. It may be wise to wait for the client to initiate or invite the use of humor before a counselor engages in the use of therapeutic wit (M. T. Garrett et al., 2005). With the aforementioned cautions in mind, counselors are encouraged to educate themselves about cultural expressions of wit and consider using humor to enhance the effectiveness of the counseling process.

Positive Reframing

Reframing consists of looking at a seemingly negative client characteristic or relationship from a positive perspective (Ivey et al., 2010). It is often a part of an overall strengths-based or empowerment strategy (Ancis, 2004a; Kim, 2005). Reframing an internalized concern by pointing out the external pressures or oppressions involved in a situation might ameliorate the sense of shame some clients might feel about seeking assistance from a counselor. For example, a counselor might reframe the acculturation tension within an immigrant family as an adaptive response for learning how to live in a new culture. Framing their concerns this way opens up the possibility of counseling as an empowering educational intervention, one that provides an opportunity for the client family to learn and educate themselves about more effective acculturation strategies.

Bibliotherapy

Bibliotherapy, that is, asking the client to read or watch culturally relevant material that might enhance her or his understanding, is recommended when counselors are familiar with a client's culture, acculturation status, and reading level. Clients' ability to see themselves and their situation in a book or video is a key component of this counseling modality (McFadden & Banich, 2003; Wehrly, 2003). Given the vicarious nature of the experience, a client may experience this technique as a safer means of exploring important issues. Reading about or watching others deal with similar issues can also assist clients to normalize the feelings or concerns that they may be experiencing. The client may feel encouraged or empowered by learning about other people who successfully resolved comparable issues. Bibliotherapy is thought to be especially effective with visual (vs. auditory) processors (McFadden & Banich, 2003).

To implement bibliotherapy, once a client's issues are identified, a counselor can select culturally and developmentally appropriate material that is salient to the specific situation or client concern. The text or film can be read or watched together or given to the client as "homework." After the reading or viewing is done, the counselor and client should process the material by analyzing the content and applying it to the client's own situation. Such processing can prevent the possibility of the experience being miseducative. Discussion of the material chosen may be a catalyst for further discussion of culture and its impact on the presenting concerns.

One example of the use of bibliotherapy with a young individual or small group is reading the children's book *Amazing Grace,* by Mary Hoffman (2007). In the text, the lead character, an African American girl named Grace, lives with her mother and nana. In aspiring to play the lead in a school production of *Peter Pan,* Grace experiences both racist and sexist remarks from peers. The story continues with Grace feeling initially discouraged, sad, and angry. With the help of her mother and nana, Grace experiences success; she is empowered to believe that she can accomplish anything she sets her mind to. One can see several potent themes in this text that can be processed and applied to the lives of elementary school–aged youth.

Intervention Strategy Three: Applying the Narrative Approach to Culture

An approach to counseling that is particularly suited to cultural issues is narrative therapy. A fundamental notion in narrative therapy is that individuals experience the realities of their lives through the stories they tell about themselves, others, and life in general (White & Epston, 1990). In narratively oriented counseling, culture is not seen as a variable that can be separated out for special attention; instead, it is the container in which a person's meanings are forged. Another word for that container is *discourse*, which was discussed in Chapter 1. Human meanings are always embedded in discourses. One category of discourse is culture. Thus, from the narrative point of view, the stories that clients tell, and live, are infused with ethnicity, gender, class, religion, and other cultural meanings (Semmler & Williams, 2000). For this reason, the narrative therapy approach is especially well suited for engaging persons who are struggling with unhelpful cultural narratives. Following is a brief description of narrative counseling.

Narrative Counseling in General

Narrative theorists begin by noting that the stories that clients bring to counseling are often problem saturated (White & Epston, 1990). These stories are dominated by what is going wrong in their lives. Many clients explain that such problems are expressions of their own inherent flaws.

A narrative counselor gently challenges this internalization of problems by helping clients externalize the problems. The counselor treats such problems as socially constructed stories rather than their being "inside" the client. The counselor helps the client see that these problem stories are constructed from cultural experience, as communicated by family, peers, ethnic group, and others.

The Case of Eduardo

Following is an example of the narrative approach as it incorporates culture. A client named Eduardo reported that he suffered from panic attacks, agoraphobia, and general anxiety. From a narrative perspective, these "disorders" are seen as culture-saturated constructions, in that the very language used to describe them and the meanings ascribed to those words are products of society. This narrative counseling description does not deny the physical experience of distress, but it offers Eduardo an alternate way of making sense of his experience, one that might be more helpful to him. Within Eduardo's traditional family and ethnic group, fear and anxiety are seen as shameful, especially in men. In his second-generation Latino American family, Eduardo has experienced powerful cultural stories about not revealing vulnerable feelings. As a result, he feels depressed, inadequate in the company of others, and emotionally isolated. Faced with negative conclusions about himself, Eduardo attempts to hide the anxiety from others and perhaps even from himself, and in so doing also avoids seeking help. A narrative approach involves the counselor's joining Eduardo in constructing an alternative account of his experience.

Strategies for Narrative Counseling

For simplicity's sake, narrative counseling is seen as having two overall processes:

The Current Story: Naming problems and their consequences and determining their foundations (deconstructing)

The Alternative Story: Joining with persons in storying their lives around their preferred, more useful purposes, values, and commitments

This depiction of two overall processes makes narrative counseling look more linear than it is in practice. To lay down a prescribed sequence beforehand would be to overlook the way that clients very actively shape the direction of the work. Narrative conversations can be seen as occasions for constructing new meanings, and clients are very active in the process of re-storying. In that sense, narrative counseling is a co-construction of meaning by counselor and client together. Nevertheless, these two overall processes can be helpful for characterizing the general flow of narrative counseling.

It can be said that narrative conversations generally start with that first process—the counselor helping clients dislodge problem stories from their sense of who they are. This separation of story from the person then "opens space" for the second process, that is, the counselor joining with clients in constructing accounts of their lives that are more in line with their preferences. What follows is a brief description of the narrative counseling process, with a highlight on cultural issues.

Phase One: The Current Story

In this phase, clients and counselors join in putting words to problems and in examining their effects. Problems are spoken of as separate from persons' identities, that is, problems are externalized. The externalizing of problems makes it easier for the client to stand back and examine how the meanings of these problems have arisen from the cultural context. This externalizing process has an interesting impact—the stories that once seemed like irrefutable truths begin to look more like influential cultural narratives.

The externalizing process is based on careful questioning by the counselor. Next we present a more explicit description of this first phase, with illustrations. It is broken into three subprocesses, which are not necessarily sequential: naming, consequences, and deconstructing the foundations. In the process, the story can be viewed as external to the client. It is a culturally induced story.

Naming

The client might first tell the problem story and give it a name. The story can then be treated as external to the client—a way that her or his community told a story that the client believed and acted on. In the case of Ayita, a working-class Cherokee woman from rural western North Carolina, her story was called "The Reservations Story." It captured her mixed feelings—pride in her heritage but her feelings of holding herself back, especially career-wise, from engaging in the wider American culture. In the previous case, Eduardo called it "Uncle Jorge's Macho Story," reflecting Eduardo's particularly stern and rigid uncle who mocked any signs of weakness in boys and men.

Consequences

A next step is to probe the existing consequences of the story. To evoke the negative power that the story has on the client's life, the counselor asks, "How is this problem affecting and/or interfering with your life/relationship(s)?" The counselor might further ask, "Does the problem have you do things that go against your better judgment?" In this process, the client becomes aware of how the problem story affects her or his perception of herself or himself and of others, and how it limits her or his actions. Clients often realize at this point how the problem story limits them. Eduardo told of "suffering in silence," pretending he was "tough" (and getting into trouble with authorities), hiding his artistic inclinations, and putting other people down in order to feel superior. Ayita acknowledged at this point that she was unhappy with her career but was not exploring options due to her acceptance of the "reservations script." Ayita reported that she "squashed" any dreams of professional work in the problem story.

The counselor might now continue to probe the consequences of the problem story by encouraging the client to evaluate its effects. The counselor might ask, "Are you comfortable with the effects or not? Which effects are most distressing?" and "Why is this such a problem to you?" Eduardo was tired of the shame he felt for being who he was. Ayita found that "The Reservations Story" trapped her into feelings of powerlessness. She said, "As a result of this story, I am beholden only to what some others think I should do and be. How can I be loyal to my people and their traditions while pursuing my dreams?"

Deconstructing the foundations

Another process is deconstruction. What has been constructed can be taken apart by looking at its foundations in a particular narrative. The foundations of the problem story can later be exposed as a particular construction among many possible ones.

Foundations of the old story

In order to probe the foundations, the counselor can ask such questions as, in Eduardo's case, "When and from what source did you first hear that men shouldn't reveal hurt or scared feelings?" or, in Ayita's case, "When and from what source did you first hear that women shouldn't aspire to professional work?" Questions are the dominant mode used in narrative counseling, with the counselor being seen as a curious inquirer.

These probes bring forth the context of the problem story. In the social constructionist vein (see Chapter 1), these patterns are not seen as self-created. Instead, they are seen as familial or cultural in nature. In that vein, the counselor asks such questions as "How did you get recruited into these ways of thinking/feeling/acting?;"Have you witnessed these ways of being in others?; and "If so, whose? And did these witnessings influence your ways of being?" Again, in this way the cultural story is unearthed. Eduardo talked of his macho uncle, one who never married but lived with his elderly mother. That uncle had called him a "crybaby." Eduardo also recognized that the boys with whom he associated in his working-class neighborhood were from disrupted home situations, unlike his, and that he was always uncomfortable being around these would-be "gangsters." He had been recruited by those discourses.

The counselor can further evoke the constructed foundations of the problem story with questions such as "How come you had a vision that your experience had to be like this? That your identity had to be this one?" Ayita responded to this question by saying, "All I knew were people who worked with their hands. Women cared for children. It was the only story I knew, except for what I saw on TV."

Foundations for a new story

The counselor can then introduce preferred possibilities with the question "What is your better judgment?" In response, Eduardo said, "I am not 'damaged goods.' I come from a loving, well-functioning family. I have fond memories of close family times in childhood. I have told myself this story of being 'damaged' because I am just sensitive to some things." He provided foundations for an alternative story with descriptions of his artistic talents, his good friendships, and his attractiveness to women. Ayita reported on her brilliance in math and science classes in high school and her continuing fascination with how nature worked. These clients' discoveries of their "better judgment" further challenged the problem story. Again, the problem story is often based in a gender, ethnic, or other cultural narrative.

In sum, naming the problem story, exploring its effects, and identifying the processes of recruitment to it undermine the essentialist fallacy that these stories are "reality." By contrast, nonnarrative approaches might identify the client as "irrational," "inauthentic," or "neurotic." These initial narrative counseling processes provide a space for the client herself or himself to take a clear position on the problem and its effect on her or his life. In Kegan's (1982) terms, the client can have *a relationship to* her or his cultural stories, rather than being subject to them. By the client's identifying the preferred story, the counselor is freed from being put into the "convincing position" as expert.

What can now be created, in the second phase of the work, is an identity that is apart from the recently externalized problem.

Phase Two: The Alternative Story

The second major process in narrative counseling follows from the Phase One naming and deconstructing of the problem story. In this re-storying phase, the counselor helps the client explore alternatives to the dominant stories. The client brings out aspects of her or his life that have not been overwhelmed by or "dictated to" by the problem, that is, experiences that don't fit the dominating patterns that surround the problem.

These aspects often consist of exceptions (e.g., times when the person felt competent, or worthy, or acted assertively). Eduardo remembered the power of revealing his fears to a friend and the help that a high school counselor had offered. He also thought of how he felt good about his "sensitive" side—the part that liked music, poetry, and reading. Ayita remembered having career dreams, passionate interests, and ideas of her own on many occasions. She further remembered her intelligent responses in science discussions in high school.

DISCOVERING NEW FOUNDATIONS

Part of the process of re-storying is to reclaim the foundations of the old story in new ways. New foundations are sought in alternative family or ethnic models, or in seeking new stories about one's group. The counselor asks, "How can you know that things could be different from the original problem story you told?" Eduardo might tell of his father's gift for music and his love of literature. He also remembered a valued high school teacher who passionately expressed feelings and words. He thought of Latino Americans who modeled nonstereotypical masculinity. In the case of an African American woman who is feeling powerless in her professional context, it might be "I saw powerful, competent African American women at my school and in my church. Plus I think about Maya Angelou and Oprah Winfrey, both of whom I saw on television recently."

This part of the work is extensive. It parallels the Working stage of counseling (Ivey et al., 2010; Neukrug, 2002). In the case of Ayita, the counselor helped her discover the stories of women who thought for themselves and held professional careers. She remembered a woman from another part of the reservation who went to college and entered law school. She learned about her grandmother's friend who had protested the sending of native people to Indian boarding schools in the early 1900s. More important, Ayita remembered times when she herself had dreams about a career as a veterinarian. She also remembered how well she had done academically in most subjects and how effective she had been in high school as a horse trainer. Eduardo thought about people who could seek help; he had seen men in movies go to therapists. He began to participate in a support group for people with anxiety problems and noted the willingness of the men in the group to reveal their feelings. He read about panic disorder and noted the possible biological dimension for it, helping him consider a medical consult.

The narrative counselor lets the client decide whether the alternative story is positive or negative and asks the client, "Why is it positive or negative?" Again, the counselor doesn't evaluate or justify. The client finds aspects of her or his experience that are constructive, and the counselor asks, "How have these achievements contributed to your life?" Eduardo found his delight in "deep conversations" with others and his "soaring" when moved by great art. He and the counselor collaboratively formed

a new story that he called "La Historia Masculina Fuerte del Artista" ("The Strong Male Artist Story"). Ayita found her academic success and her voracious interest in biology to be sources of satisfaction and pleasure. She relished stories of American Indians' relationship to nature and saw herself as carrying on that tradition in new ways. She called the new story "Ayita: A Native Woman of Science."

At this point in narrative counseling, clients might fully recognize that cultural dimensions are the foundations for the stories that they have told. Parts of the cultural stories might be useful; others can be discarded. The client is asked to find other examples of alternative cultural stories and to include them as elements of the alternative plot. In the process, the client decides the foundation for a story that works. The counselor does not advise. Activity 19.3 offers the opportunity for you to work through narrative counseling with a partner.

Activity 19.3 Trying Out the Narrative Approach

After reading the following sections, work with a partner who tells of a discrepancy or conflict in her or his life that can possibly be related to ethnicity, social class, gender, sexual orientation, or religion. Go through each of the processes of narrative counseling to work on the discrepancy, seeking out the client's cultural stories that contribute to the problem story and that can contribute to alternative stories.

I. The Problem Story

A. *Give the problem story a name.*

B. *Probe the consequences of the problem story by encouraging the client to evaluate its effects. Ask client the following:*

How is this problem affecting and/or interfering with your life/relationship(s)?

What has the problem talked you into/convinced you of about yourself and others?

Does the problem have you doing things that go against your better judgment?

What is your better judgment?

Are you comfortable with the effects or not? Which effects are most distressing?

C. *Look for the foundations of the problem story:*

When did you first hear that [fill in the theme of the problem story]?

How did you get recruited into these ways of thinking/feeling/acting (including ethnic, religious, gender, and social class bases for the story)?

How come you had a vision that experience had to be like this or that your identity had to be this one?

Have you witnessed these ways of being in others? If so, who?

Did these witnessings influence your ways of being?

II. Re-storying (Reclaiming the Foundations of the Old Story in New Ways)

How can you know that things could be different from the original problem story you told? (Probe for foundations for a new story, e.g., people in the client's life or awareness who demonstrate a different story.)

What is an alternative story? When did you witness such an alternative story for your [gender, ethnic group, social class, etc.]?

Is the alternative story positive or negative? Why is it positive or negative?

Intervention Strategy Four: Advocacy

Given the fact that many of their clients will experience inequities based on group memberships, counselors are asked to engage in social justice work as a continuing and central dimension of their practice. Advocacy for clients is described more fully in Chapter 3.

Intervention Strategy Five: Indigenous Healing Practices

Indigenous healing may be understood as an integration of the physical and the spiritual as means of helping individuals who are in challenging life circumstances. These healing practices include a wide range of interventions, including herbal remedies, rituals, faith healing, therapeutic touch, and other spiritual practices (Marks, 2006).

A counselor's developing an understanding of indigenous healing practices and the healers themselves may be essential for creating an effective treatment plan for some individuals. Members of traditional cultures often place importance on these practices and hold indigenous healers in high regard. If brought into the therapeutic process, indigenous helpers can even assume active roles and possibly partial or even total responsibility for helping individuals in their community (Constantine, Myers, Kindaichi, & Moore, 2004).

This section provides an overview of some of the indigenous healing practices and practitioners that counselors might encounter in African Caribbean, Latin American, Asian, and American Indian cultures. It should be noted that Western cultures, such as European American culture, have had, and still have, indigenous healing practices also. They include exorcism, prayer, and laying on of hands. In addition, many European Americans value such indigenous practices as yoga and acupuncture.

African/Caribbean

For many individuals who identify with African cultural values, the most powerful healing is believed to come from connection to the collective and the spiritual, rather than from individual effort and rational thought. Members of African-based cultures prominently value community, religion, and petitionary prayer (Bojuwoye, 2005; Torres-Rivera, Garrett, & Crutchfield, 2004). In these cultures, physical, emotional, cognitive, and spiritual functioning are all interrelated. Consequently, it is likely that physical manifestation would be an indicator of psychological distress (Bojuwoye, 2005; Eagle, 1998). Positive change often involves integrating physical, cognitive, and spiritual interventions. Those interventions are expressed through specific cultural healers, rituals, and positive relationships with the spirit world (Eagle, 1998; Torres-Rivera et al., 2004).

African/Caribbean cultures have many different types of traditional healers, each with her or his own specialty, focus, and methods. These include the following:

- Herbalists, who use plants and herbs as healing agents.
- Fetish men, who provide amulets, potions, and lotions that are said to be natural beneficial healing sources.
- Mediums, who have the power to communicate with the spirit world.
- Sorcerers, who have the ability to control and manipulate another person's vital force and are often connected to black magic.
- Indigenous spiritual doctors, known as diviners, who are seen as being connected to the universal therapeutic power. They use many of the same healing methods as the herbalists and fetish men, but also incorporate prayer and massage.
- Shango healers, who use communication with the spirits and dreams to find guidance for treating their patients. They lead cleansings, a practice in which a wrongdoer spends 7 or 9 days in different churches.
- Vodun (also known as Vodoun, Voudou, and Voodoo), which can be traced to the West African Yoruba people. Vodun priests focus on the relationship between the living and the dead because illness is seen as associated with evil spirits and curses. Healing comes from appeasing the dead. This practice involves dancing, offering gifts, and making animal sacrifices.

Since people from African-derived cultures, including African immigrants, are more likely to be connected to these types of healers, counselors should have a basic knowledge of all types and the location of such healers in the client's community (Marshall, 2005; Torres et al., 2004; Vontress, 2005).

Latin American

In the Latin American cultures, health and illness are often understood as a manifestation of an interaction among the spiritual, emotional, somatic, organic (environmental), and relational (social). Healers often work to understand the causes behind the suffering of individuals with mental health issues through a holistic viewpoint. Mental illness is often treated by integrating spiritual, symbolic, and physical interventions (Gonzalez-Chevez, 2005; Zacharias, 2006).

Diagnosis of physical, emotional, and spiritual problems in the Latin American tradition is done through a combination of the healer gathering the client's information, making observations, and engaging in "magic-religious" processes. The latter processes may include the healer reading objects such as an egg, corn, or cards to discover what category the illness falls into and what the best healing method may be. Consequently, treatment often includes the extensive use of spirituality, the application of altered states of consciousness, herbal remedies, or prayer to Christian saints (Constantine et al., 2004; Gonzalez-Chevez, 2005; Zacharias, 2006).

Some of the traditional healers and healing practices found in Latin American culture include the following:

- *Curanderismo*, which means to heal, is the prominent healing practice in this culture (Zacharias, 2006). Curanderos are individuals who are believed to have gained their power to heal directly from God. They involve family members in the curative process of using cleansing rituals and objects to heal by means of curanderos' own personal awareness of the suffering they can detect in those surrounding them.
- *Hot versus cold*: Diagnoses and treatments are often categorized as hot or cold. Cold conditions are treated with hot remedies, and vice versa.
- *Yerberia*, the ingestion of wild or domestic herbs, is a process often believed to restore both mental and physical imbalance.
- *Espiritistas* are believed to have the ability to communicate with spirits and the power to heal though this connection. They are considered mediums to the dead, rather than having a direct connection to a divine power.
- *Santeros* come from the religion of Santeria and are thought to be able to communicate with the saints and other spirits to resolve life situations. (Constantine et al., 2004; Gonzalez-Chevez, 2005; Zacharias, 2006)

Asian

Within this subgroup there exist many different religions, types of spiritualities, and healing practices. In this section, the East and Southeast Asian, South Asian, and Islamic traditions are discussed. It is important to distinguish the traditions from each other and not make the mistake of overgeneralizing within the overall Asian population. The common theme among them all is the focus on the interconnectedness between the mind, body, and spirit (Yeh, Hunter, Madan-Bahel, Chiang, & Arora, 2004).

East and Southeast Asian

The East and Southeast Asian cultures are strongly influenced by Chinese traditions. Within this culture there is a focus on balance resulting from the harmony of the earth, heavens, and people. The driving forces of the *qi* (pronounced "chi"), or vital energy, and the *li,* or order, are defined by the oppositional characteristics of the *yin* and *yang* (Constantine et al., 2004; Jucket, 2005; Thobaben, 2004; Yeh et al., 2004). Each of these concepts and words describes the important concept of balance. Balance is the primary goal for most indigenous healing in this cultural group. It is believed that mental illness comes from an imbalance of yin and yang in the qi and in the blood of various organs in the body.

The Buddhist tradition is common in East and Southeast Asia. In this religio-cultural schema, good mental health is the result of knowing and following the Four Noble Truths and the Eightfold Path while renouncing worldly attachments (Haque, 2010). In therapeutic healing, the four components necessary are the physician, the attendant, the patient, and the drug that must come from local herbs. In addition, yoga, worship, meditation, and prayer lay the foundation for centeredness and therefore psychological health (Haque, 2010).

Some of the common treatment modalities include the following.

- *Acupuncture* involves inserting needles into specific pressure points in the body to release pressure and pain.
- *Yoga* consists of controlled movements of the body during meditation.

- *Herbal medicine* is characterized by the prescribing of a combination of herbs and foods specific to each type of illness.
- *Qigong* is a series of controlled meditation-related physical movements.
- *Worship, prayer, and meditation* are used to find balance and promote healing. (Haque, 2010; So, 2005; Thobaben, 2004; Tseng, 1999; Yeh et al., 2004)

South Asian

In South Asia, the Indian understanding of mental health can be described by the two central concepts of *Ayurveda* and *Siddha*.

Ayurveda conceptualizes mental health as being directly related to dual harmonies: within oneself and with society. Mental health depends on the harmony among one's *karma* (actions), *vayu* (air), and *swabhay* (personal nature; Haque, 2010). Alternately, mental illness is categorized by whether the illness is of mental or physical origin, as indicated by psychological or physical symptoms (Kumar, Bhugra, & Singh, 2005). Treatment incorporates the following.

- yoga
- purification through purging, enemas, or bleeding
- meditation
- pacification through the use of ointments and ingestion of plant and/or metal combinations
- incantations
- exorcism
- changes in lifestyle and environment known as "the removal of the cause" (Haque, 2010; Kumar et al., 2005; Thobaben, 2004)

In the Siddha tradition, mental health diagnoses take into account the person as a whole, using methods such as pulse reading and urine examination. Treatment involves a restoration of equilibrium through cleansing or the application of oils and pressure on vital points (Kumar et al., 2005). There are two types of traditional healers:

- The shaman uses divine powers to heal through rituals, yoga, mantras, and exorcism.
- Mystics have unity with the deity and lead others to self-realization and transformation by example, showing the importance of sacrifice and life change through the model of their own lives. (Kumar et al., 2005)

Islamic

The sociocultural beliefs of Islamic cultures hold that it is faith that protects against bad physical and mental health. As was discussed in Chapters 10 and 16, it is through faith that Muslims handle problems when they arise. Mental illness is thought to be caused by neglect and doubt of religious values due to one's own needs or outside pressures that are counter to the teachings of the Qur'an. The will of Allah is believed to be the cause of illness and that the pain will be felt in the heart, as this is where the human psyche lives, until a deep acceptance of being in relation to Allah is met (Farooqi, 2006; Haque, 2010; Inayat, 2005).

Religious interventions are often used to heal mental distress. It is hoped that by purging the spirit through ceremony and sacrifice, balance in life can be restored (Tseng, 1999). Some of these interventions include the following.

- *sawm* (fasting)
- *taubah* (repentance)
- *recitation of the Qur'an* to ward off evil and the influences of negative thoughts in a person (Haque, 2010)

In addition, the following are important for healing in the Islamic tradition:

- Spiritual healers, who focus on restoring the balance of energy within the body by working on the *lateefa,* or energy points (Inayat, 2005).
- The shamanic *zar* ceremony, which involves having both healer and client experience a dissociated state in hopes of purging the evil zar spirit.
- Sufis, who are a type of traditional healer, applying magic to speak to the spirits of nature, performing both physical and spiritual healings (Farooqi, 2006).

Native American

Although a multitude of tribal nations compose the Native American population, there are beliefs and healing practices that are common to most. These include cultural narratives, ceremonies, and rites of passage. Native American practices are characterized by the themes of balance, harmony, and self-awareness. Health and wellness is seen as both a physical and spiritual state of being. The healer is seen as a leader, guide, and helper, someone who assists others to obtain balance and harmony (J. T. Garrett & Garrett, 2002).

Ceremonies are used as a large part of the healing process in Native American cultures. They are seen as a way to maintain balance and harmony with oneself, the group, the environment, and the spirit world, and it is through these group ceremonies that healing is found for the individual (J. T. Garrett & Garrett, 2002; Portman & Garrett, 2006; Torres-Rivera et al., 2004). Some of these ceremonies and other treatments include the following:

- *Medicine,* which refers to the essence of life or an inner power. Medicine includes physical remedies (herbs, teas) but can also be an experience, a moment, or a memory.
- *Sweat lodge,* a purification ceremony that involves a medicinal sweating experience.
- *Vision quest,* is a healing ritual that requires an individual to remove herself or himself from daily activities to go into a place where a spiritual focus can be established and an internal state of self-reflection can occur.
- *Smudging ceremony,* in which the burning of herbs is believed to create a cleansing smoke used to purify people, land, homes, and objects (Constantine et al., 2004; J. T. Garrett & Garrett, 2002; Portman & Garrett, 2006).

Concluding Thoughts on Indigenous Healing

Although each of these cultures has distinct indigenous traditions, all hold that mental health healing may come from many interrelated sources and often includes physical, psychological, and spiritual interventions. Various cultures conceptualize the source of mental health issues in various, often culturally specific ways. Therefore, counselors must remember to use assessment methods appropriate for members of a specific culture group or use standardized assessments with great caution (Haque, 2010). It is also essential to work closely with the client, family, and cultural experts to get a valid assessment resulting in better solutions to the problem (Haque, 2010). While it is never appropriate for counselors to use culturally specific treatment methods that they have not received specific training for, including culturally specific healers in the treatment process is highly recommended for clients who desire a more holistic, culturally based treatment plan. Overall, counselors must be prepared to ask questions, admit ignorance, and seek answers from any and all sources that are relevant to their clients in order to provide the most holistic treatment.

SUMMARY

This chapter has attempted to bring together the current thinking on generally effective methods for culturally alert counseling. The search for method should not, however, overshadow the dynamic dimension of any counseling work. It is only in the spontaneity of the encounter that method can be applied. The timing and manner of applying culturally alert methods are choices that each counselor must make with each client. Competency as a culturally alert counselor requires not only method, but prior cultural self-awareness and knowledge of other cultures. In Smith, Richards, Granley, and Obiakor's (2004) words, "Practicing multiculturalism means internalizing the principles of multicultural competency and acting accordingly. . . . A book or class cannot provide for multicultural competence because multiculturalism is not just a set of facts, guidelines, or principles. It is a way of life" (p. 15). It also demands a set of attitudes, including openness to narratives that are not one's own and a commitment to the work of reducing human suffering by challenging inequality and prejudice. Then, through alert action, counselors will be part of the solution.

REFERENCES

American Psychiatric Association. (2000). *Diagnostic and statistical manual of mental disorders* (4th ed., Text rev.). Washington, DC: Author.

Ancis, J. R. (2004a). Culturally responsive interventions. In J. R. Ancis (Ed.), *Culturally responsive interventions: Innovative approaches to working with diverse populations* (pp. 213–222). New York, NY: Brunner-Routledge.

Ancis, J. R. (2004b). Culturally responsive practice. In J. R. Ancis (Ed.), *Culturally responsive interventions: Innovative approaches to working with diverse populations* (pp. 3–21) . New York, NY: Brunner-Routledge.

Bojuwoye, O. (2005). Traditional healing practices in southern Africa. In R. Moodley & W. West (Eds.), *Integrating traditional healing practices into counseling and psychotherapy* (pp. 61–72). Thousand Oaks, CA: Sage.

Bolles, R. N. (2011). *What color is your parachute.* Berkeley, CA: Ten Speed Press.

Constantine, M. G. (2006). Institutional racism against African Americans: Physical and mental health implications. In M. G. Constantine & D. W. Sue (Eds.), *Addressing racism: Facilitating cultural competence in mental health and educational settings* (pp. 33–41). Hoboken, NJ: Wiley.

Constantine, M. G., Myers, L. J., Kindaichi, M., & Moore, J. L., III. (2004). Exploring indigenous mental health practices: The roles of healers and helpers in promoting well-being in people of color. *Counseling and Values, 48,* 110–125.

D'Andrea, M. (2006). In liberty and justice for all: A comprehensive approach to ameliorating the complex problems of white racism and white superiority in the United States. In M. G. Constantine & D. W. Sue (Eds.), *Addressing racism: Facilitating cultural competence in mental health and educational settings* (pp. 251–270). Hoboken, NJ: Wiley.

Day-Vines, N., Patton, J. M., & Baytops, J. L. (2003). Counseling African American adolescents: The impact of race, culture, and middle class status. *Professional School Counseling, 7,* 40–51.

Deutsch, C. P. (1967). Minority groups and class status as related to social and personality factors in scholastic achievement. In M. Deutsch & Associates (Eds.), *The disadvantaged child* (pp. 89–131). New York, NY: Basic Books.

Eagle, G. T. (1998). Promoting peace by integrating Western and indigenous healing in treating trauma. *Peace and Conflict: Journal of Peace Psychology, 4,* 271–282.

Farooqi, Y.N. (2006). Traditional healing practices sought by Muslim psychiatric patients in Lahore, Pakistan. *International Journal of Disability, Development and Education, 53*, 401–415.

Garrett, J. T., & Garrett, M. T. (2002). *The Cherokee full circle: A practical guide to ceremonies and traditions.* Rochester, VT: Bear.

Garrett, M. T., Garrett, J. T., Torres-Rivera, E., Wilbur, M., & Roberts-Wilbur, J. (2005). Laughing it up: Native American humor as a spiritual tradition. *Journal of Multicultural Counseling and Development, 33*, 194–204.

González-Chevez, L. (2005). Latin American healers and healing. In R. Moodley & W. West (Eds.), *Integrating traditional healing practices into counseling and psychotherapy* (pp. 85–99). Thousand Oaks, CA: Sage.

Haque, A. (2010). Mental health concepts in Southeast Asia: Diagnostic considerations and treatment implications. *Psychology, Health & Medicine, 15*, 127–134.

Harper, F. D., & Stone, W. O. (2003). Transcendent counseling: An existential, cognitive-behavioral theory. In F. D. Harper & J. McFadden (Eds.), *Culture and counseling: New approaches* (pp. 233–251). Boston. MA: Allyn & Bacon.

Hays, D. G., Chang, C. Y., & Dean, J. K. (2007). Addressing privilege and oppression in counselor training and practice: A qualitative analysis. *Journal of Counseling and Development. 85*, 317–324.

Hoffman, M. (2007). *Amazing grace.* London, UK: Frances Lincoln.

Holcomb-McCoy, C. (2005). Ethnic identity development in early adolescence: Implications and recommendations for middle school counselors. *Professional School Counseling, 9*, 120–127.

Holland, J. L., Powell, A. B., & Fritzsche, B. A. (2011). *The self-directed search.* Odessa, FL: Psychological Assessment Resources.

Inayat, Q. (2005). Islam, divinity, and spiritual healing. In R. Moodley & W. West (Eds.), *Integrating traditional healing practices into counseling and psychotherapy* (pp. 159–169). Thousand Oaks, CA: Sage.

Ivey, A. E. (1995). Psychotherapy as liberation. In J. G. Ponterotto, J. M. Casas, L. A. Suzuki, & C. M. Alexander (Eds.), *Handbook of multicultural counseling* (pp. 53–72). Thousand Oaks, CA: Sage.

Ivey, A. E., D'Andrea, M., Ivey, M. B., & Simek-Morgan, L. (2002). *Theories of counseling and psychotherapy: A multicultural perspective.* Boston, MA: Allyn & Bacon.

Ivey, A. E., Ivey, M. B., & Zalaquett, C. P. (2010). *Intentional interviewing and counseling.* Belmont, CA: Brooks/Cole Cengage

Jucket, G. (2005). Cross-cultural medicine. *American Family Physician, 72*, 2267–2275.

Kegan, R. (1982). *The evolving self: Problem and process in human development.* Cambridge, MA: Harvard University Press.

Kim, Y. S. E. (2005). Guidelines and strategies for cross-cultural counseling with Korean American clients. *Journal of Multicultural Counseling and Development, 33*, 217–231.

Kumar, M., Bhugra, D., & Singh, J. (2005). Southern Asian (Indian) traditional healing. In R. Moodley & W. West (Eds.), *Integrating traditional healing practices into counseling and psychotherapy* (pp. 112–121). Thousand Oaks, CA: Sage.

Marks, L. (2006). Global health crisis: Can indigenous healing practices offer a valuable resource? *International Journal of Disability, Development, and Education, 53*, 471–478.

Marshall, R. (2005). Caribbean healers and healing. In R. Moodley & W. West (Eds.), *Integrating traditional healing practices into counseling and psychotherapy* (pp. 73–84). Thousand Oaks, CA: Sage.

McAuliffe, G. J. (2007). *Key practices in culturally alert counseling: A demonstration of selected practices.* Thousand Oaks, CA: Sage.

McFadden, J., & Banich, M. A. (2003). Using bibliotherapy in transcultural counseling. In F. D. Harper & J. McFadden (Eds.), *Culture and counseling: New approaches* (pp. 285–295). Boston, MA: Allyn & Bacon.

McGoldrick, M. (2005). Irish families. In M. McGoldrick & J. Giordano (Eds.), *Ethnicity and family therapy* (pp. 595–615). New York, NY: Guilford Press.

McGoldrick, M., Giordano, J., & Garcia-Preto, N. (2005). *Ethnicity and family therapy* (3rd ed., pp. 595–615). New York, NY: Guilford Press.

Middleton, R. A., Erguner-Tekinalp, B., & Petrova, E. (2005, October). *Clinical applications of racial identity development*. Presentation to the meeting of the Association for Counselor Education and Supervision, Pittsburgh, PA.

Miville, M. L., & Ferguson, A. D. (2006). Intersections of sexism and heterosexism with racism: Therapeutic implications. In M. G. Constantine & D. W. Sue (Eds.), *Addressing racism: Facilitating cultural competence in mental health and educational settings* (pp. 87–103). Hoboken, NJ: Wiley.

Montgomery, M., Marbley, A., Contreras, R., & Kurtines, W. M. (2000). Transforming diversity training in counselor education. In G. J. McAuliffe & K. P. Eriksen (Eds.), *Preparing counselors and therapists: Creating constructivist and developmental programs* (pp. 148–169). Alexandria, VA: Association for Counselor Education and Supervision.

Neukrug, E. (2002). *Skills and techniques for human service professionals: Counseling environment, helping skills, treatment issues*. Pacific Grove, CA.: Brooks/Cole.

Paniagua, F. A. (2005). *Assessing and treating culturally diverse clients: A practical guide* (3rd ed.). Thousand Oaks, CA: Sage.

Pedersen, P. B. (2004). The multicultural context of mental health. In T. B. Smith (Ed.), *Practicing multiculturalism: Affirming diversity in counseling and psychology* (pp. 17–32). Boston, MA: Pearson.

Ponterotto, J. G., Utsey, S. O., & Pedersen, P. B. (2006). *Preventing prejudice: A guide for counselors, educators, and parents* (2nd ed.). Thousand Oaks, CA: Sage.

Rayle, A. D., Chee, C., & Sand, J. K. (2006). Honoring their way: Counseling American Indian women. *Journal of Multicultural Counseling and Development, 34,* 66–79.

Rodriguez, R. R., & Walls, N. E. (2000). Culturally educated questioning: Toward a skills-based approach in multicultural counselor training. *Applied & Preventive Psychology, 9,* 89–99.

Said, E. W. (1994). *Culture and imperialism*. New York, NY: Vintage Books.

Samhita. (2006). *Internalized colonization, beauty and Sudan*. Retrieved from http://feministing .com/2006/08/10/internalized_colonization_beau/

Samuda, R. J. (1998). *Psychological testing of American minorities*. Thousand Oaks, CA: Sage.

Semmler, P. L., & Williams, C. B. (2000). Narrative therapy: A storied context of multicultural counseling. *Journal of Multicultural Counseling and Development, 28,* 51–62.

Simcox, A. G., Nuijens, K. L., & Lee, C. C. (2006). School counselors and school psychologists: Collaborative partners in promoting culturally competent schools. *Professional School Counselor, 9,* 272–277.

Smith, T. B., Richards, P. S., Granley, H. M., & Obiakor, F. (2004). Practicing multiculturalism: An introduction. In T. B. Smith (Ed.), *Practicing multiculturalism: Affirming diversity in counseling and psychology* (pp. 3–16). Boston, MA: Pearson.

So, J. K. (2005). Traditional and cultural healing among the Chinese. In R. Moodley & W. West (Eds.), *Integrating traditional healing practices into counseling and psychotherapy* (pp. 100–111). Thousand Oaks, CA: Sage.

Stone, C., & Dahir, C. (2006). *The transformed school counselor*. Boston, MA: Lahaska Press.

Sue, S., & Zane, N. (1987). The role of culture and cultural techniques in psychotherapy: A critique and reformulation. *American Psychologist, 42,* 37–45.

Tannen, D. (1990). *You just don't understand: Women and men in conversation*. New York, NY: Morrow.

Thobaben, M. (2004). Alternative approaches to mental health care. *Home Health Care Management and Practice, 16,* 528–530.

Torres-Rivera, E., Garrett, M. T., & Crutchfield, L. B. (2004). Multicultural interventions in groups: The use of indigenous methods. In J. L. DeLucia-Waack, D. Gerrity, C. Kalodner, & M. Riva (Eds.), *Handbook of group counseling and psychotherapy* (pp. 295–306). Thousand Oaks, CA: Sage.

Tseng, W. S. (1999). Culture and psychotherapy: Review and practical guidelines. *Transcultural Psychiatry, 36,* 131–179.

Utsey, S. O., Bolden, M. A., & Brown, A. L. (2001). Visions of revolution from the spirit of Frantz Fanon: A psychology of liberation for counseling African Americans confronting societal racism and oppression. In J. G. Ponterotto, J. M. Casas, L. A. Suzuki, & C. M. Alexander (Eds.), *Handbook of multicultural counseling* (2nd ed., pp. 311–336). Thousand Oaks, CA: Sage.

Vera, E. M., Buhin, L., & Shin, R. Q. (2006). The pursuit of social justice and the elimination of racism. In M. G. Constantine & D. W. Sue (Eds.), *Addressing racism: Facilitating cultural competence in mental health and educational* settings (pp. 271–287). Hoboken, NJ: Wiley.

Vereen, L. G., Butler, S. K., Williams, F. C., Darg, J. A., & Downing, T. K. E. (2006). The use of humor when counseling African American college students. *Journal of Counseling & Development, 84,* 10–15.

Vontress, C. E. (2005). Animism. In R. Moodley & W. West (Eds.), *Integrating traditional healing practices into counseling and psychotherapy* (pp. 124–137). Thousand Oaks, CA: Sage.

Wehrly, B. (2003). Breaking barriers for multiracial individuals and families. In F. D. Harper & J. McFadden (Eds.), *Cultural and counseling: New approaches* (pp. 313–323) Boston, MA: Allyn & Bacon.

Westermeyer, J. (1987). Cultural factors in clinical assessment. *Journal of Consulting and Clinical Psychology, 55,* 471–478.

White, M, & Epston, D. (1990). *Narrative means to therapeutic ends.* New York, NY: Norton.

Yeh, C. J., Hunter, C. D., Madan-Bahel, A., Chiang, L., & Arora, A. K. (2004). Indigenous and interdependent perspectives of healing: Implications for counseling and research. *Journal of Counseling and Development, 82,* 410–419.

Zacharias, S. (2006). Mexican Curanderismo as ethnopsychotherapy: A qualitative study on treatment practices, effectiveness, and mechanisms of change. *International Journal of Disability, Development, and Education, 53,* 381–400.

Index

Asian Americans
  as a model minority, 171–172, 331–332
  communication styles, 170 (table)
  cultural values, 166–168
  factors for working with, 177–179
  immigration timeline, 162 (box)
  indigenous healing practices, 581
  intervention issues and strategies, 174–180
  mental health issues for, 170–174
  See also East and Southeast Asian Americans;
      South Asian Americans
Assessment, 487
  bias in, 527–528
  class factors to consider during, 371 (box)
  gender-neutral, 402
Assessment skills theme, 559–565
  culturally alert observation of clients, 560
  doing culturally oriented questioning, 560–561
  practicing culturally sensitive diagnosis, 561–564
  using tests in a culturally alert fashion, 564–565
Asset search, 567
Assimilation, 15, 80–81, 324
Assimilationist perspective, 97–99
Attention, disorders of, 515
Attitudes
  disability and, 509 (activity)
  toward difference, 16 (activity)
  toward diversity, 14–15
  See also Beliefs and attitudes
Autocolonization, 566
Awareness, 485–486
  bias, overcoming, 486
  spiritual self-assessment, benefits of, 486

Bainton, George, 524
Baptists, 477
Barden-Lafollette Act, 515
Behavior dimension, of enculturation/acculturation, 80
Being, sense of, 205
Being different, 429
Belenky, Mary, 15
Beliefs and attitudes, 21, 22
Bertrand, Marianne, 105
Bias
  assessment and, 527–528
  counseling and, 397, 522
  dealing with, 40
Bibliotherapy, 339, 574
Bicultural competence, 80, 81 (activity)

Bin Laden, Osama, 326
Biphobia, 433–434
Biracial, versus multiracial, 115
Bisexual persons, unique issues of, 432–434
  biphobia, 433–434
  coming-out issues, 433
  myths about, 432–433
  See also LGBT
Black achievers, 108–109 (box)
Black Church, The, 134
Black Elk, 207
Black English. *See* African American Vernacular
      English (AAVE)
Black middle class, 145–146
Black poverty, 145–146
Black Rage (Grier and Cobbs), 131
Black-white relations, contemporary, 100–101
Blood quantum, 188–189
Blumenbach, Johann Freidrich, 94
Boas, Franz, 97–98 (box)
Boone, Daniel, 237
Broaching, 556
Brown v. Board of Education, 129, 131
Bucceri, Jennifer, 171
Buddhism, 481–483
Bush, George W., 351

Caballerismo, 303
Califano, Joseph, 516
Calvin, John, 477
Calvinists, 477
Camara, Dom Helder, 58
Capabilities Approach, for individuals with disabilities,
      509–510
Capielo, Cristalis, 293
Career development journey, case summary of, 535 (box)
Careers
  African Americans and, 140–141
  class and, 358–359
  counseling for, 526–527 (box), 572
  gender and, 403
Carlisle Indian School, 199
Carpenter, Vincent D., 103
Carroll, John, 238
Cartwright, Samuel, 90
Carver, George Washington, 108
Catholic beliefs and counseling, 476 (table)
Cattell, James, 242
Channing, Stockard, 430

Hinduism, 480–481, 482 (table)

Hispanic, 83, 295. *See also* Latino/Latina Americans

Hispanic Hispanics, 297

Historical trauma (HT), 195–196, 212

Historical Trauma and Unresolved Grief (HTUG) intervention model, 212

Historical trauma response (HTR), 196

Historical unresolved grief, 196

Hoffman, Mary, 574

Holocaust, 479

Homestead Act, 239

Homosexual/homosexuality, 437. *See also* LGBT

Hooker, Evelyn, 426

hooks, bell, 58

Horton, John L., 108–109

Housing, and racism, 104

Hudson, Henry, 236

Human agency, degree of, 509

Human behavior, 37–40

Human experience, tripartite model of, 38–40

Humanism, core beliefs of, 483–484

Humanistic idealism, 470

Humility, 203

Humor, 215, 573

Hurston, Zora Neale, 98

Hwa-byung, 173

Hyphenated Americans, 238

Iceberg Concept of Culture, 27–28, 349

IDEA. *See* Individuals with Disabilities Education Act

Identity, 198
    acceptance, 431
    comparison, 429
    confusion, 429
    development model, 116–117
    phases, early, 438–439
    pride, 431
    synthesis, 431
    tolerance, 431
    See also Cultural identity

Immersion, 110

Immigration and Naturalization Act, 161, 319, 331

Implicit integration, 488

In a Different Voice (Gilligan), 58

Inclusive language, 553

Inclusiveness, 6

Indian
    blood, degree of, 188
    education policy and the achievement gap, 199–200

humor, 208
    See also Native Americans

Indigenous healing practices, 579–583
    African/Caribbean, 579–580
    Asian, 581
    East and Southeast Asian, 581
    Islamic, 582
    Latin American, 580
    Native American, 582
    South Asian, 581

Indigenous people, 189

Indigenous ways of knowing, 191–192

Individualism, 26–27, 272 (activity), 359, 363
    definitions of, 271 (table)
    isolation and, 244
    universalistic, 38

Individuality, intersection with culture and universality, 39 (figure)

Individualized Educational Program (IEP), 510 (box)

Individuals with disabilities. *See* Disabilities, individuals with

Individuals with Disabilities Education Act (IDEA), 516

Individuative-reflective faith, 467–468

Inferiority, sense of, 328

Informed consent, 487, 554–555

Insight, use of, 572

Institutional classism, 363–364

Institutional racism, 171

Integrated Analysis of Oppression, 441

Integration, 80, 324, 569–570

Intellectual disabilities, 513, 553

Interaction strain, 521–522

Internalization, 110–111

Internalized classism, 363

Internalized colonization, 566

Internalized heterosexism, 429, 441

Internalized oppressions, 52, 566–570

Internalized racism
    in nondominant groups, 102
    in South Asians, 337

Intersectionality, 29

Intersex, 434

Interventions skills theme (strategies), 566–577
    adapting common counseling approaches, 571–574
    advocacy, 579
    applying the narrative approach to culture, 574–577
    challenging internalized oppressions, 566–570
    indigenous healing practices, 579–583

Intolerance, consequences of, 244–245

Introspection, 110–111

About the Editor

Garrett McAuliffe has worked as a counselor educator, counselor, and school teacher for over 40 years. In his professional life, he has strived to increase equity in society through his counseling, teaching, and writing. He is particularly committed to empowering learners. Toward those ends, he has taught in the public schools of New York City and counseled at the community college and university levels in Massachusetts, where he also served as the director of learning assistance programs at Greenfield Community College. Since 1988, he has been a counselor educator at Old Dominion University, in Norfolk, Virginia. He grew up in a tightly connected extended family in a multiethnic neighborhood in New York City and is the grandchild of Irish immigrants. He received his Bachelor of Arts magna cum laude in English literature, with Highest Honors, from Queens College of the City University of New York, in 1971. He was named to Phi Beta Kappa for his academic performance at Queens College in 1971. He took from his undergraduate education both a love of ideas and words and a desire to turn ideas into social and personal change actions. Toward that end, he pursued his graduate counseling studies at the University at Albany and at the University of Massachusetts at Amherst, receiving his doctorate in 1985. In his time at Old Dominion University, he has produced six books, over 80 articles, more than 35 book chapters, and six training videos. His great love continues to be teaching, in all of its forms.

About the Contributors

Cristalis Capielo is currently a doctoral student in the Counseling Psychology Program at the University of Georgia. She holds a master's degree in mental health counseling from Nova Southeastern University. Her research interests include multicultural issues, Latina/o psychology, and the mental health needs of Puerto Ricans in the mainland.

Mona Danner is a professor of sociology and criminal justice at Old Dominion University. Her research and teaching expertise are in social inequality (gender, race/ethnicity, class, and nation), criminal justice policy, and globalization. She earned her PhD from the American University in 1993.

Edward A. Delgado-Romero received his doctorate in counseling psychology from the University of Notre Dame. He is currently an associate professor, training director, and program chair of the Counseling Psychology Program at the University of Georgia. His primary research interests are multicultural psychology, race and racism in the psychotherapy process, and Latino/a psychology. He is a fellow of APA Division 45 and a founding member of the National Latina/o Psychological Association.

Lynn Doyle is an associate professor emeritus in the Department of Educational Foundations and Leadership at Old Dominion University, in Norfolk, Virginia. She received her doctorate in administrative leadership and urban education from the University of Wisconsin, Milwaukee. She has served as a speech and language pathologist and special education administrator in a variety of settings. Her research interests include equity and social justice with diverse populations, pupil personnel services, special education administration, and leadership and its relationship to learning and teaching.

Karen Eriksen received her doctorate from George Mason University and her master's degree from California State University, Fullerton. She currently conducts leadership training and is the president of the Eriksen Institute. Previously she directed a counselor education department and taught at several universities. Prior to that, she practiced as a licensed professional counselor and marriage and family counselor in Virginia, Michigan, and California. She has specialties in family therapy, addictions, survivors of sexual abuse, and the intersection of spirituality and counseling. She has authored or coedited 12 books on counselor advocacy, counselor education, diagnosis, life skills, values, parenting, and creativity. Her research and publication areas are counselor preparation, constructive development, multiculturalism, and spirituality. She has been active in the leadership of several state and national professional associations.

Kathy M. Evans is an associate professor and program coordinator for counselor education at the University of South Carolina. She received her doctorate in counseling psychology from the Pennsylvania State University. Her research, publications, and national presentations address issues important to African Americans, multicultural and feminist issues, and multicultural career development. In addition to serving on the editorial board for the *Journal of Counseling & Development,* she has held national and regional offices in several professional counseling organizations.

Nallely Galván received her doctorate in counseling psychology from the University of Illinois at Urbana-Champaign and currently works as a staff psychologist for the Federal Bureau of Prisons. She works with female offenders and provides counseling services in both Spanish and English. Her research interests include multicultural issues, the mental health needs of immigrant Latinas/Latinos, discrimination and its influence on health, and health issues among underserved populations.

J. T. Garrett is a state/county health director in North Carolina. As a member of the Eastern Band of Cherokee Indians, he learned under several medicine men and women. He holds a doctorate in education from the University of Tennessee in Knoxville. He is author or coauthor of numerous articles and has written five books on Cherokee cultural ways and traditions. He has been a student and now an elder, with over 50 years studying Cherokee cultural heritage, language, and traditional teachings. His vision and life passion has always been to encourage a better understanding and appreciation of the "old ways" in American Indian cultural heritage. He is retired from the U.S. Public Health Service, Indian Health Service, where he had the opportunity to work with and travel to most of the 565 tribes in the United States.

Michael Tlanusta Garrett, Eastern Band of the Cherokee Nation, is a professor of counselor education and chair of the Department of Collaborative Support and Intervention at the University of West Georgia. He holds a PhD in counseling and counselor education and an MEd in counseling and development from the University of North Carolina at Greensboro. As author or coauthor of more than 80 professional publications dealing with multiculturalism and social justice, group work, wellness and spirituality, school counseling, working with youth, and counseling Native Americans, he has sought to advance professional understanding of working with diverse populations across therapeutic and educational settings and integrating indigenous healing practices as a way of bridging the cultural gap.

Yvette Q. Getch received her doctorate in rehabilitation education and research from the University of Arkansas in 1996. She is currently an associate professor at the University of Georgia. Her primary research interests include the impact of childhood chronic illness and disability on the family, school accommodations for children with chronic illness and disabilities, advocacy issues for children and adults with disabilities, and social justice advocacy for individuals from traditionally marginalized populations.

Edwin Gómez is an associate professor in the Department of Human Movement Sciences at Old Dominion University. He earned his doctorate from Michigan State University in parks, recreation, tourism, and urban studies. He has an MS from Rochester Institute of Technology in hospitality and travel management and an MA from Old Dominion University in linguistics, with a specialization in English as a second language. His research interests include urban recreation issues, sense of community in neighborhoods, and recreation issues related to racial and ethnic group inclusion. His most recent research looks at the relationship between acculturation processes as they relate to bilingualism, cultural identity, sense of community, and use of public spaces, such as urban parks.

Patricia Goodspeed-Grant is an associate professor in the Department of Counselor Education at the College at Brockport, State University of New York. She holds a doctorate in counseling and human development from the University of Rochester, an MS in organizational psychology from Springfield College in Massachusetts, and is a licensed mental health counselor in New York. She specializes in qualitative research methodologies. Her research and writing interests center around the meaning of work and unemployment, the loss of relationships through death or divorce, issues related to social class and counseling, and the emotional aspects of obesity and weight loss.

Lisa Grayshield, an enrolled member of the Washoe Tribe of Nevada and California, is an assistant professor in the Department of Counseling and Educational Psychology at New Mexico State University. She holds an MA and a PhD in counseling and educational psychology, both from the University of Nevada, Reno. Her research interests focus on indigenous ways of knowing in counseling and psychology, specifically the incorporation of indigenous knowledge forms as viable options for the way counseling and psychology are conceptualized, taught, practiced, and researched. She serves the local community as a board member for Indigenous Nations for Community Action.

Tim Grothaus is an associate professor and coordinator of the school counseling specialty area in the Department of Counseling and Human Services at Old Dominion University. He received a doctorate in counselor education from the College of William & Mary after serving almost 20 years as a school counselor, teacher, therapist, coordinator of a youth leadership development program, and youth minister. His primary research interests include professional development of school counselors, multicultural competence, and supervision.

Mary H. Guindon, retired associate professor and chair of the Department of Counseling and Human Services at Johns Hopkins University, holds a PhD in counselor education from the University of Virginia. She maintains a private practice as a consultant and counselor supervisor. Her areas of expertise are mental health and career management, adult transitions, relationship building, self-esteem, and occupational stress. She authored *A Counseling Primer: An Introduction to the Profession* (2011) and edited *Self-esteem Across the Lifespan: Issues and Interventions* (2010).

Julie Hakim-Larson is a professor of child clinical psychology at the University of Windsor, in Ontario, Canada. She received her PhD in life-span developmental psychology from Wayne State University, in Detroit, Michigan, and received postdoctoral training in child clinical psychology. She is a licensed psychologist in Michigan and Ontario. Her research interests include emotion and families, and

mental health and culture. Since 1997, her research has included collaborative projects involving Arab Americans in Southeastern Michigan, which has the largest concentration of immigrants from the Middle East in North America.

Shelley A. Jackson spent 10 years working as a school counselor prior to becoming a counselor educator. She received her doctorate in 1997 from Georgia State University. Since 1997 she has worked as a play therapist in addition to teaching full-time at Texas Woman's University. She has published in the areas of school counseling, expressive arts therapy, and counselor supervision. Her research and contributions to the literature in the area of bibliotherapy and counseling with children have been cited frequently. Her approach to teaching is student centered. She is mindful of the interaction between students' professional selves and their personal selves. She believes that who you are as a person is part of who you are as a counselor, therefore, her own personal interests closely follow her professional interests.

Adrianne L. Johnson is an assistant professor at the State University of New York at Oswego. Her experience includes crisis counseling, adult outpatient counseling, and college counseling. She has presented internationally on a broad range of counseling and graduate education topics and has produced scholarly publications primarily related to diversity and disability issues in counseling and higher education. She is a member of several professional organizations related to counseling, higher education, and disability advocacy. Her research interests include bias in counseling, counselor trainee competence, disability advocacy, and diversity issues in counselor education.

Barbara Kawulich currently serves as an associate professor of research and chair of the Department of Educational Innovation in the College of Education at the University of West Georgia. Her doctoral dissertation was an ethnographic study of Muscogee (Creek) women's perceptions of work, and her research with these women has continued for over

15 years. Her research and publications center on issues related to indigenous women, multiculturalism, ethics, and teaching/learning in qualitative research.

Bryan S. K. Kim is a professor of psychology and director of the MA Program in Counseling Psychology at the University of Hawaii at Hilo. He holds a PhD in counseling/clinical/school psychology (counseling psychology emphasis) from the University of California at Santa Barbara. His research focuses on multicultural counseling process and outcome, the measurement of cultural constructs, and counselor education and supervision. He is currently the associate editor of *The Counseling Psychologist* and *Measurement and Evaluation in Counseling and Development*. He is a fellow of the American Psychological Association (Divisions 17, 29, and 45), Asian American Psychological Association, and International Academy of Intercultural Research.

Gloria King is a member of the Navajo Nation whose leadership and experience in behavioral health services is with reservation and off-reservation Native Americans in rural and urban settings as a clinician and clinical supervisor as well as in administration/management. She is a licensed professional counselor in New Mexico, nationally certified counselor, and certified acupuncture detox specialist. She helped the Navajo Nation start up the first Tribal Co-Occurring Healing Center, which is a model project of national significance in Indian Country, with development of an indigenous-centered systems of care model. As a part/full-time independent consultant with rainbow star healing she provides cultural competency training, clinical supervision, technical assistance and support for behavioral health services, integration of holistic/spiritual (Native traditional and faith-based) healing and western treatment, and service and system integration. She is a speaker/presenter and advocate for indigenous-centered systems of care and social justice to eliminate health disparities. She has served on numerous regional and national boards. She has been a Substance Abuse and Mental Health

Services Administration (SAMHSA) grant consultant reviewer for 10 years and has been a SAMHSA Emergency Response Team member for the Katrina Assistance Project.

Chris Leeth received his doctorate from the University of Texas at San Antonio. His research interests include gender roles, masculinity, bullying, and health and wellness.

Susan Lester is a PhD student in counseling and a graduate teaching assistant at Old Dominion University, in Norfolk, Virginia. She earned her master's in community counseling at Saint Joseph College, in Connecticut, and has clinical experience in community clinic, religious, and private practice settings. Her scholarly and research interests include counseling as a global profession, spirituality and religion in counseling, and adult development and learning.

Karen L. Mackie is currently an assistant professor (clinical) in the Department of Counseling and Human Development at the University of Rochester. She holds a doctorate in counseling and human development from the University of Rochester and is a licensed mental health counselor and permanently certified school counselor in New York. Her scholarly and research interests include feminist and cultural studies perspectives on the work of counselors and counseling, postmodern approaches to therapy with families over the life course, creativity and improvisation in counselor education and supervision, and the intersection of social class and cultural plurality with counseling theories and practices.

Jayamala Madathil is an associate professor in the Department of Counseling at Sonoma State University, in California, where she teaches in the Community Counseling/MFT track. She received her doctorate in counseling and counselor education from the University of North Carolina at Greensboro. She has experience working in community mental health agencies, particularly with children, adolescents, and families on a wide variety of mental health concerns. Her research areas include multicultural counseling and working with families.

Sylvia Nassar-McMillan is currently a professor and program coordinator of counselor education at North Carolina State University. She has served in a variety of clinical mental health, school, and college settings over the past 25 years, and her scholarship spans multicultural, gender, and career development issues, with a special focus on Arab American acculturation and ethnic identity development. She currently serves as a member of the CACREP Standards Revision Committee and has served as a board member for the Arab American Institute Census Information Center, the National Board for Certified Counselors, and the North Carolina Board of Licensed Professional Counselors. She is past associate editor for multicultural issues for the *Journal of Counseling & Development*, for which she currently serves as senior associate editor.

Bailey J. Nevels is currently a doctoral student in the Counseling Psychology Program at the University of Georgia. She holds a Master's of Education in community counseling from the University of Georgia. Her research interests include Latina/o psychology, childhood obesity, eating disorders, college student mental health, and positive psychology.

Lori Notestine is a doctoral candidate in the Department of Counseling and Educational Development at the University of North Carolina at Greensboro. Her research interests include women's and gender issues and intimate partner violence.

Tami Ogletree, is an associate professor and program coordinator of the reading program in the Collaborative Support and Intervention Department at the University of West Georgia. She is also the site director for the Georgia Girl's STEM Collaborative Project for the National Girl's Collaborative Project. She holds a PhD in language and literacy and a certificate in interdisciplinary qualitative research from the University of Georgia. She holds an L-7 certificate in educational leadership and an MEd in early childhood and middle grades education. She has experience in public and private education from the Pre-K level to high school. Her research focus includes exploring the relationships between cohort teaching and culture, multicultural issues in the K–12 curriculum, program evaluations in K–12 settings, social justice and equity, and qualitative methodology with an emphasis in ethical research practices.

David Paré is a professor of counseling in the Faculty of Education at the University of Ottawa and the director of the Glebe Institute, a Centre for Constructive and Collaborative practice. A psychologist and family therapist, his research focuses on collaborative therapeutic practice and the postmodern turn in family therapy and psychotherapy.

Yong S. Park is a staff psychologist in the Counseling Center at the University of California, Riverside, and a research fellow in the Consortium for Multicultural Psychology Research at Michigan State University. He earned his doctorate in counseling psychology from the Counseling/Clinical/School Psychology Program at the University of California, Santa Barbara. His research interests revolve around the cultural and psychological aspects of providing professional services to Asian Americans. More specifically, he is interested in examining how relational expectations, family dynamics, and racism experiences affect the counseling process and outcome with Asian American clients.

Mark Parrish is an assistant professor and the education specialist (EdS) program director for the Counselor Education Program in the Department of Collaborative Support and Intervention at the University of West Georgia. He received his PhD in counselor education and supervision from Auburn University and his EdS and MEd in community counseling, both from the University of West Georgia. His research interests include serving the mental health needs of North American indigenous peoples along with counselor training and supervision focused on serving diverse populations in schools and in the community, and on integrating spirituality into the counseling process.

Ashley D. Paterson is currently a doctoral candidate in the child stream of the Clinical Psychology Program at the University of Windsor, in Ontario. Her research focuses on identity development and acculturation within families of ethnically diverse backgrounds. Specifically, she has examined psychological outcomes as they relate to acculturation, enculturation, and social support among Arab youth living in Canada. Her doctoral research involves identity and the role of sibling conflict in an ethnically diverse sample of youth and emerging adults.

Tarrell Awe Agahe Portman holds professional licenses as a K–12 school counselor, school psychological examiner, licensed mental health counselor, and teacher. She earned her MA in guidance and counseling from Southeast Missouri State University and her PhD in counselor education from the University of Arkansas–Fayetteville. Her research is focused on the translation of theory to practice in counseling as it interacts with the specific areas of counselor development (supervision and consultation), multiculturalism (particularly American Indians and giftedness), and education reform (action research in education).

Lee J. Richmond is a professor of education in the area of school counseling at Loyola University Maryland, where she codirects the school counseling program. She is also affiliate faculty in the pastoral counseling department. A licensed psychologist in Maryland, she is a winner of the Eminent Career Award of the National Career Development Association and has coauthored four books, eight book chapters, two monographs, and numerous articles on such subjects as spirituality and school counseling, career counseling, and women's issues. She has served on the editorial board of the *Journal of Counseling & Development,* the publications committee of the American Counseling Association, and the editorial board of the *Career Development Quarterly.* She has served as president of the American Counseling Association and of the National Career Development Association.

Edil Torres Rivera is a professor of counselor education at the University of Florida in Gainesville.

He received a PhD in counseling psychology with a concentration in multicultural counseling from the University of Connecticut, Storrs. His research interests are multicultural counseling, group work, chaos theory, liberation psychology, technology, supervision, multicultural counseling, prisons, and gang-related behavior.

Daya Singh Sandhu is a distinguished professor of research and former chairperson in the Department of Educational and Counseling Psychology at the University of Louisville. He received his doctorate in counselor education from Mississippi State University and has taught graduate courses in counseling and counseling psychology for the past 25 years. He has an interest in school counseling, multicultural counseling, neurolinguistic programming, and the role of spirituality in counseling and psychotherapy. In addition to more than 70 refereed journal articles and book chapters, he has authored or edited 12 books. He was recognized as one of the 12 pioneers in the field of multicultural counseling in the *Handbook of Multicultural Counseling* (2001). He has received several prestigious awards, including the Senior Fulbright Research Award in 2002, the Senior Fulbright-Nehru Research Award for India in 2010, and the Kentucky Counselor Educator of the Year Award in 2011. He is a past president of the American Association of Multicultural Counseling and Development (2009–2010). Most recently, he was honored as a fellow of the American Counseling Association.

Dawn M. Szymanski is an associate professor in the Department of Psychology at the University of Tennessee–Knoxville. She holds a PhD in counseling psychology from Georgia State University. Her research interests include feminist therapy and supervision; lesbian, gay, and bisexual issues; multicultural counseling; and psychology of men and masculinity.

Vasti Torres is a professor of educational leadership and policy studies at Indiana University. She holds a PhD in counseling and student affairs administration from the University of Georgia. In 2007–2008, she became the first Latina president of a national student affairs association, the American College Personnel Association. She teaches classes in student affairs administration, student development theory, diversity, and research in higher education. Her research interests center on the college experiences of Latino/a students.

Heather C. Trepal is an associate professor in the Department of Counseling at the University of Texas at San Antonio. She holds a PhD in counseling and human development from Kent State University. Her primary research interests include self-injurious behaviors, relationships/relational competencies and development (relational-cultural theory), supervision, and gender issues in counseling.

Chet Weld has been a Christian-based counselor for over 30 years. Presently, he serves as the director of pastoral counseling and the director of the Pastoral Care Department at Casas Church, in Tucson, Arizona. Licensed by the Arizona Board of Behavioral Health Examiners, he earned his BA from Ohio Wesleyan University, his MEd in counseling and guidance from the University of Arizona, and his EdD in counseling psychology from Argosy University. He is certified by the International Board of Christian Counselors as a professional Christian counselor and has published in the *Journal of Psychology & Theology* and other journals.

Kelly L. Wester is an associate professor in the Department of Counseling and Educational Development at the University of North Carolina at Greensboro. She holds a PhD in counseling and human development and an MA in criminal justice from Kent State University. Her primary research areas are in nonsuicidal self-injury and research integrity and training in counseling.

Cyrus Williams is an assistant professor in the Counseling Department at Regent University. He holds a PhD in counselor education from the University of Florida and a master's in counseling from the University of Hartford. His primary research interests include multiculturalism, advocacy counseling, addictive behaviors, and career development. Specifically, he focuses on applying noncognitive variables such as hope, resilience, and strength-based interventions to at-risk populations.

Ali Kyle Wolf received her doctorate in counseling and counseling education from the University of North Carolina at Greensboro in 2011. She is currently an adjunct professor, teaching a variety of classes for two universities, while also working in private practice providing individual, family, and couples counseling. Her research interests include leadership in counseling, developing student learning objectives for practicum and internship supervision, and utilizing technology in the counseling classroom.

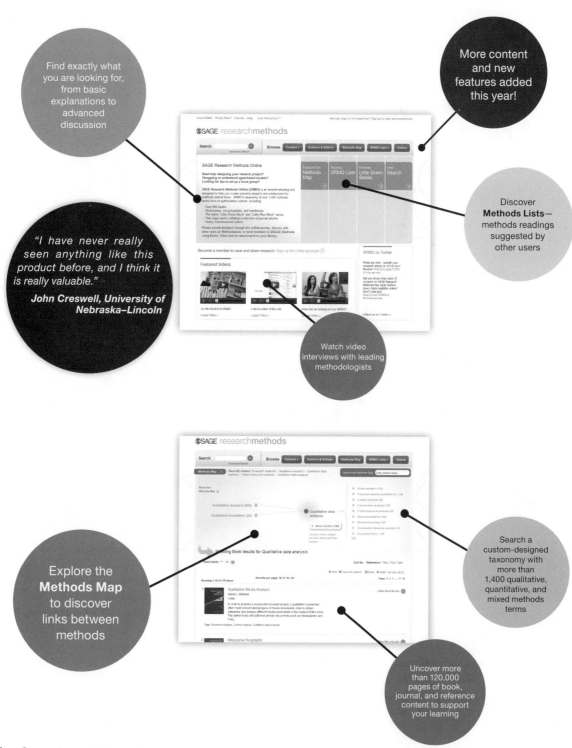

⑤SAGE research**methods**

The essential online tool for researchers from the world's leading methods publisher

Find exactly what you are looking for, from basic explanations to advanced discussion

More content and new features added this year!

"I have never really seen anything like this product before, and I think it is really valuable."

John Creswell, University of Nebraska–Lincoln

Discover **Methods Lists**— methods readings suggested by other users

Watch video interviews with leading methodologists

Explore the **Methods Map** to discover links between methods

Search a custom-designed taxonomy with more than 1,400 qualitative, quantitative, and mixed methods terms

Uncover more than 120,000 pages of book, journal, and reference content to support your learning

Find out more at
www.sageresearchmethods.com